D1351526

A HISTORY OF SWITZERLAND

The First 100,000 Years:
Before the Beginnings to the Days of the Present

The United States of America and Switzerland on the same scale

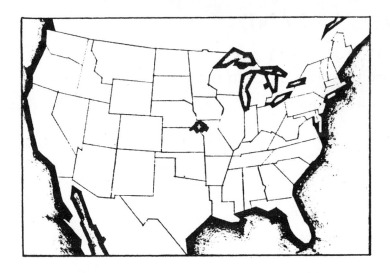

(From *Swiss in American Life*. Courtesy: Foundation Pro Helvetia)

A HISTORY OF SWITZERLAND

The First 100,000 Years:
Before the Beginnings to the Days of the
Present

By
JAMES MURRAY LUCK
Professor of Chemistry (Emeritus)
Stanford University

The Society for the Promotion of Science and Scholarship Inc.
(a non-profit corporation)
4139 El Camino Way, Palo Alto, California 94306 USA

The Society for the Promotion of Science and Scholarship Inc.
Palo Alto, California, USA

COPYRIGHT © 1985 BY THE SOCIETY FOR THE PROMOTION OF SCIENCE AND SCHOLARSHIP INC.
ALL RIGHTS RESERVED. No part of this publication may be reproduced in any form or by any means without prior written permission of the publisher. For further information, write to Permissions, SPOSS Inc., 4139 El Camino Way, Palo Alto, California 94306, USA.

ABOUT THE PUBLISHER: The Society for the Promotion of Science and Scholarship Inc. seeks to promote through its publications selected works of high scholarship in science and the humanities. The Trustees of the Society invite inquiries regarding the publication of books of appropriate quality and educational value.

International Standard Book Number: 0-930664-06-X
Library of Congress Catalog Card Number: 85-050338

TYPESET BY AUP TYPESETTERS (GLASGOW) LTD., SCOTLAND
PRINTED AND BOUND IN THE UNITED STATES OF AMERICA

TO MY GRANDCHILDREN:
Edward Nicholas Luck
Natalie Jane Calta Luck
Gregory Preyss

PREFACE

So far as I know, this work of many pages is the only comprehensive history of Switzerland in the English language to appear during the past 50 years or even during the present century.

It is the history of a small and beautiful country which, with the magnificent Alps, rises high above the rest of Europe. It is indeed small. The travelling time by train from the far west to the far east—Geneva to St. Margrethen—is about four hours and twenty minutes; from the far north to the deep south through the great Alpine massif—Basel or Schaffhausen to Chiasso—is also about four hours and twenty minutes.

Switzerland's complexities are many. Its institutions and its ways of life arouse the curiosity of the visitor, already unforgettably impressed by the natural beauty of the towering mountains, of the valleys that rise from the rivers below to the high meadows above, and of the forests buried deeply in a refreshing silence.

Its population approximates 6.4 million of whom somewhat more than one million are foreigners. Three principal languages are recognized as official and a fourth, Rhaeto-Romansh—designated as a national language—is the mother tongue of 40,000 to 50,000 inhabitants of the Graubünden. Collectively, all four languages enrich the culture and daily life of the Swiss. They may confuse the visitors from afar whose linguistic problems are compounded no end by the wealth of local dialects which in German-speaking Switzerland where most of them are rooted, are described in the aggregate as Schwyzerdütsch.

Over 20 political parties struggle for representation in the Federal Parliament. Though this may suggest political chaos, only four parties have dominated the scene in every quadrennial election since 1922. In fact, there is such a high level of humdrum stability that each of the four parties has about the same numerical representation as it had 50 or 60 years ago. Lest this be accepted as evidence that the Swiss have little interest in politics, notice that, on the average, they amend their Federal Constitution once every 14 months as contrasted with once per decade in the USA. When the Federal Government shall have acquired the political muscle or the degree of legislative competence that it would like to have, but which can only be gained by the surrender of more and more bits of sovereignty by the cantons, a political senility may descend upon the country. The Federal Constitution, far from being quite fluid, might then congeal and harden. In a hundred years or less, cantonal sovereignty may become a mere shadow of its former self. But the principle of cantonal sovereignty is cherished, and the delegation of more power to the Federal Government is regarded with misgivings, if not with open hostility, by many Swiss.

This history of the country opens before something called Switzerland, or even

Helvetia, existed. It carries us back, however briefly, to the days of Neanderthal man or to the period of time between the last two Ice Ages. The anthropological evidence, not entirely convincing, suggests that man may then have had a fleeting existence in the area within the borders of present-day Switzerland. Nine more chapters bring us to the end of the nineteenth century.

I approached the twentieth century with several misgivings. The first concerns the inability of most of us to understand current events. There are few, if any, gurus and gifted seers who know what it is all about and can explain authoritatively and accurately the happenings of the present. From a vantage point of 50 or 100 years much can be explained that at the moment defies analysis. Despite the formidable and exasperating difficulties that have to be faced when one challenges the present, I have seized upon the twentieth century and carved the subject matter into 25 sub-chapters. There are several omissions that I greatly regret but the dictates of time, space, and an occasional disinterest demanded that these lacunae be accepted. Two of these topics, admittedly important, are rendered conspicuous because of their absence: religion and the churches, covered so well by Professor Büsser in *Modern Switzerland*; and cultural activities—a subject with which I toyed in section 11.25—but which, for several reasons, could not be treated adequately.

Some Swiss institutions and practices captivate one's interest because they are so unique. The most remarkable of these is Switzerland's commitment to perpetual neutrality. It has a long evolutionary history that reaches into the distant past, long before 1814–15 when the great Powers of Europe gave it a special blessing and recognition. Because of its importance I have included a section on neutrality in every chapter from the fourteenth century on.

Industrial peace, a virtual denial of strikes and lockouts by voluntary agreements between employers and employees, is equally unique and, since its inception in 1937, has meant much in the maintenance of harmonious relations between trade unions and the associations of employers. I have described this in some detail in section 11.7.

Several other topics have been treated thematically because of their prominence and historical importance during four or more centuries: government (Chapters 5, 6, 7, 8, 9, 10 and 11); industry and commerce (Chapters 1, 3, 4, 7, 8, 9 and 10); mercenary service (Chapters 4, 5, 6, 7 and 10); population (Chapters 3, 5, 6 and 10); and public health (Chapters 1, 3, 4, 5, 6, 7 and 11).

As a nation that is extraordinarily careful to avoid any entanglement in foreign wars, Switzerland believes that she has special responsibilities that devolve upon her not only when other countries are at war but in peace time as well. Expressed in general terms, Switzerland is desirous of doing all that is within her power to alleviate human suffering wherever and whenever it may occur. Practically, this received expression when the International Red Cross—a Swiss institution—came into being. This topic is treated in section 11.19 in which Switzerland's responsibilities and those of the many national Red Cross societies, in peace and in war, are described.

The reader will understand that most of the references to source material are in

German or French. However, many descriptions of Switzerland—its people and its magnificent scenery—have been recorded in English by diligent observers who visited the country in the seventeenth, eighteenth and nineteenth centuries. A number of these reports are listed in the bibliographic references at the end of the book (keyed into the text by numbers in parentheses) so one need not despair when confronted with the many foreign language references in the Bibliography and in the "Notes" (indicated in the text by superior numerals) appended to each chapter. The work by Hertslet (in English) and the British State Papers (in English and French) help to introduce us to the world of diplomacy in relation to the stirring events of the nineteenth century.

The *Eidgenössische Abschiede*, to which frequent reference is made, consists of records of the transactions of the many sessions of the Diet and of numerous political conferences of groups of cantons. The *Bundesbriefe*, many treaties of alliance, and an overwhelming miscellany of federal documents of a parliamentary character are included in the *Abschiede*. This official collection covers the period 1245 to 1798. Then came the *Aktensammlung*—another collection of parliamentary documents from the days of the Helvetic Republic.

After 1848, when the first great Federal Constitution emerged, the *Bundesblatt* began to appear. It is also an official record of the doings of parliament. In legislative enactments, ordinances, and decrees it reports the decisions of the Federal Assembly and of the Federal Council.

Many foreign language nouns and expressions have been retained in the text without translation. Some have been explained in the "Notes." Others that may require explanation have been collected in a glossary.

In the interest of brevity, *Abschiede* has been used throughout the book instead of *Eidgenössische Abschiede*. Likewise, *Bundesblatt* has been used instead of *Bundesblatt der Schweizerischen Eidgenossenschaft*.

I wish to express my gratitude to many who, in various ways, have assisted greatly. Parts of the manuscript were read by Professors Peter Paret, Peter Stansky, and Kurt Steiner of Stanford University. Dr. Kaspar von Greyerz, then at Stanford, and Elfriede Wiesendanger of Stanford University Libraries also read several portions. To Professor Elizabeth Roemer of the University of Arizona I am indebted for information on Cheseaux's discovery of two comets. M. Marcel Ney, Director of the Secretariat for the Swiss Abroad, was able to provide biographical information on Schweppe, a very elusive person, whose name I was almost prepared to accept as a synonym for gin and tonic. O. Gfeller of the Swiss Federal Railways helpfully provided information on the history and current status of the Swiss railways and public transport facilities in Switzerland. For information on the plague and its visitations in Switzerland I am obliged, in part, to Professor Ackerknecht of the University of Zurich. Professor Josef von Ah of the Swiss Department of Agriculture helped greatly with the chapter on agriculture (11.8). To Professor Herbert Lüthy of the University of Basel and Dr. Treichler of the National Library I am grateful for memoranda on the origins of the people of Schwyz and Oberhasli.

There are many others to whom I am indebted: Dr. Raymond Probst, then Secretary of State for Foreign Affairs, for a very helpful discussion of Switzerland vis-à-vis the United Nations, and Switzerland's position in respect of human rights and basic freedoms; Dr. Lukas Burckhardt for his invaluable assistance with the chapter on industrial peace (11.7); Dr. Hans Mast, Executive Vice President and Economic Advisor of Credit Suisse and members of his staff in the Management Division for very helpful suggestions for the chapter on banking (11.12); Professor Meinrad Schär of the University of Zurich for reviewing the chapter on public health (11.3); Professor Claude Zangger, Deputy Director of the Federal Office of Energy, for his help with the section on energy developments in Switzerland (11.21) and Dr. Peter Fricker, General Secretary of the Swiss National Science Foundation for various reports of the Foundation and many helpful suggestions. Professor Ulrich Im Hof of the University of Bern read portions of Chapters 6 and 7 and offered several much appreciated comments. Professor Alexander von Muralt, Honorary President of the National Science Foundation, was a source of excellent advice during the formative years of the book.

I wish also to recognize the help afforded by various officers of the *Bundesamt für geistiges Eigentum* (Patents and Copyright); the *Bundesamt für Industrie, Gewerbe und Arbeit,* BIGA (Federal Office for Industry, Trades, and Labor); *Eidgenössisches Gesundheitsamt* (Federal Office of Public Health); *Bundesamt für Ausländer Fragen* (Federal Office for Matters Concerning Swiss Abroad); *Bundesamt für Statistik* (Federal Statistical Office)—especially Dr. Rudolf Dürmüller; the *Informationstelle für Steuerfragen* (re taxation); the Federal Finance Administration (re the public debt); and Dr. Raetus Luck, Vice Director of the Swiss National Library, together with various members of the library staff who were of invaluable aid during my annual "pilgrimage" to Bern. Mr. Cuno Jud of the Federal Parliamentary and Central Library and Hans Urs Wili of the Federal Chancellery were frequently consulted regarding access to certain documents.

And more than a word of thanks to Fritz Erne, who, as the head of Pacific Capital Resources in San Francisco, was instrumental in helping to ensure a wide distribution of the book in Europe, the USA and elsewhere. Also involved were Elton Suhrke, Theodore Rudow and William Reich whose advice and experience in marketing were invaluable.

To the staff of the American Embassy in Bern I am grateful for their help in many ways during my visits to Bern. Professor Leo Schelbert of the University of Illinois, the recognized authority on Swiss emigration, generously provided some documents from his own extensive collection. They pertained largely to nineteenth-century emigration about which I was lost in its complexity and my confusion. For his help I am greatly indebted.

I wish also to single out for special mention, the officers and the staff of Annual Reviews Inc. in Palo Alto, whose advice and material help were generously offered and gratefully received. William Kaufmann and John McNeil, in charge of the company's editorial operations and business affairs respectively, were called upon frequently to assist the author in ways too numerous to mention. Ann Polom and

Judith Mueller of the staff of Annual Reviews Inc. assumed the onerous task of typing the manuscript. Richard Burke, Production Manager at Annual Reviews Inc. aided greatly in maintaining the timely flow of copy to the compositor, the indexer, and the printer. Richard Peterson prepared camera-ready copy for the maps and diagrams in the appendix. To them and to Susan Riggs and Margot Platt as copy editors, Barbara Lee as indexer, and AUP Typesetters (Glasgow) Ltd., I express my thanks for their interest and good services. There are many others whose names escape me at the moment who came to the rescue in one way or another during the preparation of the book. I can only thank them collectively while promising to try strenuously to repair a fading memory.

I trust it is understood that those who have so kindly helped in preparation and revision of the text are in no way responsible for the final product. Errors and deficiencies must be regarded as a burden that the author alone may carry.

It is my hope that this book will contribute, primarily to the English-speaking world, a greater knowledge of Switzerland, and an appreciation of her unique position and responsibilities within the family of nations, of which she is a small but very important member.

J. MURRAY LUCK

A History of Switzerland:
from Before the Beginnings to The Days of the Present

CONTENTS

1. BEFORE THE BEGINNINGS

Introduction

A history of Switzerland might properly open with the thirteenth century, when Switzerland began to take form as a federation of autonomous districts. But it could also open in much earlier times. Hence this chapter serves as an introduction to Switzerland of the late Middle Ages. We shall pass hurriedly over the millennia of prehistory, barely mentioning the fact that a considerable body of biological, archaeological and geological evidence indicates that the territory embraced by what we now call Switzerland was thinly populated by man in the last interglacial period[1] (**20; 21; 173; 376**). The racial connections of these very early "Swiss" are totally unknown although it is generally assumed that they belonged to the Neandertal race. Indeed, the evidence of their existence is fragmentary. They disappeared during the last Ice Age and left very little of their handiwork behind. What has been found is extremely primitive. A cave at Wildkirchli,[2] near the Säntis in Appenzell, yielded crude stone implements fashioned from stone brought in from elsewhere. The cave dwellers hunted the great cave bear (*Ursus spelaeus*). Speculation alone permits one to conclude that the crudely shaped stones were used for scraping the skins of the bears and pounding the flesh. The skins were used for clothing and the flesh for food. The long bones, such as the humerus and femur, were possibly used as clubs in hunting and fighting. In the cave at Wildkirchli (1470 to 1500 meters above sea level) and in two others, Wildenmannlisloch (1628 meters) and Drachenloch (2445 meters), vast quantities of skeletal remains and teeth of the cave bear have been found, permitting a conclusion that about 1000 bears per cave are responsible for the skeletal residues (**21**, p. 101). Several other caves in Switzerland, Austria, Hungary and Poland have yielded skeletal remains of the bear.[3] In fact, less than one percent of the animal remains in the Swiss caves can have been derived from other animals (**20**, p. 179). Exceptional, perhaps, are the Basler Jura[4] and the Berner Jura.[5]

No human bones or teeth from the Old Stone Age, 120,000 to 150,000 years ago, have been found. When the glaciers of the last Ice Age advanced far into the valleys and the expanding blanket of ice rose to higher and higher levels, man retreated to higher altitudes. He found shelter in caves and under clusters of rocks with sufficient protected space for his needs. Within this increasingly hostile environment, the bears eventually failed to survive. Man likewise disappeared and did not reappear in "Switzerland" until the second half of the Magdalenian era, 12,000 to 15,000 years ago.

When the glaciers retreated, a rich forest growth gradually covered much of the land. The environment became less hostile and man reappeared. He left us much in the form of stone and bone implements and other evidence of a primitive culture. Cattle breeding, the domestication of animals, and the cultivation of plants including cereal grains presently ensued. A nomadic life in pursuit of reindeer herds gradually came to an end. Settlements appeared and, as the evidence abundantly indicates, dwellings were constructed, probably around 2500 B.C. (**132; 354**), on pilings driven into the offshore waters of some of the Swiss lakes.[6] Pilings have also been found in the deeper waters of Lake Zurich, Greifensee, and a lake in northern Italy. Doubtless other lakes will provide evidence of early man of the Neolithic or Bronze Age living in shelters constructed on pilings that were sunk some distance offshore. In Lake Zurich clay pots of the New Stone Age have been retrieved from the slime of the lake bottom. Textiles and basketry, better preserved under the slime on the lake bottom than on land, have also been retrieved. Bronze Age finds include necklaces, bracelets and pendants, looms, farming utensils, and charms made from boar fangs, bear teeth and wild boar skulls.

The depth of the pilings, which incidentally are still almost vertical, suggests that the surfaces of Lake Zurich and the Greifensee must have been at least four meters lower than at present. It is assumed that the dwellings were constructed somewhat above the lake surface to minimize the danger of flooding (**346**). In the 1960s Zurich set up a full-time professional team of divers to pursue archaeological studies in Lake Zurich. Thirty-four New Stone Age and Bronze Age sites had been identified around the lake shore by midsummer of 1981, and new finds continue to be made.

Tschumi tells us that in the cold dry winter of 1853–54 the Swiss lakes sank to levels never before known. Animal bones, implements of man and evidence of a lake-dweller culture were accumulated. Ferdinand Keller in Zurich initiated investigations, according to Tschumi, which soon gave evidence of human artifacts and lake dwellings constructed on pilings in most of the Swiss lakes or at the shores of the lakes (**372**, p. 571).

The lake-dweller culture of Lake Zurich dates from 4000 or 4500 B.C., according to dendrochronological studies. The duration of this culture is unknown, though after a long interruption lakeshore dwellings reappeared, many constructed on land at the forest's edge. Communication by a rich network of rivers and lakes permitted the transport of men and materials. We may assume that trade and commerce—the exchange of food products and of the implements and other items resulting from early handicrafts then had their beginnings. The centuries came and went and the early "Swiss" became gradually possessed of increasing skills in the handicrafts. Pottery, ceramic products, varieties of stone battle axes and jewelry appeared. Copper came into use and, with the introduction of tin, implements of bronze were fashioned.

Much of what we know about the early people of Europe results from the study of graves. Stone Age graves in Switzerland are very rare, possibly because much of the middle land was deeply covered with moraine material and rubble deposited by the glaciers during the last Ice Age. Objects found in the grave sites of later periods in Switzerland and elsewhere in Europe indicate that over many centuries vast movements of people took place. Streams of people moved from Russia, from northern Europe and from Germany. Other population groups originating in the Spain/Portugal peninsula moved into Brittany, southern France and the British Isles. Even Denmark, Poland and Hungary were eventually overrun. Around 1800–1600 B.C. the occupancy of the Swiss valleys was extended by settlement of the lower reaches of the Alps and a deep penetration of the lateral valleys. Tentatively one may conclude from available evidence that trade and commerce were actively pursued between the upper Valais and northern Italy. Between the peoples of the Ticino and Lombardy a close blood relationship developed and may in time have extended into the upper Valais.

Around 1000 B.C., after a break of centuries, lakeshore settlements again appeared. These village-type communities were favorably located for defense. Probably even more favorably located were settlements in high places which offered excellent opportunities for defense. In later years, some of these probably evolved into Middle Ages towns and villages. The findings of archaeological and anthropological interest suggest that the people of the middle land differed ethnically from those of the Alpine lands and from those of north Italy and the Ticino. Burial practices, animal bones (of horses, cattle and goats), and a great variety of skills in metal and ceramic work, as evidenced by the cups, beakers, bowls, jewelry, implements for husbandry and weapons, provide the evidence which indicates long-continued movements of people, and the intermingling or separation of different cultural groups.

In the eighth and seventh centuries B.C. a demarcation between eastern and western Switzerland became sharper. Centuries later, when the Burgundians moved down from the north, with a total penetration of the westerly parts, and Alemannian tribes from Germany dominated eastern Switzerland, an ethnic separation was clearly evident. I have said nothing about Raetia (Graubünden) and the Raetians. This is only because archaeological studies in the Graubünden have not been very rewarding thus far, except in a few places.

In the late Bronze Age (1200–900 B.C.) a great displacement of people took place and Celtic[7] tribes crossed over the Alps. Around 400 B.C. the Celts in considerable numbers appeared in the Ticino where they constituted a dominant upper layer of the people. They spread over the Swiss middle land in La-Tène times (400–58 B.C.). By the first century B.C. the Celtic-German border lay north of the middle and upper Main.

With the appearance of the Celts, prehistory fades into the past. Swiss history has its beginnings. The bountiful discoveries of the archaeologists which have given us enlightening information concerning the people of the distant past (see e.g., 376) became enriched by Celtic inscriptions. The writings of Tacitus and Julius Caesar contribute much to the beginnings of an historical record of Switzerland. Tacitus tells us of the Helvetii, a Celtic people who, according to Caesar's description, occupied the territory bounded on the west by the Jura range of mountains, on the south by the Rhone and Lake Geneva, and on the north and east by the Rhine as far as Lake Constance. This is clearly a large part of present-day Switzerland.

Helvetia and the Roman Occupation

And so we come to the days of the Roman penetration of Helvetia[8] and the ultimate occupation of the country by Roman troops and civil servants. It is important that we delve deeply into this period. One cannot appreciate the Switzerland of today and its historical evolution without being aware of the tremendous impact of the Roman occupation. Modern Switzerland is richly gifted with physical remains of the Roman occupation: at Augst near Basel;[9] at Avenches,[10] Nyon, Windisch and many other sites where excavations have revealed beautiful mosaics, sculpture, inscribed tablets, remains of buildings, and very durable city walls. And it was through several bishops from Rome and the Roman legions that Christianity entered Switzerland and spread rapidly. Many place names,[11] clearly of Roman origin or earlier, testify to the completeness of the Roman conquest. The Raeto-Romansh dialect, a mystifying language which persists in parts of the Graubünden, is partly rooted in the language of the conquerors. And, even in matters of trade and commerce, one can hardly escape the conclusion that the substantial export-import trade between Helvetia and Roman Italy was the prelude to the important role played by Italy in Switzerland's foreign trade for many centuries after the Roman occupation ended.[12]

When did the Roman occupation of Switzerland begin and what were the circumstances that led to this great northward expansion of the Roman empire? Perhaps a beginning was made in the second century B.C. (**376**, p. 52).[13,14] Certain it is that a total military occupation was achieved in 15 B.C. by Roman armies commanded by Tiberius and Drusus, the two stepsons of the Roman Emperor Augustus. The seizure of Helvetia was the fulfillment of a grandiose plan to extend the empire through a sweeping offensive operation which would carry the border as far north as the river Main or even to the Elbe.

We must go back to the days of Julius Caesar to recall a most important event in the history of the Helvetians. A huge number of these people, members of several tribes, and reported to be 368,000 in all, attempted a mass exodus in 61–58 B.C. from the Swiss middle land (**337**, pp. 68–69). The reasons are not entirely clear. Possibly they were tired of harassment by marauding tribes from the north— pressures that rendered settlement difficult, and made more and more seductive the tales of peaceful and fertile lands to the west. Apparently headed for Aquitania (southwestern Gaul), they were intercepted in 58–57 B.C. by a Roman army under Julius Caesar, the governor of Gaul. Through an impressive Roman victory at Bibracte, near Autun, the survivors of the migrating horde, now reduced to about 140,000, were driven back to their original lands, where they lived by cattle breeding and a simple agriculture. Caesar, by treaty with the Helvetians, recognized them as a free and quasi-independent people. In return for ultimate protection by Rome, the Helvetians agreed to supply troops to the conqueror when needed and to join in defense against invaders from the north. Ernst Meyer tells us that Switzerland, despite a number of successful military operations, cannot be regarded as Roman territory until several more decades had passed by. For example, no imports from Rome dating from 50 to 40 B.C., or earlier, have been found (**239**, p. 59).

In 45–44 B.C. Caesar founded Colonia Julia Equestris on the site of the Helvetian town of Novodunum (Nyon) (**337**, p. 77). It is presumed to have been a settlement of veterans of Roman cavalry drawn from several legions.[15] To the north, in the lands of the Raurics, a second military encampment, Colonia Augusta Raurica (Augst, near Basel), was founded about 44 B.C. Both encampments housed the large number of troops required to protect Gaul from a re-invasion by the Helvetians or an attack by the Rauric cavalry.

The multipronged attack on Helvetia by Tiberius and Drusus in 15 B.C. did not take place without some major and ominous preparations. Access to the pass over the Great St. Bernard was rendered secure by establishing a military post at Aosta (Colonia Augusta Praetoria), and complete control of the access routes to the Julier and Septimer passes was gained by extending Roman domination over the lands reaching up to the Alps. The Ticino, much of the Rhone valley (Valais) and part of Raetia (Graubünden) were seized well in advance. In 15 B.C. the Rhone valley was united with the existing province of Raetia.

The conquest of Helvetia by the Roman armies was accomplished in a single season. Basel, Zurich, and Winterthur were occupied by Roman troops. In fact the military occupation extended as far east as Innsbruck. Archaeological evidence proves that the area between the Rhine and the Danube was also occupied.

By 50 A.D. the whole of Switzerland had become occupied by the Romans: from Lake Geneva, the Rhone valley and the Ticino and Graubünden to the south and east, the Jura chain to the west and northwest, and the Rhine and Lake Constance to the north and east. Raetia and the Rhone valley (Valais) were united for administrative purposes. Apart from the Ticino and Narbonensis (Savoy, including Geneva), the rest of Switzerland was divided into two provinces, Gallia Belgica and Raetia (cf. **12**, map 7, specifically *Römische Provinzen im 1. Jh. n. Chr.*).

The post-Bibrachte treaty with the Helvetians seemed to portend a peaceful future for these early Swiss. But it was not to be so. In 52 B.C. Helvetian resistance surfaced and the revolt was mercilessly suppressed. Despite this incident, the local populations in time became loyal citizens and subjects of the Empire. The young men served in the Roman armies. Caesar regarded the Helvetians as the most formidable fighting men encountered in his campaigns. Burckhardt states that the Ligurians (an Alpine tribe) and the Raetians were the best and most trustworthy allies of the Roman troops to the very end, namely to the fall of Rome (**75**, p. 32).

Under Augustus, the Romans had pushed well north of the Rhine but, following upon a severe defeat in the Teutoburger forest in 9 A.D., they withdrew to the Rhine. Here two great Roman armies were posted, and watch towers and fortified places were constructed. A few years later, in 15–20 A.D., Vindonissa (Windisch) was developed into a strong military base and continued as such for a century. The Roman military policy became more and more defensive in character, with a few brief intervals when offensive operations were again resumed. In 73–74 A.D. a provincial capital, well fortified, was established by Vespasian at Aventicum (Avenches).[10] The political privileges and partial independence of the Helvetians were thereby reduced and more political power was transferred to the Roman conquerors. The military base at Vindonissa was razed in 101 and the troops were moved to defensive positions on the Danube. Basel, Zurich and Winterthur ceased to be important as military outposts at about the same time.

In general, Switzerland in the second century was peaceful. The wealth of construction at Aventicum and Augusta Raurica provides convincing evidence that this must have been the greatest period in Roman Switzerland. Class distinctions appear to have been rare, though several levels of administrative officials and Roman veterans of the wars were to be found. Many of the veterans, as well as Roman merchants and bankers, settled in Switzerland. Romanization was a purely cultural phenomenon and not the product of a massive immigration from elsewhere in the empire. Latin, the official language, was widely accepted, and displaced to some extent the Celtish and Raetish tongues. Cities, villages and agricultural estates acquired a Roman style in keeping with Roman ways of life and various trappings of Roman civilization. Excellent roadways, principally for military purposes, were constructed. Extending for almost 1500 kilometers over the lands embraced by present-day Switzerland, they almost encircled the country, with one cross-country road from the headwaters of the Aare along the river valley to Lucerne and northwards along the Reuss to Vindonissa where six of the roads converged. Some forty or more towns, villages and military forts were to be found along these roadways. By way of contrast, hundreds of individual settlements and villas dotted the countryside that reached along the great valley and middle land from Lake Geneva to Constance. These country estates varied in size from ten to several hundred hectares (one hectare being 2.47 acres). The villas, likewise, varied in size and in the luxury of their appointments. Their occupants, in the aggregate, exerted much more influence on the Romanization of Helvetia than the relatively few cities and towns.

Mosaics, sculpture, wall paintings, silverware and works of art entered the country in the latter part of the second century and the first few decades of the third. Much of this enriched the more luxurious villas. None of these beautiful Roman handicrafts were brought in during the first century A.D., as military affairs were then of prime importance.

In the third century, the peace and bountifulness of the preceding hundred years ended. Perhaps events in the preceding few decades indicated there was trouble ahead. There were disturbances of the peace in Helvetia and in neighbouring lands (**239**, p. 79, footnote 99) in the closing decades of the second century A.D. Treasures discovered many centuries later were buried, probably to escape seizure by marauders from the north.[16] Baden (Aquae Helveticae) suffered extensive destruction in 171.

The Alemannians, powerful Germanic tribes from across the Rhine, are mentioned for the first time in 212/13 (cf. **239**, p. 80, footnote 105).[17] In 254, the Alemannians in force broke through the weakening defense lines. Six years later, the invaders advanced into the middle lands. Baden was again ravaged. Augusta Raurica and Aventicum suffered massive destruction. Hundreds of villas in the path of the invaders were plundered and burned. Buried treasures and coins permit a reliable dating of these terrible incursions of the Alemannians. Only Valais remained undisturbed. Several of the Roman emperors, such as Probus, Diocletian, Constantine, Julian, and Valentinian, succeeded in driving the Alemannians back, but the victories had no lasting effect.

As conditions worsened during the third century, the Roman administrators resorted more and more to oppressive measures against the native inhabitants, who began to suffer more from their Roman overlords than from the barbarians. They were slowly reduced almost to enslavement. Bureaucratic despots took the place of the native local officials. Collection of the taxes demanded by Rome became a hated responsibility of the local authorities. The flight of officials was punished, and their positions, once held for life—or even inheritable—were lost. Torture and flogging were no longer reserved only for slaves brought in from the Mediterranean lands by the Roman conquerors. More and more forced labor, without compensation, was required of the people.

Extensive administrative changes and reorganized and reconstructed defense systems failed to halt the invaders. In 401 a great many Roman soldiers were recalled to Italy to defend Rome and much of Italy against the Goths. In 406, with many watch towers in ruins and fortresses abandoned, the Alemannians again broke through in great numbers and ravaged Alsace and the Palatinate. Crossing the Rhine, they entered the Swiss middle land and, following an ancient route through Raetia, they carried their destructive search for plunder into Italy as well. A substantial settling of eastern Switzerland by the Alemannians did not begin until the end of the fifth century and continued for the next 100 years or longer.[18] By the end of the seventh century Alemannian Switzerland consisted essentially of a wedge that divided Switzerland into three parts, since it separated Burgundian Switzerland from Raetian Switzerland to the east.

In time, the Latinized Celtic peoples of Helvetia were totally absorbed. Parts of Raetia managed to retain the Romansh language; otherwise the country became almost completely Germanized. Nonetheless it was a slow process of diffusion with intermittent periods of rather heavy migration and the establishment of many temporary settlements. People were on the move. Places of permanent abode were being sought. The old Roman communities were gradually replaced by villages that were predominantly German. Various primitive technologies survived in the villages but they were slowly intermingled with German handicrafts introduced by the incoming settlers. Agriculture and the handicrafts progressed together.

Christianity and the Church

One of the enduring side effects of the Roman occupation of Switzerland was the early introduction of the Christian religion and the accompanying power structure of the Church. The temporal rulers of the land vied with the ecclesiastical authorities in political, economic and even military affairs. The impact of Christianity as an organized religion, on Europe in general, and on Switzerland in particular, was tremendous, as the history of the ensuing centuries reveals. It was not an unmixed blessing. For the moment let us concern ourselves only with the first few centuries.

Christianity successfully penetrated some parts of the country in the third and fourth centuries, possibly even as early as the second (**229**, p. 11). A Christian bishop, Theodor of Martigny, is mentioned in a record of 381 A.D. Around 450 a monastery was founded in Romainmôtier[19] and, in 451, a Bishop of Chur is mentioned for the first time. The evidence clearly proves that Christianity had penetrated deeply into the valleys of the Rhine and Rhone by the end of the fifth century. The ancient heathenism disappeared gradually and many of the pagan practices were slowly transformed into the primitive rites of the early Christian Church. Missionaries entered from Italy and established islands where Christianity became deeply rooted. Irish missionaries also worked zealously to promote Christianity. Why the Church in Ireland possessed such missionary zeal remains unexplained. One of the Irish monks, Gallus, visited Zurich and the Lake Constance region around 610. His Irish tutor, Columban, introduced a mixture of Christianity and the worship of Wodan into east-central Switzerland. The cloister of St. Gallen is alleged to have been built over the grave of Gallus. Miracles of healing were reputed to have been wrought by the holy ones. Various bishoprics were founded during the first half of the seventh century, e.g., Basel, Constance, Lausanne, Sion, and Chur.

The Alemannians tolerated Christianity and gradually absorbed some of the Christian rites. The somewhat vague and ill-defined border between Burgundian and Alemannian Switzerland at the end of the seventh century was not only a linguistic and cultural border but also a religious boundary. Paganism persisted for many years right up to the Burgundian border.

The Church assumed economic importance as a lender of money to the needy. It also provided a modicum of care and sympathetic concern for the weak and the oppressed. The cloisters, founded as monasteries in the seventh century (e.g., St. Gallen and Reichenau), were a haven for many who sought refuge from the vexations and violence of the times. Not surprisingly, they were soon over-populated. They provided encouragement and time for meditation and various kinds of work. Monks who were interested in hard physical work engaged in construction, the hewing of trees, and in farm labor. The artistic ones pursued their skills in peace and safety. Some were remarkably gifted. Tutelo, a monk at St. Gallen who died in 915, carved from ivory a magnificent book cover. Another book cover, also carved from ivory, portrays a legendary incident in the life of the holy Gallus. Work of comparable quality was done in hammered gold leaf, silver, and stone.[20] Many gifts from donors in a vast area were received by the Abbey of St. Gallen, which became a great repository for Carolingian art. Even in the mid-800s its library housed some four hundred books, including Irish and Anglo-Saxon originals. As a center for collecting and transmitting scholarly knowledge it could be equalled only by the foundation at Reichenau. Today, little remains of the wonderful works of the artists of those early days: a few miniatures, some works of ivory, illuminated manuscripts, relief work in stone, and a few beautiful examples of the goldsmiths' and silversmiths' art.

The life of the cloister, as reflected in scholarly and artistic creativity, was possibly never greater than in the seclusion of the Abbey of St. Gallen around the ninth and tenth centuries. Monks were the literary and musical leaders of the whole of Europe. They developed melodious chants, liturgies and prayers. Balbulus, a monk from St. Gallen (circa 840–912), was the first German composer about whom anything is known. The musical and poetic forms created by him dominated the scene for a hundred years. Choral compositions and highly developed church music emerged in this period. Tutelo, who was a universal genius, pioneered in musical arrangements for several voices. St. Gallen became a great center for poetry and music as well as the handcrafted arts. It brought together German as well as Byzantine art. In both St. Gallen and Reichenau, heroic sagas of ancient German times were preserved in Latin hexameter. Most poets of the day used Latin verse, though Notker the German (circa 950–1022), used the mother tongue extensively. Notker achieved fame as a musician, poet, mathematician, and astronomer. He was the most important grammarian and writer of prose in Old High German.

Early in the ninth century the monks of St. Gallen were granted various immunities by the Bishop of Constance, as well as the precious right of free election of the abbot. In 854 the monastery was raised to a cloister and, along with the church, the school and other appurtenances, was granted the freedom of the *Romisches Reich* (the Holy Roman Empire). The abbot became a prince of the Empire with great temporal powers.

The princes of the church and the priesthood enjoyed special protection and privileges. Gifts to an abbey, an episcopate, or to the church generally could not be successfully challenged and prevented by a civil lord. Responsibility to pay tithes to the church was strengthened, and the ecclesiastical courts enhanced the power of the church and the protection of the priesthood. The inviolability of the church properties and the immunities enjoyed by the church were secured by the powers of the ecclesiastical courts. The upper levels of the clergy became great landowners. Gifts to a cloister relieved the donor of the necessity of paying tithes—a very significant fringe benefit. Gifts of one's property to the church, a monastery, a cloister, or a religious foundation assured one of a place in heaven and an income on earth. The right of asylum, which was carefully defined, regulated, and respected, testifies to the remarkably powerful position of the church vis-à-vis the civil authorities.

The organization of the churches in the three ancient valleys is obscure. We do not know whether the Alemannians were Christian or still heathen when they entered the valleys. The whole of ancient "Switzerland" was in the Bishopric of Constance. Within this bishopric the three Waldstätte belonged to the Archdeaconry of Aargau and within this to the Deaconry of Lucerne. The oldest known church on the north slope of the Gotthard was in Urseren and is mentioned in the testament of Bishop Tello of Chur in 766. In the thirteenth century, three others are known to have been in Uri. A few in twelfth-century Schwyz and Unterwalden are mentioned in early ecclesiastical records.

The Burgundians, Franks and Carolingians

One of the interesting aspects of Switzerland is its structural heterogeneity which is reflected in a three-way division into French-speaking, German-speaking and Italian-speaking areas. A fourth linguistic area exists in the Graubünden where Raeto-Romansh is still spoken by a small percentage of the people. The importance of the Roman occupation as an influential factor in shaping the future of Switzerland, at least for many centuries, is overshadowed by the lasting impact of the southward migration of peoples from northern Europe. The origin of the migrating tribes is clouded in uncertainty and is largely legendary. The southward movement began between 100 B.C. and 100 A.D. Although Denmark and the North Sea coastal areas between the Elbe and the Oder, perhaps even as far as the Weichsel, are commonly regarded as the original homelands of many of the tribes, it seems improbable that so many migrants could have come from this area within a mere 200 years.

THE BURGUNDIANS (285, I, 95–101)   As the Burgundians moved slowly to the south, they entered lands of the Alemannians and with little opposition, if any, were permitted to settle along the middle Rhine. In 406 they crossed the Rhine and resettled around Mainz and Worms. The Roman emperor, Constantine III, accepted them as confederates. However, when they moved further west into Gallia Belgica in 436, they were opposed by an army of Huns[21] under orders from the Roman commander Aetius. The Burgundians under their king, Gundahar (Gunther), were defeated and the royal family was massacred. In 443 Aetius permitted the surviving Burgundians to settle in Sapaudia (Savoy).[22] Geneva became their capital. In 451 they joined with Aetius in the great battle at Troyes against Attila the Hun. After Aetius' death in 454, the Burgundians and their Frankish successors expanded the area under their control. To the north, they reached beyond Lyon and Besançon to the plateau of Langres. Much of western Switzerland became Burgundian and Frankish. Their eastern frontier around 700 A.D., though vague and ill-defined, reached south-easterly from west of Basel to the headwaters of the Aare and the Rhone. Decades earlier it extended as far east as the Lake of Zurich. The later boundary approximated the present linguistic and cultural border between French- and German-speaking Switzerland. Not enough is known about the tribal languages of the Burgundians and Alemannians, but it is generally agreed that profound linguistic differences set the Burgundians in western Switzerland and the neighbouring Alemannians to the east well apart.

Religious differences also became manifest, almost as soon as the Romans abandoned Switzerland to the newcomers. Christianity persisted in the areas under Burgundian control. King Sigismund (†524), converted from Arianism to Christianity, displayed more interest in the founding of churches and cloisters than in extending the political power of Burgundy. Despite occasional changes in policy, the rulers of western Europe early in the Christian era, allied themselves with the Church. With political power vested in the heads of government, and authority in religious matters vested in the Church, association of the temporal and spiritual lords was soon found to be mutually advantageous. Between the two powerful classes of rulers almost total control could be exercised over their subjects.

Up to 534, the Roman influence continued to be strong and the Burgundian nobility, consisting of the royal family, powerful military leaders, principal deputies of the monarch, and holders of vast estates, were extensively Romanized. However, the Burgundians and Romans in Burgundy existed as two separate peoples, each with their own code of laws. In 534, Godomar, the last of the early line of Burgundian kings, died and the descendants of Clovis (Chlodwig),[23] the first of the Frankish kings, became the rulers of Burgundy (see Diagram 1 and Map 1 in the Appendix).

THE FRANKS AND MEROVINGIANS   In the fourth century several tribes of Germanic people north of the Main were known collectively as Franks. As a background to any account of the Franks we must recall that Julius Caesar had succeeded in annexing all of Gaul up to the Rhine, and that Tiberius in 5 A.D. received the submission of all of the tribes between the Rhine and the Elbe. At the time of Clovis, Germany as we now know it, consisted of five main districts. Its history for the next three centuries is largely that of the tribes in these areas. To the northeast between the Rhine and the Elbe were the Saxons. To the east and south lay the Kingdom of Thuringia. In the southwest were the Alemannians, confined more or less to Swabia. To their north were the Franks who occupied what later came to be called Franconia. To the southeast were the Bavarians.

It was Clovis who succeeded in 496 in forcing the Alemannians from the middle Rhine southwards into Swabia. Ten years earlier he had defeated the Roman commander Syagrius, thereby ending the nominal rule of the Romans in the lands north of the Alps. In 500 he defeated Gundobad, king of the Burgundians and, until his death in 511, Clovis dominated the rulers of Burgundy. Both the Salian and Ripuarian (or Rhenish) Franks were also under his control, as well as the whole of Aquitania which he absorbed in 507. No one could challenge his rule in the west, for all the lands to the west of the middle Rhine, western Switzerland and Burgundy were under his sovereignty. Eastern Switzerland was heavily penetrated by the Alemannians who, under a number of tribal leaders, were not well organized or fused into a single entity. They fell under the protection of Theoderich (†526), King of the East Goths, whose supremacy extended over part of Italy, Raetia, and the upper Balkans.

The dominant position of the Franks, attained under Clovis, continued through the Merovingian dynasty for almost 250 years after his death. The genealogy of the Merovingians (see Diagram 1) and the recurring "dismemberment" of the Frankish Kingdom suggest an instability that is more apparent than real. This concerns the practice of the Merovingians of dividing the kingdom among their sons: primogeniture was not prevalent. Quarrels among the heirs, violent disputes and occasional assassinations within the family characterized the times. It is amazing that the fabric of royal power held together as well as it did.

THE CAROLINGIANS   Sigebert III (†656) was the last of the Merovingians who succeeded in holding the Frankish kingdom together. His successors for the next 100 years were generally weak and ineffective. Power fell gradually into the hands of the Mayors of the Palace (Major domos)[24] as the culmination of struggles between the monarch and his nobles. The latter, at first subservient to the king and responsible to him in administering the affairs of the realm, became increasingly independent. The head of the Pippin family, powerful in the government of Austrasia, became Major domo of the whole Frankish kingdom following upon a military victory at Tertry in 678. In effect, he, his son and friendly nobles actually ruled in place of the shadow kings whose power was only nominal. Charles Martel (†741) and his successors, Pippin III and Carloman, after several campaigns against the ducal rulers of the Alemannians, succeeded in bringing eastern Switzerland totally under the rule of their family. Their control over Burgundy had, in the meantime, been tightened and secured. By 748 the Alemannian nobles had virtually disappeared from places of power. The third wife of Charles the Great was of Frankish-Alemannian parentage. Her brothers rose in social and political power. From them stemmed the Kyburg, Regensberger and Rappenswiler families who were prominent landowners in eleventh, twelfth and thirteenth century Switzerland. Through marriage and extensive possessions, a close network of relationships emerged within this high-ranking group of noble families. This cemented the kingdom together, and the successors of Pippin, the Carolingians, assumed all the power and perquisites of royalty.

Charles the Great, the most notable of the Carolingians, was crowned in Rome in 800. His father, Pippin III, had been anointed and crowned by the Pope in 754, thus bringing the temporal and spiritual heads of western Europe together in an alliance that reinforced the powers and inviolability of each. Though much has been attributed to Charles the Great which is probably legendary, he is credited with completing the integration of eastern (Alemannian) Switzerland and western (Burgundian) Switzerland. He ruled over all of France, most of Catalonia, Navarre, Aragon, Flanders, Holland, Frisia, Germany, Switzerland, Austria, Hungary, Bohemia, much of the Balkans, and all of Italy. Only a few documents that pertain to his reign have been found in Switzerland.

By gaining control over the Alpine passes he extended his rule into northern Italy and Raetia. Supported by the Church, the bishops, the heads of the cloisters and the aristocracy of nobles he apparently ruled the country with a strength that none of his predecessors could equal. The local heads of government in Raetia, responsible to the monarch, were known as counts. A number of them had extensive possessions and properties in different parts of the realm. This included Burckhardt of Swabia— a "duke"—and the heads of the Lenzburger family of whom we shall hear more in the eleventh, twelfth and thirteenth centuries.

Although we know with certainty all too little about Charles the Great, still less is known about his son and successor, Louis I (the Pious). When Louis died in 840, violent disputes broke out among his three sons and his nephews. Their quarrels continued until 870. The first accord was reached in 843 when a division of the kingdom was formalized by the Treaty of Verdun and the boundaries were defined. Charles II (the Bald) received the western portion which included Neustria, Aquitania, and part of Burgundy. Ludwig (the German) received the north-easterly or Alemannian portion of Switzerland along with Saxony, Austrasia, Bavaria and western Austria. A middle strip that extended from the North Sea to the Mediterranean, inclusive of much of Burgundy, Lombardy, and the Italian peninsula went to the eldest son, Lothar. It became known as Lotharingia and included western and southern Switzerland as well as south Raetia (see Diagram 3 and Map 2).

Ludwig the German died in 876 and was s succeeded by his son, Charles the Fat (†888)—a man who, plagued by illness and lack of vigor, was at the mercy of his counsellors. These, the nobles of the realm, though divided by their personal ambitions, managed to hold the kingdom together and to extend the sovereignty of the monarch over the east and west Franks. This was no small achievement for it was a time when the Hungarians from the east and the Saracens from the south were initiating their murderous invasions. Likewise, the Danes from the northwest penetrated deeply into France and Slavonic tribes invaded Saxony in expeditions that plundered and ravaged the countryside. The Hungarians robbed and burned many towns in the east, including Reichenau and St. Gallen. Not until 933 when Heinrich I was victorious over the marauders and 955, when Otto the Great decisively defeated them in battle, did this terrible scourge come to an end. It was even later (in 972–980) before the Saracens, who had gained control of the western passes, were driven from the Rhone valley. Prior to this (by 940–50) they had reached western Raetia and ravaged the towns from Chur to St. Gallen.

FRANCE AND THE NEWER KINGDOM OF BURGUNDY   Charles the Fat was the last of the Carolingians. He was displaced in 887 by a nephew, Arnulf, who ruled until 899 over a kingdom which was rapidly disintegrating. In the far west, France began to emerge as a kingdom separate and distinct from the Holy Roman Empire (*Romisches Reich*). From Louis II (877–79) on down through Louis V (986–987), Hugh Capet (987–996) and the Capetians we come to Charles IV (1322–28), the last of the Capetians. The Carolingians and the kings of France are listed genealogically in the Appendixes as Diagrams 3 and 4, which carry us to 1483.

The disintegration of the kingdom under Arnulf and Louis the Child was also marked by the restoration of the kingdom of Burgundy, sometimes known as the Second Kingdom of Burgundy. This came about when Boso, Count of Vienne, in 879 declared himself king of Provence and Lower Burgundy. A few years later, Rudolf I (888–912) son of the Guelph, Konrad,[25] declared himself king of Upper Burgundy including all of western Switzerland. The two Burgundies became united in 937 under Konrad I, king of Upper Burgundy, whose sister, Adelaide, married Otto the Great. As royal marriages were contracted with political and financial considerations much to the fore, there can be little doubt that this marriage was the first step in the absorption of Burgundy into the Holy Roman Empire. Rudolf III, the son of Konrad I, died without issue in 1032 and bequeathed his lands to Konrad II, Emperor of the Reich. The kingdom of Burgundy and hence western Switzerland again became a part of the Empire (see Diagrams 2 and 5 and Map 3 in the Appendixes).

It should be understood that the name Burgundy applies to several different territories with complex interrelationships. These we shall have to unravel if we are to understand a little better some of the events of considerable significance in Swiss history. First of all, the kingdom of Burgundy, as absorbed into the Empire, extended westwards to a French Duchy of Burgundy, also known as the Franche Comté or the *Freigrafschaft*. But, to add to the complexity of things, there was also a Duchy of Burgundy founded by a brother of Boso. The chief city in this Duchy was Dijon. In 1361 King Jean II of France (1350–64) gave the Duchy to his younger son Philip the Bold († 1404) who inherited the Franche Comté in 1384. His successors in a direct line of descent ended with Charles the Bold, Duke of Burgundy, who was killed at Nancy in 1477 in the last engagement of the Burgundian War.

The disintegration of the Carolingian Kingdom and the rebirth of the Kingdom of Burgundy restored the old border between Burgundian and Alemannian Switzerland as a meaningful delineation between two peoples who were linguistically and culturally apart. To the east of the border was the Duchy of Swabia which included almost all of eastern present-day Switzerland except the Ticino and a small part of the Graubünden, mostly east and south of the River Inn.

Before we concern ourselves with Swabia, and an entirely new political order that emerged when a conquering army moved southwards from Saxony, we must digress just enough to understand the role played by those members of the nobility identified as dukes and counts. This, in turn, is inextricably related to feudalism which persisted through the Middle Ages.

Feudalism

A defensive alliance in 1291 between the peoples dwelling in the valleys surrounding the southerly part of Lake Lucerne is officially accepted as the beginning of the Swiss Confederation. The alliance was formally documented about two weeks after the death of Rudolf I of the House of Habsburg, the elected head of the Holy Roman Empire since 1273. Prior to his accession there had been a long period—the Great Interregnum—during which the Empire was without a king or kaiser.[26] It was a time of turmoil and lawlessness. The strong preyed upon the weak, and pillage, robbery, and acts of violence were common. In the absence of a central authority with power and determination to protect its people against the illegal seizure of their land and possessions and the commitment of other criminal deeds, the small landowners and the freemen turned to the great landowners and the ecclesiastical foundations for solutions to their problem.

In fact, the solutions were well known. They were applied in late Roman times and lived on during succeeding centuries. When government failed to protect its people against marauders, when the public responsibilities of officialdom fell into private hands, when the kings were weak and almost devoid of power, these were the times when the solutions were found.

In retrospect the solutions appear simple, obvious and innocent. In reality they were accompanied by vast social, political and juridical changes that persisted for centuries. Freemen who were landless offered their services to a powerful neighbour in return for shelter, support and protection. Known to the Romans as a *patrocinium*, this practice survived through the Middle Ages. An adverse result was the loss of status as a freeman and reduction to that of a serf.

If he were a small landowner and poor, living in fear of losing all to his oppressors, he could surrender his land to a powerful neighbour—usually a noble, able to resist any and all marauders and, because of his political, social and military prestige, virtually immune from oppression by others. Transfer of ownership of one's land under this arrangement was originally not irrevocable. The title was transferred for a stated number of years or a lifetime. In return, the donor gained protection from the lord to whom he became a vassal. Use of the land continued to be his and he was freed of the hazards and obligations that stemmed from ownership. The arrangement was known as *precarium* tenure.

Both the *patrocinium* and *precarium* provided the means and incentive to the large landowners and nobles to build up private armies and large households of servants, retainers, craftsmen, and laborers. The vassal gave an oath of fealty to his lord. The *patrocinium* and the *precarium* were regarded as honorable relationships between the two parties, the vassal being committed to utmost loyalty to his protector and the protector's family. Under the *precarium* the vassal continued to work his land as before but he was also obliged as a first priority to render service to his lord whenever called upon. On the part of the noble lord, feudalism, with the *patrocinium* and *precarium* as the essential elements thereof, made possible the expansion of landed possessions and the creation of private armies.

The Church also resorted to both the *patrocinium* and *precarium*, thus expanding its territorial possessions and its own private reserves of manpower for military and other services. But we should note that the Church was also the recipient of quite large estates as gifts which it was not allowed to alienate. The donor, in such cases, was usually motivated by reasons of piety. When Charles Martel was in need of large sums of money to fight the Saracens with cavalry, he exploited *precarium* tenure and the vast properties of ecclesiastical foundations in an ingenious way. He seized lands of the Church under *precarium* contracts. The titles to such properties were now his. In return he made a small token payment as a symbol of ownership but derived from his newly acquired holdings a revenue great enough to care for an army. If and when the properties were returned to the Church is not clear: the sovereign (in this case the Mayor of the Palace—a *de facto* ruler) enjoyed the divine right of kings and could do no wrong.

We should note that the principal demand made upon a vassal under feudalism was military service whenever called upon by his noble lord. To minimize the threats to the State inherent in private armies, and the misuse of vassalage by the nobles,

Charles the Great[27] is alleged to have ordered that military service by the vassals of the noble lords be rendered directly to the Crown. The nobles were given the responsibility of providing soldiers when required by the king and were allowed to serve as the commanders of the contingents that they raised.

Built into feudalism were various immunities. Originally intended to benefit the Church, they became extended to the powerful families who were the great landowners. A royal immunity denied to the officers of government—the representatives of the king—the right to enter the lands of an immune proprietor to exercise any public function such as the collection of taxes in money or the equivalent, or the seizure of vassals of the noble lord for public service. Under the terms of immunity, the proprietor became, in effect, the representative of the Crown and acted on behalf of all of his tenants or vassals, free and unfree. The services to be rendered and the revenues to be received might continue unchanged. However, the transactions were not made with many individuals—vassals of the proprietor—but with the proprietor himself.

Immunities extended also to the courts and the administration of justice. Private jurisdictions developed. Private courts presided over by the noble lords replaced the public courts in civil, and even in criminal, cases. Fines were locally retained and did not pass on to the central government.[28]

The Carolingians who followed Charles the Great were generally weak. The local lords were thrown more and more upon their own resources. The higher officers of the Crown, great landowners in their own right, became increasingly independent. The duties supposedly performed on behalf of the king, were henceforth discharged for the private benefit of the great landowners as if the properties and persons under their jurisdiction were their private property. The higher nobles and the rich and powerful thus became independent of any royal authority when the kings were too weak to assert their sovereign rights. The overlords became virtual petty kings to whom the helpless freemen and small landowners came for protection when the central government was too impotent to help. The *patrocinium* and the *precarium* defined the obligations assumed by the vassal and his overlord in their respective capacities as a loyal bondman and a protective bondholder.

We should note several features of feudalism which are essential to an understanding of what it was all about: (a) Fiefs took a variety of forms. A very common fief was land, but it could also be an office (rewarding as a source of income or power), the revenue derived from specified tolls and customs duties, ownership of a mill or a craft, in general any kind of revenue-yielding property with political and social values sometimes also inherent in the fief. (b) The recipient of the fief could be at various levels of economic and political power, from the Church, the highest officers of the Crown and the nobility, down to the defenseless freeman and the small landowner. (c) Conversely, the donor of the fief could be the emperor, a king, a highly placed noble, the Church, and on down to an owner of modest landed possessions or a petty noble. (d) In the culmination of feudalism, *precarium* tenure lost its temporary character and the heir of a vassal acquired the fief and assumed the vassal obligations of his father. If the heir was a minor, the fief reverted to the lord who henceforth enjoyed the revenues that the heir would have received had he been of age. (e) Since the holder of the fief was the lord and master, judge and jury, outright expropriation of the property of the small landowner was frequently practiced. The limited duration of ownership under *precarium* tenure could be conveniently forgotten if the king were weak and all intervening vassals from the bottom to the top were as acquisitive as the fiefholder of the vassal who was wronged. (f) Multiple fiefs were common. The Count of Champagne, a peer of France with vast landholdings, held some of his lands as a fief from the emperor, some from the Duke of Burgundy, and some from two archbishops. Four bishops and one abbot also gave him land under *precarium* tenure. The great lay landowners were frequently feudal tenants of the Church. (g) The obligations of loyalty, protection and service were mutual and bound together all ranks of society from the highest to the lowest. (h) The variations found in feudal relationships between a vassal and his lord were very numerous, so much so that we cannot speak of a single feudal system. In the vast network of feudal relationships that enveloped Europe during the height of feudalism a great diversity prevailed.

Feudalism did not pass away until an enduring and effective kingship emerged. The private courts of justice, the private armies, and the private control of finance and administration gradually disappeared. The elements of feudal law, especially in respect to land tenure and transfer of ownership became the elements of public law. The private armies were replaced by military systems operated by government. The collection and administration of moneys required by the Crown became centralized under responsible public officials. Systems of government developed and professional classes emerged. By the 14th century, laws were becoming well codified, and systemization and conformity to the rules required under a stable and enduring kingship or statehood had come about. Feudalism had come to an end.

The Nobility

Dukes, counts and the like are not a part of the administrative, political, social or military structure of modern Switzerland. But this was not always so. The noble titles of duke (*dux*) and count (*comes*) which originated with the Romans at the time of Hadrian (A.D. 117–38), were adopted by the Burgundians and Alemannians although the functions associated with the titles varied greatly. In Hadrian's day the dukes were military commanders and the counts were close companions and trusted advisors of the emperor. When the Romans withdrew from their provinces beyond the Alps, Switzerland fell under the rule of a long succession of Merovingian and Carolingian kings. A few of these monarchs, notably Clovis (481–511) and Charles the Great (771–814), were outstanding in military prowess and in the skills of leadership. By conquest, marriage, and with the aid of the Church they expanded their subject territories to include virtually all of western continental Europe with the exception of the Iberian peninsula, Scandinavia, and the Slavonic border States.

The dukes continued to serve as highly placed military commanders, frequently with various civil responsibilities added to the office. The Counts of the Marches[29] functioned as military commanders. During the years of the weak Carolingians, notably after Charles the Fat, the royal power decreased. The dukes and counts gained in power, became increasingly independent and ruled the enormous territories which they held as vassals of the king as though they enjoyed ownership rights and sovereign power over the lands and people entrusted to them. Inheritance rights were exercised and for a time the title and all of its privileges came to be regarded as perquisites of the great families.

To some extent the dukes could be thought of as petty kings. Among the ancient Germans, however, the dukes were elected to command the tribal warriors in particular campaigns.[30] Military prowess was a prime requisite. Kings, however, were chosen from a royal family, believed among the credulous to be of divine descent. Some dukes, such as the Duke of Normandy, exercised for generations all the powers of a king without the royal title. Of the so-called national dukes, the Dukes of Burgundy, Alemannia, Swabia and Raetia relate most significantly to the history of Switzerland. Later (in chapter 4), the Dukes of Burgundy will receive much attention, noting incidentally that one of them, Charles the Bold (1467–77), sought unsuccessfully to have his duchy elevated to a kingdom. By the thirteenth and fourteenth centuries when the kings or kaisers of the Holy Roman Empire were beginning to be widely recognized and accepted, the ducal titles pertained to specific territories and implied no overlordship over the counts and other nobles. Vassalage, except to king or kaiser, was something of the past. All of the nobles and all freemen were, in theory, tenants of the Crown. In time the titles of nobility became merely social in significance and had no political or military connotations.

As for the counts, we learn that Hadrian's successors assigned to these erstwhile companions of the emperor a variety of duties: executive, judicial, administrative and military. In fact *comes* became a title conferred upon the high officers of government. Some were governors of provinces and others were high officials in the palace. Under the Merovingians, the counts continued to be royal officials of high rank. With the kingdom divided into areas called pagi (*pays, Gauen*)[31] it became common practice for a count (*Graf*) to be the administrative head of a pagus. In addition there were *Pfalzgrafen*, overseers of the counts, a sort of royal messenger or roving ambassador. The king made the appointments and retired the counts at his pleasure. As a royal servant of high rank, with important judicial and executive functions, a count might serve both as a prosecutor and judge. He executed the sentences of the court and typically retained for his personal use one-third of the fines which he imposed. A fraction of the revenues collected from property owners and other income sources were also his. He also exercised the right and royal obligation of protection over churches, orphans, widows and the helpless.

Over the years, the status of a count in the power and social structure of the State, and his responsibilities, varied greatly. He might be a person of much or little power, depending upon the strength of the king. Judicial, executive, and even military responsibilities might be his, or his responsibilities to the king or the people might be nonexistent. The title ultimately came to be of social significance only, usually possessed by the rich and landed gentry. Sometimes, and rather frequently in some countries, it could be acquired by purchase.

At first all counts were princes of the Empire (*Reichsfürsten*)—a title which was later restricted to a select group. All others were counts, but not princes of the Empire, and were similar in status to other free lords such as barons and even some dukes.

Among the larger landed proprietors, the counts, originally replaceable officials, succeeded in virtually freeing themselves from any royal control during the years of the weak kings. They managed to convert their office into an inheritable property which was passed down through the family like real property. Not until the eighth century did the word county (*Grafschaft*) begin to denote a specified geographical area. In some cases the boundaries of a county were fluid and ill-defined. In other cases the title had no territorial significance. For example, the title "count palatine" came to be conferred by the pope as an honor, with no territorial connotation and few, if any, official duties.

The history of Switzerland up to the nineteenth century reveals the existence of many counts. Usually they were the heads of families rich in territorial possessions and a title that passed on to their successors. Among the heads of these many noble families, the Counts of Habsburg, Kyburg, Lenzburg, Savoy, Zähringen, Rapperswil, and Toggenburg may be mentioned, for we shall hear much more of them in the pages that follow. The Habsburgs outlived all of the others and from this family came a long line of kings, kaisers and emperors. In 1416 the ruling Count of Savoy, Amadeus VIII, saw his territory raised to a duchy. Duke Victor Amadeus II (1675–1730), by conquest, became King of Sicily in 1713 and, by an exchange of titles, King of Sardinia in 1720.

Swabia and Raetia

To the east of Burgundian Switzerland lay the lands of the Alemannians and Raetians. While the Merovingian and Carolingian kings were strong enough to hold their kingdom together and to force a recognition of their kingship upon the dukes, lesser nobles, and any dissident and rebellious elements among the "great," the border between Burgundy and Alemannian Switzerland had little significance. But in the long years of royal weakness and impotence, the border of Burgundian Switzerland, though somewhat diffuse, had real meaning. To the east, a long wedge of Alemannian territory—the Duchy of Swabia—separated Burgundian Switzerland from Raetia. At the Burgundian border there was little hostility between the two peoples. The influence of the Church, favored by the kings of upper Burgundy, was strong to the west. The pagan Alemannians, who in time accepted Christianity, were tolerant of their Christian neighbors across the border.

Ancient Raetia comprised Graubünden of the present day, eastern Switzerland south of Lake Constance, most of the Tirol, and the Valtellina in northern Lombardy. The Raetians were fiercely independent people. Apart from predatory expeditions beyond their borders, cattle breeding and timber cutting were their principal occupations. Their lands were mountainous. Agriculture was restricted to the rich, fertile valleys where grain and excellent wine were produced.

In 15 B.C. the Raetians were subdued by Tiberius and Drusus. In the first century

A.D. Raetia was expanded by the addition of Vindelica to the north. Under Diocletian, the enlarged province was divided into Raetia prima, with Chur as its capital, and Raetia secunda of which Augsburg (Augusta Vindelicorum) was the capital.

We are concerned only with Raetia prima which became extensively Romanized and retained a persistent residue of Roman cultural and linguistic qualities. With the decline of the Roman authority and the rise of the Merovingians and East Goths in the fifth and sixth centuries, the governing power in the northerly part of Raetia prima passed over to the Duchy of Alemannia.

Around 600, the government of Alemannia came under a duke, Leudefred. He was more independent of the royal authority than were the Frankish dukes. As the head of the leading Alemannian family, Leudefred received the title of Duke as an honor from the Frankish king. In Raetia prima the ruling family was that of the Victorides, who headed the civil administration and the Bishopric of Chur until the eighth century when the family died out.

From the sixth to the ninth centuries the Frankish kings exerted every effort to bind Alemannia (Swabia) more closely to the rest of the kingdom. Raetia, also, was a prize worth taking. Chur commanded the easterly access routes to Italy and, for centuries to come, Italy was the scene of constant struggles for power. To the heads of the Holy Roman Empire, usually German, Italy was as much a part of the imperial possessions as Burgundy, Raetia, Swabia, and the rest of the empire.

In the tenth century a new power center appeared in the north. (To facilitate an understanding of the complicated interrelationships of royalty and of the territories involved during the tenth and eleventh centuries, refer to Diagrams 2, 3 and 5 in the Appendix.) In a determined effort to emulate Charles the Great and to restore the kingdom over which he had ruled, the German kings from the House of Ottonen and Salier drove southwards to the Alpine passes. To appreciate the sequence of events, we should recall that Rudolf I of Upper Burgundy (888–912) had succeeded in bringing Basel and the slopes of the Basel Jura under his rule. His successor, Rudolf II (912–37), sought to extend his Burgundian kingdom into Swabia but in 919 was forced to curb his ambitious plan when defeated by Burkard I, the ruling Duke of Swabia, in a battle near Winterthur. In the same year, the Emperor of the Reich, Konrad I, died. On his deathbed he persuaded the Franconian nobles to elect Heinrich, Duke of Saxony, as his successor. This was an excellent choice. Heinrich I, known in English as Henry the Fowler, overcame the opposition of the Dukes of Swabia and Bavaria. Later, the Duke of Lorraine (Lotharingia) sought his protection and recognized his overlordship. Under Heinrich I, life on solitary farms and in small villages became much more secure. In the northern territories, particularly in Saxony and Thuringia, the towns were walled and fortresses were built. The marauding Slavonic tribes were defeated and peace was negotiated in 933, following two successes in battle. To the south, marauding tribes from Hungary pillaged and plundered the lands to their west for half a century. In 909 they had driven deeply into northern Swabia, a few years later into Basel, and, following Burkhard's death in 926, they pressed through Bavaria and besieged Constance.

The cloisters at Reichenau and St. Gallen were plundered and burned. In 955 they were defeated at Augsburg by Otto the Great. A lasting peace was negotiated. The Hungarians retreated and settled down peacefully along the Danube.

In the early years of Heinrich I's rule as Emperor of the *Reich*, Burkhard I of Swabia and Rudolf II of Upper Burgundy joined forces in a common Italian policy of conquest, strengthened, if not dictated, by Rudolf II's marriage in 924 to Berta the daughter of Burkhard, and an urgent request from the nobles of upper Italy to assist in their campaign against Berengar, an unwanted ruler who had driven in from the south. Burkhard fell in battle near Novara in 926. Hermann, the Duke of Franconia, was then elevated to Duke of Swabia in a sort of coup which, consisting in his marriage to Burkhard's widow, legitimized his rule in Swabia. Rudolf II retired to Upper Burgundy. Heinrich I recognized Rudolf's rule over Basel and the Aargau in return for Rudolf's acceptance of Heinrich as his overlord. Heinrich I died in 936 and Rudolf II in 937. The Burgundian king who, by an arrangement with Hugo, the ruling Duke of Upper Italy, had received Provence as part of his possessions, was succeeded by his teen-age son Konrad.

Heinrich was succeeded as emperor by Otto I (Otto the Great, 936–73) of the House of Ottonen in Saxony. To thwart the ambitions of Hugo who, by carefully planned interfamily marriages, sought to unite Upper Italy and Burgundy, Otto took the young Burgundian king, Konrad I of Burgundy, under his imperial protection. Konrad ruled for many years (937–93). The emperor gave him a free hand in Burgundy but forbade any aggressive campaigns in Upper Italy or France. It is significant in the high politics of the day that Otto, during a great Italian campaign of his own, married Adelheid (Adelaide), a daughter of Rudolf II and the Swabian princess Berta. Hence, Adelheid was a sister of Konrad. Use of the western Alpine passes between Burgundy and Italy was made freely available to Otto by the Burgundian king.

Otto the Great was succeeded by Otto II (973–83) who, as a son of Adelheid, was also a grandson of Rudolf II of Burgundy and Berta of Swabia. It is clear that Burgundy and Swabia, by the peaceful marital route, were being drawn into the empire. Otto II was succeeded on the imperial throne by Otto III (983–1002) who, in turn, was followed by Heinrich II (1002–24), Duke of Bavaria. The King of Burgundy was then the weak, indifferent and lazy Rudolf III (993–1032) whom Heinrich II kept under his close supervision. In 1016 the emperor met, but overcame, stubborn resistance to his rule among the nobles of upper Italy. At the same time the Burgundian nobles rose in rebellion against their weakling king Rudolf III. The emperor came to the rescue and ended the rebellion, but at a price: Rudolf III was required to recognize formally the overlordship of the emperor.

Heinrich II was succeeded by Konrad II (1024–39), son of the Count of Speyer. Rudolf III, dying without issue in 1032, bequeathed his kingdom to the emperor, Konrad II, his nephew by marriage. The Burgundian nobles had other plans for the Burgundian kingdom but were defeated in battle in the winter of 1032–33. On 2 February 1033 Konrad II was crowned King of Burgundy. Rudolf III had given the comital rights and rule in the Valais in 999 to the Bishop of Sitten, and in 1011 those of Vaud to the Bishop of Lausanne. In the absence of a single power base in western Switzerland, and because of constant struggles between the bishops and the nobles, the German kings were able to profit from this endless dissension and gained a virtually unchallenged control over the western Alpine passes.

The Evolution of States and Statehood

To discuss the origin of States and statehood with a semblance of clarity obliges us to suffer through one or two definitions. Many of us would accept, perhaps with a few reservations, the concept that the word "State" connotes an independent community which exercises dominion over a determinate territory. "In its fullest form its attributes, as expressed in international law, are: (a) possession of sovereign power to pledge the community in its relations with other similarly sovereign communities; and (b) independence of all external control" (25). This is such a restrictive definition that none of the "states" of the USA, none of the fringe iron-curtain countries under USSR control, and none of the Swiss cantons could be truly regarded as a State. There are other less restrictive definitions, including the all-embracing one, also mentioned by Barclay: "the word state expresses the abstract idea of government in general, or the governing authority as opposed to the governed."

In early mediaeval times, only the second of these definitions would have any relevance; the first would be inapplicable. The earliest concept of the State derived from the general military responsibility of men to their governing authority. Among the Germanic people the authority was vested in the Teutonic tribal assembly. The paramount chief or head of the tribe was usually a mighty warrior. If possessed of the skills of leadership and hallowed by an aura of divinity, he may be thought of as a king with a title and perquisites of office that could sometimes be inherited by his descendants or family members. As early as the first century A.D., the tribes with which we are most concerned were virtually nomadic. For many years the territories occupied by the Burgundians, Alemannians, Langobardians, Sequani, Lepontii and others were ill-defined. The areas of settlement were temporarily occupied; fixed, determinate boundaries were nonexistent. This fluidity continued for several centuries during which the tribes were on the move, generally headed southwards into eastern Helvetia and Raetia (Alemannians) or south-eastern "France" and western Helvetia (Burgundians) or Italy (Langobardians).

The State, for we must use the term, would have to be identified with people, not with the territory which they temporarily occupied. It was a person State (*Personenverbandsstaat*), not an institutionally organized State within a prescribed land area (*Flächenstaat*). The person State, rarely democratic in structure, consisted of several classes: the king or tribal chieftain, a group of "noble" families, the common free—the broad masses of the army in Frankish times (*Landes*)—the royal free (*Königsfreien*), the free peasants (*Freien Bauern*),[32] the half-free (*Lites*), and the unfree or serfs (*Hörigen*).[33] The totality of the people from the king downwards to the serfs constituted the State.[34] It was structured for military purposes—defense and aggression. In time, it evolved into the feudal State with territorial boundaries that progressively became more and more sharply defined. By the late Middle Ages, the territorial State had evolved; the person State, consisting of the princely power (the king) and his body of followers, had disappeared.

Freedom, though not a factor in the development of the early Germanic States, was at the very heart of State formation in thirteenth-century Switzerland, as we shall see later.

When the Romans expanded their empire northwards and imposed their rule upon most of western Europe, they also introduced a territorial organization and a system of administration which certainly did not confer statehood upon any of the subject areas. Almost the whole of present-day Switzerland fell within the two provinces of Belgica and Raetia (first century A.D.), or Germania Superior and Raetia (second and third centuries), or finally, Maxima Sequanorum and Raetia prima (fourth and fifth centuries). From the second to the fifth centuries Geneva, the Rhone valley (Valais), and the southern Ticino were parts of three other provinces. Rivers, lakes, mountain chains and sometimes a line of milestones marked the provincial boundaries. Whether the southern border of Raetia included the Valtellina and the Levinental has not been decided to everyone's satisfaction (**239**, p. 68). Under Marcus Aurelius (circa 170), Raetia was governed by a legate of senatorial rank, although the administrative head of a province was commonly of lower rank, such as a procurator. In the times of Diocletian and Constantine the administration was tightened somewhat by further subdivisions, each under the rule of a Roman official. The whole of the far reaches of the Empire was divided into four praefectures. Each of these constituted several dioceses, and each diocese was further divided into a number of provinces. The governors of Liguria and Viennensis were of consular rank. The other provincial governors, lower in rank, bore the title *Praeses*.

May we assume that each province was a State? I think not. In the five centuries of occupation by Rome, the native people who inhabited a given province were without a political organization of their own. Independence and sovereign power at the provincial level were unknown. Administrative and military policies originated at the heart of the empire. Provincial governors represented the emperor.

By the eighth century, long after the Romans had withdrawn, regional designations such as *Ducatus* (Duchy), *Comitatus* (County), *Pagus* (*Gau*), *Centenar* (*Hundertschaft*), and *Situs* become common. These designations do not permit simple and uniform definitions, partly because they sometimes had different meanings in different parts of the country. A *Ducatus* was headed by a duke and a *Comitatus* by a count (*Graf*). In general, these two regional names pertained to the areas within which the followers or vassals of the duke or count lived; the territorial boundaries were not sharply defined. A *Centenar*, *Pagus*, or *Situs* was a stretch of land with boundaries of a sort but conceived of without any reference to the inhabitants. They were administratively convenient districts which varied greatly in their size and type of government. In Alemannian territory south of the Rhine there were two great *Pagi*—Pagus Thurgaugensis and Pagus Aargaugensis. The latter, first mentioned in the eighth century, reached as far as the Lake of Thun and represents the farthest westward advance of the Alemannians. Alsace was a *Ducatus*, once known as Baselgau or Augstgau. All of Burgundy between the Jura and the Alps was a *Ducatus* or *Pagus* headed by a duke. The rest of Upper Burgundy on the other side of the Jura had its own duke. He was appointed by the king and represented the Burgundian aristocracy—the great landowners of the region. Within a *Ducatus* or *Pagus* were towns, villages and, sometimes, extensive hinterlands which had agricultural uses and served as pasture land. Little can be said about the thinly populated high mountain valleys, which were not as inviting and habitable as the great middle land from Geneva to Constance and the broad river valley of the Rhone.

All of this suggests a fragmented regional organization and a social stratification that would be conducive to a total breakdown of the kingdom. What were the bonds that held the many bits and pieces together? In part it was feudalism. Whether the king was strong or weak he was at the center of things. In some respects all were his tenants. Beyond this, it is clear that under the system of vassalage everyone was a vassal of the king or the vassal of another vassal. This tended to bind all the subjects together in an enveloping network.

Another bond that contributed much to holding things together was interfamily marriage, especially at the upper levels. Many of the great landed families stemmed from those of royal blood. Dukes, counts and bishops were frequently blood relations of the monarch. Finally, the close alliance of the temporal and spiritual rulers served to strengthen the power of each of the parties over the subjects. It mattered little whether the subjects were noble free, middle free, the ordinary free or the unfree—the serfs and the villeins. The net of feudalism enveloped them all. Those at the bottom were the lower retainers, household servants, farm hands, and common laborers but all enjoyed the protection of someone higher in the social and economic scale. At the top there was a wealthy, powerful class of great landowners who through intermarriage, through descent from old ducal or royal families, and through alliance with the ecclesiastical powers were equally a part of feudalism— responsible for the protection of those below.

Although we may visualize a network of interrelationships that would encompass and hold together as a unit the various regions, great and small, and the people of all classes, it was still a net and not too closely knit. People of eminence came and went. Today some were in royal favor and enjoyed all the benefits of the relationship. Later, they were gone, only to be replaced by others. There was, in brief, a fluidity of class, accompanied by a fragility in the powers exercised by the nobles. At times, depending upon the strength or weakness of the monarch, the dukes and counts enjoyed almost all the fruits of sovereignty. At other times they were stripped of independence and the elements of sovereignty and were forced to recognize the supremacy of a powerful king.

One can hardly perceive in all of this, even dimly, the shape and substance of a State. "Switzerland" consisted of several large districts such as part of upper Burgundy to the west, Raetia to the east and southern Swabia between east and west. Two large *Gauen* in east central Switzerland were also conspicuous regional divisions: the precursors of the present-day cantons of Thurgau and Aargau. None of these territorial divisions can be thought of as a State, in the more rigorous sense of the word. The boundaries were fluid and the administrators (sometimes the ruler) of the various regions—a duke, a count, a ministerial (see note 33), a bishop or a petty noble—were neither independent nor sovereign. Government at the highest levels was the responsibility of kings who sometimes ruled as virtually independent monarchs, but just as frequently recognized another king or the king-emperor as their overlord.

Inner Switzerland—Lucerne and the valleys that descended to the shores of Lake Lucerne—had a remarkable history of their own. Before 685 A.D., Lucerne was an insignificant place, located in a great swamp. A lighthouse (*Lucerna*) stood where St. Niklaus chapel now stands. Öchsli (**272**), quoting Burckhardt (**75**, p. 96), who in turn, refers us to the ancient chronicle by Etterlin (**121**), claims that the lands now known as Inner Switzerland were virtually uninhabited swamps, forests, and heavily eroded mountain slopes—in short, nothing but wilderness as may be implied by the name *Waldstätte*, given to this region by the Germans, who gradually settled there.

The earliest inhabitants appear to have been Raetians. The Romans and their Alemannian successors preferred the comforts and good soil of the plains. Why subject oneself to the hard life and cruel weather of the high Alpine meadows?

The persistently repeated claim that the population of Schwyz was of Scandinavian origin cannot be satisfactorily authenticated. One of many legends with which the early history of Switzerland abounds, it derives from Nordic folk tales which are more fictional than factual.

Archaeological evidence from *Innerschweiz* suggests that the scattered finds of Roman origin pertain to a relatively small number of estates which lacked the luxurious appointments of many of the villas in the plains and lowlands. According to Stähelin, (**337**, pp. 391, 414, 417), the ruins of a Roman villa near Alpnach is the earliest evidence of the Roman penetration of *Innerschweiz*. Uri, first mentioned in 732 [according to Oechsli (**272**, p. 27)] or 853, [according to Burckhardt (**75**, p. 98)] was then "a sort of Alemannian Siberia" to which the dissidents of those early days were exiled (**272**, p. 27). Schwyz, first mentioned by this name in a document of 24 August 972 (**272**, p. 61) was probably about as uninviting as Uri. By 1150 most of the present places existed in *Innerschweiz*, but they were little more than individual estates. Not until the 13th century can one speak of a community of people in the Waldstätte—people who treasured their freedom and, in unison, strove for an actual independence from any "foreign" overlords. From the rather scanty conclusions about population that may be sifted from the confusing mixture of sagas, legends, folktales and fiction with which the early chronicles abound, and from the earliest documents of church history, and a few other acceptable records, it is hard to believe that the valley people were able to send as many as 600 men to Faenza in 1240 to give armed support to the emperor (see note 28, page 51). Even in 1315 for the crucial battle of Morgarten, it appears that *Innerschweiz* could bring together only 1300 to 1500 men (**100**, I, p. 393; **272**, p. 230).

One may well inquire about the motivations of the Germans who, in the late Middle Ages, settled in this wilderness, abandoning the less arduous environment of the plains. As Burckhardt pointed out (75, p. 109), it was only by emigration that the common people might be able to retain their personal freedoms.[35] Otherwise, plagued by banditry, violence, and related troubles, they were pressured into seeking the protection of a cloister or a powerful landowner. This carried with it their loss of status as a free people and sometimes a loss of property if not eventually returned according to the rules of *precarium* tenure. Taxes, required duties by the courts, and inescapable military service for their lord and master might well have been the final clincher. The inhabitants of these valleys were a pastoral people fiercely determined to protect their freedom while, somewhat anomalously, recognizing the overlordship of the emperor. But, as we shall see later, by the end of the thirteenth century, they refused to recognize the authority in the courts or elsewhere of any representatives of the monarch who were not from among their own valley people. For present purposes it is unnecessary to discuss further the early history of Uri, Schwyz and Unterwalden, to examine the almost endless boundary disputes between Schwyz and Einsiedeln, or to review the problems that beset these people in their relationship to the great dynastic families and ecclesiastical foundations. It is sufficient to point out that in each of these districts in *Innerschweiz*, the inhabitants tenaciously clung to their basic freedoms. They behaved in many respects as though they enjoyed sovereign rights, and were independent of all foreign powers. The fact is that their valleys and mountain slopes and meadows were the property of others. They were not totally independent as a State is independent, nor were they relieved of responsibilities to the emperor or to the families or ecclesiastical foundations that held these lands as fiefholds or in fee simple. In brief, these ancient valleys in the heart of Switzerland had not achieved statehood by the end of the thirteenth century, though in a *de facto* sort of way, as we shall see later, their inhabitants governed themselves as though statehood was already theirs.

Princely States such as those in Germany and in Italy did not exist in Switzerland.[36] Scattered throughout the country and extending into Germany were the estates of the great landowners. A number of dynastic families, headed by dukes or counts such as the Habsburgs, the Kyburgs, the Lenzburgs, and the Zähringers had vast properties, distributed somewhat chaotically. The House of Savoy had dominion over most of western Switzerland except Geneva. By marriage, by purchase, by conquest, by the deliberate enclosure of open lands extending into the mountain valleys, and by still other means the great families sought to expand their territorial possessions or to consolidate them into a few enlarged holdings. The House of Savoy sought with much determination, but without success, to possess Geneva. Expansion to the east was never vigorously pursued by Savoy. The Aare from its source in the Grimsel-Furka area to Biel in the northwest and a vaguely defined line from Biel to Basel represented for centuries to come the "border" between east and west. In the twelfth and thirteenth centuries it was about as far east as the Savoyard and Burgundian influence and power were dominant.

In the twelfth and thirteenth centuries the building of cities and towns by the Dukes of Zähringen had important consequences. For example, Bern and Freiburg, founded in the 1190s, became centers for administration, and for commerce. These cities and others founded by Zähringen were admirably situated from a military point of view: they enjoyed remarkable capabilities for defense. In the course of time, many of the cities and towns extended their rule far into the countryside but many centuries were to elapse before true statehood was attained. In 1648, the Treaty of Westphalia severed the tie that bound Switzerland to the empire. She emerged at last as a fully independent and sovereign Power. And what became of the territories, large or small, under the rule of such cities as Lausanne, Freiburg, Bern, Solothurn, Lucerne, Geneva, and the cantons of Aargau, Thurgau, etc.? Their boundaries underwent numerous changes as annexations, consolidations and administrative reshuffling proceeded with the passage of time. The *Orte* (places or districts) became more familiarly known as cantons. Though cloaked with the mantle of sovereignty, according to the Federal Constitution, many of their one-time sovereign rights have now been transferred to the Federal Government. For 300 years and more Switzerland has possessed all the attributes of a State. The cantons, however, like the so-called States of the USA and the provinces of Canada, in the interests of federal solidarity and unity, have granted to their central government many of the sovereign rights that they once enjoyed. Notably since 1848, the Swiss Federation has enjoyed international recognition as a fully independent and sovereign State.

Industry and Commerce

Much of our knowledge of industry and commerce in early "Switzerland" pertains to the first few centuries of the Christian era—the days of the Roman occupation (122). In the second century B.C., soldiers of the Raetia contingent and of a few units stationed elsewhere, were supplied from Italy with plates, cups, other utensils, clothing, and military equipment. In general, the imports were for the troops and not for the local population. Until the Roman conquest in 15 B.C., imports were not abundant. During the first century A.D., products from southern Gaul, especially ceramics such as jugs, bowls, cups, and other vessels were imported in quantity. In the second century much came in from middle Gaul and Alsace. Very few items of wood, leather, and cloth, whether of domestic or foreign origin have been found: unlike ceramic ware and metals they were biodegradable and suffered destruction by the fungi and fauna of the soil. In Vindonissa (Windisch) a few wood and leather remains of soldiers' equipment have been found. It is well known, however, that textiles and leather goods were imported in quantity, supplemented by a significant domestic production of wood and leather.

The military facility at Vindonissa had pottery ovens. Indeed potteries were rather widely distributed, the best known center being at Bern (Enge), which was a substantial producer well into the third century. Domestic pottery of the fourth century is rather rare. In general, only the pottery from Gaul and Italy was of superior quality.

In the first century bronze vessels originating in Capua were imported in quantity, especially casseroles and kettles. Good bronze items also came in from Gaul. Some bronze products, simple in form, were of domestic origin. Items of iron were also important, both foreign made and domestic.

According to the records, it is evident that luxury imports during the heyday of the Roman occupation were dominant: wine, oil, costly vessels, dried fruits and vegetables, fish sauces, oysters, spices, smoked foods, medicinal herbs, ointments, perfumes, and pigments. Tableware, vessels and other items of colored glass, textiles leather goods, brooches, bracelets, arm bands and other items beautifully fashioned from silver and gold were among the goods imported by the conquerors. Most of it came in from Italy, Spain, southern France, and the Mediterranean lands (see also note 12).

Among the domestic industries, cloth was processed by fullers and dyers and leather was produced in tanneries. There were brick and tile works, bronze works, and potteries. An iron smelter existed at Delsberg. Water-powered mills came into use in late Roman times. Spinning and weaving were home industries exclusively. Craftsmen of many kinds were to be found: carpenters, blacksmiths, waggoners, locksmiths, wheelwrights, stone masons, mosaic layers, art craftsmen, tinkers, and potters.

Conspicuous also were the peasants who farmed the land, cared for the farm animals, and, in many capacities, served their masters, the Roman military commanders, and the higher offices of the civil administration.

The Public Health

Life expectancy at birth was unquestionably very low during these early centuries. It continued to be so until modern times when the diseases of pregnancy, infancy, and childhood, deaths during childbirth, and many of the infectious and viral diseases that contributed to early death of adults were almost conquered.

In the ancient world, pandemics with startlingly high death rates have been recorded. The greatest of all was in the time of Justinian. Zinsser cited several early writers who reported upon devastating outbreaks of the plague, starting in Egypt in 540 and spreading through Palestine and on through the then known world (**406**). In Byzantium the plague continued, so we are told, for four months with 5000 to 10,000 deaths per day at the height of the epidemic. Another ancient writer, cited by Zinsser, claimed that the plague in Byzantium lasted until 590 or so. From a description of the disease—the presence of buboes and death within a few days—it is evident that the epidemic was bubonic plague, but smallpox, cholera and typhus fever may also have shared in the pestilence. Centuries were to elapse before a precise meaning was attached to the word "plague" or "pest."

In time, the black rat (*Mus rattus*)—house rat or ship rat—and its fleas were recognized as the carriers of the disease. This species of rat was firmly established in Europe shortly before 1100 (**26**). Entering from Asia and North Africa in ships that plied the Mediterranean it steadily increased in numbers from 400 A.D. on, until by

1100 it had spread over the face of Europe wherever man was to be found. By 1200 it was recognized as a menace and had heavily invaded Britain by 1300.

Tschudi, in his great chronicle, mentions outbreaks of the pestilence in central Europe in 1022, 1044, 1055, 1056, 1059, 1060, 1062, 1094, 1098, 1117, 1167 and 1190. Except for the terrible epidemic of 1348 which descended upon the whole of Europe, Tschudi makes few, if any, other references to the pestilence (**370**). Furthermore, the pest or pestilence, as recorded by Tschudi, was not always the plague. In some cases there is little doubt but that the epidemic was typhus, smallpox, cholera or some other communicable disease with a high mortality rate.

A Review

Were we to review the history of Switzerland and that of western Europe into which Swiss history is merged, from the times of the Merovingians and Carolingians to the unification of rule under Emperor Konrad II, there would be much to mention. It was a period rich in events that molded the structure of western Europe for centuries to come.

LEADERSHIP   The heads of the many ancient tribes were apparently chosen principally because of their military prowess, their ability to command, and their general qualities of leadership. When the organizational structure developed by Rome became implanted upon the subject peoples of western Europe, the recognized leaders bore the designation of kings, dukes, counts, and lesser titles of nobility. As in the Roman hierarchy, the dukes were originally military commanders. The royal title of king was something special for it connoted a divine quality which was denied to all others. This did not always imply an outstanding competence in battle. Hence, the effective leader of a tribe was not always a king, but a duke, or in exceptional cases a count. For many years the titles were not associated with specifically defined geographical areas, partly because the tribal peoples were not localized; they were swept up in great movements which finally carried the Burgundian peoples to Savoy, western Switzerland, and part of southern France— the Alemannian tribes into southern Germany and eastern Switzerland, and the Langobardians into Italy.

We shall describe the kings as petty kings, for they must be distinguished from the king-emperors who, as heads of the Holy Roman Empire, were the recognized overlords of the rulers of western Europe—at least of the Germanic areas. A few of the Merovingian and Carolingian kings, and Otto the Great of the House of Ottonen and Salier were strong enough to impose their rule over much of western Europe and to receive the homage of all the lesser kings and dukes. Pippin III (741–768) was anointed by the pope, and Charles the Great (768–814) was crowned in Rome. Coronation by the pope brought together in a symbolic act the temporal and spiritual rulers of the Holy Roman Empire. Many of the king-emperors subsequent to Konrad II participated in this rite; others refrained. A few resisted the papal authority, defied the pope, and engaged in war in Italy against the papal forces.

Many of the Merovingians and Carolingians were weak. They were unable to prevent a fragmentation of the kingdom. The dukes, counts and heads of powerful families with extensive holdings of land behaved as independent rulers who tended to exercise sovereign power over their lands and the people under their protection. The central authority weakened and almost vanished during the nominal rule of Louis the Child (899–911). Hordes of invaders preyed upon the country. Dukes reappeared in positions of power in Franconia, Bavaria, Lorraine and Swabia.

These and others, with the advent of feudalism, were in positions of special military command to protect the people and the properties entrusted to them under *precarium* tenure. In return for protection, many small landowners and lesser nobles surrendered their lands and became the vassals of an overlord. Lower-class freemen likewise became the vassals or serfs of more powerful neighbours. The dukes, and so also the counts, acquired vast possessions of land, sometimes as a royal fief but, in many cases, under *precarium* tenure. Their households and the number of their subject people greatly increased, many of whom, from serfs to lesser nobles, constituted private armies and could be called upon for military service whenever required by their lord and master.

At the height of their power, the dukes were virtually independent of any royal authority, and the title, possessions and perquisites of office became inheritable. Among them there was much dissension and constant jockeying for still greater power. When the Magyar invasions were at their height in the first half of the tenth century, the dukes realized at last that a strong central authority was indispensable. On the advice of Otto the Illustrious, of Saxony, they elected Konrad, Duke of Franconia, as the German king (911–919). Konrad, on his death bed in 919, urged the dukes to elect Heinrich, Duke of Saxony, as his successor. This was done and, in time, Heinrich (Henry the Fowler) was succeeded by the equally powerful monarch, Otto the Great, again a Saxon from the House of Ottonen and Salier. In Konrad I of the Holy Roman Empire and his immediate successors we find the beginnings of the long line of kings and kaisers who ruled the German people until the end of the monarchy in 1918 (see Diagram 5). Switzerland was a part of the empire until 1648 when her total independence was formally recognized in the Treaty of Westphalia.

Western Switzerland, with its rich Burgundian inheritance, has always been linguistically and culturally related to France which gained its own identity when separated from the Carolingian Empire by the Treaty of Verdun in 843. Throughout the centuries, the multilingual and multicultural nature of Switzerland has not been a divisive and fragmenting influence. The country has seldom ceased to enjoy a remarkable unity despite its conspicuous diversity—*mirabile dictu!*

THE CHURCH   Christianity began its penetration of Switzerland in the fourth century. The role of the Church has always been multi-faceted. In its early days in Europe and on through the Middle Ages the Church was much more involved in economics and politics than in religion. The dedication of the priesthood to promoting the brotherhood of man, peace, goodwill, and simple goodness—

however this may be defined—was greatly overshadowed by material things. Church and State were married in an alliance that was never designed for the promotion of righteousness and piety. The princes of the Church frequently exercised tremendous worldly power in their capacity as great landowners and rulers of the many subject peoples in their bishoprics and other domains. The temporal rulers, notably the king-emperors, acquired a halo of divinity when anointed and crowned by the pope, and, with this, a reinforcement of their power over the minds and bodies of their subjects.

Under feudalism, the Church, through its cloisters and other institutions, acquired lands and vassals—from penniless freemen to lesser nobles—both in search of the protection that the Church could offer.

Much was bequeathed to institutions of the Church for reasons of piety. Such gifts took the form of land, money, and other kinds of property. Extensive landed possessions came to the institutions and princes of the church as outright gifts of a royal house. Other properties were held as royal fiefs. These acts of royal largesse were not without a price. The recipient used his enormous power to solidify the position of the donor in the area involved, to ensure obedience of the people and to promote the political ambitions of the royal house. Kings, dukes, counts and others of the high nobility busied themselves in founding churches, convents, cloisters and religious institutions as a means of ensuring and strengthening support by the Church. For centuries, lay investiture was widely practised and relatives or faithful friends of the heads of government were installed as bishops, abbots, priors, etc. This continued until the reform movement of the tenth and eleventh centuries finally brought an end to lay investiture.

The movement, which spread far out from the cloister of Cluny in Burgundy, was directed against secularization of the churchly institutions and their exploitation by princes and nobles in their constant struggles for power. Marriage of the priests, sale and purchase of office, and other such transgressions were inveighed against. The Church, through its alliance with the worldly powers, had lost its sense of mission and had become transmuted in its priesthood and in its functions into something remote from saving the souls of the unbelievers. The king-emperors of the time, and especially Heinrich III, lent their support to reform. Pope Leo IX (1048–54) and Gregory VII (1073–85) were strongly reform-minded. Under Pope Gregory lay investiture was forbidden by an edict of 1075. The whole reform movement within the Church was one of the very significant events of the Middle Ages.

Notes and Comments

1. Artifacts and other evidence of man's presence in "Switzerland" in Neolithic times have been found at literally hundreds of sites. By contrast, not more than twelve or thirteen sites containing items of archaeological importance and dating from the beginnings of the last Ice Age or earlier had been located by 1957 [ref. **12** (Maps 1 and 2)].

2. Wildkirchli may indeed have been the oldest prehistoric human settlement in Switzerland. But see note 5, below.

3. In the Swiss caves, only one skeleton, almost complete, has been found. It approaches three meters

in length and, since 1910, has been housed in a museum in Kirchhoferhaus, Museumstrasse 27, St. Gallen.

4. The principal remains from the early Ice Age in the Basler Jura are those of the mammoth, rhinoceros, ox, deer, ibex, and chamois: bear remains are rare.

5. A human incisor tooth found at St. Brais (canton Jura), believed to be 40,000 years old, may have belonged to the "first Swiss." The tooth goes back to Neandertal times and possibly constitutes the first unequivocal evidence of man's presence in prehistoric Switzerland. St. Brais is at an elevation of 975 meters above sea level, in a part of the Jura which remained ice-free during the last Ice Age. Bones of the great cave bear and of other animals were also uncovered in the diggings (295).

6. 2550–2500 B.C. is the date assigned by Suess and Strahm (354) to a lake dwelling in Auvernier, known as Auvernier I. Immediately beneath Auvernier I are the posts or pilings of an earlier, undated settlement known as Auvernier II. One may not conclude that throughout Switzerland the construction of lake or lakeshore dwellings proceeded contemporaneously. A thorough study of a site near Thayngen (Schauffhausen canton) fixes the date of the settlement at about 3700 B.C. (132).

7. The Celts may be described as an ancient people originally from the Baltic, Scandinavian and North Sea areas who migrated into central and western Europe. In general, all of the people with very fair hair, light blue-grey eyes, and who were long-headed, thin-faced, and tall in stature were described by the ancient writers as Celts. The Greeks called them *keltoi.* Modern writers usually referred to them as Teutons (generic for Germans). A second group had round heads, broad faces, hazel-grey eyes, and chestnut hair. They were of medium height. They fell midway between the Teutonic Celts and the dark-skinned, dark-haired Mediterranean people. The Celts of ancient Switzerland, north of the Alps, are generally considered to have been of the Teutonic type. They were the original Helvetians, coming into "Switzerland" from south "Germany" in the fifth and sixth centuries B.C. This Helvetia, at the time of Caesar, had some 400 villages and 12 cities. The Celtic languages may have been confused by philologists with Gaelic—the languages of the ancient people of western Scotland and Ireland (308).

8. First described as "ager Helvetiorum," later Helvetia.

9. Augst (Colonia Augusta Rauricum) was developed by the Romans into a military encampment. An impressive excavation project has revealed the magnificent remains of a great amphitheater, temples, and baths. A small but excellent museum has been built beside the remains of the ancient city to house many of the beautiful pieces of sculpture, mosaics, silver plate, drinking vessels, intricate golden jewelry, etc. recovered during the excavations. For instance, discovered in the late 1970s, at a depth of 11.5 meters, was a beautiful necklace of 24 carat gold, about 34 centimeters in length. A samovar, a bronze lantern, ceramic articles, and human bones have also been unearthed at about the same depth. The remains at Avenches are more extensive but were despoiled during many centuries until government intervened to protect the site.

10. Avenches (Aventicum) became the provincial capital, and military base. The name given to it by Vespasian in 73–74 A.D. was Colonia pia Flavia . . . Foederata, soon shortened to Colonia Helvetiorum. It was richly provided with a great amphitheater (112 × 98 meters), an arena, public halls, many monuments, and a city wall 6 kilometers long with some 80 towers. At the height of its greatness its population approximated 50,000.

11. For example: Avenches (Aventicum), Basel (Basilia), Chur (Curia), Lausanne (Leusonna), Moudon (Minnodunum), Orbe (Urba), Sion (Sedunum), Solothurn (Salodurum), Vevey (Viviscus), Windisch (Vindonissa), Yverdon (Eburodunum) and Zürich (Turicum). Andolfingen, Rudolfingen and Waltalingen are *Stammvater* designations of pre-Roman villages and refer to the early heads of separate family lines. Rüschlikon (Ruocksilinghofa), Bendlikon (Pankilinghofa), Wollishofen (estate of Wolo) and Dubendorf (Dubilo's village) remind us of one-time manorial estates in Roman or pre-Roman times.

12. Cloth, raw wool, vegetable oils, oysters, wine, Oriental spices, Asiatic silk, jewelry and works of art passed over the communication routes to Switzerland. Salt was also an essential, even an indispensable, import item. The Helvetians, in turn, exported to the land of the conquerors, their small milk-rich cows, cheese, honey, beeswax, wood, cereal grains and fish. It is improbable that this trade was significant prior to 15 B.C.

13. The Tigurines, a Celtic tribe to the south of Lake Neuchâtel and around Aventicum, defeated a military force under the Roman Consul, Lucius Cassius Longinus, in 107 B.C. (376, p. 51).

14. Among 472 Roman coins found at Nyon, 22 are coins of the Republic, minted in Rome from 205–195 B.C. to 45 B.C. Twelve of these date from 205–195 to 100–95 B.C. (**228**). Nyon (Colonia Julia Equestris) did not become a Roman military post until 45–44 B.C. We could conclude that Nyon experienced a Roman penetration, civil or military, long before its conversion into a military base or, alternatively, that old coins remained in circulation for a surprisingly long time.

15. The date of founding is not precisely known. Meyer (**239**, p. 57) gives 50–45 B.C. as the date, but others have proposed several different dates between 58 and 44 B.C. (**281**).

16. In 1975, the remains of a Roman temple were discovered at Martigny (Valais canton). Known as Octodurum by the Romans, the place became an important crossroad between Rome and the northern provinces occupied by the Roman armies. The approach to the Saint Bernard pass was hazardous because of winter avalanches, hurricanes and sub-zero temperatures. The large quantities of gold and silver coins, jewels and sculptures found in the temple excavations suggest that officers and administrators returning to Rome may have offered these precious things as gifts to the gods to insure a safe passage over the Alps. Leonard Giannada established a Foundation in memory of his brother Pierre, who died in a most tragic accident. The Foundation has preserved the temple remains by building over it a remarkable museum with the temple and a statue of Jupiter, found nearby, as the centerpiece. The museum, with two levels of galleries for exhibitions, also hosts concerts by soloists and orchestras of international renown. The great vaulted interior is noted for the acoustical purity that it provides for such musical events.

17. The Alemannians, as a union of several west German tribes, came into being at the end of the second century A.D. They enjoyed a dubious reputation derived from their savagery in combat and their tribal restlessness—expressed in repeated incursions into neighbouring lands (especially Gaul, Romanized Helvetia, and northern Italy) which they plundered and ravaged. In 277 or so, Dekumatenland (corresponding to present-day Baden and Württemberg) became their home base until Clovis, two centuries later, forced them into Swabia.

18. In Baden, Switzerland, eight Alemannian sepulchers were found in 1978–79. At least one of the skeletons was from the sixth century A.D.

19. According to an inscription in a building adjacent to the beautiful old Abbey in Romainmôtier (Vaud).

20. Excellent photographs of some of these artistic treasures from the tenth to the twelfth centuries are to be found in Gagliardi's history of Switzerland (**146**, Vol. I, plates 17 to 22).

21. Huns—At least four peoples of uncertain identity have been described as Huns. Our interest is in the Huns, who, possibly originating farther east, were settled for a time to the north of the Caspian Sea and in the southern Urals. The Magyars who reached Hungary in the ninth century are said to have been from a closely related stock. About 372 A.D. the Huns moved westwards from their Russian homeland. In 374 they invaded the lands of the Ostrogoths. The Visigoths were next defeated in battle and in 376 were allowed to settle in Thrace. The Romans, around 430 to 450, paid heavy tribute to the Hunnic kings for leaving them in peace. The most famous of the Hunnic kings was Attila who pushed southwards as far as Constantinople and, subsequently, westwards across the Rhine to the Rhone valley and on into the lands of the Burgundians. Attila died in 453. Within a few years the empire he had amassed fell apart amid the quarrels of his many sons. The Huns dispersed after several defeats in battle and many returned to southern Russia.

22. From the death of Gundahar in 436 to that of Aetius in 454, the Burgundians were probably under the rule of Roman officers.

23. Clovis, remarkable as a warrior, was also reputed to be a "monstre vainqueur et inhumain, honteusement parjure..." (**247**, p. 23). We also learn that Clovis united the Salian and Ripuarian Franks by a typical bit of treachery. Sigebert (the Lame) was king of the Ripuarian Franks. Chloderic, who had aided the Salian Franks in a battle in 507 was his son. Clovis persuaded Chloderic to assassinate his father and next arranged for the assassination of Chloderic. The Ripuarian Franks then accepted Clovis, who was ruler of the Salian Franks, as their king (**286**).

24. Described by Saint-Pierre (**313**) as a "visier" who "used to be called a Mayor of the Palace and sometimes was in fact selected by a mistress or a flatterer of the king."

25. The Guelphs (*Welfs*) consisted of a powerful German family with extensive holdings of land. In

the eighth century, part of the family settled in Swabia. In 1070, Welf IV was Duke of Bavaria. In 1137 the family also acquired the Duchy of Saxony. Kaiser Friedrich I acquired both of these great possessions from his cousin, Henry the Lion, in 1180.

26. The head of the Holy Roman Empire, after election by the princely Electors, received the title of king. If subsequently anointed and crowned in Rome by the pope, he became designated as kaiser.

27. Feudalism may not be considered as an economic and political institution which served a purpose only during the rule of weak kings unable to protect their subjects. Charles the Great used vassalage, and vassals of vassals, as a means of organizing and administering his vast empire. Because of his omnipotence he could protect his many vassals. They needed him. Later kings needed the vassals—a trend that grew under a succession of weak kings whose power was little more than nominal.

28. The administration of justice and protection through the courts of the several classes of people in the days of feudalism was very complex. External to the State, and on the manorial estates of the landlords an endless number of private courts arose, serving the needs of a large class of people, and offering their sole protection against violence and despotism (**272**, pp. 126 ff.). With the supervention of various immunities the whole "system" became even more complex. In effect, manorial courts (*Hofgerichte*) with regulations that applied to all the free and unfree within the manorial estate, came into being. External to these were the courts administered by the State (*Volksgerichte*). Apparently the main purpose of the manorial courts was to lessen the authority of the State over the inner manorial affairs of the landlords (*Grundherrn*).

29. The Marches: border territories where defense against marauding tribes was a recurring problem. Examples: Nordmark, Ostmark and Thüringian Mark—all three bordering on Poland (circa 1000).

30. During the reign of Guntram (†592), we hear of dukes for the first time in the territory on the other side of the Jura. Four, who served the king in that region, are mentioned by Peyer (**285**, p. 101). One of these, Theudefred, was the conqueror of the Langobardians in Valais. An Alemannian duke, Leudefred, is mentioned at about the same time.

31. For administrative purposes, "Switzerland" underwent many divisions. Under the Helvetians the whole of the Swiss middle land was divided into four *Gauen*. The Romans reconstructed the *Gau* structure and established many small local units with much local administrative authority. In the first century A.D. when most of western Europe was a part of the great Roman Empire, all of Switzerland north of the Alps was a part of Gallia Belgica except for Raetia which then included the Rhone valley (Valais). In the reconstruction during the second and third centuries, most of Switzerland became a part of Maxima Sequanorum. The crescent-shaped western boundary of Raetia remained unchanged. It extended from Lake Constance to the head waters of the Rhone, the Aare, the Reuss and the Rhine. Geneva, the Rhone valley and much of the Italian part belonged to three other Roman provinces.

32. Later known as *Gotteshausleute* (people attached to a religious establishment) or peasants who bought their freedom.

33. According to Öchsli (**274**) "The unfree originally had no more claim to rights and jurisdiction than the farm animals." But they still enjoyed the protection of their feudal lord. Among the unfree was a strongly differentiated group known as ministerials. They were given important responsibilities in peace and in war, and had the possibility of rising into the lower nobility. Unlike the rest of the unfree, they served their lord and master, the *Graf*, in combat. The gift of a single village as a fief to a faithful ministerial was not uncommon. He might also be entrusted with various judicial functions. In the early days of feudalism, the concept of nobility almost defied definition. A distinct class of people—the nobles—sharply separated from the masses of the people did not exist. The boundaries between the many classes, especially in the lower nobility, were fluid. "It was principally by the nature of its wealth, by its exercise of authority, and by its social habits that this group was defined" (**274**).

34. A simple analogy to the early mediaeval state is a colony of bees. The ruler is the "queen." Her "subjects" are divided into several classes with well-defined functions. The whole constitutes a "bee state" (let us call it *Bienenverbandsstaat*) and exists as a migratory tribe or society, until finally settling down in an area with boundaries recognized by members of the colony.

35. How free were the free? From a ducal domain, Uri, for example, became the property of the Frankish kings and was an annex to the royal estate in Zurich. The few inhabitants, including the descendants of Roman deserters, were mostly unfree. In 853, Ludwig the German gave these properties,

including the Fraumünster in Zurich to his daughter Hildegard. She died in 856 and much of the property came into the possession of her priest and finally to the Cloister of St. Felix and Regula.

Title to the soil carried with it ownership of the people. By the thirteenth century, Uri was the property of several landowners, possibly many, including the Fraumünster of Zurich as the principal owner. Formally there were no free peasants. Whoever did not belong to some other lordly proprietor, belonged to the Fraumünster. The status of those who gradually emigrated into Uri from the tenth to the twelfth centuries, largely to retain their freedom, is not at all clear. But apparently they were not quite as free as they had hoped to be. Through gifts to the Abbey some became free. Finally, in 1232, by purchase, Uri itself became *Reichsfrei* and owed allegiance to the king alone: the former district representatives of the king were no longer recognized.

36. The principality of Neuchâtel (eighteenth century) was an exception and so also the several territories ruled by princes of the Church (and of the Empire) such as the Bishopric of Basel and the Abbey of St. Gallen.

2. THE BEGINNINGS

Introduction

In the preceding pages, we have visited a "Switzerland" of the distant past. How may one date the beginnings of present-day Switzerland? From the time of the last Ice Age or earlier—ten thousand years or more? From the days of the tribes that preceded the Romans, or from the Roman occupation itself? From the earliest documents that are still extant? Or much later?

Switzerland, within the framework of all that follows, was nonexistent until the people within specific geographical areas, with their separate and independent governing bodes, formed a network of alliances for their mutual protection and for other matters of common interest. After many long years this intricate structure evolved into a rational federation of its constituent parts. This we call the Swiss Confederation. The Swiss call it a *Bund* or an *Eidgenossenschaft*—a federation of peoples (*Eidgenossen*) bound together under a solemn oath (*Eid*). From an original defensive alliance of three neighboring peoples it expanded eventually into a federation of over twenty regional groups, which are now known as cantons. This is Switzerland. When did it come into being? What is the date of that first regional alliance?

The First Alliance. When?

9 DECEMBER 1315? Histories of Switzerland and semi-historical descriptions recorded by travellers, if written prior to the closing decades of the eighteenth century, declare in unison that the Swiss Confederation had its formal beginnings in a covenant between Schwyz, Uri, and Unterwalden dated 9 December 1315 (see Chapter 3, note 9). This was essentially a defensive alliance between the peoples of the forested valleys that reach downwards to the Vierwaldstättersee (Lake of the Four Forest Districts, commonly called Lake Lucerne). The three regions were known collectively as the *Waldstätte* (forest districts). The very important alliance into which they entered is documented as the *Bundesbrief*[1] of Brunnen.

A point of unusual interest is that signing of the treaty followed by only three weeks a remarkable victory of the valley people, heavily outnumbered though they were, over a powerful Austrian army at Morgarten (14 November 1315).[2] The Confederates were acutely aware that the Habsburgs would not permit them to enjoy the fruits of victory for long. A strengthening of the bonds between the *Waldstätte* was clearly necessary if the ancient rights of their people were to be preserved. And there was another reason for acting promptly. The victory at Morgarten created a sensation throughout Europe. Even the House of Austria gained respect for the indomitable courage and skill in battle of these men from the *Waldstätte*. The right moment had arrived to capitalize on their victory and to declare through the terms of their alliance that they would tolerate no interference from any outsiders, including the House of Austria. Hence the apparent haste in negotiation of the treaty.

1 AUGUST 1291?   But if the Swiss Confederation had its beginnings in December 1315, why does Switzerland festively recognize 1 August 1291 as the day of her birth? The awakening came in 1758 when a Latin document dated 1 August 1291, which carried the seals of Schwyz, Uri, and Nidwalden, came to light. It was first published in Basel in 1759. Copies of this document and of a translation made in Stans were placed at the disposal of Schwyz and Stans (in Nidwalden). They were first studied by Johann Heinrich Gleser of Basel, who at once recognized the Latin document as the oldest *Bundesbrief* between Schwyz, Uri, and Nidwalden.[3] The contents of this important document are discussed in the next chapter.

The story of its discovery, possibly a little too colorful, is fascinating and carries within it a warning to all archivists, librarians, and custodians of records, which will become apparent as we unravel the story. The existence of such a document was suspected even in the sixteenth century. Werner Steiner in his *Liederchronik* of the early sixteenth century declared "they knew well of a treaty written in Latin and contracted some years ago"[4] (**182**). However, in the summer of 1569, Aegidius Tschudi[5] visited the archives of *Innerschweiz*,[6] and neither in Schwyz nor in Stans, the capital of Nidwalden, was anything revealed to him about a *Bundesbrief* of 1291.

This is what had happened (**182**).[7] Since the middle of the fifteenth century Schwyz kept her State archives in an old tower behind the Council House. In 1560 the documents were moved from the tower into the house of the *Seckelmeister* (Finance Minister). There they remained for many years until the *Seckelmeister* complained that he should be free of all responsibility for custody of the documents: he was a financial officer, not an archivist. In June 1595 four officials were instructed to prepare a register of all the freedom documents (*Fryheiten, Freibriefe*). The register that they presumably prepared has long since disappeared and is considered to be irretrievably lost. In 1616 mention of the 1291 document came from Unterwalden where it was rumored that someone in Stans saw a German translation of a document "H" described as "the ancient instrument of the oldest federal alliance with Uri and Schwyz, year 1291".[8] During Easter 1642 a serious fire in the town of Schwyz[9] burned the Council House and the upper part of the archives tower (reconstructed about 1600). The old documents were rescued and for safekeeping were dispersed in several different houses. In 1660 the Council agreed to reassemble the official documents in one place and a new tower was built to house the precious records. By 1672 the task was completed and the documents found themselves in the cupboards in the tower. An archivist was appointed in 1688 and, a few years later, an assistant archivist. The State recorder (*Landschreiber*) was henceforth relieved of the responsibility of being custodian of the records. In 1740 the then archivist (former Landschreiber Frischherz) prepared a two-volume register of the documents in his possession and assembled them in an orderly fashion. The register itself was misplaced in 1906 and was not found until March 1953.[10] In 1758, Johann Anton Felix von Balthasar of Lucerne was informed of the existence of the 1291 *Bundesbrief* in a letter from the deputy archivist Josef Anton Reding. Then it was that the archivist, his deputy, and a third party from Nidwalden prepared copies of the Latin document and made the Stans translation available to Schwyz.[11]

AN EARLIER ALLIANCE?   And here the story would end were it not that the document of 1 August 1291 is really not the oldest treaty of alliance; it is merely a renewal of an earlier *Bund*. The pertinent portion of this great document reads as follows: ". . . and each community promises on every occasion whatsoever . . . to take revenge for injuries, and by a high oath concerning these things and, without deceit, renewing the old (or ancient) form of the Confederation."[12]

The *Bundesbrief* of 1 August 1291, to which we shall return, is a masterly presentation of political goals. Partly because the document carries the seals of the three States it has the highest level of credibility. Hohlenstein (**182**) and others regard it as a political document of the greatest significance. As a defensive treaty it was clearly directed against any enemies from beyond the valleys and mountainous slopes of the *Waldstätte*. The allies constituted an *Eidgenossenschaft*, which as explained earlier, is a community of places and of people bound together by a solemn oath.[13] Many of the alliances and associations of States and of people that were concluded in Europe in ancient and medieval times were sworn agreements (*Schwurverbände*). The oaths were not *pro forma*; they were seriously entered into and the breaking of an oath commonly carried very severe penalties. Finally, unlike any earlier alliance, that of August 1291 was declared to be in perpetuity ("*in perpetuum duraturis*").

Now we come to the earlier alliance of which the *Bundesbrief* of 1 August 1291 is merely a renewal. What were its contents? Who were the contracting parties? And, above all, when was it negotiated? These questions, of obvious importance to the historian, have commanded the attention of many scholars during the past two hundred years. However, the questions have permitted little more than mere speculation because the document itself has never been found nor was it listed in any register that is known to modern historians. Even the documents that might suggest some answers are regrettably few in number. The ravages of time and human frailties have wrought incalculable damage. Fire (accidental, from natural causes, or deliberate), carelessness in storage, theft, and destruction are among the obvious reasons for the lack of documentary evidence. We must also recognize that before the days of printing all documents were written and copied by hand. Latin was the *lingua franca* for documents of the Middle Ages and there were few, except among the clergy and the scholars, who had adequate competence in Latin. Town and State recorders (*Stadtschreiber* and *Landschreiber*) with the desired facility in language were relatively few in number. Perhaps because of this, but also as a characteristic of the popular legislative assemblies of the early days (primitive *Landsgemeinde*), many unwritten and unrecorded agreements were concluded. Though oral (*mündlich*), they were entered into under binding oaths and had all the force of law. The contents of such agreements were passed on from father to son and from one generation to the next. From some of these agreements, legends, sagas, and early historical writings (frequently of doubtful credibility) had their origin.

1245–52, 1273?   With these reservations it is perhaps sufficient to point out that two schools of thought have proposed two different datings: there is no consensus. Two of the great scholars of Swiss history, Kopp[14] and Wilhelm Oechsli,[15] concluded that the earlier alliance was entered into between 1245 and 1252 (**207**; **208**; **272**). Others, notably Meyer (**240**) and Bresslau (**64**), argued in favor of 1273.[16] Both schools of thought agree that the contracting parties were probably the same for the 1291 agreement and its predecessor, although the possible adherence of Obwalden to the earlier alliance cannot be excluded. Peyer concludes that the available evidence is insufficient to pinpoint the date of the earlier alliance. "The oldest alliance was probably concluded between 1239 and 1291, but we cannot be more precise" (**285**). Tschudi, without citing any supporting evidence, states that the oldest *Brief* was dated 1231 (**370**).

While the mid-thirteenth century was a troublesome time and the pressures to form defensive alliances must have been great, it is difficult to understand how Schwyz, Uri, and Nidwalden could then have concluded an alliance. The emperor, Friedrich II, was at war in Italy against Pope Gregory IX. The emperor had initiated the war in 1236 in an effort "to bring the cities of north and middle Italy back into the 'unity of the *Reich*'" (**272**, p. 252). The pope realized that this was a war in which the temporal lord of the earth (the king of the *Römisches Reich*) could endanger the supremacy of the spiritual lord (the pope). On Palm Sunday, in 1239, Pope Gregory IX declared a ban against the king. The purpose of the war was almost certainly an effort by Friedrich II to regain control of the passes and the southern approaches to the profitable Gotthard route to and from Italy. According to Bresslau (**64**), Schwyz and Obwalden supported the emperor, while Nidwalden and Uri sided with the papal party. Hence an alliance between Schwyz, Uri and Nidwalden would appear to be most improbable.[17] Yet all three "cantons" honored their obligations to the Empire by providing troops in 1240 to assist their emperor in his siege of Faenza.

Is 1273 more acceptable? True, it was a time of great uncertainty and concern for the future. The Great Interregnum of 1256 to 1273, plagued by violent disturbances, plundering, and an absence of imperial authority over the nobles and regional governors, had led to regional associations for defensive purposes throughout the Empire. The election of a powerful and acquisitive Habsburg [Rudolf IV of Habsburg (Rudolf I of the Holy Roman Empire)] as king aroused fears within the *Waldstätte* for the peace and security of their people.

To understand the anxiety of the valley people we must go back to 1232. In that year Count Rudolf II (the Elder) of Habsburg died and his extensive possessions were divided between his two sons, Albrecht IV (the Wise) and Rudolf III (the

Silent). The latter ruled over Laufenburg (on the Rhine between Basel and Schaffhausen) and enjoyed comital rights over Zurich and the lands known as Zurichgau. Sovereignty over Schwyz and Nidwalden, which were a part of the Zurichgau inheritance, followed. In the spring of 1273 Count Eberhard of Habsburg-Laufenburg (son of Rudolf III) was obliged to sell his possessions and private rights in central Switzerland to his powerful cousin Rudolf IV (son of Albrecht IV) of the main Habsburg line.[18] The people of the forest cantons had lived under the administration of Rudolf III with a minimum of interference, but Rudolf IV was a new, ambitious, and acquisitive ruler whose policies toward his subjects were unknown and aroused the greatest apprehension. Note that Rudolf IV in that same year was elected Emperor.

Uri was deeply disturbed for a reason that was uniquely hers. In the early thirteenth century she had succeeded in bridging the deep and formidable chasm cut by the river Reuss.[19] In so doing, access to the Gotthard pass was opened up and a profitable traffic between northern Europe and Italy developed. Use of the route was totally under the control of Uri and the revenues were hers. The Urners were well aware of the ambitions of the House of Habsburg and of their desire to acquire control of this important communications link and the rather considerable income that it generated. Uri was also an enclave, a foreign island, in the midst of Habsburg possessions. A persuasive argument can certainly be made for the entry of Schwyz, Nidwalden, and Uri into a binding defensive alliance on election of this formidable head of the Habsburg dynasty to the imperial throne.

THE TWELFTH CENTURY OR EARLIER?   And now, as we probe into the early history of the Swiss Confederation, another problem arises. It pertains to the adjective "antiquam" as used in the Latin document of 1 August 1291. Thus far we have accepted *alten* (old) as the correct translation into German. But let us now proceed upon the premise that *uralten* (very old, possibly ancient), as used by von Ah (**8**), is the meaning that the writers of the document intended to convey. This leads us back to Tschudi's chronicle (**370**) and to a series of events which strongly suggest that a defensive alliance between the valley people may have been contracted in the twelfth century or even earlier. Several of the early chroniclers state that such an alliance existed and was renewed every ten years, evolving into a perpetual alliance years later. The treaty of 1 August 1291 and the succeeding alliance of 9 December 1315 were directed primarily against the Habsburgs, but it would be a mistake to assume that they were the first to make life difficult for the strongly independent people of the ancient cantons. This brings us to a long-continued, early, and inflammatory dispute between the Schwyzers and the Abbey of Einsiedeln from which one may possibly infer that the elements of an alliance existed very early between the peoples of the *Waldstätte*.

The Einsiedeln-Schwyz Dispute

In 1114 Abbot Gero of Einsiedeln initiated a long and bitter dispute with Schwyz, whose people occupied the valleys and mountain meadows southwest of the abbey

(**370**, I, p. 49). The quarrel involved Abbot Gero with his *Schirmvogt* (protector), Count Ulrich of Rapperswill, on the one hand, and on the other, the peasant farmers of Schwyz and the brothers Arnolf and Rudolf, Counts of Lenzburg and lords of the city and district of Zug. According to Tschudi, the counts of Lenzburg were joined in "a special alliance with the three forest districts of Schwyz, Uri, and Unterwalden." Tschudi states that the men of the three *Orte* (places) were free people of the Empire, responsible only to the emperor himself. Of their own free will they had chosen the counts of Lenzburg as their *Schirmvogt*. The date of this agreement is given as 1110.

The dispute with Abbot Gero was over land, the ownership of which had not been clearly defined. It broke out anew in 1114 but had been simmering ever since the Abbot called for a settlement. He had tried to force Schwyz to appear before the imperial *Reichsvogt* (the local representative of the emperor), but his insistent demands were refused or ignored. The Schwyzers declared themselves to be free people who could not be required to appear before the local courts of justice: they were subject only to the emperor. In 1114 it happened that Kaiser Heinrich V (1106–1125) was in Basel and from there he ordered the two parties to appear before him (**370**, I, pp. 51–55). Schwyz argued that by common knowledge, over many years, the borders of its lands had been well defined and established. But they had no *Brief* to support this assertion. The Abbot claimed that before the days of Kaiser Otto the Great (936–973) and of Duke Hermann of Alemannia, the abbey had acquired through gifts and purchases all of the wild and mountainous territories in dispute. The abbot submitted a document from Kaiser Otto which recorded the gift by Duke Hermann of lands in the disputed area.[20] Schwyz pointed out that the letter said nothing about the transfer of lands to the Abbey, as Gero had alleged, except of Meinratszell:[21] it pertained in no way to the *Landmarchen* (border lands) which were in dispute. The abbot then submitted a *Freibrief* dated September 2, 1018, from Kaiser Heinrich II (Heinrich the Holy, 1002–24)[22] in which the borders of the lands of the abbey were defined in detail. It also stated that lands were given, and "overgiven," as a permanent possession of the abbey.

The emperor issued judgment against Schwyz or the Lenzburgs. He ordered that 100 pounds be paid to him personally and that the borders of the abbey's possessions be defined anew—essentially as given in the ancient *Freibrief* of 1018.

Schwyz was greatly aroused. "For almost a hundred years her people had peacefully occupied these lands. They had caused trouble to no one. They had rendered service to the emperor. But now this Abbot Gero raises a storm of trouble and the Kaiser does not help them." With the support of Uri and Unterwalden, according to Tschudi, they refused to accept the judgment of the emperor. They refused to move one step from their ancient lands and *Landmarchen* and to this end they pledged their land, their bodies, their goods, and their blood (**370**, I, p. 56).

According to customary law which prevailed through much of the feudal period (**42**, I, pp. 109–122; **43**), the Schwyzers had a strong case, despite the documentary evidence which was used so effectively against them.

Two litigants go to law about a field . . . no matter which of them is the present holder, that one will succeed who is able to prove that he ploughed the land . . . during previous years, or, better still, that his ancestors before him did so. For this purpose . . . he will invoke as a rule "the memory of men as far as it extends." Title-deeds were hardly ever produced save to assist memory. . . . Once the proof of long usage had been adduced, no one considered it worthwhile to prove anything else. . . . The word 'ownership' as applied to landed property would have been almost meaningless. . . . Fixed proprietary exclusiveness belonged to the concept of ownership in Roman law. (**43**, pp. 69, 70).

The Schwyzers clung tenaciously to their position in this war of words: they were a stubborn people.

The abbot continued to appeal to King Heinrich V and his successors for help. Tschudi's chronicle indicates that the emperor wrote several times to the Schwyzers urging their compliance. They, in turn, insistently pointed out that forcing them from lands which they had peacefully occupied for many years was quite wrong and unjust. The kaiser did nothing further and the tension, with occasional violent confrontations between the Schwyzers and the monks, dragged on. A ten-year pledge of support was given by Uri and Unterwalden[23] to their brothers in Schwyz, each promising to help and protect the others (**370**, I, p. 56). More specifically, Schwyz was assured of assistance in the defense of its lands against the emperor and the abbot.

Thirty years passed by. It was now 1144 and Abbot Rudolf of Einsiedeln sought the intervention of Konrad III (1138–52) in support of the abbey's claims against Schwyz. The emperor ordered both parties to appear before him at Strassburg. A considerable number of dignitaries—bishops, abbots, dukes, and other nobles— appeared as witnesses (see **207**, III, p. 318). The original judgment of Konrad's predecessor was sustained.[24] Schwyz stubbornly refused to submit. As free people, the Schwyzers no longer sought the protection of king or kaiser.[25] "If the Kaiser will give to the unjust monks the inheritance from our forefathers it is useless to remain under his protection: from henceforth our right arm is our protector" (**255**, I).

It is clear from the history of the next five hundred years that the people of the Waldstätte continued to recognize the sovereignty of the emperor. Yet, paradoxical as this may seem, they never ceased to consider themselves completely free within their own borders and without obligations to the Empire. They regarded themselves not as Habsburg subjects, but as members of a *Reichsgemeinde*, responsible only to the emperor. In 1146, the abbot urged the emperor to write sharply to the Schwyzers. This was done and the use of other means to force submission was threatened if Schwyz would not yield (**370**, I, 71). But the Schwyzers and their allies were a determined people. The abbot threatened them with war and the emperor ordered Uri and Unterwalden to help the abbot, not the people of Schwyz. Zurich, Lucerne and others were likewise instructed to aid in forcing the Schwyzers to submit. Schwyz described to its neighbors the unjust judgments of the two emperors and begged them to refrain from aiding the abbot (**370**, I, 72–74). By 1150, Konrad III was tired of the whole affair and of the constant complaints of the abbot: there were more important matters before the emperor. Schwyz was declared an outlaw and her people were excommunicated. The three ancient lands promptly declared themselves free of all obligations to the Empire which "constantly levied taxes and claims for damages and did nothing in return" (**370**, I, p. 73).

Konrad III died in 1152 and was succeeded as emperor by his nephew, King Friedrich of Frankfurt, commonly known as Barbarossa (Kaiser Friedrich I, 1152–90). He was a good friend of the Lenzburgs—a family that for several generations had served Schwyz as protector under a special type of friendship pact. They were advisors to Schwyz and had a variety of responsibilities for which they were reimbursed from tax revenues. The old Count Rudolf of Lenzburg who died in 1136 was a Schwyz countryman and his descendants continued to be firm supporters of the Schwyzers against Einsiedeln. Through conciliatory efforts of the Lenzburgs, the kaiser in 1152 lifted the ban on the *Waldstätte* and asked the Bishop of Coblenz to terminate the excommunication and to absolve the Schwyzers. He also urged the abbot to return to a peaceful relationship with the *Waldstätte* and to wait patiently for a lasting solution which the future would surely bring.

For some decades, the troubles were minimal. The Schwyzers cultivated the forest lands, laid out meadows and fields in the disputed area and built huts. But in 1213, the abbot called for help from his *Schirmvogt*, the Count of Rapperswil, who with his retainers burned the huts and stalls, destroyed the plantings and seized the cattle, implements and utensils. Fighting between the Schwyzers and the defenders of the abbey continued for several years, aggravated by the burning of abbey properties and the theft of horses and cattle by the Schwyzers. The latter called upon Rudolf (the Old) of Habsburg to adjudicate the dispute. The claims of the Schwyzers were respected subject to an agreement regarding the use in common of certain of the disputed areas (**272**, p. 116).

On the death of Rudolf the Old (1232), Zurichgau and the valleys around Lake Lucerne passed to Rudolf the Silent († 1249) founder of the Habsburg-Laufenburg line. The Aargau possessions were inherited by Albrecht IV, father of the later King Rudolf.

The battle of Morgarten, precipitated by events in 1314, was aggravated by an attack upon Einsiedeln by the men of the Waldstätte who seized cattle and took as prisoners many of the monks and lower personnel of the cloister. There was already a ban against the Schwyzers to which the latter had replied by placing a bounty on the head of the abbot. The abbot extended the ban and interdictum to include Uri and Unterwalden and at the same time called for help from King Friedrich (1314–30), the official protector (*Schirmvogt*) of Einsiedeln (**272**, pp. 338 ff.).

The Freedom Letters (Freibriefe)

The years passed and another Friedrich was head of the Holy Roman Empire [Friedrich II (1212–50), grandson of Barbarossa].[26] In 1240 he was at war with Pope Gregory and, being under a papal ban, was having trouble at Faenza, Ravenna, and elsewhere in Italy. In collecting an army, Friedrich requested the three *Waldstätte* to send contingents of troops to help "tame this obstreperous Pope"[27] and to join in the siege of Faenza. The *Waldstätte* replied affirmatively and agreed to send six hundred well-armed men.[28] In turn they requested that they be made free subjects of the Empire responsible only to the emperor, and that they be under his direct protection and rule. Kaiser Friedrich was greatly pleased by the arrival of the troops from the *Waldstätte* and on 14 December 1240, he sent to Schwyz a special *Freibrief* under the seal of the Empire granting to its people the freedom requested (**370**, I, pp. 134, 135). The letter acknowledged the devotion and loyalty that all the people of Schwyz had expressed to him by letter and by messenger. They are free people, and the kaiser, in reaffirming their status, assures them that they are placed under his and the Empire's protection. At no time will they be alienated from the Empire. He "gives to the people the assurance of his complete mercy and goodness toward them if they continue in their devotion to him and in their willingness to render service to him."

The letter to Schwyz, in Latin, is reproduced by Tschudi and translated. According to Tschudi, identical letters of the same date were sent by the kaiser to Uri and Unterwalden—a point that has been questioned by some historians. Businger[29] reproduces the letter allegedly sent to Unterwalden (**79**, I, p. 456). As for Uri, we learn from Schmid[30] (**324**) that "the Kaiser was so pleased with the performance of their men at Faenza that he ceremoniously confirmed their ancient freedom."[31] There are in Tschudi's text many slight changes which suggest the existence of the alleged *Freibrief* or a careless copying and adaptation by Tschudi of the original documents. Kopp[14] has expressed the opinion that Uri and Unterwalden (or the rulers of Stans and Sarnen) received no such letter (**207**). It may seem surprising that such a rich source of documentary material as the *Quellenwerk* (**296**) reproduces Friedrich's letter to Schwyz but does not mention the letters allegedly sent to Uri and Unterwalden. But we should not forget that a great many of the early documents pertinent to the history of the Confederation have been lost. For example, the archives of Uri were largely destroyed by fire during the battles of resistance to the French in 1799 and Unterwalden suffered heavy losses of its archives in 1713.

AN ALLIANCE EARLY IN THE TWELFTH CENTURY? And here we must return to the twelfth century. Is there any additional evidence to support the thesis that the three ancient cantons had indeed formed a quasi alliance by 1114, if not earlier? Documentary proof is lacking. Petermann Etterlin, historian (*Geschichtschreiber*) of Lucerne, in his famous chronicle (**121**) consistently refers to the three forest states as *die dry lender* (the three lands) and writes of them as if they were one.[32] Regrettably, no dates appear in the chronicle until much later. The first dated event is the election of Rudolf of Habsburg as king in 1273. No mention is made of any early formal alliances, written or oral. Justinger (**199**, p. 61), in his *Berner-Chronik*, which was written in about 1430, mentions that "long ago, even before Bern was founded,"[33] the three *Waldstätte* were at war with the Kyburgs and then with the Habsburgs. "The people of Uri long ago had been allied with the other two forest states."[34] War was their problem and a united front against their rulers—the regional governors appointed by the Crown, and various officials—appears to have been their defense. These foreign officials busied themselves in seeking ways to extend the authority of the rulers and to strengthen the bonds that held the people firmly attached to the ruling dynasty. Again, the alleged early alliances between the three ancient cantons are not dated. Johannes Stumpf, a gifted chronicler who wrote on a variety of subjects, mentions, all too vaguely, several old *Bundesbriefe* between the ancient cantons and presents a mere suggestion of the contents (**352**).

Stumpf mentions briefly the alliance of 1315 which, we are told, was arranged by Stouffacher of Schwyz (**352**, p. 224). Next, an earlier accord in 1251 is described, whereby Uri, Schwyz and the city of Zurich entered into an alliance of several years' duration for the purpose of taking counsel together, and of helping one another in defense against those who would do harm to any of them (**352**, p. 279). Later in his Chronicle (p. 457), Stumpf returns to the 1251 alliance, this time dated October 16, mentioning that Konrad ab Iberg (the Landammann) and the people of Schwyz bound themselves together with Uri and Zurich. Could Stumpf have been misinformed, careless in his dates, or the victim of printer's errors? On 16 October 1291 an alliance between Schwyz, Uri and Zurich is known to have been entered into and hence we can only infer that a little mischief was innocently committed by Stumpf or his printer (**370**, I, p. 104).

I suspect that we find ourselves in that shadowy era of quasi-history where much of the evidence derives from sagas and legends passed down by word of mouth from generation to generation.[35] A keen and meticulous observer from England, Archdeacon William Coxe, who made four tours through Switzerland in 1776, 1779, 1785, and 1786, mentions that "during the twelfth century, various disputes between these three cantons and the emperors, united them more firmly than ever; and they were accustomed, every ten years, to renew formally their alliance" (**95**, I, p. 280). Coxe did not cite the source from which this statement was derived but it might easily have been Tschudi's *Chronicon Helveticum*, which mentions an alliance in February 1206 between Uri, Schwyz and Unterwalden,[36] subject to renewal every ten years (**370**, I, p. 104).

Allegedly this was not the earliest, for we read that from olden times the people of these three valleys entered into these renewable alliances of stated duration, and that meetings were held (*Tagsatzungen*) to discuss matters of common interest. These short-term alliances continued to be entered into, so we read, until "1315 or 1316 when a permanent everlasting alliance" was agreed to. Confusing perhaps is Tschudi's mention of Wernher von Attinghusen, then *Landammann* of Uri, as the one who proposed the 1206 alliance, for it was also a Wernher von Attinghusen, Landammann of Uri, who joined in negotiating the alliance of 16 October 1291 between Uri, Schwyz, and Zurich. Von Liebenau's genealogy of the lords of Attinghusen mentions a Werner I of Attinghusen (1248–76) and his son Werner II (1275–1321), Landammann of Uri (**217**). Earlier Werners of Attinghusen or Schweinsberg, if they existed, are not mentioned in the genealogy. Werner II of Attinghusen apparently became Landammann of Uri in about 1295 and held the office until his death some 25 or 30 years later. As Landammann, he is mentioned in documents of 1301, 1303, and 1308 (**272**, p. 319).

This brings us back to Tschudi, his status as an historian, and his credibility. Johannes von Müller described the *Chronicon Helveticum* as "not simply one among other sources but beyond question the chief source." Müller noted discrepancies between Tschudi's work and other chronicles, including mistakes in dates and in facts, but he explained these away, at least to his own satisfaction, and continued to regard Tschudi as the greatest of the early recorders of Swiss history. His chronicle was described by Müller as the "fundamental work on the history of Switzerland" (cf. **48**, pp. 237–54). Bonjour, among the great present-day historians of Switzerland, describes von Müller as "the intellectual heir of Aegidius Tschudi"—a great compliment in itself. And, finally, von Wyss, a highly regarded Swiss historian in the mid-nineteenth century, made a similarly favorable appraisal of von Müller (**396**). von Wyss and others have expressed an equally high regard for Kopp (**207**). Kopp, however, insisted on complete documentation and was one of Tschudi's most severe critics. In the third book of his remarkably detailed history, Kopp reports with meticulous care on the twelfth-century quarrels between Schwyz and Einsiedeln and discusses the reputed alliance of the three forest States in 1114 or earlier. Several of the footnotes on p. 319, and pp. 326–329 draw attention to a number of statements by Tschudi which Kopp insists are erroneous.

What more can be said about Tschudi's credibility and that of other chroniclers who made extensive use of sagas, legends, folk tales and, possibly, of documents which have long since disappeared without even a trace of their alleged existence? Tschudi, it should be noted, is credited with reproducing, and thus saving, in his great chronicle some seven hundred documents (**48**). He studied Swiss and foreign archives and looked into ecclesiastical records. He made rich use of decrees, letters, yearbooks, inscriptions, folksongs, and the heroic sagas and legends of his day. Through fire, wanton destruction, carelessness,[37] theft and the ravages of time much of the material available to Tschudi has long since disappeared. The weight of evidence, undocumented though some of it appears to be, strongly suggests, though it does not prove, that the three ancient cantons were allied for defense against the oppressors of any one of the three far back in the twelfth century, if not even earlier. Whether such an ancient alliance, possibly unwritten, is the predecessor referred to in the *Bundesbrief* of 1 August 1291 is, however, an open question.

We should recall that much of the history of Europe, before printing was invented and before ability to write were common, rested on folk songs, legends, sagas, and tales from the past. Much was transmitted by word of mouth. Schiller, possibly with tongue in cheek, certainly departed from the truth when he wrote "Everything happened as I have told you." Nevertheless we must respect the following:

> Man will narrate Tell's apple-shoot
> As long as the mountains stand their ground.

Notes and Comments

1. *Abschiede* I, pp. 243, 244, 9 December 1315: Tschudi (**370**, I, p. 276). A *Bundesbrief* is literally a letter that sets forth the purposes and terms of an alliance entered into by the contracting parties. It would seem more appropriate to use the word *Bundesvertrag* to designate a treaty rather than a letter, but it should be noted that any legal document or charter was commonly described as a *Brief*. Perhaps without exception, each of the many intercantonal alliances into which the members of the Swiss Confederation entered in many long years is known as a *Bundesbrief*, rarely as a *Bundesvertrag*.

2. The Habsburg forces, under command of Duke Leopold, in the vicinity of Morgarten numbered 2000 to 3000 against 1000 Schwyzers inclusive of contingents from Uri and parts of Unterwalden (**308**, pp. 189, 190; **146**, I, p. 208). A second Austrian cavalry force under Count Otto of Strassburg, numbering 6000, attacked from the Brunig pass and overran Obwalden. On learning of the Austrian defeat at Morgarten the army of Count Otto hastily retreated (**247**, p. 76).

3. Obwalden joined shortly after 1291. Hence, it is customary to describe this early alliance as having been contracted between Schwyz, Uri, and Unterwalden, which consisted of two half-cantons, Nidwalden and Obwalden.

4. "Sy hand wol darvor (or "darvon") einen pundt ghan in latin gschriben, vor ättlichen jaren ufgricht [erste Erwähnung des Bundesbriefes (**243**, p. 174)"].

5. The two volumes of Tschudi's chronicle, covering the period from 1000 to 1474 A.D., are invaluable: they are enriched by the reproduction and translation (from Latin into German) of many historically important documents. Some of his interpretations and recorded events have been questioned by historians. However, even though the Chronicle is not fully documented, it is nonetheless a valuable record of five of the most exciting centuries in Swiss history. Johannes von Müller (1752–1809), himself a great historian, described Tschudi's chronicle as "the fundamental work of Swiss history." It draws heavily upon witnesses of the past, folksongs, sagas, decrees, letters, yearbooks, inscriptions, and other chronicles, of which there were many.

Tschudi belonged to an old Glarus family. Though he lived from 1505 to 1572, his great work was not published until the eighteenth century. He was a one-time disciple of Zwingli but became a vigorous opponent of the Reformation. He tried in vain to establish the five inner *Orte*, the heart of Swiss Catholicism, as a separate confederation, but the "*Tschudikrieg*" of 1559–64 was unsuccessful and he lost much support. At various times he served as *Obervogt* of the Abbey of St. Gallen, *Landvogt* of Baden, and a representative of Glarus in the Diet. As an historian of Switzerland of the Middle Ages, he was the first to make extensive use of original documents in Swiss and foreign archives, many of which were lost in later years by fire, wanton destruction, and carelessness. In 1559 he was sent on a federal mission to the *Reichstag* in Augsburg. On this occasion he was elevated to the nobility by Kaiser Ferdinand I— at least it is so alleged by Tschudi, but denied by some of his critics, such as Gallati (**147**). Tschudi was prone to "correct" documents, to round off the description of events with details foreign to the documents themselves. This has been partly explained by practices common among other contemporary humanists. "The document-attested truth was frequently subordinated to humanistic subjectivity and personal emotions" (**381a**). But Iselin, who wrote the foreword for the *Chronicon Helveticum* in 1734 still thought of Tschudi as the "Swiss oracle of his times" (Introduction to Vol. 1 of the Chronicon).

6. Usually Schwyz, Uri, and Unterwalden, but occasionally Lucerne and Zug are included.

7. For a more detailed account of the troubles that Schwyz encountered with her archives, see Benziger (**34**).

8. ". . . uralte Instrument der ältisten eidtgnoszischen Puntnuszen mit Ury and Schwyz, anno 1291" (**182**, p. 127).

9. Capital of the canton of Schwyz.

10. J. C. Benziger, in an article on the archives of Schwyz (**34**) reported that the register was still available ("*heute noch erhalten ist*") (**34**, p. 114). Hohlenstein wrote that the misplaced register was found on 25 March 1953 in a totally unexpected place ("in einem gänzlich unerwartenten Platz") (**182**, p. 130). Benzinger's sources include the Council's Protocolls for Schwyz, the *Seckelmeister's* accounts for Schwyz, and six other sources including the cantonal archives (**34**, p. 99).

11. The *Bundesbrief* of 1 August 1291 and that of 9 December 1315, along with many other treaties of alliance, are now housed in an attractive new archives building in the town of Schwyz.

12. In the original document, ". . . ac in omnem everitum quelibet universitas, promisit alteri accurrere, cum necesse fuerit ad succurendum; et . . . injurias vindicare, prestito super hiis corporaliter juramento, absque dolo servandis, antiquam confederationis formam juramento vallatum, presentibus innovando . . ."

The Stans translation the concluding portion of the above excerpt: "Die alten wisz der gelüpte mit dem eyde umbgeben mit disem brieff ze nüwrende."

Von Ah (**8**, p. 16) gives a free translation in modern German, "Sie erneuern hiedurch und stärken den uralten Bund mit heiligem Eide."

Several other translations into German (medieval and modern) and French differ slightly but all refer to the renewal of a pre-existing alliance.

13. The Swiss Confederation is referred to in many legal documents, past and present, as the *Schweizerische Eidgenossenschaft*.

14. Joseph Eutych Kopp (1793–1866) was a philologist, poet, politician, and historian. Starting in 1819 he was a professor in Lucerne. His great History (**207**), terminated by his death in 1866, covers only the period from 1273 to 1341. The volumes are enriched with copies of relevant documents from 1168 to 1341 and with references to a few others that reach back to 972. Kopp was extraordinarily cautious and insisted on documentary proof of historical "facts." He was very critical of Tschudi (**370**), whose remarkable *Chronicon Helveticum* goes deeply back into the 11th century.

15. Wilhelm Oechsli (1851–1919) was Professor of History at the Federal Institute of Technology from 1887 to 1893 and Professor of History at the University of Zurich from 1893 to 1919.

16. Meyer pointed out that the judicial clause in the 1291 pact appeared in its primitive form in the first penal code of Uri (circa 1250) and was probably transposed in 1291. Bresslau focuses on the same clause and resorts to a different argument. The verbs in this clause are all in the first person—quite unlike the rest of the document which is cast in the third person. Hence it may be inferred that this clause was an afterthought; it is assumed to be of different authorship than the rest, and in 1291 was inserted into a pre-existing treaty of alliance, the date of which is now the subject of inquiry. So runs the argument.

17. Although one may agree with Bresslau (**64**) that Schwyz and Obwalden supported the kaiser in his war against the pope and that Uri and Nidwalden were on the papal side, the popular support of one side or the other was not clear cut. Throughout the 1240s there was a great deal of internal dissension. In Uri there were popular uprisings against the Church, specifically against the cloisters. In Schwyz there was an appreciable number of adherents to the papal party who were subject to plundering, property confiscation and violent attacks. Bresslau refers to a document of 28 August 1247 constituting an order of Pope Innocent IV to Schwyz and Obwalden to return to the Church's side or be severely punished.

Rudolf III of Habsburg-Laufenburg, following a policy of expediency, shifted his allegiance from one side to the other two or three times during these troublesome years. Friedrich II died in 1250 and a rather tenuous peace began to emerge in Innerschweiz by 1252. The *Reichsfrei* cities, hitherto dependent on their king/emperor for protection, turned to others for help. Bern and Freiburg, allied in 1218 and again in 1243 for reasons of trade and commerce and mutual defense, sought the protection of the Count of Savoy. Zurich turned to the House of Habsburg and Schwyz and Obwalden accepted the protection of the Count of Habsburg-Laufenburg. These were the early years of the Great Interregnum (1256–73) when there was neither king nor kaiser to protect the places that had received the enviable status of freedom of the empire (*Reichsfreiheit*).

18. Eberhard, under the persuasive influence of Rudolf IV of Habsburg, had but recently married Anna of Kyburg (daughter of Hartmann V), and promptly received from Rudolf IV a huge bill to cover his expenses as administrator of her lands while she was a minor. To satisfy his creditor, Eberhard then sold the whole of his possessions in central Switzerland to his cousin for 14,000 marks (**240**) and reduced the Kyburg properties to the Burgundian holdings. Rudolf now had absolute rule over eastern Switzerland, for the sale included Zurichgau, much of Aargau, Zug (city and surrounding lands), towns in Schwyz and Nidwalden, people and properties in the Waldstätte (*"lute und gut in den Waltstetten"*) (**298**, p. 493, Item 1092, 5 May 1273). His sovereignty extended from Lake Lucerne and the inner mountains northwards to the Rhine. His goal was expansion of the Habsburg possessions into a closed

principality reaching from the upper Rhine (above Basel) to the Alps, and from Lake Geneva (*Genfersee*) to Lake Constance (*Bodensee*).

19. James Fenimore Cooper (**90**, p. 228) visited Switzerland in 1828. A new bridge over the Reuss was then in the first stages of reconstruction. The first stone bridge, probably constructed in 1218–26, was preceded by a wooden structure called the *Stiebende Brücke*. The name suggests that the bridge was heavily enveloped in the spray or drizzle from the nearby falls. Its successor, the *Teufelsbrücke* (Devil's Bridge) derived its name from a legendary claim that only with the help of the devil could the bridge have been built.

Prior to bridging the Reuss, the gorge could be crossed by an old detour around the upper Schöllenen and over the Bäzberg. This was long long ago. A thousand years were to pass before the gorge was bridged and packhorse traffic became possible. With the bridging of the Rhine in 1226 (the first fixed river crossing between Lake Constance and the North Sea) a great stream of traffic developed from Italy, over the Gotthard pass, the Devil's Bridge, and through Lucerne and Basel to north and western Europe (**394**).

Cooper used the older bridge which had been greatly damaged in 1799 in a battle with the French. After passing through a "dark gallery—two hundred feet long and called the 'Hole of Uri'" (the *Urnerloch*, tunnelled in 1707), the party came at once to the bridge.

> Abutments were the living rock; its thickness but a thread; the span of the arch was about eighty feet; its width might have been fifteen; the height above the Reuss, a hundred; and there was no railing. The wind blew so furiously that I really wished for a rope to hold on by . . . *the* Devil's Bridge . . . Beelzebub himself is thought to have had a hand in this . . . fifteen thousand persons, it is calculated, go into Italy, or return by this route, annually . . . three hundred packhorses or mules cross the mountain, weekly, for a portion of the year.

Andreas Ryff (cited by Wyss, **394**) reported the old bridge to have been about five feet in width! He crossed the bridge in May 1587.

> One comes directly and unexpectedly to the Devil's Bridge . . . on the right hand the waters of the Reuss rush and thunder down upon one from high up among the rocks and just below the bridge, they gust away down over more rocks . . . and the bridge no more than five or six shoes (feet) wide . . . no one seeing it [the bridge] for the first time, is so manly that he is not frightened out of his wits when he comes so unexpectedly round the corner and over this high narrow bridge—especially as there are no handrails and no wall alongside and no handrails can be made for the following reasons [Ryff then gives the reasons].

Another description of the bridge, somewhat similar to Cooper's though less poetic, has been given by Lewis Agassiz (1793–1866) who appears to have crossed it about the time of Cooper's visit (**5**, p. 172). See also (**318**, p. 10). A quaint account is given by Sir Edward Unton (1563–64):

> ". . . from olsera [andermatt] aboute ii englyshe myles is a brydge which is calld ponte inferno; it standeth in a straite betwene the mountaines the beginynnge of the ryver of redin [Reuss] cometh from mount gadard and at this brydge hath such a fale among the huge stones that is merveylous . . . (**397**, p. 112).

The Gotthard pass may have been in use as early as 1004 (**205**). A hospice and chapel, in honor of St. Godehardus, are known to have been built between 1166 and 1176 on Mt. Ursare, as the mountain was then called. The pass was used frequently by Duke Berchtold IV of Zähringen between 1154 and 1177 when sending troops to the aid of Kaiser Friedrich I (Barbarossa).

20. Otto's letter, dated 946, is reproduced by Tschudi; a German translation of the original Latin document is also included. See also items 1058 (3 February 961) and 1099 (14 August 972) in Hidber (**174**). Abbot Gero's formal complaint appears as item 1581 in the Hidber collection.

21. The Abbey or cloister was founded by a canon of Strassburg, Eberhard or Benno by name (**272**, p. 109; **99**, I, p. 148), in 934 (according to Oechsli). Tradition has it that an Irish monk, Meinrad from Reichenau, had been murdered in 861 on the site chosen for the cloister. Meinrad had built a hermit-like

cell which received the name Meinratszell. Einsiedeln, as the name of the abbey, dates from 1073 or earlier.

22. Tschudi's chronicle (**370**, p. 52) reproduces the Latin *Freibrief* and a German translation, also to be found as item 1255 in Hidber's work (**174**). A *Freibrief* was a greatly valued document issued by an emperor to a city, an ecclesiastical State, or a temporal State. Such a letter conferred freedom upon the State and its people and made them responsible only to the emperor. In the case of ecclesiastical establishments, freedom from taxes and customs duties was a common additional benefit. The freedom of Einsiedeln was confirmed and reconfirmed at least seven times between 1004 and 1134. [The following documents in the Hidber Collection (**174**) pertain to the dispute between Einsiedeln and Schwyz, the confirmation of gifts and immunities to Einsiedeln, the freedom of the monks to elect their abbot, and the granting of royal protection against robbers and all intruders: Documenta *1058*, Feb. 3, 961 A.D.; *1080*, Jan. 23, 965; *1099*, Aug. 14, 972; *1100*, Aug. 19, 972; *1110*, Dec. 28, 975; *1137*, Oct. 27, 984; *1203*, June 17, 1004; *1255*, Sept. 2, 1018; *1288*, Aug. 19, 1027; *1313*, Feb. 4, 1040; *1393*, Feb. 23/24, 1064; *1414*, May 24, 1073; *1565*, Oct. 2, 1111; *1581*, Mar. 10, 1114; *1698*, July 15, 1136; *1732*, May 28, 1139; *1797*, July 8, 1143/44 A.D.].

23. Es hattend ouch die von Schwitz mit denen von Uri und Underwalden/dero Zit ein Jars-Püntnuss/wie si dann von Alter har ein lange Zit gehept/dieselbigen Jar-Püntnussen warend nit ewig/giengend allweg ze 10. Jaren umb uss/und dann so richt man ein nüwe uff/mit mer oder minder Artickel/nach Gestalt der Löuffen/in disen Püntnussen was allweg der fürnemist Artickel/dass Si einandern solten schützen und schirmen/bi Iren Ländern und Landmarchen/aber ussterthalb waren Si einandern nützit verbunden (**370**, I, p. 56).

24. Item 1797 (8 July 1144) in the Hidber collection; also see Tschudi (**370**, I, pp. 68–71).

25. The elected head of the Holy Roman Empire received the title of king. If subsequently crowned in Rome he became kaiser. I have frequently used emperor as an acceptable synonym, because as king or kaiser he was head of the Empire.

26. Friedrich was elected king in 1196 but did not displace the counter-king Otto IV until 1212. In 1220 he was crowned in Rome as kaiser. He was twice banned by Pope Gregory IX who damned him as a heretic and an anti-Christ. His military campaigns almost succeeded in unification of the whole of Italy.

27. "diss Pabsts Ungestümme ze temmen." (**370**, I, p. 134).

28. Six hundred? Probably a Tschudi exaggeration.

29. Joseph Businger was canon of Grossglau in Prussian Silesia.

30. Franc Vinzenz Schmid (1758–1799) was *Oberwachtmeister* in 1782, commander of artillery, a member of the War Council of Uri, and *Landschreiber* (cantonal recorder). In 1799 he was killed in battle against the French, who destroyed by fire the precious archives of Uri.

31. Uri had bought its freedom in 1231 but in so doing had claimed the freedoms possessed in much earlier times. According to Oechsli (**272**, p. 246) the Habsburgs held the *Reichsvogtei* over Uri from 1218 to 1231. In 1231, Heinrich, acting as a representative of his father, Emperor Friedrich II, bought back the *Vogtei* over Uri from the Habsburg Count, Rudolf the Old, and gave to the people of Uri documentary assurance that he had bought their freedom from the Count and that their land would never again become enfeoffed nor would it, by pawning, ever again be separated from the *Reich*. By this act, Uri gained its freedom, becoming responsible henceforth only to the emperor. But was this a gift? One must suspect that Uri, enjoying substantial revenues from all who used the Gotthard route, paid plenty in return for this generosity. Whether the sale of Habsburg Uri to the *Reich* was initiated by Rudolf the Old, Friedrich II, or his son Heinrich, or at the request or Uri, is unknown. Heinrich, mentioned here, must not be confused with Count Heinrich of Luxembourg who was elected head of the *Reich* as King Heinrich VII in 1308 and served until his death in 1313.

32. v. Müller, going back to the days of the Roman occupation, tells us that "The Romans found in these valleys people who never united with their neighbors in other valleys. They were a disunited people." Later on, possibly leaping forward to the thirteenth century when much may have changed, he writes "All in all there appears to have been only one people in the three lands." (**255**)

33. I.e. before 1191.

34. "Nu hattent sich die von Ure von Altem har verbunden zu den andern zweyn Walstädten" (**199**, p. 61).

35. What can one accept as factual in the chroniclers' descriptions of "Switzerland" in the first few centuries of this millennium? Several leaned heavily on Tschudi. von Müller, in the first few chapters of his first volume (**255**, I), describes with a little more color than Tschudi, but with almost total agreement in substance, many events of those early years. Both include Tell's apple-shoot, the Scandinavian origin of the people of Schwyz and Hasli, and other legends which very few scholars accept as factual. Note that Burckhardt (**75**) contends that *Innerschweiz* was very thinly populated in the thirteenth century, while v. Müller tells us of overpopulation problems in the valleys. We learn that two solutions were in vogue: voluntary emigration (but not into neighbouring valleys) or a forced emigration in which some were driven out by the remaining established inhabitants.

36. But von Wyss (**396**) tells us that the first alliance was in *Hornung* (February) 1306, when "the three lands . . . made a *Bund* and swore together."

37. A. Ochsenbein (**271**) gives a specific example with a new twist. Many documents pertinent to the early history of Solothurn are missing. A raging fire in 1459 destroyed the city clerk's house and the chancellery. Many valuable documents—manuals, missives, and account books—were destroyed in the flames. But there was another cause of loss. The members of the Council and employees often kept documents at home, loaned them to others, and eventually lost some or carried them off elsewhere and into oblivion. In 1666 the city clerk required that henceforth all documents in his custody be retained at all times in the council building.

3. THE THIRTEENTH AND FOURTEENTH CENTURIES

Introduction

Let us now review the salient events of Swiss history during the thirteenth and fourteenth centuries. And this we must introduce by a brief return to the eleventh century.

After the conquests by the Alemannians and Burgundians, the royal Houses of Germany and Burgundy held dominion over central Europe. When the House of Burgundy died out in 1033, Konrad II, King of Germany and Italy and Roman Emperor in the west, also became the King of Burgundy. His kingdom embraced the whole of modern Switzerland (Burgundy east of the Jura chain; the Duchy of Alemannia; and the valleys extending from the Alps). For 400 years, the lands of present-day Switzerland were bound closely together—politically and economically—to the Germany of the Middle Ages. To hold these lands and people together as a political entity and to administer such a geographically disparate area constituted a formidable challenge to the authority and power even of kings. Representatives of the crown and numerous feudal lords established noble dynasties and exercised virtually sovereign rights over their lands. The supremacy of the temporal head of the Holy Roman Empire over these many territories and fiefdoms which made up the German States was nominal.

During the two centuries that followed the days of Konrad II the control of the *Romisch* king over the mountainous areas of central Europe progressively weakened. External preoccupations, such as struggles with the papacy from 1076 to 1122 and attempts of the German kings to extend control over the whole of Italy only added to the power of the nobles and the local lords. After Friedrich II's death in 1250 the crown passed briefly to weak and incompetent successors. From 1256 to 1273, the period of the Great Interregnum, neither king nor kaiser occupied the throne. Law and order suffered an almost total breakdown. Armed bands, frequently under commands of the lower nobility, plundered the towns and villages and robbed the merchants and traders. Feudal lords sought to expand their lands by conquest and pillage. The weak were swallowed up by the strong, and the period came to be known as *die kaiserlose, die schreckliche Zeit* (the terrible times without a king).

A Search for Protection

Communal organizations developed slowly and gave little protection to the people. In defense of their lives, property, and traditional rights, many of the free farmers and town and village communities placed themselves under the protection of powerful feudal lords. Bern and Freiburg, both founded in the last decade of the twelfth century by Berchtold IV, Duke of Zähringen and royal Rector of Burgundy, received by treaty the protection of the House of Savoy. The alliance of Peter II of Savoy with Bern in 1265 or thereabout was renewed by Amadeus V of Savoy. In some instances, monastic houses expanded their lands and their influence by the acquisition of farms and villages in return for the security they could offer to the former owners. Although these developments tended toward the restoration of order, they also ushered in a partial return to serfdom since the former freemen became bound as laborers to the lands they had previously held in fee simple.[1] In the flat lands and the lower reaches of the valleys, despite the violence and the disorder of the times, the mediaeval communities based on agriculture managed to persist. Agriculture required an orderly kind of management. Times for ploughing and harvesting had to be regulated, and cooperation in cutting of the forests and construction of buildings was necessary. Common lands had to be defined and used in the general interest. Freemen and serfs worked side-by-side, and together developed in these evolving social communities a sense of political responsibility. Between neighboring communities defensive alliances came into being and a higher order of political organization emerged.

The Principal Dynastic Houses

The ecclesiastical territories in the area of present-day Switzerland, with the possible exception of the Abbey of St. Gallen, of the Bishopric of Basel, and of two or three other bishoprics, never succeeded in exercising the political power of the principal dynasties, nor were they able to emulate the feudal lords in aggressive expansion of their domains. Justice at the lower levels was commonly administered by the bishops, abbots and the local *Ammänner* but high justice was meted out by the civil lord (see also note 6). It was he who, also on behalf of the sovereign, extended protection and security to the many dependants—farmers and villagers alike—and exacted a tax for his services. Of the ten or more powerful families that exercised the powers of lordship over most of present-day Switzerland, we need mention only four which, in the thirteenth century, were of unusual importance in the struggle for power: the Houses of Zähringen, Kyburg, Savoy, and Habsburg. To tighten their mastery over the Swiss plateau and to increase their tax revenues, the Zähringers founded towns and sold various privileges to towns already in existence: Bern,

Freiburg, Thun, Burgdorf, Laupen, Rheinfelden, and even as far west as Yverdon and Moudon. During the century, the number of towns in German Switzerland founded by several of the dynasties increased from sixteen to eighty with the Zähringers initiating the process and three other Houses strenuously following their example.[2]

The Zähringer dynasty died out in 1218. Many of the Zähringer holdings went to the Kyburgs to whom the Zähringers were related by marriage.[3] The Kyburgs with their principal holdings and seignorial powers centered in Thurgau now exercised their lordship over the northwesterly part of the Swiss plateau. In the middle of the century, Hartmann IV of Kyburg, while retaining for himself the ancestral possessions of the family in Thurgau and around Zurich, gave to his nephew Hartmann V the rest of the Kyburg territories. But this dynasty, and with it all the ambitious schemes of the Kyburgs, ended with the death of Hartmann V in 1263 and of his uncle Hartmann IV in 1264, the last of the male line. The latter was married to Margaret of Savoy who died without issue.

Peter, the reigning Count of Savoy, whose family domains extended over the whole of the great valley and mountain slopes north of Lake Geneva, now dreamed of taking over the Kyburg territories and attaining dominance over most of the Swiss plateau. But the powerful Habsburg family with proprietorial or protectorate rights over central Switzerland from Alsace and Aargau down to the valleys of Schwyz, Uri, and Unterwalden had similar plans of conquest. The hopes of the Savoyards were encouraged by the townsmen of Bern, Freiburg, and Murten who, to escape the Habsburgs, and to obtain greater security, placed themselves under the protection of Savoy.[4]

The House of Habsburg

The Habsburg dynasty which, from 1273 on, ruled over much of central Europe for the next six and a half centuries encountered little difficulty in expanding its territories and sovereign rights except in Switzerland. Indeed, it was their mistrust of the House of Habsburg, their fear of trouble in the uncertain and violent times which would surely follow upon the death of King Rudolf I (July 15, 1291), and their desire to join in defense against the common enemy which, as much as anything else, caused the villagers and peasants in the valleys of Uri, Schwyz, and Nidwalden to form the binding alliance which was concluded two weeks later. It might be noted that on the death of Count Rudolf II of Habsburg in 1232, his extensive possessions were divided between his two sons. The younger of the two, Count Rudolf III, ruled over Laufenburg with comital rights over the lands around Zurich. This included sovereignty over Schwyz and Nidwalden.

The Laufenburg branch of the Habsburgs ultimately sold their rights and their dynastic holdings in central Switzerland to the other side of the family, specifically to Rudolf IV,[5] nephew of Rudolf III. It is clear that Rudolf IV was outstanding among the heads of the European dynasties. His competence in expanding, retaining, and administering the Habsburg territories was widely recognized. To the surprise of no one he was elected King of Germany and Emperor of the Holy

Roman Empire in 1273. His extraordinary thirst for conquest, combined with negotiating skill and exercise of royal prerogatives, enabled him in the late 1270s to dispossess the King of Bohemia of the duchies of Austria, Styria, and Carinthia. Acquisitions by purchase were also made, for example the lordship over Freiburg, bought from the Kyburgs in 1277, and the town of Lucerne, purchased from the Abbey of Murbach in 1291. To his sons he gave Austria and Styria in 1282. From then to the shattering events of the early decades of the twentieth century, Austria became totally identified with the Habsburgs.

The Alliances of 1 August and 16 October 1291

But it was in Switzerland, where lay the ancestral home of the dynasty, that the Habsburgs encountered the troubles and military defeats with which we associate the beginnings of the Swiss Confederation. Part of the resistance of the early "confederates" is attributable to the success of those from Uri who, at the end of the twelfth century, succeeded in bridging the *Schöllenenschlucht* over the river Reuss, thus facilitating traffic between central Switzerland and Italy via the St. Gotthard pass. The importance of this commerical route by mule train which now developed and grew in economic importance was not lost on the Habsburgs who coveted the income through customs tolls and rights of passage derivable from control of this north-south route. Only the valley communities of Uri, the peasants and the villagers appeared to stand in their way.

Of equal concern was the administration of justice, for this involved all of those over whom the Habsburgs exercised the rights of lordship. High justice (judgments of blood) was administered by the king, and justice in matters of less consequence by his local representatives. Each valley had one or more of these *Ammänner* who eventually were appointed by the inhabitants of the valleys from among their own number.[6] The principal *Ammann,* with somewhat superior powers was known as the *Landammann.* Judicial functions were also assigned to certain vassals of the counts, specifically to *Ritters* and *Ministerialen*[7] who, in return for these and other services, were commonly given single villages as a fief. The extent to which the overlords, whether appointed by the king or his *Reichsvögte,* interfered with the *Ammänner* or the *Landammänner* varied greatly from valley to valley.

Initially, the troubles with the Habsburgs and the Hohenstaufens[8] were not too serious, although of sufficient concern that the people of Schwyz implored Friedrich II that they be placed directly under the Crown instead of its agents. This concern is evidenced by a letter from Friedrich II in 1240 in which the Kaiser placed the Schwyzers under his direct royal protection. To the inhabitants of the Waldstätte in general, their troubles with the overlords began, or were aggravated, when these "governors" or regional administrators came to be appointed from among nonresidents of the valleys. It is reasonably certain that these "foreigners" preyed upon the peasants and villagers and failed to administer justice with the fairness, honesty, and local understanding that were considered to be a reasonable expectation. Although many ancient documents are missing, it may be assumed that representations were made by the peasants and villagers to their sovereign, the first after the long Interregnum, Rudolf IV of Habsburg (Rudolf I of the Holy Roman Empire). Before 1282, the King assured the Schwyzers that no foreigner would sit in judgment over them: judges would be appointed only from among their own people. Shortly before his death in 1291 he promised never to appoint a serf or an unfree person to a judicial position over the people of the Waldstätte (**285**, I, 178). After the death of the king, the inhabitants of *Innerschweiz* saw to it that these promises of their late sovereign were formally recognized in a perpetual covenant. As victims of the banditry, the pillaging, and the disorders that grew in volume during the Interregnum and, harassed as they were by foreign overlords, the men of Uri, Schwyz, and Nidwalden subscribed to a Convention of 1 August 1291,[9] whereby, *inter alia*, they solemnly declared their refusal to accept as judges and local governors any who obtained their office by purchase and any who were not from among their own numbers.[10] Otherwise this covenant renews an earlier alliance (see Chapter 2), *"Erneuerung des alten, eidlich bekräftigten Bundes"* (**81**, p. 39), among those who inhabited the valleys of Innerschweiz. The document of 1291 concerned itself with crime, punishment, justice, the maintenance of internal peace, and a common defense against enemies: an attack on one of the cantons to be judged as an attack on all three. It was in no way revolutionary, it did not propose the overthrow of tyrants and to the contrary, stated that each subject, according to his status, should render proper service to his master.

Dear to the Habsburgs was a centralization of power and a totem-pole line of command in the power structure. The prince, as head of the dynasty, was the sovereign lord. Next came the *Vögte* who as judges, tax collectors, and conscribers of military levies, served as representatives of the prince in the local communities and regions subservient to the Habsburgs. However, the emperor–ruler of the Holy Roman Empire was not always a Habsburg, and it was the emperor whom the people of the embryonic Swiss Confederation recognized as their overlord. They were stubbornly resistant to the centralized power structure of the Habsburgs and struggled for a grass-roots type of government with as much authority as possible vested in local people. This explains two of the early victories of the *Waldstätte* in their struggle for self-determination. The first was the *Freibrief* of 1240 from Frederick II to Schwyz and the inalienable rights granted by the Crown to Uri in 1231. In effect, these forest communities were placed directly under the protection of the emperor, as was already the case with Hasli.[11] The second was a victory in the making, spelled out in the tricantonal covenant of 1 August 1291, whereby the "Confederation" refused to recognize the authority of "foreign" *Vögte*. The inhabitants of the *Waldstätte* demanded that only their own people, locally elected as *Ammänner*, should administer justice in the lower courts, collect taxes for local needs, and discharge the responsibilities of the Habsburg *Vögte* and *Reichsvögte*.

The Landsgemeinden

And here, expanding upon an earlier reference to *Ammänner*, and *Landammänner* (note 6), something must be said about *Landsgemeinden* and the important grass-roots democracy of early Switzerland. In so doing we must recall the differences between the cities and the countryside. The cities tended to be populated by people who differed from those in the country in their day-to-day activities, in culture, and in government. The cities, quite uniformly, developed centralized forms of government in which decision-making was commonly the exclusive right of some of the old families noted for their wealth and high social position. But in the countryside, the real groundsoil of the Swiss Confederation, centralism in government was totally foreign. Here, the people were the sovereign power. Administration and decision-making rested in their hands and were directly exercised: elections, legislative decisions, intercantonal alliances, decisions on peace and war. Once a year the people of the "canton" came together for these exercises in self-rule. They convened as a country community—a *Landsgemeinde*, practicing a form of government which had its roots in the tenth or eleventh century, and even savored of the Athenian democracy. Any who have had an opportunity to witness a *Landsgemeinde* at work, as in Glarus, cannot fail to sense the unforgettable drama of such an occasion.

In the fourteenth century all inhabitants of the area, except bondsmen, were eligible to participate and vote if fourteen years of age. But a hundred years later, Schwyz, Glarus, and Appenzell, deciding that greater maturity was required, increased the minimal voting age to sixteen. The younger ones, however, were encouraged to witness the proceedings as a means of political indoctrination.

In the earlier days of the *Landsgemeinde* the assembly exercised functions of a court of justice, and passed judgment in criminal matters: the guilt or innocence of the accused, his punishment or his pardon.

As Dändliker points out, the *Landsgemeinde*, wherever it has survived the inroads of rule by councils, is a living and sacred monument to a noteworthy system of government (**100**, I, 544–47). It reached its peak in the fifteenth century. Somewhat as an inheritance from the past, it helps to explain the aversion of the Swiss toward centralism in government.

And now we return to 1291, the death of the emperor on July 15, a rapidly developing anti-Habsburg movement throughout the empire and widespread unrest that combined to precipitate the Covenant of 1 August 1291. This historically important alliance was soon followed by another; indeed many more covenants, some quite fugitive, and some in seeming contradiction with other solemn covenants, were negotiated as the Swiss Confederation painfully grew in stature. On 16 October 1291, Uri, Schwyz, and the royal city of Zurich formed a loose three-year defensive alliance.[12,13] Following upon the election of two emperors by a bitterly divided electorate of princes, a war of succession broke out. The Habsburgs, again at war, defeated the Zurchers at Winterthur and forced Zurich to denounce the treaty.

Morgarten and the Covenant of Brunnen

Albrecht of Habsburg, elected Emperor in 1298 on the death in battle of Adolf of Nassau, turned to diplomacy in his first efforts against the Swiss. He ratified the provisions of the early *Freibriefe* but supported the Abbey of Einsiedeln in its disputes with Schwyz. Albrecht, murdered by his nephew Johann in 1308, was succeeded by Henry VII of Luxemburg as king and emperor. The new monarch, equally disposed toward duplicity, confirmed the *Freibriefe* for the three *Waldstätte* but, in an act of reconciliation with the Habsburgs, permitted the heads of the dynasty, Friedrich and Leopold, to test their rights against the *Waldstätte*. Henry VII died in 1313. Taking advantage of a divided electorate and a second war of succession, Schwyz turned against the Abbot of Einsiedeln, plundered the Abbey, and took prisoners.[14] War with the Habsburgs was now inevitable: the spiritual overlordship of the Bishop of Constance and the civil authority of the Habsburgs as protectors of Einsiedeln had been challenged. The *Waldstätte* threw their support to Ludwig of Bavaria, the opposing contender to Habsburg for the throne.

The economic sanctions which the Habsburgs forced against the *Waldstätte* were a mere prelude to the war that speedily followed. The three cantons "neutralized" Glarus by a nonaggression pact and Uri and Schwyz made a similar pact with the Habsburg town of Arth. The Swiss, through effective roadblocks, picked the scene of battle—a narrow pass between the Aegerisee and the towering mountain of Morgarten. The Austrians were totally defeated. Stumpf (352) tells us that 1500 mounted Austrians were forced into the Aegerisee and drowned. A second column of Austrians approached Unterwalden over the Brünig pass and overran Obwalden. They learned of the disaster and were speedily forced to retreat into the Bernese *Oberland*. This victory of the Swiss farmers and peasants at Morgarten on 14 November 1315, was heralded throughout Europe as a military sensation. A few weeks later (9 December 1315), the historic covenant of 1 August 1291 was renewed and strengthened by the so-called Morgarten *Bund*. As a treaty of defense, it was pointedly directed against the Habsburgs, and it contained a new and important clause denying to a member of the Confederation the right to negotiate peace or to enter into other alliances without the consent of the others. From a legal point of view this additional Article, though frequently violated in the years that followed, constituted a first concession on the part of almost totally autonomous "cantons" in the interests of federal unity. In the spring of 1316 an assembly of the princes of the realm conceded that their historic rights in the *Waldstätte* were lost, and Ludwig, the emperor, confirmed the *Freibriefe*. Town and country communities in *Innerschweiz* sought alliances with the young Confederation, and in July 1318 the House of Austria entered into an armistice with its former enemies.

Lucerne and Zurich join the Confederation

Lucerne had sided with the Habsburgs in the battle of Morgarten and in attacks on Schwyz from the lake. These hostile acts came to be outweighed by some very practical considerations. An alliance with Lucerne would strengthen the hold of the *Waldstätte* on the very important north-south communications route from the Gotthard to Basel and beyond. This route, after crossing the lake, continued northwards by river from Lucerne, an important trade center and industrial town, and ultimately to the Rhine.

At this time in its history the Habsburg influence was dominant, with an Austrian *Vogt* in Baden as the overlord. After Morgarten the anti-Habsburgs gained in strength with resultant limitations in the office of the *Vogt*. His powers were reduced, and Lucerne received the right of selection. Also, the *Schultheiss* (mayor) henceforth had to be chosen from among the *Burgers*. In brief, following upon Morgarten, a long series of events conspired to strengthen the efforts of the city to free itself from Habsburg domination and to resist the increasing demands of the Austrian overlords.[15] After exercising its good offices in 1320 to mediate a recurrence of the strife between Schwyz and the cloister of Einsiedeln, Lucerne concluded a perpetual alliance with the forest cantons on 7 November 1332. Predictably, the Habsburgs were angered, and Karl IV denounced Lucerne's breach of faith. The emperor refused to confirm the *Freibriefe* and promises of moral support given to the *Waldstätte* by Emperor Ludwig.

The forest cantons, sensing another war with the Habsburgs, reached out to extend the scope of the Confederation. On 1 May 1351, an alliance with Zurich was negotiated. Zurich, hitherto pro-Habsburg in its sympathies, was an important commercial city. Like Lucerne it sought a secure access to the north-south route for transport in place of the long and circuitous route to Italy through the Graubünden. In the 1330s the city came under the leadership of Rudolf Brun whose policies further incited the Habsburgs to war. Brun was a dictator—a shrewd, if not unscrupulous, politician. He gave to the city a new constitution which established a city council made up of the 13 masters of the craft guilds and of 13 nobles and merchants. Brun was elected *Burgermeister* for life. His opponents, now banned from the city, sought refuge near Rapperswil under the protection of the ruling seigneur (an offshoot of the Habsburg family) who, in February 1350, organized an attack on Brun and Zurich. The attack was aborted but Brun, foreseeing the troubles ahead, attacked and destroyed the castle of Alt-Rapperswil. The Habsburgs besieged Zurich at least three times between 1351 and 1355 but were unsuccessful in their efforts to force Zurich to renounce its alliance with the embryonic Confederation whose contingents had rallied to the support of their new ally. From the tenuous Peace of Regensburg (1355) the *Waldstätte* made a few gains: recognition of the Confederation by Austria and a questionable cessation of Habsburg's claims of dominion over Schwyz and Unterwalden.

Compared with the basic document of August 1291, the treaty with Zurich was admittedly curious in the following respects. Zurich reserved the right to honor existing alliances and to negotiate others: Brun demanded this. But, by the same token, the Confederation and Lucerne were also free to honor their various alliances. Both sides expressed their loyalty to the emperor as their sovereign lord. Perhaps it was this continuing recognition of the emperor that weakened the many intra-Swiss alliances of the next 300 years. These were frequently rich in potential confusion and contradiction, for example, a pact of friendship and mutual help entered into by Zurich and Austria in 1356. Though contrary to the spirit of the alliance of 1351 with Lucerne and the *Waldstätte*, the treaty of 1356 did not imply a withdrawal of Zurich from the young Confederation. Also, the expansion of the

Confederation to include Bern, consummated in March 1353, was surely a violation of the agreement (fall of 1352) between the Confederation and the Habsburgs unless the thrust of the Bern alliance with the Confederation was in no way anti-Habsburg.

Throughout the second half of the fourteenth century, every effort by the Confederation to expand its area of influence and to increase the freedoms of its people incited the Habsburg House of Austria to renewed measures of suppression. At issue were many different causes of Austrian concern, including a desire to avenge the humilating defeats at Morgarten and Sempach, other military frustrations, the loss of revenues from hitherto subject territories, and the stubborn insistence of Austria on centralization of authority and administration. Also, Austria's policy of expansion was directed toward south-east Europe and Hungary, with buffer states to its west—a policy which could not be effectively implemented if the Swiss continued to foment unrest in areas of Habsburg influence by expanding the Confederation through diplomatic finagling and anti-Habsburg measures.

Alliances with Glarus and Zug

While the Habsburgs were engaged in their military adventures against Zurich and Rudolf Brun, the *Waldstätte* negotiated an alliance with Glarus. Here, the Habsburgs held the right of high justice through inheritance from the Counts of Kyburg. The *Landammann* was also an appointee of the Habsburgs but possessed little control over the Glarners. They were a very independent people and proud of the democratic structure of their local government. All Glarners were equal before the law. There was no social stratification and of noble families there were none. They had refused to provide a levy for the Austrians at the time of the Morgarten battle. In return, Albrecht united Glarus with the districts of Weesen and Gaster—a move which was designed to strengthen his control over Glarus. This did not rest well with the Glarners whose increasing show of stubborn independence angered Austria and led to an open break, with an Austrian division moving in from Weesen in February, 1352. On 4 June 1352, a covenant between Uri, Schwyz, Unterwalden, Zurich and Glarus was signed. Glarus agreed to help its allies by providing troops if needed for the defense of the Confederation. This agreement was not entirely mutual since the assistance to be expected by Glarus when in need was not unconditionally assured, and Glarus was denied the freedom to form other alliances without consent of the Confederation.

Zug, a city that controlled the area to the north of Schwyz, after passing through the hands of various feudal lords, finally became a Habsburg possession and stronghold. It was an effective barrier between Zurich and the *Waldstätte* and useful to the Habsburgs as a well-fortified place and staging area from which attacks against the *Waldstätte* could be launched. When the first of the Austrian wars against Zurich was seemingly ended, the Confederates attacked Zug. It fell in June, 1352, and capitulated two weeks later. The fight was largely symbolic since the city contained a vigorous faction which supported the Confederation. An act of federation, the *Zuger Bund*, was signed 27 June 1352. This included Lucerne and recognized certain of the rights of Austria as the overlord.

Bern's Expansionism and Alliance with the Confederation

Meanwhile, much had been happening in Bern, an ancient city to the west, which would have profound effects on the Confederation. The city, founded by the Zähringers in 1191, with an existing small town (Nydegg) on the Aare serving as the nucleus, had grown rapidly.[16] It was a military outpost at the interface of the Habsburg and Savoyard areas of influence. The democratic social structure of the *Waldstätte* and of Glarus was lacking; it developed into an aristocratic city with positions of authority firmly vested in the families of wealth and social importance. When the Zähringers died out, Bern placed itself directly under the protection of the emperor and received from Friedrich II in 1218 a *Freibrief* which granted royal status to the city. Beyond this, Bern negotiated protective alliances with Freiburg, Murten and the Bishop of Sitten (Sion) against the great feudal lords. It also sought the protection of the House of Savoy against the Counts of Kyburg. When Rudolf of Habsburg became emperor he confirmed the *Freibrief* of 1218 but only after he had taken Freiburg. The Habsburg policy toward Bern was one of encirclement which presently led to two sieges, a military defeat, and the imposition against the city of a very heavy fine. The anti-Habsburg factions in Bern became dominant and an alliance, later known as the Burgundian Confederation, was entered into with Freiburg, Murten, Payerne, Solothurn, and the Bishopric of Sitten.

The city went through a long and difficult period of economic and social unrest. A new constitution, toward the end of the thirteenth century, gave to the mediaeval craft guilds representation on the ruling Council of Two Hundred, but the aristocracy continued to retain the positions of leadership and authority. In the next 50 years diplomatic manoeuvering and military activities proceeded at a feverish pace. Existing political alliances and pacts of friendship were renewed. An alliance with Oberhasli was negotiated and, in 1334, Bern acquired a lien on the Haslital and, hence, the lordship over the valley. This acquisition and the alliance with Oberhasli were of great importance for they gave access to Uri, to Unterwalden via the Brünig pass, and to the upper part of the Rhone valley. Thun, a fortified town which might have stood in the way, was purchased from the Kyburgs. Two small wars, the Gümmenen and Weissenburger, and the acquisition of a lien on Laupen increased Bern's possessions in the direction of Freiburg and into the Bernese Oberland. This aggressive policy of expansion in the area between the Rhine and the Rhone rivers and the Jura and the Alps alarmed the remaining feudal lords of *Kleinburgundy* to the west. The civil and ecclesiastical lords of the affected area formed an alliance, to which Freiburg, now disturbed by Bern's aggressive expansion, adhered. Seeking by diplomatic means to avoid conflict, Bern endeavored to neutralize her neighbors. Her most faithful allies were in the Oberland and the *Waldstätte*. It is significant that the House of Savoy adopted a policy of neutrality toward the *Waldstätte*.

War had become inevitable. In the spring of 1339 the counts of Aarburg and Valangin attacked the border areas to the northwest. The Bernese forces overran Aarburg and attacked Laupen. Joined by contingents from the Oberland and the

Waldstätte, and under the supreme command of Rudolf von Erlach, the coalition of feudal lords was totally defeated in the historic battle of Laupen on 21 June 1339. Bern's authority was now widely respected. Though balancing on a diplomatic tight-rope, the city entered into a ten-year pact of friendship with Austria and simultaneously renewed an earlier friendship pact with the young Swiss Confederation. It also concluded treaties of peace with the authorities of the Burgundian lands to the west. Reluctantly, by virtue of the pact with Austria, it sent contingents of troops to join the Habsburgs in their war against Zurich but it also tried to mediate the dispute. The outcome of the war persuaded Bern, on strategic grounds, to ally itself more closely to the *Waldstätte* and their friends—hence the perpetual alliance of 6 March 1353 and additional treaties of alliance with Lucerne and Zurich.

In 1356, Karl IV gave to his empire a new constitution, the "Golden Bull." One of its provisions forbade the cities of the realm to form alliances among themselves. As we shall see, this repressive article was totally ignored by the *Waldstätte* and their allies. The House of Austria, meanwhile, had become diverted by its efforts to expand its possessions and its influence in Italy. When Archduke Albrecht II, the head of the House, died in 1358, his three sons were too young to rule; these two events combined to give the Confederation some 20 years of peace. Bern promptly resumed its policy of alliances, for example, with the towns of Gersau and Weggis away to the east (on the *Vierwaldstättersee*), and Schwyz and Zug again entered into a military pact (1364–65).

An incident that involved Rudolf, one of the Kyburgs, proved important to Bern in her desire to expand further. In quest of more *Lebensraum*, Rudolf and his allies among the nobility planned a secret attack on Solothurn in early November, 1382. But a farmer, Hans Rot, spied on the count's War Council and alerted the city in time [**100**, I, p. 492; **108**, p. 50]. Solothurn, now allied with Bern and with aid from the Count of Savoy, seized Burgdorf, the most important of the Kyburg cities. Rudolf, desperate for funds, agreed to sell Burgdorf and Thun to Bern and pledged never again to start a war without permission from Bern and Solothurn.

The Sempach War

Bern was now at the very border of Austria's Aargau possessions. As tension with the Habsburgs increased, Bern endeavored to strengthen its bonds with the *Waldstätte* where frustrations imposed by the Peace of Regensburg were mounting. The two surviving sons of Albrecht II of Austria were now of age and in 1379 they divided their inheritance. Albrecht III retained Austria and surrendered the Italian possessions, the Tirol, and the Habsburg territories in Switzerland to Leopold III who strengthened his position by purchase of the fortified towns of Nidau and Büren on the Aare.

Mention has been made of the "Golden Bull" of Karl IV. Despite its prohibitions, many intercity alliances were negotiated during his lifetime. Some were for the regulation of common economic interests while others were for protection against the repressive and expansionist policies of the feudal lords—especially the

Habsburgs. Thus, in February 1385, Bern, Zurich, Zug, and Solothurn formed such an alliance, and Lucerne and Constance entered into a friendly agreement on matters of mutual concern. Lucerne, in 1386, extended its area of control into Entlebuch and the entire valley. The city also took over the Habsburg town of Sempach and appropriated to itself the right, hitherto an Austrian privilege, of appointing the chief magistrate of Lucerne. All of these acts constituted an open challenge to Leopold. Although personally disposed toward a settlement by negotiation, his nobles wanted to finish off the "rebels" and advised him to resort to arms. Leopold assembled his army at Brugg, drawing upon the nobles, their vassals, and troops from half of Europe. On 9 July 1386, his army approached Sempach while a second detachment moved toward Zurich. The defending Swiss were mainly from Lucerne and the *Waldstätte*. Bern and Zurich stood aside for reasons of their own. Again, the Austrians were defeated and Leopold was killed in battle. The impressive victory of the Swiss had repercussions over the whole of Europe and was glorified in various sagas and heroic poems. Shortly thereafter (April, 1388) the Austrians turned against Glarus to separate it from the *Waldstätte*. It was a surprise attack but the Glarners reassembled their forces and at Näfels won a stunning victory over the Austrians. This ended the Sempach war. As a valid generalization, it should be noted that the wars with Austria were eventually between the knights and nobles on the one side and the Swiss burghers and peasants on the other (274).

A 20-year treaty of peace between Austria and the Swiss Confederation was signed on 16 July 1394. By its terms, Glarus and Zug were again free to re-enter the Confederation. The conquests made by Schwyz and Bern were formally recognized and confirmed. Lucerne was freed from Austrian domination and its seizure of Sempach, Wolhusen, the Entlebuch, and other Habsburg possessions was recognized. The treaty was signed and sealed by the members of the Confederation and also by Solothurn. The bonds of fealty to the Emperor were not severed.

The Confederation of 1291 had now evolved into an eight-member alliance of near-autonomous districts. It is not surprising that the Confederation had also developed a very complicated legal structure. In reality, it was a network of intermeshed alliances with a mutual and united defense against their enemies as the principal element in common.

The Pfaffenbrief and the Sempacher Brief

The allies were also bound together by two important supplementary agreements, the *Pfaffenbrief* of 7 October 1370, and the *Sempacher* Brief of 10 July 1393. The first of these carries the seals of Zurich, Lucerne, Zug and the three *Waldstätte*. It was designed to clarify the status of ecclesiastical courts. At the time of the *Pfaffenbrief* many difficulties had arisen because of the increasing independence of ecclesiastical lords who were subject in matters of law only to ecclesiastical courts. The *Pfaffenbrief* declared that throughout the Confederation the competence of the civil courts alone would be recognized. This ruling applied to all inhabitants including the ecclesiastical foundations as persons before the law. Other clauses dealt with police protection of the most important routes of travel and transport. Armed undertakings, pursued without the permission of the competent authorities were forbidden. The document was a milestone in the development of Swiss constitutional law in that it provided for amendment of any of the sections by the desire and approval of the majority.[17]

The *Sempacher Brief* constituted a first attempt to codify and define military law. It was an all-Confederation document to which Solothurn also adhered. The requirements for strict military discipline, the rules and regulation of plundering, the division of booty, the protection of women, children, and religious establishments, and the punishment of deserters were all defined. In other ways the *Brief* pertained to a loose, defensive alliance of free cities and rural communities, seeking freedom from subjection to the feudal lords, above all the House of Habsburg-Austria. It was not a declaration of independence from the Empire but a statement of freedom within the Empire. It called for recognition of the fundamental rights of self-determination and self-administration, the collection of taxes and the dispensing of Justice to be the responsibility of officials, judges, and courts of their own choosing. On a democratic and regional basis, the members of the Confederation sought recognition of the right of self-administration, in contrast to the nobles who had striven for control of their territorial possessions on dynastic grounds. The Sempach war made the Confederates of the eight allied regions conscious that, in spite of the diversity of their individual interests and goals, they were closely united, though to different degrees, in a common opposition to the House of Austria.

The "Bund of the Upper Lands"

The Swiss Confederation proved to be stronger and more durable than other semi-independent regional federations that came into being at the time, notably in France and England. To what may we attribute the strength and endurance of the "*Bund* of the Upper Lands", as it was commonly called? First of all in importance was the geographical compactness of the region; it fitted neatly into the area between the Rhine and the Rhone and between the Alps and the Jura. Note that the central core of Uri, Schwyz, Unterwalden, and Lucerne surrounded the *Vierwaldstättersee* (Lake Lucerne) which facilitated inter-communication and transport. Also the main transport routes within the Confederation, over the Gotthard to Italy, and the principal river valleys, were of unusual importance for trans-European traffic and as a source of revenue to various member States of the Confederation. The most surprising quality of the *Bund* was its human heterogeneity: free cities, agricultural and forest communities, peasants, free men, burghers and many within the lesser nobility. In common was an unfailing determination to win and maintain their communal independence—subject only to the Emperor. Officially, this recognition of the Emperor lasted until the Peace of Westphalia in 1648, but the bonds of attachment steadily weakened with the passage of time.

Freedom of communication, of travel, and of domicile were becoming of increasing importance. Centers of culture existed in northern Italy, Paris, South Germany, and in England. An active cultural exchange was in progress between Zurich, Bern, Basel, Lucerne, Italy and Germany. Material well-being increased, and order in the towns and on the highways gradually replaced the disorder which reached its height during the *Interregnum*. Acts of violence such as highway robbery were curbed by inflicting very severe penalties.

Population

The population grew very slowly during the fourteenth century, principally because of the catastrophic effects of bubonic plague,[18] commonly called the pest or the Black Death, which, with other pestilential diseases, decimated the land during that period. The population of Zurich City has been reported to be as follows: in 1357, 6000–7200; in 1408, 5250–6100; in 1467, 4540–4960; in 1529, 4615–5540; in 1637, 8621; in 1682, ca. 11,000; in 1762, 11,452; in 1799, ca. 10,000 (342). The fifteenth-century decrease in population is attributed to the Old Zurich war. The late eighteenth-century decrease, observed also in other Swiss cities, may have been due to civil warfare (confessional) and the impact of the French Revolution. The population of the area embraced by present-day Switzerland is assumed to have approximated 600,000 in 1300 and possibly a few thousand more in 1400. Leprosy, introduced during the Crusades, and other new diseases which assumed epidemic proportions called for strong hygienic measures.[19] Leprosy, itself, had little effect on life expectancy and, hence, did not have any adverse effect on population growth in the fourteenth century.

Significant in respect to population was a policy adopted by the towns, quite without exception, to increase their population. The newly founded cities, many of which originated in the twelfth and thirteenth centuries, sought to increase as rapidly as possible the number residing within their city walls. This policy was dictated by the need to enhance their defense capability and to compensate for the attrition caused by high death rates, the outflow of their men into foreign military service, and war-time losses. The most privileged citizens were the burghers. Admission to the *Burgerschaft* was an alluring bait. The burghers alone held positions in government. They alone could become bailiffs. Communal property rights, and privileges therefrom, such as use of the meadows, forests, common lands and other communal properties were enjoyed only the burghers. At first one became a burgher by mere residence within the city for a year and a day. Others, on return from battle, almost automatically were admitted as burghers. Basel accepted as burghers several hundred of its men after each of the thirteenth- and fourteenth-century battles. Sometimes whole villages on the outskirts were absorbed by the larger cities and the families were added to the *Burgerschaft*. This added to the political and military power of the city and correspondingly weakened that of the countryside. The records show that Basel took in 5000 burghers, exclusive of women and children, between 1356 and 1500, and 2000 more between 1530 and 1600.

The Cities and Towns

In the Alps, cities were completely lacking, though open market places such as Altdorf, Glarus, Sarnen and Schwyz had each approached the size of a small city.

The number of cities failed to increase in the late Middle Ages and the existing cities, on the average, did not increase in size. Thus Basel changed but little from 10,000 inhabitants. In the fourteenth century Bern, Freiburg, Constance and Zurich each had a static population of about 5000. A few cities had 2000 or so inhabitants, while many towns throughout the century had even less than 500 (**285**, p. 225). This cessation in population growth can be attributed to bubonic plague which, notably in 1348–49, caused the death of up to 50 percent of the inhabitants of some cities. The many wars of the fourteenth and fifteenth centuries also took their toll. With this stagnation in the growth of the towns, an accompanying economic stasis was in evidence. In contrast, the twelfth and thirteenth centuries were periods of population growth and economic development. The guilds which came into being in the Brun period and, later, may be have contributed to the economic difficulties through policies that limited production and imposed a variety of restraints on free economic activity.

It should be noted that the failure of city populations to grow, and the decline of industrial production in the late Middle Ages were phenomena in the economic history of the whole of Europe and were not peculiar to Switzerland alone (**285**, p. 226; see also note 2).

The Economy

Grain was an important product of agriculture in Innerschweiz in the thirteenth and early fourteenth centuries—even fairly high up on the mountain slopes. By the mid-fifteenth century the cultivation of cereal grains in the Alpine areas became almost totally displaced by a grass economy. This led, for a time, to an economy based on milk and a thriving export of cattle, accompanied by a steadily increasing importation of grain. Documents of the thirteenth and fourteenth centuries mention many farms in the *Waldstätte*. Grain was raised in the valley bottoms and on the lower slopes of the mountains. Oats, barley, rye, beans, peas, beets and hemp received specific mention among agricultural products. Viticulture was also practiced on the mountain slopes. Fruits were important throughout the *Waldstätte* and nuts were cultivated for oil production. In addition to cattle for milk and beef, horses, sheep, and swine were raised. It is alleged that the Schwyzers seized a herd of 400 horses from the meadows of Einsiedeln during the feud of 1308–11.

Forests were also important to the economy. Unlimited cutting was not permitted. Certain forests which gave protection against avalanches or served to reinforce the defense of borders could not be cut. All houses were of wood, except the stone towers and houses of high officials such as the *Vögte* and the *Ministerialen*. Construction was a do-it-yourself activity though some early records mention carpenters.

Mills for the grinding of grain are mentioned in the twelfth- to fourteenth-century records. Smiths and cobblers are mentioned in the oldest records of Engelberg and Einsiedeln, and a tailor is mentioned in Sarnen (Obwalden).

Of great importance, especially for Uri, was transport. Hundreds of muleteers used the Gotthard route from which Uri derived substantial revenues in tolls. The passes, of outstanding commercial and military importance to "Switzerland" were the Great St. Bernard in the west and the Lukmanier, Bernhardin, Splügen and Julier—satellites of the Septimer—in the east. The Gotthard, eventually the most important of all, was extensively used in the early thirteenth century after bridging the river Reuss at the *Schöllenenschlucht*. For many years, until the Gotthard route took over, much of the traffic to and from Italy passed through Lucerne and Raetia. Uri was responsible for maintenance and repair of the "Devil's" bridge which constantly suffered damage from avalanches and rockfalls. Labor was free because Uri could conscript its people for such public works. Charges, specifically for bridge repair and replacement, were imposed on all who used the bridges except the fellow countrymen from Schwyz, Unterwalden, and the Ursern valley.

Transportation and marketing possibilities improved, more and more roads throughout Western Europe were built, and market fairs increased. All of this ushered in a period of prosperity for the pastoral peoples who occupied the pasture lands (*Hirtenland*) from Appenzell and *Innerschweiz* to Freiburg. Incidentally, these were the people who, for some centuries from Morgarten on to the 1800s, provided a high proportion of the Swiss mercenaries whose services were greatly in demand by foreign governments.

Associated with the increasing export-import economy was a steady growth in financial affairs and the inevitable need for more money in circulation. This was followed by a gradual devaluation of silver currency in relation to the gold guilders (*Gulden*), a trend which was evident even in the fourteenth century. The purchasing power of the guilder also began to decline as the prices of merchandise in the towns and of cattle from the mountain meadows steadily increased. The cost of living increased, and noble families and great landlords, whose income, frequently in the form of rents, was fixed, were forced to borrow from the business people of the cities. Mortgage indebtedness increased, and properties were sold or so encumbered that the hinterlands became increasingly dependent on the cities. This had a profound impact throughout the land and accounts, in part, for the disappearance in *Innerschweiz* of large landholdings by the Church and the nobility. Within the cities a small upper layer of rich nobles and merchants grew in prosperity.

A few cities developed a thriving export business and international commercial relations. The linen industry and export of linen products characterized the areas around Schaffhausen and St. Gallen. Silk weaving, an art imported from Italy, developed in Zurich. Even in the fourteenth century, Freiburg had built up a widely known cloth manufacturing industry. In the countryside, especially among the farmers of the Lake Constance region, the cultivation of flax and the spinning and weaving of linen were important economic activities. They provided the raw linen which in Constance and St. Gallen was dyed, manufactured into lace and other products, and exported. In the Alpenlands, cattle were raised, cheese and leather were manufactured and, in part, exported.

If one may generalize, the Swiss towns and villages of the thirteenth and fourteenth centuries had few, if any, who lived in abject poverty, a thin layer of the very rich, and many with very modest possessions who constituted the middle class.

This was a time when the nucleus of later "Switzerland" consisted of Schwyz, Uri, and Unterwalden whose people had entered into the important alliances of 1291 and 1315. Who were the landlords and who were the tenants? Did the landlords impose any rules upon their tenants that went beyond their obligation to pay rent? And how were the rents paid?

The last question permits a simple answer. Money was a nuisance. Each "canton" had its own currency. A coinage acceptable throughout "Switzerland" was virtually nonexistent until the Federation introduced a federal currency in 1850. And so it was that rents were paid partly in money but more generally in natural products (*Naturalien*)—grain, nuts, fish, cattle, goats, goat skins, sheep, felt, wood for building, cloth, wool, leather, cheese, eggs, apples, meat, etc.

The other questions require a canton-by-canton treatment. Uri, Schwyz, and Unterwalden were originally a part of Thurgau. They became a part of Zurichgau when the westerly part of Thurgau was administratively severed from its parent. Uri was a "sort of Alemannian Siberia" (**272**, p. 27) in 732 when the region was first mentioned. It was to Uri that the Duke of Alemannia banned Abbot Eto of Reichenau for being too friendly to the Carolingian Karl Martel. But the duke soon "went to his reward" and Uri became a property of the Carolingians. Ludwig the German, in 853, gave to his daughter Hildegarde a cloister in Zurich and much surrounding property including the land of Uri. But she, on her deathbed in 856, gave much of this to her priest from whom it reverted to the cloister—better known as the Fraumünster of Zurich.

By the thirteenth century there were several landowners in Uri, possibly many, and it is not established that the whole of Uri was ever a possession of the Fraumünster. The Abbey also "owned" most of the unfree peasants, for whomsoever did not belong to some other landowner became the property of the *Gotteshaus*. Through gifts to the Abbey some of these became free and the whole of Uri became free (*Reichsfrei*) in 1231 by a substantial payment to the emperor. The original gift to the Abbey diminished in size but in the thirteenth and fourteenth centuries the Abbess was still the principal landlord in Uri. In the late thirteenth century we know that she received a part of the tithes (*Zehnten*) collected by the churches. The properties of the Abbey were widely scattered throughout Uri, and purchases, gifts, and exchanges of holdings proceeded constantly. By the beginning of the thirteenth century there were many temporal landowners in Uri. Among them were the local governors or overseers (*Vögte*) and, later, the counts of Rapperswill who, up to 1238, were also the imperial governors (*Reichsvögte*) in Ursern as tenants of the emperor. The counts of Lenzburg (from Schwyz), the Habsburgs, and other noble families had properties in Uri. There were also many small holdings owned in fee simple by free farmers. In Wettingen there were many free, whose relationships to the landlord were regulated by locally devised statutes.

A common unit of land area was the hide (*Hufe*). A hide of land, equal to ten hectares (twenty-five acres), was indivisible in Carolingian times. Later, division among the sons of a deceased owner was permitted, so also the acquisition of additional *Hufen*.

In 1359 the cloister sold its entire possessions, the income derived therefrom, and the rights that pertained, to the land of Uri for about 100,000 francs. Along with Wettingen, three other foundations of the Cistercian order sold their possessions to the land of Uri. It is tempting to infer that the "canton" of Uri must have enjoyed a considerable income from the transit tolls imposed on the many who used the approach through Uri over the Devil's Bridge to the Gotthard and northern Italy. Hence, she had the money to buy her freedom from the emperor and to acquire the landed possessions of a number of temporal and ecclesiastical landowners.

In the mid-thirteenth century the four communities Altdorf, Bürglen, Erstfelden, and Silenen were each placed under the administrative control of a mayor (*Meier*). The communities were, in effect, estates (*Meierhöfe*) which the Abbey entrusted to the four *Meieren* as perquisities of the office. The principal task of the *Meieren* was to oversee these properties and to ensure that the rights and income of the Abbey suffered no loss. Originally, they probably had police and juridical functions which came to an end when the communities began to administer their own affairs through their own appointees. The *Meieren* were men of local importance. Konrad, *Meier* of Erstfelden (1275–97) was one of the fathers of the *Eidgenossenschaft* in 1291, while Arnold, *Meier* of Silenen, also said to be a father of the embryonic confederation, became *Landammann* of Uri in 1291. As local government evolved, a *Meier* came to be known as an *Ammann*.

In the thirteenth century, the lower subclass of the *Ritters* (a knightly class in the lower nobility) and *Ministerialen* were heavily represented in the *Waldstätte*. The Ritter of Silenen in Uri was also the *Ministerial* to the Abbess of the Fraumünster in Zurich.

Bordering on Schwyz, first mentioned in 972 in a document whereby Otto II confirmed various gifts of his father, was the great cloister Einsiedeln—the center of almost endless border disputes with the Schwyzers. Whether the Einsiedeln people, apart from the monks, were serfs or free small farmers is not stated in early documents. The monks of Einsiedeln were mostly *Ministerialen*. Many of these are identified by name in Oechsli's very detailed description of the times (**272**, p. 165). They also had the title of *Herr* which could be used only by the nobility. In the thirteenth century, only clerics and *Ritters*, among the lower nobility, had the *Herr* title. In general, the *Ritters* of Schwyz were either in the service of the cloister or of the Habsburgs. In 1289, many Schwyzers supported King Rudolf in his march on Besançon. It is certain that some of these were already *Ritters* or were later elevated to the *Ritterschaft* through military service to the Habsburgs.

The possessions of cloisters in Schwyz were not very great; and all were eventually purchased by the "canton" for much less than Uri paid for the Wettingen properties. Among the noble families, the Lenzburgs were prominent landowners who played a conspicuous role in the Schwyz-Einsiedeln dispute. Count Eberhard of Habsburg-Laufenburg was another great landowner in Schwyz—eventually selling his properties to his cousin, King Rudolf I, to settle a rather enormous claim for the cost of caring for Eberhard's wife when she was still an unmarried minor. The Kyburg and Froberg families are also known to have been owners of extensive properties in Schwyz. But there was also a predominance of free peasants who lived on their own ground and soil—probably more than in any other "canton" of *Innerschweiz*.

In Unterwalden, some 15 manorial estates (*Höfe*) existed in quite early times. Each was administered, typically, by a *Meier* and a *Kellner* (service employee). Each was entitled to a *Hof*—a *Meierhof* or a *Kellnerhof*. Sometimes the two offices were combined and only one *Hof* served as the official premises. Police and juridical functions over the people in the community were exercised by the *Meier* unless the authority had already been vested in the abbot or prior of the *Murbach Abbey* (in Lucerne) which since 840, at least, owned extensive holdings in Unterwalden. The *Kellner* was required to collect the ground rents and any other income and revenue to which the *Hof* was entitled.

The people serving the estates of the Abbey were mostly unfree and in the thirteenth century constituted a tightly closed society. If any of these married an outsider, the children of such a union lost all property rights. If a serious delinquency, such as three years default in payment of rents was encountered, the properties involved fell into possession of the Abbey. Those who rented any land from the Abbey paid lower rents than others and, by virtue of immunities enjoyed by the Abbey, none of its properties were taxable by the king or kaiser.

Later in the century, the Abbey ceased to be the sole possessor of its Unterwalden properties. Much of the income and property rights belonged to the Abbot, the prior, or the administrative officers of the four cloisters; a division of the Abbey's properties had taken place. Certain political rights were sold to Austria—a fact of significance to the *Waldstätte*. The Abbot, of course, retained the seignorial and sovereign rights of the Abbey, though he rented out much of the property rights to a long list of others—from the prior on down to the monks in the cloisters. By a purchase treaty of 16 April 1291 all the rights which the Abbot of Murbach had in 16 *Höfe* in Lucerne, income and all, were sold with few exceptions to Austria (**272**, p. 76).

The counts of Lenzburg, based in Schwyz, had extensive properties in Unterwalden. The family had established the prebendary foundation in Beromünster (Lucerne "canton") to which Count Ulrich (the Rich) of Lenzburg gave a number of Unterwalden *Höfe* in the eleventh and twelfth centuries. The workers in these estates were unfree servants who farmed the lands, did the housework, and took care of the properties—all of this in return for their personal maintenance and protection. They were at the bottom of the social scale and were subject to many rules and restrictive regulations imposed by Beromünster. The free were a minority, and were also strictly controlled by Beromünster though their property rights were usually inheritable through several generations.

Within Unterwalden, there is also the famous Engelberg cloister which enjoyed a long-continued connection with a nunnery (*Frauenkloister*). The leading families of the Lake Lucerne area were accustomed to send their daughters to the nunnery for shelter and upbringing. The novitiates customarily brought money or other gifts to the *Frauenkloister* which added to its wealth. Engelberg also possessed a number of churches and other landed properties. The larger manorial estates were administered, as was customary elsewhere, by a *Meier*.

Unlike Uri and Schwyz, the church was the economic and political "head" of Unterwalden. We may think of the region as consisting of many small pieces which in the mid-thirteenth century had no formal political bond, but which were much more closely associated with the cloisters and religious institutions than with a central political authority. It was, in effect, an ecclesiastical state. Whether the name "Unterwalden" was in use at that time is even in doubt (272, p. 266). In thirteenth-century documents, the people were called *Waldleute* (the forest people). By 1261, a corporate entity called the *Gemeinde der Waldleute des unteren Tales*—viz. Nidwalden—had been established. By 1291, the parishes of the upper valley were united into a single sovereign corporate entity—viz. Obwalden. The two valleys soon came together into a single unit (Unterwalden), though sovereignty continued to be divided between the two halves—Nidwalden with its capital in Stans, and Obwalden with its capital in Sarnen.

Ministerialen were most numerous in Unterwalden. Some were in the service of the cloister Murbach-Lucerne, in the management of its extensive properties in Unterwalden. Engelberg had many *Ministerialen* in its service. The *Meier* of Stans and the *Kellner* of Sarnen also belonged to the *Ministerial* class.

By the end of the thirteenth century most of the noble families in Unterwalden had disappeared or suffered a considerable diminution in their holdings. The House of Habsburg, however, survived and expanded its Unterwalden properties considerably, sometimes by purchase, sometimes by exchange.

Raetia

As the fourteenth century came to an end, Bern hastened to extend its influence into the *Oberland* by an alliance with Wallis (Valais). She perceived the immediacy of a new war with Austria, now threatened by the alliances being forged by the *Waldstätte* on the approaches to Raetia.[20] Glarus, as an intermediary, concluded a permanent alliance with the Upper or *Grau Bund* in Raetia on 24 May 1400.

Raetia as a whole belonged to the German Reich. Politically, it was split into a number of territories, some falling under the control of feudal lords and various nobles, such as the Count of Toggenburg, or of ecclesiastical foundations—the Bishopric of Chur and the Cloister of Disentis—for example. An extensive alliance of peasant communities, the *Gotteshausbund*, came into being in 1367 and extended over the whole of southeastern Raetia to the Austrian border. A second comparable alliance, the *Grau Bund*, was formed in 1395. It consisted of the whole of western Raetia and bordered on Glarus, Uri, and what is now known as Ticino. The *Gotteshausbund*, though adjacent to Austria, was oriented politically against the Habsburg—more so than the *Grau Bund* which was really a defensive alliance against all invaders from beyond the borders of the alliance. The Glarus—*Grau Bund* alliance of 1400 was an important entering wedge by which the Swiss Confederation hoped to extend its influence to the very borders of Austria.

Appenzell and St. Gallen

More important in the early 1400s were the associations of the Confederation with Appenzell and St. Gallen, their immediate neighbors to the northeast. And here we must digress somewhat to consider the early history of these complex communities. The Abbey of St. Gallen, founded in 854 or earlier, possessed unusual rights arising from its antiquity. The Abbot was a Prince of the Reich. He was not only the spiritual head of the Abbey and administrator of its extensive landholdings but also a feudal lord with great political power. His word was law. He levied the taxes, controlled expenditures, and raised troops as needed for his military objectives. But there was also a second power, the town of St. Gallen, with which the Abbot was in more or less constant conflict. Perhaps this was inevitable for the town was completely surrounded by the lands of the Abbey.

The early thirteenth century was a time of much misfortune for the Abbey and relations with the town were at a low ebb. The struggle for self-determination which was characteristic of the times made much progress in the town, such that by the end of the century St. Gallen had obtained the status of a royal town subject to none but the king. The Abbot who hitherto administered justice in the lower courts of the town was now excluded. The town developed an administrative structure with a *Burgermeister* and guild representation on the council. It became a member of the League of Seven Cities in the Lake Constance region but, as yet, was without any ties to the emerging Swiss Confederation.

In the eleventh century, the Abbey of St. Gallen possessed the land now known as the Canton of Appenzell. It brought in new settlers, and germanized the area (the earlier language was a dialect of Romansh). Later, some of the village communities acquired a number of rights from the sovereign and, by the second half of the fourteenth century, had progressed far toward independence. The principal route to the Vorarlberg, which was of much importance to St. Gallen, fell through several of these towns and villages. To restrain St. Gallen and the Appenzellers from a rapprochement which might have serious political consequences, the Abbot entered into an accord with representatives of Austria in the Rheintal. Fearful of an armed conflict with Austria, Appenzell in 1401 sought a defensive alliance with the town of St. Gallen. This led to the expected result, a counter-alliance in 1402 between the Abbot of St. Gallen and the Austrian governor of the Rheintal. The League of Royal Cities of which St. Gallen was a member persuaded St. Gallen to renounce its alliance with Appenzell.

Appenzell then turned to Schwyz in 1403 and negotiated a similar pact. This quickly led to a war in the opening stages of which, the Abbot, joined by contingents from the League of Royal Cities, marched against the Appenzellers and their new allies from Schwyz. The Abbot suffered a humiliating defeat in the battle of Vögelinsegg and with his fleeing troops was driven back to the gates of St. Gallen. The alliance of the Abbey and the League of Royal Cities fell asunder and the member towns concluded treaties of peace with Appenzell. Unfortunately this did not end hostilities, since Friedrich IV of Austria entered the scene and ordered the Abbot to join an Austrian army in a march on Appenzell. The Swiss Confederation was promptly reminded of its 20 years' peace with Austria which forbade any member States of the Confederation to assist Austria's enemies. The reminder was pointedly directed at Schwyz which now withheld its support from Appenzell. However, St. Gallen now placed itself openly on the side of Appenzell. It is significant that Zurich, Bern, Lucerne and Solothurn, though ordered by Friedrich IV to lend him their support, refused to do so. The Duke suffered a modest defeat in an initial effort to conquer St. Gallen. In the meantime a second powerful Austrian column moved against the Appenzellers who had taken position at a narrow pass by Stoss. In pouring rain and on slippery ground, the mounted forces of Austria were helpless against the Appenzellers. The Austrian forces were decimated and Friedrich IV, now discouraged, gave up the fight. In 1406, Austria negotiated an armistice and in 1407, the Abbot of St. Gallen placed the cloister under the protection of Appenzell! With encouragement and renewed support from Schwyz, the Appenzellers advanced on the Vorarlberg and urged the farm communities to resist the nobles. Some of the neighboring feudal lords, including the Counts of Werdenberg and Toggenburg, hastened to declare their friendship with Appenzell. In late 1407 the invaders attacked Bregenz, suffered a bloody defeat in January 1408, and in humiliation retreated homewards.

Defiantly, Appenzell now sought recognition by the emperor, in effect requesting a *Freibrief* which would place the State directly under royal protection. It also negotiated an alliance with the Swiss Confederation.[21] This was concluded on 24 November 1411, with seven of the member States as signatories. Aristocratic Bern remained on the outside, largely because she had little self-interest in the alliances then being negotiated by the cantons to the east.

Like Glarus, Appenzell was admitted to the Confederation as an unequal. Without the consent of the Confederation she agreed not to engage in war. In foreign relations, the advice and consent of the Confederation must be sought in matters of high policy. In 1412, St. Gallen entered into a ten-year pact with the Confederation—again with restricted membership rights.

An uneasy peace, lasting only a few years, followed. Appenzell meanwhile opposed every effort of the Abbot to regain his rights and in 1426 the Abbot placed the stubborn Appenzellers under the ban and interdiction of the church. The acrimonious disputes led to renewed warfare. The feudal lords now sided with the Abbot and the Confederation stood aside. The first two engagements were won by the Appenzellers but the third and decisive battle, at Herisau, was lost. Appenzell was now forced to accept arbitration of the dispute by the Swiss Confederation. The rights of the Abbot were upheld but Appenzell gained more independence in tax matters and in the composition of the courts. By this time (1429) the Confederation had developed a real depth of interest in the political problems of the area between the Bodensee (Lake Constance), the Zurichsee, and the Walensee. Schwyz sympathized with the views of Appenzell, shared its aspirations, and was eagerly desirous of opening up communications between Zurich and Raetia along the flat lands of the Linth valley. However, not until 1513 was Appenzell admitted to full membership in the Confederation.

Expansion to the South

While this move to the east was under way, the Swiss were fast becoming involved in developments to the south. Uri, above all, sought to strengthen its control over the Gotthard route. Jointly with the people of the Ursern valley, agreement was reached on an ordinance governing transport over the route, including taxes, tariffs, and police protection. On crossing the border of Uri at the Gotthard ridge, the route continued into the Duchy of Milan. In 1402, the death of the reigning Duke whose son was a minor led to bitter inter-party fighting and serious threats to the security of the Gotthard route, including recurring fighting between the Swiss and Italian muleteers. The Swiss intervened under the guise of restoring order. Forces from Uri and Unterwalden crossed over into the valley of Leventina, which in 1403 gave up without a struggle. It became a subject of Switzerland, with the Leventines swearing fealty and putting themselves under the protection of Uri and Unterwalden. In a sense the Swiss regarded themselves as liberators who responded to the call of the Leventines, just as Schwyz had responded to the call of Appenzell. To secure the Gotthard route, the freedom and the friendship of those on the other side of the Gotthard were important. The Leventines were given the full rights of selfadministration under Swiss protection but the district was not admitted to the Confederation.

Uri and the Ursern valley now used their strengthened political position and resources to purchase Bellinzona. In common with Obwalden they thereby held an important approach to the plains of Lombardy and the road to Milan. Was the Swiss Confederation in sympathy with this movement to the far south? It was clear to all that the Duchy of Milan would regain its strength, and the rights attached to control of the Gotthard route would be the subject of dispute and future strife. Indeed in April 1422, a Milanese general suddenly attacked Bellinzona and brought it under his control. When he moved on to the Leventine, Uri and Unterwalden, now thoroughly alarmed, sought reinforcements from their fellow members in the Confederation. Zug and Lucerne responded, Zurich procrastinated, and Schwyz decided to attack through the Eschental toward Domodossola. Bern remained outside of the fray. Uri and its allied forces, eager to retake Bellinzona, took up a position at Arbedo. In the battle that followed on 30 June 1422, both sides suffered enormous losses. Many of the Swiss leaders were killed in battle, including a third of Lucerne's governing council. "Was the contest worth the price?" was a question which the Swiss would have to ask themselves again after the bloody battle of Marignano in September, 1515. The famous dictum of Brother Klaus, "Don't meddle in foreign wars," was never again forgotten (see Chapter 4).

Neutrality

One of the most unique aspects of Switzerland and her institutions is her status as a perpetual Neutral. This is recognized and respected throughout the world and was even guaranteed in 1814–15 by the signatory Powers of the Treaty of Paris. It is appropriate that we inquire into its beginnings. Neutrality in the Middle Ages was so far removed from the present concept of neutrality that some historians and students of international law refuse to recognize that it was ever observed before the seventeenth century. But neutrality is a thing of many parts and we must ask ourselves whether any part of the whole was practiced in the early days. Did "neutrality" in the Middle Ages mean that a neutral State would totally abstain from any participation in a war then raging or about to begin—sit quietly (*stille sitzen*),[22] as they used to say? Did a neutral State deny to the armed forces of belligerents the right of passage through its territory? Did it refuse to provide mercenaries to warring Powers? Did it refuse to permit recruiting within its borders by representatives of the belligerents? Did it defend itself against trespass by belligerent forces to prevent extension of the fighting into its own territory? Did it treat both sides equally and impartially, not extending any favors to one that were denied to the other? Did it sedulously avoid provocative behavior toward a neighboring State?

All of these questions would have to be answered in the negative. The early history of central Europe is rich in agreements between States, communities, feudal lords, kings and emperors in which neutrality (*stille sitzen*) by one or more of the contracting Powers is pledged in any war involving the others. The agreements were frequently defensive alliances, sometimes deliberately unilateral to maintain friendly relations between the Neutral and one of the parties at war. The dispatch of troops to aid a friendly Power was clearly a form of mercenary service and was widely practiced in Europe for centuries. Swiss mercenaries were greatly in demand, an inevitable result of the sensational victories of the Swiss at Morgarten (1315), Laupen (1339), Sempach (1386), Näfels (1388) and Stoss (1406). The Swiss were universally esteemed for their courage in battle and their loyalty to those into whose service they entered.[23]

The sanctity of prior agreements was universally recognized, and assistance given by a Neutral to one party to which it was bound by treaty was not considered a breach of its neutrality, provided only that it did not go too far. Thus, no one seriously questioned the right of a Neutral to send troops to support its ally. If the number was not excessive, if the troops were used defensively to protect the frontiers of their ally and to provide internal security, and if they were not obliged to engage in offensive operations, the neutrality of the State was not compromised. In fact, this interpretation of the rights of a Neutral prevailed through the seventeenth and eighteenth centuries.

Even the right of passage of armed troops of a foreign Power through a neutral State was recognized. We need only examine a political map of Europe to realize that in the good old days this right was entirely reasonable. Germany was a conglomerate of relatively small autonomous States. Switzerland was also an aggregate of near-autonomous States which owed their allegiance to the *Romisch* king. All contained pockets or islands of foreign possessions. The many dynastic holdings were not neatly consolidated in large blocks but were scattered in bits and pieces. In time, a measure of consolidation came about through interdynastic marriages, conquest or purchase. In the days of scattered possessions, of enclaves within a foreign territory, the defense of such holdings required the free passage of armed troops through the intervening territory of a Neutral. The right was never questioned until agglomeration had proceeded far and many of the foreign enclaves had disappeared.[24]

In the Middle Ages, little, if any, effort was made by a Neutral to treat both belligerents equally. But the time soon came when a Neutral, notably Switzerland, declared its intention to be impartial (*unparteiisch sein*).[25] This is not the time or place to inquire critically into the practicality of according equal treatment to both belligerents. Schweizer described it as a theoretical fiction which in reality never did exist and is not possible (**328**, p. 46). Over a century earlier, Emerich de Vattel (1714–67), one of the greatest authorities on international law, declared such theoretical impartiality to be absurd since it would be impossible for any State to render equal aid to two belligerents (**374**, III, 104). In this context, aid to a belligerent could then take the form of mercenaries, food, supplies for the civilian population, war materials and money.

What evidence do we have in the early history of Switzerland of agreements that savor of a primitive sort of neutrality and involved the members of the emerging Confederation? There are several such agreements that deserve mention.

In May, 1308, Albrecht I, the Emperor, was murdered near Oberrieden by his nephew John of Swabia. Dukes Friedrich and Leopold of Austria,[26] bent on revenge, prepared the way by a neutrality pact with Zurich in 1309. The treaty permitted the Austrians to march through territory controlled by the city, and to enter Zurich, unarmed, for purchase of supplies. The Austrians in turn agreed to respect the neutrality of the valleys of the Limmat, the Sihl and the Zurchersee from Dietikon to Wadenswil, and to pay damages to Zurich for any infringement of the pledge (**370**, I, p. 248; **328**, p. 24). The treaty, by virtue of its unilateral character, denied any favors whatever to the other party—in this case not at all surprising.

Between 1382 and 1385 Bern and the Counts of Kyburg were at war. Duke Leopold III of Austria promised Bern to remain neutral (*stille sitzen*) even though the Kyburgs were his vassals and were related to the House of Habsburg. Nor would the Duke grant to the Kyburgs the right of passage of their armed retainers through his territories. Leopold's declaration of neutrality was totally unilateral.

In 1394, eight years after Sempach, Austria and Zurich concluded a friendship pact of 20 years duration.[27] Zurich promised to remain neutral in case of another war between Austria and the Swiss Confederation, while Austria pledged herself to come to the aid of her ally if Zurich should be attacked by other members of the Confederation. A popular uprising within Zurich and vigorous complaints by the other members of the Confederation soon brought an end to this diplomatic victory of the Austrians.

A five-year treaty between Bern and Solothurn on the one hand and Rudolf of Hochberg, Count of the Marches,[28] on the other, was signed on 31 May 1399. This was a straightforward agreement to ensure mutually the free movement of goods and people between the territories of the two parties. If one party should go to war with a third, the second party promised to remain neutral. The second party was also required to seek, by peaceful intermediation, a restoration of the peace. If such a friendly offer was refused by the third party, the second party was pledged to intervene by force—provided that the third-party attack was unjust. Significant in the evolution of foreign policies was an exclusion from the terms of the pact, of other parties with whom other alliances had been negotiated or some special relàtionship existed. Thus the Reich and Austria were excluded by both. The Count of the Marches excluded his fiefholders and his bosom friends. Bern and Solothurn excluded member "cantons" of the Swiss Confederation and their associated cities and States.

In 1406, Rudolf of Hochberg promised to remain neutral in any war in which Basel might be engaged during the following year.[29] Six months later the pact was renewed for another year.[30] A pledge was included whereby Basel promised to remain neutral in any war in which Rudolf of Hochberg might be involved. By virtue of earlier agreements to provide military assistance if needed, Basel excluded through a reservation clause, the Bishopric of Basel and the cities of Bern, Strassburg and Solothurn.

A somewhat involved treaty, a ten-year pact, was concluded in 1405 between Appenzell and St. Gallen on the one hand and a number of towns in the "Gasterland" on the other.[31] The latter agreed to protect Appenzell and St. Gallen from attack by any dissident elements in Gasterland. In return, the people of the towns were granted the freedom of trade and commerce in Appenzell and St. Gallen and certain travel privileges. Enemies of the towns, however, were to be excluded from entry into Appenzell and St. Gallen and were to be denied any aid whatsoever. The two "cantons" agreed to avoid carrying any wars with others into the Gasterland. The right of peaceful transit of troops through Gasterland by the one party and through Appenzell and St. Gallen by the other was agreed to.

A short but excellent treatment, in English, of Swiss neutrality, including its disorderly and faltering beginnings, is by Bonjour (56), whose major work on the history of Swiss neutrality comprises nine volumes (49).

The Closing Years of the Fourteenth Century

As the fourteenth century ended, Austria controlled, through ownership or other rights, Thurgau, Aargau, the largest part of what is now the canton of Zurich, and the district of Willisau. The Dukes of Austria also exercised the rights of a liege lord over small scattered feudal areas and as administrators of the law over ecclesiastical lands and holdings. The Habsburg influence was also strong in the west. Freiburg was a center of influence. Austria's policy clearly sought for control along the Rhine from Constance to Basel and, through the Bishopric of Basel, on into the Bernese Jura.

Meanwhile, Bern took advantage of the 20 years of peace with Austria to extend her control far and wide. By purchase and by diplomacy she acquired parts of the Simmental, the Emmental, and Frutigen. From the Kyburgs, who were heavily in debt, the city purchased Wengen, Aarwangen, and Herzogenbuchsee. She became exceptionally strong economically. In 1393, Zurich and Austria concluded a special friendship pact which applied to a very extensive area from Lake Constance to Freiburg and from Schaffhausen to the Grimsel Pass. Most of this region was not even under Zurich's control. Of great interest is the fact that Zurich pledged itself to remain neutral in case of a new conflict between Austria and the Swiss Confederation. Austria, in turn, promised to help Zurich if attacked by her fellow members in the Confederation. This diplomatic victory of the Austrians was short-lived. Within a few weeks a popular revolt broke out in Zurich and the pro-Austrian mayor was overthrown and forced to flee from the city. This led to important constitutional changes in Zurich—more political power to the craft guilds and the right of the city to appoint its own *Reichsvogt*, the representative of the king.

Notes and Comments

1. The free and the partially free, such as those attached to abbeys and other religious establishments, constituted the great majority of the *Innerschweiz* population in the thirteenth century. The emancipation of the unfree went on during the next two centuries, but is believed to have made substantial progress even by 1291. To describe the people as either free or unfree would be an oversimplification. Numerous gradations existed (see e.g. **272**, p. 189). An impression of the social complexity of the times can be gained by mentioning some of the classes: the *Ministerialen* and the *Ritters* (see note 7); the *Hintersassen* (free farmers of a low status) who farmed lands owned by others and paid ground rents to their landlords); the *Knechte* (servants and farm hands); *Hörigen* (those who were in bondage to the Church and to the worldly great and were virtually the property of their protector, the landowner), several kinds of *Vögte* (in general, administrative officials with the functions of an overseer) including representatives of the emperor, i.e. *Reichsvögte*; administrative officials of the church (Churchwardens) with the added responsibility of ensuring protection—so called *Kirchenvögte*. The number of *Vögte* of one kind or another in a province (*Gau*) such as Zurichgau or Thurgau was almost countless (**272**).

A multiplicity of regulations which defined the relations between the landlord and his serfs, his tenants and retainers was also characteristic of the times. Some of this was designed to make sure that the State did not interfere in the affairs of the landowners. Thus, in every manorial estate there arose a set of detailed rules applicable to those attached to the manor; also an estate court (*Hofgericht*) to administer the rules. In these courts all of the personnel of the manor, free and unfree, were obliged to appear. And the people, not the landlord or the administrator of the estate, passed judgment on the matters that came before the court. In disturbed times, the people met weekly to discharge this judicial function. In times of peace they met biweekly, usually with the *Graf* (count) serving as chairman but not as a judge. In a sense this was similar to the workings of the courts for established communities (*Volksgericht*) where the people of the community (*Gemeinde*), not the count, determined the verdict.

Thus there arose, external to the State, and on the estates of the landlords, regulations in infinite detail which governed the conduct of the free and the unfree and gave to the unfree an assured existence. The unfree were denied this paternal sort of protection in the public courts of the State. The numerous private courts served the needs of a large class of people by offering protection against violence and despotism. Originally these courts had no competence in affairs external to the estate. In time, some of the authority of the public courts was transferred to the landlords, and the manorial courts acquired some of the qualities of the State courts. It should be noted that the *Graf*, responsible to the king, was originally the uppermost official in a *Gau* (province). He exercised multiple functions as head of the military, police, fiscal, and judicial officials. With the passage of time, his responsibilities diminished and, by the fourteenth century, were frequently only nominal.

2. In the thirteenth century, the foundation of cities proceeded much more rapidly than in preceding centuries. For reasons that are not obvious this was a time of significant population growth. Bickel

assumes, on the basis of several studies, that the population of the area embraced by present-day Switzerland, around 1300 or 1400, approximated 600,000 to 650,000 (**40**, pp. 39, 48). In the fifteenth and sixteenth centuries the population increase was small because of the heavy loss of life attributable to war and visitations of the bubonic plague. In a number of cases, such as Bern and Freiburg, the cities served as fortified centers, well located for defense. They functioned as regional capitals for centralization of administration and political control over the surrounding lands or, in some cases, for collection of tolls at important river crossings and transport centers. Typically, the cities founded in the Middle Ages exercised economic, political and military functions. Some attained the status of a royal city (*Reichsfrei*) and enjoyed a large measure of independence in political and juridical affairs.

Toward the end of the Middle Ages, the cities in the area of present-day Switzerland, exclusive of the Ticino, numbered about 140. All but 22 of these were located on the shores of a lake or a river (**40**, p. 58). Others had been founded but failed to survive.

Many of these were very small, consisting of little more than a castle, a few houses, other buildings and the surrounding city wall. Insofar as the city exercised control over the people of the surrounding countryside, as was frequently the case, the problems that arose between the two parties became more and more difficult to resolve, and persisted in part even to modern times.

It will be understood that some of the cities of present-day Switzerland were founded in Roman times or even earlier. In general they centered around religious foundations, being in several instances the seat of a bishopric. For example Basel, as the first city of the Bishopric of Basel, was founded at the beginning of the seventh century, Chur in the middle of the fifth century, Zurich around 929, and Lausanne around 906. The economic and cultural life of these cities was in active development in the eleventh and twelfth centuries, but one must emphasize the fact that unlike most of the cities originating in the twelfth and thirteenth centuries, they came into being as the site of important religious foundations such as, in Zurich, the Fraumünster founded in 853 by Ludwig the German, and the Grossmünster—a prebendary foundation; St. Peter's Church in Lausanne and several bishoprics. Such cities for many years depended for their existence on their close association with a cloister, a church, an abbey, etc. Peyer, however, points out that some cities and market towns, founded by the Romans in the seventh and eighth centuries, were strictly centers for economic enterprise, trading places located on important transport routes (**285**, p. 155).

3. Ulrich III of Kyburg (†1227) was married to Anna of Zähringen.

4. Under Peter II (1263–68), his brother Philip I (1268–85), and Amadeus V (1285–1323), the House of Savoy controlled the territory from Lac Leman (Lake Geneva) to the Aare. Their influence extended northwards to Lyon. Except for scattered possessions of other dynasties the counts of Savoy ruled the whole of western Switzerland. The dynasty, however, never vigorously sought to expand east of the Aare.

5. The mother of Rudolf IV of Habsburg was Heilweg, a daughter of Ulrich III of Kyburg. Through her, Rudolf inherited a substantial part of the Kyburg holdings. When elected head of the Holy Roman Empire as King Rudolf I, he retained the title Count of Kyburg and Habsburg.

6. In the valleys of *Innerschweiz* all the people participated in the decision-making process. In these assemblies (*Landsgemeinden*) only foreigners were excluded. The serfs of the House of Lenzburg and of the cloisters were entitled to participate. The free and the unfree worked together and the welfare of all demanded that both take part in these assemblies. Democracy was not introduced: it came by itself. At the head was the *Ammann* (a word known to the Lombards, signifying at the time a military leader). According to Öchsli an *Ammann* corresponded to the old Carolingian *Centenar* (**272**, p. 123). He was chosen by the people "who listened only to whom they wanted and not to whom they must." Free birth and a good name were necessary for election. Bondsmen were ineligible because their obligations consisted only in service to their master (a conflict-of-interest situation). They were not free to be equally fair to all. The judges, by custom, were from old well-settled families. They were impartial because they were rich enough in their own right (plenty of cattle and other possessions) to be nondependent on foreign payments and life annuities. The uppermost judge, superior to all the other judges, was called the *Landammann*. In the natural development of their grass-roots democracy the valley people fashioned their own judicial system and laws based on plain common sense. The *Landsgemeinde* was the important decision-making body.

Whatever troubles these people had were seldom internal but stemmed from the different customs and unrest of neighboring peoples, and the persistent efforts of ruling dynasties—notably the Habsburgs—to force acceptance of foreign overlords (255, I, pp. 21–24).

7. The *Ministerialen* belonged to a strongly differentiated group of the unfree who were enabled to rise into the lower nobility. They were given important responsibilities in peace and in war. In combat, they served their lord and master, the Count. A *Ritter* seems to have been slightly higher in the lower nobility. He served in war, his principal function, and could rise into higher levels of the nobility.

8. The Hohenstaufens descended from the Swabian family of Staufer. Friedrich II, King of Sicily and Emperor of the Reich, was the son of Kaiser Heinrich VI (1190–97), the conqueror of Sicily. The Hohenstaufen Emperors were Konrad III (1138–52), Friedrich I (1152–90), Heinrich VI (1190–97), Friedrich II (1212–50), and Konrad IV (1250–54). There is disagreement between Tschudi (370) and Ploetz (293) in the numbering of the Heinrichs. It is clear, however, that the first Heinrich was Emperor from 919 to 936 and four other Heinrichs served as Emperor before we come to Heinrich VI.

9. Prior to 1800 or so, historians dated the beginnings of the Confederation from 1308 or 1315. For example, see *Délices de la Suisse* published in 1714 (311) under the authorship of Abraham Ruchat. Ruchat refers to an offensive and defensive alliance of 1308 between Uri, Schwyz and Unterwalden, inspired by the tyranny of two Austrian governors appointed by Albrecht I (1298–1308). Rudolf I, the King, and father of Albrecht, had died July 15, 1291. Reference is also made by Ruchat to the perpetual alliance of 9 December 1315, between the three valley communities (ultimately known as cantons) of Uri, Schwyz, and Unterwalden. This Convention, later confirmed by the German Emperor, Ludwig of Bavaria, extended and solidified the terms of earlier agreements between these three forest cantons around Lake Lucerne. Stanyan, also in 1714, likewise unaware of the covenant of August 1, 1291, assigns 1308 or 1315 to the formal beginnings of the Confederation (339).

It should be noted that during the troubled years around the turn of the century, localized rebellions against the Habsburgs and their agents broke out elsewhere in the lands of present-day Switzerland, in south Germany and in several of the Austrian provinces in which the Habsburgs had extensive holdings. It is uncertain whether these scattered uprisings were spontaneous and identical in cause, or whether the nucleus of revolt lay in the three ancient cantons from which the contagion then spread rapidly through the Habsburg holdings. Whatever may have happened elsewhere, only the stubborn insistence of freedom by the people of the three ancient cantons led to an enduring Confederation.

10. "Wir haben auch einhellig gelobt und festgesetzt, dass wir in den Tälern durchaus keinen Richter, der das Amt irgendwie um Geld oder Geldeswert erworben hat oder nicht unser Einwohner oder Landmann ist, annehmen sollen" (81, p. 39).

11. Hasli is a district in the Bernese Oberland reaching up to the high mountains where the Aare and the Rhone originate. To its east is the canton of Uri with Obwalden to the north. Hasli has a complicated and curious history. It is believed to have enjoyed freedom under the Reich from the time of Charlemagne (771–814), who received the help of its people in his efforts with the sword to spread the Christian religion. Settlement of Hasli probably began in the seventh century, though this is undocumented. Around 1124 much of Hasli was essentially a province of Burgundy—perhaps the only part of transjura Burgundy which was recognized as part of the Reich.

In 1296 Bern and Hasli executed a mutual defense pact. Prior to this the Houses of Kyburg and Savoy were involved successively in protective agreements with Hasli. Its troubles began in 1310 when Kaiser Heinrich VII became indebted to the Weissenburg family and pawned the land of Hasli, its properties, and its people as security. The pawn was never redeemed and passed through several ownerships. The people lost the freedoms and immunities they had enjoyed under the Reich and were exploited by their rulers. Bern came to the rescue and laid siege to Wimmis, the family seat of the Weissenburgs who once again owned the pawn "ticket." After several indecisive efforts, the Weissenburgs were defeated. In August 1334, Hasli was absorbed by Bern and the old freedoms of Hasli were partially restored. This followed because Bern became a royal city in 1218, enjoying the direct rule and protection of the emperor. Hasli, as a subject land, was required to pay annually to Bern 50 "pfunden Pfennigen." This payment of 50 pounds, designated as a Reich's tax, was paid to Bern every year until 1798 (251).

12. Tschudi (370, I, pp. 148, 149). (Tschudi gives to this the year date of 1252—surely an error. *Abschiede* I, p. 3, Item 3 and *Beilage* 2, p. 242, give the year date of 1291.)

13. This treaty of alliance is of unusual interest since it permits identification of the fathers of the

Confederation—assuming only that the men mentioned in the October treaty were equally involved in the "conspiracy" that inspired the manifesto of 1 August 1291. They were the political leaders in Schwyz and Uri: Konrad ab Iberg (*Landammann*), Rudolf Stoufacher, and Konrad Hunn—all three from Schwyz; and from Uri, Werner von Attinghusen, Burkhard Schüpfer (a former *Ammann*), and Konrad, *Meier* of Oertschon (now Erstfelden) (*Abschiede* I, **242**, 16 October 1291).

Gagliardi (**146**, I, p. 195) emphasizes the point that early alliances were really agreements between persons bound together under oath (*Schwurbünden*), not alliances of regional governments. However, by 1291, the agreements were inter-governmental. He adds to the list of "conspirators" two sons of Rudolf Stoufacher (or Stauffacher), and Arnold, *Meier* of Silenen (*Landammann* of Uri). Others, unnamed, were certainly involved. But, despite the beauty of the saga, historians are loath to accept a William Tell, as one of the fathers of the Confederation. We are now assured by the *Nebelspalter* (a Swiss weekly publication devoted to humor and political satire) that, though there was no such man as William Tell, the fact that he killed the tyrannical governor Gessler is firmly established!

That the "conspirators" met in secret at Rütli to organize the overthrow of foreign tyrants is also given short shrift. Nonetheless the legends are beautiful and inspiring. They have played an important and continuing role of great significance in maintaining a fervent national pride.

14. The long-lasting disputes between Schwyz and Einsiedeln ended in 1386 when the *Reichsvogtei* of Einsiedeln was terminated by absorption into the canton of Schwyz.

15. The nucleus of Lucerne may be regarded as the cloister, founded in the eighth century by the Carolingians. In the middle of the ninth century it became annexed to the great Alsatian cloister, Murbach, around which the Murbach possessions in the vicinity of Lake Lucerne were centered. Since 1135 or earlier these properties were under Habsburg rule. The city itself is alleged to have been founded around 1180 or 1200 when the opening of the new transport route over the Gotthard was speedily followed by the development of the city, at the end of Lake Lucerne, as an important commercial center for the processing of goods headed to the north, south to Italy, or east to the Zurich–St. Gallen area. A rapid growth of the city appears to have taken place, for we read that "around 1250 it already approximated its nineteenth-century size" (**285**, p. 203)!

16. "Bern is one of the finest and historically interesting cities from the point of view of development. It is a witness of the Staufer or Zähringer art of building. The City is an historic legal monument equivalent to a document of stone giving us information on city building while other sources remain silent" (**349**).

The basic building unit was uniformly 100 feet by 60 feet but the parcels were almost always a fraction thereof, e.g. 1/4, 1/5, 1/6, or 1/8 of the 100-foot frontage. Most of them in the old city were 1/5 or 1/6 and are still so. The old city (to 1152) ran from the beginning of Gerechtigkeitsgasse to Nydegg, which was still older. Junkerngasse and Postgasse were part of this old city. An expansion in later years carried the city limits as far as the Zytglogge and included Kesslergasse, Kramgasse and Metzgergasse. The third extension of the city brought it to the Käfigturm. The outer part of the newer section ran from there to the Christoffelturm (which used to face the end of Spitalgasse). The Schanzen and Bollwerke date from 1623–46 (**349**).

The name, Bern, is possibly of Celtic origin (**285**, p. 217), though one must be aware of the fanciful tale according to which Berchtold of Zähringen decided to name his city after the first animal which his hunters killed or captured in the environs: a bear, of course.

17. Swiss law for many years has required that changes in the Federal Constitution receive approval by a majority of the cantons and a majority of the total popular vote.

18. Especially the terrible epidemic of 1348–49. We must remind ourselves that in the early literature, the words plague and pestilence were loosely used. Frequently typhus, smallpox, diphtheria, dysentery, enteric fever, etc. in epidemic proportions were included in the statistics of bubonic and pneumonic plague. The inclusion of deadly pneumonic plague, in which the disease spread through inhalation of infected sputum, is understandable. The victims were bluish-black on death, hence the term "black death."

In the mid-fourteenth century the European population was completely susceptible and the death rate was almost catastrophic. Zinsser (**406**, p. 88) reports that in 1348, two-thirds of the population contracted the plague and almost all died. In 1361, one-half became afflicted and a few of these survived. In the epidemic of 1371, one-tenth of the population fell victim to the plague but many survived. In 1382, the plague struck about one-twentieth of the people, but almost all survived. Zinsser draws attention to the progressive weakening of the disease as it occurred in a population which, by 1382, had become thoroughly saturated.

The cause of the plague was unknown. A French surgeon attributed the great plague of 1348 to a conjunction of Saturn, Jupiter, and Mars in the sign of Aquarius. The rabble blamed the nobility. The nobility (and others) blamed the Jews who in Basel, Strassburg, and Mayence were mercilessly burned and slaughtered. Gravediggers were blamed because they profited from the dead. Cripples and beggars were blamed, being charged with causing the disease out of envy and malice (380, pp. 54–63). Many others believed that the Black Death signalled the second coming of Christ, the end of the world, God's displeasure with man and His punishment for their sins. Flagellation by hordes of people attended or followed upon the plague. Such terrible events as the Black Death would only end with the redemption of the sinful world: the end was approaching. For a scholarly treatment of this aspect of the Black Death, see Lerner (214).

The number of deaths reported by Wain and by Zinsser, is astounding—allegedly 25 million in Europe. One-fourth to one-half of the population of England is believed to have died from the great plague. On the Continent, the pope consecrated the Rhone to permit a Christian burial for those whose bodies were thrown into the river.

Two important things were learned; (1) the disease spread over trade routes and by sea; (2) quarantine measures were gradually introduced. In 1377–1403 the chief Mediterranean ports held vessels for 40 days before they were permitted to dock (380). Hence the word quarantine from the French *quarante* for 40. Whether the real culprit, the rat, which became established in Europe about 1100, was recognized as somehow or other responsible, appears to be unlikely. By the sixteenth century, the rat was suspected to be the carrier of the disease and, in England during Shakespeare's time, rat-catchers were important officials (406). We are reminded by Ackerknecht that, possibly as early as A.D. 224, the Chinese suspected that rats were involved; the disease was known as a rat pestilence (1, p. 11).

19. "This country is extremely full of leper-hospitals, and the roads are quite full of lepers" [Eastern Switzerland (Thurgau) in 1580, as described by Montaigne (250, p. 39)].

20. Essentially, the Canton of Graubünden, which derived its name from one of the three principal parts of Raetia—the *Grau Bund.*

21. "Burg- und Landrecht der Appenzeller mit Zürich, Lucern, Uri, Schwyz, Unterwalden, Zug and Glarus," *Abschiede* I, 341, Item 45 (1411). Also in Tschudi (370, I, p. 657).

22. Archidamus III (King of Sparta in the fourth century B.C.), when he saw that the Eleans were leaning to the side of the Arcadians, wrote a letter containing only this, "It is a good thing to remain quiet" (277, p. 35).

This advice may reflect one of the earliest concepts of neutrality, usually expressed by the injunction "*Stille sitzen.*"

23. The betrayal at Novara (1500), compounded by an engagement in which Swiss were arrayed against Swiss, is an unpleasant exception (see Chapter 4).

24. In present-day Switzerland, the small town of Büsingen, a short distance up the Rhine from Schaffhausen, is a German possession though completely surrounded by Swiss territory. The enclave is 16.8 kilometers in circumference. Another enclave, this time Italian, is on Lago di Lugano in the southern Ticino. It is the small town of Campione (7.1 kilometers in circumference), and shelters a gambling casino.

25. The Hague Conventions of 1907 impose impartiality in the treatment of belligerents as an obligate requirement of a neutral State. However, the impossibility of treating both belligerents impartially and equally is now well recognized. It is a well meant and noble declaration toward which a Neutral might aspire but cannot faithfully and unswervingly observe.

26. Friedrich the Beautiful († 1330) and Leopold († 1326) were sons of the murdered emperor, reputed to be the father of twenty-one children.

27. *Abschiede* I, pp. 87f., Item 196, 26 June 1393. See also *Abschiede* I, pp. 329 ff., Item 42.

28. A count of the Marches or *Markgraf* was somewhat higher than a *Graf* in the nobility of the day.

29. *Abschiede* I, Item 390 in the *Regesten*, p. 465, 14 January 1406.

30. *Abschiede* I, Item 390 in the *Regesten*, p. 465, 20 July 1406.

31. *Abschiede* I, Item 388 in the *Regesten*, p. 464, 5 November 1405.

4. THE FIFTEENTH CENTURY

Expansion to the South Continues

The battle of Arbedo (1422) in which both sides suffered very heavy losses was indecisive. The Duke of Milan, impressed by the tremendous resistance of the out-numbered enemy, offered Uri a high ransom if she would renounce any claim to Bellinzona. This ancient and stubbornly determined canton was more interested in revenge and in the income to be derived from Gotthard-Bellinzona traffic. Three years later, supported by troops from other cantons, the Urners again laid siege to Bellinzona. The invaders were disunited in matters of policy and military tactics. Serious dissension arose and resulted in delays that threatened the success of the venture. The transalpine policies of Uri were deemed of little importance to the allies from other cantons, and many returned to their homeland. Bellinzona and the Leventine were lost. Apart from the lack of any common interest among the Swiss in Uri's desire to expand across the Alps, Uri suffered also from her own inadequacies in men and weaponry and the dispersal of her forces in another area of combat, the Eschental.

This important valley, possessed by the Duke of Milan, was of interest to Uri. For decades the Urners had led their cattle into its meadows only to have them driven out by the subjects of Milan. Uri's complaints were without effect and in 1410 a volunteer force from Uri and Obwalden invaded the valley, expelled the Milanese governor and set up another government. The Eschental became a subject land of Uri, Obwalden, and Lucerne which, in turn, appointed a resident governor of their choice in Domodossola.

The valley was of strategic importance. Access to the valley of the Rhone was provided by a well-established route over the Griespass. Farther on, the Gemmi pass led to Kandersteg, and the Grimsel opened out on the Bernese Haslital. The routes over these passes had been secured in 1397 by an agreement between Bern and Upper Wallis (Valais). While these routes connecting the Eschental with a segment of 15th-century Switzerland were of importance to the Swiss they meant much less to the farmers and peasants of the Eschental. They desired only to be left alone but in so far as they had loyalties to a State, the inhabitants of the Eschental were more in sympathy with Milan than with Uri or Bern; rich and famous Milan would be more helpful to the dwellers of the valley than the "peasants and cowhands" to the north. In 1410 they rose against their Swiss overlords and expelled the Swiss-appointed governor in Domodossola. It was a short-lived victory, for in 1411 the valley was reconquered by a Swiss army drawn from seven of the cantons. For a second time a governor appointed by the Swiss was the ruling authority in Domodossola. A resident of the valley was chosen for this high office. The Confederate army was withdrawn to the homeland to support the forces engaged in the conquest of the Aargau. With their departure, the Milanese faction of the Eschental again seized control. In 1416, forces from Uri and Obwalden returned to the valley for the third time. There was little opposition to the reconquest. The Maggiatal and the Verzascatal, two valleys running northwards from the eastern end of Lake Maggiore, were also seized by the invaders. In 1417, they appointed a governor (from Nidwalden) and in 1418 induced the Emperor of the German Reich, King Sigismund, to confirm their title to the three valleys.

Expansion into the Valais

These conquests gave to Uri and Obwalden certain rights in Upper Wallis (Valais) which immediately brought these ancient cantons into confrontation with the Bishop of Sitten, the overlord of much of the Rhone Valley. Lower Valais belonged to Savoy with local powers in the valley exercised by families of freemen and officials from the lower nobility. Upper Valais consisted largely of farming communities with common interests but interspersed with a scattering of feudal possessions. A revolt in lower Valais in 1375 had threatened the lordship of the Bishop. Intervention by Savoy, motivated by a desire to secure a foothold in Upper Valais, led, after much fighting, to a negotiated peace. The Bishop and the freemen of the valley, to strengthen their own position, entered into a defensive alliance in 1403 with Uri, Unterwalden and Lucerne.

The pact had the inevitable result of drawing Valais into the transalpine policies of Uri which were certainly suspect to the feudal lords and the House of Savoy. The intervention of Bern was sought and given—Bern being now concerned over the security of its own route into the Eschental. From 1418 to 1420 Bern was involved in constant feuds, marked by repeated episodes of plunder and pillage. By the terms of an uneasy peace in 1420 the feudal lords were required to return to the lords of Raron (the Bishop) the lands they had taken, and to pay damages. This coincided in time with the slaughter at Arbedo and the loss by Uri of its transalpine possessions. The Italian valleys were left in peace temporarily, Uri with several other cantons having turned to conquest of the Aargau.

Policy Considerations

Questions of high policy were now descending upon the young Confederation. The persistent search for freedom and independence from foreign Powers continued unabated. Without any concerted agreement among the cantons, a conscious effort to expand the power and lands of the members of the Confederation was evident. Territorial expansion, principally at the expense of Austria, and a redirection of purely defensive alliances into military pacts pointedly aimed at reduction of the powers and possessions of the various dynasties became policies of high priority within the Confederation. Could such policies be pursued by common consent and action without aggravation of rivalries and friction among the member cantons? There was an obvious danger of splitting the Confederation: Bern, driving with determination toward the north and west, the *Waldstätte* toward the south and, in alliance with their neighbours, to the east. On the diplomatic front, the 20-year peace between the Confederation and Austria, negotiated in 1394, was renewed in May 1412 for fifty years. Friedrich IV, the reigning Duke, relinquished any claim to taxes by Glarus and ceded the middle March to Schwyz.

Conquest of Aargau

A series of unrelated events led, by a concatenation of circumstances such as characterized the history of the Middle Ages, to the conquest of Aargau by the Swiss. Two popes in militant conflict—one in Rome, the other in Avignon—threatened the peace of Europe. A church council had been convened in Constance charged with resolving this vexatious if not scandalous situation. Sigismund, as Emperor of the *Römisches Reich*, intervened and forced Pope John XXIII to abdicate; the rivalry of the two popes and the recurring acts of violence and repeated threats of excommunication had to be ended. To the dismay of the emperor, all of the dynastic interests including the Duke of Austria supported the deposed pope who, now encouraged by these developments, renounced his forced abdication. The kaiser promptly placed the House of Austria under the ban of empire which meant that the Habsburg possessions were outlawed and, without any royal protection, were open to seizure. The German princes and towns were not summoned to war against Austria, it being evident that the Swiss would seize upon this opportunity to acquire any Habsburg territory within their areas of interest. In July 1414, the kaiser made a state visit to Bern and received assurances of Bernese support in the royal campaign against the Duke of Austria. Some months later the 50-year treaty of peace with Austria (signed two years earlier) was denounced by the Confederation and, with royal encouragement, the Swiss moved against the ancient holdings of the Habsburgs in the Aargau. In 1415, Zofingen fell and many other cities surrendered in rapid succession. When it was over, Bern found itself master of a great area extending northwards to the confluence of the Aare and the Reuss; Lucerne acquired Sursee and territory around the cloister of St. Urban. Zurich seized Dietikon and other towns. Finally, Baden fell to a united Swiss army, and administration of this important city and surrounding territory came to be shared by all eight members of the Confederation, each in turn appointing the local governor. The privileges enjoyed by the Aargau cities were confirmed by their captors who extended to these towns the precious right of self-administration.

The month-long conquest of the Aargau had barely ended before Duke Friedrich appeared humbly before the kaiser. A reconciliation followed and the Swiss were ordered to return to Austria all of the territories acquired in the recent campaign. The Swiss refused and the conquered areas remained firmly in their possession with no serious effort by the kaiser to enforce the royal command. In fact, the kaiser was constantly plagued by a shortage of money and was heavily in debt to Bern and Zurich, to whom a part of the Aargau had been mortgaged. Years later, Duke Friedrich renounced all claims to the Aargau, doing so on his own behalf and on that of his successors.

The Toggenburg Inheritance

Meanwhile, a fraternal quarrel with serious consequences broke out between Schwyz and Zurich over the estates of the Count of Toggenburg. The head of the House was childless and, despite the pressures of many possible heirs that he make a will, the lord of Toggenburg died intestate in April 1436. Many small feudal lords related to the Count or to his wife were among the claimants to his possessions. Schwyz and Zurich held treaties of friendship and alliance with Toggenburg but were at cross purposes in their claims upon the estates. Zurich was interested in Gaster because of a desire to control and secure the approach to Italy through the Graubünden. But the Gasterland was also important to Schwyz which already possessed the adjacent territory of the March. Zurich tried to occupy the Gasterland but the villagers refused the oath of allegiance. However, alliances with Zurich were concluded by a number of towns on the Walensee. Schwyz formed similar alliances with communities in the heart of the Toggenburg and, in December 1436, Schwyz and Glarus concluded an alliance with the Gasterland. Zurich interpreted this as a deliberate provocation and retaliated by mobilizing her troops and placing an embargo on the shipment of foodstuffs to Schwyz.[1]

Intervention by the Confederation failed to bring the two parties to a reconciliation of their dispute and both prepared for war. An arbitration court of nineteen men urged without success a return to the status quo. Time appeared to favor Schwyz which by now had been granted possession of Uznach by Toggenburg. Austria had pledged to Schwyz the territories and towns of Gaster, Windegg, Amden, Weesen, and Walenstadt. Communities in the Raetisch portion of Toggenburg had also formed an alliance of their own, the League of the Ten Jurisdictions (*Zehngerichtebund*) patterned after the *Graubund* and the *Gotteshausbund*. Zurich's hopes for expansion in southern Toggenburg and the Graubünden were vanishing.

War with Zurich

In November 1440, Schwyz formally declared war on Zurich and, supported by troop contingents from Uri and Toggenburg, laid waste the Zurich countryside. Crops were systematically destroyed and, by fire and sword, the communities were ravaged.

Zurich, now suffering greatly, proposed an armistice and arbitration of the dispute by joint mediation of the other five cantons. A most uneasy peace was the result—a calm before the storm. Frustrated in their efforts to expand, and eager for revenge, the majority in Zurich had forced a return to the policies of 50 years earlier and the conclusion of a treaty of mutual help and friendship with Austria. Despite the consequences of this alliance, Zurich was not in full contempt of her obligations as a member of the Confederation. Her alliance of 1351 with the other Swiss cantons reserved for her the right to conclude other alliances. However, this alliance with Austria was certainly not compatible with her obligations to the other seven members of the Confederation.

Friedrich III of Habsburg-Austria (Duke Friedrich V of Steiermark prior to his election as Emperor of the Reich in 1440) saw in the new alliance with Zurich, concluded on June 17, an opportunity to settle the old scores of his House with the *Waldstätte*. Zurich promised the kaiser a free hand in the Aargau in any attempt by the Habsburgs to regain their lost possessions.

She also returned to the kaiser almost all of the Kyburg holdings which had come into her possession. In turn, Zurich was promised Uznach and the original Toggenburg territories to the northeast. It also followed that Zurich, with Austrian support, would be recognized as the leading canton and city in a reconstructed Confederation to reach from the Black Forest to Raetia. Military support and a provision for arbitration of disputes between the two parties were spelled out in a second document. In September the kaiser made a ceremonial and festive visit to Zurich.

During a hundred years, bonds of common interest and of mutual economic and political value had been slowly forged between the Swiss communities. The other cantons warned Zurich that the alliance with Austria violated the sense and the spirit of the treaty of 1351 whereby Zurich entered the Confederation. At the same time the kaiser denounced the old freedoms granted to the Swiss cantons which previous emperors had confirmed. His purpose was clear—destruction of the Swiss Confederation. Negotiations with Zurich by the other cantons in conferences at Baden and Einsiedeln failed to persuade Zurich to abandon the Austrian alliance, and war broke out anew.

Parenthetically, it should be noted that Friedrich III (1440–1493) was the most hostile of the Habsburg emperors. For 50 years he tried to destroy the Swiss Confederation. He refused to confirm the *Freibriefe*. He sought desperately to induce Zurich to secede from the Confederation, and, in so doing, was instrumental in precipitating civil war (the Old Zurich War) and finally summoned the French to come to the rescue of Zurich. The terrible battle of St. Jacob on the Birs followed. In the Burgundian war his actions toward Switzerland savoured of treachery. He repeatedly declared the ban of Empire against the Swiss. His subjects generally, and the Swiss in particular, knew from Friedrich III only threats of war, of litigation, and of punishment—never an offer of help.

In May 1443, Schwyz and Glarus threw down the gauntlet and received the complete and firm support of the other cantons. Their forces descended from all sides on the territory of Zurich. Again the harvests were destroyed and the countryside ravaged. Bremgarten and Baden fell to the Confederates. Bern and

Solothurn laid siege to Laufenburg. The siege of Rapperswil, a well fortified town, was unsuccessful. Rumor has it that troops penetrated the city through a breach in the wall but tarried too long in the public wine cellars and were easily driven back.

In August, agreement was reached on another armistice subject to abandonment by Zurich of her lost territorial possessions. Eight months later a conference of the cantons was held at Baden, attended by representatives from Savoy, Württemberg, the imperial cities and ecclesiastical States. The *Waldstätte* and their allies insisted that Zurich denounce the Austrian alliance, otherwise the conquered territories would not be returned to Zurich. When the pro-Austrian party in Zurich, still dominant in influence, heard of the terms they summarily rejected the opportunity for peace. Several leaders of the peace party were executed and the war was continued.

Zurich implored the kaiser to send troops, even foreign legions, to her aid. In the meantime, and for reasons that are obscure, the Confederates laid siege to Greifensee. Though defended by only 100 men the town resisted for three weeks. On entering the city the Confederates forced surrender of the fortress and, despite a promise of amnesty, they promptly slaughtered over 60 of the defenders—only old men and young boys were spared. This is an example of the extent to which hatred had by now arisen among the forces at war.

In May, Zurich was surrounded and besieged. Friedrich III tried feverishly to muster support for the relief of Zurich and appealed to the Duke of Burgundy. But the duke, a vassal of the French king, declared his State to be neutral. Finally, assistance was sought from Charles VII, King of France. The request came at a most fortunate time for Zurich and Austria. The Hundred Years' War with England had just ended with the armistice of May 28, 1444. France, with a huge force of soldiers about to join the unemployed, gladly agreed to support Austria. The French army, though experienced in war, was made up largely of ruffians whom the French king was relieved to send from the country on a foreign expedition. Under the command of the Dauphin they entered Switzerland from Alsace—40,000 in number. By now the war was developing into a contest in which the Austrian nobles and their vassals were arrayed against the farmers and peasants with all the old enmities again coming to the surface. One of the nobles, Thomas von Falkenstein, seized Brugg and thus enabled the French army to cross the Aare. Bern replied by attacking Farnsburg, the seat of the Falkensteins in today's Basel area. The Dauphin then moved his army in the direction of Basel, and the Confederates with only 1,200 to 1,500 men, though greatly outnumbered, decided to pursue the enemy. The French fought a delaying action at Pratteln, at Muttenz, and up to the river Birs. Once across the river, retreat for the Swiss was difficult. Could they but reach Basel, help from that source might be expected. As it happened, a detachment of 3,000 men set out from the city to join the Confederates but, fearful of the huge army in the distance, they withdrew without joining battle. The Confederates were forced into a frontal attack and within four hours lost 900 of their men. An offer to surrender was refused. When it ended almost all of the Swiss had been killed.[2] The dead were buried in three mass graves. Such was the battle of St. Jacob on the Birs.[3]

Was anything learned from such a dreadful contest? Again, the raw courage of the Swiss in hand-to-hand conflict left an unforgettable impression upon the French and much of Europe. The Swiss were defeated by an overwhelming horde but also by firearms. The impact of this new kind of weaponry and combat was not speedily comprehended. The Swiss still had faith in their pikes and halberds and in hand-to-hand fighting in which they were almost invincible. Slowly they acquired firearms by purchase, by manufacture, and as booty. Perhaps most importantly, they began to lose the urge for territorial expansion by offensive warfare. But even this lesson was not fully learned until the battle of Marignano in 1515. Not until then did Swiss foreign policy reflect the intention of the Swiss to restrict their military actions to defensive warfare only.

The sieges of Zurich and Farnsburg were raised, and the Dauphin with his mission accomplished moved northwards into Alsace. He had done for Zurich all that had been promised. Many of his troops who lingered behind were killed by the Swiss, others lost their lives at the hands of the Alsatians. The rest were gradually reabsorbed in France.

In October 1444 at Ensisheim in Alsace a treaty of peace was signed between France on the one side and Basel, Solothurn, and the seven confederate "cantons" (Zurich was not included in the pact) on the other. It provided for improvements in trade with France, protection for any Swiss in French territory, and a promise from France to be the mediator in arranging a peace settlement with Austria. Incidentally, the relations between France and Austria had cooled appreciably and there began to emerge between France and Switzerland a friendly relationship which would prove to be of long duration. The peace treaty with France has been reported by Dürrenmatt (108) to be the first treaty negotiated by the Swiss with a Power outside of the German Reich.

A formal peace between Zurich and the seven federated cantons[4] was finally concluded at Constance on 9 June 1446. In the preceding two years the war with Zurich had been slowly coming to an end amid numerous border incidents, robbery of cattle, burning, and plundering. The formal peace did not bring an immediate end to the old hatreds, and the bitterness of Schwyz toward Zurich lingered on. The friendly intervention of the mayor of Augsburg helped eventually in effecting a reconciliation. Zurich was pressed into renouncing her alliance with Austria. Schwyz retained its stronghold on the Zurichsee—its approach to the plain of the Linth. The territories of Zurich, lost by conquest, were returned and Austria tacitly renounced any claim on the Aargau. Basel, determined that Austria must abandon its claim to Rheinfelden, fought the Austrian armies in 1448 and 1449. Bern and Solothurn sent troops to assist Basel in a final attempt in April 1449 to drive the Austrians from Rheinfelden. A treaty of peace was signed at Brisach in May 1449. Austria retained possession of Rheinfelden, and Basel received a few rather minor territorial benefits.

Expansion to the East

An overall result was a strengthening of Switzerland's hold on the areas west of the Rhine. More and more independent States in this important region sought alliances with the Confederation. In August, 1451, the Abbot of St. Gallen, formerly pro-Austrian, concluded an alliance with Zurich, Lucerne, Schwyz, and Glarus. The Abbot thereby came under the protection of these cities and cantons but did not become a member of the Confederation. As an ecclesiastical State, the Abbey and its territories became somewhat of an associate member. The alliance with Appenzell had been recently renewed and in 1454 an alliance of 25 years' duration was negotiated by Schaffhausen with Zurich, Bern, Lucerne, Schwyz, Zug and Glarus. This was a most important pact for it brought into close association with the Confederation a city and territory which had enjoyed the protection of the emperor of the Reich since the 12th century. It had been consistently pro-Austrian in the supply of troops to Austria, though it did not participate in the Old Zurich War. In July 1454 St. Gallen concluded a permanent alliance with Zurich, Bern, Lucerne, Schwyz, Zug and Glarus. Even the Swabian city of Rottweil in 1463 associated itself temporarily with the eight-membered Confederation.

Expansion was thus proceeding closer and closer to the Rhine. It was a time of incessant fighting and of resort to violence for the attainment of trivial objectives. The young were prone to rise against their masters. The peasants and lower vassals frequently were in conflict with their masters and feudal lords, some of whom they imprisoned, others they beheaded, commonly in revenge for various wrongs.

It was in such an environment that the "*Plappart* war" with Constance broke out in 1451. In August of that year Constance held a shooting competition and a competitive sportfest: stone throwing, running and jumping. Visitors and contestants came from various cantons, especially from Lucerne. Trouble arose on trivial grounds; the Lucerners claimed their honor had been impugned and sought Swiss support in their demand for redress. An army of 4,000 Swiss appeared but were bought off by the people of Constance through a payment of 3,000 gulden. The money was divided among the 4,000 and peace was restored. But Constance did not forget this unfortunate indicent and her feelings toward the Swiss cooled considerably.

Thurgau Enters the Confederation

However, to the north in the areas west of the Bodensee (Lake Constance), the territory of Thurgau was about to come under Swiss control. It happened that in 1460 Pope Pius II was in serious disagreement with Duke Sigismund of Austria. The pope held over the duke the threat of excommunication. Prepared to resort to war, the pope invited the Swiss to seize the Thurgau—an Austrian possession. In 1460, in the space of three weeks, the towns of Frauenfeld, Walenstadt, Sargans and Diessenhofen and the rest of Thurgau fell to the Swiss. Winterthur resisted the siege and remained an Austrian possession. In 1461 the conquest was confirmed by Austria who renounced her claims to the Thurgau. Like Aargau and Baden, the new canton was administered as a possession of all of the federated cantons in common. Meanwhile, Appenzell had acquired much of the adjacent Rhine valley by purchase and, from 1460 on, the Rhine came to be regarded by the Swiss as their rightful border with Austria.

Mülhausen

North of the Rhine in ancient Alsace is the city of Mülhausen.[5] In the Middle Ages it enjoyed the status of a free city, administratively independent of Austria to which Alsace belonged. In 1466 the city proposed an alliance with Bern and received a cordial and affirmative response, for a move in that direction would strengthen Bern's hold on the Aargau. Mülhausen was motivated both by fear of Austrian aggression and by the quite unpredictable policies of France and Burgundy. The negotiations resulted in a 25-year pact between Mülhausen and Bern and Solothurn jointly. Austria was angered and encouraged the Austrian nobles in Alsace and south Germany to terminate all trade relations with Mülhausen and Schaffhausen. In 1467 an Austrian noble, von Heudorf, seized several burghers of Schaffhausen and imprisoned the *Bürgermeister*. Bern quickly responded, after first making peace with the bishops of Constance and Basel. Bern's intervention terminated the troubles only briefly, for in 1468 Mülhausen took to the field and burned to the ground the manor of an Austrian noble. Immediately the entire Austrian nobility in Sundgau (Alsace) marched on Mülhausen and prepared to lay siege to the city. Again at the request of Mülhausen, Bern came to the rescue, joined by troops from Schaffhausen and St. Gallen. It appealed to the Swiss as a welcome opportunity again to take to the field against Austria and to solidify their hold on a long stretch of the Rhine including even Waldshut on the north bank far west of Schaffhausen. For this enterprise the Swiss were well prepared. They moved into the Sundgau and toward Waldshut but could find no enemies who were willing to engage in battle. Hence they turned to robbery, wanton killings, plunder, and destruction by fire— the ruthless wartime practices of the Middle Ages. Basel, fearful of what might happen to her, remained neutral in the shelter of her city walls. The Swiss troops began to return homewards but had barely left the Sundgau when the Austrians reappeared and invested Mülhausen. The Swiss returned to the scene and besieged Waldshut for five weeks, but in vain. Both sides had by now tired of the fighting and agreed to a peaceful settlement. In the treaty, Austria promised to leave Mülhausen in peace and to resume trade. She also agreed to pay to the Swiss 10,000 gulden, and, as security for the payment, Duke Sigismund pawned Waldshut and a part of the Schwarzwald, redemption to be within one year.

Freiburg becomes "associated"

If we now turn to the west we come to Freiburg (in Switzerland), an ancient city torn between its responsibilities and loyalties as an Austrian possession and its increasing desire for independence. Bern, a very powerful neighbour, was vigorously expanding its territories and its political power. It was in frequent conflict with Freiburg. A crisis arose in 1447 when Freiburg, under pressure from Austria, attacked Savoy. Bern, coming to the support of Savoy, invaded Freiburg territory and pursued the usual practice of pillage, plunder and destruction. In the following year Freiburg sought peace and was compelled to pay heavy damages to Savoy. This precipitated an inner revolt and led to Freiburg's secession from Austria in 1452. To the annoyance of Bern, she now turned to Savoy as a protector but in 1454 endeavoured to improve her relations by a *Burg- und Landrecht* with Bern. Such agreements, common among the Swiss of the Middle Ages, gave to the Freiburgers a status somewhat below that of the people of Bern. Freiburg received an associate status under the protection of Bern but was denied a number of rights and freedoms which equality would confer.

Economic and Social Developments

The end of the Old Zurich War was also the advent of a new era of economic growth and prosperity. True, recovery from the widespread destruction in and around Zurich could not proceed speedily. Villages had been burned, crops and farm animals destroyed or carried off, and the people had been robbed and pillaged. As was true of wars in the Middle Ages the objective of the Schwyzers and their allies among the Confederates had been total destruction of the enemy—revenge for the boycott of foodstuffs which Schwyz had suffered at the hands of Zurich. But Zurich did recover and presently experienced the beginnings of the prosperity that was spreading through most of Europe.

This economic growth probably received its greatest stimulus in 1425 when the pope lifted the ban on interest. Such charges for borrowed money ceased to be regarded as usury and the Church no longer discouraged the practice. Money flowed more freely and with this a credit system evolved. Although this emerging financial system of credit on purchases and interest on loans originated in Italy, international financial and commercial organizations soon appeared in the major cities of Europe. In Switzerland the most famous was the Diesbach-Watt Society named after the Watt and Diesbach (Goldschmid) families in Bern. This financial house and Basel were the sources to which Bern usually turned to finance her programs of expansion and reconstruction. Although completely destroyed by fire in 1405, Basel was totally restored in the next 50 years. Some of the more noted families occupied comfortable estates, villages, or small palaces and were on friendly terms or in blood relationship with distinguished families in other countries.

Basel, which did not become a member of the Confederation until 1501, was becoming a great transport and commercial center. It was situated at the crossroads of Europe and gained popularity as a European center for international conclaves, notably the famous ecclesiastical Concilium which began in 1431 and lasted for 17 years. The city had been totally destroyed by the great earthquake of 1356, yet Piccolomini[6] 80 years later described it as a beautiful and modern city (**288**). Many houses had gardens, windows were common, and travellers were prone to compare its beauties and charms with those of Florence.

The usual concept of the Middle Ages as a time of darkness and gloom is certainly misleading as far as 15th-century Italy, France (Burgundy) and parts of Switzerland are concerned. It is doubtful whether the laboring class in the towns, and the many who were poor, were in desperate straits although their needs were admittedly great. Daily and weekly markets appeared in the cities. Bread and also pastries could be found in the shops. Meat was common and its quality and display became subject to police regulations. Wines from Burgundy and Italy were imported for the connoisseur. Bread and a sort of compote prepared from vegetables or fruit formed the staple diet. Meat, fish, game and cheese (in the mountain areas) and wine were occasional supplements. Grain was largely imported. Salt was seriously lacking for it had not by then been discovered in Switzerland.[7]

France saw in these shortages of salt and grain opportunities to profit by satisfying these needs in return for economic and political gain.

Geneva which was to become of great importance as a part of Switzerland was a wellknown center for fairs and markets of expanding interest. But Lyon was a French competitor and in 1463 Louis XI sought to stifle the Swiss competition by forbidding his subjects to visit the Geneva fairs. Some of the German States also began to circumvent Geneva—an economic irritation which only served to strengthen the determination of Switzerland, Bern particularly, to solidify her position in the west. But more of this later.

Public baths, important in the social life of the towns, were common in the Middle Ages but were not an unmixed blessing, for Switzerland is in the heart of Europe and use of the public baths by the many travellers from other countries brought into Switzerland a variety of hitherto unknown diseases. The baths were also centers of depravity which led the governing bodies of the cities to prescribe rules of conduct. Basel in 1431 began to require separate baths for the two sexes and in 1439 Zurich ruled that operation of a public bath in the city would henceforth require a license from the governing body. The pleasures of the bath came to an end only in the seventeenth century when rivers and lakes replaced the public bath—offering their pleasures without charge and providing a more sanitary environment (see also chapters 5 and 6).

The late Middle Ages were marked by a considerable amount of travel. Scholars communicated with each other by letter but also by personal visits to their counterparts in other countries. Merchants, craftsmen, apprentices, military men, priests, and students met on the pilgrimage routes which extended to Jerusalem and the Middle East. The pilgrimages were made by rich and poor alike.

River traffic in Europe was highly developed and this enriched communications and facilitated the movement of people. For example, one could travel from Bern to Brugg, by descent of the Aare, in one day but the return trip by boat was impossible and the boatman had to return on foot.

Descriptions of other countries, their people, and their customs served as the beginning of a voluminous literature in geography, history, descriptive biology and geology. It was the heroic period in Switzerland in the sense that the great military victories of her people and her heroes in battle were immortalized in songs, sagas, and chronicles. Dubious accounts of the origin of the Swiss appeared, notably in the famous White Book of Sarnen,[8] which attributed their origin to Nordic settlements in Schwyz and Oberhasli.[9]

Education

Education of the people and scholarly inquiry received little, if any, encouragement in the fifteenth century. Ignorance and mysticism were rife and any challenges to religious dogma were vigorously repressed by the ecclesiastical courts. The bio-medical sciences, as an example, developed slowly in the midst of a hostile authoritarian environment. The deplorable state of affairs may be illustrated by the judgments of the secular and ecclesiastical courts in matters pertaining to entomology. Various insect pests such as locusts, cockchafers, and caterpillars were the defendants in many trials throughout Europe in the second half of the century. Initially the proceedings consisted in little more than the hearing of complaints, but by 1478 a method of prosecution had been developed in which the judges appointed counsel to defend the pests which had been indicted. A trial usually ended with an extradition order which required the defendants to leave the country within a stated time. If they remained longer the insects were threatened with malediction and excommunication. At this point the ecclesiastical courts were in charge of the proceedings against the defendants.

Sinner (**335**) reports upon a specific case in 1479 before the Bishop of Lausanne. His diocese was heavily infested with cockchafers which ravaged the foliage of trees and, as larvae, destroyed the roots of plants. At the request of Frikart, Chancellor of Bern, and in the name of the republic the insects were tried before the tribunal of "their" bishop. This advocate, a man named Perrodet, was reputed to be full of chicanery. Neither the advocate nor the accused appeared in court. The ecclesiastical court passed judgment and pronounced "a contumace," a severe sentence. The insects were excommunicated, proscribed in the name of the Holy Trinity, and condemned to leave forever the entire territory of the diocese of Lausanne. Sinner also cites the judgment of an ecclesiastical court at Troyes, France, 9 July 1516: "at the request of the inhabitants of Villenoce, the caterpillars are admonished to leave within six days, failing which they are declared to be banned (*maudites*) and excommunicated" (**335**, II, p. 154). In a number of cases, after a solemn judgment by the justice, some of the insects were executed in the presence of the court. Not until the end of the seventeenth century was the excommunication of insects forbidden. The practice, however, died out slowly: the last ecclesiastical judgment against insects was made in Europe in 1733. It is suspected, and with good cause, that the insect extradition orders were issued with the real purpose of strengthening respect for the courts and impressing the masses with the profundity of wisdom possessed by the judges of high rank. In most cases they were quite learned men who knew that plagues of insect pests were of short duration. Nevertheless, the impression was created that the judgments of the courts caused the disappearance of the pests (**22**).

A National Consciousness?

Whether or not a national consciousness was beginning to emerge in Switzerland is certainly open to debate. Throughout the fifteenth century and well beyond, the bonds that held the Confederation together were forged from the common interest of the cantons in defense against their enemies. The defensive alliances grew stronger as the foreign policies of the cantons became unified and became more and more clear as to who was the common enemy and who were the friends. A unifying force that contributed to a national consciousness was victory in war, in battles fought by contingents of troops from various cantons. Another was the occasional repressive policies directed by the kaiser, and by Habsburg-Austria especially, against some of the cantons. Such irritations and wrongs, focused upon a few, served only to bring others within the Confederation to the rescue.

But there were also strong divisive forces that greatly inhibited the growth of a Swiss national consciousness. Basically, and for years to come, the cantons owed their allegiance to the German *Reich*. The Swiss felt themselves a part of the empire, perhaps a very special part, and the pressures to separate from the *Reich* were not strongly apparent. As members of the empire, despite their growing association as a federation of their own, they existed as distinctly separate autonomous States. Each had its own coinage and each was fenced in by customs barriers that impaired the intercantonal flow of agricultural and industrial products. Each of the cantons had foreign policies of its own and enjoyed almost total freedom in negotiating alliances and military capitulations with foreign Powers. For many years the city cantons and the agricultural cantons were at loggerheads. The peasants and "cowhands" of the country were despised by the aristocrats and the merchants of the cities and, soon, religious differences from canton to canton were to have profoundly divisive effects. Indeed many of these forces that ran counter to a national consciousness persisted until the constitution of 1848 was accepted by the cantons as the basic document necessary to define their common obligations and restricted freedoms. Even today there is the widely circulated half truth that a Swiss is only a Swiss when he is outside Switzerland. Within the country he is a Berner, a Zurcher, or a Genevoise, etc., etc.

Foreign Powers

Austria, despite her mistakes in relations with the Swiss and her repeated defeats in battle, had become by 1460 the leading power of southeast Europe. She had, through loss of territory, been reduced to a more compact nation. Switzerland had grown in the east and north at Austrian expense. In 1453 the Turks took Byzantium by storm and several years later drove the Venetians out of the Peloponnesus. The English, on conclusion of the Hundred Years' War, withdrew to their island kingdom. Louis XI, succeeding to the French throne in 1461, sought to stem the feudal dissolution of his kingdom and also to gain a clearly defined eastern border. Of equal importance was a strengthening of his hold on Burgundy which, during the Hundred Years' War, had managed to establish itself as an increasingly in-dependent feudal State. To the east, Burgundy had acquired territory which once belonged to the German *Reich*. Dijon and Besançon constituted the heart of the duchy, but by conquest, marriage and inheritance, cities in Lorraine and the Low Countries had become Burgundian possessions. Flanders and Brabant were of great importance to the duchy in trade and commerce. The homeland, in an area with favorable soil and climate, produced an abundance of grain and wine. The House of

Burgundy was wealthy and ambitious. Its policy was to become a third Power strategically located between France and Germany.

Expansion Renewed

The Swiss, by the 1460s, had extended their territory eastwards to the Rhine and had no intention of inviting more trouble with Austria by attempting conquests farther to the east in the Vorarlberg. The Rhine was a natural border which could easily be defended. But to the south toward the Duchy of Milan, and to the west toward Burgundy, Savoy and France, opportunities for expansion and improvement of the frontiers presented themselves. Under the leadership of Bern the Swiss began to enter into active diplomatic relations with foreign Powers. Whether so small a country should endanger its independence by trying to outmanoeuver its powerful neighbours did not disturb the Swiss of the fifteenth century. Growth of population presented problems which pressed for solution, and expansion into the great fertile areas to the west appeared as a partial answer. The higher reaches of the voralpine zones had become more accessible and, in part, rendered arable, but food shortages were becoming more frequent.

The surplus manpower could not be absorbed by industry, for this was virtually nonexistent. Military employment in the service of foreign countries attracted many who would otherwise be unemployed. Indeed, France and others had been so impressed by the tremendous courage of the Swiss at the battle of St. Jacob on the Birs and their great victories in the past that Swiss mercenaries were constantly in demand. Not until 1848 did Switzerland, by its first Federal Constitution, deny to its people the right to engage as mercenaries in military service under foreign Powers. Even so, these military capitulations did not actually terminate until 1870, when the service contracts with Naples and the Papal State came to an end and most of the mercenaries returned to the homeland.

Fifteenth Century Bern

Bern had become a wealthy and aristocratic city. Among its burghers were the Bubenbergs, the Scharnachtals, the Erlachs, the Mülinens, and the Hallwyls. As quasi-feudal lords, and despotic in their power, such families ruled the city and determined its politics. In addition, there were the commercial and banking families—the Ringoltingens (originally Zigerli) and the Diesbachs (Goldschmid) who, with affiliates and intimate contacts throughout Europe, helped to finance Bern's purchases of territory and her military engagements.

Around 1470 a movement of some importance developed in the city which deserves mention because it was the beginning of a slowly developing effort by the common people to curb the despotic powers of the leading families among the burghers. The movement was known as the *Twingherrenstreit* (or *Zwingherrenstreit*)[10] and was led by Peter Kistler, a master butcher and, later, the *Schultheiss*. Kistler succeeded in transferring to the city some of the powers which had been practically vested in the leading families as virtual feudal lords, some of whom had jurisdictional claims over lands outside of the city. Their powers were greatly weakened, to the great satisfaction of the city's craftsmen and artisans. Kistler also won the support of the Great Council which passed a clothing ordinance directed against the nobles and leading burghers. This condemned the wearing of shoes with buckles and of dresses with ostentatious trains, and subjected such clothing practices to police regulation. In a counter-demonstration the noble ladies and men gathered in the cathedral wearing the forbidden dress. They were promptly fined by the courts. But such demagoguery could not survive and Kistler's influence declined. The clothing ordinance was revoked and the rights of the city over its feudal lords were defined in new regulations.

Prelude to the Burgundian War

In June 1467, Philip the Good of Burgundy died and was succeeded by his son, Charles the Bold (1433–77). The man had grown up in a rich and ostentatious environment, sheltered from the harsh realities of life in the Middle Ages. His was a world of fantasy and the power of the duchy to which he had fallen heir was a facade that covered a great deal of internal weakness. He was eager to elevate the status of the duchy to that of a kingdom, an aspiration of which his liege lord the King of France was well aware. To win the favor of the kaiser, who alone could elevate the duke to royal status, would require money which the House of Burgundy had in abundance. The ever-penurious Duke Sigismund of Austria, a cousin of the kaiser, negotiated a loan of 50,000 gulden from Burgundy. With 10,000 gulden he paid off the Swiss and redeemed his title to Waldshut and the Schwarzwald. He again pawned Waldshut and the neighboring part of the Schwarzwald, this time to Burgundy. Rheinfelden, Sackingen, and various Alsatian possessions were added to the package. At the same time, by the Treaty of St. Omar (May 1469), Charles the Bold promised to Sigismund his protection and help against the troublesome Swiss. Bern realized that it had suffered a defeat in this pawnshop diplomacy and decided that Charles of Burgundy would have to be regarded as her prime enemy. She turned to France in an effort to restrain Burgundy, in the full realization that Louis XI, a clever but thoroughly unscrupulous monarch, had good cause to be suspicious of Burgundy's foreign policy. In the diplomatic warfare, now getting under way, Duke Sigismund had the full support of his cousin the Kaiser, Friedrich III.

On the Swiss side several notable statesmen emerged, especially Niklaus von Diesbach from the Bernese Emmental and Adrian von Bubenberg[11] from the Bernese Oberland. After Kistler's downfall both had become leaders of some consequence. Diesbach had travelled much and was highly in favor at the French Court. As we shall soon see, the policy he pursued would lead inevitably to war with Burgundy. He was a loyal Bernese and was pro-French for political reasons only. Perhaps it was his hope that Bern, with Switzerland, would become a great Power, an effective balance between the conflicting aspirations of France and Germany. If this was really the basis of his policy it would obviously bring the Swiss into conflict with Charles the Bold who was dreaming the same dreams for Burgundy. Bubenberg was about the same age as Diesbach and was also well educated and had travelled extensively. Also a loyal Bernese, he was initially pro-Burgundy on purely political grounds—certainly not because, by inheritance, he was the recipient of a Burgundian pension. He was more conservative than Diesbach and was not disposed toward the intimate political associations, intrigues and superficialities of the French Court which Diesbach deliberately cultivated to gain the desired support. Diesbach regarded Bubenberg as a rival and an opponent of his political aspirations for Bern.

Louis XI, incited by Diesbach, planned now to bring about the fall of Charles the Bold and for this purpose foresaw a possibility of using the Swiss, to whom the Treaty of St. Omar had brought grave forebodings. The Diet, commonly suspicious of the ambitions of any neighboring ruler, mistrusted the Duke of Burgundy but was very hesitant to resort to war over Burgundy's foreign policies. Bern also knew that Austrian support for Charles the Bold was a reasonable expectation, since the Treaty of St. Omar constituted an alliance for certain purposes between Austria and Burgundy.

Charles now focused his attention upon the lower Rhine. In 1469 he appointed Peter von Hagenbach as Burgundian governor in the pledged Austrian territory in Alsace and Breisgau. Hagenbach applied extremely rigorous rules for the maintenance of order and discipline and quickly aroused the anger and hatred of the people by his tyrannical practices. Mülhausen reported all of this to Bern and earnestly requested that representations be made to Burgundy to recall Hagenbach. Bubenberg, a family friend of the duke, was sent to discuss the problem with Charles but was given a cold and unfriendly reception. Hagenbach and his policies were fully endorsed by the duke. Diesbach, expecting this rebuff, urged upon the Diet a closer association with France. The result was a treaty of neutrality signed by France and the *Vorort*[12] on 13 August 1470. By this treaty each party was pledged to deny any help to Burgundy in the unhappy event of war with the other of the two signatories.

Meanwhile, the necessity of a secure relationship with Austria became of great importance to the Swiss, for in case of war with Burgundy she required guarantees of security against any Austrian intervention on the side of Burgundy.

The Austrian-Swiss Treaty of 1474

As it happened, Sigismund was becoming alarmed by the wars of aggression and was being urged by the lower nobility in the Sundgau (south of upper Alsace) to enter into an alliance with the Swiss. Philip the Good (1396–1467), father of Charles the Bold, through the Treaty of Troyes with the English in 1420, had united the possessions of the Burgundian Duchy in the Netherlands. By purchase, inheritance, conquest, and with help of the pope, he greatly enlarged his possessions in the north and brought the duchy to the height of its power. The policy of his son Charles was to establish a bridge between his holdings in the south and those in the Netherlands by acquisition of Alsace and Lotharingia (Lorraine). The Treaty of St. Omar in 1469 gave him a tentative hold on the Austrian possessions in Upper Alsace, Breisgau, Pfirt and various Austrian territories on the Rhine. In 1473 he conquered additional territory and pressured the Duke of Lotharingia (René II) into signing the Treaty of Nancy, by which Charles obtained important possessions in this duchy and also the right of passage of his troops through the rest of the duchy. This aggression was pursued further in 1475 by the Burgundian conquest of Lotharingia and banishment of René II.

In the preceding year, events had taken their course in Alsace and Breisgau: an angry people had seized and beheaded Hagenbach. Even before this incident and its incitement to further aggression and acts of revenge by Charles, Sigismund of Austria initiated diplomatic negotiations with the Swiss. In January 1474 the Swiss Diet, meeting in Lucerne, was advised that Austria sought a permanent peace with Switzerland and proposed that the King of France act on behalf of both parties in the final negotiations. Initial discussions were limited to the pledged Austrian possessions on the Rhine—threatened as they were by Burgundy. Basel, at the same time, urged a formal defensive alliance with the most powerful *Reich* cities on the Rhine. In February the majority of the Swiss cantons expressed agreement for continued negotiations with Austria, looking toward a permanent peace and also a friendly alliance with the "*niedern Herren und Städten.*" In March, the Swiss, the city of Basel, and the Bishop of Strassburg concluded a defensive alliance of ten years with four of the Austrian cities on the Rhine. In return for 80,000 gulden the cities were in effect pawned, subject to redemption on repayment of the loan. The money was placed on deposit in Basel pending the fulfillment of certain conditions. The Swiss confederates and Basel were undoubtedly building up an additional defense against Burgundy by negotiation of this secondary alliance. In the peace negotiations with Austria the Swiss demanded unbreakable guarantees of an assured and permanent peace. By May 30 the treaty was ready for approval, subject to a final rewording by the King of France.

The possessions of both sides were to be formally confirmed and honored by both parties without return of any of the Swiss acquisitions obtained by conquest or otherwise. Arbitration of disputes was carefully provided for, as demanded by the Swiss. The Swiss expressly agreed to refrain from the absorption of more Austrian territory and Austrian subjects. Austria agreed to support the Swiss in the Waldshuter Peace. The northern border would be protected through recognition of the permanent peace by the Austrian subjects in the Schwarzwald and along the Rhine, who were solemnly sworn to respect the treaty. The Swiss agreed to provide Austria with troops (mercenaries) at the request and cost of the duke, provided that such requests did not contravene other Swiss obligations. There was mutual agreement on the free and safe passage of goods and people through territories of the two parties.

The Duke of Austria still hoped that several provisions of the permanent peace would be altered in his favor by the King of France. But Louis XI was not interested in pleasing Austria. In fact the Austrian ambassador, to his painful surprise, was informed that the treaty would be binding both on Sigismund and his successors in the duchy. The document was signed 11 June 1474.

I have described the events incident to the treaty, and its principal provisions, at some length, for up to that time it was the most important treaty negotiated by the Swiss with a foreign Power.[13] All earlier peace agreements with Austria had been provisional, of limited duration, and sometimes capriciously entered into. The document, usually known as the *Ewige Richtung*,[14] made a deep impression on the Swiss. Their enemy of 200 years had now reconciled himself to peaceful relations with the Swiss for all time, and it was also a defensive alliance since each party promised help to the other if attacked by a third party. Bells rang out and celebrations of the event were held throughout Switzerland. The duke himself came through Switzerland, accompanied by a brilliant retinue, to attend the Easter festivities at Einsiedeln. His old adversaries in city and country gave him a hearty reception en route to the Abbey.

War with Burgundy

But now Burgundy and France presented problems to the Swiss which had soon to be solved. One week after the *Ewige Richtung* had been signed, Sigismund denounced the Treaty of St. Omar with Burgundy. By this act Austria was relieved of all responsibility to give aid to Burgundy in the war which Burgundian policy would inevitably provoke. Sigismund also assumed that France would remain neutral in such a war, leaving Burgundy and Switzerland as the sole belligerents. Charles the Bold, meanwhile, promoted a plan to ensure nonintervention by the Emperor, Friedrich III. He proposed that Maximilian, son of Friedrich, be married to his daughter, Maria of Burgundy, and that the duchy be elevated to a kingdom with himself as the first monarch. The marriage eventually took place, but not the coronation. Charles, however, who loved parades and grand military manoeuvers, assembled his army for a great and memorable demonstration on the occasion of his expected coronation. Disappointed by the termination of his negotiations with the kaiser, he led his army into upper Alsace in a great show of force and to the alarm of Sigismund of Austria. The Alsatians only shortly before had risen against the Burgundian governor, Hagenbach, whom they beheaded on 9 May 1474. One should note that these events coincided in time with negotiations for the permanent peace between Austria and Switzerland. There can be little wonder that Sigismund, disturbed by Burgundian aggression in his Alsatian possessions, was ready to make peace with the Swiss and to denounce promptly his treaty with Burgundy.

In the meantime, preparations by the Swiss for war with Burgundy went on apace under the aggressive political leadership of Diesbach. Bubenberg steadily objected to Diesbach's incitement to war. Having thrown at Diesbach all responsibility for provoking a war with Burgundy, Bubenberg was dismissed from the Council in fear that his known pro-Burgundian inclinations would lead him into espionage on behalf of Burgundy. In Bern, most of the noble families and the common people favored Diesbach's pro-French policies. Bubenberg, in disfavor, was out of it all. We know that in 1475 he no longer went to the Distelzwang Guildhall but to the Red Lion *Stube* (restaurant). The Distelzwang patrons were pro-Diesbach and the Red Lion patrons, including a few of the nobles, were pro-Bubenberg.

In October, 1474, Diesbach succeeded in negotiating a treaty of alliance with France, a pledge in case of a Swiss-Burgundian war to give full military support to the Swiss or, in lieu thereof, a payment of 80,000 gold francs and a yearly pension to the eight cantons plus Freiburg and Solothurn—an extraordinary agreement. In return, Louis XI received the right to recruit Swiss mercenaries as needed for his own campaigns.[15] Diesbach now felt confident of success, secure in a good treaty with France and in the permanent peace with Austria. The war could begin.

Bern moved her troops to the west and north, seized Erlach and Hericourt, and moved on into the northerly part of Vaud. Bern by now had penetrated Savoy which was ruled by Iolantha, sister of the French King. The Duke of Savoy (Amadeus IX), husband of Iolantha, was dying obscurely and was incapable of governing the duchy. Savoy was internally in dissension and, for some time had sought help from Bern. The Duchess, however, had made the serious political error of giving permission to Burgundy to move troops from Lombardy through her territory. Bern interpreted this as an excuse for large troop movements of her own into Vaud. The Swiss overran the south shore of Lake Neuchâtel and in an equally ambitious move seized control of Valais—the entire valley of the Rhone. By October 1475 they had reached the Genfersee (Lake Leman).

The emperor, disturbed by this sudden and extensive military activity of the Swiss, made peace with Burgundy in May 1475. In September, Louis of France, who became equally disturbed by the vigor of the Swiss campaign, renounced his alliance with the Swiss and agreed to recognize Burgundy's claims in the Sundgau and Upper Alsace. As Sigismund of Austria had anticipated, Burgundy and Switzerland thus came to be pitted solely against each other. Charles, following his conquest of Alsace, moved on into Lorraine, seized control of the duchy and banished the duke. In January 1476, with a great army, Charles headed for the Jura, seized Grandson and, in fearful vengeance, killed the defenders. Not until March 2 did a Swiss relief force arrive—18,000 men in all. The Burgundians, though defeated, managed to escape. They left behind a vast amount of booty including their artillery of 400 guns. The duke, shaken by this reverse, nonetheless reformed his army at Lausanne and pushed northwards. He stopped at Morges to display his army in all is splendor to the Duchess of Savoy. Within three weeks the march to Payerne and Murten was resumed. Bubenberg, following the death of Diesbach, was now restored to favor and commanded a Bernese army which moved to Murten (Morat). Bubenberg decided that Murten would probably receive the main thrust of the Burgundian attack. On June 9, the advance forces of the Burgundian army arrived and commenced the siege of Murten.[16] In the meantime, troops from all eight of the Swiss cantons plus Alsace, Lorraine, and Thurgau assembled in Bern—an army of 25,000 under the command of Hans von Hallwil of Bern, Hans Waldmann of Zurich, and Kaspar von Hertenstein of Lucerne. On June 18 Bubenberg reported that Murten could hold out for only a few more days—the Burgundians had already breached the walls. On June 19 the Swiss army got underway, made the difficult crossing of the Saane at Gummenen, and in good order reached Murten on June 22. Despite days of anxiety, nervous waiting, and repeated sounding of the call to arms, the duke was surprised by the arrival of the enemy. The Swiss attacked at once, outflanked the Burgundian army, and in successive waves of attack drove the enemy into disorderly flight. But there was no escape, they were either killed in battle or forced into the Murtensee and drowned.[17] The Swiss imprisoned the Duchess of Savoy at Tours[18] and systematically plundered her territory, except Lausanne.

Louis XI, pleased by the turn of events and the defeat of Burgundy, negotiated a peace settlement between Switzerland and Savoy. Bern obtained Aigle while Erlach, Murten, Grandson, Orbe, and Echallons were placed under the joint sovereignty of Bern and Freiburg. Very heavy damages were levied upon Savoy which was forced to pledge the whole of Vaud as security for payment.

Burgundy tried to continue the war and soon invested Nancy the seat of the Duke of Lorraine. The Swiss sent a relief force under the command of Hans Waldmann which arrived in the winter of 1476–77. On January 5 the Burgundian army was destroyed and Charles was killed in battle. His successor as Duke of Burgundy was his son-in-law, Maximilian of Austria.

The southern Burgundian possessions were coveted by Bern. The canton, with an increasing need for salt, grain, and wine, proposed occupancy of the conquered territory. The other cantons feared Bern's ascendancy to power, but the spoils of war and the hard cash derived from the settlement with Burgundy and Savoy brought immediate satisfaction and minimized the displeasure arising from Bern's ambitious dreams of expansion. The other cantons could foresee only difficulties and trouble in the common overlordship of such a vast area. Furthermore, their interest in expansion, at least that of the *Waldstätte*, was transalpine.

At this point Louis XI intervened and proposed that in return for 150,000 gulden Maximilian be permitted to retain Burgundy. The king also promised to purchase the services of 6,000 Swiss soldiers to assist him, defensively, in his recurring wars. In early 1477, a peace treaty with Maximilian was signed in conformity with the terms of settlement proposed by France. Money appealed to the Swiss, and gold from those who would purchase their favors, especially from France, flowed into town and country. War had become an important industry and the principal source of income from abroad. The peasantry and the artisans liked it because of the ever-present promise of booty. The threat to their lives was no deterrent. Politicians and statesmen, the country's leaders, were debased by rich payments and gifts from foreign princes and nobles. Various families became wealthy and of great influence through war, specifically those who recruited, organized, and commanded the mercenaries—if only by proxy.

But the old feuding between town and country constantly recurred and despite some superficial evidences of prosperity and contentment, there was much internal discontent. The rural cantons hated the cities and insisted that no more city States be admitted to the federation. The region of Entlebuch sought recognition as a separate canton. The cities were unhappy because the Burgundian war yielded only 150,000 gulden which were dissipated about as soon as received. They also wanted an extensive revision of the federal structure and of the laws upon which the Confederation rested.

The Agreement of Stans

Dissension between town and country, between the city members of the Federation and the *Länder* (the agricultural cantons, principally the Waldstätte) cropped up repeatedly from the fifteenth century to the nineteenth. In the fifteenth century two causes were conspicuous. One was the domination of the country cantons by the cities—newly aggravated in 1481 by the prospective admission of two more city cantons (Freiburg and Solothurn) to membership in the Federation. They were almost forced upon the country cantons by the great power of Bern, Lucerne and Zurich. The second difficulty was the lack of a mutually acceptable policy regarding the division of booty from war.

The constitutions of the *Länder* rested on the free people of all the communities— a widely diffused democracy. In the cities, government was not popularly based. It was centered in the two councils (The *Grossrat* and the *Kleinrat*) where only the uppermost families among the burghers had a voice. The legislative powers extended, nonetheless, into the rural areas of the city cantons, such as Bern, despite the lack of representation of the farmers and peasants in the Councils. In every way the cities were more powerful and richer than the *Länder*. The cities insisted that wartime booty be divided according to the number of warriors that each city or rural community could provide. According to von Müller (**255**), as cited by Bluntschli (**45**), Zurich, Bern and Lucerne together could summon 39,000 men to battle; the *Länder* could provide only 14,000 but with equal insistence demanded that booty be divided equally between the two parties. They argued that they, principally the valley people of *Innerschweiz*, were the ones who had founded the Confederation and for years defended it with their own blood.

An incident early in the century should be described to illustrate further the serious gulf between the cities and the peasantry. In Zug, a bitter rivalry between the town and the rural communities had developed. The peasantry in the countryside endeavoured to have the cantonal capital moved from Zug to a rural district. On 23 October 1404, the Confederation was astounded to learn that a large number of Schwyzers, in support of the Zug peasantry, had invested the town and intended to realize their demands by force. Zug's entry into the Confederation in 1352 had been formalized by a pact which clearly put town and country on the same level and on a par with Schwyz. The seizure of Zug indicates that class solidarity was stronger than federal solidarity and could threaten the survival of the Confederation. The War Council promptly sent a contingent from Lucerne to occupy the town. Troops from several other member cantons assembled nearby. As a result, the Schwyzers and the Zug peasants quietly withdrew. Two weeks later, the Diet, whose judgment Schwyz agreed to accept, imposed upon Schwyz a heavy penalty for property damage in Zug and for the cost of mobilizing the federal contingents. The special alliance that joined the Zug peasants to those of Schwyz was formally dissolved.

Incidents such as that of Zug and Schwyz, between the bourgeoisie and the peasants, broke out from time to time within the Confederation. They serve to illustrate the hate and hostility between town and country that continued for centuries and expressed itself in several violent outbreaks. Class solidarity could be understood but national solidarity was something abstract, diffuse and theoretical. The intervention of Bern and Glarus, strongly federalistic cantons, as mediators in the dispute, publicized the dangers of the Zug affair. A powerful show of force added strength to their role in mediation and conciliation and brought the affair to an end **(213)**.

In 1481, the serious differences that separated the city cantons and the peasantry, mostly of the *Waldstätte*, surfaced once again, more dangerously than ever. The proposed admission of two more cities (Freiburg and Solothurn) was the last straw. An ugly civil war was imminent between the two parties. And so at Stans near Christmas, 1481, there was an almost irreconcilable deadlock with the parties preparing to adjourn and fight it out. At the last moment, the priest of Stans, Heinrich am Grund, appeared with a message from Niklaus von Flüe (Brother Klaus).[19] Brother Klaus pleaded for unity among the Swiss. Conversations began anew, so the story goes, and ended in a peaceful and harmonious understanding. Thereupon, on December 22, Freiburg and Solothurn were admitted as members of the Confederation and the Agreement of Stans (*Stanser Verkommnis*) was signed.[20] The message of Brother Klaus was simple and direct: "Do not become involved in the affairs of foreign Powers. As brotherly *Orte*, come to each other's help when domestic strife breaks out." For all time the rural *Orte* should prevent the country subjects (farmers and peasants) of the city *Orte* from striving for an independent political status. The Lucerne chronicler Diebold Schilling, 1460–1515 (not to be confused with his uncle Diebold Schilling, 1430–86, the great chronicler of Bern), reported upon the tension between the cities of Zurich, Bern, Lucerne, Freiburg and Solothurn on the one hand and the three lands of Uri, Schwyz and Unterwalden on the other. A few pages later on we are told "How this subject was at last resolved through Herr Heymen or Heyne or Heini, pastor of the church at Stans. The priest spent hours at night in conversation with Brother Klaus and next day brought the advice of Brother Klaus." He had told Klaus that war was imminent. By noon the priest had returned to Stans. All of the delegates were preparing to leave, but the message made such an impression that within one hour all was done and the agreement was approved. It was signed and sealed by delegates of all the *Orte* and sworn to as a permanent accord. Klaus made no personal appearance.

It seems that Brother Klaus had given similar advice a month or so earlier, and a spirit of reconciliation was possibly somewhat in evidence at the Diet of November 25–30 when a preliminary draft of the *Verkommnis* was prepared. The Diet sent an official letter of thanks to Brother Klaus for his help.

Waldmann and his Troubles

Social and political unrest followed the Burgundian war and Hans Waldmann, the politically gifted mayor of Zurich, did a few things that added to the troubles.[21] He married a rich widow and was financially independent. This inspired the envy of his associates who were well aware that money alone did not elevate one to the aristocracy. Honored by nomination to the *Konstafel*, the guild of aristocrats and leading businessmen, he was rejected from membership. He did not forget this insult and turned to support of the craft guilds. When elected *Bürgermeister* of Zurich in 1483 he gained the hatred of the former mayor and of others. He tried to build the city State into a more austere and rigid structure. The feudal system of government was to be replaced with a centralized and logical system. Country folks should be restrained from entering employment as craftsmen. They should work exclusively in agriculture, thus complementing the artisan-commercial activities of the city residents. By clothing mandates, much like those of Peter Kistler in Bern, he tried to lessen the influence of the aristocrats. This was petty but possibly politically motivated. His clothing regulations angered the aristocracy but won the approval of the lower social orders. He forbade the hiring of mercenaries by Zurich. This promptly aroused vigorous protests from *Innerschweiz*. Waldmann received the protests of a commander of mercenaries who visited him in Zurich. The conversation went far beyond pleasantries and Waldmann, feeling that he had been insulted during the vigorous dialogue, ordered that the man be arrested and beheaded. But this was also to be the end of Waldmann. The country folk rose against him and, aided by Waldmann's enemies in the city, had him condemned to death and beheaded. This was an ignoble, if not shameful, fate for one who in the Burgundian war had contributed much to its victorious conclusion.

While Brother Klaus had urged the Swiss to keep to themselves and to avoid entanglement in the affairs of other States, adherence to this sage advice was not easy. The fighting prowess of the Swiss was now so universally recognized that they were courted by all the princes of Europe. The destruction of Burgundy brought to the fore a steadily developing Franco-German confrontation. It was also a time of growing nationalism in Europe which manifested itself in Switzerland by a desire to be free of the German Reich.

An Imperial War against Switzerland

In 1483, Charles VIII, son of Louis XI, succeeded to the French throne. Dynastic troubles around him convinced him of the desirability of foreign conquests. He directed his campaign against South Italy and in 1495 he reached Naples victoriously—but not without arousing very powerful opposition: the pope, the kaiser, the Duke of Milan, Schwyz, Uri, Bern, (and several other *Orte*). Money flowed from both France and the kaiser in an effort to draw the Swiss in on one side or the other. Could the rather fragile bonds of union between the Swiss *Orte* stand the test?

In 1493 Friedrich III died and was succeeded as emperor by his son Maximilian I. He was a romanticist, as his father-in-law, Charles of Burgundy, had been before his military adventures turned disastrously against him. One of his ambitions was to restore the trappings of finery and ostentation that gave richness, colour, and an air of chivalry to those who ruled as princes of the realm. Knighthood was again to be in flower! To restore these outward suggestions of greatness, money was of first importance. A tax, the common penny (*der gemeine Pfennig*) was levied throughout the Empire, ostensibly as a military assessment for defense against the Turks.[22]

Maximilian also centralized the judicial system by introducing an Imperial Chamber of Justice.

Both the tax and the centralization of the administration of justice were offensive to the Swiss. For 250 years they had struggled for freedom from the jurisdiction of any who were not of their own choosing and who were not of their own people. Even in 1493 taxes were repugnant, especially as payment to the treasury of an empire which had not assisted the Swiss in their military campaigns against Burgundy and against the French Armagnacs in the Old Zurich War. They refused to pay the tax and to accept as administrators of justice the emissaries of any centralized chamber.

In a strategic political move, the Swiss negotiated a treaty with Charles VIII, whereby France was assured of Swiss mercenaries as needed, and the participating Swiss cantons would enjoy a renewed inflow of French gold. The treaty was signed 1 November 1495. Shortly thereafter, the emperor sought 8,000 Swiss mercenaries for war against Charles VIII. The request was denied.[23]

St. Gallen and Schaffhausen, in a stubborn dispute with the new Imperial Chamber of Justice, fell under the ban of Empire. In south Germany, pamphlets and poems insulting to the Swiss appeared, and the name *Schwabe* (cockroach), with contemptuous overtones, found its way about. To protect themselves against Austria, the *Graubund* in June 1497, the *Gotteshausbund* in 1498, and Chur shortly thereafter, allied themselves to the seven easterly Swiss *Orte*. The Articles of Association provided for economic and military assistance and such other help as might be expected in bonds of mutual friendship and respect. Several days later, war with Austria broke out.[24] The Austrians invaded the Münstertal and occupied the cloister at Münster. The kaiser was then in the Austrian Netherlands. Austria turned to him and to the Swabian League of Cities for aid. Thus the Swabian war had its beginnings.

Eastern Switzerland and the Graubünden were the centers of resistance against the kaiser's plans. The military alliance between Austria and the kaiser (also of the House of Habsburg—Austria) was publicly apparent. The first phase of the war in the Graubünden and the Tirol consisted solely of pillage and destruction. The losses on both sides were small and the Swiss acquired Klettgau and Hegau. The second phase was fought in south Germany and northern Switzerland. In April 1499 the kaiser himself arrived to lead the campaign. He proclaimed his enemies under the ban of Empire and called for an imperial war against Switzerland.

The Austrians, in the meantime, assuming the Swiss to be tied down by the kaiser in Thurgau, assembled a large army at Calven, the gate to the Münstertal. But the Swiss forces were more mobile or more numerous than assumed, and on May 22 they attacked the Austrians and after a fierce struggle forced them into retreat. The Austrian losses were heavy, and the Swiss lost their leader, Benedikt Fontana. Shortly thereafter, the imperial army under the immediate command of von Fürstenburg crossed the Rhine from Sundgau and with 16,000 men—largely Dutch and Walloons—laid siege to the Solothurn fortress of Dornach. On July 22, the Swiss approached from the Jura, well armed, in good order and ready for battle. It was a hot day and many of the enemy forces were bathing in the Birs. The Swiss attacked at once. The enemy was defeated with heavy losses and von Fürstenburg fell in battle.

The kaiser realized that his cause was lost. He called for an armistice and concluded a peace treaty at Basel on 22 September 1499. The independence of the Swiss *Orte* received a *de facto*, though not a *de jure*, recognition. All of the Swiss cases before the Imperial Chamber of Justice were put aside and the union between the Swiss cantons and the three leagues in the Graubünden received Imperial recognition.[25] The Common Penny tax was quietly abrogated and any jurisdiction of the Imperial Chamber of Justice over Switzerland was disclaimed.

A Thirteen-Member Confederation

An unexpected result of the Swabian war was Basel's entry into the Swiss Confederation, on 9 June 1501. Basel had provided to the Swiss, to Bern especially, much of the money needed for construction, for territorial expansion by purchase, and for the ever-recurring wars of the preceding century. The Swiss in turn, by their courageous and sacrificial stand at St. Jacob on the Birs had saved Basel from conquest and destruction by the French Armagnacs. The Swiss promised security to Basel, despite its exposed position on the frontier, and complete freedom in economic development. Should war ever break out among the other *Orte*, Basel agreed to remain neutral and to offer her services as a mediator in any dangerous intercantonal disputes. On 10 August 1501, Schaffhausen was sworn in as a member of the Confederation, and on 17 December 1513, Appenzell became a full member.

Events to the South

In our preoccupation with the Burgundian War in western Switzerland and the Swabian war to the north and east, we have passed over the changing face of Switzerland to the south. Much was happening. Uri was reaching far to strengthen her hold on the southern approaches to the Gotthard pass while the people of Upper Valais sought secure possession of the Eschental to provide more room for their farm population. On the plains of Lombardy the warning of Brother Klaus against foreign adventures would soon be vindicated in bloody combat.

By January 1467, after four win-and-lose campaigns, Uri held the Levinental and enjoyed toll-free privileges right up to the walls of Milan. The duke at this time was Galiazzo Maria Sforza who had given some troop support to Charles the Bold in the opening phases of the Burgundian war. As the war came to a close, dissension between town and country in Switzerland rose to the surface. The duke's viceroy in Bellinzona wrote sarcastically to his master about the problems of the Swiss and expressed the hope that they would tear themselves apart. The word soon reached Uri whose people were now sufficiently provoked to prepare again for war.

In December 1476 the Duke of Milan was murdered. His widow, eager to avoid more conflict with Uri and *Innerschweiz*, signed an agreement with all eight *Orte* and St. Gallen in which she promised to pay the Confederation 32,000 gulden. She also confirmed the possession of the Levinental by Uri. This was July 1477. In the winter of 1478, despite all attempts to appease the Swiss, Uri with 10,000 men laid siege to

Bellinzona. They were joined by other Swiss, notably Hans Waldmann and von Bubenberg. Like several other sieges undertaken by the Swiss this one was a failure, even though the defenders were known to be miserably equipped. Discipline suffered amid the Swiss who turned to plunder and pillage. They ravaged the villages and towns in the area, almost up to Como and Lugano. December came with cold and hunger. A retreat was ordered with a small rearguard left behind to delay an approaching relief force of Milanese—actually a mercenary force of 10,000 men. The advance was slow, hindered by snow, ice, and bitter cold. Suddenly the Swiss, under the command of Teiling, turned and in a bloody battle forced the Milanese into a disorderly flight. It was now 24 December 1478. In January, 1479, the Urners seized the Bleniotal and Biasca. At this point the French intervened and negotiated a treaty of peace with Milan. By its terms the Swiss retained the Levinental but restored possession of the Bleniotal and Biasca to Milan.

In Italy at this time there were four important and powerful States: the Kingdom of Naples, the Papal State, the Republic of Venice, and the Duchy of Milan. Smaller principalities and free cities such as Florence and Genoa completed the political structure of the Italian peninsula. In art, natural science, and the social and philosophical sciences, Italy was a leader in Europe. It had an irresistible attraction for those sovereigns in Continental Europe who were afflicted with a thirst for power. Charles VIII of France, continuing the policy of his father, laid claim as an inheritance to the Kingdom of Naples. In a military expedition with 8,000 Swiss mercenaries he sought to bring the Kingdom under his rule. Indirectly the Swiss supported this ambitious project, being the source of the mercenaries, in return for a rich flow of French gold in to the various *Orte*. In 1495, when tension with the German Reich was again rising, all of the *Orte* except Bern concluded a new alliance with France, thus giving formal support to the French campaign against Milan. Ludovico Moro was then the vice-regent of the young duke. His well-publicized sympathy toward the kaiser encouraged the Swiss to lend their support to the French. Bern, however, along with Obwalden and Schwyz, had concluded an economic treaty with Milan, hence Bern's refusal to give any military aid in support of France's aggressive policy toward Milan.

Charles VIII died in 1498. He was succeeded by Louis XII of the House of Orleans who announced publicly his right of succession to the Duchy of Milan. Moro, as regent for the young son of the murdered Sforza, now sought aid from the Swiss, especially from Bern. Through Bern's efforts, and in association with Lucerne, Schwyz, and Unterwalden, a new capitulation (the seventh) was signed with Milan in the fall of 1498. The other *Orte* stood aside. Through agreements and much French gold, Louis XII so effectively pleaded his case that in March 1499 all of the *Orte* signed a new treaty with France. By this they agreed to provide 5,000 troops for the French war against Milan. With this strong support Louis marched on Milan, drove Moro out of the city, and declared himself to be the new ruler. The whole dubious affair, this haggling over the price of mercenaries, this willingness of the Swiss to sell their men to the highest bidder, and the ultimate betrayal at Novara were among the several ignoble and shameful phases of Swiss history.

In the spring of 1500, Moro succeeded in reconquering the duchy. In this the behaviour of the Swiss was infamous and was not soon forgotten. Six thousand Swiss mercenaries, principally from the Valais and the Graubünden, had been recruited by the Milanese while 10,000 were in the pay of the French. In April, 1500, both forces met at Novara,[26] with Swiss engaged in the defense of the city, and others hired by the French besieging it. The Swiss Diet at last intervened and tried to mediate the dispute. The mercenaries themselves realized that the situation in which they had been placed was intolerable. Over the heads of their comrades-in-arms the two Swiss forces negotiated with each other, and those under Moro's command received from Louis XII the right of safe passage through his lines if they left the city. Moro was to be smuggled out of the city with the departing Swiss but one of the Swiss from Uri (Turmann by name) broke his oath and betrayed Moro. The regent was seized by the French and imprisoned. This unseemly affair disgraced the Swiss throughout the whole of Europe. The ease with which the Swiss could be swayed from one side to the other by offering enough money was widely recognized as a disgrace. Mercenary service, from then on, though it continued for many years, was a less honorable profession.

The Early Chroniclers

Many chronicles, records of events in "Switzerland," were written during the fourteenth, fifteenth, and sixteenth centuries. Some of the chroniclers were commissioned by cities such as Bern, Lucerne and Zurich. A few of the chronicles have a broad sweep and record items of historical interest from within all of the allied *Orte*. Feller and Bonjour, in their two-volume work on Swiss historiography, recorded biographical and other information of interest on a host of Swiss historians and chroniclers from the earliest times (**131**). Beyond biography, sketches of the lives and doings of the following selected chroniclers give us a picture of the human environment which deserves inclusion in a history of Switzerland.

KONRAD JUSTINGER (ca. 1370–ca. 1438)   The *Schultheiss* (Mayor) of Bern commissioned Justinger to write a history of Bern. This was not the first because the *Chronica de Berno*, possibly the first, appeared in 1325–40. Justinger was not a Berner, apparently coming from Rottweil, but in 1391 he is mentioned in the records as a burgher of Bern. He became the city recorder in 1399 and a notary in 1400. Later, as a notary in Zurich, he had responsibilities pertaining to certain seasonal books of the Grossmünster. In writing his history of Bern he used the *Chronica de Berno* and various documents in the city chests. As source material, other than the strictly Bernese sources, he depended on other chronicles and on events related to him by word of mouth. He made little use of sagas. Feller and Bonjour considered Justinger to be frequently inaccurate and guilty of overlooking important items. The original of Justinger's chronicle ("Die Berner Chronik des Conrad Justinger") no longer exists.

In 1408 he bought a life annuity in Basel, based on property ownership. In 1414–15 he was engaged by the city to prepare the great civic reception for King

Sigismund of the *Romisches Reich* on the occasion of his state visit to Bern. He left Bern for Zurich, apparently in a huff about something, and lived for a time in Basel also.

DIEBOLD SCHILLING OF BERN (1403?-86)   This man, uncle of Diebold Schilling of Lucerne, was probably the most important fifteenth-century historian of Bern. He belonged to a Solothurn family which for generations had been interested in intellectual and political affairs. From 1460 to 1476 he was the assistant city recorder in Bern, and from 1476 to 1481 served as a recording clerk for the city treasurer. For the next four years he served as a clerk of the court.

In 1462 he entered one of the most famous guilds and at once became the secretary, later the treasurer, and master of the Guildhall. Here he met a number of the great ones of the day including Diesbach and Bubenberg. In 1468 he became a member of the Council of Two Hundred (the *Grossrat*) though not a politician and never a delegate to the Diet (*Tagsatzung*). In 1474 the Council commissioned Schilling to prepare a history of Bern. Though he participated in the Burgundian War he managed to finish the Chronicle (*Die amtliche Chronik*) in 1483 when this monumental three-volume work, handwritten on parchment and richly illustrated, was presented to the *Grossrat*. The Chronicle contains about 600 pictures, in color, which Schilling himself is believed to have drawn.

Schilling wrote in a simple and straightforward style and included almost everything. The Chronicle is not restricted to political events. He was not highly educated and resorted to a simple moral in appraising his great work: "Virtue preserves; evil destroys". His description of the Burgundian War is of prime historic value. Charles the Bold, the Duke of Burgundy, is described as the real culprit and is depicted as a ruthless, bloodthirsty tyrant—his friends as despicable villains. Schilling relied on his own experiences and observations as source material, not on the writings of other chroniclers.

DIEBOLD SCHILLING OF LUCERN (1460?-1515), A NEPHEW OF THE BERNER SCHILLING   Diebold and his brother Hans worked as illustrators and writers in Lauber's publishing house in Hagenau (or Hegnau?). After working with his father in the Chancellery in Lucerne, and in Bern as an illustrator, he was appointed assistant recorder in Lucerne, finally achieving the title of notary. In the Franco-Milanese war he sided with Milan against the pro-French mayor, Seiler, and others. Ultimately he was richly rewarded by Ludovico Moro of Milan. He participated in the battle of Nancy in January 1477—the last engagement in the Burgundian war. In 1487, because of untrustworthiness, he lost his position in the Lucerne chancellery. In the following year, he appears to have visited Vienna in the company of the chronicler, Melchior Russ.

His chronicle includes the founding of Lucerne and its history to 1509/13. He was less critical than Petermann Etterlin but drew upon Etterlin's chronicle for at least three-fourths of his own. He used other chronicles but not that of his uncle in Bern. Otherwise he wrote from his own experiences and made no effort to make of his chronicle, a history of the Federation. Feller and Bonjour consider the work to be a good source for the battle of Giornico and especially valuable as a record of the *Tagsatzung* of Stans which he witnessed. The period 1503 to 1509, not reported upon by Etterlin, is described in detail. The chronicle contains about 440 illustrations, mostly full page, and of excellent quality. In these, and in the text, he describes the daily life of the Swiss at work and at play. Many of the pictures portray the Swiss as warriors. Schilling died in Hungary in 1515.

PETERMANN ETTERLIN (1440/50–ca. 1509) Etterlin's father, Egloff, was city clerk of Lucerne from 1427. Petermann took part in the Waldshuter and Burgundian Wars. He fought at Grandson, Murten and Nancy. In between these military engagements he became an attorney and, in 1495, the clerk of the court in Lucerne. He wrote his famous chronicle (121) in 1505/07. Unlike earlier chronicles, Etterlin's embraced the whole of the *Eidgenossenschaft* ("Switzerland"). After the Burgundian War, there was a revival of an all-Swiss feeling within the Confederation and this is the spirit expressed in his writings. To a friend in Basel he wrote that he did this work because of his love for the *Eidgenossenschaft* and the joy he found in old chronicles. It was the first printed Swiss chronicle. As sources, he drew upon earlier chronicles including the White Book of Sarnen.[8] He also drew upon his father's memory in his description of the battle of Arbedo and the Old Zurich War. The chronicle is considered by Feller and Bonjour to be good source material for the Burgundian War, especially for the final battle of Nancy. For this period (1468–77) he used archival sources supplemented by his personal observations and experiences.

The first four or five pages pertain to Einsiedeln and Meinrat. Next comes $1\frac{1}{2}$ pages about Charlemagne. "Ury, Switz and Underwalden" are referred to as the first areas to be settled. Throughout the book, the three are mentioned as if they were one—"die dry Lender" [the three lands] treated as a unit. There is no mention, however, of any early formal alliance subject to renewal every ten years, as reported by Coxe (95, I, p. 280) and by Tschudi (370, I, p. 104).

THE WHITE BOOK OF SARNEN[8] It would be important to know the extent to which the early chroniclers used the White Book. Justinger, Petermann Etterlin, and Johannes Stumpf are believed to have used it (297). Tschudi possibly drew upon its contents, though many details in Tschudi's chronicle appear to come from Etterlin.

The book itself was discovered in Sarnen in the early 1850s. It aroused at once the interest of a number of historians. Kopp (see ref. 207 and note 14, Chapter 2) reported the lack of any documentary proof of the existence of *Vögte* named Gessler and von Landenberg. He questioned also the Tell legend and the alleged settlement of Schwyz and Hasli by Swedes and Fresians; both legends appear in the White Book of Sarnen. The book was discovered by Gerold Meyer von Knonau (1804–58) while reorganizing the archives of Obwalden. Georg von Wyss (1816–93) also shared to some extent in the discovery and a heated dispute over priority arose between the two men. Von Knonau wrote a brief announcement of this important find for the *Neue Zürcher Zeitung* (22 May 1856) and von Wyss (395) published a 22-page description of the book.

JOHANNES STUMPF (1500–77/78)   Stumpf was born of poor parents but with persistence and hard work derived a good education in Frankfurt, Heidelberg and Strassburg. In 1520 he entered the religious order of St. John. In 1522 he became the prior and preacher in Bubikon. He joined Zwingli and was at the center of the baptism dispute. He tried to expand the Reformation though he lacked a vigorous argumentative and fighting nature. After the battle of Kappel, in which Zwingli was killed, Stumpf became Dean of Oberwetzikon. In 1529 he married, and later became the priest in Stammheim and Dean of the Chapter in Stein am Rhein. He was a great historiographer and was honored by Zurich where he was created a burgher. In 1540 he started his main work, including therein a report on his travels through Switzerland, mostly on foot, in 1544 (**353**). In 1586, his extensive chronicle was published (**352**). In its preparation he received support and remarkable collaboration from Tschudi, Vadian, and Bullinger, and gave full expression to his great talent as a writer. In 1564, he published a more popular and reorganized chronicle as a handbook for the young, to instruct them at little cost in the history of the *Eidgenossenschaft*. It was patriotically oriented against the princes of the *Reich*. He also prepared large maps of the country which were much in demand and were ultimately collected into an atlas.

AEGIDIUS TSCHUDI (1505–1572)   Please refer to note 5, Chapter 2.

HEINRICH BULLINGER (1504–1575)   Bullinger was born in Bremgarten (in Aargau), as the son of a deacon, and studied at the University of Cologne. From 1520 on, he buried himself in the new learning and the great religious disputes of the Reformation times. In 1522 he became a teacher in the cloister at Kappel. By 1525, the Reformation was accepted in the cloister and the monks discarded the robes of their Order. Bullinger then became the priest at Bremgarten and a friend of Zwingli. After the second Kappeler War, Bremgarten again turned to catholicism and Bullinger fled to Zurich where he became priest in the Grossmünster and successor to Zwingli who was killed in battle in 1531. He was a forceful preacher. As Myconius said "Zwingli is not dead but, like the Phoenix, has risen again." His strength lay in his peace of mind, security, and political tact. He formulated ordinances for the Church, instruction in the schools, and sponsored social legislation for the poor. Under his calm and conservative leadership, the Reformed Church gained in strength and acceptance. His conservative approach pleased the Swiss. Although he was not a battling zealot like Zwingli, he was of the same mind and fought against mercenary service and, in consequence, a mercenary-supply treaty between Zurich and France. He was an effective and voluminous writer, with correspondents throughout Europe. He was the author of 100 or more theological tracts, e.g. on heresy; a humanistic drama came from his pen, and an exhaustive diary to 1574. Weather and crop reports, miracles, and incidents pertaining to the hated mercenary service were included in his encyclopedic interests. He wrote many small localized histories (e.g. the cloisters of Kappel and Einsiedeln; the counts of Habsburg) and labored for 40 years in the collection of material for his great Swiss chronicle (**68**). In this he carefully cited his sources. Stumpf, a contemporary, drew heavily upon this chronicle. The literature concerning Bullinger is enormous. A vivid impression of this is provided in the report of a symposium edited by Gäbler and Zsindely (145); especially pertinent is the paper by Fritz Büsser (145, pp. 7–19).

ALBRECHT VON BONSTETTEN (1441/45–1503/05)   Among the Swiss humanists of the fifteenth century, Bonstetten was possibly the greatest. After his first student years in Freiburg (Breisgau) and Basel, he studied canonical law in Pavia (1471–74). In 1475 he became Dean of Einsiedeln. Travel throughout "Switzerland" was extensive and more than a mere past-time, for in 1479 he prepared, in Latin, the first Swiss geography. He knew the country thoroughly and described places, the people (their culture and character), commerce, trade, army strength, and the battle of Giornico. He included the first description of the coats of arms of the eight *Orte* which then constituted the Federation. He also wrote a biography of Niklaus von Flüe whom he had visited. In 1480 came the legends of the Holy Meinrad and, in 1494, a description in Latin and German of the cloister Einsiedeln. Much of his correspondence—101 letters are known—covers science, learning, politics and student problems in Pavia. His writings are free of bombast and pompousness, his style being simple and direct, though somewhat dry.

VALERIUS ANSHELM (1475–1547)   Anshelm came from Rottweil, located in the Schwarzwald. Since 1463, Rottweil had been an associated State of the Swiss Confederation. After two or three years of study (1492/93–1495) in Cracow, Anshelm entered the University of Tubingen, followed by study in Dijon in 1501. We next hear of him in Bern where he became head of the Latin school. In 1509, he was appointed city physician of Bern at a salary of 100 pounds per annum, plus wood, grain, and the right of private practice. He vigorously opposed the pension system, as did others of prominence who accepted the Reformation and the teachings of Zwingli. Both Vadian and Zwingli were among his friends. He expressed his doubts about the effectiveness of the Mass for the Dead, and his wife was fined by the authorities for similar indiscretions in which she questioned current beliefs concerning the "Mother of God." In anger, Anshelm returned to Rottweil, only to be driven from the city with 40 others who had accepted the Reformed faith. They complained bitterly to the *Tagsatzung* but without result. He soon returned to Bern as the official chemist and with the right to pursue his private medical practice. In 1520, Anshelm was commissioned to prepare an official chronicle of Bern. In 1507/09 and 1510, he had published two historical works and was well prepared for the assignment. His life work was his great chronicle (16) which gives principal attention to the period 1477 to 1536. He sought to improve on Justinger for the years 1030 to 1298, and to describe the Burgundian War from a quite different point of view than that of Schilling. His account almost serves as a counterpoise or *Gegensatz* to Schilling's. He made extensive use of documents and of reports of eye witnesses. Although his chronicle focuses on Bern, it reaches out into a history of the *Eidgenossenschaft*, and may even be regarded as an approach to a history of the world—from Adam to 1536. Common things, such as weather, harvests, accidents, catastrophes and miracles, of interest to ordinary people, are included. He lived in a very dynamic time with an abundance of great happenings. Because of his broad intellectual interests and his skill as a writer, he portrayed the exciting events of his time very effectively. He had great respect for, and an abundant knowledge of, the ancients—Caesar, Livy, Plutarch, Plato, and Virgil. As a physician, he departed from other chroniclers by including a history of disease. Unlike the usual practice of historians, Anshelm's value judgments were numerous. His moral judgments were those of the protestants; as sins he mentions mercenary service, the pension system wherein the few enriched themselves at the expense of those whom they rounded up as mercenaries, and the mercenary-supply agreements, especially with France.

JOACHIM VON WATT (VADIAN) 1484–1551   In 1501, Vadian was sent by his father to the University of Vienna. There he studied humanistic literature but also science, especially astronomy and geography. From being a student he soon became a teacher, with great abilities as a speaker, poet and author. Kaiser Maximilian created him Poet Laureate. In 1516 he became professor of Latin and Greek in Vienna. He strengthened his knowledge of geography by extensive travel and independent observations. In 1534, he published his own geographical work on the three parts of the earth: Asia, Africa, and Europe. Like Copernicus he believed the earth to be a sphere. In Vadian's opinion, Amerigo Vespucci was the discoverer of America. In 1517 he became Rector Magnificus of the University of Vienna. Next, we hear of him as a student of medicine, of his return to his homeland (St. Gallen), and his appointment as the city physician. In 1526, he became *Bürgermeister* and held the office for many years. The city sought to merge the Abbey with its great landholdings, and the city into a single State (canton). During these religio-political struggles, Vadian was an energetic and accomplished statesman. In his writings he supported the claims of the city over the Abbey and the countryside, partly by pointing out how the monks and the papacy had fallen away from the true faith. After several preliminary publications, his chief work appeared in 1529/31 as "Die grosse Chronik der Äbte" and covered the years 1199–1490. In 1531, a great mob plundered the cloister and destroyed many documents but Vadian managed to collect some 600 of the precious documents. His own chronicle, fortunately, was already widely distributed. In the 1540s he supplemented his great chronicle by a "Kleine Chronik der Äbte" for the years 720 to 1531. The second part of the great chronicle covers the growth of St. Gallen and the *Eidgenossenschaft*—their alliances and their wars—and the history of the German *Reich*. The small chronicle is limited to St. Gallen and eastern "Switzerland." Vadian was the lone historian in St. Gallen though he shared some of his interests in history with Johannes Kissler (1502–74). Scholars were not abundant in the city; linen manufacturing and trade were "the thing." Vadian had an uncanny ability to separate the true from the false, historical facts from legends and fables. Hence he considered Tschudi's account of the freeing of the ancient Swiss as a mere saga—a legend. He regarded Erasmus highly and placed him with Zwingli among the great reformers. He was religiously tolerant in so far as State policy, and his own hatred of the papacy, permitted. Feller and

Bonjour summed it all up: "He was the greatest humanistic historian of Switzerland" (131).

KONRAD TÜRST (1455–1509) Türst is credited with preparing the earliest of the maps of Switzerland. Not surprisingly, the map contains many errors, especially in distances. His early desire was to be a prebendary in the Zurich Fraumünster, like his father, but an ordinance of 1476 did not permit this because "enough were there already." He became a student of medicine and was presently appointed city physician. In 1499 Emperor Maximilian called him to be his personal physician and astrologer. As somewhat of an historian, his chief work was his description of the ten-member Swiss Confederation (die Beschreibung der zehnörtigen Eidgenossenschaft) in 1495/97.

THURING FRICKER (FRICKART, FRICKARD) (ca. 1429–1519) As a student at Heidelberg, Fricker received his baccalaureate degree in 1458, and his Master's degree in 1460. He studied subsequently in Pavia and, in 1470, succeeded his father as Stadtschreiber (City Clerk or Recorder) of Bern. Having served frequently as a representative of Bern in the Diet and in a variety of other Councils, including membership in the Grossrat and the Kleinrat, he was a recognized authority on the inner and outer politics of Bern and the Confederation. His description, unfortunately unfinished, of the Twingherrenstreit appeared in 1470. He also wrote many volumes of the Bern Council's Manual.

BENEDIKT TSCHACHTLAN (†1493) AND HEINRICH DITTLINGER (†1478/79) These historians collaborated in writing a chronicle of Bern. The volume has many illustrations in color. The original copy of the chronicle is in the Central Library, Zurich. Tschachtlan died of the plague in 1493.

MELCHIOR RUSS (killed in the Swabian War in 1499) Russ was the author of Eidgenössische Chronik, written in 1482 and first published in 1832–34 by Joseph Schneller (Jenni, Bern, 1834, 272 pp.). Fourteen documents dating from 1386 to 1405 are included in an appendix. Russ and his father before him, were cantonal recorders of Lucerne. The chronicle is largely restricted to Lucerne's history and does not contain anything about the origins of the Confederation.

The Public Health

The few examples that follow are indicative of public awareness, in the fifteenth century, of the infectious nature of pestilential disease. Thus, in January 1479, the Bishop of Valais was advised not to visit Bern because of the pest in that region (Abschiede III. 1, p. 22). Next, we learn that in the cantons of Schwyz, Glarus, and Unterwalden, meetings of local communities (Gemeinden) could not be held because of the pest (Abschiede III.1, p. 76). In August, 1484, the Duke of Milan closed the market in Bellinzona because of the pest (III.1, p. 188). In September he closed the market at Barisi for one year because of the pest (Abschiede III. 1, p. 192). But he hastened to add that this closure of the market did not mean that the Swiss (Eidgenossen) were frobidden to travel in his country (Abschiede III. 1, p. 196).

Again, in August 1493, the Duke of Milan closed the market in Bellinzona because of a recurrence of the pest (*Abschiede* III. 1, p. 441).

Neutrality

In the preceding chapter a number of alliances or agreements were described which suggest that something which we must call "neutrality" was beginning to emerge. Lasserre's excellent treatment of the origins of Swiss neutrality really begins with the late fifteenth century, for only then did events transpire which, in his opinion, are sufficiently relevant to deserve consideration (**213**, pp. 257–275). The Swiss Confederation evolved through an expanding and interlocking network of alliances between independent, sovereign States. These alliances were frequently in conflict with one another but this never seemed to bother the Swiss, partly because, in a reservation clause (*Vorbehalt*), they excluded any obligations stemming from pre-existing alliances. Despite the built-in conflicts and contradictory responsibilities in these agreements they tended in the aggregate to lead steadily toward a neutral posture for the whole Confederation, since each alliance was for defense against aggressors.

Lasserre reminds us of a 1479 treaty with the king of Hungary—essentially a treaty of friendship with specific relevance to neutrality. In this document, wherein the Swiss agreed to furnish no military aid whatever to any enemy of the king, the concept of neutrality or friendly passivity may have received its first diplomatic expression. The king, Matthias Corvin, had dreamed of seizing part of Austria or even acquiring the imperial crown, and would have much preferred a firm military alliance with the courageous Swiss who had just emerged victorious from the Burgundian War. But the Swiss were on friendly terms with Duke Sigismund of Austria and his son Maximilian. They stubbornly refused any military alliance which would rupture the relations with these two Austrian nobles. But Corvin accepted the inevitable and paid the Swiss handsomely for entering into the treaty of friendship with Hungary.

The fifteenth century was a time of almost constant warfare. Very few engagements were defensive operations against a foreign aggressor. The most noteworthy of these was the battle at St. Jacob on the Birs against the French. The many other engagements in the Old Zurich War were strictly in the nature of civil warfare between Zurich and her fellow members within the Confederation. The Burgundian war consisted mainly of heroic efforts to defend the Confederation, especially the extensive territory ruled by Bern, against the efforts of Charles the Bold to expand the Duchy of Burgundy. But it was also a determined effort by Bern to seize more territory to the west.

On the contrary, the seizure of Aargau and Thurgau from Austria, the southward expansion, with its conquest of the Leventina and Bellinzona, and the campaign in Valais were brazen acts of violence by the Confederation or some of its member cantons against neighbouring territories.

The neutrality of a State is certainly not compromised by defensive warfare. Defense against an aggressor is an elementary right. However, the wars of conquest, undertaken largely by Bern and Uri, cannot possibly be regarded as compatible with a neutral posture and an avoidance of provocative acts toward neighbouring States. It can be argued, however, that the fifteenth-century Swiss regarded their seizure of Aargau and Thurgau and other conquests to the East in a different light. To them, all of this was nothing more than an extension of their thirteenth- and fourteenth-century policy of defense against Austria and the Habsburgs. Even more to the point is the omission of any declaration of neutrality toward foreign Powers from each of the intercantonal treaties of alliance which bound the member cantons together in the Swiss Confederation. Many years were to elapse before the central government began to issue such proclamations.

A number of the early decisions on neutrality policies concern relations with Austria. Winterthur, until absorbed by Zurich in 1467, was an Austrian possession. The Old Zurich War (1440–1450) found Zurich entering into an alliance with Austria, to the great displeasure of all the other federated Swiss cantons. In 1407 Zurich and Winterthur negotiated a "permanent" alliance. Winterthur, understandably, made sure that the alliance did not contravene her obligations to Austria. If Austria were to go to war against Zurich or her Swiss allies, it was agreed that Winterthur would give help to neither side but would remain neutral (*Stille sitzen*). Zurich promised to protect Winterthur and to defend her against any attackers, and Winterthur, reciprocally, promised to counsel and help Zurich in case a corresponding need arose.[27]

Another agreement provided that, in the event of a war between Zurich and Austria, the fortified towns of Feldkirch and Jochberg would not turn against the fortress at Grandeck but, with the forces at their disposal, would remain neutral.[28]

An agreement in 1417, involved Schwyz and the Duke of Toggenburg. The latter was pledged to observe and respect any peace treaty which Schwyz and Austria might conclude. Furthermore, if Schwyz should go to war against Austria, the people of Gaster, Sargans, Walenstadt, Amden, Weesen, Windegg and Nidberg— all of these places having been pawned—must remain neutral.[29]

In 1411, Appenzell turned to the Confederation for a protective alliance. The response was favorable and Appenzell was admitted to the *Bund*, somewhat as an associate, not as an equal among equals. The Confederation had a determining voice in matters of high policy. Appenzell was denied the right of engaging in war and was thus neutralized. This explains her nonparticipation in the Old Zurich War of 1436 to 1450 in which she would otherwise have been allied, almost certainly, with Schwyz. Bearing in mind the tension and constant threat of open conflict between the cities and the peasants of the agricultural areas, it is significant that the alliance of 1411 required that Appenzell refrain from aiding either side in any such conflict (e.g. a peasant revolt). Instead, she must attempt to mediate the dispute.

Appenzell and the Abbot of St. Gallen were in open conflict in 1421 but the remaining seven members of the *Bund* refrained from involvement except as peacemakers. They attempted to mediate the dispute.

Appenzell's neutral status was terminated in 1452 by a new treaty which brought the canton into closer relations with the seven easterly cantons. She was thereby enabled, if not required, to join the majority of the federated cantons in any intercantonal or foreign war in which the Confederation might be plunged. Not until 17 December 1513 was Appenzell admitted to full membership in the Confederation, qualified by the requirement that she must remain neutral in case of intercantonal conflicts wherein peaceful mediation had failed.[30] Similar clauses are to be found in the treaties of alliance of 1501 with Basel and Schaffhausen whereby these two cantons were admitted to membership in the Confederation.[31] In all three cases, the cantonal government promised to give help to none, should war break out between the other members of the Confederation. Rather, the covenants obliged them to make every effort to mediate any intercantonal disputes that might lead to a rupture of the peace.

When the principal cities and towns in Aargau fell to the Swiss in 1415, Baden and areas under its control became a subject land. Peace was delicate and fragile, and with the advent of the Old Zurich War, Baden begged to be allowed to remain neutral. The Confederation agreed to the request with the rather remarkable response that she must remain neutral (*ruhig sitzen* or "sit quietly") through all wars between members of the Confederation. Similar requests came in from others and quite a number of subject cities were neutralized: Uster and the Grüningeramt,[32] Wetzikon, Kempten, Ettenhausen and Medikon.[33]

Foreign enclaves in the cantons were almost invariably required to remain neutral in the event of war. Certain Toggenburg possessions were neutralized by pacts with Zurich in 1416 and with Schwyz in 1417.[34] In the armistice of 1460 between Austria and the Swiss Confederation, the Austrian city of Winterthur (in Zurich territory) promised to remain neutral if war were to be resumed between the two Powers.

A host of treaties designed to preserve the peace were negotiated following the Old Zurich War. In 1452 a treaty of the Confederation with France declared the permanent friendship of the two countries, evidenced by their agreement never to oppose each other in battle or to help any who might attack the other of the two parties.[35] Of singular interest was the pledge of both parties to deny an enemy of one the right to pass with his troops through the territory of the other. A similar disavowal of the ancient right of the *Durchzug* is found in a neutrality treaty of 1487 between Maximilian of Austria (Emperor of the *Römisches Reich*) and the Swiss Confederation.[36] As time passed, Switzerland became increasingly alarmed whenever a foreign army operated near her borders. She was in constant fear, not so much of an attack upon herself, as of an unpermitted shortcut by one army (e.g. Austrian) through Swiss territory to permit attack on the enemy beyond (e.g. a French army).

Other neutrality treaties negotiated during the closing decades of the century were designed to provide a protective shield of neutral States among Switzerland's immediate neighbors. All of these treaties denied the right of the *Durchzug* to any enemy of the contracting parties. Parties to the treaties included Württemberg (in 1469 and 1500), the Bishopric of Constance (in 1469), Strassburg (in 1474 and 1479), Bavaria (in 1491), and Savoy (in 1512).

If Switzerland was moving at all toward true and total neutrality, there is little evidence of it in respect of mercenaries. The Swiss cantons continued to provide them to almost all comers. But there were exceptions. Emperor Maximilian in 1495 requested 8,000 Swiss mercenaries to assist him in his war against Charles VIII of France. It was denied, presumably because of the 1452 treaty with France which had been reaffirmed by Louis XI in 1463 and by Charles VIII only a few weeks prior to the Austrian request. A request by France to recruit Swiss mercenaries for use in the Anglo-French war had been refused in 1452. This action of the Diet angered the *Waldstätte* whose people had long since approved of foreign military service as a source of employment and income. The Diet made a gesture of appeasement by ruling that Swiss neutrality would not be impaired if men of military age voluntarily entered France for military service. The French request and the involvement of the Diet were unusual, because agreements for supply of mercenaries were negotiated at the time between individual cantons and the foreign government concerned.

The century ended with the battle of Novara in 1500. This was a glaring example of a violation of the typical basic agreement for mercenary service which required that Swiss soldiers would be used only in a defensive operation. At Novara, Swiss were fighting Swiss. This disgraceful happening was intolerable but it was repeated again and again in the ensuing 250 years.

During the closing years of the fifteenth century, religious dissension which had become so prominent in the sixteenth century, began to emerge. On the wall of an old charnel house at Leuk in Upper Valais is inscribed "Oh godly Christ may you be protected from Lutheran deception and trickery." Within the charnel house, under old human bones and skulls, archaeologists discovered in the late 1970s some 25 Gothic wooden statues dating from the thirteenth to the fifteenth century. Still older statues are expected to be found. It is assumed that the statues were hidden in the charnel house to protect them from those vandals who were intent on destroying sacred images and sculptures of the Catholic Church. The find is described as the most important art treasure of the century in Valais—to be retained in the village, if possible.[37]

Notes and Comments

1. Häne has stated that the men of military age in Zurich in 1442–43 numbered 4,000 to 5,000. Of these, about one-half could be called into active service, leaving an equal number for civil defense duties (**163**). The population of the canton of Zurich at this time was probably 25,000 or less (**40**, pp. 43, 45).

Zurich committed a grievous error in not agreeing, at the very beginning, to a proposal of Schwyz that the dispute be arbitrated. The federal pact of 1351 with Zurich required that arbitration be employed in settling disputes with members of the Federation. This means of solving litigious disputes was used more than 100 times in the first two centuries of the Confederation. Confessional disputes were exceptional: they were rarely, if ever, arbitrated. When an arbitration court finally recommended a solution of the Schwyz-Zurich dispute, Zurich stubbornly refused to accept the judgment of the court. The Federation recognized the equality before the law of two parties in arbitration irrespective of their economic or military potential. This egalitarian principle, commonly expressed as "the equality of the unequals," was unacceptable to Bürgermeister Stüssi of Zurich who looked down upon Schwyz as a canton of simple-minded peasants, not to be regarded by proud, rich and powerful Zurich as an equal in an arbitration procedure or in any other circumstance (**213**). But the Schwyzers, equally proud and stubborn, hated

Zurich—in part an expression of the deeply rooted sentiment of peasants against the cities and city cantons. To Zurich's surprise and consternation, all of the other cantons supported Schwyz and agreed that Zurich was the guilty party—a conclusion which was reflected in the final judgment of the Augsburg arbitrator. In the preceding years of the dispute, the towns in general favored Zurich, as opposed to the "peasant cantons," but it was an alliance of Zurich with Austria in 1449 that finally turned even the towns against Zurich.

2. Tschudi (**370**, II, p. 425) reports that only 32 survived and were thereby disgraced: "they preferred the life of cowards more than the honor of an heroic and noble death." The military code of the Swiss required that their men die in battle rather than be captured by the enemy or seek safety in flight.

3. The Dauphin never forgot the remarkable courage of the heavily outnumbered Swiss in this battle. Later, as Louis XI, he strove for a friendly alliance with the Swiss, obviously to have their help as mercenaries in his various wars. This was finally accomplished in the Franco-Swiss treaty of October 1474.

4. Appenzell was not involved. She was not a full member of the Confederation and the *Burg- und Landrecht* of 1411 required her to remain neutral in any conflict between member cantons. She had however kept watch over Austria which did not itself participate actively in the Zurich war, and in 1452 (November 15) the seven easterly cantons negotiated a new pact which brought Appenzell into closer association with the Confederation. Her neutral status was terminated and in any future disagreements and troubles involving the Confederation she would be obliged to follow the majority. But again she was not permitted, without the consent of the Confederation, to begin any war or to form any alliance with other cities or with feudal lords. [*Abschiede* II, pp. 870–72, *Beilage* (15 November 1452), "Bundesbrief der VII Orte mit dem Lande Appenzell"]; see also Dierauer (**103**, II, p. 142), Tschudi (**370**, II, pp. 570–72), and *Abschiede* (II, 200–01, 16 May–June 1446, and Beilage 21, 811–14). This peace agreement might more accurately be described as an armistice which ended hostilities between Zurich and the rest of the cantons. The remaining issues were settled by arbitration. On 13 July 1450 the alliance of Zurich with Austria was ruled to be a grievous error and the Zurich burghers voted to renounce the alliance. In a solemn ceremony, Zurich was readmitted to the Confederation. The Old Zurich War, as it is usually called, is fully described by May (**232**, III, pp. 5–212). A second valuable treatment of the war, stripped of almost all descriptions of the military engagements, is by Lasserre (**213**, pp. 59–90).

5. Montaigne (**250**, p. 17) erroneously placed Mülhausen in the canton of Basel.

6. Aeneas Silvius Piccolomini (1405–64). Elected Pope Pius II in 1458, he was a great friend of Basel and founder of its University (1460). In a long letter to Cardinal Julian St. Angeli, the papal legate, Piccolomini described the city of Basel and its people at the time of the Great Church Council of 1431–48 (**288**). Aeneas Silvius said little about the lives of ordinary people but he gave a fascinating description of the burgher class, the nobles, and the rich merchants. Their houses were well arranged and furnished and fully as beautiful as those of Florence. They were pleasantly white and most were painted. Some had gardens, fountains, and a lodge. They had heatable rooms in which the household ate, lived, and slept. Facilities for steam baths were also to be found. Floors were covered with tan bark, sometimes with carpets. Tapestries adorned the walls. Birds lived in the houses in winter for it was too cold outside, and they were protected because of their beautiful singing. On the roofs of the houses were the storks. There they nested and cared for their young, always enjoying the protection of the householder who believed that "If one takes the young, fire will break out in the house." The streets were described—wide enough for carts to pass, and with fountains in every street. The city was protected by a stout wall with an encircling moat. The wall was topped with flat stone plates which bore Hebraic characters and were taken from Jewish cemeteries. The Basler, however, believed that the strength of the city was in the unity of spirit of its people, "for when the people are thus united they cannot be conquered by a large number of the enemy. When the people are not united the smallest attack can be disastrous." The city squares were well ornamented with shade trees and there the children played (fighting games, archery, and stone throwing) while the women sang, danced and gossiped.

The letter describes the administration of justice in some detail. Even in worldly matters the bishop was the supreme authority. He had the power of the sword and administered justice over the greater criminals. In return for his labors he received annually four pfennigs from each family. Punishments were

The Drachenloch (Swiss National Museum, from Heinz Bächler "Die Ersten Bewohnern der Schweiz")

A Swiss Lake-Shore Settlement (Swiss National Library, from "Urgeschichte der Schweiz" by Jakob Heierli)

Andiron of Grey Clay—circ 1000 B.C. (Swiss National Museum)

Golden Bowl, circ 600 B.C., found in Canton of Zurich in a 1906 Excavation (Swiss National Museum)

Hydria—Greek Water Vessel of Bronze, 51 cm in height; about 590 B.C., from Meikirch-Grächwil/Be (Bern History Museum)

Dea Artioni—Queen of the Bears; A most important piece of Roman bronze. Found in 1832 in Muri/Be (Bern History Museum)

Roman Vessels of Glass (Swiss National Museum)

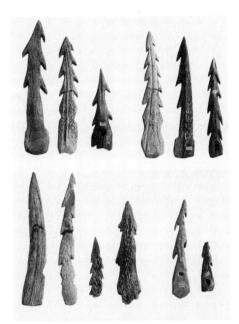

Harpoons from several sites in Bern Canton (Bern History Museum)

The man from Prilly (Vaud Canton). Bronze with olive-green patina. Found in Prilly in 1704. Identity unknown. Probably Celtish or Roman. Late Trojan times (Bern History Museum)

Mosaic from Roman times depicting the planets and gods of the sea. Each medallion is 67.5 cm in diameter. (Swiss National Museum)

Golden Jewelry, circ 200 A.D. From Obfelden (Zurich canton). (Swiss National Museum)

Romainmôtier—South facade of the collegiate church with remains of the Gothic cloister (Swiss National Tourist Office)

Ivory Relief, illustrating Psalm XXVI. Believed to have decorated the Prayer Book of Charles the Bald (Swiss National Museum)

Painted Wood Ceiling, 12th century A.D., St. Martin's Church, Zillis, Graubünden. (Swiss National Tourist Office)

Remains of the Roman amphitheater at Aventicum (Avenches)—Capital of Helvetia (Swiss National Tourist Office)

The Devil's Bridge (Swiss National Library)

Aegidius Tschudi, "Gilg Tschudi of Glarus,"
(Swiss National Library)

William Coxe (Swiss National Library)

The Battle of Sempach, 1386. The legendary Swiss hero, Winkelried, is at the left with an armful of
Austrian lances piercing his body. (Swiss National Library)

A citizen of Appenzell expressing agreement at Trogen Landsgemeinde (Open-air People's Parliament/ Northeastern Switzerland. (Swiss National Tourist Office)

Swiss Open-air Parliaments. Every year on the first Sunday in May, the voters gather together for the Landsgemeinde in the "ring" at Glarus. In the background: the Glärnisch massif may be seen./Eastern Switzerland. (Swiss National Tourist Office)

The Battle of Morgarten, 15 November 1315 (Swiss National Library; from Tschachtlan's Berner Chronicle)

The Chapel of Morgarten built in the 16th century to commemorate the victory over the Austrians in 1315. (Swiss National Tourist Office)

The Countryside surrounding the battlefield of Morgarten. (Swiss National Tourist Office)

cruel and very severe; some died during the punishment; others had their limbs broken on the rack; some were drowned in the Rhine; some were burned or buried alive, or sealed in the wall, or given only bread and water until they died of hunger and thirst. The people were said to observe scrupulously all religious services, masses and fasts. They refrained from any heathen literature and never heard of Cicero or other Roman and Greek orators. Grammar, dialectics (logic) and music were the subjects of study. The nobles were reported to have summer and winter palaces and to regale themselves with fancy balls. The beauties of the city appeared in festive clothing ornamented with jewels of gold, silver, and precious stones. Much time was spent in eating: "gladly they keep their feet under the table for a long time," "(*Sie halten die Füsse gern lang unter dem Tisch*)." The common people were said to be satisfied with their lot, except for those who had too little bread. Fish were abundant, especially salmon. Indeed, there was a rule that no servant might be obliged by his master to eat salmon more often than three times each week.

One remarkable fact about Basel is its total destruction by an earthquake in 1356 and its restoration. Not 100 houses remained and these were destroyed in subsequent tremors and by fire in the inner city. Wackernagel (**378**) wrote that "It lay in ashes like Sodom and Gomorrah." Yet, 50 years later at the time of the Great Council the city had been completely rebuilt.

7. The first Swiss source of salt to be industrially developed was at Bex (canton Valais). It was never of major importance. Even by 1906, the Bex works produced only about one-fifteenth of the country's yield of salt (**128**, p. 96). For many years, Switzerland was heavily dependent on France and Germany for this indispensable substance. Only when salt deposits, discovered in the Rhine basin, were adequately exploited did Switzerland's dependence on foreign sources greatly decrease. Her production of salt in 1976 was 311,611 tons against a consumption of about 340,000 tons [**341**, pp. 159, 163 (1979)].

8. The White Book of Sarnen, discovered in the archives of Obwalden by Meyer von Knonau, has been the subject of a number of studies. I shall refer only to those of von Wyss (**395**), Wirz (**392**) and Meyer (**241**). The book is of unusual interest because it is among the oldest of the Chronicles and contains what appears to be the original version of the Tell legend. The Tell legend, as found in the White Book of Sarnen, was reproduced in an appendix (*Beilage*) to the *Neue Zürcher Zeitung* in 1856. Thanks to Meyer von Knonau, Tschudi's version of the legend appears in the same appendix alongside the White Book's version. The 258 sheets, of which 233 are hand-written documents and 25 are devoted to the origins of the Swiss confederation, are bound together in bright yellowish-white pigskin. The hand-written documents were assembled between 1435 and 1478 or possibly between 1470 and 1472. Most of the documents were written by the same hand, apparently that of the *Landschreiber* (analogous to County Clerk) of Obwalden, mentioned in the documents as Hans Schriber but from other sources believed to be Hans Schälly. The book appears to have served as a guide to the public law and as such was of use to the *Landschreiber*. A few comparatively late documents (up to 1607) were added by others. Several of the 15th- and 16th-century historians (Konrad Justinger, Johannes Stumpf, and Petermann Etterlin) appear to have used the White Book of Sarnen extensively in preparing their own chronicles.

The book goes far beyond the events of local Obwalden interest. It starts with the *Bundesbrief* of Brunnen, dated 9 December 1315, and describes in documentary fashion the growth of the Confederation from the original triple alliance to a federation of eight member States. The 25 pages of running text are a curious and fascinating mixture of historical facts and legends, the latter enriched by some spicy tales about the two hated governors, Gessler and von Landenberg, and their henchmen.

As for the historical facts, we are told that "Count Rudolf von Habksburg," a friend of the Count of Tirol, became king and took to himself "turgöw, zürichgöw and ergöw." He imposed a tax that the people must pay to the *Reich* and to no one else. If they helped the *Reich* when needed, and they swore their fealty to no one else, they could enjoy their rights and freedoms. The king kept his word, but he went away and appointed *Vögte* who were very bad, Gessler in "Switz" and Uri, and von Landenberg in Unterwalden.

The spicy tales are much too fanciful to accept. The reference to Stauffacher's house and Gessler lacks credibility. I include it because it leads into an account, possibly dubious, of the origins of the anti-Habsburg conspiracy of 1307 (or 1291?). A man named Stoupacher (Stoufacher or Stauffacher) had built a beautiful house which was coveted by Gessler. In fact the governor demanded the house and all of Stauffacher's possessions. This was going a bit too far, so Stauffacher's wife urged her husband to meet secretly with brave, resourceful men from all three valleys and organize a conspiracy to drive the hated tyrants and their retainers from the land. Allegedly one of the conspirators was Tell, Thall, or Tall. The story then continues by easy stages into the swearing of the oath at Rütli, the "apple shoot," the killing of Gessler at Hohle Gasse, and the *Bundesbrief* of Brunnen.

The authenticity of the "apple shoot" is difficult to accept, since closely comparable events are described in the legends and heroic sagas of Norway, Denmark, Sweden, the Faeroe Islands, Iceland, and England. The Anglo-Saxon ballad, "The History of William Cloudesly," is one of the Robin Hood type and first appeared in 1536.

There is also some doubt whether men named Gessler and von Landenberg ever served as *Vögte* (governors), and the existence of a man named Tell, Tall, or Thall at the time and place of the "apple shoot" is also in question. A number of the sagas and legends that lend color to any history of early Switzerland are related (in English) in the *Swiss American Review*, 25 July 1979 (Swiss Publishing Co., 608 Fifth Avenue, New York, N.Y. 10020).

9. I am indebted to Professor Herbert Lüthy of the University of Basel and Dr. W. Treichler of the *Landesbibliothek* in Bern for information on the alleged Swedish origins of the people of Schwyz and Oberhasli. The following is largely a summary of their memoranda.

That Schwyz was originally settled by emigrés from Sweden and East Fresia is somewhat of a legendary tale which was current in the fifteenth century. The canon of Upsala, Ericus Olai, who was present at the great Concilium of Basel (1431–48) recorded the alleged migration in his *Chronica Regnis Gothorum*. In rather broad terms, Switzerland and Austria were treated as Swedish or Gothic foundations. Indeed the great church councils of Constance and Basel may have played a role in the exchange of the old Norse and Swiss migration sagas. The first written evidence of this legend can be traced to the fierce polemics which raged between Zurich and the forest cantons during the war of 1436–50. The Zurich canon, Felix Hemmerlin, reviled the people of Schwyz as rustics of the lowest possible sort, descended from rebellious heathen Saxons who had been banished by Charlemagne into the desolate valleys of the voralpine regions around the southern part of the Vierwaldstättersee (Lake Lucerne). The *Landschreiber* (cantonal secretary) of Schwyz, Hans Fründ, rose to the defense of his people by claiming that they were noble descendants of Swedish and Fresian forbears who emigrated at a time of famine in their homeland when no less than ten percent of the population migrated. Six thousand Swedes and 1200 Fresians were said to have ascended the Rhine and, having fought the Franks, were permitted by the Alemannians to settle around Mt. Pilatus, in Schwyz, and in the upper Aare Valley, which they named Hasli. They helped the pope, the kaiser, and the king of the West Goths storm Rome about 400 A.D. As the legend continues we are told they were richly rewarded and both the Schwyzers and the people of Hasli received the freedom of the *Reich*. Their heroic deeds, as described by Fründ, appear to have been copied from legends localized in the ancient "free valley" of Oberhasli.

The literary evidence may rest simply on a typical humanist's pun with a play on the homonymy of "Swycia" and "Swecia." The White Book of Sarnen gave credence to the legend and gave to it a halo of authenticity. The story was common to Swiss and Swedish historiography and constituted a part of the rhetoric and diplomacy of Swedish-Swiss relations in the Thirty Years' War. The government of Schwyz in 1531 decreed that all of its inhabitants should remember in prayer the great food shortage and the resulting migration from Sweden. The whole story was upheld by the Swedish historian Erik Gustaf Geijer in his great history of the Swedish people, "De Colonia Suecorum in Helvetiam deducta" (dated 1828). If one attempts to weigh the "evidence," the theory of the Swedish origin of the people of Schwyz and Overhasli must be regarded as nothing more than one of the many sagas that enriched the literature of the Middle Ages. Tschudi disposed of it as a mere fable. See also "*Herkommen der Schwyzger und Oberhasler.*" The original (ca. 1460) is lost, but anonymous copies prepared in the fifteenth and sixteenth centuries remain.

10. *Twingherrenstreit*, (or Zwingherrenstreit) may be translated as "struggle against the despots."

11. Adrian von Bubenberg (1431?–1479). von Bubenberg was probably born in the castle at Spiez (the entire city and its surroundings were purchased in 1338 from King Heinrich III by Johannes von Bubenberg, Schultheiss (Mayor) of Bern.

For many years, the Bubenbergs and the House of Burgundy had been friends. A Burgundian pension to the Bubenbergs was inherited by Adrian who, allegedly, went to Philip the Good or Charles the Bold as a Bernese envoy to collect the proceeds. From 1453 to 1458 he served as the *Landvogt* of Lenzburg. This was followed by eight years of foreign service as a commander of Swiss mercenaries in Germany. In 1464, on the death of his father, Adrian inherited the family properties and became a member, virtually by inheritance, of the *Kleinrat* (small or executive council) in Bern. In 1467 he was sent by Bern as an envoy to renew the alliance with the Duke of Savoy. In 1468, he became *Schultheiss* of Bern, almost as an inherited right. He was then in command of a Bernese army of 7,000 men engaged in the defense of Mülhausen and Schaffhausen against the Austrians.

The Waldshuter Peace of 1468 was disadvantageous to Duke Sigismund of Austria. In 1467, Charles of Burgundy had concluded a neutrality pact with Bern, Freiburg, Solothurn and Zurich (*Abschiede* II, *Beilage* 42). Despite this, and at the request of Sigismund, Charles took the Austrian duke under his protection and warned the Swiss to undertake no hostilities against Sigismund. Succeeding events, leading finally to the war with Burgundy and Bubenberg's stubborn defense of Murten, are described in three of the sections in this chapter.

12. In between sessions of the Diet, one of the *Orte*, chosen in accordance with a predetermined system of rotation, served as the executive agent of the Confederation and was known as the *Vorort*.

13. See J. Dierauer, (**103**, II, pp. 210–217).

14. Literally, "permanent direction or course"; in the present context it means "permanent peace."

15. This was probably the first Franco-Swiss treaty for the supply of Swiss mercenaries to France. The treaty was renewed a number of times in the following three centuries with only minor variations. The principal provisions were the granting of recruiting facilities in Switzerland to the French; the promise of French help to Switzerland in case of need; and substantial annual payments by France to each of the cantons. The Swiss did not use their widely recognized military prowess for their own aggrandizement but "preferred to squander it in military service for the advantage of others" (**274**, p. 5).

16. Bubenberg, in one of the most remarkable decisions in military history, ordered that the gates of Murten be left open day and night (Diebold Schilling (**321**, II, p. 35); Ziegler (**405**, p. 61). By this device the defenders were kept constantly on the alert against any attempt by the Burgundians to break into the city, and Charles the Bold, already quite nervous, became even more jittery in trying to determine the meaning of such tactics. Gingins La Sarra (**151**), however, referring to a dispatch of 13 June 1476, quotes the envoyé of Milan "C'est pour laisser les communications libres d'un ouvrage à l'autre, dans l'intérieur de la ville, et non par bravade que les portes de Morat restèrent ouvertes."

It was not until Murten was almost lost that the combined Swiss army of 24,000 men from other cantons arrived on the scene. Despite fatigue and pouring rain they attacked the enemy at once. It was a great victory for the Swiss. Bubenberg was honored in several ways. He was restored to the *Kleinrat* and, in 1478–79, was confirmed for the fifth time as *Schultheiss* of Bern. He died early in 1479. His burial place is unknown. Bern, belatedly (in 1897), erected a monument in his honor.

17. In 1825, Lake Murten, the first of the Swiss lakes to become seriously polluted, was invaded by a red alga, *Oscillatoria rubescens* de Candolle. When the algae became conspicuously visible to the people of the region, the word soon spread that this was the blood of the Burgundians, at last coming to the surface after the slaughter of 1476.

18. Released the same year by her brother the King of France.

19. Niklaus von Flüe (1417–87), also known as Brother Klaus, was born in Sachseln, Obwalden. When 14 years old and entitled to vote, he attended his first *Landsgemeinde*. From 1443 to 1460 he appears to have participated in the Old Zurich War, probably in a non-military capacity as an administrator. In 1467 he left his large family and, becoming a hermit, lived an ascetic life in a "cell" in the Ranft not far from Sachseln. A small chapel, the Marienkapelle, was erected adjacent to his cell in 1468. He was visited by many important people of his time—political leaders, princes, and ecclesiastical lords—and numerous gifts, including donations from the kaiser, came to support and adorn the chapel. Several of his visitors who later gained acceptance as writers of chronicles were Heinrich von Gundelfingen (ca. 1445–1490), Hans von Waldheim (ca. 1422–79), Johannes Trithemius (1460–1516), and the humanist Albrecht von Bonstetten (1441/45–1503/05). They perpetuated the legend, which had

been widely circulated, that Brother Klaus neither ate nor drank during the 19 or 20 years of his life as a hermit (cf. Welti, **385**).

He became deeply interested in matters of political concern. His program for Switzerland was "Peace and Neutrality." He spoke out against foreign influence, Swiss involvement in the affairs of foreign countries, the pension system, mercenary service in the aid of foreign princes, and the "blood money" which was derived. The indomitable spirit of Unterwalden, long committed to freedom and to the political and economic independence of the valley people, accounts for his worldly political interests.

A document of 1474 says that Brother Klaus, when questioned on the subject, earnestly spoke and urged that the *Eidgenossen* (Swiss) remove themselves from foreign lords and their money. They should remain on their lands and continue in freedom, unity, justice, and friendship.

The influence of Brother Klaus was so great that Obwalden, for many years, maintained a strong position against pensions and gifts from the House of Habsburg-Austria in return for providing military assistance through mercenary service. The policy of the Confederation in these matters was debated at every session of the Diet for many years in an effort to gain a consensus. Much of the opposition came from Schwyz which was very dependent upon the income from pensions and capitulation agreements for foreign military service. Robert Durrer (**109**) writes that Brother Klaus appeared in person before the Diet at Stans in 1481 to urge acceptance of his program. He was so convincing that all eight *Orte* accepted his advice and Freiburg and Solothurn adhered to the agreement and became members of the Confederation. Solothurn even sent its official thanks, accompanied by 20 gulden for a permanent Mass. Others report that only a message from Brother Klaus, delivered by the priest of Stans, was presented (see e.g. **120**). Diebold Schilling (1460–1515), the famous Lucerne chronicler, though he and his father witnessed the proceedings at Stans which is described in his Chronicle, makes no mention of Brother Klaus.

Though Brother Klaus had sought retirement from the world (or his large family) and could neither read nor write (**109**), he had a sustained interest in worldly questions. Politics and mysticism together flowed through his veins. The house in which he was born and lived for some years still stands and is visited by thousands of people every year.

20. *Abschiede* III. 1, 109–10, 22 December 1481; *Beilage* 12, 696–98.

21. Hans Waldmann (1435?–1489). The date of Waldmann's birth is uncertain. The *Biographie Universelle* gives 1426 while the *Historisch-biographisches Lexikon der Schweiz* records the date as "*spätestens* 1435" (not later than 1435). This is also accepted by Walter Schaufelberger (**317**, p. 331). Waldmann, a tailor in Zurich, later a tanner, and then an iron merchant, achieved success in military affairs (at Murten in 1476 and Nancy in 1477) and in diplomacy. He was honored by election to the highest office in the guilds of Zurich in 1480 and as *Bürgermeister* in 1483. His greatest diplomatic success was in concluding the treaty of 1487 with Austria—in effect a renewal of the Austrian-Swiss treaty of 1477. But he also authored the hated clothing mandate and a second order that required the killing of the large dogs owned by farmers (the dogs damaged the sport of hunting). Finally, he endeavoured to centralize authority in his own person. His avowed purpose was to restore the balance of power in western Europe, dominated for centuries by the Princes and heads of the Holy Roman Empire.

22. The Ottoman Empire under Suleiman I (1520–66) approached the zenith of its power. It extended almost from the German frontier to Persia. The Black Sea was practically a Turkish lake. The whole of the Euphrates valley, including Bagdad, was conquered. Almost the whole of the Balkan peninsula except Montenegro (Albania) and a part of the Dalmatian coast, had fallen to the Turks. The north coast of Africa from Egypt to Morocco came under Turkish rule. Suleiman's war on Hungary which continued fitfully from 1521 to 1562 was a disaster to Ferdinand I (brother of the Emperor Charles V). The Treaty of Prague in 1562 stripped the House of Habsburg of Transylvania, almost all of Hungary, and required the payment of heavy indemnities to the Turks. By 1683, the Ottoman Empire included almost all of Hungary, Moldavia, Bessarabia, and much of the north shore of the Black Sea from Odessa eastwards through the Crimea. An attempt by Suleiman II to conquer Vienna failed. In the light of later concerted efforts by the heads of state to maintain a balance of power in Europe it is of interest that Francis I, King of France (1515–47), alarmed by the vastness of the empire over which Charles V was the sovereign authority, encouraged Suleiman in his wars against the Habsburgs.

23. The denial can be only partly attributed to the anger aroused among the Swiss by Maximilian's Common Penny Tax and his Imperial Chamber of Justice. The Swiss could not afford to tolerate the use of their people in the military service of both belligerents (Charles VIII had already contracted for his supply). The obligations of a neutral Power in times of war require that any favors or services extended to one belligerent be made equally available to the other. But in 1500 the concept and practice of neutrality as something that went beyond mere abstention from war was only beginning to be accepted as a basic element in the foreign policy of any State, and the Swiss were not yet ready to question seriously the morality and decency of selling their people to foreign Powers. However, the presence of Swiss soldiers in opposing armies, of Swiss fighting Swiss, was frowned upon. The practice was in popular disfavour—a factor which would also lead to a denial of the emperor's request. Impartiality in the policies of a neutral State toward neighbouring belligerents was almost unheard of.

24. This was not a violation of the Permanent Peace of 1474 between the Swiss Confederation and Austria, for Austria's invasion of the Münstertal and her military campaign generally were directed against the *Graubund* and the *Gotteshausbund* which were not then members of the Confederation.

25. Strictly speaking, the treaties of 1497 and 1498 were between the seven easterly cantons and two of the three leagues in the Graubünden. The third component of the *Graubünden*, the League of Ten Jurisdictions, was nonetheless associated with the other two and it came to be entitled to the same rights and responsibilities as the two signatory leagues.

26. A second battle at Novara, in which the Swiss in the service of Maximilian Sforza defeated the French, took place on 6 June 1513.

27. *Abschiede* I, 121, 2 September 1407.

28. *Abschiede* I, 164, 9 September 1416.

29. *Abschiede* I, 169, 24 January 1417.

30. "Der Appenzellerbund," *Abschiede* III. 2, 1361–64, 17 December 1513.

31. "Der Baserlerbund," *Abschiede* III. 2, 1291–97, 9 June 1501; "Der Schaffhauserbund," *Abschiede* III. 2, 1297–1300, 10 August 1501.

32. *Abschiede* II, 175 f, 22 March 1444.

33. Schweizer, P. (**328**, p. 141).

34. Schweizer, P. (**328**, pp. 142, 143); Tschudi (**370**, II, p. 69).

35. *Abschiede* II, 869–70, 8 November 1452.

36. *Abschiede* III. 1, 726–29, 14 September 1487.

37. Ref. **266**, 12 February 1979.

5. THE SIXTEENTH CENTURY

After the fall of Novara, the Duchy of Milan came under the sovereignty of France. Territorial gains were made by the Swiss: the Bleniotal, Bellinzona and several other towns were ceded to them by Louis XII under the terms of the Treaty of Arona. But the betrayal at Novara in April 1500 disgusted many and, indeed, Turmann was tried and hanged as a traitor.

Foreign Pensions and Mercenary Service

The sale of mercenary service, now in disfavor, received a measure of control through new restrictions on recruiting. At Baden on 20 July 1503, the Diet agreed on several controls of the pension system including a denial to the subjects of all the *Orte* of the right to accept foreign pensions. It also provided for punishment of Swiss mercenaries. Zug would not agree to the proposed punishment and Solothurn then withdrew its adherence to the ordinance because of lack of unanimity (*Abschiede* III. 2, pp. 234, 235h). The agreement, expanded, appears also as a supplement (*Beilage* 10). It includes the punishment approved for violators: a fine of five guilders; if the guilty one has no money, five weeks in prison on bread and water only; if he refuses to return to his homeplace or to "Switzerland", and if others help him remain away, those involved will not be allowed to return to "Switzerland" (*Abschiede* III. 2, *Beilage* 10, pp. 1314–16). To this there is a long addendum (pp. 1316–17) by the three leagues in the Graubünden pertaining to an earlier pension agreement of 25 February 1500.

On August 30 in Lucerne, the Diet, with all the *Orte* represented, entered into another agreement concerning pensions, punishment of mercenaries, and foreign service:

> We the above-mentioned *Eidgenossen* ... from this day forward with no princes or lords, as have the name ... alliances, unions, agreements, or other obligations, as might be

proposed, make, take, conclude, . . . without our above-named *Eidgenossen* in common or the majority of us favor, know and want . . . (*Abschiede* III. 2, pp. 240–42).

As an example of the difficulties encountered in giving any force to the pious resolutions of the Diet we note that at another session in Zurich on 9 September 1505, the delegates from Lucerne complained that Zurich and Solothurn would neither seal nor swear to the agreement of Baden concerning pensions and mercenaries. Because Lucerne only sealed and swore to the Baden agreement on condition that all of the *Orte* accepted it, she therefore requested that all seal and swear or she, for her part, would not be bound by the same . . . (*Abschiede* III. 2, pp. 319, 320 (f)).

Hence, it is not surprising that the basic agreement of 20 July 1503 was not faithfully observed; the lucrative system of pensions from foreign princes had enriched many who received from their cantonal government the contracts to raise and command the contingents of Swiss mercenaries. The system had lasted for years and it brought a rich flow of money into the country. The restrictions imposed by the Diet were acceptable to few of the cantons. One after another freed themselves of the limitations in the *Pensionenbrief*. Indeed, it was not until the nineteenth century that mercenary service came to an end. In the eighteenth century Swiss troops served with the French, the kaiser, Naples, Austria, Piedmont (including Sardinia and Savoy), Prussia, Spain and Venice.

France, now in possession of the Duchy of Milan, sought an understanding with Kaiser Maximilian. Together with Spain, the two entered into a military alliance through the League of Cambrai (1508). They had a common enemy in the Republic of Venice which had to determine whether the Triple Alliance was a threat to the support enjoyed by Venice from the supreme head of Christendom, the exceptionally warlike statesman and general, Pope Julius II. The friendship of the Swiss was sought, Franco-Swiss relationships having cooled somewhat. Louis XII, all too confident that the greed of the Swiss would make them submissive to his seductive proposals, had tried to renew the old mercenary treaties but was unsuccessful.

Renewed Warfare in Upper Italy

In Switzerland, Mattäus Schiner, Bishop of Sitten (cardinal after 1511), was then the competent and politically astute representative of the pope. He was not only the spiritual head but, very effectively, the worldly lord of Wallis (Valais). He was strongly anti-French and he regarded with grave concern the expansionist policies of the French king. He had interceded in favor of Milan and Moro and vigorously supported Julius II, the lord of the Papal State. With equal vigor he energetically opposed the objectives of Spain, Austria, and France as could be easily deduced from the League of Cambrai. On 14 March 1510, Schiner with much energy and tact managed to effect a five-year alliance of the 12 *Orte* and Valais with Julius II. The Swiss promised to protect the Church and the Holy Sea, to make 6000 troops available to the pope, and to withhold any such military support from other Powers. Julius II, in turn, agreed to make annual payments of money to each of the *Orte*. The agreement was a notable event in Swiss-Papal relations, recognized by the papal gift of a silken banner to each of the *Orte*.[1]

In 1511 Schiner succeeded in drawing Emperor Maximilian into an alliance with the Confederation. In the so-called *Erbvereinigung* with the Swiss, each of the parties agreed to remain neutral in any war in which the other might be engaged. There was little if anything in this alliance which provided for military support by one if the other were attacked from without. The kaiser also promised to each of the *Orte* and their associated states (*Zugewandte*) an annual payment.

This master-stroke by Schiner was hardly finished before the Swiss seized upon an opportunity to attack the French in Lombardy. A rather trivial incident involving two Swiss representatives in Lugano gave an excuse for a wild punitive expedition into the Italian plains. The Swiss army reached the gates of Milan. In proper perspective the incident was little better than an atrocious act of brigandage. It is alleged that the behavior of the Swiss was so disgraceful an Upper Italian mother had only to say to her naughty child, "If you do not behave the Swiss will get you."

Maximilian, the Swiss Confederation, the Papal State and Venice were now allied in a common cause. Opportunely, the King of England declared war on France. The Swiss were destined to play a central role but after a few years of fame and glory suffered a humiliating descent from their venture into "Great Power" politics.

In the spring of 1512, the Swiss marched against Pavia. At the end of April the Diet met in Zurich and proclaimed throughout the Confederation a general call to arms. At the end of May a well-equipped army of 18,000 assembled at Chur and marched through the Münstertal to Verona. Here they were greeted by Cardinal Schiner in the name of the pope, and joined by their Venetian allies. The army attacked Pavia, took the city by storm and moved on to Milan which was soon captured. By a stroke of the hand, the whole of Lombardy was almost freed of the French. The Swiss were not to be deprived of the fruits of victory; *Innerschweiz* took possession of the lower Ticino and the Eschental as far as Domodossola while the allied *Orte* seized the Valtellina, Bormio and Chiavenna. With the French now in full retreat, the victorious allies restored Maximilian Sforza, son of Moro, as Duke of Milan.

Seizure of Neuchâtel

In 1512, Bern seized the Principality of Neuchâtel which had been held since 1504 by the Count of Orleans-Longueville (a bastard line of the French monarchs of the House of Orleans) and declared it to be subject to the rule of Bern. The seizure was justified by Bern on the grounds that the Count was then fighting for France and was therefore an enemy of the Confederation.[2]

War with France Continues

Swiss rejoicing over the victories at Pavia and Milan was tempered by the news that Louis XII in 1512–13 had placed a new and well-equipped army in the field supported by a hard core of German mercenaries. In 1513 the French entered Lombardy and again seized Milan. In the meantime, Julius II died and the

Venetians switched sides and allied themselves with the French. Swiss reinforcements numbering some 8000 men joined in the defense of Novara which was under siege by the French. The French withdrew to a fortified position and, immediately attacked by the Swiss, were put to flight. The victory on 6 June 1513 was complete (**65**); again the French departed from Lombardy. But French emissaries in Switzerland endeavoured through bribes to foment unrest and to establish a strong pro-French party.

The Diet responded by raising an army of 15,000 men to carry the war to France itself. In 1513 the Swiss forces entered Burgundy and took up positions before Dijon and Besançon. They were reinforced by imperial troops under the Duke of Württemberg. In September the French negotiated a Swiss withdrawal by promising in the name of the king a payment of 400,000 gulden, a renunciation of the French claims to Lombardy, and a cessation of recruiting on Swiss soil without the express permission of a majority of the Diet. The Swiss had hardly withdrawn before Louis XII, a few months before his death, declared the agreement to be null and void.

Early in 1515 his successor, Francis I (1515–47), decided upon a new campaign against Milan, despite the opposition of a new army of 18,000 men which the Swiss sent into Lombardy. Eager to avoid another costly and possibly humiliating war, the French king made to the Swiss a substantial offer of money to permit his peaceful acquisition of Milan. The Diet responded by sending another contingent of 7000 men into Lombardy. On crossing the Alps, the Swiss reinforcements met many of their countrymen who were on their way home, disappointed by long waiting and bored by inaction.

Although Francis I had in the field an army of 55,000, he was not eager to engage the Swiss in battle. In September 1515 he was successful at Gallarate in persuading the Swiss to accept a negotiated settlement. France would pay damages to Sforza, and Switzerland would receive one million crowns, including the 400,000 gulden promised at Dijon. In return, the Swiss would abandon their claim to all territory south of Bellinzona. The Swiss from the westerly *Orte* and Valais accepted the offer but Zurich and *Innerschweiz* refused to do so. The former returned to their homes, the latter moved on to Milan. The French advanced from Marignano and suffered a slight setback when one of their patrol forces was driven back by the Swiss. Although it was late in the day and their leaders advised caution, the Swiss stormed the main French position in the face of heavy artillery fire. By nightfall the outcome was still in the balance. Friend and foe were forced to lie down on the battlefield and wait for daybreak. Early in the morning the Venetians arrived to aid the French. When the tide seemed to turn in favor of the Swiss, their leader ordered a retreat to Milan. This was done in good order but by the time they reached Milan half of their troops lay dead or dying on the battlefield. On the fifteenth day they retreated northwards to the Alpine passes, leaving a small rearguard to hold the castle in Milan. Courageous as they were, the Swiss could not stand up against the newer artillery and technical equipment with which the French were supplied. Through the House of Savoy as mediator, conversations were held to terminate the war, and in

November 1516 in Geneva a perpetual peace, an *Ewige Friede*,[3] with France was negotiated and peaceful relations were resumed. Despite the many Swiss declarations in the preceding two decades against mercenary service and the pension system, 12 of the 13 *Orte* (but not Zurich) formally agreed on 5 May 1521 to provide King Francis with many mercenaries and military equipment (*Abschiede* IV. 1a. *Beilage* 1, pp. 1491–1500). This treaty of "peace and friendship" was to continue in effect until the death of Francis and three years more. The king, for use in France, Milan, Genoa or elsewhere, was permitted to contract for not less than 6000 of more than 16,000 armed Swiss footsoldiers. All of the recruits were required to remain in the service of France as long as she shall be at war, unless troubles in Switzerland required their return for defense of the homeland. The Swiss and any recruited from the associated places (*Zugewandte*) were not to be distributed among a number of army units but were to be kept together as a unit. As long as France was at war, the two parties agreed that neither would enter into a separate peace with an enemy of the other.

In addition to the substantial payments that were promised, the Swiss were permitted to buy salt from France at a very favorable price—an important fringe benefit.

Neutrality was emerging as a Swiss policy and distinctions were drawn between wars of defense, which clearly were permissible to a neutral, and offensive combat, which was certainly not consonant with neutrality. There was nothing in the treaty with France that limited the use of Swiss troops to defensive operations only. Many instances of the use of Swiss mercenaries in offence by the French and others caused frequent complaints by the Swiss authorities and were a continuing concern as long as mercenaries were provided to other Powers.

In 1549, an alliance or treaty was concluded between Henri II of France and eleven of the cantons (not Bern and Zurich). In all essential respects it was merely a renewal of the treaty of 1521 with Francis I to provide Swiss mercenaries for French service (*Abschiede* IV. 1.e 1385–90).

The treaty of peace was unexpectedly favorable to the Swiss. They received from France economic concessions for trade with Milan and Lyon, and France paid the 400,000 crowns promised by Louis XII to cover Swiss expenses and losses in the siege of Dijon, and for Swiss renunciation of all claims on the Duchy of Milan. Bellinzona, Locarno, Lugano, and the Leventine remained with the Swiss, who surrendered possession of the Eschental. France also settled with all the cantons the problem of pension payments.

Thus the efforts of the Swiss to retain Milan came to an end, and the inner unrest, dissension and violence which had been breaking out within Switzerland with terrible elementary force did not terminate. The fifty-year interval between the beginning of the Burgundian war, the end of the war over Milan and the utter defeat of the Swiss at Marignano led into a period of great change, with social and religious transformations that upset and rent the country with rudimentary and passionate outbreaks of violence.

The Swiss as Soldiers

More than a word should be added about the Swiss as soldiers, and the opinions current in the sixteenth century about the Swiss generally. Their courage in battle was recognized throughout Europe. "There is no one quality so universally allowed to the *Switzers*, as that of valour" (**339**, p. 128). Indeed in every engagement from Morgarten (November 1315) onwards, the Swiss displayed a tactical skill and a primitive disdain of death in combat that knew no equal in the warfare of the Middle Ages.[4] Huldrych Zwingli,[13] a military chaplain from Glarus during the Italian war, wrote a colorful description of the course of the war to his friend Vadian in St. Gallen. He described the exploits of a small band of young men from the Swiss vanguard who swam across the Po and, against the opposition of 800 of the enemy, managed to establish a bridgehead. They were followed by the entire youth of the army who swam the river, halberds in hand. This was a tribute, according to Zwingli, to the studied training of the Swiss youth in swimming, running, and jumping, etc. Although verging on the overcolorful, Zwingli's account of the elementary valor and fighting spirit of the Swiss is essentially confirmed by Correro, an ambassador of Venice to the French court. He describes an incident in which a Swiss regiment under Colonel Pfyffer brought the French king and his retinue safely back from Meaux to Paris. This was in 1567 during the religious war in France and the battles with the Huguenots. Correro's wonderment over the fighting ability of the Swiss was qualified by his unsavory observation that the Swiss soldiers were most offensive, unpleasant, and personally disgusting. They turned on an enemy, so we are told, like a pack of mad dogs.

In the travel reports which began to appear in the sixteenth century, the Swiss as a whole were rarely described in flattering terms.[5] The German humanist, Trithemius,[6] reflecting on the Swabian war, wrote that the Swiss were by nature over-presumptuous, rebellious, and enemies of the princes. They were described as arrogant and as people who found delight in deceit and trickery. His colleague, Wimpheling[7] from Schlettstadt, composed a long prayer for the "God-forgotten Swiss" who had hearts of stone, no humanity, and were worse than the Turks. Other observers wrote about their love of war and their primitive violent tendencies—a sort of explosiveness into rage on little provocation. Oechsli reminds us that "the Swiss were regarded as 'lordless peasants' and as 'rude cow-milkers' but the whole of Europe feared their pikes and halberds. 'They want to become Swiss' was the proverbial expression in Germany about all those who sought independence from their lawful lords" (**274**, p. 7).

Background of Religious Dissension

Marignano was hardly over before these "undisciplined" people and their governments were swept up in the tremendous upheaval of the confessional war. Although it started in Germany and Italy, the conflict spread over the whole of Europe. The causes of dissension between the Church and its people were to be found throughout the land. Some of the causes originated in the distant past.

Changes, deeply rooted in thought, in social customs and in the inner feelings of the people had been in progress from the beginnings of the Confederation. The association of the forest people into a defensive alliance, the expansion of the Confederation to include such city cantons as Bern, Lucerne and Zurich, and the development of trade and commerce with other States carried with it the seeds of far-reaching change. From about 1500 on, the pace was accelerated, largely because of Zwingli. The religious schism that punctuated the Reformation with violence and hate was an unfortunate accompaniment.

The Reformation, even the violent resistance to reform, was inevitable. Quite apart from the dramatic effect of Zwingli's preaching it was a predictable product of improved and greatly expanded communication which facilitated the exchange of ideas, of improvements in printing, the production of books and the initiation of schooling. Knowledge of reading and writing reached farther out among the people and an exchange of experiences, of knowledge, and of opinion were broadening developments that penetrated all social layers.

Demographic Aspects

Socio-economic and demographic changes were not without their effects. Complete census counts were not made by the cantons before 1600. But from church records and various assumptions the population of the area embraced by present-day Switzerland has been reported to be about 600,000 people in 1300 (Bickel, **40**). Because of the great plague of 1348–49 (known in Northern Europe as the Black Death) which decimated almost the whole of Europe,[8] it is most improbable that the population of Switzerland increased during the fourteenth century. From the 1400 base of 600,000 (assumed), the population is believed to have increased to about 850,000 by 1500, despite a return of the pestilence in 1438–39 when again, people fell "like leaves in the forest after the first frosts of autumn" (*Wie beim ersten Herbstfrost in den Wälden die Blätter fallen*). By 1600 the population of the area embraced by present-day Switzerland appears to have increased to about one million.

The life expectancy of males at birth has been reported (**40**) as 21.2 years in 1600. Half of the newborn were dead before attaining the age of eight. Almost inevitably, the responsibilities of an adult had to be assumed by the very young. The events of a lifetime were packed into a few years. In 1500 marriage of women at the age of 12 or 13 was common. At the age of 14, in Basel, men were subject to military duty, liable to payment of taxes and active politically. In 1514, the age at which these duties were assumed was raised to 16, as in most of the other cantons. Boys of 10 to 15 carried weapons.

Zwingli entered the University of Vienna at the age of 14. The "youthfulness of adults" continued through the seventeenth and into the eighteenth centuries. Albrecht von Haller entered the University of Tubingen as a medical student at the age of 15. His friend, Johannes Gessner, was equally young when he began his academic life. Leonhard Euler, already Professor of Physics in Basel, was 20 when called to the Petersburg Academy of Science by Catherine I, widow of Peter the Great. Daniel Bernoulli was invited to membership in the Academy at 25. Johann Bernoulli III became Astronomer Royal in Berlin at the age of 19. At the age of 13 he had already become a Doctor of Philosophy. H. B. de Saussure was only 22 when elected to a chair at Geneva. Charles Bonnet was only 16 when he made his famous study of caterpillars, and 20 when he discovered the phenomenon of parthenogenesis.

Although life expectancies at birth were low (32 to 34 in the eighteenth century) it is apparent that if one managed to survive beyond the age of 20 his chances of survival to the Biblical "three score years and ten" were good. The average age at death of the best-known 35 Swiss scientists and technologists of the eighteenth century was 70 (**221**). The average age at death of the 20-year survivors was probably lower in the sixteenth and seventeenth centuries when wars and pestilence took a heavy toll of the adult male population.

Man still lived by the fruits of agriculture, even in the cities. The estates of the rich were very large. The holdings of the peasants and the small farmers were too restricted in size and quality. In the mountain meadows and valleys the yield of the soil was inadequate and food had to be imported. Despite the relatively small number of people, population pressures were serious and Bern tried to alleviate the plight of her people by expanding westward. In the early 1430s inflation also added to the troubles of the poor: food prices rose rapidly and exorbitantly.

Montaigne's Observations on the Public Baths

Public baths continued to have a socializing influence, if one may draw conclusions from the sometimes colorful accounts of travellers. On his celebrated visit to Germany, Switzerland and Italy in 1580–81, Montaigne seized every opportunity to drink the waters at various hot springs and baths. He spent ten days at Plombières in France and five days at Baden in Switzerland. His diary (**250**, pp. 10–15 and 25–28) gives us a detailed description of the hot springs and baths at Plombières and Baden respectively. The physical facilities, the social customs, and regulations governing the conduct of guests are set forth: "Some take their meals in the bath, where they usually have themselves cupped and scarified." Montaigne, at Plombières, customarily drank, about four pints of the hot spring water each morning at seven. "People from the Franche Comté, and many French, have been coming here in crowds. . . . A singular modesty is observed; and yet it is indecent for the men to bathe otherwise than quite naked saving a little pair of drawers, and for the women, saving a shift." Mixed bathing was quite the thing. A joyous spirit pervaded the baths. Some of the guests sang, others played instruments, some ate, others slept, some danced, and the time passed all too quickly. "All prostitutes and immodest girls are forbidden to enter the said baths, or to approach the same within five hundred paces under penalty of being whipped at the four corners of the said baths . . . all persons are forbidden to use towards the ladies . . . and girls . . . any lascivious or immodest language; to touch their persons indecorously. . . ." The Master of Baths at Plombières was required to examine the bodies of all persons to ensure that no one with "various contagions and infections" entered the baths. At Baden, there were two or three uncovered public baths for use by the poor. The many other baths were fully enclosed, covered, and separated like private cells which were rented out with the guest apartments. "The inns are very magnificent . . . where we lodged there have been seen, in one day, three hundred mouths to feed . . . and quite a hundred and seventy beds . . . for the guests who were there." "Anyone escorting ladies who wish to bathe with respect and delicacy, may bring them here, for they are also alone in the bath." "The people of the country use the waters principally for bathing, during which they have themselves so severely cupped and bled that I have sometimes seen the water in the two public baths looking like pure blood."

Class Distinctions

Class distinctions were then far less pronounced, except in the aristocratic cantons, than elsewhere in Europe. In the country towns and the rural cantons the plain people exercised an appreciable influence through the grass-roots democracy of decision-making by the *Landsgemeinden* (annual voting assemblies of the people). Free men from the lower classes could become burghers, in whom government of the cities was vested. They could move, at least by marriage, into the nobility. Social distinctions meant little. After a battle, the gentlemen and nobles were commonly buried with the peasants (*Die Herren sollen bei den Bauern liegen*).

And for some this was even a prosperous time. The cities sought to establish as a political and economic policy for the Confederation the capture of profits. The country folk turned to mercenary service. It satisfied the restlessness of the young and their spirit of adventure. Money and booty were its rewards. The cantons profited from the pensions of foreign States which contracted for the services of Swiss soldiers. The money derived from these sources covered most of the expenses of the cantons. France absorbed yearly some thousands of Swiss mercenaries. Although the returning veterans frequently came back to their homeland crippled or sick and incapable of any heavy work, the peasants and servant class were unwilling to accept a termination of the system. Town and country were divided on the issue, at first because the cities wanted to regulate and control by improved administrative procedures the organization of mercenary service. Later, the cities became opposed on ideological grounds. It should be pointed out that the mercenaries were sometimes quite young and unaccustomed to well-disciplined behaviour. A man voted and carried weapons at the age of 14—a product of the low life expectancy of the times and of the need to accept adult responsibilities at an early age.

In the war against France, agents of Francis I had a black market going in the recruitment of soldiers. It developed into a scandalous affair since the Swiss mercenaries fought for France, yet Swiss army leaders who participated in the recruitment pocketed substiantial payments from France—their enemy. In an aggravation of the scandal, Swiss fought Swiss, a result of the presence of their countrymen in the French service.

Revolt of the Peasants

In 1513 a social crisis came to a head and the peasants revolted. Since the early Middle Ages social and economic crises fell heavily upon the peasants. The money in circulation increased too rapidly and the purchasing value of the currency decreased. Land costs went into an inflationary spiral. Non-replaceable farm hands left the plough for military service at home and in foreign States. Expenses in connection with the Confederation's military campaigns soared. Military duties through levying of troops increased. The peasants, now in revolt, marched on Bern, Solothurn, Lucerne and other cities. They plundered the cloister of St. Urbans. Taking the law into their own hands they punished the *Kronenfresser*, those who accepted the despised pensions. The unrest was finally contained and the local and cantonal governments wisely avoided any attempt to punish their rebellious subjects who had been swept into the revolt.

Various interpretations have been placed upon the peasants' revolts in the sixteenth century. In part they certainly expressed resentment against mercenary service. The young men left the farms for the excitement and rewards of foreign military service. Serious shortages of farm labor resulted, and only those who organized the regiments of mercenaries, and in turn received substantial pensions, benefitted. Others saw in these rebellious movements an expression of political-economic discontent such as one might witness even today, perhaps akin to an uprising of the masses against their alleged oppressors in the privileged classes.

The religious reform movement of Luther and Zwingli unquestionably played an important role. Within the "common people," religious observances and adherence to the teachings of the Church were deeply rooted. The Reformation brought about extraordinarily rapid and fundamental changes in religious beliefs and practices. The social implications led to much disquietude and inner turmoil. The confusion which resulted produced an almost revolutionary climate which was incompatible with the unquestioning acceptance of the conservative and dogmatic teachings of the past.

Agricultural production decreased because of the labor shortages. Prices of necessities purchased in the towns increased greatly. More and more vehemently the farmers demanded an end to all pensions. "Only to fill their moneybags do the masters sell the peasant mercenaries to the meatbank"—a cry which was heard throughout the land (Bonjour, 53). The gulf between city and country, between the towns and their subjects, widened, and verbal abuse heaped upon the farmers aggravated an already serious situation. The city governments imposed upon their country subjects many irritating restraints such as a ban on hunting and fishing, and closing of the forests. Superimposed was a confusing financial burden: tithes, duties, taxes, and interest charges. A certain amount of contributed labor to the community came to be compulsory such as helping with the harvests and aiding in the production of wine and grain for the community—all of this at the expense of the precious time required in food production for their own needs. The peasants' anger against the governments of city and town spread to the churches and the cloisters because of the taxes to which the church was entitled and the demands of the cloisters for more and more serf labour.

The cities were fearful that the deadly virus of revolt in the countryside might spread to the towns and infect the lower classes. Led by Bern, a number of cities in other cantons set aside for the moment the problems of confessional disagreement and united in a common policy designed to suppress domestic revolt. A solidly united *Burgerschaft* was the objective. In time, Bern yielded on many points such as freedom to hunt bears, wolves, foxes, and wild pigs, but the country subjects were still forbidden to cut wood in the forests. Some community services continued to be compulsory such as bridge building, maintenance of the roads, and reforestation.

One of the objectives of the countryside was a return to the good old days when the troublesome and heavy financial burdens of which they complained fell only upon the landowners. In Bern, for example, serfs could not be taxed, which accounts in large measure for the desire of government to abolish serfdom and, thereby, to widen greatly the tax base. Religion, insofar as Christian charity, humanity and justice were concerned, played an insignificant role in these politico-economic issues.

Similar revolts broke out among the peasants of Germany. Violent manifestations of discontent were frequent but were less evident in sixteenth-century Switzerland. In Germany the peasant farmers were still treated as slaves, chained as serfs to the estates of their masters. Rebels in south Germany sought to recruit in Switzerland adherents to their cause. Rumors of early help from the South German Peasants' Confederation reached the Swiss peasantry. In Germany, dissatisfied elements in the cities sympathized with the peasants, while in Switzerland there was a constant fear that city dwellers who possessed no property might at any time join peasants in violent disturbances. In the Münster valley a great crowd of rebels did threaten the cloister but the Bern government intervened in time. It was a different story in the Laufental where the peasants burned the Cloister Kleinlützel.

Peasant refugees from South Germany were received in parts of Switzerland. However, Aargau refused to accept peasant refugees from Alsace and Sundgau. The canton had enough trouble with its own peasantry and based its negative decision on the old adage "One cannot put out a fire with straw."

Government

Attempts were made to improve the relations between government and the governed. At the federal level there was little that could be done. The Diet could legislate reforms, but enforcement was cantonal and was always subject to policy decisions by the individual sovereign States. There was no Federal Constitution, and attempts to bring the cantons more closely together and to legislate for the whole were constantly frustrated by the reluctance of the people to accept a central authority.

The Federation was held together by an interlocking network of alliances and various *Briefe* (charters of accords)—notably the *Pfaffenbrief*, the *Sempacher Brief*, and the *Stanser Verkommnis*. True, the Diet was the uppermost legislative authority, constituted of representatives from each of the cantons (who were required to vote in accordance with instructions from their cantonal government), the associate members (*Zugewandte*), and subject territories.[9] Decisions had to be unanimous. Even when an agreement was reached, implementation did not necessarily follow because of cantonal sovereignty.

The executive authority (*Vorort*) alternated between Bern, Lucerne and Zurich. The Diet itself met usually in Baden.

Playing a less obvious role in the maintenance of a federal unity, however tenuous such bonds might be, was the army. This was not a truly federal organization but an interesting mixture of more or less independent contingents from the various cantons drawn together for a specific war. But inherent in its structure and its purpose was something that strongly contributed toward federal cohesion. The close association in battle of men from different parts or the Confederation who fought, suffered, and even died together fostered a strong spirit of brotherhood and oneness. Even the returning mercenaries who shared the experiences of life abroad in the service of foreign princes contributed toward a federal unity. Oddly enough the Ambassador of France, the only foreign Power at the time with diplomatic representation, had a unifying influence. By various means, but most successfully with French gold, he managed to dampen the disruptive effects of the threats, quarrels, and dissension that frequently arose between some of the *Orte*. He had no special interest in maintaining domestic peace and in fostering Swiss unity. The money that flowed from his coffers was to assure the recruitment and flow of soldiers to France. But the Swiss knew quite well that if their bread was to be buttered they must minimize internal discord and observe respectfully their capitulation contracts with foreign Powers, especially France.

Although the Diet was democratic in spirit and in structure, political, military, and diplomatic decisions—real government authority—had become centered in each of the cantons in a few influential families. At first this social layer was not exclusive. There was room for gifted newcomers, for parvenus like Hans Waldmann in Zurich. They were enabled to hold positions of authority. Only in the seventeenth century did this ruling class become exclusive. In the city cantons the cities owned the governing rights. The individual village and city communities and government entities enjoyed varying degrees of self-government as defined in their charters. And this in turn was a cause of tension between the cities and their subjects. The city authorities tried ceaselessly to unify the legal relationships and to dispense with a great variety of special rights. These efforts constantly aroused resistance since the subject communities would not part with the ancient freedoms and rights conveyed by their old *Freibriefe*.

The forms of government in the different cantons were different. Although properly and meticulously defined in each case, none was democratic, unless it be the ancient forest cantons (the *Waldstätte*). The members of the Great Councils (usually 200 in each canton) frequently served for life. From the Great Council, the governing bodies of a canton were selected. In Basel and Zurich the Great Councils drew most of their members from the handicraft guilds and commercial bodies. In

Bern, Solothurn, and Lucerne the nobles and aristocratic families exercised a determining influence in government. Political activity made heavy demands upon honorary office holders. Local governors and bailiffs enjoyed lucrative positions and were often able to keep such positions within the family, as if by an unstated right of inheritance. Their powers were such that many events within their circles of influence and authority could be turned to their advantage. They prospered.

The Reformation

The Reformation was more than a challenge to the Catholic Church. The religious schism that led to extraordinary changes in the practices of organized religion and in the beliefs of its adherents came about in an environment of intellectual ferment and of constant challenge to dogma. Intellectual life with its deep interest in learning was centered in the cities, especially in Basel. There the Great Council of the Church (1431 to 1448) had been held and a famous University had been founded in 1460. The art of book printing was beginning to flourish.[10] Wood cuts and copper plates of very high quality were to be found, among them the magnificent works of Albrecht Dürer (1471–1528).[11] The famous Dutch humanist Erasmus described in 1516 the intellectual life of Basel in a letter to a friend in Alsace: "a city with a stimulating University in which not one but many scholars are protected by the city walls. All fields of knowledge are represented, and Greek, Latin and even Hebrew are understood by most."

Of the many scholars, artists and humanists in Basel, contemporaries of Erasmus, were the brothers Auerbach, Thomas Platter from Wallis, Paracelsus (Theophrastus Bombast von Hohenheim—the remarkable physician from Schwyz), Jakob Meyer, Hans Holbein the younger, Konrad Witz, Felix Platter (son of Thomas)—one of the most famous physicians in Europe—and Heinrich Loreti (also known as Glareanus).

To understand more fully the days of the Reformation, let us inquire into the lives of Thomas Platter (1499–1582), Glareanus (1488–1563), and Paracelsus (1493–1541).[12] Thomas Platter was born near Visp in 1499. An undersized and slender boy, he was sent at the age of six to live with relatives in Stalden. His father had just died. He worked as a goatherd, several times being trampled down by the goats, his diminutive size offering no protection. His relatives beat him from time to time because the goats got into their fields of grain. His breakfast was usually cheese and rye bread; a rich portion of whey constituted his dinner. In summer he slept in the hay mow and winter in a straw sack. At the age of nine or ten he was given to a woman whose cows he was required to tend. From the village priest he hoped to learn reading and writing, but the priest was impatient with the boy and Platter learned neither. Unexpectedly, a distant relative, Paulus Summermatter, appeared and offered to take the boy on a travel tour of German schools. In his day, Summermatter was regarded as a leading scholar. Filled with great expectations, Platter joined the nine other students in the group. Most of these were called *Bacchanten* while the three remaining, including Platter, were the *Schützen*. They were obliged to serve the *Bacchanten* and to beg for their maintenance. The hoped-for freedom was lacking. Summermatter proved to be a tyrant and thoroughly exploited his young charges. Though Platter learned neither reading nor writing, he saw much of Germany and became acquainted with the heights and depths of life in those days. His thirst for knowledge, thus far frustrated, became greater. Finally, he ran away from Summermatter. In Ulm he was befriended by a butcher girl who had become acquainted with Swiss in the Swabian war. She provided him with food and shelter until he fled from Ulm and went to Münich and then to Constance. His wanderings next took him to Zurich where he was sheltered and helped by the humanist Myconius. He also became acquainted with Zwingli[13] and the beginnings of the Reformation in Switzerland. Allegedly he helped Zwingli in the Baden disputation by bringing him reports from Zurich every other day. He married a penniless orphan, Anna Dietschin, who was a maid in Myconius' household. In his spare time Platter studied Greek and Hebrew, Myconius being his teacher. He learned ropemaking and later, in Basel, was employed as a ropemaker and teacher of Hebrew. He also became acquainted with Erasmus, who offered him financial help which he declined. On return to his hometown of Grächen he opened a rope-making shop and also became schoolmaster in nearby Visp. The Bishop of Sitten (Sion) took a liking to Platter and offered to appoint him as the cantonal school director in Sitten, with a firm salary. The young man declined the offer and, ever-restless, returned to Basel where in 1540 he became director of the cathedral school after an interim period as a student of medicine and a doctor's helper in Pruntrut. He also opened a rope-making business and soon thereafter a printing establishment. He grew in wealth and honor. His wife died in 1572. At the age of 73 Platter again married and fathered six more children before his death nine years later in 1582. All of this describes the life of an unusual person of the sixteenth century whose intellectual life was pursued in parallel with his material concerns.

Unlike Platter, Glareanus (Heinrich Loreti, 1488–1563) came from a family of comfortable means. His father held high office in the government of his town and was determined to provide for his son a good education. As a student in Rottweil, and later in Cologne, he was not subjected to the cruel experiences of the *Schützen* which Platter was forced to endure.

Glareanus finally settled in Basel in 1514, where he taught Latin and Greek, attracted to the city by the fame of Erasmus. Later, during the turmoil of the Reformation, he went with Erasmus to the *Hochschule* (University) in Freiburg/Breisgau as professor of classical literature (1529). There, as in Basel, Glareanus was active among the humanists and enjoyed a wide reputation as a scholar. Kaiser Maximilian I crowned him poet laureate. It is worth noting that Platter, though of humble origins and deprived of the advantages and encouragement that Glareanus enjoyed, succeeded in attaining a comparable high level of regard among the intelligentsia and humanists of the day.

Paracelsus (Theophrastus Bombast von Hohenheim) was born in Einsiedeln in 1493. His father, a doctor, came from Württemberg and himself taught the young man reading, writing, arithmetic, and a foundation in medicine. Like Platter, Glareanus, and others who eagerly sought a good education, Paracelsus travelled widely. He wandered over the length and breadth of Europe and became a virtual encyclopedia of medical knowledge and practice. His travels took him to many European universities and finally to Basel. There he accepted appointment as city physician and, later, as professor of medicine in the university. Among his patients were the printer and humanist, Froben, and the great humanist, Erasmus of Rotterdam. Most of his fellow professors turned against him because of his unorthodox theories (he believed in nature, natural forces, and herbal medicines, and had little patience with book-trained doctors) and, perhaps also, because of envy: he was very popular among the students. His lack of orthodoxy was reflected in his many deep theological and philosophical writings concerning illness of the soul. He also made enemies among the city officials and intrigues against him grew. All of this enmity culminated in dismissal from his positions. In 1528 he left the city in haste and anger. His disappointment was great. He resumed his travels among the European universities and died in Salzburg in 1541.

We should now turn to Bern and Zurich for an added understanding of the environment in which the Reformation made its way in Switzerland. Bern differed much from Basel. It was a city with an aristocratic government, quite unlike Basel and Zurich, and with ambitious policies of territorial expansion. Its population in the fifteenth and sixteenth centuries could not have exceeded 5000, perhaps half that of Basel. It was neither a busy commercial city like Zurich nor as great a center of humanism as Basel, though it was in Bern that one of the early historians of Switzerland, Konrad Justinger, commenced his professional career. An interest in history was characteristic of the Renaissance, and it was Justinger who in 1420 was commissioned to write a history of the city and its relations to the Swiss Confederation (**199**).

Bern was also the home of Niklaus Manuel Deutsch (1486–1530)—poet, diplomat, soldier, and painter. He was of Lombardian origin and was gifted in politics and diplomacy. In the French war against Milan he led a Bernese contingent of mercenaries and later served as a local governor in Erlach. By 1528–29 he had discontinued painting and sketching and had gained recognition as the foremost representative of those arts in Switzerland. In the last two years of his life he devoted himself almost exclusively to politics. In 1528 he was elected to the small council, the uppermost governing body in Bern. He served repeatedly as a Bern delegate to the Diet. Bern also sent him on many diplomatic missions to other important and influential places in Switzerland. His remarkable career ended by his death in 1530 at the early age of 45.

Because of its favorable location in respect of transportation, Zurich acquired importance, quite early, as a trade center. Published population estimates indicate that the cities of Zurich and Bern were approximately equal in size, each numbering about 4500 to 5500 inhabitants during the fifteenth century (**40**). The government and people of Zurich proved to be remarkably receptive to the new ideas of reform that were flowing in from Germany and Italy. Streams of thought and proposals for reform of the church, of religious belief, and of the social order converged on Zurich.

During Reformation times, Switzerland produced an astonishing number of humanists and historians. Germany, very much larger, produced relatively few. Even by 1500 the separation of Switzerland from the *Reich* was beginning to develop. Intellectually, however, the bonds between Germany and Switzerland were closely knit.

Zurich had its own circle of humanists who had formed around the printer Froschauer. Great as their influence in the promotion of reform might have been, there is little doubt that Huldrych Zwingli[13] was the inspired and tireless leader in Zurich, if not throughout the whole of the area embraced by present-day Switzerland.

Huldrych Zwingli and the Reformation

For 40 years, 1378–1417, there were two popes, each in dispute with the other, one in Rome and one in Avignon. Each was busily engaged in fighting, banning and excommunicating the other. This was a sorry sight for the believers, the faithful of the Church. Cruelty, selfishness and worldliness were manifest among the fifteenth-century popes. They had all the human weaknesses and little of the Christ-like qualities of humility, mercy, and kindness. It was against such evils in the Church and its priesthood that Zwingli inveighed. The attitude of the Church, formally, was to label many of the complaints as outright heresy. Its expenses were great because of its lavish displays and costly ceremonial occasions. To cover expenses the Church sold indulgences quite shamelessly. Those who lived out their days in the cloisters were subject to much public rebuke and condemnation. They were accused of immoralities and, with no thought of serving the poor and the oppressed, sought only comfort, security, and escape from the hardships of life in the outside world.

Much of the income from the sale of indulgences went to Rome to support the very expensive political intrigues of the papacy, which involved itself in diplomacy, warfare, and the purchase of support through bribery. According to the amount paid, one could be absolved from different categories of sins. Those who sold the letters of indulgence themselves prospered from this low and shameful trade. It was, in part, against this practice that Martin Luther directed the 95 charges which he nailed to the church door at Wittenberg in October 1517. This brought on the theological strife and, as much as anything else, introduced the Reformation to central Europe. The pope, immersed in his worldly political concerns, at first regarded the movement for reform as a trivial irritation. By the time he recognized that very basic questions were at issue it was too late; the movement, leading to new religious teachings and observances, was now far advanced.

The Reformation was a response to the great need for a religious awakening. Besides a readiness to submit to God's will in daily life arose a hunger for truth. As mentioned earlier, this hunger was an inevitable result of an increase in learning and the diffusion of new and challenging ideas throughout Europe. Searchers after God claimed to have found in the Bible the religious truths they were seeking. The school of humanists in Basel responded to the need with the first critical edition of the New Testament in the vernacular. This, in turn, led to an inquiry into religious observances. Were the lives of the priests in harmony with the spirit of the evangelists and the letters of the Apostles? Questions speedily arose about the biblical justification of monasteries, the position of priests in the community, and the form of the Mass. Soon, the papacy itself was declared to be unbiblical.

The strife of the theologians was at first remote from the causes of the dissension over religious belief. People became interested in the relation between God and man, and between God and the world in which man lived. In the middle was the concept of divine grace and mercy. The old Church held firmly to the belief that the pope was Christ's representative on earth. It was the Church, so the argument went, that administered the infinite treasure of divine grace symbolized by Christ's death on the cross. The Church claimed to be the fully empowered and sole mediator between God and man. But Luther argued from Paul's epistle to the Romans that Christ, as the son of God, was the only intermediary, and renounced the contention of the Church that the priesthood had a special and unique position between God and man. Zwingli meanwhile, with political reform uppermost, used the New Testament in support of an evangelical-moral base for his fight against pensions and mercenary service. He declared this to be the position of Christ.[14]

In the spring of 1522, the printer Froschauer and his friends in Zurich demonstrated against the Church of Rome in a way that was then fairly common, by deliberate violation of the rule of fasting in Lent. Zwingli was among them; they enjoyed a meal of sausage. Zwingli was rebuked by the Bishop of Constance, who instructed the authorities of Zurich to take some decisive action against him. However, the majority of the Great Council (*Grossrat*) defended Zwingli who next called for a public debate between himself and his supporters on the one side and representatives of the Church on the other. The Council approved and in January 1523 the first debate took place. Over 600 people from city and country, from the laity and the priesthood, were present to hear the arguments of Zwingli against those of Johannes Faber, the vicar-general of the Bishop. The religious dispute, now fast spreading in Europe, had become outstanding in importance. After some hours of disputation between Zwingli and Faber, the Council decided to support Zwingli. The Reform Movement then swept the country like an avalanche. In October 1523, a second debate attended by a much larger audience was held. Again Zwingli received the official support of the cantonal government, and the introduction of reforms followed.

In October 1524 the Council prohibited the sale of indulgences and soon thereafter abolished pilgrimages, the confessional, and religious anointings. Finally, icons, images, and religious relics were banned from the cantonal churches. Later, the convents were closed and in 1525 the Masses were replaced with a sacred meal— the celebration of the Last Supper. At the same time the Great Council removed Zurich from the jurisdiction of the Bishop of Constance and severed the relationship with the hierarchy of the Church of Rome.

These radical reforms affected deeply the lives of many whose practices in formal religion had evolved in over 1000 years of Christianity as interpreted and ordered by the papacy. In Zurich the reforms were effected in little more than $2\frac{1}{2}$ years. For the people, the impact on their daily lives and on their submissiveness to the authority of the Church of Rome was upsetting and even frightening. They were now aboard a ship with neither a rudder nor a captain and in the midst of a stormy sea. Much that had been taught as religious truth was now declared to be in error and was replaced by completely new teachings. Even the age and structure of the physical world were in question. Until then the geocentric theory of Ptolemy, based on a flat disc-like earth, had been universally accepted. But the new learning declared the earth to be a sphere which revolves around the sun. Such a teaching conflicted with religious dogma and verged on heresy. To those who cherished orthodoxy such teachings were deeply disturbing, not only to the laity, but to the Church and to established authority generally.

The Reform Movement confused the clergy, released new demands and desires and unleashed the pent-up, widespread forces of social dissatisfaction. One of its immediate results was an opposition movement against Zwingli, initiated by the Anabaptists, who were declared to be fanatics and heretics. The Anabaptists promoted a literal interpretation of the gospel and a total acceptance of the Sermon on the Mount.

All this disturbed the State since much of the teaching was anarchistic: a social order in which the Church would be completely replaced by free Christian communities which would develop unmolested by pressures from the State. In addition to their unorthodox ideas on baptism, the Anabaptists believed in the innate purity and sinlessness of man. From this stemmed the Anabaptist opposition to military service, to the death penalty, and resort to violence; officials of the government should be guided by the Sermon on the Mount. To its teachings, government should literally adhere, and even interest and tithes should be abolished. This revolutionary social-political movement spread quickly from city to country, and made heavy inroads through much of Switzerland. Zwingli perceived the dangers in this radicalism and attempted to restrain the leaders. In a third debate in 1525 he tried to convince the proponents of adult baptism of the error of their beliefs by express biblical proof.

From its birthplace in Germany the reform movement spread to Switzerland and established itself in Zurich. It was not entirely an expression of religious extremism; it originated partly in the heresy movements of the Middle Ages. The general religious upheaval and shattering of faith in the old religious practices breathed a new life into age-old anti-Church forces. Some of these divisive influences had become manifest even in the twelfth century. In western Switzerland they expressed themselves as opposition to the teachings of a Church founded on dogma. The Church itself was not the object of their fight but rather the prevailing concepts of the Church of Rome.

Violence, following upon a general peasant uprising in Germany, broke out in the district of Grüningen where the peasants plundered the convent of Rüti and sought to force their demands upon the authorities. They succeeded in obtaining a prompt abolition of tithes, of serfdom, and of ground rents. Freedom to hunt and fish, as well as the free election of clergy by the communities soon followed. Zwingli's great influence was a powerful factor in persuading local government to accept some of the demands and to promise serious consideration of the others. In the Zurich area the main points of dispute between the peasants and the civil authorities were resolved and the restoration of peace and quiet was festively celebrated. Elsewhere, rather heavy-handed methods were used to suppress the rebels.

Zwingli was finally obliged to leave to the civil authorities the resolution of the troubles with the Anabaptists. His theological arguments were ineffective against the fanaticism of his opponents. Apart from their opposition to baptism, they refused to take the oath, to bear weapons, and to pay taxes. Government responded with severe punishments. Their leaders were drowned in the Zurichsee, hung, or banned from the city. Around Bern the fight against the Anabaptists continued into the seventeenth century as a sad chapter of official cruelty. In the seventeenth and eighteenth centuries they migrated to more hospitable parts of Switzerland such as the Bernese Jura where they were at least tolerated. Anabaptist colonies were also established in the Bishopric of Basel and in Moravia.

Meanwhile the Reformation continued to spread through much of Switzerland. In *Innerschweiz* it encountered mounting resistance on both religious and political grounds. As for the latter, there was no support in the three most ancient cantons for Zwingli's efforts to abolish mercenary service and the pension system. To the Confederation and the individual cantons these were important sources of income. Two subordinate governors in Thurgau became involved in the religious turmoil through defending the "wrong side" in a dispute. They fled to Zurich, were extradited to *Innerschweiz* which they had sharply condemned, and were hung. This created a frightening precedent for the punishment that religious "rebels" could expect in the ancient cantons. And now the inner *Orte* went much further and concluded with Austria an agreement which pledged the united efforts of both parties to protect the old beliefs and practices of the Church of Rome. The treaty was short-lived since the head of the House of Austria, the Emperor Charles V, angered by the presence of Swiss mercenaries in the French service in the Franco-Austrian war in northern Italy, and the return of thousands of them to *Innerschweiz*, terminated the agreement.

The cantons that sought to remain true to the old beliefs did not abandon their determined efforts to resist the religious reforms. They proposed to the Diet that a public debate, broad in its scope, be held in Baden. The debate lasted from 19 May to 8 June 1526 with Dr. Eck, Luther's most vigorous opponent, as the champion of the Catholic cantons. Zwingli refused to participate because it was clear that the debate would not be limited to interpretation of the scriptures, but would reach far into political issues. The debate ended with Eck victorious. From canton to canton positions were taken by government, either to remain with the Church of Rome, to adopt the Reformed religion, or to leave individual towns or districts within a canton free to adopt either position.

In some parts of the country the religious issues became complicated by the infusion of social and political issues: e.g. the disunity between townspeople and country folk, and the tensions between the craft guilds, tradesmen, and the aristocracy. Also, abolition of the convents was not to be decided on religious grounds alone. The arguments were based on simple economics. In the cities, the convents, as producers, competed with the artisans and craftsmen. The monks did not live only in quiet contemplation, away from tilling the soil or working at handicrafts. In the countryside, they were considered to be little more than troublesome collectors of the tithes which farmers were obliged to pay. All of these considerations had political repercussions which were reflected in social cleavages with increasing hostility between opposing groups.

In Basel, the craft guilds were supporters of reform, of the new beliefs; the nobles and the wealthy sought to preserve the old. The political influence of the guilds was great—almost a determining factor in elections of the government, of the Great Council and of the Small Council (the Executive Body). On the night of 8 February 1529 the Great Council met to consider specific demands of the guilds. Meanwhile, a great crowd assembled in the marketplace. Many were armed. Suddenly, large groups from the mob, inflamed by the tensions of the occasion, marched upon the churches and destroyed all religious images, relics, crucifixes, and statues in sight. In a few hours the destruction was complete. The bishop had long since fled from the city, now to be followed by the old believers from the ruling class and a large number of scholars from the university. The guilds seized political power without effecting any significant political reforms. In the churches, however, major changes were immediately instituted and from 1 April 1529, new ordinances went into effect. By these decrees which were meticulous in detail the Reformed religion was officially introduced.

In Bern also, officialdom, in the form of the Great Council and with the support of the guilds, ordered that the Reformed religion must replace the old. The transformation was achieved without the violence that Basel unhappily experienced. And Zwingli's untiring attacks on mercenary service and the related pension system fell upon sympathetic ears, for Bern had suffered heavy losses among its men who fought in Italy during the Franco-Austrian war. The adherents of the Reformation won the Great Council elections of 1527 and thereupon placed the convents under civil administration.

Early in 1528, in an apparent attempt to nullify the impact of the Baden disputation of 1526, the Great Council called for a debate of the social and religious problems that continued to be in dispute. The debate, attended by some 500 theologians and over a hundred of the laity, continued for three weeks. The proponents of the Reform Movement were numerous and were effectively represented. The adherents of the old faith failed to receive sufficient support, notably because of the failure of the leading bishops and representatives from *Innerschweiz* to attend. This great drama, an effort to resolve by debate the relations which should exist between man and God, and man and his human environment led to no definitive results but unquestionably accelerated the movement for reform.

Four years passed before the Reformed Church received its new constitution— the so-called Synod. Meanwhile, the authorities moved cautiously, guided by Zwingli's counsel, in an endeavour to prevent violent resistance to the great changes that were underway. But in the *Oberland* the people would have nothing to do with the new religion. Those of Oberhasli, free people of the *Reich*, associated themselves with Unterwalden in armed resistance. The incipient uprising was pitilessly repressed and the more uncompromising adherents of the Church of Rome were constrained to leave their homeland for a more hospitable environment. This only served to widen the breach between the believers of the old and the adherents of the Reformed religion.

Bern, with a vigorous foreign policy of its own, was feared by the ancient cantons. Since the Burgundian war, Bern had grown mightily in military power and had now struck an impressive blow among the most influential cantons in favor of the Reformation. *Innerschweiz* feared the political consequences of the Reformation, perhaps as much as the confessional changes. The possibility of an unfavorable political restructuring appeared to the ancient cantons to be dangerous and imminent. Political and social reforms were becoming inseparable from the religious reformation. In Zurich the State was evolving into an authority that exercised both ecclesiastical and temporal powers. Austria, a powerful adherent to the old beliefs, appeared to the ancient Catholic cantons no longer as an enemy but as a friend. Zwingli proclaimed the fusion of civil and religious authority in the government of the State to be an elevation of a worldly government into a godly State and a protector of the Reformed Church.

To Zwingli the more dangerous opponent was not *Innerschweiz* but Austria. With this in mind he endeavoured to build his own Federation, presumably as a structure to be superimposed upon the Confederation of the 13 cantons. Thus, Zurich concluded a Christian *Burgrecht* with Constance as an alliance for protection of the Reformed faith. Bern joined the alliance and so also did the towns of St. Gallen, Biel, Mülhausen, Basel and Schauffhausen. As members or allies of the Swiss Confederation these five had been expressly denied the right to enter into additional alliances. Zwingli defended this treaty of alliance by arguing that the new *Bund* was not a political union in the narrow sense of the word but an alliance for protection of the faith. On 22 April 1529, the five inner cantons, now greatly disturbed by the turn of events, signed and sealed a so-called Christian Alliance (*Christliche Vereinigung*) with Austria. The treaty provided that Austria would send 10,000 troops to aid the Catholic cantons in the event of a civil war. Austria was promised a free hand, in such a case, to seize Constance. The alliance appealed to the kaiser, who was also the Grand Duke of Austria, as a part of his own ambitious scheme of forming powerful leagues against the protestants.[15]

Political Relationships in Europe

The events in Switzerland cannot be isolated from the reform movement in western Europe as a whole. The political relationships of the Powers need to be clarified since the Reformation was almost as political as religious in its impact. The emperor was Charles V, a grandson of Maximilian I. He ruled over a European empire consisting of Spain, the ancient lands of Habsburg-Austria, the Netherlands, and Germany. It was a loosely knit federation held together by fealty to the emperor.

Charles of Habsburg, educated in Flanders, succeeded Ferdinand as King of Spain in 1516 (Charles I of Castile and Aragon). By virtue of his birthplace (Geneva) and the homeland of his youth (Flanders) the 19-year-old monarch was neither Spanish nor German. He was in fact Dutch and Burgundian. He saw little of Spain and regarded the kingdom and the Netherlands principally as rich sources of money to be used in his behalf to bribe the Electors of the Empire. In this he succeeded, for in 1519 he was elected Emperor of the Reich (Charles V, 1519–56).

Charles V was a militant catholic who opposed the Reformation because of the catholicism of Spain and because the tidal wave of protestantism in Germany threatened his concept of imperial power. The treaty of mutual support which had been signed by Austria with the five catholic cantons of Switzerland harmonized with his vigorous opposition to the Reformation. The opponents of his policy, other than the protestant cantons and affiliates of the Swiss Confederation, were the German protestants and France and England. For political reasons these two great Powers felt threatened by the ambitions of the emperor. Zwingli saw his efforts in Zurich to achieve reforms seriously threatened by the power of Austria and the emperor. To him, resort to arms and a quick military victory over the catholic cantons seemed to be the only way to bring about an annulment of the Austrian-*Innerschweiz* accord.

The Confessions at War

Many isolated incidents brought the Confederation perilously close to civil war: the hanging of a catholic sergeant in Thurgau because of his opposition to the official introduction of the Reformed religion by Zurich; the burning in Schwyz of a Zurich preacher who was convicted of heresy in expressing the new beliefs; and other such incidents. In June 1529 Zurich declared war on the five catholic *Orte* and assembled its troops at Kappel. *Innerschweiz* rallied its forces at Baar, only four or five kilometers to the south. At this critical moment Glarus sent its *Landammann* to attempt a resolution of the quarrel and to press for peace and tolerance. Äbli succeeded in persuading the two parties to agree upon an armistice. The First Kappeler Peace was signed—a truly remarkable document, for it gave to each local community, by majority vote of its inhabitants, the right to accept the new religion or to adhere to the old. In various respects it provided for a degree of tolerance which ran completely counter to the spirit of the times. Religious belief was still not regarded as a personal matter to be decided only by the individual conscience. But the Peace of Kappel at least gave to a community of people, rather than to a cantonal government, the right to decide upon the religious observances and beliefs which they, as a community, preferred to accept—the Reformed or the old-time religion. The Christian Alliance of *Innerschweiz* was tacitly recognized but it was agreed that its alliance with Austria should be dissolved. This action was in harmony with other provisions of the peace treaty in which the acceptance of pensions was declared to be unlawful and alliances with foreign States were denounced.

Unfortunately, the Peace of Kappel was of short duration. Charles V no longer concealed his intention to restore the old order and to destroy the gains of the reformers, especially in Germany. The German protestants, now on the defensive and hopeful that the bitter hostility between Luther and Zwingli attributable to disagreement over biblical interpretation could be overcome, proposed an agreement with the adherents of the Reformed faith in Switzerland for their common defense against oppression. Zurich's leadership, with Zwingli, in seeking to have the new faith adopted by the entire Confederation, aroused the old fears and mistrust of the ancient cantons. They had not forgotten the Old Zurich War, and now the proposals of the German protestants, directed primarily to Zurich, deepened the gulf between the catholic cantons and the adherents of the Reformation. Count Philip of Hesse, seized with a desire to bring the leaders of the Reformation together to resolve the Luther-Zwingli dispute, arranged a religious debate in Marburg. This took place in October 1529 with the participation of Luther, Zwingli, and the leading scholars of the Reformation. The hoped-for reconciliation was not achieved. Luther and Zwingli held tenaciously to their doctrines. In 1530, Zurich and Basel (later joined by Strassburg) entered into a defensive religious alliance with Hesse. Meanwhile, the *Reichstag*, assembled at Augsburg by order of the emperor, declared the repressive measures enacted by an earlier *Reichstag* at Worms (in 1521) to be in full force. The new religion was now seriously jeopardized by the might of the emperor. Without respect for the Peace of Kappel, Zurich forced a new Reformed Church ordinance upon Thurgau, and St. Gallen violated the peace by a similar forced introduction of the Reformed faith into the Rheintal.

On 27 February 1531 the Schmalkaldic League was organized in Germany to defend the adherents of the evangelical faith against the militancy of the catholic Emperor, Charles V. The members of the League were prominent leaders in several of the German States and in three lower- and eight upper-Germany Reich cities.

The Swiss protestant cities were excluded, principally because of the scriptural differences between the Lutherans of Germany and the Zwinglians of Switzerland, and the mutual dislike and distrust that separated Luther and Zwingli. In 1530 Zwingli had tried to bring Hesse, Württemberg and the German towns, including Constance and Strassburg, into an all-European Christian alliance with its roots in the evangelical alliance of St. Gallen, Mülhausen and Biel which linked these towns to the Confederation. But Zwingli's grandiose scheme was unrealistic and encountered the powerful opposition of Luther.

In 1534, Württemberg was reconquered by the League and Duke Ulrich was appointed Head of State. Charles V, in 1538, approved the formation of a catholic counterorganization—the Catholic Reform Movement. In 1541 the kaiser declared war on the League. In 1546 he placed two of the most vigorous leaders under an imperial ban. The kaiser was victorious in the campaign against the protestant forces in the Danube basin. Southern Germany then went over to the kaiser and in 1547 the League was dissolved. The victory was short-lived and incomplete: the protestant movement survived and grew. Charles V abdicated in 1556, crushed and disappointed by his failure to wipe out the Protestant Reform Movement.

Farther to the east, the Milanese seized the strategic entrance to Graubünden's

Adda valley. This was the culmination of a long series of border skirmishes. Graubünden, pursuant to the treaty of 1497 with the seven easterly cantons, now turned to them for aid against the Milanese. The five catholic cantons denied the request because Graubünden had accepted the new beliefs. Its people were described contemptuously as traitors. Zurich and Zwingli regarded the Milanese attack as a crusade against the Reformation—a campaign against heresy. The refusal of the five ancient cantons to assist in the defense of Graubünden was taken to be convincing proof of an intention of the catholics to overcome Zurich by encirclement.

Zwingli's anger and his unconcealed preparation for war alarmed the city and met with a cool reception among the other Reformed cantons. Bern found itself in the middle—serious differences in the canton and a foreign policy oriented toward the west. To Zwingli the religious struggle was paramount. Bern, while accepting the Reformed religion, was opposed to a war with *Innerschweiz*. Zwingli went too far, in the judgment of the Great Council, to overcome resistance to his policy in Zurich, and he was requested to resign as parish priest of the Great Münster. But this shocked the people and he was urged to remain. His position now appeared to be strengthened. However, the five catholic cantons had not been inactive and in October 1531 they mobilized their troops. The two forces met in battle at Kappel on October 11. The modest-sized army from Zurich was defeated and 500 of its people, among them Zwingli, lay dead on the battlefield. Ten days later forces from Zurich and the Reformed cities suffered a second defeat. In November, under pressure from other cantons, an armistice was concluded. Then came the Second Peace of Kappel.[16] This accord, considering the spirit of the times, was tolerant and forgiving in its provisions: each party was to be left free and unhindered in the practice of its religion; whoever wished to return to the Catholic Church must not be prevented from so doing, and the Mass was to be restored in any community which so desired. The Free Districts (*Freie Ämter*)—six were specified—were to be included in the Peace.

The military defeats and Zwingli's death constituted a significant setback for the adherents of the Reformed Church. Zwingli had long been recognized as the spiritual head of the entire German-Swiss Reformation, not simply as the leader in Zurich. His influence was felt in Germany and in France. His uncompromising attitude in religion had been expressed also in his politics—a quality which occasionally had aroused much opposition even among those of the Reformed faith. In his passion for social justice and in his efforts to awaken in man a sense of responsibility for the public weal he was far ahead of his times.

The Second Peace of Kappel

The Peace of Kappel, which was followed by a return to peaceful relations, although sometimes tense, defined firmly for almost 200 years the basis of accord between the believers of the old and of the new. Communities returned to the Catholic Church or remained with the Reformed religion, as they chose. Because of past repression and cantonal-wide adherence to one faith or the other, such freedom of decision at the local level was hitherto unknown. In Thurgau, which had been "reformed" by Zurich, 14 districts became catholic, 18 remained with the Reformed Church, and 30 decided upon a policy of equality. Elsewhere in the Confederation the results were similar. In Solothurn, for example, evangelical services in the city came to be forbidden and many of the Reformed faith migrated to neighbouring towns in the canton of Bern. In Zurich and Bern, religious and political unrest was an inevitable result of the military defeat. In the country, the citizens demanded the right to share in decision-making on matters of high policy, especially on questions of war and peace. In both cities the relations between the old and the new believers were again defined in response to popular demand. In Bern, a Synod was agreed to, the first basic law to define the relations between Church and State. It served also as a political-pedagogical instrument. In 1536 the first "Helvetic Confession" was adopted by representatives of a number of cities and cantons.

Events in Geneva and Vaud

To the west the Reformation pursued a different course than in German-speaking Switzerland. Bern was politically involved because her expansionist policy had extended her influence and interests to Lake Leman and to Savoy. The Reformed religion acquired the doctrinal principles espoused by Calvin,[17] a follower of William Farel (1489–1565) who came from the French Dauphiné and was a Zwingli disciple. With encouragement from Bern, Farel preached "the word" in the principal towns of the former Burgundian Switzerland. In 1532 he moved on to Geneva but, in 1538, was forced out of the city by the "old believers." Waadtland (Vaud) was partly under the sovereignty of Savoy, and at times Bern had served as arbitrator in the recurring quarrels between the Duke of Savoy and the towns of Vaud. In the early 1500s Savoy was ruled by Duke Charles III (1504–53) who opposed the new ideas of his time, sought to centralize the administration of his duchy, and to reduce the special rights and privileges which over the years had been won by the cities and countryside. Bern's policy was twofold: a continuation of her westerly conquests and the union of much of Vaud with Franche Comté. Of great importance, because of defense considerations, was the compactness of Vaud—an area enclosed by such natural frontiers as the Jura, Lake Leman and the westerly stretches of the Alps.

In the Burgundian war the easterly part of this region had fallen under the joint administration of Bern and Freiburg. The westerly part had suffered much through plundering and fire in the anarchical period that followed the Burgundian War. The various temporal and ecclesiastical rulers in this fragmented area were in a constant struggle, each seeking to extend his power and his possessions. Nominally, the Duke of Savoy was the ruler, subject only to the emperor of the *Reich*. However, Charles of Savoy had delegated much of his authority in Vaud to the noble families and the bishops of the Church. Of these the most important was the Bishop of Lausanne, whose holdings were scattered in seemingly random fashion from Lake Leman to Avenches. In Lausanne, the burghers had gradually acquired most of the powers formerly exercised by the Bishop in government of the city. In 1525, Lausanne signed a friendship pact and quasi-alliance (*Burgrecht*) with Bern and Freiburg, thus protecting the city against the acquisitive pretensions of the Duke of Savoy. Bern, however, conquered Vaud in 1536, absorbed it into itself, and thus reduced Lausanne to a sort of subject city. It almost did the same to Geneva. Bern was exceedingly strong. It tended to dominate, its equals becoming in effect its subjects. Not until the Congress of Vienna in 1815 were Vaud, Freiburg, Geneva, and Neuchâtel fully liberated from Bern through their re-establishment as separate cantons, equal before the law to Bern. The Emperor, Charles V, shortly after the *Burgrecht* of 1525 had declared Lausanne to be a free imperial city, subject only to the imperial authority.

Bern's military interest in Vaud has already been mentioned. Economic considerations were also of prime importance. Grain and salt, available in Vaud as export commodities, were in constant demand in Bern which for years had been handicapped by shortages of these necessary products. And it is clear that Vaud would benefit by a close association with Bern. Her people derived no benefit from the fragmentation of the country and from the constant power struggles between the families in which government was factually vested.

Religious and Political Dissension

More or less in the middle of Savoy was Geneva, a free city since the late Middle Ages. The House of Savoy tirelessly attempted to strengthen its influence in the city, if not to absorb it within the Duchy. Savoy had succeeded since the fourteenth century in placing a member of the family on the Bishop's throne. Justice was administered by a representative of the House, almost as an inherited right. In fact, the House of Savoy sought to strengthen its hold on Geneva just as the Habsburg dynasty constantly endeavoured to strengthen its tenuous grasps on Zurich and Lucerne, and with similar results—vigorous resistance by the citizenry. The burghers, accustomed to self-government of the city and possessed of the right to choose the local officials, were actually divided into two factions—a Savoyard party and those who sought a close association with the Swiss Confederation.

Geneva had also to be on the alert against the ambitions of France. French policy sought to weaken Geneva economically. To this end France forbade her people to participate in the great fairs in Geneva; instead of these, the fairs at Lyon began to receive the blessings and favor of the monarch, with seriously adverse effects on Geneva. Savoy and France were allied by a treaty of friendship but after the defeat of France at Pavia, the alliance fell apart. Bern and Freiburg had quickly seized the opportunity to negotiate a mutual treaty of defense and commerce with Geneva. It was in the nature of a *Burgrecht* which was signed in February 1526 and was similar to the 1525 pact with Lausanne. The alliance was joyously celebrated by both parties within Geneva. The Duke of Savoy, now alarmed by this close accord, attempted military action against Geneva, only to be repelled and defeated by a combined force from Bern, Solothurn, and towns in eastern Vaud. In the Peace of St. Julien, the Duke renounced all claims to Geneva and pawned the whole of Vaud to Bern and Freiburg as security that his promise would be honored.[18]

This happened at about the time that Farel was expelled from Geneva. Faced with Bern's threat to denounce the Peace, Geneva permitted Farel to return and to preach the Reformed religion. In 1536 the new faith was officially accepted and endorsed by the city. Early in the year war broke out between France and Savoy. Seizure of the north shore of Lake Leman by the French appeared to be imminent. In response to a poll of its people, Bern ordered its troops into Vaud. There was little resistance by Savoy, and Bern speedily occupied Geneva and seized Lausanne. The Bernese also moved from lower Valais into upper Savoy, seized the towns on the south shore of the lake, and even penetrated the Pays de Gex. It was a poor country and the whole of the conquered territory was declared to be a subject land under the sovereignty of Bern. Beyond this military and political conquest, and in vigorous support of the Reformation, Bern decreed that the Reformed religion was to be recognized and accepted throughout the conquered territories. This decree followed upon a great disputation in Lausanne in which Farel and Calvin led the proponents of the Reformation.

In 1537 Bern founded an Academy in Lausanne (later to become the University of Lausanne) which had as its principal function the training of priests and theologians in the Reformed religion. Conrad Gassner (1516–65), a great Swiss universalist, was appointed to the professorship of Greek in the new Academy. In the whole of Europe the Reform Movement had entered a phase in which religion and politics alike were subject to almost convulsive upheavals.

The Catholic Church, now strongly on the defensive, initiated its own reform movement, known in protestant terminology as the Counter Reformation and in the language of the Catholics as the Catholic Reform Movement. In Spain, Ignatius Loyola founded the Society of Jesus, the Jesuit Order, deeply committed to propagation of the old beliefs and practices of the Church. Charles V sought to crush the spread of protestantism in Germany by force of arms. Though he won the Schmalkaldic War of 1546–47 he failed to destroy the Protestant Movement. When he abdicated in 1556, enfeebled and disappointed, the *Reich* broke asunder into the Spanish Habsburg line and the centuries-old Austrian inheritance. Philip II, the only son of Charles V, succeeded to the Spanish throne, and Ferdinand I (1556–64), brother of Charles V, became head of the House of Habsburg-Austria. He was also elected Emperor of the *Reich*. France, in her foreign policy, was forced by the succession into an awkward position. She sought to be the protective Power for the Catholic faith but was confronted by strongly Catholic Spain with the same ambition. France's position in foreign affairs was weakened by Spain's newly acquired sovereignty over the Duchy of Milan, an inheritance from Charles V.

In central and eastern Switzerland the Second Peace of Kappel was not observed with the tolerance that had been envisaged. Protestant families expelled from *Innerschweiz* and Ticino obtained refuge in Zurich. Dissension in Glarus rose to such a pitch between 1556 and 1564 that the five inner cantons resorted to armed intervention to protect the rights of their fellow Catholics. Aegidius Tschudi, the great historian and politician, was the principal leader on behalf of the Catholics in the so-called Tschudi war of 1559–64. The war ended indecisively and a fragile peace was restored. Glarus returned to the policy of accepting both confessions on an equal basis.

At the same time, Bern was having her troubles, political and confessional, aggravated by the mistrust and jealousy of *Innerschweiz* in respect to Bern's power politics and economic strength. Through Spain's generosity Duke Emanuel Philibert of Savoy had regained his duchy.[19] He now demanded of Bern the return of Vaud and the rest of the Savoyard possessions that Bern had acquired by conquest. In these demands, Spain was supported by *Innerschweiz* which went so far as to form a "permanent" alliance with Savoy in 1560 and to declare Vaud to be the rightful possession of Savoy. This diplomatic strategy isolated Bern since her own allies among the Reformed cantons were not ready to go to war because of Vaud. Basel entered as a mediator and in 1564 persuaded both parties to negotiate a peaceful settlement.

By the Treaty of Lausanne, Bern returned to Savoy the conquered territory on the south shore of Lake Leman and also the Pays de Gex. However, the Bern-Geneva accord (*Burgrecht*) remained in effect. Hence, without a war, *Innerschweiz* managed to weaken somewhat the power of Bern.

An even greater threat to Bern arose from the civil war in France between the catholics and the French protestants—the Huguenots. The catholic faction, essentially the French government, urged Savoy to revive its claim on Geneva and to make every effort to destroy the independence of the city. At the same time the catholic çantons of Switzerland were urged to support the cause of French catholicism by providing mercenary troops. This they were glad to do. A similar request to provide troops in support of the Huguenot cause was addressed to the Reformed cantons. Though the request was denied, recruiting of troops by representatives of the Huguenots was finally permitted. This led to regrettable episodes of Swiss soldiers in combat with their own countrymen on foreign soil. Though not isolated incidents in the tarnished record of mercenary service, they also reflect the bitterness of the confessional schism within the Swiss Confederation.

The leaders of foreign policy within *Innerschweiz* were Ludwig Pfyffer of Lucerne and Melchior Lussy[20] from Stans in Unterwalden. Pfyffer, sometimes known as the Swiss king, was a dedicated defender of the "old-time" religion. He was a soldier of outstanding competence, and the regiment that he raised for the French King's war on the Huguenots distinguished itself by its disciplined behaviour, bravery, and skill in combat. Although the people of Lucerne resented the entrenched positions and power of the leading families which ruled the city, they solidly supported Pfyffer. In fact, he was elected *Schultheiss* in 1571 and confirmed in office every two years until his death in 1594. Politically, Pfyffer directed the support at his command to French catholicism. Lussy, on the other hand, leaned toward support of the Papal State and Spain. Equally devoted and zealous in defense of the catholic faith, he was more conciliatory in temperament than Pfyffer. Lussy's efforts and his appeal to the Archbishop of Milan succeeded in 1574 in the installation of a Jesuit center in Lucerne for the catholic priesthood.

Relations with France and Spain

Meanwhile, the religious conflict elsewhere in Europe, especially in France where all hope for a peaceful solution had almost vanished, added to the tensions between the two confessions in Switzerland. The bloody massacre of Huguenots during the night of 23 August 1571 in Paris had tremendous repercussions. Bern, Zurich, and Geneva accepted thousands of Huguenots who fled from France. The five cantons of *Innerschweiz* reacted by strengthening their alliance with Savoy. They promised that they would never oppose the policies of the duchy in respect of Geneva and Vaud.

France, however, changed its political orientation and, despite the confessional differences, drew more closely to Bern and did not oppose Bern's sovereignty over Vaud and Geneva. This angered Pfyffer who now turned to Spain and sought support of the "Holy League" in an effort to prevent Henry of Navarre, a Huguenot, from ascending the French throne. Several thousand troops from *Innerschweiz*, according to Pfyffer's plan, would be made available to the catholic party in France. In Switzerland, he sought to bring the catholic cantons more closely together in matters of policy by negotiating in 1586 a special alliance called the Christian Union or also the Golden Borromaic Federation. Its sole purpose was alleged to be protection of the faith but, implicit in such a league, was a *de facto* separation from the Swiss Confederation. In 1587, in defiance of their sworn responsibilities as members of the Swiss Confederation, the five catholic cantons and Freiburg formed an alliance with Spain.[21] The treaty contained the usual provisions for friendly understanding and for improvement in commercial and political relations but also, and quite uniquely, granted to the King of Spain freedom of passage of his troops through their respective territories. Should a religious war break out in Switzerland, Spain would assist the catholic cantons and would be free to seize the Valtellina.[22] Each of the signatory States would receive from Spain a yearly payment of 1500 crowns. This alliance was essentially complementary to a treaty between the six catholic cantons and Savoy.[23]

That the treaties with Spain and Savoy were at cross purposes to the alliance with France appeared to be of little concern. Thus the catholic cantons were pledged to help defend Milan (against Spain) as soon as it was returned to the French Crown. But they were also obliged by the treaty with Spain to protect Milan as a Spanish possession against its enemies. In the treaty with France, the catholic *Orte* agreed to deny the *Durchzug* to any of the enemies of France. However, the Spanish alliance of 1587 specifically granted to Spain *Durchzug* rights over the Gotthard.[24]

The Christian Union and, especially the alliance with Spain, had serious repercussions in Appenzell where both the Reformed and the catholic faiths were permitted. The catholics urged that Appenzell join the catholic cantons in the Spanish alliance—a proposal that was firmly resisted by the protestants. To avoid a bloody conflict the cantonal government decided in 1595 to divide the State into two half-cantons—a catholic half with Appenzell town as the capital, and a protestant half with Herisau as its capital.[25] Since each half canton now enjoyed the independence and autonomy of a whole canton, the catholic half was free to join the Spanish alliance. But one must ask whether the treaty with Spain was anything more than a paper tiger—a threat which might instil caution in the Reformed cantons and restrain them from any belligerent act. The question is very much to the point if we recall that in 1588 the great Armada of Philip II of Spain was defeated by England, and the remnants of the fleet were destroyed by fierce Atlantic storms. This historic event so weakened the position of Spain as a great European Power that some of her allies redirected their foreign policies away from Spain.

In France, Henry of Navarre ascended the throne in 1589. Although he himself renounced the Reformed faith in 1593 he extended to the Huguenots freedom to practice their religion. In the wake of this enlightened policy the protestant cantons of Switzerland joined in a friendly alliance with France. Indeed, the alliance took the form of an all-Swiss friendship pact in which the catholic cantons equally participated. The catholic alliance with Spain was not renounced but the pact with France was unquestionably attractive to *Innerschweiz* for two reasons: (i) through adoption of the catholic faith by Henry IV, France again became a catholic Power; (ii) the treaty with France permitted the King once again to purchase the services of Swiss mercenaries, most of whom came from the economically distressed forest cantons of *Innerschweiz*. For this the French agreed to pay one million gold *Talers*. [26] The protestant cantons benefitted by the resumption of lucrative pension payments. And thus, the defeat of the Spanish Armada indirectly averted a civil war in Switzerland and brought together, in respect to Franco-Swiss foreign policy, two powerful factions which had become perilously separated by confessional differences.

As the sixteenth century came to an end, an unstable peace had settled upon Switzerland. The threat of civil war was averted but only temporarily. A lasting solution to the religious problem had not yet been found and years were to pass before catholics and protestants could live harmoniously and peacefully together. Savoy had not abandoned her hopes of absorbing Geneva into the Duchy. In upper Italy, the treaty between Spain and the catholic cantons was still in force. Oddly enough, this helped to maintain the peace in Switzerland, since the initiation of warlike acts by the Reformed cantons could conceivably lead to the loss of the Valtellina to Spain and war in the Graubünden.

The Public Health

The earlier section on demographic aspects should be referred to as somewhat of an introduction to the present section. Here we shall concentrate on the terrible epidemics of typhus and bubonic plague which swept through armies and frequently decided the outcome of wars. In the 1520s, the Emperor Charles V, who ruled Spain as a part of the Holy Roman Empire, was at war in Italy with Francis I, king of France. At issue was northern Italy. With the aid of his forces from Germany, Italy fell to Charles V and in 1525 the French king was imprisoned in Spain. Milan and Naples were now held by Spain and the Papal State of Rome was completely encircled. In 1526 the French king was liberated and Pope Clement VII joined the

French in opposing the overweening ambitions of the emperor. The League of Cognac in May 1526 drew together, as a militant union, Pope Clement VII, King Francis I, Sforza of Milan, and the rulers of Venice. But in the following year the imperial army under Frundsberg and the Duke of Bourbon sacked Rome and imprisoned the pope. Then came the plague and devastated the city. Enormous numbers of the residents died, including two cardinals and others in their retinue. Lannoy, an imperial general, was also among the victims. A French army under Lautrec advanced from the south. The Spaniards, pressed for time, endeavoured to fortify Naples. Here too, the plague intervened and the imperial army was reduced to less than 11,000 men. The city was placed under siege by Lautrec and his army of 28,000. By June of 1528, after $1\frac{1}{2}$ months, Naples was exhausted by near-famine. The city was saved by typhus which decimated the French encampment. We are told that in 30 days Lautrec's army was reduced to about 4000 (**406**). On August 29, Lautrec called off the siege and began to retreat. His forces were pursued by an imperial army under the Prince of Orange and were slaughtered. "In 1530, Charles V was crowned ruler of the Roman Empire at Bologna by the power of Typhus Fever" (**406**, p. 253).

Another epidemic of typhus in 1552 forced the emperor to abandon the siege of Metz. In a single month, more than 10,000 of his men died of the disease and many others died in military prisons. Villages in the area were also struck by the disease which did not terminate its ravages until the summer of 1553.

Typhus had also participated in the Turkish-Hungarian war of 1542 in which a supporting army from Germany and Italy lost 30,000 men. In 1566 Emperor Maximilian II marched into Hungary with his great army only to encounter an even more severe epidemic of typhus. Though striving to protect his eastern possessions he was finally forced to abandon his campaign.

The *Abschiede* also contain a number of references to matters of public health. Thus, in August 1502, Bern regretted that it could not send its delegates to participate with others in a meeting with the king, because of the sickness that then pervaded the city (*Abschiede* III. 2, p. 174). In July 1506, Schwyz was urged to speak in a friendly way with the authorities of Glarus, to request that their people refrain from visiting the market in Bellinzona because of the illness that ruled the city (*Abschiede* III. 2, p. 352). In 1514, it was reported that the local governor of Domodossola had not gone to the city to collect dues and taxes because of the pestilence. He had little news from the city because half of the people had fled (*Abschiede* III. 2, p. 772). Finally, we learn that the commissioner of the city recommended, in April 1514, that the public accounting office be closed for the year because of the *Death* (*Abschiede* III. 2, p. 785).

Nutrition

Montaigne's diary (**250**) has a wealth of information on sixteenth-century Baden, Constance, and Lindau. His observations on public baths have been reported upon in an earlier section, but he also had much to say about other aspects of life in these towns.

The village people give their labourers for breakfast very flat *fouaces* (a thick cake, hastily baked on a hot hearth by hot embers laid on it, and burning coals over them), in which there is fennel, and on the top of the *fouaces* little bits of bacon very small, and heads of garlic (**250**, p. 39).

They grow a great abundance of headed cabbage which they cut up small . . . and they put a great quantity of it into tubs with salt, of which they make soup all winter (**250**, p. 41).

An abundance of provisions; many kinds of messes to diversify their courses (e.g. made of quinces, or with baked apples, sliced and placed in soup), sauces, salads (e.g. of headed cabbage), broths from which they all fish in common (for they do not serve it out individually); an abundance of good fish which they serve with the meat course. They disdain trout and eat only the roe. Plenty of game (woodcocks . . .). They mix stewed plums, pears and apple tarts with the meat course. The only dessert is pears, apples, walnuts and cheese. [They use] four different sorts of pounded spices. Also caraway or something similar (biting and hot) which they mix with their bread, and their bread is mostly made with fennel. After the meal, 2 or 3 courses of things to provoke thirst (**250**, p. 42).

It is a crime to see an empty goblet and not to fill it at once; and never any water, even if it is asked for, and only then if the person is held in great respect (**250**, p. 44).

After the cloth was removed, other fresh courses among the glasses of wine: first, *canaules* (gateau in the shape of a crown), then gingerbread; for the third, a loaf of delicate white bread . . . into the interstices of which they had put plenty of spices and plenty of salt (**250**, p. 39).

Montaigne dined well, his food and wine were superb: "they cover the tables very sumptuously—at least ours" . . . "the least meals take up three or four hours . . . and they ear less hastily than we do" (**250**, p. 24) . . . "they never serve eggs except hard-boiled, cut into quarters in the salads, which are very good and made with quite fresh herbs" (**250**, p. 51).

Hauser (**167**) has described foods and meals which have been detailed in many records from the sixteenth to the nineteenth century. Although the book focuses on Zurich, one may assume that the same foods and eating habits applied to other parts of Switzerland, with the exception of some inhospitable areas including the high mountain meadows.

Originally, the ways of living differed greatly from canton to canton. The housing, clothing, and food of the burghers differed greatly from that of the nobles and of the peasants: A festive meal, as described by Hauser, appears to have been much the same in the early sixteenth century as the sumptuous meals which Montaigne enjoyed. Geese, hens, capons, pheasants and pigeons must be ready. For meat courses, hot fat sausage, fried sheep brain, tripe, swine heads, pigs' feet, leg of veal and of pork were served. As a side dish, fat collected as the residue during the cooking of meats was recommended. White bread served with a hot, fat sauce was also a dainty addition. All food had to be well-salted and spiced. This caused a great thirst which then called for wine or *sauser* (partially fermented juice of grapes and other fruits). Dessert at the best tables consisted of cherries, strawberries, grapes, apples and sometimes nuts.

Much fat was used at meals. Food cooked in fat, like cheese fritters, was served at festive meals. Up to the sixteenth century food was usually eaten from the hand. Sometimes it was rolled in, or baked with, a pasta for ease in handling.

Cheese was widely used, sometimes as an appetizer or a dessert. Soup made from a cottage cheese, or fried cottage cheese, was a common dish in the fifteenth and sixteenth centuries.

Eggs were eaten in the households of the burghers. They were either fried or served as a soup. Omelettes, cooked in butter, not oil, were also used. Soft-boiled eggs, then as now, were commonly used as a food for the sick.

Meat was then more important than it is today. Cows and swine walked along the streets of Zurich and every well-fixed burgher had a stall beside his house. In the poorer classes in the seventeenth and eighteenth centuries meat, usually pork, was eaten once or, at the most, twice per week. Some was smoked and kept for the entire year. Sauerkraut was served with pork, and cabbage or lettuce with bacon. Boiled beef was common in the sixteenth and seventeenth centuries. Goat meat was less used.

In April and May salmon swarmed in the Limmat and other rivers. These and crabs graced a festive table. Pike was also eaten. Even in the seventeenth century, the fish catch was so abundant that many people maintained themselves on fish throughout the year.

A *brei* or porridge made from millet or oatmeal was a very common foodstuff in the Middle Ages; in fact, the word *brei* was synonymous with *Nahrung* (nutrition).

Up to the end of the eighteenth century, a fruit purée was the most common breakfast food, especially of craftsmen and unskilled workers. The vegetables varied greatly, by season and locality, but beans, cabbage, fennel, beets, and peas are frequently mentioned.

Bread was originally prepared by the *Hausfrau* but, even in the thirteenth century, bakeries, regulated by various ordinances, were in existence. The regulations pertained to the quality of the bread, operation of bread shops, hours of sale, and prohibition of bean meal and hops as admixtures with the flour. Rye, oats, and spelt flour were used in the baking. Raised bread (with yeast) was a specially privileged food. Such breads could easily be broken, and should not be confused with the hard bread used by the mountain people.

Sugar, potatoes, rice, and coffee were not introduced until the seventeenth and eighteenth centuries. Spices were "worth their weight in gold." Pepper and saffron were not common and were very expensive.

Figs, dates, oranges and lemons came in from the south but only the rich could afford such imports. The rich also had sugar even in the sixteenth century, but the poorer people used honey instead. Tea came in from Holland, first in 1630, and was prized by doctors. The Swiss also made their own "tea" from a mixture of various dried herbs.

Obviously, no information is available on nutritional deficiencies other than goiter (iodine deficiency), which was very common in the Rhone valley, and scurvy which must have been very rare. Some anemias, attributable to certain nutritional deficiencies, must have existed but many years had to pass before their causes were recognized.

Niklaus von Flüe (Brother Klaus) expressed some interesting views on health and nutrition.

> Much food causes many illnesses. A full stomach weakens the spirit and endangers life. Do not eat so much as will fill the stomach or cause nausea on rising from the table. We should not eat as much as we can but only as much as Nature requires (**109**, I).

Trithemius, describing Klaus as an example of holiness, said that now the hermit had lived 20 years without food! "This, my dear brothers, have I told you, that nothing is so difficult but with persistent practice can become easy." And hence we learn that Klaus gradually reduced his food intake until he ate nothing. "You my brothers, do likewise" (**109**). When asked by the Abbot of St. Stephan if it was true, as rumored, that he had eaten nothing during many years, Klaus allegedly replied "I have never said and I do not say that I eat nothing" (**109**).

Neutrality

The discussions within the Diet and the decisions that were reached in the early years of the sixteenth century strongly suggest a determination of the Swiss to be strictly neutral, to avoid any military entanglements with neighbouring countries, and to bring Swiss mercenary service to an end. In March 1500, alarmed by the distressing fratricidal conflict in Italy (6000 Swiss in the service of the Duke of Milan opposing thousands more in the army of Louis XII of France), the Diet ordered the opposing Swiss regiments "not to allow themselves to be drawn into combat against each other" (**213**, p. 261).

When the Diet met in Zurich (30 September 1507) nine of the cantons informed the kaiser that they would not join in his contemplated march on Rome; likewise, they would not help the king of France or send troops to any foreign land. Each of the nine expressed their determination to remain neutral. The record mentions that an agreement is in preparation under which the cantons would bind themselves to send no mercenaries to foreign princes and to disallow the acceptance of pensions by any Swiss who, otherwise, might agree to raise the requested number of mercenaries.[27]

There were many other comparable incidents in the years to come, leading to agonizing discussions in the Diet. And from these arose the firm determination to remain neutral in any wars that involved Switzerland's neighbours. The policy evolved very gradually and not without intense opposition from the ancient cantons of *Innerschweiz*. The poverty of their soil, and the increase of a population that could not be sustained, led inevitably to vigorous pressure by the heartland cantons for continued Swiss mercenary service. There was also the demonstrated valour of the Swiss in combat, and the disturbing fact that many peaceful occupations were open only to those who enjoyed privileged positions of birth and family—obviously to the virtual exclusion of the peasant population of the *Waldstätte*. The last consideration was enough in itself to force their young men into military service with the French, the Germans, the Austrians and several other nations. Paradoxical as it may seem, this wide dispersion of Swiss mercenaries, combined with a firm policy of avoiding fratricidal conflicts, contributed mightily to the evolution of Swiss neutrality. The great influence of Niklaus von Flüe in the late fifteenth century, and of Zwingli in the sixteenth, had an influence on the statesmen of the day that cannot be over-emphasized. The policy of non-involvement in the affairs of other States was approved with but little opposition. Defensive warfare was accepted. The Swiss had no trust in the promises of their neighbours and any approach of foreign armies toward the Swiss frontiers was invariably countered by a strengthening of the border defenses.

The disruptive effect of foreign wars, the return of sick, wounded and maimed mercenaries, of men incapable of work, of men whose morals were shaken by the degrading aspects of warfare—savagery in combat and a lust for booty—were recognized as unhealthy to the country, and a very heavy price to pay for peace at home.

At Baden on 20 July 1503, and Lucerne on 30 August 1503, the Diet condemned the entire pension system and the recruitment of mercenaries (*Abschiede* III. 2, p. 241). The defeat and loss of life at Marignano caused the Swiss to ponder seriously whether it was all worthwhile. Passionate polemics followed. The struggle had its confessional aspects since the cantons of the *Waldstätte* were solidly catholic and ardent advocates of continued military capitulations. Zurich and Bern, however, urged on by Zwingli, were determined to end the whole business. In fact, it was Zwingli who persuaded Zurich in 1521 not to join the other twelve cantons in the military alliance with France.

Zurich, under a law of 1522, interdicted all foreign pensions. When one of the principal magistrates broke the law and allowed himself for a price to work for the French alliance, Zurich, to set an example, condemned him to death. For almost a century and a half no one in Zurich dared to advocate foreign military service.

In 1546 war broke out between Charles V and his catholic forces against the Protestant Schmalkaldic alliance. Neither confessional group in Switzerland, fearing civil war, would render aid. Requests for military aid addressed to the Diet by either the emperor or the Protestant League were declined. The catholic cantons refused to send support to Constance, then protestant and under attack by the emperor, even though the refusal would cause difficult economic problems for Switzerland.[28]

But it must be emphasized that, despite the many noble resolutions, the great influence of Zwingli, and the convincing arguments against foreign military service and the pension system, anything akin to strict neutrality throughout Switzerland was far from attainment. The Diet was little more than a forum for debate between representatives of the cantons. The resolutions were without effect unless the delegate support was unanimous. And the delegates were obliged to obey the specific instructions of their cantonal governments; they were not free to be guided by their private opinions. The cantons, treasuring their individual sovereignty, were not prone to recognize a central authority for all Switzerland. To make matters worse, the enforcement of most decisions of the Confederation devolved entirely upon these highly individualistic sovereign cantons.

To illustrate the difficulties we learn that in the session of the Diet at Lucerne (5 January 1508), several representatives from certain cantons had not yet appeared. Those present were irritated because of their embarrassing position between two opposing rulers (the emperor and the king of France), each seeking Swiss military support. The delegates also realized that "we must act unanimously in such matters, as our forefathers did."[29] They declared they would remain neutral and hoped for a final decision at the next meeting of the Diet. On January 26 they replied to the kaiser and the king of France. "The Swiss will give no help to either side but will remain neutral." In replying to France, the Diet stated that they remembered well the Swiss military alliance but since France was not being attacked there was no reason for the French king to demand Swiss military help.[30] But France claimed Milan as French territory and demanded that the Swiss honor the terms of the alliance by providing troops to aid in its defense. At the session of the Diet on 15 March 1508, Zurich reported that she would remain neutral and would send no troops to aid the French. But France, acting through a French bishop and a Frenchman of the lower nobility who were in Switzerland, actively recruited for the French cause. The bishop was ordered to leave the country. The second party was ordered detained in Lucerne, and at his cost, until the Swiss men in French service were returned home. Pressures had arisen to recall the Swiss in foreign military service. Bern declined to make any reply to France pending the return of her own mercenaries. Schwyz declared her intention to send her men to assist the kaiser if the French failed to return the Schwyz mercenaries. Other cantons declared they would do "this or that"—several different courses of action were proposed.[31]

The kaiser made forceful demands upon his Swiss subjects for military aid, even threatening them with war if they were disobedient. Some of the cantons declared they would remain neutral (Zurich, 13 October 1507). Lucerne (a catholic canton) wavered. Several delegates had not arrived, others had not received instructions from their government. Finally, the intentions of the kaiser and the French king were not clear (Zurich, 8 December 1507). One persistent report alleged that the two belligerents were, in reality, equally determined to march on Rome and seize the papal throne. A variant of this claimed that the kaiser was only interested in protecting Rome and the papal throne from conquest by the French.[32]

Despite many such pious declarations within the Diet, it should be noted that much of the sixteenth century was marked by an extraordinary amount of Swiss belligerence. For the first few decades of the century, Switzerland's behaviour toward her neighbours was clearly provocative. There is little evidence of any genuine desire to adhere to a Confederation-wide policy of neutrality until well into the century. The papal alliance of 14 March 1510, the war on France, the belligerent campaign in upper Italy, and the seizure of Neuchâtel, are examples of aggressive warfare lacking any of the qualities of defense of the Confederation against foreign Powers. Territorial expansion by several of the cantons was very much in evidence.

The Confederation and its member cantons trod a most dangerous path. It is little short of miraculous that it managed to survive. Through diplomacy and war it succeeded in fending off its powerful neighbours. It also benefitted through a slowly developing respect by the major European nations for the still unformulated balance-of-power principle.

Then came the Reformation, religious dissension, catholics arrayed against protestants, and civil war. For years, Switzerland was to be a country divided against itself. But with the aggressive campaigns of the first fifteen years behind them, the Swiss gradually became united in a policy of neutrality abroad. This may be surprising for in their domestic religious wars both the confessions "fought like dogs." It should be noted that Basel and Schaffhausen, although strongly pro-Zurich and pro-Bern in their sympathies, did not participate in the Kappeler war (1529–31). They observed faithfully the restrictive clauses in their *Bundesbriefe* of 1501 which required them to remain neutral in wars between other members of the Confederation.

Expansion of the territorial boundaries of the Confederation beyond reasonable limits began to fall into disfavor in the late fifteenth century and was politically frowned upon throughout the sixteenth. The important policy questions came to be "Will the newly conquered territory enhance our defensive capability?" "Will it give us a better frontier with a strong natural barrier which enemy forces could not easily cross?" It was considerations such as these which persuaded the Swiss not to retain their conquests in Burgundy and the Franche Comté. In 1513, when Swiss seizure of Dijon and Besançon appeared imminent, the invaders readily agreed to withdraw in return for Louis XII's promise of four million francs (**103**, II, 521–23)—a very nice supplement to the moneys promised by Louis XI in 1477 in return for permitting Maximilian and Maria of Burgundy to receive the Burgundian inheritance (**103**, II, 287–88). Continued retention of the area against the aspirations of neighbouring France would have been impossible. Pursuant to the Italian campaign, and with similar considerations in mind, the Swiss were quite willing to yield possession of the Eschental in return for retention of Bormio, Chiavenna and the Valtellina. To the north and east, the Rhine was regarded as a satisfactory frontier. The Jura became a part of the north-westerly defense system when the Principality of Neuchâtel was seized in 1512. A broad policy against further conquests and intervention in foreign strife was beginning to emerge.

Treaties with foreign Powers frequently invited so much discord within the Confederation that perceptive-minded leaders began to speak out against all foreign alliances. In so doing they re-expressed the thoughts of Niklaus von Flüe (Brother Klaus) who in 1481 had inveighed with great effect against entangling involvements of his countrymen in the affairs of other countries (see Chapter 4, Note 19). Hans Waldmann, the gifted but unfortunate mayor of Zurich, had also urged a similar policy of restraint.

An incident, whereby Swiss mercenaries in the service of the French were employed against the forces of the emperor in Italy, had a remarkable result. The kaiser made pressing representations to the Swiss against this French duplicity—a breach of contract with the Confederation—addressing his complaint to the "permanent and natural friends of the Holy Empire." In September 1504 he wrote to all of the cantons and requested that they remain neutral, they they help no foreign State, that they forbid their vassals and all subjects to serve any king, prince, or lord, and "that they not go against us in any foreign land." The proposal was not generally approved but the kaiser persisted and made further representations against foreign alliances and foreign military service by the Swiss. Finally, all the *Orte* represented in Lucerne on 26 January 1508 wrote to the kaiser that they would obediently accept his proposal to remain neutral.

The Diet then resorted to the strongest of measures. They denied to the French king any troop reinforcements, and denied to both the kaiser and the king of France permission to engage in recruiting in Switzerland without express and prior approval. Neither France nor the *Reich* honored faithfully this prohibition and the cantons were reminded that they should punish all who violated the order. In view of the internal conflict that split the Confederation during the Reformation into two irreconcilable factions, it was partly Swiss restraint from entrance into foreign alliances and their refusal to join in foreign wars that permitted the Confederation to survive.

Mercenary service, which Zwingli so strongly opposed, was a never-ending source of problems to the Confederation. In the Peasants' War (*Bauernkrieg*) of 1525 in Germany, the Duke of Württemberg began recruiting in Thurgau and Aargau to raise troops to aid the peasants. It was impossible to prevent occasional mercenaries from joining one side or the other and any who were caught were punished. The German peasant leaders were earnestly requested to send back any Swiss soldiers of fortune who had joined their forces. In the war of 1536 between the emperor and France, the Confederation was implored by the emperor to forbid its subjects to serve in either of the two belligerent forces. The delegation sent by Charles V urged that Switzerland remain neutral and impartial in the dispute, continuing to maintain with strict impartiality friendly relations with both parties. The Diet replied by declaring that troops would not be sent to the aid of foreign princes. Zurich urged upon her fellow Swiss a policy of impartiality and neutrality (*Unpartyschung und Neutralitet*),[33] declaring that the time had come for all Swiss to be called home from military service for foreign Powers.

In the Schmalkaldic War (1546–47) the Swiss were urged to be friendly toward those of the protestant faith and not to allow any of their subjects to join the forces that were moving against the protestant States. Bern, Basel and Zurich replied sympathetically and declared they would not permit any of their subjects to give support to the opponents of the Schmalkaldic League. All of the cantons represented at the October session of the Diet denied transit of prospective combatants through their territories. Likewise, the transport of weapons and war materials to the areas of combat was denied. Much of this was being smuggled in from Italy as ordinary commercial goods. The local governor of Baden pointed out that if all Swiss would be true to the Fatherland, then with the help of God all violence would be prevented. Without formulating theories or formalizing basic principles, the leaders of the day understood well some of the essential aspects of neutrality as guiding principles of foreign policy.

In 1545, the Diet adopted a policy of unconditional neutrality. Transit rights (the *Durchpass*) were denied to foreign troops and the transport of war materials through the federated cantons was also forbidden.[34] The Diet informed the emperor of the intention of the Confederation to remain impartial and neutral and to punish any who entered foreign military service.

But as long as Switzerland was deeply divided within itself by its own confessional strife, it was extremely difficult to unite on all-Swiss policies relevant to foreign religious wars and domestic policies with strong religious content or overtones. Many decisions of the Diet failed to be observed faithfully by the cantonal governments. Divisiveness was more common than unity. In the French wars of religion, mercenaries from the catholic cantons went to the defense of the French Crown (catholic) against its enemies. But when the Catholic League turned against Henri III and his Huguenot successor (Henri of Navarre) the catholic cantons and all Switzerland were again divided. Cantons of the Reformed faith withdrew their opposition against a foreign alliance and permitted the Huguenots to recruit among the Swiss. Bern in 1582 renewed its alliance to the French Crown and sent 7500 troops to aid the Huguenots and the Huguenot monarch. Glarus, Basel and Schaffhausen sent a second regiment, and Zurich in 1587 followed through with a third. Swiss were again drawn into warfare against their own countrymen—a terrible situation which ended only in 1593 when Henri IV became a catholic and the Swiss protestant mercenaries returned home.

The new monarch adopted an enlightened policy toward the Huguenots. Though he became a catholic, oppression of the Huguenots ended, and friendly relations with the protestant cantons were resumed. The catholic cantons were gratified by the return of the French monarchy to the catholic faith. Once again, though not deeply rooted, harmonious relations and something of unity were again superficially evident in the Confederation.

Neutrality had its ups and downs. Well-meaning and noble declarations emerged from time to time, punctuated however by numerous violations and failure of observance at the cantonal level. However, as the century came to a close, Switzerland and her cantons had ended their wars of conquest. Territorial expansion, if any, would have to be achieved by diplomacy and not by war.

The problems of developing and maintaining a neutral posture in sixteenth-century Switzerland were many, as we have seen, and mention must be made, in this connection, of the Franche Comté. This "province" for many years was the subject of a good deal of diplomatic pulling and tugging that involved Spain, Burgundy, France, the Emperor of the *Reich,* and Switzerland. In the sixteenth century, Switzerland regarded the Comté as hers, almost as an inheritance. But the French king regarded the Comté covetously, as the Swiss well knew. The Diet sought to exact from the French king a promise that he would engage in no hostile acts against the Franche Comté and would regard it as an associate of the Confederation.[35] The King then assured the Swiss that he would not infringe upon the Comté and would leave its people in peace provided only that the people of the Comté would be equally peaceful toward France.[36]

Kaiser Maximilian and his wife Margaretha now entered upon the scene to urge the Swiss to remind the French king that they, Maximilian and Margaretha, were related to the Swiss through the lands they inherited (Austria and Burgundy), and the inheritance agreement, which, it was claimed, protected them against hostile acts in the event of a war between France and other Powers. They sought a renewal of the agreement which, as originally intended, should be renewed every ten years. The kaiser requested that a date be set for this renewal. The French king replied that he would do whatever was conducive to peace and quiet so long as the kaiser was likewise inclined.[37]

International relations quickly became confused because of the war in Italy, with Swiss mercenaries in the service of France engaged in military operations in Milan, the Franche Comté and the Netherlands. The kaiser, now actively opposed to the French, asked for Swiss help in the Comté, at least 10,000 Swiss mercenaries to serve the kaiser, and permission to recruit the Swiss officers and men.[38] The Duchy of Burgundy must be told to refrain from hostilities against the Comté.[39] Nine complaints were cited by the Comté and renewal of the peaceful inheritance agreement, now overdue, was again urged.[40] Next we learn that Burgundy asked that trade and commerce between the Comté and the duchy be permitted to go on unhindered. Burgundy and the Kaiserin (Margaretha as Archduchess of Burgundy) reported that no decision would be reached without the knowledge and desire of the Swiss![41] At last the delegates from the Comté announced that a continuance of the inheritance agreement for three years had been agreed upon by the Comté, the duchy, various castles, cities and towns, with the consent of the kaiser and Margaretha.[42]

Part of Switzerland, as seen by Sir Edward Unton

Before leaving the sixteenth century, we should take note of the observations of a distinguished visitor from England. The following is from the diary of Sir Edward Unton, as written by "his gentleman servant, Richard Smith" (397). Much of the diary pertains to Italy, but eventually the travellers entered Ticino from Milan and Como and continued on to Basel.

> the whole dukdome of myllane is under king phillip/from thence the firste of October xxv myles to bed to a cytie of the same dukdome called como not faire standinge at the fotte of the mountaines and farthest cytie towards zwechary [Swetzarria (Switzerland)]/in this contry of Lombardie is indefferent good vitaille for travailers the people notwithstanding very subtill and craftie gyven as the rest of Italians to deceive strangers/ffrom Como the 2 of October to Lugano xxi myles Italian/entringe the mountayns at Como and entrynge the zwychers domynion viii myles from Como/takinge bote at a Lago called co de lago [Capolago] in the mydd way betwen como and lugano/from lugano the 3 of October to berlinzona [Bellinzona] xvi myle Lugano a market towne of the zwichers berlinzona is a littell towen of theirs also not withstandinge the people speake Italian for the most parte to mounte godard from berlinzona the 4 of October to a borgo caled Rolo

[Airolo] at the fote of monte san godard vi leags from berlinzona/after we were passed como aforsayde our way laye amongest mountaines mervelous straite in dyvers places and wonderfully to behold for that they ar made for most parte with mens hands forced with stones uppon the sydes of the mountaynes and also hewed oute of the gret rocks in many places so that in many places ii horses may not well mete without daunger/very stony: from Rolo the 5 of October to a littell towne caled torffo [Altdorf?] att the fote of the said mounte san godard on the other syde 7 leages from Rolo this mountaine is from the fote to the topp 2 leages and very stepe the way narow stony and dangerous snow lyenge upon the mountaine both winter and somer/uppon the top of this hil is an osterye [hospice]/al our way unto this mountaine the hills ar very full off chestnutt tres very abundante of chestnuts/but this montaine bereth nothinge but snow and stones/we ffound extrem cold upon this hill/we descended this hill still untill we came to a littell towne called olsera [?] from there rose an enlyshe myle plaine ground and descended again from olsera aboute ii enlyshe myles is a brydge which is called ponte inferno [Devils' bridge] it standeth in a straite betwene the mountaines the beginynnge of the ryver of rehin [Reuss] cometh from mount gadard and at this brydge hath suche a fale amonge the huge stones that is merveylous/aboute xvi enlysh myle from torfo we toke bote and passed the lake of lucerna the 6 of October and so come to lucerna which is vii leages by water lucerna is a pretie toune of the zwichers standing on the lago whereoute runneth the ryver of the rehyne [Reuss/ffom thence we to horses the 8 of October and came to basylea [Basel] the 10 of October the waye in dyfferent/the country more lyke unto the woodland contry in England then any other that I (have) sene their vilages some what lyke also/ffrom lucerna to basill 9 leages basilea is a fair cytie of the zwichers upon the ryver of rehine [Rhine]/ther is buried Erasmus Roterodamus/ther we toke bote the 11 of October to Strosborogh [Strassburg] 14 leages/ . . . this kind of travaill is not very plesaunt but rather very paynfull bothe by reson of colde/and also because we wer forced to lodg in most places in villages and blynd osteries wher we found ill chere and worse lodginge/ . . .

Notes and Comments

1. A few of these banners are still to be found in Swiss museums.

2. In 1530, the overlordship of Neuchâtel passed to the House of Nassau-Orange, the direct line of which ended in 1702 in the person of William III, King of England. In 1532 the ruling Count assumed the title of Prince.

3. *Abschiede* III. 2, 1406–15, 29 November 1516.

4. For a more modern, and blunt appraisal of the Swiss as soldiers we find the Earl of Minto reporting as follows to Viscount Palmerston on 15 January 1848: "The nominal strength of the Papal army, in regular and police force, is I believe between 18,000 and 20,000 men. Its actual strength does not exceed 12,000 or 13,000, of which about 3000 Swiss alone are good for anything" [*Br. State Papers* 37, 829 (1848)].

5. Montaigne (**250**) is surely an exception. He was not an ordinary traveller. He belonged to the French nobility and was accustomed to travel with a "handsome retinue," which in his journey of 1580–81, numbered about a dozen—including servants and muleteers. He was, in general, favorably impressed by the Swiss. He was greeted by "officers of the different municipalities with presents of wine; on which occasions there would be speech-making on both sides. Similar gifts of wine, fruit and game were frequently made by private individuals, sometimes mere strangers." "In truth, in all these parts . . . they show us all possible courtesy . . . They are a very kindly people, especially to those who conform to their ways . . . In Switzerland he suffered no inconvenience therefrom, except that at table he had only a

little clout of half a foot for a napkin . . . and never is a Swiss without a knife with which they pick up everything, and they seldom put their hands into the dish. The exaction of payment is somewhat tyrannical, as is the case in all countries . . . but besides, they added many little tricky charges, contrary to their custom. It is a pity that, however much you exert yourself, it is impossible for a stranger to gain information from the people of the country, unless you happen upon somebody more intelligent than the ordinary, with regard to the noteworthy things of each place; they do not know what you are asking them." In Constance, Montaigne suffered one of the few unpleasant experiences recorded in the Swiss and near-Swiss portions of his diary. This led to a not unexpected generalisation "we were badly lodged at the *Eagle*; and we got from the landlord a sample of the barbaric independence and arrogance of the Teutonic character, over the quarrel of one of our footmen with our guide from Basel." In Lindau, we are told "they are vainglorious, choleric and given to drinking; but . . . they are neither traitors nor thieves." Regrettably, Montaigne's diary records little about the ordinary people of Switzerland (i.e. in Basel, Hornüssen, Baden, Schaffhausen). His associations were with the upper classes whose social customs, eating and drinking aroused his interest and are described with limitless attention to trivial details—wooden spoons, goblets of silver, the courses of food served at a meal, the warmth of the rooms, the dress of the women, and the courtesies to be observed in meeting ladies. Montaigne suffered from "the stone." He even records how much water he drank at each hot spring, how frequently and how much urine he passed, and the nature of his bowel movements.

6. Johannes Trithemius (1460–1516). Abbot of Spanheim by Kreuznach in the Rheinland. One of many distinguished people who visited Brother Klaus in search of advice.

7. Jakob Wimpheling (1450–1528). German patriot, writer, theologian, historian, and politician. Studied in Freiburg, Erfurt, and Heidelberg. Served as catholic priest in Speyer (1484–98), and Professor of Poetry, Eloquence and the Greek language in Heidelberg (1498–1500). From 1500 to 1515 he lived in Strassburg, then returned to Schlettstadt (Alsace)—his birthplace. He believed in only one *Reich* and one kaiser whose temporal power extended over the entire world. He hated the Swiss and despised their type of republican government, which he did not understand. To him, the Swiss were barbarians who lived outside the principles of law and order.

8. Wurstinen, in the *Basler Chronik* (**393**), states that the deaths in Basel alone numbered 14,000 but a cautionary editorial footnote on page 118 points out that this number is greatly exaggerated since Basel's population at that time did not exceed 10,000; Bickel (**40**) put it at 8000 to 10,000. When the first census was taken in 1779 the population of the city was reported to be 15,040. At no time in the 15th century could the population have exceeded 15,000—in contrast to "guesstimates" of 40,000 to 50,000 which were widely circulated. Even the "Schweizer Brevier" for 1971 (Kummerly and Frey, Bern) cites the same inflated estimate of 14,000 great-plague deaths in Basel. The book of the Great Council, the *Ratsbuch*, gave an estimate of 5000 Basel deaths in the plague of 1438–39 (Wackernagle, **378**). The population estimates given by Bickel (**40**) report the following for Zurich: 1357 (6000–7200); 1408 (5250–6100); 1467 (4540–4960); 1529 (4615-5540); 1637 (8621); 1682 (10,800–11,400); 1799 (ca. 10,000). The decrease in estimated population during the fifteenth century may be attributed to the return of the pestilence in 1438–39, and the wars in which Zurich was heavily engaged.

9. Such as Thurgau and Aargau; the transalpine territories were also represented.

10. About 1000 incunabula were published within the towns of present-day Switzerland. From Basel alone, 804 works are reported to have appeared. In the last three decades of the century 46 printers were located in Basel. Between 1501 and 1550 the presses of Basel produced about 3500 works, while Geneva and Zurich, each with 8 presses, printed some 1000 and 500 works respectively (**202**).

The transition from incunabula (early printed and hand-written works from about 1480 on) took place about 1500 but cannot be accurately dated because incunabula continued to appear even after the printing of books was well under way. One-tenth of all known incunabula concern medical history. About 4500 items pertain to the natural and exact sciences, and of these about 3000 are strictly medical. Roughly 220 medical incunabula are known to have appeared in Europe before 1481 (**206**). Second only to Basel, Geneva was the most important city in Switzerland in which books were being printed. Book-printing in Switzerland antedated its production in France; a cloister in Aargau is alleged to have had a press in 1470, and the priory of Rougemont (Bern canton) had one by 1481 (**335**, II, p. 77).

11. *Albrecht Dürer.* This great artist was born in Nürnberg in 1471. After some years (1490–94) in Strassburg, Colmar, and Basel, he spent a year or more in Italy with a long sojourn in Venice (1505–06). Subsequently he was active in the service of Kaiser Maximilian and, later, lived in the Netherlands. In artistry, his works are unsurpassed. He is credited with about 350 wood-cuts, and at least 100 copper engravings. Dürer died in 1528.

12. Drawn from Dürrenmatt (**108**) and Feller and Bonjour (**131**).

13. Huldrych Zwingli (1484–1531). Born in Wildhaus (Toggenburg), Zwingli received his elementary schooling and, in accordance with the custom of the times, attended various universities as a scholar. In 1502 and again in 1506 he returned to the University of Basel where he acquired a basic knowledge of the humanities and matriculated as a Master of Liberal Arts. He then became a priest in Glarus but for several years he displayed little interest in the religious dissension of the day. As a military chaplain in Italy during the war of 1512 to 1514, he became greatly concerned about the evils of mercenary service and the system of pensions based on the sale of such military assistance to foreign States. His political sympathies were strongly anti-French.

Not until 1519 or 1520 did Zwingli become deeply involved in the confessional disputes. In 1516 he went as a priest to Einsiedeln where, in the peace and quiet of the cloister, and with encouragement from Erasmus, he studied the New Testament in the original Greek. In 1518 he was called to the Great Münster in Zurich and entered upon his duties when the religious revolts had already broken out in Germany. Zurich was struck by the plague in 1519 and Zwingli, who insisted on visiting the sick, himself fell ill. His almost miraculous recovery gave him a moral rebirth. He renounced the annual salary he had received from the papacy and threw himself wholeheartedly into the struggle against the church of Rome. He lost his life, along with 500 of his compatriots from Zurich, at the battle of Kappel in October, 1531.

14. The scriptural disputes between Luther and Zwingli were aggravated by linguistic differences. Zwingli used local forms of expression in speech and in his biblical translations while Luther turned to the ordinary written German of the day. He regarded the Swiss dialect of Zwingli with hostility and this may have prejudiced him against the Swiss reformer and his theological arguments. Luther is alleged to have remarked in 1529, following a doctrinal discussion with Zwingli: "Such bad German; one has to sweat before he can understand it." The related problem did not arise in western Switzerland where the language of the people adhered fairly closely to the rules of composition and grammar which had developed in France under the influence of the French court.

15. Because of their protests against the reactionary decrees of the Reichstag in matters of religious faith and practice, the adherents of the Reformed religion came to be known as "Protestants."

16. The so-called "Second Peace of Kappel" is a misnomer. Though it pertains to the agreements which followed upon the second battle near Kappel, it is described in the basic documents as the "Second National Peace" (*Zweiter Landfriede*). This title is found in two separate documents which differ in several respects. The first of the two (*Abschiede* IV. 1b, pp. 1567–71), signed on 20 November 1531 at Deinikon and Zug, constitutes the treaty of peace between five catholic cantons (Lucerne, Uri, Schwyz, Unterwalden and Zug) and Zurich. Negotiations appear to have involved only the representatives of the six cantons mentioned. The second document (*Abschiede* IV. 1b, 1571–75), signed on 24 November 1531, at Bremgarten, is the corresponding treaty of peace between the same five catholic cantons and Bern. A singular feature of these negotiations resides in the affiliations of the participants. Although the representatives of the two principals are not named in the document it is clear that Bern and the five catholic cantons were heavily represented. The named participants were from the cantons of Appenzell, Glarus and Freiburg and, somewhat curiously, a number of representatives of the King of France, the Duke of Savoy, and of several other heads of state (for example, the Duchess of Longueville and Neuchâtel).

Two other documents that are certainly germane, though not designated as part of the *Zweiter Landfriede*, are the declarations of peace between the same five catholic cantons and protestant Basel and Schaffhausen. The two documents are said to be almost identical in wording. Only the *Friedbrief* with Basel is reproduced in the *Abschiede* (IV. 1b, 1575–77). The Basel document was signed at Baden in Aargau on 22 December 1531 and the corresponding declaration between these five catholic cantons and Schaffhausen was signed at Baden on 31 January 1532. Only the catholic cantons and the governing body of Basel (or Schaffhausen) participated in the discussions. The peace that now descended upon the country did not settle the recurring disputes and violence between the protestants and catholics. Almost two centuries were to elapse before the two parties managed to overlook their religious differences and begin to live together in an enduring peace [see Chapters 6 and 7 for the third and fourth *Landesfriede* (National Peace Accords)], by which the civil wars of religion at last almost came to an end. See Chapter 9 for the last of the religious wars—the *Sonderbund* War.

17. Jean Calvin (1509–64), born in Picardie, studied theology, law, and various aspects of humanistic philosophy in Paris and French universities. In Basel, 1535, he soon became a leader in the Reformation and at the age of 27 wrote his famous book, "Institutions of the Christian Religion" in which the whole of the reformed doctrine was meticulously, logically, and with remarkable clarity, laid out. After a rather stormy sojourn in Geneva, during which he met Farel and was encouraged to accept a teaching post, he and Farel in 1538 were forced, for a span of two or three years, to leave the city. During this time he carried on his work, first in Neuchâtel, then in Strassburg. Returning to Geneva in 1541 he established a new structure for the Reformed Church which, divided into four orders, would be headed by a consistory of priests and elderly laymen. In cooperation, the State should help the Church in disciplinary matters and the Church should exercise its best efforts to strengthen the State. Calvin's union of Church and State appealed to the leaders of industry and commerce who became the chief proponents of protestantism in Holland, France and Scotland. Geneva itself became a pillar of the protestant faith.

He was tireless in his efforts to insure strict adherence to the doctrine and practical aspects of his teachings. In this he was certainly a zealot who would not tolerate the "free-thinkers" and their heretical teachings. Witch hunting, hangings, and burnings-at-the-stake were expressions of the religious intolerance of early Calvinism, later to be carried out with fanatical zeal by those of his followers and emigrants from England who migrated to New England in the sixteenth century. In 1559 Calvin initiated a course of lectures in the Geneva Academy which became a center for students from many lands, who wanted to learn from the "master." Active politically, he was greatly influential in strengthening the independence of Geneva by opposing inroads by Savoy, France, and even friendly Bern. The city conferred upon him in 1559 the honor and status of a burgher.

Calvin died in May 1564, just two years before his followers in the Netherlands suffered the burnings, hangings, banishment and cruelty of the Spanish rulers—Philip II and his governor in the Netherlands, the Duke of Alva. (See also J. R. Sinner, Chapter 7.)

18. *Abschiede* IV. 1b, 1501–05 (Par. 3,4), 19 October 1530.

19. By the Treaty of Nizza (1538), Savoy had been divided between the Emperor Charles V and Francis I, King of France.

20. Melchior Lussy (1529–1606). A very interesting biography (in English) written by a direct descendant of Melchior Lussy has appeared in *Swiss American Review*, 13 February, 27 February, and 5 March 1980.

21. *Abschiede* V. 1, 1829–40, 12 May 1587.

22. Valtellina is a part of present-day Italy, bounded on the west by Lake Como and by Graubünden to the north. In the sixteenth century it was of great military importance, for it controlled the passes leading from the south to the valley of the upper Rhine, Graubünden and the Austrian Tyrol. In 1512 the Valtellina and the adjacent counties of Bormio and Chiavenna were ceded by Mastino to the Bishop of Chur in whose castle Mastino had sought protection and died in exile. The territory was briefly occupied by the French who were driven out in 1513 by troops from Graubünden and the Bishopric of Chur. Maximilian Sforza, newly elevated to the ducal throne of Milan, ceded the Valtellina, Bormio and Chiavenna in perpetuity to the Bishop of Chur and Graubünden. In 1530 Graubünden acquired dominion over the whole of the territory—thus excluding the Bishop of Chur. Apart from continuing intrigues, struggles for possession between France and Spain, and occasional forays into the Valtellina by enemy troops, the area remained in the possession of the Swiss and their Graubündian allies until 1797. In that year the three provinces were joined to the newly created Cisalpine Republic. The Congress of Vienna in 1815, under pressure from Metternich, ratified the transfer of the territory to the Duchy of Milan (under Austrian control), thus stripping from Switzerland an important protective bulwark to the southeast.

23. *Abschiede* IV. 2, 1541–51, 8 May 1577.

24. Montaigne **(250,** p. 28) reports on his conversations in Baden concerning the involved relationships between France, Savoy, Spain and some of the Swiss cantons during the 1570s. "In all these parts they receive the name of the king of France with respect and friendship. . . . The Spaniards are in bad odour here."

25. The two half cantons still exist (Appenzell Inner Rhoden and Appenzell Outer Rhoden) each with but one representative in the Council of States, instead of the usual two. Because of a disagreement over taxation, Unterwalden in 1150 had reconstituted itself into the two half cantons of Nidwalden and Obwalden, sometimes described as *Unterwalden ob und nid dem Wald* **(370,** I, 71). Basel also became divided into half cantons (in 1830) known as Baselland and Baselstadt, thus terminating the subjection of the countryside to the city.

26. A German coin, no longer in circulation, equal to about three marks.

27. *Abschiede* III. 2, 397f, 412–13; Zurich, 30 September and 8 December 1507.

28. The emperor and his House were strongly catholic. The declaration of the Diet was important because it indicated the intention of the catholic cantons to refrain from participation in this religious war against the protestant States of South Germany. However, in 1658, the government renounced the interdiction against foreign military service.

29. *Abschiede* III. 2, 414–16; Lucerne, 5 January 1508.

30. *Abschiede* III. 2, 417–20; Lucerne, 26 January 1508.

31. *Abschiede* III. 2, 421–24; Zurich, 15 March 1508.

32. *Abschiede* III. 2, 403, 411–14; Zurich, 15 October, 8 December 1507.

33. Schweizer **(328,** p. 201) states that this expression, as used by Zurich in the instructions to its representatives in the Diet, apparently appeared for the first time in Swiss documents in 1536 (*Abschiede* IV. 1c, 710g, 26 June). In the reports of the following session of the Diet it was replaced by the weaker exhortation, "disengage yourselves from foreign Princes" (*sich aller fremden Fürsten und Herren zu müssigen*), (*Abschiede* IV. 1c, 738v, 31 July 1536).

34. *Abschiede* IV. 1d, 488f, 16 June 1545; 546q, 19 October 1545; 582, 24 October 1545.

35. *Abschiede* IV. 1a, 55; Bern, 1 and 2 July, 1521.

36. *Abschiede* IV. 1a, 59, 60; Dijon, 18 July 1521.

37. *Abschiede* IV. 1a, 150; Lucerne, 1 January 1522.

38. *Abschiede* IV. 1a, 160–162; Zurich, 7 January 1522.

39. *Abschiede* IV. 1a, 168; Baden, 31 January 1522.

40. *Abschiede* IV. 1a, 172; Baden, 11 February 1522.

41. *Abschiede* IV. 1a, 193; Neuenburg, 19 May 1522.

42. *Abschiede* IV. 1a, 223; Bern, 23 July 1522.

6. THE SEVENTEENTH CENTURY

Introduction

In the seventeenth century, the Swiss cantons and their associated city States were held together by an intermeshing network of alliances, and a loose sort of constitution was respected, none too faithfully, by the thirteen members of the Confederation. From outside it probably appeared to be an integrated whole. The Diet met regularly and debated both domestic and foreign policy. It negotiated treaties with foreign princes and potentates and, piece by piece, it slowly added to its strength and influence over the proudly autonomous cantons.

Throughout Europe the century was one of turbulence and strife. When it ended, many areas of Germany were devastated and villages destroyed. Some of these in Southern Germany were resettled by Swiss immigrants. France had also suffered during its sixteenth-century religious strife and its wars in Italy and with Spain. But in the seventeenth century she rose to the zenith of her power under Richelieu and Louis XIV. And the French court became a most significant intellectual and literary center.

For Switzerland, the century was one of comparative peace and quiet. The wounds of religious strife were not healed but there was less violent conflict. It was even a period of progress. The thirteen cantons and their subject and associated peoples managed to avoid any direct involvement in the Thirty Years' War, although the associated three States to the east, now known as the Graubünden, were caught in the middle between two powerful belligerent groups, and suffered all the horrors of war. The members of the Confederation practiced the delicate art of living side by side in peace and tolerance and learned much in the process.

Observations of Foreign Travellers

A LAND OF WELL-BEING   Foreign travellers, probably with poetic license and some exaggeration, described the then Switzerland as a land of well-being whose inner peace and security were proverbial, and where the good burghers administered the affairs of town and country unselfishly and well. Thus Burnet[1] (78, pp. 15 ff.) in a description of Bern reported that the "Peasants are generally rich . . . they pay no duties to the publick . . . I was showed some who . . . had of Estate to the value of 100,000 crowns, but this is not ordinary, yet 10,000 crowns for a Peasant is no extraordinary matter." Again we read "Switzerland is extream full of people and in every place in the Villages, as well as in their Towns one sees all the marks he can look for of plenty and wealth . . . people are well Clothed and every one lives at his ease . . . though France and Italy are both richer than Switzerland—yet the countries are depeopled and in both countries people appear to be in misery and poverty" (78, p. 42).

Stanyan, in a general description of Switzerland, mentions that the peasants are excellent husbandmen. "Some of them arrive at great Riches for People of that Rank, it being no extraordinary thing to see a Farmer worth forty or fifty thousand Crowns . . . The other [peasants] of the Païs de Vaud have not so good a reputation; they are accused of Laziness and of being given to Stealing," (339, p. 138).

Burnet describes an interesting institution in Geneva: the Chamber of Corn.

Citizens may buy their corn where they wish. But the city has on hand always a 2-year supply. The Bakers are required to buy from the Chamber at a fixed price. This gives a good income to Geneva for public houses also must buy from the Chamber. If one buys too much he may return it at the purchase price. In Rome the Pope buys all the corn of his patrimony at 5 Crowns a measure and even that is slowly paid. In fact he then owed the farmers 800,000 Crowns. He sells it at double the price after first reducing the measure by 1/5. That is buys for 5 and, in effect, sells for 12. The Bakers must buy predetermined quantities. Any they return is credited at only 5 Crowns per measure.

Geneva manages to pay 300 soldiers, maintain an arsenal, pay 24 ministers and professors, besides all the charges of government including honoraria for council members out of the corn revenues.

There is a great number of Ministers and Professors in all 24, payed out of it, besides all the publike charges and offices of the Government. Every one of the lesser Council of 25. having a 100. Crowns, and every Syndic having 200. Crowns pension. The salarie for the Professors and Ministers is indeed small, not above 200. Crowns . . . which was a more competent provision when it was first set off 150 years agoe (78, pp. 7–9).

And notwithstanding their neighbourhood to the Switzers, drinking is very little known among them (78, p. 10).

Burnet also reports on the prosperous condition of Zurich:

. . . their subjects live happy for the Bailifs here have regulated appointments, & have only the hundredth penny of the fines, so that they are not tempted as those of Bern are, to whom the fines belong entirely, to strain matters against their subjects. . . . One of their chief Manufactures is Crepe, which is in all respects the best I ever saw (**78**, p. 47).

GOVERNMENT   Most of the cantons were governed by a Great Council (*Grossrat*) of about 200 and a small council (*Kleinrat*) which served as the executive body. The members of the small council were selected from the Council of 200. In the aristocratic cantons such as Bern, Lucerne and Solothurn the governments in fact were oligarchies, since the governing bodies were constituted of family members from the propertied and noble classes whose tenure of office was frequently for life. From among themselves they selected the bailiffs and other officers who enjoyed positions of honor, prestige, and enviable incomes.

> There are six noble Families in Bern that have still this priviledge, that when any of them is chosen to be of the Council they take place before all the Ancient Councellours, whereas all the rest take place according to the Order in which they were chosen to be of the Council (**78**, p. 62)

Burnet tells us that in Bern "the chief Magistrates are two Advoyers who are not annual as the Sindics of Geneva, but are for life" (**78**, p. 15).

> The City of Bern is divided into four Bodies not unlike our Companies of London which are the Bakers, the Butchers, the Tanners, and the Blacksmiths, and every citisen of Bern does incorporate himself into one of these Societies, which they call Abbeys . . . every one of these chuses two Bannerets, who bear office by turns . . . & every one of them has a Bailiage annexed to his office which he holds for life (**78**, p. 24).
>
> The Chamber of the four Bannerets that bear office, has a vast power . . . they have so absolute an authority in shutting men out from imployments, that their office, which is for life, is no lesse considerable than that of the Advoyer, tho they are inferiour to him in rank . . . (**78**, p. 25).
>
> and yet there is so much intrigue and so great a corruption in the distribution of these imployments, that the whole business in which all Bern is ever in motion is the catching of the best Bailiages, on which a family will have its eye for many years before they fall . . . (**78**, p. 17).
>
> . . . in many of their Bailiages, of which some are Abbeys, the Bailifs not only feed on the Subjects, but likewise on the State, and pretend they are so far super-expended, that they discount a great deal of the publick revenue, of which they are the receivers . . . (**78**, p. 24).
>
> There are 72 Bailiages . . . in every one of these there is a Bailif named by the Council of 200, who must be a Citizen of Bern and one of the 200, to which Council no man can be chosen till he is maried (**78**, p. 15).
>
> . . . the Bailiffs have all the confiscations & fines so that drinking being so common in the Countrey and that producing many quarrels . . . The exactions of the Bailif are the only Impositions or charges to which the inhabitants are subjected (**78**, p. 16).

THE PEOPLE   Colorful descriptions of the people are to be found in the reports of the seventeenth and early eighteenth centuries. Burnet continues his description of Bern:

> The men are sincere but heavy, they think it necessary to correct the moisture of the Air with liberal entertainments . . . The women are generally imploied in their domestick

affairs . . . and are so much amused[2] with the management at home, and enter so little into Intrigues that among them . . . they know not what vapours are, which he (an eminent Phisitian) imparted to the idleness and intrigues that abound elsewhere . . . The women do not amuse themselves with much thinking, nor did they know what amours were (**78**, p. 20). The men are robust and strong . . . and have generally an extream sense of liberty (**78**, p. 21).

We are also told that in Zurich

their women do not converse familiarly with men. It is only strangers that put off their Hats to Women, but they make no Courtesies: and here as in all Switzerland Women are not saluted, but the civility is expressed by taking them by the Hand (**78**, p. 48).

ADDISON'S COMMENTS   Addison (2) described the Swiss in similar terms:

Were the Swiss animated by Zeal or Ambition some or other of their States would immediately break in upon the rest . . . but the Inhabitants of these Countries are naturally of a heavy phlegmatick Temper . . . as soon as any publick Rupture happens, it is immediately clos'd up by the Moderation and good Offices of the rest that interpose (**2**, p. 285).

It is the great Endeavour of the several Cantons of Switzerland to banish from among them everything that looks like Pomp or Superfluity. To this end the Ministers are always preaching, and the Governors putting out Edicts against Dancing, Gaming, Entertainments, and fine Cloaths . . . Should Dressing, Feasting, and Balls once get among the Cantons, their Military Roughness would be quickly lost, their Tempers would grow too soft for their Climate, and their Expences out-run their Incomes . . . Geneva is much politer than Switzerland, or any of its Allies, and is therefore looked upon as the Court of the Alps (**2**, p. 286).

We also learn from Addison that in the Graubünden

the people are much more livelie than the Switzers, and they begin to have some tincture of the Italian temper.

JOHN EVELYN'S VISIT   John Evelyn (1620–1706) who spent a few weeks in Switzerland in 1646 left a very readable description of his journey from the plains of Lombardy over the Alps, down the Rhone valley to Sion, into Savoy, and finally to Geneva and on into France (**123**, Vol. 1, pp. 335–51). First, he dwells on the ruggedness of the mountains as he and his friends ascended toward the Simplon.

The next morning, we mounted again through strange, horrid, and fearful crags and tracts . . . and only inhabited by bears, wolves, and wild goats . . . Some of these vast mountains were but one entire stone, betwixt whose clefts now and then precipitated great cataracts of melted snow, and other waters, which made a terrible roaring.

He writes of "narrow bridges made only by felling huge fir trees . . . athwart over cataracts of stupendous depth." He mentions "a few miserable cottages . . . amongst these inhabit a goodly sort of people, having monstrous gullets or wens of flesh, growing to their throats . . . some as big as a hundred-pound bag of silver hanging under their chins."

Evelyn attributed the cause of such goiters to the drinking of melted snow,[3] but added

> The truth is, they are a peculiar race of people . . . it is a vice in the race, and renders them so ugly, shrivelled and deformed, by its drawing the skin of the face down, that nothing can be more frightful; to this add a strange puffing dress, furs, and that barbarous language, being a mixture of corrupt High German, French and Italian.

He described the people as "of great stature, extremely fierce and rude, yet very honest and trusty." On the summit of Mount Simplon they found a few huts and a chapel. After a meal of cheese, milk, and "wretched wine" they "went to bed in cupboards" in a room where the ceiling was "strangely low for those tall people". It was an uncomfortable night and was followed by an incident that throws a little light on the administration of justice. As they were mounting their mules, they were approached by a "huge young fellow" who affirmed that their dog had killed one of his goats. The party "set spurs and attempted to escape" but were soon stopped by a "multitude of people" on their way to early Mass. They were disarmed, confined to one of the rooms "in their lodging" and watched over by a guard. After the Mass came "half a score of grim Swiss" who "sate down on the table and condemned us to pay a pistole for the goat, and ten more for attempting to ride away." If not paid immediately they would be "imprisoned for a day of public justice and might have their heads cut off . . . for amongst these rude people a very small misdemeanour does often meet that sentence." They paid the fines, "and with fierce countenances had our mules and arms delivered to us."

Late at night, after a preciptous and hazardous descent, they reached Brig. The Rhone valley, rich in grass and grain, delighted the weary travellers. By nightfall they reached Sion, the capital of Valais, where they paid their respects to the principal citizen who appears to have provided hospitality for the night. The next day they reached Martigny and noted that the "people were very clownish and rusticly clad . . . with little variety of distinction betwixt the gentleman and common sort, by a law of their country being exceedingly frugal. Add to this their great honesty and fidelity, though exacting enough for what they part with."

In St. Maurice, they paid their respects to the Governor who was eager to send a contingent to the Simplon area to "most severely punish the whole rabble" who had caused such trouble to the travellers over a wretched goat. The next day the party entered Savoy and reached Beveretta by evening. Evelyn was "extremely weary" and promptyly went into a bed from which "one of the hostess' daughters had just been removed." It was pleasantly warm, the linen was not changed, and unfortunately for Evelyn the young woman had just recovered from smallpox. The next day they hired a boat and sailed the length of the lake to Geneva. There, a "very learned old man" who claimed he had once been physician to King Gustaf of Sweden, suspected the smallpox, "bled me, purged me, and applied leeches." For sixteen days in a warm bed he was "tended by a vigilant Swiss matron, whose monstrous throat . . . would affright me." "The pimples came forth" and "By God's mercy, after five weeks keeping my chamber, I went abroad." He dined with a number of important and very hospitable people, rowed about the lake, and visited a fish conservatory where the trout, allegedly numerous in the lake, were sometimes "six and seven feet long."

Evelyn describes Geneva as a "strong, well-fortified city." "Here are abundance of booksellers; but their books are of ill impressions; these, with watches, crystal, and excellent screwed guns, are the staple commodities." The Savoy side of the town was under continual watch; "but, in case of any siege the Swiss are at hand."[4] Outside of the town was a spacious field (Campus Martius) where, every Sunday, the young men practiced with guns and long- and cross-bows. Adjacent to the field was a place for bowling and another for the public execution of criminals. Fugitives from other countries, seeking to escape punishment, were summarily executed. "Amongst other severe punishments here, adultery is death." As for goiter, Evelyn noted that "this town is not much celebrated for beautiful women, for even at this distance from the Alps, the gentle-women have something full throats."

MILITARY STRENGTH   Travellers to Switzerland also commented on the military strength and zeal of the Swiss, with pertinent observations on mercenary service and the pension system. Evelyn had noted that in the western part of Valais

> Every man goes with a sword by his side . . . It is a frequent thing here for a young tradesman, or farmer, to leave his wife and children for twelve or fifteen years, and seek his fortune in the wars in Spain, France, Italy, or Germany, and then return again to work.

Burnet (78, p. 21) reported that Bern was "always ready for war. All the men are listed and posted and she could easily raise 80,000 men." Zurich, we are told, was smaller than Bern "yet the publick is much richer: they reckon that they can bring 50,000 Men together upon 24 hours warning" (78, p. 47).

Addison, some fifteen years later, outdid Burnet in his report on Bern's military capability. "They can send a hundred thousand Men into the Field, tho' the Soldiers of the Catholick Cantons, who are much poorer, and therefore forced to enter oftener into Foreign Armies, are more esteemed than the Protestants" (2, p. 277).

> Meldingen in the center of the canton of Bern[5] is a little Roman Catholick Town with one Church. . . . It is a Republick of itself under the protection of the eight ancient cantons. There are in it a hundred Bourgeois, and about a thousand Souls. . . . Though they have very little business to do, they have all the Variety of Councils and Officers that are to be met with in the greater States . . . the several Councils meet every Thursday upon Affairs of State, such as the Reparation of a Trough, the mending of Pavement, or any the like Matters of Importance. The French Ambassador uses their bridge and gives the Town a pension of twenty pound Sterling. Hence, the Republick is extremely industrious to raise all the men they can for his Service, and keeps this powerful Republick firm to the French Interest (2, p. 277).

Zurich, we learn from Addison, "had arms for 30,000 men in its arsenal," while the Abbot of St. Gall "can raise an army of 12,000 Men well armed and exercised," (2, p. 279). "The king of France distributes pensions throughout Switzerland." "The town of St. Gall gets 500 crowns/year; the Abbey, 1,000 crowns." "The Ministers in particular have often preached against such of their Fellow-Subjects as enter into the troops of the French king; but so long as the Swiss see their Interest in it, their Poverty will always hold them fast to his Service" (**2**, p. 290). Finally, Stanyan on the same subject, reports that in Bern, "the whole body of the People, from 16 to 60, is enrolled in the Militia" (**339**, p. 193). In the war of 1712 about 80,000 men were in arms, of whom 40,000 were from Bern and 20,000 from Zurich (**339**, p. 193).

The Administration of Justice

The administration of justice and the punishments that were meted out reflect the severity of the times. Cruelty and barbarity characterized the judgments by the courts, both ecclesiastical and civil. Burnet reports "a third Adultery is punished with death—also the fifth act of Fornication" (**78**, p. 20). Heresy hunts, burnings at the stake, drownings, executions, and confessions by torture were common throughout central Europe, Italy, Spain, England, and the colonies of the New World.

"Judgments of God"—tests to determine the guilt or innocence of an accused person—some of which went back to pagan times, were applied through the twelfth century and lingered on to a reduced extent in succeeding centuries. Some of the "judgments of God" were Christian in origin:

> Among them was the Carolingian ordeal of the Cross, in which the litigants held their arms out from their shoulders in the shape of the cross; the first to let his or her arms drop lost the case. Diverse as these customs were, all were founded on a belief that such means revealed a divine judgment on the question at issue (**299**).

Religion

Mention has been made of the peace accords of 1529 and 1531–32 by which the cantons or even the communities within a canton could determine their religious future by declaring adherence to the Catholic or to the Reformed faith. Burnet tells us that

> the Popish Cantons made laws that it shall be capital [punishment] to any to change his Religion; once a year on a set day at Mass all masters of families swear to continue true to the State and firm in their religion to their lives end. So heresy is punished with death and confiscation of goods. In Protestant Cantons any who turn are merely obliged to leave the Canton. In Appenzell and Glarus both are tolerated and have equal privileges. But in the year 1656 some of the Canton of Schwitz, changing their Religion and retiring to Zurich, their Estates were confiscated, and some others that had also changed but had not left the Canton, were taken and beheaded . . . Schwitz demanded back its subjects and wanted to proceed against them as delinquents—an old law which requires a canton to deliver up the incoming criminals from another canton if demanded. Then followed a war between the Catholic and Reformed Cantons. Bern and Zurich raised 25,000— commanded by Mr. d'Erlach, advoyer[6] of Bern. The Catholics had not above 6,000. Both sides soon ran off the field. Bern left its cannon and so the next day Lucerne carried them off causing a great tumult in Bern (**78**, p. 26).

D'Erlach was rebuked and the war was soon ended. Burnet reports,

> There was also a feeling in Switzerland that the other cantons should not have intervened in this dispute solely between Schwiz and Zurich[7] (**78**, p. 27).

Before we concern ourselves with the political and economic history of the seventeenth century we should return to the early 1600s to develop as a background further information relevant to various aspects of the social history of Switzerland—the day-to-day lives of the people. In so doing we shall necessarily select those features of the human environment which come vividly to one's attention—qualities which impress one because they differ sharply from the familiar.

As the history of the Reformation makes abundantly clear, religion played an important role in the lives of the people. Rarely, if ever, did this mean a personalized type of religion in which one's relationship to his God was solely a concern of the individual. The Church and the State decided what their people were permitted to believe, including much of what is now considered to belong to the natural and physical sciences. Dogma reached far and wide. Right and wrong were defined as absolutes. There was little room for the skeptic and no place in the social structure for the disbeliever, certainly not for those who openly declared their disbelief in any of the "eternal verities" as defined by the Church. Religious practices and observances were highly formalized and deviations from the rules were not lightly or mercifully regarded. Transgressors endangered the Church, the State, and the people—this was widely accepted; hence, the Spanish Inquisition and the heresy hunts which went on throughout Europe and the New World for many years. The mind may not pursue its inquiries unfettered. The unknown must be approached and studied with the greatest caution lest one might call into question the everlasting truths.

Schooling

Schooling at the elementary levels was far from universal and the subjects that were taught were not such as to encourage and develop the inquisitive mind. In the universities of the Middle Ages and on into the seventeenth century the subjects of study were fairly safe: Latin, Greek, mathematics, logic and sometimes chemistry, physics and medicine. But the Galileos had to be prepared for hostility toward their findings and punishment by the secular and ecclesiastical authorities.

Witchcraft and Superstition

In such an environment, ignorance and superstition were rife. Spirits of all kinds abounded, devils were a part of reality, and the incarnation of devils and evil spirits was widely accepted. Witches were everywhere and witchcraft and sorcery were practices of the devil that had to be rooted out. Heresy was often believed to share a common origin with witchcraft, both being attributed to machinations of the devil within. Trials and punishment of witches were almost a daily occurrence in the late sixteenth and early seventeenth centuries. Dürrenmatt (**108**) tells us that in the present canton of Vaud some 650 witches were consigned to the flames between 1591 and 1665, usually after terrible tortures. In Calvinistic Geneva there were 58 such deaths by burning between 1542 and 1546. Among other charges, witches and Jews were accused of responsibility for the plague epidemic which swept the country at that time.[8] Elsewhere in Switzerland, convictions of persons charged with witchcraft were frequent although the specific accusations varied. Events of unexplained origin, mishaps which one was powerless to prevent, a sudden death of unknown cause, destruction of a building by an outbreak of fire, a crop failure, and sometimes even the simple jealousy of an ever-successful rival were among the many alleged evidences of witchcraft. In Zurich, the Anabaptists suffered under such charges. Although proceedings against persons charged with witchcraft were never formally abolished, the trials, the torture and the burnings at last came to an end: in Vaud in 1680; Geneva in 1642; Zurich in 1714; and Glarus in 1782.

Several studies of European witchcraft in the sixteenth and seventeenth centuries have claimed that the witch hunt was peculiarly a phenomenon of western Europe, not to be found in Russia where Orthodox Christianity was the dominant religion. Zguta, however, cites a body of evidence which suggests that the witch hunt may have been pursued almost as vigorously in Muscovite Russia as in western Europe (**404**).

Monter, in his excellent treatise on witchcraft in France and Switzerland, has provided a checklist of witch trials in Geneva from 1527 to 1681 (319 trials in all), in the Franche Comté between 1559 and 1667 (203 trials), and in Neuchâtel between 1568 and 1677 (331 trials). The three lists are incomplete but other records from Vaud, Fribourg, Montbéliard, and the Bishopric of Basel are still more fragmentary and incomplete. Several panics in Geneva, associated with outbreaks of the plague in 1545, 1567–1568, and 1571, attributed to witchcraft, were included by Monter. Of 319 trials in Geneva, 68 of the accused were executed. In the canton of Zurich, 220 persons were tried between 1533 and 1714; 74 were executed. In the canton of Lucerne, 505 persons were tried between 1550 and 1675; 254 of these were executed. Of those who escaped execution (usually by burning), most were banished, and a small percentage were liberated. Pre-Reformation Geneva suffered a terrifying form of diabolical activity recorded in confessions of plague-spreaders who gave themselves to the Devil, and in return were taught how to prepare quintessence of plague which was used to kill people in order to obtain their clothing and personal effects (**249**).

Population

The population of the area embraced by present-day Switzerland increased but little during several centuries. There can be no doubt that the recurring epidemics of the plague took a very heavy toll. Combined with high infant and child mortality and a short life span there was necessarily a very low rate of population growth.[9] From a base of about one million in 1600 the population by 1700 had increased to only 1,200,000 or so (Bickel, **40**). Nonetheless, Switzerland as a whole experienced a considerable ebb and flow of her population. As many as 40,000 to 50,000 of her people were lost by emigration as compared with 20,000 to 25,000 in the sixteenth century. When the Thirty Years War ended in 1648 a heavy emigration into the decimated areas of South Germany and Alsace took place.

After the alliances of 1603 and 1706 between Venice and the Graubünden there were two significant waves of emigration from the Graubünden to Venice. The emigrants were mostly pastry cooks, but shoemakers, brandy merchants and scissors grinders were also among the emigrants. As early as the twelfth century pastry makers from the Graubünden had moved in appreciable numbers into the Venetian republic. They were well received and, in 1493, formed their own guild.

A seasonal emigration from the Ticino into Italy should also be mentioned. These were the builders of churches and palaces—men who practiced their skills in Italy as early as the thirteenth century. Thousands of Ticinesi made these annual seasonal migrations. They were the builders of the grandest palaces in the cities of Lombardy, Venice and Tuscany. Later they carried their skills into the rest of Italy, other Mediterranean lands, and into Germany, France and even Russia. Others from the Ticino migrated seasonally into Milan where they developed a specialty business in roasted chestnuts, and later in sugar pastries and chocolate (**40**, p. 102).

Balancing the population loss attributable to emigration, was a considerable influx of Huguenot refugees from France. The Edict of Nantes in 1598 terminated the oppression of the Huguenots and ended the first wave of incoming refugees. However, in 1685, when Louis XIV lifted the Edict, oppression of the French protestants was resumed and a great many Huguenots, possibly 100,000 to 150,000, fled to Switzerland. For many, the stay in Switzerland was relatively brief. Nine-tenths of the total eventually moved north into the Protestant States of Germany. Geneva, from 1685 to 1720, had a Huguenot population of 3000 or so. In 1693, Lausanne and Bern are believed to have had 1510 and 1053 Huguenots within their respective city populations. Much of Swiss industry (watches and textiles) owe their origins, not to economic causes but to religious oppression in neighbouring countries, especially France, for the refugees from France and Italy brought with them invaluable skills and "know-how".

Restrictions on Growth of the Burgerschaft

We should also note the seventeenth century restrictions on the admission of burghers. These were widely imposed for two compelling reasons. When the space within the city walls became filled, population growth had to be restricted or the city's area had to be expanded by extending the defensive barrier represented by the city walls. The latter was much too expensive. The second reason was the determination of the small circle of ruling families within the *Burgerschaft* to prevent any dilution of the rights enjoyed by the existing burghers.

Some cities increased the residence requirement: Bern, for example, in 1598 imposed a six-year period of residence before one could become a burgher. In 1635 new burghers were excluded from public offices. After 1650, handicraft workers were denied admission to the *Burgerschaft*. In 1660 a ten-year moratorium was declared on new admissions. Lucerne in 1638 declared that no more burghers would be admitted during the ensuing 50 years.

Admission fees were imposed by most of the cities as time went on, and the cost to prospective burghers rose gradually to almost prohibitive levels. Solothurn, in 1690, not only terminated the acceptance of additional burghers but ordered that anyone who even raised the question of relaxing such a hard policy would lose all his rights and would be expelled from the city.

Smaller towns followed the examples and practices of the large cities. Their restrictions became just as severe. The reason was transparently clear: to restrict the use of communal property—fields and forests, meadows and arable land—to the existing burghers.

Health Resorts

Visits to health resorts to drink the waters from mineral springs, rich in hydrogen sulphide, sodium sulphate and lithium salts, were believed to be highly desirable. Rheumatism, arthritis, paralytic conditions, digestive and metabolic disorders, fevers, and "congestion of the brain" were advertised as curable by certain of the magic waters. Many *Kurorte* (literally, "cure places") still flourish in Switzerland and, in the vicinity of vile-smelling mineral springs, in many other countries. A few years ago during a visit to the Engadine in Graubünden, the director of a *Kurort* assured me that people with diabetes mellitus had been cured by the *Kurort's* dietary care and copious drinking of the thoroughly unpleasant water that emerged from the springs!

In the seventeenth century these *Kurorte* and their hot-spring baths had other very important functions. They served somewhat as holiday resorts and thereby brought together whole families, their relatives and their friends. They had a much more significant socializing influence than the public baths of the fourteenth and fifteenth centuries. The high and the low visited these baths—sometimes separated according to social status, but frequently intermingled. These were festive occasions with much eating, drinking and singing. Stories were told, ballads were sung, the glorious events of the past were related, and the heroic legends and sagas of the early days came to life. Men who had returned from foreign military service told of their experiences in other countries and of the ways of life in Italy, France and elsewhere. With all of the bitterness of the confessional disputes vividly in mind, discussion of religious questions and singing of religious songs were usually strictly forbidden. Attendants were sometimes on hand to prevent fist fights and the use of daggers and knives when quarreling broke out. In some places, discipline was enforced by the guests themselves who arranged courts of their own to adjudicate the problems raised by the trouble-makers and the unruly. Marriage markets flourished. Visits to these baths provided those rare occasions when women could escape from the house. Serious efforts were made to display the young women to advantage and to arrange matrimonial contracts. Although men saw much of the outside world as soldiers, students, travelling craftsmen and itinerant laborers, the women were virtually confined by the customs of the day, from youth to old age, in the homes of their parents or, later, in those of their husbands.

Geneva and Savoy

As mentioned earlier, the seventeenth century was comparatively peaceful and quiet for the Confederation and its close associates—Raetia (the Graubünden) being a striking exception. But the times were by no means uneventful. In 1571, Geneva, threatened from without, sought membership within the Confederation and the protection that this would ensure. However, under pressure from the catholic cantons which were unwilling to accept Geneva and its "heretics" into the Confederation, the request was denied. The Duke of Savoy, well aware of the disappointment and irritation of Geneva over this rebuff, turned events to his own advantage. Numerous attempts of Savoy to strengthen its hold on Geneva eventually led in 1589 to war. Geneva sought the support of France but the war reduced itself to minor skirmishes and ended indecisively in a dubious peace. Savoy did not abandon her objective and in 1602 made a renewed effort to seize the city. In late December, the Savoyards scaled the city's walls by night. Vigorous street fighting ensued and the attackers were beaten back over the walls or killed in the streets, In July 1603, Duke Karl Emanuel of Savoy promised to build no fortresses or to maintain garrisons anywhere near the city: a neutral zone at the border, "four leagues deep," was agreed upon. He also promised Geneva free transport of goods through his territory.[10] The city from then on enjoyed almost 200 years of peace, terminated only by the fall of Geneva in 1792.

The Graubünden

Events in Raetia proved to be more serious and threatening. Indeed the Confederation barely escaped being drawn into the fray. Raetia was torn by the confessional disputes and the attendant violence. It was also weakened by a political constitution which gave a mere suggestion of power to the central administration. Three States or provinces constituted Raetia: the League of God's House (*Gotteshausbund*), the League of Ten Jurisdictions (*Zehngerichtebund*), and the Grey League (*Graue Bund*).[11] The first two adopted the reformed religion, the third adhered to the catholic faith. An unusual degree of democracy prevailed in the Graubünden. In each of the three member States the central administration had but little authority. Real power rested in the various communities which enjoyed a remarkable freedom from the decisions and pressures of any higher authority. Each community (*Gemeinde*) elected its own priest, determined its level of taxation, and its military responsibilities. This state of affairs, the ultimate in political freedom, verged on anarchy and rendered almost impossible, even within a single League, a common policy in domestic matters and in foreign relations. In religious matters, disputes between neighbouring communities were bitter and frequently punctuated by violent disturbances. "The two valleys of the upper and lower Engadin are pointed out by the Papists, as little less than Cannibals towards such Catholicks as come among them" (**78**, p. 72).

August the First—Swiss National Day. The facade of the Swiss Federal Archives in Schwyz in Central Switzerland, with its huge wall scene of the swearing of allegiance to the pact, painted by Heinrich Danioth in 1936. (Swiss National Tourist Office)

The Chapel at Sempach (Lucerne canton) built in memory of the battle of Sempach on July 9, 1386, when the Swiss again defeated the Austrians. (Swiss National Tourist Office)

State Visit of Kaiser Sigismund to Bern, 3 July 1 (Swiss National Library)

Appenzell joins seven of the federated cantons as a limited member of the Confederation (Swiss National Library)

The Founding of Bern in 1191. (Burger Library, Bern; from Diebold Schilling's Chronicle). The illustration shows Duke Berchtold V of Zähringen on the left and Bubenberg on the right.

The "Apple-Shoot" by Tell. (Swiss National Library; from the Etterlin Chronicle)

The three founders of the Confederation join together in a defensive agreement sworn to by a solemn oath at Rütli (Swiss National Library)

The three founders and several fellow conspirators meet secretly at Rütli (Swiss National Library; from Etterlin's Chronicle)

Tell leaps to safety from the boat of his captors. (J. H. Füssli, Swiss National Library)

The Rütli meadow on Lake Lucerne. Here is 1291 Uri, Schwyz and Unterwalden signed an alliance which later became the Swiss Confederation. (Swiss National Tourist Office)

Battle of Arbedo, 30 June 1422. (Swiss National Library; from Diebold Schilling)

Extension of Bern from the Zeitglocke to the Käfigturm. The Count of Savoy in foreground. (Burger Library, Bern; from Diebold Schilling's Amtliche Chronik)

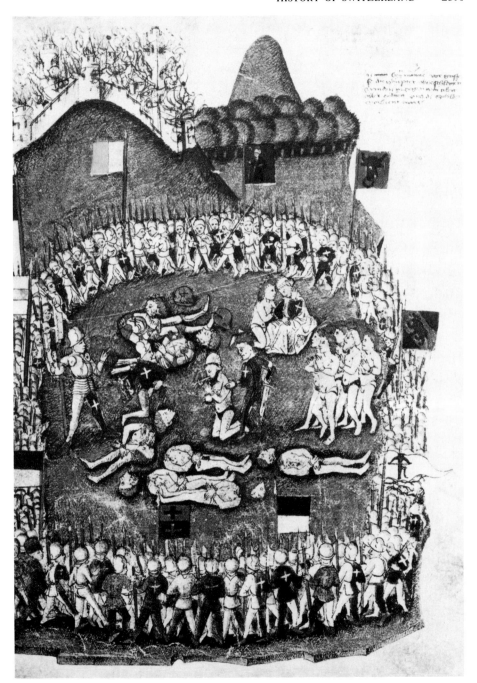

Slaughter of the Greifensee defenders, 28 May 1444. (Swiss National Library)

Battle of St. Jakob on the Birs, Basel in background. (Swiss National Library; from Tschachtlan's Berner Chronik)

Wilhelm Snell (Swiss National Library)

Louis XI of France (Swiss National Library)

Battle on Lake of Zurich at Männedorf, 29 October 1445. (Swiss National Library)

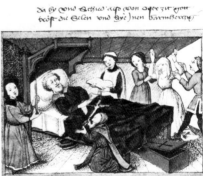

Death of Count Friedrick VII of Toggenburg, 30 April 1436. (Swiss National Library)

The Battle at Murten (Swiss National Library; from Diebold Schilling's Berner Chronik)

Medieval double-walled city of Murten; founded by the Zähringers, circ 1176. (Swiss National Tourist Office)

Niklaus von Flüe at the Ranft visited by the priest from Stans—Heinrich am Grund. (Swiss National Library)

The Diet at Stans receives the message from Brother Klaus. (Swiss National Library)

Hans Waldmann (Swiss National Library)

Execution of Hans Waldmann in 1489. (Swiss National Library)

Execution of the traitor Turmann in Uri, 1500. (Central Library, Lucerne; from Diebold Schilling's Luzerner Bilderchronik, 1513)

Basel is sworn in as a member of the Confederation, 13 July 1501. (Central Library, Lucerne; from Diebold Schilling's Luzerner Bilderchronik, 1513)

Fifteenth Century Executions (Burger Library, Bern; from Diebold Schilling's Berner Chronik)

Beginning of Construction of the Cathedral in Bern, circ 1420 (Burger Library, Bern; from Diebold Schilling's Berner Chronik)

Burning of heretics in Schwarzenburg. (Swiss National Library; from Diebold Schilling's Spiezer Bilder-Chronik, 1485)

The Diet of the ten cantons; Zürich, 23 July 1499. (Swiss National Library)

The great fire in Bern, 1405. (Burger Library, Bern; from Diebold Schilling's Berner Chronik)

A meteorite falls at Ensisheim, 7 November 1492.
(Swiss National Library)

In Lucerne, 1499; a rare dragon in the river and a
steer's head in the sky. (Swiss National Library)

Deliberate drowning of a boy in Lucerne, 1470. (Central Library, Lucerne; from Diebold
Schilling's Luzerner Bilderchronik, 1513)

Burning of Johann Huss in 1415 in Constance, as a heretic. (Burger Library, Bern; from Diebold Schilling's Berner Chronik)

Destruction of the Burg Schwanau (Burger Library, Bern; from Diebold Schilling's Spiezer Bilder Chronik)

The mint of Uri, Schwyz, and Nidwalden in Bellinzona (Central Library, Lucerne; from Diebold Schilling's Luzerner Bilderchronik, 1513)

Fifteenth Century Games (Swiss National Museum)

Cherrywood desk of the 15th century, presumed to have been made in Basel, circ 1440, for the convent in Wettingen (Swiss National Museum)

Pope Martin V visits Bern and is festively received, 1478. (Burger Library, Bern; from Diebold Schilling's Berner Chronik)

Johann Frobenius (1460-1527) of Basel, a famous book printer. (Swiss National Library)

Johannes Stumpf (Swiss National Library)

Battle of Novara 3-6 June 1513. (Swiss National Library; from Stumpf's Chronicle)

Battle of Marignano, 1515. (Swiss National Library; from Stumpf's Chronicle)

Archery contest in Altdorf, 10 September 1503 (Swiss National Library)

Erasmus of Rotterdam, 1467-1536 (Swiss National Library)

Battle at Kappel, 11 October 1531 (Swiss National Library)

Shrovetide festivities in Schwyz, February 1508 (Swiss National Library)

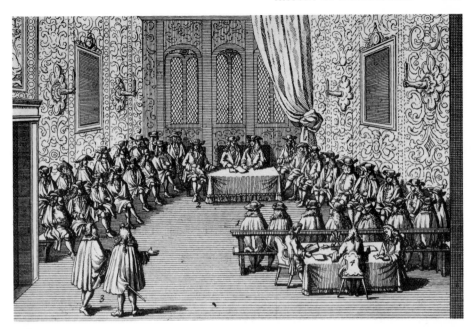

Session of the Diet of the 13 cantons in Baden, 1531. (Swiss National Library)

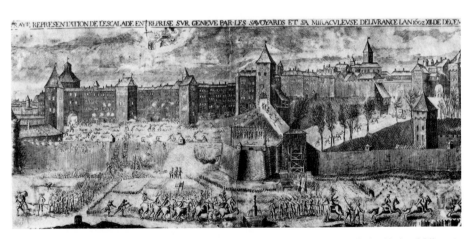

The *Escalade;* an attempt by the Savoyards in December 1602 to seize Geneva (Swiss National Library)

de Saussure's ascent of Mt. Blanc, 1788 (Swiss National Library)

The Peasants' Revolt in 1653. The last of the free men of Entlebuch (Swiss National Library)

Ulrich Zwingli (Swiss National Library)

H. B. de Saussure, 1740-99 (Swiss National Library)

Johannes Bernoulli, 1667-1748 (Swiss National Library)

Daniel Bernoulli, 1700-1782 (Swiss National Library)

A Gobelin tapestry portraying renewal of the French alliance between the Swiss Confederation and Louis XIV of France, 18 November 1663 (Swiss National Museum)

Niklaus Leüwenberger, leader of the peasants' revolt, 1653 (Swiss National Library)

Leonhard Euler, 1707-1783 (Swiss National Library)

Charles Bonnet, 1720-1793 (Swiss National Library)

Abraham Stanyan, 1669-1733 (Swiss National Library)

Johannes Scheuchzer, 1672-1733 (Swiss National Library)

Konrad Gessner, 1516-1565 (Swiss National Library)

Karl Ludwig von Haller, 1768-1854 (Swiss National Library)

Emer de Vattel, 1714-1768 (Swiss National Library)

Johannes von Müller, 1752-1809 (Swiss National Library)

Abraham Ruchat, 1678-1750 (Swiss National Library)

From J. J. Scheuchzer's "Natur-Historie des Schweizerlandes"

Cheese-making in an alpine dairy, circ 1700 (Swiss National Library)

A very conservative force that frequently balanced off the disunity among communities resided in a number of noble families with large estates and great influence in domestic and foreign affairs. Some were allied by marriage or by close friendly relations with different royal houses. For example, at two opposite poles were a group of families headed by the Plantas with their sympathies directed to Spain and Austria, and a second group headed by the Salis family whose support was directed to France and Venice. At the beginning of the century, Austria was allied with Spain—ruler of the Duchy of Milan—while the aristocratic Republic of Venice was an ally of France. These alliances were disturbing to the Graubünden, split by its own internal divisions, yet dependent for trade and commerce on the maintenance of its age-old passes between Austria and the Spanish Duchy of Milan on the one hand, and Venice on the other.

Both of the great European Powers endeavoured to win the favour of the Graubünden because of the necessity to secure their communications over the Alps between Austria and Italy. In 1603 Venice negotiated an alliance with the three Leagues which gave to Venice the right to recruit 6000 men from within the Graubünden. The three Leagues received suitable pensions in return, and all of their people, catholic and protestant alike, were given the right to engage freely in trade and commerce with the Republic of Venice. In case of war, each of the two parties promised to deny the use of the Alpine passes to any enemy of the other. Spain reacted promptly to the provocations inherent in the treaty. The Spanish governor in Milan began construction of a fortress on the border of Valtellina, closed the approach to the Splugen pass and placed an embargo on grain shipments to the Graubünden. A hard bargain was eventually struck. The Spanish authorities agreed to lift the embargo on grain shipments but the three Leagues were required to promise that any movement of foreign troops, obviously Venetian, would not be permitted without the consent of Spain. Trouble at once broke out in the Graubünden. In 1607, adherents to the Spanish cause marched on Chur and through a military court inflicted a bloody punishment on the pro-Venetian leaders. The Venetian party soon replied with similar violence against the adherents of the Spanish cause. The wave of executions ended with a transitory victory of the pro-Spanish party which succeeded in 1617 in preventing renewal of the alliance with Venice.

But all of the incidents and all that had gone before in the history of the Three Leagues were minor in comparison with the major events that were now beginning to unfold. In 1618 the Thirty Years War commenced. The Graubünden became the scene of a companion, and not totally unrelated, struggle that involved several of the Great Powers. The beginnings are obscure although the complaints of the reformed Synod of Bergün against the political stance of the Planta family as supporters of Spain and Austria led to their condemnation as traitors. Their castles were destroyed and the two brothers who headed the family were driven from the country. At the same time, a preacher of the Reformed Church, Jürg Jenatsch,[12] rose to prominence in the political affairs of the Graubünden.

The bloody punishments ordered by the Synod of Bergün created a precedent. In the Valtellina,[13] a conspiracy was formed among the catholic majority who, in one night in July 1620, murdered in Tirano and in the entire valley, some 500 of the Reformed faith, including leaders of the politically active protestants. Only a few escaped. Bern and Zurich each sent troops to support the cause of the protestants—an act which almost led to civil war in Switzerland. This near calamity came about when the five catholic cantons sent troops to Chur to support the catholic party, after first closing off at Mellingen the access road of the two regiments from Bern and Zurich. The Spanish party, now strongly supported, concluded an agreement with the Duchy of Milan for return of the Valtellina to the Graubünden. The agreement provided that only the catholic religion would be tolerated and that the Plantas could return to their castles, allegedly destroyed.

But Jenatsch was not to be outdone. He passionately encouraged the French-Venetian party to new resistance. On 25 February 1621, with a small band of conspirators, he attacked the castle of Rietberg and murdered the leader of the Spanish party—Pompejus Planta. This kindled the flames of battle anew and the followers of Jenatsch rose to a man. Jenatsch himself quickly changed from a priest to a leader in the field of war. The *Innerschweiz* troops in Chur were put to flight and the Graubünden was induced to disavow its agreement with Milan. In October 1621, with 6000 men in arms, Jenatsch attempted to reconquer the Valtellina. The campaign was unsuccessful: in a few weeks the troops returned to their home valleys in the Graubünden.

A political and military catastrophe followed immediately. An Austrian army moved into the Graubünden and occupied Prättigau, the lower Engadine, the Davos area and Chur. The Spaniards seized the county of Chiavenna. The leaders of the French-Venetian party, including Jenatsch, fled the country. The Graubünden was required to yield in perpetuity possession of the Valtellina and Bormio and to cease their closure of the Alpine passes. Chur and Maienfeld, it was agreed, would be occupied by the Austrians for 12 years. Severe restrictions were imposed upon members of the Reformed faith who wished to visit their homeland in the Valtellina. But in April 1622 the people of Prättigau, suffering under Austrian oppression, succeeded in overthrowing the enemy and forced them from their valleys. The protestant cantons of Switzerland hastened to send help to Prättigau. Strengthened by troops from Venice, Chur and Maienfeld were liberted and the Austrians were driven from the valleys. But in the fall of 1622 the Austrians placed a new army in the field. The country was ravaged by severe and bloody fighting and the lost territories were reconquered by Austria. The principal local and district governments were forced to swear allegiance to Austria. Terrible punishments followed. Only a return of the plague brought an end to the acts of revenge. Famine speedily came next to throw an added burden of suffering upon the oppressed.

At about the same time, with the Thirty Years War in progress, imperial forces overran the Palatinate. France, under the leadership of Richelieu, regarded this act, coupled with the Austrian-Spanish successes in the Graubünden and the transalpine possessions, as a threat and decided to intervene in the Graubünden. The Swiss Confederation was itself threatened by the war which now raged near its borders. It was unable to intervene directly in defense of its Graubündian neighbours and associates, but the reformed cantons placed mercenary troops at the disposal of Richelieu. In the fall of 1624, the French army under the command of the Marquis of Coeuvres drove the papal troops, the Spaniards and the Austrians from the occupied valleys of the Graubünden and the transalpine territories of Chiavenna and the Valtellina. Many leaders of the French party, including Jenatsch, who had fled abroad returned to their homeland.

Unfortunately, Cardinal Richelieu was now reminded that his responsibilities to the pope took precedence over his political allegiance to the King of France. The Raetisch regents who governed the Valtellina during the earlier years were unpopular and this facilitated Richelieu's return of the Valtellina to the Papal State. Ferdinand II, whose troops under the supreme command of Wallenstein had been victorious in a series of engagements, now turned against the French in a contest over the succession of rule in northern Italy. The negotiated settlement with France over the affairs of the Graubünden was promptly broken as the imperial troops, en route to Mantua, marched through the valleys of the Graubünden to the Alpine passes. It was not a peaceful *Durchmarsch* but was characterized by pillage, destruction of property and slaughter of the people. At its worst it came abruptly to an end with a return of the plague in the winter of 1629–30. Allegedly, a fourth of the population of the Three Leagues died from this dreadful visitation of the pest.

As the winter ended, the kaiser suddenly and unexpectedly faced a new foe, King Gustav Adolf of Sweden, who entered the war to support the German protestants. The kaiser withdrew his troops from the Graubünden which at once found itself subject to occupation and rule by its saviour—the French. Richelieu appointed the Huguenot Duke, Henri de Rohan governor of the territory;[14] Rohan also assumed supreme command of the French-Graubündian forces. Jenatsch who in the meantime had been engaged in military service in the Palatinate became a high military officer and trusted adviser of Rohan. In 1635, with growing impatience in the Graubünden, Rohan decided the time had come to free the Valtellina of its Spanish overlords. Jenatsch led the campaign and in a brilliant series of engagements drove the Spaniards from the valley. But the peace of 1636 was incomplete. Though rights of sovereignty were returned to the Graubünden, Richelieu insisted that the reformed religion must not be recognized or practiced in the Valtellina.

Jenatsch, determined to free the Graubünden and its transalpine possessions of all foreign rule, suddenly revealed an astonishing capacity for duplicity. While continuing as the trusted adviser of Rohan, he secretly became a catholic and made appropriate overtures to Spain. Still escaping any breath of suspicion by Rohan, he conspired secretly with the Austrians at Feldkirch for such help as might be needed. With equal cloak-and-dagger skill he organized an internal revolt against the French and brought the leaders of both confessions from all parts of the Graubünden together in a so-called "*Kettenbund*." In early 1637 all was in readiness for the uprising. On March 19 Maienfeld was seized under the leadership of Jenatsch. The duke was completely surprised by Jenatsch's treachery and a few days later, confronted also by impending Swiss intervention, capitulated. Rohan and the French troops, by agreement with Jenatsch, were granted free withdrawal from the territory. By the terms of capitulation, the Valtellina, Bormio and Chiavenna were to be returned to the Graubünden as subject lands.

Jenatsch, now supreme commander of the Raetisch troops and governor of Chiavenna, immediately entered into negotiations with Spain to secure to the Graubünden its old transalpine possessions. He did not refrain from terrifying acts of revenge, and with unconcealed threats and with all the means at his disposal he forced his will upon the Spaniards. His tactics and harsh dictatorial ways could not be tolerated even by his closest friends. Resistance against him quickly grew and, in a dramatic Brutus Caesar-like scenario, Jenatsch was murdered during the shrove-night festivities in Chur. On 3 September 1639, the Graubünden concluded a "permanent peace" with Spain. The Valtellina was formally returned to the sovereignty of the Graubünden and Spain was granted free use of the Graubündian Alpine passes. It was also agreed that while the Reformed confession would continue to be forbidden in the Valtellina, the Inquisition with all its terrors would no longer be allowed in the valley.

The possessor of the Valtellina was sometimes Austria, sometimes Spain, and, prior to 1639, sometimes the Graubünden. In 1618, it was as much a part of the Graubünden as could be expected in such chaotic times.

On 25 August 1618, a remarkable disaster overtook Pleurs, a wealthy town near Bormio—a disaster remote from turbulent politics and attributable only to Nature. It was a town of 2200 inhabitants with many noble buildings, possible only in a town of great wealth. According to Burnet, on the date indicated, an inhabitant rushed through the town and told the people "to be gone, for he saw the mountains cleaving. At the hour of Supper the Hill fell down and buried the town and all the Inhabitants" (**78**, pp. 96–97). The disaster has been reported by others and was probably not exaggerated by Burnet.

Not until 1649 was peace with Austria restored. Her claims on Prättigau, Davos, Churwalden, etc. were renounced through payment of a heavy ransom. Austrian claims on the lower Engadine were satisfied a few years later by another substantial payment. If one reflects upon the terrible events that transpired in the Graubünden during the troubled years of the wars with Austria, Spain and France, the conclusion is almost inescapable that if Switzerland had permitted herself to be drawn into the Thirty Years War she would have suffered a corresponding fate; the theater of warfare would almost certainly have reached far into the territories of the Confederation. At the same time, it is regrettable that she did not come actively to the defense of the Graubünden. And yet before one passes judgment it is fair to ask how she could have given effective assistance. The confessional disputes had so split the Confederation that the Diet would be totally unable to unite the cantons in support of either the French-Venetian or the Spanish-Austrian party. Also, what we now call Switzerland was then totally lacking in strength at the center. The jealously cherished autonomy of the cantons frequently prevented any concerted action by the Confederation as a whole. It should also be noted that, if the Swiss had a common policy, it was becoming more and more directed toward noninvolvement in the affairs of the Great Powers.

The Thirty Years War

The Thirty Years War ended in the Peace of Westphalia in 1648, the concluding years being nothing less than a destructive and ravaging war of attrition between the contending parties. Southern Germany was decimated and many of its villages were almost totally depopulated. France and Spain, except for the squandering of resources in war, suffered less. The principal theater of war was Germany since the conflict started as a contest with the kaiser and the catholic House of Austria arrayed against the protestant princes of the German Reich. Switzerland escaped any physical destruction, but the sentiments of the people swayed from side to side with every turn in the fortunes of war. In the early years, with the catholic forces of the kaiser and the House of Austria in the ascendancy, the catholic cantons would willingly have entered the war. They regarded as wasteful any proposal of the Diet to strengthen the border defenses.

In 1628 an imperial army of 28,000 men was assembled near the Swiss border to the north. Though Bern and Zurich were alarmed, *Innerschweiz* showed little concern over a possible invasion. However, in the face of threatening expressions directed by the Austrian forces against the "rebellious Swiss," the catholic cantons finally joined with the evangelicals in an agreement to occupy the passes into the Rheintal, Thurgau, and the county of Baden and to strengthen the defensive installations on the border.[15] In Thurgau a 10,000 man force was assembled from a number of cantons for protection of the long Thurgau border. Meanwhile, the catholic cantons reminded the evangelicals that faithful observance of neutrality required them to avoid any provocation that might induce the Austrian army to initiate an unfavorable action against the Confederation.[16] As events unfolded it became clear to the catholic cantons that a new source of danger was emerging that could prove catastrophic—the entry of Sweden into the war and the imminent danger that the evangelical cantons might enter into a military alliance with the Swedes.

Relations with Sweden

The King of Sweden in 1631 brought his army to assist the German protestants and endeavoured, though unsuccessfully, to persuade the Swiss Confederation to unite with Sweden in a grand alliance against the kaiser. Gustav Adolf did not understand Swiss neutrality and regarded it with contempt. The alliance which he naively proposed was vigorously opposed by the catholic cantons. They saw in the proposal a clear intention of the Swedish king to wage a religious war. In his letter of 13 September 1629 directed to the "freedom-loving and courageous Swiss" he designated Austria as their common enemy. The bearer of the letter, Philipp Sadler, decided that a paragraph or two concerning the catholics was so insulting that he refrained from its delivery. Undeterred by this action of Sadler, the king sent a second representative, Count Rasche, to appear before the Diet and in all obedience to carry out the royal instructions. The letter described the Swedes and the Swiss as blood relations (see Chapter 4, note 9), as people who should be in closest friendship. The count attacked the House of Austria and proposed an alliance of the Republic (Switzerland) with King Gustav Adolf, "the protector of freedom against all despotic monarchs."[17]

In February 1632 the Diet replied to Rasche in the negative; in view of older alliances and especially of that with Austria, the Confederation, while appreciating the proffered friendship of the Swedish king, would enter into no additional foreign alliances. Rasche returned the reply as unacceptable and condemned the "monstrous" *Erbeinung* with Austria. He described neutrality as an expression of "national cowardice, laziness, and treachery. Much better, more wholesome and more conducive to the general welfare, and to the preservation of freedom would be a policy of openness, of frankness and of not acting as if ashamed of your behaviour." In April 1632 the King himself wrote to the 13 *Orte* and offered a halfway sort of neutrality, namely that the Swiss Confederation allow neither the *Durchpass* nor any favors and advantages to the enemy (Austria and Spain). To this was added a royal threat, that of marching through Switzerland against his enemy and thus embroiling the Confederation in a war on its own soil.

The debate in the Diet continued for ten days with ambassadors from Sweden, Austria and France in attendance. It was a moment of grave concern since the Swedish proposal was essentially an ultimatum. In May, the Diet replied to the king that all *Durchpass* requests would be denied, and all threats to the peace and tranquility of their beloved Fatherland would be disregarded. They demanded respect for their neutrality and for their desire to treat the two belligerent factions impartially. The reply had the character of a formal declaration of neutrality. Despite the re-emergence of the old confessional hatreds of the previous century, this decision to *Stillsitzen*—to remain neutral—was finally reached with near unanimity. As determined as ever, the king, assisted by the Duke de Rohan, on behalf of France, proposed a four-year neutrality pact[18] which, from its renewed unilateral provisions, would have abrogated the old Austro-Swiss *Erbeinung* during the life of the proposed treaty. Austria complained bitterly and urged the Swiss not to accept such a proposal.[19] All representatives of the seven catholic *Orte* agreed that the policy declaration of May should remain as an adequate definition of the Swiss position. When King Gustav fell in battle in November 1632, tension within Switzerland diminished and another crisis almost passed by.

Actually, a serious violation of Swiss neutrality in 1633 at Stein am Rhein and a subsequent involvement of the protestant cantons, especially Zurich, in a bitter quarrel with the catholic cantons of Innerschweiz almost precipitated a civil war. The difficult situation that was emerging was compounded by fear that the Swedish army intended to seize the four principal Austrian-occupied cities on Switzerland's northern border. France, urging a strict Swiss neutrality toward the two belligerents, Austria and Sweden, proposed that the cities on the Rhine be occupied by the Swiss. The cities concurred, and requested removal of the Austrian troops and inclusion under the protective shield of Swiss neutrality.[20]

Bern and Solothurn Clash

There were other crises. In September 1632, a contingent of troops from Bern attempted to march through the Jura to strengthen the defenses of Mülhausen, an "affiliated" city in the heart of Alsace, which feared an attack by the kaiser's army. Troops from Solothurn, a catholic city, decided to prevent the advance of the Bernese contingent. A few of the Bernese were killed and about 30 were taken prisoner. The governor of Solothurn may have acted rashly, impetuously, and with excessive religious fervor. Bern protested vigorously and threatened Solothurn with reprisals. A serious conflict was imminent and the outbreak of a full-fledged civil was was feared by many. It was only through the skillful intervention of Johann Rudolf Wettstein[21] of Basel, and the French Ambassador to Switzerland and the Graubünden, Henri de Rohan, that the anger of Bern was appeased.

A Swedish Army Violates Swiss Neutrality

A more serious incident took place in the Thurgau. A Swedish army of 6000 men, under General Horn, crossed the border at Stein am Rhein on 7 September 1633 and marched across the canton toward Constance in an effort to attack the city, held by forces of the kaiser, from the Swiss side. More was involved than a violation of the frontier and the march of a belligerent army through neutral territory. Zurich, which had a defensive force of 300 men stationed in Stein am Rhein, withdrew the troops only a few weeks before the Swedish march through Thurgau. The catholic cantons promptly accused Zurich of being privy to a protestant conspiracy to permit the Swedish army to march through Thurgau for the relief of a city held by the catholic forces of the kaiser. Indeed it was reported to be an open and shameful invitation to the Swedish general to enter Thurgau.

Why was not even a hand raised against him? On September 14, General Horn wrote apologetically to Zurich to explain that the *Durchzug* had been necessitated by the overriding demands of the war against Austria. Did the general request a *Durchpass* from the Swiss? Were his explanations and apologies in good faith?[22] Actually, he violated even the elementary rules of a *Durchzug* in that he fired upon Constance from the neutral soil of the Confederation, not from Austrian territory.

The catholic cantons immediately charged Zurich, which was responsible for defense of the Stein am Rhein border, with complicity. It was widely believed that Zurich had conspired with the Swedish commander, and that the invasion had been planned with Zurich's knowledge and approval. The position of the evangelical *Orte* in general aroused constant suspicion within the catholic cantons, largely because their policy in affairs of state differed frequently from that of the Diet. In 1612 Zurich and Bern had concluded a treaty with the Markgraf of Baden and, in 1613, they entered into a military treaty with France. In 1628, Zurich, it was claimed, was pressing toward alliances with foreign military Powers from which it had earlier abstained. At the Evangelical Conference of 1629, Zurich and Bern, in spite of Basel's protest, urged the creation of a special defensive ordinance for the evangelical *Orte* on the grounds of necessity for protection of the true faith and

Christian charity. Their objective was to vest the War Council with full power to assist foreign princes and leaders of government with men and money. Hans Ludwig von Erlach of Bern, then commander of the Zurich forces, was himself regarded with suspicion by the catholic cantons. He had been in the service of German protestant princes and had also been quartermaster-general for Gustav Adolf from 1623 to 1627. He was known to be a trusted military adviser of the Swedish monarch.

Swiss Neutrality During the Thirty Years War

Without adhering closely to chronology, it may be well to explore some of the incidents of the ensuing ten years that had an important bearing on Swiss neutrality and on the maintenance of peace within the Confederation.

Rasche was soon to disappear from the scene. Because an accord with the entire Confederation could not be reached, Rasche proposed in March 1632 a formal alliance between Sweden and the evangelical cantons whereby the latter would provide men and money to the Swedish army but would deny any help to Sweden's enemies, also denying to Austria and Spain any transit of troops and supplies over the passes from Italy. If only because of the treaty with Austria and the exclusion of Basel and Schaffhausen, as required by the terms of their entry into the Confederation, the proposal was disapproved. But its nonacceptance was facilitated by the arrogant and offensive spirit of Rasche's letter and the contempt and lack of understanding which he displayed toward the Swiss policy of neutrality. Above all it was a most dangerous proposal in that its acceptance would certainly invite a more intensive division of the country along confessional lines. Nonetheless there was strong support in Zurich for unilateral aid to the Swedish army. In May 1632 Zurich wrote to Rasche and held out hope that in the near future a favorable outcome might result—a reply that was inspired and urged by the pro-Swedish party.

Several pamphlets were in circulation at the time, purporting to report on various discussions, actual or fictional, on the problem of maintaining a real or a sham neutrality. The man on the street was reminded of the Biblical injunction, "He who is not with us is against us," which was interpreted in the present instance as, "failure to support Sweden can only mean we are against her."

The most persistent and effective champion of the Swedish cause in Zurich was Johann Jakob Breitinger who became *Antistes* (dean in the Church ministry) in 1613. He led the War Party with the fanatical zeal of one impelled by a sense of divine mission. In his early days, and in the Zwingli tradition, he had enjoyed the reputation of a man of peace, opposed to all foreign alliances. But in the 1630s he preached the doctrine that neutrality expresses a disgraceful national laziness. He opposed the principle of federal solidarity and unity against outside forces. He became a skillful theocratic dictator in the government of Zurich and unhesitatingly exposed publicly all those who, following private exhortations, continued to oppose his pro-Swedish policy. He triumphed brilliantly when his harangues against the authorities went much too far and the heads of government decided to put him in his place. Their reprimands ended in an embarrassing defeat for the statesmen who were no match for Breitinger's brilliance in speech and rhetoric. He scolded them like errant schoolboys. Beyond question, he was very gifted politically and had he not been such a religious fanatic he might have become a truly great statesman.

In July 1629 Breitinger addressed the Great Council of Zurich over the apparent danger of war and indulged in a tirade against the catholic *Orte* "who plan to fall upon us from all sides." The members of the Peace Party were alleged to be entering into traitorous understandings with the catholics. His concept of neutrality was similar to that of Rasche. In October 1632, in a speech before the Synod, he turned to the Biblical injunction (Revelation III, 16) for support, "Because thou art lukewarm and neither cold nor hot, I will spue thee out of my mouth." He urged those of the reformed faith to "make use of the triumphant and victorious Swedish army and put an end to the papist affairs . . . we are bound before God to assist the king."

A close associate of Breitinger from 1627 on was a remarkable military adventurer, Georg Hans von Peblis. Although alleged to be a Scotsman from Peebles County (hence his name), his early history is unclear. At various times he was in the service of James I of England, the Duke of Buckingham, King Charles I, and the King of Denmark. He became closely associated with the Chancellor of Sweden, and was intimately acquainted with the generals of these Powers. After some years of service with Count Mansfeld he and von Salis in 1622 entered the military service of Zurich. In that same year the two went to the Engadine where von Salis, a Graubündner, named Peblis commander of his troops in the Graubündian war. In September 1622, after the defeat of the Graubünders at Saas, Zurich placed Peblis in command of a Zurich regiment assigned to the defense of Sax—a Zurich possession. In July 1629, the Great Council of Zurich, fearing an imminent outbreak of war, commissioned Peblis to a high position in its service.

From 1627 on, Breitinger carried on a lively correspondence with Peblis who seemed ever to be on the move, sometimes in Paris, London, The Hague, Heidelberg, Frankfurt, or at the Swedish army headquarters. Peblis' wife, a German, lived for some years in Zurich and appears to have been an intermediary in the exchange of letters. She had strong political opinions; she shared Breitinger's religious fanaticism and frequently told him what he should preach. Breitinger, in turn, had the utmost confidence in the advice and military competence of Peblis. He urged the Great Council to accept completely Peblis' advice.

Immediately after his appointment by the Great Council, Peblis proceeded to assemble the militia and to instruct the men and their officers in the newer methods of warfare. New artillery, munitions, and other weaponry were procured and cavalry units were organized. He inspected the border defenses and reported that those at Stein am Rhein were quite inadequate—a significant fact in view of General Horn's entry into Swiss territory at this point a few years later. In 1631 he was granted a leave of absence to undertake a mission for the King of Sweden. Peblis was soon able to report that Gustav Adolf wished to express his friendship to the people of Zurich and to offer his help in case the city should be attacked. The king proposed to station an army near Basel as a diversion to Zurich's enemies and as a help to

Zurich in case of need. Peblis accompanied the king and his army on their march to Magdeburg and on to Frankfurt.

Gustav Adolf's death in November 1632 at the battle of Lützen did not bring an end to the determination of the War Party in Zurich to draw Switzerland into the conflict. The secret negotiations that were in progress were only briefly interrupted. By August 1633 the plans for Horn's invasion of the Thurgau were moving rapidly forward. On August 21 Horn moved his army by a forced march from Donauwörth toward Stein. Hans Jakob Grebel, commandant in Gottlieb, entered the conspiracy and in company with a Swedish engineer inspected the defenses on the south side of Constance. Within a few days, Horn, by letter, informed the Swiss border guard of his intention to make a sudden attack on Constance from the Swiss side and requested a pass. Although the facts are by no means clear there is good reason to believe that Grebel failed to deliver the letter until a day or two after the invasion. Captain Ulrich, a courier of sorts, appears to have been equally at fault. He and Colonel Schavalitzki who in 1632 transferred from the service of Zurich to that of Sweden, were advisers to Horn in laying out the best route for the march through Thurgau.

The purpose of the invasion was not simply to attack Constance, but more importantly, to involve Switzerland in the war. The invasion only makes sense if Horn was convinced that it would ensure a military alliance with the evangelical cantons. Indeed in October 1633, Horn sent to Zurich, through Schavalitzki, the draft of a proposed alliance with Sweden.[23]

Breitinger's role as the chief actor in this fast-moving drama of plots and counterplots is quite clear. Apparently he did not know exactly when the Swedes would invade Thurgau and did not expect it so soon. Though surprised, he was delighted, as indicated in letters to his friends in Bern. In a feverish effort to gain the support of Bern in a military alliance of the evangelical cantons with Sweden he reported the mood of Zurich to be far more favorably disposed toward war than it actually was. He alleged that, from burghers to subjects, no one was against war and among the upper classes a remarkable unity existed in support of the cause.

Horn's march on Constance and his plan to attack the city from the Swiss side proved to be of no avail. The Swedish troops returned to Stein am Rhein on October 3 and re-entered Germany. The circumstances that attended this violation of neutrality, some of which have been mentioned in preceding paragraphs, raised the greatest concern within the catholic cantons. Zurich tried to place the blame on the catholic commander of the military posts at Eschenz and Steckborn. Kesselring, commander of the guards in Thurgau, an appointee of the Diet, was of the Reformed faith. He was accused by the catholics and charged with complicity in the Swedish violation. Partly to appease the catholics, Kesselring was made a scapegoat. He was arrested by the catholic governor (*Landvogt*) of Thurgau, tortured, heavily fined, and imprisoned. This severe treatment aroused among the protestants in Bern and Zurich immediate counter-measures. Kesselring, a native of Thurgau, was also a burgher of Zurich and therefore enjoyed the protection of the city. Basel and Schaffhausen attempted to restrain the authorities in Zurich who, along with Bern, decided upon a direct approach to General Horn, seeking his military help in a punitive expedition and at the same time appropriate measures in south Germany to hold the kaiser in check.

The Diet met for ten days in early September. The representatives of Zurich insisted they had had no advance knowledge of Horn's plans. This disclaimer was not accepted by the representatives from the catholic cantons who urged that immediate measures be taken to drive the Swedes out of the country. The Diet condemned the invasion as a violation of neutrality for which there were no extenuating circumstances. In advising Horn of this action they requested assurance that such an event would not recur and that Horn's army would speedily leave. Zurich refused to accede to the catholic plan to drive out the Swedes and the War Council sent Ulrich and Grebel on a secret mission to Horn to ensure Swedish help in case the catholic cantons, now deeply aroused, should form a military alliance with the Austrians. Adding to the anger of the catholics was Zurich's tactless supply of the additional powder and cannonballs to the besiegers of Constance.

On 6 September 1634, the Swedish troops suffered a severe defeat at Nordlingen. This curbed the militant proposals of Bern and Zurich. Otherwise, civil war would certainly have broken out and, with equal probability, Switzerland would have been drawn into the war between the Great Powers. Kesselring was released from prison in 1634 and a restoration of internal peace appeared to be more promising.

The catholic cantons, however, were enraged over Zurich's delivery of munitions to Horn, also by hostile pamphlets stemming from the siege of Constance, and by the persistent assertions of the War Party in Zurich about the inevitability of war. The complaints focused on the War Council in which Breitinger, Peblis, and three others exercised dictatorial power. Despite their apparent success in driving the whole country toward a military alliance with Sweden, the peace-seeking elements of the population, even in Zurich, were not without strength. They were shocked by the actions of the War Council and the threats of the catholic *Orte*. The remaining evangelical cities were equally dismayed by the arbitrary decisions of the Zurich War Party. On 23 January 1634, the Zurich War Council met with representatives from Bern and with von Erlach to plan the details of a war on the catholics—so it was alleged by the five *Orte*. A large Swedish army would be joined by forces from Zurich, and from territory on the German side of the Rhine a cavalry regiment would be recruited and organized by Schavalitzki. Staging areas were decided upon. Lucerne and Schwyz would be invaded and, with anticipated assistance from Rohan's French army in the Graubünden, Uri would likewise be attacked.[24]

Had this plan been carried out, the Confederation would have fallen apart. Most important to all of the federated cantons was the preservation of the Fatherland and not a renewal of warfare between the confessions coupled with direct involvement in the war beyond its frontiers. Serious differences over various aspects of the plan arose among the strategists and between the evangelical cantons. Horn and Peblis tried to persuade Bern to sign an alliance with Sweden. This she refused to do and, finally, all of the evangelical *Orte* refrained in unison. The general Diet of 21 May 1634, put the stamp of approval on this decision and catholics and protestants alike united in a policy of peace within and continued friendly relations with their powerful neighbours. The strong inner neutrality of the various *Orte* saved the country. All of the cantons joined in a reaffirmation of their historic policy of neutrality and impartiality toward the belligerent States beyond their borders.

Another Violation of Swiss Neutrality

Another threatening incident occurred in January 1638 when the troops of the Duke of Weimar, though denied permission to do so, marched from Delsberg through Basel territory for an attack on the Austrian cities of Säckingen, Waldshut, and Laufenburg. It was alleged that the Bernese colonel, von Erlach, who was also a member of the cantonal government, was involved in this bit of military strategy. Bern was now accused of complicity and a situation again arose which threatened domestic peace. Erlach resigned from the government and entered the service of the duke. The Diet, deeply troubled by this questionable behaviour of von Erlach, and finally convinced that something must be done to strengthen the neutrality of the land, resolved in 1638 that the movement of foreign troops through the territories of the Confederation must be forbidden forever.[25] At last, the threat to her neutrality, inherent in the passage of foreign troops through the country, was recognized.

The Defensionale of Wyl

In January 1647 the important *Defensionale of Wyl* was unanimously adopted.[26] This stemmed from a decision that there be a Federal Council of War and that arrangements be made immediately for the defense of the frontiers by an all-Swiss army. Each of the cantons and associates was pledged to provide a stated number of troops and of equipment—700 men in all—500 to be stationed immediately at assigned places along the Thurgau border and 200 in the Rhine valley. Twelve thousand men, fully armed and equipped, contributed by 20 *Orte* (cantons and associated city States) were to be in readiness against any possible invasion. They were assigned as two army corps, each of 6000 men, for rendezvous at Frauenfeld and Bischoffzell. After these troops were dispatched, the *Defensionale* provided that 24,000 men contributed by each *Orte* in the same proportion as before, be in readiness as a reserve force. The *Defensionale* fixed the size of each company, defined the necessary equipment, the number and rank of officers, and arrangements for payment. The *Defensionale* should be regarded as the most important intercantonal or all-Swiss agreement since the early defensive alliances of the young Confederation, for it constituted the first major step toward an effective Federal Government at the expense of a small portion of cantonal autonomy. Defense of the frontiers now became a federal responsibility. No longer was it incumbent upon each and every border canton to defend its own stretch of the frontier with strictly cantonal troops.

The *Defensionale* was renewed in 1668 but was seriously endangered in 1677 when the catholic cantons of Appenzell Innerrhoden, Obwalden, Uri, Schwyz, Zug and the catholic part of Glarus withdrew from the Federal Pact. In so doing they were motivated by the unending religious dispute with the reformed cantons, by fear of dominance by the large cantons, by displeasure with the rigidity of organization necessary for the federal army, and by their own economic weakness. Fortunately the rest of the cantons stepped into the breach and the defensive capability of the Confederation was not weakened.

Switzerland becomes Independent of the Empire

As the Thirty Years War drew to a close, the Swiss Confederation sought representation in the negotiations between the Great Powers. Their first objective was to be set free from the juridical authority exercised by the Supreme Court of the Reich to which all member States were subject. After many difficulties and frustrations, Rudolf Wettstein[21] was formally permitted to participate in the negotiations at Münster, but only as the representative of Basel and of the protestant cantons. In fact, however, he served impartially on behalf of the entire Confederation. He worked patiently with two objectives in mind: freeing of the Confederation from the juridical authority of the Supreme Court of the Reich, and formal recognition of Switzerland as an independent State among the treaty-making Powers. His patience and persistence were ultimately rewarded. In October 1647 the supreme authorities of the Reich, with the confirmation of the emperor, decreed that Basel, the thirteen Swiss cantons, their associated city States and territories held in common, were no longer to be subject to the Reich and the Imperial Courts. The final document appeared under the date of 16 May 1647, and constituted Article VI of the Peace of Westphalia which was concluded in October 1648. This gave to the Swiss Confederation total independence from the empire which it had factually enjoyed since the Swabian War. Of great importance was international recognition of the severance of all ties with the empire and the elevation of the Confederation as a whole to the status of a treaty-making Power. From this, one can only conclude that the right of individual cantons to enter into treaties and agreements with foreign States was tacitly diminished.

The Peace of Westphalia was not a complete answer to Switzerland's problems with her neighbours. Lotharingia (Lorraine) and the Franche Comté were excluded from the Peace, and Spain continued at war until 1659. In the spring of 1652 undisciplined forces from Lotharingia and Brandenburg overran Alsace; Mülhausen, bound by treaty to the evangelical cantons, was threatened. Territory belonging to Basel and Solothurn was overrun. The danger was significant and the *Defensionale* was called into play.

Louis XIV Seizes the Franche Comté

Louis XIV's campaign of 1667 and 1668 was directed against the distant Spanish Netherlands but the Franche Comté also became involved through its relationship to Spain.[27] The decision of the Diet in 1667 to defend energetically the Comté could not be effectively implemented because the catholic *Orte* were allied to Spain. Hence, in 1668, the French were able to seize the Franche Comté without Swiss resistance. This unexpected act of the French led speedily to a revision and strengthening of the *Defensionale*.[28] The French withdrew their forces but reoccupied the Comté in 1674. (The annexation was confirmed and recognized by the Treaty of Nimeguen in 1678.) Spain was unable to put up much resistance although Austrian troops under Count Stahremberg tried to support the Spanish defenders. This effort of Stahremberg required passage through Basel territory. The force of 550 men marched from the Birs bridge down the west bank of the Birs into the Bishopric of Basel. This was done without Swiss permission but, fortunately, there were no grave consequences. At Basel's request 2000 Swiss troops arrived on the scene. However, they were much too late.[29] Austria apologized for Stahremberg's transgression and claimed that he had acted without knowledge of the government and against his given word.

The Confederation's War Council which met frequently from 1674 to 1676 had full powers and even received foreign diplomats. Naturally there were complaints about the power exercised by the War Council. Schwyz was a center of agitation against the Council and the *Defensionale*. Mistrust, rumors, and lies were so damaging that by 1679 most of the catholic *Orte* withdrew from the *Defensionale*. The remaining *Orte* filled the gap with additional men and weapons and the federal strength in defense was not significantly weakened. It is of interest that the catholic cantons, despite their formal withdrawal, promised that if any Swiss territory was invaded, they would come to the defense with all their strength in accordance with the terms of the ancient alliances.

While neighbouring States, especially South Germany, Northern Italy and the Graubünden were greatly weakened by the prolonged war, the Confederation enjoyed prosperity—commercial and agricultural.[30]

The Search for Security

Many of its people were affluent and the well-being, now experienced, brought with it a desire for increased security. The city and the country—peasants, laborers, artisans, craftsmen, and merchants—were all eager to protect themselves against the hard times that were sure to come, and to maintain possession of what they had won. There was much uncertainty about the political well-being of the country.

The tremendous task of reconstruction in south Germany, of repairing the damage wrought by the war, was left to the German princes and heads of States. In France, thanks to Sully and Richelieu, it was more of a national undertaking. In Germany it was a time when much power, lost by the monarchy, was appropriated by the heads of States who henceforth enjoyed a greatly increased independence in government.

In Switzerland, the struggle for increased security took several forms not all of which were in the national interest. In the cities, efforts were made to limit the number of families invested, *de facto*, with the power of government. At the same time determined efforts were made to tighten the control exercised by the cities over their subject country areas, and to render much more difficult elevation of those who moved into the cities to the status of a burgher. Recognized as a haven of security and a country of prosperity, many foreigners emigrated to Switzerland, the beginnings of a long-continuing penetration by foreigners. In time this added helpfully to the work force but created a variety of problems. Acquisition of land by foreign speculators, and an eventual *Überfremdung* by a multitude of foreign workers who were not all eligible for citizenship and who were not assimilated into the native population, have been recognized in recent years as the most troublesome.

Class distinctions, which meant little in the early days of the Confederation, began to play an important role in political and social life. In the cities, the right to occupy offices in government and in the army became more rigidly restricted to certain families. In Bern, Lucerne, Freiburg, and Solothurn this class took form as a real patriciate. Below the patricians a nondescript class of citizens existed who were, in effect, ineligible for political and military office. At the bottom of the scale a large proportion of the city's population was denied all political rights. In the rural towns, class distinctions also became more evident, especially in the rights and privileges of different levels of the citizenry. In the days of the Reformation, government tried to be receptive to and to encourage popularly-supported initiatives. The times had hardened and the practice of trying to ascertain the popular will gradually vanished. The subjects had to obey and government felt under no obligation to listen first to popular demands.

In economic matters such cities as Basel and Zurich, among others, with a substantial representation of the guilds in city government took appropriate measures to protect themselves from competition by the people of the rural areas. Restriction of the rural areas to agriculture and animal husbandry was a popular device, thus forcing the countryside to turn to the cities for the purchase of most nonfarm items. Inevitably this heightened the tension between city and country. Quarrels at government level and bitter misunderstandings arose. In the early 1650s a sudden fall in prices brought the quarrels to a head and precipitated the second Peasants' War.

The Second Revolt of the Peasants

The first Peasants' War during the days of the Reformation was a determined effort on the part of a poorer class in the population to improve their economic lot—of people who knew repression and suffered all the miseries of hunger and extreme need. The war in the seventeenth century was of an entirely different cause. It concerned the peasants and small farmers who had profited greatly during the Thirty Years War. They had experienced affluence and a new prosperity which were now threatened by a severe reduction in farm income. Government, in its attempts to enhance the security of the Confederation and to ensure the well-being of its people, was alleged to be devoting its efforts to the special interest of the cities, ignoring the needs of the countryside. Government was also accused of limiting the ancient freedoms of the small farmers by restrictive measures. The internal dissension was aggravated by the consequences of the *Defensionale*. There was general agreement that at least minimal precautions must be taken for protection of the borders. But this cost money, especially since repeated calls for the levy of troops were made. The principal cities faced up to the problem by the imposition of special taxes. Initially these fell only upon the burgher class, but in the concluding phase of the Thirty Years War the villages and towns in the countryside were told that they must share the burden. There was immediate opposition, principally because the decision was unilateral. Unlike the practices of the past, no opportunity was given to the villagers, the peasants, and the small farmers to participate in the decision-making. The situation was almost parallel to the complaints of the colonists in the days leading up to the American Revolutionary War—"Taxation without Representation." There was in this breakdown of communication a lack of adequate explanation to the newly taxed, and no financial accounting—both conducive to·mistrust and bitterness. The governments, meanwhile, tried to compensate for the increased expenditures, attributable to the war, by debasing the currency and by continuing the special wartime taxes even after the war was a thing of the past. Late in 1652 the authorities of Bern suddenly reduced the purchasing value of the batzen[31] to one-half of its former value and allowed three days only during which the old currency could be used as legal tender.

The first manifestation of deep unrest was in the Lucerne town of Entlebuch, where the farmers and peasants of the area were acutely conscious of their age-old freedoms. Dear to them were the traditions and practices of the old *Landsgemeinde* in which a grass-roots democracy flourished. Though subject to Lucerne, the people of the countryside were also accustomed to enforcement by their own people of administrative measures decided upon at their *Landsgemeinde*. A three-man delegation was sent to Lucerne to urge the authorities to annul the terrible ordinance of 1652 concerning currency devaluation, to remove the tax on salt, and to permit payment of property taxes with goods instead of money. The delegation was completely unsuccessful. The firm denial was even accompanied by threats of military action—an indication of the depth and extent of ill-will that had arisen. It led, inevitably, to more insistent demands for increased rights of self-determination by the people of Entlebuch and of the valley. In February, 1653, a *Landsgemeinde* of the peasantry, now supported by ten other districts subject to Lucerne, assembled in Wolhusen. A properly prepared document of alliance for the common cause was prepared and sworn to. Many priests and clerics appeared on the side of the country folk.

Initial attempts at peaceful settlement of the dispute were unsuccessful. Lucerne invited the catholic *Orte* to mediate the quarrel but the efforts failed. Three thousand armed peasants marched on Lucerne. The city closed its gates and the peasants pitched camp outside the city. At this point, further efforts by the catholic *Orte* led to an armistice under which some of the peasants' demands were granted. The peasants dissolved their alliance and returned home, satisfied with the assurances of the authorities at Lucerne. But peace had not been restored. An influential element in Lucerne disagreed with the settlement and called upon the Diet to consider the problem. The discontent of the peasants had by this time extended into several other cantons. The Diet, putting aside all confessional differences, decided to make an example of the "rebels". Under the authority of the Stanser *Verkommnis* of 1481 which pledged the cantons to act in concert against rebellious subjects, the Diet issued an open letter—a manifesto—which labelled the peasants and their supporters as wicked disturbers of the peace and warned them of the punishment to be expected if their rebellion continued.

The warning served only to kindle again into flame the anger of the peasants. In many parts of the Confederation the peasants were stirred into renewed action. To them the widening gulf between the peasants and the gentry reflected the serious differences in policy between the peasant communities and the Diet—regarded as an assembly of the gentry, the rich and powerful families. In the disputes which raged and the class war which threatened the Confederation, confessional differences were for the moment forgotten. Serious attempts to effect a reconciliation were unsuccessful. The peasants, called together to organize a formal alliance of the farming areas, met at Sumiswald in April 1653 and appointed three of their number to military and political leadership in the movement. Assembled again, three thousand strong, at Huttwil one month later, the peasants formed a binding alliance and, under oath, united for ten years in their common cause. In seven Articles, the document which was signed and sealed recognized the necessity of maintaining the Confederation as such, but pointed to the governing authorities as enemies of the small farmers. The measures to be taken against traitors were defined and the responsibilities of the peasant communities in the interests of mutual assistance were spelled out in some detail. The authorities, now thoroughly alarmed, tried to renew negotiations in the interest of achieving a peaceful solution of the continuing dispute. Disillusioned by previous experiences and filled with mistrust of government, the peasants marched on Bern. They were under the command of Niklaus Leüwenberger who was not gifted with the qualities that the movement needed. This siege of the capital city was easily possible only in Switzerland because within the whole of Europe there was no other country in which all men of military age would have combat weapons in their possession at all times[32] (see Häne **163**, p. 6). The city closed its gates and immediately entered into discussions with the peasants. Within a week a treaty was signed—the so-called Treaty of Murifeld. The peasants yielded to the authorities and dissolved their League. Fifty thousand pounds were promised the peasants as war damages and assurances were given that various complaints would be sympathetically examined and the leaders would not be subject to any acts of revenge. Leüwenberger recommended acceptance of the government's proposal and, naively, failed to ask for firm guarantees of performance. The peasants' army of 16,000 men was dissolved and the men returned home.

At this point, the Diet again intervened and with renewed determination to put the peasants in their place, set aside the Bern accord and resorted to military action. Troops were raised from among those districts in which the peasants had little strength and where the authorities were clearly hostile to the demands of the peasants. Several armies under the command of experienced officers took to the field. In district after district, the peasants were completely defeated. The Bernese authorities nullified the promises given in the Treaty of Murifeld and the authorities demanded punishment of the leaders of the rebellion. Leüwenberger was arrested, tortured and executed. Some were executed by the sword, others were strangled, and many were ruined by the imposition of crushing fines. In some cases, various precious freedoms were withdrawn from the rebellious rural communities. Some of the complaints of the peasants were recognized, especially in the administration of justice. Among the reforms, it might be noted that sale of convicted persons to Venice for service as galley slaves was no longer permitted.

A curious observation by Burnet is relevant to any discussion of peasant revolts:

> [In Solothurn] the fortifications cost about 2 million livres and they often resent the expensive undertaking . . . it is certain that a fortification that is able to resist the rage of their Peasants in the case of a Rebellion is all that is needful (**78**, p. 46).

The Waser Proposal for Federal Reform

An important proposal concerning federal reform was set forth by *Bürgermeister* Waser of Zurich. He recommended to the Diet that the various *Bundesbriefe* under which the cantons were joined together as members of the Confederation be consolidated into a single document of 29 Articles. This would ensure a uniformity of action, from canton to canton, on matters of broad importance between government and its subjects. The proposal was not accepted. One might well infer that it would be regarded as an unwarranted trespass upon cantonal autonomy. Some reforms did result, such as a redefinition of the obligations of local governors and an urgent recommendation that they be more friendly and understanding in their relations with the people.

The First Villmergen War

The peasants' revolt had hardly come to an end, before the confessional quarrels broke out anew. The basic tensions, subdued during some years of tenuous peace, had not been resolved and again threatened the Confederation with civil war. France made determined efforts to prevent such a war, not because of any interest in a peaceful Europe. Rather, Louis XIV and his minister Mazarin sought to strengthen the position of France as the leading European Power. Civil war in Switzerland would certainly cut off the flow of Swiss mercenaries which France urgently needed and which had been assured by the treaty of 1614 with Switzerland. The agreement expired in 1651. Its renewal was of the utmost importance to Louis XIV.

The mediation efforts of France were unsuccessful. The catholic cantons, mistrustful of the policies of Zurich and Bern, decided to draw more closely together and to restore the bonds of catholic unity. In 1651 they renewed the treaty of 1560 with the Duke of Savoy. This accord seriously threatened the close relations between Bern and Geneva. Four years later they extended their alliance with the Bishop of Basel, focusing its impact against the cantons of Bern and Basel and the associated city State of Biel. Later in the same year (October, 1655) the members of the Golden Borromaic League reaffirmed their alliance and added the catholic communities in Glarus to their number. On their side, the protestant cantons invoked the support of Oliver Cromwell, the Lord Protector of England, doing so by means of a special agreement to protect the protestant faith. As an instrument of foreign policy it was clearly directed against France which was fearful of English intervention.

An isolated incident in the canton of Schwyz led to another civil war, the so-called "First Villmergen War." Since the wars of the Reformation, Schwyz was totally dominated by a heavy catholic majority and catholicism was the official and only acceptable faith. Under the leadership of the town of Arth, a few protestant communities continued to adhere to the reformed church. They were repeatedly warned by the Schwyz authorities, who in 1655 forced the protestant dissenters into flight. Zurich, by request of the oppressed minority, acted as their legal representative and urged the Schwyz authorities to refrain from confiscation of the properties of the accused. The dispute soon involved other cantons and intervention by France in the role of a mediator. The rumor spread among the catholic cantons that Zurich sought war in order to divide, to the benefit of the protestants, the sovereignty over certain jointly administered territorial possessions—the *Freie Ämter* (free districts). The rumor was not securely founded but it added to the increasing bitterness between the two confessions. Renewed efforts at mediation were fruitless and, early in 1656, Zurich turned to war. With the help of Bern, she was confident of success. A number of the cantons refrained from participation because any such involvement in disputes between the other cantons would be entirely contrary to the terms of their Articles of Association (*Bundesbriefe*) as members of the Confederation. The armies of Bern and Zurich alone were now faced with the united opposition of forces from five or six catholic cantons. It was widely assumed abroad that the protestant armies would be victorious. Confident of victory the protestant forces marched into the *Freie Ämter*. The Bernese army, isolated from that of Zurich and unprepared for battle, was overtaken at Villmergen in the early morning of 24 January 1656 by the forces from *Innerschweiz*. The result was disastrous to the Bernese army. Almost 600 of their men were killed, 400 were wounded, and many were taken prisoner. The Zurich army which besieged Rapperswil, failed to take the city.

Thus, the First Villmergen War ended triumphantly for the catholic cantons. The two parties met in conference and concluded an agreement that temporarily ended the war. The third Confederation-wide peace was signed in Baden on 7 March 1656.[33] This reaffirmed the sovereignty of the cantons in confessional matters and declared that confessional disputes within the territory of the *Freie Ämter* were to be arbitrated by a Court in which the two confessions would be equally represented. Some of the Articles in the treaty concerned purely military affairs. Agreement prevailed that the weaponry and methods of war employed by the Swiss were completely outmoded. A decision to introduce modern weapons and improved methods of warfare was soon implemented by Zurich and Bern but the pike, the morning star, the halberd and the tactics of the past continued for some time in *Innerschweiz*. The delay proved to be disastrous to the Catholic cause.

The Absolutism of Louis XIV

As we return to questions of foreign policy we enter upon a period of great importance in European history. Louis XIV, a man skilled in diplomacy, ruled a powerful kingdom which under his direction became an outstanding example of absolutism in government. The all-powerful head of State was the monarch, an apostle of the doctrine "I am the State." The limited monarchies of England and the Netherlands were anathema to Louis XIV. With a highly centralized government and all the powers of an unlimited monarchy, with a weakened Germany to the east and a greatly enfeebled Spain to the south, France had little to fear. She went far to increase her exports and to develop an even more favorable balance of trade. Money flowed into the country. The death of Cromwell restored a monarchy in England with powers greatly limited by a Parliament possessed of the constitutional guarantees and strength introduced by Cromwell. Louis XIV looked upon the English system of government with disdain and as evidence of internal weakness and governmental impotence.

The absolutism of Louis XIV had repercussions within the small and cautious neighbour, the Swiss Confederation, which was ever-fearful of the frequently volatile nature of French foreign policy. Since Marignano and the wars of the Reformation, friendship with France had become weakened even though pious assurances of France's enduring amity were frequent during the seventeenth century. The Swiss regarded the power politics of Louis XIV and the economic and military strength of France during his long reign (1643–1715) as an overshadowing threat to their neutrality in European affairs. Yet it is also clear that the proponents of the theory of the divine right of kings saw in the absolutism of Louis XIV support for their efforts, most evident in the reformed cantons, to win a Confederation-wide acceptance of the reformed faith.

In June, 1658, as a result of the diplomatic skills of the French Ambassador in Solothurn, a renewal of the French agreement with the reformed cantons, providing for the purchase of mercenary service, was achieved. As a by-product, the position of the Franche Comté in relation to France and the Confederation remained clouded in obscurity. The Swiss claimed sovereign rights over the county but it was still loosely chained to France.

The Treaty of 1663 with France

In 1663, the agreement for the purchase of Swiss mercenary service was extended to all thirteen cantons and the associate members of the Confederation (**103**, IV, 93). The signing of the treaty was festively celebrated in Paris following upon administration of the oaths in the Church of Notre Dame. Over 200 representatives from all of the cantons participated in the ceremonies. Of great importance to France was the right to recruit 16,000 Swiss troops. In return each canton was to receive from France a yearly payment of 3000 francs and each of the associated city States 1500 francs. The Confederation was also given the right to buy salt and grain, duty-free, from France. The eastern cantons tried unsuccessfully to persuade the French to permit duty-free export into France of the products of their developing textile industry. Their fellow Swiss were satisfied with the restoration of pensions and gave no support to the representatives from the eastern cantons. Again, and to their shame, the Swiss proved that they could be corrupted by money and that their high resolve to terminate their dependence on foreign pensions could be easily compromised. The Swiss policy in respect of mercenary service was bitingly described in 1703 by the ambassador from Savoy: "Les Suisses vendent au plus offrant et au dernier enchérisseur . . . n'ayant aucun profit plus assuré que celui qu'ils font par la vente de la chair humaine" (50). Ruchat (311) was even more severe in his castigation of the Swiss mercenaries: "they do not weigh the reasons but only the money." To this he added an old French proverb, "Point d'argent, point de Suisse."

In 1689, France paid a total of over 200,000 livres in pensions to Swiss cantons and several other suppliers of mercenaries (128, p. 92).

French Territorial Expansion under Louis XIV

Louis XIV had already entered upon an ambitious policy of expansion, encouraged by the weakness of the rest of Europe. His ambitions led to him to reach out toward the Netherlands, Lorraine, and even Austria. The Swiss mercenaries were essential to his plans. The Confederation soon had cause to regret their treaty with France. In 1668 Louis occupied the Franche Comté over which the Confederation claimed protective rights. The Comté had reverted to Maximilian of Austria after the Burgundian War and then to the Spanish line of the Habsburgs when the emperor, Charles V (grandson of Maximilian) divided sovereignty over his vast territorial possessions between his brother Ferdinand and his only son Philip II, who received the Spanish inheritance. During the Thirty Years War the catholic cantons, then warmly sympathetic toward Spain, had agreed to protect Spain's claims on the Franche Comté in return for Philip's assurance of military support should civil war with the protestant cantons again break out. But an earlier treaty with France, urged by the Confederation, had provided that the Franche Comté would be neutralized should Spain and France find themselves at war. To the dismay of the Swiss, French troops marched in and occupied the Comté.

The Swiss had good cause to be alarmed by Louis XIV's seizure of the Franche Comté. The county had been restored to Spain by the treaty of 7 November 1659 between France and Spain and its seizure by France was also contrary to the Act of Renunciation of 1660. Not only was the Swiss Confederation alarmed by the expansionist policies of Louis XIV but so also were Great Britain, Holland, Sweden, Portugal (with Spain), and the Empire.

Laying aside all of their past disputes over confessional differences, all 13 cantons and their associated States now displayed a remarkable unanimity, proving that the needs of the Confederation took precedence over religious disputation. They realized at once that Louis' seizure of the Franche Comté posed a threat to Geneva, to Vaud, and even to Swiss possessions on the Rhine.[34] In March, 1668, the Wyl agreement on defense (*Defensionale von Wyl*) was renewed and a Confederation-wide levy of 13,400 infantrymen and several squadrons of cavalry was proclaimed in accordance with the *Defensionale*.

The Peace of Aix-la-Chapelle of 2 May 1668 restored the Franche Comté to Spain. Louis recalled his troops but it was a short-lived peace. Within a few years France and Spain were again at war. France again seized the Franche Comté in

1674, drove the imperial forces out of Alsace, seized the Duchy of Lorraine, Freiburg in Germany, and various portions of the Spanish Netherlands. The Peace of Nimeguen (17 September 1678) confirmed the Franche Comté with all of its towns and dependencies as a possession of the King of France. The catholic cantons were now determined to fight and requested of Bern, proudly jealous of its rights as a virtually autonomous State, permission for their troops to pass through the canton. The permission was not given. The Diet then united on the momentous decision to declare Switzerland in its entirety to be a neutral State which would defend its own rights and integrity, by force of arms if necessary, and would no longer become involved in disputes between other countries. By virtue of this policy decision, Strassburg, which for over 100 years had been a close associate of Zurich, found itself isolated. The city was seized by France in September 1681. Shortly thereafter, Louis converted the Alsatian village of Hüningen into a heavily armed fortress. It lay in close proximity to Basel and was an obvious threat to that city.

Abuse of Swiss Mercenaries by France

Louis' war of expansion now turned to the Netherlands. In 1682 he entered upon the conquest of the territories around the lower Rhine. Contrary to all earlier agreements he used his Swiss mercenaries in this campaign for offence, despite a clear understanding with all governments which contracted for the services of Swiss troops that they would be used only for defensive purposes. The Confederation, approached by Holland, protested to Louis but to little avail. Several of the Swiss officers refused to continue in the service of the monarch and returned home, but many remained in the French service. Just as Louis had been given the right to recruit troops in Switzerland, the Confederation now gave permission to his enemies, England and Holland, to recruit Swiss troops. This equality of treatment extended by a Neutral to the two belligerent forces, an essential policy in the new neutrality, led to another repetition of the intolerable situation in which Swiss were in battle against their fellow countrymen.

Permission to England and Holland to recruit Swiss mercenaries was granted in 1688, shortly after the beginning of Louis' third war of conquest, this time directed against the Palatinate. Ignoring all objections from the Swiss, Louis repeated his violation of capitulation agreements and sent Swiss mercenaries into service in Germany. The war was to last over ten years and was to confront the Confederation with the imminent danger that Swiss might again be in combat against their countrymen, this time in German territory. Swiss casualties in the battle of Malplaquet, 1709, during the Spanish War of Succession, were very heavy. To the Swiss, the war with their fellow countrymen was not simply another phase of their own confessional war, different only in that they fought their battles on foreign soil. Surprisingly, the allied Powers in combat with catholic France included catholic Austria and catholic Spain.

Treaties of Friendship and Defense Sought by the European Powers

Various proposals from European Powers for treaties of friendship and defense were considered by the Confederation during the closing years of the century. Most of these requests were very questionable because of ulterior motives. In some cases a proposed alliance was based on the obvious desire of a Power to secure transit rights for troops and supplies through Swiss territory. The Diet made its position clear; the Confederation was not prepared to alter its declared policy of using its armies solely for the defense of its borders, and of denying *Durchzug* rights to all the Powers. Recruiting by foreign Powers within the territories of the Confederation was also declared to be incompatible with Swiss neutrality and would not be permitted, although in 1691 the Confederation allowed recruitment of troops to aid the kaiser in defending the Vorarlberg. It is evident that the Swiss, disturbed by Louis XIV's determined efforts to expand the territories and the power of France, were inclined to interpret quite liberally the terms of the Austrian *Erbeinung* and to bend her own policies to favor France's enemies. Pressures on Switzerland to enter the war against France were relentless and unending. But the allies (Lorraine, Austria, most of the German States, Spain, and the Netherlands) were seriously divided among themselves in matters of policy and could not act harmoniously together. Had Switzerland have joined this multiheaded alliance, she would almost certainly have been attacked by the French.

The concept of impartial treatment of belligerent States grew in strength as the war ended. Both sides had to be treated equally and the members of the Confederation were repeatedly urged to refrain from provocative acts toward either party. At the same time fixed responsibilities toward neighbouring Powers, as defined in old alliances, permitted the Confederation to be seemingly more generous in the provision of troops to France's enemies—e.g. Strassburg and Austria—than to France itself, always insisting, however, that they be used only for defense.

Foreign Military Service

A fine line of distinction was drawn between permitting the use of any part of the *Defensionale* forces by a belligerent, and allowing recruiting in Swiss territory on behalf of a foreign Power where such recruitment appeared to be compatible with old alliances. Recruiting by the French was generally confined to several stated cantons. It was not an all-Swiss affair and the Confederation hastened to point this out when defending itself against frequent complaints and charges of duplicity.

War was then a curious profession, curious because of the practices and the motivations of those involved. Swiss officers and their men were only partly motivated by religious affiliations. The payments and fringe benefits were of prime importance and were frequently the determining factor.[35]

The Confederation and its member cantons had two powerful means of control. The Swiss officers and men in foreign service were subject to instant recall if their government determined that their use in specific cases contravened the agreement under which they were permitted to serve a foreign Power. The penalties for disobedience toward a recall order were very severe. Steps could also be taken, in the interest of impartiality, to adjust the numbers of Swiss subjects in military service so that a rough numerical equality was maintained—16,000 Swiss in French service would mean that about the same number should be permitted to serve with the allies.

Little if any control could be exerted over the non-Swiss, the foreign adventurers resident in Swiss territory who fought for whomsoever they chose. Finally, there were entire foreign regiments under the command of Swiss officers who fought on one side or the other, and motley companies of adventurers recruited by Swiss agents in foreign countries and sometimes commanded by Swiss officers. It is not without interest that Switzerland did not effectively put an end to mercenary service by her subjects until far into the nineteenth century.

Prelude to the Spanish War of Succession

The war in Holland which ended with the Treaty of Ryswick in 1697 was followed in August 1698 by a Treaty between England, France and Holland, commonly called the first Treaty of Partition. King Charles II of Spain was about to die without issue. Emperor Leopold had claims through the Spanish Habsburg line on the crown of Spain. The Treaty of Partition, designed to forestall a union of Spain and the Empire, gave the Duchy of Milan to Archduke Charles, Leopold's second son—a sort of consolation prize. France, in turn, was supposedly separated from Spain forever by the Act of Renunciation signed by the Infanta Maria Theresa prior to her marriage to Louis XIV. The treaty contained the usual noble sentiments which reflect the concept of a balance of power. No prince shall "disturb the order settled by this treaty . . . and so aggrandize himself to the detriment of the others" (Jenkinson, ref. **198**, Vol. I, p. 312, Article XIII of the First Treaty of Partition).

The Second Treaty of Partition of 25 March 1700 confirmed the substance of the preceding treaty and was soon followed (September 1701) by the Second Grand Alliance or Treaty between the emperor, the King of Great Britain, and the States General of the Netherlands. Charles II of Spain had died childless and the emperor, as expected, claimed the Spanish inheritance for his family. Louis XIV had not only claimed the crown of Spain on behalf of his grandson, the Duke of Anjou, but speedily invaded the Spanish Netherlands and opened a military campaign on a broad front to enforce his claim. Europe was again in turmoil. Thus the Spanish War of Succession which was to last for thirteen years, the result of Louis XIV's thirst for a universal monarchy, burst into flame and ravaged the face of Europe. It was Louis' last war.

Treaties of peace and friendship were signed at Utrecht in 1713 between Austria, England, France, Holland, Prussia and Spain. Switzerland became involved through the provisions of Article XXXVII of the Treaty of Peace and Friendship between Louis XIV and other signatory powers. Thus, we find in Volume III of Du Mont (**107**, pp. 366–71) that

> In this present Treaty of Peace and of Alliance will be included on the part of the said Seigneur Christian King [Louis XIV] all those who will be named before the exchange of

ratifications and in the space of six months after they will have exchanged: The States General, the Queen of Great Britain, and all their other allies . . . as also the 13 Cantons of the Swiss League . . .

A similar statement is to be found in the *Abschiede* (VII. 1, p. 24b; Beilage 10, pp. 1407–10). Here we find that his Majesty will include "as a mark of his affection to the Helvetic Body, all 13 Cantons of the Swiss League, the Abbey and town of St. Gall . . . and all the allies and co-allies of the Helvetic Body." Eventually the 13 cantons, their allies and associated States were included but not without much wringing of hands, and debate among the Swiss: 1. The catholic cantons refused to recognize the protestant Anne as the rightful Queen of Great Britain; 2. A letter to the kaiser from the Swiss government failed to address him as "his Catholic Majesty" and was returned; 3. The election of Charles VI as kaiser had not yet been reported to the Confederation, which would, according to protocol, be obliged to congratulate him before discussing business; 4. Some of the cantons stubbornly refused to recognize his second title "King of Spain"; 5. The intermediation of Count von Trautmannsdorf to resolve the problems with the kaiser, could not be invoked since his mandate as ambassador ended with the new election.

These problems of diplomatic protocol were ultimately resolved and Switzerland, her allies and associated States were included. The Treaties of Utrecht (1713) and Rastadt (1714) were distinguished by a recarving of the territories of several of the signatory Powers, all in the interest of restoring a Balance-of-Power. Switzerland's exceptional and unique position as a Neutral was implicitly recognized by the Powers. This recognition and a final (?) solution to the power struggles that had been troubling Europe during much of Louis XIV's long reign meant much to the Swiss Confederation.

The Huguenot Immigration

As the end of the century approached, Louis revoked (in 1685) the Edict of Nantes, under which French Protestants had enjoyed the right to practice the religion of their choice. Persecution of the Huguenots was renewed. Among the protestants this could only be regarded as the final act of a vengeful monarch whose adherence to policies of absolutism and the divine right of kings had led to nothing but trouble during his long reign. Thousands of Huguenots fled to the protestant cantons of Switzerland in search of peace and security. Despite the heavy financial burden and the difficulties encountered in the rapid absorption of a flood of refugees, Switzerland benefited greatly over the long term. The Huguenots brought new skills and eventually added much to the economic strength and well-being of their adopted country.

Emigration to North America

The records reveal a series of emigrations, partly from Switzerland to the New World, as early as the sixteenth century. Some of the emigrants were motivated by a determination to seek a haven where freedom to practice the religion of their choice could be assured: Anabaptists, Mennonities, Amish, and Huguenots. In 1525 a group of Anabaptists in Zurich went to America in search of religious freedom. A significant number of Swiss joined a group of English emigrants in 1607 and, in three ships, finally reached the James river. There the settlers founded Jamestown in Virginia, the oldest English colony on the American mainland. Thus the Swiss took part in the founding of Virginia which, along with Massachusetts, struggled most passionately in the late eighteenth century to launch the independence movement. The revolutionary Virginia Declaration of Rights in 1776 may indeed have influenced the Union's Declaration of Independence as well as the French Declaration of Human Rights (159, p. 230).

A search for freedom from religious oppression was not the only reason for emigrating to the New World. There were economic reasons as well. In the mountainous parts of the Protestant cantons, especially in the Bernese Oberland, overpopulation was much in evidence. There were also the hunger years, little rain or too much. Food for the people was insufficient. Finally, life for the young was dull. Mercenary service, even in the seventeenth century, was losing favor among many. It no longer offered a means of sopping up the excess population. The catholic cantons of *Innerschweiz* suffered acutely but despite the grave doubts of their people about migrating to a new land that was known to be heavily protestant and sectarian, some joined in the emigration movement. Bern finally became concerned by her loss of population and between 1641 and 1660 imposed some difficult regulations and virtual prohibitions of emigration. But it was not so in Geneva, and in 1670 the Genevois, Carteret, founded a Swiss colony at Charleston in South Carolina. Small groups, largely from Geneva and Neuchâtel emigrated to North and South Carolina, joining groups of French Huguenots in flight in 1685 after revocation of the Edict of Nantes. At about the same time (1683) Georg Wertmüller of Bern arranged with William Penn for use of a large piece of land near Philadelphia for Swiss colonization. Dr. Heinrich Zimmermann (1673–1750) from Wattenwyl led an emigrating group of Swiss in 1698 who settled in Germantown, a suburb of Philadelphia, where a small Swiss colony already existed (159, p. 231). In 1729, the Zimmermann family was naturalized under the name Carpenter. In 1800, members of the family moved to Ohio where they founded the city of Lancaster and the village of Bern (179).

Neutrality

The Diet met in Baden on 3 May 1674 and declared the Swiss Confederation to be a neutral State—an important decision in its long and rather tempestuous struggle toward a united policy in foreign affairs.[36] The history of the Swiss is not that of a people who were consciously directing their domestic and foreign policies over the centuries toward a strict avoidance from any entanglement in the affairs of other States. Except in defense against foreign aggression, the Confederation had little authority over the autonomous cantons, and the instances of cantonal exercise of the full rights of a sovereign State are numerous.[37] Disunity between the cantons was conspicuous through much of the century. The wars of religion reveal most strikingly the depths of intercantonal discord. Equally revealing, and in the same vein, are the conflicting foreign agreements or alliances with England, France, Spain, Savoy, Holland and Austria (or the Holy Roman Empire). These were frequently negotiated by some cantons in order to strengthen their position against an opposing group of cantons, or by the Diet to ensure an appearance of unity and impartiality.

The status of the *Durchzug*, the passage of foreign troops through the territory of a neutral or friendly State, received a searching examination in seventeenth century Switzerland. In the late Middle Ages, the *Durchzug* was almost an unquestioned right. How else, in heavily fragmented central Europe could any of the dynastic Houses keep in touch with their scattered possessions, dotted about amid the holdings of other Houses? As territorial consolidations were effected, the right of the *Durchzug* came into question. More and more, permission had to be sought, and more and more reluctantly were such requests granted. The pressures on the Confederation were severe. The kaiser sought permission to bring his forces stationed in Italy to the theater of conflict in central Europe by a march through Swiss territory. Spain, in 1614, sought permission for a similar *Durchzug* from Italy to Germany. The *Durchzug* was occasionally permitted by some cantons and just as often disallowed. The complaints were numerous. There were four border transgressions by the major Powers through Basel territory, one through Bernese territory, and one through Thurgau. However, the heart of the Fatherland escaped penetration by foreign troops. Serious efforts were made to be impartial toward belligerent forces beyond her borders. For example, the evangelical *Orte*, despite Zurich's protests, denied the *Durchzug* to the protestant army of the Markgraf of Baden-Durlach because of conflicts with the long-standing treaty with Austria. At the same time a similar request from catholic Austria was denied.

The Swiss policies, cantonal and federal, toward the *Durchzug* definitely hardened. Acceptance of the restrictions by foreign Powers was rendered difficult by the appearance in 1625 and 1631 of the first two editions of the great work by Grotius on international law (**154**). Grotius claimed that the innocent passage and repassage of foreign troops through neutral territory was not a violation of neutrality. Belligerent forces, forthwith, began to invoke the *Durchzug* as a right that could not be challenged. Finally, the Diet decided that the passage of foreign troops through the territory of the Confederation was such a serious threat to her peace and security that the *Durchzug* by foreign troops must be ended forever.[38] This official termination of the *Durchzug*, except for a single violation during the Spanish War of Succession, was faithfully honored until the unhappy days of the late eighteenth century when the armies of Napoleon Bonaparte invaded the country.

Almost from its infancy, the Confederation imposed upon its members the responsibility of serving as peace-seeking intermediaries in disputes between other members of the Confederation. In the seventeenth century attempts were made to serve as intermediaries in the attainment of peace between belligerent foreign Powers. In June 1636 the Diet discussed the question of peaceful intercession between the principals in the Thirty Years War. A resolution to this effect was passed unanimously and appropriate letters were sent to the Holy See and the heads of government of the warring Powers. Without replying directly, the kaiser explained that he did not seek destruction of the kingdoms of this enemies but, rather, "the return of all Christendom to a precious peace." He also urged the Swiss to recall their subjects serving in the French military forces.[39] In 1638, and again in 1639, a universal armistice was proposed before the Diet.[40] The peace-making efforts were fruitless, but a notable result was achieved. Both confessions expressed in common a unity of action and purpose, and the policy of peaceful intercession in foreign wars gained in strength throughout the Confederation.

The dispatch of mercenaries by the Swiss cantons to aid foreign Princes in their numerous wars became a subject of increasing concern. The capitulation agreements were numerous. They continued to be an important source of revenue, especially to the ancient forest cantons, and a solution to their chronic unemployment problems. The evils of the practice were increasingly evident, notably the many instances in which Swiss soldiers were forced to engage in the attack rather than in defensive operations only. Although there was a general awareness of constant violations of the capitulation agreements, mercenary service continued to be permitted and encouraged by various seventeenth century treaties, notably that of 1663 with Louis XIV.

Another problem that received attention and some clarification concerned contraband.[41] A difference existed in Swiss policy toward the procurement or transit of goods in ordinary commerce as opposed to weapons and military supplies. In March 1638 the French complained that a ship carrying powder and foodstuffs for the army of Bernhard of Weimar had been seized at Klingnau by the provincial governor (*Landvogt*) of Baden. Investigation established that the cargo had been falsely certified, and that powder, artillery matches, oil, fish and cheese constituted the cargo. The Diet, in April, awarded the entire cargo to the fiscal authorities in lieu of customs duties, and ruled that the transport of munitions to a foreign Power required the express approval of government. The Diet also decreed that the belligerents must be treated equally and impartially in matters of trade and commerce. More specifically, provisions must be made available to the Swedish army across the Rhine just as freely as to the armies of the kaiser.[42]

A related problem concerned neutral shipping on the Rhine and Lake Constance. Schaffhausen complained of acts of piracy by a commander in the service of Bernhard of Weimar. Cargoes were being seized and charges levied on the ships. Schaffhausen and Zurich introduced a convoy system to protect their shipping. Ultimately, Swiss ships were no longer molested—they were treated as Neutrals—but other shipping continued to be plundered. This and related incidents constitute a part of the early Swiss experience in respect to the rights of asylum granted to enemy shipping when driven into neutral waters.

A similar right of asylum for troops on land was quite unknown. The question arose, however, before the Evangelical Conference in February 1644. What should be the policy of the Confederation toward a fleeing army that sought asylum in

Swiss territory? The seventeenth century answer was to disallow entrance and asylum because of possible pursuit by a victorious army and continuation of the fighting on Swiss soil. What a contrast to the nineteenth century policy and the internment of an entire French army during the Franco-Prussian War!

A device that was used increasingly in the seventeenth century to provide a protective shield between Switzerland and its neighbours is to be found in the neutralization of border zones. In 1603, the Duke of Savoy, after an ignominious failure to seize Geneva, agreed to the establishment of a neutral zone at the border, "four leagues deep." After a great deal of diplomatic wrangling, an accord which neutralized a stretch, "two hours deep,"[43] on the right bank of the Rhine was signed in 1689 by the accredited representatives of the kaiser and the King of France.[44] The kaiser stubbornly refused ratification until the Spanish War of Succession broke out some twelve years later. In a sense this was a real triumph for the diplomatic efforts of Switzerland since Austria at last recognized the principle of neutralization and of restraint from armed intervention in the affairs of neutral cities and States—a policy which the Confederation had espoused for many years.

The neutralization of border territories farther to the west encountered numerous problems. Neuchâtel, which had been associated with Bern since 1406 or so in a pact of everlasting friendship, was formally neutralized in 1683 and 1695 when the clouds of war were again darkening the horizon. The Principality had been seized by Bern in 1512, unquestionably to extend its defensive bulwark to the crest of the Jura. Neuchâtel's status in respect to Bern and the Confederation was nonetheless curious and potentially dangerous because of her dual loyalties. As a Principality, the sovereign head in the latter part of the century was the Abbot of Orleans, who was succeeded in 1694 by his sister. Events subsequent to her death in 1707 involved the King of Prussia who, by election in 1707, became Prince of Neuchâtel and sovereign head of the State. All in all, Neuchâtel's relations with the Confederation were peaceful and problem-free, except for a tiff with France in 1708,[45] until the closing years of the eighteenth century and the great dispute with Prussia in the 1850s.

The Franche Comté, separated from Neuchâtel and Vaud by the crest of the Jura was a constant source of diplomatic strife between France, Spain and the Confederation. The complicated series of events, brought into prominence by Louis XIV's duplicity and thirst for conquest, came to an end in 1678 when the Peace of Nimeguen confirmed the Franche Comté as a French possession. There had been countless infringements of the Act of Neutralization of 1522. Switzerland made no serious effort to intervene. She regarded the Comté only as a buffer State, useful in protection of her own neutrality, but impossible to defend against neighbouring France. The confessional strife which split the country into two discordant groups of cantons would also have made it exceedingly difficult to unite the Confederation in any military action designed to defend the Comté against either France or Spain.

South of Lake Geneva (Lac Leman) lay the Duchy of Savoy. It is of unusual interest that Savoy, so frequently at odds with the Confederation in previous centuries, proposed that protection under the banner of Swiss neutrality be granted to much of the Duchy. This was discussed at length at the Diet of 9 December 1703 in Baden (*Abschiede* VI.2, 1107–20). In principle, Switzerland would have been agreeable to the proposal if defense of this large area, especially against France, would have been feasible. The Alps to the southeast would have provided an effective barrier against an invasion from Piedmont. But the area was much too large for defensive occupation by Swiss troops in the event of attacks on Savoy by a powerful aggressor. Eventually Chablais and Faucigny in upper Savoy were placed under the protection of Swiss neutrality. The agreement with Savoy was confirmed by the Congress of Vienna in 1815 and the Treaty of Turin in 1816. France, meanwhile, had given solemn assurances of her intent to refrain from any attempt to annex Savoy.

The policy of encirclement by an almost unbroken chain of neutralized zones on the other side of the Swiss border was dictated by more than political and military considerations. It also was deeply rooted in economics. It was of utmost importance to protect from the ravages of war those areas, such as the Franche Comté, which were essential to the Confederation for her indispensable imports of salt, grain, other foodstuffs and wine.

Efforts to maintain a political equilibrium were vigorously pursued in the seventeenth century and were of profound significance to Swiss neutrality. The maintenance of a balance of power on the Continent had become the most important element in the foreign policies of European statemen. We shall not attempt to explore the beginnings of the concept of the balance of power. It was well understood in the early days of the seventeenth century. Sully (**355**) who lived from 1559 to 1641, served as Ambassador to England during the days of Henry IV of France (1589–1610), whom he had known as a teenager. He had this to say about the balance of power:

> There are none of these Monarchies in Europe but whose Destruction will require a Concurrence of Causes infinitely superior to all human Force. The whole, therefore, of what seems proper and necessary to be done, is to support them all in a kind of Equilibrium.

As for the Great Design of Henry IV, "The equilibrium of Europe would be maintained by the principal Powers acceding to and becoming the Guarantors even of particular Treaties." Queen Elizabeth of England, with whom Sully discussed the Great Design, favored the idea. Basically, she and Henry IV of France wanted to humble the House of Austria. In essence, it was a plan to redivide Europe, cutting and trimming here and adding there, in order to provide a balance of power, and to permit all Europe to be governed and regulated as one great family.

Pertinent also are the instructions to Oliver Fleming of England on his assignment as resident agent with the protestant cantons (**133**):

> They, the Swiss, are invironed (as we see) with the three potent countries of Germanie, France and Italie, & may rightly feare danger from anie of theis that shal grow great above the rest. It concerns them therfore to indevor by al meanes to keep the balance equal. . . . Then the Helvetian bodie, by the advantage of seate and armes, may again balance the greatest kings (as hertofore they have donne) & live at home secure & richt.

In Aglionby's final report[46] we read this sage observation (6),

> They say it is true they may be shutt up by France on one side and the house of Austria on the other; but they doe not thinke that those two powers will combine easily to their ruine and either of them may save them against the other.

When the struggles between her neighbours were fairly evenly contested, Switzerland's neutrality was respected and violations were essentially limited to infractions at the border. Thus, both in peace and war, the principle of a balance of power, as understood by Switzerland's powerful neighbours, contributed effectively to the preservation of her neutrality.

The Public Health

The earlier section on health resorts pertains to those diseases which, allegedly, could be cured by copious drinking of the evil-smelling mineral waters that emerge at various places on the earth's surface. The section also focuses on the social functions of the public baths. Here, we shall turn to the plague and other epidemic diseases which wrought havoc for centuries—in fact until modern medicine began effectively to bring them under control. The Thirty Years War was less of a struggle between opposing armies than between man and disease. As Zinsser has mentioned, referring to wars prior to present times:

> Soldiers have rarely won wars. They more often mop up after the barrage of epidemics. And typhus with its brothers and sisters—the plague, cholera, typhoid, dysentery—has decided more campaigns than Caesar, Hannibal, Napoleon and all the inspector generals of history (**406**, p. 153).

In the Thirty Years War, typhus was the main scourge from 1618 to 1630. For the remainder of the war, plague took over and was more terrible than typhus. In 1625–26, Mainz, Metz, Nuremberg and smaller towns were struck. Gustavus Adolphus commenced the siege of Nuremberg in 1632. After 11 weeks, food and other supplies gave out. Typhus hit the town and the besieging army. "In seven weeks, 29,000 men died" (**406**, p. 276).[47] On September 3, the Swedes, decimated by disease, abandoned the siege and retreated, Wallenstein's army, also attempting to capture Nuremberg, marched away to escape further ravages of the pestilence. Deaths in Germany due to the plague and typhus far exceeded the deaths in battle, During the Thirty Years War, the population of Württemberg is said to have fallen "from 400,000 to a mere 48,000" (**1**, p. 35).

The great epidemic of 1348 was probably pneumonic plague in which the victims, dying within a few days, became blue-black in colour—hence the term "Black Death." The destroying angel could hardly have been more devastating. Deaths in Europe have been estimated at one-fourth to three-fourths of the population. The Black Death ravaged Europe for 300 years with epidemics in 1360, 1369, 1372, 1382, 1400, 1409, 1437, 1460, 1473, 1482, 1492, 1509, 1514, 1527, 1532, 1560, 1576, 1593, 1603, 1622, 1630, 1654, 1655, 1675, 1679 and 1694. Several accounts by English writers, descriptive of the epidemics of 1630 and 1655, report the death of 60,000

Traité de la Peste showing the costume worn by doctors and others who visit victims of the plague. Note the mask with eyes of crystal and a long nose filled with perfumes (Swiss National Museum).

people in London alone (**370**). Three mass phenomena, psychopathological or religious in origin, followed upon the Black Death: flagellation, St. Vitus dance, and persecution of the Jews. The mass episodes of flagellation were noted in Europe in 1260, 1296, 1333, 1354, 1414, and sporadically to 1710 (**370**). Jews were persecuted on every possible occasion. Many emigrated to Poland. If there was a shortage of Jews upon whom to blame any severe epidemic, the populace turned against lepers, gravediggers and alleged witches. The charges were the same, but the Jews, as the only money-lenders in the Middle Ages, were widely hated and hence persecuted.

The last European pandemic, from 1663 to 1668, reached Austria and Switzerland at the end of this period. Thereafter, epidemics of plague were localized, the last to strike part of Switzerland being in 1721.

The typhus and bubonic plague epidemics of the seventeenth century were caused by rats and rat fleas which transmitted the disease. In the early eighteenth century, hordes of ferocious brown rats (*Rattus decumanus*) almost exterminated the black rat *(Rattus rattus)*—the principal troublemaker. (See also notes 8 and 9 in this chapter.)

Notes and Comments

1. Gilbert Burnet (1643–1715); 1669—Professor of Theology in Glasgow; 1674—Priest in London.

2. Occupied.

3. It was a widely and tenaciously held theory in Switzerland that goiter was caused by drinking "snow water." Coxe treated the subject at length and convincingly disposed of this theory of the etiology of goiter and replaced it with one of his own. To Coxe, goiters were caused by an accumulation of "tuf," an insoluble deposit of calcium salts derived from hard water and known to every housewife as the hard greyish deposit that forms eventually in tea kettles. Not until 1820 was it established (by Coindet) that common goiters were caused by a shortage of iodine. In 1917, Marine and Kimball proposed that iodine prophylaxis be widely used in the USA. Soon thereafter Hunziker and Eggenberger proposed that Switzerland also resort to similar measures (1). The universal preventive is iodized salt which has gained worldwide acceptance.

In the Valais, Coxe observed a high incidence of goiters and idiocy. After discussing this at length, he concludes "all that with truth can be affirmed, is, that goitrous persons and idiots, are more abundant in some districts of the Valais than perhaps in any other part of the globe." "They call them 'Souls of God, without sin'; and many parents prefer these idiot-children to those whose understanding are perfect; because, as they are incapable of intentional criminality, they consider them as certain of happiness in a future state" (**95**, Vol III, pp. 397–409).

4. This refers to the treaties of protection between Bern and Geneva (beginning with 1526) whereby Geneva was assured of aid from Bernese militia if attacked by Savoy or other Powers.

5. Meldingen: now known as Mellingen. At the time of Addison the canton of Bern was much larger than at present, since it included Aargau and bordered on the Freiämter in which Mellingen was located. Zurich canton was immediately to the east. The Peace of Aarau (1712) gave to Bern and Zurich administrative authority in common over the Freiämter. (Prior to 1712 the Freiämter were administered by the eight cantons jointly.) The French Ambassador, who resided in Solothurn, on his journeys to Baden for meetings of the Diet, would have been obliged to pass through Mellingen.

6. *Bürgermeister*, mayor, or a chief magistrate in local government.

7. This is an interesting comment since the feeling reported to exist surely stemmed from long lasting agreements that intercantonal disputes must not involve other members of the Confederation except as mediators. Thus, the armed intervention of Bern and Lucerne would have been improper since only Schwyz and Zurich were at war.

8. Switzerland suffered from four visitations of the plague in the seventeenth century: 1608–12; 1628–29; ca. 1650; and 1667–70. Of the total population, numbering little more than one million, thousands succumbed. During the great plague of 1348–39, the Jews had to bear responsibility for causing it all (**95**). Under torture they were forced to confess that the devil induced them to poison the fountains, the streams, and the food of the Christians. Bags of poison were alleged to have been found in the fountains. In January, 1349, large numbers of Jews were rounded up in Basel, driven into a large wooden building on an island in the Rhine and burned to death. Others who fled the cities were hunted down by the villagers and burned. In some instances whole families burned themselves in their own homes for there was little chance of escape. A few weeks later, 2000 Jews were burned to death in their synagogues. As in Basel, the authorities in Bern, Constance and Strassburg claimed to have proof that the Jews had poisoned the drinking waters and thereby caused the plague. When the supply of Jews was exhausted, a number of Christians who were alleged to be plague carriers, and a variety of "suspicious characters," such as witches, were burned.

Albrecht Burckhardt (**74**) reported 16 epidemics of the plague, probably including cholera, typhus, smallpox, diphtheria and other epidemic diseases, in Basel alone during the fifteenth and sixteenth centuries. The four most serious epidemics in the seventeenth century were probably bubonic plague. That of 1610–11 (or 1608–12) was the worst of the four and is described in the literature of the day as the "great death" (*das grosse Sterbend*).

As might be expected the mortality rates from the plague were highest in the cities because of high population density. But some cities, once they learned to impose a quarantine against visitors from plague-stricken areas, succeeded in escaping some of the epidemics entirely. Thus the epidemic of 1667–68, which struck Basel and parts of Bern canton, left Zurich, Geneva, and *Innerschweiz* completely untouched.

Although the seventeenth century literature and earlier reports tend to give exaggerated mortality rates for the plague, one must not underestimate the significance of bubonic plague, and especially pneumonic plague, as a terrible killer. Felix Platter (1536–1614), reporting on the epidemic of 1610–11 in Basel, noted 3968 deaths among 6408 who came down with the plague—a 60 percent mortality. His data were derived from Platter's house-to-house visits following the epidemic. We learn from Bickel (**40**, p. 82) that out of 41,276 deaths in seventeenth century Basel, 9500 were from the plague. In Geneva, three plague epidemics in the century caused 3400 deaths out of a total of 55,000 deaths—a much lower percentage than in Basel.

By the 1660s some of the cities had learned a few important lessons. If the plague struck, schools, churches, and courts were closed. Markets and fairs were suspended, the sick and attendant personnel were isolated, and funeral ceremonies were severely restricted. By the imposition of a strict quarantine against traders and merchandise from southern France, Switzerland escaped the terrible epidemic which struck Marseilles in 1720. The plague visitation of 1721 was localized and was the last to strike Switzerland.

9. In seventeenth and eighteenth century Zurich, of every 100 deaths 48 to 59 were children. During the same period, in Geneva, 20 to 24 percent of all deaths were of infants under one year. In 1550–1600 more than half of all live births died before the age of five years (**40**, p. 80). Because of the high mortality in infancy and childhood, life expectancy at birth was only 21.2 years in the sixteenth century, and 25.7 in the seventeenth. It rose gradually to 40.7 in the period 1814–33. These statistics, cited by Bickel (**40**, p. 86), are from the mortality tables of Geneva. Physicians and surgeons of the day were too few in number and were not equal to the challenges imposed by ignorance of physiology and bacteriology, lack of sanitation, pollution of drinking water, and poor nutrition of their patients in childhood.

Because of European wars in which many Swiss were killed, a marked excess of women prevailed, even into the eighteenth century. In the city of Bern in 1764 there were 7987 females and 5694 males—a sex ratio of 140 to 100.

10. Treaty of Peace concluded at St. Julien, 21 July 1603. See Du Mont (**107**).

11. The three are known collectively as the Graubünden (the Grey Leagues).

12. Jürg Jenatsch (1596–1639). Son and grandson of priests of the Reformed Church. Studied theology in Basel and Zurich. A priest for three years in the Graubünden and Valtellina.

13. The Valtellina had a long and troubled past. It was conquered and briefly occupied by the Three Leagues in 1486–87 and again seized in 1512 along with Chiavenna and Bormio. Between France, Spain, Austria and the Three Leagues there was a constant tug-of-war over who ruled this great valley that continued until 1797.

14. Rohan, faced with the awkward problem of moving his army from Alsace into the Graubünden, solved it brilliantly. He dared not move through the southern German States because the Duke of Lorraine with a strong army held the towns on the right bank of the Rhine and would resist Rohan's passage. If he led his army through Switzerland and without permission of the Diet he would alarm the cantons. If he asked permission of the Diet he would obviously divulge his plan of operations. Instead, Rohan, as he entered each territory in succession, applied for permission to pass and excused himself for lack of time for not applying to the Diet. By this device he was able to lead his army through Basel, Aargau, Baden, Zurich, St. Gallen and finally to Chur, passing mostly through Protestant cantons.

15. *Abschiede* V. 2.1, 541, 12 March 1628; V. 2.1, 543–47, March–April 1628.

16. *Abschiede* V. 2.1, 547–48, 12–13 April 1628.

17. *Abschiede* V. 2.1, 664f, 9 December 1631.

18. *Abschiede* V. 2.1, 713d, 716 par. 5, 7–16 October 1632.

19. *Abschiede* V. 2.1, 719–28, 7 November 1632.

20. *Abschiede* 5.2, 754–60 (Baden 3–21 July, 1633).

21. Johann Rudolf Wettstein (1594–1666). Elected master of the guilds in Basel in 1635 and

Bürgermeister in 1645. Represented Switzerland during the negotiations which culminated in the Treaty of Westphalia (1648) and the formal separation of the Swiss Confederation from the German Reich.

22. *Abschiede* V. 2.1, 770–77, 14–29 September 1633.

23. *Abschiede* V. 2.1, 785d, 8–9 October 1633.

24. *Abschiede* V. 2.1, 811–16, 23–25 January 1634.

25. *Abschiede* V. 2.1, 1068f, 2 February 1638. de Vattel (**374**, Vol III, Chapter VII, Sect. 119), while conceding that the innocent passage of foreign troops through a neutral State is a right to be enjoyed by a friendly State, recognized that the Neutral still retained the right to deny the passage if it considered the grounds for such a denial were sufficient.

26. *Abschiede* V. 2, 1410d 17–31 January 1647; 2255–60, January 1647.

27. *Abschiede* 6.1, 913–999, Baden, 28 March 1674.

28. *Abschiede* VI, 1675–98, 18 March 1668 and later alterations to 13 November 1678.

29. One must also infer that the Swiss troops sent to strengthen the border defenses along the Rhine on the occasion of the Choiseul *Durchzug* of 28 June 1678 were also much too late to be of appreciable help. The Diet had to be summoned (July 3) and five more days elapsed before the *Defensionale* contingent of 2650 men got underway. Nonetheless the *Defensionale* proved to be an effective deterrent against border transgressions, though it seldom happened that their forces were engaged in actual combat along the border.

30. The Thirty Years War ended with Switzerland, as a whole, in a prosperous state and much of the country comparatively peaceful and quiet. But were we to assess the overall effects of the war on Switzerland, a summary such as the following would be in order. In addition to the border violation by General Horn which had serious political repercussions and the several other transgressions of Basel territory which have been mentioned earlier, there were many trifling violations, frequently by groups of cavalry who were unaware of the precise location of the border. This led to plundering, devastation of neutral places at the border, seizure of property of neutrals and even the taking of prisoners. In 1632 forces of the kaiser attacked two Schaffhausen towns which, fortunately, were fairly well defended. In September 1633, Bernhard's army plundered several Schaffhausen villages. General Altringer's army also burned and plundered several villages until driven off by 2000 troops from Zurich which came to the rescue. Trouble arose through erection of forts and gun emplacements close to the border and in positions of threat to Swiss territory. Under Swiss protest, some of these were destroyed, though a menacing fortress erected by the Austrians at Hüningen, just outside of Basel, remained for years. Border violations such as these were the basis for Swiss diplomatic efforts to secure her frontiers by a neutralized zone extending over most of her perimeter.

31. In the Middle Ages, the *dinar* (penny) was the most common coin in circulation. The period 750 A.D. to 1300 was known as the *Pfennigzeit* (penny time). Originally, the penny was a silver coin. Later, the *Plappart* (or *Blaffert*), *Batzen, Dicken, Groschen, Gulden, Heller, Kreuzer, Schilling*, and *Taler* appeared. It is tempting to tabulate the relative values of these coins as Ochsenbein and several encyclopedists have attempted. The attempt failed because Bonaparte's Act of Mediation returned to the cantons their former autonomy and rights of coinage, previously centralized by Napoleon in the "one and indivisible" Helvetic Republic. Later, the central government was enabled to introduce a uniform system of coinage. The franc was again fixed in value at ten *Batzen* and one *Batzen* was declared equal to ten *Rappen* (or centimes). The Federal Constitution of 1848 was soon followed by the law on currency (in 1850). This law transferred the exclusive right of coinage from the cantons and others to the Federal Government. The Swiss and French francs were declared to be of equal value. Until then, as many as 56 different authorities had the right to stamp out their own coins. At one time as many as 700 different pieces of money were in use in Switzerland (**257**). The *Batzen* was long ago withdrawn from circulation.

32. I am indebted to Colonel Reichel, Chief of the Federal Military Library, for the information (transmitted by Colonel Freedman, then Defense Attaché at the U.S. Embassy in Bern) that "this custom is as old as Switzerland itself." Every male Swiss, from age 16 on, was subject to military duty, continuing, in general, to the age of 60. (At the present time compulsory military duty begins at age 20 (recruit school) and continues to age 50 with a total of 52 weeks of military training spread over the 31

years of obligatory service.) With a few exceptions the man had to provide his own weapons. This requirement lasted until the constitution of 1874. In the early days, from Morgarten in 1315 to Marignano in 1515, the weapons were the halberd, the long spear (5.5 meters), the sword and the crossbow.

The morning star (a club, heavily covered with iron spikes) came later, apparently around 1620. The halberd and the long spear were favored in the fourteenth and fifteenth centuries. Young boys (400 in number and 8 or 10 to 15 years of age) carried the military equipment of the men returning from the Burgündian war. This was an introduction to their military training. Then came the drills, learning to march in good order and to carry weapons properly (163, pp. 7–12).

33. The Third National Peace entitled "*Friedenschluss zwischen Zürich und Bern und den Katholischen Orte (dritter Landfriede)*" was signed at Baden on 7 March 1656. This accord came about through the intermediation of Basel, Freiburg, Schaffhausen and Solothurn. All thirteen cantons were represented in the negotiations: the seven principals and the six remaining members of the Confederation (*Abschiede* VI. 1, 1633–37).

34. In 1687, two of the high-ranking officers, Escher of Zürich and Daxelhofer from Bern, were sent under diplomatic status and protection to seek a clarification of French policy toward Switzerland and Geneva. They refused to accept the lavish gifts that were offered by the King. Other favors were declined. Louis must have been impressed by the uncompromising rectitude of the Swiss special ambassadors, for he refrained from any further threats to Geneva.

35. Swiss officers in foreign service moved about quite freely. Heinrich Bürkli, since 1669, was in the military service of the Palatinate. In 1688 he participated in the defense of Heidelberg against the French. He entered the service of the kaiser in the following year and in 1691 became a regimental commander of Swiss troops assigned to protection of the Austrian cities on the Rhine. In 1724 he was promoted by the kaiser to the rank of Field Marshal General. This is but one of many examples of the "itinerant" nature of the service of Swiss army officers in the seventeenth century.

36. "In order to ensure the peace and neutrality of the Fatherland, Basel and Zurich are fully empowered to summon the War Council on the approach of an army and to arrange for troops, weapons and all necessary supplies..." (*Abschiede*, VI, 1, 921a, 3 May 1674). Both Basel and Zurich were alarmed by the closeness of belligerent forces to the Rhine, their boundary to the north. The document (*Abschiede*) in the archives of Basel and other cantons is a more strongly worded declaration of neutrality which may have suffered from editing when transcribed into nineteenth century German. It permits one to regard the action of the Diet in 1674 as the elevation of Swiss neutrality to a guiding principle in foreign policy, as Bonjour has pointed out (49, I, p. 19).

37. The Constitution of the Swiss Confederation refers to the 22 members as sovereign cantons which in their totality constitute the Confederation. Article 3 states explicitly that "the cantons are sovereign insofar as their sovereignty is not limited by the Federal Constitution, and as such they exercise all rights which have not been given over to the Federal Authority."

38. *Abschiede* V. 2, 1068f; Baden, 2 February 1638. Note the exceptional permission granted to France for a special *Durchpass* in 1703 (*Abschiede* VI. 2a, p. 1062, Baden, 20 May).

39. *Abschiede* V. 2, 1003b, September 1636.

40. *Abschiede* V. 2, 1072, 16 March 1638; 1140h, June/July 1639.

41. For quite some time contraband was not well defined. General terms alone, no specifics, were used in the "Articles of Peace between France and Spain" (7 November 1659; Articles XII, XIII), in the "Treaty of Commerce between England and Holland" (17 February 1668; Articles II, III, IV) and in "A Declaration of War against France, and a Placart of the States General of the United Provinces, concerning the Commerce of the Inhabitants of the said Provinces; as also of neutral Powers in the Ports of France..." (9 March 1689, Article II). See Jenkinson (198, I, pp. 113, 190, 209, 273).

42. *Abschiede* V. 2, p. 1418, Baden, February–March 1647.

43. The distance a man would walk in two hours, approximately six miles.

44. *Abschiede* VI. 2a, pp. 244–47, Baden, 6–14 December 1688; VI. 2a, pp. 268–73, Baden, 25 April to 7 May 1689. From the beginning of the Spanish War of Succession, Louis XIV favored Swiss neutrality and neutralization of the banks of the Rhine, specifically Rheinfelden, Laufenburg, the Fricktal,

Waldshut, Sackingen, and one mile north of the river and of Lake Constance. In this matter he was generous, agreeing to pay the costs of occupation by neutral Swiss forces. Later, he warned the Swiss of the imminent *Durchzug* by General Mercy, but Switzerland did nothing to protect the Rhine crossing points. The Swiss ignored the French warning (**128**, p. 109).

45. In April 1708 Switzerland urged that commerce be restored between France and the Principality, and that the people of this border territory be left in peace. The King of France was also assured that under guarantees of the Confederation the inhabitants of the city and province of Neuchâtel would not disturb the peace and repose of his land and people. These proposals and assurances were ratified and approved by Louis XIV (*Abschiede* VI. 2, p. 1431, 2 May 1708).

46. William Aglionby was appointed by Queen Anne of England as "Envoye Extrdry to the Confederate States of the Suisse Cantons." His instructions in some 20 "Articles" were very detailed and, in themselves, informative about the state of affairs in Switzerland. Aglionby reported with even greater detail on each instruction. Aglionby was instructed "to reside at Zurich or Berne as you shall find most expedient for our service."

> The Canton of Berne being the powerfullest of all the Cantons seemes uneasye at the preeminence wch Zurich has of having the directorye and chancerye of all the Cantons wch gives that Canton a kind of superiority in their councils; but this being settled from the beginning Berne cannot hope to alter it, but I found that they thought that if they could make their Canton the constant Residence of all protestant Ministers it would in some measure equall them to Zurich . . . I resolved to settle at Zurich as the center of all the deliberations of the helvetick body. (**6**)

The fourth article of his instructions, as interpreted in a subsequent paragraph, directed Aglionby to "compasse an Allyance with the Cantons and an offensive league against france." But he discovered that the Swiss "still avoyd disobliging france unnecessarily; that their circumstances would noe wayes allow them to depart from an exact neutrality" (**6**).

47. This estimate can hardly be reconciled with a statement on page 159 of Zinsser's book that typhus and scurvy killed 18,000 soldiers.

7. THE EIGHTEENTH CENTURY TO THE END OF THE OLD CONFEDERATION

Introduction

The wars of religion within the Confederation might appear to have ended with the third nationwide peace of 1656 which settled the first Villmergen War. But much dissension remained, one constant source of friction between the catholic and Reformed cantons being in their joint administration of Baden and the *Freien Ämter* (Free Districts). These parts of the Aargau had fallen to the eight members of the Confederation in 1394 and in 1415. Population trends in favor of the Reformed cantons, industrialization, and development of economic power by the Reformed *Orte* left the catholic cantons in a relatively weakened state, lacking in the strength to play a decisive role in decision-making on matters of importance to the whole Confederation. The death of Louis XIV in 1715, a friend and virtual protector of the catholic cantons, also deprived them of strong support from a very powerful neighbour. Urgently in search of assistance from others, the catholic cantons had renewed in 1695 and 1696 their alliances with Valais and with the Bishop of Basel. Beyond moral support for the catholic cause there is no evidence that these alliances effectively strengthened the catholic position.

The Toggenburg Problem

The increasing influence of the Reformed cantons, if related to the tenacity with which the two sides in the religious conflict held to their ideological positions, was doomed to lead to a renewal of stubborn and violent confrontation. Trouble soon arose when the Abbot of St. Gallen, a prince of the Empire, decided to construct a road from Wattwil in Toggenburg to Uznach (near the Schwyz border) with the declared intention of improving the communications between Schwyz and St. Gallen. This seemingly innocent proposal aroused considerable opposition in Toggenburg where the protestant faction regarded the proposed road as a military highway to facilitate the movement of troops from catholic Schwyz. Toggenburg was a subject territory of the abbot and at the same time enjoyed the benefits of an old protective treaty with Schwyz and Glarus and certain rights of self-government. The abbot was not inclined to yield in his determination to build the road and, indeed, decided to absorb part of the costs which the community of Wattwil would otherwise be obliged to pay.[1] The Toggenburgers continued in their opposition and the autocratic abbot with stubborn resolve began to impose fines, to arrest and to bring to trial his opponents in Toggenburg. The small "war" soon assumed a greater dimension when the Reformed cantons joined in opposing the abbot. The abbot replied by negotiating a treaty of protection with the Kaiser, Leopold I—an act which aroused great concern within the Confederation. While Glarus, true to its old treaty, continued to support Toggenburg, Schwyz was sharply divided: one faction urged that the protective treaty with Toggenburg be terminated, but others used their influence in urging that Schwyz assist the Toggenburgers in their drive for independence. The decision was not easily made but in the summer of 1703 the *Landsgemeinde* agreed that Toggenburg would continue under the protection of Schwyz and a so-called Peasants' Law was agreed upon with Toggenburg. With the influence and power of Louis XIV now declining, Bern and Zurich boldly proposed to the abbot in 1707 that freedom of religion be granted in Toggenburg with equal recognition of the right of all of its people to practice the religion of their choice. This was coupled with demands for greater freedom of self-government in Toggenburg—hence, an implied increase in freedom from the oppressive authority of the Abbot of St. Gallen. Leodegar, the Abbot, promptly and decisively denied the proposals. With equal alacrity, the *Landsgemeinde* of Toggenburg declared for its people freedom in their adherence to either the catholic or the reformed faith. This declaration converted the Toggenburg problem from a political to a confessional-oriented dispute. Schwyz, faithful to the catholic cause, terminated its alliance with Toggenburg and switched its support to the abbot. Louis XIV protested against the intervention of Bern and Zurich and, though it was an empty threat, declared his intention to invade Vaud. The Toggenburgers in 1710 seized several castles of the abbot and threatened the income of the abbey with expropriation of its assets in the subject State.

Civil War

War broke out in 1712 between the cantons of the catholic and reformed faiths. Basel, Schaffhausen, and Appenzell stood aside from the conflict because of the neutrality requirement imposed upon them when they entered the Confederation. Freiburg, Solothurn, and the Bishop of Basel refused to become involved because of political considerations. Glarus also refrained from any further involvement in the dispute. The armies engaged in combat at Bremgarten in Aargau. It was an unequal contest for the primitively organized troops of *Innerschweiz*, still mainly equipped with the lance, the halberd and the "morning star".[2] They were no match for the well organized and disciplined troops of Generals von Tscharner and de Sacconay, supplied with more modern weaponry and better trained in military tactics. The hoped-for support from France was not received and the catholic forces suffered a major defeat. The army of the reformed cantons pressed on through Thurgau and the Rhine Valley and occupied Toggenburg. The abbot fled to south Germany, and the forces of Generals von Tscharner and de Sacconay conquered Baden. The war might have ended in June 1712. Both sides were tired of the conflict but only Lucerne and Uri were prepared to accept the terms of peace proposed by Bern and Zurich, especially the requirement that the catholic cantons be denied any right of participation in the government of Baden and the *Freien Ämter* which for many years had been governed in common by all members of the Confederation.

The negotiations terminated and the war continued. A new army of 9000 men from *Innerschweiz* engaged their enemy, about equal in number, at Villmergen in late July. Both sides suffered heavy losses and by the end of the day the forces led by Bern emerged victorious.

The Peace of Aarau

The war was concluded with the fourth national peace, the Peace of Aarau, 11 August 1712.[3] Catholic domination came to an end, and basically equal rights for both confessions were granted throughout the Confederation. Each *Ort* could continue in the confession of its choice and in Baden and the *Freien Ämter* the catholic and reformed religions were granted equal recognition. The Second National Peace Treaty of 1531 which was oriented in favor of the catholic cause was declared null and void and surrender to Zurich of the pertinent documents of 1531 was ordered.

Political adjustments were also a consequence of the Peace of Aarau. The county of Baden and the northerly part of the *Freien Ämter*, including Mellingen and Bremgarten, were transferred to the jurisdiction of Bern and Zurich. Bern, from then on, participated with Zurich in the administration of Thurgau, the Rheintal, Sargans (east of Glarus—now a part of the canton of St. Gallen) and the remainder of the *Freien Ämter*: the catholic cantons were henceforth excluded. Presumably the intent of this political readjustment was to achieve a more balanced division of territory between the catholic and reformed cantons.

The Peace was not conciliatory and tended only to perpetuate dissension and political strife. The catholic cantons demonstratively assembled their people on the Rütli to swear the ancient oath of mutual defense and to renew the Borromaic Alliance of 1586. Eager to seek the help of France, the catholic cantons and associated places (Lucerne, Uri, Schwyz, Appenzell Inner Rhoden, the catholic part of Glarus, Unterwalden, Zug, Valais, Freiburg and Solothurn) persuaded Louis XIV, now old and weary, to renew an alliance with them. This he did unwillingly, for he had no desire to jeopardize the chances of renewing the agreement of 1663 with the entire Confederation. The treaty had assured him of a continuing inflow of Swiss troops essential to his imperialistic ambitions. Officially, the new alliance with the catholic cantons and their associates, signed in May 1715, was for protection of the faith, but the French Ambassador in Solothurn, Count du Luc, who acted on behalf of the monarch signed a separate and secret agreement—concealed from the King— which committed France to provide military aid in case of a renewed religious war in Switzerland. Du Luc's activities behind the backs of Bern and Zurich were certainly known to the British government through the reports of Stanyan, the British Ambassador in Bern. However, France drew back from any direct provocation of the protestant cantons (**236**, p. 40). The aging monarch died shortly thereafter and the so-called "Truckli Bund" lost its importance in the new political arena.

Domestic Peace

For the next 80 years, in spite of the religious discord which the Peace of Aarau only served to perpetuate, Switzerland enjoyed internal peace. Perhaps it was only superficial but the years were of great importance in the development of the Confederation. The turmoil and constitutional upheavals of the Napoleonic years that followed were shattering in the extreme yet political restructuring in those dreadful years provided the kind of experience in government that was an indispensable foundation for the period of reconstruction (1815–48).

Wars continued to be fought with but little interruption in other parts of Europe, but they had little direct impact upon Switzerland. Russia developed into a great European power. Austria brought together the independent duchies, the almost autonomous provinces, and subject lands of which she was constituted, and rose to be the most powerful State in southeastern Europe, challenged only by the Ottoman Empire which reached far into the Balkan peninsula and northwards to Austria. Prussia had risen to greatness and was recognized as a powerful neighbour by Russia, the other German States and Austria. France had lost her extensive possessions on the North American continent to Great Britain. The revolutionary unrest within the thirteen colonies and the American War of Independence which soon followed were a part of the ferment which found its ultimate expression in Europe in the French Revolution. But through it all, until the contagion of unrest and the Napoleonic wars spread into Switzerland, the country enjoyed an inner peace.

Science and Scholarship

Science and scholarship began to flourish, notably in Basel and Geneva where the liberalizing influence of humanistic studies created an academic freedom in which dogma could be challenged and new and unorthodox investigation in the sciences could be pursued without repression. The border cities, unlike Bern and Zurich, were heavily penetrated by French refugees to whom the old orthodoxy was completely foreign. In addition to the brilliant work of the Bernoullis, Leonhard Euler, and Lambert in pure and applied mathematics, many studies were directed toward the practical needs of the people. Higher education and fundamental research into basic questions were regarded as luxuries which could be ill afforded.[4] In applied mathematics, for example, attention was directed to such projects as navigation problems on the high seas, the optimum position for a ship's mast, calendar making, and land measurement.

Science Organizations

Science organizations also came into being (142). Possibly the earliest was the *Collegium Insulanum* which existed through the brief four-year span 1679–83. It was founded under the inspiration of Johann Jakob Wagner of Zurich, a physician and natural scientist. The *Collegium Insulanum* was soon followed by the *Gesellschaft der Wohlgesinnten* (1693–1703) with a small membership of officials, military officers, theologians, and merchants.

To a considerable extent, much of science and scholarly study was then an avocation of the *Liebhaber*—the dedicated amateur whose intellectual pursuits were in theology, philosophy, and the humanistic sciences. The distinction between research and dilettantism was vague, and the supreme authority in answering the provocative questions raised by the science of the times was the Bible, the writings of the ancients, or the pope. The Society is reported to have interested itself in such intellectual exercises as "whether witches can really go by air from one place to another," "where the soul of Lazarus rested from his death to his raising from the dead," and "whether Samson was guilty of suicide."

Two societies with special interests in mathematics, were the *Gesellschaft der Feuerwerker*, founded in 1686, and the *Mathematisch-militarische Gesellschaft*, founded in 1765. The first of these is still very much alive. Under its new name, *Artillerie-Collegium*, it holds regular meetings and publishes every January a *Neujahrs Blatt*.

An attempt was made, at the end of the seventeenth century, to found an all-Swiss polyhistorical society under the presidency of the theologian Samuel Werenfels. The idea originated with the physician and botanist Theodor Zwinger who made the proposal to a group of scientists in Basel in 1702. Nothing came of the plan, evidently because of the general preoccupation with the Spanish War of Succession and the beginnings of the Toggenburg troubles.

In 1745, the physician Heinrich Rahn proposed to Johannes Gessner, Professor of Physics and Natural Sciences in Zurich, that a Physical Society be organized. With the support of various "gentlemen," the *Physikalische Gesellschaft* was founded. Lectures and laboratory studies were arranged. Gessner hoped that from this would emerge a College for Experimental Physics and Natural History. The Society did undergo a transformation, at least in name, and in 1746 became the Natural Science Society (*Naturforschende Gesellschaft*) of Zurich. The Society, which met every 14 days, was the recipient of many valuable gifts, especially books and instruments.

Several years later, in Basel, at the suggestion of the printer Johann Rudolf ImHof, the *Societas Physica-Mathematico-Anatomico-Botanico-Medica Helvetica* was organized. In 1751 ImHof published at his own expense the first volume of the

Acta of the Society. The ninth and last volume appeared in 1787. Among those whose papers appeared in the volume were Albrecht von Haller of Bern,[5] J. G. Sulzer of Winterthur, J. H. Lambert of Mülhausen, Leonhard Euler of Basel, Daniel Bernoulli of Basel, and Jacques Barthelemy Micheli du Crest[6] of Geneva.

An *Ökonomische Gesellschaft* was founded in Bern in 1759 under the initiative of Johann Rudolf Tschiffeli. This, in turn, was the forerunner of the Natural Science Society of Bern, which was founded in 1786 by Samuel Wyttenbach. A medical society, the first in Switzerland, was founded in 1713 in Geneva by Daniel Leclerc and reorganized in 1775 as the *Société des Médecins de Genève*. One year later H. B. de Saussure[7] of Geneva organized the *Société des Arts* for scholars, artisans and craftsmen. After reorganization by the government in 1786, the Society provided courses of public instruction in metallurgy, applied mechanics, and watch- and clock-making.

Many societies, cultural and technological, were organized during these times. Most were quite ephemeral. But as the century was coming to an end, one of the most important of all was conceived. This was the *Schweizerische Naturforschende Gesellschaft* (Swiss Society for Natural Science) which came into being in 1815. The purpose of its two founders, Jakob Samuel Wyttenbach of Bern and H. A. Gosse of Geneva, was to organize an all-Swiss Society of Natural Science which would unite in a single body the scientists and interested laymen of the two main lingustic regions of the country, *Suisse allemagne* to the east and *Suisse romande* to the west. In October 1797 an organizing group met in Herzogenbuchsee but the time was not quite right for consummation of their plans: Geneva was already occupied by Napoleonic troops and only a few months more were to elapse before the whole country fell before the French invaders. With the end of the Napoleonic wars, Geneva became a Swiss canton in September 1814 and the Society was at last established one year later. The important role of the Society in the scientific affairs of present-day Switzerland has been described elsewhere (**219**).

Swiss Scientists and Technologists of Note

THE BERNOULLIS   The three most famous of the Bernoullis were certainly Jakob (1654–1705), Johann (1667–1748)—a brother of Jakob—and Daniel (1700–82), the second son of Johann. Their earlier studies, enriched by travel to centers of learning in Europe, were in theology or medicine, but their natural aptitude and love for mathematics led them irresistibly into mathematics,[8] physics and, sometimes, into seemingly unrelated fields.

LEONHARD EULER   Leonhard Euler (1707–83)[9] was the favorite pupil of Johann Bernoulli. He became one of the great universalists of his day with remarkable achievements in pure and applied mathematics, physics, mechanics, technology, philosophy, and religion. His assembled works, in the course of publication by the Euler Commission of the Swiss Society of Natural Science, are expected to fill 80 quarto volumes.

LAMBERT   Johann Heinrich Lambert of Mülhausen (1728–77), coming from very humble beginnings, pursued his interest in mathematics with considerable difficulty. He developed a great reputation in Europe in mathematics, mathematical astronomy, optics and philosophy. Kant, with whom he had an extensive correspondence, regarded him highly.

VON HALLER   Albrecht von Haller was possibly the greatest universalist of the century. His intellectual interests covered all fields of scholarship. He was a famous botanist, a geologist, a physiologist, a grammarian, and a poet. Under "Notes and Comments", a more detailed sketch of his life is presented.[5]

DE SAUSSURE   Horace-Benedict de Saussure contributed tremendously to geology, geophysics, exploration of the Swiss Alps and the development of instruments useful in mountaineering and indispensable in meteorology. A biographical sketch[7] is given in "Notes and Comments".

GOSSE   Henri Albert Gosse (1755–1816) of Paris and Geneva studied chemistry, anatomy, surgery and physiology. He did some good experiments on digestion which were published by Senebier [*Oeuvres de Spallanzani* II (1787), pp. 378–891]. The study was facilitated by Gosse's ability to vomit at will. Next, he turned to pharmacy and established himself in Geneva in 1788. Not content with mixing potions he was soon immersed in activities that were far removed from ointments, herbals and elixirs: a study of glaciers, the composition of potters' clay, the bleaching action of chlorine, problems in botany, and in geology. With Schweppe[10] he invented artificially carbonated water. He was also active in political affairs and was sent to France officially to oppose the efforts of those who were urging that Geneva be annexed to France. He managed to escape all the hazards of the revolution despite his friendship with some who were guillotined. Perhaps his most notable achievement, shared with Wyttenbach, was the founding of the Swiss Society for Natural Science.

WYTTENBACH   Jakob Samuel Wyttenbach (1748–1830) of Bern was Gosse's counterpart in *Suisse allemande*. Though a theologian, by virtue of his early training and as pastor of the Church of the Holy Ghost, his interests in natural philosophy knew no bounds. Botany, mineralogy, crystallography, geology, glaciology, and the Swiss Alps all fell within the compass of his scientific curiosity. In the Academy of Bern he held a teaching position in mineralogy together with an appointment in materia medica in the Medical Institute.

CHÉSEAUX   Jean Philippe Loys de Chéseaux (1718–51), a native of Lausanne, is another example of the gifted amateur, the true *Liebhaber*, who in his short lifetime established a lasting reputation because of his astonishing erudition. Apart from painting and music his early predilections led him into classical literature—Latin, Greek and Hebrew—and Arab, Chinese, Syrian, and Egyptian antiquities. His knowledge of geography astonished his contemporaries. He became interested in comets and was essentially a co-discoverer of the Klinkenberg-Struyck comet in

December, 1743. Three years later he discovered, without contest, a second comet, the Comet Chéseaux (82). His publications were numerous and diverse. He became a corresponding member of the four most distinguished scientific societies in Europe. Like many of his great contemporaries he was deeply religious and accepted the authority of the Bible. Fortunately for his peace of mind, his own studies never led him to challenge its prophecies and its explanations of the origin of the earth and man.

DU CREST   Jacques Barthelemy Micheli du Crest (1690–1766) was born into a famous refugee family which was hospitably received in Geneva a century or so prior to his birth. The family was honored by election into the burgher class. Jacques Barthelemy served as an officer in the French army but from 1738 on pursued his acquired interest in science. He moved within French scientific circles and later spent some time in Basel in association with Daniel Bernoulli. He made important contributions in geodetics, physics, thermometry, and cartography, and was among the first to use trigonometry in land surveying. In Geneva his competence in civil engineering was recognized. His services were employed in bridge construction and in reconstruction of the city's fortifications, but not without rigorous objections by du Crest to various policies of the government.[6] It is rather extraordinary that his most important work in science was done during his long political imprisonment (1747–66) in Aarburg.

KAPPELER   In Moritz Anton Kappeler of Lucerne (1685–1769) we find a man who spent many years in the practice of medicine but distinguished himself at home and abroad by his great contributions to mineralogy, crystallography, geology, the methodology of surveying, cartography, and the study of mountains. His five-year study of Mount Pilatus, published as a monograph in 1767, was unsurpassed for many decades in its quality, precision, and devotion to detail. His famous work on crystallography, published in 1723, was soon followed by Kappeler's election to the Royal Society (London).

J. J. SCHEUCHZER   Perhaps the first to publish anything of real substance on the natural history of the Alps was Johannes Jakob Scheuchzer (1672–1733) of Zurich who, along with Conrad Gessner (1516–65),[11] Leonhard Euler, and Albrecht von Haller, were the four greatest Swiss universalists. His intellectual pursuits penetrated deeply into medicine, natural history, mathematics, geology, paleontology, geography, cartography, history, theology, and philosophy. Of interest also is his book on dragons—an historical document based on the writings of others and on the tales told to him in the course of his travels. The book appeared, in Latin, under the imprimatur of the Royal Society of London of which he was a foreign member. Isaac Newton was then the President of the Society. Scheuchzer carefully avoided any personal judgment of belief or disbelief in the existence of dragons, although Conrad Gessner, in his book on snakes, had classified dragons within the snake family. Belief in the existence of dragons in the caves and deep chasms of the Swiss mountains was widespread, even in the eighteenth century. This is evident from the folklore and the names of some Alpine communities, such as Drachenberg, Drachenloch, and Drachenried. Six of the eleven dragons in Scheuchzer's book have been recently reproduced in an article by Müller (254).

BONNET   At least two Swiss biologists, in addition to the great von Haller, should be mentioned. Charles Bonnet of Geneva (1720–93) devoted himself to the classical languages while in college. He had no real interest in "dead languages" and left college with the reputation of being a poor scholar. His natural bent was in biology, stimulated by a memoir by Réaumur which came to his attention. At the age of 16 he made a study of caterpillars which received the commendation of Réaumur. At the age of 20 he discovered the phenomenon of embryonic development without fertilization, later known as parthenogenesis—a most important discovery which led to his election as a corresponding member of the French Academy of Science. Later he turned to botany, but his greatest contributions to science were in zoology. His complete works, assembled by himself, comprise eight volumes (1779–82) followed by eighteen published between 1779 and 1788.

HUBER   François Huber (1750–1831) came from an old Schaffhausen family which moved to Geneva and became burghers in 1654. His father awakened in the son a deep and persistent interest in science. At the age of 15 he completed his examinations in chemistry and physics with instruction from H.-B. de Saussure and Charles Bonnet. He became blind at 19 but carried on his remarkable studies on bees with the aid of his wife, his son (Jean Pierre) and another assistant. Noteworthy among his achievements was the discovery that the queen bee becomes fertilized while in flight and thereafter remains fertile for the rest of her life. He described the development of the queen bee from the larva of an ordinary worker through special feeding. He reported upon the building and architecture of the honey comb, and proved that the wax was not derived from pollen as had been previously believed. His research on bees was published both in Geneva and Paris. Huber is still regarded, worldwide, as one of the most important investigators of bees—a remarkable achievement for a man who was blind for all but 19 years of his life (143, p. 169).

JEAN ANDRÉ DE LUC (1727–1817)   de Luc, born in Geneva, developed an interest in geology and meteorology. In science he determined a relationship between barometric pressure and the height of mountains. With his brother he made a number of trips into the Faucigny Alps. He is best known for his letters about mountains, morals, and the history of the earth and of man. Six volumes of these letters were addressed to Queen Charlotte of England, wife of George III.

The great explorers and geologists of eighteenth century Switzerland have been mentioned: J. J. Scheuchzer, H.-B. de Saussure, M. A. Kappeler, and Albrecht von Haller. Of course there were others, but these four are mentioned because of their all-encompassing interest in natural phenomena and their great contributions to the natural history of the Alps.

This was a time when training in one field of learning opened the way to the pursuit of research in other quite distant subjects. Science and the entire world of learning, though well on the way to a seemingly orderly type of compartmentalization, nonetheless enjoyed a delightful fluidity such that the barriers between disciplines were nonexistent. The initial and formal training of the Bernoullis and of Leonhard Euler was in theology or medicine. Professional chairs were shuffled about with ease to accommodate the changing interests of the incumbent. Daniel Bernoulli became Professor of Anatomy in Basel in 1733 but did his research in hydrodynamics, and in 1750 succeeded in exchanging his chair in anatomy with that held by the Professor of Physics, and this he retained to the end of his life.

Foreign Visitors

There were also the travellers who published fascinating descriptions of the country. Their ventures into Swiss history, their descriptions of the towns, of the people, of government, of the majestic beauty of the Alps and of the awesome ruggedness of the mountains constitute an invaluable record of eighteenth century Switzerland. William Coxe in his three-volume *Travels in Switzerland* described with a wealth of detail the four extensive journeys that he made through Switzerland in the years 1776, 1779, 1785 and 1786. His letters to his patron, William Melmoth are the writings of a careful diarist and a keen observer (**95**). A. Yosy, who lived in Switzerland for a number of years, 15 or more, published in 1815 a two-volume work, *Switzerland, as Now Divided into Nineteen Cantons*, based largely on her travels into various parts of the country (**400**). The volumes are embellished with 50 colored engravings, illustrating the dress typical of different cantons, regions, and classes of people. They are rich in extravagant descriptions of the Alps, in horror stories, lurid tales, and "vulgar errors" (as Sir Thomas Browne described many curious beliefs that were then current in England). There is, however, sufficient solid substance in Yosy's writings to make the work a valuable record of eighteenth century Switzerland.

At least four other English travellers have left us fascinating descriptions of Switzerland and fairly good, but brief, accounts of her political history. The best of the four, in my judgment, is that of Abraham Stanyan (1669–1732), who spent a number of years in the British Foreign Service as Ambassador to Venice and, from 1705 to 1714, as Ambassador to the Reformed Cantons of Switzerland (**339**). A curious feature is that his name appears nowhere in the book—either on the title page or elsewhere therein. His description of the cantonal government of Bern, where he resided for eight years is excellent, though his description of the people, patronizing in the extreme, is hard to accept (e.g. pp. 134–39) despite its apologetic qualifications. Joseph Addison (1672–1719), an English statesman (**2**), also published a good and well-balanced account of his travels. As the title implies, most of the book is devoted to his observations in Italy but the section on Switzerland, from which I have taken a number of excerpts, is well worth reading. I believe that one would also enjoy the oldest of the four—the book by Gilbert Burnet (**78**) which was published in 1686. It is the most gossipy of the four, it contains many lurid tales, and is somewhat rich in extravagances. Burnet (1643–1715) was Professor of

Theology in Glasgow in 1669, a protestant vicar in London in 1674, and later Bishop of Salisbury.

While mentioning the travellers from England, we should not overlook John Evelyn, even though his famous diary pertains to the previous century. In the company of several others he made a "Grand Tour" of the continent which lasted some three years. Part of the tour in 1646 took him from Lombardy over the Simplon, down to Brig, and through the Rhone valley to Sion, Martigny, St. Maurice and into Savoy. From there the party went by boat to Geneva and finally entered France on their homeward journey. The Swiss phase of the journey lasted a few weeks only. In an earlier chapter I have described some of Evelyn's observations but it is appropriate at this point to write a few lines about the diarist himself. He lived from 1620 to 1706, entered Balliol College in Oxford in 1637, but was an indifferent scholar. Among his Balliol friends was Nathaniel Conopius from Greece who introduced Evelyn to coffee drinking,[12] carefully noted by Evelyn in his diary. After two journeys to the Low Countries in 1641 and Rome in 1643, he set out with a few companions on his so-called Grand Tour of 1644 to 1646. His diary covers the years 1641 to 1705–06 and was first printed in 1818. The Dobson edition (123) covers three volumes. The diary contains many inaccuracies (for example he places Brig in the Valtellina instead of Valais) which suggests that unlike his famous contemporary, Pepys, who made his entries day by day, Evelyn appears to have written up his observations and described his experiences much less frequently. Never again did Evelyn visit the Continent as a bona fide traveller. Writing on a great diversity of subjects, including "Fumifugium; or the Inconvenience of the Air and Smoke of London dissipated," was a passionate interest, expressed in dozens of notable publications, many of which did not appear until many years after his long life had ended. His diary is a chronicle, descriptive of great events and famous people during an unbroken span of sixty years.

Swiss Travellers

Of the Swiss travellers in the eighteenth century, Ruchat and Sinner are among the most interesting. Abraham Ruchat (311), who published his *Délices de la Suisse* in 1714, used the pseudonym Gottlieb Kypseler de Munster. The four volumes are given over, in large part, to a survey of the history of the Confederation. But they are not without many generalizations and contemporary observations. In the introduction, Ruchat bemoans the fact that Switzerland is poorly known even by her own people. The Swiss from the German-speaking part are poorly instructed about the French-speaking Swiss (the *Romandes*) to the west. And these in turn know even less about the German-speaking Swiss (the *Allemans*). One cautious (?) generalization by Ruchat: "the language of the Swiss Allemans is just as barbarous as it is believed to be in the heart of France." The French, Ruchat added, regarded the Swiss as rough, crude, simple, barbarous, heavy, and devoid of good manners. But, today, he explains, things have changed and the Swiss officers are possessed of good manners and have none of the qualities of a "simpleton." He continues his harsh criticism by mentioning a French lady who proposed to retire in Switzerland but feared at first to do so because she understood that in such a country, people lived in caves and the lairs of wild animals.

He was ecstatic about the mountains and the glaciers. The waters that run from the glaciers is the best imaginable. The peasants drink them as a sure cure of diarrhoea, dysentery, and some fevers. The are also recommended for the relief of toothache (no mention of snow water as a cause of goiter—a popular theory). "But one must not seat himself, nor sleep beside a fountain or in the snow. Otherwise one will not wake up, at least most will not. It is necessary to resist the temptation." He relates a story from the canton of Lucerne of a great bird with a wing spread of twelve feet that lived upon "young children, fish, fowls, and various kinds of quadrupeds." The same story was related by Yosy a hundred years later (**400**, I, p. 183) who attributed it to Father Lysat, Juriste de Lecrores. Yosy also describes (Vol. I, p. 111) the therapeutic qualities of the waters from glaciers and the dangers that attend sleeping "near the spot whence these waters issue," repeating, with no substantive change, the description given by Ruchat.

Ruchat concerns himself with a few other trivia such as the great age to which the people lived, mentioning that many live to 100 and more. This he attributed to the extensive use of milk, cheese and dairy products as their principal foodstuffs. Cheese was eaten in place of bread, which they baked only once or twice a year. Their longevity was also attributed to the purity of the mountain air and abstinence from luxuries such as coffee, tea, chocolate and various foreign liquors. Ruchat claimed that these were unknown in Switzerland before 1690 and their present consumption was leading to degeneration of the solid and sturdy Swiss.

The war of 1712 was fought during Ruchat's time. While noting that Bern and Zurich, arrayed against five of the Catholic cantons, were winning, he cautiously pointed out that there was no use in prophesying the final settlement, for there was no consensus as to how Bern and Zurich would divide their conquests and change the government of those territories (Baden and the *Freiämter*), jointly administered by the eight oldest cantons. In discussing political matters Ruchat made the sage observation: "The Swiss lack only one thing. They are not united. They are bound together by perpetual and inviolable treaties, from which they should regard themselves as brothers. But they are divided and the cause of their division is religion." As for the catholics of Uri or Schwyz "one may doubt whether the pope himself is more papist than they are" (**311**, p. 792 et seq.).

Ruchat was born near Vevey. After periods of study in Bern, Berlin and Leyden he became a pastor in the Reformed Church and then Professor of Elocution in the Academy at Lausanne. Next he became principal and finally Professor of Theology. As the first post-Reformation historian of the "Pays de Vaud," then a part of Bern, he searched the archives and libraries thoroughly for source material. At the age of 30 he published an ecclesiastical history of the Pays de Vaud. Later he completed a history of the Swiss Reformation, much of which remained unpublished until 1835.

Johann Rudolf von Sinner (1730–87) who travelled about western Switzerland gave more attention to libraries, book printing, and centers of learning than most of his contemporaries. (In 1748 he had been appointed chief librarian in Geneva.) In an interesting section on Calvin and Calvinism, Sinner states that the library in Geneva contains 344 letters written by Calvin and 2023 of his sermons bound in 44 volumes! As a center of book printing in Switzerland Geneva was second only to Basel in importance, so we are told by Sinner (**335**, II, pp. 70, 76).

It is well known that at least 50 different printers, engaged in book manufacture, were located in Basel up to 1600 and at least 17 more in the seventeenth century. Of course, not all of these were contemporaries. By 1799, with improvements in technology and increased output of individual establishments, the number had greatly declined. In all Switzerland the number of printing establishments and paper factories had decreased by the year 1799 to 39 and 33 respectively.

Several Notable Scholars

In so far as travellers through Switzerland left diaries, letters and books, descriptive of their travels, they served also as historians. Among the more professional eighteenth century historians one must mention Johann Jakob Bodmer of Zurich (1698–1783) and Isaak Iselin of Basel (1728–82). Both were historians of social movements, gifted in literature, poetry and philosophy but with little interest in economic and political history. Iselin's greatest work was his *History of Mankind*, published in 1768.

JOHANNES VON MÜLLER   The greatest historian in eighteenth century Switzerland was certainly Johannes von Müller (1752–1809). From 1796 to 1771 he studied theology and church history in Göttingen. Then, with encouragement from Professor August Ludwig Schlözer, he turned to profane history which he pursued for the rest of his life with dedicated single-mindedness despite other responsibilities and high appointments. At the age of 20 he became Professor of Greek in his home town of Schaffhausen. Later he served in Mainz (1787) and Vienna (1792) as a librarian, diplomat and publicist. In 1804 he became an historiographer in Berlin. After the 1806 reconciliation with Napoleon he was appointed as State Secretary and Minister to the Kingdom of Westphalia. This gave him little satisfaction, his health began to fail and he sought retirement from the position. In 1808 he was appointed by the King to the Council of State and General Director of Education. It is quite clear that he suffered under such honorable but, for von Müller, quite unrewarding positions. He lived a very simple life and much preferred his studies and his writings. He was the author of some 28 books, of which the most famous is his history of the Swiss Confederation (**255**), of which five volumes, ending with 1489, appeared between 1780 and 1808. The work was continued by others who added an additional thirteen volumes. Bonjour (**48**), a Swiss historian of the present day, speaks of von Müller as the intellectual heir of Aegidius Tschudi—a great compliment in itself. Von Müller, incidentally, attached tremendous importance to the balance-of-power principle which dominated the political policy of European States from the days of William III of Orange onwards. Britain was a great champion of the idea since, from her insular position, she could not afford to be jeopardized by a too-powerful neighbour on the mainland. As a young man, von

Müller vigorously advocated adherence to this policy in the political strategies within Europe. He was well aware of the constant struggle between the Bourbons and the Habsburgs for attainment of a universal monarchy. He lived in fear of an hegemony under Kaiser Joseph II who, Müller wrote, would destroy the small States of Europe: Holland, Switzerland, Venice, Geneva, and many small German States. "Since the barbarians from the north destroyed the throne of the Caesars, was Europe never so close to reunion of all administrations under a single despot." He noted with approval how the European States broke the power of France (Louis XIV). Strangely enough, despite all of his fears and pessimism, he did not look upon the rise of Napoleon as ushering in the end of the world (**51**).

VATTEL   Eighteenth century Switzerland also gave birth to one of the greatest students and European authorities in the field of international law. I refer to Emmerich de Vattel (1714–67) of Neuchâtel. His three-volume work, *Les droits des gens ou principes de la loi naturelle*, published in London in 1758, is a model of clarity (**374**). Many of his concepts of neutrality and of the rights and responsibilities of a neutral State have been accepted by later authorities in international law and are incorporated in the reports of the international conferences at London and the Hague. His statement on national sovereignty is simple and direct:

> No nation has the right to meddle in the government of another. . . . It is a manifest consequence of the liberty and independence of nations, that all have the right to govern themselves as they choose, and no one has the least right to intrude himself (se mêler) in the government of another. Of all the rights which belong to a nation, its sovereignty is without doubt the most precious . . . (Book II, Chapter IV, p. 21).

Vattel, also interested in the balance-of-power, provided a legalistic definition: "a description of things by means of which no Power finds itself in a state of absolute predominance and of making the law for others (Book III, Chap. III, pp. 496ff).

DUMONT   Etienne Dumont (1759–1829) of Geneva was not an authority in jurisprudence, but his views on the philosophy of government have been of lasting importance. Actually, from the age of 22, he served for some years as a pastor in the reformed church. But his years in England where he was a close associate of Jeremy Bentham, and in France where he was equally close to Mirabeau, gave him an insight into government that permitted him to present with authority his own philosophy of government. Depressed by the emerging terrorism in France as the Revolution grew from more to more, Dumont returned to Geneva. There, as a member of the administrative committee created by the new revolutionary regime, he was unable to counternance the excesses of the government and, in 1793, returned to England where he remained until 1814. His strong religious convictions, his firm belief in Christian charity as a basis for government, his passion for liberty and for order within the law, were basic to his philosophy. He was not a revolutionary and, having witnessed the French Revolution from within and from without, he endeavoured to set forth the rules which ought to regulate the conduct of affairs of state.

KARL LUDWIG VON HALLER   Karl Ludwig von Haller (1768–1854) of Bern, a grandson of the great Albrecht von Haller (1708–1777), was Professor of State and International Law in Bern. He witnessed the fall of his city to the armies of Napoleon and the complex developments in the philosophy and form of government imposed by Napoleon upon the Swiss people. On becoming a catholic in 1820 he was excluded from the Great Council of Bern and was virtually obliged to leave the city. He moved to Paris and served under Charles X as a publicist and diplomat. With the fall of the Bourbons he returned to Switzerland. Between 1816 and 1834 his life's work "Restoration of the Science of Government or Theory of the Natural State of Society" appeared as a six-volume publication. His concept of government was simple. The weak seek the protection of the strong and, in turn, serve them. Thus the father rules over his wife and children, the leader over his followers, and the lord of a House over his servants and retainers. He voiced the political desire of the Bernese patricians to restore the ancient regime. His patrician concept of government gained popularity among the intellectual and political leaders of France, Italy, Prussia, Austria, and Spain.

Corruption in High Places

Although Switzerland was seemingly at peace with herself and with her neighbours, we might well ask whether the morality of the people and the extent of social justice were any different than in France where events during the days of Louis XV and Louis XVI led inexorably to the revolution of 1789. The French court and the upper layers of society, so brilliant in various ways, were deeply steeped in corruption. They were generous patrons of literature, of science, and of the arts. They were also morally decadent. The acquisition of wealth, of position, of favors at the court were ruthlessly and shamelessly pursued. There were also the great writers who in the novels of the eighteenth and nineteenth centuries depicted the luxurious lives of the rich in contrast to the wretched lives of the poor. Social injustice was rampant and the penalties heaped upon the poor for trivial offences were frequently excessive in cruelty. Only a few spellbinders and a strong underground were needed to bring on a revolution.

As contrasted with France, Switzerland stands out in bold relief. It lacked a ruling monarch, a court, a central government rich in the resources and power upon which an aristocracy could feed. The division of power among the thirteen sovereign cantons and their subject and associated States was not conducive to the growth of corruption, open or ill-concealed, such as was to be seen in the French capital. There were families of great wealth, it is true, but the ostentatious display of riches was not regarded with favor, and perhaps never has been. Switzerland of the eighteenth century, like that of the twentieth, was a country of hard-working people where toil and assiduous use of one's talents were virtues. This was not the kind of environment in which indolence, corruption, and depravity could flourish.

Frugality and the Simple Life

Frugality and outward simplicity in life were encouraged. In Zurich, government maintained the strictest economy. It was not only free of debt but reserves of money were carefully husbanded to provide against any sudden emergency. The entire cost of the war of 1712 against the catholic cantons was paid from accumulated reserves without the imposition of an additional tax (95). To minimize ostentation, Zurich disallowed the use of carriages in the town—except by strangers. The edict was not designed to reduce traffic congestion in the public thoroughfares. In Basel, it took a different and rather peculiar form. The use of carriages was not prohibited, but citizens and inhabitants were denied the privilege of having a servant at the rear. In some of the towns e.g. in the Valais, many responsible citizens persistently opposed all improvements, motivated by frugality but also by the fear that improvements would invite visitors to the towns and "a concourse of strangers would only serve to introduce luxury among the inhabitants, and destroy that simplicity of manners for which the *Vallaisans* are so remarkably distinguished" (95). There were no standing armies, and this, as decades passed, together with an official dedication to frugality permitted Bern, Zurich, and Basel as well as other towns to store away relatively large amounts of gold which was seized by the French and shipped to Paris when Napoleon conquered the country.

Religion

One should not overlook the role of religion. The persistence of confessional hatreds from the early days of the Reformation far into the eighteenth century reflect the depth of religious feelings and the firm grip of religion upon the Swiss. Hatred of one confession toward the other was common enough but there was also to be found a great diffusion of pious attention to the rules of religious behaviour and observance of rituals. Though one may argue that much of this was only formal, superficial and devoid of Christian humility, tenderness and love, it must be conceded that the environment did not favor gross corruption and depravity.

Social Injustice and Class Distinctions

Certainly there were occasional instances of malfeasance within the bureaucracy; there were lapses in the integrity of high officials, and violations of trust within the people's representatives, but such instances of wrong-doing appear to have been few and far between. But, according to present day standards, there was social injustice, some of it in a form that may have been uniquely centered in the aristocratic and oligarchic city cantons of Switzerland. A rigidity of class developed which was totally foreign to the fourteenth and fifteenth centuries, for example. In those early years it was possible for one to rise from serfdom into the class of the free. Social distinctions tended to disappear as the serfs were emancipated. Thus a serf who dwelt for a year and a day within the walls of a town could no longer be claimed by his lord. In the *Waldstätte* the numerous serfs of the ecclesiastical and temporal lords became free peasants either by revolt or by purchase. From 1413 onwards, Bern steadily abolished serfdom by means of purchase of one's freedom. In 1485 the city declared that hereditary serfdom would no longer be tolerated. Marriage into the nobility, at least the lesser nobility, was perfectly possible. Class distinctions meant little. Those of the lower social classes still enjoyed the opportunity and right to become burghers, the social layer in which government at all levels was vested. By 1500 there were only two classes in Switzerland: (a) the burghers of the sovereign towns and the country folk of the sovereign rural cantons; (b) inhabitants of the subject domains. Later on a patriciate class emerged in some of the cantons. Until then a subject could enter a town and for a few *gulden* could become a citizen. Honors and offices became as open to him as if he was a burgher by birth. "How could any rule against their will a people, each of whom had a pike and a halberd in his home?" (**274**)

But by the seventeenth century a hardening of class distinctions and a rigid separation of rights and privileges became manifest. Exclusivity of class in the aristocratic cantons was by now one of their distinguishing features. No longer was it possible for anyone born into the lower class, the subject families, to become a burgher, to enter into the ranks of government. We read, for example, that in Zurich "on the 7th of January, 1661, the [Sovereign] Council determined to make no "more burghers; which resolution has been invariably followed" (**95**).

That such exclusivity was uniformly and rigidly observed throughout the Confederation was certainly not the case. As with many other laws, ordinances, and customs there were differences from canton to canton. Purchase of burghership was a common practice. Sometimes it was conferred as an honor in recognition of public service, or to confer status upon an important and distinguished foreigner who had become an inhabitant of the town. In Neuchâtel, 138 were accepted as burghers between 1760 and 1785. Of these 38 were foreigners, i.e. German, French, or Swiss.[13] In Geneva also the burghership could be readily acquired by purchase.[14] Within the burgher class of the larger towns, luxury and opulence, but little ostentation, were fairly common. Population statistics for Zurich indicate that in 1780 not less than 20 per cent of the population consisted of servants, who had steadily increased in number though the population of the city had remained rather constant at 10,000 to 12,000 for several centuries. This suggests either an increase in the opulence of the "upper classes" or various economic pressures that expanded the servant class (principally female) in the towns. The possession of wealth was by no means confined to certain classes within the cities and towns. Farmers, throughout the fertile valleys, frequently were very prosperous. Coxe in his *Travels through Switzerland* noted that in the Emmental "many of the farmers are extremely rich." Burnet (**78**) who travelled through Switzerland in the preceding century made similar observations about the wealth of the peasantry. Stanyan described the peasants as "honest, robust, and laborious people . . . by Application and Industry, some of them arrive at great Riches for People of that Rank, it being no extraordinary thing to see a Farmer worth forty or fifty thousand Crowns" (**339**, p. 138).

Government

The government of eighteenth century Switzerland requires description. In large measure, for there were few changes until the French occupation, the government was also that of seventeenth century Switzerland. It is a complicated story, for it concerns a weak central government and the separate governments of thirteen sovereign cantons allied by interlocking treaties for their mutual protection and defense. Linguistic, confessional, and ethnic differences add to the complexity. Then we have the problems stemming from the deeply rooted differences between the rich, industrialized, urban-dominated cantons and the old, rather poor, rural cantons, based on agriculture and lacking in centers of manufacture and trade. The former were generally aristocratic oligarchies or guild-dominated, and the latter were democracies of a pure and primitive type.

Contributing to the weakness of the central government was its lack of authority and of administrative organs to exercise such powers as it did possess. Its most visible instrument was the *Tagsatzung*[15] or Diet which may be thought of as a parliamentary body. Ordinary sessions were held regularly and special sessions were called occasionally. Both concerned matters of common interest to the members of the Confederation and their associated and subject States—problems such as war, peace, and alliances. Maintenance of internal order was a subject of constant concern and also defense against belligerent foreign Powers. The Diet had neither legislative power nor the centrally available means to effect some decisions. These were binding upon the member States only when unanimity prevailed. For many years it had no fixed place of meeting and any *Ort* had the right to call the Diet into session. Hence, the special sessions were held only as the need arose and usually lasted only one or two days.[16] Later, Zurich, Bern, Lucerne, Baden, Frauenfeld, and Aarau became the accepted places of meeting, with Frauenfeld serving as the place of meeting from 1712 until the French invasion. The general Diet consisted of two representatives from each of the thirteen *Orte* and one from each of the associated States (the *Zugewandte*) the latter being invited but not required to attend. The French ambassador, who resided in Solothurn, was usually invited. The business of the Diet, in between its sessions, was transacted by the officers of the *Vorort*, the particular *Ort* in which the Diet had last met.

There was much rigidity in protocol. All details of sitting in rank order had to be meticulously observed, the representatives of the eight oldest *Orte* occupying elevated places. Each *Ort* had one vote and the representatives were not permitted to express their personal opinions. They were required to present the official and collective action of the legislative body of the *Ort* which they represented.

After the confessional split the catholic *Orte* met in Lucerne and the evangelical *Orte* in Aarau. These were recognized as special sessions of the *Tagsatzung*. After 1815 the *Vorort* and the place of meeting were one and the same, rotating every two years between Bern, Lucerne, and Zurich (**179**).

The aristocratic cantons were seven in number. Each was centered around a city and originally included very little of the surrounding territory. Hence, government was vested in the citizens and even when the cantons became quite large through territorial expansion only citizens of the ruling town had any voice in government.

The government of Bern can be regarded as typical of the aristocratic cantons. Sovereign power was vested in the Council of Two Hundred[17] (also called the Great Council). The Council was responsible for declarations of war, enactment of treaties of peace and of alliance with other cantons and foreign Powers, coinage, the treasury, civil employment in positions of any consequence, and in fact, the exercise of all other rights of absolute sovereignty. The filling of vacancies in the Council of Two Hundred was the responsibility of the Small Council or Senate, consisting of 27 members from the Council of Two Hundred, sixteen *Seizeniers* drawn by lot from among the older bailiffs, and two Envoys who presided over both Councils.

The government was clearly aristocratic, even oligarchic, because the sole right of filling vacancies in the Great Council was vested in the Small Council. Relatives and friends were almost invariably chosen, with the common citizens and tradesmen virtually excluded from government. The elections were held only once in nine or ten years, vacancies being permitted to accumulate until the Council was reduced in number to only about 100 active members. By this device and other peculiarities in the electoral procedure maximum opportunity was given to the remaining members to receive appointments as bailiffs, to be chosen for other lucrative positions of trust and to posts of ecclesiastical preferment, since only members of the Great Council qualified for such positions. Not uncommonly, an elector, of whom there were 43, would nominate his eldest son, or if he had daughters only, a prospective son-in-law. In practice, only three or four days elapsed between election of the *Seizeniers* and the elections to the Great Council. Hence, lovers in abundance appeared at the door of a newly elected *Seizenier* during those few days.[18] Sometimes the first words that were spoken between a lover and his prospective bride were the words of the marriage contract. This, we are told (**339**, p. 79), was the favored procedure for election to the Great Council, since few indeed gained admission by virtue of outstanding competence for such service. We are told by Coxe that since 1682 there were no constitutional checks of any kind[19] on the powers of the Great Council, "as a general assembly of the citizens is never convened on any occasion" (**95**, II, p. 221). The Great Council which met twice weekly was, in effect, the legislative body and the Small Council which met daily exercised executive functions.

Lucerne, also oligarchic, had a membership of only 100 in the Great Council and 36 in the Small Council. The sovereign power of the former was only nominal since in practice it actually resided in the latter. The Small Council was completely self-perpetuating because it filled any vacancies in its membership without the necessity of confirmation by the Great Council or the citizenry. A son generally succeeded his father or a brother succeeded his brother. Thus the power of government was vested in a few patrician families and the right of succession to council membership and to various positions of emolument and trust was virtually hereditary. But, unlike Bern, only an assembly of the burghers could declare war, execute treaties of peace or of alliance with other cantons or foreign Powers, or impose taxes.

Solothurn, after 1681, permitted only its "ancient" burghers to enjoy eligibility for membership in the Great Council and participation in the affairs of government. The ancient burghers were defined as those old and illustrious families "whose ancestors had, by their valour and prudence, laid the foundation of the republic" (**95**). Thus, by edict, eligibility for offices in government was restricted to the burghers of 1681 and to the families of their descendants. Various foreigners and others who were subsequently admitted to burghership were designated as "new" burghers and were denied the right of enjoying governmental positions of honour, trust, and emolument. Supreme power was thus vested in the ancient burghers of the Great Council to which others could not be elected until the number of member families was reduced to 25. It was also decreed that "any burgher who should make any proposition contrary to this law, should be banished from the canton, and that his goods should be confiscated" (**95**, I, pp. 224, 225).

In Zurich, Basel, and Schaffhausen, where the guilds were heavily represented in government, the "meaner sort of citizens and tradesmen" were eligible for membership in the Great Council.

In sharp contrast to the guild-dominated and the aristocratic-oligarchic governments of several of the cantons were the primitive democracies of the ancient *Waldstätte*. A fierce love of independence, of freedom from the rule of foreign Powers and a passionate determination to manage their own affairs under the leadership of magistrates from their own valleys were outstanding characteristics of these people. Somewhat anomalously they considered themselves throughout the centuries a part of the Empire until the total independence of the Swiss Confederation was granted by the Treaty of Westphalia in 1648. While recognizing the overlordship of the "Romish Emperor" in all civil or worldly matters the people of these ancient valleys consistently refused to accept, as local or regional governors and administrators of justice, any foreign officials appointed by the emperor. From time to time in each of these three ancient cantons the people assembled in the public square of the principal town and, by voice vote, or show of hands, elected their principal magistrates and their *Landammann* or governor. Every burgher, fourteen years of age and over (fifteen years of age in Schwyz) had the right to vote. Matters of general concern such as war, peace, military capitulations, alliances and taxes were likewise subject to popular vote. The loyalty of these valley people to the emperor, though qualified by their refusal to accept any of his officials as intermediaries or administrators, ran closely parallel to their unswerving allegiance to the pope whom they recognized as the supreme authority in all religious matters.

The Confederation

The government of the Confederation in the early eighteenth century and of its constituent parts may now be summarized as follows. The Confederation itself rested on the ancient treaties of 1291, 1308, 1315, the intercantonal treaty of 1446, the Sempacher Brief (1481), the Convention of Stans (1393), the Defensionale of Wyl (1647) and the Treaty of Aarau (1712). Considered in their entirety, these agreements defined the Confederation as a perpetual defensive alliance between the 13 cantons with a few special privileges and powers vested in the eight most ancient cantons. The specific responsibilities of each of the 13 in provision of men and armaments for the defense of the country were defined in detail. The fundamental articles of alliance were paramount and could not be superceded by other agreements between any of the 13 contracting parties. Each was free to contract foreign alliances, to grant troops to foreign Powers, to accept or reject the moneys of other cantons, to impose taxes, to collect duties on products from other cantons or foreign countries, to have their own courts of justice, and, in brief, to exercise every other right of sovereignty. Beyond the seven aristocratic and the six democratic cantons mention must be made of nine associated cities and States which were, in general, free of foreign dominion and enjoyed a neutral status which was respected by the Powers and protected by the Swiss. These were the Abbey of St. Gallen, the towns of St. Gallen, Biel, and Mülhausen, and the federated States of Valais, Geneva, Neuchâtel, the Bishopric of Basel, and the Three Leagues of the Graubünden.[20]

The Administration of Justice

The administration of justice and the judgments handed down by the officers of the law played a very important role in the lives of the people. In Switzerland, as in most of Europe, the confession of one charged with a crime was an absolute necessity before judgment could be made and punishment inflicted. This carried in its wake the practice of trial by torture. In the absence of a more humane code of criminal jurisprudence and a prompt confession, the suspected criminal was usually put to the rack. Where the judgment of the court required that a fine be paid, an important question is: who received the fines? In some cantons, the fines went to the community and the judges were paid from public funds. This was the practice in some parts of the Graubünden where neither the governor, the judges, nor baillifs received any part of the fines. During the reign of Maria Theresia in the long years of Austrian domination, the empress received the fines for criminal offences and paid the expenses of the judges and the courts. The judges, in turn, were usually elected by the people. Trial by jury was also common in many communities in the Graubünden. In the Valtellina, which was subject to the Graubünden, there was much corruption. Two-thirds of the fines went to the local governor who was permitted to examine the accused in secret and in the absence of any counsel for the defense. The case could then be passed on to a lesser official or settled by a fine imposed by the governor. Although some of the officials discharged their duties honorably and with no trace of venality, the system was conducive to corruption by extortion. The salary of the governors was trifling but could be handsomely enriched by the threat of torture, by the imposition of heavy fines, and by communication of sentence in return for a substantial payment. As mentioned both by Burnet and Coxe, many crimes went unpunished if the persons who committed them had either acceptable credit or much money; fining an offender was always more advantageous to a judge than a sentence of capital punishment, torture, or imprisonment.

Within the Swiss Confederation proper, the guardians of the law and the dispensers of justice, usually received a portion of the fines levied against the guilty. In the many bailiages the chief official was the bailiff. His was a lucrative position and was coveted by members of the Great Council who alone were eligible for the office.

> There are 72 Bailiages into which the whole canton of Bern is divided . . . these Bailiages are imployments both of Honor and profit . . . & the Bailifs have all the confiscations and fines . . . & in the 6 years of his Government according to the quality of his Bailiage he not only lives by it, but will carry perhaps 20,000 Crowns with him back to Bern: on which he lives till he can carry another Bailiage. . . . The Citizens of Bern consider these Bailiages as their inheritance and they are courted in this State perhaps with as much Intrigue as was ever used among the Romans in the distribution of their Provinces (**78**, p. 15).

> The Bailiffs may live splendidly during the six years of their Government, and yet put in their Pockets Five and Twenty, or Thirty Thousand Crowns, which is a great Sum in a Country, where the Law retrenches all Superfluities in Equipage, Apparel and Furniture (**339**, p. 88).

Sometimes the income of the bailiff was derived from tithes, from customs duties received by the cantonal government, or from a portion of the estate of a deceased person. Not infrequently, this estate tax was oppressive and it was widely resented.

In the city of Bern a novel system of correction was used for those found guilty of misdemeanors. They were committed to a House of Labour, were reportedly well fed and clothed, and every morning were sent in companies to sweep and wash down the streets.

> In harvest time, any gentleman may engage as many of these delinquents as he pleases; and some who were formerly very ill disposed, became good members of society, after having lived two or three years in this manner. They are compelled to attend divine service every Sunday morning when both men and women are very cleanly dressed; but all of them have a broad flat iron under their chins to prevent their escape (**400**, I, p. 58).

"At other times they are taught to read and write, and are instructed in various trades . . . and are constantly employed. . . . By these means the expence of the establishment is nearly supported" (**95**, II, pp. 215, 216).

In Lausanne a quite unique system prevailed in passing sentence in criminal cases. If found guilty by the courts, sentence was passed by the burghers who resided in the principal street of the city. Two magistrates acting as counsels for the defense and prosecution presented the evidence and the citizens by majority vote determined the sentence (**95**, II, p. 66, 67). The practice bears a resemblance to trial by jury.

Industry

To understand eighteenth century Switzerland more fully, a description of the day-to-day work of the people, their food, and their social customs is appropriate. Swiss industry in the eighteenth century was predominantly agricultural. Cheese, cattle, butter, and hides were produced in sufficient quantites in the canton of Freiburg to permit export. Valtellina and Bormio, both subject to the Graubünden, also exported these products of the farm. From the valley of the Leventina similar products were exported. From July to October about 300 horses per week, loaded with cheese, made the difficult transalpine trip from Airolo (south of the St. Gotthard) to Münster in the Upper Valais. Thousands of horses were exported from several cantons, principally to France, during the War of the Spanish Succession (**128**, p. 99).

Cotton and linen, as thread or cloth, and spun silk also loomed large as products of Swiss industry. We are told that in the late eighteenth century two-thirds of the people of Zurich earned their livelihood by spinning thread and silk and making linen for the town. Much of this was a home industry, for most families had a loom which was almost as common and indispensable as a table and benches. Zurich began to be threatened economically by the growth of competition in Winterthur, a city which was a protectorate of Zurich. By edict, Zurich decreed that the spinning of silk and, consequently, the weaving of silk, must be terminated in Winterthur. As might be expected, much ill-will and litigation between the two parties resulted.

The silk industry in Zurich originated in the confessional disputes, which went on endlessly in the southern part of the Swiss transalpine territory where silk spinning and manufacture had long been practiced. Many who were driven from the region by a law against adherents of the reformed faith fled to Zurich where they were hospitably received. They brought with them the necessary skills and introduced the silk industry into their new homeland. Appenzell also had a lively industry in the spinning of thread which was exported to the canton of St. Gallen by which Appenzell is completely surrounded. St. Gallen is still noted for the beautiful lace which is manufactured in the canton. Silk was also spun in the Valtellina and exported in quantity to Zurich and Basel. About 3000 pounds of the highest quality silk were shipped annually to England. Chiavenna was also a rich source of raw silk for export, though its principal industry was transport for it served as an important communications center between Milan and Austria and Germany.

Trade relations with France appear to have been good until 1781. Swiss citizens living in France enjoyed a favored-nation treatment. But in that year they were required to pay a poll tax and all of the imposts levied against French nationals. Increased duties on Swiss imports, except on cheese and linen, were suddenly imposed. Finally, in 1786, the importation of linen was prohibited. The economies of Zurich, Glarus, and Appenzell were threatened by this ban that exports to France continued, either in contraband trade or through sale by contract with the French East India Company.

Small iron foundries existed in two or three villages but the industry never became important. In fact, metal ores and coal have never been found in sufficient quantities in Switzerland to support a viable mining industry.[21]

Salt has also been an important item of commerce. The quantities in Switzerland were inadequate for the needs of the country, until rich deposits in the Rhine basin were exploited. In 1978, 390,591 tons were produced from Swiss sources, almost enough to satisfy the needs of the country (**341**, 1979, p. 159). In the eighteenth century, brine pits at Aigle, Bex and Bévieux were exploited. They were the only source of salt in Switzerland and the annual production in the 1780s amounted to little more than 500 tons. The country's needs were satisfied by importing from France. By virtue of a very favorable treaty the Swiss were enabled to buy French salt at about one-fourth of the price that prevailed in Paris. Most of the money expended on imports was for the purchase of salt and grain (**128**, p. 196).

The manufacture of watches and clocks, an industry for which Switzerland became deservedly famous, developed to something of economic importance in the eighteenth century. In the beginning it was highly localized in Geneva and from there it spread to Le Locle and La Chaux-de-Fonds. It is still the principal industry in the canton of Neuchâtel. It is said to have originated in that area in 1679 when Daniel John Richard of La Sagne undertook to repair a watch which one of his nieghbours had obtained in London. After almost two years spent in fashioning the necessary instruments and obtaining the materials, he succeeded in the manufacture of a complete watch designed from the model before him. Somewhat more of the art was learned during a visit to Geneva. On returning to his home he engaged in watchmaking and instructed several assistants. Richard died in Le Locle in 1741, leaving five sons who followed in their father's occupation. Watchmaking gradually spread throughout the area and became, in time, the principal business of the inhabitants. In the 1780s the annual production of watches amounted to about 40,000.[22] Coxe was much impressed by the industry of these people who numbered about 6000 in the area around Le Locle and La Chaux-de-Fonds. Their inventiveness and skill in the mechanical arts appear to have been quite remarkable. Besides watch- and clock-making, they engaged in the manufacture of lace, stockings, and cutlery for export. Villagers developed skills as painters, enamellers, engravers, gilders, and instrument makers. "Such perfect ease and plenty reigns throughout these mountains that I scarcely saw one object of poverty" (**95**, II, p. 113). Yosy reported that the merchants of the canton were "very rich and lived sumptuously" (**400**, II, p. 167).

Employment in industry presented a variety of problems in eighteenth century Switzerland. In Basel, strangers—i.e. foreigners—were not permitted to engage in commerce or to follow any trade—a policy which originated partly in the very special and exclusive privileges accorded to the burghers. In aristocratic Bern "those families who enjoy any influence in public affairs would hold themselves degraded, by engaging in any branch of commerce" (**95**, II, p. 213). The profitable and respectable employments were in the bailiages or as officers in the service of foreign Powers. In Valais there was no industry of any consequence. Travellers complained that the people of the canton were ignorant and indolent while Coxe made the very general observation that "In regard to knowledge and improvements they are some centuries behind the Swiss" (**95**, I, p. 396). To some, the backwardness of Valais was attributable to the high incidence of goitre and mental retardation, especially in the lower part of the Rhone valley around Sion. The cause of goitre, which was then a serious problem, was totally unknown but was the subject of many fanciful theories.

Nutrition

Apart from the writings of Verzar who prepared an authoritative report on the nutritional status of the peasantry in the mountain villages in 1960 (**375**), there is little historical material available on the food of the common people, despite their numerical superiority. An earlier report in 1938 on the peasants of the Eifischtal (better known as Val d'Anniviers) is very pertinent (Schleiniger, **322**). Travellers to Switzerland belonged to the gentry and, in general, had little to report about the lives of the peasants. A few interesting observations about the food and lives of the peasants were reported by Coxe, that astute observer who made four very extensive travels through Switzerland in the late eighteenth century (**95**). From him we learn that around Chiavenna the principal food of the peasants consisted of salt meat, rye bread, milk, cheese and polenta. The latter was a mush made of ground chestnuts, boiled with milk, and usually admixed with bread crumbs. In the upper Engadine, salted meat, bread, milk, and cheese were the staple items of diet. Bread was baked only two or three times a year, and, when served, was usually broken up with a hatchet and soaked in warm milk. Butter was also made in some of the mountain villages and was preserved by melting down and pouring while hot into bottles—a homely procedure that appears to have been long employed for delaying the onset of rancidity and the growth of microorganisms. Yosy (**400**, II, p. 32) describes an unusual food preparation which was used by goatherds in the high mountain meadows near the head waters of the Rhine. It consisted of a pasty mixture of flour and honey. Schleiniger (**322**) reports that a mixture of marmot fat, honey, and wine boiled together was commonly fed to children in the Val d'Anniviers during their early years; the healthy survived, the others died. A comparable preparation of marmot fat with wine and secret decoctions was a common remedy prescribed by the medical quacks (*Kurpfuscher*) for internal or external use.[23] After the first few years the children received corn bread, goat milk, cheese, possibly some meat, a very little fruit, and some boiled vegetables, also wine. A typical diet for the older children and adults consisted of coffee, black tea, or cocoa water with a little milk, some cheese and bread. The bread was baked every three or four months—a maize-wheat-rye type—which was stored in the cellar. After a month or so it became hard as stone and was broken up with an axe and soaked in water or milk. The midday meal typically consisted of boiled potatoes, pasta, cheese, and coffee or tea, and wine. The evening meal was usually of cheese and a vegetable soup—the latter being made by boiling together leeks, cabbage, beetroot, potatoes, and pasta. Although Schleiniger's report pertains to the year 1938, it is probable that the food of the peasants was similar two centuries earlier. An exception would be potatoes and coffee, which were not introduced into Europe until the seventeenth century. Goat milk and cheese were also used as common foodstuffs. A goatherd and a boy, as his helper, commonly lived in a rude hut among their sheep and goats and were quite isolated from other people. This resulted, as might be expected, in a sharply limited vocabulary such that conversation with visitors was restricted to matters that pertained to sheep and goats.

Where conditions were favorable for cultivation, potatoes were used abundantly as a foodstuff. Grain could seldom be raised and the mountain meadows were usually given over to pasturage. The provisions for a family of seven have been described in some detail (95, I, p. 353): stored away for the long and dreary winter months in the mountainous regions of Uri were seven cheeses, each of 25 pounds; 108 lb. of hard bread; and 1000 lb. of potatoes. There were also seven goats which were fed with the boughs of fir trees, and three cows that lived on hay collected during the summer, and fir boughs also when the hay harvest was poor. A part of the ground was used for the cultivation of flax. During the winter months many mountain families busied themselves in spinning thread and weaving linen cloth.

In the alpine regions, goats, kids, and marmots were commonly used as sources of meat. Bread was somewhat of a luxury[24] among the peasants in the upper valleys since the regions were too cold for the cultivation of cereal grains. Carrots, turnips, and cabbages were raised for family consumption where climate and soil permitted. The real riches of the peasants were their cattle. Cheese from the mountain meadows of Bern was sold in the city market. After the cheese was prepared a residue of curd was collected which was dried in the chimney and eaten in the winter instead of bread. The remaining whey was boiled down to an amorphous mixture of milk sugar and protein. This was used instead of beet sugar which was expensive and was usually considered to be inferior to the product from whey. Travellers in the Graubünden report that the meals served in the inns seldom consisted of more than macaroni or other "pasta" and wild fowl boiled in oil. The clergy and other privileged persons had in private storage quantities of dried fruits which were not generally available.

Public Health

Epidemics of the plague ceased to be pandemic by the eighteenth century. In 1711, an epidemic in Brandenburg claimed 215,000 lives and in the Austrian epidemic of 1721 about 300,000 died. These were the last in western Europe even though rats infested with fleas were plentiful and ubiquitous. Russia suffered a severe epidemic in 1770–72 (10) but it failed to move westward. By 1820, plague, except for an occasional case, disappeared as a health problem from all of Europe (406).

The rat is also a carrier of typhus and trichinosis and is "more dangerous to man than the vaunted tiger" (1). "The Seven Years War, the French Revolution, and the Napoleonic campaigns in Europe were all more destructive of life by one disease [typhus] than by the power of cannon, rifle and bayonet" (406, p. 287). In November, 1741, Prague was surrendered to the French army because 30,000 of the Austrians opposing the French died of typhus.

The disease was finally conquered in the twentieth century through the use of DDT. This remarkable insecticide, used in Italy during World War II, rapidly brought an epidemic of typhus to a halt (1).

Smallpox, also, wrought terrible havoc in the eighteenth century.

> One tenth of all deaths in Europe in the eighteenth century, as well as the majority of all cases of blindness were attributed to smallpox. In the Middle Ages and sixteenth century

the disease was mild. Hence it was called small pox. Syphilis which was concurrent was called 'big pox' (1, p. 62).

Jenner, in 1798, triumphed over the disease, by the development of vaccination against smallpox through inoculation with cowpox. Its efficacy was proven in the Franco-Prussian War of 1870–71 when only 278 of the thoroughly vaccinated Germans died of smallpox, as compared with 23,000 deaths from smallpox among the French forces. Smallpox is now considered by the World Health Organization to be eliminated throughout the world. Yellow fever also wrought its havoc. To illustrate the point we need only be reminded that this disease killed 29,000 of the 33,00 men sent by Napoleon to Santa Domingo to conquer that island first and then to carry the campaign of conquest to the Mississippi valley. Yellow fever ended his great plan and may have induced Napoleon in 1803 to sell Louisiana to the USA (1).

Napoleon's armies in Russia, including 9000 Swiss who were forced into service, were decimated by the Russians. The greatest killer, however, was known as spotted fever or petechial typhus. It was also called "war and famine plague," but bubonic and pneumonic plague, typhoid fever, malaria, cholera, dysentery and scurvy were probably embraced by this sweeping name for a miscellany of diseases that were common in war. Napoleon's "Grande Armée" shrank from 500,000 men to 80,000 by the time he reached Moscow.

It was in Poland that the Grand Army first suffered enormous losses from disease. Insect-infested hovels, poor nutrition, hot days and cold nights began to inflict havoc on the troops. Respiratory infections (pneumonia principally), dysentery, enteric fevers and typhus greatly reduced the number of "effectives." On entering Moscow no food could be found. Typhus and dysentery were now the chief enemies. The retreat began on 19 October 1812 with mounting losses en route from disease and the pursuing Russians. Only 5000 are said to have reached Wilno alive, as the disastrous retreat approached an end (1, p. 36). Many of these were ill, injured, and so impaired as to be incapable of work. Marshal Ney reached Wilno with only 20 soldiers—the sole survivors of the Third Army Corps.

By 1813, Napoleon was able to raise a new army of 500,000 men. Most of the recruits, because of their youth, were susceptible to the usual epidemic diseases. Disease and prior battles at Bautzen, Dresden and Karlsruhe reduced his army to 170,000 men by the time Napoleon faced his enemies at Leipzig. His defeat, according to Zinsser, was brought about by the terrible inroads of disease rather than by the enemy soldiery (406).

The virus of typhus fever has been found in the rat flea. The transmission of the disease appears to be from rat to rat by the rat louse and the rat flea and then on to man with the flea carrying the virus in between the human epidemics. Sanitary facilities were inadequate in military encampments and body lice and rat fleas, well imbedded in the underclothing, thrived (406, p. 189).

The brown rat (*Rattus decumanus*), more ferocious than the black rat (*Rattus rattus*), was unknown in western Europe until the eighteenth century. It came in from China or east of Lake Baikal. "It did not dare to enter Switzerland until 1869, and has never done very well among the Switzers." It also had a hard time in another thrifty country—Scotland. "It took it from 1776 to 1834 to get from Selkirk to Morayshire" (406, p. 201). The brown rat carries such epidemic diseases as plague, typhus, trichinella spiralis, rat-bite fever, and infectious jaundice.

Robert Southey once suggested that the first requisite to successful rat eradication was to make the animal a table delicacy.

Pestalozzi, von Fellenberg, and Education

Johann Heinrich Pestalozzi (1746–1827) was born in Zurich and attended the Zurich *Hohe Schule*. Rousseau's "Émile", published in 1761, and his dramatic call for a return to Nature struck a sympathetic chord in young Pestalozzi. He spent the year 1767–68 on the famous experimental farm of Johann Rudolf Tschiffeli (1716–80) at Kirchberg near Burgdorf. He soon tried his hand at agriculture—first in attempting the cultivation of *Rubia tinctorum* (a member of the madder family used as the source of the dye madder) and next in dairy farming. Both of these ventures ended in failure.

His greatest desire was to provide education for the poor. Many peasants and labourers in the cities had never received any schooling and couldn't care less. They were not interested in things of the mind. Elementary and middle-level schools were few in number in eighteenth century Switzerland, which also lacked a sufficiency of competent and dedicated teachers. Whatever interest was displayed by the authorities in promoting education was directed toward the universities and the educational desires of the upper classes. There was no place in the scheme of things for education of the poor. Such schooling would only serve to excite the interest of the young in activities remote from the farm and hard physical labor. The idealism, simplicity and emotional quality of Rousseau's writings, especially "Émile," elicited a remarkably favorable response among intellectuals wherever the book was read.

In 1779, Pestalozzi opened his educational facility for poor, neglected, and wayward children, with financial support from Zurich, Basel and Bern. The Helvetic Society, with encouragement from the very influential Isaak Iselin, was much interested in Pestalozzi's undertaking. His plan called for a combination of formal teaching of the usual fundamentals and physical work in the fields, because a return to Nature through farming was at the heart of his program. The children were 30 to 40 in number. Work in the fields was the summer activity while spinning and weaving kept the children occupied in winter. But the money ran out in a year or two despite financial help from relatives and his wife's inheritance. He returned with his family to Zurich. Eighteen years were spent in writing, expressive of a determined intention to lay out his concepts of education. In *Die Abendstunde'eines Einsiedlers* he described his entire program. Basically, in Nature he saw economic order, an understanding of the interrelationships of man, and of a behaviour pattern that rested on the general laws of morality.

The most remarkable of his works was *Lienhard und Gertrud*. This was about the common people. Gertrud represented the old sort of womanly virtue. Lienhard, a drunkard, typified human weakness. A third character exemplified the common sense of enlightened despotism and the fatherly ruler in human society. The book was a startling success and Pestalozzi was hailed as the creator of a new form of literature. Phillipp Albrecht Stapfer (Chapter 8, note 14), the Helvetic Minister for Arts and Education, became a patron and protector of Pestalozzi. Despite the chaos and troubles of Napolenoic rule in Switzerland, there was a widespread search for beauty, goodness and nobility of character.

The French National Assembly proclaimed Pestalozzi a French citizen. The Directory, in December 1798, placed him in charge of the orphanage at Stans in Unterwalden where, three months earlier, there had been a great loss of life and property resulting from the French victory over a desperately resisting people. Pestalozzi served as father and mother to the children in his care. They were the greatest days of his life. He was poor among the poor. In 1799–1800, with a young assistant, and support from Stapfer, he was moved from Stans to Burgdorf. The castle was made available to serve as a seminar, a school, and an orphanage. In 1801, *Wie Gertrud ihre Kinder lehrnt* appeared. This, with Gertrud as the model, added another dimension to Pestalozzi's concept of education: the basis of a sound education is the loving concern of the mother for her child from the very day of its birth. Gratitude, love, and trust are the highest of attributes.

In 1803, the Burgdorf institute had over 100 children. The teaching staff included two men of great reputation—Johannes Niederer and Johannes von Muralt. Visitors came from near and far to see the institute and to study the Pestalozzi method. In 1804, the Mediation government in Bern required him to move elsewhere. He started in Münchenbuchsee, a few miles from Bern. Nearby was the estate of Philipp von Fellenberg who, much influenced by Pestalozzi's teachings, initiated a comparable, but much more complicated and extensive, enterprise of his own. Soon, the castle at Yverdon was made available to Pestalozzi who was not in full accord with von Fellenberg. His Burgdorf colleagues, also out of tune with von Fellenberg, joined him at Yverdon in 1805. Children and teachers came to him from east and west Switzerland, and from other countries, notably from Prussia and Russia. The teaching staff grew to 50.

In 1809, a Commission sent by the Diet reported on the Pestalozzi method. In brief, it should not be made a part of the official school systems but must remain under private initiative. In 1814, Pestalozzi went to Basel to request that troops be sent to protect his school and the town (Yverdon). He met some of the representatives of the Great Powers and urged Tsar Alexander I to improve the school system in Russia and to end serfdom.

Pestalozzi never ceased to emphasize the sanctity of the home and the blessings of a true family life as the basis of a fruitful human society. His wife died in 1815. In the next two years, quarrels and tension within the staff at Yverdon caused many to leave. The institute was dissolved in 1825 and Pestalozzi, wearied and ill, died in 1827. A monument to his memory has been erected in Yverdon.

I have drawn heavily upon Hürlimann's article (**190**, pp. 380–92) for much of the above.

In Philipp Emanuel von Fellenberg (1771–1844) we find a gifted Bernese who, in the revolutionary times, served his government for a short while as legation secretary in Paris. Unlike many aristocrats he was attracted to Pestalozzi's efforts to educate the poor. His own program which he implemented at Hofwyl included almost everything, and still more, that might be relevant to education of the poor. Pictet (**290**) visited Hofwyl and concluded that Fellenberg's program was too gigantic, too expensive, and lacking in sufficient means of execution. It included a model farm, an experimental farm, a farm-implement factory, a shop to perfect mechanical aids, a school of industry for the poor, a boarding school for the children, a theoretical and practical agricultural institute, a normal school, and an educational facility for sons of the upper class citizenry—"perhaps all too much for one man to direct." Pictet concluded that the model farm was good, the experimental farm was fair, and the school of industry for the poor was a very essential part. Some children, from families with means, could and did pay. The moneyed children enjoyed more diversity in their education; the poor, less so "but sufficient for their class." Those in charge of instruction had a sort of missionary zeal and were convinced that the enterprise should spread throughout the land.

Fellenberg's motive, so we are told, was to produce happy people who would be useful in society. Hence his practical program was supplemented by moral and religious education.

The children were generally 8 to 13 years of age. At the time of Pictet's visit (December, 1811) there were 14 poor children and plans to increase the number to 30. All arrived in a miserable state. Vehrli (a responsible and good associate of von Fellenberg) kept a complete record on each child. He talked with them, read to them, sang with them, and told them stories. He was their constant companion. Two other teachers for drawing and music were also attached to this elementary institute. Natural history, botany, and gymnastics were also taught. Instruction in Greek was followed by Latin. Whether these languages were taught in the elementary school is not clear from Pictet's report.

The institute observed none of the usual means of encouragement or special recognition: no firsts, no second, no prizes, no medals. Every Saturday evening, the instruction of the week was recapitulated for the pupils. The firm but gentle tone of the professors, and their paternal sentiments which inspired remonstrances and exhortations to greater effort greatly impressed the children. Their little weaknesses and little sources of pride were all exposed in these sessions. Pictet, though critical of much, tells us that there was probably no other educational institute in which there were joined together so much pleasure in work, so much freedom under rule, and where the pupils had more occasion to prepare themselves for their adult life through the example of decent and polite manners. In general, they were confident, open, gay, and happy because they felt that they were loved.

The school for the poor had been planned for 13 years but had been operating for only two. Here the objective was to assure to the indigent of the land a happy and industrious existence, and to ban from the villages laziness, misery, and vice. Ordinarily, children from poor but honest families were accepted, but some children were received whose past was colored by misfortune; a child of eight years whose peasant father was reduced to utter misery; a youth and his parents picked up by gendarmes in Alsace as vagabonds; the child was sent to Hofwyl by a friend who knew about Fellenberg's program. Another child, abandoned by his parents, was found by a forest guard. Life for these children was stripped of all but the bare essentials. Their food was largely potatoes and milk. Piles of straw constituted their bedding.

Most of the above on von Fellenberg is drawn from Pictet's report (**290**) with a few items from the chapters by Daniel Frei and Jean-Charles Biaudet in Volume II of the *Handbuch der Schweizer Geschichte* (Zurich: Berichthaus, 1977). Much has been published about Pestalozzi but relatively little about von Fellenberg. The principal work is by Kurt Guggisberg (**157**).

Social Customs

The social customs of eighteenth century Switzerland throw considerable light on the social graces, the conventions, and the entertainments of the people. Much of the story, as recorded by travellers, is restricted to the families of the gentry. In Zurich, life was generally simple and tranquil. Dinner was served at noon, after which, in winter, the men visited their clubs in town to smoke, drink wine, and eat fruit and cakes. In the summer they passed their time in country villas. The women were not fond of visiting and were engaged in the usual household occupations and instruction of their children. They rarely appeared when strangers were received. Occasionally they went out in small groups with close friends and relatives.

Bern, "the first diamond in the Helvetic Confederation," is reported to have been more lively and sociable than any other town in Switzerland. Men and women met together socially, the women being "the life and ornament of the daily assemblies". Dancing was a frequent amusement in Bern and other towns. Public balls were held fortnightly in Bern. Throughout the country such entertainment commenced early, usually at 4 or 5 o'clock, and terminated by 10 or 11 in the evening, commonly because of strict ordinances which fixed the hour of closing. English country dances were well known, but the waltz was most common. Summer dances were in open pavilions "amid scenes of rural festivity." We are told (**400**, I, p. 59) that in Bern the "lightness of the air gives a sprightliness to the wit of the young women which was not to be found in the women of other countries. They would be shining characters if more attention was paid to their understandings." Despite the lavish praise that Bern received, Yosy, with pardonable extravagance, reported (**400**, II, p. 130) that "the inhabitants of Basel are the most polite and accomplished people in the world, and pay the greatest attentions and civilities to strangers. . . . The ladies are handsome, and all of them good musicians."

In part of the Graubünden, adjacent to the Rhine, Sunday evening parties were held in the village of Haldenstein[25] where friends assembled "to eat cream and dance to the glimmerings of the moon." In the Lausanne area, dancing was also very popular, and Sunday parties were held by the lake, with chestnuts and cream, boiled together, as the favorite refreshment. Sunday dancing in Basel, by peasants, was not permitted and all card parties had to break up by ten in the evening. Cards, music, and conversation appear to have been the principal amusements in and about Geneva. It was reported by Yosy (**400**, II, p. 184) that in Ferney-Voltaire, a few miles north of Geneva, "the public walks by elegant ladies and gentlemen were as brilliant as in Kensington Gardens. The ladies, dressed in the French fashion, were more beautiful and splendid than in Paris." In winter, sleigh rides were the preferred amusement, not uncommonly in parties of 20 or 30 with two to a sled. The lady, wrapped in blankets, sat in the sled while her gentleman companion stood behind and drove.

Music was widely appreciated and enjoyed. Singing by all enlivened festive occasions throughout the country. The harp, piano and guitar were favorite instruments. Great importance was attached to music in the upbringing of young people.

Travel

Travel in Switzerland presented many problems because of the mountainous terrain that constitutes much of the country. In the great valleys of central Switzerland there were no difficulties; travellers used the same kinds of conveyance as were employed throughout Europe. In the 1780s, a carriage travelled weekly from Lucerne to Basel and from Basel to Zurich. A diligence for six persons went three times a week from Bern to Thun, Bern to Basel, and Bern to Lausanne and Geneva. The inns along the principal roads were very clean and dinners cost about 20 batzen (two francs). Travel by carriage was also possible on some of the principal mountain roads, for example over the Simplon Pass into the Ticino and Italy. Otherwise travellers over the Bernese Oberland into Valais or over the great Alpine barrier into Italy were obliged to go on foot, or on horses or mules. "Delicate" travellers in the more rugged ascents were carried in armchairs supported by poles slung over the shoulders of bearers.

Accommodations were plain, if not primitive. Coxe reported (**95**, I, p. 333) that a few miles south of the Grimsel Pass a small "hovel" existed for the convenience of travellers. Beds, alone, were lacking. He and his guide had a meal of "excellent cheese, butter, milk (the usual fare), some good wine, a small portion of kid, and a boiled marmot." The host, appointed by the canton of Bern, was on duty for nine months each year. When he left, the hut remained open and a supply of cheese, hard bread, and salted meat was kept in the hut for the occasional wayfarer. A similar "hovel" was reported to be at the top of the Grimsel and there his guide and a peasant "danced to music played on a rebec by a shepherd."

Travellers from Kandersteg into Valais went over the Gemmi and by a very steep descent, hewn from the solid rock in 1735 or so, reached the town of Leuk. Despite the difficulties in travel, the area was very popular. It was famous for its hot springs, reputed to be of great therapeutic value. Visitors bathed and drank the waters for the treatment of gout, rheumatism, "obstructions," and cutaneous disorders. An avalanche in 1719 had destroyed many houses in the area. The public accommodations were inferior, the houses were "miserable," but "the people from different quarters of Switzerland [were] very affable and obliging. . . . Several of them invited us to their respective houses; and this invitation was made with that openness and unaffected frankness so peculiarly characteristic of the Swiss" (**95**, I, p. 376). Hot springs and mineral baths in various parts of Switzerland were much frequented, not only by invalids but by parties of friends and relatives who came for pleasure. If access to the hot springs south of the Gemmi by the Kandersteg route was not sufficiently trying to the eighteenth-century traveller, what about the difficulties that beset those who visited the mineral baths at Pfäffers? For many years there were no roads—construction would have been prohibitively expensive. Invalids were lowered by ropes from one rock to another, a distance of 1000 feet. Even so, the baths were frequented by the Swiss and also by people from Germany, Italy and Holland.

Fanciful Tales

Miraculous cures were attributed to these waters. A boy of fourteen, suffering from a severe nervous disorder since infancy, is alleged to have begun recovery of his faculties with the first bathing and drinking of the waters. "He became completely cured and lived to be one of the most learned men of his age." At the mineral springs of Hallau, a man of 40 who was almost blind is reported to have so improved his vision by the faithful application of the waters that he was able to dispense with spectacles. These and other fanciful tales embroider the two volumes by Yosy. Her description of Switzerland and its people is fascinating and greatly enlivened by the innumerable "old wives' tales," tall stories, and superstitions related to her in her travels: a deadly poisonous paper given to Mr. Alet by the Jesuits; the fatal effects of sleeping near the waters emerging from glaciers; mountain flowers fatal to the touch; Lake Colondri whose waters emit volumes of smoke with a noise like thunder; Lake Lauerzer which, following the great Mt. Rossberg avalanche in September 1806, threw "flames of fire" at intervals for several days; the bones of a giant 19 feet in height; the monk who lived 186 years and experienced a second growth of hair and teeth; the dragons in the ancient cantons; two soldiers who were beheaded and thrown into the river Aare, who were subsequently "seen with their heads in close conversation;" the ghost-ridden castle with its nightly clamor of "perpetual noises, dismal groans, clanking chains, and clashing swords" so terrifying that "all the young women of the village were afraid of going out." Yosy adds the comments: "such was the supersition of the times, and such, indeed, is the credulity of country people even to this day;" "ignorance and superstition predominate over the people."

The Helvetic Society

A very important society, organized in 1762, was the *Helvetische Gesellschaft* (Helvetic Society). Its importance rested in the fact that it sought to bring together from the entire Confederation all those concerned people who were interested in a peaceful resolution of the many problems that were beginning to threaten the unity, if not the continued existence, of the country. The circumstances leading to organization of the Society are not without interest. Many Swiss from throughout the Confederation had assembled in Basel to celebrate the tercentary of the founding of the University. Among them was Isaak Iselin who, as a typical representative of the prominent Swiss in the days of the "Enlightenment," and with encouragement from two leading citizens of Zurich, seized upon the idea of renewing year by year an assembly, such as that of 1760 in Basel, where constant high-level discussions among the many concerned citizens who were present fired his imagination and resolve. The Society, founded at Schinznach, met annually from 1761 to 1797 to debate the issues which confronted the people and to organize work programmes devoted to specific problems. The study of Swiss history to identify and appraise the divisive changes in government and in the relations of government to the governed was an important concern of the Society. So also, reform of the military organization was a subject of study. The very existence of the Society and the issues that seized its attention reflect the breadth of the gulf that had arisen between the fast-moving demands of the people for reform and the lethargy of government in even recognizing that reform was needed.

The Society brought together in its membership people of all classes. Men from all levels of government, protestants and catholics, and intellectual leaders from the various cantons came together in a spirit of good-will and deep concern for the welfare of Switzerland and her people. Government itself, notably of the aristocratic cantons, soon came to regard the "Schinznach Circle" with distrust and disfavour. Its open criticism of the existing state of affairs, and its advocacy of change caused the Society to be identified by the ruling families as a hostile center of unrest. The Society held its last assembly in 1848.

Its successor, equally dedicated and high-minded, was organized in Bern early in 1914. Tensions were then rising in Europe and a major war which threatened to engulf the entire continent was imminent. Unlike the late eighteenth century, Switzerland was at peace within itself but beyond its borders, as had happened so frequently in the past, the delicate equilibrium between the great Powers was likely to be upset. The *Neue Helvetische Gesellschaft* (New Helvetic Society) came into being in this clouded political environment. Its founders were acutely aware of the dangers that threatened Switzerland. The purpose of the new Society was to bind together the various linguistic groups and to strengthen Swiss unity. The Society vigorously promoted the entrance of Switzerland into the League of Nations—a venture into international political collaboration from which the Confederation, sorely disappointed, ultimately withdrew. The Society issues a monthly publication and, since 1930, an excellent yearbook of multiple authorship, *Die Schweiz*. An English-language edition, *Switzerland*, is also published.

A Summary Description

If we were to attempt a summary description of eighteenth century Switzerland we would be able to start with several plusses. The violence of the wars of religion that tore the country apart came to an end in 1712 and the Swiss gradually learned to submerge their confessional differences and to acquire the fine art of living harmoniously together. The Spanish War of Succession (1702–13) which raged around her borders did not demand of her people massive involvement in defense. The violations of her border, as viewed in retrospect, were not serious. Economically, the country benefitted through the export of supplies to the belligerents, including an undetermined amount of contraband. Miraculously, the country was spared from further visitations of bubonic plague, though it was not until 1894 that the causal organism was identified by Yersin and a satisfactory form of prevention by vaccination was discovered (**165; 398; 399**).

The population of the area embraced by present-day Switzerland increased during the century from about 1,200,000 to 1,700,000. This may seem surprising in view of all that imperilled the life of a woman. Deaths at childbirth were high because of poor sanitation and the lack of competent doctors. The risk of death in childbirth was enhanced by numerous pregnancies. Stanyan (**339**) reported that families with nine to ten children were very common. Because of stillbirths and high mortality in infancy and early childhood there must have been many more pregnancies which the mothers of large families had to endure. Poor nutrition of the less privileged, and the widespread excessive consumption of alcohol were additional hazards.

As the population increased, the food requirements of the country also swelled. With this, the voices of those who sought a more intensive exploitation of the soil came to be heard. Research in agriculture, the use of manure as a soil fertilizer, the introduction of the potato and its use as a food for people emerged. The teachings of the Physiocrats spread from France over the whole of Europe and a belief in the unlimited capacity of the soil to provide food in quantities sufficient to sustain vast numbers of people was widely accepted. "The wealth of a nation is in its soil" was seized upon by the agricultural cantons as a fundamental precept and as a counterweight to the growing strength and influence of the cities in which industrial and commercial power was slowly emerging. One of the great landowners in the canton of Bern, Rudolf Tschiffeli (1716–80), pioneered in the introduction of improved methods of agriculture. His farm was, in effect, a museum piece visited by many who were interested in applying the new concepts of agronomy. Pestalozzi, especially, but also von Fellenberg, with encouragement from many public-minded individuals, attempted to educate the underprivileged children from poor families by novel methods which included farming and other practical skills as substantial supplements to formal instruction in the recognized basic subjects of the elementary schools.

EMIGRATION   Any account of emigration from Switzerland in the eighteenth century is not likely to radiate much good cheer. All in all, it is a rather sad story— more of a minus than a plus—but it should not be omitted and is best related at this point. The increase in population during the century would have been much greater were it not for losses by emigration. The Anabaptists, unwelcome in the Emmental, continued to leave the country. Many resettled in Brandenburg, in Prussian Lithuania, in Pomerania and the Palatinate. Others, usually for political and economic reasons, accompanied by quite a number who had settled temporarily in the Palatinate, migrated to the English colonies in North America—mostly to Pennsylvania and the Carolinas. Bern, Zurich, East Switzerland and Basel contributed to the exodus. Some, unable to pay their transportation costs to America, found themselves bound in virtual slavery to the colonial immigration agents until their debts were paid. Unwilling to support any who might return because of distressed circumstances, some of the cantons took defensive measures against any returning emigrants who would normally be entitled to local support if penurious. Bern welcomed the exodus of Anabaptists, and, in fact, paid the emigration agents for each Anabaptist they succeeded in moving out of the canton.

In the canton of Bern the Anabaptists had given the authorities endless concern. The aristocratic government did everything possible to get rid of such troublesome dissenters. The East India Company was urged to ship some to the East Indies.

Throughout the century, the story is the same. In 1701, a Bernese patrician, Franz Ludwig Michel (1675–1720) sought land in Pennsylvania and Virginia for Swiss settlers. Michel joined forces with Johann Georg Ochs and Georg Ritter in 1702. Through the Great Council of Bern, the cooperation of the British government was sought. With the help of Aglionby, British "Envoye Extrdry [Extraordinary] to the Confederate States of the Suisse Cantons" (6), arrangements were finally completed to settle 400 to 500 in the two colonies. Bern seized upon the opportunity to get rid of Anabaptists and the dependent poor. Ritter & Co. were to be paid 45 *thalers* a head for every *Taufer* they succeeded in carrying off to America and 500 *thalers* more for another group of about 100 paupers who desired to go to America (**124**, p. 3). In 1710, Christoph von Graffenried (1661–1743) of Bern joined in the act. As a man of considerable influence, he managed to obtain 17,500 acres of land in North Carolina on which he settled some of Michel's emigrés, with still more from the Palatinate. He founded the town of New Bern, apparently assisted by Michel and Georg Ritter & Co. Battles with the Indians made life in New Bern precarious. von Graffenried, with the help of Michel and the English authorities, prepared for a new settlement at Potomac Falls in Virginia. The difficulties were insuperable and von Graffenried faced financial ruin. His misfortunes continued. He went to England in search of financial help, only to find that his principal patrons, (the Duke of Beaufort and Queen Anne) had died and King George I declined to give the requested support. von Graffenried returned to Bern and broke completely with his past as a colonial entrepreneur (**159**, pp. 234, 235).

Bern's policy hardened. The troublesome sectarian dissenters, better known among the emigrants to America as Mennonites and Amish, and the dependent poor were eagerly transported elsewhere. They left without any right to return. Should this be attempted they would be punished by death (**159**, p. 235). In 1718, despite the displeasure of Manning, the British Resident in Bern, Captain Merveilleux of Neuchâtel enticed numbers of Swiss to Pontarlier and the Pays de Gex—for ultimate shipment to Louisiana. The whole enterprise was ill regarded by the authorities; the project, misrepresented to the innocent victims, commonly involved their seizure by force and transport abroad. Many of the men ended up in

French military service in a Swiss colonial regiment commanded by Franz Adam Karrer of Solothurn.[26]

In 1734, Jean Pierre Pury (1675–1736) of Neuchâtel, who had grown rich in the service of the East India Company, obtained 24,000 acres in South Carolina for 600 emigrants. The settlement that followed was named Purrysburg. It was ultimately abandoned and is now an object of archaeological study (215). In the 1730s, Switzerland was flooded with brochures, rich in misrepresentation and fraud, advertising the attractions of the New World. Pury was an adventurous and unprincipled entrepreneur, charged with dishonesty and unscrupulous behavior. Again, Bern issued proscriptions and warnings.[27] She had had enough of this pro-emigration "stuff." Letters from the colonies were opened and unfavorable items in such letters were published to discourage any who contemplated emigration. Emigration agents were seized and imprisoned. An existing emigration tax of five percent on one's property was riased to 10 percent. But permission to emigrate was readily given to the poor, the cripples, criminals and the hostile unpleasant "troublemakers." The climate of South Carolina was considered unhealthy by many who then resettled in Georgia.

The last organized colonization in the eighteenth century for settlement in the New World was that of 1751—New Scotland (Nova Scotia) being the promised land. Thereafter, emigration was that of families and individuals doing so on their own. The great organized Swiss ventures in settlement abroad had come to an end (159, p. 238).

In 1768 many catholics emigrated to Spain on invitation of the Spanish government, but usually against the advice of their cantonal government.

The number of Swiss who emigrated to the United States between 1700 and 1800 has been estimated at 20,000 (34). Between 1820 and 1925 the number may have been as great as 300,000 (35, p. 17; 159, p. 240). By 1930, the total number of Swiss emigrants and their descendants in the USA approximated one million. About two-thirds of these had become American citizens. Of the total emigrants from Switzerland, Benziger estimated that up to one-fourth returned to the homeland (35, p. 18). The number of Americans who, by 1930, had settled in Switzerland may not have exceeded 1600 (35, p. 23). By year-end 1980, the number totalled 9165 (341, [1981], p. 90).

A few remarks should be added about the participation of Swiss in the French-English wars in North America. Karrer and Merveilleux (see note 26) recruited the first Swiss colonial regiment, known for its service in Louisiana in 1734–39. Later the commanding officer was Franz Josef von Hallwyl (1719–85) who reportedly fought against the English in the colonial war of 1754 to 1763. He attained the rank of field marshal in 1762 and was pensioned off in 1763 on dissolution of his regiment following the Paris Treaty of Peace.

Several Swiss officers attained distinction in the service of England. Among these was Henri Louis Bouquet (1719–65) from Rolle in the canton of Vaud. As a soldier of fortune he had served in the mercenary forces of Holland, Sardinia and France before accepting a position of command with the English forces in North America.

Early in his carrer he met Frédéric Haldimand (1718–91) of Yverdon who was Bouquet's close friend for life and executor of Bouquet's estate—a man whose military service in Canada with the English was of the greatest distinction. Both Bouquet and Haldimand joined 46 Swiss and other European officers who contracted for service with the Royal American Regiment—a motley collection of English, Scottish, Irish and American colonials (German, Dutch and a few Swiss). This unusually large regiment, consisting of four battalions and, if possible, 4000 men when at full strength, had endless problems in administration and command. Bouquet became commander of the first battalion. With other units from the regiment and native colonials, who passed in and out of the enlisted ranks, Bouquet's responsibilities focused first on the French and their Indian allies in Pennsylvania, Maryland and South Carolina. The last stronghold of the French in Pennsylvania was burned and abandoned by the French commander who marched his forces back to Canada. The French never returned to Pennsylvania after 1759 when they also abandoned their remaining posts in the colony.

The Indians from then on were Bouquet's only remaining official enemy despite the strength of the French to the west. In a noteworthy expedition against the Indians who were becoming increasingly belligerent, Bouquet fought a decisive engagement at Bushy Run (near Fort Pitt) in early August that virtually wiped out the Indian warriors to the last man. The Pennsylvania frontier settlements were safe once again. Bouquet had further successes in the Ohio valley in 1764 with a minimum of actual combat. In 1765, promoted to the rank of brigadier-general, Bouquet was sent to Florida to reorganize the British forces, but in August, shortly after his arrival, he came down with yellow fever and died at Pensacola on 2 September (**379**).

Bouquet was succeeded in Florida by Haldimand, who had distinguished himself in 1758–60 in the war against the French in Canada. He held the post in Florida until 1770, when he was transferred to New York as Commander-in-Chief of the British forces. In 1776, King George III promoted him to lieutenant general and in 1778 named Haldimand Captain General and Governor-in-Chief of Quebec in succession to Sir Guy Carleton.[28] In 1786 he returned to Switzerland and died in 1791 in his native Yverdon (**101; 117**).

Two other Swiss remain to be mentioned. Augustin Prevost (1723–86) served as an officer in Sardinia, transferring to the English military service as major general. He became governor of Georgia and distinguished himself in the American War of Independence. One of his sons, George (1767–1816), born in New York, entered the British army and served in the West Indies during the Napoleonic Wars. As military governor of St. Lucia, 1798–1801, he succeeded in establishing good relations with the French population of the island and became its civil governor in 1801. In 1805 he was created a baronet and in 1808 became Lieutenant Governor of Nova Scotia with the rank of Lieutenant General. In 1811 he was transferred to Quebec as administrator of the government of Lower Canada. In November, 1811, he took office as Captain General and Governor-in-Chief of Upper and Lower Canada[28] (**117**). As Commander-in-Chief of the British forces in Canada he was personally responsible for two humiliating episodes during the war of 1812–14. He left Quebec in April 1815, on recall to England, and died one week before he was to face court martial for the disastrous defeat at Plattsburg (**117**).

As mentioned in Chapter 10, many Swiss, either as mercenaries or as settlers in the country took part in the American Civil War (1861–65). Three of the generals in the opposing armies were Swiss.

MISCELLANEOUS   Industrial development within the Confederation and its associated States, perhaps favored by the population increase, proceeded rapidly. By the end of the century, between 150,000 and 200,000 were employed in the textile industry (cotton, linen, and silk). In Toggenburg half of the population found employment in the cotton industry.

The watch industry, by 1800, had become the most important of the Swiss industries. Geneva had been making pocket watches since 1500 or so, but by 1685 only 100 masters of the craft and 300 helpers were employed in the industry and produced about 5000 watches per year. A hundred years later, employment in the industry in Geneva had risen to 6000 and about 85,000 watches were produced. The corresponding statistics for the Principality of Neuchâtel were 4000 and 40,000 to 50,000 respectively (**301**). An astonishing amount of industrial production came from the homes of the people. Factory production was on the increase but many years were to pass before the home industries were completely displaced.

Among the rewards of domestic peace was an outburst of scholarly activity which could hardly have flourished amid the distractions of war. Many societies for scientific and scholarly purposes were organized, and many scholars of international fame added luster to the country. Indeed, at one time, most of the members of Friedrich II's new Prussian Academy were of Swiss origin.

Although the impediments to travel were numerous, the country became an object of great interest to foreigners some of whom made very extensive journeys. The forbidding Alpine massif was studied by a number of scientists, mostly Swiss, and the extraordinary beauty of the high, rugged mountains and the charm of its valleys began to be known to the outside world. One may even venture to date the beginnings of the tourist industry in Switzerland from the eighteenth century.

Personal incomes and possessions, as reported by travellers, suggest that the peasants and farmers were richer than in previous centuries. The burghers and the citizens of the towns were also well off. They enjoyed, exclusively, positions of emolument in government and, in most of the cantons, a monopolistic position, as a class, in trade and commerce. Some families became quite rich through high office, in mercenary service, or as the prime beneficiaries of capitulation agreements with foreign Powers.

The food of the common people was also adequate if not abundant. Milk and cheese loomed large as principal components of the diet throughout Switzerland: the quality and quantity of the food proteins were consequently excellent. Vegetables, such as cabbages, turnips, beets, carrots and potatoes were common items of food. By way of contrast, the consumption of fresh vegetables in England during the seventeenth and eighteenth centuries appears to have been very small. The upper classes in Switzerland, as in most countries, were abundantly fed, though not always wisely.

MERCENARY SERVICE   Mercenary service, more of a minus than a plus, rose to a very high level in the eighteenth century when the nations of Europe, save the Swiss, were for many years at each others' throats. The number of Swiss who served in the armies of foreign Powers was surprisingly great, if related to the population of the Confederation: the 1690 total was about 65,000; in 1701 it approximated 53,000; the peak level of almost 79,000 was reached in 1748; and by 1787 the number had decreased to about 40,000. Most of the eighteenth century Swiss mercenaries were in the service of France, Holland and Spain.[29] As in previous centuries the incomes of the participating cantons were substantially increased by the sale of mercenary services but at a terrible price. From the fifteenth to the eighteenth centuries inclusive, the Confederation is believed to have lost between 600,000 and 750,000 of its men—killed, disabled, or missing. Another estimate for the same period gives a total population loss, through mercenary service, of 900,000 to 1,000,000 men. There was also a loss by normal emigration of about 110,000 which was fully compensated by immigration. Somewhere between 100,000 and 150,000 Huguenots are believed to have found refuge within the Confederation during the religious terror in France.

OTHER MINUSES OF EIGHTEENTH CENTURY SWITZERLAND   Among the minuses of eighteenth century Switzerland one would be obliged to include education. In spite of the gifted amatures—the *Liebhabers*—in all fields of learning, and the many great ones in science and scholarship generally, education as we understand it was restricted to the families of the rich and influential. Few there were who advocated schooling for the "lower classes." Although it was the "Age of Enlightenment," it was also a time when the working class and the "subjects" were not encouraged to become clever and to develop their minds. They must be content to do the mundane work of the world. Such teaching as did exist rested on the authority of the Bible. The catechism, the Bible, and the Book of Psalms constituted the core of learning to which were added the elements of reading, writing, and arithmetic.

Some of the other minuses of eighteenth century Switzerland would be regarded by an outsider as trivial, especially when viewed in retrospect from a twentieth century vantage point. Some would be described as amusing. But, in the aggregate, they loomed very large indeed and they set in motion a rising tide of frustration, irritation and anger that led eventually into what must be described as the Swiss Revolution—more or less contemporaneous with the French Revolution. Perhaps the troubles stemmed from the nature of government in some of the cantons, specifically those that were aristocratic, oligarchic and patrician. The disenfranchisement of many, exclusion of subjects from many positions of trust and emolument, and denial of the right to engage in various gainful occupations were grossly unfair according to later concepts of human rights and, in themselves, would inevitably have led to violent revolution if not remedied in time by peaceful reform. The trouble that this exclusivity of class was certain to engender was compounded by numerous ordinaces that fell with severity upon the common man. Many of these were paternalistic—rules of conduct such as a father might lay down for his children—inspired possibly by a paternal sense of responsibility on the part of the "upper classes" toward the "lower classes." Thus the "subjects" were forbidden to visit friends or relatives during the hours of religious services; meal times and behavior at meals were strictly regulated; the permissible jewelry of women was defined; smoking, drinking, and dancing were strictly regulated; and in some cantons female servants were denied the right to wear corsets or to dress themselves at any time in clothing items made of silk. Bern, in 1661, issued a public ordinance or mandate against all sorts of current vice. The order was arranged like the ten commandments. It contained as number 7 an absolute prohibition of tobacco smoking. A violation of the order was punishable by a heavy fine or, if insolvent, placement in the pillory. A special tribunal of seven members from the two Councils administered the mandate. It was called the "Chambre du Tabac" and survived until about 1750. The ordinance included, among other punishable offences, adultery, lewdness, drunkenness, baptismal banquets, dancing and arrogance or ostentation (**335**, p. 276).

Many of these strictures and the widespread invasion by government into the regulation of social customs, morals, and personal behaviour were a carry-over from the puritanism and the rigorous rules of conduct that emerged in the previous two centuries.

Beginnings of a Revolutionary Movement

The Helvetic Society, acutely aware of the dangers inherent in government regulation of morals and social conduct, came to be regarded by government, more specifically by the entrenched ruling families, with suspicion and hostility. Suppression of dissent and punishment of the dissenters was the policy of government. Two or three of the great writers of the time gave to the revolutionary movement a powerful philosophical and literary base that threatened the establishment. The first of these, Voltaire,[30] was not a Swiss. He lived for many years in Ferney, now known as Ferney-Voltaire, which lies just a few miles from Geneva on the French side of the border. Voltaire wrote with extraordinary clarity. He was probably the strongest critic of the French monarchy and, through his writings, the most articulate exponent of the social ills behind the revolution in France.

ROUSSEAU   Jean-Jacques Rousseau (1712–78), born in Geneva, was the author of two famous books which, along with his other writings and those of Voltaire, provided a powerful intellectual base for the revolution in France and parallel revolutionary movements in Switzerland. In *Social Contract* he developed the concept of the ideal State in which man was supreme and the State was subservient. The relations between government and its people were to be defined by contract, essentially a Constitution, always subject to change by will of the people. In *Émile* we have the story of a man who grew up in such an ideal State and, by virtue of this, expressed the personal and social virtues which are to be cherished. In the ancient States, Rousseau wrote, men were free and equal and government was the servant of the people. But the history of government through the centuries is that of a progressive pre-emption of individual rights, loss of historic liberties, and the rise of a monstrous parasitic organism that feeds upon the people it is supposed to serve. Rousseau challenged the dogma of the ruling families that the State derived its authority from God and that its subjects were not empowered to change the laws by which they were governed. Such writings were as a gauntlet thrown at the feet of government—an open invitation to the people to resist the encroachments of government upon their rights and liberties. The authorities of Geneva, of many of the cantons, and of foreign countries regarded Rousseau with increasing distrust and hostility. In 1762 he fled to Bern, where for a short time he had a sort of curiosity value. Though granted asylum on St. Peters Island in the Bielersee his residence permit was presently revoked and he fled to Neuchâtel. The governor at that time was a friend of Friedrich II, King of Prussia, who displayed no hostility toward either Rousseau or Voltaire. After a brief stay in the Principality, Rousseau moved to England and finally to Paris where he died in 1778.

Serious confrontations in Geneva between the burghers and the ruling aristocracy were frequent throughout the eighteenth century. About 1760 the aristocratic families of the city won back some of the rights which the burghers had painfully regained in the earlier decades. The "victory" of the ruling class was marked by a public burning of the books of Rousseau before the Geneva Council House.

Rousseau's philosophy spread far beyond Switzerland. In 1783 the Peace of Versailles gave international recognition to the independence of the thirteen British colonies in North America, newly designated the United States of America. The victory of the colonials was the triumph of a political philosophy embodied in the Declaration of Independence. It was probably the first time that any State subscribed to the doctrine of the equality of man and of man's basic right to liberty and the pursuit of happiness. A prime function of the State is to secure and preserve these rights. The Constitution, which followed, was based on the sovereignty of the people. It was essentially a social contract. What could be more expressive of Rousseau's philosophy than the Declaration of Independence and the Constitution of the USA! In France, the call of the revolutionaries for "Liberty, Equality, and Fraternity" rang out as a slogan which expressed the three basic rights of man as defined by Rousseau.

UNREST IN GENEVA   Throughout the century Geneva was in almost constant unrest. Troubles between the burghers and the ruling families continued with only brief intermissions of peace. The confrontations between the burghers and the ruling aristocracy became increasingly serious. Through the Assembly of Burghers—the General Council—the burghers demanded the return of certain specific rights which they once possessed. Among others, they sought return of the right of pardon and the right of confirmation of new taxes imposed by government. Unable to restrain such pressures the government turned to Bern and Zurich for support. With the help of troops from these cantons the government in 1707 succeeded in suppressing the beginnings of revolt. The leaders were either banned from the city or summarily executed. In the 1730s, the burghers renewed their demands upon the government. Delays, hesitation, and timorous responses by the rulers were the result. In the face of such temporizing, the movement among the burghers gained ground. Street fighting erupted and Bern and Zurich again intervened, this time as mediators who hoped to resolve the problems. In 1738 a compromise was reached and an Act of Mediation granted to the burghers several of their demands: the General Council of burghers was granted the right to elect the governing authorities, to participate in the enactment of legislation by the State, to make the final decisions over taxation proposals, and to make any declarations of war or peace. It also was empowered to settle the vexing question, with its costly financial implications, of rebuilding the city's fortifications. Recognizing that the ruling aristocracies of the day were disposed to legislate in secrecy, it is noteworthy that the Act of Mediation specified that the laws of the State were to be assembled and published. In a sense such a code was a constitution that defined the relations between the government and the people. The next 25 years were unmarked in Geneva by any serious disturbances of the peace, although the rulers of the city continued in growing discontent with the restrictions imposed upon them by the burghers. After the bookburning episode of 1762, tensions steadily increased and by 1766 revolution was again imminent.

In a Pacification Edict of 11 March 1768, the burghers obtained the right to elect one-half of the Great Council (Council of 200). The Natives[14] now demanded additional rights and finally won the right of eligibility for election to the burgher class. In 1782 a serious uprising broke out, the government was put to flight and the top authorities functioned as a security council. In July 1782 troops from France, Bern, and the Kingdom of Sardinia-Piemont (formerly Savoy) entered the city, put down the resistance and restored the officers of government to their former positions. All of the rights won by the burghers since 1738 were declared null and void. Only the "natives" were permitted to retain their equality of rights with the burghers. This triumph of the aristocracy was brief, for only a few years later the great revolution broke out in France and brought with it a resurgence of unrest in Geneva. The constitution of 1768 was restored but all was destined to change when annexation by France came about in 1798. Geneva, though a protectorate of Bern since the 1530s—one might almost describe it as an associated State—was not an integral part of the Confederation until 1815. It was adjacent to France and was susceptible to the revolutionary doctrines that came from the pens of Rousseau and Voltaire and from the writings and widening influence of French emigrés and visitors. For a description of the earlier history of Geneva, and its eighteenth century structure and problems, the work by Keate (**203**) can be warmly recommended.

It is important to know something of the unrest that arose among the subject peoples within the Confederation proper and other associated States. The troubles of the ruling class and the unrest of their subjects assumed different forms in the several cantons.

UNREST IN LUCERNE   In Lucerne the unrest expressed itself in basic disagreements between the Church and the State, between the city and the countryside, and between the clergy and the common people. The patrician families within the ruling class were themselves divided on superficial issues. As elsewhere within the Confederation, the rulers failed to understand the strivings of their subjects and were resistant to their demands. In the country town of Entlebuch where the Second Peasants War of 1652–53 originated, the spirit of revolt was still alive. The town demanded of the cantonal government in Lucerne the right of self-government, equality, and an amelioration of the severe penal code that followed upon the Peasants' War. Other towns in the canton made similar demands. Though the clergy were divided in their sympathies, many of the priests understood and supported the strivings of the country folk for relief from the tyrannies of Lucerne. Rome intervened and made it quite clear that any priest who went too far in opposing the ruling class would be recalled. Within the patricians themselves a united and common front failed to emerge. Some held fast to the principle of exclusivity of rights in the ruling class while others wavered before the urgings of their priests for a more Christian understanding and appreciation of the improvements sought by their subjects. The fight between Church and State began with trivia. A local governor ordered a ban on dancing within a certain village in his area of responsibility. The local priest pointed out that for ages the right of permitting or of forbidding dancing in the community belonged to the priest. He declared that the governor exceeded his authority and thereupon lifted the ban. The central authorities now intervened, admonished the priest and ordered him to reverse his ruling. This he refused to do and was promptly deprived of his office. The papal nuncio protested against this arbitrary action of the cantonal government, left Lucerne and moved his office to Altdorf. A public outcry followed and both the pope and the King of France entered the fray. The countryside was aroused and Lucerne became alarmed. The government requested Bern and Zurich to provide military aid in case the matter got out of hand. The result was a deep rift within Lucerne which was sealed over by a compromise that settled nothing

DISSATISFACTION IN BERN   Events in Bern were not unrelated to those in Geneva. Not only do we find dissatisfaction among the burghers essentially comparable to that among the burghers of Geneva, but also drawn into the troubles in Bern was a famous refugee from Geneva, Micheli du Crest.[6] A number of the burghers formed a conspiracy to unseat the ruling families, by force if necessary, and to restore to the burghers a number of rights which had gradually been pre-empted by the oligarchy. The plot was also known as the Henzi conspiracy, Samuel Henzi being the principal in the case. Henzi appears to have been an idealist, not entirely in tune with his more vigorous and violence-prone associates in leadership of the plot. When the conspiracy was exposed some 60 men were found to be involved. The authorities acted promptly and decisively. Henzi was arrested on 4 July 1749 and a few days later he and his two principal associates were led to the scaffold. Others, among them Micheli du Crest, were sentenced to life imprisonment. In its beginnings, the conspirators, then 27 in number, had sought reform through the proper channels. A memorial submitted by these burghers in 1744 merely requested that the government examine the complicated electoral procedure to determine if simplification were possible. Admittedly it was hoped that such electoral reforms would again permit burghers, other than the ruling families of the time, to gain representation on the Great Council.

In 1735, a member of the newly elected Great Council of Bern had presented for study and consideration by the Council, a long and detailed list of desirable reforms—a political memorial. The author of this important document was actually Albrecht von Haller,[5] then a 27-year-old physician in his home city of Bern. Very astutely, Haller described the evolution of aristocratic governments. Historically they had developed into either oligarchies or democracies. Regretfully, Bern was emerging as an oligarchy—a conclusion supported by a statistical summation of the number of ruling families in the government. Prophetically, he warned of the dangers of an oligarchy which would prove to the free burghers to be more unbearable than foreign submission. The memorial called upon the "noble gentlemen" to dissociate themselves from the emerging oligarchy. The recommendations were rejected in the Great Council by a small majority (116 to 84). Von Haller was not himself a member of the Great Council. Disappointed by the negative position of that body, he accepted an invitation to a professorship in Göttingen where he remained from 1736 until his return to Bern in 1753.

Somewhat earlier, in the 1720s, an incident arose involving Bern and its subject territory of Vaud which throws further light on the temper of the times. A Major Davel who had distinguished himself in the second Villmergen war was a highly regarded officer in the Bernese forces. After the Peace of Aarau he was placed in command of a military district in Lavaux. The post was a sinecure with a good pension, little work and much free time. Davel read deeply and devoted himself to solitary religious contemplation. He developed a deep concern over the disinterest of the people in religion and in what he regarded as a widespread moral depravity. Deliverance of the people from their waywardness and their liberation from oppression became an obsession. In March 1723 he mustered his troops for the usual military exercises, placed himself at their head, and marched to Lausanne. To the startled city fathers, Davel explained respectfully that he had come to set them free. He was quickly seized, his troops were dismissed, and a report was dispatched to Bern. Davel was ordered for trial at Lausanne on a charge of high treason. It was established that he had acted alone and no evidence of a conspiracy was presented. In April, Davel was beheaded in the public square. Bern passed over the matter lightly and continued to disregard the widening unrest among its subjects and its burghers. Of 450 families in Bern eligible in 1700 to occupy positions of trust and authority in government, the Great Council (about 200 in number) stemmed from only 100—approximately two Council members from each family.

UNREST IN SCHWYZ   In Schwyz, popular unrest originated for reasons that were quite unique. The cantonal government was a democracy of the purest type and the problems arising from a deeply rooted aristocracy and an oligarchy separated from a subject people were unknown. The troubles arose when the French Minister of War amended the arrangements under which the Swiss regiments in the pay of France served the monarchy. The Swiss leaders in this mercenary service lost the right of independent administration of their companies and the retention, as entrepreneurs, of any excess in fiscal appropriations. Schwyz protested vigorously: in the future no Schwyzer would serve the French. Oblivious to this decision, the wife of Nazar von Reding, a high-ranking Schwyzer in command of troops in the French service, continued to recruit for France. The income of the Redings from French pensions was clearly in danger; one must suspect a conflict of interest. The *Landsgemeinde* of Schwyz then voted to forbid, subject to severe penalties for violation, enlistment by Schwyz men for service in the French forces. And von Reding's wife was fined six thousand *thalers*,[31] a sum probably designed to compensate for loss of revenue from France. The King of France promptly retaliated by dismissing the Schwyz regiments then in his service, terminating the annual payments to the cantonal government, and placing an embargo on shipments of grain and salt from Burgundy to Schwyz. For six long years, the "Tough" faction, so-called, held stubbornly to their anti-French position. By then their fellow countrymen were tired of it all. In 1771 the "Soft" faction won out in the *Landsgemeinde* elections. von Reding was elected *Landammann* and capitulation agreements for service to the French monarchy were resumed.

TROUBLES IN THE LEVINENTAL   In the Levinental, which for three centuries had been subject to Uri, serious unrest was coming to the surface attributable to the heavy taxes imposed by Uri to meet the costs of the Villmergen war. This was aggravated by a hardening of the policy of Uri toward her subjects in the Levinental. Charges by Uri of corruption and irregular practices in the local government led to punishments, acts of revenge and threats against the liberties of these subject people. Violence broke out and in May 1755 a military expedition from Uri occupied the valley and punished severely the leaders of rebellion. The liberties of the people were cancelled, they lost the precious right of self-government, and they began to suffer under an almost tyrannical rule by Uri.

AND IN NEUCHÂTEL   The Principality of Neuchâtel also had its troubles. As we have seen, a wave of unrest was spreading across the entire face of Europe, here attributable to certain popular grounds of complaint, and there resulting from still others. In Neuchâtel the popular discontent appears to have stemmed from the system of tax collection. In much of Europe the taxes were farmed out. In return for a fixed and contractual sum, the State sold to an entrepreneur the exclusive right of collecting the taxes. The excess revenue, over and above that which he must pay the State, constituted his profit. In Neuchâtel, this system was unknown until introduced in 1767 by Frederick the Great of Prussia, the ruling prince. The people of Neuchâtel saw in this change, an expression of a centralist policy which was totally unacceptable to those who cherished their right of local government. The city of Neuchâtel declared that any one who contracted with Prussia to collect the taxes would lose his citizenship. The Principality was already split politically into three factions: a Prussian party, a French party, and a faction that sought total independence. The political unrest which this division encouraged, now aggravated by the tax problem, provoked the King of Prussia to request the help of Bern in restoration of order in the Principality. General Scipio von Lentulus, a citizen both of Prussia and Bern, was commissioned in 1768 to accept this responsibility. By his strength and his wisdom, peace was restored within the Principality and no further troubles of any consequence arose until the Napoleonic wars swept over Europe.

TROUBLE IN FREIBURG   In the canton of Freiburg, more specifically in the district of Gruyère, the immediate incitement to unrest is to be found in several impolitic acts of government, vexatious actions by the bailiffs, and the vigorous but seditious leadership of Peter Nicholas Chenaux who inflamed the peasantry to revolt. As elsewhere, one observes again a people who were jealous of their liberties and very sensitive to any trespass by government or any of its agents upon their freedoms. The troubles arose early in the century. Between 1726 and 1739 the peasants of Gruyère rose in rebellion against the aristocrats of Freiburg and the princely Bishop of Basel whose officials failed to respect the ancient rights of various communities and used little if any tact in their dealings with a sensitive people. The Bishop sought help from his allies among the catholic cantons of the Confederation. When this failed, he turned to France and with her help succeeded in repressing a violent uprising in 1739. This desperate resort to military aid from a foreign Power must be interpreted as a dangerous tactic which invited more trouble in the future.

In April 1781 insurrection broke out again in Gruyère. The convent of Valsainte had been secularized and several fasts and religious festivals had been abolished. The monks were friendly and were well regarded by the people. The intrusion of government into the affairs of the Church angered many of the peasants. The authorities turned to the code of social conduct which they strengthened by increased punishments and greater severity of interpretation in matters of social behaviour and morals; the peasants were alleged to be too exuberant and care-free in their behaviour.

Chenaux, a native of La Tour de Trême, aided by John Nicholas Andrew Castellaz, a burgher of Freiburg, had risen to leadership of the rebels. Chenaux was a man of good appearance and gifted with the eloquence needed to inflame the spirits of the mob. Castellaz was an advocate, well-versed in the law, alert to infractions by the bailiffs and to any trespass by the authorities upon the immunities of the people. It was quite a team and of course there were others active in leadership. They did not hesitate to bend the truth to their own purposes and before large assemblies of the peasants declared that the government was about to impose heavy taxes on their cattle and horses, that the annual present of salt which they shared with the burghers of Freiburg was to be withheld and that the settled policy of the government was to overturn the religion of their ancestors. In May 1781 an armed mob of peasants, some thousands in number marched on Freiburg. The terrified rulers of the city temporized with promises and appeals for negotiation.

Meanwhile they called upon Bern for help. Summoned by von Erlach, the 85-year-old advoyer, the Great Council responded immediately. Over a thousand troops reached Freiburg within a day and reinforced the garrison. The undisciplined rebels soon dispersed in panic. The leaders fled. Chenaux was apprehended and killed. Nothing came of the promises of immediate relief by the rulers of Freiburg. Chenaux was treated as a martyr and crowds assembled in his honour, bearing crosses, singing hymns and chanting requiems. The meetings were tumultuous and signalled renewed rebellion. They came to an end when the Bishop of Lausanne forbade such demonstrations under pain of excommunication.

Other cantons were fearful that France would seize upon these disorders as a pretext for interference, possibly with troops, in the affairs of Freiburg. "Woe upon that republic in whose internal politics foreign powers interpose," declared the champions of Swiss independence. With such a background of rebellion by the peasantry, and with widespread fears of French intervention, it is remarkable that the ruling authorities in many of the cantons still failed to respond sensitively and wisely to the urgent need for reform. The basic causes of unrest among the burghers and the subject classes of the federated cantons and their associated States were almost totally misunderstood. The concept of divine right as the policy by which government ruled was deeply imbedded in the ruling families of the aristocratic cantons. When three of the cantons were called in to mediate the Gruyère-Freiburg disputes the decision of the mediators was exactly what one might expect. They, the mediators, would defend and protect the existing form of government and would never permit an appeal relating to the amendment or alteration of the constitution by other than the supreme council of the republic. This, for the time being, put an end to any attempts by the burghers and others to institute reform in the topmost echelons of government.

France and the Prelude to Revolution

Meanwhile events in France were carrying the country headlong into revolution with an increasingly serious impact on Switzerland. In France the monarch enjoyed absolute power with no restraints imposed by any institution of government. Corruption was widespread, despotism was manifest in government and in the courts of justice, and finances were out of hand. Her wars had been extremely costly and the extravagance of the monarch had brought the State to the verge of bankruptcy. All credits were exhausted. In May 1789 the Estates General met in Versailles. The House of Representatives, consisting of one-third of representatives of the clergy, one-third of nobles, and one-third of burghers (the so-called Third Estate) was, by this time, totally inept and unable to cope with the progressive deterioration of the country. The atmosphere was highly charged with political concern, with the revolutionary ideas of Rousseau and Voltaire, and with an influx of revolutionary sentiments from North America. Issues were passionately debated in political clubs that came into being almost spontaneously. The contrasts between reality and the ideals for which the people were groping became clarified. Instead of the freedoms of which Rousseau wrote there was only the despotism of an absolute monarchy. Instead of equality, France knew only a highly privileged nobility, a church with enormous riches and possessions, and an exploited, politically deprived, Third Estate which paid the taxes to support the clergy, the nobility, and the monarchy. Fraternal relations between the citizenry (the burghers) and their ecclesiastical and civil lords were nonexistent.

FRANCE AND THE THIRD ESTATE   Events moved rapidly. Only two months after the assembly of the Estates General, the Third Estate declared itself to be the only constitutional body with legislative powers. In July the mobs stormed the Bastille, and opened the gates of the State prison. In August, the Third Estate nullified all prior rights of the representatives of the nobility and denied to the clergy the tithes to which they had hitherto been entitled. For a time the idealists triumphed, there was a minimum of violence, and high were the hopes that lasting political and social reforms would be peacefully achieved. The aristocracy and the ruling class were terrified by the rapidity of change, by the loss of power and privilege, and by the economic jeopardy into which they were thrown. These fears were contagious and quickly crossed the border into Switzerland with which there was a long history of economic, social, political and military (via capitulation agreements for Swiss mercenaries) association. The ruling aristocracy was terrified, as in France, with the realization that the fiery demand for liberty, equality, and fraternity could lead to widespread revolution and might even destroy the political and social structure of the Confederation.

SWISS EMIGRÉS IN FRANCE   In Paris many Swiss emigrés were to be found. A goodly number were political activists who had sought in France a haven where their liberal ideas and crusading spirit would be tolerated and where they could hope to escape from the sometimes puritanical restrictions that had emerged in parts of the Confederation. In 1770 a Swiss Patriots' Club was founded in Paris and a Swiss Correspondence Bureau was opened, the latter to transmit to the liberally inclined folks at home political information, literature from the pens of the revolutionaries, and instructions from political agitators. Vaud, Geneva, and the towns of the entire area around Lake Geneva became centres of revolutionary activity. Intellectuals and leaders within the Helvetic Society were among those who gave inspiration and direction to the movement, always in the hope of nonviolent reform.

Two men played a special role and were of great importance in influencing the revolutionary movement in Switzerland. One was Peter Ochs,[32] the head of the guild masters in Basel. The other was César de la Harpe,[33] an emigrant from Vaud. They were uncritical admirers of the French Revolution who waited impatiently for the citizens of Switzerland to rise up against their rulers. Their actions and inflammatory provocations bordered on treason. Peter Ochs, in his youth, had travelled extensively through the French-speaking part of Switzerland. He was intelligent but vain and sought, through associations with political leaders, to become popularly known and to establish for himself a place in history. De la Harpe belonged to a noble family from Vaud which, despite the respect it enjoyed among the aristocracy of Vaud, was treated as lower-class subjects by the patricians of

Bern. He himself had been humiliated by the Bernese aristocrats. Though a political idealist, his eagerness to see an end to the tyranny of the ruling class was almost certainly enhanced by his personal resentment toward the Bernese patriciate. He had the unusual experience of serving some years in St. Petersburg as tutor to the Tsarevich, later Alexander I of Russia. His political ideas and ideals developed unhampered and were passed on to his pupil. He maintained a vigorous correspondence with political leaders in Vaud and the revolutionary leaders in France. He hoped passionately for a liberation of Vaud from political domination by the government of Bern.

Such revolutionary ideas were widely disseminated among the Swiss who served as mercenaries in France. A Swiss regiment stationed at Nancy mutinied in August 1790. Meanwhile the power of the monarch had been sharply curtailed by the Third Estate and under a new constitution the limitations of royal power were defined and the rights of parliament were substantially increased. In Basel, in December 1790, under the influence of Peter Ochs, the Great Council swept away the last vestiges of serfdom. In September of that year the people of lower Valais had risen against their rulers, the lords of Upper Valais. The two reached an accord which seemed to end the troubles, but within a year rebellion broke out anew and the rulers resorted to military measures to suppress the revolt and to punish the leaders.

Reforms in Bern

Bern resolved to introduce the reforms which were now so vigorously demanded. But it was by token only and came too late. The Great Council resolved in 1790 that in a space of four years they would admit as burghers some 25 or 30 families from the city and countryside including five from the subject territory of Vaud. Through the services of a competent journalist, hired for the purpose, Bern was promptly informed of the progress of events in France. It is doubtful, however, that this foreign news service was of much value. The rulers of Bern were not prepared to recognize the similarity of provocations among the people, and identity of objectives of the intellectuals both in France and Switzerland. There was also a lack of unanimity in the course to be pursued. In fact the unrest in Vaud and the strengthening reform movement had reached such a point that the tidal wave of revolt threatened to engulf the capital city itself. Among the intellectuals of Vaud, a national self-consciousness had developed. Some hoped for a union with France. Others sought the freedom to remain Swiss. Much of this was a surprise to Bern because the strength of the common-language bond which existed between France and Vaud had been underestimated and the effectiveness of the treaty of alliance, annually renewed between Bern and Vaud, had been overestimated. The situation was confusing, even to the French, who later "liberated" Vaud, for the people still subscribed to the basic concept of the Confederation—the indivisibility of the Fatherland.

In the confusion of the day various incidents served to intensify rather than to decrease the unrest of the Vaudois. In 1790 a pastor in Mézières urged his people to demonstrate against the domination of Bern and to refuse payment of the potato tithe. The small council in Bern ordered that the pastor be arrested and transported to Bern for imprisonment. This trespass upon the freedoms of Vaud had its repercussions both in Bern and Lausanne. The result was that pastor Martin was set free, was reinstated in his pastoral office and received a payment of damages for the arrest. The "Patriots" of Vaud regarded this as a signal victory.

A more troublesome incident followed. In July 1791, the "Patriots" arranged a memorial celebration, an anniversary festival, to commemorate the fall of the Bastille on 14 July 1790. Speeches and revolutionary songs aroused the fervor of the Vaudois. Bern decided in a mood of anger and fear that a show of strength was necessary. Two thousand troops were sent to Lausanne and the town councillors of a number of communities in Vaud were ordered to appear in Lausanne on a stated day. Before a long line of Bernese soldiers, drawn up in the principal streets, the Vaudois councillors were required to march bareheaded to the castle. There the humiliation continued. Representatives of the Small Council from Bern reminded the councillors of their duties, reprimanded them severely, and threatened the leaders with charges of high treason. This ceremonial dressing-down was not soon forgotten.

The Revolution in France Moves On

In France, meanwhile, the initial idealism of the revolutionaries was giving way to a terrible wave of violence as men committed to a bloody purge assumed the leadership of the reform movement. The motivating idea was the sovereignty of the people. The king, no longer trusted by the leaders, tried to escape to the Austrian Netherlands. He was seized at the border and returned to Paris as a prisoner. The fury of the mob now turned against the monarchy and the nobles. Acts of violence against the great landowners in the provinces were no longer punished. Many of the nobles fled abroad where they attempted to arouse the princes and rulers of foreign countries to join in a movement to suppress the French revolutionaries. The rest of Europe was fearful that the revolution would soon engulf the entire continent and a coalition movement against the French revolutionaries began to take form. In the meantime the new rulers of France anticipated events and declared war on Austria. Prussia, shortly thereafter, joined the Austrian side.

The Swiss Dilemma

In Switzerland, the leaders were sharply divided. One faction urged that the Confederation hold fast to its time-honored policy of neutrality. Few there were who advocated a military alliance with Austria and Prussia, despite the desire of the ruling families and the various cantonal governments to see the revolutionary government of France defeated. They had seen how Austria, Prussia, and Russia in an era of peace had arbitrarily divided the independent Kingdom of Poland among themselves. And Austria's position as the historic enemy of Swiss liberation could not be forgotten. The 50-year alliance of 1777 between France and the Confederation was still in force and even though the entire European system of alliances was now thrown into chaos, there were those who believed that the

Confederation still had certain responsibilities to the old government of France that must be honored. Whatever course the Diet might choose to follow required a strong and well-equipped militia. And this was lacking. The ancient cantons of *Innerschweiz*, defeated in the second Villmergen war, had done little to modernize their equipment and military tactics. Bern's army, which in 1712 was modernized and good, had aged considerably in the meantime. Much the same could be said of the armies of the other cantons where, without exception, nothing had been done to replace obsolescent and outmoded equipment. The cost of modernization had been the great deterrent and this, coupled with the dubious security afforded by the Franco-Swiss alliance, totally immobilized the cantonal governments, now faced by the greatest danger that had ever confronted the Confederation.

It was the only country in Europe that required military service of all of its men and obliged them to have at home in instant readiness their uniform and rifle. The strength that might be inferred for such a system was however deceptive. The organization was that of an army to be deployed for defense of the borders, its tactics were outmoded and the system of troop supply and ordinance spelled out in the Defensionale of Wyl was no longer effective for the kind of warfare that was emerging as the eighteenth century came to an end.

By 1792 the Swiss borders were endangered on the east by the advancing armies of the allies. To the west, Porrentruy in the Bishopric of Basel was already occupied by French forces. Freiburg, with its own share of troubles, had long demanded a *Tag* which was at last convened in May, 1792. Bern, Solothurn and Basel had already declared their neutrality and had initiated the necessary defensive preparations. Von Steiger, the *Schultheiss* of Bern, and a strong advocate of Swiss neutrality, set forth the Swiss position to Louis von Marval (Prussian Ambassador to Switzerland, 1792–95) who was posted in Neuchâtel. Steiger emphasized the impossibility of Switzerland joining the concert of Powers against France. There were the treaties of peace and friendship with France; Swiss troops were in the French military service; there was a real danger that Switzerland would become a theater of war; the country, while determined to defend its borders vigorously, had no taste for a foreign war: Switzerland would be split into several parts because of the diversity of opinion among the cantons on the issue of peace or war; and an offensive alliance, as proposed by the allies, would be most questionable among the Swiss. Moreover, Bern had to watch out for a separatist movement in Vaud, it had also to protect its own borders and to give help to the Bishopric of Basel, to Neuchâtel, and to Geneva for their own defense. Finally, Bern had heavy expenditures for military facilities and grain procurement (63). Büchi also quotes from a letter (21 June 1792) by Stürler von Altenberg to Johannes von Müller which throws light on the temper of the times:

> Unfortunately they believe here (Schaffhausen?) as in Coblentz that the French nationals are only a band of scoundrels—riffraf—who will not defend themselves for one minute, and that the counter-revolution will proceed easily from one end of the kingdom to the other, in four days of time as the revolution itself went on, and it has only to march to send the National Assembly to the gallows and re-establish the former government.

France at War, and the Reign of Terror

The pro-French party in the Confederation soon found their position untenable and turned speedily into opposition as a new government in France changed completely the ways of the old. The new government of France declared war against Austria and Prussia on 20 April 1792, and in September a National Convention seized power in France. A reign of terror descended upon the country as opponents of the revolution were hunted down in Paris and the provinces. Thousands were beheaded or drowned. A few weeks earlier, on August 10, the royal palace in Paris had been stormed by an armed mob. When the action ended, the regiment of Swiss guards entrusted with defense of the palace had been slaughtered by the hundreds, partly because the King ordered the regiment to cease firing when the action was far from complete. The National Convention, soon after its assumption of power, terminated the contracts of all Swiss subjects in the military service of France, doing so without the compensation and payments due under the various capitulation agreements. Except for the mutiny of a Swiss regiment stationed in Nancy it is remarkable that the remaining eight or nine regiments stationed in Paris and provincial cities held firm to their contractual obligations until finally recalled to their home cantons. Their morale was reasonably good in spite of their constant exposure to revolutionary propaganda. It was strengthened, unquestionably, by the revulsion aroused from the slaughter of their countrymen before the Tuileries. The Diet, with characteristic indecision and hesitancy, did not recall the Swiss regiments immediately after the terrible incident of August 10. Within the counsels of the Confederation were those who urged that the Swiss soldiers in France, relieved now of any responsibility to protect the monarch, should undertake a defense of France against the terrifying violence of the revolutionary mobs. For almost three weeks (September 3 to 22) the Diet struggled with the problems that had arisen but could not agree on the action to be taken.[34] The Bishopric of Basel, threatened by the approach of French troops, sought assistance from the catholic cantons on the basis of treaty obligations. These, in turn, requested help from Austria. The Confederation gave its approval and was even disposed to grant permission for Austrian troops, if sent to aid the Bishop, to cross Swiss territory. A French army under General Custine seized that part of the Bishopric which was subject territory of the German Reich but refrained from crossing into the cisjura part which enjoyed the protection of Swiss neutrality. Assurances were given that the neutrality of this portion of the Bishopric would be respected[35] but it is evident that Switzerland, nonetheless, was greatly concerned: her defenses had been breached and a French army, if so inclined, could probably beat down any resistance and enter the great central valley.

Swiss Indecision and Neutrality

The time for indecision was now past. The relatively few concessions that the Confederation and the cantons might have made to their own subjects passed by, and urgent reforms and improvements to enhance the Confederation's military preparedness escaped attention. What was done was too little and too late. The Switzerland of the past was headed irretrievably toward its downfall. Bern, the most powerful of the cantons, assumed a position of leadership in defense of the Confederation against disruptive forces within and the threatening movements developing to the north. The Confederation bravely declared its intention to adhere firmly to its historic principle of neutrality, to allow no warring Power to set foot on the soil of Switzerland and to pass through its territory. Should this be attempted, force would be opposed with force, and any trespass upon her territory would be most vigorously resisted.[36]

France urged the Confederation

> to take all necessary measures in order that the most exact neutrality would be observed by each of the States which constitute the Confederation . . . and keeping under surveillance those most cruel enemies of France, those French conspirators who in the past two years have fled into the States bordering on the Rhine and into all other neighbouring States of France . . . and some of the refugees should be expelled. Further, you should take all necessary measures to avoid assistance in any way to the House of Austria.[37]

Bern followed through with an expulsion decree (17 June 1796) applicable to all immigrants who were provocative in conduct and guilty of acts against the State. Lies, vicious propaganda, and hostile behaviour were charged against many. At the time of the decree, Karl Ludwig von Haller reported the presence of 618 French emigrés in Bern. Six months earlier there were only 114, all of whom were old men, women and children. The number expelled is not stated. Because of the troublesome French emigrés, Bern found the introduction of a passport system to be necessary. This was new and an unpleasant restriction against the original freedoms of the Swiss, which were deeply rooted and anchored in traditions of freedom of the individual. The French idea was a rationalistic concept based upon State supremacy: the good of the State was paramount.

Austria, whom Switzerland feared the most, indicated in an ambiguous reply to Switzerland's proclamation of neutrality that France had already violated Swiss neutrality, and, should the emergency arise, the armies of Austria would not hesitate to cross Swiss territory. England, also in the coalition against revolutionary France, made persistent efforts to persuade Switzerland to overlook provocative acts by French emigrés and others, that compromised her neutrality. The English Ambassador, Wickham,[38] was finally recalled in 1797. His predecessor, Fitzgerald,[39] was equally guilty of political intrigues and of involvement in the internal affairs and foreign policy of the Confederation.

von Steiger who was a man of unblemished character and basically conservative was entrusted with the military and political power that the deteriorating situation required. Unfortunately the gift of dynamic and inspired leadership was not his. Could he have rallied the people against the mounting perils to the Fatherland, could he have inspired the faint-hearted and irresolute to unite in a determined effort to save the country, the outcome might have been different. He had long been suspicious of France, disliked the frivolity of the French court, and had opposed the Franco-Swiss alliance of 1777. Steiger became the head of a War Party which drew its strength principally from Bern, Freiburg and Solothurn. The Party was quite prepared to have Switzerland join the coalition against revolutionary France because Steiger concluded that, with the monarchy swept away, the flood of revolution would not be stemmed merely by Swiss neutrality and respect for the Swiss border. An all-Swiss conference, convened in Aarau by the War Party, was on the verge of committing the Confederation to join the coalition in the war against France. Zurich's representatives, in accordance with their instructions, insisted on an unswerving re-affirmation of neutrality and Bern satisfied itself for the moment with the termination of diplomatic relations with France. The Diet repeated its declaration of armed neutrality and again asserted its determination to defend the Fatherland with the blood, the bodies, and the possessions of its people.

Countering Steiger's War Party was a party dedicated to peace at almost any price. The leaders of the Peace Party assumed that the mob violence and anarchy prevailing in France could not continue for long. It would end in the foreseeable future and if so it would be shamefully wasteful to spend for military preparedness the large sums of money that the War Party sought to have appropriated. A significant number of the ruling families adhered to the Peace Party because of their wishful thinking that the deterioration in France would soon end and the former ruling class of nobles and aristocrats would be restored to power.

Revolution in Geneva

In the fall of 1792 French troops invaded Savoy. Geneva, fearing that her safety was threatened called upon Bern and Zurich for help. Almost 2000 troops were sent in response. Negotiations with the French led to assurances that the city would be spared from invasion. The Swiss troops withdrew and soon thereafter revolution broke out in the city under remote direction by the French revolutionaries. Government of the city was exercised by a French leader of the powerful minority of insurgents. A reign of terror followed and continued almost unabated until 1795.

Louis XVI of France was executed in January 1793. The power of government passed into a "Welfare Council," a resolute executive body which ruled as despots and continued with even greater vigor the policy of exterminating the former aristocratic rulers of France. This strengthened the coalition of foreign Powers now beginning to assemble their forces in expectation of war. Under the leadership of Edmund Burke, England's foreign policy turned vigorously against the bloody tyranny of the French revolutionaries and the threat imposed by their dictators to the principles of freedom treasured by the English people. England, Naples, the Netherlands and Spain joined the coalition against France for the movement in France now posed a threat to the peace of all Europe.

Geneva was now firmly under the control of a revolutionary government. France had seized a large part of the Bishopric of Basel and in March 1793 had absorbed it into France as the Department of Doubs. Important segments of the Swiss defense bulwark were now lost: Geneva to the west and the Jura defense line to the northwest. Armies of the French Revolutionary Command were poised on the Jura slopes. Why did France continue to respect the neutrality of the Principality of Neuchâtel and of the southerly part of the Bishopric of Basel? Why did the revolutionary army not move at once into the great central valley of Switzerland to facilitate its campaign against Austria?

France Depends on Switzerland for Supplies

The answer has nothing to do with military strategy, nor is it to be found in any genuine intention of the revolutionary command to honor its repeated assurances of respect for Swiss neutrality. To the contrary it is to be found in economics. Since early 1793 France found herself opposed by a coalition consisting of England, Holland, Spain, Naples, and the German States as well as her earlier enemies: Prussia, Austria, and Sardinia. The resulting economic blockade would have had a devastating effect were it not for the open border with Switzerland.[40] From the Swiss cantons France imported grain, cattle, horses, weapons, copper, saltpeter (an essential ingredient of black powder), leather, shoes, and cloth. When their own domestic supplies ran low, Swiss merchants and wartime speculators imported vast quantities from Austria, south Germany, Italy, and Hungary and funneled them through to France. Austria justified its action, knowing full well what was happening, by claiming that, otherwise, revolutionary forces would rise to the surface in Switzerland and the French would move in. In the winter of 1793–94, 9000 horses entered Schaffhausen from south Germany for trans-shipment to France. About 30,000 rifles of German origin were re-exported to France. The profits accruing to the Swiss were enormous. The President of the French Convention complained of the "unheard-of" prices at which cattle, horses, and powder were supplied by Swiss exporters. It is little wonder that the French showed little if any hesitation in seizing, a few years later, the gold reserves of the cantonal governments, notably of Bern.

Renewed Discord in Switzerland

In 1795 tensions relaxed somewhat, the reign of terror in Geneva came to an end and Prussia and Spain concluded a separate peace with France. For Switzerland, there was only a temporary respite. France continued to exert unrelenting pressure in this direction and that. She demanded extradition of the French aristocrats who had sought asylum in Switzerland and were politically active in their support of the Swiss War Party. The Diet, as well as the authorities in the various cantons, found their freedom of action fast disappearing because of continued French interference. They could hope only for an early end to the revolutionary movement in France. Threats of invasion by the French, unless major concessions were made, plus the lack of unity within the government, and divisive influences at work among the people, totally demoralized the country. It is doubtful whether any serious resistance could have been mounted had the French chosen to invade the territories of the Confederation.

The government of Zurich was confronted with new demands in the form of a memorial prepared by Heinrich Nehracher: constitutional reforms, increased freedom in trade and commerce, and in reduction of censorship. Freedom of discussion, of publication, and of intellectual activities focussing on political dissent and the problems of the day, were sought. The government responded promptly. The memorial was regarded as an incitement for a popular uprising. The document was publicly burned, Nehracher and his principal associates were punished, centers of potential revolt were occupied by government forces and severe punishment was promised the "troublemakers." Bern took appropriate precautions by having a contingent of troops in readiness to send to the aid of Zurich should the necessity arise.

In the lands of the Abbot of St. Gallen, unrest, as elsewhere in the Confederation, rose to threatening dimensions. The abbot succeeded in appeasing his people by cancelling certain taxes and imposts which were the subject of much complaint. In 1795 he subscribed to a so-called treaty which granted relief from certain other financial burdens related to serfdom, through payment of a rather modest sum. It was also conceded that the people should themselves elect the officials of their own communities. The abbot was far-sighted and wise in the institution of these reforms, thereby setting an example which had an impressive effect on neighbouring jurisdictions.

The French Directory

Meanwhile, in France, an important change in the government came about. Power passed into the hands of a five-membered "Directory" which included in its number François de Barthélemy, former ambassador to the Swiss Confederation. Although the Diet in 1792 had severed diplomatic relations with France, Barthélemy had remained in Solothurn and continued to serve his country by promoting the cause of France within the leadership of the Peace Party. The leaders of government within the Confederation were persuaded to minimize the dangers arising in the western parts although it was becoming increasingly clear to some that the turn of events in France was more threatening than ever. Out of the violence and disorder of the preceding few years the new regime in France was gaining a popular acceptance, at least an acquiescence in the form of government that emerged on dissolution of the monarchy and loss of power by the aristocrats.

More Indecision in Switzerland

That the rulers of the old Swiss Confederation and of its member States would eventually be displaced and a more democratic structure would emerge was recognized by many of the Swiss intellectuals. Others, with less insight, believed that the Peace of Basel between France, Prussia, and Spain ended the threat of a French invasion and signaled a return to peace and order within the Confederation. They subscribed to the opinion that the crisis had passed. In retrospect one must conclude that this belief could only have been entertained by those who blindly accepted the propaganda of the Peace Party, who believed the belligerent Powers would respect Swiss neutrality, or who were too terrified to face up to the facts. It soon became evident that the borders were not well defended and that incidents in the vicinity of Basel raised serious doubts about the efficacy of the border guards and the determination of the authorities to enforce rigorously the neutrality of the country. At Basel's border where France and Austria were separated, the armies of the two Powers faced each other in the fall of 1796. The French held a bridgehead in the powerful fortress of Hüningen. The Austrian plan called for capture of the bridgehead. At the last moment the Diet sent a Bernese regiment to strengthen the border and to frustrate any attempt by the two belligerents to trespass on Swiss soil. Bern, fearful of the great expense in maintaining the regiment assigned to the Basel border, soon reduced the size of the force. Austria, in the night of November 29, attempted a surprise attack on Hüningen by a column of troops which crossed unhindered over Swiss territory. The attack on Hüningen misfired and the Austrians fled before the pursuing French, again crossing over Swiss territory. The border guards eventually rose to the occasion and cleared the Swiss territory of the "invaders." As a curious aftermath, both the French and the Austrians re-buked the government because of its negligence in failing to protect its borders adequately, as expected of a neutral country. Basel dismissed the commander of the Basel unit, and France and Austria, with weightier problems before them, appeared to be satisfied.

In general, the duties of the border guards proved to be quite perfunctory. Had they have possessed the strength that adequate protection of the border required, the story might have been different; presumably, the Austrian *Durchzug* could have been prevented. One rather unexpected duty that fell to the border guard concerned the many deserters and adventurers in foreign service who crossed into Switzerland. In the first three years of the war almost 25,000 of these were led through Basel territory into an Austrian depot at Lorrach.[41] They were, in the main, French who deserted or were cut off from their regiments: the rights of asylum and the practice of internment of belligerents by a Neutral had not been established even by 1796.

Prelude to the Conquest of Switzerland

France, meanwhile, as later events proved, was advancing its plans of conquest which included Switzerland. There can be but little doubt that the Directory, apart from political motivations and military strategy, coveted the reserves of gold which were known to be stored in Bern and Zurich. Switzerland was flooded with pamphlets, satirical poems, leaflets, and well-planted rumors, the whole campaign against the War Party being planned by French agents commissioned to carry out this insidious and subversive campaign. The government, now unable to meet on common grounds with its own people, was totally incapable of stemming the agitation and mounting troubles in these last days of the old Confederation. The purpose of this vicious campaign of propaganda, lies, and rumors was to weaken the resistance of the Swiss to the coming invasion. The French Directory probably overestimated the military capability of the Swiss defense organization and failed to appreciate the weakness of the Swiss armies at that time. Austria was the principal opponent but to subdue this historic enemy of French aggrandisement, conquest of

Switzerland and control of the Alpine passes into Italy and the Valtellina, and thereby into Austria, were important to France. A Swiss corridor into upper Italy would also greatly facilitate communication between France and her areas of occupation and control in northern Italy.

Intrigue continued at an accelerated pace. The English Minister in Switzerland who had used his influence against the rise of the revolutionary government in France was expelled or recalled in 1797.[38] True, he had abused his office by endless efforts to bring the Swiss into the war against revolutionary France. Sheltered by the security of neutral soil he had used English gold to bribe army officers, government officials, and influential Swiss in a determined effort to swing popular sentiment in favor of the War Party. With an abundance of money provided by the British government he had supported and encouraged many revolutionary Franco-Swiss agents who were steadily undermining the Swiss resistance by persistent propaganda.

Many Swiss emigrés had settled in Paris. A significant number had been expelled from their homeland because of their declared sympathies with the rebellious subjects at home and with the revolutionaries in France. César de la Harpe, returned from Petersburg and again living in Paris, addressed a memorial to the Directory, in which military intervention in Switzerland was requested. He proposed that the lower part of the Rhone valley (lower Valais) be absorbed by France, that the Principality of Neuchâtel be joined to France, and the southern slopes of the Jura be occupied by French troops. In a second memorial, to which a number of his fellow Vaudois also subscribed, the Directory was urged to send a contingent of troops into Vaud to "liberate" its people.

De la Harpe was the enemy from without while Ochs, as a high official in Basel, pursued a traitorous policy from within. His weakness was his vanity and his determination to play a leading role in overthrow of the government. In November 1797 he was sent to Paris, commissioned by the government to negotiate with the Directory over transfer of the Fricktal, formerly Austrian territory, to Basel. The Directory seized upon this opportunity to use Ochs for their own plans to overthrow the Confederation. Napoleon Bonaparte, now in command of the armies of France, instructed Ochs to draft a new Constitution for the Switzerland of the future, a clear indication that war against the Confederation had been decided upon. In accepting this assignment Ochs clearly engaged in a treacherous act against his Fatherland. Napoleon's designs against Switzerland were now evident to all. The thirteen cantons of the Confederation became the victims of a squeeze play which they were powerless to resist.

In October 1797, Austria was forced to conclude peace with France. In the Treaty of Campoformio, Austria surrendered her Belgian provinces to France and gave formal recognition to the Cisalpine Republic forged by France from the former Austrian territory around Milan. The Swiss Confederation, now too weak to do more than protest, was also deprived of its sovereignty over the Valtellina which became fused into the Cisalpine Republic. Geneva was already occupied by the French.

The fateful progress of these events shocked and dispirited many within the counsels of the Confederation. In December, much of the territory governed by the Bishop of Basel was occupied by French troops who overran the Jura slopes as far south as the town of Biel.[42] Bonaparte journeyed to Italy and, humiliating as it was to the Swiss, he received military honors en route. On a visit to the battlefield of Murten he declared publicly that should he be forced into a military confrontation with the Swiss his troops would not be driven into the Murtensee—the fate of the army of Charles the Bold in the fifteenth-century Burgundian war.

In late December, 1797, the Diet was summoned to an extraordinary session at Aarau. Little more was accomplished than a patriotic proclamation and a show of defiance towards the French. Catholics and protestants alike joined in the patriotic gestures. A few weeks later the members of the Diet, with many thousand onlookers, assembled to subscribe to the historic oath of allegiance, and to reaffirm the covenants which solemnly bound together the member cantons. The bells of the city rang out and cannon were ceremoniously fired. In retrospect, there was nothing festive about the occasion. It was, in effect, a funeral or a wake. The great crowd of onlookers was divided in its sympathies. Quietly, the dissatisfied majority refrained from any emotional outburst against this last-minute attempt at a show of solidarity. The Diet closed its eyes to the ill-concealed internal strife that divided the country.

Last-Minute Reforms in Switzerland

At the last moment, only a month or two before the fall of the Confederation, the governing bodies of most of the aristocratic cantons and associated States offered to their subjects many of the reforms which had stubbornly been denied throughout the century: equality of rights for the burghers in the country towns with those in the cities; equality before the law of subjects and the burgher class; restoration of many freedoms and liberties to subject classes in town and country alike; and surrender of the right of self-election by the ruling class to election of its representatives by the governed. Several of the regions which had suffered much from internal discord and oppression from without seceded from their former ruling State and declared themselves to be independent self-governing republics. Revolutionary agents from France had penetrated all the States embraced by the Confederation and openly led the movement in some regions for separation from the Confederation or from the rule of outsiders. Schwyz, for example, yielded its sovereignty over Uznach and Gaster, St. Gallen recognized the new republic of Toggenburg, and Uri, with French troops now in command of the plains of Lombardy, abandoned its governing rights over the Leventine.

Most of the districts and States within the territory of the Confederation were now enfeebled and deprived of any effective government. France now focussed its campaign on the city of Bern and the large area under its rule. The Great Council of Bern had elected Karl Ludwig von Erlach as the general in command of its troops and summoned its people to the colours. Several of the battalions from the Lake Geneva area refused to take the oath of allegiance. It was suspected and feared that the French attack would be directed first against Vaud. Franz Rudolf Weiss, a man of doubtful competence for such a difficult task, had been placed in civil and military command of Vaud. The province fell without a shot being fired. The general in command of the French army poised on the Bernese border proclaimed the freeing of Vaud and its re-establishment as the independent Republic of Leman. Weiss fled to Yverdon and the Bernese governing officials in Vaud retired from office. A small body of troops, loyal to Bern, retreated into Bernese territory. Lausanne was occupied by the French, without resistance, on 28 January 1798. French troops were promptly dispersed through the whole of Vaud and another French army occupied the Bernese town of Biel.

The Fall of Bern

Within the governing Councils of Bern conflicts on matters of policy arose anew between von Steiger of the War Party and the leaders of the Peace Party. The government was paralyzed by this inner strife and was unable to make any decisions on which there was evidence of unity. The French took advantage of the situation with half promises, veiled threats, and subversive measures designed to weaken further the resistance. The Great Council sent a delegation to Payerne in mid February to request of the French General Brune a 14-day armistice. The French agents, focussing their activities on the Bernese, spread the rumor that the members of the delegation had been bought off and were engaged in treasonable acts. Various units of the mobilized troops, dispirited by the breakdown of morale, deserted the army and went home. As February was coming to an end, von Erlach demanded that the government grant to him full emergency powers or accept his resignation. The power was granted. When the armistice was about to expire, the Directory ordered Brune to open an attack on Freiburg, Solothurn, and Bern. Possibly to spare further bloodshed, or to break down the last vestiges of resistance, Brune sent an ultimatum to Bern, demanding resignation of the government, release of all political prisoners, and demobilization of the troops. Whether it was possible at this critical moment to restore the morale of the people and of the army, through a strong and heroic leadership is doubtful. Instead of an immediate rejection of the ultimatum, the authorities in Bern, in common with the governing body of Zurich, advised General Brune that they were ready to accept the ultimatum in principle. Rumor-mongering was renewed and the earlier rumors of traitorous behaviour by the agents of government appeared to be confirmed. Troop contingents from other cantons, required by the terms of defensive agreements to come to the defense of Bern, attempted to be of aid, but false rumors of surrender or of the capture of Bern, and incredible delays in mobilization within some of the cantons defeated the attempt to render effective help. Small contingents arrived from the ancient cantons. On March 2, Brune repeated his ultimatum and, without resistance, entered Solothurn with his army. von Erlach retreated with his army to a stronger position behind the Aare, Saane, and Sense rivers. Not accustomed to retreat, the morale of the Bernese forces was certainly not enhanced by this manoeuver. On March 4, the Great Council of Bern abdicated, and Frisching, leader of the Peace Party, was installed as head of a provisional government. But Brune declined to show any respect for this "man of peace" and fought his way through Neuenegg, Laupen, and on to Bern. Fraubrunnen had also fallen to a second army. von Steiger, meanwhile fled over the Brunig Pass into the uplands.

On March 28, Lecarlier, a high French official, informed his government that he had assumed the full power of government over the whole of Helvetia. He announced to the Swiss that a new constitution had been prepared in Paris under which the country would be ruled, and ordered its acceptance by all the cantons. The money which, over the years, had been so carefully husbanded and stored in the ancient cellars under the council houses was seized by the French and shipped off to Paris.[43] Thus ended the old regime. But enough courage, resolve, and national pride remained to provide the foundation upon which a united Switzerland would again arise.

Neutrality

The European wars of the eighteenth century posed more serious problems to the maintenance of Swiss neutrality than might be suspected. The invasion of Switzerland by the armies of revolutionary France was the final blow, but the earlier wars of the century were not without their challenges to the Confederation. The Spanish War of Succession (1702–13) posed almost every type of problem to the Swiss, bent on maintaining their neutrality and impartiality toward all belligerents. The Polish (1733–38) and Austrian (1741–48) Wars of Succession added few if any challenges that were new or unique.

Even before the war of 1702–13 broke out, the Powers tried to persuade Switzerland to adhere to the Second Treaty of Partition (1700) as a guarantor.[44] They used the seductive argument that it is the duty of all neutral States to join in preventing war, in particular the war that now threatened as a result of the impending death of the King of Spain (Charles II) without issue.[45] The proposal conflicted sharply with Confederation policy to avoid all such dangerous guaranties which could so obviously draw Switzerland into a European war.

There were two contenders for the throne of Spain: Duke Philippe of Anjou who, as the grandson of Louis XIV, was supported by France; and the kaiser who claimed the inheritance because of the Habsburg origin of the King of Spain. When the grandson of Louis XIV gained recognition by Naples, Milan, Florence, Genoa, and the Papal State as King of Spain (Philippe V) the balance of power was completely upset. Philippe V was also the Duke of Anjou, and Spain and France henceforth became firmly bound in a political and military alliance. A seriously aggravating factor was the return of the Duchy of Milan to Spanish sovereignty[46] and the obligation then thrust upon Swiss mercenaries in the service of the Duchy to defend Milan against the kaiser and his allies. With the outbreak of war, the enemies of France became united in a single objective: to end the efforts of Louis XIV to establish France as the dominant Power in Europe and the center of a universal monarchy.

Large forces of the belligerents were soon encamped near Switzerland's northern border along the Rhine. Attempts were made to persuade the Powers to neutralize the cities on the right bank and a wide strip of territory beyond.[47] The negotiations which went on for months were futile since both Louis XIV and the kaiser encumbered their provisional acceptances of the proposal with numerous reservations and conditions that could not be resolved. In these negotiations, the Confederation declared its determination to observe a strict neutrality in the impending struggle.[48] The Elector of Bavaria (allied with France) gave explicit assurance that his troops would not trespass upon Swiss soil. In December 1703, France gave written assurances that throughout the war the entire stretch of the Rhine from Lake Constance to Basel would be spared from any hostile acts by French and Bavarian forces provided that the Swiss refrained from any hostilities against France or Bavaria. Each of the two belligerents finally assured the Confederation that Swiss neutrality would be respected so long as the opposing Power continued to honor this pledge.[49] The assurances were renewed by both Powers in July 1708.[50]

Early in the war the kaiser sought permission to recruit Swiss troops for defense of the Austrian border. The request was supported by Britain and Holland in the hope that the recruits would join the allies in preventing a union of French and Bavarian forces in South Germany. Active participation in the general defense of the *Römisches Reich* was also contemplated. Although a number of Swiss regiments were ultimately made available to the kaiser to defend several Austrian cities on Lake Constance and others on the right bank of the Rhine, the Confederation refused to be drawn into an overall defense of the *Reich*. This would certainly involve the Swiss in full scale military operations on the side of the allies and would invite French retaliation.

Both sides complained of many transgressions in the use of Swiss mercenaries. In the Netherlands they were engaged in offensive operations by both the French and the allies. Five Swiss regiments that fought under Marlborough and Prince Eugen in the victorious battle at Höchstädt[51] in August, 1704, were not employed solely in defense. Incidentally this victory over the French ended a situation in South Germany which appeared threatening to Switzerland.

In April, 1705, Lucerne proposed to the Diet that the warring Powers be urged to call a peace congress to seek an end to the war. Bern and Lucerne were lukewarm to the proposal: they considered that the effort would be utterly futile. However, the catholic cantons regarded Lucerne's initiative as an "idea inspired by Heaven." Neither the Diet nor the kaiser accepted this appraisal of Lucerne's proposal. The kaiser was especially embittered because, while "imploring his Majesty to listen to their respectful desire for peace" and pointing out that "*the Eidgnosschaft* at this time is almost the only place in the world which by the Grace of God stands apart in true neutrality and peace from the warring Powers," the catholic cantons had the temerity to renew a military capitulation with Philippe V of Spain. This treaty promised *Durchzug* rights through the catholic cantons and 4000 to 13,000 soldiers to help in the campaign in upper Italy against the Kaiser. Allegedly, the document was signed while negotiations were in progress over the Lucerne peace proposal.

Now we come to 1709 and an incident which caused a tremendous furor and saber rattling within Switzerland. On 20 August, the Austrian Lieutenant Field Marshal, Count Mercy, with a large cavalry force—possibly 4000—crossed into Swiss territory at Rheinfelden and, avoiding the main road, sped through Pratteln and Binningen to the French-Alsatian town of Hägenheim. From there he continued north on the left bank of the Rhine and joined forces with his infantry division opposite Neuenburg.[52] Three hours or so appear to have been required for the 16 km crossing through Basel territory. The elderly and much-disturbed *Bürgermeister* of Basel, on receipt of news that the *Durchmarsch* was under way, reminded the Austrian Commander-in-Chief of the neutrality treaty with the kaiser. He was advised in reply that Mercy's crossing would be fully justified in a forthcoming letter.

This trespass upon Swiss territory was compounded by a second violation. Severely defeated by the French in an engagement near Neuenburg, about 500 of Mercy's cavalry managed to escape and retraced their access route toward Rheinfelden. Some were fired upon by the Swiss but the larger groups escaped. A few small groups were intercepted and led to Basel-Augst for questioning. The victorious French general, du Bourg, accused the Swiss of failure to intercept the fleeing Imperial troops at the westerly border where they should have been driven back into French territory.

Several glaring weaknesses in the neutrality practices of the day stand out in bold relief. There was no provision for the internment of troops of a belligerent Power on their escape into a neutral country. Disarmament at the point of entry was not an accepted practice nor were the laws governing the right of asylum developed. Furthermore, contrary to the principles of neutrality, Mercy did not use the first crossing on 20 August to permit passage into Austrian territory, but, on the contrary, into that of his enemy.

Just as disturbing as the Mercy violation of Swiss neutrality were events in the shadowy areas of back-room diplomacy, of rumors, conspiracies, intrigues, deception, and espionage. Count du Luc, the French Ambassador, had warned Basel in August 1709 (!) that the kaiser intended to order the Rheinfelden crossing. The Diet responded with a unanimous decision to adhere strictly to its historic neutrality.[53] Instead of deciding upon a firm course of action in case du Luc's warning should prove to be correctly founded, the Swiss, already torn by inner dissension and strife between the two Confessions and the mounting belligerence of the Toggenburg problem, lapsed into indecision, inaction, and a sort of Dietary paralysis. Time passed by and official concern over the French warning vanished. Then came the *Durchzug*, the usual recriminations and efforts to focus the blame on the kaiser, the Austrian Commander-in-Chief, Count Mercy, Basel, and possibly Bern.

As early as 1706, after the French defeat at Ramillies, Bern established a Commission which was instructed to negotiate secretly with the Powers about the difficult and sensitive questions that would have to be resolved at the end of the war. Zurich, somewhat reluctantly, was persuaded by Bern to set up a similar commission to cooperate with Bern which assumed, almost by default, a position of leadership in the secret negotiations that were initiated. Territorial rearrangements were of paramount importance. Bern was eager to have the French expelled from the Franche Comté. Basel and Schaffhausen, also involved, hoped that the peace treaty would provide for French expulsion from Alsace. All this was of little concern to Zurich, which, along with Basel, sought to have the great French fortress at Hüningen and several other threatening fortifications levelled. The reformed cantons were unanimous in the belief that the allies would emerge victorious. For this reason they excluded the catholic cantons, whose sympathies were pro-French, from the secret negotiations which soon were extended at the ambassadorial level to Great Britain, Holland, and Prussia.

Bern's ultimate objective was neutralization of the Franche Comté, and international recognition of Swiss protectorship over the Comté, Savoy and the Duchy of Milan. Undoubtedly, she was playing with fire. If her secret gamesmanship became known to France, her own position and that of the reformed cantons would be seriously compromised. War with the catholic cantons would be a possible consequence. The allied Powers could also argue that if Bern were so eager to have the Franche Comté removed from French sovereignty she should join the allies in military action against France.

The fact that negotiations between the reformed cantons and the allied Powers were in progress could hardly be hidden. There was an excess of diplomatic activity and the stakes were high. Peculiar as it may seem, the Bern Peace Commission in 1708 chose Baron St. Saphorin,[54] a diplomat in the service of Austria to represent Bern in the preliminary peace negotiations conducted by the allied Powers at the Hague. His overriding objectives were to achieve the defeat of France and to advance the protestant cause. The secrecy of the negotiations could not be preserved. It was not long before France learned of the real purpose of St. Saphorin's mission in the Hague. The so-called peace negotiations were a cover for something quite sinister—an invasion of the Franche Comté by Count Mercy's army and a second force from upper Italy which would descend through the Aosta valley and enter the Comté from the west. The invasions would be timed to coincide with an uprising of the people in the Franche Comté incited by agents dedicated to the allied cause.

The hazardous and dubious aspects of Swiss involvement were the secrecy with which the Peace Commissions negotiated, the vast amount of lying that ensued, the representation of only a segment of the Confederation—the reformed cantons—in the negotiations, and, as a consequence, discussions with only one of the belligerents. A Colonel Braconnier, who at one time played a dubious role in the French diplomatic service, laid before the British Ambassador Stanyan and Metternich of Austria the detailed plans for seizure of the Franche Comté. St. Saphorin suspected Braconnier to be an adventurer of dubious credibility. His suspicions were fully justified for Braconnier subsequently informed Du Luc, the French Ambassador (1709–16), of the planned uprising in the Franche Comté. The plan, allegedly involving St. Saphorin, called for conquest of the Franche Comté through an Austrian *Durchmarsch* across Basel canton to seize the lightly guarded bridge at Neuenburg, and at the same time an attack on the Franche Comté from Savoy. Willading[55] was also involved as a director of the *démarches* of St. Saphorin. Willading "had promised that his canton will declare itself against France as soon as the allies will have occupied a secure position in the Comté." Apparently, some secret papers concerning the plan were found in General Mercy's briefcase which, having been lost, came into the hands of the French. This incriminating incident was reported by Du Luc who proposed to urge the cantons, represented at the next *Tagsatzung* at Baden, to protect their points of entry with utmost care, as they were obliged to do by alliances and by the Treaty of Neutrality of 1702. The Swiss replied, 7 August 1709, that they intended to observe scrupulously and exactly all the relevant treaties. Subsequently, Du Luc stated that on August 17 he learned that Mercy would make the Basel *Durchmarsch* during the night of August 20.

It happened as predicted and Du Luc, holding Bern and Basel responsible, urged the Swiss to take up arms against the Empire and seek satisfaction for this violation of their neutrality. If this was refused, Du Luc went on to invite the Swiss to join arms with France.

Du Luc wrote to the French king a highly critical description of the Swiss:

> Please forgive me it I blow hot and cold from my mouth; but it is necessary that you have complete knowledge of these people who have totally changed, if it be true that at one time in Switzerland a healthy, straight-forward understanding and honest sincerity prevailed (**403**, p. 35).

In April, 1713, Du Luc wrote to the French court on the general subject of "How to weaken Bern."

> Install Conti as Prince of Neuchâtel and Valangin. Next seize Vaud and annex it to France. This will cut Bern down to a modest size and make her easy to manage. The Comte will be protected with no chance of Germans [Austrians?] ever marching through Vaud—part of France in the future (**142**, p. 300 et seq.).

Du Luc's appraisal of the Swiss is counter-balanced by a devastating description of Du Luc's character:

> He was a master in all the arts of deception and intrigue . . . a very hot-headed and avaricious rascal (St. Saphorin to Prince von Salm, 6 March 1709 (**148**)).

Cunning, mendacity, trickery and hypocrisy were the most outstanding qualities of the Graf du Luc. He understood diplomacy well. His understanding of a subject, his intentions and his many deviations and turns in policy were always exceptionally well concealed (**148**).

A second traitor to the allied cause and to the Swiss was Hieronymus von Erlach (1667–1748), son-in-law of Willading, who, after resignation from the French military service in 1697, became commander of one of the two Swiss regiments made available to Kaiser Leopold for defense of the Austrian command at the battle near Neuenburg at which one of Erlach's officers and a number of his men were captured by the French. Erlach rose in favor with the kaiser but continued to receive generous pension payments from France. He became a trusted source of information to Du Luc about Austrian plans for conduct of the war and the secret "negotiations" of St. Saphorin. Zellweger (**403**) quotes many passages from Du Luc's correspondence that prove how deeply involved Erlach became in passing information to the French. Despite his services to Austria and France, Switzerland also held Erlach in high regard. This is difficult to understand. His conduct was dishonorable if not traitorous. Schweizer (**328**, pp. 447, 448) builds a case against him as one who played both sides against the middle and enriched himself immensely in so doing. In 1715 he retired from foreign service with the reputation of one of the most accomplished generals of his time. In the terminal years of his life he served as *Schultheiss* of Bern (1721–47).

All of the armies in the Spanish War of Succession were made up of professional mercenaries with fugitive loyalties, hired by kings, princes and heads of government who sought favorable realignments of their country's frontiers and shifts in the balance of power that would strengthen some and weaken others. Swiss fought for France and Spain and were also heavily represented in the allied armies. Money, booty and adventure were the rewards.

At the highest levels, deceit, lies, diplomatic finagling, sacred understandings and treaties-of-today-to-be-broken-tomorrow, bribery and treachery were instruments of war as valuable to a belligerent as swords and bullets.

Did anything emerge to the benefit of Switzerland from her venturesome entanglement during these years in the affairs of the Great Powers, highlighted by the quasi-secret manoeuvering of St. Saphorin on behalf of several of the Reformed cantons? The Franche Comté, not even mentioned in the various treaties of peace that ended the war, remained under the sovereignty of France. Perhaps the most profitable result of these years of intrusion into power politics was the realization once again that the Confederation had little to gain and much to lose by any departure from the hands-off policy so earnestly advocated by Brother Klaus (see Chapter 4).

In November 1733, on the outbreak of the Polish War of Succession, an extraordinary session of the Diet was convened. Significantly, the Diet issued a proclamation of neutrality to all of the Powers participating in the war:

> As a further means of preserving the peace and quiet that we desire, a complete and exact neutrality towards all of the warring Powers will be observed. . . . No party at war will be allowed to make a stand on Swiss soil and to this end to attempt a Durchmarsch. . . . Force will be repelled with force.[56]

For the benefit of Austria and France she also reaffirmed her neutrality in July 1735 "to remain unswervingly neutral and in all emergencies to protect the borders against any possibility of a surprise attack by the forces of the Great Powers."

Much of the war was fought in southern Germany, Alsace, and upper Italy. A troublesome problem arose because of the many deserters who fled to Switzerland. In general, their uniforms and weapons were seized at the border but internment practices, applicable to deserters and escaping foreign mercenaries, had not been developed. Usually, the deserters were granted exit passes, ordered out of the country and told never to return.[57]

The Austrian War of Succession, seemingly intended to settle a challenge by Charles of Bavaria to the widely accepted agreement that Maria Theresia of Austria succeed her father (Charles VI) as head of the Holy Roman Empire, was little more than a territorial dispute. It was essentially an endeavour by Prussia to expand her territories and influence in the affairs of western Europe, then dominated by France and Greater Austria. In August 1743 belligerent forces again began to assemble north of the Rhine. The Diet issued to the heads of the warring States a declaration of Switzerland's neutrality. The proclamation may be regarded, in substance, as a reaffirmation of the declaration of 13–17 November 1733. The war ended with the Peace of Aachen (Aix-la-Chapelle) in 1748. Nothing happened during the eight-year struggle which strengthened or impaired the total and exact neutrality that Switzerland so persistently proclaimed.

Switzerland's resolute policy of total neutrality disturbed the British government. Throughout the century a succession of British Envoys and/or Ambassadors to the evangelical cantons,[58] from Stanyan in 1705 to Lord Robert Fitzgerald in 1792, received instructions which were strikingly similar in content (236). For example, the instructions to Burnaby (22 January 1743):

> ... establish such an influence with the cantons, as may make them of effectual service to Us and Our Allies, and to destroy the credit which the House of Bourbon has, for many years, kept up in that country, particularly that we may be enabled to raise a body of troops there.

Stanyan was required to propose to the cantons a military alliance with Great Britain and that they join the coalition against Louis XIV.[59]

To Great Britain, the *bête noir* of Europe was Louis XIV. His dream of a universal monarchy lived on, somewhat abated perhaps, in the aspirations of Louis XV and Louis XVI. The British Government was firmly convinced that the overweening ambitions of France must be suppressed.

Why did Britain fail in her seductive efforts to persuade Switzerland to join in the military alliance against France or to provide Britain with a few thousand mercenaries? The reasons are many, but two, in particular, deserve mention: (a) The Swiss had decided long before the wars of the eighteenth century that the dictates of such a great geographical separation would make it quite useless to invoke any military aid from Britain in the event of a crisis. On the Continent, Britain was also regarded as a sea Power with colonial interests across the Atlantic that constantly absorbed her attention. And Switzerland well knew that any military aid to Britain in her campaign against France would only invite an instant invasion by France and civil war within the Confederation. (b) Switzerland was heavily dependent upon France in trade and commerce. Salt, grain, wine and other essential commodities were supplied by France in adequate amounts and under favorable terms. Switzerland also enjoyed a favored nation treatment in respect of textile exports to France.[60] Beyond this economic dependence, there was a long history of treaties of friendship and of military capitulations, especially with the catholic cantons. The political relationships reflected a real fear of France. Steiger, as *Bürgermeister* of Bern, admitted to Burnaby "this country is under the power of France. The people here are too timid . . . they all fear the French King's resentment" (Burnaby to Newcastle, 22 April 1743). Five years later Burnaby reported to Newcastle "of all the cantons, Basel is the most subject to France, Solothurn [seat of the French Ambassador] not excepted." He mentioned also "its slavish subjection" to France.

In May, 1777, the ancient Treaty of Perpetual Peace (1516) between France and the Confederation was again renewed.[61] The sixth Article, drafted by the Diet, was a most impressive declaration of neutrality to which the two Powers gave their assent:

The King and the Helvetic Body regard as a consequence and necessary effect of their alliance that the engagement which they renew shall not suffer their enemies and respective adversaries to establish themselves in their respective countries, lands, and seignories, nor to accord them any passage through their said countries for the purpose of attacking or molesting the other ally, promising reciprocally to oppose them even with force of arms if necessity so requires; and as the present absolutely defensive treaty must not prejudice nor derogate the neutrality of the parties, the respective cantons here declare in the most express manner their desire to observe and maintain it [their neutrality] in every case and without distinction towards all the Powers.

The first Article expressed with equal determination the purpose of this defensive alliance "which has no other intention than to further mutual protection and security without offence to anyone." The peaceful intentions of the two parties were expanded upon in the third Article which describes the "strictly upright union as a defensive alliance for the peace, defense, and preservation of the persons, states, lands, and rights which they then possess in Europe."

This was a remarkable document which favored Switzerland in several respects and which might have had consequences of enduring value had the revolutionary government of France, a few years later, not brought an end to the peace which was at last descending upon Europe: (i) If Switzerland were to be attacked by a foreign Power, France would come to the rescue with its own forces and at its own cost, but only if this help were requested. (ii) However, if France were attacked, Switzerland was not obliged by the treaty to come to her aid; the Confederation agreed only to permit the royal government of France to recruit troops from within the signatory cantons without guaranteeing the success of such efforts. (iii) All treaties, capitulations and agreements which the Confederation had hitherto subscribed with other Powers were not to be nullified by this treaty with France, it being agreed that the reciprocal declaration of neutrality which constituted the basis of the treaty did not conflict with Switzerland's agreements with other Powers.

The treaty of 1777, described as a renewal of the treaty of 1516, must also be considered in relation to the treaty of 1663. The treaty of 1777 was the product of debates within the Diet which appear to have been initiated in 1731, if not earlier.[62] At a conference of the evangelical and associated *Orte* held in Aarau in 1731, the treaty of 1663 was reviewed, Article by Article. Subjects such as the following were discussed:

1. The lands to be protected should be defined; do we mean the land held by the French Crown in 1663 or those of present-day France which would also include Alsace and the County (*Grafschaft*) of Burgundy?

2. The duration of the treaty: a few years or quite a long time.

3. Does the stipulated size of the mercenary force (not less than 6000 and not more than 16,000) include Swiss troops already in France?

4. The stipulated force should be raised by voluntary enrollment and not by compulsion.

5. The troops may be used only for defense (*Schutz und Schirm*) of the specified lands and may not be led over the border or otherwise used under any pretext whatever.

6. Payments to be made in Swiss money.

7. In place of pensions (*Pensionen*), the yearly payments (*Jahrgelder*) should be designated by some other name (of which several were proposed).

8. Existing delinquencies in payments should be settled and provision made for promptness in future payments.

9. Purchases of salt from France should be free of all taxes. Fruit, wine, fish, cattle, other foodstuffs, and wood, hay, and straw also to be free of customs duties and other taxes on importation from France.

10. The treaty must be purely defensive and unrestricted by reservations or qualifying conditions.

As an addendum to the treaty, religious freedom was considered: no one, because of religion, may be excluded from an office in the army; members of the evangelical faith must be granted free exercise of their religion; admission to hospitals to be free of any religion discrimination; priests in the field may not be denied admission to the sick and the imprisoned.

The alliance of 1777 proved to be the last treaty of peaceful association negotiated between France and the Swiss Confederation.

Rumors were rife that Austria, involved in the rape of Poland,[63] was bent on seizing her ancient possessions in eastern Switzerland: the Aargau, Thurgau, and much additional territory. Convinced that she had more to fear from her ancient enemy Austria, than from France or Prussia, the Confederation entered willingly and with high hopes into the new treaty with France.

Enough has been written in the preceding sections descriptive of events in France and Switzerland from 1789 to the fall of Bern in 1798 to indicate that the strict observance of neutrality in Switzerland during those turbulent years was clearly impossible. The patrician families, 600 in number according to de la Harpe, had exclusive possession of the instruments of government—a tremendous power which they were determined to retain. Added to the dissension between the War Party and those who insisted upon peace at almost any price was the persistent and seemingly unbridgeable gulf between the patricians and the common people. Many members of the old families in France—patricians whose numerous rights and privileges had been guaranteed by the pre-revolutionary government—managed to escape across the border into the neighbouring States of the Swiss Confederation. Until it was too late to do anything to end the revolution and restore the old order to power, the refugees exhausted every means of drawing Switzerland into military action against the revolutionaries. The French Ambassador, Barthélemy, in a letter to the French Foreign Minister LeBrun, reported that the refugees—French aristocrats—furious that the State of Bern had not led Switzerland into war against the Republic, were openly making tirades against Bern and seeking every possible means to harm her. The Swiss granted the right of asylum to all and sundry, at least until they caused trouble to the State. The inability or failure even to attempt to screen the incoming refugees at the border aggravated the problem. Peter Ochs and de la Harpe added fuel to the fires of discontent in Vaud, in the upper Jura, and in Geneva. The patrician class in Switzerland, accused of many wrongs against those whom they ruled, should be brought to justice, and the revolutionary government of France should intervene on behalf of the common man.

Haasbauer, in a study of the historical writings of Karl Ludwig von Haller, has analyzed at length the views of von Haller on Swiss neutrality, especially in relation to events in Switzerland during the last few years preceding the fall of the old Confederation (160). As the permanent secretary of the Small Council (the *Kleinrat*) in Bern and as a member of many missions, von Haller was thoroughly informed. The French claimed, so we learn, that Switzerland, though officially neutral, was conducting a secret war against the French Republic. He avoids any mention of the severe attacks by France on Swiss neutrality, while pointing out, however, that the terrible events of 1792 (August 10 and September 2 and 3) aroused a storm of resentment in Switzerland and added greatly to the popular support of the policy of strict neutrality declared by the Diet in May 1792. Not surprisingly, the tragic events of 1792 strengthened also the hands of the War Party in its insistent demands that Switzerland join the European military alliance that was forming against the armies of the French Republic.

Recruiting in Switzerland on behalf of the revolutionaries, and also on behalf of the tottering monarchy, appears to have been tolerated despite its violation of the exact and strict neutrality that the Diet proclaimed. Equally in violation was the permission granted to Austrian and French soldiers to pass through Switzerland during the retreat of Moreau's army.

Though heavily damaged by the Austrian campaigns in Switzerland, by the French occupation and by all the untoward events of the war, von Haller attributed Switzerland's economic health to neutrality. The health of the economy, alleged by von Haller, is surely hard to reconcile with the tremendous costs involved in trying to maintain a neutral posture: the loss of revenue resulting from the return of the Swiss guards, the costly maintenance of the Swiss border guards and later of the French forces of occupation, the loss of credit balances in Germany, and the greatly increased prices for imports.

And yet, to von Haller, Swiss neutrality was a transitory thing. It was not anchored in the Constitution,[64] and the possible participation of Switzerland in future wars, had to be reckoned with: it could not be cast aside. But he held fast to arbitration as the preferred method of settling disputes—internal or international. The procedure was well understood by the Swiss for it was deeply rooted in the oldest alliances between the member States of the Confederation.

Of course, a heavy price must be paid for neutrality. A neutral State loses its friends and receives inadequate protection against its enemies. "He who in times of need will help no one must not count on the help of others for himself." Neutrality was certainly not a protective mantle behind which Switzerland could enjoy the restfulness of peace, of an undisturbed social order and of economic prosperity. For a long time, as the only neutral neighbour of France, she paid heavily, so von Haller claimed, for the blessings of being spared the horrors of war. One must assume that the huge income accruing to Switzerland through the sale of horses, other supplies and mercenary services was more than compensated for by the loss of many killed in combat, and the physical and social damage to those who returned from foreign service.

Because of her neutrality, Switzerland made possible the development of France into a power State. In time she, herself, fell victim to this overpowerful neighbour and natural enemy. In a letter to von Müller, von Haller wrote that because of her central position in Europe, her three linguistic groups, and her abundant traffic, Switzerland, more than any other land, was open to unfriendly propaganda and machinations of all kinds. And then, he adds the extraordinary statement, "In its finest times Switzerland was never neutral." "Switzerland," so we learn, "can thank neutrality for its conquest." "In neutrality one finds the causes of the Swiss revolution of 1798 and the revolts of 1830 and 1831." Von Haller's personal views, according to Haasbauer, were such as to deny to neutrality any justification and any value. He went even further, so we are told, and held that the neutral position of Switzerland was responsible for the downfall of the old *Eidgenossenschaft*. Finally we come to a message from Bonaparte himself—a letter addressed to two representatives of the Swiss Confederation, meeting in Lugano.

> I have received today your letters of 29. August. I beg you to remain persuaded of the pleasure that I have had in being able to again to testify to the sentiments with which you have inspired me and to thank you, myself, for the sagacity with which, during your government, you have contributed to the tranquility of our frontiers. The nation that you represent has a reputation of wisdom, that one loves to see confirmed by the conduct of its representatives. Believe especially that I will regard always, as one of the happiest moments, that when it will be possible for me to do something that can convince the 13 cantons of the esteem and the very special consideration that the French have for them.[65]

The outbreak of the French Revolution and the invasion of Switzerland effectively nullified all treaties of assistance and mutual declarations of lasting friendship and neutrality that existed between the French monarchy, other Powers and the Swiss Confederation. The dissension within Switzerland between the War

Party and those who urged a firm adherence to peace and neutrality almost totally paralyzed the Confederation. The ultimate invasion by the armies of Napoleon Bonaparte ended the old *Eidgenossenschaft*.

Notes and Comments

1. Ruchat (1680–1750), as an observer of events in Switzerland during the late seventeenth century, gives a detailed description of the accumulating provocations that led to the war of 1712 ("Mémoire instructif sur les causes de la guerre arrivé en Suisse l'an 1712" (**311**, p. 805 et seq.).

Under Ulrich, a beneficent Abbot of St. Gallen who had bought the seignorial rights over Toggenburg from the ruling family, all of the ancient privileges claimed by the Toggenburgers were confirmed: the right to enter into mutual defensive alliances with other States (e.g. Schwyz and Glarus); the right to enter into capitulation agreements with foreign Powers for sale of mercenaries; freedom of trade and commerce with other States; and complete liberty of conscience in religion. In 1532, a new Abbot, Diethelm Blaarer, denied the right of freedom of worship. In 1634 and 1642 the Reformed cantons intervened in an effort to restore the ancient religious freedoms of the Toggenburgers—but to no avail. By 1664 persecution of the protestants was widespread: Jeremy Braun, a minister from Lichtenstieg, the capital of Toggenburg, was imprisoned and then banned from the country for having wrongly explained the catechism. Conditions worsened and even the catholics were abused. The local governor, representing the abbot, was apparently determined to end the spiritual and temporal liberties of the Toggenburgers. In 1685, Schwyz and Glarus tried, without success, to renew the treaty of common burghership which for 250 years had served to join them in alliance with Toggenburg. Ruchat agrees that the Abbot of St. Gallen in his day was a very unpleasant fellow of the "common sort" whose self-interest and overweening ambition caused increasing provocation. He imposed fines for all sorts of trivialities, such as smoking tobacco, marrying without buying his permission, and complaining about his high-handed actions.

But, by what right may the Toggenburgers' allies (Schwyz and Glarus) intervene? "By no right, whatever," said the abbot. Toggenburg, he claimed, was a fief that he held from the emperor, and he, the abbot, as a prince of the empire would permit no meddling of outsiders in the affairs of Toggenburg. The problems were compounded by an old alliance of 1451 between the Abbot of St. Gallen and the four cantons of Zurich, Lucerne, Schwyz and Glarus. In 1706 the Swiss Diet was "struck dumb" on hearing a report of the abbot's contention that he had no responsibilities to the cantons. It was then that the abbot's deputy dared to tell the cantons that they may not intervene in the affairs of Toggenburg. Zurich became alarmed because of the proximity of Toggenburg and, with Bern, made further representations to the abbot but to no avail.

In 1707, the Toggenburgers made seven specific demands of the abbot including freedom of worship. This was too much for Rome and the catholic cantons. The abbot sought the formal support of the emperor, and the Swiss cantons, again divided into two confessional groups, prepared for war. Solothurn and Freiburg, afraid of Bern, stood aside and Schwyz, renouncing its role as a protector of Toggenburg, joined the catholic forces.

2. A club heavily fitted with iron spikes.

3. *Abschiede* VI. 2, 2330–37, 18 July, 9–11 August 1712.

4. The founding dates of the Swiss universities may suggest an impoverishment of the cantons during the seventeenth and eighteenth centuries or a lack of interest in higher education in much of the country. The civil wars of the seventeenth century drained the resources of the country, and the wars beyond her borders forced the Confederation into constant obsession with problems of defense. The eighteenth century offered considerable respite: civil warfare ended with the Peace of Aarau and the cantons quickly recovered from financial exhaustion. The University of Basel was founded in 1460, Bern in 1528, Lausanne in 1537, Geneva in 1559; and then a long gap, followed by Zurich in 1833, Neuchâtel in 1838, Freiburg in 1889, and the *Hochschule* St. Gallen for Economic and Social Sciences in 1898. The Federal Institute of Technology in Zurich was established in 1855. There are no universities in *Innerschweiz*,

Appenzell, Glarus, Zug, Valais, Solothurn, Ticino, the Graubünden, Aargau, Schaffhausen and Thurgau. Since 1966 the cantonal universities have been partly supported by federal subventions.

5. Albrecht von Haller (1708–77). One can do scant justice to the great von Haller in the lines that follow. Born in Bern, he studied medicine and science in the Universities of Tübingen, Leiden and Basel. Remarkably precocious, he could translate from Greek at the age of 10, and composed for his own private use a Chaldaic grammar, and a Greek and Hebrew lexicon. As a young man he made many botanical and geological excursions into the Alps and published in 1742 a two-volume illustrated flora of Switzerland, later expanded to three volumes and descriptive of almost 2500 plants. Seventeen years of his life were spent in Göttingen as Professor of Anatomy, Surgery, and Botany in the new university. Otherwise his years of research and scholarly publication were spent in his homeland. Botany, anatomy, and physiology were the sciences to which he contributed the most. His studies of the blood vessels, the mechanism of respiration, of muscle contractility, and of the properties of nerve were classics in his day. His textbook of physiology, first published in 1747, reappeared in many editions and translations. His bibliography encompasses almost 600 published works, some of these being entire volumes.

Beyond his fame as a scientist, he enjoyed a reputation as a poet of some consequence. In his early twenties he became the "poet of the Alps," and described the beauty and majesty of the Alps and the simple ways of the mountain people. His poetry gave to von Haller an enduring place in the world of literature. In his later years he turned to comparative studies of government and published also a number of religious writings. He declined several pressing and tempting invitations to accept distinguished positions abroad. The honor that gave him singular satisfaction was his election to the Great Council of Bern.

6. Micheli du Crest of Geneva was more than a physicist and civil engineer. He opposed the plan for financing the work on bridges and fortifications and other aspects of the program. He was soon expelled from the General Council of the burghers and banned from the city. Du Crest suddenly appeared in Bern where he was at once identified as one of the leaders of the Geneva revolutionaries. Later he was charged with participation in a burgher conspiracy against the ruling families of Bern. On arrest and conviction he was condemned in 1749 to life imprisonment. He was released in 1766 and died three months later.

7. Horace-Benedict de Saussure (1740–99). At the age of 22, de Saussure was elected Professor of Philosophy in the academy of his native Geneva, with responsibilities for instruction in the natural sciences also, for philosophy embraced natural philosophy as well. As was the custom of the times he made many journeys abroad to expand his knowledge and to enrich his acquaintanceship with the intellectual leaders of Europe. Savoy, Switzerland (Geneva was not then a part of the Swiss Confederation), France, Belgium, Holland, England, and Germany, were the countries in which he travelled. Accompanied by a party of considerable size, he climbed Mont Blanc in August 1788 (first ascended by Balmac and Paccard in August 1786), and made a number of observations of scientific interest. His interest in mountaineering stemmed from his love of the Alps and his passionate desire to study their geology and glaciation. His skill in instrumentation led to development of instruments for studying the transparency of the atmosphere, atmospheric electricity, humidity (the hair hygrometer), and wind velocity (the anemometer). Together with instrumental improvements in thermometry, his contributions to geology, geophysics, glaciology and meteorology identify de Saussure as one of the greatest of the early students of these sciences. His "Voyages dans les Alpes" continues to be the basic work on the geology and physical geography of the Alpine massif.

De Saussure also participated in the pioneer studies on hot air balloons. In January 1784 he visited the Montgolfier brothers and initiated experiments on the nature of the gas in these balloons. He concluded that the "Montgolfier Gas" was merely ordinary air reduced in density through expansion by heat. It was Priestley's work "On the different Kinds of Air" that inspired Etienne Montgolfier and his brother Joseph with the idea of using balloons filled with a light gas as a means of travel. Their famous demonstrations of 1783 were epoch-making. To de Saussure, such balloons which could be made to lift hundreds of kilograms would be of military value, even though he doubted that they could even be used for flights into the high Alps (332, p. 96).

The oldest son of H.-B. de Saussure was Nicolas Théodore (1767–1845), whose studies on the respiration and metabolism of plants proved to be fundamental to the emerging science of plant physiology. "De Saussure was the first to strike a balance sheet which indicates the unity of the photosynthetic quotient . . . and he was the first to show that water and salts, as well as carbon dioxide, were essential for the nutrition of the green plant" (175). He and Jean Senebier of Geneva (1742–1809), who made notable studies of assimilation by plants, were among the leading investigators of the eighteenth century in the new discipline of plant physiology.

8. Three of the Bernoullis held in succession, for 103 years in all, the Professorship in Mathematics at the University of Basel: Jakob (from 1687 to 1705), his younger brother Johann (1705 to 1748), and Johann's third son Johann II (1748 to 1790).

9. Incidentally, Paul Euler, the father of Leonhard, was a pupil of Jakob Bernoulli—a further indication of the close intellectual relationship between the Eulers and the Bernoullis. A granddaughter of Leonhard Euler married Jakob Bernoulli II (1759–89), a grandson of Johann Bernoulli.

10. Jakob Schweppe (1739–1821). Schweppe was born in Witzenhausen in Hessen-Kassel, Germany. He settled in Geneva in 1768 and established himself as a jeweler. In 1790 he invented artifically carbonated water and commenced its manufacture in Geneva, in association with an Englishman, William Belcombo. He moved to Bristol in 1794 and later to London where he successfully introduced his "soda water" to the medical profession. His special "stand-up" bottle was familiarly known as the "drunken bottle." He started a subsidiary in Derby, sold his rights in London, made a fortune, and returned to Geneva (date unknown).

It should be noted that the priority of Schweppe in the invention of artificially carbonated water may not be firmly established. In the Encyclopedia Britannica one reads that such waters appeared in England and Sweden about 1775–80. Factories and bottling plants were opened in Geneva, Paris, London, Dublin, Dresden, etc. from 1789 to 1821, and in 1807, Benjamin Silliman of Yale University began producing bottled soda water on a commercial scale.

I am indebted to M. Marcel Ney of the Auslandschweizersekretariat der Neuen Helvetischen Gesellschaft for this information about Schweppe. See also Gerbel (150) for the role of H. A. Gosse in the soda water invention.

11. The Academy (later, the University) of Lausanne, founded in 1537, appointed Conrad Gessner in that same year to the Professorship of Greek.

12. Coffee was introduced in England in 1641. It had reached Constantinople around 1550 and spread to the Continent in the 1640s. It was known in Venice around 1645 where it was sold at high prices in apothecary shops as a medicinal agent. Some 30 years later, coffee houses run by Graubündians, and still later by Armenians and Arabs, came to be common in Venice. The Valtellina, then a possession of Graubünden, bordered on the republic of Venice. A number of Graubünden families are credited with founding the bread, pastry shops and associated coffee houses in Italy, the German States, and eastern Europe (200).

13. In the eighteenth century the Principality of Neuchâtel was closely affiliated to Bern but it was not a member of the Swiss Confederation. Technically, the Swiss were foreigners. The ruling Prince from 1707 to 1857 was the King of Prussia, except during the Bonaparte period. The treaty of Schönbrunn had given Neuchâtel to France. From 1806 to 1813 it was ruled be General Berthier to whom a grateful Bonaparte had given the Principality. On reunion with Prussia, Friedrich Wilhelm III in 1814 gave it a constitution which conferred upon the Principality a dual status, that of a Prussian possession and, rather paradoxically, recognition as the 21st canton of Switzerland.

> How singular soever this Practice may appear in other countries, of allowing the Subjects of one Prince of State to live in Alliance with, or under the Protection of another; yet it is very common in Switzerland (90).

This conflict in status led to a revolution of royalists. In late 1831 the republicans tried to overthrow the government and dissolve the ties with Prussia but not until early 1848 was a republican government firmly established. The king objected and his rights were confirmed by a London Protocol of 1852. This achieved nothing and in September 1856, under Count Friedrich Pourtales, a Putsch was attempted but collapsed two days later. Napoleon III intervened to prevent war with Prussia. Switzerland extended amnesty to all political prisoners and the king in 1857 surrendered all of his rights over the canton. In

1815, though somewhat anomalously, it was described as a cantonal Principality of the Swiss Confederation.

14. The population classes of Geneva consisted of five distinct groups: citizens, burghers, inhabitants, natives and subjects. Citizens were the children of burghers who acquired the status of burgher by birth or by purchase at a high price. They alone could be in the Council of 25, in the magistracy, and in offices of authority. Only the citizens and burghers could engage freely in commerce. Inhabitants and natives could do so on payment of an annual fee. The "subjects" were required to be protestants and enjoyed the sole benefit of living under a mild government (203). Only the first two classes could hold positions in government. The "inhabitants" were strangers who purchased the right of protection and permission to live in the city. Their presence was encouraged by a few special privileges. "Natives" were the sons of inhabitants and they enjoyed additional advantages.

15. From *Tag* (a coming together of delegates or accredited representatives for a parliamentary conference) and *Satzung* (resolutions emerging from a *Tag*). *Tagsatzung* has come to mean the conference itself.

16. The longest *Tagsatzung* lasted from 6 April 1814 to 31 August 1815. It was faced with the heavy responsibility of forming a new structure for the Confederation in place of the constitution which derived from the Napoleonic Act of Mediation (1803). The last *Tagsatzung* was held in Bern, 4–22 September 1848. It was convened to report the results of voting on the new Federal Constitution.

17. More accurately, a Council of 299 members. However, almost 99 held appointments as bailiffs and were resident in the many bailiages scattered far and wide over the countryside. When membership of the Council was complete only about 200 were available for attendance on the sessions.

18. "It is pleasant to see what Numbers of passionate Lovers start up in three or four Days time" (**339**, page 79).

19. This may require qualification. According to Stanyan and Burnet the two youngest members of the Great Council were "Guardians of the People's Liberty." They could convene a meeting of the Great Council whenever anything was proposed or was being done which might be "prejudicial to the Rights and Liberties of the People or Citizens" (**339**, p. 72; **78**, p. 15).

20. Neuchâtel was not entirely free of foreign domination, nor was the Graubünden. The Principality of Neuchâtel was, in fact, subject territory of the King of Prussia, while the Graubünden, despite its ancient alliances with some of the Swiss cantons, was also closely allied to the House of Austria. From 1639 to 1726 the Graubünden had been allied to Spain by virtue of the Treaty of Milan in 1639. When the Spanish branch of the House of Austria died out and the Spanish War of Succession came to an end, the Duchy of Milan became a part of the Empire under Charles VI. The emperor prevailed upon the Graubünden in 1726 to renew the Treaty of Milan. By this diplomatic conquest, the House of Austria assumed almost unlimited authority in directing the affairs of the Graubünden. In return for the service of soldiers from the Graubünden, Austria paid liberal pensions regularly, gained the favor of leading members of the Diet by substantial bribery, and guaranteed to the Graubünden continued retention of the Valtellina. Indeed, from 1726 until 1815 the Graubünden was subject to Austrian domination.

21. Ruchat (**311**) regarded favorably the lack of precious metals (silver and gold) in commercially exploitable amounts. "They only excite the cupidity and avarice of men and of neighbouring (or other) countries; hence the sad fate of Mexico and Peru which were ravaged by foreigners."

22. In 1974, by comparison, approximately 59,000,000 watches were exported from Switzerland, together with a large number of watch movements without cases.

23. Until 1924 there were no doctors in the Val d'Anniviers. The nearest physicians were in Siders at the base of the valley.

24. Coxe, in reporting that the peasants in the mountainous parts of Switzerland lived chiefly upon milk and potatoes, pointed out that bread in the mountain areas was more expensive than cheese and butcher's meat (**95**, I, p. 351).

25. The village of Haldenstein, about two miles north of Chur, was part of a small State of approximately five square miles. Since 1568 it had been an independent sovereignty under the protection of the Graubünden. In the 1780s it was ruled as a barony by the von Salis family. The inhabitants, numbering between 300 and 400, were serfs or vassals until 1701 when they were granted several

immunities. The baron enjoyed the right of coinage, the exclusive privilege of hunting and fishing, and a claim for two days of work and one load of manure annually from each of his subjects. He appointed the judge in the criminal court, received the fines that were levied, and served as the last judge of appeal in criminal and civil cases.

26. Karrer was not the first Swiss officer to enter the colonial military service in the New World. Diebold von Erlach (1541–65), a Bernese Swiss, died in 1565 in Florida as a captain in the military service of France (**124**). Schelbert tells us that Diebold von Erlach was attached to a French Huguenot expedition that planned to establish a settlement (New France) on the coast of Florida—a part of the Spanish domain in the New World (**319**).

27. The Diet met in Baden in 1734. Bern and the Zurich delegates ask what kind of regulations against the large exodus of people to Carolina "in Westindies" can be issued. In Bern and Neuchâtel the sale of a *Booklein* by Herr Pury of Neuchâtel has been forbidden. In spite of all warnings, over 200 persons have gone and a mandate against further emigration has been issued. But it is a disease and still more have left. In spring, others intend to go. A commission is named to study the problem. The Commission agreed unanimously that the ringleader should be kept under surveillance and punished. The emigrants must be hindered in every possible way. (*Abschiede* 7, 1, 506, 1 December 1734.)

28. Haldimand has been described, erroneously, as Governor (**124**, II, p. 50) or Governor-General of Canada (**379**, p. 37; **224**). The first Governor-General of Canada was Viscount Monck, appointed in 1867 when the Canadian Act of Confederation came into being. Both Haldimand and Prevost were honored erroneously by the equivalent title: generalgouverneur (**159**; **35**, pp. 4, 5: **409**) or gouverneur général (**101**).

29. Switzerland was not the only source of troops available to foreign Powers. England, for example, purchased the services of many mercenaries from several German States for assistance in its wars in North America.

30. François-Marie Arouet (1694–1778). In 1718 he adopted the name Voltaire. In 1717, Voltaire wrote a satire about Louis XIV, who had died two years earlier, which landed Voltaire in the Bastille for almost a year. His release is largely attributed to his great literary work, *Oedipus*, which he finished in 1718. This gained for Voltaire immediate recognition as a man of great literary promise. From 1726 to 1729 he lived in England which he described as the freest of all lands. In the early 1730s, again in trouble with the ruling class, Voltaire fled to Lorraine where his friend Mme. du Châtelet gave him the protection of her castle at Lunéville. He returned to Paris in 1744 and received the signal honor in 1746 of election to the Académie française. A few years later he moved to Potsdam on invitation of Friedrich II of Prussia (Frederick the Great), who was equally generously disposed toward Rousseau. From 1755 to 1760 he lived near Geneva and, though well received at first, he presently found the intolerance and bigotry of the ruling class to be unbearable. He left the city and retreated to his chateau at Ferney which he had acquired in 1758. In 1778 he returned to Paris and was triumphantly received, only to die two months later. Voltaire's many writings are frequently expressive of his long-continued fight against religious intolerance as he had experienced it in Calvinist Geneva and against the social and political privileges of the French nobility, clergy, and ruling class.

31. A coin, no longer in circulation, equal in value to about three German marks.

32. Peter Ochs (1752–1821). Born in Nantes, grew up in Hamburg, and came to Basel in 1769 where he became Doctor of Jurisprudence in 1776. In 1778 he resumed his studies in Leyden and was appointed *Ratsschreiber* (Recorder to the Council) of Basel in 1782. He was a frequent delegate to the Diet and was elected a member of the Great Council of Basel in 1794 and head of the guild organizations in 1796. He befriended the French revolutionaries and was the recognized head of the Swiss sympathizers with the revolutionary movement in France. He journeyed repeatedly to Paris as Basel's minister delegate on economic and political questions. On 12 April 1798, as President in Basel of the National Assembly, he proclaimed the Constitution of the Helvetic Republic. He became the first president of the Helvetic Senate and, later, a member and president of the Helvetic Directory. From 1802 to 1803 he was a member of the Consulta in Paris and, during the days of the Mediation, a member of the Great and Small Councils of Basel. In 1813 and 1816 he was *Bürgermeister* of the city. He was the author of an eight-volume work on the history of the city and canton of Basel as well as the writer of some poetry and of several publications in the fields of drama and law.

33. Frédéric César de la Harpe (1754–1838). Like Ochs, de la Harpe was trained in the law and became an advocate in 1778. From 1784 to 1795 he lived in St. Petersburg as tutor to the Tsarevich. On return to Switzerland he was banned from Bern because of revolutionary brochures which he published in 1795. He found refuge in Paris where he prepared an essay on the Constitution of Vaud. In 1797, de la Harpe urged the French Directory to invade Vaud and convert it into a free State under French protection. He also sought a virtual annexation of the southern slopes of the Jura, Neuchâtel and the lower Valais by urging their separation from Switzerland and their conversion into French protectorates. After the Swiss Confederation became the "one and indivisible Helvetic Republic," de la Harpe returned to Switzerland and served as a member of the Directory until its dissolution by the Helvetic Councils in 1800. He soon fled to France where he lived until 1814, continuing his fight for an independent Vaud, no longer in subject status to Bern. In this he succeeded, and in 1816 he became a member of the Great Council of the canton.

34. *Abschiede* VIII, pp. 184–91, 3–22 September 1792.

35. *Abschiede* VIII, pp. 168, 169, 172m, 14–30 May 1792.

36. *Abschiede* VIII, p. 170g, 14–30 May 1792.

37. *Abschiede* VIII, p. 174, 2–27 July 1792. Excerpts from a letter by the French Ambassador Barthélemy, written as instructed by the King of France.

38. William Wickham (1761–1840). Wickham graduated from Oxford in 1782. He studied civil law in Geneva and in 1788 married into the Bertrand family of that city. In 1794 he was sent by the British Foreign Office on a secret mission to Switzerland where he became Chargé d'Affaires during Fitzgerald's absence. In 1795 he was appointed Minister Plenipotentiary to the Swiss cantons and the Graubünden, in succession to Fitzgerald. In 1797 he was recalled to England as Undersecretary of State in the Alien Department but in 1799 was ordered back to Switzerland and was attached to the allied armies as Envoy Extraordinaire. From 1794 to 1797 he was under instructions to organize a network of trusted adherents to the royalist cause in France who would keep him constantly and promptly informed of events in France. He was to keep in touch with these informants by messenger, by secret correspondence, and by personal visitation—all in the hope of strengthening the royalist cause. He was also to use every effort to swing the Swiss around to the royalist cause and to that of the Austrians and others who opposed the revolution.

Wickham carried out his instructions well, so well in fact that in 1797 he was obliged to leave. We learn (Wickham, **387**, II, p. 44) that the French Directory sent a messenger (Menaud) to the advoyer of Bern (Steiger) "requiring in the name of the Directory, that I should receive immediate orders to quit the Swiss Territory" (Wickham to Lord Grenville, 10 October 1797). Notice the peremptory order of the French Directory:

> The Executive Directory, convinced that the mission of Wickham to the Helvetic Cantons has no reference whatever to the respective interests of England and Switzerland; and that his sole object is to excite and encourage plots against the internal and external security of the French Republic, charge the citizen Menaud to invite and require the government of the canton of Berne, and also the other Helvetic Cantons, if necessary, to give directions for Wickham's immediate departure from the territories of Switzerland.

On 3 November 1797 Wickham was instructed by Grenville to withdraw the Mission altogether from Bern, because "His Majesty wishes for tranquility and peace of the Swiss Cantons." In the early 1800s Wickham was named British Ambassador to Berlin and later to the Austrian Court, but both Prussia and Austria refused to accept him because he was "personally obnoxious to the French Government."

39. Lord Robert Stephen Fitzgerald (1765–1833)—Fifth son of the first Duke of Leinster. Appointed Minister Plenipotentiary in Switzerland in 1794 (replacing Louis Braun, a Swiss subject, who had been serving as Chargé d'Affaires). In 1795 Fitzgerald was transferred to the British Embassy in Copenhagen.

40. Both Robespierre and Talleyrand spoke in glowing terms of the important service rendered to France by neutral Switzerland. In April 1801, Stapfer said to Talleyrand that "Switzerland through its neutrality had saved France" [cited by Bonjour (**49**, I, 134)]. But when Swiss neutrality ceased to be of any

value to France, the "free sons of Tell," "our necessary allies," came to be described as "oligarchs, vassals of princes, and friends of England."

41. *Abschiede* VIII, 226i, 4–28 July 1796.

42. To no avail, the Diet reminded the French Directory that the neutrality of the "Swiss portion" of the Bishopric had been assured under the terms of the Franco-Swiss covenant (*Abschiede* VIII, 278e, 27 December 1797–31 January 1798).

43. In 1800, Napoleon and his army passed through the tiny Alpine village of Bourg-St. Pierre on their way to Italy. Napoleon signed a note in which he promised to reimburse the tiny community "in full" for all damage caused by his men and for help of the villagers with their mules in getting his cannon over the Great St. Bernard pass. The bill was not promptly paid and has been revised annually. Inclusive of interest it amounted to $73.3 million in 1983. The bill includes the felling of 2037 trees at six francs each; provision of 188 cooking pots (80 were never returned); 3150 logs; local labor at three francs daily for each man; and rental of mules at six francs each per day. The Mayor of the village, stating "It is only right that he should honor a debt of France" sent a delegation with the bill for $73.3 million for presentation to Francois Mitterand during a 1983 visit of the French President to Switzerland (**357**, 30 April 1983). S fr. 45,000, or so, were accepted in 1984 in settlement of the debt.

44. *Abschiede* VI. 2, 861i, 4 July 1700.

45. *Abschiede* VI. 2, 881i, 19 September 1700.

46. A victory of the Kaiser's army at Turin in 1707 changed the situation completely and restored the duchy to Austrian sovereignty.

47. *Abschiede* VI. 2, 908, 919, 921, 926, 955, April 1701 to January 1702.

48. *Abschiede* VI. 2, 925c, 4 July 1701; 2288–89, ¶s 1, 2, and 3, 7 September 1702.

49. *Abschiede* VI. 2, 1415c, 15 January 1708.

50. *Abschiede* VI. 2, 1457i, 1 July 1708.

51. Usually described as the battle of Blenheim to distinguish it from another battle fought near Höchstädt on 20 September 1703, in which General Styrum's army, with heavy losses, was defeated by the French under Villars and the Elector of Bavaria. Höchstädt is a small town on the left bank of the Danube, a few miles from Ulm.

52. On the Rhine, northeast of Mülhausen; not to be confused with Neuenburg (Neuchâtel) in Switzerland.

53. *Abschiede* VI. 2, 1458l, 1 July 1708; VI. 2, 1530i, 7 July and 29 August 1709.

54. François Louis de Pesme, Baron St. Saphorin (1668–1737), was born in the canton of Vaud. As a Swiss officer, he served in Holland and Prussia, and transferred to the service of Austria in 1688. Under Prince Eugen of Austria he participated in the war on the Turks, and in 1696 became vice admiral of the Austrian fleet in the Danube. Emperor Leopold created him major-general. He continued to serve Joseph I and Charles VI, sometimes in the army but more often in diplomacy. On return to Switzerland he was named minister to the Elector of the Palatinate. In 1706 he became Austrian Ambassador to the Evangelical cantons. In 1707 he negotiated the transfer of Neuchâtel to possession of the King of Prussia and for the next five or six years was entrusted by Bern with several delicate diplomatic negotiations. In 1713 he represented Bern at the Congress of Utrecht and in January 1714 signed the treaty of alliance at the Hague whereby Bern agreed to provide Holland with mercenaries. In 1737, he died in his chateau at St. Saphorin, Vaud.

Puysieux, a French Ambassador, had a bitter opinion of St. Saphorin who, skillful in management, "must run the show in whatsoever he is involved." St. Saphorin, in turn, wasted no words in describing the French Ambassador, Franz Karl du Luc, who succeeded Puysieux. He is "a master in all the arts of deception and intrigue . . . a very hot-headed and avaricious rascal" (St. Saphorin to Prince von Salm, 6 March 1709) (**148**). But France was down on St. Saphorin for two reasons. As Bern's representative, he championed the King of Prussia, instead of Louis XIV's candidate Prince Conti, in election of the ruler of the Principality of Neuchâtel. Again, on behalf of Bern, he opposed election of the Duke of Anjou as King of Spain in succession to the childless Charles II. Incidentally, this opposition cost Bern an annual loss of 70,000 ecus of salt (an ecu is an obsolete French coin equal to three francs) and another 70,000 ecus to maintain Swiss troops in protective occupancy of cities on the Rhine (St. Saphorin to Prince Karl

Theodor von Salm, first minister of the Vienna court, 7 December 1708 [**403**, vol. II]). He had a sharp, penetrating mind, and could appraise well the current problems in foreign affairs. He was deeply committed to the protestant cause in Europe. Whether or not he had any respect for Swiss neutrality in the Spanish War of Succession is a moot question. By virtue of his birth, St. Saphorin was a Swiss or, perhaps more precisely, a vassal of Bern. In 1716, then in England, George I appointed him British Ambassador to Austria with the rank of Lieutenant General. He served in Vienna for six years.

55. Johann Friedrich Willading, Schultheiss of Bern and one of the wealthiest men of his day; father-in-law of Hieronymous von Erlach.

56. *Abschiede* VII. 1, 453d and e, 13–17 November 1733; VII. 1, 523h, 4–21 July 1735.

57. *Abschiede* VII. 1, 454l, 456h, 8 December 1733 to 13 January 1734.

58. The catholic cantons refused to recognize the House of Orange (protestant) as the legitimate successor to the catholic Stuarts in the British monarchy. For quite some time the British Ambassador to Switzerland was accredited only to the "Evangelical Corps." Later, the expression "Helvetic Body" was used in Britain's diplomatic correspondence.

59. Note Stanyan's perceptive observation "Indeed I cannot see how they [Bern and Zurich] can any way side with us, without immediate danger of ruin by an invasion of French troops, and having at the same time a war with the catholics [the catholic cantons], who are entirely at the devotion of France" (Stanyan to Sunderland, 16 April 1707).

60. Most of these economic benefits were suddenly and unexpectedly abolished by France in 1781 with a most serious impact on Switzerland's textile industry.

61. *Abschiede* VII. 2, 475–95, 12–31 May 1777. The treaty embraced all 13 cantons and their associated and subject States. The Principality of Neuchâtel was thereby included, to the great satisfaction of Friedrich II of Prussia, the sovereign *de jure*. Switzerland was pleased because with the Bishopric of Basel, included as a protectorate of Switzerland (since 1743), the westerly buffer States essential to her defense reached to the crest of the Jura.

62. *Abschiede* VII. 1, 395–400, 12 December 1731.

63. This refers to the partitions of 1772, 1773 and 1776, when Prussia and Russia in three vigorous strokes seized the country and divided it between themselves and Austria.

64. The Federal Assembly has a stated responsibility for preserving the independence and neutrality of Switzerland (Article 85, par. 6, of the Federal Constitution). The Federal Council must watch over the preservation of Switzerland's independence and neutrality (Article 102, par. 9 of the Federal Constitution). The only mention of neutrality in the Federal Constitution of 1980 is found in these two paragraphs.

65. *Abschiede* VIII, June/August, 1797, p. 253.

8. FROM THE FALL OF BERN TO THE TREATY OF TURIN, 1816

Even before the fall of Bern, a new constitution drafted in France was ready for submission to the Swiss, but not for discussion and possible amendment. It was handed down by Bonaparte under the principle of *force majeure*: acceptance was mandatory. The alternative was annexation to France—an ever-present threat. An earlier draft, drawn up in Paris by Ochs in November 1797, had been summarily rejected by Bonaparte. Though it followed in most respect the pattern set by the French Directory of 1795, it would have permitted the Swiss to vote its acceptance and, in accordance with other provisions, to amend the Constitution in the future. Napoleon would have none of this.

The Helvetic Republic

The Constitution, thus forced upon the Swiss by their conquerors in March, 1798, less than a month after the fall of Bern, was foreign in every respect and was doomed from the start to invite hostility and resistance. Inspired by revolutionary ideology, it was doctrinaire in character and oblivious to the lessons of hundreds of years of Swiss history. The changes in government were sudden and dramatic.[1] Consider, for example, the first Article: "The Helvetic Republic is one and indivisible." This was thrust upon a people who for centuries had treasured cantonal autonomy and independence, who had little respect for federalism but a profound distate for centralism, and could hardly be expected to bow down to the highly centralized government that the rest of the Constitution particularized. In fact, the cantons were preserved for administrative convenience only. They were stripped of all legislative power and rights of sovereignty.

Having said this much, it is now necessary to describe briefly the setting, to look again at the old Confederation upon which the new constitution was implanted. It is

305

no exaggeration to say that the cantons had lost much of the feeling for collective security which was really the fundament upon which the Confederation rested. Frequently ignored or circumvented was the requirement in the old *Bundesbriefe* to render military assistance, each to the other, in case of danger. The cantons fell to the invader, more or less one by one. Collective, coherent and integrated resistance was lacking. Even the mechanism by which the provisions of the Defensional were implemented and troops were "rushed" to the danger points was much too ponderous and time-consuming.

Despite the Peace of Aarau in 1712, confessional discord lived on and bitter hostility between the catholic and evangelical cantons frequently rose to the surface. And still another disruptive force was the never-ending disharmony between town and country. Ultimately, but all too late, it became clear that the dominance of the town over the peasantry of the countryside had to give way to new relationships.

There were still other aspects of the old Confederation that were incompatible with the changing times and which seemingly found a remedy in the new constitution. Much personal servitude, vestiges of the days of feudalism, persisted in the old Confederation. In the patrician and oligarchic cantons the ruling class denied to many of the people the right to enjoy positions of trust and of emolument. There were many privileges of birth that were enjoyed by the few but were not permitted to the many. Large property owners and the employers of labor tended to exploit the peasantry and the working class. The rack and torture, used for centuries to force confessions of guilt, were no longer compatible with the spirit of the times and had to be abolished. The new constitution sought to eliminate any social parasitism and to introduce the concepts of equality of opportunity, equality before the law, and equality of political rights to all citizens of the State. The Confederation was a complexity of virtually autonomous cantons, of allied and associated States, of protectorates, and jurisdictions which were subject to several cantons or to one alone. The social and political structures that had evolved during the centuries, characterized by much that was desirable and at the same time rich in inequities, were abolished or completely transformed in April 1798 by a stroke of the pen. Or were they? To answer this we must first look at the new political structure of the Confederation and the sequence of events that followed during the next few years.

In its first few paragraphs, the new Constitution emphasized the unity and indivisibility of the Helvetic Republic. The interests of the country as a whole must be considered paramount. The citizens in their totality are to be sovereign. No part or no right of sovereignty may be detached from the whole to become a particular and exclusive property—of an individual, a class, or a region. The form of government shall always be that of a representative democracy.

As in France, executive power was henceforth vested in a Directory of five which, in fact, had virtual dictatorial power. The members were inexperienced. Though honorable men they knew nothing about an efficient exercise of their new responsibilities. It was said of Begoz, ministre des affaires étrangères (minister of foreign affairs), that he was generally called ministre étranger aux affaires (minister, stranger to affairs of State; **105**, I, p. 77). These men were not traitors: they knew their countrymen well and realized that the Swiss people would never accept and honor the constitution now forced upon them.

Legislative power was exercised by two Councils, distinct, separate and independent of each other: a Senate with four deputies from each canton and a Great Council made up of eight deputies from each canton. Below the Councils in this pyramidal structure were the electoral bodies in which rested the responsibility of electing the legislative councils, the judges of the cantonal tribunals, the judges of the supreme tribunal and members of the administrative chamber. Provision was made for one elector from every hundred citizens of voting age who, in turn, constituted a primary assembly. The primary assemblies were to meet from time to time, with the responsibility each year of naming the members of the electoral bodies. Every citizen of 20 years and over was required to sign the civil register of his canton and to declare under oath that he would serve his country in the cause of liberty and equality.

Switzerland, as a whole, was divided into cantons, districts, communes, and sections or quarters of the large communes. These served as elective, judiciary, and administrative divisions. Because of territorial realignments, the thirteen cantons of the old Confederation became eighteen in number. One quite noteworthy change was a fusion of the old cantons of *Innerschweiz* into a single canton, appropriately named *Waldstätten*. Being stripped of all associated and allied States, subject territories, and fringe possessions, the republic with which we are concerned in April 1798 was considerably diminished in size. Geneva, Mülhausen, and the Bishopric of Basel were now absorbed by France. The Valtellina, Bormio and Chiavenna were annexed to the new Cisalpine Republic and the Valais was soon to be shorn from the Helvetic Republic to permit the armies of Napoleon to have unhindered communication with Italy via the valley of the Rhone and the Simplon pass. A few years later (1806) Neuchâtel was also to be detached from the Helvetic Republic.

The official language of the old Confederation had been German. The Constitution of April 1798, through declaration of the unity and indivisibility of the new Republic converted it into a multilingual State with equal recognition of the French, German and Italian languages. This we may consider as evidence of "unity in diversity" of which many examples could be drawn from any faithful description of the Swiss people and their country.

In March, 1798, Brune was replaced by Lecarlier as Commander-in-Chief of the French forces of occupation. Shortly after his appointment, Lecarlier summoned representatives of the cantons to Aarau and presented the new Constitution with instructions that it be promptly accepted. The Grand Scheme, thus foisted upon the people, was destined to have but a short life. New forces were set free but the practices of the past, the memories of the *Landsgemeinden* and the traditional democratic processes could not be forgotten. Likewise, attachment to the Church—catholic or reformed—and to religious institutions was very strong and, unlike France, the bonds could not easily be served. It is also self-evident that still others who had enjoyed special privileges of class and social position were unable to accept gracefully the new social and political order. The new Republic, "one and indivisible," was more commonly described by the man on the street as "one and invisible."

Oppression and Swiss Resistance

The French, purporting to be friends of the newly liberated Swiss, were friends in name only. Their policies were ruthless and punitive. Upon the freed people of Vaud, General Menard levied a war payment of 700,000 livres. Bern was assessed 6.7 million francs in gold and an additional four million were seized from the treasury. Nine million francs were paid by the other cantons. If account be taken of the goods that were plundered, the French seized from Bern alone some 14 million francs. The moneys demanded by France, apart from that in the public treasuries, were levied against the ruling families, individuals highly placed in government, the bailiffs and those who had enjoyed the right of suffrage. Only those who had served the "cause of liberty" would be exempted but there would be no reduction in the total to be paid: To ensure payment the French selected twenty hostages—twelve from Bern and eight from Solothurn. The burdensome costs of the French army of occupation were also charged against the Swiss. In March and April 1798, two months only, the "liberated ones" were forced to provide to the French army more than 500,000 kg of bread, 180,000 kg of meat, and 50,000 rations of oats. The people complained bitterly and even the Directory joined the voices of protest. The Directory appealed to General Schauenburg in May 1798 to recognize the economic distress and popular resistance that were becoming manifest.

Appenzell had already refused to recognize the Constitution of April 1798 and resistance movements began to spread through the ancient cantons of *Innerschweiz* (and in Valais). But weakness and indecision prevented any concerted action by the Swiss. The French forced the rebellious cantons into submission, first Obwalden, then Zug, Luzern and finally Schwyz, the center of resistance. It was not long before resistance flared up again in Schwyz and Nidwalden. The Directory now intervened by dispatch of an ultimatum to Schwyz and Nidwalden. Schwyz soon terminated its active resistance but Nidwalden rejected the ultimatum. The Directory ordered Schauenburg to move his army against the stubborn Nidwaldeners. The fighting continued for three days and hundreds were killed. The French suffered heavy casualties and, in revenge, plundered and burned Stans—the capital. Five thousand French troops remained in occupation of the land.

Switzerland, still stubbornly endeavoring to convince itself and others that it was independent and neutral, next became a theater of warfare between the continental Powers. It was an inevitable result of a new alliance with France which, like the Constitution of April 1798, was forced upon Switzerland under threat of annexation to France. The alliance, signed on 24 August 1798, replaced the old series of defensive alliances which had culminated in the promising treaty of 1777. On paper, the advantages of the alliance were mutual, but in fact the treaty favored only the military policies of the French Directory.[2] Switzerland was forced to accept Article 2, which described the alliance as offensive and defensive, and to yield to France unlimited use of a military road from Basel to Lake Constance and of a second which ran along the valley of the Rhone from Lake Geneva to Brig and over the Simplon pass to Italy. The alliance involved nothing less than a total surrender of Swiss neutrality and independence.

The Powers Declare War on France

In the fall of 1798, acting in response to a call for help, Kaiser Franz of Austria sent an army into the Graubünden. The adherents to the French cause, and the French resident, fled. The coalition of European Powers arrayed against France (Austria, England, Prussia, Russia) declared war on France in March, 1799, following Bonaparte's declaration of war on Austria in February. France promptly invoked the terms of the treaty of alliance with Switzerland and called upon the Republic to provide 16,000 men for the war against her enemies, but the "great neighbour and friend" was by now so universally hated that recruitment yielded only 600 men. Many of military age fled over the borders in spite of the severe penalties if caught and convicted. The government, under heavy pressure by the French, passed a law of compulsory military service applicable to men of 20 to 45 years of age.

The war was fought in south Germany, Switzerland and upper Italy. The coalition planned for the Austrians to seize the most strategic mountain passes while a second army was to advance over the Gotthard from Italy through Switzerland and on into south Germany, although this important pass, following the capitulation of Schwyz and Nidwalden, was firmly under French control. The primary objective was to drive the French from eastern Switzerland. Meanwhile the French defeated an Austrian army in the Graubünden in April 1799 and forced the government into a formal alliance with the Helvetic Republic. Shortly thereafter, the French suffered two defeats by the Austrians. The Swiss, hoping for the best, were now encouraged to believe that the tide had turned and the French would soon be driven from their country. They were supported in this by the knowledge that their General von Steiger was waiting in Augsburg with an army of emigrant Swiss to join in the final victory over France and restoration of the old regime in Switzerland.

Renewal of Swiss Resistance

Popular resistance increased and armed uprisings broke out in eastern Switzerland and in the ancient cantons. As the position worsened, the Directory resorted to extreme measures to subdue the revolts, even raising troops and placing them at the disposal of the French. In May an Austrian army moved into eastern Switzerland and in early June defeated the French in an engagement near Zurich. At this point a Russian army under Korsakov relieved the Austrians in eastern Switzerland. A second Russian army in Lombardy, under Suvarov, was ordered to cross the Gotthard into Uri and Schwyz, and to join forces with Korsakov. The strategy failed with Korsakov's defeat by the French in the second battle of Zurich on 25 September 1799 and Korsakov's forced retreat into south Germany. Not until Suvarov had crossed the Alps did he learn of Korsakov's defeat. He was forced to withdraw before the French. In doing so he accomplished an arduous retreat, famous in military history, over a most difficult route into Glarus. After a few days of rest for his exhausted army he led them over the Panixer pass in early October to Ilanz and ultimately to Russia.[3]

Meanwhile, all was not well in the Directory. Ochs, who along with de la Harpe had been made a member of the Directory in 1798, was dismissed from government under the charge of transmitting state secrets to the French. Actually the Councils had had enough of his total servility toward the French. In early January, 1800, de la Harpe and two other members of the Directory were dismissed. On 9 November 1799 Bonaparte had been declared First Consul of France, with virtual dictatorial powers. De la Harpe, who had become more and more of a tyrant and despot while in the Directory, had not failed to conceal his hopes of assuming in Switzerland a position of power comparable to that of the First Consul. The Swiss quickly put an end to any such aspirations.

Pressures began to develop for radical changes in the Constitution. The activists became polarized into two political parties, the Unitarians and the Federalists who sent petitions for reform and drafts of new constitutions to the First Consul in Paris. Coincident with the dismissal of de la Harpe and others on 7 January 1800, the Councils dissolved the Directory and replaced it with an executive council of seven members. Some months later the two legislative councils were dissolved, only to be replaced by a smaller body of 50 members who acted without the authority of a constitutionally established body. But the people were apathetic. As long as their country was occupied by a foreign army what could they do but send deputations and petitions to the First Consul?

In 1799 foreign armies had converted eastern Switzerland into a virtual battleground. Between the Austrians, the Russians and the French, villages were burned, meadows were laid waste, roads were ruined and forests were devastated. Those who fled the country, and they were many, complained with conviction that the surrender of Swiss neutrality resulting from the alliance of 24 August 1798 had brought fearful suffering upon the land. The Swiss ambassador in Paris sought out Talleyrand[4] and impressed him with a description of the "immeasurable sufferings" of the Swiss people resulting from the loss of their neutrality for a war of which they wanted no part. Talleyrand discussed these complaints with Napoleon and reported on the scandalous behaviour in that unfortunate country of many French military and civil agents who needlessly aggravated the misfortunes of the revolution by pillage, plunder, theft, brigandage and trampling upon the elementary rights of both the middle classes and the poor.[5] It was, however, made quite clear to the Swiss that France would not withdraw her troops until Switzerland proved that she could and would protect her borders against the Austrians. Until then the Swiss need not entertain any hope that their neutrality would be restored.

The Peace of Lunéville

By the end of 1800, Austria was tired of the war and again negotiated a separate peace with France. The Peace of Lunéville did little for Switzerland. She received the Fricktal from Austria, thus greatly improving her border near Basel. Supposedly she was also granted the right to draft a new constitution.[6] In this, however, Napoleon was not to be outdone. He proposed a constitution which the Unitarians considered was much too federalistic. Soon, and with an impressive display of French troops, Napoleon ordered the Council of 50 to accept his Malmaison constitution. At the head of government a *Landammann* of Switzerland must be elected. Alois Reding was chosen.[7] The Unitarians tried again and through an assembly of 47 of their party drafted still another constitution which was more centralistic than ever. Though rejected by a vote of the people, the so-called second Helvetic Constitution in these days of political turbulence remained in force anyway.

Annexation of Valais by France

On 16 May 1802 Napoleon declared Valais to be an independent republic under the protection of the French, Italian, and Helvetic Republics. And to the Swiss, somewhat in compensation for this *de facto* annexation of the Valais, or in token response to their many complaints of the misbehaviour of French troops, Napoleon withdrew his occupation forces from Swiss soil.[8] The leaders of government realized at once the imminent danger of civil war—Unitarians against Federalists. They knew equally well that the French army was still necessary to maintain order. In its absence the Swiss army would probably be incapable of preventing internal revolt and Switzerland's weakness would be exposed to the whole of Europe. The Swiss ambassador to France, Stapfer, called on Napoleon for help. The emperor drew from Stapfer the frank admission that his government was unable to stand alone. Presumably, this is exactly what Napoleon wanted to hear for it was a clear sign of approval of French intervention if and when the emperor chose to send troops into Switzerland.

In the meantime the Diet had concluded a friendship pact with England, Austria and Russia—an act which aroused the anger of the emperor. He issued a proclamation to the Swiss which said in effect, "For three years we have quarrelled without you understanding . . . your history proves above all that your domestic wars could never have been ended without the active intervention of France . . . I shall be the Mediator [of the Swiss Confederation]."[9] A representative of the Federalists hurried to Paris and heard the ultimatum, "Either a well-ordered Switzerland with a solid government friendly to France or no Switzerland."[10]

The "War of Sticks"

On withdrawal of the French army the Swiss rose in open protest against the hated constitution of the Helvetic Republic. Without a fight, Bern won this War of Sticks (*Stechlikrieg*). In many cantons the *Landsgemeinden* met, denounced the existing constitution and declared themselves to be the ruling bodies as in the glorious days of cantonal sovereignty. The deposed leaders of government fled to Lausanne and later to Savoy. On 27 September 1802 the Diet convened in Schwyz and debated adoption of an extreme federalistic constituion: the Unitarians and Centralists were in total disfavor. Bern, eager to return to its past territorial dominance, attempted to place Aargau and Vaud again under its rule, but without success. Napoleon, angered by these displays of defiance, sent General Ney with 12,000 troops back into Switzerland on October 21. The leaders of the revolt against the Helvetic Republic were imprisoned in Aarburg.

The Act of Mediation

In November some 60 delegates, principally Unitarians, went to Paris to advise the First Consul on the drafting of a new constitution. Napoleon ignored the delegation and on 19 February 1803 imposed a new constitution of his own making—the so-called Act of Mediation or Mediation Constitution. This was much more federalistic than the Malmaison Constitution. He understood the Swiss well. In the Act of Mediation he restored a large measure of independence to Switzerland but retained the dominance of French influence. It was a compromise between the aspirations of the Unitarians and the Federalists and between those who sought a return of special privileges for the few and those who demanded liberty and equality for all. It responded to the necessity of change and was a constitutional answer to the universal dissatisfaction that prevailed. It restored federalism, a large measure of independence was guaranteed, the Directory and the legislative councils of the past few years disappeared and were replaced by the long familiar Diet in which decisions by vote of the majority were to prevail. To the thirteen old cantons and six new ones much of their old autonomy was restored and many of their local institutions were re-established. The office of *Landammann* of Switzerland, rooted in the experiences of the past five years, was continued. Napoleon, who by his acts had little respect for democratic processes, preferred to have in a position of final authority only one man—the *Landammann*, whose responsibilities were very great and whom he could take to task if Switzerland ever strayed from the pathways of French foreign policy.

Provision was made that the seat of government between sessions of the Diet should be in Basel, Bern, Freiburg, Lucerne, Solothurn, or Zurich—each serving in turn. The *Schultheiss* or *Bürgermeister* of the *Vorort* automatically became *Landammann* of Switzerland during the period of time that his canton served as the seat of government.

All of the cantons, though ceasing to be mere administrative units, and though much of their former autonomy was restored, were denied the right to negotiate alliances with foreign Powers or among themselves. Intercantonal customs barriers disappeared; the right to collect duties on imports became vested in the Diet (the Federal Government) which controlled all traffic over its national frontiers. The Diet alone could enter into military capitulations and these, in turn, could be with France alone (a few minor exceptions), never with any of the enemies of France. Also the cantons were not permitted to recover any of the subject territories that were theirs prior to establishment of the Helvetic Republic.

Four types of cantonal government emerged during the Mediation, each canton being free, in principle, to rule itself as it pleased. The ancient cantons in the heart of the country, plus Glarus, Zug, and both the Appenzells returned to pure grass-roots democracy with a *Landsgemeinde* as the governing body; Bern, Lucerne, Freiburg and Solothurn adopted patrician-aristocratic styles of government which were significantly milder than in the pre-revolutionary days. The countrysides, henceforth, were to be represented in the Great Councils, and the disenfranchisement of some classes of citizens was terminated by the Act of Mediation. Also, subject classes disappeared and all privileges of place, of birth, of person, and of family were disallowed. This could only mean that the unique privileges once vested in the ruling families of the patrician-oligarchic cantons had to be relinquished. The cities of Basel, Schaffhausen and Zurich had been accustomed for many decades to substantial representation of the guilds in their ruling Councils. This became broadened by providing for some representation from the countryside. The new cantons of Aargau, St. Gallen, Ticino, Thurgau and Vaud established democratic types of government in accordance with the spirit of the Enlightenment and the doctrines of emancipation and equality which infused the Act of Mediation and the Constitution of the Helvetic Republic. Some of the rights in the new order were enjoyed only by those burghers who owned landed property, which tempered somewhat the concept of equality in an otherwise democratic order. Graubünden, the sixth of the new cantons, returned to the constitution of the old Raetia as a federation of three quite autonomous States.

The rights of settlement and of trade and commerce remained protected—a carryover from the Helvetic Republic. But some of the disadvantages of the past few years continued under the Mediation and were destined to invite unending bickering with France and a barely concealed anger among a people who were determined to regain their independence and recognition as a neutral State. Switzerland was obliged to conclude with France a military alliance that gave to Napoleon the right to recruit 6000 Swiss who could be used anywhere in Europe for any type of military service. The principle of restricting their use in combat to defensive operations only, though expressed in a 50-year alliance, was totally foreign to the ideas and plans of the First Consul who also had the right to recruit an additional 8000 Swiss if any part of France were attacked. Related to military matters was Napleon's requirement that supervision of the roads and bridges and responsibility for their maintenance must be vested in the Federal Government, not in 19 semi-autonomous cantons.[11] The roads and bridges were of greater importance to France and to Napoleon for military purposes than to the Swiss themselves.

It is worth noting that Napoleon was determined to maintain Switzerland in a weakened position, ever dependent upon France. He saw to it that the Swiss army was small and that the Diet was virtually powerless. In 1804 when the Diet proposed that a Swiss war chest, a military school, and a general staff be established to meet her needs as an independent and neutral State, Napoleon promptly forbade these innovations. He insisted that Switzerland's neighbours were duty-bound to afford protection in any national emergency. In December 1802, Napoleon had explained to a Swiss delegation that the neutrality of their country was now safely assured because of a new equilibrium of power between France and Austria. France held the

Simplon and its approaches while Austria had the Tirol. Switzerland, in the middle, was safe from either of her neighbours "because she held the middle of the arms of the balance".[12] He insisted that Switzerland must admit to herself the impossibility of defending her land without French help.

Some Consequences of French Policy

The First Consul further weakened Switzerland by his economic policies. Freedom of trade was granted in name only. Swiss industry was tied closely into the French economic system and commercial policy. The Confederation was required to buy its salt, 200,000 hundredweight per year, from France at a fixed price, well above the prevailing price for salt from Germany. She was also compelled to pay to France 28 million francs, alleged to be the cost of the French army of occupation which "defended" Switzerland during the war that ended with the Peace of Lunéville (9 February 1801).

Proposals to separate Church and State were resisted by both confessions. Attempts to imitate some of the radical results of the revolution in France failed in Switzerland; for example, the abolition and expropriation of monasteries. Attempts to abolish religious processions were more successful but were productive of increased tensions within the country. Provocative also was a program for the introduction of civil marriage. However, the plan was not implemented and, indeed, the legislative approval of civil marriage did not come about until late in the century.

Napoleon signed a separate peace with England (Peace of Amiens) in 1802. The shift in the balance of power on the continent was seriously disturbing to the British Crown, so much so that the peace was in fact nothing more than an armistice and in 1803 Anglo-French hostilities were resumed at sea. The French ships of war suffered total destruction. England celebrated the glorious victory at Trafalgar while Napoleon publicly attributed the loss of his ships to "terrible storms at sea." A few years passed by without much active warfare on land and Napoleon used the breathing space to advantage. In 1804, in the presence of the pope he crowned himself as emperor, with the title Napoleon I, Emperor of the French.

In 1805 the third war of the coalition against France broke out with serious economic consequences for Switzerland. Napoleon proclaimed, 21 November 1806, a continental blockade against trade with England which resulted in a boycott of all exports from the continent to England and the imposition of very high import duties on goods of British origin. The Swiss textile industry was at once threatened with collapse. It was rescued only by a slight relaxation in French policy to permit the import of English machine yarn without which the textile industry would have been ruined. Goods were also smuggled in from Italy, some of the items originating in the newly emerging American republic and the British colonies. Even before the continental blockade, Switzerland found that her industry was becoming seriously weakened by French economic policy. Early in the days of the Mediation, and in spite of Napoleon's promises to protect Swiss industry, France suddenly raised to intolerable levels the duties imposed on Swiss exports to France. The obvious purpose was to weaken Swiss industry and to strengthen that of France. The duties on English cotton goods exported to both France and Switzerland were raised enormously in a determined effort to cripple British industry. Finally came the total blockade followed by enormous activity in smuggling. England replied to Napoleon's continental blockade by orders of 7 January and 11 November 1807 which imposed a blockade of all ports that excluded English merchandise. All vessels that tried to run the blockade would be seized unless they had previously put in at an English port and paid a substantial tax (**170**).

Although the Swiss textile industry managed to maintain a precarious existence many famous firms became bankrupt. Unemployment, hunger, and severe deprivation became the lot of many who were dependent on a viable domestic industry. Beggars were numerous and the government appealed to the generosity of the bourgeoisie to help the poverty-stricken unemployed. In some cases entire communities broke into rebellion and order had to be restored through the use of troops ordered into action by the Diet. The terrible effects on industry resulted in a heavy emigration from eastern Switzerland in which the textile industry was largely located. Among these were many skilled weavers and spinners.

Emigration from the homeland was also attributable to French military policy. On 24 August 1798, the mutual defense alliance of 1777 with France had been replaced, under pressure from the French Directory, by an alliance which would permit the use of Swiss troops in offensive combat. There were those among the Swiss who predicted that abandonment of the principle of defensive agreements would prove to be the grave of their freedom. It could only mean the end of Swiss independence and neutrality. It was not long before Napoleon, invoking the terms of the alliance, called upon Switzerland for 18,000 recruits to fight for France. Recruitment was a total failure and great numbers of men of military age fled the country. Later, when Napoleon decided to carry the war to Russia (in 1812) he demanded every man permitted by the capitulation agreement with Switzerland. Again recruitment failed miserably. The Swiss had no desire to fight for Napoleon but they entered the Spanish and English armies in considerable numbers. Although the capitulation agreement provided that recruitment must be "voluntary and without pressure" Napoleon insisted that Switzerland provide 12,000 men. The government resorted to various devices to satisfy the demand. Finally a motley crowd of 12,000 was made available to the dictator, many being of the sort that Switzerland was glad to get rid of: thieves, other petty criminals, and persistent troublemakers of various kinds. The cantons joined in the act. Schwyz rounded up a goodly number of men who mocked at religion. Solothurn specialized in supplying smugglers. Lucerne provided night revellers, spendthrifts, shirkers of work, and fathers of illegitimate children. Ticino contributed those who were guilty of carrying forbidden weapons and St. Gallen supplied an appreciable number of medical quacks and wife beaters. As a sequel to this forced recruitment, Switzerland was next forbidden to permit any recruiting on behalf of the enemies of France.

In May 1807, Napoleon wrote to Reinhard about the recruits (**259**, p. 479). After addressing Reinhard as "my very great and dear friend," he commented on the courage and loyalty of the Swiss in battle. He wanted foreigners (Spanish, Dutch, etc.) to be excluded from the body of recruits. In concluding the letter "Your good friend, Napoleon," he asked that the cantons be assured of his friendship and of his constant protection (**259**, p. 480). Reinhard appears to have enjoyed such flattery and was unfortunately influenced, to the detriment of Switzerland, by Napoleon's friendly (?) salutations.

Napoleon Resumes War with Austria

In 1805, Napoleon resumed the war with Austria; The Peace of Lunéville was, like the Peace of Amiens, nothing more than an armistice. Napoleon, now at the height of his power, determined to use Swiss neutrality to his benefit. Austria promised to respect the neutrality of Switzerland if France would also give a similar assurance. Napoleon stubbornly declined to do so because, so he claimed, this recognition by France had already been solemnly subscribed in the Franco-Swiss treaty of 1798. Switzerland, on 23 September 1805, declared its neutrality in the war.[13] It proclaimed its intention to man its frontiers with federal troops and to adhere strictly to a policy of impartiality toward both belligerents, refraining however from use of the century-old expression of its intention "to resist force with force." To France no advantage was to be found in sending her armies across Switzerland to attack Austria, but it meant much to Napoleon to know that Switzerland would defend her eastern border against any Austrian forces. The French won a stunning victory over Austria at Austerlitz, and to the consternation of the rest of Europe forced the Kaiser (Franz I) into concluding the Peace of Pressburg (26 December 1805). This again gave formal recognition to the independence of the Swiss republic under the government prescribed by the Act of Mediation (de Martens, **227**).

War against Austria broke out again in 1809. Once again Switzerland declared her neutrality and sent troops to defend the Vorarlberg border. The *Bürgermeister* of Zurich, Hans Reinhard, hastened to Regensburg on an official mission to seek from Napoleon a confirmation of his intention to respect the neutrality of Switzerland. The emperor was in such a bad mood that Reinhard could not determine whether he would approve the request or condemn Swiss neutrality to death. "As for me, this neutrality is an empty word devoid of any sense. It will be of service to you only as I may wish" (Steiner, **345**). Later, and evidently in a calmer mood, he said to Reinhard "How would it be if I were to unite the [Austrian] Tirol with Switzerland? The land is similar in mood and physical properties. It has the same thirst for freedom and would fit in well under your Constitution . . . all other States enlarge themselves . . . yours remains weak and small." The Diet took the offer seriously and concluded that annexation of the territory would arouse the lasting enmity of Austria and increase Switzerland's dependence on France. The principle to be observed: a neutral Switzerland must not annex the property of other States and, in turn, must surrender no territory of its own. Napoleon was probably puzzled by the declination of his offer and in the Peace of Vienna in 1809, the possible enlargement of Switzerland was not mentioned.

Switzerland's Territorial Losses

Thus far Switzerland had experienced only a progressive reduction in size through the policies of the emperor. Bornio, Chiavenna, and Valtellina had been made a part of the new Cisalpine Republic. The gift of the Fricktal had been more than nullified by Napoleon's conversion of the Valais, eight times the area of the Fricktal, into an independent republic in May, 1802. In February 1806, Prussia had been forced by Napoleon to surrender the Principality of Neuchâtel which was given by the emperor to his marshal Alexandre Berthier. For centuries, Bern and Neuchâtel had been closely associated and even the King of Prussia recognized that his distant possession was, in fact, a protectorate of Bern. Although its Jura defense system had broken down when the French army of General Brune seized the southern slopes of the Jura in 1798, Switzerland was greatly alarmed by Napoleon's formal seizure of the Principality—a *de facto* annexation by France. Vaud and Geneva had long since been lost. In October 1810 the Ticino was occupied by Italian-French troops, allegedly to prevent the smuggling of goods banned by Napoleon's continental blockade and boycott of British exports. This occupation carried with it the imminent danger of the annexation of Ticino to the Republic of Milan—rumored to be a near certainty. That this annexation did not come about can be attributed to internal resistance by a people who preferred to remain, despite the foreign occupation, as a part of Switzerland. Not until the fall of Napoleon was the Ticino again recognized as an undisputed part of the Swiss Confederation. On 12 November 1810 the Republic of Valais was annexed to France as the Department of Simplon and placed under the rule of a French prefect. The annexation of Valais bound together, by the Simplon route along the Rhone valley, France and French-held Italy. To Napoleon this was a military necessity although he attributed the seizure publicly to the need to maintain order in a State which had fallen into anarchy.

The representations and protests directed to Napoleon in respect to these many seizures of territory and violent trespasses against "independent" Switzerland were timid and even obsequious. Her people were exhausted and weary in soul and body. For 12 years their country had suffered military occupation, political harassment, industrial bankruptcies, severe unemployment, food shortages, emigration of her menfolk and the forced service of others in Napoleon's armies. The spirit of resistance to the dictator and her pride as a nation had almost disappeared. The Diet went to extremes in observing diplomatic courtesies and in extending congratulations to their oppressor on numerous occasions, always in the hope of winning his favour and in gaining some relief from his ruthless economic and political policies. In early June, 1804, a special courier was sent to Paris by the Diet to convey the good wishes of the Swiss republic following the First Consul's coronation on May 25 as Napoleon I, Emperor of the French. Congratulations were again extended by a special delegation of the Diet in 1805 when the Emperor of the French declared himself King of Italy. Another delegation travelled to Paris in June 1810 to congratulate Napoleon I, Emperor of the French and King of Italy, on his marriage to Marie Louise, Archduchess of Austria. The emperor acknowledged warmly the letter of congratulations and expanded his imperial title by a third designation "Mediator of the Swiss Confederation." His grateful acceptance of the Swiss adulation did not deter the emperor a few months later from sending his Italian troops to occupy the Swiss Ticino and from annexing the Valais to France, two quite hostile acts which aroused in many the very understandable fear that the annexation of all Switzerland would soon follow. The final act of servility came in April 1811 when another delegation conveyed to the emperor and empress the congratulations of the Swiss on the birth of a son, the King of Rome.

Napoleon's War with Russia

War with Russia commenced in the late summer of 1812. The Grand Army reached Moscow only to find the city deserted and burned. In October the great retreat to the west was ordered. The storms of winter descended early, the weather was unusually severe, and the retreat was catastrophic. Nine thousand Swiss had been forced to serve with the French in this disastrous campaign. Only 700 returned and many of these were crippled and incapable of work.

Prussia and the German States rose in arms against Napoleon. The Russian Tsar, Alexander I, was hailed as the saviour of Europe. Great Britain called for a new European alliance against Napoleon. In the summer of 1813 Austria once again declared war on France and a few months later the armies of Napoleon were severely defeated in the battle of Leipzig (16–19 October). Paris fell in March 1814, and Napoleon abdicated and was banished to Elba. The major Powers assembled after the memorable Peace of Paris to proceed with the territorial and political reconstruction of Europe.

Beneficent Results Under the Mediation

Before continuing with a résumé of the historic events of 1814 and 1815—a rather dim chapter in the history of Switzerland—we should review some of the gains to Switzerland achieved during the days of the Mediation. Many men were enfranchised who had previously been denied any equality of political rights. Vestiges of feudalism disappeared and the right to enjoy positions of trust and emolument could not be denied on grounds of class or social distinction. Equality of the citizens before the law and denial of any special privileges attributable to birth were among the gains, on paper at least, which came to the Swiss citizenry in the days of the Helvetic Republic and in Mediation times. In the Graubünden the special privileges of the ecclesiastical and temporal lords were abolished. In the old cantons any job holders in public office who had been engaging in petty thievery were summarily dismissed. Zurich improved her school system and Basel issued a school ordinance for the benefit of children in the countryside. In general, schooling was actively promoted in much of the Confederation although responsibility in education, with the popular disapproval of centralism, became cantonal and not all of the cantons responded to the changing times. Promotion of education grew out of the *Aufklarung* but it was also an inevitable expression of the growing recognition of people's rights. A leader in the movement for universal schooling was Philipp Albrecht Stapfer[14] who sought uniformity above all. He demanded for both sexes compulsory education which would be, through heavy subsidies from government, inexpensive for all and free for the poor. Boys were to recieve an introduction to military training and instruction in handicrafts. Girls would be taught domestic sciences. Teachers would be pensioned at age 65, a Swiss School of Education for teacher training would be founded and, as the culmination of Stapfer's great scheme, a national university would be established. He was years ahead of his contemporaries. His visionary plans came to naught, virtually all remained on paper, wrecked by the great cost of implementation and the opposition of cantonal universities and academies.

Several more cultural societies came into being, a product of the rebirth of intellectualism: the "Swiss Society for the Public Good," "Swiss Society for Education," and the "Swiss Society for Historical Research."

The Diet encouraged development of its military establishment. The Linth from the Walensee to the Zurichsee was straightened out and a canal was built from Mollis to the Walensee—a project which was started in 1807 and finished in 1828. It was the first notable all-Swiss undertaking and it increased greatly the country's resources in arable land. Hans Konrad Escher, the principal in charge of the project, was ultimately honored by the noble designation "von der Linth", perhaps the only time in Swiss history that nobility was conferred by the Swiss government upon one of its people.

During the later days of the Mediation, preparations were under way for the Restoration, the period which would follow the fall of Napoleon. The intention was clear and laudable—to absorb the best from the days of the Helvetic Republic and to unite it with the precious values of the past. On one hand, we have Karl Ludwig von Haller, grandson of Albrecht von Haller, and his *"Restauration der Staatswissenschaften."* On the other, we have Benjamin Constant of Vaud. Haller saw in the State and its various authorities something ordained by God, including the patrician concept of human inequality and the Middle Ages' idea of society as a corporate structure. Constant saw in freedom and the free society something which must eventually degenerate into an authoritarian State ruled by a dictator. He observed that in France the revolution began with freedom, but a freedom that was finally lost in the despotism of Napoleon. Haller became the theoretician of the reactionaries, of the patrician class, while Constant emerged as the exponent of conservative liberalism. Thus, two new political theoreticians of European stature, each with a wide and influential following, arose in Switzerland.

Switzerland after the Battle of Leipzig

Now let us return to the last two months of 1813 and the two years that followed. Leipzig had been won by the coalition army, the French were on the run, and the pursuit was on.[15] Did the Swiss join in the chase? No. They were exhausted and broken in spirit. Their leaders were neither creatures of Napoleon's making, blindly devoted to him, nor were they gifted diplomats who had ably striven to stave off the worst. In fact there was no place for the strong and resolute; the requirements for effective popular resistance were lacking. In 1813, Zurich was the *Vorort* and her chief magistrate, Hans von Reinhard was *Landammann* of Switzerland. Unfortunately he possessed an ill-concealed admiration for Napoleon and an extreme timidity in the presence of the emperor. Even the catastrophe of the Grand Army in Russia seemed to Reinhard to be only an inconclusive misfortune. He expressed no vigorous determination to terminate the alliance with France nor would he have Switzerland join the coalition against Napoleon. Had he have followed either course aggressively and with resolve it is probable that the former Swiss territory annexed to France and the subject States separated from the Swiss cantons would all have been returned. He and his counsellors behaved as if they had no intention of shaking off French domination. A division of opinion also existed among the people. Some sought a return to the old Switzerland of pre-revolutionary days. A minority of this faction in *Innerschweiz* and in the aristocratic cantons were ready to rise in revolt. While the rest of Europe rose against Napoleon there was no strength of leadership in Switzerland and no evidence of a vigorous resolve to regain territories and rebuild a strong Confederation. There was no popular uprising and no national will.

The Diet assembled in extraordinary session in Zurich on 15 November 1813. They declared a state of armed neutrality[16] in the Swiss Confederation, named Rudolf von Wattenwyl general of the armies[17] and issued a stirring appeal (20 November) to the Swiss people to stand firm in maintaining the neutrality, the freedom and independence of the Fatherland. Napoleon was advised that the people had declared their desire "to observe this same neutrality toward all the Powers in the most absolute and most impartial sense; on this rests our political existence." Similar declarations of neutrality and impartiality toward all the belligerent States were sent to the Austrian, Prussian, and Russian monarchs.

The Diet called 15,000 to 20,000 men to the colours but did not recall their men who were then in French military service. They also formally terminated the Confederation's participation in Napoleon's continental blockade. The Diet assumed that the allies would respect the neutrality of Switzerland and they knew quite well that Napoleon need not be feared since a neutral Switzerland was essential for the protection of his flank.[18] The princes and heads of government among the allies were inclined to regard Swiss neutrality with good will. But not so with the generals who wanted to reserve the right to march through Switzerland to attack the French in Burgundy and elsewhere. Metternich, the powerful leader of Austrian political affairs, sided with the generals. On political grounds, he also urged a military occupation of Switzerland to ensure a restoration of the pre-revolutionary leadership and conservative cantonal governments. After centuries of exposure to French policies and French domination in her foreign affairs, Switzerland was not to become a bastion of anti-French influences and events.

She was too weak to resist a *Durchmarsch*. One can hardly be surprised that the allied generals took full advantage of Switzerland's military plight and decided on 15 December 1813 to lead their armies through Switzerland to attack the French.

von Wattenwyl knew that the Federal army was inadequately trained, that it was lacking in fighting strength, and was only of symbolic value. A few days later the commander of the Swiss border guards at Basel signed a capitulation agreement and on December 21 a force of 195,000 allied troops—Austrians and Russians—headed for the several Rhine bridges and entered Switzerland (**201**).

Occupation of Switzerland by the Allied Armies

The entry of the allied armies was preceded by several declarations and proclamations by the allies: to the *Landammann* of Switzerland from the Austrian and Russian plenipotentiaries (20 December); to the Swiss people from the Commanding General of the allied armies, Schwarzenberg (21 December); an Order-of-the-Day to the Grand Army from Schwarzenberg (21 December); and a General Declaration by the allied Powers on entry of the army into Swiss territory (21 December).[19] Despite some plundering and other transgressions the *Durchmarsch* was reasonably well conducted and discipline was fairly well maintained. In the meantime, the Swiss army of 12,000 men under Wattenwyl had retreated before the advancing allied army without offering any resistance. Several columns of the allied army marched against Porrentruy, high up in the Jura, while others, moving to the west, advanced on Neuchâtel, Besançon and on to Lake Geneva. Bern and Freiburg were soon liberated, the French were driven from the Valais, the high passes leading to Italy were seized, and Geneva was taken over by a victorious Austrian army. Again, as in 1799, Switzerland was overrun by foreign armies but in 1813 they were received as liberators and friends rather than as enemies of the people. Basel became for a time a military headquarters and served as a meeting place for the crowned heads of Austria, Prussia and Russia during the latter part of January 1814.

Though liberated from the French, Switzerland paid a heavy price for the surrender of her neutrality. In all fairness to her, despite the price to be paid, she was virtually forced to abandon her commitment to neutrality. Her own weakness and the overwhelming size of the allied army presented her with no alternative. And what was the price she paid? Enormous numbers of troops and supporting civilians had to be quartered. Diseases, such as typhus, broke out and spread through the Swiss population. Additional hospital facilities had to be improvised, the existing hospitals being filled to overflowing. The initial relief that was felt on expulsion of the French soon gave way to renewed fears and anxiety as the Austrians and their allies took over the country. Offsetting the troubles attributable to the occupation were the assurances of the allies that all of the lost territories and additional areas would soon be returned to Switzerland.

The cantons began to stir into action to end the Mediation, to remove the framework of the Helvetic Republic and to restore the "good old times." The ensuing 18 months, up to mid-August 1815, were not among the great days of Swiss history. It was as if nothing had been learned during the preceding 15 years. The leaders were unprepared for the Congress of Vienna and unclear as to what they hoped to accomplish beyond a return to the ways of the past and a system of 13 cantons with associated States. It is worth noting that none of the European statesmen agreed to reconstitution of the new cantons as subject territories of the thirteen.

Switzerland Prepares for Freedom and Independence

On December 23 Bern declared the end of the Mediation and set up a Commission of the States as a provisional government. The Diet assembled in Zurich and agreement was reached on the basis of a new constitution. Bern and four other recalcitrant cantons yielded on the question of subject States. On 6 April 1814 the Diet of the 19 cantons was convened. It devoted many sessions to the constitution of the new Confederation and went down in history as the longest Diet ever (6 April 1814 to 31 August 1815).

There is no reason to doubt that the Diet would have been convened sooner or later to prepare a new Constitution appropriate to the needs of an enlarged nation, proud of its long heritage of neutrality, freedom and independence. It was preceded however by gentle diplomatic prodding from the Austrian and Russian plenipotentiaries in a letter (31 December 1813) to the *Landammann* of Switzerland (Reinhard):

> "The time has arrived when Switzerland . . . is called to reassume its place among the free and independent nations of Europe. . . . A subject which merits its particular attention [is] the formation of . . . a Constitution. . . . Their Majesties promise Switzerland not to lay down their arms until its complete independence, and the Constitution which it will freely adopt and be freely accepted, have been placed under the guaranty of the European Powers. They repeat that at the same time they are firmly resolved to achieve the restitution of those parts of the Confederation's territory usurped by France."[20]

In his reply (4 January 1814), the *Landammann* gave formal notice of the termination of the Act of Mediation and assured the plenipotentiaries of the intention of the Diet to engage itself in the preparation of a new Constitution:

> "The deputies of the cantons adopting the Convention of 29 December 1813, have given notice of the dissolution of relations founded on the Act of Mediation. . . . The new Act of Confederation is to be based on simple and just principles which the great majority of the cantons has already approved and to which one can hope that the others will soon adhere. This Federal Act on which will rest the liberty and independence of Switzerland is a task in which the Diet principally is called to engage. The formation of each particular Constitution is within the competence of each canton, and is subject to approval by the Diet."[21]

The Convention referred to above stated specifically that there are to be no subject territories: "there will be established no relations of subjection incompatible with the rights of a free People."

The Federal Pact

Let us now take a look at the new Federal Pact which the Diet accepted on 16 August 1814, noting first of all that it applied to an enlarged Confederation of nineteen cantons (the former thirteen plus St. Gallen, Graubünden, Aargau, Thurgau, Ticino and Vaud):

I. The cantons guaranteed reciprocally their Constitutions, such as will have been decreed by the supreme authority of each canton, in conformity with the principles of the Federal Pact. The territories of the respective cantons were likewise reciprocally guaranteed.

II. To defend the neutrality of the country, a federal militia of 30,000 men was established and the number of troops to be provided by each canton was specified.

III. The estimated annual costs, including "other general expenses of the Confederation," were determined to be S.fr. 490,500 which were charged in specified amounts against the various cantons. A war chest of at least S.fr. 981,000 was approved with part of the income to be derived from a federal tariff on imports of luxury items.

IV. Any canton, menaced from without or within, had the right to call for federal assistance. In the case of menacing actions of a foreign country, the endangered canton was to notify the *Vorort* (the canton in charge of affairs between sessions of the Diet: Zurich, Bern or Lucerne) which must convene the Diet. The latter was then required to do whatever was necessary for the security of Switzerland.

V. Intercantonal disputes were to be settled by arbitration.

VI. Intercantonal treaties which prejudiced the rights of other cantons and the terms of this Federal Pact were not allowed.

VII. There was to be no class favoritism in the enjoyment of political rights.

VIII. The Diet, which directs the general affairs of the Confederation, was to be composed of deputies of the nineteen cantons who must vote according to instructions from their governments. The power to declare war and to conclude peace was vested in the Diet. The Diet also negotiated treaties with foreign Powers and concluded commercial treaties. The cantons retained the right to conclude military capitulations with foreign Powers and the authority to negotiate agreements concerning economic and police matters provided that the Conventions entered into did not violate the Federal Pact or the constitutional rights of other cantons.

IX. Federal representatives of the Diet, appointed for the discharge of specifically designated responsibilities and to serve for stated times, were to be nominated by the cantons.

XII. The existence of the convents and chapters and the preservation of their properties . . . were guaranteed.

XIII. The National Debt, as of 1 November 1804, continued to be recognized as S.fr. 3,118,336.

XIV. Existing intercantonal Conventions and accords, concluded since 1803, were to remain in effect if not contrary to the terms of the Federal Pact. The status of decrees promulgated by the Diet between 1803 and 1815 was to be determined by the Diet.

This Federal Pact may be thought of as an Act of Union which supplemented and combined in a single document various Articles contained within the many intercantonal alliances of previous years. A second edition of the Pact, necessitated by enlargement of the Confederation to twenty-two cantons, otherwise with few substantive changes, was signed and sealed on 7 August 1815.[22] The three new cantonal members of the Confederation were Geneva, Neuchâtel and Valais.

The Federal Pact accomplished less than a strong viable Confederation required. It added little to the strength of the nation. It provided a federal militia, and a war chest. The former replaced the cantonal militia, each under the ultimate control of its cantonal authority. Unquestionably there resulted a strengthening of Switzerland's military capability. But otherwise the cantons regained most of their autonomy and many of the rights of a sovereign State. The embryonic nation had a long way to go before enough authority was surrendered by the cantons to permit us to speak of a federation with enough power at the center to function effectively in intercantonal and foreign affairs.

The new order of things was really decided by the cantons, each of which tended to go its own way. The patrician families of Bern, Lucerne, Freiburg, and Solothurn regained the right, lost during Mediation times, of holding the positions of authority in the political and military departments of government. In the guild cantons the modest liberalization achieved during the Mediation continued. In the new cantons, equality before the law, qualified by the vesting of certain electoral rights in the property-owing families, continued as in the Mediation.

Preparations for the Congress of Vienna

Napoleon abdicated in the spring of 1814 and the first Peace of Paris was signed on May 30. The Powers assembled in Vienna in October. The long Diet sent an official delegation which represented the Federation as a whole. Cantonal delegations were also present. Preparations within the delegations were inadequate. Leadership was divided and there was no consensus on priorities and procedural matters. The requests on which there was the greatest unanimity were: return of lost territories and redefinition of the national frontier; international recognition of the independence and neutrality of Switzerland; advice to the Powers of the new Federal Constitution; and demands for the payment of damages by France as compensation for plundering and for many expenses incurred by Switzerland because of the French occupation.

One of the great disappointments was the failure of their representatives to achieve return of Bormio, Chiavenna, and the Valtellina to Swiss possession. If a Swiss army had moved promptly into this part of the Cisalpine republic after Napoleon's defeat at the decisive battle of Leipzig there is little doubt that return of this territory to Switzerland would have been accepted by the Congress as a *fait accompli*.[23]

Even so all need not have been lost. The Powers would have approved reorganization of most of this territory as a new canton and its return to Swiss jurisdiction. Indeed the people of the Valtellina were eager that this be done; they wanted to be a part of the Swiss Confederation. Reinhard, still the *Landammann* of Switzerland, refused to accept this solution. He stubbornly opposed others within the delegation, admittedly because the people of the Valtellina were predominantly catholic. The acceptance within the Confederation of another catholic canton was too much for Reinhard and he would not yield. Publicly he argued for return of the entire package—Bormio, Chiavenna, and the Valtellina—to the Graubünden and he refused the proposed compromise of returning Bormio and Chiavenna to the Graubünden and accepting the Valtellina as a new canton. Metternich, speaking for Austria, convinced the Powers that the best solution, pursuant to dismantling the Cisalpine republic, would be incorporation of the provinces within the Duchy of Milan. This solution was accepted by the Powers and the whole of this area, deemed to be important to Switzerland for several reasons, thus fell under Austrian hegemony.

Part of the Bishopric of Basel was added to the canton of Basel and the rest became a part of Bern with the formal understanding that the catholic faith in the Jura would be protected and the people would enjoy equality before the law as in the rest of the canton. It was also agreed that various feudal burdens, removed in 1798, would not be reimposed. Neuchâtel was returned to Prussia in June 1814 with a rather curious constitution which recognized the Principality as Prussian territory but which also admitted it as a canton within the Swiss Confederation. This dual relationship was approved by the Powers. Military service was required of all "subjects and inhabitants of Neuchâtel without exception" between the ages of 18 and 50 "but they may be used in war only to maintain public order, to defend the State and in fulfillment of treaty obligations with Switzerland."[24]

Geneva and Savoy

The problems posed by Geneva and Savoy were among the most difficult to resolve and, at the same time, of very great importance to Switzerland. Playing a decisive role in the sequence of events was Charles Pictet de Rochemont,[25] Geneva's principal delegate to the first Congress of Paris (April–June, 1814).[26] Pictet arrived in Paris on April 18 and promptly busied himself with the great project of uniting Geneva to Switzerland as a canton, not merely as an allied State. In April 1798 Geneva had been absorbed into the Republic of France and recognized as the center of Napoleon's newly created Department of Leman. By 1814 the city and State had freed themselves of the bonds to France. Pictet, whose influence grew from day to day, endeavoured to convince the Powers that additional territories must be ceded to Geneva to make it contiguous to Vaud. It was then separated by a French corridor extending to Versoix on Lake Geneva and a number of troublesome French customs ports. Pictet established excellent relations with Sir Stratford Canning—the 26-year-old British minister, accredited to Switzerland in 1814, also with Clausel de Coussergues—the French delegate and friend of Geneva, and equally warm relations with the Russian and Austrian representatives. Pictet's persuasive yet friendly approaches had significant results despite the fact that the Swiss delegates failed to arrive until May 26 when the Articles of Agreement were signed. By the First Treaty of Paris, the Powers recognized the independence of Geneva and promised that it would be made a part of the Swiss Confederation as another autonomous canton.[27] In the meantime toll-free use of the road through Versoix seemed to be assured. The Pays de Gex which Geneva had conquered in 1589 but which, like Geneva itself, had been absorbed by France was to be ceded to Geneva by an Act of May 12, but this decision was rescinded in the closing hours of the Congress. As for Savoy, nothing was accomplished, but much was discussed.

Though the future appeared to be promising, Geneva, now assured that it would become a part of Switzerland, was still separated from the neighbouring canton of Vaud by the Versoix corridor. The Austrians were also a problem. They had moved in from Italy after the fall of Napoleon and occupied the city, avowedly as friends of Switzerland. But the Swiss met with no success in attempting to persuade the Austrians that they were no longer the masters. The civil governor, the Count of Ugarte, continued to requisition clothing and supplies for the Austrian troops as though it were a conquered country. Pictet urged upon Metternich the necessity of recalling Ugarte and pointed out to Prince Schwarzenberg, Metternich, and Castlereagh (British Foreign Minister)

> that all the mic-mac we have seen here and around us—things given, taken back, contradicted, and purposely embroiled . . . conceals the project of the House of Austria . . . to take all or part of Savoy, and Geneva, as a means of encircling and governing Switzerland (**84**, pp. 32, 33).

An important associate of Pictet during his years as a diplomat was François d'Ivernois, a former Genevois who had been banished from his country by its aristocratic government after the turbulent events of 1782. He went to England, served the British Crown well, became a citizen and was knighted. d'Ivernois was a convinced adversary of the French Revolution. A brief visit to Geneva in 1792 permitted him to witness the acts of terror and, subsequent to his visit, to be condemned to death. The deed of annexation of Geneva by France in 1798 specified that d'Ivernois was to be excluded forever from French nationality. Though living in England, he was a Genevois at heart and when the Republic of Geneva was reconstituted as an independent State, the provisional Council entrusted him with the delicate mission of persuading the British government of the necessity of uniting Geneva with the Swiss Confederation.

The Congress of Vienna

The Congress of Vienna, convened in October 1814, was attended by 216 princes, heads of States, chiefs of missions, and official delegates. Geneva was represented by Pictet de Rochemont, François d'Ivernois and a secretary. The Diet of the Swiss Confederation sent three delegates and two secretaries. A few cantonal representatives were also present.

The interests of the small States were of little concern to the Great Powers except as they contributed to the two principal objectives of the Powers: to readjust national boundaries in such a way as to create a new balance of power—in effect to re-establish an equilibrium between the European States in light of the shattering events of the French Revolution and the Bonaparte era; and to resist any re-awakening in France of ideas of conquest, by surrounding her with States of sufficient strength to resist invasion—the Pays-Bas to the north, Germany to the east, and Switzerland to the southeast.

Pictet and d'Ivernois urged that the provinces of upper Savoy be united with Switzerland. As far back as 1611 Savoy had sought an agreement assuring her of Swiss protection in the event of invasion by an unfriendly Power. In 1699 new approaches were made by Savoy in an endeavour to have Savoy declared a Neutral by the Powers and placed under the protection of the Swiss cantons. France entered vigorous objections and continued to do so in 1703, 1713 and 1748. In the first year of the French Republic (1792) all seven provinces of the Duchy of Savoy were annexed by France. After the decisive defeat of Bonaparte in the Battle of Leipzig and his subsequent abdication, the States which he had seized lost no time in declaring their regained freedom. The neutralization of Savoy and its possible "helvetisation" had been discussed earlier in diplomatic circles, the idea being encouraged anew by the Sardinian plenipotentiary accredited to the Congress of Vienna and in accordance with the expressed wish of King Victor Emmanuel. Savoy, a part of Sardinia, was almost totally separated from the rest of the kingdom by the formidable Alpine massif. Switzerland had balked at earlier proposals that the whole of Savoy be placed under the protection of her neutrality since effective defense of such a large area would put an impossible strain on her resources.[28] Geneva and the Swiss Confederation agreed that neutralization of the northerly provinces of Chablais and Faucigny was highly desirable. Geneva realized that this would enhance her security to the south and east and the Confederation was confident that defense of these two provinces for which she would then be responsible was militarily feasible. Pictet and d'Ivernois worked tirelessly to achieve the neutralization of the two provinces. Geneva as a whole did not support Pictet and d'Ivernois as unanimously as one might expect. Geneva was strongly Calvinistic and there were many who regarded with trepidation, or even open hostility, any treaty that might permit the strongly catholic provinces of Savoy, even as buffer states, to exert any influence in the affairs of the emerging canton of Geneva. Even more vigorous was their opposition to the absorption by Geneva of a number of catholic communities to the south of the city. With the support of Wellington and the tacit approval of Talleyrand, the proposal of neutralization received the formal acceptance of the conferees in the Protocol of 29 March 1815, and confirmation by Article 92 of the Final Act of the Congress of Vienna. The published diplomatic correspondence of Pictet and d'Ivernois (Cramer, **96**) strongly suggests that the three representatives appointed by the Swiss Diet were ineffective in the Savoy problem and did nothing up to the last moment in the negotiations initiated by the Geneva delegates.

Switzerland's Demands

The Swiss delegation, in accordance with their instructions, sought the following: recognition of Switzerland as an independent State; formal recognition of Switzerland's neutrality by the Powers; establishment of a good frontier amenable to adequate defense; accession of the Bishopric of Basel and the town of Biel; reunion of Constance with the Swiss Confederation; return of the Valtellina to the Graubünden; re-establishment of the former Italian frontier; indemnities for the retention by Austria and the Grand Duchy of Baden of various properties belonging to Swiss religious foundations; and the disenclavement of Geneva and provision of free communication with neighbouring Swiss cantons (Vaud and Valais).

The Powers first attempted to exclude France from the deliberations concerning Switzerland. Talleyrand was furious. Wieland (*Bürgermeister* of Basel), speaking for his delegation, replied that Switzerland did not approve of the exclusion of France from discussion of the problems at issue. France, represented in the debates by the Duke of Dalberg, was soon admitted. Dalberg advised the conferees that he was authorized to agree to the cession of part of the Pays de Gex to Switzerland provided that Aargau was given to Bern. And then he added the significant remark: "It is necessary to close this country entirely and to protect it completely from war. Switzerland ought to be everybody's Fatherland."[29]

Much that Switzerland desired was granted by the Powers represented in the Vienna Congress, in some cases as promises or declarations of intent which would require subsequent ratification or reconsideration by the Powers. Unanimity prevailed that the independence and perpetual neutrality of Switzerland must be recognized and guaranteed, that the Bishopric of Basel must be restored, partly under the sovereignty of Basel and partly under Bern, and that certain indemnities must be granted to the Confederation. Geneva was united with her various enclaves, free communication with Vaud was assured; corresponding freedom of access to Valais was granted by the Simplon route. The neutralization of Chablais and Faucigny and certain concessions with respect to the Pays de Gex helped to round out Geneva's frontier and to provide a protective shield in the event of war. Her admission to the Swiss Confederation as the 22nd canton was formally approved. Valais was likewise admitted to the Confederation and Neuchâtel's admission was approved by the Powers and agreed to by the sovereign prince, the King of Prussia, whose ties to the canton were not completely severed until 1857.

But there was much that was lost and requests that were denied. Most painful of all was the loss of Bormio, Chiavenna and the Valtellina which were torn from the Graubünden and, in effect, transferred to Austria. With this, the former Italian frontier was not re-established except for the Ticino-Italian frontier, Ticino having already been restored to Switzerland. The Swiss request to admit Constance, already joined to Thurgau by the bridge at Kreuzlingen, to the Swiss Confederation fell upon deaf ears.

The Hundred Days

With alarm and fear of catastrophe, the conferees learned that Napoleon had escaped from Elba on March 1 and, after landing at Cannes, had speedily raised an army for a march on Paris and overthrow of the restored Bourbon monarchy. The Powers issued a declaration of war on March 7 and the Confederation, a few days later, sent 15,000 men to protect her borders to the west. Deeply worried over the unexpected turn of events and the uncertain position of the Swiss Guard regiment, the Diet sent another contingent of 15,000 men to the western frontiers and named the 75-year-old Niklaus Franz Bachmann as General and Commander-in-Chief.

In realization of the overwhelming importance of putting an end to Bonaparte, the Diet finally departed from its historic policy of strict neutrality to which it had stubbornly adhered almost to the very end. It accepted a formal military alliance with the Allies.[30] In June, with the *Durchmarsch* now permitted, the allies sent an army through the Valais and other contingents through Basel territory into Alsace. The Diet next empowered General Bachmann on 3 July 1815 to cross the northwesterly frontier in a move against the fortified city of Besançon. The instructions to General Bachmann contained no reference to Swiss neutrality: offensive military action against the French was to be initiated—clearly incompatible with the behaviour of a Neutral. Of principal importance appeared to be a strengthening of the security of regained Swiss territory, and preserving untarnished the independence and the honor of the Confederation.[31] Six of the cantons voted against this action of the Diet for any of several reasons: deep reluctance to abandon even temporarily the time-honored policy of strict neutrality; opposition to the march of allied forces (largely Austrian) through their particular canton; and, finally, the news of Napoleon's decisive defeat at Waterloo some two weeks earlier gave to the prospective siege of Besançon the less-than-honorable appearance of beating a man who is already down and out.

Furthermore the army was miserably prepared.[32] The country's defenses were disorganized and deplorably weak. The arsenal at Chur was empty, Schwyz lacked munitions and the Ticino suffered both from depleted arsenals and a lack of munitions. According to Chapuisat (**84**) a Swiss officer wrote from Valais, "We lack rifles and cannon." The campaign added nothing of lustre to Switzerland's military history. The Doubs river border had hardly been approached before a brigade mutinied rather than cross the river into France. After the troublesome mutiny was settled the troops were used only for the occupation of the Pays de Gex and a town in the French Jura. Bachmann was recalled and he and Castella (his chief of staff) were dismissed.

Other units of the army participated in the siege of Hüningen in mid-August. At the end of the month the garrison of the fortress surrendered. The buildings were occupied by the victors and eventually razed to the ground. Napoleon was taken prisoner shortly after the battle of Waterloo (June 18). In the meantime, after ruling for 100 days, he abdicated in favor of his son (June 22) and was banished to the island of St. Helena.

The Final Act of the Congress of Vienna (The Second Treaty of Paris)

The Congress of the Powers, interrupted by the return of Napoleon from Elba, reconvened in Paris in August 1815. Apart from the final confirmation of a number of tentative decisions and the disposition of many detailed matters carried over from the two previous sessions in Paris and Vienna, the most important acts involving Switzerland pertained to the formal recognition of its independence, its perpetual neutrality, and the inviolability of its territory.

The importance of the final Act is apparent from the following excerpts taken from the translation laid before the British Parliament (Hertslet, **172**).

> The Accession of Switzerland to the Declaration published at Vienna the 20th March, 1815,[33] . . . having been duly notified to the Ministers . . . there remained nothing to prevent the Act of Acknowledgement and Guarantee of the perpetual Neutrality of Switzerland from being made conformable to the above-mentioned Declaration . . . the Powers who signed the Declaration of Vienna of the 20th March declare, by this present Act, their formal and authentic Acknowledgment of the perpetual Neutrality of Switzerland; and they Guarantee to that country the Integrity and Inviolability of its Territory in its new limits, such as they are fixed, as well by the Act of the Congress of Vienna (No. 27) as by the Treaty of Paris of this day (No. 40), and such as they will be hereafter. . . . The Protocol of the 3rd November . . . stipulates in favour of the Helvetic Body a new increase of Territory to be taken from Savoy, in order to disengage from Enclaves, and complete the circle of the Canton of Geneva.
>
> The Powers acknowledge likewise and guarantee the Neutrality of those parts of Savoy designated by the Act of the Congress of Vienna of the 20th May, 1815 (No. 19), and by the Treaty of Paris of this day (No. 40), the same being entitled to participate in the Neutrality of Switzerland, equally as if they belonged to that country.
>
> The Powers who signed the Declaration of the 20th of March (No. 9) acknowledge, in the most formal manner, by the present Act, that the Neutrality and Inviolability of Switzerland, and her Independence of all foreign influence, enter into the true interests of the policy of the whole of Europe.
>
> . . . no consequence unfavourable to the rights of Switzerland . . . can or ought to be drawn from the events which led to the passage of the Allied Troops across a part of the Helvetic States. This passage, freely consented to by the Cantons in the Convention of the 20th May, was the necessary result of the free adherence of Swtitzerland to the principles manifested by the Powers who signed the Treaty of Alliance of the 25th March.
>
> . . . in fine, Switzerland has deserved the advantages which have been secured to her, whether by the Arrangements of the Congress of Vienna (No. 27), by the Treaty of Paris of this day (No. 40), or by the present Act, to which all the Powers in Europe are invited to accede.[34]

The Declaration was signed 20 November 1815 by the accredited representatives of Austria, France, Great Britain, Prussia and Russia.

It is of considerable interest that the important section on Switzerland (third paragraph above) was drafted by the Swiss delegate, Pictet de Rochemont. How this came about is not entirely clear. One interpretation says in effect that the delegates of the Powers became so bogged down in trying to reach an accord on the wording of the draft that they entrusted the task to Lord Castlereagh (Great Britain) and the Count of Capo d'Istria (Russia). These two turned to Pictet, apparently because they found themselves under the heavy pressure of other obligations. Obviously they had great respect for Pictet's integrity and competence, realizing also that Pictet had sat in on all of the debates and must have sensed quite well what the conferees were trying to achieve. From Pictet's correspondence (Pictet, **291**) we learn (pp. 316–17) that "in the declaration of March 20, they [the conferees] promised to prepare an authentic instrument for the solemn recognition of the neutrality of Switzerland . . . Castlereagh, in agreement with Capo d'Istria has requested me to prepare a draft of this solemn Act." The next day Pictet added "My draft of the Act carrying recognition and guarantee of Swiss neutrality is approved. . . . I have introduced in it a phrase intended to firmly establish that it is in the interest of the whole of Europe that no foreign Power [enjoy the right] to exercise any influence in Swiss affairs."

Something must be said about the guarantee by the Powers of the "Integrity and Inviolability of [Swiss] Territory" and the guarantee of her perpetual neutrality. Pictet and his colleagues probably had their doubts about such guarantees which could be construed as an open invitation to the Powers to intervene in Swiss affairs whenever they believed that Swiss domestic and foreign policies endangered the balance of power and the harmony of the European States. Had Pictet excluded these guarantees from his draft of the final Act, he would have thrown open the whole question of the recognition of Swiss independence, territorial integrity, and neutrality to renewed debate. The guarantees, in fact, had already been determined and agreed to by the Powers in their Declaration of 20 March 1815.[35] On 19 December 1814 Capo d'Istria of Russia drafted a proposed treaty by which the Powers would promise "to recognize the independence and neutrality of the Helvetic Body." This followed upon a Swiss request to the Powers "that the independence and neutrality of Switzerland be recognized." A "final" report by the Powers of 16 January 1815 included a pledge to "recognize the perpetual neutrality of the Helvetic Body." But Austria—unquestionably Metternich was the responsible party—included in a counterpledge in February 1815, the idea of a guarantee by all of the Powers. In any case intervention, on any grounds whatever, was exactly what the Swiss wanted to avoid, as we shall see later.

The Treaty of Turin

The Second Treaty of Paris still left open some of the problems pertinent to Savoy, Geneva and the Swiss Confederation. The Swiss Confederation and the Canton of Geneva appointed Pictet de Rochemont as their envoy plenipotentiary to meet in Turin with the accredited representatives of the King of Sardinia in an effort to resolve these problems. Partial or provisional solutions had been agreed upon between the Powers in Protocols of 30 May 1814 (No. 1), 29 March 1815 (No. 10), and 3 November 1815 (No. 38). Discussions had also taken place between Geneva and Sardinia prior to the Turin Conference. The Treaty of Turin, concluded 16

March 1816, established the political frontiers of the canton of Geneva. They have remained almost unchanged since that date. The canton still has sovereignty over two small enclaves, Céligny and La Coudre, in the canton of Vaud. Free trade zones were established reaching into Savoy at least three miles beyond the political frontier.[36] The Acts of the Congress of Vienna (29 March 1815) and of the Second Treaty of Paris (20 November 1815) relative to the neutrality of the upper Savoy provinces of Chablais and Faucigny were also made a part of the Treaty of Turin. The parts of Savoy so designated were to enjoy the benefits of Swiss neutrality "in the same manner as if they belonged to Switzerland." The Treaty provided also for freedom of communication, of travel, and of commerce between Savoy and Geneva. Of considerable importance was the agreement on protection of the rights of the many catholics, absorbed into Geneva on cession of numerous Savoy communities, to continue to practice freely and unhindered the catholic religion, subject only to the external authority of the Holy See. Privileges hitherto granted to charitable foundations and institutions for public instruction, existing within the territories ceded by Savoy, were to be preserved. Public debts referable to the ceded territories were henceforth to be a public charge against Geneva. It was further agreed that 100,000 pounds be paid by Geneva to Sardinia to permit construction or improvement of the route between lower Savoy and Chablais.[37] The Treaty, consisting of 24 Articles, was signed on 16 March 1816. The next day King Victor Emmanuel of Sardinia gave to Pictet a handsome golden box decorated with the King's portrait and diamonds (Chapuisat, **84**).

Neutrality

What can be said about the neutrality of Switzerland, her independence, the integrity and inviolability of her territory, and her relations with the European Powers during these extraordinarily difficult years? For fifteen years everything appeared to be lost. The Confederation was totally at the mercy of a foreign despot whose policy was to break the spirit of its people, to impair its capability of defense, and to weaken drastically its economic and military potential. Early in 1793, the northern half of the Bishopric of Basel was occupied by the troops and administrative officers of Napoleonic France. True, this territory had not been within the protective embrace of Swiss neutrality and for six years the Swiss were lulled into the belief that Napoleon intended to respect their neutrality.

Why did Napoleon finally invade Switzerland? And, why did he temporize until 1798 before striking the fatal blow? Actually, he had no respect for Swiss neutrality. On several occasions he declared that he would use the Swiss and their neutrality to the advantage of France whenever he saw fit to do so. But he had good reasons in 1793 for preferring a neutral Switzerland. By the spring of that year the original coalition of Prussia, Austria and Sardinia against Napoleon had greatly expanded. Only from the Swiss side could be procure the vast quantities of supplies needed to sustain France and to supply his armies: the allied Powers had already imposed such a strong blockade that a "neutral" Switzerland in the service of France resulted. A neutral Switzerland had served Napoleon well for five or more years and a neutral

Switzerland, committed to the defense of her borders, would be of continuing value as a great protective shield against those enemies, especially Austria, who might otherwise be disposed to attack France through Swiss territory.

In 1797, Austria made a separate peace (Campoformio) with France.[38] Other considerations that spelled an end to any lip service by France to Switzerland's neutrality now became paramount. Although the whole of Vaud had fallen under French influence and partial occupation, and Savoy, Piedmont and lower Valais were also in the hands of the invader, and Geneva fell in April 1798, it was clear to the French and Swiss alike that the occupation of all Switzerland would facilitate the annexation by France of several strategically or economically important areas. Finally, through the occupation and subjugation of Switzerland this small and sometimes troublesome neighbour would come under Napoleon's total control. The economy of the country, its military potential and its foreign policy could then be manipulated and managed to the exclusive advantage of France.

In falling under the "protection" of France, Switzerland became a vassal State. Only five months after the fall of Bern, the firm and long-continued commitment of the Confederation to neutrality suffered a severe blow. On 24 August 1798 she was forced to sign a treaty whereby Napoleon was enabled to use Swiss troops in warfare in any way he saw fit. The important principle of restricting the use of Swiss mercenaries to defensive operations was shattered. Realistically, Switzerland suffered a total loss of both her independence and her neutrality. To suggest that any vestige of either remained would be pure fiction. Amendment of the treaty by stripping it of Article 2, which permitted the use of Swiss troops in offense, and of Article 5 which required, for French army use, Swiss construction and maintenance of two military highways leading to Austria and to Italy, was widely and insistently demanded throughout the Confederation. But these demands of the people and representations to Napoleon by the Swiss Ambassador in Paris were to no avail. With the Act of Mediation in February 1803 the "one and indivisible" Helvetic Republic became a thing of the past. Whatever betterment this brought to Switzerland was insufficient, if not trivial. Her independence and neutrality continued to be an illusion, since she and the constituent cantons could enter into capitulation agreements and foreign treaties only with France.

The military campaigns in Europe, beginning with the first declaration of war against Napoleon, did not constitute a single war that went on and on until its formal termination in 1815. What we have seen was a series of wars, interrupted by treaties of peace of brief duration. They provided the combatants with breathing periods and opportunities to prepare for the next round. Switzerland, professing stubbornly that she was still a Neutral, as she had been for 300 years, kept pace with the belligerents' affirmations of their return to peace and friendship by issuing declarations of neutrality in 1796, 1805, 1809, 1813, 1830 and 1870. These declarations, affirmations and re-affirmations of neutrality differed little in content from the proclamations of the Diet in 1702, 1733, 1735 and 1743. In general, they declared the intention of the Confederation to treat the belligerents impartially, to maintain an exact neutrality, to deny *Durchzug* rights to the armies of all foreign

Powers, and to defend her borders vigorously against forced entry by any belligerent. The integrity of her territory and its inviolability would be stoutly defended, and, as appears in several of the proclamations, "Force will be met by force."

The declarations issued during the days of Napoleon meant nothing to the Emperor of the French. He was a ruthless despot. His armies entered Switzerland, occupied Swiss territory, or returned to France whenever he chose. His political agents imposed their will upon the Federal and cantonal governments. His prefects governed the annexed territories. The several proclamations of Swiss neutrality were regarded by Napoleon as "empty words." Nonetheless he tolerated, and probably approved of, the declarations for he knew they would impose no restraints on his own freedom of action but they might be helpful in restraining his enemies from launching through Switzerland an attack on his southeastern flank.

By 1813 the fortunes of war had changed mightily. The Russian campaign of 1812 had come to a disastrous end. The Swiss neutrality declaration dated 18 November 1813 followed by only a few weeks the decisive defeat of Napoleon at Leipzig.

The Swiss ambassadors in Paris and Vienna received instructions to advise the Emperor of the French and the allied monarchs, respectively, of the November declaration of Swiss neutrality. This unusual resort to personal missions at the ambassadorial level was probably designed to indicate Swiss determination to be impartial toward the belligerents. One can hardly escape the conclusion that however polite the allied monarchs may have been in their acknowledgements, they knew quite well that Swiss foreign policy was not strictly impartial and that the complete and exact neutrality alleged to be in force was in fact a mere shadow of the real thing.

What is to be found in this Declaration of Neutrality that would cause the belligerents, especially the Allied Powers, to write it off as of no importance? Let us consider the Declaration:

> "The Swiss Confederation . . . envisages as its most sacred duty to remain absolutely neutral in the present war, and to carry out loyally and impartially the obligations of this neutrality towards all the belligerent Powers. In order to sustain this neutrality and to maintain order in the full extent of Swiss territory, the Diet has determined to occupy its frontiers with Confederation troops and to defend through [force of] arms the security and inviolability of its territory. . . . The Diet is inspired with full confidence that they [the Imperial and Royal Courts] will give to the generals commanding their armies the most precise orders to leave Swiss territory intact, and not to permit in any case . . . passage through Swiss territory."[16]

The Allied Powers and their generals, with an enormous army, knew perfectly well that the troops of the Confederation, greatly inferior in numerical strength and in weaponry, could not prevent the allies from marching through Swiss territory. And the Swiss general staff was also fully aware of its unpreparedness to put up an effective resistance. Furthermore, the Declaration was signed by Reinhard as *Landammann* of Switzerland, who was well known to be so pro-Napoleonic, possibly through timidity and fear, that any pledge of absolute neutrality and impartiality issued over his signature and under his leadership would be honored only in the breach. The Declaration would be nothing more than a scrap of paper.

Why did the Diet even bother to issue such a Declaration if it knew full well that the proclamation could have no deterrent value against the belligerents? It was certainly influenced by strong public opinion that Swiss neutrality be preserved as in the past 300 years: the Declaration, according to its prefatory paragraph, was issued as a unanimous decision of the Diet, which was probably guided by historical precedents. Every war in the seventeenth and eighteenth centuries in which the Confederation's powerful neighbours were involved led to a prompt declaration of neutrality by the Diet.

The generals of the Allied Powers were under no illusions as to the real state of affairs in Switzerland and, determined to bring the war to a speedy and decisive end, resolved to lead their armies through Swiss territory. In this top-secret decision they had the moral support of large elements of the population of the German States among whom it was being said that the "do-nothing neutrality of the Swiss was ridiculous; it was a state of nullity rather than neutrality, a form of political sleeping sickness" (quoted by Bonjour, **49**, I, p. 174). Writers and publicists within the German States described Swiss neutrality as something despicable which Switzerland, to its everlasting shame, had used to protect it from the hard realities of existence as a nation. Some clamored for absorption of Switzerland within the German *Reich* as another member of the family of German States (**169**). This idea of annexation to Germany received no support from Metternich who nourished the hope that Austria in the post-Napoleonic period would replace France as the great ally, protector and friend of Switzerland.

Neither the Proclamation of 21 December 1813 addressed to the Swiss people by the Commander-in-Chief of the Grand Allied Army nor his Order-of-the-Day addressed to his troops has anything to say about neutrality. In contrast it is worth noting what the Austrian and Russian plenipotentiaries had to say about the subject in their Declaration of 20 December to the Landammann of Switzerland:

> The sovereigns require that . . . Switzerland, through the re-establishment of its former boundaries, recover the means of maintaining [its] independence; but they are unable to recognize a neutrality which, in view of Switzerland's political relations, exists only in name. . . . Their Majesties will not involve themselves in the internal government of Switzerland, but they can no longer permit it to remain subject to a foreign influence. They will recognize its neutrality from the day when it will be free and independent.[39]

In their Declaration of 21 December the Allied Powers had much more to say:

> Switzerland is so little in this state [legitimate and true neutrality] that all the principles of the Rights of Man authorize [us] to regard as nul that which today she calls her neutrality. . . . The pretended neutrality of a State which is not casually directed, but which is regularly governed by a foreign influence, is in itself a word devoid of meaning . . . this fictitious neutrality serves as a rampart of injustice, and becomes an obstacle to the projects of those who want to establish a better order of things; it ought to disappear at the same time as the source of the evil that it protects . . . Switzerland, under the

Constitution [Act of Mediation, 1803], which was presented to it has become . . . a veritable province of the French Empire . . . a Declaration of Neutrality which issues from such a source loses every right to the name by which it wishes to protect itself. . . . The Allied Sovereigns declare that as soon as the moment will have arrived, at which they will be able to negotiate the General Peace, they will devote all their attention and all their care to the interest of the Swiss Nation, and will not regard as satisfactory any Peace in which the future political state of Switzerland will not be ruled according to the principles which have just been set forth, assured for the time to come, and formally recognized and guaranteed by all the European Powers.[40]

After the Battle of Leipzig, and again following the final defeat of Napoleon at Waterloo in 1815, political activity between the Allied Powers and Switzerland rose to fever heat. On both occasions the Allies spared no efforts, including diplomatic subterfuge, lies, and ill-concealed cover-ups, either to draw Switzerland into the war as a military ally or to cast Swiss neutrality to the winds and carry the war into her territory. By the same token, the Swiss, faced with conflicting pressures from all sides—within their country and from without—and caught in the middle of political turmoil, repeatedly compromised their status as a professed Neutral.

Can we draw up a meaningful balance sheet in which gains and losses are weighed against each other for these two decades of Swiss history? Were one to attempt such a task he could only conclude that the gains, in the retrospect of almost 200 years, far outweigh the losses. Territorial changes may have little to do with neutrality, except from the not unimportant problem of capability for defense on which the security, independence and territorial inviolability of the Neutral may depend. Nonetheless, we must recognize that a Confederation of thirteen cantons in the 1790s became greatly expanded into one of twenty-two federated cantons in 1815. True, the Valtellina, Bormio and Chiavenna and several peripheral and isolated possessions such as Mülhausen were lost.

The political gains were enormous. The formal recognition by the allied Powers in 1815 "that the Neutrality and Inviolability of Switzerland, and her Independence of all foreign influence, enter into the true interests of the . . . whole of Europe" was a great and enduring victory[41] for which Charles Pictet de Rochemont deserves much of the credit. The guarantees mentioned elsewhere in the Final Act of 20 November 1815, and again in the Treaty of Versailles, were not to Switzerland's liking. But not many years were to pass before the implied threat and fears of possible interference by the great Powers in Switzerland's foreign and domestic affairs subsided.

It can be argued that the Declarations of Neutrality issued by the Diet during this period were not what they purported to be and that Switzerland might better have suffered in silence. Admittedly she did not observe a strict and exact neutrality, behaving impartially toward both sides and not favoring one over the other. But between 1798 and 1813 she was so chained to France that her foreign and domestic policies were dictated by Napoleon Bonaparte and her economy was forced into the exclusive service of France. And she was quite incapable of mounting an adequate defense of her frontiers, despite her piously declared intention to do so.

The capitulation of von Wattenwyl in 1813, his failure to resist to the death the allied invasion, was not the act of a Winkelried or of any legendary hero of the past. The surrender of neutrality in 1815[30] and the dubious effort of Bachmann to lead an army into France after Napoleon was already beaten added nothing to the honor and glory of Switzerland. If these were errors in judgment they reflect a distressing, but almost inevitable, lack of strong leadership in a country which was fatigued, exhausted, despoiled and deliberately weakened by almost two decades of enslavement to Napoleonic France. The events cited have long since been forgotten and the extent to which they lastingly tarnished the honor and reputation of the country is almost negligible.

It is also self-evident that the Swiss learned much, and this was a real gain, during those difficult years. Perhaps they had to suffer through the five years of the "one and indivisible Republic" to learn that for Switzerland, federalism rather than centralism is a far better form of government, appropriate to a people divided by language, by origin, and by deeply rooted cultural differences. Perhaps also these years of travail were necessary to abolish some of the social injustices attributable to an excess of special privilege. As we shall see, the Swiss still had much to learn in the fine art of living harmoniously together, in maintaining internal peace, and in gaining the full respect of other nations near and far.

Notes and Comments

1. *Aktensammlung aus der Zeit der Helvetika* I, 567–587, and addendum (pp. 587–92), 28 March 1798.

2. *Aktensammlung* II, 884–89, 19 August 1798.

3. The Earl of Minto in a letter (4 December 1799 to William Wickham, then the British Envoy Extraordinaire attached to the allied armies) described Suvarov in most unflattering terms: "Instead of a great general and a great man, I find an ignorant designing mountebank, besides being very mad and very mischievous as madmen generally are" (Wickham, **387**, II, 340). The letter expresses the anger and disappointment in British government circles over Suvarov's return to Russia with his army and the resultant serious weakening of the Austro-Russian forces in combat with the French.

4. Charles Maurice de Talleyrand (1754–1838). Created Duke of Talleyrand-Périgord in 1807. Studied theology and became Bishop of Trèves, later Archbishop of Lyon and Bishop of Autun. Gifted in financial matters and interested in speculations, he became Agent General of the clergy, and Administrator of the Properties of the Church of France. With even greater skills in diplomacy he served as deputy of the clergy to the Estates General of 1789. Talleyrand eulogized the new "social contract" of 1791 and was sent to England in the name of Louis XVI to gain British neutrality. This he failed to achieve and was equally unsuccessful in a second mission in the following year. He was forced to leave France in 1792 because of his suspected friendliness with the dethroned King of France. He went to England and lived briefly in London in exile. After the death of Louis XVI, Pitt declared war on France. Talleyrand, then in London, stayed on for a time but eventually had to leave, as did all French citizens who were officially suspect. He went to America in exile and spent his time in financial speculations. In late 1796 he was permitted to return to France.

As the most worldly of all prelates, lively, vivacious, and a "big spender," Talleyrand frequented the balls, the gay affairs, and enjoyed the friendship of the ladies surrounding the Directory. Madame de Staehl had him appointed Minister of Foreign Affairs in 1797. He raised vast sums of money for the Directory, using any means whatever, usually unscrupulous in the extreme. He praised and extolled Napoleon, flattered and fawned upon him, and carried out the political and administrative preparations for Napoleon's Egyptian campaign. He negotiated the Peace of Lunéville with Austria, the Peace of Paris with Russia, and the Peace of Amiens with England. During Napoleon's splendid years (1805, 1806)

Talleyrand completed with consummate skill the groundwork for the Confederation of the Rhine: Bavaria, Baden, Württemberg, etc. And while Napoleon fought Austria, Talleyrand succeeded in maintaining Prussia in a neutral position. Despite his proneness to associate only with conquerors he foresaw the end of Napoleon and, in good time, collected around himself an influential group opposed to the Emperor of the French. After Napoleon's downfall Talleyrand bent his efforts to achieve a return of the Bourbons. He solidified France's position at the Vienna Congress and succeeded in minimizing her loss of territory. He served as Foreign Minister during the "Hundred Days," but was forced by Louis XVIII to retire in 1815. In 1830 he supported Louis Philippe's claim to the throne and served from 1830 to 1834 as ambassador to the Court of St. James. The successful outcome of Anglo-French collaboration in establishing the Kingdom of Belgium through separation of the territory from Holland was largely due to Talleyrand's skills.

He should not be confused with his cousin, Count Augustin Louis de Talleyrand (1770–1832), a contemporary, who was appointed by Napoleon as Minister plenipotentiary in Baden and subsequently as Ambassador to Switzerland.

5. *Aktensammlung* V, 829–32, 6 March 1800, "Rapport du ministre Talleyrand au premier Consul sur la mission du cit. Reinhard en Suisse."

6. Napoleon discussed with a Swiss delegation the constitution proposed by the Swiss. After stating that he did not believe very much in the usefulness of constitutions, Napoleon is reported to have said: "You are independent; you are able to constitute yourselves as you believe to be appropriate." Napoleon went on to say that the constitution they proposed was bad. It would be alright for China, France, or any other country but it was not appropriate for a country as unique as Switzerland (**259**, p. 457).

7. Alois von Reding (1755–1818). Retired as a colonel in the army in 1788 and became *Landammann* of Schwyz. In 1798 the French forces swept over Lucerne and Zug and menaced the whole of Schwyz. Six hundred men from Uri and some from Zug joined the 650 from Schwyz. Under the command of Reding all swore solemnly to fight to the death—never to retreat. The French, in superior numbers, were driven from the field. Though the victory was only temporary, the courage of the defenders so favorably impressed General Schauenburg that an armistice under terms favorable to Schwyz was arranged. In return for formal submission to the new Helvetic Constitution, Schwyz was assured under guarantees of France that there would be no levies of men or of money in the canton. Freedom to practice their religion, safety of its persons, conservation of its arms, and preservation of property and property rights were all guaranteed. In November, 1801, von Reding was named *Landammann* of Switzerland which meant head of government for the Helvetic Republic. Disillusioned by the intrigues of those of his countrymen who favored the one and indivisible government which had been forced upon the Fatherland, he headed once again the confederates in Schwyz. Troops were sent against them several times by the central government of the Helvetic Republic and were defeated by the Confederates on each occasion. Reding and others were arrested by the French General Ney and imprisoned in the fortress of Aarburg. He was set free after a few months. The Act of Mediation came in 1803 and ended some of the worst abuses. Reding was again elected *Landammann* of Schwyz and named as its representative in the Diet. After the events of 1812 and 1813 he no longer concealed his hatred of Napoleon and joined with many of his countrymen in endeavours to end forever any resumption of power by this tyrant and oppressor.

8. *Aktensammlung* VII, 365, 8 July 1802.

9. *Aktensammlung* VIII, 1437–38, 30 September 1802.

10. *Repertorium der Abschiede der eidg. Tagsatzungen* (1803–13), 2nd Edition, pp. 395–494. This includes the Act of Mediation, the Constitutions of the 19 cantons and the Constitution of the Confederation.

11. *Aktensammlung* IX, 10, Beginning of October 1802.

12. *Aktensammlung* IX, 882, 12 December 1802.

13. *Repertorium* (1803–13) pp. 785, 786, 23 September 1805.

14. Stapfer, Philipp Albrecht (1766–1840); Studied in Bern and Göttingen; 1798–1800. Minister of Public Instruction in the Helvetic Republic; 1801, Appointed Swiss Minister Plenipotentiary in Paris; 1804, Retired to private life in Paris; 1815, Elected to the Great Council of Aargau; 1817, Returned to Paris.

15. The Russian army wanted only to get to Paris. It has been said (Pictet, **291**) that the soldiers knew only two words of French: "*bruler Paris*" (burn Paris).

16. "The Diet has concluded . . . to man the Swiss borders with federal troops and to defend with arms the security and the inviolability of its territory . . ." (*Repertorium* (1803–13) p. 786, 18 November 1813).

17. Switzerland appoints a general, a Commander-in-Chief of its armies, only when endangered by a war in neighbouring countries.

18. From the time of François I, neutrality was a fundamental principle of the alliance of the Swiss with the French Crown. The treaty, concluded in 1803, reaffirmed and consecrated it anew; "we remain ever faithful to our national precepts in declaring today to observe toward all Powers, in the most absolute and impartial sense, this same neutrality, on which rests our political existence" (*Repertorium* 1803–1813, p. 787, 18 November 1813).

19. *British State Papers* **1**, 1162–69, 20–21 December 1813.

20. *British State Papers* **1**, 1170–71, 31 December 1813.

21. *British State Papers* **1**, 1171–72, 4 January 1814.

22. The two Federal Pacts referred to are set forth in *British State Papers* **1**, 1172–77, 16 August 1814 and **3**, 803–09, 7 August 1815.

23. Switzerland was on the point of moving an occupation force into the disputed areas but was "outfoxed" by the Austrians (**259**, Appendix 17). On 6 May 1814, the Diet named Colonel von Hauser as commander of the forces who were to occupy Bormio, Chiavenna and the Valtellina. The Diet also requested the high officers of the allied forces to recognize Colonel Hauser in the capacity stated. On the same day, von Reinhard, as President of the Diet, advised the ministers of the Allied Powers (Austria, Prussia, Russia) by letter that Colonel Hauser's command was en route through the Graubünden; further that "in consequence of declarations of the high Powers that Bormio, Chiavenna, and the Valtellina should be restored to Switzerland, the Diet has decided upon a military occupation of these territories." A few days later the government received the unexpected news that a large Austrian force had moved into the disputed area. On May 11 the ministers of the Allied Powers were informed by the Swiss that there must surely be a misunderstanding since the sovereigns of the high Allied Powers had expressly invited Switzerland to occupy these provinces with their forces. On May 17 the Austrian commander advised Reinhard that he and his troops would leave as soon as he received the necessary orders from his king and emperor (**259**, Appendix 17). Needless to say the orders were not received and the Austrians continued in occupation of the provinces. The question remains whether it might not have been wiser for the Swiss to have moved their troops into the area without any prior declarations of intent, the first of which was in April. There was too much talk, too little action, and excessive caution by the Swiss. The Austrians had acted promptly and without prior warning or diplomatic niceties.

24. *British State Papers* **2**, 1060–63, 18 June 1814.

25. Charles Pictet de Rochemont (1755–1824). Pictet's father (Charles senior), a colonel, was active in military affairs, notably in organizing an army corps of 3000 of his countrymen for service abroad under a typical capitulation agreement which carried a personal honorarium of seven guineas per man. The son, Charles, was in military service from 1775 to 1785 and retired with the rank of major.

In 1762, Rousseau's *Contrat social* and *Emile* were published. Both in Paris and Geneva, and later in Bern, the authorities ordered that the books be burned. The district attorney of Geneva in 1763 described them as "bold, scandalous, impious and tending to destroy the Christian religion and all governments" (**27**). In the meantime, Rousseau found himself obliged to flee in all haste from France. He took refuge in Môtier, in the Principality of Neuchâtel. Although the father of Charles Pictet criticized parts of *Contrat social* he vigorously deplored a decree of the *Petit conseil* of Geneva whereby these works of Rousseau were condemned as being inflammatory and revolutionary. One month later (23 July 1762), the Council censured Colonel Pictet and ordered that his letter in defense of Rousseau be destroyed in his presence, that he be suspended for two years from membership in the Grand Council of 200 and from the bourgeoisie and that he be fined. The letter was not destroyed and is still in the archives of Geneva (**368**). Rousseau wrote a touching letter of gratitude to Colonel Pictet and then renounced his Geneva citizenship.

For 12 years, with a single exception in February 1770, Colonel Pictet refused to participate in the meetings of the Council of 200.

The son, Charles, married in 1786. Within the family, the father (Colonel Pictet) was a strict disciplinarian and was accustomed to unquestioning obedience. He attached a high value to a good education and provided for his children the best schooling that was possible. The children were required to be diligent and to make profitable use of their time.

In 1792 Geneva surrendered to the armed revolutionaries among its citizens and on 27 December the Small Council held its last meeting. Charles Pictet (the son), then the auditor, and the other officers of State were dismissed by the citizens with the *bonnet rouge*—the revolutionary egalitarians. He retired from public life for the next 20 years and devoted himself to agriculture, with a special interest in raising pure-bred Merino sheep. This was a profitable enterprise. He sold 900 to Alexander I of Russia who agreed to advance 50,000 roubles and to provide Pictet with 13,000 hectares of land near Odessa for use as a breeding ground.

In 1796 Pictet founded the *Bibliothèque britannique* which was devoted to inventions and discoveries of practical importance to mankind. Two collaborators assisted in the enterprise: Marc Auguste Pictet (brother of Charles) and Frédéric Guillaume Maurice. The three worked together for 29 years. The publication was eventually split into two: *Archives des sciences physiques et naturelles* (which was changed to *Archives des sciences* in 1948 and continues to appear) and the *Bibliothèque universelle* which experienced several minor changes in name and terminated its long career in 1930. By promising to refrain from politics, the *Bibliothèque britannique* was permitted to continue publication throughout the French occupation and Charles Pictet was allowed to visit England from time to time to collect material for publication.

In 1814 Pictet returned to politics as Geneva's delegate to the Congress of Vienna. He represented Switzerland as minister plenipotentiary at Paris in 1815 and Turin in 1816. He published anonymously in 1821 a remarkable article entitled "De la Suisse dans l'intérêt de l'Europe," designed as a reply to a provocative, if not threatening, speech by General Sebastiani, the French Minister of War. French newspapers were not allowed to print or to mention the Pictet article. Two years later it appeared over Pictet's name with an expanded title (**289**).

26. In early January, 1814, the Diet and several of the Cantons sent delegates to Basel for a preliminary conference with various heads of State. Alexander I of Russia was received with enthusiasm by the Swiss as he expressed to the delegates his displeasure that the neutrality of their country had been violated by the army of the allies (which included his own divisions). He urged the Confederation to present before Europe a stable internal organization and a Constitution adapted to the new circumstances within a rapidly changing Europe. The emperor's views carried great weight and he was hailed in Geneva as a protagonist of the city's hopes and aspirations. On the Swiss side the tsar was supported strongly by Frédéric César de la Harpe (his one-time tutor), representing Vaud, and Charles Pictet de Rochemont. Geneva sent two other delegates to Basel—Saladin de Budé (secretary) and the syndic, Des Artes. Pictet promoted the ideas of those who favored a liberalization and modernization of the country. Des Artes, a reactionary, was a representative of the past.

27. Swiss troops entered Geneva on 1 June 1814 and were enthusiastically greeted by the people. On 12 September 1814 the Diet voted to accept the Republic of Geneva within the Swiss Confederation. The Act of Union, consisting of six brief Articles, was signed by the two parties on 19 May 1815, having already received approval by the Powers in a Declaration of 20 March 1815 and the Protocols of 29 March.

28. *Abschiede* VI. 2, 347h, 2–18 July 1690; 355g, 4–24 August 1690; VI. 2 1140–41b, 13 April 1704; VI. 2,1143a,14–15 May 1704.

29. "Il faut fermer entièrement ce pays et la mettre tout à fait à l'abri de la guerre. La Suisse doit être la patrie de tout le monde" (Chapuisat, **84**).

30. A Declaration by the plenipotentiaries of the eight Powers assembled at Vienna states their readiness "to give to the King of France [Louis XVIII] and to the French nation, or to any other government which will be attacked . . . all the assistance necessary to reestablish tranquillity, and to make common cause against all those who attempt to endanger it" (*British State Papers* **2**, 665—66, 13 March

1815). On March 25, Great Britain, Austria, Prussia and Russia signed a formal military alliance ". . . against the designs of Napoleon Bonaparte and . . . agreed to keep constantly in the field, each a force of 150,000 men complete . . . and to employ the same actively and conjointly against the common enemy" (*British State Papers* 2, 443–449, 25 March 1815). In response to an invitation (25 March) by the four Powers, the royal government of France acceded to the Treaty of Alliance two days later. Urged by the "Big Four" (25 March) to join the other European Powers in adhering to the alliance, the Diet responded (12 May) by pointing out that their most effective assistance would be through the energetic defense of their own frontiers, and in so doing it would not be isolating Switzerland from the common cause. But on 20 May, Switzerland signed a Treaty of Accession. A proclamation of the Diet on 10 June called the Swiss soldiers "brothers-in-arms of the Allied troops" (**139**).

By this treaty, Switzerland, which already had 30,000 men in the field to protect her frontiers, was promised assistance by the contracting parties if she were attacked and requested assistance. "In case of urgency, or where the common interest requires a momentary passage of Allied Troops across some parts of Switzerland, recourse will be had to the authority of the Diet."

We should note that the Treaty authorizes only a *momentary* passage of allied troops and even this is subject to some sort of further authorization by the Diet. Implicit in this paragraph is Switzerland's approval of a march of allied troops through her territories, if so requested. The Diet also promised that Switzerland would "hinder, of its side, every enterprise that could hurt the operations of the Allied Armies." Convinced of the necessity of defeating Napoleon, Switzerland, by these engagements, abandoned for the duration of hostilities her time-honored policy of neutrality. *British State Papers* 2, 472–76 (1815).

Württemberg acceded to the same Treaty on 30 May 1815 and agreed to keep 20,000 men in the field to assist the Allies.

Chapuisat (**84**, p. 65) has reproduced the substance of a conversation between Eynard (one-time secretary of Charles Pictet de Rochemont) and Lucien Bonaparte (Prince of Camino and brother of Napoleon I) which is not without interest:

> Eynard—"If the Allies do not make war, they will be obliged to remain under arms and a state of peace without disarming is worse than war." Lucien B.—"I understand the force of this argument and, if war should ensue, I fear then for Switzerland: it will become the theater of the war." Eynard—"Why is that? Does the emperor want to attack Switzerland?" Lucien B.—"Certainly not. Neutrality suits his purposes and he will maintain it, but I believe that it is in the interests of the Allies to occupy Switzerland, and if they once enter, the war will be fought on its territory."

31. *Repertorium 1814–1848*, **III**, #29, pp. 300–308; #28 D and E, pp. 263–288. #29 concerns political and military plans of the Diet. #28 D and E, 12 May to 26 July 1815, pertain to General Bachmann's military operations.

32. The Diet was acutely aware of the sad state of Switzerland's military preparedness. Napoleon had deliberately contrived to weaken the Confederation in every possible way: seizure of the gold reserves of the principal cantons; imposition of heavy fines, penalties, and financial charges; forcing her industries to the verge of bankruptcy; stripping the country of agricultural products and supplies required by France; and refusing to allow the Confederation to build up a military chest, to organize a school for the training of officers, or to strengthen her military establishment in any way. One is forced to conclude that one reason for the Diet's determined effort to preserve Swiss neutrality during the "One Hundred Days" was the common knowledge within the officers' corps, the War Council, and within the ruling Councils of the cantons, of the country's unpreparedness for any vigorous military campaign.

33. *British State Papers* 2, pp. 148–49:

> "The Diet accedes, in the name of the Swiss Confederation to the Declaration of the Powers reunited in the Congress of Vienna . . . 20 March 1815, and promises that the stipulations of the Transaction inserted in this Act will be faithfully and religiously observed. The Diet expresses the eternal gratitude of the Swiss nation towards the High Powers who through the said Declaration . . . promise solemnly to recognize and to guarantee the Perpetual Neutrality that the general interest of

Europe requires in favor of the Helvetic Body" [Annex XI.B to the Declaration of the Eight Powers at the Congress of Vienna, 20 March 1815; signed at Zurich 27 May 1815].

34. "Act signed by the Protecting Powers . . . Guarantee of the Perpetual Neutrality of Switzerland, and the Inviolability of its Territory" Paris, 20 November 1815 (**172**, I, pp. 370, 371).

35. "As soon as the Helvetic Diet will have given its accession to the stipulations set forth in the present Transaction, an Act will be made carrying the recognition and guarantee, on the part of all of the Powers, of the perpetual neutrality of Switzerland in its new Frontiers" [Annex XI.A to the Declaration of the Eight Powers concerning the Affairs of the Helvetic Confederation; signed at Vienna 20 March 1815], (*British State Papers* **2**, p. 143).

36. In 1815 the Powers had agreed upon a second free trade zone which extended deeply into the Pays de Gex beyond the political frontier which separated France from the Canton of Geneva.

37. On 3 November 1815, the Powers agreed that the King of Sardinia would receive from France a payment of ten million francs to fortify the Franco-Sardinian frontiers. This conformed with a general policy for "strengthening of the line of Defense of the States bordering upon France," under which Austria and Prussia would also receive pecuniary indemnities (Hertslet, **172**, I, p. 329).

38. Concerning which, William Wickham, the British Ambassador to Switzerland had made the prophetic comment "If peace with Austria be concluded, this country is immediately gone" (Wickham to Grenville, British Minister for Foreign Affairs, 15 October 1797). A few months later the invasion was under way.

39. *British State Papers* **1**, 1163, 20 December 1813.

40. *British State Papers* **1**, 1165–69, 21 December 1813.

41. Article 435 of the Treaty of Versailles (28 June 1919) to which about 100 nations adhered begins as follows: "The High Contracting Parties . . . recognize the guarantees stipulated by the Treaties of 1815, and especially by the Act of November 20, 1815, in favour of Switzerland, the said guarantees constituting international obligations for the maintenance of peace . . ."

9. THE BIRTH OF A NATION (1816 to 1848)

The Times of the Restoration, the Regeneration and the Constitution of 1848

As the name suggests, the Restoration was to be a return to the "good old pre-Napoleonic days." The war was over and Switzerland's 15 years of travail were now in the past. The final Act of the Congress of Vienna restored much of her lost territory, improved her boundaries, abolished the subjection of her associated States, and gave her nine new cantons. Her independence, territorial integrity, and perpetual neutrality were recognized, confirmed, and guaranteed by the Great Powers and other lesser States. And a new constitution—the Federal Pact—had been accepted by the cantons and by the Powers. The cantonal constitutions, in turn, had been approved by the Diet. God was in His Heaven and all was well. Or was it?

Economic Difficulties

All was not well. Napoleon had succeeded, as was his policy, in greatly weakening the country. She had been depleted of foodstuffs and of cattle, horses, and livestock in general. Industrial products, useful to France and to Napoleon's armies, had been trans-shipped to France by Swiss tradesmen or confiscated by the French armies. Supplies remaining for use by the Swiss were vanishingly low. Economic boycotts, imposed by one side and then by the other, had almost ruined the Swiss textile industry. The fall of Napoleon was followed speedily by a policy of the English that proved to be as ruinous to the Swiss textile industry as the earlier boycotts. English textiles that had accumulated in Britain during the continental blockade were "dumped" on the continent and so flooded the market that several years were to pass before the Swiss textile industry, which was gradually being mechanized, could effectively compete. The difficulties of Swiss industry were further aggravated by prohibitively high tariffs that were imposed by most of her neighbours against Swiss exports—textiles, watches, and the products of her small struggling metal-working industries. The tariffs were unquestionably punitive, reflecting the anger of neighbouring countries against the outrageous practices and profits of the Swiss traders who had supplied Napoleonic France during the years of the allied blockade. The import restrictions also constituted an effort by Switzerland's neighbours to protect their own industries and conserve their finances. The royalist government of France totally interdicted the importation of Swiss agricultural products. The Diet sought an all-Swiss solution to the problem but failed to procure the required majority of votes. Out of this came a Concordat of $13\frac{1}{2}$ cantons determined to act in concert against France. They failed, however, to maintain any unity of action and the Concordat ceased to function in the following year.

The serious industrial crises were aggravated by a succession of bad harvests. Heavy snowfalls and flooding were of such severity in 1816 as to ruin the harvests. The crops of vegetables, fruit, hay, and grains were pitifully small. The price of bread rose eightfold and in some cantons much of the population had to depend on public assistance. Food shortages were common and areas where severe privation, even starvation, occurred were all too numerous during the hunger years of 1816–17. The suffering in the eastern cantons because of food shortages was heightened by the industrial crisis. We need only recall that over a hundred thousand spinners had been employed in the textile industries of eastern Switzerland at the end of the eighteenth century. Mechanization of the industry, which began in Switzerland in 1801 with the introduction of hydraulic power, progressed at a good pace, possibly too rapidly in view of the reduction in markets. A shift from linen to cotton spinning and weaving helped for a time, but only temporarily. Massive unemployment followed, wages were reduced, and poverty and emigration from the affected areas were the inevitable result. The federal authorities introduced relief programs, soup kitchens, and other palliatives but the government had little power, and the cantons, where the real authority resided, could not coordinate their efforts and failed totally to introduce effective measures.

The Federal Pact

On the constitutional front, the Federal Pact was not without its virtues, few though they were. The 22 cantons contracted to act as one in defense against enemies from without and revolution from within. They assigned to the Federal Government, i.e., the Diet, the sole right to declare war, to conclude peace, to negotiate alliances and commercial treaties with foreign Powers,[1] to establish a Federal Militia, and to charge the costs against the various cantons. Intercantonal treaties which trespassed upon the rights of other cantons were disallowed. The Diet alone could name the federal ambassadors and elect, in case of war, the general, his chief-of-staff, and the federal colonels.

Otherwise, there was little change. The cantons enjoyed almost all the rights of sovereignty. The cantonal delegates to the Diet were required to vote according to instructions from their cantonal governments. Within the Diet, a simple majority was sufficient for a federal decision—admittedly a great improvement over the days when enactments of the Diet required unanimity. But the majority had not the means of forcing the minority to respect its decisions. The Diet continued as a debating forum. It could not guarantee the liberties of its people, their freedom of religion, their freedom to practice their profession in any canton of their choice, the right of association, and the freedom of the press. The rights of determination on matters such as these remained with the cantons. Penal codes varied from canton to canton. The right to enter into capitulation agreements with foreign Powers continued to be cantonal.[2] The Federal Government, consisting of but a single chamber, represented the cantons only. A second chamber, to express the wishes of the people on a population basis, was not to be created until 1848. In consequence, we must visualize a situation in which the 12,000 people of Uri had an equal voice in the Diet with the 300,000 people of the canton of Bern (Biaudet, **38**, p. 44).

Many intercantonal problems in the early 1830s resulted from the weakness of the Federal Pact, which permitted the cantonal governments to return to their old ways and failed to recognize that the charter of the "one and indivisible" Helvetic Republic did have a few virtues. To give credit where credit is due, we must admit that the Helvetic Republic of 1798 to 1803 enshrined the concepts of equality of opportunity in employment, equality before the law, and the right of establishment. It ended temporarily the disenfranchisement of many people of voting age, the subject status of country to town, and the lordship of some cantons over subject territories and States. Most of the cantonal constitutional reforms for which the Swiss struggled during the 1820s and the 1830s focused on the failure of the Federal Pact to preserve these social and political gains, as well as on the inability of the Federal Government to bring an end to the economic chaos that impaired the interrelations of the 22 member States.

As a source of revenue for the Federal Government the duties on foreign imports, collected by the border cantons, were transmitted to the federal authorities.[3] Additionally, the interest on funds in the war chest and emergency contributions by the cantons supported the operations of the Confederation. Rights of coinage, specification of standards of weights and measures, the post, and transport continued to be cantonal responsibilities. Nothing but chaos and an intolerable confusion resulted. Intercantonal Concordats were of little help. Free trade or protectionism between these 22 little sovereign States, was frequently discussed. We read that it was less troublesome to ship the linen goods of St. Gallen through Strassburg than across Switzerland, and transport from Basel to Zürzach[4] was less costly through the Grand Duchy of Baden than through Switzerland (**310**, p. 389). Most foreign shipments detoured their way around Switzerland rather than attempting to cross any of the 22 cantons which constantly competed with each other and seldom cooperated. In sum total there were over 400 taxes—local, communal, cantonal, and federal—on the transport of goods. Whenever a bridge or a road was built a toll was imposed against all who used it. The Ticino managed to levy 13 taxes along the Gotthard route and at each tax station required the merchandise to be unloaded and weighed. The cantons were so angered by the imposts levied by neighbouring cantons that, in retaliation, even more tolls and assorted charges were dreamed up. And so it went, from bad to worse and from confusion into chaos.

The exclusive right of coinage was not granted to the federal authorities until 1848–50. Before then, cantons, cities, and temporal and ecclesiastical lords enjoyed the right to issue their own currency. The 56 different authorities that exercised this right circulated *in toto* over 700 different pieces of money: gold, silver, copper, and bronze. Beside the Swiss franc (equal to ten batzen) and other Swiss coinage, French francs, the French écu (equal to six Swiss francs), and the écus of Brabant, Bavaria, and Württemberg were also in circulation as legal currency. The standards of weights and measures that were in use were equally variable, if not unpredictable, from canton to canton. Were we to go back to 1580 we would learn from Montaigne (**250**, p. 9) that "from Bar-le-Duc [in eastern France] the leagues resume the measure of Gascony, and become longer and longer as one approaches Germany, until they are doubled and even trebled." But we need not go back to 1580. In 1815, Switzerland had to tolerate no less than 11 foot measures, 60 different units of length for measuring cloth, 81 measures of volume for liquids, and 50 different measures of weight. There was no improvement until the cantons did the sensible thing in 1848 and permitted the Federal Government to impose a single set of standards on all 22 cantons.

The recognition of cantonal autonomy, or even sovereignty, in internal matters constituted a rather questionable blessing bestowed by the Federal Pact on some cantons; questionable because popular unrest of the past would almost certainly recur in the future. Most in evidence was the return to power of the former ruling families in the aristocratic patriciates of Bern, Freiburg, Lucerne and Solothurn. In the first few years of the Restoration, a return to legitimacy was perhaps the most basic and conspicuous policy that the conservative leaders of the Great Powers shared in common. They had had enough of revolution, of popular unrest, and of dissent by the governed.

Relations with Austria

Switzerland came to be a focus of interest and of policy decisions by Russia, Prussia, and Austria for two reasons. The first in importance stemmed from the guarantee by the Powers of Switzerland's neutrality, independence, and territorial inviolability. This guarantee was destined to cause almost endless friction with the Powers and resulted in their serious meddling in internal matters that the Swiss were loath to regard as anyone's business except their own. The second reason was a reflection of the extreme conservatism of the continental monarchs, especially of Austria where Prince Metternich was the author and exponent of foreign policy. He had not abandoned hope that Switzerland could be fashioned into an Austrian protectorate, just as she had been a virtual protectorate of France during two centuries of pre-Napoleonic Europe.

Jean-Jacques Rousseau, 1712-1778 (Swiss National Library)

Albrecht von Haller, 1708-1777 (Swiss National Library)

César de la Harpe, 1754-1838 (Swiss National Library)

Peter Ochs, 1752-1821 (Swiss National Library)

The triumphant entry of the French into Bern, 5 March 1798 (Swiss National Library)

The French in Switzerland, 1798; collection of plunder (Swiss National Library)

The King of Prussia elected Prince of Neuchâtel and Valangin, 13 November 1707 (Swiss National Library)

Napoleon's war in Russia. Swiss forces cover the retreat of the French over the river Dwina, 20 October 1812 (Swiss National Library)

James Fazy, 1794-1878 (Swiss National Library)

Charles Pictet de Rochemont, 1755-1824 (Swiss National Library)

Jakob Stämpfli, 1820-1879 (Swiss National Library)

Giuseppi Mazzini, 1805-1872 (Swiss National Library)

J. C. Kern, 1808-1888 (Swiss National Library)

General Dufour (Swiss National Library)

The First Consul, Napoleon Bonaparte, visits the hospice on Mt. St. Bernard, 1799 (Swiss National Library)

Suppression of the Aargau convents, 1841 (Swiss National Library)

Conrad Escher von der Linth (Swiss National
Library)

Albert Bitzius (Jeremias Gotthelf) (Swiss National
Library)

The last session of the Diet, 4 to 22 September 1848 (Zentralbibliothek, Lucerne)

The First Federal Council (Swiss National Library) Bottom row (L to R): Stefano Franscini, Friedrich Frey-Hérosé, Wilhelm Naef; Middle row: Ulrich Ochsenbein, Jonas Furrer, Henri Druey; Top: Josef Munzinger.

Dr. Alexander Yersin, discoverer of the cause of the plague. Photograph taken at Nahtrang, Annam (Viet-Nam), in March 1892. (From Bernard, N, ''Yersin et la peste,'' Lausanne: Rouge et cie, 246 pp. 1944)

Metternich of Austria, 1773-1859 (Swiss National Library)

Disarmament of Bourbacki's army, February 1871 (Swiss National Library)

A weaver's cellar in Appenzell, circ 1820/30 (Swiss National Library—from a painting by J. Schiess)

Albert Gallatin, 1761-1849 (Swiss National
Library)

Louis Agassiz, 1807-1873 (Swiss National
Library)

In this portion of the Rhine, Friedrich Miescher II
(1844-1895) fished for salmon; from the sperm he
prepared a nucleic acid, now known to have been
a crude DNA. Miescher's discovery serves as an
important part of the foundation stone of
molecular biology. (Courtesy of Staatsarchiv
Basel)

Alfred Escher, 1819-1882 (Swiss National
Library)

The Christoffelturm in Bern. A magnificent tower in Bern, torn down in 1865, following a slender majority vote in the municipal council (Swiss National Library)

The hospice and chapel on Mt. St. Gotthard (Swiss National Library)

125th Anniversary of Swiss railways (1972). The Bernina train from St. Moritz in the Engadine to Tirano in the Italian Veltlin crosses the Alps at a height of 2,257 m without a summit tunnel and is the highest through train in Europe. Without the aid of a rack rail it covers a height difference of 1,828 m. On the Lake Bianco at the top of the Bernina Pass. (Swiss National Tourist Office)

Scheduled Postal Buses, in 3 hours, take tourists from Chur in the Grisons through the San Bernardino road tunnel to Bellinzona in the Ticino, N 13 Motorway on southern ramp of the San Bernardino road above Mesocco. (Swiss National Tourist Office)

This aerial cablecar conveys 40 passengers from Wengen to the Männlichen area in 8 minutes. Left, the Jungfrau massif; right, Lauterbrunnen Valley and the Breithorn/Bernese Oberland. (Swiss National Tourist Office)

The Lavaux wine district on the shores of the Lake of Geneva; criss-crossed by walls which absorb and retain the warmth and prevent the soil from being eroded. (Swiss National Tourist Office)

It is clear that Metternich understood neither the Swiss nor the forces that were emerging in Switzerland for social, political, and religious reform. Otherwise, how could he possibly hope that the Swiss would temper their fiery love of independence, accept any form of Austrian domination, and adopt his own arch conservatism? He had several good reasons which, superficially at least, might appear to be well founded. He was confident that the patricians of the aristocratic cantons were deeply conservative, for they were born into conservatism and the privileges they enjoyed as the ruling families were only possible in the kind of State and social order that Metternich was resolved to preserve. Even in the guild-structured cantons of Basel and Zurich he might find support in the cities, where government was localized and where a rigid policy prevailed of ensuring that the countryside be kept in a state of dependence. As for the population at large that had suffered so cruelly during 15 years of occupation, pillage, plundering, and economic ruin by France, how could there remain even a vestige of trust in such a country and in such people? Was it not Austria that had driven the French armies out of Switzerland, and was it not Austria that had befriended the Swiss? And would it not be Austria that would be Switzerland's friend in the future, prepared to protect her from enemies without and from dissident forces within? This is exactly where Metternich misjudged the Swiss. Much as they had suffered under the French, they would brook no alliance, association or concept of government that would permit a foreign Power to meddle in their internal affairs, either to suppress the advocates of change or to support the champions of the *status quo.*

We should, of course, understand that Metternich was not without support among the Powers. His reactionary conservatism appealed to Alexander I of Russia and to Friedrich Wilhelm IV of Prussia. The leaders of government in Great Britain, while conservative in a British sort of way, were not deceived by Metternich and understood better than others that Metternich, if he had his way, would soon upset the balance of power in Europe by elevating Austria to a dominant position on the continent.

The Holy Alliance

Britain's refusal to join the Holy Alliance, conceived by the Russian Tsar and subscribed to eagerly by Austria and Prussia, arose not so much from fear of holiness in international affairs as from the suspicions that Metternich generated in the leaders of Britain's government. The Holy Alliance was based on a principle, sacred to any monarch who believed in the divine right of kings, that a prince was the father of his people. He must keep them in the straight and narrow path of righteousness and they, as the governed, must not question the judgment of the prince. Switzerland, subjected to heavy diplomatic pressure, joined the Holy Alliance in 1817.[5] Publicly, the three monarchs talked only of the maintenance of peace. How could the Swiss or anyone else possibly find this objectionable? Privately, the triumvirate made every effort to preserve the *status quo.* The Holy Alliance was, in fact, a political instrument and Switzerland, so unpredictable to the continental Powers, so willing to grant asylum to malcontents and "troublemakers," had to be closely supervised and directed. It would be easier to keep the Confederation in line as a member of the alliance—something that the reluctant Swiss suspected from the very beginning to be behind the diplomatic manoeuvers of the monarchs.

Paramount Authority of the State vs Direct Democracy

Karl Ludwig von Haller, grandson of the great Albrecht von Haller and an eminent theoretician of the science of government, provided intellectual support to those of the Metternich School. von Haller would have nothing to do with the doctrine of human equality. To him, human inequality was a biological fact, divinely ordained. Society consists of the governed and those who govern. The State and the authority of the State are paramount and must be so recognized. His great six-volume work on the theory of government presented *in extenso* a philosophy which was welcomed by the arch conservatives and the proponents of a patrician type of government.

In an opposite camp we find Benjamin Constant[6] of Vaud who championed the ideas of democracy and of direct government by the people. But he saw in the history of the French Revolution a freedom-dedicated government, which purported to be representative of the popular will, degenerate into a dictatorship. Such a retrograde evolution, he feared, might be the unfortunate fate of any democracy. While von Haller was the theoretician of the most reactionary conservatives, Constant was the leading advocate of a conservative liberalism.

Complaints of the Continental Monarchs

At this point we might well ask what, if anything, was happening within Switzerland that might be extremely unsettling—a nightmare—to the conservative monarchs who treasured the *status quo* above all else, and who had guaranteed Switzerland's independence and perpetual neutrality. Only one of the 22 cantons was monarchical (Neuchâtel), insofar as it continued to be a Principality of the King of Prussia. The remaining 21 were suspect. Their popular governments, their independence of action, and the absence of a strong central authority suggested to the monarchs that anarchy was rampant. Switzerland also became a haven of refuge for the many discontented, and the political exiles who fled into Switzerland from the neighbouring countries. If a refugee became *persona non grata* in one canton because of unfriendly political activities, he had only to cross the border into a neighbouring canton. The Diet, itself, was loath to intervene. Because of this weakness at the center, abuses of the right of asylum by political activists among the refugees continued until 1838 with a recurrence in the Ticino in 1848.

The refugees included a high proportion of intellectuals, some of whom, to the great displeasure of the conservative monarchs, received professorships within the Swiss universities. Ludwig Snell,[7] a German refugee and Professor of Government in the University of Bern from 1834 to 1836, was a conspicuous leader of the intellectual wing of the political activists. Within the lecture halls of the university, through pamphlets, and in radical publications he raised anew the call for freedom of thought and freedom of expression. He defended the advocates of political reform and, as might be expected, brought down upon his head the wrath of those who were dedicated to preserve the *status quo*. His brother Wilhelm took part in the civil war of 1833 in Basel and, later, was appointed to a university professorship. He was a leader of the most combative wing of the advanced radicals.[8] He profoundly influenced his son-in-law, Jakob Stämpfli, a well-known Swiss radical and advocate of a thorough-going reconstruction of the Federal Constitution.[9]

The early 1820s were a time of popular unrest in the German States, of revolution in Spain, and of troubles in Italy. The monarchs saw revolutionaries wherever they turned. The Swiss cantons were inundated with spies and foreign agents hired to observe, to report, and to create provocations which would justify foreign intervention. Reports from their spies flooded the offices of foreign governments. It mattered little if the truth was distorted and the information was fictitious. The Diet was virtually forced by the pressures from abroad to adopt stringent measures against trouble-making foreigners and against the Press. The *Conclusum* of 1823 on the Press and foreigners did much more than was intended. It revealed the servility of the Diet before the Great Powers and fired the radicals, the student organizations, and other groups into renewed activity. The *Conclusum* was virtually an order to the cantons to refrain from any acts which might incite hostility abroad and have dangerous political consequences in foreign affairs. Specifically, they were ordered to deny the right of asylum to any criminals and those who through provocative acts menaced internal peace.

The Helvetic Society was reborn and resumed the efforts initiated at Schinznach (see Chapter 7) to serve as a forum for men of goodwill interested in debating the problems that continued to fragment the country. A dozen other all-Swiss societies came into being, most of them apolitical. Yet their very existence served as a protest against the do-nothingness of the conservatives.

Federal societies for singing, shooting, gymnastics, and various professional societies served to bring together their members from all parts of the Confederation. The problems that beset the Confederation certainly came under discussion in the informal gatherings that accompanied the formal sessions. Conservatives within, and the suspicious monarchs without, complained repeatedly that these societies were merely covers under which pernicious propaganda was spread and conspiracies against the established order were fomented. To some extent these societies were infiltrated with both spies and conspirators, the latter using such country-wide organizations as a means of spreading the contagion of revolt. Such were the complaints directed against the Federal Government. Prince Metternich of Austria and Prince Hardenberg of Prussia wrote to the *Vorort* in November 1820 with a specific complaint about gymnastic societies (*Turnanstalten*), which "engage not in gymnastic exercises but in political intrigues against the public tranquility. Such conspirators menace all governments. . . . They want to replace them with political chimeras and they tend to subvert the whole order" (v. Tillier, **366**). A *Turnanstalt* at Chur in the Graubünden was reported to be made up of refugees and "bad heads" from different countries, including the brothers Snell, several other professors and named individuals who had fled from Germany, and had "acquired a sad notoriety through their aberrations."

The princely communications, identical in content, were placed before each and every cantonal government, and all 22 cantons pronounced themselves forcefully in favor of the established order. A typical reply from one of the cantons (Lucerne) is quoted by von Tillier.

> Such a disposition of spirit which admits no thought of innovation is sufficient perhaps by itself alone, to paralyze every pernicious influence. But there is also the profound conviction that the best political policy for Switzerland consists in not involving itself in affairs abroad. It is also the instinct of an honest and judicious people: the more it cherishes its independence the less it is inclined to carry outside of itself its cares and its solicitude. All of this gives little opportunity for seduction. Neither the effervescence of distant agitations nor the ramifications of dissatisfaction in some states against the legitimate authority would be able to affect them. The existing forces of vigilance of the authorities, the power of each canton, and the federal bond plus the lessons of experience suffice to repress every dangerous enterprise (**366**).

The Free Masons were heavily suspect. Karl Ludwig von Haller saw in freemasonry a secret society dedicated to the overthrow of the Catholic Church and the State. "In large measure, the schools are in its hands, soon it will blow up the Federal Assembly in Frankfurt, soon fall on Savoy, soon attempt to destroy the catholic cantons, soon the chief seat of Christianity will be violently attacked . . ." (v. Haller, **162**). Wilhelm Öchsli (**275**) reported on a list of about 25 secret societies with headquarters or branches in Switzerland that had in common the overthrow of existing governments. The preparation of the list was the work of the Paris police. One of the societies, the Free Masons, was said to be directed uniquely against religious and monarchical institutions. Hence its total suppression, in the troubled 1800s, in Russia. The police described the Order of the Templars in detail and claimed that the prescribed oath referred to the despotism of kings, the spread of obscurity by catholic priests, and the desire of tyrants to re-establish feudalism. Even Pictet and d'Ivernois, who rendered such outstanding service to Geneva and to the Confederation in 1815, were regarded by the Paris police as dangerous: "Especially with their pen, Councillors of State Pictet and d'Ivernois . . . seek to propagate destructive principles" (Öchsli, **275**, p. 29). The same report declared that a Swiss catechism published by the "too celebrated" La Harpe teaches the youth that insurrection is the most "saintly" of its duties and "one of the first precepts that man can desire is that of knowing how to keep a secret" (Öchsli, **275**, p. 45). Despite such "witch hunting," or possibly because of it, liberal movements on many fronts increased in activity. Among the liberals, a left-wing grouping of radicals became more and more assertive and more and more demanding of social and political reform. Sympathies for the people of Greece who rose in rebellion against the Turks were widespread. Physicians, surgeons, military officers and others volunteered for service in the cause of the Greek patriots. A Geneva banker, Gabriel Eynard,[10] extended such generous financial aid to the Greeks as to evoke from Metternich the comment "Monsieur Eynard is one of the men who has troubled me the most in this world." As might be expected, the conservative monarchs and their agents and advisers who watched over Switzerland in search of evidence of the deadly virus of radicalism and reform were greatly disturbed by the wave of philhellenism. However, control of the press weakened, more newspapers were founded, and many of the cantonal governments began to publish their proceedings. The *Conclusum* was ignored and in 1829 was formally abolished. In Basel, St. Gallen, Thurgau, Zurich and Vaud the movement for peaceful reform grew rapidly. In the Ticino, popular demands forced the cantonal government to draft a more liberal and democratic constitution.

Mechanization Begins

The Regeneration, rather arbitrarily dated from 1830 to 1839, was ushered in by two notable events, the introduction of steam power and the French and Polish revolutions of 1830–31. Switzerland, with an abundance of mountain lakes, rivers, and fast-flowing streams, had learned years before to harness hydraulic power for industrial purposes. In so doing she gained a brief advantage over her competitors, which she lost with the advent of the steam engine. Within a few years, however, Swiss industry seized upon the new source of power. Transportation companies came into being and, from 1825 on, steamships began to ply the waters of the Swiss lakes on regular schedules. At first these strange ships that travelled without sails, and moved faster than boatmen could row, were believed to be the work of the devil—manifestations of sorcery and witchcraft. In the 1840s steam-powered trains began to appear, and the horse, the carriage, the sailing vessel, and the large heavily-manned rowboat were soon to lose their status as hitherto irreplaceable necessities in freight and passenger transport.

The great changes in industry brought about by introduction of the steam engine were accompanied by rapid mechanization of industrial processes, a flight of agricultural labourers into industrial employment, and a gradual improvement of working conditions. It was a period characterized by many changes which penetrated deeply into many aspects of life in Switzerland.

Revolutions of 1830–31

Political change in Switzerland which continued unabated until 1848, had profound effects, partly because of the outbreaks of violence which preceded the reforms and partly because of the constant threat of intervention, by force if necessary, by all of Switzerland's neighbours great and small. This was greatly accelerated by the so-called revolution of July 1830 in Paris, which was not a true revolution in the sense of armed conflict but, rather, the forced termination of the ultrareactionary regime of Charles X. Thus the post-Napoleonic period of legitimacy in the monarchy ended after 15 years. France was not alone in experiencing a serious political upheaval that might conceivably have ushered in another period of violent revolution by the people. To the north, the Netherlands underwent a separation by which the Powers established the kingdom of Belgium. Poland experienced a bloody repression by Russia, the downfall of the monarchy, and the exodus of many who sought refuge wherever it could be found. Portugal, dominated by Spain, was suffering a period of oppression. Greece was locked in a life-or-death struggle with Turkey from which it sought liberation. Brazil overthrew its constitutional monarch, initiating a wave of political unrest that spread throughout the ever-volatile South American States.

Demands for Reform

Throughout the Swiss Confederation, the cantonal governments yielded to the demands for constitutional reform and accepted revisions in their constitutions which gave recognition to the sovereignty of the people in elections to the Great Councils, to the principle of equality before the law, and to the right of petition. A more just distribution of charges imposed by government on the citizenry, and the possibility of redemption of tenure were additional gains sought by the people. In most cases the popular demonstrations were peaceful, and assumed, as in the cantons of Bern and Zurich, the form of a massive *Landsgemeinde*. In Thurgau, St. Gallen, Solothurn, Bern, Lucerne and Ticino violence was lacking. Though the popular demonstrations in Freiburg, Schaffhausen and Vaud were tumultuous, there was no bloodshed. The governments of Schwyz and Basel were resistant and refused to yield to the demand for reform. Intracantonal warfare followed. Schwyz came very close to a division into two half-cantons, and federal troops were ordered into the District of Küssnacht, a part of Schwyz which retained its loyalty to the Federal Government and had been invaded on 31 July 1832 by cantonal troops from the rest of Schwyz. In Basel, civil war erupted between the town and the country peasants. When peace was restored it was agreed that the canton be divided into Baselstadt and Baselland each with its own liberalized constitution acceptable to the people.

The League of Sarnen

This internal dissension had created a most serious problem for the Confederation. In November 1832, Uri, Schwyz, Basel, Neuchâtel, Valais and Unterwalden entered into a federation of their own, known as the *Sarnerbund* or League of Sarnen. The member States, either intensely conservative, or stubbornly determined to retain all the rights of independent sovereign States, or harboring still other resentments against other cantons, agreed to abstain from sending delegates to the Diet as long as deputies from Baselland and outer Schwyz (the District of Küssnacht) were admitted. The Diet did not hesitate to act. Federal militia in early August were ordered to occupy the entirety of Schwyz and of Basel cantons. The dissolution of the League of Sarnen was ordered. By the end of August all of the dissidents except Neuchâtel yielded to the inevitable, tacitly admitting that the League was separatist in spirit and contrary to the Federal Pact. They took the federal oath and henceforth sent delegates to the Diet. Neuchâtel delayed, claiming a privileged position because of its status as a Prussian Principality though also a Swiss canton. Federal troops moved into the canton which abandoned its isolated position in September. All 22 cantons were once again reuinited and solemnly committed to participation in the business of the Diet.

The Guarantee by the Powers

Already a movement was on foot to revise the Federal Pact. Attempts were made to draft a new constitution but were twice rejected. The ancient cantons, which treasured their sovereignty far more than life under a Federal Government possessed of more power than was in the Federal Pact, were adamant. They also had strong support from the continental Powers who declared insistently that their guarantee of Swiss neutrality and independence was inseparable from their guarantee of the Pact itself. Karl Ludwig von Haller (cf. Winkler, **391**) argued that the Powers had in no way guaranteed the Federal Pact of 1815, which concerned Swiss domestic affairs alone except for a superficial approach to a unitary Constitution. The Powers did assure the continued existence and territorial integrity of Switzerland and its status as a peaceful and neutral mid-European State. But they could not be expected to honor such a guarantee if Switzerland became a workshop for revolution and an assembly point for all the German, French, and Italian conspirators. von Haller supported the right of intervention by the Powers if Switzerland were unable to maintain an internal peace. The right of intervention is, said Haller, merely the right to help one's neighbour whether or not aid is requested. For example, to rush in to prevent a neighbour's house from burning to the ground is a friendly and neighbourly responsibility. But intervention by the Powers should not be by force of arms, said Haller. First, by diplomatic means they should express their concern over any internal disorder, presumed to be contagious. Next the Powers could use financial pressures in respect to payments to persons, corporations and foundations. Passport denials and temporary suspension of commercial relations would also be in order—but not an armed intervention. He considered Metternich to be definitely in error in regarding the Federal Pact, Swiss neutrality and territorial integrity as a single political package.

The Refugee Problem

Now we must return to the refugee problem which worsened greatly when the Polish insurrection of 1830–31, brutally repressed, was followed by the flight of Polish refugees. Bern received over 400 in 1833, provided them for a time with food and shelter, and even permitted them to retain the weapons which they possessed on entry. Had the newcomers been content to remain quietly in the background and be absorbed gradually in the general population there might have been few, if any, complaints from foreign governments. In fact, however, the Poles conspired openly with other refugees, with revolutionaries from Italy, Austria, the German States, and elsewhere.

By late 1833 the Swiss perceived that greater troubles with the refugees were developing. They were also finding burdensome the costs of supporting the refugees, most of whom were in need of maintenance. Most of the Poles had entered from France in April 1833, doing so without formal permission from the border cantons through which entry had been made. In October and November 1833, an exchange of notes between the Federal *Vorort* (Zurich) and the French Ambassador expressed the desire of Switzerland that France permit the Poles to re-enter France, either to find asylum in that country or to be allowed to pass through for entry into any country where they might be enabled to settle. France agreed to permit passage through France and agreed to pay the transportation of the Poles from French ports to England, Portugal, Egypt or Algeria.[11] France, the Netherlands and Germany were in sharp disagreement, however, on procedural matters and on disposition of the refugees once they came under their particular jurisdiction. Germany, for example, intended to ship them on to America. Bern, on the other hand, was unwilling to be a party to any convention "which would deprive the Polish refugees in the canton of Bern of a free choice of their future place of sojourn."[12]

The spiritual head of the movement was Mazzini,[13] the founder of "Young Italy" and the recognized father of the Italian Confederation. From his base in Geneva he conceived a plan to invade Savoy and to overthrow the King of Sardinia. Poles, Italians, and Germans assembled at Rolle and in February 1834 arrived on the south shore of Lake Geneva. Most of them were disarmed by the Geneva militia but 50 or so armed men got through. Joined by French and a few other adventurers, a motley force of over 200 men, including Mazzini, marched on Annemasse, and after seizing the contents of various treasuries abandoned the plan of a further penetration into Savoy.

The repercussions were immediate. Threatening notes poured in to Bern from Austria, the German Diet, Russia, the Grand Duchy of Baden, Bavaria, the Kingdom of the Two Sicilies, Württemberg, Prussia and Sardinia.[14] Bern responded by ordering the expulsion of all foreigners who had participated in the madcap hostilities against Savoy. In the preceding month, the *Vorort* had replied to the Powers by proclaiming bravely a sound statement of policy:

> Every independent State, without contradiction, has the right to accept refugees whose conduct is peaceable. Switzerland at all times has recognized this and will continue to do so in the future. On the other hand it has a duty to see that those refugees who abuse their asylum in order to disturb the tranquillity of other States are rendered unable to renew their hostile deeds. . . . The troublesome refugees will be expelled as soon as other obstacles (independent of the will of government) have been overcome.

The statement was later clarified: "and the return of any expelled refugees will not be allowed."[15]

There were interminable delays in completing the expulsion. Bern, in defense, pointed out that agreement on the procedures to be followed required not only workable arrangements with other countries but coordination with other Swiss cantons that had refugee problems. The cantonal governments were many and it was not easy to reach a consensus. Austria replied "that the internal legislation of a country cannot be adduced as a justification of the mischievous consequences resulting therefrom to other States."[16] And the Grand Duchy of Baden demanded "the removal of those refugees who, without having been personally present in the expedition against Savoy, have nevertheless, directly or indirectly, participated in the revolutionary attempts against the neighbouring States."[17] Furthermore, guarantees were demanded from Switzerland to ensure that persons expelled would not be permitted to return and resume their former hostile acts.

Bern's responses did not satisfy the complaining governments, and Metternich, in reprisal, ordered the recall of all Austrian workmen from the canton. With support from Russia and the German States, and confronted by an adamant Bern, Austria broke off diplomatic relations with the cantonal government which became the federal *Vorort* on 1 January 1835. The German States, Russia, Sardinia, and even France, complained about Bern's failure to expel the remaining foreign refugees who, with hardly an exception, were regarded by Switzerland's neighbours as dangerous troublemakers who threatened the very foundations of the established order.[18] Even in May and June 1834, Switzerland's neighbours, one and all, were threatening some sort of concerted action to force Switzerland to expel the remaining troublemakers—proven or potential.

On June 24 the *Vorort* issued a policy statement which for a time appeared to solve the refugee problem to the satisfaction of foreign governments. Almost in unison the foreign diplomats expressed approval and announced the resumption of friendly relations with Switzerland.[19] Unfortunately, expulsion of the refugees dragged on until, as we have seen, Austria, the German States, Russia, Sardinia and France renewed, with more menacing diplomatic manoeuvres, their paper warfare with Bern.

From the letters sent by the *Vorort* to the cantons and from the contents of correspondence with France we find that the refugee problem continued to embarrass Switzerland through 1835 and 1836. A circular letter of 22 June 1836 reminded the cantonal governments of the urgent necessity of completing the expulsion of all refugees who continued to abuse asylum in Switzerland, and to disturb the tranquility of other States. Of those expelled, some managed to return. There was a continuation of vicious propaganda, of meddling in the internal affairs of Switzerland and of assorted activities that seriously compromised the Confederation and individual cantons. Plots against the Grand Duchy of Baden were uncovered.

France agreed to accept the expelled refugees, to grant temporary asylum under close surveillance, and to provide means of subsistence until they could be shipped off to other countries willing to receive them. By mid-November 1836 the two governments appeared to be satisfied that the refugee problem was settled and the amicable relations of the past were again restored.

Among the many noteworthy refugees, of whom I have named very few, the one of greatest concern to Switzerland's neighbours was Prince Louis-Napoleon (nephew of Napoleon Bonaparte) the future Napoleon III of France. Following the exile of his father, King Louis of Holland, the son spent his younger days in Thurgau. He became an honorary citizen of the canton and served as an artillery captain under Dufour.[20] Nonetheless he did his best to re-establish the Napoleonic dynasty in France. In 1836, involved in an unsuccessful *coup d'État* against Strassburg, he went briefly into exile in America. On return to Switzerland he instigated the publication in Paris of a widely distributed inflammatory brochure against the "bourgeois King" of France. Thousands of copies were spread among the ranks of the French army. In August 1838 the royal government of France demanded of the Diet the extradition of the prince.

Switzerland regarded the demand as totally improper, if not outrageous. The prince, even though a nephew of the Napoleon who had ravaged their country, was nonetheless under Swiss protection as an honorary citizen of Thurgau. Popular sympathy for the prince ran high, and the Diet, refusing to yield to the demands of France, brought the country to the brink of war. With encouragement from Austria, Prussia and Russia, France mobilized an army of 25,000 men, and the Diet, in preparation for an armed conflict, named a general to command its forces and dispatched two army corps to the frontier. Fortunately for all concerned, Louis-Napoleon left the country voluntarily in October 1838 (**30**). Another crisis disappeared into the past, and Switzerland's neighbours appeared to be satisfied.

Suppression of the Aargau Convents

The suffering into which Switzerland was plunged from 1816 to 1820 or so spawned an extraordinary interest in pietism and in religious sects of many different flavors. It was a recrudescence of a similar wave which Bern experienced from 1802 to 1810. None of this is surprising because the Napoleonic revolution, with its devastating effects, tore people away from many of the beliefs and practices of the Church in which they were accustomed to find comfort in times of tribulation. The days were soon to come, however, when two great movements directed against the catholic church were destined to have a far greater effect upon Switzerland than religious cultism. Pressures began to develop to suppress the convents, notably in Aargau, and to expel the Jesuits. Together they had an extraordinary effect, for they culminated in a confessional war and had political overtones sufficient to advance the cause of liberal radicalism and the adoption of a new federalistic constitution in place of the Federal Pact. As we shall see, the fact that the existence of the convents had been guaranteed by the Federal Pact was without effect on the trend of events.

In 1832, seven of the cantons (Bern, Baselland, Aargau, Thurgau, Lucerne, Solothurn, and St. Gallen) formed a Concordat with the intent of achieving unity of action in economic matters and in other areas of common interest; it had become hopeless for 22 cantons to reach a consensus on questions that came before the Diet. In 1834 the Concordat of seven moved into the supersensitive problems stemming from confessional differences in the Confederation. All seven subscribed to the Articles of Baden which were clearly anti-clerical. The foundation of a Swiss archbishopric, the creation of local synods and the control of seminaries and religious orders by the State were high on the list of proposals. The taxing of convents and the approval by Church and State of mixed marriages were also recommended. In an encyclical of 1835 addressed to the Swiss clergy, the pope condemned the Articles of Baden. Troubles broke out in the *Freiämter* which required the intervention of troops to restore order. A petition of protest with over 7000 signatures from the catholic Jura in the canton of Bern was ignored by the Great Council of Bern. Again, military intervention was required to restore order and prevent further aggressive demonstrations by a rebellious populace. Vienna expressed its displeasure at the turn of events, and France threatened direct intervention, even a military occupation of the Jura, if Bern did not disavow the Articles within 48 hours. Humuliated, Bern yielded to the French demands in June 1836 and endeavoured to mend its relations with the Holy See.

Still greater troubles attended by violence broke out in the new canton of Aargau. In 1839 the newly adopted revision of the cantonal constitution gave to the radical liberals enough power to break, in their favour, the equilibrium in representation in the governing council that then existed between the two confessions. The conservative forces united in vigorous protests over control of the convents exercised by the State. In 1841 another partial revision under Radical-Liberal leadership aroused the open resistance of the catholics against the liberalized government of the canton. Military assistance from Bern, Baselland and Zurich was required to suppress the incipient rebellions. When order was again restored, the leaders of the catholic opposition were arrested, and final responsibility for stirring the people into revolt was attributed by the Liberals to inflammatory actions by the convents of Aargau, widely regarded as centers of resistance to the dissemination of new ideas and any advocacy of change. The convents were alleged also to be storing arms and ammunition for the insurgents (153).

The cantonal government promptly ordered the suppression of the eight convents then existing in the Aargau. The repercussions were more serious than ever anticipated. The Papal Nuncio and the Austrian Ambassador intervened in favour of restoration of the convents, and even protestant Prussia expressed its displeasure over the action of the government. A number of the cantons, principally catholic, demanded a convocation of the Diet, which, in April 1841, declared that suppression of the convents was incompatible with Article XII of the Federal Pact which guaranteed the rights of the convents. The Great Council of Aargau offered, as a compromise, to reopen three of the convents—a proposal which the Diet refused to consider. In 1843, a proposition that re-establishment of a fourth be approved was accepted by the Diet in a close majority vote. The hope of the majority that this would be widely approved as a reasonable compromise proved to be in vain. Indeed the conservative opposition insisted that the Diet was without constitutional authority to decide religious questions by a simple majority vote.

At this point we might well pause to ask for some of the outward evidence of rebellious behaviour against which the "establishment" complained. In a "Memorandum on the Affairs of Switzerland"[21] we read:

> Complaints are made especially of the progressive tendency of the youth of the canton [Aargau] to mutiny and insubordination. The adult scholars particularly are distinguished by their rebellious spirit and the rudeness of their manners and character. . . . The people have too often been excited to insubordination. Too much has been said to them of natural rights and not enough of their duties. The public newspapers of the canton have too often inflamed their minds with the pompous words of 'light', and 'progress' so that we are now . . . reaping what has been sown. The citizens no longer acknowledge any authority. The youth of the canton . . . relying on their physical force,

incline to break through every restraint which could check their presumption. . . . The public journals preach up the unlimited sovereignty of the people. . . . It is high time that all the citizens of the canton, old as well as young, got upon more solid ground, in order to be able to resist the spirit of irreligion and infidelity which threatens to overrun the country.

Lord Cowley in a report from Paris to the Earl of Aberdeen, and with apparent reliance on Guizot (French Minister) as his source of information, wrote

> . . . the disorders at Lausanne are fomented and encouraged by the radicals of Berne, who parade the streets of Lausanne, singing the seditious songs so much in vogue in the worst times of the French Revolution and inveighing in terms of great violence against aristocrats and persons possessed of wealth.[22]

Aargau and Lausanne were not atypical. Similar incidents were reported from other towns and cantons.

The catholic cantons, which began in 1841 to hold sessions of their own to decide upon questions of strategy, held several meetings in Lucerne. There emerged from these debates a programme which provided for the creation of a central catholic authority, a continued vigorous struggle against radicalism, and possible joint action with other conservative cantons. Most serious of all was a clear threat to withdraw from the Confederation if all of the convents were not re-established in Aargau. A committee on political affairs was authorized to encourage the interested governments to take such preliminary military measures as appeared to be indicated.

It should be noted that in 1841 the radicals of Ticino succeeded in overthrowing the recently established conservative government. Solothurn, long recognized as catholic and conservative, had fallen under the influence of Joseph Munzinger[23] a vigorous and effective leader of the radical party. Almost single-handed he suppressed all attempts to return the government to the conservatives, and did not hesitate to imprison the leaders of the opposition. Bern had also fallen to the radicals whose most effective and demonstrative leaders were Ulrich Ochsenbein[24] and Stämpfli.[9]

The Jesuit Problem

The seriously divisive troubles over the convents might still have been resolved peacefully were it not for an equally vexing problem which pertained to the Jesuits. This religious Order which had been suppressed by Pope Clement XIV in 1773 was reconstituted in 1814, and Jesuit colleges were reopened in Freiburg and in the Valais. The reappearance of the Order was welcomed in several of the catholic cantons which suffered under widespread and chronic poverty. The Jesuits were prepared to undertake, in such depressed areas and elsewhere, much of the responsibility for higher education. They were accepted gratefully in Schwyz in 1836, even by the protestants. Opposition developed in Lucerne, although the question of inviting the Jesuits to re-establish their Order would appear to be within the competence of the canton. The political storms which broke out with renewed vigor on a wide front focused on the Jesuits as the cause of mounting dissension. The Articles of Baden, strongly anti-clerical, had been adopted by the Concordat of Seven only shortly before the Jesuit problem added to the flames of controversy between the radicals and the catholic conservatives. The peasants of rural Lucerne, led by their fellow peasant Joseph Leu,[25] demanded of the cantonal government that the Jesuits, vigorous defenders of the Faith, be invited to Lucerne as teachers and priests. The issues were becoming resolved into a power struggle between the anti-clerical radicals and those who would at all costs defend the Faith. The Jesuits themselves, recognizing the seriousness of the opposition, delayed taking any action on Lucerne's invitation. In February 1844, the Great Council decided to defer a further study of the Jesuit question. On the surface, the ticklish problem appeared to have been put to rest. But it was not to be so. The resolution of the issues that sharply divided the people and the cantons defied any peaceful solution.

A small scale civil war was fought in Valais in 1844. The Jesuits were numerous and were blamed by many for inciting the people of Upper Valais into open revolt. A small army of rebels marched on Sion. In connivance with a faction of the government in lower Valais they easily seized power and became masters of the government; but not without several violent encounters including a bloody battle on the river Trient. According to Grote (**153**) the public considered the Jesuits to have been responsible for these intrigues and violence. The Jesuits, in turn, busily denounced the rebels as impious and hostile to religion. The political leaders in several of the cantons soon came to regard the Jesuit activities as embittering the relations between the catholic and protestant cantons. In the Valais, as well as in Bern, Solothurn and Ticino the radical governments resorted to extreme measures to overcome the resistance of the catholic conservatives and to maintain a semblance of order. In May 1844, Augustin Keller,[26] himself a catholic, opened a debate on the Jesuit question in the Great Council of Aargau, and in August demanded of the Diet the expulsion of all Jesuits residing in Switzerland.

In February 1845, Guizot, the French Minister-President, was reported to have instructed the French Ambassador in Rome "to represent to the Papal Government the urgent necessity of their recalling the Jesuits from Lucerne, since their continuance in that canton will inevitably occasion a civil war in Switzerland." It appears that Metternich had made similar representations to Rome.[27] Although all of the Powers concerned, including the President of the Swiss Diet (Ochsenbein), agreed that if Pius IX would recall the Jesuits the occasion for civil war would disappear, the matter dragged on interminably. As late as 28 November 1847 when the war was almost ended, we find Britain proposing that the seven *Sonderbund* cantons, in the interest of restoring peace, "address themselves to the Court of Rome" to urge "that the Order of the Jesuits be interdicted from having any establishment within the territory of the Swiss Confederation."[28]

The catholics closed their ranks protectively as hostile demonstrations broke out in various places and inflammatory brochures, articles in the radical press, and speeches by the radical leaders menaced not only the existence of the Order in Switzerland but catholicism itself.

Along much of the Swiss border to the north and east several of the Powers assembled their armed forces either to scare the Swiss into repression of all anarchical activities of the radicals or to be prepared themselves for any contingency that might require military action. In early March 1845, Vienna ordered 4000 men into the Vorarlberg to strengthen the military forces posted on the Swiss frontier. Similar measures were taken by Württemberg and the Duchy of Baden.[29] Metternich, however, considered that armed intervention by the Powers was quite impracticable since "100,000 men would be required to render it efficient."[30] And certain it was that any advance of an Austrian army into Switzerland would unite the entire country in all-out resistance to such a violation of their territory and independence.[31]

Two ill-conceived and poorly-organized attempts by volunteer detachments of radicals to invade Lucerne in 1844 and 1845 failed miserably but added greatly to the deep concern of foreign governments and fears of the catholic conservatives. Radicals from several of the cantons had joined in these unfortunate adventures. The second misadventure in March 1845 was led by Ochsenbein. Of the 2500 radicals under his command, 105 were killed and 1800 were taken prisoner. The French Ambassador warned that France would not hesitate to intervene if it were deemed necessary to restore peace and order. Austria, Prussia and England urged Lucerne to postpone a renewed invitation to the Jesuits. Lucerne refused to yield and with the approval of Pope Pius IX a small number of Jesuits came to Lucerne in 1845 and quietly entered upon their duties as teachers and preachers.

The Sonderbund

Beginning in 1841, representatives of the catholic cantons had met from time to time to discuss their problems and to plan the means of defending their religious freedom and their political independence. With the passage of time, increasing evidence of the spread of radicalism, and the armed attacks on Lucerne, caused the meetings to be held secretly. A formal defensive alliance, a separate federation of the seven catholic cantons, conceived in 1843–44, came into being in December 1845. This was the *Sonderbund*. The five Articles which set forth the purposes of this special federation describe it as a defensive alliance, pure and simple, with a leadership of seven, one drawn from each member canton, possessed of plenipotentiary powers. Two rather sinister paragraphs describe this body of seven as a War Council "charged with top-level direction of the war." (**310**, p. 420). The Articles contain not a word about secession from the Confederation although it is hard to believe that Constantin Siegwart[32] would have opposed a separate conservative Catholic Federation if reconciliation with the protestants and the radicals could not be achieved.

In retrospect, formation of the *Sonderbund* was unwise. Even among the conservative catholics there were those who described it as a serious political error. But beyond question the catholic cantons considered they were seriously menaced by the aggressive anti-clericalism of the radicals whose influence appeared to be increasing in the more liberal protestant cantons.

In June 1846, the *Sonderbund* and the secret preparations of its War Council became known when all was divulged before the Great Council of Freiburg. Although Freiburg was one of the *Sonderbund* cantons, internal opposition was articulate and vehement. Some in Freiburg saw the *Sonderbund* and its plans as the death knell of the Swiss Confederation. It immediately became a federal affair of prime importance and totally overshadowed for the moment the Jesuit problem. The debates before the Diet resulted in August 1846 in a vote of ten cantons and two half-cantons for dissolution of the *Sonderbund*. This was only two votes short of a majority. In October, a revolution in Geneva brought the Radicals to power under the leadership of James Fazy.[33] To the surprise of all, a political upset in St. Gallen in May 1847 gave to the Liberals a majority in the governing council. When Ochsenbein assumed the presidency of the Diet as chief of government in the *Vorort* and opened the session of 5 July 1847, he knew that the votes were in hand. On 20 July, the Diet, by an affirmative vote of twelve cantons and two half-cantons, ordered the dissolution of the *Sonderbund* as incompatible with the Federal Pact.

While awaiting a reply from the *Sonderbund* cantons, the Diet took several actions that were clearly necessary in view of the dangers that now threatened the very existence of the Confederation. The dissident cantons were ordered to cease their preparations for war. Officers, under threat of total demotion, were ordered to refrain from entering the military service of the *Sonderbund*. Munitions from France and Austrian Lombardy, under transport to the dissidents, were seized. As a constructive measure, the Diet appointed a commission of seven to study and report upon the problems that were of deepest concern to the *Sonderbund* cantons. A commission was also formed to undertake a study of the Federal Constitution: its revision was insistently demanded by the radicals who were acutely aware of the weaknesses inherent in almost total cantonal sovereignty. Some of the powers of the cantonal governments had to be surrendered to the central authority if the Confederation was to survive. The final act of the Diet, prior to adjournment, was to order expulsion of the Jesuits and to deny to the Order the right of establishment in Switzerland. This resolution of the Diet fell heavily upon the catholic cantons and struck them at their most sensitive point. Until then, there was some question whether the *Sonderbund* would go to war or would yield to the demands of the Diet. Now, no doubt remained that war was inevitable. Seriously considered by Guizot of France and Metternich of Austria was a partition of Switzerland between the two Powers in the guise of offering protection to the *Sonderbund* (Grote, **153**).

Metternich tried to rally several of the Powers to come to the aid of the catholic cantons. France, faced with a strong liberal opposition, declined. England would have nothing to do with Metternich's plans and, while strongly desirous of maintaining the peace, refrained from lending support to either side.

The Diet reassembled on 24 October, with the seven dissident cantons refusing to participate. The mobilization of 50,000 men was ordered and Henri Dufour,[20] of Geneva, appointed as general, was placed in command of the federal army. This was a fortunate selection for Dufour possessed not only good military experience and outstanding competence as a soldier but he was also dedicated to protection and preservation of the Confederation at any cost. On November 4, the Diet, by formal resolution, decided to dissolve the *Sonderbund* by force of arms.

From the beginning there could be little doubt of the final outcome. Dufour had under his command a larger army. It was better equipped, supplied, and led. The commanding general of the *Sonderbund* army, Ulrich von Salis-Soglio,[34] led a smaller army (30,000 men) with inadequate equipment and, from the beginning, short of munitions. Serious differences in matters of tactics and strategy between him and his chief of staff contributed to his impending defeat.

Freiburg, detached from the other six cantons and most divided in respect to the policies of the *Sonderbund*, was surrounded by four divisions of Dufour's army and surrendered on November 14 without resistance and renounced its alliance with the remaining six. Zug capitulated on November 21. Lucerne provided the strongest defense but, outnumbered and outfought, the *Sonderbund* army was forced back to the city itself. The leaders of the *Sonderbund*, including Constantin Siegwart, Bernard Meyer, Prince Friedrich von Schwarzenberg (an Austrian volunteer in the service of the Alliance) and a few clerics, had already fled. Uri, Unterwalden, Schwyz and Valais were ready to lay down their arms. The war of the *Sonderbund* was over. It had lasted only 26 days. A total of 128 killed in action and 435 wounded was the cost in lives of this, the last civil war in the history of the Confederation. All of the dissident cantons agreed to renounce their alliance and to accept the decision of the Diet to expel the Jesuits. The financial costs of the war were charged against the *Sonderbund* cantons, Neuchâtel and Appenzell Inner Rhodes, which remained neutral throughout, were assessed rather nominal sums to be added to a federal fund for the disabled. Contrary to an order of the Diet, these two cantons had refused to abandon their declared neutrality and failed to join in the war against the dissident *Sonderbund* cantons.

More on the Guarantee

The Great Powers, with the exception of England, resisted for some time any acquiescence in the consequences of the federal victory. They knew that the Liberals and Radicals now in power were committed to reform of the constitution, to structural changes which would consolidate into a Federal State the 22 little republics known in their entirety as Switzerland. The Diet was informed that the guarantee of the territorial integrity and perpetual neutrality of Switzerland, accorded by the signatory Powers of the final Act of the Congress of Vienna (20 November 1815), was conditioned by Swiss retention of the constitution then in force (the Federal Pact). Metternich's principle of government was simple and obvious: divide and rule. A country fragmented into 22 small pieces could be dominated by the continental Powers more easily than a united Switzerland. The Diet refused to yield.

Finally a second note, more threatening than the first, followed. It was signed by the representatives of France, Austria, Prussia and ultimately approved by Russia. The Swiss were amazed and shocked by the peremptory tone of the message. In reply they courteously but firmly reminded the Powers that Switzerland, as a sovereign State, had every right to reconstitute its internal structure as Switzerland and its people considered best.[35] The pretensions of the Powers in this matter were rejected outright. Both France and Austria were disturbed by the turn of events in 1848. To France, the new Swiss constitution would no longer permit France to behave as if she had some sort of dominion over Switzerland. Austria was troubled because she had lost her old friends in Switzerland and had gained no new ones. Metternich believed that the Powers enjoyed the right of "police supervision" over Switzerland, a concept that was incompatible with Switzerland's new constitution and, to the Swiss, was equally repugnant and untenable under the Federal Pact. Metternich was constantly fearful that any unitary constitution would draw Switzerland once again into the French orbit. In fact he argued insistently that if Switzerland became something other than the kind of State which the Powers guaranteed in 1815, the solemn guarantees would consequently become null and void.

Intervention by the Powers came abruptly to an end with the revolutions of 1848. In Paris, Louis-Napoleon was toppled from his throne, while in Vienna the arch conservative Metternich was forced to flee the country in haste. He found refuge in England, then in Belgium, ultimately seeking retirement in his Johannisberg castle. In 1851, at the age of 78, he was recalled to Vienna to serve as an adviser to the young king, Franz Joseph.

Problems in the Ticino

Switzerland almost escaped the upheavals of revolution but not entirely, for in the Ticino a host of refugees and political activists caused the greatest embarrassment to the Confederation. The Ticino became the headquarters of a movement directed against Austria in which Mazzini and Garibaldi were conspicuously in the forefront. As Peel, the British Ambassador in Bern, reported to Viscount Palmerston on 14 August 1848 an invasion of Austrian territory from the Ticino would not be in harmony with Swiss neutrality and would give Austria a substantial pretext for armed intervention in this Swiss canton.[36] In a later dispatch, Peel reported that as many as 15,000 Italian refugees, many of them armed, were in the Graubünden. "Great numbers" of refugees were also reported to be in Lucerne, Baselland and Bern. "Incredible numbers" were reported to be on relief. The Italians were mostly conscripts and "nothing could induce them to return to Lombardy . . . while they showed the greatest repugnance to enter Piedmont." The *Vorort* begged Austria to proclaim an amnesty to encourage these "poor refugees" to return to their own country. France was requested to issue passports to those desirous of entering France.[37] On August 30, Peel reported to Palmerston that Marshal Radetzky, military governor of Austrian Lombardy, had urged the government of Ticino to disarm the organized bands of refugees, to see that they are dispersed and otherwise restrained from invasion of Lombardy. Two armies of insurgents, each of 4000 men, under the command of Garibaldi and four others were reported to be harrassing the Austrians in guerilla warfare and in proclaiming an Italian Republic in Bormio.[38]

Because of the failure of the cantonal governments in the Ticino and in the Graubünden to take any effective action against the militant refugees and because Radetzky had threatened to take measures which were strictly within the sole competence of the Federal Government, federal troops were sent into the Ticino and the Graubünden. Refugees were disarmed and some were transported into the interior of Switzerland. Others were expelled to Piedmont. Their weapons were sent to the armory in Lucerne.[39] Troops under Garibaldi's command were disarmed and dispersed.

The measures threatened by Radetzky (19 August) against Ticino were put into effect on September 18: all citizens of the Ticino, resident in Lombardy or in the Venetian State, were ordered to return to the Ticino; all postal and commercial communications between Lombardy and the Ticino were terminated; and passports issued by the Ticino authorities were not honored for entrance into Lombardy unless they carried the visa of the Austrian Ambassador in Switzerland.[40]

The Confederation, considering Radetzky's note to the government of Ticino as hostile, insulting, provocative and founded on false or exaggerated reports, replied promptly in a vigorous protest directed to the Austrian government. The actions taken by the cantonal and federal governments were defended as fully compatible with Switzerland's international obligations. The *Vorort* demanded an immediate revocation of the vindictive actions taken by Radetzky, including, incidentally, his termination of salt exports to the Ticino which were assured and protected by treaty. With pardonable exaggeration, the *Vorort* declared this suspension to be "hostile and without example in the history of civilization." The Austrian government was reminded that in late July an entire Italian army corps had been forced to retreat into Swiss territory, there to seek temporary refuge. The granting of asylum, in conformity with the principles of humanity, was stated to be a longtime policy of the Confederation in its status as a neutral land. It was also said to be the policy of the Confederation "to observe a rigorous neutrality *vis-à-vis* neighbouring States, of not meddling in any way in the affairs of a foreign State, all this in conformity with the constantly observed principle that each nation must be free to regulate its internal affairs according to its needs."[41]

Though the government of the Ticino objected to the intervention of 2000 federal troops, it is quite clear that the problem at issue had become a federal matter which lay outside the competence of the cantonal government.[42] By mid-November 1848 order had been restored and amicable relations between Austria and Switzerland had been renewed—at least diplomatic correspondence was again couched in cordial terms. But see Chapter 10, Introduction.

The Constitution of 1848

Apart from the short-lived war with the *Sonderbund* and the unfortunate troubles on the Ticino–Lombardy border and in the Graubünden, Switzerland was the only continental country that was not drawn into the turbulent waters of the revolutions of 1848.[43] This was a blessing. In comparative peace and quiet she could devote herself to the important constitutional reforms which were on everybody's mind.

The original commission, appointed in 1847 to initiate extensive amendment of the Constitution was enlarged in the interest of broad cantonal representation. The leaders, all of a liberal or radical tendency, proved to be men of outstanding competence: Ulrich Ochsenbein,[24] Jonas Furrer,[44] Robert Steiger[45] from Lucerne, Joseph Münzinger,[23] Henri Druey,[46] Friedrich Frey-Hérosé from Aargau, and Johannes Conrad Kern.[47]

The Commission gave itself wholeheartedly to the project and succeeded in completing their great assignment in less than two months. One must not underestimate the difficulties of the task: demands by the most extreme radicals for a highly centralized government—a close approach to that of the "one and indivisible" Helvetic Republic of 1798; demands by the representatives of the strongly conservative cantons to preserve the *status quo* and to respect the ancient principle of cantonal sovereignty; the fears of the catholics that they would suffer from protestant repression; and the suspicion of the cantons with small populations that they would be rendered powerless against heavily populated Bern and Zurich. The final document, as presented to the Diet, was written and edited by Kern and Druey. It was a remarkable series of recommendations, founded, not on high-sounding abstract principles, but derived from almost six centuries of struggle as an evolving Confederation and from the hard lessons of the preceding 50 years. The Diet made few changes in the document and in June approved the Constitution by majority vote. The final session of the Diet was held in Bern which was to become the capital of Switzerland. On 12 September 1848, an electoral commission was able to report that the new Constitution had been approved by $15\frac{1}{2}$ cantons and by a popular vote of nearly 1,900,000 against 292,400. The new Constitution was then declared to be accepted and recognized as the fundamental law of the nation.

Furrer prepared a preliminary draft (*Entwurf*) of the Constitution which was widely distributed in Zurich. It concluded as follows:

> If the Swiss people accept this proposal, so ought it with truth be said 'we are the only people in Europe who have carried out in these stormy times, in peace and quiet and by legal means, the difficult work of its political restructuring' (**196**, p. 100).

Haas claims that Burlamaqui of Geneva and especially Rousseau had a far greater influence on formulation of the Declaration of Independence and the American Constitution than Locke, Montesquieu, Blackstone or Coke (**159**). In turn, the two-chambered government provided for in the American Constitution, appealed to James Fazy of Geneva, with strong support from Bluntschli in Zurich, as a good model for use in structuring the Federal Parliament of Switzerland. The Swiss constitutions of 1848 and 1873 were certainly modelled after the main elements of the American Constitution (**369**).

We need not examine the Constitution of 1848 in detail but it may be well to remind ourselves of its salient points.[48] First of all it had to be a compromise, the only realistic way of resolving the conflicting demands of different pressure groups. The least disagreement concerned the introduction of a bicameral type of government. This was a great achievement. There was to be a Council of States (the

Ständerat) which, like the Diet of preceding years, represented the cantons—two delegates from each of the 19 cantons and one from each of the six half cantons. As something quite new to Switzerland, provision was made for a complementary body, the House of Representatives (*Nationalrat*) which represented the people on the basis of population. The canton of Uri which, in the Council of States, commanded the same number of votes as Bern or Zurich, was, henceforth, counterbalanced by the votes of delegates in the House of Representatives where Bern with its population of 300,000 or more was entitled to more delegates (hence votes) than lightly populated Uri.[49] As time went on, the voice of the people, as expressed through the House of Representatives, progressively became more significant than that of the cantons.

Much of the Federal legislation to come had to receive the approval of both the House of Representatives and the Council of States. The two bodies were to meet together from time to time as the Federal Assembly (*Bundesversammlung*), defined in Article 71 as the supreme authority of the Confederation. The Federal Assembly was specifically empowered to elect the Federal Councillors, the members of the Federal Tribunal, the Federal Judges, the Chancellor, the general in command of the federal army and his chief-of-staff.

The executive body, responsible for carrying out the decisions of the Assembly, for proposing to the House of Representatives and the Council of States matters which should be enacted into law, for watching over the cantonal legislation, for seeing that the Federal Constitution was faithfully observed in all respects, and for many other subjects of importance in domestic and foreign relations, was established as a seven-membered body known as the Federal Council (*Bundesrat*).

As an important innovation the new constitution called for a Supreme Federal Court or Tribunal of eleven members. Except that federal judges were to be elected by the Federal Assembly, this tribunal was to operate independently of the publicly elected political bodies.

In matters of procedure it is worth noting that members of the Councils were henceforth to be free from the cumbersome restriction of voting according to cantonal instructions—a long-standing requirement which weighed heavily upon the transaction of business by the Diet during the many years of its existence.

The overriding purpose of the Confederation was stated to be "maintenance of the independence of the Fatherland against the outside, preservation of peace and order within, protection of the liberty and rights of the Swiss people and enhancement of their common welfare."

Of considerable significance is Article III which recognizes the sovereignty of the cantons, insofar as it is not limited by the Federal Constitution. The cantons are to continue to exercise all the rights which they have hitherto enjoyed which have not been given over to the Federal authority. This says a great deal, for, were we to examine the Federal Constitution in detail, we would find that the most essential rights of a sovereign state were transferred to the Federal Government. We would find that the Federal Government alone may declare war and peace; enter into treaties, commercial and otherwise, with foreign States; declare, collect and retain for federal purposes the income derived from import and export duties at the national frontiers. Intercantonal duties, transit charges and other impediments on trade were abolished. The cantons were denied the right to conclude political treaties and alliances between themselves (Art. VII). Secessionist movements were expressly forbidden—a grim reminder of the *Sonderbund* and of the threats inherent in the Borromaic Federation of 1586. The rights of coinage, and of operating the postal services were transferred to the Federal Government. Weights and measures were at last to be standardized and unified under federal jurisdiction.

Of great importance are Articles 89 and 121. The former states that federal laws and federal decrees must be approved by both Councils (par. 1) and that federal laws and generally binding decrees must be submitted to the people for approval or rejection if 50,000* Swiss citizens entitled to vote or eight cantons so demand (par. 2). Article 121, which deals with amendments to the Constitution states that partial revision may be brought about by means of a popular initiative or according to the forms laid down for federal legislation (par. 1). The popular initiative consists in the request, presented by at least one hundred thousand* Swiss citizens entitled to vote, aiming at the introduction, setting aside, or modification of specified articles of the Federal Constitution (par. 2).

The referendum (Art. 89) provides a means for the people to set aside decisions approved by parliament. The initiative provides for collaboration in changing the Federal Constitution. Sometimes there is a feeling that participation by the people is excessive; there are very many votations on matters submitted to the referendum or initiative. Is democracy abused (**55**, p. 327)?

We may well ask, what was left within the competence of the cantons and how did the new constitution benefit the ordinary citizen? First, let us consider the man on the street, as we commonly designate the ordinary citizen. Article IV harks back to the Constitution of the Helvetic Republic. We are told that "All Swiss are equal before the law. There shall be in Switzerland no subject status, and no special privileges attributable to place, birth, family or person." Elsewhere in the constitution we find that minorities are to be protected in their rights and a number of precious freedoms are constitutionally guaranteed: freedom before the law, freedom of settlement, of association, of trade and industry, freedom of the press and freedom of worship. Nevertheless, the Jesuit Order and all of its affiliated organizations were denied the right of establishment in any part of Switzerland (Articles 51, 52), an inevitable sequel to the disputes described earlier (this constitutional proscription against the Jesuits was abrogated in May, 1973).

And the cantons, what did they gain and what rights did they retain? The several Articles that concerned military matters and provisions for defense of the State and the member cantons added much to cantonal security. The British envoy in Bern reported in 1859 to Lord Russell that "in the winter of 1856–57, during the crisis of the Neuchâtel affair, this country [Switzerland] placed on foot within a month an

---

* As amended in 1977. Prior to 1977, 30,000 citizen requests were sufficient for a referendum and 50,000 for an initiative.

army of 200,000 men, well provided with artillery, and confidently prepared to cope with the invading armies of Prussia."[50] Advanced training of the militia became a federal responsibility. The Federal Government also assumed increased and clearly defined responsibilities to ensure defense of any canton that was threatened with violence from without or which might find itself unable to suppress internal violent revolt with the quite small military force that it was still permitted to have at its beck and call.

Income for cantonal expenses was assured. Initially at least, the cantons retained possession of the salt monopoly, of a stamp tax, a tax on alcoholic beverages, and the right to levy a certain amount of direct taxation. Education continued to be a local and cantonal responsibility, except that Article 27 gave the Confederation the right to establish a university and a polytechnic school.[51] As the years have passed the expenses of the Federal Government have increased more rapidly than those of the cantons. New sources of revenue are not open to the Federal Government without amendment of the constitution and this requires legislative approval by a majority of the cantons and majority acceptance by the people through a national referendum. If the economic health of a country and its people is not at its best we know quite well that increased taxes and new devices to add to the income of government are abhorrent to the ordinary citizens who, in Switzerland, have frequently denied through a referendum the requests of government.

Although the cantons, over the years have transferred in bits and pieces some of their powers as Sovereign States to the Federal Government, an effective operational compromise has evolved. In short, the Federal Government enacts a hosts of laws applicable to the entire federation, but frequently concludes the text with the statement that enforcement is a responsibility of the cantons. This "throws the door wide open" for non-enforcement by a canton if the law is not pleasing to the cantonal authorities—a result which can be detrimental to the best interests of the Federation.

Relations with Great Britain

The political posture of Great Britain during the three decades under review should be reported upon for it was far removed, with respect to Switzerland, from the policies of the continental Powers. This was partly attributable to Palmerston's[52] suspicions of Metternich and general disapproval of his policies, especially with respect to Metternich's obvious desire to convert Switzerland into an Austrian protectorate. The revolutions and popular unrest of 1830 passed England by. Public opinion became liberalized and this was reflected in government. Palmerston consistently rose to the defense of Switzerland not so much in the cause of liberalism but to maintain peace in Europe, without which Britain's economy could not hope to flourish. It was important to Britain that Switzerland serve effectively as a buffer to nullify the ambitions of Austria and France, each of which sought a dominant political position on the continent. This meant, in turn, that Switzerland's independence must be safeguarded. She must be constantly assured of her territorial integrity and inviolability.

To defend the cause of Swiss independence and neutrality against the machinations of the continental Powers, Palmerston named Robert Peel[53] as British Ambassador accredited to Switzerland. Peel fraternized with the Radicals and freely expressed his sympathies with their program for social and constitutional reform. The diplomatic representatives from the rest of Europe regarded him as an *enfant terrible.* He and the French Ambassador were the only foreign diplomats who lived in Bern. The others had been ordered by their governments, in protest against Bern's liberalism, to live in Zurich.

When the refugee problem was most vexatious to the continental Powers, Metternich proposed that Switzerland be surrounded with a military cordon until she had expelled all of the troublemakers. Neither France nor Britain would agree to such a policy. Friedrich Wilhelm IV of Prussia sought agreement among the Powers to mobilize against the "lawless and godless" radicals. He contemplated a military occupation of Neuchâtel which enjoyed the dual but ambiguous status of a Swiss canton and a Prussian Principality, whose neutrality, so he claimed, had been infringed upon by Switzerland. But Palmerston pointed out that the Treaty of Vienna required the Powers to respect Swiss neutrality, hence the military occupation of any part of the Confederation was out of the question. Britain disapproved of Metternich's constant threats against Switzerland, and France, for a time, defended the *Vorort* in its replies to Metternich's menacing demands. But when a French spy and *agent provocateur* was arrested by Bern, Switzerland immediately declared herself outraged and released an anti-French brochure— thousands of copies being distributed in Paris. France responded by sending troops to the Swiss frontier and closing it against the passage of people or goods from Switzerland. Bern protested against any foreign interference in her internal affairs and strenuously objected to the hostile blockade.

Palmerston did not consider the radicals in Switzerland to be a serious danger to the European States, and he reminded the Powers at a Paris conference that they were bound by treaty to respect the independence and neutrality of Switzerland. France appeared to be satisfied and lifted the blockade. In fact, neither Austria nor France attempted intervention by force, possibly because liberal movements in their own countries were coming to the surface. Ochsenbein's speech in July 1847 was favorably received by Palmerston who sent his congratulations to Ochsenbein. But he also cautioned Switzerland against a repression of the *Sonderbund* by force of arms because it might invite a dangerous intervention by the Powers.

The Diet declared war on the *Sonderbund* on 4 November 1847. A few days later the Duc de Broglie proposed to the five Powers that they join in offering their services as mediators between the two warring parties. The political aspects of the interrelations between the 22 "Sovereign Cantons"—not the religious questions— were proposed for discussion.[54] It is interesting to note that Palmerston, in agreeing that the Powers should offer to mediate the dispute, attached three important conditions to Britain's acceptance:

the refusal of such an offer, if it should unfortunately be refused, is not to be made the ground for armed interference in the internal affairs of Switzerland;[55] that the Diet should confirm the declarations which it has frequently made of its determination to respect the principle of the Separate Sovereignty of the Confederated Cantons, which form the basis of the Federal Compact;[56] and not to allow, the case arising, the insertion in the Federal Compact of any new Article without the consent of all the members of the Confederation.[57]

In proposing that amendment of the Federal Compact required unanimity of consent by all 22 cantons and in stressing the principle of cantonal sovereignty, Britain clearly agreed with Metternich and with the position of the *Sonderbund* cantons as set forth at great length by Constantin Siegwart-Müller of Lucerne.[58,32] Nonetheless Britain considered the separate alliance of the seven dissident cantons to be at variance with Article VI of the Federal Compact and Palmerston expressed the hope that France would so remind the leaders of the *Sonderbund*. Prussia also maintained that the separate alliance was generally admitted to be illegal. Though Palmerston accepted the principle of cantonal sovereignty, he asserted that one would push the principle too far by claiming that the occasional temporary occupation of one or more cantons by federal troops is incompatible with such sovereignty.

One need hardly add that the *Vorort* "refused most positively all intervention from abroad in this purely internal affair," and later (December 8) reaffirmed their rejection of peaceful mediation by the Powers not only because hostilities had already ceased, "but even on principle."[59] Ochsenbein went still further in declaring that "the Federal Authorities . . . will not recognize that any Power or any minority of the cantons has the right to interpret the Federal Pact—a right which belongs only to the Confederation itself."[60] To concede even an iota to the demands of the *Sonderbund* cantons or to the proposals of foreign mediators was too much to expect of the tough-minded Ochsenbein.

Palmerston was wrongly accused by various diplomats of intervening in the *Sonderbund* war through representations to Dufour. The general denied the charge. In describing the campaign against the *Sonderbund* he wrote that no foreigner was permitted to approach the general staff, and that no British agent did so (**106**). The British premier sent Canning to Switzerland to offer his services in achieving a peaceful solution to the affair but the war was over by the time Canning arrived on the scene. Friedrich Wilhelm IV of Prussia, Louis-Napoleon of France, and Metternich were angered by Palmerston's desire to bring the deeply divisive dispute to a peaceful end. They had hoped for a *Sonderbund* victory and were visibly soured by the triumphant rise of the radical left and the ultimate emergence of a truly federated nation.

In July 1849, the Federal Council had an opportunity to flex its muscles on behalf of the people of this newly emerged nation. Ten thousand revolutionary troops from Baden, beaten by Prussia, crossed the Swiss frontier in good order and sought asylum. The Federal Council promptly ordered the cantons to expel the leaders of this horde of rebels in search of asylum. For years, Switzerland was a sanctuary of agitators and rebels from other States. Many of them continued to disturb the peace and quiet of Switzerland's neighbours despite regulations designed to prevent such behaviour. Admittedly these rules of conduct for Switzerland's "guests" were poorly enforced and Switzerland was repeatedly compromised (**196**).

Were we to look forward to the 1860s we would find problems arising, such as that of mixed marriages and the 1864 treaty with France, that were not easily solved by the Constitution of 1848. Some of the federal councillors were prepared to stretch the constitution to cover any troublesome problems, but to the older councillors and to many of the people the constitution of 1848 was as sacred as the ten commandments: everything must be solved within the rigid and narrow limits of the *Verfassung* (**330**). The revisionists sought to strengthen the military capability and efficiency of the State because of the growing federation of the German States to the north and a united Italy to the south. Politically there were two forces: the centralists and the federalists, with increasing pressure (that never ends) for much greater respect for cantonal sovereignty. See also Chapter 10.

Neutrality

The thirty or so years that followed the Congress of Vienna were destined to expose Swiss neutrality to challenges fully as serious and as threatening as any that faced the Confederation during the two centuries that ended with the French Revolution, the invasion of Switzerland and the "one and indivisible" Helvetic Republic of 1798. The whole of Europe enjoyed a decade of comparative peace and quiet after the final fall of Napoleon. Everyone was tired of war. The continental States were on the verge of bankruptcy. Commercial blockades by one side or the other had almost ruined the economies of all.

Switzerland suffered severely. Hard work, a Spartan existence by many, restoration of her industry and a gradual return of her export markets ultimately paid off. And during these years of recovery there was also a widespread satisfaction, almost triumphant, that the Powers at last had given formal recognition to her total independence, her territorial integrity, the inviolability of her borders and her perpetual neutrality. Indeed, all of this was conceded to be in the best interests of all Europe, and all of these diplomatic triumphs were even guaranteed by the Powers. But as we shall soon see, the deepest disagreement existed between the two parties—Switzerland *vis-à-vis* the Great Powers—as to what, in fact, was guaranteed.

One of the first threatening incidents that disturbed the repose which Switzerland was at last beginning to enjoy came only five years after the final Act of the Congress of Vienna was signed. On 17 July 1820, the French Minister of War, General Sebastiani, introduced in a budget speech before the Chamber of Deputies a few remarks that were overtly menacing to the Confederation. "The time has passed when we can entrust to a secondary Power, however brave, an important portion of our eastern frontiers . . . if France found herself engaged in a serious war with Germany, she would be forced to occupy with her troops this same Power." Two days later another French general expressed the same point of view. Charles Pictet de Rochemont replied in 1821, anonymously, in a publication entitled "De la Suisse dans l'intérêt de l'Europe." Its distribution in France was banned and French newspapers were not permitted even to mention its existence. Two years later it was republished under Pictet's name and with an expanded title (**289**). He destroyed Sebastiani's thesis point by point.

The early 1820s ushered in another and much more serious menace to Switzerland's peace and neutrality than the provocative rhetoric of a few French generals. Indeed, it was a new and totally unanticipated danger, never before experienced during the many years of Swiss neutrality. We refer to the influx of refugees from the German States, from Piedmont, and to some extent from Spain, who were received most hospitably by several of the cantons. There they escaped oppression. The political activists, who were mostly intellectuals such as the Snell brothers from Germany, renewed their clarion call for extensive political reform, distributed revolutionary brochures and founded left-wing newspapers. The radical left of the Liberal party gained in strength and dominated the governments of several of the cantons. Disturbing as this was to the conservatives throughout Switzerland, it was the repercussions abroad from this progressive drift into a radical liberalism that created a crescendo of complaints from Switzerland's neighbours. The Confederation was accused of tolerating the dissemination of vicious propaganda into neighbouring States, and of serving as the center of an infectious political process from which the deadly contagion of revolt would spread into all of Europe. Threats of intervention in the internal affairs of Switzerland began to darken the communications that reached the *Vorort* from neighbouring States. The Confederation, as a neutral State, was accused of acting irresponsibly in not suppressing the troublemakers. In guaranteeing the independence and neutrality of Switzerland, the Powers, so it was claimed, had every right to intervene if provocations arising within Switzerland disturbed the peace and quiet of her neighbours.

Although there was plenty of fuel in the fire, much more was added by a second wave of refugees who fled to Switzerland following the revolutions of 1830. The Confederation was alarmed by the turn of events. It sensed that Europe was again on the brink of war. On 27 December 1830, the Diet issued the following Declaration of Neutrality:[61]

> The Diet of the Swiss Confederation . . . declares in the name of the 22 federated Cantons, that if war should break out between the neighbouring Powers, it is firmly resolved to maintain a strict Neutrality. It has the right to this as an independent State, and this right has been guaranteed by the most solemn treaties. It declares again that to ensure respect of this [Neutrality] it will use all the means that are in its power. . . . With trust in the God of their fathers, the Confederates await events with calm and solidarity. They unite all their efforts to defend the integrity of the soil, the independence of the nation and their ancient liberty. No sacrifice will be too great to attain this noble end. In these grave circumstances, the Diet entrusts the destinies of the State to the patriotism, the courage and the perseverance of every Swiss whom it will call to arms to protect the frontiers against every external attack from whatever side it may come.[62]

We should note that this is much more than a declaration of neutrality. It is a declaration of Switzerland's intention to call upon her men, the federal militia, to respond to an imminent call to arms to defend the country against any possible attack. Switzerland had already learned that international guarantees of the inviolability of its territory and of its neutrality were little more than scraps of paper. Prussia and Great Britain together—an odd couple—had urged Switzerland in 1815 to strengthen its armed forces since the only sure defense of its independence and its neutrality must come from within. It was Stratford Canning (the British Ambassador) who persuaded the Swiss to centralize the administration and control of military affairs, to organize a military school for officer training and to establish a war chest. Prussia's concern stemmed without doubt from her concept of the balance of power in Europe. Were war to break out once again between the two ancient combatants, Austria and France, a well equipped, well manned, and well organized Swiss army committed to the defense of a neutral Switzerland would be an effective restraining wedge against either Austria or France. This would leave Prussia free to pursue her own plans of aggrandisement at the expense of the other German States.

Switzerland retreated slowly, and perhaps reluctantly, from her stubbornly held position on her right as an independent State to grant asylum to incoming refugees from foreign countries as she, and she alone, might determine. Was she right in insisting that her neighbours may not intervene? Her recognized independence, guaranteed by the Powers, would seem to permit her to resist any intervention in her internal affairs but her neutrality, equally recognized and guaranteed by the Powers, would surely not permit her to tolerate and condone within the territory of the Confederation any activities that could be provocative to another State and disturbing to its peace and tranquility. How a provocative activity is to be defined and who is to be the judge of an alleged provocation is another matter. The armed attack upon Savoy by a band of adventurers based on Swiss soil was surely a provocation to Sardinia, to which was added the embarrassing twist that Switzerland, by the Vienna Treaty of 1815, was the protector of Savoy's neutrality. Whether inflammatory propaganda by individuals who describe a neighbouring State as an enemy of elementary human rights and an oppressor of its people justifies intervention in the affairs of a neutral State may be open to question.

Why was Switzerland so slow in achieving the arrest, expulsion and deportation of those among the refugees and among its own people who were guilty of criminal acts, however such acts may have been defined by the Diet when it conceded that the right of asylum was being abused, and agreed that any violent intrusion into neighbouring territory was an illegal act against a friendly State? The answer to this resides in the near total cantonal sovereignty which was enshrined in the Federal Pact. Not until the dissolution of the *Sonderbund* and adoption of the Constitution of 1848 was enough power vested in the Federal Government to permit the enactment of legislation on important matters of consequence to the whole of Switzerland.

Lest we conclude that the Confederation and several of its cantons were alone guilty of violating neutrality through provocative acts to its neighbours in which political activists seemed freely to indulge, it is appropriate to examine the other side of the coin. In the war of the *Sonderbund*, who supplied arms and weapons to the *Sonderbund* cantons? Who helped to finance their campaign against the federal authority? Austrian Milan, France, and Sardinia provided weaponry, and Austria granted the financial aid. Were these not unfriendly and provocative acts toward a neighbouring State? Had the *Sonderbund* emerged victorious, Switzerland would have been ruinously divided and a second *Sonderbund*, consisting essentially of the protestant cantons, would have arisen.

Throughout the history of nations, neutrality as a fundamental principle in foreign policy has been a target of abuse as well as of praise. The period we are considering was no exception. The negative comments, not unlike those of earlier years, should be mentioned for they frequently carried a good deal of conviction and were often expressed by men of goodwill and of judicious temperament:

(a) Neutrality is inherently negative; it is expressed in abstention from something, viz. from war and from acts conducive to war; it is lacking in positive values; (b) It is an admission of weakness; (c) It is a fad of Swiss diplomats who, if they were realistic, would recognize that the treaties of 1815 which include the principle of perpetual neutrality are not in harmony with the present political system in France, on which the fate of Switzerland depends; (d) It is immoral and expressive of national selfishness; (e) A free and independent people should be ashamed to hide under a cloak of neutrality when people in neighbouring States seek to rise against their oppressors. The Swiss should join, in the name of elementary justice and human rights, in overthrowing rulers who exploit and victimize their people. In other words, Switzerland has a revolutionary mission within Europe; (f) Neutrality is a snare and a pitfall conceived by the Powers as a means of separating Switzerland from the rest of Europe.

Others indulged in emotional tirades, slogans, and inflammatory outbursts originating within Switzerland or within neighbouring States:

(g) This "timid outsider" . . . has tarnished our spiritual (*seelische*) position. The Swiss has become resigned, skeptical and indifferent. He goes cautiously out of the way of any action, holds back from decisions, criticizes all happenings as a Pharisee. Through neutrality the Swiss national character has experienced an unfortunate imprint. Switzerland is merely an intellectual place of refurbishment; it is no longer a creater of unique values; (h) Neutrality has converted Switzerland into a servile maid in the service of foreign Powers; (i) It signals the death of everything Swiss; (j) People! Neutrality is your death![13]

Mazzini went further and, though totally in error, proclaimed to all that neutrality was forced upon Switzerland in 1815 against her will. The Powers, so he said, were determined to seal it off hermetically to protect their own countries from the infectious democratic principles that flourished in Switzerland.[63]

A few words must be added about the guarantee which Metternich had managed to sandwich into the declaration by the Powers concerning Switzerland's perpetual neutrality, her independence, territorial integrity, and the inviolability of her frontiers. At first sight the guarantee of these precious rights by the signatory Powers of the Final Act of the Congress of Vienna would seem to be innocent and free of all mischievous intent. But, in retrospect, and bearing in mind the revolutionary activities of the political refugees and their impact upon the ultra-conservative monarchies of Europe, the Powers of eastern Europe used the guarantee as a justification for the many threatened interventions in the internal affairs of Switzerland. Within limits the Swiss conceded, though reluctantly, that the neighbouring States had cause to complain.

However, another aspect of the guarantee led only to a total standoff between the two parties. The Federal Pact which had served as the constitutional structure since 1815–17 deprived Switzerland of sufficient strength at the center to legislate effectively on most matters of any consequence. The drafting of a new Constitution became the loudly proclaimed objective of the radical left. Metternich, with corresponding determination, championed the cause of the reactionaries and declared in unison with Prussia and Russia that the guarantee in the Vienna Treaty of November 1815 was tied indissolubly to the then constitution of the Swiss Confederation. In other words, replacement of the then Federal Pact by a new Constitution would render null and void recognition by the Powers of the independence, territorial integrity and perpetual neutrality of Switzerland. A majority of the cantons refused to accept this interpretation and the designated leaders within the country proceeded with their appointed task of drafting a new constitution. This was completed and the constitution of 1848 became the law of the land.

The year 1848 was also a time of political turmoil and of popular revolt throughout the continent. These convulsive events, including the fall of Metternich, ended the argument, and Switzerland, now a nation, entered upon the future with new hopes, aspirations, and confidence in her internal strength. She learned much about the dangers of involvement in international party politics and, most important of all, became convinced that the 1815 guarantee by the Powers was a delusion and a snare.

Ochsenbein, in his opening speech before the Diet in July 1847, explained in a few words Switzerland's interpretation of the troublesome guarantee:

> ... foreign Powers have absolutely no right to inject themselves in our internal affairs for it is not by virtue of the Treaty of Vienna that the Confederation has the right itself to draw up its constitution but it is by virtue of its sovereignty; it is not the Federal Pact of 22 cantons which has been guaranteed by the contracting Powers, it is rather the territory pertaining to the Confederation by virtue of the Treaty of Vienna.[64]

Observations of Fenimore Cooper

Before bringing this chapter to a close it may be of interest to include some observations by a distinguished American—James Fenimore Cooper (1789–1851), who, with members of his family, travelled in Europe from June 1826 to October 1833. Several months in 1828 and again in 1832 were spent in Switzerland. He was a diligent traveller and a keen observer, covering parts of the country with the same thoroughness and zeal that Coxe had displayed in the late eighteenth century. His observations and comments are recorded in several publications (**89** to **93**). They contain much trivia, some gossip, and many reflections on a host of matters that stirred his interest. His descriptions of the scenery are almost poetic in their beauty: "The lake was covered with boats, whose tall sails drooped in pure laziness" (**91**, p. 186); "The lake of Brienz . . . is imbedded among mountains that divide the clouds" (**92**, I, 221); to the south from the Rigi Kulm "rose the mountains in a crowd and confusion . . . the peaks, hoary, grim and awful; a congress of earthly giants" (**92**, I, 191); "As picture after picture broke upon us, the old *toozy-mouzy* was awakened, until we . . . felt ourselves in a perfect fever of mountain excitement" (**91**, p. 187). And also, "lake of Lungern . . . looking blue and dark, laved the side of one of the most exquisitely rural mountains eye ever beheld; the whole of its broad breast being in verdant pastures or meadows, and teeming with brown châlets" (**92**, I, 230).

He had relatively little to say about the political upheavals, the refugees, the activists and the *agents provocateurs*. In August 1832 he wrote "Europe is in a very unquiet state. The governments like to crush the spirits of the people, and the people begin to see the means of extricating themselves from the grasp of their taskmasters" (**89**, p. 274). Later in the same month, we learn "The agitated state of Europe . . . had kept the usual class of travellers at home . . . though the cantons are said to be pretty well sprinkled with Carlists, who are accused of assembling here to plot" (**91**, pp. 185, 186). In Brienz "An Englishman at a nearby table began to cry out against the growing democracy of the cantons . . . 'instead of one tyrant, they will now have many'" (**91**, p. 193). "I soon felt a suspicion that the man was an employé of the Carlists, and that his business in Switzerland was connected with political plots" (**91**, p. 194). In Bern (1832)

> many arrests had just taken place, and a conspiracy of the old aristocracy had been discovered, which had a counter-revolution for its object. . . . This very day is said to be the one selected for the effort, and rumour adds that a large body of peasants from the Oberland were to have crossed the Brunig yesterday, with a view to co-operate in other sections of the country . . . the Austrian government and the French Carlists, are openly accused of being concerned in this conspiracy[65] the plot had been betrayed, some were already arrested, and some had taken refuge in flight (**91**, p. 199).

Finally "Schweitz[66] is in dissension and may soon split into two" (**93**, II, 195).

Cooper made an astute observation on the interest of the Powers in maintaining Swiss neutrality; "The cantons are equally good, as outworks, for France, Austria, Bavaria, Wurtemberg, Lombardy, Sardinia and the Tyrol. All cannot have them, and all are satisfied to keep them as a defence against their neighbours" (**93**, II, p. 168). A related comment: "The Confederation has been formed and will be kept together more by outward pressure than by any natural cohesion. . . . It would be sadly troubled to make head against a vigorous combination, like that which partitioned Poland" (**92**, I, 215). Two interesting comments about his own country and its people: "Americans [have] an impertinent interference with the concerns of others" (**91**, p. 269); "Americans are great talkers on political subjects; you would think they were about to fly to their arms, and just as you expect a revolution, they go home and drink tea" (**91**, p. 231).[67]

I suspect that Cooper had a puritanical complex against alcoholic beverages and drunkenness. In the Valais "here I have seen a great deal of it, even among the females. I met one of the latter staggering drunk in the road . . . I repeat for the eleventh time . . . there is less of this disgusting practice at home . . . than in any other country I have visited" (**92**, I, 112). In Paris "you will judge of my surprise when first I saw a platoon of the royal guard . . . staggering drunk, within plain view of the palace of their master . . . passed thirteen drunken men during a walk of an hour. Many of them were so far gone, as to be totally unable to walk" (**91**, p. 219). "I asked a labourer if he ever got *grisé* [drunk] and he laughingly told me—'yes, whenever I can'" (**91**, p. 220). "Official reports show ten thousand cases of females arrested for drunkenness, in Paris, during the past year" (**91**, p. 221).

Cooper had a curious attachment to quantitation—the number of windows in houses, population estimates for almost every town and canton he visited and data such as the following: "I counted 158 of them [chalets] from the windows of the inn" (**92**, I, 83); of 110 passers-by in the vicinity of Bern "97 had different shades of auburn [hair] from very light brown to very fair, none had red hair and scarcely any black" (**92**, I, 111). He also reports that in a single hay field there were 23 laborers of whom 16 were women" (**92**, I, 111).

As many others had reported, Cooper noted the high incidence of thyroid goitres. "Goitres? They are seen by thousands; nay, few people here are absolutely free . . . quite usual to see them of hideous size . . . Valais, the very focus of goitreism" (**92**, I, 112). In St. Maurice, canton of Valais, he noticed many cretins in the streets and mentions the prevalence of "hideous goitres" (**92**, II, 193).

In the Thurgau, Cooper encountered a number of well-dressed beggars. Later he learned that young mechanics after apprenticeship travelled about on foot from place to place to learn still more of the trade: "On these professional pilgrimages, they are permitted to beg, by general sufferance" (**92**, I, 137). Near Altstätten he met more beggars, "commonly little children," who called out "*Bitte, bitte*" which Cooper heard as "Pity, pity"[68] (**92**, I, 152). Later, as he approached Zug, "children rushed out to beg" (**92**, I, 176). In "Tockembourg"[69] he met many "sleek, well-fed, and sturdy beggars with well-filled knapsacks . . . a questionable mode of commencing life" (**92**, I, 161).

Cooper's writings on Switzerland are richly sprinkled with entertainingly amusing, and sometimes snobbish, observations presented in his inimitable style. With respect to Schaffhausen "Prior to 1798 its government was *aristo-democratique* . . . which, I presume, means that the aristocrats ruled, while the democrats thought they ruled" (**92**, I, 135). In St. Gallen we learn that a high wall surrounded the Abbey and separated it from the town "Most probably to keep the holy celibates home at night" (**92**, I, 157). The female pilgrims [on their way to Einsiedeln] "seemed respectable and more human than usual" (**92**, II, 35). "Beauty in the sex is scarcely to be looked for here, or indeed, anywhere else among mere peasants" **(92, II, 82)**. *Voiturier*, defined by Cooper as "a class of men . . . who deal in horses, wines, lamp-oil and religion" **(91, p. 184)**.

And to conclude we find a delightful generalization about the Swiss: "Notwithstanding one or two instances of roguery that I have encountered, I would as soon depend on a Swiss, a clear bargain having been made, as on any other man I know" **(91, p. 303)**. This reminds one of a much earlier generalization by a famous English naturalist, John Ray, who travelled through parts of Switzerland in 1665: they [the Swiss] are so honest that "one may travel their country with a bag of gold in his hand" (Ray, **303**).

Notes and Comments

1. The cantons remained free to carry on direct negotiations with foreign agencies in economic and commercial matters, and in matters of a juridical and police nature. They were, however, restrained from entering into agreements that impaired the rights of other cantons or were not in harmony with the Federal Pact.

2. France, generally in disfavour in Switzerland, tried to restore something of the old time good-neighbour relations of pre-Napoleonic days. She entered into capitulation agreements for more than 12,000 Swiss mercenaries. The Confederation, determined to practice the impartiality required of a neutral State, provided Holland's armies with over 10,000 men. Spain, the Papal State, Naples and England contracted for about 5000 more, hence a grand total of about 25,000 Swiss mercenaries. Prussia also maintained in Berlin a regiment of Swiss guards drawn from the Principality of Neuchâtel. Because of the rapidly spreading wave of liberalism and politically radical movements in Switzerland, the supply of mercenaries to foreign governments was soon to decline rapidly. Their use in support of ultra-conservative monarchies raised many questions in Switzerland.

3. The border cantons resented this loss of income. They lost no time in inventing charges of their own which were not designated as duties but were nonetheless superimposed on the federal tariffs.

4. Zürzach is on the left bank of the Rhine about 75 km east of Basel.

5. *Abschiede.* 10 July 1817, Art. XIX, p. 124.

6. Constant de Rebecque, Benjamin (1767–1830). Constant travelled in England and Germany in his youth. Stimulated by the revolution in France, he went to Paris in 1794 and became a member of the Tribunate in 1799. Banished by Napoleon in 1802, Constant lived first in Weimar and later in Coppet as a guest of Mme. de Stael. He returned to Paris in 1816 and became a member of the liberal opposition party and, in 1830, a Councillor of State. In a number of writings on the theory of government, he accepted as an ideal the limited constitutional monarchy of England.

7. Snell, Ludwig (1785–1854). Born in Idstein (Hesse), Snell attended the gymnasium of which his father was director. He studied in the University of Giessen and returned to Idstein gymnasium as a professor in 1809. After suppression of the Idstein gymnasium in 1817, Snell became director of the new gymnasium in Wetzlar. However, his liberal ideas were unacceptable to government. Dismissed from his position, Snell moved to Switzerland and in 1824 went to London where he eked out a living by giving lessons in German language and literature. In 1827 he returned to Switzerland to a teaching position (Greek literature and ancient philosophy) in Basel. Politically active, his writings were widely distributed throughout Switzerland. In 1831 Snell became director of the *Républicain*, the principal organ of the liberal movement. Zurich conferred its citizenship upon him and elected him to the Great Council of the canton. He became a professor in the Zurich gymnasium, but soon moved on to Bern where he lectured on public law, political economy, and the history of the Swiss Confederation. However, the aristocrats of Bern would not tolerate his too-liberal ideas. Again in Zurich and then in Nassau he continued to expound the ideas of radical liberalism. Toward the end of 1847, Snell returned to Switzerland. The Radicals were now entering upon a period of triumph. Tired of the fray, he retired to Küssnacht (Zurich) and to the study of socialism. Many of his writings proved to be ephemeral but were very influential in the 1830s and 40s.

8. Snell, Wilhelm (1789–1851). In May 1845, Snell was dismissed from his professorship of jurisprudence by the governing council of Bern. He was charged with excessive drinking, drunkenness and leading the students astray by such habits. According to Feller (**129**), no less a person than Gotthelf called Snell a corruptor of the youth "who uses the lecture theater as a saloon and the saloon as a lecture theater." Stämpfli rose to Snell's defense. In a leading article in the *Berner Zeitung* he wrote "Reaction has devoured its first victim." He vigorously attacked the authorities who "condemned him [Snell] not because of his weakness but because of his virtues." Others described Snell as a generous and almost childlike person who would give away his coat to one in need. He was deeply religious in a personal sense and totally unselfish. In the advocacy of liberal and radical causes "he could stir up his hearers as if fiery lava flowed from his heart and soul" (Weiss, **383**). Young people were entranced by his words and his spirit. In preaching representative democracy he so impressed his student audiences that they spoke often of a Law School for the Youth, to be founded by Snell.

Whoever knows Professor Snell knows he is a man of extraordinary spirit (*Geiste*) and character, but also has his weaknesses. Herr Snell is born a man of the opposition, who, especially when his feelings are aroused, recognizes no one beside and over him, and who would oppose the highest government authority even if this were the dear God himself. But, likewise, everybody who knows him knows that secret plots or intrigues are foreign to him and that he would be the most incapable man for the founding or execution of a conspiracy. (*Berner Zeitung*, 29 May 1848, unsigned).

In time, the Superior Court (*Obergericht*), in accordance with decisions of the governing council of Bern and of the lower courts, awarded Snell substantial damages—one year's salary and continuance of this as a yearly payment. In February 1849, after being rejected for two years, he became professor of Natural Law, French Civil Law, and Bernese Criminal Law.

9. Stämpfli, Jakob (1820–79). Born into a farming community, Stämpfli was raised in the restricted limits of farm life. At the age of 12 he was sent to school in Lausanne and Neuchâtel. He became interested in the study of law in his early teens and was admitted as a student of jurisprudence by the University of Bern in 1840. Among his professors was Wilhelm Snell, Stämpfli's most stimulating teacher, and whose daughter ultimately married him. In 1844, he passed his State examinations in law and opened an office in Bern. In the same year he founded the *Berner Zeitung*, the purpose of which was to promote direct democracy, greater responsibility among State officials, reform of popular education, improvement of the judicial system, and uniting of the liberal-minded men (*Freisinniger*) of all cantons. From 1846 to 1850 Stämpfli was a member of the governing council of Bern. In 1848 he was elected to the *Nationalrat* (Federal House of Representatives) and became its president in 1851. At the age of 34 he was elected to the Federal Council by the Federal Assembly and served until 1863. He was President of Switzerland in 1856, 1859, and 1862.

In many ways he was a simple man and lived a simple life. He was blunt, direct, and free of affectation. When asked, while a Federal Councillor, why he always travelled third class he replied "Because there is no fourth class." He was taciturn or laconic in company and abhorred small talk. His speeches were clear, informative, and remarkably precise, but his superior ability sometimes caused his colleagues in the Federal Council a little discomfort in his presence.

From 1855 on, he was the recognized leader of the Radical party. He advocated a military occupation of North Savoy at the time of its annexation by France but was not supported by his colleagues in government. He also joined with Druey in supporting the defensive and offensive alliance proposed by the King of Sardinia for military action against Austria in Lombardy but was outvoted by his fellow Councillors.

His great preoccupation was the Swiss railroads. This soon led to a power struggle between Stämpfli who advocated public ownership and Alfred Escher—a man of great wealth and political power—who championed private ownership. The railroads, at first greeted with suspicion by the people, sprung up like mushrooms; several of the companies were founded by Escher. Stämpfli retired from politics in 1863 and founded the *Eidgenössische* Bank with the obvious purpose of fighting Escher (head of the largest Swiss bank) on his own ground.

After the American Civil War, Stämpfli was named a member of an international tribunal to adjudicate the USA's claim against England for damages—England having equipped the southern Confederates with arms and a warship, the *Alabama*. This proved to be his last public service (129). He died in 1879.

10. Eynard, Jean Gabriel, of Geneva (1775–1863). Businessman in Genoa and financial adviser to the Queen of Etruria and the Grand Duke of Tuscany. After 1810, he lived in Rolle and Geneva where he built the Palais Eynard and the Athenaeum. He accompanied Pictet de Rochemont and d'Invernois as a Geneva delegate to the Congress of Vienna in 1814, and used all of his strength and a part of his financial resources in the case of Greek independence.

11. *British State Papers* 24, 981–82, 8 November 1833.

12. *British State Papers* 24, 979–81, 31 October 1833.

13. Mazzini, Giuseppe (1805–72). Italian patriot and a leader of the European revolutionaries. His philosophy is clearly set forth in the following excerpts from his writings:

> Then began the exile hunt. For a space of four months diplomatic notes fell as thick as hail upon poor Switzerland, or like the swarms of crows and flies that surround a corpse. Notes came from Naples, from Russia, from all four points of the compass . . . bidding her expel the exiles . . . they were but two hundred, and yet, seized with terror and hatred at the sight of them, old Europe has donned her antiquated armour of notes and protocols and, determined to do battle against them, has put in motion her whole body of diplomatists . . . prefects, troops, and spies (234).
>
> People! Neutrality is your death. When, in the cabinets of the despots the Pact was prepared which the Congress of Vienna produced, a sarcastic smile broke over their lips which said: Switzerland will be neutral! And the kings spoke: again a dead people . . . neutrality is nothing other than death. It is this word . . . which bans your sympathies, which closes your heart to pity, to indignation, and to hope . . . you reply: I am neutral! Eh bien! be neutral! People, do not deceive yourselves. This is not neutrality . . . Neutrality such as your fathers understood it was nothing other than a hatred for all kings and a love without limits for the people. Your fathers were neutral when they caused the crowned heads to fall. . . . They were neutral at Giornico. They were neutral at Marignano. They were neutral because they abhorred equally Louis XI, Charles the Bold, the Duke of Milan, and François I. . . . They fought for the people, for liberty, for themselves (235).

14. The notes of protest were similar in content. Excerpts from two of these are sufficient to indicate the concern and fears of Switzerland's neighbours:

> The first appearance, some years ago, of formidable numbers of Poles, who forcibly entered Switzerland from France . . . had already created uneasiness in the Bavarian Government. . . . It cannot escape the acute sagacity of the High Directory [*Vorort*], that this danger must still impend, so long as Foreign refugees, whose criminal designs admit of no doubt, are allowed to remain in Switzerland (*British State Papers* 24, 994–95, 8 March 1834).
>
> . . . fugitives and conspirators from every country have been able to choose Switzerland for their place of reunion, and from there, through public and secret conspiracies, they have organized revolutionary propaganda which embraces every country, propaganda which can lead to the assassination of princes and to uprisings of the people, through the principles that it professes, and which have been spread most recently into Germany and Italy, through incitements of every kind. . . . In the first days of February, an invasion of Savoy, prepared and directed by the Poles, the Italians and several German fugitives, and . . . the audacious conspirators and participants in this criminal *attentat* have been able to return to Switzerland as into a place of secutiry (*British State Papers* 24, 992–93, 6 March 1834).

15. *Abschiede* pp. 239–42, 18 March 1834; p. 283, 24 June 1834.

16. *British State Papers* 24, 1013–15, 23 April 1834.

17. *British State Papers* 24, 1032–33, 1 June 1834.

18. The fiery spirit among the "rebellious ones" (refugees and some citizens), is evident from the following letter written to the editor of a paper in La Chaux-de-Fonds:

> You have not forgotten that following a shooting which took place last 6 September . . . two citizens were arrested. The one had sung "Le Chant du départ," and the other, my word it is necessary to tell

you, the other was accused of having *pissé* in the pocket of a royalist. I have just seen the list of expenses entailed by those two crimes of lese-aristocracy. Total 20 francs. 'You have sung a patriotic song: 20 francs for the mayor. You have *pissé* or sneezed or spit in the face of a royalist. 20 francs for the mayor.' I almost forget to tell you that the expenses of the trial for singing the song and for . . . amounted to 68 francs, after taking off 20 francs for the mayor. [*Le Proscrit (Journal neuchâtelois)*] 15 March 1835.

19. *British State Papers* **24**, 1042–48, 7 July–21 August 1834.

20. Dufour, Guillaume Henri (1787–1875). One of the most famous Swiss generals. He was born in Constance of an old Geneva family. In 1807 Dufour was sent to the École polytechnique in Paris where he worked for an entire year in a military hospital. He also studied botany under H. A. Gosse, then in Paris. In 1809 Dufour was sent to Corfu to assist in defense of the island against the English. He was taken prisoner but was released when Corfu was regained by the French. In 1817 he returned to Switzerland and acquired anew his Swiss citizenship. In 1827 Dufour became a Federal colonel and in 1830 was posted at Thun where Prince Louis-Napoleon served under him as a junior officer. In 1831, honored by France as a Companion of the Legion of Honor, Dufour declared "I will use all my efforts and influence to defend a neutrality which is nearly as much in the interests of France as in that of Switzerland. It is a task in the accomplishment of which I have dedicated my life." In 1847, and again in 1857, Dufour was elected General by the Swiss parliament. He conducted the war against the *Sonderbund* with conspicuous skill and humanity. He ordered his troops to refrain from any "overkill" and to show the utmost compassion toward the defeated enemy: they too were Swiss and sons of the Fatherland. Some foreign papers had insinuated that Palmerston had influenced Dufour in his campaign. In fact, neither a British minister nor any diplomatic agent accredited to Switzerland had any contacts with Dufour. He confided in no one **(106, p. 78)**.

21. Submitted to Viscount Palmerston (*British State Papers* **57**, 865–66, 18 February 1845).

22. *British State Papers* **57**, 835–36, 21 February 1845.

23. Munzinger, Joseph, of Solothurn (1791—1855). Politician. In December 1830 he proclaimed the sovereignty of the people of Solothurn and thereby initiated the political regenerationof the canton. He held various high political offices in Solothurn from 1831 onwards, including presidency of the cantonal government. He served also as Federal Councillor (1848—55) and President of Switzerland in 1851.

24. Ochsenbein, Ulrich (1811–90). Politician and one-time leader of the Radicals in the canton of Bern. He was elected to the governing council of Bern in 1846, and was President of the Diet in 1847. In 1848 he was elected to the Federal Parliament and subsequently to the Federal Council. After 1850, Ochsenbein became increasingly conservative and in 1854 withdrew from the Federal Council. He went to France and became a brigadier general in the French service. He returned to Switzerland in 1856 and was recalled to France in 1870. As a general in command of a division he served under Bourbaki, whose army, in January 1871, retreated into Switzerland and was interned. In 1855 Ochsenbein recruited two regiments of Swiss to enter the service of France in the Crimean war. Six recruiting bureaus were established in France just across the Franco-Swiss border, thus circumventing the strictly enforced Swiss law. [Recruiting within Switzerland for military service on behalf of foreign Powers was strictly forbidden by the Federal Parliament (*Bundesblatt* 7, 4 August 1855; and additional enactments in 1859).] On eventual return to Switzerland, Ochsenbein vigorously fought the policies of his former colleagues within the Radical party. In 1844 and 1845, he led two expeditions of volunteers in unsuccessful attacks on Lucerne, the center of the catholic opposition to the anti-Jesuit policies of the Diet. Although Ochsenbein used all of his efforts to bring about the war against the *Sonderbund* he opposed Druey and Stämpfli in their attempts to induce the Federal Council to join Sardinia in a defensive and offensive alliance directed against Austria.

25. Leu, Joseph (1800–45). Catholic democrat. Opposed vigorously the politics of the aristocrats and anti-catholics. Active in cantonal politics. Assassinated 20 July 1845.

26. Keller, Augustin, of Aargau (1805–83). Active in Aargau politics and education. Served in the cantonal government and as a member of the Federal House of Representatives 1854–66. President of the Assembly 1858. Although a catholic he initiated the action against the Aargau convents. He was a leader

of the anti-Jesuit movement and an outspoken opponent of the doctrine of infallibility enunciated by Pope Pius IX in 1870.

27. Cowley to Aberdeen, *British State Papers* **57**, 833, 3 February 1845.
28. *British State Papers* **57**, 948, 27 November 1847.
29. Sir Robert Gordon to Aberdeen, *British State Papers* **57**, 840, 8 March 1845.
30. Sir Robert Gordon to Aberdeen, *British State Papers* **57**, 841, 22 March 1845.
31. Minto to Palmerston. Report of a conversation with Ochsenbein, *British State Papers* **57**, 898–901, 4 October 1847.
32. Siegwart, Constantin (1801–69). Born in Ticino. Settled in Lucerne. Very active as a conservative politician. Chairman of the *Sonderbund* War Council. On defeat of the *Sonderbund* army, he fled to Valais, then Lombardy, Innsbruck, Strassburg and Köln. Returned to Switzerland (Altdorf) and published several volumes of his memoirs.
33. Fazy, James (1794–1878). Publicist and statesman. Educated in France in business and commerce but soon turned to literature and journalism. In 1825 he founded the *Journal de Genève*. Returned to Paris in 1827 and participated in the revolution of 1830. Founded several papers and fought strenuously for freedom of the press. Returned to Geneva in 1833, and in 1842 founded the *Revue de Genève*—the organ of the Radical party. In October 1846 the Radicals took over the cantonal government with Fazy at the helm. During several years of authoritarian leadership he accomplished much in modernizing Geneva and in constructing the new city. In 1871 he became a cantonal senator and was appointed Professor in the University of Geneva. Died in poverty in 1878.
34. von Salis-Soglio, Ulrich (1790–1874). In the Alliance War of 1813–14; Dutch military service in Belgium (1830–39); Swiss Colonel, 1842, stationed in the Valais to restore order; General of the *Sonderbund* army, 1847.
35. On 1 January 1847, Bern succeeded Zurich as the *Vorort* for the ensuing two-year period. The governments with which Switzerland enjoyed diplomatic relations were so advised. Austria, on January 10, reminded Bern that the authority from which the *Vorort* derived its power was the Federal Pact. Bern was advised that this power must "not be invaded in its essence or violated in its spirit . . . which can only be satisfied by faithfully upholding the Cantonal Sovereignty guaranteed by the Confederation, and only limited as regards specified Federal objects" (*British State Papers* **35**, 1135–36, 10 January 1847). On the following day Prussia sent a note of similar tenor to Bern. Russia joined in the act on January 10. Bern acknowledged promptly the Austrian and Prussian notes and, without mincing its words, advised the Austrian and Prussian diplomats that in matters relating to the internal

affairs of Switzerland they [the *Vorort*] are solely responsible to the other Confederated Cantons . . . and they are equally determined carefully to defend the independence of the Swiss Confederation and of its Federal authorities, and resolutely to resist every possible attempt to interfere in any manner whatever in the internal affairs of the Confederation (*British State Papers* **35**, 1137, 14 January 1847).

To all of this, Ochsenbein, as President, in his opening speech before the Diet on 5 July 1847, added a thought of his own ". . . it is not the Federal Pact of 22 cantons which has been guaranteed by the contracting Powers; it is the territory belonging to the Confederation by virtue of the Treaty of Vienna" (*British State Papers* **36**, 1119, 5 July 1847).

36. Peel to Palmerston, *British State Papers* **41**, 1275–76, 14 August 1848.
37. Peel to Palmerston, *British State Papers* **41**, 1312–13, 26 August 1848.
38. Peel to Palmerston, *British State Papers* **41**, 1327–28, 30 August 1848.
39. The *Vorort* to the Government of Ticino, *British State Papers* **41**, 1331, 23 August 1848.
40. Marshal Radetzky to the Government of Ticino, *British State Papers* **42**, 637–38, 15 September 1848.
41. The *Vorort* to the Austrian Government, *British State Papers* **42**, 662–67, 23 September 1848.
42. Peel to Palmerston, *British State Papers* **44**, 759–60, 13 November 1848.
43. A localized disturbance broke out in Neuchâtel where the Royalists, suffering a popular defeat,

were displaced from government and the formal ties with the nominal sovereign, the King of Prussia, were apparently severed.

44. Furrer, Jonas, of Winterthur and Zurich (1805–61). Born in Winterthur. His father was a locksmith, the youngest of 14 children fathered by a gravedigger. During his early schooling he aspired to be a physician but accepted his father's advice and studied law. As a novice he came under the tremendous influence of the great Kaspar von Orelli. Subsequently, he continued his study of law in Heidelberg and Göttingen with finishing touches in Berlin, Dresden, Prague and Zurich. In 1827 he took his final examinations and qualified in Zurich private law. Göttingen, apparently interested more in the past than the present, evoked critical comment by Furrer. "If [in Göttingen] a student found in an old yellowed law book a comma that had never before been mentioned, he would be among the most fortunate and could write a learned paper about it" (**196**, pp. 9, 14). Furrer soon became active in politics and served at all levels in city, cantonal and federal governments. After adoption of the new Federal Constitution, he became a Federal Councillor and first President of Switzerland (again in 1852, 1855, and 1858). He was of great service to Switzerland in the Political and Justice departments where his leadership in foreign affairs (the refugee and Neuchâtel-Prussia problems) was outstanding. He was highly regarded by his colleagues because of his great ability, his honesty and his freedom from intrigue. An extensive and warm biography of Furrer is that by Isler (**196**).

45. Steiger, Jakob Robert (1801–62). Doctor of medicine and liberal politician. Took part in both of the ill-fated expeditions against Lucerne in 1844 and 1845. Captured and condemned to death. The trial aroused international interest. Freed from prison, he went to Zurich and practiced medicine in Winterthur until 1847. Then returned to Lucerne and re-entered politics. A member of the Federal Parliament 1848–52. A prolific writer on political subjects. Also author of a book (1860) on the flora of Lucerne canton, the Rigi and Pilatus.

46. Druey, Henri (1799–1855). From an old family in Faoug (Canton of Vaud) which provided the mayors of the town for two centuries (until 1753). Statesman. First supported the conservative government of Vaud but later (1830) became a Radical. Participated at all levels in the cantonal government. Contributed greatly to revision of the Federal Constitution of 1848. Elected to the first Federal Council. President of Switzerland in 1850. Favored military support for the democratic movements in Italy and Germany. Retired from politics after his military-intervention policy failed to receive support of the Council and Parliament.

> Druey, a leader in the Federal Council, was a puzzling phenomenon whose powerful influence on the whole of French Switzerland struck the quiet Germans as inexplicable. . . . To the German liberals he was considered a stormy element whom one must keep within bounds. But basically they were guided by all of his impulses. He was the bond (*Bindeglied*) between the older magistrates and the young elements, who pressed forward between the liberals and the radicals. His personal influence kept Vaud firmly for federal affairs on the road to a centralized liberalism. . . . Furrer, Munzinger, Franscini, the men of the old school kept the train on the rails, but he was the driver who at any given time indicated the direction (**330**).

In a speech before the Diet, Druey is reported to have said "My Shirt is nearer to me than my coat" (**153**, p. 31) which may be interpreted to mean "my canton is closer to me than the confederation"—a reflection of the prevailing sentiment throughout Switzerland.

47. Kern, Johannes Conrad (1808–88). Politician, lawyer, diplomat. President of the Justice Commission—a "triumvirate" which in effect ruled Thurgau from 1837–49 in matters of justice, legislation, and politics. In 1849 he became President of the cantonal government, in 1850, a bank president and director of Escher's North-East railway (Zurich) in 1853. Supported the anti-Jesuit movement and the *Sonderbund* opposition. President of the Federal House of Representatives (*Nationalrat*) in 1850 and of the Federal Court of Justice in 1853. As President of the *Schulrat* he organized in 1854 the newly established Federal Institute of Technology. Ambassador to Paris 1857–83.

48. The complete constitution of 1848 is to be found (in French) in *British State Papers* **47**, 1245–65, 12 September 1848.

49. Article LXI provided for one representative in the House of Representatives (*Nationalrat*) for each 20,000 of total population with not less than one representative for each canton or half canton. The amended and updated Constitution of 1963 provides for a total membership of 200 with the seats divided among the cantons and half cantons in proportion to their population (Article 72). Again each canton or half canton is assured of at least one representative.

50. *British State Papers* **50**, 460, 21 November 1859.

51. The exercise of this right came about in 1855 when the Federal Institute of Technology at Zurich was opened. In 1874 a constitutional amendment empowered the Confederation to establish . . . a University and other institutions of higher education, or to support such institutions. The Confederation has never exercised its right to establish a university. The Federal Institute of Technology at Zurich and its sister institute at Lausanne are almost entirely supported by the Federal Government. However, within recent years the Federal Government, through grants to the university cantons, has participated substantially in sharing the capital- and operating costs of the universities. It also now exercises much control over professional education, e.g., in medicine, dentistry, agriculture and veterinary science. Education and training for a great many trades fall under federal control, and secondary education at the gymnasium level is also in large measure regulated by the Federal Government through its right to pass upon the qualifications of those who seek admission to the universities.

52. Palmerston, Viscount (1784–1865). Statesman. Elder son of Henry Temple, the second Viscount Palmerston. Educated in Italy and England. His alliances with political parties were fugitive: he was a true independent. He held many high offices in government including Secretary of State for Foreign Affairs (1830–41 and 1846–51) and Prime Minister (1854–58 and 1859–65). One of his great diplomatic triumphs was in obtaining the independence of Belgium despite much opposition from Holland, France and Belgium itself. He mediated so many European disputes that he was commonly called "the great meddler"—actually a tribute to his skill in diplomacy and his frank honesty in foreign affairs. His knowledge of Europe's problems was encyclopedic. He was disgusted by Louis Napoleon's annexation of Savoy, and his plans for the further aggrandisement of France. "Louis Napoleon's mind," he said, "is as full of schemes as a warren is full of rabbits." His policy toward Switzerland in respect of the refugee problem, the Savoy annexation, and the *Sonderbund* affair was friendly, sympathetic and generous. As much as anyone he prevented Austria and France from waging war on Switzerland in 1847/48.

53. Peel, Sir Robert (1822–95). Third baronet, politician, eldest son of the great Sir Robert Peel (1788–1850). Secretary of the British legation in Switzerland, May 1846, and Chargé d'Affaires in November 1846. Resigned in July 1850 and returned to England. Possessed of a fine presence, gaiety of manner and rich oratorical abilities. His character was volatile and he used his great abilities fitfully. He enjoyed the confidence of Viscount Palmerston but not of Lord John Russell to whom Peel's failings were obnoxious. He was a great friend of Switzerland, and his speeches before the House of Commons on the cession of Savoy to France were rich in factual information. He deplored the duplicity of France and the outright falsehoods of the French diplomats concerning French foreign policy. [Cf. Peel's two great speeches on the Savoy question: 30 March and 22 June, 1860 (**100**); refer also to the next Chapter.] Later, he lived for many years at Villa Lammermoor on Lake Geneva. In the winter of 1871, he personally witnessed the crossing of Bourbaki's army into Switzerland and their disarmament at the border.

54. Duc de Broglie to Palmerston, *British State Papers* **57**, 911, 9 November 1847. As early as February 1845, Guizot had proposed a Conference of the five Powers on the affairs of Switzerland. The proposal, in which Metternich also had a hand, was the subject of a flood of communications among the Powers for the next three years. There was little objection to having such a conference, but the seed fell on stony ground and failed to germinate. Why? Principally because of disagreement on the meeting place for such a conference—London, Baden, or Neuchâtel. The war ended on 1 December 1848, leaving the question of a place for the conference as unresolved as ever. The Alice-in-Wonderland world of diplomacy has not changed. Remember the almost interminable discussion in Paris in 1968–69 between the representatives of South Vietnam, North Vietnam, and two other delegations before they got down to business? It lasted for ten weeks (shall the conference table be circular or rectangular?).

55. Palmerston to Marquis of Normanby, *British State Papers* **57**, 918, 16 November 1847.

56. Draft of identic note to the British Chargé d'Affaires at Bern for presentation to the President of the Diet and to the official organ of the *Sonderbund*. *British State Papers* **57**, 920, November 1847.

57. Draft of identic note to the Diet and to the *Sonderbund*. *British State Papers* **57**, 948, November 1847.

58. Siegwart-Müller, Constantin, to Baron von Kaiserfeld. *British State Papers* **57**, 888–898, 6 September 1847.

59. *British State Papers* **57**, 922, 980, 6 November 1847.

60. *British State Papers* **57**, 874, June 1847.

61. *British State Papers* **18**, 1372–73, 27 December 1830.

62. Six months later, the President of the *Vorort* was able to report to the Diet that the people of Switzerland had responded as one to the call to arms.

> This appeal, dictated by the prudence and dignity of a free nation, made by the inviolability of Swiss territory, has been unanimously received throughout Switzerland . . . it has inspired confidence and reunited the people and the government in a noble end, and has become from this time forward, for one and for the other, the polar star which will guide them through the labyrinths with which the whole of Europe is now encumbered. (*British State Papers* **18**, 1373–76, 4 July 1831).

63. For a remarkably distorted concept of neutrality, read what Mazzini said about it (see Note 13).

64. *British State Papers* **36**, 1119, 5 July 1847.

65. The conspiracy referred to by Cooper was a backlash of the strife in Neuchâtel over the League of Sarnen.

66. The canton (Schwyz), not the nation (Schweiz).

67. Cooper attributes this comment to the Abbé Correo.

68. *Bitte* = Please.

69. Toggenburg.

10. THE SWISS NATION

The Years of its Youth (1848–1914)

Introduction

The Diet met for the last time in September 1848. The first session of the Federal Assembly was held in Bern in early November 1848. Bern had already been selected as the capital of the Confederation. It was well located in the great central valley and on the linguistic border between the French-speaking and the German-speaking parts of Switzerland. It had a long history of leadership in the affairs of the Confederation. There were few to question the wisdom of the choice though a strong case was made for Zurich. The troubles with the *Sonderbund* cantons were too recent to permit any serious consideration of Lucerne.

The adoption of the new Constitution was a great and triumphant moment in the affairs of the Swiss Confederation. A solid base was laid for strengthening at the center with a corresponding decrease in the sovereign power of the cantons. This constituted a first and very important step in the direction of political unification of the 22 federated cantons. Without this, significant progress toward an urgently needed economic unification could not have been achieved.

However, the Constitution of 1848, the innovative governmental structure which it introduced, and the high quality of the first Federal Council did not usher in decades of peace and quiet. The Grand Duchy of Baden was the scene of several popular revolts which broke out in succession in 1848 and 1849. The radical governments of the northerly Swiss cantons did little to control the demonstrations of sympathy and support within these bordering areas. Active recruiting of volunteers in these neighbouring cantons was carried on, as leaders of the revolt, virtually unhindered, sought to widen the base of support and seek military aid among sympathizers in Switzerland. Refugees also streamed in from Baden as troops from Hesse and Prussia entered the Duchy to suppress the uprisings. The Federal Council urged the cantonal authorities to maintain a strict surveillance of the refugees, and ensure the preservation of order by forbidding armed assemblies and expelling any insurgents who had participated in the earlier revolts. The Federal Council called 24,000 men to arms and prepared to mobilize the entire army if the neutrality and territorial integrity of the Confederation were endangered.

In December 1851, Prince Louis-Napoleon, through a *coup d'État*, ascended the throne of France as Napoleon III. This top-level political upset suggested to the Powers that something akin to a reversal in political sympathies at the lower levels could be reasonably expected. No longer, so the argument ran, would radicals and "troublemakers" be permitted to raise their voices or actively foment insurgence against the conservative, aristocratic, and patrician governments of Austria, Russia, Prussia and the other German States. Never again should Switzerland be permitted to be a sanctuary for leaders and activists of socialist doctrines.[1] Within France a party of interventionists demanded that France rush to the aid of the catholic minority, allegedly oppressed following their defeat in the *Sonderbund* war.

Louis-Napoleon was angered by the Swiss press which, at times, tended to ridicule his person and his government. Nonetheless, remembering the good treatment he had received in the Thurgau in earlier years, he curbed his royal wrath. And this was all to Switzerland's good. Austria had tried to tempt the Emperor of the French to occupy Vaud and Geneva while she would move into the Ticino—all of this in the interests of repressing the demonstrations and hostile activities of the radical left and the troublesome refugees. The French Cabinet, however, none too sure that the new emperor knew his way through the maze of foreign affairs, made several peremptory demands upon the Swiss Confederation: (i) that freedom of establishment be granted to French Jews resident in Switzerland:[2] the Constitution of 1848 conceded this right only to persons of the Christian faith; (ii) that a French journalist who wrote unfavorably of the emperor and his government be delivered to the French authorities by direct administrative procedures without submission of the case to the Swiss judiciary; (iii) that the Federal Council give formal assurance that it would expel all refugees designated by the French Ambassador as hostile and undesirable residents. This demand was accompanied by threats of an economic blockade and military occupation.

The Federal Council replied that these extraordinary demands constituted a serious and unwarranted intervention in the internal affairs of a sovereign State and an affront to the dignity and the liberty of the nation. England advised France to cool down: she was making demands upon an independent and neutral State that were unreasonable and improper. Furthermore, neither France nor Austria had the right of military occupation of Swiss territory without the formal accord of the signatory Powers of the Treaties of 1815. On 27 March 1852, the Federal Council put an end to the whole affair by declaring its firm resolve to defend its neutrality and to tolerate on Swiss soil no refugee who was guilty of dangerous machinations against the Swiss Confederation or any foreign Power. Napoleon III, meanwhile, rebuked his ambassador by disavowal of the ambassador's meddling in the internal affairs of a friendly neighbour and by declaring that he never had any intention of undertaking any enterprise hostile to Swiss independence.

The Ticino-Lombardy Affair

This brings us to 1852 and to a renewal of troubles in the Ticino and unhappy relations with Austria. A law enacted in May 1852 restored to the State responsibility for secondary education in the canton. In implementation of the law, the cantonal authorities abolished several religious institutions dedicated to instruction of the youth. The Bishop of Como and the Archbishop of Milan promptly complained to the Austrian authorities, insisting that the cantonal government had violated the law and existing treaties. The Federal Council, with sole responsibility for the conduct of foreign affairs, failed to act with sufficient dispatch, and on 22 November 1852 the Ticino government expelled 22 Lombardian Capuchin monks who were charged with pernicious conduct against the well-being of the State. Lombardy was then an Austrian province. Hence it is not surprising that in December the Austrian Ambassador in Switzerland demanded the re-installation of the monks or, failing this, all Ticinesi resident in Lombardy would be expelled by the Austrian authorities. The Federal Council rose to the defense of Ticino: As a sovereign canton the Council of State had the right and the responsibility of policing the activities of foreigners and of taking such action as was deemed necessary. Privately the Federal Council pointed out to the cantonial government that the measures it had taken were a little imprudent, if not provocative. Ticino was prepared to reimburse the monks by payment of a pension and the affair might have soon ended if the two parties could have reached an agreement on the financial settlement.

Unexpectedly, a revolt against Austria broke out in Milan on 6 February 1853. Leaders of the revolutionary party living in the Ticino were suspected of inciting the uprising. The Milanese authorities closed the Ticino–Lombardy and the Graubündian borders in a move designed to prevent the passage of insurgents into Lombardy. The military commander of Milan followed with measures that forced 10,000 Ticinesi to flee from Lombardy. A diplomatic paper war ensued. Britain, Austria, the cantonal government and the Federal Council were all involved. Austria stubbornly refused to terminate the measures of reprisal and Switzerland, with equal stubbornness, refused to consider Austria's behaviour as other than arrogant. Especially irritating to the Federal Council was Austria's insistence that she had a right to participate in the regulation and control of Ticino's problems with troublesome refugees and revolutionary insurgents. Austria recalled her Ambassador to Switzerland and the Federal Council issued the necessary military orders which the dangerous situation required.

Lájos (Ludwig) Kossuth (1802–94), an Hungarian statesman who led the liberal opposition in Hungary and was forced to flee the country in 1848–49, wrote to Federal Councillor Druey in June 1853 urging that Switzerland take up arms against Austria. It may be recalled that Druey favored military intervention by Switzerland in support of the democratic movements in Italy and Germany (see Chapter 9, Note 46). Kossuth argued that popular uprisings by the many adherents of Mazzini, and revolt within the Austrian army, would facilitate the enterprise.

"The power of Austria is more imaginary than real. It has to employ the first half of its forces to keep the other half in submission. Hungary and Italy are volcanoes ready to erupt at the first opportunity." Kossuth claimed that Croatia, Serbia and Roumania would join in a war on Austria. Furthermore, the German States would not rise to defend Austria because France would then intervene against Germany. Finally, a naval blockade of Austrian ports, e.g. Trieste, can be assured (209).

In realization that a storm was arising in the near East (the Crimean war), France and Britain worked feverishly to prevent a Swiss·Austrian war. Just as the cantonal government of Ticino, radical and anticlerical in its political philosophy, was about to resign because of its failure to solve the local problems arising from the expulsion of the Ticinesi, the Austrian government accepted a payment of 115,000 francs in settlement of the dispute over expulsion of the Capuchin monks. At the same time Austria permitted the return of the expelled Ticinesi to Lombardy, provided only that they scrupulously observed all local ordinances. Thus the Ticino–Lombardy affair came to a peaceful end.

The Neuchâtel Problem

If one recalls the good relations that had existed between Bern and Neuchâtel for some hundreds of years it might seem paradoxical that a situation could arise in the Principality which would expose the Confederation to its greatest danger since the French Revolution. Her very existence was threatened, not so much because of any displeasure with the Confederation arising within the people but because of a curious and ambiguous state of affairs which set Neuchâtel uniquely apart from the other 21 cantons. Not only was it a full fledged member of the Confederation, recognized as such by the signatory Powers of the Treaty of Vienna in 1815, but it was also a Principality, subject to the overlordship of the King of Prussia who was elected sovereign in 1707–08. Despite the potential conflicts inherent in this dual attachment to two totally dissimilar governments, peace and harmony prevailed within the canton—and for a very simple reason. The King of Prussia, resident in Berlin, was far removed from Neuchâtel. He was content, year by year, to receive his share of the taxes levied within the canton, and to leave high-policy decisions to Bern or the Swiss Confederation under whose protection the Principality had been placed at the request of the king himself. His person was also protected by a regiment of Swiss guards recruited from within Neuchâtel and paid from the royal purse.

For many years the political troubles of Neuchâtel were trivial, mere ripples on the surface of rather quiet waters. Then came 1848. This was the year of revolutions and of tumultuous political upheavals throughout Europe. Switzerland had its war with the *Sonderbund*, and many of the cantons elected governments of a radical-liberal complexion. Neuchâtel experienced a republican revolution. The new government declared its ties with reactionary Prussia to be severed, preserving however its status as a member of the family of 22 cantons joined together as the Swiss Confederation. The King of Prussia complained loudly and bitterly to the Great Powers and to royalist parties within the canton. The complaints continued until they became tiresome to the Powers who in the London Protocol of 8 May 1852 gave formal recognition to the new state of affairs in Neuchâtel.

But this was not to be the end of the diplomatic warfare. On 2–3 September 1856, some hundreds of royalists in Neuchâtel seized control of Le Locle and the castle of Neuchâtel. It was a short-lived victory. On the following day, the cantonal militia stormed the castle and captured the ringleaders and 600 of their followers. Bern had hoped to mediate the dispute but direct action by the forces of the republic carried the day. Friedrich Wilhelm IV, furious over the turn of events, demanded that the prisoners be unconditionally released and be granted amnesty. The Confederation, which alone was empowered by the Constitution to negotiate with foreign governments in matters involving the federated cantons, declared that the prisoners would not be released until prior assurances were received from Prussia that the independence of Neuchâtel would be acknowledged and formally confirmed.

The Neuchâtel question immediately became a matter of grave concern to all the principal European Powers. The French position was set forth verbally to the President of the Confederation on September 30: the prisoners should be released. France would then use its good offices with the other Powers to obtain from the King of Prussia firm assurances that the independence of Neuchâtel and its freedom from all foreign bonds would be conceded. Russia and Austria lost no time in joining in. They urged upon the Federal Council the immediate and unconditional release of the imprisoned insurgents. Britain, implying that a joint effort with France to resolve the problem might not succeed, requested of the Federal Council a precise statement of the Swiss position and the Confederation's concept of an honorable solution. Her intention was to seek an agreement among the Powers which would permit a united front in negotiations with Prussia.

By mid-October it became clear that Prussia was preparing to enforce her demands upon Switzerland by military intervention. A huge army, believed to number between 100,000 and 150,000 men, was about to be mobilized and the south German States had given permission to the Prussian command to advance with the army to the Swiss border through Baden and Württemberg. The Emperor of France addressed himself directly to General Dufour on October 24 to remind him of the extreme gravity of the situation. That France intended to make every effort to prevent a Prussian invasion of Switzerland was self-evident. She was motivated only partly by benevolence toward Switzerland. Her own self-interest demanded that Prussia be kept in check. Austria, likewise, was not prepared to accept a serious threat to the balance of power which would be the inevitable result of a Prussian victory in a central European war. She rejected Prussia's call for a common military action against the "Swiss demagogues" and would hinder, if she could, the menacing increase in Prussia's military might.

Both Prussia and Switzerland adhered stubbornly to their positions: Prussia demanding unconditional release of the prisoners in advance of a negotiated settlement of the issues in dispute; refusing to indicate her position with respect to the Swiss conditions for an honorable settlement and "refusal to recognize that Switzerland had any right to change without the King's assent the Constitution of

Neuchâtel," for it is a matter of "honor that he support those [the royalists] who had wanted to re-establish the former order of things."[3] Switzerland, in turn, refused an unconditional release of the prisoners; Prussia must give adequate assurance that the prisoner release and amnesty which she demanded would be immediately followed by Prussian recognition of the total independence of Neuchâtel, free of all bonds to any foreign State. France and Britain gradually moved closer to the Swiss position but Friedrich Wilhelm IV, even by the end of December, had said "not a word either with respect to the base on which negotiations could rest, or of the conditions which he felt able to propose as indispensable for the renunciation of his pretended rights."[4]

Instead of an indirect approach through France or Britain, the Confederation proposed direct negotiations with an accredited representative of the king for the purpose of achieving Prussian recognition of the independence of Neuchâtel. This suggestion was not only summarily rejected but, accompanying this rebuff, came an immediate closing of the Prussian legation in Bern. The king had had enough and was determined to resort to added military pressure. Bern responded in the same vein and with the full cooperation of all the cantons, the students of the universities and academies—the country's youth—declared Switzerland's firm intention to resist the threatened invasion. Thirty thousand of the first line troops were assembled on the frontier and reserves were ordered to be in instant readiness if called.

At this point delegates of the Powers, in conference over the serious threats to the peace of Europe that were now emerging, endeavoured to present a united front in negotiations for a peaceful settlement. They agreed that Switzerland as a sovereign Power had final jurisdiction over the prisoners. Favorable also was the circumstance that the United States of America declared itself prepared to join in such a collective action. The Federal Council, now counting on the moral support and diplomatic intervention of the Powers on Switzerland's behalf, declared itself ready to recommend to the Federal Assembly that the prisoners be released but that they be required, in the interest of public order, to leave the canton until the entire Neuchâtel problem was resolved. This very considerable concession was still encumbered by the demand that Prussia at the same time give positive assurance relative to the absolute independence of Neuchâtel.

The Federal Assembly formally approved the report of the Federal Council, approved the levy of troops for defense of the Fatherland, approved unlimited credits for the expenditures involved, and initiated election of the general and his chief of staff. The Federal Assembly, in January 1857, approved the proposal of the Federal Council that the prisoners be released subject to their temporary expulsion from the canton. They were set free on January 17 and 18 but the threatening gestures and hostility of an embittered Prussia continued for many more months. Not until 26 May 1857 were the last of the matters in dispute settled and a treaty relative to Neuchâtel was approved and signed by the representatives of Great Britain, Austria, France, Prussia, Russia and Switzerland.[5] Several of the Articles might well be summarized. By Article I, the King of Prussia renounced in perpetuity for himself, his heirs and successors all sovereign rights over the Principality of Neuchâtel and the County of Valangin. By Article II, the State of Neuchâtel, henceforth independent, shall continue to form part of the Swiss Confederation on the same footing as the other cantons. Article V declared that a full and complete amnesty would be granted to all of the political insurgents and military prisoners associated with the September uprising. It was also agreed that no action, criminal or correctional, would be taken by the canton or by any other corporation or person against the participants in the events of September.

The signatory Powers also ratified a Protocol, separate from the Treaty, by which the Kings of Prussia were enabled to preserve in perpetuity the title "Prince of Neuchâtel and Valangin," it being understood that the use of this title would not confer upon the Kings of Prussia any rights whatsoever *vis-à-vis* Switzerland or the Canton of Neuchâtel. The king was also granted an indemnity of one million francs.

Why did Switzerland make such a fuss over the Neuchâtel affair? Why did she wait for four and one-half months before releasing the prisioners? Was not the incident a tempest in a teapot that would not have blown into a tornado if Switzerland had only swallowed her pride and acceded to the royal demand? To answer these questions we must think of the rather difficult and potentially explosive situation that inherently confronts any State with divided loyalties and re-sponsibilities. Imagine Louisiana as one of the 50 States of the USA and also as a colony of France, or the State of California continuing, somehow or other, to be under Spanish sovereignty, or Alaska as both a republic of the USSR and the fiftieth state of the USA. The Alaskan analogy is by no means ridiculous for we must think of Neuchâtel in 1856 as a canton administered by a government that was committed to democracy, to freedom, and to the preservation of basic human rights but, also a Principality—a sovereign possession—of one of the most reactionary Powers in Europe. If we agree that a USSR sovereignty over Alaska would lead to trouble, it surely follows that Prussian sovereignty over a Swiss canton in the 1850s would be certain to menace the peace of Europe.

Retention of the royalist prisoners increased enormously the bargaining position of the Confederation in its efforts to bring to an end the ambiguous status of Neuchâtel which presented few if any problems to the Confederation during the many years of cantonal sovereignty and to aristocratic oligarchic governments in several of the most powerful cantons. The prisoners were, in effect, hostages. They were under the full political control of the Federal Government which used the 600 hostages as pawns in a dangerous game with Prussia. As one reads the several messages of the Federal Council to the Federal Assembly in 1856 and 1857 and scans the vast amount of diplomatic correspondence pertaining to the Neuchâtel question, he is certain to be impressed by the ever-recurring insistence of the Confederation that Neuchâtel must henceforth be independent and free of all foreign ties. This was Switzerland's objective and this is what it was all about. In its message of 13 January 1857, the Federal Council summed it up in a few words: "Le point capital est toujours d'obtenir la reconnaissance de l'indépendance de Neuchâtel de toute influence étrangère."[6]

In November 1858 the revised Constitution of the canton was adopted.[7] In view of the events of the preceding two years much is summed up in the first two Articles. "Article I. "The canton of Neuchâtel is a democratic republic and one of the States of the Swiss Confederation; Article II. The sovereignty resides in the people. . . ."

The Unification of Italy

The Italian war of unification should not escape mention, for it came to bear upon Switzerland in a way that was important and unexpected, specifically through the annexation of Savoy by France. Moreover, the Ticino, Switzerland's Italian-speaking canton, reached southwards into northern Italy, bordering on the States of Piedmont and Austrian Lombardy. To the east of Lombardy was the Venetian State, also under the sovereign power of Austria. The serious refugee problem in the Ticino in 1848 and the troubles with Austria on the Lombardian border, attributable to political activists and revolutionaries have been described in the preceding chapter. From 1848 to 1858 the Italian States were the scene of unending warfare, now here, now there. Political skulduggery and ever-changing ephemeral alliances were the order of the day. The Papal State, France, England, Austria, Spain, Piedmont, and Sardinia were all involved as principals in the unfolding drama. Mazzini and Garibaldi, as leaders of the swelling ranks of those who called for the defeat of Austria and formation of a united Italy, pressed steadily forward. The Italian desire for unification and for independence from Austria was deeper and more universal than many realized, especially among those who were shielded from the common people. Cavour, a skillful Piedmontese politician, was exceptional in understanding fully the growing pressure for liberation from Austria and for unification of the Italian States. He was the principal architect of the struggle for freedom and the most gifted tactician among the Italian statesmen of the 1850s. He was also a skillful practitioner of the dubious arts of deceit and duplicity.

Cavour, then prime minister of Piedmont, saw in Napoleon III of France a person with Italian sympathies with whom an alliance might be formed to isolate Austria and force her out of Lombardy and Venetia. An agreement was reached at Plombières in July 1858 between Cavour and Napoleon III whereby France would supply 200,000 men and Piedmont 100,000 for a united effort to expel Austria and to expand Piedmont into a kingdom of North Italy.[8] Central Italy would later become a separate kingdom to be ruled by one of Napoleon's relatives. Southern Italy would become a third kingdom and, if the emperor won out in this game of kingsmanship, would be ruled by another relative of the Bonaparte family. Cavour's agreement, assuming that Napoleon III revealed his plans, reeked with subterfuge and deceit. His heart was set on a united Italy with Rome as the capital. It should be noted that the agreement between Cavour and the French envoy was verbal. No written agreement appears to have been signed and recorded.

Napoleon set an additional price on cooperation with Piedmont. In return for French assistance, which was to continue until Austria was driven from both Lombardy and Venetia, Sardinia would cede Savoy and Nice to France. And now, we must ask whether this prospective annexation was secretly agreed to between

Cavour and the Emperor of France? Except for rumor-mongering, one must conclude that the arrangement was top secret. Let us look at some excerpts from the diplomatic correspondence of the day for the whole question is germane to Switzerland's relations to Piedmont, Sardinia and Savoy and the security of her southwestern frontier.

1 July 1859: Concerning "the rumour of the projected annexation of Savoy to France . . . the Sardinian minister here [Bern] positively denied that there was any such engagement."[9]

4 July 1859: "Count Waleski [French minister in Paris] stated, indeed, that he could give me the positive assurance that there was no understanding whatever upon the subject between France and Sardinia."[10]

8 July 1859: "Count Waleski . . . said that I might give your Lordship the assurance that the emperor had abandoned all idea of annexing Savoy to France."[11]

10 February 1860: "His Majesty, however, disclaimed all intention of annexing Savoy against the will of the Savoyards themselves, and without having consulted the Great Powers."[12]

10 February 1860: "M. de Cavour . . . told him [the Swiss envoy in Turin] that no engagement subsists between Sardinia and France for the cession of Savoy to France, and that Sardinia is not disposed to sell, cede, or exchange Savoy to France."[13]

22 March 1860: "The King of Sardinia received a Savoyard deputation and said the ties which bound his dynasty to Savoy were too ancient to be rent asunder" (**280** p. 129).

Need we add that Napoleon III, his ministers, the King of Sardinia, and Cavour spoke with forked tongues. On 24 March 1860 the "Treaty of Annexation of Savoy and Nice to France" was signed.

Sir Robert Peel, who spent many years in Switzerland and served as Chargé d'Affaires at the British Embassy in Bern from 1846 to 1850, made a number of passionate speeches in the House of Commons deploring the annexation of Savoy to France (cf. also Chapter 9, Note 53). Among his remarks before the House we find the following:

13 February 1860: The Cession of Savoy would be "a most scandalous and iniquitous proceeding";

28 February 1860: "The French talked about correcting their geographical frontiers — a most serious matter because the frontiers were fixed by the great Powers in 1815 as being those that existed in 1792. Only in conference with the Powers could the frontiers be changed . . ." "The independence of Switzerland depended upon its neutrality and its neutrality would be destroyed by the annexation of any part of Savoy to France". . . . "These treaties [1815, and all previous treaties between Switzerland and Savoy] went even further than a guarantee of neutrality, for the House of Savoy engaged never to detach these provinces of Chablais and Faucigny otherwise than to Switzerland";

2 March 1860: "This question of Savoy . . . involved handing over the liberties of many thousands of people like so many slaves to the will and pleasure of the Emperor of the French."

30 March 1860: "France says she wants only 'un territoire de très peu d'étendue.' But this is Savoy which for 230 years has been considered necessary to the welfare of Switzerland. . . . In 1814 she was prevented by the Powers from taking it but now she

takes it without asking. . . . And how could the King of Piedmont part with those provinces which abut upon Switzerland and which he is bound either to keep or to return to Switzerland. He has no more right to dispose of Savoy than our Sovereign would have to part with Gibraltar."

22 June 1860: "On three occasions (February 10, March 1, March 6) France gave assurances that the Powers would be consulted before the contemplated annexation went into effect. . . . It is insulting and degrading for the annexation to take place without even consulting the seven Powers which have solemnly guaranteed the neutrality of this territory under Swiss protection."

5 July 1861: "They all said they were . . . to meet in a conference last year. But none was held. Why? . . . M. Thouvenal . . . said they must recollect that the whole of Savoy was irrevocably attached to France, and they could not, therefore, treat that subject. . . . Thus the only reason for holding the conference was excluded by France. Hence a conference was of no use." [Regarding Louis Napoleon]: "His policy will only have the effect of rousing every man in Switzerland to engage in a patriotic struggle, and of causing the brave people of that country to spurn unanimously the smiles and flattery of a despot. . . . Louis Napoleon wrote 'not only will Savoy augment the French territory but it will open the great Simplon road and give to France the freedom of the Alps and, in case of war, a great battle field for an offensive and defensive contest.' "

The events in the Italian peninsula during 1859 need to be considered *in extenso* because of the determined efforts of Italian insurgents to separate the Ticino from Switzerland and reconstitute it as a part of a new and united Italy. Insurgents in Milan addressed to the people of Ticino a proclamation which was clearly seditious:

An Italian heart beats in your breast . . . we love you as brothers and regard you as our fellow citizens. . . . Oh, let us unite in a beautiful brotherhood all the people of the land encompassed by the sea and the Alps. . . . Everything binds you to us: the Heavens, the land, language, belief, customs, commercial interest, historical traditions, misfortunes and hopes. Everything which is most holy to a people, which determines one's life, which you have in common with us—not with Switzerland. . . . Tichinesi . . . we want to unite with our brothers, we want again to be Lombards and Italians.

The Federal Council reminded the cantonal government of Ticino that the proclamation was an invitation to Ticino to secede from the Confederation—an act of high treason. But the Federal Council believes the Ticinesi to be too intelligent and patriotic for such a treasonable act. The distribution of the leaflet is an unfriendly act which the government of Sardinia should prevent.[14]

Between 24 April and 22 May, 1859, troops from a number of cantons, including Ticino, had been sent by Switzerland to guard the Ticino–Lombardian border. The troops were warned to be on the alert for Italians (refugees or recruiters) attempting to enter Ticino. The border guards must remember that traffic in weapons and munitions is not allowed: weapons, powder and munitions brought in by refugees and deserters must be seized. Old people, women, children and the sick may remain in Ticino but all others must be interned elsewhere in Switzerland. Troops of the warring Powers who cross the border because of enemy pressure or for safety must be disarmed and sent off with military escorts for internment in Chur (Austrians) or Lucerne (French and Sardinians).

The mercenary troops in Naples and Rome were then designated as Swiss regiments, not as foreign regiments. Since they were there to protect despotic governments they aroused great enmity among the local inhabitants against Switzerland and her people. However, it was pointed out that the capitulation agreements run out this year—1859. Henceforth, they may not be called Swiss regiments.

Austria declared war against Sardinia on 28 April 1859 and after several serious defeats on the battlefield, ceded Lombardy to Sardinia under terms of the Peace of Zurich (10 November 1859). By the end of 1860 most of the Italian States were united with Sardinia–Piedmont into the Kingdom of Italy under Victor Emmanuel who was proclaimed King of Italy on 18 February 1861. A Prussian—Italian alliance concluded in April 1866, led to the final defeat of Austria at Königgrätz and the ultimate absorption of the Venetian State into the Kingdom of Italy. In July 1872, after defeat of a papal army almost two years earlier, King Victor Emmanuel entered Rome and declared the ancient city to be henceforth the capital of Italy.

In 1862, shortly after the unification of Italy was completed and Victor Emmanuel was declared King of Italy, the governments of Italy and of Switzerland made a number of declarations designed to extend to all of Italy the provisions of international treaties entered into in prior years between Sardinia and Switzerland:[15]

(a) That of 16 March 1816 concerning the right of establishment by the citizens of one country in that of the other, and abolition of the ancient rights concerning reversion of private property to the State (escheatment).
(b) That of 28 April 1843 on the extradition of criminals.
(c) That of 8 June 1851 pertaining to establishment and commerce.

Switzerland and the Savoy Problem

To appreciate the background of the Savoy problem, which descended heavily upon Switzerland in 1859 and 1869, reference should be made to the Savoy Section in Chapter 9 and to the preceding Section in this chapter. Although a major episode in the paper warfare of Europe's diplomats, the possible annexation of much of upper Savoy by France existed only as a rumor which boiled and bubbled for almost two years before the Treaty of Annexation suddenly came to the attention of the startled Powers. The extraordinary climate of deceit in which the rumors thrived has been described.

When the rumors reached Switzerland, the President of the Swiss Confederation lost no time in impressing upon the British government, Switzerland's influential and constant friend, the vital importance of upper Savoy to Switzerland's safety and independence. Its annexation by France would seriously threaten the security of Geneva and the Valais. On several occasions the President expressed the fear that the role played by the King of Sardinia in formation of the Italian Confederation might impinge unfavorably upon the arragements made in the Treaties of 1815 for protection of the southwestern frontier of Switzerland—viz. neutralization under Swiss protection of upper Savoy.

The questions that had to be resolved were several. Three were clearly of prime importance.

1. Would the status of the affected provinces of upper Savoy *vis-à-vis* Switzerland be essentially modified if these provinces were to become part of the Kingdom of Italy or, alternatively, were they to become part of France through annexation?
2. In the case of a war involving Italy or France, as the case might be, would Swiss troops be able to enter the provinces of upper Savoy to protect their neutrality in accordance with the Treaties of 1815?
3. In such a case would Italy or France have the right to withdraw her troops, stationed in these provinces, by passage through the Valais to Piedmont—a right and a duty hitherto granted to Sardinian troops in the event of a war involving Sardinia?

As long as the ancient Kingdom of Sardinia was the sovereign power in upper Savoy, Switzerland entertained few fears if any for the security of her southwestern frontier. The absorption of Sardinia into the Italian Confederation changed the complexion of things considerably, since the new Italy with a population of about eleven million had to be regarded as a Power of the first order. The Federal Council of Switzerland assumed that there would be no change in the status of the provinces of upper Savoy without the prior consent of the signatory Powers of the treaties of 1815. It was also assumed that in all such discussions, Switzerland would necessarily participate. As late as January 1860 the Swiss Minister in Paris was assured by Baroche, a French Minister, that "this question [the rumored annexation of upper Savoy by France] has no interest, either at present or in the future . . . but," he added, "should any change occur . . . it should only be made after a complete understanding between France and Switzerland. . . ."[16]

The assumptions of the Federal Council proved to be misplaced: the Treaty of Annexation of Savoy to France was signed at Turin on 24 March 1860 by the accredited representatives of Sardinia and France without any prior consultation with Switzerland or the Great Powers. Four days later the Swiss minister at Turin laid before the Sardinian Minister for Foreign Affairs the official protest of the Swiss Government. The treaty of annexation was deemed to be perfidious.

> As this Treaty has been concluded without the concurrence of Switzerland, who had, however, applied to be allowed to participate in it as one of the principal parties concerned . . . this official publication cannot be considered by the Federal Council but as a preliminary act of menace against the rights of which the Confederation is possessed by virtue of former Treaties. Consequently any act of appropriation by France in the North of Savoy, whether civil or military, as long as no understanding shall have been come to with Switzerland on the subject, will be regarded by her as a flagrant violation of her rights. . . . The defence of Switzerland's neutrality in time of War making the occupation of Faucigny, Chablais, and the Genevese by Federal Troops indispensable, the Federal Council has been obliged to address the Powers. . . .[17]

Would the annexation of upper Savoy by France have been nipped in the bud if Switzerland had exercised her right to occupy the neutralized provinces when Sardinia in 1859 entered the war against Austria and joined with Piedmont in the cause of unification of Italy? Would Napoleon III who vacillated repeatedly in his support of Piedmont and was, in fact, a most uncomfortable and irresolute ally, have pressed for the cession of Savoy to France if upper Savoy had been occupied by the armed forces of Switzerland? A strong case can be made for the belief that the emperor would have refrained from the annexation if Switzerland had occupied the neutralized provinces. Napoleon had been well treated by the Swiss when he lived as an honorary citizen in the Thurgau. He had also served as an artillery captain under Dufour and he knew first hand that the Swiss militia deserved the respect of any Power that might engage it in combat. Also, his diplomacy was rich in indecision, suggestive of a weakness that was foreign to the character of his uncle, Napoleon I. He must also have known that Austria, Britain, Prussia and Russia would protest the territorial expansion of France resulting from the annexation of Savoy.

All of this must have been self evident to the Swiss Federal Council, which leads us into the obvious question. Why did Switzerland refrain from occupation of the neutralized provinces of Savoy, her well-recognized right under the treaties of 1815? Was it because of timidity? Was she being cautious, perhaps excessively so? Timidity, no. One can recall few occasions when Switzerland displayed timidity in foreign policy. The facts suggest that the Federal Council yielded to excessive caution, committed a political blunder or succumbed to lethargy. Caution, because it would be in harmony with Swiss foreign policy to make sure that her military occupation of upper Savoy, despite the rights granted by treaty, would not be offensive to the Great Powers. Many months could be expended in reaching a consensus. And, admittedly, Napoleon III was totally unpredictable. Military action by France against Swiss forces in the neutralized provinces could not be excluded. Caution was indicated.

But may one conclude that Switzerland made a political misjudgment in failing to occupy the provinces? Recall that when the tide turned against Napoleon Bonaparte in 1813, the Swiss could almost certainly have occupied the Valtellina, Bormio and Chiavenna, thereby forestalling Metternich's diplomatic triumph in persuading the Powers to transfer the whole of this former Swiss (Graubündian) territory to Austria. Rapid-fire decision-making in such matters was not a characteristic of Swiss political action, always deterred by respect for cantonal sovereignty and the strong desire, if not the necessity, of cantonal unanimity in the formulation of federal policy. The situation in Savoy was somewhat parallel to that in the Valtellina. In both cases important losses of territory, actual or potential, resulted from the failure of Switzerland to act swiftly and confidently when the opportunity came her way.

In 1859, Switzerland was presented with a second golden opportunity to regain the Valtellina. The whole of Lombardy was enmeshed in revolution. Its sovereignty was in a state of flux, with Austria on the losing side. One can safely assert that Austria would probably have preferred to restore the Valtellina to Switzerland than to see it pass with all the rest of Lombardy into the possession of her Sardinian enemy. All that the Confederation had to do to enforce a demand for restoration of her one-time territory was to occupy it at the right moment with her armed forces. Since she had never abandoned her claim on the Valtellina, torn from the Graubünden by Napoleon I, the occupation could hardly be regarded as an unneutral act. Resistance by the weakening Austrians, well on their way to defeat, would not have been encountered. The local population with its strong pro-Swiss sympathies would have welcomed the troops from Switzerland with open arms and rivers of wine.

Her failure to move into upper Savoy was not entirely attributable to procedural delays or lethargy in exercising her rights of occupation when Sardinia and France became involved in the Italian wars. This follows from the fact that France transported troops by rail through a portion of the neutral territory, and Switzerland, far from lodging a protest against this violation of neutrality, condoned the act. The President of the Confederation stated "it was not the intention of his government to prevent the passage of troops by that portion of the Victor Emmanuel Railway which traverses the neutral territory. . . ."[18] The Savoy question was also clouded by the Swiss decision that military occupation of the neutralized provinces by Switzerland was not mandatory under the treaties of 1815 but was optional. The Confederation claimed the right to exercise, or not to exercise, the option and to enjoy the sole right of deciding whether Swiss armed forces would occupy any part of the neutral territory they think proper, in the event of a war in which the neighbouring Powers would be engaged.[19]

Finally we must consider the reaction of France to the Swiss protest of March 28 and to an earlier warning of March 15 addressed to the King of Sardinia whose rumored cession of Savoy to France was believed to be imminent. France responded with perfect aplomb; her *sang-froid* remained undisturbed. On 20 June 1860 the French Minister for Foreign Affairs, in a proposal to Lord Russell of Great Britain, and without mention of the Swiss protest, declared as follows:

> The moment is come for the Government of the Emperor to conform to the obligation which it has incurred of coming to an understanding, as well with the Powers who signed the General Act of Vienna as with the Swiss Confederation, on the subject of the contingent neutralisation of a portion of Savoy. The object of this understanding . . . should, in our opinion, consist in reconciling Article 92 of the Act of Vienna with Article 2 of the Treaty of Turin 24 March 1860.[20]

Article 2 of the Treaty of Turin conceded that the King of Sardinia could not transfer the neutralized provinces of Savoy "except on the conditions upon which he himself possesses them."[21] The Article also declared that the Emperor of France was obliged to reach an understanding on this subject, both with the Great Powers represented at Vienna and with the Swiss Confederation. Of the several means of attaining the desired understanding, a conference of the Powers in which Sardinia and Switzerland would be invited to participate appeared to be the favored procedure. A few days later, the British Minister for Foreign Affairs (Lord Russell) approved the proposal that the Powers confer.

It should be noted that the conference was not held. The status of the neutralized portions of Savoy continued to be a subject of dispute between France and Switzerland for many years. In Annex I to Article 435 of the Treaty of Versailles (1919) an abrogation of the stipulations set forth in the Treaties of 1815 regarding the neutralized zones is stated to have been accepted in principle by both France and Switzerland. A number of reservations by the Federal Council did not permit a final resolution.

France had recourse to an extraordinary argument in an attempted justification of her annexation of Savoy and Nice. The King of Sardinia, through enlargement of his dominions by inclusion of all the Italian States would become the sovereign head of 11 million subjects. This expansion, we are told, would so jeopardize the security of France that the annexation of Savoy and Nice was necessary to restore a semblance of balance. Britain, through Lord Russell, ridiculed this argument by pointing out that France, so rich, populous, and military, with its 36 million inhabitants (exclusive of her colonies), could not conceivably be endangered by a country of 11 million people, on the other side of the Alps, joined together in a fragile federation of which the cement was not yet dry. As we shall soon see, Prussia's Bismarck did not accept the French explanation and balanced off the French territorial gains by seizing Alsace and Lorraine in 1871.

The Vallée des Dappes

France and Switzerland for over 40 years had left unsettled a seemingly minor problem inherited from the Treaties of 1815. At issue was a relocation of the border between the two countries, involving a small strip along the north-westerly frontier of Vaud. In 1815 the Powers agreed that territory seized from Switzerland by Napoleon should be restored. However, a secret agreement, arrived at in the smoke-filled rooms of hush-hush diplomacy, assured the French that the Powers would restore to France some of the territory taken from them by the Treaties. The Swiss government learned of the agreement and refused to be bound by any such secret promises. Switzerland stubbornly resisted and France procrastinated, the Swiss becoming increasingly miffed. The relations between the two countries were already strained by the French annexation of Savoy. Possibly as an appeasement, France, in 1862 agreed to a settlement of the border problem.

In December 1862, a treaty was signed that finally put an end to the long-continued bickering and quibbling.[22] The agreement was nothing more than a compromise. Switzerland ceded to France 704 hectares (1,760 acres) at the extreme westerly end of the area under revision, while France ceded to Switzerland 703 hectares, consisting of a long narrow strip eastwards. Although the new boundary in the latter portion was moved northwards, France still retained an important road, the Route de Bois d'Amont, which connected one part of the canton of Vaud (the Vallée de Joux) with another part of the canton served by a connecting road, the Route de St. Cergue. The two parties agreed that this corridor through France would be free from all transit, toll or customs dues.[23]

The treaty required no transfer of populations and permitted those who lived on either side of the new border to retain their present domicile and nationality or to change their citizenship to French or Swiss if they individually chose to do so.

The International Red Cross

The battle of Solferino in 1859 was one of the bloodiest combats of the Italian wars of unification. A Franco-Piedmontese army defeated the Austrians and left some 40,000 dead and wounded on the field of battle. Henri Dunant of Geneva, a witness of the slaughter, was vividly impressed with the horror of it all and the incredible suffering of the victims. Seized with missionary zeal and the conviction that a humanitarian medical and hospital service must be organized which would impartially render aid to the victims of war, he laid the foundation for what ultimately became the International Red Cross. A brochure by Dunant, entitled "Un souvenir de Solferino," described poignantly the agonies and sufferings of the Solferino casualties. This widely read work appeared in 1862 at a time when Europe was unusually receptive to humanitarian appeals. Individual citizens, government, the press, religious organizations, and health services responded to the message.

In February 1863, the International Committee of the Red Cross, initially a group of five, met in Geneva and laid the foundation for the organization. It was nongovernmental, entirely Swiss in its composition, and financed by voluntary contributions. In time, the committee was expanded to a membership of 25. The First International Conference of the Red Cross was held in October of the same year under the presidency of Henri Dufour. The Federal Council, sensing the necessity of leadership by neutral Switzerland, invited foreign governments to participate in a diplomatic conference designed to recognize and define the status of the International Red Cross. The conference in which the delegates of 12 countries participated was convened in Geneva on 22 August 1864. A remarkable unanimity prevailed, and the Convention which was concluded received the adherence of all European nations by 1868.

The Convention was restricted to military matters, specifically to the amelioration of those wounded in battle. Ambulances and military hospitals were henceforth to be recognized as neutral and, as such, protected and respected by the belligerents. The neutrality of the services would cease if a military guard were provided. Those engaged in these Red Cross services, even after occupation of the territory by the enemy could continue to fulfill their functions in the field hospitals or ambulances wherein they served or they could retire and rejoin the Corps to which they belonged. Provision was also made for the evacuation of sick and wounded to their homelands under Red Cross protection.

In the years since 1864 the responsibilities assumed by the International Red Cross have greatly expanded. Wherever large scale suffering occurs—through fire, flood, earthquakes, pestilence, famine or other misfortunes—the Red Cross is to be found.

The role of Switzerland must be emphasized. The services of the International Red Cross are carried out as a great humanitarian effort under the protection of a neutrality which receives world-wide recognition. The organization is based in Switzerland—the first country in the world to pursue a policy of perpetual neutrality. The activities of the International Red Cross give to this a quality which is rich in positive values and imposes upon Switzerland a continuing responsibility of a most humanitarian character. Her neutrality has evolved into something which is far removed from the negative and over-simplified concept of mere abstention from war.

Significantly, the emblem of the Red Cross—a red cross on a white field—is the exact reverse of Switzerland's national emblem—a white cross on a red field.

The Franco-Prussian War of 1870–71

In 1870, the relations between France and Prussia became suddenly strained by the news reaching Paris that the Crown of Spain had been offered to Prince Leopold of the House of Hohenzollern, and had been accepted by the Prince. The Prussian Ambassador was promptly advised by the French Minister of Foreign Affairs that France would not tolerate the establishment of the Prince of Hohenzollern, or any other Prussian prince, on the throne of Spain. On the following day (June 6) the French position was explained to the diplomatic corps. The Foreign Minister made much of the desire of France to remain strictly neutral in the internal affairs of another sovereign Power. But, in so doing, acceptance of this policy certainly did not oblige France to allow a foreign State to upset the balance of power in Europe by placing one of its princes on the Spanish throne.[24] The declaration, we are told, was "received with loud applause from all parts of the Chamber."

Britain was asked by France to intercede in the matter, using her best efforts both with Prussia and Spain to urge upon them the gravity of the problem. Her Majesty's government succeeded—at least Prince Leopold renounced his candidacy for the Spanish throne. France remained dissatisfied and enlarged the boundaries of the dispute with Prussia by next demanding guarantees for the future that the Prince would not again renew his candidature, and that no member of the Hohenzollern family would ever accept an offer of the Spanish Crown. The King of Prussia informed the French Ambassador that he could not bind his heirs and successors by acceptance of the second condition imposed by France.[25]

Admittedly there was more to the Franco-Prussian dispute than appeared on the surface. France was unquestionably alarmed by the growing power of Prussia. Under Bismarck's leadership, Hanover and Hesse had entered into a federation with Prussia, and the absorption of all the remaining German States into a powerful German Confederation was only a matter of time. France was eager to bring Prussia to her knees and thus put an end to the emergence of a united Germany which would be a much greater threat to France than the disunited family of sovereign States which hitherto existed.[26] The invitation to a Hohenzollern to accept the Crown of Spain gave to France the pretext for war against Prussia.

An impasse had been reached and both France and Prussia resorted to war as the last extremity. France called out its reserves on 15 June 1870 and declared war on

Prussia. The same evening the King of Prussia in the presence of his Council of Ministers and Generals ordered a mobilization of the entire army of the North German Confederation.

Fortune turned against the French with punishing results. By mid-October, Toulon and Strassburg had fallen before the German army, Paris was closely hemmed in and German troops had extended their operations as far as the river Loire. The destruction by France of the railways, bridges, and canals in the neighbourhood of Paris did not arrest the advance of the German army. Continuation of the war by France would have been senseless and hopeless. The government fell and administration of the country became the responsibility of a Provisional Government for National Defense which was established at Tours. Because of its instability and the impending defeat of France, Britain withheld recognition of the provisional government despite urgent pleas from France.

In September 1870, Prussia began to clarify the terms under which an armistice would be granted to France. The principal demand was cession of Alsace and Lorraine to Germany, by right of conquest. Bismarck supported this by a very pointed argument which could not have been lost upon France: "The cession . . . we are striving for, involves, in its territorial relations, a diminution of the French dominion about equal, in its superficial extent, to its increase by the addition of Savoy and Nice. . . ."[27] On 28 January 1871, this senseless war came to an end on signature of an armistice by the representatives of France and Prussia.

Of more immediate concern to us is the impact of the war on Switzerland which borders on France, on Alsace, and on the southern German States which fell under the expanding influence and ultimate sovereignty of the Prussian Federation. The ink on the French Declaration of War was barely dry before the Federal Council of Switzerland took appropriate action. It called to arms the general staff and the elite of five divisions, 37,000 men.[28] All the rest of the elite forces of the Swiss militia were placed on alert. The Federal Council addressed a message to the Federal Assembly and proposed adoption of the following decree:[29]

> 1. The Swiss Confederation, during the war which is breaking out, will defend the neutrality and the integrity of its territory by every means at its disposal. The Federal Council is charged with making a declaration to this effect to the Governments, to the belligerent States, and to the Powers which guaranteed the Treaties of 1815.
> 2. The mobilization of troops, ordered by the Federal Council, is approved.
> 3. The Federal Council is further authorized to make additional levies of troops, and to take all other measures that it believes necessary to maintain the neutrality and defense of the territory.
> 4. An unlimited credit is extended to the Federal Council to satisfy the expenses it will entail by virtue of the full power accorded by the preceding Article. . . .
> 5. The Assembly will proceed immediately to nominate the General-in-Chief and his Chief-of-Staff.

The Assembly unanimously accepted the proposals without discussion and named Johannes Herzog[30] from Aarau as the General.

A few days later the President of the Confederation addressed a note to the signatory Powers of the Treaties of 1815 in which he declared the intention of Switzerland to occupy, if circumstances required, the neutralized portions of northern Savoy.[31] The fact that Savoy had been ceded to France by Sardinia in 1860 did not, in the judgment of the Federal Council, nullify that portion of the treaties of 1815 which extended to Chablais and Faucigny the protection of Swiss neutrality, and gave to Switzerland the right to occupy these areas in the event of war by neighbouring Powers. The purpose of the note was to advise the Powers of Switzerland's firm resolve to occupy northern Savoy if deemed necessary for defense of the neutrality and territorial integrity of the Swiss Confederation.

The war was rapidly coming to an end when Switzerland was caught up by the fast moving events in a most unexpected way. General Bourbaki, commander of the French army of the East, with almost 100,000 troops, was driven back in defeat to the Swiss frontier. Herzog at once (late in January 1871) ordered that another division be called to arms for concentration around Biel. The Federal Council hesitatingly consented. Meanwhile, in desperation, Bourbaki committed suicide. The command passed to General Clinchant who lost no time in negotiating with Herzog about a possible internment of his army in Switzerland.

The French position was desperate and Clinchant's options were few. He could engage the Prussian army in a battle which would degenerate into a senseless slaughter. He could surrender his army or retreat into Switzerland and accept the internment of his troops. The morale of the army was gone. It was a spiritless, sick and fatigued body of men with only one desire—to save themselves. The German army of Manteuffel had cut off retreat into France and was pressing toward the Swiss frontier near Pontarlier. The situation was dangerous for Switzerland since pursuit of the French army into Switzerland could not be excluded as a threatening possibility. In all haste, battalions from Vaud and Neuchâtel were rushed to the border. Herzog arrived at the Swiss frontier facing Pontarlier at midnight January 31, and dictated to the emissaries of General Clinchant the conditions for internment: total disarmament on entry into Switzerland, surrender of all weapons, munitions, military equipment, all funds in possession of the army, and the mails— all to be returned to France on conclusion of the war. The next day at 5:00 A. M. the French soldiers, beaten, humiliated, and suffering from the cold, began to cross the frontier with 12,000 horses and about 300 pieces of artillery. The internees were distributed into 186 camps scattered throughout most of Switzerland. The newly organized Red Cross was called into action and discharged creditably its first noteworthy assignment in helping to care for the sick and suffering among the interned soldiers.

The internees were repatriated in mid-March and France paid 12 million francs, the costs of the internment.

The war was over and Switzerland's environment had changed greatly. Her neighbours were no longer the ones she had known at the end of the Napoleonic war. To her south was a united Italy, a potential threat to the Ticino. Upper Savoy, previously a neutralized buffer zone over which Switzerland enjoyed a protectorship, was now a province of France. Geneva was exposed defenseless. To the northwest, humbled by her recent defeat, France faced an uncertain future. Napoleon III had fallen. A republic had emerged. The small and independent German States to the north of the Swiss border had been fused by Bismarck with the many other German States into a powerful empire.

Whatever may have been the fears engendered in Switzerland by the awesome power of a united Germany, it is worth noting that some in Germany openly expressed their disdain of the Swiss. A German writer is quoted by Bonjour (55):

> For centuries Switzerland has hung from our body like a paralyzed limb and sucks our juices without itself moving for them. To cut it off would be damaging to the limb and destructive to the body; it will again survive only through close associations with the body.

Prussia, always a militant and aggressive Power, and recently irritated by the loss of the Neuchâtel Principality, had become the heart of the empire. Alsace, a French province since 1798, had been torn from France and was now a part of Germany. Basel was now three-fourths surrounded by the new Germany. The face of Europe had altered and the balance of power had changed mightily. Switzerland, ever cautious, feared the worst.

In 1882, Bismarck negotiated a Triple Alliance of Germany, Austria, and Italy. Austria, somewhat weakened by the successful Franco-Italian campaign against Austrian Lombardy and Venice, had turned her attention to the Balkans and sought to dominate politically and economically the disunited peoples of the Balkan peninsula. Bismarck's Triple Alliance was countered, a few years later (1891) by a mutual defensive pact between republican France and Tsarist Russia. The *Entente Cordiale* of 1904 between England and France, followed by much diplomatic and military shuffling about, expanded inevitably into the Triple Alliance of England, France, and Russia. Germany, dynamic, proud, restless, industrially strong and impatiently aggressive was hemmed in. Her commercial penetration and conquest of foreign markets was disturbing in the extreme to Great Britain and to the industrial nations of the west. The stage was being set for the World War of 1914–18.

And how did Switzerland regard the new Germany? She was greatly concerned, a concern that developed through successive stages of suspicion, distrust and political coldness into an ill-concealed animosity, if not hatred. She realized all too well that political unity, economic strength, military preparedness and a sense of oneness among her own people were essential for the salvation of Switzerland. Divided into three linguistic groups, and barely recovered from the confessional wounds of the *Sonderbund* war, there was a real fear that German imperialism might precipitate a terrible European war. This could tear Switzerland apart with a possible total dismemberment running the lengths of her linguistic frontiers.

But western Switzerland was not uncompromisingly francophile. The annexation of Savoy by France and the defenselessness of Geneva, now deeply thrust into French territory, had chilled considerably the friendliness toward France that had been slowly returning after the years of suffering under Napoleon Bonaparte.

The Germans in the Southern States of the New Germany Empire could not understand why the Swiss did not rejoice over the fall of France, while Garibaldi in Italy was bitter because of Switzerland's failure to assist France in her struggle against the armies of a united Germany. The Swiss position was admittedly difficult and the circumstances were unusual: the two combatants were her neighbours and historic bonds of origin directed her sympathies to both France and Germany. Whatever Switzerland, as a Neutral, might have done would have been mis-interpreted by either or both of the combatants and she would have received no thanks whatever: the price of neutrality.[32]

Central and eastern Switzerland were anything but well disposed toward Germany and the Germans. No less than 172,000 German nationals settled in Switzerland between 1860 and 1910—mostly in the towns. The German annexation of Alsace and Lorraine did not rest well with the Swiss. Her industrial aggressive-ness, her pan-German imperialism and the absolutism of the Prussian-dominated Empire were reflected in the jingoism and world-conquering spirit of many of the German immigrants. In sharp contrast were the strongly democratic Swiss who cherished their ancient institutions, and valued beyond words their freedom and their independence—a people disinclined to meddle in the affairs of other countries and equally determined to be left in peace by the neighbouring States. It was inevitable that the new Germany would be coldly received and her people, settling in Switzerland, would be frequently accepted with displeasure, if not unconcealed hostility. However dubious this generalization with its many exceptions may be, it is essential to an understanding of the mood of the Swiss people as the Confederation moved into the stirring events of the twentieth century.

The End of Mercenary Service

The War Minister, Marquis de Louwois, said one day to King Louis XIV in the presence of the Colonel of the Swiss Guard Regiment, Peter Stuppa:

> "Sire, If your Majesty still had all the gold and silver that you and your royal forefathers gave to the Swiss you could pave a road from Paris to Basel with Talers". "Sire", added the Swiss colonel "that can be so, but if, besides, all the blood that flowed through the veins of those members of our nation who served your majesty and your royal forefathers, were collected one could fill with it a canal between Paris and Basel".

The Federal Constitution of 1848 provided the State with the competence to end mercenary service. Existing capitulation agreements had to run their course to the expiration dates specified in the cantonal treaties, but Article XI of the Constitution forbade all future military capitulations. Lest one be surprised by this abrupt termination of an ancient institution it may be well to review some aspects of the Swiss experience.

For many years it was regarded as a glorious institution. The remarkable success of the Swiss in defeating almost all opponents in the many battles of the fourteenth and fifteenth centuries testified so conspicuously to the bravery, tenacity and combat skill of the Swiss soldiery that their services, as mercenaries, were eagerly sought by virtually all the crowned heads of Europe. In the forest cantons especially, overpopulation and unemployment continued for many long years. Stanyan (**339**, p. 144) noted that:

> if they did not continually drain their country by keeping troops in Foreign Service, they would soon be so much overstocked in proportion to the Extent and Fertility of it, that in all Probability, they would break in upon their Neighbours in Swarms or go further to seek out new seats.

Service in foreign armies, arranged through capitulation agreements, certainly alleviated the problems of unemployment. It also appealed to the adventurous spirit of the young. Frequently the booty was considerable and this compensated in part for the small pay received by the common soldier. The cantons received pensions from the foreign Power, and those who were assigned to procure the volunteers and organize the companies, were handsomely rewarded. The commanding officers were also generously paid.[33] The patrician cantons favored mercenary service because it provided appropriate employment for men of high rank to whom military service for a foreign Power was rewarded with a good income and social distinction. In the eighteenth century as many as 700 generals in foreign armies were Swiss (**40**, p. 97).

But there was much to be said against the practice. Niklaus von Flüe (Brother Klaus), a very wise hermit of great influence among many, had denounced mercenary service on all counts. He described the money derived from the interlocked system of pensions as "blood money." Haggling over the price to be paid, and an inclination to sell the services to the highest bidder were degrading. Of those who returned to the Fatherland many were crippled, sick and incapable of heavy labor. There were also many who did not return. From the fifteenth to the eighteenth centuries inclusive, the Confederation lost between 600,000 and 750,000 of its men—killed, disabled, or missing. Another estimate places the population loss through mercenary service at 900,000 to 1,000,000 men. At one time (1748) as many as 79,000 Swiss were in foreign military service. To maintain the numbers at the levels stipulated in the capitulation agreements, more and more men were constantly fed in to replace the killed and missing.

The young Swiss from the mountains had flocked into mercenary service hoping to satisfy their desire for new experiences, booty, wine, women and an end to poverty. However, many Swiss were loath to have the young men used to support despotic absolute monarchies (e.g. in Naples). From 1831 on, the cantons in their own constitutions began to forbid mercenary service. In Italy the Swiss found themselves in the service of tyrants who used their mercenaries to repress popular uprisings of people in search of freedom.

The worst aspect of mercenary service and the subject of frequent complaints was the repeated violation of the basic stipulation in all capitulation agreements: that Swiss soldiers in the service of a foreign Power may be used only in defensive operations, never on the offense. That Swiss were fighting Swiss was repeatedly established, an intolerable situation that arose from the sale of mercenary services to both of the belligerents. One of the earliest, most shameful, and most publicized incidents was in 1500 at the battle of Novara but there were many other similar incidents that helped to pave the way for ending the system: in France, at the time of Henri of Navarre, when Swiss from the Catholic cantons found themselves in combat with Swiss from the reformed cantons in the service of the Huguenots; in the German States during Louis XIV's third war of conquest; in the Netherlands during Louis XIV's attempt to conquer the territories around the lower Rhine; and during the Spanish War of Succession (in the battles at Höchstadt in 1704, at Ramillies in 1706, at Malplaquet in 1709, and in the Duchy of Milan). When the Crimean War was drawing to a close, a "Swiss legion" of 3300 men (including many Germans), recruited for service with the British, was in training at Dover. Part of the legion got as far as Smyrna. The war had already ended with the Peace of Paris on 30 March 1856, so the men saw no combat service (181).[34] Although France received a favored-nation treatment in the procurement of Swiss mercenaries, she was also the greatest offender. Many protests directed to Louis XIV against the misuse of his Swiss soldiers went unheeded.

It is quite impossible to understand some aspects of mercenary service, unless we realize that until the last few decades of the nineteenth century European wars were fought by professional armies with the combat units drawn from various countries. For example, a regiment of 1293 men in Perugia during the Italian War of Unification consisted of 640 Swiss, 45 French, 23 Italians, 55 Austrians, 180 Bavarians, 98 Württembergers, 70 from other German States, 155 Belgians, 10 Savoyards, 6 Poles and 1 Spaniard.[35] Marlborough's army, at one time 60,000 strong, numbered only 12,000 British.

In the American Civil War (War of the States), Swiss were in the combat forces of both the North and South. At least 6000 were in the Union army in 1862 and three of the generals in the two armies were Swiss (253, p. 22). The common soldiers fought not as professionals but as conscripts. Many Swiss had emigrated to the USA (many of these were naturalized) and, on the outbreak of war, became subject to the conscription laws to which both sides had recourse. Some, not wanting to participate, tried ineffectually to escape military service by attempts to renounce their citizenship.

Lincoln's plans for the ending of slavery were eulogized by the Radical press in Switzerland. After his assassination he was described as a martyr for the cause of freedom. Incidentally the words of Lincoln in his great Gettysburg address—"of the people, by the people, for the people"—were used a generation earlier by Zurich Dr. Schenz before the Helvetic Society at Olten: "Alle Regierungen der Schweiz müssen es erkennen, dass sie bloss aus dem Volke, durch des Volk und für das Volk da sind" (253, p. 41).

In the late 1700s something entirely new cast a shadow over mercenary service. This was the very real fear, not without cause, that Swiss serving in France would become infected with the revolutionary ideas that were current. The revolution against the establishment was promoted not only by the French sympathizers but by adherents to the "Swiss Patriots Club" in Paris and by such influential Swiss as Ochs and de la Harpe. In 1790, a mutiny of a Swiss regiment stationed at Nancy had serious political repercussions though it was not really political in origin. It might just as well have been political, because the after-effects did much to generate among the Swiss soldiery real sympathies for the revolutionary cause. In this general context, the incident that created the greatest concern about mercenary service was the slaughter of the Swiss Guard before the Tuilleries on 10 August 1792. The Guard was an elite corps assigned to defend the person of the French monarch. To the revolutionaries, the Swiss Guard was as much an enemy of the people as the king himself. After this terrible event one might have reasonably expected that the remaining eight or nine Swiss regiments in Paris and several provincial cities would have been called home. However, they remained for several more years but any taste they might have acquired for the ideas of the revolution was blunted by the revulsion over the slaughter of hundreds of their compatriots on August 10.

Another historical event that contributed mightily to bringing mercenary service to an end was the Italian War of Unification. Swiss mercenaries served the heads of several of the Italian States. In defending these reactionary, sometimes despotic, rulers the Swiss created a great deal of ill will. The mood of the day stemmed from the widely disseminated teachings of Mazzini and Garibaldi in the cause of liberty of the masses. Notably in Naples, but also in Rome and Milan, the Swiss were derided and defamed for the military support given to despotic rulers who lived parasitically upon the common people and contributed nothing to public welfare. At least this was essentially the substance of the complaints directed against the Swiss mercenaries then serving in Italy. In Milan one heard the cry "Morte al papa, morte agli Svizzeri!" In Florence, a number of Swiss shops had to be closed because of violent demonstrations against Switzerland.

Obviously the time had come for official action by the Swiss government. The outcry of the Italian people against Swiss mercenaries was escalating into popular demonstrations against everything Swiss. This also evoked a remarkable amount of support within Switzerland, all focussing upon the evils of capitulation agreements, the pension system, and recruiting for military service in the armies of foreign Powers. The only surprising aspect of the practice was that so many years had to pass before it was ended.

While the memories of Novara (1500) were still troubling the minds of many, the Diet issued a strong proscription against mercenary service and the acceptance of pensions, even decreeing the death penalty for those who violated the ordinance. This action of the Diet was precipitate and politically untimely. It was followed in 1503 by a milder decree which in spirit denied its subjects the right to accept foreign pensions. This *Pensionbrief* was not faithfully observed and the cantons, one after another, freed themselves of its limitations. When Zurich in 1508 returned to the old pension system, the action of the Diet in 1503 in forbidding the acceptance of pensions lost all meaning. Its supporters had vanished. Under the persuasive influence of Zwingli who throughout his life proclaimed mercenary service and the pension system to be intolerable evils, Zurich forbade her subjects to accept pensions or to enter the military service of foreign Powers and held fast to this policy against foreign alliances until well into the seventeenth century except for a "fall from grace" in 1582 and 1587. Several other cantons that enacted legislation similar to that of Zurich were not so steadfast and succumbed much sooner to the seductive solicitations of France and the tempting promises of rich financial rewards.

In May 1849, pursuant to Article XI of the new constitution, the Federal Assembly passed a law forbidding military capitulations. Recruiting on behalf of foreign Powers was forbidden. Swiss and foreign agents who engaged in recruiting within the Confederation became subject on conviction to fines and imprisonment.[36]

This was not the end. It was only the beginning of the end. In those cantons where capitulation agreements were still in force recruiting was permitted to continue, but only until the dates of expiration.

Recruiting beyond the Swiss frontiers could not be prevented. In 1855, Ochsenbein, then a general in the French service, established six recruiting bureaus just across the Swiss border with the intent of organizing two Swiss regiments for France. Ochsenbein, meanwhile, remained in his headquarters in Besançon. The British, not to be outdone, opened a main recruiting bureau in Schlettstadt with several others adjacent to the Swiss border. The Austrians tempted the young Swiss to come to Bregenz and Feldkirch for enlistment in the service of Naples and Rome. Holland also had recruiting bureaus in Baden near the Swiss border. Two Russian agents from St. Petersburgh were reported to be recruiting for the Russian artillery forces but after a brief appearance near the border they vanished. The British, seeking 5000 men, made the most enticing offers and by May 1855 over 1000 men had crossed the border at Basel en route to Schlettstadt.[35,37]

The cantons cooperated in enforcement of the law. In 1852–54 St. Gallen convicted and punished over 80 recruiters and Basel meted out punishment to a few. Some of the cantons, even as early as 1830, had enacted legislation against military capitulations. The federal law of 1849 extended the ban on mercenary service to all of its citizens in Switzerland and imposed several restrictions on those who were resident in foreign countries.

In 1853 and 1859, the federal government tightened the law against recruiting for foreign Powers, even to the punishment of its citizens who aided in any way whatever, such as paying a prospective recruit's travel expenses to the border. At the same time the law against foreign military service can be said to have been relaxed. In special cases a canton could approve a request for entrance into foreign military service but such approvals required confirmation by the Federal Council.[39] Approvals by the Federal Council appear to have been granted to regimental and company commanders, and to officers of lower grade if the service in a foreign army would enhance the military competence of these men. The Federal Council reserved the right of recall if Switzerland's need for their services became paramount.

In July 1866 the Federal Council issued a decree which prohibited the export of weapons and materials of war, especially to the bordering States and to any collecting depots in the vicinity of the border. The order provided also for the confiscation of weapons brought into the country by refugees, and deserters.[40]

As reported by a commission of the House of Representatives (*Nationalrat*) in

1859, it was generally conceded throughout the Confederation that since the middle of the eighteenth century the ideas of freedom, equality and human rights had been making an increasing impact on all classes of the population.[41] At the same time military service for foreign Powers was being subjected to increased scrutiny and criticism. Economic, agricultural and industrial pursuits, and the fine arts were now accepted as best for the country and for the individual. In the councils of government it was also becoming more and more evident that Swiss mercenaries, because of their military competence and the numbers involved, had an indirect influence, sometimes decisive, on the fate of a country or neighbouring State. In short, mercenary service by the Swiss resulted at times in a very unpleasant meddling in the affairs of another country. Mercenary service came completely to an end in 1870 when the foreign regiments in the service of the Vatican terminated their engagements. Only the ceremonial Swiss guard on duty at the Vatican remained. The Swiss military law of 1927 affirmed all previous prohibitions against the service of its citizens in foreign armies.[38] By this action the posture of Switzerland as a neutral State was greatly strengthened. It is nothing short of amazing that for many decades, mercenary service by the Swiss was never officially regarded as being incompatible with the country's neutrality. See also Bonjour (**54**).

Revision of the Constitution

The Constitution adopted in 1848 was a great step forward, but only a few years had to elapse before it became clear to many that it had not gone far enough. More power had to be surrendered by the cantons to the federal authorities—parliament and the courts. Some of the responsibilities which reasonable people would expect to be assumed by government could only be discharged properly if competence in such areas was transferred from the cantons to the Federal Government.

There was little argument about the desirability of giving the central authorities constitutional authority to legislate on railway construction and operation. By 1860 a number of small railway companies, constructed under cantonal and community legislation, had fallen into bankruptcy. Others, inadequately capitalized or of proven inefficiency, were bought up by two or three of the large companies and merged into their operating systems. There were many disappointments, and substantial losses were suffered by those who invested in the small companies. The railway business had to be a concern of the Federal Government, not of the cantons or of local government. On this there was general agreement.

The times were also favorable for substantial revision of the constitution on purely political grounds. Democratic movements, originating in the cantons, expressed themselves in insistent demands for more direct democracy and for a greater participation of the people in the decision-making process. Carried forward to the federal level, we find that much of the outcry for constitutional reform focused on the referendum and the initiative. The referendum on constitutional questions was already in practice. It was obligatory under the constitution since amendments to the constitution required for their approval majority votes of the cantons and of the people. If acknowledged as a popular right, the optional referendum would permit the legislative acts of the Federal Assembly to be approved or vetoed by the voters. Through the right of the initiative the people would be enabled to propose new laws and amendments of the constitution. The optional referendum would give the people the right to reject newly enacted laws. The initiative, a more positive right, would permit the people to legislate.

In 1869, the canton of Zurich adopted a constitution which paved the way for similar action by other cantons. Hitherto, the political power of the people was restricted to voting on amendments to the constitution and in electing representatives to the legislature. This was not enough and only about one-fifth of the electorate ever bothered to vote. Wealth and economic power were concentrated in the few and they continued to constitute the ruling class. They provided the members of the ruling councils, the directorates of corporations, and were the leaders of commerce, industry, and capitalistic enterprise. Economic and political leadership were closely allied and concentrated in the few. Alfred Escher, who personified this concentration of power, was singled out by a few vigorous pamphleteers as the target: "he and his kind must be dethroned; participation of the common man in the legislative process must be assured." The new constitution was a result of this growing desire for a greater measure of direct democracy. It recognized recourse to the referendum and the initiative as fundamental political rights of the people. It also provided for popular election of the government and of the councillors of State. A wave of similar reforms at the cantonal level was touched off in Bern, Aargau, Lucerne, Solothurn and Thurgau.

Where did the Radicals stand? Governments dominated by the Radical party, which was in the ascendancy in many cantons, uniformly pressed for revision of the Federal Constitution. Concern for popular democracy was not the issue. Although the platforms of the Radical party differed somewhat from one canton to the next, there was one demand which was at the heart of Radical programs wherever found, namely centralism. Far more power must be vested in the central government and cantonal autonomy must be sacrificed wherever it appeared as an obstacle to the national well-being. For half a century (1874–1920) the Radical party was dominant in Switzerland. Although the Radicals of Geneva, of Vaud, and of Suisse-Allemagne differed here and there in political philosophy, the party as a whole cut across all distinctions of class and region. The party drew its strength from agriculture, commerce, and industry. It absorbed ideas from the right and from the left—somewhat conservative on some issues and far to the left on others. The Liberal party was bourgeois and industrial in outlook. The Socialist party represented the proletariat. The Catholic party had only a denominational base and suffered from a too-restricted political philosophy. To some extent it could only be nourished by a continuing distrust of any ideas that originated within the evangelical cantons.

In military affairs, General Herzog could only report to the Federal Government that the structure of the army, its organization, its training, equipment and combat capability were totally inadequate. Without mincing his words he reminded government that the war of 1870–71, in which, fortunately for Switzerland,

Herzog's army was not drawn into combat, revealed weaknesses in the army that necessitated immediate correction. Much of this was publicly known before the Franco-Prussian war but it was an unpleasant subject for general discussion. Until Herzog's report was made public any dust that was raised by the well-informed was swept under the carpet. The weaknesses were uniformly attributable to the constitution of 1848 which stated that the federal army was to be made up of contingents provided by the cantons (Article XIX). Military instruction of the infantry continued to be a cantonal responsibility (Article XX.3) subject, however, to federal surveillance of both instruction and weaponry. Herzog's report to the government enumerated *inter alia* the following defects: a serious lack of uniformity among the cantons in military instruction and training. In general, it was totally inadequate; the weaponry and equipment provided by the cantons left much to be desired; some of the cantons took their responsibilities all too lightly, and, almost without exception, all of them restricted their military expenditures to sub-minimal levels; auxiliaries such as the sanitary corps and the veterinary services were quite unsatisfactory.

This was a shocking state of affairs which permitted only one remedy: centralization of military affairs in the Federal Government. This required amendment of the constitution and a new body of federal laws pertinent to structure, training, and equipment of the federal army. The centralists, eager for total revision of the constitution and reduction in the power of the cantons called for "One law, one army." When this slogan became expanded to "One law, one army, one God," the Catholic party became more suspicious than ever of the political intentions of the Radicals. To them, the slogan could only mean a determination of the Radicals to subordinate the Church to the State and to strip the Church of much of its power. The *Kulturkampf*, with its closing of the Aargau convents and expulsion of the Jesuits, was regarded with foreboding as a token of even more restrictions to come: evil days seemed to lie ahead if the Radicals had their way.

In 1866, Parliament approved a totally revised constitution. In some ways it was a grab bag—a catch-all. It provided for a sweeping centralization, even transferring to the Federal Government some powers which might just as well have been left with the cantons. The referendum which followed—obligatory on constitutional matters—resulted in a popular veto. Some provisions, such as the optional referendum on legislation enacted by the Federal Assembly, were defeated in Parliament and never reached the people. A curious combination of catholic Conservatives, Democrats from the French-speaking cantons, and a majority from Liberals of eastern Switzerland managed to put an end to the 1866 revision.

A few years later, the Federal Assembly returned to the problems of the constitution. It appointed a commission to study the many proposed amendments and to submit specific recommendations to Parliament. The leader in this renewed effort to revise an outmoded constitution was Emil Welti, one of the most capable of the Federal Councillors. He was known to be an effective proponent of the Radical cause and highly centralistic in his political philosophy. Somewhat paradoxically he was opposed to any extension of people's rights in the federal sphere, presumably because the referendum on legislative matters would give to the federalists a weapon which could be used to thwart the programs of the centralists. The catholics of *Innerschweiz* were conservative and strongly federalistic. They opposed any extensive tampering with the constitution: cantonal sovereignty must be preserved. The Swiss from the French-speaking cantons, though democrats to the core, disliked many of the amendments that were being proposed by the commission. The opposition in French Switzerland was led by Louis Ruchonnet of Vaud—a man of great ability who was well known and highly respected. Though a Radical Democrat he defended both federalism and the principle of cantonal autonomy. To Ruchonnet goes much of the credit for the happy compromise which was reflected in the constitution of 1874—supreme legislative power vested in the Federal Assembly but enforcement of the legislation, whenever feasible, by the cantons. Opposed to Emil Welti was Federal Councillor Jakob Dubs, who gave his great abilities to the cause of federalism. In the end the federalists won out, but not until 1874. The draft accepted by the Assembly in March 1872 was voted down by the people: it was too centralistic but a significant improvement over that of 1866. The defeat was real but not overwhelming. The strength of the opposition was greatly reduced. In 1870 the doctrine of papal infallibility had been proclaimed by Pius IX and the Vatican Council. This extraordinary dogma reawakened confessional strife, divided the catholics and created a rift in the Catholic party. The formidable opposition to the revised constitution which was expressed in 1866 was now greatly reduced though not entirely overcome.

Parliament returned to the problem at once. The people called insistently for revision of the constitution, while elections to the House of Representatives (*Nationalrat*) convinced Parliament that greater moderation in the proposed amendments was demanded. The revision of 1874 adopted by the Federal Assembly was approved by substantial margins both by the people and the cantons.

The new Constitution of 1874 stripped the cantons of much of their power in military affairs and centralized the organization, training and equipment of the Swiss army—the federal militia. A body of laws stemming from this part of the constitution was enacted in 1875 and provided a greatly improved organization for defense of the country. The constitution also gave to the Federal Government the much-needed competence for construction and operation of the railways.

The most important innovations were the referendum and the initiative. Amendments to the constitution proposed by Parliament, and legislative enactments of the Federal Assembly henceforth ran the risk of veto by the people. In Switzerland, by virtue of the popular referendum and the initiative, it is the people who have the last word. Parliament dare not be capricious, nor may it go too far in centralization—in adding to its own power at the expense of cantonal sovereignty. The referendum on constitutional matters was made obligatory in 1848. The right of the referendum on legislative enactments, introduced in 1874, is optional. Thirty thousand concerned voters were to be enough to force a nation-wide referendum on a newly enacted law.[42] Since 1921 international treaties have also been subject to the optional referendum.

The 1874 amendments to the constitution did much more. They provided a base for federal legislation in commerce, and in some aspects of corporation affairs including bankruptcy proceedings. Civil marriage was approved. This was part of the "new look" in government. Civil powers had to be supreme in the land even if they encroached on ecclesiastical authority or on the powers of any religious establishment.[43] The Jesuits were obliged under the new constitution to leave Switzerland, and the federal competence in expulsion was widely extended to apply to other religious orders "whose activities are dangerous for the state or disturb the peace among the different creeds." Likewise "the establishment of new convents or religious orders and the re-establishment of those which have been suppressed[44] are forbidden" (Art. 52). And in matters of law "ecclesiastical jurisdiction is abolished" (Art. 58.2). All political and civil rights of the citizen were henceforth to be independent of the churches. At the age of 16 one became free to choose the religion that he preferred or to declare his intention not to join either confession or religious sect. Nonmembers of a confession could not be required, henceforth, to pay the ecclesiastical imposts to which the church administrations had been entitled. The maintenance of peace between the confessions and the settlement of disputes concerning the property of the churches became cantonal and federal responsibilities. And no longer could religious or economic considerations be invoked to prevent a marriage. Virtually total freedom was granted to men and women of marriageable age to select a spouse.

Responsibilities in education and the necessary constitutional competence emerged with a few complications. At the primary level, schools no longer were permitted to have a confessional dependence or quality. They were instruments of the State, and government no longer would recognize the right of churches to influence the character of public education. The centralists had their way with respect to the universities. Though the six universities (*Hochschule*) then in existence[45] continued to be cantonal in respect to financing and overall supervision, the centralists saw to it that the constitution permitted the central government to establish "a federal university and other institutions for higher education or to subsidize such establishments."[46] Primary education, compulsory and free (in public schools), continued to be a constitutional responsibility of the cantons[47] — not without objections from the ardent centralists who finally conceded that centralization of this responsibility would require a small army of federal inspectors. The constitution, as revised, also required the Federal Government to grant subsidies to the cantons "to help them carry out their obligations in the field of primary instruction" (Art 27 bis.1).[48] Finally, in the field of education "the Confederation is entitled to legislate on vocational training in the fields of industry, crafts, commerce, agriculture, and domestic service." To this end, much legislation has been enacted. The Federal Government prescribes in detail the kind of training, supervises the examinations of the trainees, and publishes from time to time the names of those who are professionally qualified to engage in various occupations.

The constitution of 1874 extended the competence of the Federal Government in many other areas: the last of the intercantonal tariffs disappeared; collection of the customs duties and the revenues derived became exclusively a federal concern and benefit. Working conditions in factories became subject to federal legislation. Gaming tables and casinos were forbidden and lotteries came under federal control. The issuance of bank notes became a federal monopoly.

The constitution went far in respect to the courts. The Federal Court of Justice was established as a permanent institution of the State, with its seat in Lausanne. It was empowered to adjudicate disputes in civil commercial law between the Federal Government and the cantons. The Federal Court is not permitted to pass on the constitutionality of a federal law, unlike the Supreme Court of the USA, but it can rule against cantonal laws which are not in harmony with federal legislation or which trespass upon the rights of other cantons. In the interests of uniformity among the cantons it also has regulatory powers in matters of trade and traffic.

Many of the provisions of the constitution of 1848 were embodied in the constitution of 1874 with little, if any, change. To mention only a few: customs affairs, post and telegraph, coinage, weights and measures, supervision over roads and bridges, the bicameral system of government with a Federal Council and a Chancellory (federal secretariat).

Constitutional history reveals that seven partial revisions of the federal constitution were made between 1874 and 1891. Until 1891 partial revisions could only be introduced by the Federal Assembly. However, on 5 July 1891 the right of the initiative was granted to the people, thus making it possible for amendments to the constitution to be introduced by the people, rather than the parliamentarians, for legislative action. Between July 1891 and December 1962 a total of 62 partial revisions were approved. Seven of these came about through exercise of the initiative. During the same period 56 amendments were rejected in the obligatory referenda that followed their submission to the people. On the average, the Constitution during those 71 years was amended every 14 months. In sharp contrast, the US Constitution was amended only 24 times in its first 175 years and ten of the amendments were adopted almost before the ink was dry on the basic document. The Swiss constitution is a living document which constantly undergoes change. Of the 121 Articles in the constitution of 1874, 92 survived the ensuing 71 years virtually without change. Thirty-nine new Articles were introduced and others were changed significantly. Of the 61 partial revisions since 1874, 36 were designed to extend the competence of the Federal Government, principally in respect to the economy, transport, and traffic. The current edition of the federal constitution is that of 1 April 1977. A total revision of the constitution is under way. It can be achieved only in piecemeal fashion and the end of the process is not in sight.

One should note, in conclusion, that constitutional amendments and legislative enactments, if rejected by the people, frequently receive popular assent on a second or third re-submission. Either a modification of the original act is called for, or the government finds itself obliged to explain things to the people more clearly and fully—in short to do a better selling job. If one may generalize on such matters it is quite clear that the Swiss people are prepared to accept personal sacrifice and increased financial burdens imposed by government when they are convinced of the necessity or reasonableness of the proposals. Increases in tax rates, the introduction of new sources of tax revenue (which require approval by the people), and approval of salary increases requested by members of Parliament are simple cases in which the people ultimately approved the proposals of Parliament. In matters of personal freedom and property rights they are stubbornly resistant to encroachment by government. A capital levy proposed in 1922 was so heavily snowed under in the referendum that Parliament has not voted since then in favor of such an unwelcome invasion of property rights. The people are likewise resistant to any proposed restrictions of cantonal sovereignty which they consider to be superfluous, capricious, or unnecessary. The long years of popular democracy have resulted in a sustained and deep interest in political affairs. The people have an uncanny ability to ferret out and to reject any proposals of Parliament which they consider to lack precision, to be too sweeping in character, and perhaps even designed to add excessive power to the central government. It is not easy to catch the Swiss voters in a somnolent state or in a rubber-stamping mood.

The Railways

Invention of the locomotive by George Stephenson in England was followed in 1825 by construction of a railway line from the coal center of Darlington to the ocean port of Stockton. Thirty years or more were to pass before Switzerland took advantage of this new system of transport. One reason for the long delay was unquestionably the same as in England where the common man greeted the invention with total mistrust. He feared these smoke-exhaling iron monsters that raced across the countryside at "terrifying speeds." "The devil himself must have inspired the invention." Eduard Schütz has quoted an opinion expressed by an English "expert":

> The locomotive exhales a poisonous smoke, which pollutes the atmosphere, which kills birds, and makes men ill. The heavens will be so darkened by the smoke that the sun can no longer shine through; the houses in the vicinity of the line [Manchester to Liverpool] will catch fire through sparks from the smokestack. The hens can no longer lay their eggs in peace, the cows can no longer eat grass, agriculture must come to an end since it can no longer provide hay for the horses. But the travellers at all times are in the greatest danger; the exploding boilers will tear them in pieces, and their relatives will no longer be able to prepare for them an ordinary Christian burial (**325**).

Richard Feller has pointed out that in Switzerland most of the people were opposed at first to railway transport. Travel by train, so we are told, would make people sick. The clouds of black smoke would pollute the air. The prices of agricultural products would be lowered to disastrous levels and farm lands would be devalued. The trains would facilitate a great influx of foreigners and immorality would follow (**129**). It was, in fact, the industrial north and east, where economies in transport costs of imported raw materials and in delivery times, were eagerly sought, that the greatest demand for railways was centered. The agricultural west rightly foresaw the disastrous effects that railways would have on agricultural prices and opposed the railway schemes. von Segesser expressed a different kind of concern, essentially that of an environmental conservationist. Regarding a railway over the Lukmanier or the Gotthard, which was then under discussion, he wrote "I want rather that permanent silence rule in these regions, where today the eagle still spreads its wings in freedom, than that I at this price, the price of our honor, would want the locomotive to travel the road over our passes" (v. Segesser, **330**). von Segesser's opposition, however, included additional concerns that pertained to more than the environment. He visualized a railway crossing of the Alps evolving into the political and military axis of Europe. The Gotthard railway would become a great channel for the flow of foreign troops and war material. Swiss neutrality would thereby become endangered, even the very existence of Switzerland herself (**330**, vol. 3, pp. 272–282).

But Switzerland had other problems, uniquely hers, that delayed development of transport by rail. The lack of coal as a natural resource was an impediment. Equally important was the total lack of any enabling legislation which would be applicable to the whole of Switzerland and would permit construction of transcantonal railway systems. Not until 1846 did a national spirit begin to emerge. Before 1848, very few Swiss would think of Switzerland as his native land. His loyalties and his *Heimat*-Consciousness focused upon his canton and his local community. But it would be ridiculous to think of 22 separate railway systems serving 22 separate cantons with the legislation, and possibly the technology, differing from one canton to the next.

Not until August 1847 did the first intra-Swiss railway commence service. It extended from Zurich to Baden—a distance of 22 km, a travelling time of 45 minutes and at a passenger cost of 1.60 francs for first class accommodations. This constituted the first stage in the Swiss Northern Railway system, which would presently continue through Aarau to Basel and there connect with a line through Freiburg and Karlsruhe to Frankfurt (16 hours travel time from Zurich). A French Company after several years of negotiations had previously received permission to construct a line which connected Basel with St. Louis, an Alsatian town about 1800 meters to the north. Its trains penetrated Switzerland only as far as the old French railway station in Basel. Service was commenced in June 1844, a memorable event which climaxed some years spent in resolving the Swiss political, financial and legal problems (**28**). The line was important, not simply because it was for Switzerland a first, but because St. Louis was the junction point for the *Chemins de fer d'Alsace* which since 1840 had operated a service between St. Louis and Strassburg—5 clock hours apart.[49]

In 1849, after the Federal State came into being, the Federal Council was instructed by the Assembly to develop a plan for a Swiss railway network. Two English engineers were engaged by the Federal Council to provide expert advice and to lay out plans for a Swiss railway network. In 1850 an expropriation law was passed which empowered the Federal Government to acquire such lands as were deemed necessary for a country-wide national railway system.

Although the experts advised against construction by private companies, a sharp struggle promptly ensued between the advocates of a privately owned system, led by Alfred Escher, and those, under Stämpfli's leadership, who strongly urged a system developed and owned by the Federal Government.

Politically, the careers of Escher and Stämpfli ran for a time in parallel. Before becoming the leader of the Radical party in the Federal Government, Stämpfli served as president of the governing council (*Regierungsrat*) of Bern, while Escher at 29 was head of the Zurich government and later President of the House of Representatives (*Nationalrat*) in the Federal Government. Until the railway question came to the fore the two men were good friends in spite of differences in background and in economic philosophy. Stämpfli spent the early years of his childhood in the confined environment of a farming community. Escher came from an aristocratic family of considerable wealth. He was well educated, versatile, a born leader and possessed of a commanding appearance. As soon as Parliament became entangled in the involved question of private vs State ownership a bitter rivalry arose between the two men. At the politico-philosophical level, Stämpfli was an uncompromising advocate of ownership of the railway systems by the Federal Government. He was a centralist through and through. Escher believed with equal conviction in the virtues of private enterprise and in the private construction and ownership of the railways. Both realized that the investment required would be tremendous. Some opposed railways in general. They voiced the opinion that railways were totally unsuited for such a mountainous country as Switzerland.

In 1852, Parliament decided in favor of private construction: the financial and political risks were too great to justify construction by the State. Under Escher's direction and with the financial resources of private investors, and Escher's *Kreditanstalt* (which invested ten million francs in the West Switzerland Railway), the building of the railroads quickly got under way. The North-East Railway, the Central Railway and the West-Switzerland Railway eventually emerged. Between them, service by train was provided from Geneva to Lake Constance—the East-West span of Swiss territory. From the beginning they operated profitably. They were a demonstrated success. The early fears of the doubters were dissipated and in the feverish excitement that ensued many small lines, frequently ill-conceived, were built. Almost every valley of any consequence demanded a railway. Some of these small companies disappeared in bankruptcy; some lines were merged into the major railways, and a few survived. The ultimate survivors of major size were four or five in number: the three already mentioned, the South-East Railway based on St. Gallen, and the Gotthard Railway[50] which was somewhat of a late-comer. Of the nonsurvivors, the National Railway Company which had been built with financial support from various cantons and communities and intended as a competitor to Escher's North-East Railway began to slip into bankruptcy. It was acquired in 1880 by the North-East Railway at a knockdown price of four million francs and a loss of 28 million francs—quite a tidy sum—by the original investors.

Escher's power and influence in finance and industry began to surpass that of Stämpfil in the political arena. Stämpfli, with characteristic vigor attacked the "railway barons." The substantial dividends paid by the profitable companies came from the people, so he contended, and should be returned to the people. He tried to do battle with Escher's financial–industrial complex by urging the Federal Government to construct a secondary system of lines from Lausanne to Bern to Lucerne. Stämpfli dominated the Federal Council and convinced his fellow councillors that the growing strength of Zurich, and the power and influence concentrated in Escher and his railway companies had to be fought to a finish. The Federal Government invested and lost $2\frac{1}{2}$ million francs in the railway that Stämpfli impetuously and unwisely proposed. The government of Bern, interested in becoming the transportation center of Switzerland, also invested and lost two million francs. The company had to be liquidated while construction was under way. Stämpfli was heavily criticized on all sides. After serving as president of Switzerland in 1862, he left the political sphere and became head of a newly founded bank in 1863. A line from Bern to Lucerne was eventually constructed but not by the government. Stämpfli's weaponry for the battle with Escher was not exhausted. He continued the fight after his retirement from politics. Stämpfli persistently pointed out that the railway companies were rivalling the government itself. They exercised, so Stämpfli argued, an uncontrolled economic power and political influence. "Almost beyond the reach of government, their policies were antisocial. They exploited the people. They were responsible to no one."

In 1898, 19 years after Stämpfli's death, the main railway companies were bought out by the Federal Government which thus acquired 2830 km[51] of track and the rolling stock for 1044 million francs (**384**). In 1902 the nationalized railway system was entrusted to a separate administrative and operating division in the Federal Department for Transport, etc.

The nationalization of the railways, as one might surmise, was not accomplished with ease. First, there were legislative problems. On revision of the federal constitution in 1874 an Article was included[52] which gave to the Federal Government the necessary competence to legislate on railway questions. A law of 1875 established a Department of Railways in the Federal Government, while a number of laws in the following years increased the competence of the government and paved the way for nationalization.

For some years there had been intense opposition to State ownership on many different grounds. All in all, the service rendered under private ownership was good. The cost of acquisition by the State would be a staggering burden for the nation to bear. Nationalization would strengthen the forces of centralism, doing so at the expense of cantonal sovereignty and a healthy federalism. Perhaps this argument, with its broad appeal to the Swiss of every canton, was the most powerful of all. It united the conservatives wherever they were to be found. It also appealed to the catholics, for the papacy, already disturbed by the unification of Italy and the fusion of the German States into a powerful Republic, saw in the vigorous efforts of the Radicals an attempt to achieve a total centralization of government in Switzerland. As the power of the European States increased at the center, the power of the Church in its worldly concerns decreased. Rome feared, with good cause, that the

Church itself would suffer increasing restraints imposed by powerful centralized governments.

And so we find the catholics uniting with the conservatives to constitute the principal organized opposition to nationalization of the railways. There were also those, not insignificant in number, who were so upset by the failure of many small railway companies and the mounting costs of the Gotthard construction that they convinced themselves and others that the railways were doomed to be totally uneconomic. It is not surprising that the first attempt at nationalization failed. The legislation enacted by the Federal Assembly, on recommendation of the Federal Council, was defeated in an ensuing referendum. In December 1891 the act of Parliament was supported by only 131,000 votes against 290,000 in opposition. Federal Councillor Emil Welti, an ardent and vigorous advocate of nationalization of the railways, regarded this negative declaration by the people as a personal defeat. The day following the referendum vote he resigned—unquestionably a great loss at the cabinet level.

But it may well be argued that the dominance of the Radicals in the Federal Council had to be tempered. This was soon achieved by the election in December 1891 of Joseph Zemp, the new leader of the conservatives in the canton of Lucerne—an able successor to von Segesser who had died in 1888. Zemp helped to formulate a new law in 1897 for purchase of the railways. The draft was approved by the Federal Council and enacted into law by the Federal Assembly. With the passage of time, the Catholic-Conservative opposition had become completely divided on the issue, the Radicals in government had become weaker numerically and the cautious Swiss voter had decided there was less to fear from nationalization in 1898 than in 1891. The referendum followed enactment of the law and was resoundingly approved: 386,000 votes in favor to 182,000 in opposition. All of the principal railway companies except the Gotthard were purchased by the Confederation and merged into the Swiss Federal Railways. The Gotthard company which was partly owned by Germany and Italy was not acquired by the State until 1909 when the international treaties pertinent to foreign government investment ran out. Many private companies which provided some unusual type of service such as up the slopes of the Niessen, or to the Rigi Kulm or from the Lauterbrunnen valley to the Jungfraujoch have continued under private ownership. The Rhätische Bahn of 394 km and the Bern-Lotschberg-Simplon Bahn of 251 km are the largest of the private railway systems. In fact, on a kilometer basis, the private lines in 1944 approximated in total length those of the federal system: 150 private lines totalled about 3000 km and those of the Swiss Federal Railways approximated the same total mileage.[53]

If we return to the earlier years of the Swiss railways, and after the initial fears of the iron monsters had been dispelled, we might note that the federal network expanded from 38 km in 1854 to 1300 km in 1864 and to 2913 km by 1970. All but 15 km or so are now electrified.

Development of the railways suffered a setback during 1914-18. The usual wartime difficulties that plagued transportation facilities, even in neutral

Switzerland, were seriously aggravated by the lack of coal (in 1914 less than 1 percent of the Swiss railway mileage was electrified; hence, almost the entire system was dependent on imported coal). Financial problems descended heavily upon the country and were not solved until 1922–23. As the decade came to an end the railways were enjoying the taste of prosperity: they virtually monopolized the major transport services. Then came the automobile as a serious competitor. The Second World War, unlike the first, provided the responsible officers of the Swiss Railways with few headaches. Electrification had proceeded far in the intervening years and transport by the competing autos suffered a temporary decline because fuel and rubber were in very short supply. When the war ended the old problems returned and a bevy of new ones arose.

To strike a satisfactory balance between the auto, the train, the ship, and the aeroplane in the transport of goods and people is extremely difficult and demands constant study. The solutions are unusually hard to find in Switzerland where government, despite an endless flood of legislative enactments, intrudes but little in the affairs of industry. Though most of the railways are nationalized, they come under a separate business management which is on the periphery of government control. Fortunately it is a country where patience and compromise are as enduring as the Alps; and where arbitration has long been practiced in the settlement of problems that arise when irresistible forces meet immovable objects.

The excellent and far-reaching railway network (federal and private) in Switzerland is supplemented by a post-auto service which provides transportation to a multitude of villages that are inaccessible by train. The total length of the post-auto lines administered by the postal department approximates 7522 km. In addition, about 3450 km are serviced under concessions to private auto companies.

If one were interested in the leisurely travel of the good old days it is worth noting that in 1859 the trip from Zurich to Bern required $4\frac{3}{4}$ hours.[54] The present running time is 1 hour 12 minutes. Members of Parliament travelling from Zurich to Bern were reimbursed (*Entschädigung*) on the basis of 24 hours for the round trip.[55] From the schedules of the North-East Railway it appears that the fashion was to leave Zurich at 7 : 27 P.M., to travel as far as Aarau, there to spend the night, or seven hours of it. At 4 : 15 A.M. the traveller entered a train of the Central Railway and reached Bern at 7 : 15, alert and eager for the work ahead. Almost 12 hours will have passed by since he left Zurich. In 1859, the trip from Samedan in the Graubünden to Bern also figured in the reimbursement authorizations. The one-way trip, calculated from the schedules of the day required 36 hours. Today, only $5\frac{1}{2}$ hours of travel, inclusive of 30 minutes of stopover time in Chur and Zurich, are required. Dr. O. Gfeller of the Swiss Federal Railways, to whom I am greatly indebted for much of the material in this section, suggests that the *Bundesblatt* (an official publication of the Federal Government) used *Wegstunden*[49] instead of clock hours. The round trip from Zurich to Bern equals 56 *Wegstunden* which cannot be reconciled with the train schedules of 1859 or with the authorized 24-hour travel reimbursement.

The Gotthard

This great Alpine massif, by virtue of the pass and the two tunnels may well be regarded as the center of the most important north–south traffic route in Europe.[50] At the expense of some repetition, I include this section as an historical overview. Described in the earliest documents as Mt. Ursare, Urserenberg, Mons tremolus or Mons elvelinus, the Gotthard is referred to in Habsburg records of 1303 to 1309 as St. Godhardsberg. This name, in turn, is derived from St. Godehardus in whose honor a chapel and hospice had been erected on the mountain in 1166–76 or in the early 1200s. In time the name of the mountain and the pass became transformed to Saint Gotthard or merely Gotthard.

The fame of the mountain must be attributed to the pass which may have been in use as early as 1004 (cf. **2**, Note 19) and became accepted by traders and travellers as the most important route over the Alps for traffic between Italy and northern Europe. According to Kipfer (**205**), the first clear documentary evidence is to be found in *Annales stadenses* by Albrecht von Stade who crossed over the pass in 1236 on returning from Rome to his home in Germany. This manuscript or diary pertains to travel from the north to Rome and from Rome northwards. The records of customs duties indicate that in 1299 a much used route was from Jougne (in France, near Vallorbe) to Rothenburg near Lucerne, and finally over the Gotthard to Italy.

Uri was especially interested in the Gotthard Pass especially after the Devil's Bridge (*Teufelbrücke*) over the Reuss was built (cf. **394**). Uri controlled the northern access to the pass and collected tolls from travellers and merchants. Equally important to Uri was the use of the pass by her soldiers who conquered, lost, and conquered again the Leventina and Bellinzona (see Chapters 3 and 4).

The original hospice and chapel at the top of the pass were dedicated by the Archbishop of Milan in August 1230. The hospice and chapel have quite a history in their own right if one may base such a conclusion on the eminence of visitors. In 1567 and again in 1570 and 1581, Archbishop Borromäus visited the St. Gotthard hospice. In 1623 a new benefice (*Pfründe*) was constructed but remained unoccupied from 1648 to 1682. H.-B. de Saussure was a visitor in 1775 and for several days made a number of scientific observations. Goethe made at least three visits, in June 1775, November 1779, and October 1797. The Englishman, Greville, on a wager, crossed over the pass in 1775 in a small one-horse carriage en route to Rome. The famous Russian general Suvarov with his army crossed the pass in September 1799. Charles Dickens and his family crossed over the St. Gotthard pass in 1845. [Schazmann has written a fascinating account of Dickens' experiences in Switzerland (**318**)]. In the winter of 1800, the hospice was occupied by French soldiers who, to keep warm, burned much of the woodwork from the building.

The hospice was not restored until 1834. Airolo, which then exercised the rights over the hospice, transferred all rights to the hospice in 1841 to Felice Lombardi. A hospital of sorts and a so-called inn stood beside the hospice. The innkeeper was required to provide shelter to impoverished travellers without exacting any payment. He had also to see that the sick were cared for, kept warm, and, if proper hospitalization was needed, he was required to transfer them to Italy or Germany by means of a sled or *Saumpferd* (pack-horse). In dangerous weather, the innkeeper had also to ring bells, or make other signs to minimize the possibility of travellers losing their way. He was permitted to keep 45 cows and 80 or 90 goats to feed upon the scanty pasturage available in the short mountain summer. The pastor in Airolo had the right to make an annual collection throughout Switzerland to support facilities for the poor, especially on the Gotthard.

The number of travellers over the pass and the amount of freight transported each year, even in the Middle Ages, were very great. According to Kipfer, the customs duties collected at the Gotthard in 1300 amounted to 1108 Basel pounds (in today's currency, about one million francs). In the sixteenth century, the annual traffic reached 12,500 quintals of merchanidise, 9000 horses and 15,000 travellers. In 1770, 20,000 travellers crossed over the Gotthard. After substantial road improvements, the traffic increase was almost incredible: 40,000 quintals of merchandise in 1833; 80,000 quintals and 79,000 travellers in 1880.

As early as 1494, the Gotthard road to Milan was a postal transport route. In 1653, the journey by post from Lucerne to Milan required four days. In 1850, operation of the post became a federal responsibility. A traveller, with patience, could then go from Basel to Milan in 38 hours. Before this, horses bred at Einsiedeln were used for the Gotthard post. In the winter months, long columns of sleds were employed, the travellers being tied down, with faces covered to minimize frost-bite. A lead horse, with a bell on its neck, led the column. The sound of the bell indicated to the travellers that they were still on the roadway. Avalanches of snow were all too frequent. In 1624 a column was submerged by an avalanche and 300 lives were lost.

As the road improved, so did the number of poor who stopped off at the Gotthard facilities. Aided by Felice Lombardi, who was known as "father of the poor," over 10,000 of the poor made the trip. In 1876, the number rose to 17,847. The hospice ran out of money and continuance of support depended on voluntary payments by the canton and by individuals.

Felice Lombardi died in 1860. His son, Felice Lombardi, Jr., continued the work of his father, and in 1866 built the hotel Monte Prosa beside the hospice.

Industry and the Economy

The only natural resource that Switzerland has been able to exploit significantly is water. Because the rivers originate from glaciers high in the ice-clad mountains, she has used these fast-flowing streams as a source of power. During the early years of industrial development factories were usually built near the rivers from which water could readily be diverted into mill streams for paddle-wheel generation of power.[56] When the steam engine came to be exploited for industrial use, an entirely new era, the industrial age, was ushered in.

THE TEXTILE INDUSTRY   The textile industry was the first to be developed on a large scale in Switzerland. It already had an important place in the economy since spinning and weaving constituted a widely dispersed home industry that helped to supplement the family income. It also contributed significantly to Switzerland's exports. A special type of middleman played an essential role in home industry. His was the responsibility to distribute the necessary raw materials, to provide the machinery (e.g., looms) that might be required, and to collect the finished products. These were next readied for domestic sale or for export. Some products, such as parts for watches and clocks, were assembled in factories into the finished products.

Early in the nineteenth century the industry began to shift into centralized factory operations. This followed upon the invention of mechanical spinning machines, first imported into St. Gallen from France in 1801, and which soon appeared in the cantons of Appenzell and Zurich. Several important consequences followed. Some of the early textile mills developed workshops for repair and maintenance of the equipment and these, in some instances, expanded into machine construction. The firm of Escher-Wyss, founded in Zurich in 1805 as a cotton-spinning mill, expanded into machine construction and achieved throughout Europe an enviable reputation. The 204 spindles introduced in St. Gallen in 1801–02 was a modest beginning. By 1827 the number of spindles in Switzerland had increased to 400,000, to one million or so by 1850 and to approximately two million by 1872. The Confederation was second only to England in the manufacture of thread and yarn. The mechanical loom, developed by Gaspard Honegger, received a wide acceptance and the textile industry was able to progress into the second stage of mechanization—weaving. Here, the invention of the fast shuttle, of the satin-stitch embroidery technique, and other technical improvements in the 1820s and 1830s soon outdistanced production by the home-weaving industry.

FACTORIES   This brings us to a second important consequence of mechanization. Throughout the country, the home manufacture of textiles found itself on the decline. Home spinning and weaving could not compete with the increasing efficiency of the machine and the centralized factory operation. Weavers and embroiderers found themselves displaced by the machine. Massive unemployment followed as the primitive procedures of the early factories were replaced by sophisticated machinery. In November 1832, workers in Uster destroyed by fire one of the large factories. It was an emotional rebellious outburst expressive of indignation over labor practices and fear of the power that the factory had over their lives. There was much about factory employment that had to be remedied. The hours of labor were long and the wages were low. The employment of children created abuses similar to those in England. The social conscience was aroused when it became widely known that the textile industry in east Switzerland employed some thousands of children six to eight years of age on work schedules as long as 16 hours per day. In Zurich in 1815 the employment of children under nine years of age came to be forbidden. In 1837, the minimal age of employment was raised to 12 years and night work was prohibited to all under 15 years. Both the employer and the parents objected to these restrictions. Legislation designed to improve the factory employment of women was also restrictive and was opposed by both parties.

There was still another important consequence of industrialization and centralization of production in factories. This concerns the migration of agricultural laborers to the growing centers of industrial employment. Although the country experienced several severe industrial crises resulting from foreign competition, flooding of markets and other causes, there were also agricultural crises. In some of the agricultural cantons overpopulation and unemployment of the young presented continuing problems. Home industry was on the decline. The prices of farm products moved erratically. Adversities of weather and every European war introduced fresh cycles of ups and downs in agricultural prices and peasant income. To the young, life on the farm was hard, monotonous and narrowly restrictive. Just as service in foreign armies had had its appeal in the past, so it was the town that now beckoned the young.

The demands of Switzerland's industry could not be satisfied by Swiss alone. A steadily increasing influx of foreigners added to the employment rolls of the railroads and the factories. This was a totally new phenomenon. From 72,000 foreigners in 1855, the number increased to about 230,000 in 1888 (7 to 8 percent of the population). Most of the immigrants were German and French. By contrast, the foreign population numbered about 585,000 in 1960, of whom 93,000 were German and 346,000 were Italian (almost 11 percent of the total population was foreign). In 1974, foreigners numbered 1.1 million (almost 17 percent of the total population).

The War between the States (the American Civil War of 1860) had profound effects on the Swiss economy. By 1860, Switzerland's cotton industry had reached a level of prosperity which was the greatest ever. It was a serious competitor of the British cotton industry. Cotton came in from the southern States in ample supply until the Civil War erupted. The blockade set up by the Union fleet cut off the source of raw cotton and seriously reduced Swiss exports of cotton products. Raw cotton imports fell from 294,000 quintals in 1861 to 189,000 in 1862 and the price of cotton increased fourfold by 1864 over the 1860 price. When peace was declared in 1865, the price fell drastically. Industry lost heavily and the Radical press seized upon the crises to thunder against the "cotton barons."

Political effects also accompanied or followed upon the war. By drawing an analogy from the secession of Lombardy and Venice from Austria in the Italian War of Unification, the Swiss were somewhat puzzled by the inability of the southern States to secede from the Union. An anonymous Swiss author urged in a brochure that Switzerland intervene in the war as a mediator. This simple and commendable proposal was complicated and ruined by the added suggestion that Switzerland sponsor a great colonization project to the benefit of both Switzerland and the Union. Swiss unemployed would be sent to America to fight on the side of the North. This would implant a large Swiss colony and would promote Swiss-American trade (**253**).

EMIGRATION   The influx of foreigners mentioned above was more than counter-balanced by emigration which continued at a high level during most of the century. Between 1798 and 1888 about 160,000 foreigners settled in Switzerland but 387,000 Swiss emigrated, mostly to the USA, Brazil, Argentina, Uruguay and Paraguay. A significant number emigrated to Russia, especially to the Crimea. The reasons for this heavy emigration—over 4000 per year—were many. Occasional agricultural crises did their bit in causing sufficient despair to induce the farmers and peasants to emigrate. The misery induced by the terrible weather of 1816—repeated snowfalls throughout the year, flooding, loss of all crops, and catastrophic increases in the price of bread—is impossible to imagine.[57] Public assistance, soup kitchens, and the tremendous efforts of philanthropic organizations were not equal to the needs of a sick and starving population. Also in the first half of the century the Malthusian doctrine was widely disseminated by Swiss demographers, of whom the most distinguished were in Geneva. Early marriage was declared by some concerned people to be a vice. They urged that marriage of people under 40 be prohibited—the purpose being to reduce family size to two or three children instead of the usual six. Needless to say, such a law was not enacted, although there was a widespread fear of overpopulation, and mercenary service—the time-honored method of facing up to excessive population burdens—was sbout to end.[58] The thinly populated Americas welcomed the newcomers and usually made generous grants of agricultural land.

The nineteenth century was marked by a very considerable emigration from Switzerland to the USA. In 1816–18, widespread hunger in the homeland caused many Swiss to emigrate to the Midwest where they settled along the Ohio and the Mississippi rivers. Between 1860 and 1890, California was the favored destination of the incoming Swiss, especially those from Ticino and Innerschweiz. In the first half of the eighteenth century only about 15,000 Swiss emigrated. In contrast, it has been estimated that 300,000 Swiss emigrated to the USA between 1820 and 1925. The motives for emigration were largely economic, with farmers and artisans constituting the emigrating majority. Glarus suffered greatly when power-looms replaced hand-looms. Emigration was accepted by many as an unwanted but inescapable solution. Nicolas Dürst and Fridolin Streiff, representing a Glarus emigrants' association, set out for the New World in March, 1845, to search for land and a site for settlement. They bought 1200 acres of land in Wisconsin on which the town of New Glarus (1970 population: 1454) was founded. The first settlers, 119 in number, reached New Glarus in mid-August 1845, after a journey of 124 days. Other Swiss settlements in the New World include New Bern (1970 population: 14,660) in North Carolina, founded in 1710 by von Graffenried, Michel, and Ritter; Lucerne in Pennsylvania; and Lancaster and Bern in Ohio.

Seldom mentioned is the almost forgotten Swiss emigrant, Heinrich Lienhard (1822–1903?) from Glarus canton, who, with four companions, was among the first of the adventurous pioneers to cross the continent to California. He left a diary which in great detail describes his travels (**218**). Leaving Le Havre in 1843, he landed at New Orleans and continued by river steamship up the Mississippi to St. Louis. In search of farm land he went northwards to St. Paul where, it was rumored, good land could be bought for $1.25 per acre. He was too late, land was unavailable at the right price; he turned back to New Helvetia in southern Illinois. A variety of jobs failed to satisfy him. Hence we learn that in April 1846 he renewed his westward trek—by ship to Independence and Indian Creek in western Missouri. After continuing the journey with a large group of emigrants from the Indian Creek assembly point, he and four others, eager to reach California before winter set in, separated from the large wagon train and continued by themselves as the five "German Boys." They reached Fort Bridger in south-west Wyoming in July. Taking a short-cut over the desert lands of Utah (then Deseret)—and reaching the Great Salt Lake a full year ahead of the Mormon settlers, they finally came to the end of their journey—Sutter's Fort in Central California—by mid-October (**266**, 7–8 March, 1981—a full page article by Alfred Christiansen).

Johann August Sutter (1803–80), having obtained land from the Mexican governor of California, established a settlement near the Sacramento River. He probably did more than anyone else in encouraging and facilitating the immigration of Swiss into California. Unfortunately for Sutter, gold was discovered on 28 January 1848, in a ditch leading to his saw mill. The rush was on. Hundreds of gold seekers poured into the area. They overran his land, seized his cattle, and, bit by bit, stripped him of his land. His workmen deserted him. Though appointed a major-general of the California militia in 1853, he was soon ruined by the depredation of his properties. An unfavorable decision of the Supreme Court in 1858 legalized the loss of his lands.

New Glarus, more than any other Swiss settlement in the USA, has retained many Swiss characteristics: choral societies, cheese and embroidery industries, use of the Swiss dialects by her older citizens, and Swiss names for her streets and hotels.

After 1850, commercial people—traders, shopkeepers, and bankers—made up most of the emigrants. They were financially better off than their predecessors of the eighteenth century and than those who left the Fatherland in 1818 (**159**).

Swiss settlers also participated in the Civil War and the war against Mexico (1846–48). In the Civil War, two Swiss fought, as generals, with the Confederate army, and one, General Hermann Lieb from Thurgau, served in the Union army of the North. The two with the southern forces were General Felix Zollikofer (whose forefather had emigrated in 1710 with Christoph von Graffenried of Bern) and General Nägeli (**159**).

Switzerland was not always willing to encourage the exodus of young able-bodied men. The poor, as they became a burden on their communities, were told of the golden opportunities in the lands across the seas. In addition, thousands of people who were incapable of work—invalids, cripples, the victims of war (the one-armed, the wooden-legged), the blind, and large numbers of cretins and homeless strays were unloaded by the communities and shipped off to the "promised land." In time the emigration practices were improved, the emigrants received some legal protection and the emigration agents, who commonly were paid through capitation grants by the host countries, were placed under proper supervision.

By the 1870s, fears of underpopulation seized the country, coinciding with a period of rapid industrial growth. Between 1888 and 1914, 290,000 foreigners settled in Switzerland and only 123,000 of her people were lost by emigration.

Of the nineteenth-century emigrants to America who achieved distinction only a few need be mentioned. Albert Gallatin (1761–1849), born in Geneva, is best known as a statesman and diplomat, serving under Presidents Jefferson and Madison as Secretary of the Treasury. Interested in banking and finance, he became president of the new National Bank of New York (1832–39) and subsequently, though briefly, president of the new New York University.

Jean Louis Badollet (1758–1837), also from Geneva, was less distinguished in public service than his Geneva classmate and close friend, Gallatin, who had come to America in 1780. Badollet followed a few years later. The extensive correspondence between the two friends continued until 10 months before Badollet's death. The published correspondence (**364**) makes it clear that each was a sounding board for the other and each gained in strength from their enduring friendship and exchange of ideas.

Louis Agassiz (1807–73), born in Neuchâtel, came to the USA to accept appointment as a professor of natural science at Harvard University. He was among the leading natural scientists of his day, with a world-wide reputation; two others, Martin Henni (1805–81) and Philip Schaff (1819–93), were distinguished theologians.

It is appropriate to mention the heavily documented and authoritative treatment of Swiss emigration by Leo Schelbert (**319**). Two fascinating descriptions of experiences of Swiss emigrants in the American colonies in the 1820s are by Johannes Schweizer (1785–1831) and Jakob Rütlinger (1790–1856). The English translations constitute the contents of a book by Billigmeier and Picard, editors, (**41**). Also in English is an unusual book, edited by Faust and Brumbaugh (**124**) — unusual because it consists mainly of lists of eighteenth-century emigrants to America from the cantons of Zurich, Bern and Basel. The lists are enriched by such details as age, date of baptism, marital state and other minutiae. The first section, (Zurich, 1734–44) of 122 pages, is introduced by a brief preface and an introduction of 25 pages by Faust. This is scholarly and very informative as to the changing policy of government toward emigration. The section lists about 2300 emigrants but, with reasonably plausible assumptions concerning the rest of Switzerland, Faust arrives at an estimated total of 25,000 emigrants to the American colonies during the entire eighteenth century. This is trivial if compared with an estimated Swiss emigration to the USA of over 250,000 between 1820 and 1910. A period of great economic distress in 1816 to 1818 (the hunger years) initiated the nineteenth century flow of emigrants.

The section of 79 pages on Bern begins with a very excellent 25-page introduction by Gottlieb Kurz, the State Archivist, and his associates who give us a summary sketch of Swiss emigration to America in years preceding the 1734–44 decade. The decade is of unusual interest because of the heavy Swiss emigration in that period.

The final section of 131 pages on Basel is entirely the work of Adolph Gerber who, like Kurz, consulted almost all available sources — a more thorough job than that of Faust. The lists for each year from 1734 to 1792 are introduced by helpful information provided by Gerber.

The book concludes with a ten-page analysis by Schelbert. Here one will find many corrections and additions to the lists and a well-deserved paragraph of praise to Gerber for his outstanding contribution.

THE MACHINE INDUSTRY   By 1870 or so, the machine industry of Switzerland had expanded considerably. Shoe factories, paper mills, straw-weaving factories, the railways, and the chemical industry created new challenges and new markets for the machine industry. Swiss industry in general expanded greatly from 1850 on. Branch factories were opened in Austria, Italy, Hungary and Russia. Clothing for export to the Balkans and Asia Minor, and sarongs for the East Indies were manufactured in Glarus.

The roller mill for grain, though not a Swiss invention,[59] contributed much to the development of the machine industry in Switzerland.

The most successful of the early roller mills was constructed in Pest. It was the first of its type in Hungary. The company was organized in June, 1839, but for a number of years encountered almost insuperable difficulties.

A unique feature of the Pest operation was the inclusion of a foundry and machine works in Szechenyi's company. Hungary was barely entering the industrial age in the 1840s. The foundry and machine work were indispensable adjuncts to the mill. It was a great success, thanks to Abraham Ganz from the canton of Zurich who ultimately set up his own company, which became world-famous in the machine-construction industry. The Swiss firms of Escher, Wyss & Co. and Ganz & Co. were leaders in the manufacture of roller mills (**312**, p. 153).[60]

Although milling machinery was constantly improved, nobably by J. J. Sulzberger (1802–55), the modifications were insufficient to overcome major technical defects. Beyond such problems, were the competition of the old stone mills and the almost prohibitive cost of shipping in grain and transporting meal and flour to distant markets: railway companies did not even commence operations until the 1850s.

The real break-through in the technology of roller milling came with the introduction of porcelain cylinders, developed by Friedrich Wegmann of Zurich, manufactured in Oerlikon, and first marketed in 1873. Like the case-hardened castings which came later, the surfaces of the porcelain cylinders were much harder than those used by Sulzberger. They resisted damage by hard foreign particles that sometimes entered with the grain.

Wegmann's discovery served as a stimulus to many subsequent improvements in roller-mill technology and to growth, in its early years, of the Swiss machine industry (**312**, p. 169).

TRADE POLICY   Benefitting greatly from a free trade policy, Swiss industry managed to penetrate the European markets heavily. Beginning in 1860 the extension of free trade to France, Belgium and Japan opened up additional lucrative markets for export. Between 1850 and 1870 Swiss trade in the world markets tripled. The growth of Swiss industry is truly remarkable if we recall the dearth of natural resources in the country: coal, iron, nonferrous metals and petroleum are lacking. From imports of raw materials, and, by emphasis upon precision and quality in manufactured products, she has been able to compete effectively against other highly industrialized States. Tourism and the banking industry, exports of pharmaceutical products, of chocolate and dairy products, all originating in the nineteenth century or earlier, have greatly supplemented her income. Nor should we fail to mention the world-famous Swiss army knives, of which President Reagan recently ordered 2000 specials (*Connoisseur*, Dec. 1984).

In 1891 Switzerland abandoned reluctantly her free-trade policy. She was virtually forced to erect defensive tariff walls because of the protectionist policies of her neighbours. A tariff war with France promptly ensued and, as might be expected, escalated with every revision of the tariffs. This Franco-Swiss economic warfare, oddly enough precipitated by Germany's industrial expansion in the late 1800s, lasted from 1893 to 1895. The defeat of France in the Franco-Prussian war of 1870–71 and the subsequent consolidation of the German States into Bismarck's German Empire made Switzerland almost totally subject to German influence for 40 to 50 years until the First World War ended Germany's economic and political domination of western Europe.

POPULATION   The distribution of workers among various industries in Switzerland is shown in Table 1. The data become more meaningful if related to population and to the number of workers in the home industries.

The population of the area embraced by the 26 cantons of modern Switzerland has been estimated at 600,000 to 650,000 in 1400, at 800,000 to 850,000 around 1500, about 1,000,000 in 1600, and possibly 1,200,000 in 1700. The census of 1798 gave a population of about 1,646,000 (inclusive of Mülhausen and the Valtellina). The country's population by actual count increased to 2,393,000 in 1850, to 2,832,000 in 1880, to 3,753,000 in 1910, to 6,270,000 in 1970 and to 6,329,000 in 1980. Prior to 1798, the population estimates are gross approximations but appear to be of the right order of magnitude.

In 1850, the eight largest cities and their respective populations were as follows: Geneva 31,238; Bern 27,558; Basel 27,513; Lausanne 17,108; Zurich 17,040; La Chaux-de-Fonds 12,638; St. Gallen 11,234; and Lucerne 10,068 (**40**, p. 142). These eight cities alone had more than 10,000 inhabitants each. By 1888 the number of cities (10,000 inhabitants or more) had increased to 18, and, by 1970, to 92 (**341**).

The ten largest cities by the end of 1945 were Zurich 357,100; Basel 168,600; Bern 136,700; Geneva 135,500; Lausanne 99,300; St. Gallen 63,600; Winterthur 61,300; Lucerne 57,300; Biel 43,800; and La Chaux-de-Fonds 31,800 (**40**, p. 199).

HOME INDUSTRIES   The number employed in home industries almost defies calculation. We learn from Hirzel (**178**) that toward the end of the eighteenth century a third of the population depended on industry for a living. If so, about 500,000 people would have been industrially employed. Possibly this is an over-estimate. The point is that in many homes of the farmers and peasants, and also within the towns, the entire family—men, women, children and the old folks[61]—occupied their spare time and supplemented the family income by spinning, weaving, doing embroidery, manufacturing jewelry and parts for the watch and clock industry,[62]

Table 1 Numbers employed by industries and in handwork at home

Industry	1850[a]	1870[a]	1910[b]	1968[c]	1975[i]
Textiles[h]	160,000	180,000	188,000	64,000	43,000
Watches and Jewelry	38,000	73,000	56,000	77,000	62,000
Metals			41,000	120,000	176,000
Graphic arts	2,500	3,000	15,500	51,000	53,000
Chemicals	500	800	8,300	60,000	69,000
Food and beverages	8,700	11,800	69,000	56,000	103,000
Clothing and leather	32,700	35,500	136,000	68,000[d]	46,000
Building and building materials[j]	29,000	34,500	205,000	356,000[e]	252,000
Wood and furniture processing			73,000	44,000	64,000
Paper, rubber, leather			16,500	39,000[f]	38,000
Machines			60,000	263,000[g]	254,000
Electricity, gas, water			9,800	38,000[i]	22,000

[a] From Gruner (**155**, p. 130).
[b] From Bickel (**40**, 128).
[c] **341**, 1969, p. 144.
[d] Includes shoes and bedding.
[e] 1965 statistics.
[f] Exclusive of shoes.
[g] Includes vehicles.
[h] Artificial fibres, silk, cotton, wool, linen, embroidery, woven goods, and stockings.
[i] **341**, 1979, p. 144.
[j] 116,000 in 1888; 174,000 in 1900 (**40**, p. 128). These are totals, inclusive of building materials (wood; paper, rubber, leather; machines; stone and earth. Gruner's data for 1850 and 1870 cover only the building and wood industries (*Bau-und Holzgewerbe*).

etc. A great diversity of products for domestic use and for export could be made by home industry.

Prior to the advent of the machine the data on industrial production pertain to home industry almost exclusively. In the last decade of the eighteenth century and in Zurich alone, there were over 34,000 spinners and 6500 weavers. St. Gallen counted 80,000 to 100,000 spinners, weavers and embroiderers. At the same time, Basel's population included over 2200 silk-band weavers, almost all of whom lived in the countryside. Around the turn of the century (circa 1800) the cotton industry employed about 100,000 hand spinners. By 1814 the infant mechanized industry employed about 6000 machine spinners—half of these in the canton of Zurich (**40**, p. 120). It should be noted that the Huguenot refugees of 1690 must be credited with introducing into Switzerland the technology of weaving muslin. A French refugee, Pierre Bion, is generally believed to have brought the art of cotton spinning and weaving to St. Gallen.[63]

THE WATCH INDUSTRY While eastern Switzerland (Zurich, Zug, St. Gallen, Appenzell, Glarus) pioneered the textile industry, western Switzerland, even earlier, had developed a thriving watch industry. Pocket watches are known to have been constructed in Geneva since the beginning of the sixteenth century. Around 1685, the 100 master watchmakers and their 300 helpers produced about 5000 watches annually. A hundred years later about 6000 were employed in the industry and annual production rose to around 85,000 watches. The industry spread into the Jura, where it became broadly dispersed, with the most intensive centers of production in Le Locle and La Chaux-de-Fonds.

URBAN DOMINATION   The cities which for many years dominated the countryside did not hesitate to strengthen their industrial position by imposing restrictions on their competitors in the country. Zurich in 1683 denied Winterthur (population in 1700, about 2800) the right to do any printing. In 1717 it forbade the introduction into Winterthur of the silk and certain other industries. Though such measures had a paralyzing effect on the subservient towns in the canton, they helped to disperse the embryonic textile industry into the homes of the farmers and peasants. Parenthetically one might add that in the eighteenth century when Bern had a population of about 10,000, it governed almost despotically a rural population of 400,000 or so. The four protestant cities (Zurich, Bern, Basel and Schaffhausen) with about 40,000 inhabitants in all, ruled with firm hands a rural population totalling about 600,000. Likewise, four catholic cities (Lucerne, Zug, Freiburg and Solothurn) with a combined population of 19,000 legislated for (and against) 190,000 subjects in the countryside.

Table 1 reports only on those employed by industry, either in factories or as handworkers at home. Table 2 presents supplementary information on the numbers employed in other occupations.

FARMING   The decrease in farm workers after 1888 fails to indicate the significant trends in domestic food production during the century. Around 1850 when some 300,000 hectares were given over to the raising of grain, agriculture supplied about 80 percent of the country's food requirements. By 1875 the corresponding figures were 240,000 hectares and 70 percent of food requirements. Early in the 1880s the figures fell to only 212,000 hectares and 45 percent of requirements; by 1895, to

Table 2   Numbers employed in various occupations[a]

Occupation class	Numbers		Index, 1888 = 100
	1888	1910	1910
Land and forest economy	488,500	477,100	98
Industry, handwork	543,000	811,000	149
Commerce, banking, insurance	59,700	118,000	196
Hotels, guest facilities	32,600	78,200	240
Trade and transport	35,400	84,700	239
Public and private service	51,200	86,900	170
Housework; day laborers	94,400	115,000	121

[a] From Bickel (40, p. 127).

196,000 ha and 20 percent of requirements; and in early 1914 to 110,000 ha and 15 percent of requirements.

This drastic decrease in cereal production requires an explanation. It was only partly due to the competing demands of industry. More to the point was a continuing fall in the price of grain which was attributable to heavy imports of inexpensive cereals from Russia and North America. From 1872 to 1881, German wheat brought to the farmer S.fr. 15.08 (yearly average) per *malter*[64]. By 1882 to 1891 the price averaged S.fr. 9.59, and in 1892–99 one *malter* yielded only S.fr. 7.88 (**40**, p. 125).[65] Many farmers fell heavily in debt and still others became bankrupt— 900 in Zurich canton alone (**40**, p. 125). Even by 1885 agricultural land had fallen by one-third in price from the prevailing prices of 1872–81. Some who had the necessary capital and knowledge turned to cattle raising and the production of hay, clover and fodder generally. This permitted stall-feeding of cattle in winter. Others attempted the transition and failed in the effort. It was a slow development accompanied by much financial distress. Ultimately, agricultural crises led to the imposition of protective tariffs by the Confederation. The farmers, involved in a desperate, losing battle on the economic front turned also to political action, but with less concerted action than industrial workers were able to summon. Farmers are inherently conservative, and radical socialism which, late in the century, captivated the leftist elements in the Socialist party did not appeal to the farmers. Their votes were generally split among the parties in the center and to the right. They vented their spleen when they could against the privileged classes in the towns: traders, bankers, and any others—God excluded—whom they could blame for agricultural crises, for low farm-product prices, the fall in value of farm land, and for farmer bankruptcies.

Fortunately, for all concerned, a gradual improvement set in around 1890. As a whole, Switzerland enjoyed economic prosperity from then until the outbreak of the First World War in 1914. The old system of crop rotation had become supplemented, if not replaced, by extensive ferilization with manure. Lands of marginal fertility were brought into use. The cultivation of potatoes and other root crops also greatly increased. The dairy industry which grew in importance with the decline of cereal production led to the emergence of cheese factories in abundance throughout the valleys. In 1900, cheese constituted 36 percent of Swiss exports. The farmer and farm-dependent industries were again coming into their own.

On balance, however, Switzerland was emerging as an industrial State. By 1913, 80 percent of her exports were products of her manufacturing industries. In that year exports amounted to S.fr. 1,376 million as compared with 653 million in 1887. In 1914 the factories numbered more than 8000 and the factory workers more than 500,000. By 1967 these had increased to over 13,000 and 880,000 respectively.

BANKING (BACKGROUND)   The lending of money to individual persons or to organized institutions is as old as money itself. Financial services for credit and loans probably originated in Italy but even in the fourteenth century were to be found in the major cities of Europe. In Switzerland the Diesbach-Watt Society, located in Bern, did much to finance Bern's wars in the fifteenth century, and her programs of reconstruction. Bern and Basel were the principal financial centers in early Switzerland. The charging of interest on loans was regarded as usury by the church and, until 1425 when the ban on interest was lifted, the money lenders were non-Christian. After 1425, money on loan became more available and the economy prospered (see also Chapter 4).

In the sixteenth century, the craft guilds, which were to be seriously at odds with the nobles, the aristocracy, and the wealthy, came into being and assumed political power in Basel and Zurich. The policies and social attitudes of the craft guilds hindered the operation of banking and financial services in Basel and Zurich. In Geneva, during the days of Calvinism, the pastors used their influence against the interest rates on money borrowed at less than the ten percent that the city was obliged to pay on its borrowings.

The Thirty Years War ended in 1648 and was followed by some decades of favorable economic developments. Calvinism ceased to be a serious deterrent to money lending. Geneva, beginning to serve as a center for financial services, is credited with establishment of the earliest banks in Switzerland. According to notarized records, Turretini in 1698 was the first of the Swiss bankers (Iklé, **191**). Iklé goes on to tell us that by 1709 there were a dozen families that became famous in Geneva's financial history. Louis XIV of France obtained vast sums from Geneva and Amsterdam to pursue the Spanish War of Succession, which, it is estimated, cost the king about seven million livres per month, with Geneva providing for several years about one half of the king's needs.

Bankers served as intermediaries between the king and private money lenders. The principal lender of the funds for Louis XIV was bankrupt by 1709 but the war continued for another four years.

In 1714–16, 44 bankers from Geneva and elsewhere in Switzerland lived in Paris and were involved as the losers in one of the earliest and worst of Europe's banking scandals. A company organized by John Law issued shares of stock to people in exchange for government securities. The plan, had it succeeded, would have converted the entire public debt into shares of the Société des Indes, but it collapsed in 1720 and John Law escaped to Amsterdam. A severe liquidity crisis and various bankruptcies followed in 1720–21. After the crisis, banking developed anew in Geneva. Solid Huguenot contracts were made with correspondents throughout Europe. The role of Switzerland as an important banking center in the eighteenth century is impressively pointed out in a quotation from Mast's excellent chapter on the Swiss banking industry (**230**, pp. 113–28): "From His Imperial Majesty in Vienna and the Kings of France and England right down to the most obscure German princelings and the towns of Germany and France, every governing authority was in debt to the cantons and towns of Switzerland."

The Geneva banks, after 1770, were heavily oriented toward France. The French Crown raised money through interest-bearing bonds. Originally, the interest was to continue in perpetuity. Later, the interest was to be paid until the death of the holder, at a uniform rate based on an average remaining life expectancy of 15 years.

In effect this meant that bonds were paid off 15 years after issue. With the American War of Independence, the French treasury incurred such huge debts that the government defaulted on interest payments and the currency fell into disrepute. In 1789 the Geneva banks were overloaded with 20 million livres for which there was no market. Many banks defaulted on payments.

The French occupation of Geneva lasted from 1798 to 1813. The economy suffered greatly, with the exception of the clock and watch industry. Private banks, the prevailing type, financed watch exports and prospered. In 1848, Fazy of the famous Geneva family founded the Banque de Genève, and in 1853 established a sort of universal bank which liquidated in 1865.

A St. Gallen family, the Höggers or Hoggeur, became involved in banking during its early years. Three brothers in the family migrated to Lyon, joining many other Swiss, and engaged in the sale of St. Gallen linen. The family owned a bank in Paris from about 1700. With this as a base, the brothers imported silver, had it coined, and made it available to the king in exchange for bankers' papers and short-term bonds. They also financed Charles XII of Sweden. They were almost ruined in the financial crisis of 1709 but were rescued by St. Gallen relatives. Another Hoggeur founded a bank in Amsterdam in 1722 which floated loans for Benjamin Franklin in the American War of Independence and gave credit to American entrepreneurs.

Basel in mediaeval times had its share of money changers and lenders. During the Great Ecclesiastical Council of 1431 to 1448 many foreign money changers came to Basel. In 1530, however, the craft guilds reserved all banking operations to the city government. The public agency that henceforth provided the banking services eventually fell into disfavor because of its monopolistic position and privileges. It lived on until 1746 when it was dissolved because of some bad credit transactions. Late in the century at least a dozen banks were organized and still others came into being in the nineteenth century.

Around 1700, Zurich was a small town of 10,000 to 11,000 inhabitants (**40**, p. 62) and banking got a late start, though the city was a money lender in mediaeval times—usually to permit the payment of mercenaries. In 1570 the city loaned money to Charles IX of France so he could pay off his mercenaries who were mostly Swiss. It was a two-year loan of 150,000 livres at 5 percent interest. Unlike France, neither Bern nor Zurich helped finance the Spanish War of Succession (1702–13). Surplus funds accumulated. By 1709 Bern had invested one million thaler in England and Holland. Zurich in 1727 invested 100,000 guilders in English government securities and bought 20 shares in the South Sea Company.

In 1755 a new organization was set up by the Great Council of Zurich to accept deposits and invest abroad. The bank was named Leu & Company after the city treasurer. It was strictly a government agency and issued bonds bearing 3 to $3\frac{1}{2}$ percent interest. The foreign investments were losses to the bank and Leu defaulted on the interest payments. Foreign investments fell in value from 2.7 million to 700,000 guilders in 1822. Business was transferred to the homeland, and Leu & Company became a private mortgage banker in Zurich. A few others carried on banking and exchange transactions with commodity trading or silk manufacturing as well. They were relatively large enterprises and had no need for the services of private bankers. Hence no really old bank exists in Zurich.

In 1850 the franc, with a fixed value relative to gold, became the national currency throughout Switzerland, replacing the many cantonal currencies that then existed. Basel, even before 1850, had become a great storehouse of capital for Switzerland, upper Baden, eastern France and Alsace. Bank notes were issued by the Bank of Basel (1843–44), which merged with the Swiss Bank Corporation (*Schweizerische Bankverein*) when the National Bank was founded.

The Swiss Bank Corporation is one of the three big Swiss Banks, each with a balance in 1982 in excess of 73 billion francs. It originated in Basel, somewhat as follows: In the mid-nineteenth century six private banks formed a syndicate to spread the risk in the issuing business and to conduct major transactions. After the Franco-German war of 1870–71 the syndicate founded the *Basler Bankverein*, pursuant to another merger. The post-war years suffered an economic crisis and banking losses were appreciable. In 1895, the *Basler Bankverein* merged with the *Zürcher Bankverein* and, two years later, took over the Union Bank of St. Gallen. Thus the Swiss Bank Corporation was born, which, as might be expected, absorbed still other banks in the years that followed. In 1899, the Cantonal Bank of Basel, fostered by political organizations, came into being. By 1977 it was the twelfth largest bank in Switzerland.

In 1856, Credit Suisse (*Schweizerische Kreditanstalt*) was founded in Zurich by Alfred Escher. Along with the Swiss Bank Corporation and the Union Bank of Switzerland (*Schweizerische Bankgesellschaft*) it is a member of the big three.

In 1862 the Bank of Winterthur was founded. It merged in 1912 with the Bank of Toggenburg. From this merger grew the Union Bank of Switzerland which is the largest of the big three with balances, in 1983, in excess of 100 billion francs.

The Nineteenth Century Factory Worker

Almost all that follows pertains only to the factory worker. The problems of the working man may be summarized in almost a single sentence. The work day was very long and, in most of the trades, the income of the worker fell far below the family budget. Deficit financing (loans when possible; use of family savings if any) was out of the question as a solution to a continuing problem. How was the problem solved? Only by all members of the family being gainfully employed. A textile worker in Zurich in 1840 would typically receive in wages about 400 Swiss francs per year; his wife could earn 225 francs and each of his two children about 150 francs (**155**). The family income would total 925 francs and the budgeted expenses 967 francs. In St. Gallen in 1868 a textile worker earned about 640 francs, his wife in household service 380, and the two children about 300. The family income thus increased to 1320 francs per year and the year's expenses to something between 965 and 1470 francs (Gruner, **155**, pp. 141–42). One answer to the budget-deficit problem was found in the large family. As Gruner points out, six children of working age permitted an almost princely life style: yearly wages of 3345 francs against a family expenditure of 2405 francs for necessities. In the Zurich *Oberland* four to six working members of a family were needed to make life bearable.

As will be mentioned later, the cantonal and federal governments enacted a number of laws to control and restrict the factory employment of women and children. The legislation was also designed to prescribe the maximum permissible length of a "normal" work day. Oddly enough, but for quite different reasons, both the employers and the employees were opposed to the laws. The employer sought to maximize his profit and the employee sought to maximize his income. "Rather a spoonful more of soup than a half-hour less of work" was to be heard in Zurich on introduction of the factory law of 1870. The average length of the work day in factories of the nineteenth century is given by Gruner (**155**, p. 131): 1815, 14 to 15 hrs/day; 1830, 14 to 15; 1840, 14 to 15; 1850, 12 to 14; 1860, 12 to 13; 1870–77, 11 to 13 hrs/day. Finally, the Factory Act of 1877 established the elevan-hour work day throughout the Confederation. Wages, expressed as a weighted average, based on the number of workers in each of the six largest industries, increased about 120 percent between 1830 and 1875. Competition in the larger industries was countered in the early days by wage reductions or a lengthening of the working day or both. In time, social pressures and factory legislation put an end to such practices.

How was the income of a working man's family expended in the nineteenth century in order to provide the necessities of life? The data reported by Gruner pertain to the period 1830 to 1875 (**155**, p. 134). Before 1850, about 17 percent of the expenditures, instead of 14, was for clothing; heating and lighting required about 12 percent of the total instead of 7. Expenditures on food in the earlier years of the century constituted about 59 percent of the total instead of 62.

Informative also are the data on the costs of specific items embraced by the items in Table 3. These are set forth in Tables 4 and 5.

The data in Tables 4 and 5 must be regarded as country-wide averages. As such, regional deviations from the average are not shown, and short-term fluctuations in any given locality are obscured. Thus, in Bern in 1847 the price of bread was 28 rappen per pound but in 1849 it fell to 14 rappen. A kilogram of potatoes which cost 4 rappen in 1845, rose to 9.3 rappen in 1846 and to 12 to 17 rappen in 1847. In general, potatoes were inexpensive and whenever a family was forced to economize on expenditures for food, this was almost accomplished by eating less bread and more potatoes. As might be expected living costs were lower in the countryside than in the towns. Incomes were lower but foodstuffs and some other necessities were cheaper than in town. Early in the nineteenth century as much as 60 percent of the expenditures of a family of four would be for food. In 1971, on the average, only 25 percent of the factory worker's income would be expended for food.

With respect to annual wages (salaries) the following information pertains to nonfactory workers in 1859 in several towns: a wagon washer and assistant packer (in Yverdon), S.fr. 640; postman and letter carrier in Brienz, 500; chief letter carrier in Chaux-de-Fonds, 1000; postman, letter carrier, and telegrapher in Teufen (Appenzell), 1140; postal employee in principal post office in Neuchâtel, 1020;

Table 3   Household expenditures of a factory worker's family[a]

	1830 to 1875	Percentage of total
Foodstuffs		62.0
Bread	17.5	
Potatoes	7.4	
Milk	9.4	
Butter	4.0	
Meat	9.8	
Coffee	2.4	
Other foodstuffs[b]	11.5	
	62.0	
Clothing		14.0
Housing		13.5
Heating and lighting		7.0
Miscellaneous		3.5
		100.0

[a] Gruner (**155**, p. 134).
[b] Cheese, vegetables, fat, fruit, flour, spices, etc.

secretary of the customs bureau in Geneva and cashier of the 6th customs district, 2800.[66]

In Table 6 some of the data on living costs are presented in a form that relates the cost of a few necessities to the hours or minutes that one would be obliged to work to permit purchase of a unit quantity. The data, recalculated, are drawn principally from Gruner (**155**) and Hauser (**167**).

Table 4   Typical prices of various foods consumed by a factory worker's family[a] (averages for nineteenth century Switzerland) [prices are in rappen (centimes)]

Year	Half-white bread (kg)	Potatoes (kg)	Milk (liter)	Butter (kg)	Beef (kg)	Coffee (kg)	Eggs (each)
1830	36	4.3	9.0	135	58	157	—
1835	32	2.8	12.0	144	63	222	—
1840	—	4.5	9.9	151	56	160	3.0
1845	34	3.6	8.3	152	69	135	4.3
1850	32	7.0	8.5	133	61	150	3.5
1855	—	9.0	10.0	164	84	170	—
1860	40	8.5	12.7	178	95	180	5.0
1865	33	6.6	11.3	188	98	240	5.4
1870	45	7.0	12.5	216	119	240	6.0
1875	43	8.6	16.0	244	—	270	8.1

[a] Gruner (**155**, p. 132).

Table 5   Typical expenditures for clothing, housing and heating by a worker's family[a] [prices in rappen (centimes)]

Year	Beechwood (cord)	Shoes (pair)	Cotton cloth (meter)	Stockings (pair)	Man's shirt	Woman's skirt	3-Room apartment (year)
1830	—	—	—	85	—	—	—
1835	—	—	—	—	120	540	—
1840	2500	500	250	63	—	470	15,000
1845	2810	—	210	—	—	—	15,000
1850	2280	640	—	55	275	500	—
1855	2590	—	—	—	—	—	—
1860	3750	510	—	—	225	550	—
1865	4260	—	250	—	—	550	27,500
1870	4660	1100	190	—	285	—	—
1875	5050	1050	190	50	—	—	24,000

[a] Gruner (**155**, p. 133).

The Rise of Socialism and Trade Unions

It was inevitable that the factory workers would eventually seek political solutions to their problems. In retrospect, one is not surprised by the formation of trade unions and the importation from England of the strike strategy, as organized measures of defense against exploitation by their employers. Nor is one surprised that the city factories were the principal focal points of mounting unrest. The proletariat was to be found in the towns. The employees of small factories in the rural areas had kindred complaints but their problems had less serious impacts. Unlike their brothers in the cities, they had two strings to their bow: they were factory workers but they were also farmers. In 1840 about 80 percent of all Swiss owned their bit of land. They could raise their own fruit and vegetables and sometimes had a surplus for sale in the towns. Nonetheless the poorer people throughout the nineteenth century had to expend about 60 percent of the family income on food. From 1827 to 1842 for every 100 male adults employed by the cotton industry, 50 children under 16 were also employed. The proportion fell to 10 or 12 percent by 1882 as legislation throughout the cantons focused on the child-labor problem. The employment of women by the cotton industry continued high throughout the century. For every 100 adult males employed, as many as 50 to 70 adult women worked in the cotton industry.

Industrialization was destroying the social structures that had evolved during the centuries: communities of independent self-reliant people, conservative, God-fearing, subservient to civil and ecclesiastical authority and, at the lower economic levels, accustomed to long hours of hard work. Family income was supplemented, and brought up to maintenance levels by various means: women were employed as domestics in the homes of the upper classes; men and boys had ancillary

Table 6 Working time required for procurement of various necessities[a] [in hours and minutes (0/00) unless otherwise stated]

Year	Average wage (rappen/hr)	Bread (kg)	Potatoes (kg)	Milk (liter)	Butter (kg)	Beef (kg)	Eggs (each)	Beechwood (cord)	Shoes (pair)	Man's shirt	Woman's skirt	One year's rental of 3-room apartment
1830	10	3/40	0/25	0/50	12/30	5/50	—	10 days	55/00	—	—	—
1840	10	3/30	0/25	1/00	15/00	5/20	0/20	7½ days	50/00	12/00	47/00	4½ months
1850	13	2/30	0/30	0/40	10/00	4/40	0/15	10 days	32/00	21/00	31/00	—
1860	16	2/30	0/30	0/50	11/10	6/00	0/20	9 days	52/00	14/00	34/20	—
1870	21	2/10	0/20	0/25	10/20	5/40	0/20	7 days	35/00	13/30	—	—
1875	30	1/20	0/17	0/20	8/10	—	0/15	—	—	—	—	2½ months
1880	45	1/00	—	—	6/30	3/25	—	—	—	—	—	—
1970	720	0/10	—	—	1/50	2/20	—	—	—	—	—	—
1979[b]	1273	0/10	0/03	0/05	1/40	1/45	0/02	—	6/45	3/00	7/00	2 months

[a] The Table indicates the remarkable extent to which real wages (expressed as purchasing power) have increased since 1830. The data for the nineteenth century are taken from Gruner (**155**, p. 133).
[b] Calculated from *Die Volkswirtschaft* 53, August 1980 (ref. **72**, pp. 555 and 559).

employment on the estates of the rich; and home industries acquired an increasing importance as textile manufacture, clock making, etc. came to be farmed out to handworkers at home.

The rise of the factory eventually brought an end to much of this. The independence and self-reliance of the people came to be replaced by factory dependence of such dimensions that an industrial crisis, let alone the avarice of some industrialists when times were good, created desperate suffering among the poor.

Many fumbling efforts and much groping about for feasible solutions to the mounting problems of the factory worker were characteristic of the times. Journeymen's associations and provident societies grappled with the problems. Co-operative societies of the Rochdale type came into being. Socialized communities of the Robert Owen type were advocated. French socialist doctrine, as advocated by Charles Fourier and Proudhon, was vigorously promoted. In 1838, in Geneva, the first section of the Swiss *Grütliverein* was organized by the Swiss members of a Swiss–German workers' organization which was having an overload of doctrinal dissension within the ranks. Albert Galeer (1813–51) formulated the program of the *Verein* and gave it its socio-political orientation. In demanding that the State see to it that no citizen who devotes himself diligently to a lifetime of hard work and industry should ever be reduced to starvation, Galeer was an early advocate of the welfare State. The *Grütli* movement satisfied a need and spread quickly throughout Switzerland. Branches were formed in many cantons. The movement had inherited a flavor of communism which in many places aroused the mistrust of government. In 1852, the conservative government of Bern banned any *Grütli* activity in the canton as a threat to security of the State. In general, the *Grütlianers* were politically to the left of the Radicals and Democrats. The Radicals were never really dramatically radical. The principal demands of the Radicals were for centralism in government which was always a challenge to the advocates of federalism. If the Radicals had had a far left philosophy they would never have been able to dominate the Swiss political scene and control Parliament for 46 years (1874 to 1920). The program of the *Grütli* movement which motivated its members for 50 years focused on adult education, publicly supported workmen's health insurance (*Krankenkasse*), a people's bank, financially secured by the State, and the establishment by government of a labor secretariat. Its political orientation was seemingly diffuse but it had much in common with the Social Democrats. It played a leading role in organization of the first Swiss Federation of Workers (1873). Fifty years later the *Grütliverein* merged with the Social Democrats and disappeared from the political arena.

Unencumbered with political ideologies were the early associations of workers and unions for provident purposes, education and self-help through foundations of their own making. Later, as trade unions came into being and work stoppages began to play a role in enforcing demands, the workers' foundations gave financial support to the strikers. The watchmakers in Geneva became unionized and instituted the first large strike. The tailors, furniture makers, shoemakers, and typographers became organized into unions and struck successfully to gain wage improvements.

Metalworkers' organizations were solidly established in the 1880s and the Swiss Metalworkers' Association was formed in 1888. Years later (1915) it merged with the Swiss Watchmakers' Association and formed a powerful union (84,000 members in 1919). In its infancy, the union, thoroughly combative in spirit, proclaimed as its objective "the preparation, in collaboration with the international proletariat, of the workers' takeover of production and the elimination of class domination."

There was no dearth of intellectuals who, in their writings, propounded the doctrines of socialism and communism. The workers who introduced socialist and communist ideologies into Switzerland in the 1800s were relatively few. Wilhelm Weitling (1808–71)—a German journeyman tailor who lived in Switzerland from 1841–1844—propounded the philosophy of communism and quickly aroused the anger of the establishment.[67] Weitling was a contemporary of Karl Marx (1818–1883) and appears to have preceded Marx and Engles in championing the concept of the class struggle, in trumpeting the demand for abolition of private property, and in insisting on the responsibility of work by everybody. Privilege and social parasitism had to go.

A rather remarkable man who was at first heavily influenced by Weitling's ideology was Johann Jakob Treichler (1822–1906) who came from a poor family near Zurich—his father, a small farmer and handworker. At 12, Treichler became a factory worker, later a teacher, and in 1844 a student of jurisprudence. His philosophy of State socialism elicited in the government of Zurich a reaction similar to that of a red cloth to a bull. Though harrassed by a cantonal law of 1836 (the *Maulkrattengesetz*) he was elected to the Great Council of Zurich in 1850 and in 1852 to the National House of Representatives (*Nationalrat*)—the first Socialist to achieve such recognition in Switzerland.

Karl Bürkli (1823–1901), a tanner by trade, was attracted to socialism through the writings of Fourier. Weitling's belligerent advocacy of communism was not to Bürkli's liking. He promoted the idea that capitalism should be replaced gradually, and by peaceful evolution, through consumer cooperatives in collaborative agreements with associations of producers. Along with Treichler, Bürkli in 1851 founded the Consumers' Association of Zurich. Mention should also be made of Pierre Coullery (1819–1903) who founded in 1851 the Bern Reform Association. He was an early advocate of socialism which he interpreted as brotherhood and justice, the right to live and work, and political and economic equality—but not the abolition of private property rights.

The most important and effective leader of the workers, and proponent of the socialist cause in the closing years of the nineteenth century, was unquestionably Hermann Greulich (1842–1925).[68] He never subscribed to the communist doctrine of a dictatorship of the proletariat for he believed in the attainment of a social democracy through the gradual evolution afforded by the legislative process. Greulich and Bürkli in 1870 founded the Social Democratic party which had but a brief existence. A second attempt in 1880 was equally unsuccessful. Not until 1888 when a Bern patrician, Albert Steck, joined in the effort was the party securely founded. Its political philosophy was untinged by communism for it advocated the transition to a Socialist State by the slow evolutionary process of social reform through legislation.

Socialism and communism were of foreign origin. The deeply rooted belief of the Swiss in the sanctity of private property rights was totally incompatible with any native Swiss movement toward establishment of a full-blown socialist State, especially if cloaked with any of the vestments of communism. In general, the advocates of communism and of far-left socialism entered Switzerland from Germany, France and Italy. They were burning with passionate zeal for the programs they proposed. Their first converts were not the native-born Swiss but the refugees who had fled to Switzerland to escape persecution in their home country. Many of these harbored ideas about politics and industry that disturbed the Swiss, especially the privileged class, and, by neighbouring governments were interpreted as open invitations to rebellion by their subjects.

The Wohlgemuth affair of 1889 illustrates the problem (177). August Wohlgemuth, a police inspector from Mülhausen was arrested in Rheinfelden, carrying a batch of incriminating letters to Anton Lutz, a German subject from Bavaria, then living in Basel. The letters invited Lutz, in return for a monthly payment to serve as an agitator, a spy, and an informer in certain labor circles in Basel, Alsace-Lorraine, and the Grand Duchy of Baden. Part of the money received by Lutz went into the coffers of the Socialist party. Hilty describes Wohlgemuth as "one of the clumsiest and most bungling of police inspectors" (177). Bismarck demanded the right to place Germany's properly accredited police officials in Switzerland to watch over and report upon anarchists and revolutionary socialists who endangered the security of Germany.

Numa Droz, in an exchange of letters, presented the official Swiss point of view, doing so as a member of the Federal Council: (a) Switzerland believes in and shall continue to grant the right of asylum to any whom she chooses; (b) Germany's demand constitutes a direct infringement of Switzerland's sovereignty and independence; (c) the Act of 20 November 1815 [subscribed to by the heads of State in Europe] declared *inter alia* that Switzerland's independence of any foreign influence is in the true interest of the whole of Europe.

Similar letters were sent by the Federal Council to Russia and to Austria whose conservative monarchs were being urged by Bismarck to join in putting Switzerland in her place. However, Wohlgemuth was expelled from Swiss territory, having been found guilty of engaging an *agent provocateur* to agitate in the workers' circles in Alsace-Lorraine and Germany—thereby endangering the security of the Swiss Confederation.[69]

The first all-Swiss Federation of Workers (*Schweizerische Arbeiterbund*) of 1873 survived a mere seven years. It was a conglomerate of disparate elements which attempted to achieve reform by a variety of programs which, in the aggregate, lacked a unity of procedure and were sometimes hopelessly conflicting. There were the militant Communists, determined to achieve a dictatorship of the proletariat, the Social Democrats with a liberal but moderate program of social reform, the

Trade Unions, Radicals bent on achieving more power in the central government, and the advocates of grass-roots reform through cooperatives, provident societies, and self-help organizations. In 1887 the Swiss Federation of Workers was reorganized as a central all-Swiss Federation of Trade Unions—a central *Gewerkschaft* which gave a common purpose and direction to the trade unions which were coming into being. The Federation, joined by the Radicals, the Democrats, the Socialists (in 1888), Social Democrats and other proponents of reform, was able to summon the necessary support to effect much of the legislation which was insistently demanded. In the last few decades of the century, much had already been accomplished: the Factory Law of 1864 which brought about the 12-hour day, abolished night work, and gave protection to pregnant women; the Factory Law of 1877 which established the 11-hour day, forbade employment of those under 14 years of age, and assured adequate government inspection of factories. Interestingly enough, the people voted down, through an 1882 referendum, a federal ordinance which was designed to establish a federal secretariat of schools. Why was this seemingly inocuous measure rejected? Only because it would have meant an intrusion into cantonal affairs—a needless sacrifice of cantonal responsibility in education and a delegation of more power to the central government at the expense of cantonal sovereignty.

Militancy characterized the many labor disputes of the 1890s and the first few decades of the twentieth century. Strikes were numerous (520 between 1860 and 1894) and repressive measures were common. To government, to the leaders of industry, and to the uncommitted, strikes were totally incompatible with the traditional spirit of the Swiss people. Troops were called out on at least a dozen occasions to maintain the peace and to break up the demonstrations by workers. Not until 1937 did the ugly confrontations of class warfare come to an end. Under wise leadership within the largest of the trade unions and the corresponding association of employers, industrial peace was finally born (see Chapter 11.7).

Treaties of Friendship, Commerce, Reciprocal Establishment, Etc.

It is a diplomatic nicety and a gesture of international courtesy that treaties between two Powers shall be introduced by a declaration of friendship—past, present, or future. Though such a declaration usually has a pro-forma quality, the treaty of 1850 negotiated between the United States of America and Switzerland[71] has a very genuine ring to it. The preamble tells us of "the bonds of friendship which so happily exist between the two Republics."

In Article I we learn that citizens of the two countries

> shall be admitted and treated upon a footing of reciprocal equality. They shall be at liberty to come, go, sojourn temporarily, domiciliate, or establish themselves permanently ... acquire, possess, and alienate therein property ... exercise their profession, their industry, and their commerce ... they shall have free access to the tribunals, and shall be at liberty to prosecute and defend their rights before courts of justice in the same manner as native citizens. ..."

Article II tells us that the incoming citizens of the other country shall be free

> from personal military service; but they shall be liable to the pecuniary or material contributions which may be required, by way of compensation, from citizens of the country where they now reside, who are exempt from the said service. In case of war, or of expropriation for purposes of public utility [they are also to] be placed on an equal footing with citizens of their host country with respect to indemnities for damages sustained.

Article V takes care of real estate which foreigners shall be entitled to hold or inherit. It pertains also to the disposition of personal property "by sale, testament, donation, or in any other manner." The American or Swiss foreigners shall be treated equally in such matters with the citizens of, and according to the laws of, the host country.

In matters of commerce, we learn from Articles VIII and X that the two countries "shall treat each other reciprocally as the most favoured nation," meaning thereby that neither party shall "grant any favour in commerce to any nation . . . which shall not immediately be enjoyed by the other party."

Articles XIII to XVII pertain to the extradition of fugitive criminals from the USA to Switzerland, and vice versa. The applicable crimes are listed. It is of some interest that offenses "of a political character" are specifically excluded. Neither country appears to have had any qualms over the provision of hospitality to political refugees from the other country, such as those who assailed Austria, Prussia and Russia in the 1830s.

Five years later a similar treaty was concluded between Switzerland and Great Britain "to maintain and strengthen the ties of friendship which happily subsist between the two countries."[72] Unlike the treaty with the USA, it does not cover the extradition of fugitive criminals.

In 1876, the German Empire, newly forged by Bismarck from many independent States, entered into a treaty of establishment with Switzerland.[73] Friendship is not excluded, for again we read of "the desire to maintain and to strengthen the bonds of friendship existing between Switzerland and the German Empire." The rights of establishment as defined in the treaties between Switzerland, the USA, and Great Britain are set forth in the present treaty somewhat more concisely, with less detail, and with a few changes. A protocol expands upon the question of military service. The expulsion of undesirables is briefly treated, and extended by an agreement of each party to accept any of its citizens who are expelled by the other as undesirables.[74]

In June 1864, France and Switzerland concluded a treaty of establishment which gave to French nationals in Switzerland and to Swiss nationals in France an equality of rights with citizens of the host country, and an exclusion from military service in the case of war.[75] The preamble breathes the air of friendship "which unite the two peoples." This treaty is of unusual interest for Switzerland became thereby morally obliged to extend to Swiss Jews in Switzerland the rights of establishment hitherto restricted to Christians.[2,70]

Neutrality

By the end of the nineteenth century, the principles and practices of neutrality adopted by Switzerland had almost fully evolved into what we might describe in the 1980s as a fully rounded picture of the rights and responsibilities of Switzerland as a perpetual Neutral. Even so, we must recognize that Swiss neutrality in the twentieth century has expanded in scope, has altered in points of emphasis, and the country has faced a host of problems attributable to her neutral status. We need only read the Tables of Contents of volumes II to VIII of Bonjour's encyclopedic work (49) on Swiss neutrality to become aware of the almost innumerable events in the past eight decades of Swiss history that pertain to Switzerland's efforts to live the life of a neutral State in a rapidly changing world.

As a background to much of this we shall have to carry our story to 1914, to the dawn of World War I. Our starting point will be 1848, the year of the first Swiss constitution that had some real significance as an expression of a federalistic spirit and structure for the association of 22 cantons. To get a feeling for what it is all about I must suggest to the reader that he take a good look at the excellent article by Barclay (24) which will help to put us in tune with the state of the subject in 1910 or so. It would also be well, by way of contrast, to read again the section on neutrality in Chapter 3. This will give us a picture of the state of Swiss neutrality, if there was such a thing, in Switzerland of the late Middle Ages.

In 1907, at an international conference convened at the Hague, agreement was reached on many of the rights and responsibilities of a neutral State. The first Article of one of the Conventions that emerged from the conference states that "The territory of the neutral Power is inviolable" (161). How does this relate to the Swiss experience between 1848 and 1914? There was rarely a year when all four or five of her neighbours were simultaneously at peace during the last five decades of the nineteenth century. Swiss policy for many years back called for the issuance of a declaration of neutrality on the outbreak of each and every war which might threaten the peace within Switzerland, her independence, and her territorial integrity. Between 1848 and 1914, the Confederation issued at least three proclamations of neutrality. Without exception, these proclamations declared the firm resolve of the Confederation to defend her neutrality and territorial integrity. In implementation of these declarations the Federal Council adhered consistently to a pattern which was generally effective. Troops were mobilized and sent to defend the border where an incursion into Swiss territory had to be guarded against.

From the vantage point of the present we may well ask whether the border guards and their reinforcements could have held back a foreign army, superior in numbers, determined to invade the country. Whatever the answer to this question may be, the Swiss were lucky: they enjoyed the blessings of the Almighty on two counts. Although there were occasions when a foreign army was uncomfortably close to the border there is little if any evidence that either an invasion of the country or a *Durchzug* was seriously contemplated.

A second and most important reason for Switzerland's good fortune resided in the principle of territorial equilibrium to which the heads of State in the major European countries tacitly subscribed. An invasion of Switzerland by France would certainly invite an invasion of France by Germany. Were Germany to seize a part of Switzerland, France would probably respond by invading Germany. Italy could not seize the Ticino without inviting an almost certain attack upon North Italy—the former Austrian Lombardy. The continental Powers were not restrained from acquisitive or punitive invasions of Switzerland by visions of Swiss military superiority or by the knowledge that the Swiss were committed to defend their country by mass participation of the population. It was well known that older men and boys, women and children, all of their own volition, would join in defense of their homes and country if the emergency arose. The real deterrent to the Powers was mutual jealousy, distrust and fear of each other, and an inability to forge a common policy which might have been directed toward the dismemberment of Switzerland along her linguistic boundaries. This would have harmonized with the nationalistic aspirations which were widely expressed in the 1860s and the 1870s. Western Switzerland would go to France, the Ticino to Italy, central Switzerland to Germany, and the Graubünden to Austria.

To consider further the question of territorial integrity and inviolability of the frontiers of neutral Switzerland we must be aware of other very pertinent considerations. The first is that Switzerland had long since ceased to place any trust whatever in the guarantees of the Powers to defend Switzerland's independence and territorial integrity. The guarantees were clouded by an assumed right of intervention in Swiss affairs if Switzerland became a haven of security for hostile elements committed to an overthrow of conservative, reactionary, and despotic monarchies. Switzerland knew full well that her defense against an aggressive Power was not to be found in scraps of paper with pious assurances of protection by others, but only in her own internal strength and correctness of behaviour.

As we look into other aspects of the inviolability of her territory we should recognize that Switzerland's border problems were essentially of two categories: those that originated from without and those that were generated within. Here we shall limit ourselves to the activities of those concerned individuals whose political philosophies were denounced and feared by the continental monarchs.

Switzerland's border to the north required a variety of defensive measures in 1848. Politically active refugees from the Grand Duchy of Baden streamed into the northern cantons. They were close to many of the Swiss radicals through language, origin and political sympathies. Tales of despotism and oppression under the monarchs were widely circulated and political solidarity was placed above neutrality. Revolutionary doctrines flowed freely and were countered by a widely distributed statement of the Federal *Vorort* on Swiss policy. This said in effect that Switzerland, under all circumstances, must remain neutral.

The Federal Council declared, much to the point, that Switzerland would not tolerate foreign refugees who, on Swiss soil, conspired and plotted hostilities against a neighbour. Refugees were to be disarmed on crossing the border and warned against abuses of asylum. During a second revolt in September, 1848, the entering refugees from Baden were not permitted to remain in the border cantons but were moved farther into the interior. A third uprising broke out in Baden and the adjacent Palatinate in May 1849. The Federal Council sent 5000 men to defend the border. Recruiting in Switzerland for the rebel cause was strictly forbidden and the export of weapons to the rebels was prohibited. The insurgents were defeated and subdued by a large Prussian army. In July, 9000 of the beaten troops with much war material crossed into Switzerland. They had been preceded by many Baden civil officials and officers who fled with their families to seek refuge in Switzerland.

A related problem stemmed from the rebels' sympathizers in Switzerland who, in person and through smuggled weapons, tried to aid the insurgents. German workers employed in Switzerland, newly naturalized Swiss from Germany, and many Swiss activists were eager to jon the rebels. "Save Europe from the despots" rang out as their battle cry. The Swiss border guard succeeded in stopping most of them at the border and confiscated weapons and munitions which were on their way to the duchy. At one time as many as 25,000 of the militia were posted on the northern border. The political and military chiefs of the third Baden uprising and of the revolt in the Palatinate were soon deported. The remaining refugees, 10,000 or more, were distributed among the cantons where sympathetic radicals were not dangerously numerous. Although the Powers contended that Switzerland was a workshop for revolutionaries and the center of a spreading political disease that would destroy every well-ordered State, they appeared satisfied that the Confederation was doing everything possible to restrain the troublesome political activists. At least they felt so until the days of Bismarck.

Switzerland became disturbed, as did other countries, by the aggregation of power in the new German Empire. Bismarck was feared, for the Swiss saw in him a man who knew neither legal nor moral restraints. Legislation had been enacted, under his insistence, against social democracy and social democrats. Many of the German socialists fled to Switzerland. In Zurich they published the *Social Democrat*, deliberately tailored for export to Germany. The paper, distributed in large numbers, repeatedly assailed Bismarck and the Prussian royal family. The left wing of the Swiss Radical party and the German Socialists were united in a friendly alliance. German *agents provocateurs* infiltrated the ranks of both groups. The Federal Council finally suppressed the *Social Democrat* because of its provocative policies, and deported the four editors.

Other incidents involving an anarchist organization and more German spies and *agents provocateurs* greatly imperiled the relations between Switzerland and Germany. Bismarck contemplated intervention by placing a German police force in Switzerland to restrain the "troublemakers." Numa Droz, head of the Swiss Political Department, replied, undaunted, that Switzerland would share its police responsibilities with no one. If the Federal Council yielded to such a request it would be vigorously opposed by the Federal Assembly and by public opinion throughout Switzerland. Turning next against Swiss neutrality, Bismarck invoked the guarantee by the Powers of Swiss neutrality and, as Metternich had done before, he threatened Switzerland with active intervention by the Powers. If Switzerland continues to harbor and protect German revolutionaries who threaten the peace and security of Germany, the question must be asked, according to Bismarck, as to how far Swiss neutrality is compatible with guarantees of peace and order. The protection of Swiss neutrality by the Powers requires Switzerland not to tolerate anything that endangers the peace and security of the Powers. In his campaign against Switzerland, Bismarck sought the support of Russia, Italy and Austria, but without success.

In June 1889, Switzerland established a special federal agency (*Bundesanwaltschaft*) to sharpen the Swiss police measures against anarchists and disturbers of the peace. Bismarck did not indicate that he was now satisfied and he set up a strong border control against the inflow of inflammatory literature. He did not mention again the neutrality question. Much of the German press opposed Bismarck's threats against Switzerland. Whether Bismarck really wanted to provoke a war with Switzerland and whether an absorption of his small neighbour was part of his plan for a greater Germany has never been answered. However, it is quite evident from the record that Bismarck feared that a southward expansion of the new German Empire into central and eastern Switzerland would throw Switzerland immediately into the arms of France.

Some years earlier, Metternich threatened Switzerland even more vigorously and directly than Bismarck had done. Austrian Lombardy was under attack by revolutionary troops determined to free the province from Austrian rule. Milan had fallen to the rebels on 19 March 1853. About 700 irregulars from the Ticino who had crossed the border in small groups participated in the liberation of Milan. In January, Metternich had reported to the Austrian Kaiser that if an invasion by volunteers from the Ticino took place, he would pursue the enemy into their homeland and occupy the Ticino with Austrian troops. The threatened invasion came dangerously close and might have taken place if the Austrians had not been fully engaged in their efforts to hold Lombardy against the fanatically inspired rebels. The cantonal government of Ticino sent troops to the border to prevent numerous volunteers from crossing into Lombardy to join in the attack but the cantonal troops at heart sympathized with the rebels. Lugano was the center of revolutionary activity in the canton. Recruiting for the rebel cause went on virtually unhindered by government. A company of volunteers organized in Zurich and the Thurgau marched in good order through the Ticino and crossed the border with little more than a slap on the wrist. Recruiting for the cause was carried on in the Valais and in Vaud, even with encouragement from Stämpfli.

Two series of events speedily ensued. The Austrian commander in Lombardy, Radetzky, ordered all the Ticinesi out of Lombardy. The Federal Government quickly took control of the situation. It reminded the cantonal government that foreign affairs, under the new constitution, fell exclusively within the competence of the Federal Government. The federal authorities were greatly disturbed by the border incidents, the failure of the cantonal authorities to prevent gross violations of Swiss neutrality, and the stream of Austrians flowing in from the south to seek refuge in the canton. All Italian males over 18 years of age, then in the Ticino, were moved into more distant cantons for internment. Their weapons were seized. New arrivals from Italy were permitted to remain only one week. The Swiss irregulars in Lombardy were ordered to return instantly. Only the vociferous minority in Parliament—the Radicals and some of the intellectuals—wanted Switzerland to join the revolution against Austria in Lombardy. Jonas Furrer, the Federal Councillor in charge of the Political Department, demanded adherence to strict neutrality.

In an 1859 report of a Commission of the Ständerat (Senate) we read that

> unanimity prevails among the Swiss people that neutrality must be maintained at any price. This firm resolve is found to override all other matters on which differences of opinion exist. The Swiss people will gladly sacrifice their blood and their possessions to prevent the Fatherland becoming an area of combat between foreign armies.[76]

The Franco-Prussian war of 1870–71 presented Switzerland with the problem of interning an entire French army, originally of 120,000 to 150,000 men.[77] About 90,000 men reached the Franco-Swiss border at Verrières and, in the early hours of a bitterly cold 1 February, crossed the border into Switzerland. They were disarmed on entry and distributed throughout Switzerland in churches, schools, assembly halls, hospitals, and other buildings—186 places in all.

The internees were demoralized and dispirited. There was much sickness, and infectious diseases were widespread. The newly established International Red Cross was called upon to assist in the care of the sick and wounded. They performed their task with great devotion and served a humanitarian need of unusual dimensions. The Geneva Convention, supplemented by an additional Article in 1868, provided for the neutralization of hospitals in belligerent territories. Switzerland, aware of its duties as a Neutral, sent many of its army doctors to serve in the military hospitals of both belligerents.

Representatives of 27 governments assembled at the Hague in 1899 and 1907 to codify an internationally acceptable set of rules descriptive of the rights and responsibilities of a Neutral. It is difficult to escape the conclusion that some of the Conventions must have been derived from Switzerland's long experience. Note, for example, the rules regarding internment:[78]

> Section IV. Art. 57. The neutral State which receives on its territory troops belonging to the belligerent armies, will intern them, insofar as possible, far from the theater of war. It shall guard them in camps, and, even confine them in fortresses or in places appropriate for this purpose. It will decide if the officers may be permitted freedom within the neutral State subject to verbal assurance that they will not leave the neutral territory without authorization.
>
> 58. In the absence of any special Convention, the neutral State will furnish to the internees food and other necessities, clothing, and the care demanded by humane considerations. Reimbursement will be made, on resumption of peace, of the expenses occasioned by the internment.
>
> 59. The neutral State may authorize the passage over its territory of the wounded or sick belonging to the belligerent armies, provided that the trains which carry them shall transport neither personnel nor material of war. . . . The wounded or sick transported

under these conditions . . . by one of the belligerents . . . ought to be guarded by the neutral State to the end that they shall not be permitted again to take part in the military operations. . . .

60. The Geneva Convention applies to the sick and wounded interned on neutral territory.

On several occasions in the nineteenth century, Switzerland found herself in paper warfare with the continental Powers because of the political activists from other countries to whom Switzerland had granted asylum. The refugees who stirred up the trouble waged ceaseless attacks on the conservative and reactionary monarchies bordering on Switzerland. Swiss sympathizers joined in the fiery barrage of epithets and inflammatory tirades designed to encourage rebellion against tyrannical governments that oppressed the masses. It is important to know the bearing that all of this has on Swiss neutrality. First of all it appears to have no formal bearing in the sense that problems of this sort are not covered by the rules of conduct for neutral States as spelled out at the Hague. There is, however, a widely understood and accepted precept in international law that a sovereign State must not behave in a provocative and threatening way to other sovereign and independent States. Obviously this must be interpreted to include provocative behaviour by the residents of a State as distinguished from provocations by government. The latter may be more serious in their impact but the noisy outbursts and inflammatory tirades of many "activists," supported by a revolutionary Press, can and did build up to threatening volumes of very disturbing onslaughts against Switzerland's deeply conservative neighbours.

Switzerland reluctantly conceded that the refugees who engaged in these activities were abusing the asylum which had been granted to them. Appropriate measures were eventually taken against these disturbers of the *status quo*. Basically, Switzerland resented the threatened meddling of the Powers in her internal affairs. She made it clear that, as a sovereign independent State, she would grant asylum to whom she chose and she would reject the right of asylum to others whom she did not choose to accept within the shelter of her territory and the protection of her government. As Numa Droz pointed out to the Federal Assembly, Switzerland's guiding principle must always be her own best interests, with proper regard to the well-being of her neighbours. The supervision and repression of anarchistic and revolutionary elements was not uniquely a Swiss responsibility, deriving from its neutrality. Rather, it was a responsibility of every State, neutral or not. The Swiss policy concerning asylum is not a consequence of Switzerland's neutrality but an attribute of her sovereignty.

Numa Droz benefitted greatly from the advice of Carl Hilty,[79] Professor of Federal and International Law at the University of Bern, whom he frequently consulted. Hilty, citing some of the requirements of international law which a Neutral, like any other State, must observe, remarked that a State must not permit within its territory the incitement of violence and disturbances against the peace of other States. It must be inoffensive in its conduct toward others, and always on the alert against troubles stirred up by the Press and by assemblies of organizations which seek the overthrow of another government. The right of asylum and of hospitality in Switzerland must not be granted to criminals and to those who incite riots and revolution and imperil the security of another State. Observance of this provision of ordinary international law is even more necessary in the case of a Neutral whose neutrality, integrity and inviolability are guaranteed by other States **(176)**. Hilty reports on a conversation of Charles Pictet de Rochemont[80] in September 1815 with Archduke Johann of Austria in which Pictet pointed out that Switzerland must be able to grant the right of asylum to honest but persecuted men from other countries and to those whose ideas are not tolerated elsewhere **(176**, p. 57). Apparently, the Archduke nodded approval.

The neutralization of North Savoy and the ultimate annexation of Savoy by France have been discussed in previous pages. In the post-annexation years much happened that involved Swiss policy toward North Savoy. Switzerland held firmly to her rights in Savoy as granted by the Powers in 1815.[81] True, much had changed. Originally, the occupation by Swiss troops was deemed to be of crucial value to Switzerland's security, for in the event of war involving her neighbours Switzerland had the right to move in her forces and thereby cut off troop movements between Italy and France over the Simplon or the Great St. Bernard passes. However, in 1882 the railway through Mt. Gotthard was completed and this altered military strategies completely. Italy began to think of the ease of access to the north and the greatly improved communication with Germany, her partner (with Austria) in the new Triple Alliance forged by Bismarck. Were France to invade Switzerland, German and Italian forces could rendezvous in Switzerland and launch a war against France on Swiss soil. Switzerland would thus be drawn into the Triple Alliance. Bismarck was not impressed by the argument and the Swiss press ridiculed the idea. There were several variations of the same theme including the possible cession of Savoy to Switzerland in the event of a Franco-German war which, in 1886, loomed up as a real possibility. Bismarck took it for granted that Germany would emerge victorious and the carving of additional territory from France, for the benefit of both Switzerland and Germany entered into the thoughts of the military and political strategists.

But there was another important consideration that Switzerland dare not overlook. Following upon the French annexation of Savoy the neutralized areas to the north were permanently occupied by French troops. It was inconceivable that they would withdraw from Faucigny and Chablais in the event of war. And it was clear to the Swiss that were Switzerland to exercise her right of occupation of the area with Swiss troops, war with France would almost certainly follow. France, as the legal successor of Sardinia, in Savoy, believed that she, not Switzerland, had the right to occupy the neutralized provinces. Switzerland tried, unsuccessfully, to persuade France to lay out in great detail the procedure to be followed should the eventual occupation of North Savoy by Swiss troops become necessary under the Treaty of 1815. At the heart of the request was a desire to define adequately the relations between the Swiss occupation troops and the French administrative authorities. To these approaches, France made no reply, probably because she wanted complete freedom to determine her course of action by events of the moment. By the same token Switzerland reserved for herself the right to decide if and when the occupation of North Savoy would be to her advantage; it must be an *ad hoc* decision. From the military point of view the possible occupation came to be of vanishing importance, but Switzerland adhered tenaciously to the legality of her demands; in the future, it might strengthen her bargaining position in the diplomatic world of give and take.

Throughout the century Switzerland was troubled by the smuggling of weapons, munitions, and other items of contraband to belligerent forces across her borders. She knew full well that this sort of traffic compromised her neutrality, and long before the problem of weapon exports by Neutrals, or transport of materials of war through neutral territory, was codified by the Hague Conferences she took measures of her own to put an end to such assistance to belligerents. Strong decrees were issued against weapon shipments to foreign countries, and the Federal Council, supported by the cantonal governments, took especially severe measures against weapon smuggling.

The problem rose to the surface during the Boer War (1899–1902). Illegal sale of weapons from official agencies or by private firms to the Boers was widely believed to be taking place, but, though carefully investigated, such transactions were never proved. Swiss fought on both sides in numbers that have never been credibly reported. A great deal of secrecy surrounded Swiss participation, both in the alleged smuggling of weapons and in the illegal recruiting that was carried on for the Boer cause. No one in official circles wanted to arouse the anger of Great Britain, a great Power which for centuries had supported the Confederation in her recurring disputes with the continental Powers. However, everyone knew that Swiss sympathies were largely with the Boers, farmers almost one and all, fighting for their freedom against industrially powerful Great Britain. The Swiss press was intemperate in its condemnation of British policy and incurred the rebukes of Swiss industrialists and other influential citizens. Money was raised for the Boers. Queen Victoria was petitioned to end the war and an offer to mediate the conflict was tendered. The British, by now, were irritated by the course of events in Switzerland and replied, testily, that any effort by the Swiss to mediate the Anglo-Boer dispute would be regarded as improper meddling in the affairs of others. Switzerland thereafter refrained from joining other countries in a united and common effort to persuade Britain to end the war.

Military alliances of a Neutral with a foreign Power have always been suspect. The various *Bundesbriefe* which describe and define the purposes and terms of alliance between the cantons on joining the Swiss Confederation always emphasized mutual defense against an enemy as one of the principal purposes of the alliance. In the early days, the enemy was the House of Habsburg-Austria. The enemy also came to be recognized as belligerent forces beyond her borders which, with evil intent, might be planning a trespass upon or a seizure of part of her territory. Throughout the centuries, defense of her borders against an actual or potential enemy, was a constantly recurring problem.

These demands upon her defensive capability were supplemented by military activity of another sort, namely territorial expansion by resort to war: expansion to the west as pursued so vigorously by Bern; to the south, with Uri initiating the trans-Alpine conquests; and to the east with the fifteenth-century conquest of Aargau and Thurgau. These several waves of expansion did not involve the help of foreign Powers. There were no foreign alliances negotiated for purposes of conquest. On the contrary, some of the territorial expansion resulted from defensive combat, notably in the Burgundian War. Some alliances were compromising, questionable, and of relatively short duration. With a number of exceptions, a part of the Confederation, but not the whole was involved. Zurich entered into an alliance with Austria in 1440 (see Chapter 4)—a treaty with dangerous implications. The alliance was extended to include France. It was obviously not a confederation-wide alliance. Nor was the treaty of alliance between Spain and the catholic cantons (see Chapter 5) which was totally incompatible with the principles of neutrality that the Confederation endeavored to observe. One important exception would be the alliance of the entire Confederation against Napoleon in the closing days of the long struggle of the Powers against the "Emperor of the French."[82] One must exclude the treaty—an offensive alliance with the French—which Napoleon forced upon Switzerland in 1798.[83]

If one may generalize, the nineteenth-century policy of Switzerland with respect to alliances eventually reflected the following considerations. Alliances with foreign Powers shall be enacted, if at all, only in times of war: they have little meaning, and are of questionable merit, in peace. Any war-time treaty of alliance will, in principle, be directed against that particular belligerent which first violates the territorial integrity of the Fatherland. Were France and Germany to be at war, whichever of the two made a deliberate trespass upon Swiss territory would be immediately identified as an enemy. An alliance with the other belligerent or with one of its other neighbours would probably follow. Switzerland, throughout the latter part of the nineteenth century, declared unambiguously, that decisions in such matters could not be made in advance—the result of inflexible policies. A position would be taken on an *ad hoc* basis and only when the emergency arose. And the Federal Assembly alone was empowered to decide such questions. The military commands of the various Powers speculated between themselves in the hush-hush atmosphere of secret diplomacy, upon the probable policies of their governments in a variety of hypothetical situations. Switzerland moved steadily toward a policy that would condone a war of offense. She could not continue to sit quietly behind her frontiers and wait for an enemy to strike.

When the dispute with the King of Prussia over Neuchâtel had risen to fever heat, Switzerland's General Dufour, with unlimited credits voted for the army, was prepared to post a substantial force in the canton of Schaffhausen. If war were declared by Prussia, an immediate invasion of the south German States would follow. Democracy and much sympathy for Switzerland existed in these border areas which had not yet been absorbed by Prussia into the German Federation. As World War I approached, the military command in Switzerland was virtually committed to offensive strikes, with support of a neighbouring ally against any belligerent which deliberately violated her territory.

It is worth noting again that Switzerland placed little if any trust in the guarantees by the Powers of her neutrality and territorial integrity. She had learned that her defense against aggression was to be found only in her own internal strength. At the Hague Peace Conference in 1899, Switzerland, with this consideration in mind, refused to agree to an arms-limitation policy. In respect to defense, she argued that a small nation requires unlimited freedom of action. National defense by the small States, the argument continued, is not a danger but a security for European peace. This incident serves to illustrate the dubious worth that Switzerland attached to guarantees by the great European Powers. Hence we may well ask why Switzerland, on every possible occasion, especially in her proclamations of neutrality, reminded all and sundry that her neutrality and the inviolability of her territory had been guaranteed by the signatory Powers of the several treaties of 1815. When the First World War was about to begin, Switzerland issued the expected declaration of her neutrality.[84] After an introductory high-sounding paragraph we are told that

the Swiss Confederation will maintain and defend by every means at its disposal, its neutrality and the inviolability of its territory such as they were recognized by the treaties of 1815; she herself will observe the strictest neutrality vis-à-vis the belligerent States. Relative to . . . the act of recognitiion and of guarantee of the Swiss neutrality [20 November 1815].

For the Final Act of 20 November 1815, see reference **85**. As another example of the seeming importance attached to the guarantee we read in an earlier declaration:[86]

The Federal Council, therefore, declares in the most formal manner, that, if the Peace of Europe should be disturbed, the Swiss Confederation will defend and maintain, by all means at her disposal, the Integrity and Neutrality of its Territory, to which she has a right in her character as an Independent State, and which has been solemnly recognized and guaranteed to her by the European Treaties of 1815.

One may conclude that it was good policy to remind the Powers, whenever it was appropriate to do so, of the solemn guarantees they had made to Switzerland in 1815; no harm was done by such reminders. Some increase in bargaining power also accrued to Switzerland if any of the guaranteeing Powers threatened to violate her neutrality and territorial integrity.

Swiss neutrality, unlike that of any other Nation, is described as "perpetual" in contrast to "ordinary" or "occasional" neutrality. Perpetual neutrality imposes obligations upon the Neutral both in peace and war. Occasional neutrality, in its simplest form, is little more than abstention from a specific war, usually a conflict between neighbouring States. In wartime, the rights and responsibilities of a Neutral, set forth in the Hague Conferences of 1899 and 1907, are identical for both the perpetual and occasional Neutral. On conclusion of the specific war toward which the occasional and perpetual Neutrals proclaim their neutrality, the occasional Neutral resumes, in her domestic and international affairs, her pre-war status as an ordinary member of the world family of nations. The responsibilities of the perpetual Neutral continue.

And here we should remind ourselves that these peace-time responsibilities of the perpetual Neutral have never been codified. They have never been the subject of an international conference such as those convened at the Hague. Nor is such a conference likely to be held so long as only one nation—Switzerland—may be described as a perpetual Neutral. Switzerland's neutrality is of her own choosing. It evolved through the centuries. For three hundred years at least, she has tried, not always with success, to discharge the recognized duties of of a neutral State. Several other neutral States, such as Belgium and Luxemburg, had their neutrality forced upon them by the Powers. They were neutralized. Their neutrality is of comparatively recent origin (i.e., Belgium in 1831 and Luxemburg in 1867) and, sad to say, it had no deterrent value against Germany in the Franco-Prussian War and in the two World Wars of the twentieth century.[87]

Nothing more need be said about Swiss neutrality in times of war, those numerous occasions when Switzerland's neighbours were really at it, tooth and nail. What Switzerland did about it, not always in unanimity and with success, has been discussed in this and preceding chapters.[88] However, it is appropriate to look into Switzerland's unique responsibilities in times of peace, her duties to her neighbours and to the world as a perpetual Neutral. Some of these are of nineteenth-century origin and have been greatly added to and expanded in the twentieth century. No one forced these upon her. They are of her own doing. Some are humanitarian in motivation and function. The most striking example is the International Red Cross, strictly Swiss in origin, headquartered in Geneva, and with world-wide ramifications. Wherever the terrible scourge of war breaks loose and wherever a great catastrophe strikes, the Red Cross is sure to be found.

International organizations, in great numbers, have established their headquarters in Switzerland. Geneva in course of time became more of an international city than a city dominated by a native Swiss population.[89] The International Post and Telegraph organization settled in Switzerland early in the twentieth century and many more international organizations followed. Most of these established themselves in Switzerland after the two World Wars. The Palace of the League of Nations (post-World War I) still stands in Geneva and is used for many international conferences. It is a monument to the hopes for an enduring world peace that were entertained by men of goodwill throughout the world.

Were we to proceed farther into the twentieth century we would find a Europe desperately in need of integration. It is a Europe that has much to learn from Switzerland, a belief that was prophetically envisaged in 1815 when the signatory Powers of the Treaty of Paris declared in unanimity "that the Neutrality and the Inviolability of Switzerland, and her independence of all foreign influence, enter into the true interests of the policy of the whole of Europe." Some of us interpret this to mean that what is good for Switzerland is good for Europe. We can at least dream of a Europe wherein the diversity of nations and of ethnic groups will still permit a unity of the whole. Hundreds of years were required for the fiercely independent and sovereign cantons of Switzerland to sacrifice portions of their independence and to subordinate some of their cantonal rights and privileges for the greater welfare of each and all in a federated State. May one dream of the day when the nations of Europe will subordinate some of the treasured rights of an independent State in the interests of a comparable European federation? European federalism means much to Switzerland. Although she scrupulously avoids membership in any international organization wherein the member nations are committed to military action against an aggressor, she joined the European Common Market as an associate member. This permits economic cooperation devoid of any politico-military commitments. Whether she would join in economic warfare (e.g., a blockade) against a member State or a nonmember nation is dubious.

No one can take even a sweeping look at Switzerland in the past century or so without being impressed by the unswerving determination of the Swiss to adhere to their neutrality and to demand respect for their independence and their sovereignty. Switzerland's foreign policy requires that she avoid any meddling in the affairs of other independent States, demanding by the same token that there be no interference by others in her own internal affairs. If there be any exception to this policy it resides in her willingness to serve as a mediator, on invitation, in international disputes that threaten to interrupt the peace. The advice of Brother Klaus (see Chapter 4, Note 19), and the principle of international law laid down by Emer de Vattel (**374**), continue to be basic precepts in Swiss foreign policy:

> No nation has the right to meddle in the government of another. . . . It is a manifest consequence of the liberty and independence of nations, that all have the right to govern themselves as they choose, and no one has the least right to intrude himself in the government of another. Of all the rights which belong to a nation, its sovereignty is without doubt the most precious . . . (Book II, Chapter IV, par. 54, p. 21).

DIPLOMATIC RELATIONS AND NEUTRALITY   Switzerland's diplomatic relations with foreign Powers were cumbersome until well past the middle of the century. For many years France was the only country that maintained an embassy in Switzerland. Located in Solothurn, the French Embassy was headed by an Ambassador. Great Britain sent representatives of her foreign ministry to Switzerland throughout the eighteenth century from Fleming in 1702 to Wickham in 1795. Their titles varied considerably: "Resident Agent with the Protestant Cantons" (Oliver Fleming); Envoy Extraordinary to the Confederate States of the Swiss Cantons (Wm. Aglionby); Minister Plenipotentiary (Lord Robert Fitzgerald and Wm. Wickham); Ambassador to the Reformed Cantons (Abraham Stanyan) and Ambassador accredited to Switzerland (Robert Peel). Most of them were assigned to Switzerland on a specific mission which was usually that of trying to persuade Switzerland or the protestant cantons to join with Britain in opposing France and her overweening ambitions.

Switzerland, in turn, throughout the eighteenth century and earlier maintained a diplomatic corps of very modest size.

Up to well past the middle of the last century, diplomatic missions were limited to its four neighbours—France, Austria, Prussia-Germany and Piedmont-Italy. Washington became a fifth diplomatic post in 1882, even ahead of London (1891). Much of Switzerland's foreign contact was discharged by consuls and consular agents. To fill the gap in her diplomatic establishment, Switzerland made use of the foreign services of Germany and of the United States.[85]

Diplomatic relations became more complicated as various Powers accepted responsibilities in representing the interests of various belligerent or other countries which had terminated for the time being diplomatic relations with other Powers.

The outbreak of war in 1914 . . . thrust the greater part of belligerent interests on American shoulders, including Allied affairs in most of the Central Powers, and German and Austrian interests in Russia. When the United States entered the war in 1917, these protective mandates had to be redistributed among the remaining neutrals, with Switzerland taking a substantial share. At this time the Swiss maintained nine full diplomatic missions, the last additions having been at St. Petersburg and Tokyo in 1906, plus consular missions under *chargés d'affaires* at Madrid and Buenos Aires. A number of Swiss envoys discharged plural missions, that is, they were accredited to several countries concurrently. . . . In 1917, a separate mission to The Hague was split off from its parent London, ostensibly to help spark some badly needed Dutch raw materials for pinched and land-locked Switzerland (85).

Notes and Comments

1. The President of the Swiss Confederation in an address to the Federal Assembly on 3 April 1850 reminded his audience that Switzerland was not to be thought of as a fortress from which troops spring to defend the liberties and rights of man wherever they are trampled upon. This was obviously a thrust at those of the radical left who sought to persuade others that the Confederation had a noble responsibility to use its armed forces not simply to protect human rights within the State but to aid in freeing from their bondage the oppressed masses in neighbouring countries.

2. In 1864 the Confederation concluded a treaty of establishment with France. In so doing, Switzerland was obliged to permit French Jews to settle freely in Swiss territory. In 1866, by popular vote, the same right was extended to Swiss Jews who thenceforth were permitted to settle anywhere they chose in Switzerland.

3. "Message du Conseil Fédéral à la Haute Assemblée Fédérale . . . *British State Papers* 47, 822, 26 December 1856.

4. Ibid. *British State Papers* 47, 831, 26 December 1856.

5. Hertslet 172, II, 1316–19 (in English); *British State Papers* 47, 40–42, 26 May 1857 (in French).

6. *British State Papers* 48, 913, 13 January 1857.

7. *British State Papers* 48, 993–1001, 21 November 1858.

8. Estimates published in the *Neue Zürcher Zeitung* (20 June 1859) suggest that the two belligerents (Austria vs France and Piedmont) each had about 160,000 men in combat.

9. Captain E. A. J. Harris (British diplomat) to Lord Russell, *British State Papers* 50, 456, 1 July 1859.

10. Earl Cowley to Lord Russell, *British State Papers* 50, 457, 4 July 1859.

11. Earl Cowley to Lord Russell, *British State Papers* 50, 458, 8 July 1859.

12. Earl Cowley to Lord Russell, *British State Papers* 50, 491, 10 February 1860.

13. Sir J. Hudson to Lord Russell, *British State Papers* 50, 495, 10 February 1860.

14. *Bundesblatt* 2, pp. 151–155, 8 July 1859.

15. *British State Papers* 61, 1043, 11 August, 10 September 1862.

16. W. G. Grey to Lord Russell, 9 January 1860, *British State Papers* 50, 465.

17. Hertslet, **172**, II, 1435, 28 March 1860.

18. E. A. J. Harris to the Earl of Malmesbury, *British State Papers* **57**, 172, 7 March 1859.

19. *British State Papers* **57**, 173, 6 March 1859.

20. Hertslet **172**, II, 1448, 20 June 1860.

21. Hertslet **172**, II, 1430, 24 March 1860.

22. Hertsler **172**, II, 1525–27, 8 December 1862.

23. If interested in the amusing consequences of the border reshuffling, one should visit La Cure where at least three commercial buildings, including a hotel/restaurant, are split into Swiss and French sections. La Cure is easy to reach by train or car from Nyon in Switzerland.

24. *British State Papers* **60**, 785, 6 July 1870.

25. *British State Papers* **60**, 832, 854, 855, 904, 13 to 16 July 1870.

26. *British State Papers* **60**, 896, 897, 19 July 1870.

27. *British State Papers* **61**, 839, 1 October 1870.

28. The Prussian army, well trained and fully equipped, quickly seized the advantage and drove the French, who were ill-prepared for the war, from the Rheinland. The theatre of warfare moved to the north. The Swiss border between Basel and Schaffhausen was no longer endangered and on August 17, demobilization was ordered by the Confederation. General Herzog and his Chief-of-Staff were placed on leave. Economy continued to be a determining factor, even in war. Herzog prepared two reports for the Federal Council based on his observations during mobilization of the defense force of 37,000 men. He emphasized the slowness of assembly of the troops and commented unfavorably on their equipment and weapons. Herzog did not resume command until the last moment, viz. 19 January 1871. In the meantime, troops from the Duchy of Baden moved into Alsace and Lorraine, and the panic-stricken inhabitants fled *en masse* toward Switzerland.

29. *British State Papers* **60**, 868, 15 July 1870.

30. Herzog, Johannes (1819–94), 1847, participated in the *Sonderbund* war; 1860, Chief of Federal Artillery; 1870–71, General in command of the border occupation troops; since 1874, active participation in army reform.

31. *British State Papers* **60**, 909, 18 July 1870.

32. *Bundesblatt* 3, 789–828, 8–17 December 1870.

33. In France, around 1700 or so, the payments were not made directly to the common soldier but to the company commander who retained one half. The Swiss private was entitled to 20 livres per month less the cost of his bread ration. Of the gross amount, the company commander retained 10 livres which amounted to 2100 livres per month for a full company of 210 men. Part of this was passed on to under-officers, bandsmen, orderlies, etc. To maximize his profit a company commander typically tried to maintain a full complement of 210 men and to require a capitulation agreement of not less than three years. Occasionally, the regimental commander (a colonel or *Oberst*) would name himself as commander of each of the companies in the regiment, which in turn would be actively commanded by salaried deputies appointed by the *Oberst* (Feller **128**, pp. 18–20).

34. *Bundesblatt* 2, 329, 4 August 1855.

35. *Bundesblatt* 2, p. 173, 13 July 1859.

36. *Bundesblatt* 1, p. 563, 22 May, 1849: 1, 565–569, 19 May 1849.

37. The Swiss policy with respect to mercenary service did not permit her citizens to serve on the lakes or oceans. Service overseas was also excluded. If the Federal Council had strictly enforced the restrictions on recruiting for foreign service, it is improbable that this legion could have been raised. Apparently, Federal Councillor Furrer was not opposed to recruiting for the British cause if it were done secretly and with no involvement of the Federal Council. Von Segesser complained bitterly that British recruiting in Switzerland was carried on openly and without any official restraint. The police of Basel reported in a similar vein **49**, I, p. 335 (footnotes, 45, 46).

38. *Bundesblatt*, 1, 761–821, 22 June 1927; *Militarstrafgesetz*, 13 June 1927, Art. 94.

39. *Bundesblatt* 2, 217–21, 19 July 1859.

40. *Bundesblatt* 2, 224–25, 9 July 1866. Similar prohibitions against the export of weapons and materials of war were decreed in 1870–71 (Franco-Prussian War), 1914 (World War I), 1935 (Italian-Abyssinian War) and 1936 (Spanish Civil War).

41. *Bundesblatt* 2, 449–58, 19 September 1859.

42. Increased to 50,000 in 1978.

43. "The exercise of civil or political rights may not be restricted by any proscription or condition of an ecclesiastical or religious nature" (Art. 49.4).

44. For example, in Aargau. The constitutional proscription against Jesuits and convents was abrogated in May, 1973.

45. The University of Freiburg and the Hochschule of St. Gallen were not founded until 1889 and 1898 respectively.

46. The federal government has refrained from establishing a federal university. Instead, the fine art of compromise to which the Swiss are dedicated and in which they have displayed a remarkable aptitude, came into play. A federal university has not been established nor is one currently under consideration, but the breadth of the Federal Institutes of Technology (ETH Zürich, ETH Lausanne) has been greatly expanded by including the humanities and social sciences in the institutional structure. Thus an institute of technology achieved a partial metamorphosis into a university.

47. In fact, we read "The autonomy of the cantons in the field of education shall *always** be upheld" (Art. 27 quater.3).

48. Legislation enacted in 1965–66 also provides for annual federal payments to the cantonal universities to relieve the respective cantons of part of the heavy burden of operating costs and of capital expenditures.

49. The older Swiss literature is replete with references to pedestrian hours (*Wegstunden*). One Swiss *Wegstunde* was equal to 4.808 km, the distance a man would ordinarily walk in one hour. The distance from Zurich to Bern is 28 *Wegstunden* or 134.6 km. The actual distance (by rail) is today 129 km.

50. The Gotthard Railway was a great personal triumph for Escher, shadowed, however, by the shameful treatment he received as the project came to completion. Technically it was a challenge; a long tunnel (15 km) had to be drilled through the Alps. Louis Favre of Geneva, the engineer in charge of construction, pursued the Gotthard project with outstanding success. Financially, it was in constant peril until construction was completed and service was commenced. Germany, Italy, the North-East Railway, the Central Railway, 15 cantons and many private investors participated in the financing. When, on two occasions, still more money was needed the Federal Government invested a modest sum (12.5 million francs in all, as required by a law of 1878). Alfred Escher, tha target of mounting hostility and under great pressure from political and financial interests, resigned the presidency of the company. In March 1882, after ten years of construction, the project was completed at a cost of 307 men who were killed and 877 others who were injured during construction of the tunnel. Escher, tired and ill, was not invited to the unveiling festivities and died a few months later—a disappointed and lonely old man. The Gotthard Railway revolutionized traffic between Milan and Lucerne. A transit time of several days was reduced to 8 to 10 hours. Austria in 1867 had opened a line to Italy through the Brenner, and France in 1871 completed the Mount Cenis tunnel. The Gotthard line soon established itself as the preferred transport route, being much more direct than the competing lines. A second tunnel, for motorized road traffic, was completed in September, 1980. It extends from Goeschenen in Uri to Airolo in Ticino.

51. Including the Gotthard Railway Co., acquired in 1909.

52. Article 26.

53. In 1974, however, the privately owned railway companies numbered 83 with a total of about 2090 km of track. Most of these are highly localized, and many are designed to carry the visiting tourist to points of great scenic interest. This total does not include about 735 km of specialized lines (cogwheel, funicular, and aerial cable), familiar to many tourists.

54. *Neue Zürcher Zeitung* 20 June 1859 (North-East Railway advertisement).

55. *Bundesblatt* 1859, I, pp. 442–44.

56. Around 1400, the territory of present-day Switzelrand embraced about 140 towns and villages. With the exception of 20 or so, all of these population centers were on river banks or the shores of lakes.

---

* Italics are mine. The official German text of April 1977 reads "*in allen Fällen*"; "Dans tous les cas" in the official French text.

Availability of water power, ease of transport, and military considerations (defense) were the most important factors that determined their location.

57. The period 1813–1817 was marked by climatic conditions that can only be described as quasi Ice Age. The Alpine glaciers reached down almost to the terminal moraines of 1600. The year 1816 was commonly known as the *Jahr ohne Sommer*, the year without summer. The entire five-year period is also designated as the Little Ice Age—one of the coldest and wettest periods in Swiss history (**287**).

58. The dire predictions of Malthus influenced the intellectuals, but probably were almost unknown to the peasants. The rural population was certainly not receptive to any proposals to reduce family size. In 1843 and 1846–47 agriculture suffered from widespread outbreaks of potato disease and a series of bad harvests in the early 1850s. Food shortages were common and drastic increases in food prices were just as frequent. These considerations outweighed Malthusian doctrine in causing the emigration waves of the 1850s and 1860s.

59. The first roller mill for grain, of which any record exists, was probably invented by a mechanic, Juanelo Turriano, during the reign of Emperor Charles V (1519–56). Another source cited by Rutz (**312**, p. 6) credits an Italian watchmaker of Charles V who later was condemned to death because he allegedly had made his invention in league with the devil. The first patent on a roller mill appears to have been issued in 1753 to Isaac Wilkinson of England, who constructed a functional mill entirely of iron which, so it was claimed, "would crush, coarsely grind, or finely mill malt, oats, beans, sugar cane, or any kind of grain." Other eighteenth-century rolling mills came into use in England but most of these were experimental. An important exception was one designed by Boulton in 1780. This large "Albion Mill" was powered by steam instead of wind or water and soon led to the construction in England of other steam-driven roller mills (**312**, p. 9).

60. Escher, Wyss & Co. was already a well-established firm, having been founded in 1805 by a group of Zurich merchants. The company was headed by Johann Caspar Escher (not to be confused with Johann Conrad Escher von der Linth). A factory known as *Neumühle* was purchased. Machinery was installed for the spinning of cotton. Prior to this, Escher, who was not only an able promoter but keenly interested in technology, had succeeded in constructing a mechanical spinner operated by hydraulic power. By 1807 the Company had successfully entered a long and triumphant career: its cotton thread was immediately recognized as a superior product. A few years later the Company manufactured spinning machines for sale—even to competing enterprises (**301**).

61. "During the winter months, the straw-weaving industry occupies 65,000 to 70,000 persons, for the most part women, children and old people. The great majority work at home" (**40**, p. 212).

62. Franscini (**136**) reported that the cotton industry employed 50,000 to 90,000 persons around 1850. This included individuals of both sexes who spent a good part of each year in spinning and weaving but a still greater portion of their time at work in the fields. The number of spinners of *Schappe* (a by-product of silk manufacturing, from which silk yarn could be made) around 1850, was reported by Franscini to be 2500 factory workers and 4000 to 5000 in home industry. Rappard (**301**, p. 214) estimated the number employed by the watch industry in the mid-1850s at 40,000, of whom 30,000 worked at home.

63. The linen industry in St. Gallen is believed to have had its origins in the twelfth century. Linen weaving in the villages of Bern appears to be equally old, while the spinning and weaving of wool are known to have been pursued in Basel, Freiburg, Geneva and Zurich in the thirteenth century (**40**, p. 47). As the home industry in textiles gradually developed, the export of thread, yarn, and woven products became increasingly important as sources of revenue to the towns and cantons. Toward the end of the Old Zurich War (1436–50) weapons manufacture had also become an important home industry.

64. Grain measures in Switzerland (**312**, p. 198). Considerable differences in the standards for weights and measures existed throughout Europe.

Before 1837:	*After 1837:*
1 Malter = 4 Mütt	1 Malter = 10 Viertel
1 Mütt = 4 Viertel	1 Viertel = 15 Litres
1 Viertel = 20.5 Litres	

The Mütt was abolished in 1837.   1 Liter of grain = about 1.59 pounds   1 pound = 468 gm.

65. One Swiss Franc equals 100 Rappen (or Centimes). During the nineteenth century the Swiss franc approximated in value 19.3 USA cents. In 1934 the USA dollar was devalued and the Swiss franc rose to 32.1 cents. Later revaluations brought the franc to 22.9 cents, 24.5 cents and, in 1971, to 26 cents. In 1980 and mid-1981 the franc, which had risen gradually to 62 cents, declined to 46 cents. By early 1985, the Swiss franc had declined to about 36 cents. The strength of the US dollar against many foreign currencies militated seriously against US exports.

It is appropriate to mention the confusion in Switzerland, prior to 1850, in the standards for weights and measures and the relative values of various coins in common use. The confusion was attributable to the sovereignty of the various cantons and to special privileges in coinage that were enjoyed by various institutions and highly placed persons. In the canton of Vaud, for example, there were, in 1814, 18 different measures of length, 25 measures for dry fruit, and 32 for moist fruit. Vaud introduced a law in 1822 to provide uniformity within the canton in systems of mass and weight.

In 1792, France adopted the meter (one forty-millionth of the circumference of the earth) as the unit of length. Systems of mass, weight and currency were also decreed, all stemming from unalterable units. *Hofrat* Horner, a burgher of Zurich, proposed that the Swiss foot (*Fuss*) be declared equal to 30 centimeters, and the pound (*Pfund*) equal to one half kilogram. At the time, the Swiss pound was the average of 24 pound weights from most of German-speaking Switzerland.

In France, despite tne new meter, there were those who preferred to use the old *pied de Roi* which equalled 12 *Zoll*. There was also the Paris *Aune*, equal to 44 *Zoll*, and the Lyon *Aune* of 42 to 42¾ *Zoll*. Note that 1 *Zoll* equals 1 inch and 1 Aune equals 1 ell. The meter was seven *Zoll* shorter than the Paris *Aune*. Napoleon, who had decreed that one meter shall equal three metric feet, was annoyed by the existing standards and commented "Ils ont fait une bêtise" ("They have done a stupid thing").

In Switzerland, in 1838, a concordat of 12 cantons proposed a uniform system of mass and weight but they got nowhere until 1850 when the newly born Confederation introduced all-Swiss standards of mass, weight, and coinage. In 1836, an expert commission had proposed that one Swiss franc be equal to 10 batzen and one batzen to 10 rappen. Historically, the French and Swiss systems of coinage had been closely linked. In the old French system:

1 Louis d'Or equalled 48,24 and 12 livres.

1 thaler equalled 6 livres (later, equalled 5 livres).

1 livre equalled 20 sous and 1 thaler equalled 100 sous.

A six-livre coin was in common use for many years.

In 1798 or so, in west (French) Switzerland, one French franc was equal to 7 batzen. In Milan in 1804, Napoleon introduced the French Münzfuss in place of the Milanese korrentlivre, followed in 1816 by the Austrian livre. As for the Italian lire, Austria introduced an Austrian lire in place of the lire correnti. In Geneva there was the lire Piemontese, but in the Valtellina a common coin was the *Bündtner Blützger* (from Chur). Most of the above is from a paper by Leonhard Pestalozzi (**283**, pp. 4–25). See also Chapter 6, Note 31.

66. *Bundesblatt* 2, pp. 158, 248, July 1859.

67. In 1841, Weitling was sent by the communist leadership in Paris to Geneva to promote the communist party in Switzerland. He succeeded in organizing many local units, and in Zurich in 1843 promoted the communist cause with evangelical zeal. He was arrested by the local authorities and in 1844, following a trial of international interest, was expelled from the country.

68. Greulich, originating in Breslau, settled in Zurich in 1865. He founded the newspaper *Tagwacht* and in 1887 became head of the Workers' Secretariat. Active politically, he served successively as a member of the City and Cantonal Councils of Zurich and later as a member of the Federal House of Representatives (*Nationalrat*).

69. *Bundesblatt* II, p. 685, 30 April 1889; II, p. 686, 3 May 1889; *Bundesblatt* III, pp. 651–55, 15 June 1889. Ten members of the *Nationalrat* requested a report from the *Bundesrat* on the present difficulties between Switzerland and other countries. Numa Droz responded to the request.

70. The Swiss Constitution of 1848 guaranteed freedom to practice their religion to "Christian confessions throughout the Confederation" (Art. 44). Article 48 required all of the cantons to accord equal treatment in legislative and juridical matters to Swiss citizens of Christian confessions whether

Table 7   The population of Switzerland according to confessions (1837 to 1970[a,c])

Confession	1837	1860	1888	1910	1970	1970 Percent
Protestant	1,300,000	1,479,000	1,716,000	2,108,000	2,992,000	47.8
Catholic	889,000	1,022,000	1,184,000	1,594,000	3,117,000	49.7
Jewish	1,360	4,200	8,070	18,000	20,744	0.3
Other[b]	—	5,866	9,309	33,479	140,423	2.2

[a] Bickel (**40**, p. 140).
[b] Includes other protestant sects and other non-Christian religions.
[c] 1970 Data from ref. **341**, 1977, p. 28.

already settled in the canton or newly entering—the so-called right of establishment. These specific references to citizens of Christian confessions do not appear in the Constitution of 1874 which guarantees the right of establishment to all citizens and declares that freedom of conscience and of belief is inviolable.

71. "Convention of Friendship, Reciprocal Establishments, Commerce, and the Surrender of Fugitive Criminals, between The United States and Switzerland", (*British State Papers* **38**, 285–90 Bern, 25 November 1850).

72. "Treaty of Friendship, Commerce, and Reciprocal Establishment, between Great Britain and Switzerland," *British State Papers* **45**, 21–9 Bern, 6 September 1855).

73. "Traité d'Établissement entre la Suisse et l'Empire Allemagne," (*British State Papers* **67**, 534–37 27 April 1876).

74. A new Treaty of Establishment with Germany was signed in 1890. In this same year, Bismarck fell from grace. One may suspect that the new treaty was designed to restore the once cordial relations that existed between Germany and Switzerland prior to the difficult years of Bismarckian threats (1876–78 to 1890). This was replaced in 1909 by a more explicit agreement (*British State Papers* **102**, 439–43, 13 November 1909).

75. "Decret de l'Empereur Français, pour promulgation du Traité concernant l'Etablissement des Français en Suisse et des Suisses en France, conclu le 30 Juin, 1864" (*British State Papers* **54**, 1101–03, 28 November 1864).

76. *Bundesblatt* 1, 525–28, 5 May 1859.

77. For the conditions of internment which the commander of the French army was obliged to accept see Hertslet (**192**), III, pp. 1907–08, 1 February 1871.

78. *British State Papers* **91**, 1001, 29 July 1899.

79. Carl Hilty (1833–1909). Carl Hilty, born in Werdenberg, was the son and grandson of practicing physicians. From 1844 to 1850 he attended the Evangelical Cantonal School in Chur. A second catholic school in Chur was also cantonal up to the union of 1850. As for religion, Hilty found much in the rituals, forms, and beliefs taught in the cantonal school that was quite impossible for him to accept intellectually. But he had an inner sort of piety and religion that was very real to him. On the death of Carl Hilty's mother in 1847, his father, Johann Ulrich Hilty (1793–1858) returned to Werdenberg from Chur to occupy the very beautiful house, the former Landvogtei Schloss, which he had bought in 1835. The Hilty family held this until 1956 when it was sold to the Canton St. Gallen for representation purposes. In 1851 Carl Hilty became a student in Göttingen, excluding theology from his studies because of his unpleasant experiences with formalized religion in the cantonal school in Chur "*obwohl dies eigentlich mein rechter Beruf gewesen wäre*" (**231**). Having a hearty skepticism of the medical sciences, he decided against the study of medicine. Law became the center of his program at Göttingen. From Göttingen he went to Heidelberg and continued his studies. In 1854 he journeyed to England. On return to his homeland, he practiced law in Chur from 1855 to 1873. Then, to his great surprise, "equal only to being named

Emperor of China" if such had happened, he was elected Professor of Federal Law in the University of Bern and held the chair until his death in 1909. Apparently, in the professorship, he succeeded Munzinger who, on his deathbed, urged that Hilty be his successor. Hilty's election, as described by Mattmüller, was rammed through the Faculty by the cantonal director of education, Ritschard, who at the age of 28, had just been appointed to the post.

80. See Chapter 8, Note 25.

81. Art. XCII of the Treaty of Vienna, 9 June 1815 [Hertslet (172), I, p. 262].

82. "Treaty of Accession of Switzerland to the Treaty of Alliance of the 25th March, 1815, between the 4 Powers." *British State Papers* 2, 472–76, 20 May 1815.

83. *Aktensammlung* 2, 884–89, 19 August 1798.

84. *British State Papers* 108, 839–40, 4 August 1914.

85. Hertslet (172), I, 370; *British State Papers* 3, 359, 20 November 1815.

86. Hertslet (172), II, 1356, 14 March 1859.

87. In the 1960s, Belgium became a member of NATO, thus ending her status as a Neutral, to which she had returned in 1934 after renouncing her postwar military accord with France.

88. Switzerland's concept of neutrality, as summarized by the Political Department in November 1954 (*Verwaltungsentscheide der Bundesbehörden,* fasc. 24, p. 9–13) appears in English as Appendix One to Christopher Hughes' excellent book *The Parliament of Switzerland* (London, 1962).

89. A pertinent statistic is the high percentage of foreign students in the University of Geneva in 1962/63: 55.4 percent of the total student body (219). The native population of the city is also engulfed by the large number of foreigners attached to the many missions and international organizations based in Geneva.

11. THE TWENTIETH CENTURY

11.1 SURFACE FEATURES

"On less than 2% of our land surface there are about 60% of the active population, more than half of the industrial production facilities and about 3/4 of the service facilities (*Dienstleistungsbetriebe*)". **(377)**

By way of an introduction to the twentieth century, let us take a brief look at the surface area of Switzerland and its functional divisions. Its total area approximates 4,129,000 hectares,* where it has held fast with but little change since 1815. Expressed otherwise, Switzerland is about half the size of the State of Maine. Of the total area, 2,019,000 ha (49 per cent) consist of pasturage and agriculturally productive land; 1,052,000 ha (25.5 per cent) are forested, while the remaining 1,057,000 ha (25.6 per cent) are unproductive **(341**, 1979, p. 91).

Are they really unproductive? They consist of the great mountain chains, the rivers and lakes, the overbuilt lands of the cities and towns, and the communications network of highways and railroad lines. The mountains are of extraordinary touristic value because of their intrinsic beauty and attractiveness to thousands of hikers and skiers. They are also a source of several varieties of game, in which almost all Swiss restaurants specialize in the appropriate season. But most importantly, the high mountains, eternally covered with ice, husband Switzerland's greatest natural resource—water. From the imposing central massif, the Rhine, the Rhone, the Reuss, the Aare, and the rivers of the Ticino and northern Italy have their origin.

The rivers and lakes, reported as unproductive, are the home of the domestic fishing industry and are of some importance in transportation.[1] Currently (1977) about nine million passengers (between nine and ten million per year since 1955) and 3300 tons of merchandise (658,000 tons in 1960) are transported on the Swiss lakes. The current income of Sfr 42 million just nicely approximates the current expenses **(341**, 1981, p. 251). This equivalence of income and expense has been maintained year by year since at least 1948 when income and expense each amounted to about eleven million francs.

Some 28 natural lakes exceeding 0.5 km^2 are to be found in Switzerland. Of these, the largest is Leman (Lake Geneva) with a surface area of 581 km^2 and the smallest is Mauensee (0.55 km^2 and a maximum depth of only 9 meters). The deepest is Lago Maggiore (372 meters) in the Ticino. It is also quite large (212 km^2). High up in the Alps at an altitude of 2205 meters above sea level is little Daubensee (0.67 km^2). Five of the natural lakes (Geneva, Constance, Maggiore, Lugano, and Lac des Brenets) are on the frontier with a sizeable portion of each being in France, Germany, or Italy **(341**, 1979, p. 7).

In addition, there are 38 artificial lakes resulting from the construction of dams.

* 1 hectare (ha) = 2.471 acres.

The largest of these is the Sihlsee (10.9 km²) but with a capacity of only 92 million cubic meters. Much more impressive is Lac des Dix (4.0 km²) with a capacity of 400 million m³. The dam has the distinction of being almost the highest (2364 m above sea level) of all 38. Eleven of the group were natural lakes originally and were altered in surface altitude and capacity by dam construction.

The principal function of the dams and artificial lakes is the production of hydroelectric power. For many years the power so produced was adequate for Switzerland's needs. By the early 1970s, potential sources for additional development practically ceased to exist and the Confederation turned to nuclear power. In 1981, five nuclear reactors were in operation, and five others were under study or the sites were approved (see also reference **401** and section on Energy—11.21). As has happened elsewhere, the whole program is subjected to troublesome and very expensive delays as the result of opposition by many who express their hostility in demonstrations, legislative activity, and occasional violent attempts to damage installations or other property.

The forests are largely concentrated on the slopes of the Jura in the northwest and in the Ticino to the south. Still heavily forested are the ancient cantons of Uri, Schwyz and Unterwalden in the very heart of Switzerland. The present distribution of forests remains practically unchanged since the Middle Ages.

The forests are of unusual importance to the Swiss. Their value as a source of wood for construction and fuel is obvious. But beyond such uses, a rich forest cover on the mountain sides is an effective protection against the winter avalanches that threaten any villages that hug the lower slopes. They also help to prevent soil erosion and they aid immeasurably in preserving the ground-water resources. Their intrinsic value as peaceful, quiet and beautiful places in which to retreat, as hikers and lovers of nature, is not lost upon the Swiss. Any who have wandered through such magnificent forests as those of the Bremgarten, the Könizberg, the Schüpfenberg, and others in the Emmental, will never forget the berries, the mushrooms, the neatly arranged stacks of firewood, the beautifully colored autumn foliage, and the grey low-hanging mists and frost-decorated conifers of early winter.

Over 70 per cent of the forest land is publicly owned and rarely passes into private ownership. The forests must be managed on a sustained yield basis and the land area devoted to forests must be maintained. The law also provides for the rigid control of forests under private ownership. The laws, federal and cantonal, recognize the forests as an asset to be treasured and much of Switzerland's forest policy is directed toward increasing the forest land, and reforesting (if at all possible) slopes denuded by avalanches, and increasing the total yield and quality of the forest products.

As a relic of original communal ownership is the continued right of access to forests. None may be denied the right the right to tramp through the forests and gather berries, mushrooms, pine cones and the like. Enclosures may be made temporarily on the grounds of silviculture (e.g. newly reforested areas) but may not be made permanent. Since 1878 there has been a federal forestry service, but the day-to-day management of the forests is largely a responsibility of the cantonal forestry services.

A School of Forestry was established in 1855 as a division of the Federal Institute of Technology, and a Federal Institute for Forestry Research followed in 1885. Largely because of the denuding effects of avalanches and overgrazing, the timber line on many mountain slopes in the Alps has been seriously lowered in the past few hundred years. The re-establishment of forests on high mountain slopes and in climatically difficult situations is a major research project of great importance. A representative area under study is high up on the Dischma valley above Davos. Climatological conditions are unfavorable in the extreme. Typical of other high Alpine slopes, the mountain side has been denuded by erosion, rock and land slides, avalanches and mountain torrents.

A study of forestry in eight European countries, published in 1967, reported that Switzerland made profits from her forests that exceeded those of any other country in the group of eight (**94**).

Notes and Comments

1. The traffic on the Rhine, specifically the tonnage of goods entering the port of Basel, deserves mention. In 1980, about 8,762,000 tons of merchandise were received—mostly petroleum. In contrast, the outgoing tonnage down the Rhine was only about 257,300—mostly products of the machine and metal industries.

11.2 POPULATION

Introduction

Now that we have been introduced to Switzerland's surface and its functional divisions, let us become acquainted in a very general but quantitative way with those who populate the land. As in many other countries, a decennial census is the rule in Switzerland. That of 1980 took place on December 2 at an approximate cost of 55 million francs and 130 tons of paper. In intervening years, annual population estimates are made by the Federal Statistical Office.

Table 8 gives the census data and population estimates for 1850, 1880 and various years of the twentieth century, Zurich Canton is the most heavily populated (1,120,200) of the 26 cantons, and the city of Zurich with a population of 711,600 (end of 1978), inclusive of its suburbs, is the largest of the Swiss cities. The city proper, exclusive of its suburbs, with a population of 379,800 is twice as large as its runner-up (Basel). Principally because of a flight to the suburbs, all four of the largest cities (Zurich, Basel, Geneva, Bern) have experienced a steady population decrease of 12 to 15 percent since 1965.

The Foreign Population

"Foreignization" (*Überfremdung*), a persistent and troublesome problem in Switzerland, will be partially discussed later in this chapter. As an introduction, the state of the problem at its height should be mentioned. The foreign population in 1974 (the peak year) and 1980 consisted principally of the following (1980 in parentheses): Italian 555,000 (421,000); German 111,000 (86,000); Spanish 122,000 (97,000); French 53,000 (46,000); Austrian 43,000 (32,000); Jugoslav 35,000 (44,000); Turkish 27,000 (38,000); Greek 11,000 (8,800); Czechoslovak 13,600 (13,900); British 13,535 (14,000); USA 11,111 (9,200) (**341**, 1975, p. 118; 1981, p. 90). Table 9 presents the corresponding data, and a little more, for selected years in the past century. Until the second World War, immigrants from Germany were the most numerous. After the war, Italian immigrants greatly exceeded in number those from any other country. See also Table 10 on naturalization.

473

Table 8

Year	Population[a] Total	Aliens Number[d]	Percent of total	Cities[b]	Towns & villages[c]	Households
1850	2,392,740	74,782	3.0	8	3196	485,087
1880	2,831,787	211,035	7.4	17	3173	607,725
1900	3,315,443	383,424	11.6	21	3143	728,920
1930	4,066,400	355,522	8.7	31	3087	1,002,915
1950	4,714,992	285,446	6.1	42	3059	1,312,204
1960	5,429,061	584,739	10.8	65	3030	1,594,010
1970	6,269,783	982,887	17.2	92	2980	2,062,438
1974	6,442,800	1,064,526	17.2	—	—	—
1975	6,405,000	1,012,710	15.8	—	—	—
1976	6,346,000	958,599	15.1	—	—	—
1977	6,327,000	932,743	14.7	—	—	—
1978	6,337,000	898,062	14.2	—	—	—
1979	6,356,300	883,837	14.0	—	—	—
1980	6,365,960	892,807	14.2	96	2933	2,446,360
1981	6,384,349	942,038	14.8			
1982	6,423,106	960,324	15.0			
1983	6,436,500	956,100	14.9			
2000 (Est.)[e]	6,750,000	1,090,000	16.1			
2020 (Est.)[e]	6,661,000	990,000	15.0			

[a] Total population data are from **341**, 1979, pp. 14, 31; 1981, p. 33. Ref. **377**, 1983, Vol. 56, p. 629; Ref. **266**, 10–11 March 1984, p. 36.

[b] With over 10,000 inhabitants, Source **341**, 1981, p. 14; 1951, p. 10.

[c] With less than 10,000 inhabitants. Source **341**, 1981, p. 14; 1951, p. 10.

[d] 1970 et seq. Seasonal workers, border-crossers and international functionaries with their families are not included. Populations of seasonal workers and border-crossers vary greatly during a year. The numbers of seasonal workers plus border-crossers at the end of 1974 and at the end of 1978 were reported to be 117,295 (**341**, 1975, p. 113) and 92,667 (**341**, 1979, p. 85), respectively. If these totals are added to the alien population figures for 1974 and 1978, as given above, we arrive at revised totals for the alien population of 1,181,821 in 1974 and 990,729 in 1978—a four-year decrease of 191,000. But if we use mid-year averages (April, August) we could conclude that the seasonal workers plus border-crossers numbered, more realistically, 245,400 for 1974 and 149,000 for 1978 (**341**, 1979, p. 82). By so doing we arrive at revised totals for the alien population of 1,310,000 in 1974 and 1,047,000 in 1978—a four-year decrease of 263,000. Alien population data for 1850 and 1900 are from ref. **327**, p. 80.

[e] Prognosis of the St. Gallen *Zentrum für Zukumftsforschung.*

In recent years there has been a small but significant increase in the total population. This is principally attributable to an excess of births over deaths.

Citizenship and Population

A change in the law concerning Swiss citizenship has contributed somewhat to the decrease in the alien population. Prior to amendment, the law provided that Swiss citizenship descended only through the father. The present law recognizes an equal right of the mother. Formerly, children born of a Swiss father and a mother of foreign nationality acquired Swiss citizenship as a birthright. Under the present law,

Table 8a Some international comparisons[a]

| Country | Population[b] | | | Surface area thousands of sq. km | Population in absolute numbers per sq. km |
	Census date	On census date	Estimated 1.7.78		
Switzerland	2.12.80	6.365	—	41.3	154
Australia	30.6.76	13.548	14.249	7686.8	2
Canada	1.6.76	22.993	23.499	4976.1	2
Monaco	1.2.75	0.025	0.026	0.01	17,450
New Zealand	23.3.76	3.129	3.107	268.7	12
United Kingdom[c]	25.4.71	55.506	55.822	244.0	229
USA	1.4.70	203.235	218.059	9363.1	23
USSR					
European	15.1.70	182.503	—	5571.0	33[d]
Asiatic	15.1.70	59.245	—	16,831.0	4[d]

[a] Source: **341**, 1981, pp. 569–74.
[b] Population in millions.
[c] England, Wales, Scotland, and Northern Ireland.
[d] As calculated.

Table 8b Some international comparisons. Population of several countries according to age groups[a,b]

| Country | Year | Age in years | |
		0 to 4	60 and Over
Switzerland	1979	56	180
Australia	1977	85	132
Canada	1977	75	128
Mexico	1975	184[d]	48[c]
New Zealand	1977	89	138
Sweden	1976	66	212[d]
United Kingdom			
England & Wales	1976	66	200
Northern Ireland	1977	85	158
Scotland	1977	65	188
USA	1977	70	152
USSR	1974	166 (0 to 10)	131
West Germany	1977	50[c]	200

[a] Source: **341**, 1981, p. 578.
[b] Per thousand of total population.
[c] Lowest of all 38 countries listed in the Yearbook.
[d] Highest of all 38 countries listed in the Yearbook.

Table 9   The foreign population of Switzerland (excluding, in general, international functionaries and their families)

	1860	1880	1910[a]	1950[a]	1980 Total number[b]	1980 Number employed[f]
Total number	114,983	211,035	552,011	285,446	892,807	602,420
Civil state						
Unmarried (adults)			344,449[c]	164,406[c]	183,028	
Married			183,550	96,506	452,970	
Widowed			21,807	19,932	20,000	
Divorced			2205	4602	18,788	
Children under 16 yrs					218,021	
Nationality						
German	47,792	95,262	219,530	55,437[e]	86,331[e]	63,329[e]
Austrian	3654[d]	13,309[d]	41,422	22,153	31,736	25,918
French	29,603	53,653	63,695	27,470	46,177	69,236
Italian	13,828	41,330	202,809	140,280	420,700	261,788
Greek	—	—		—	8824	4791
Jugoslav	—	—		—	43,898	32,721
Spanish	—	—		—	97,232	63,127
Turkish	—	—		—	38,073	20,720
Belgian	361	500	833	—	4098	1942
British	1202	2812	4118	—	14,050	6753
Dutch	128	438	1363	—	9957	4576
European Russian	560	1285	8457	—	—	—
Rest of Europe	17,350	624	5220	—	33,892	—
American (USA)	425	1111	2994	—	9165	3392
Asian			1072	—	—	—
African	—	—	417	—	—	—
Australian	—	—	81	—	—	—
Other	80	711	—	40,106	48,674	44,127
Religion			1910	1950	1970	
Protestant			142,463	63,936	136,967	
Catholic			383,424	204,056	865,611	
Jewish			12,187	8313	8767	
Other or none			13,937	9141	68,731	

[a] From **341**, 1979, pp. 20, 24, 28; 1920, pp. 62, 63: Excludes border-crossers and seasonal workers.
[b] **377**, 1981, pp. 120, 123. Excludes border-crossers and seasonal workers.
[c] Includes children under 16 years.
[d] Includes Hungary and Liechtenstein.
[e] West Germany.
[f] **377**, 1981, p. 131, Includes border-crossers and seasonal workers (i.e. all four classes of employed foreigners).

Table 10 Nationality of foreigners acquiring Swiss citizenship[a,b]

	German	Austrian	Italian	French	Other	Total	Wives & minor children	Grand total
1893	462	38[e]	62	194	19	775	1733	2508
1889–1910[i]	1652	168[f]	368	551	120	2859[g]	—	2859[g]
1900	557	57[e]	162	253	47	1076	2255	3331
1950	1351	148	1702	317	472	3990	—	3990[g]
1980	2653[c]	734	3095	727	2866[h]	10,075[d]	—	10,075[d]

[a] Source: **377**, 1981, p. 117; **341**, 1916, pp. 258, 259; 1920, p. 32; 1951, p. 105.
[b] Includes ordinary naturalization and renaturalization of those who had previously been naturalized but later lost their Swiss citizenship.
[c] From West Germany (**377**, 1981, p. 117); includes East Germany (**341**, 1981, p. 71).
[d] Excludes 3867 children who acquired citizenship through recent legislation.
[e] Austrians and Hungarians.
[f] Austrians, Hungarians and Czechoslovaks.
[g] Wives and children included.
[h] Includes: 135 British and 114 from USA.
[i] Yearly average.

children born of a Swiss mother, married to an alien, are also entitled to Swiss citizenship. When the new law came into effect, a number of children born of Swiss mothers (but married to aliens and living in Switzerland) became Swiss citizens. This necessarily increased the Swiss fraction of the total population at the expense of the resident population of aliens. Actually, the revised rules on citizenship present a number of complications and still conflict with the principle of equal rights for men and women. The law on citizenship is to be revised once again for simplification and removal of inequities.

A favorite game of demographers is forecasting population. In reality it is a very important task because an expanding population requires that the infrastructure be ready in advance of the increasing burden of people. More housing, hospitals, schools and transport facilities are among the obvious requirements to which the planners must give attention. If population estimates are much too high, if the assumed growth rate of the population is seriously in error, an inflated building boom can be the result. There was indeed, an elevated rate of residential building construction in the 1960s which continued to 1973 and then declined. Thus in 1960, the number of newly constructed residential units was 38,991. The number rose steadily to 81,865 in 1973 and then fell to 34,464 in 1978, due largely to a *Baustopp* ordered by government.

Overbuilding

The obvious conclusion of overbuilding during a few hectic years is supported by the number of vacant lodgings. The number in 1973 was 11,477 or 0.6 percent of the total of lodging units in all Switzerland. But by 1976, with 51,231 vacancies, 2 percent of the total lodging units were vacant. By 1978 the vacancy rate had receded to 1.12 percent, to 0.74 percent in 1980 (**341**, 1980, p. 171) and to 0.5 percent in 1981, low enough to be regarded by experts as an emergency state. Building activity of all kinds has been decreasing since 1973 but new projects have been in the planning and early construction stages since 1976. In 1980, the five largest cities, inclusive of suburban towns, added a total of 3,132 residential units and issued 4,001 building permits. For all 92 cities the corresponding totals were 11,883 and 15,796 respectively (**341**, 1980, p. 170).

Apartments

We should also be aware of the change that has gone on in the number of people who occupy an apartment. In 1960 the average was 3.3, compared with 2.9 in 1970, and 2.3 in 1980. We are reminded that if in 1980 the occupancy were 3.3 as it was in 1960, the current vacancy rate would be as high as 20 percent and half a million living units would be vacant (**266**, 11/12 July, 1981). All of this results from an expressed desire of people for a little more "elbow room," from the determination of young people to occupy as soon as possible their own apartment, and probably from an increased divorce rate whereby families are split, each half with a need for less living space. But increases in the cost of rentals and other cost-of-living increases can have an opposite effect in the sense that younger people may double up or triple up to reduce their occupancy costs—hence a hypothetical return to the 3.3 per apartment of 1960, or even higher.

Population Growth

In the 1960s, Switzerland experienced a growth euphoria with extraordinary consequences. The number of foreign workers increased steadily in the 1950s and 1960s until by 1970–74, over a million aliens were in Switzerland, about 17 percent of the total population. For years, unemployment was unknown and foreign workers were readily absorbed. A population of 10 million by the year 2000 was regarded by planners as a reasonable estimate, stemming largely from the rate of growth between 1960 and 1965 (**266**, 31 January 1970). But a study by the Federal Statistical Office, including appropriate demographic principles, gave a more reliable estimate of 7.3 to 7.5 million. In 1977 the Federal Statistical Office reported an even more conservative forecast—a population of 6,537,500 by the year 2006. The obvious determinants are the birth rate, the death rate, and immigration/emigration.

As for emigration, we are here concerned with the exodus of Swiss citizens from the Fatherland and of resident foreigners also (cf. Table 11). We should note that in the eighteenth century, Switzerland lost, principally through emigration and mercenary service, between 340,000 and 390,000 of her people (almost a fifth of the population) (**40**, p. 55). Of these many emigrants, 89 percent were mercenaries in the military service of foreign Powers. In the nineteenth century, the loss totalled about 153,000 (**40**, p. 159). A net loss of her citizens by emigration has continued through the twentieth century. In 1958, for example, the net loss was 2742 and in 1974 the loss totalled 1755. Part of the detailed information for these two years is presented in

Table 11 Emigration[a]

Years	Overseas		To European countries	
	Swiss	Foreigners	Swiss	Foreigners
1868–75	31,860	—		
1881–85	50,490	3098	—	—
1891–95	24,350	5295	—	—
1901–05	18,760	5550	—	—
1914–19	9355	1977	—	—
1921–25	25,121	4275	—	—
1931–35	4783	1862	—	—
1939–45	2446	2919	—	—
1946–50	8865	4795	—	—
1963–67[b]	32,499	—	56,384	—
1970–74[b]	37,418	—	42,902	—

1971–75 (Destination not reported) 48,834 Swiss of military age[c]

	Destination of overseas emigrants[d] (Swiss)						
	USA[e]	Canada	Brazil	Argentina	Oceania[f]	Africa	Asia
1887–90	27,076	20	440	3988	92	40	12
1901–05	21,660	150	225	1485	295	170	120
1911–15	16,970	1090	810	3365	405	220	200
1916–20	10,820	225	915	1145	45	780	550
1921–25	16,975	2860	2175	2800	605	2130	950
1931–35	1910	160	400	800	100	1785	905
1936–40	3110	525	830	2150	305	1015	785
1941–45	865	10	250	120	—	170	70
1946–50	6926	1101	807	1421	564	1064	396
1963–67	10,363	5402	613	305	2746	7068	3859
1970–74	8079	4601	1124	396	4830	10,561	5357

[a] Source: **341**, 1951, p. 95.
[b] Source: **341**, 1977, pp. 76, 77.
[c] Swiss citizens subject to military control—viz. males of military age. Source: **341**, 1979, p. 79. The net population loss of citizens subject to military duty was 9078 in 1971–75: returnees numbered 39,756.
[d] Source: **341**, 1951, p. 94; 1932, p. 93; 1977, pp. 76, 77. Central America (and much of South America) not included.
[e] Mexico included in data for 1887–90 and 1901–05.
[f] Principally Australia and New Zealand.

Table 12. If we include all the intervening years (1959 to 1973) the total net loss for the 17 years amounted to 38,723 (**341**, 1969, p. 73; 1975, p. 103).

Effects of the Two World Wars

Population data, as reported by the Federal Office of Statistics, permit the conclusion that in each of the two World Wars many Swiss who were residents of the countries at war, returned to the homeland—as might be expected. In each of the five years, 1941 to 1945, the number of Swiss who returned to Switzerland exceeded

Table 12   Migration of Swiss citizens in 1958 and 1974[a]

Country or continent	Year	Emigrants (*Auswanderer*)	Returnees (*Rückwanderer*)	Net loss
Europe	1958	9504	8360	1144
Argentina	1958	78	105	−27
Brazil	1958	185	140	45
Canada	1958	966	249	717
USA	1958	1709	1001	708
Other countries in the Americas	1958	390	306	84
Africa	1958	850	899	−49
Asia	1958	534	568	−34
Oceania[b]	1958	254	100	154
Total net loss in	1958			2742
Europe	1974	7366	6538	828
Argentina	1974	72	74	−2
Brazil	1974	389	153	236
Canada	1974	975	688	287
USA	1974	1497	1367	130
Other countries in the Americas	1974	531	486	45
Africa	1974	2000	2051	−51
Asia	1974	1060	1004	56
Oceania[b]	1974	929	703	226
Total net loss in	1974			1755

[a] From **341**, 1969, p. 72; and 1975, p. 102.
[b] Principally Australia and New Zealand.

the population loss through emigration, the five-year net increase being 5005. But in every subsequent year, 1946 to 1977, Switzerland has experienced a net loss of those of her citizens who were subject to military service, the grand total for the 32 years being 65,590 (**341**, 1969, p. 77; 1979, p. 79). If family members were to be included (no data available), the loss would be much greater.

For the foreigners in Switzerland we should note that in the 30-year span, 1880 to 1910, there was an increase in their numbers of 322,360. However, the following 40 years, 1910 to 1950, which included the two World Wars, witnessed a foreign population decrease of 266,565. An extraordinary increase of 299,293 in the foreign population followed in the ensuing decade, 1950 to 1960. The population decrease from 1910 to 1950 is almost entirely attributable to the recall, by the countries at war, of their male citizens of military age then residing in Switzerland. This resulted in the exodus of entire families. Table 13 reports on the number of Swiss citizens who were settled in foreign countries in 1928, 1940 and 1977. Two classes of Swiss citizens are included: those who have Swiss citizenship only and those who are citizens of Switzerland as well as citizens of the country of residence (dual citizenship).

Swiss Citizens Abroad

There are many reasons why the Swiss, at one time or another, have left their homeland. Religious persecution (e.g. of the Anabaptists and other Sectarians in the sixteenth, seventeenth and eighteenth centuries) caused several waves of emigration. Mercenary service in the armies of foreign nations attracted many who were lured by dreams of an exciting life elsewhere, or of the richness of the booty and spoils of war that fell to a victorious army. In the nineteenth century an occasional heavy exodus could be explained by crop failures (e.g. lack of rain or too much rain)[1] or disastrously low prices for farm products. Some will remember the "brain-drain" years of the 1960s when significant numbers of scientists, engineers and scholars of other persuasions emigrated from Great Britain, Switzerland and western Europe generally, to the USA—then the land of golden opportunity.

Table 11 reports on emigration from Switzerland during the years 1868 to 1974, both with respect to numbers involved and overseas destinations. The favorite overseas destination has been the USA, except in recent years (1970–74) when Africa received about 2500 more Swiss emigrants than the USA. Table 11 also reports on the substantial decrease in emigration during 1914–19 and 1939–45, the years of World War I and II, respectively.

A total of 354,000 Swiss were settled in foreign countries at the end of 1980 (341, 1981, 79). Switzerland subsidized 19 schools for Swiss children abroad. The schools use the Swiss system of education and are of special importance to children whose residence in foreign countries is temporary.

Immigration and Foreign Workers

The immigration/emigration rates in Switzerland present the greatest uncertainty in any population estimates for the future, the number of immigrants being subject to changing political policies and economic conditions in Switzerland and in the homeland of the migrants. The immigrants fall into three categories: (1) seasonal workers who, as the name implies, are admitted into the country for a few months at a time (a nine-month maximum), never for a full year; (2) the non-Swiss border-crossers who live in Italy, France, Germany, Austria, or Liechtenstein, but who enter and leave Switzerland, where they are employed, for a day at a time; (3) the year-long aliens whose work permits allow them to remain in the country for a full year. In April 1979, these three groups, all of whom are subject to immigration controls, numbered 277,609 (525,304 in 1974). About one-third of these were Italian citizens and were mostly men (approximately two-thirds of the total). But beyond this three-membered group there is a large fourth group of immigrants. This consists of those aliens who have been in the country for some years—a result of repeated renewals of their year-long work permits. They are known as the *Niedergelassene* and in April 1979, totalled 351,007. The number of seasonal workers varies considerably from month to month while the year-long permit holders (*Jahresaufenthalter*) and the *Niedergelassene* (no longer subject to the controls) constitute more stable population groups from month to month in any given year. The decrease in foreign worker population from 1974 to 1979 can be largely accounted for by the decrease in numbers of seasonal workers (71,852) and of "year-longers" (157,583, April data). As a generalization it should be mentioned that the established aliens (*Niedergelassene*) have been steadily increasing in number over the years while the year-long permit holders have been decreasing since the mid-1960s (**341**, 1979, p. 82). At the end of 1978, within the gainfully employed, the year-long permit holders numbered 145,130 and the *Niedergelassene* 334,296 (**341**, 1979, p. 87). Data for the seasonal workers, the border-crossers and the international functionaries are not available as of the end of 1978. In April 1979 the seasonal workers numbered 49,374 and the border-crossers 89,642 (**341**, 1979, p. 82). Employment of the foreign workers is reported upon in Table 14.

For the benefit of those who enjoy burying themselves in statistical information, I have included Table 13 (Swiss Citizens Resident in Selected Foreign Countries), Table 15 (Population Balance), Table 10 (Nationality of Foreigners Acquiring Swiss Citizenship) and Table 16 (Miscellaneous Data Pertaining to Swiss Citizens). See also item 2 in "Notes and Comments."

The most recent piece of federal legislation pertaining to the foreign population was enacted 19 June 1981 (*Ausländergesetz*) (**329**, 1981, II, 568–93). The law has been challenged and will be settled by a popular referendum.[3]

Just as Switzerland is eager to maintain the number of resident foreigners at acceptable levels, so also is her good neighbour, Liechtenstein, similarly inclined. At the end of 1979, the foreign population of Liechtenstein numbered 8944 which was about 35% of the total population! Of the 8944 aliens, almost half (4004) were Swiss. The number of Liechtensteiners resident in Switzerland was somewhat over 1800.

The foreign workers in Switzerland are not completely happy with their lot. Six hundred representatives of about 200 organizations concerned with the problems met in Bern early in 1980 to talk things over. They concluded that the present foreign-worker policy tends to isolate the aliens and to envelop them in an atmosphere of disfavor and prejudice. The fact is that most of the foreign workers have been employed in work which the Swiss themselves prefer to avoid: e.g. the hard and dirty work in hotels and heavy labor in construction. The Swiss are spoiled: a nation of hard workers is being converted into a nation that prefers an easy life with the hard, dirty or unpleasant, and menial tasks performed by foreign workers. This is not to deny the fact that many foreign workers because of their industry and know-how contribute a great deal to the welfare of Switzerland. However one may regard the foreign worker, he is now indispensable in Switzerland. All that remains to be determined is the number of aliens the country is prepared to absorb—and the rate of inflow.

Late in 1980 between 10,000 and 15,000 people, brought to Bern by 10 special trains from throughout Switzerland, assembled in front of the Parliament buildings to demonstrate the solidarity of Swiss trade-union members with the immigrant

Table 13 Swiss citizens resident in selected foreign countries[a]

	1928	1940	1977
Austria			6492
Belgium	5720	5000	7227
France	144,000	80,000	92,267
Germany	55,810[b]	52,500[b]	42,146[c]
Great Britain	15,060[d]	17,000	14,046
Irish Free State		60	300
Italy	18,900	16,650	20,345
Spain	3200	2500	5910
USSR	1100	900	100
Other European countries	8090	6580	17,211
Europe (total)	251,800	181,190	206,044
Algeria	3020	1910	839
South Africa	500	1200	8458
Other African countries	3571	5308	9615
Africa (total)	7091	8418	18,912
Asia (total)	2470	3309	9092[e]
Oceania (total)	1470	1900	12,646
Argentina	15,960	12,000	11,899
Brazil	4370	4900	9857
Canada	8390	5200	20,759
USA	49,900	44,000	37,550
Other countries in the Americas	4520	5480	14,464
Total for the Americas	83,140	71,580	94,529
Grand total	346,051	266,397	341,223

[a] Source: **341**, 1979, pp. 76, 77; 1940, p. 118; 1942, p. 95.
[b] Inclusive of Austria and Danzig.
[c] Both Germanies.
[d] Includes the Irish Free State.
[e] Including 2132 in Israel.
Note that Swiss citizens only are included in the data for 1928 and 1940 except in Russia where the *Doppelburgers* were included.

seasonal workers. "Never before on the *Bundesplatz* were so many nationalities represented. Above the immense crowd of demonstrators towered banners in Italian, Spanish, Jugoslav, Portuguese, and Turkish languages." The speakers protested a statute which allegedly discriminates against the seasonal workers. "Our foreign workers are also human beings and have the right to equal treatment with the Swiss . . . we speak no longer of foreigners and Swiss but only of colleagues" (**373**).

Table 14   Employment of the foreign workers

The working population	February, 1960[a]	August, 1980[a]	Resident foreign population December, 1981
Border-crossers	33,578	100,404	
Seasonal workers	27,428	109,873	
Year-longers	214,285	125,439	215,904
Established residents	—	370,593	694,002
Total	275,291	706,309	909,906

It will be noticed that while the foreign population at the end of December 1980 totalled 892,807[b] (Table 8), the working population among all four of the above classes in August 1980 equalled 706,309. Men were employed mostly (above 15,000 per category) in (a) the machine and metal industries, (b) construction, (c) commerce, (d) hotels and restaurants. Women were employed mostly (above 15,000 per category) in (a) physical therapy and beauty salons, (b) hotels and restaurants (c) commerce, (d) machine and metal industries, (e) the textile industry, and (f) clothing, laundry and shoe industries.

Seasonal workers were employed almost entirely in hotels and restaurants. The border-crossers found employment mostly in commerce and the machine and metal industries. The other two classes (about 83% of the total) were distributed as follows in their sources of employment: 120,000 in the machine and metal industries; 54,000 in construction; 46,000 in commerce; 36,000 in textiles, clothing, laundry and shoes; 35,000 in hotels and restaurants; and 39,000 in physical therapy and beauty salons (**377**, 1981, pp. 133, 135).

[a] Source: **341**, 1981, pp. 82, 84; **266**, February 6–7, 1982.
[b] The "resident" foreign population consists only of year-longers (*Jahresaufenthalter*) and established residents (*Niedergelassene*). Border-crossers and seasonal workers are not included.

Table 15   Population balance[a] (yearly average per decade)

15a. The Swiss

Census period	Excess of births[b]	Increase by marriage[c]	Increase by acquisition of citizenship[d]	Net increase through immig./emig.[e]	Total increase
1888–1900	22,761	−140	2119	−4414	20,326
1900–10	28,697	−34	3462	−5199	26,926
1941–50	36,792	1675	3339	1238	43,044
1960–70	28,423	4297	4165	−2346	34,539

15b. The Foreigners

Census period	Excess of births[b]	Increase by marriage[c]	Increase by acquisition of citizenship[d]	Net increase through immig./emig.[e]	Total increase
1888–1900	4203	140	−2119	10,591	12,815
1900–10	7164	34	−3462	13,123	16,859
1941–50	−723	−1675	−3339	12,164	6877
1960–70	22,211	−4297	−4165	35,785	49,533

[a] Source: **341**, 1979, p. 29; 1932, p. 41.
[b] Births minus deaths.
[c] Decreases if a Swiss woman marries a foreigner.
[d] Includes ordinary naturalization and renaturalization of those who had previously been naturalized but later lost their Swiss citizenship.
[e] Excess of immigrants over emigrants.

Table 16 Swiss citizens

	1880[a]	1910	1950	1970
Total number	2,846,102	3,201,282	4,429,546	5,189,707
Civil State				
Unmarried	1,736,021	1,915,502	2,169,941	2,418,031
Married	919,137	1,069,326	1,932,811	2,452,194
Widowed	181,403	198,773	259,538	314,977
Divorced	9541	17,681	67,256	104,505
Birthplace				
Switzerland	2,635,067	3,118,271	4,225,511	4,931,511
A foreign country	211,035	83,011	204,035	258,196
Religion				
Protestant	1,667,109	1,965,351	2,591,439	2,854,727
Catholic	1,160,782	1,210,114	1,783,558	2,232,311
Jewish	7373	6275	10,735	11,977
Other or none	10,838	19,542	43,814	71,692
Mother tongue				
German	2,030,702	2,326,138	3,285,333	3,864,684
French	608,007	708,650	912,141	1,045,091
Italian	161,923	125,336	175,193	207,557
Romansh	38,705	39,349	49,979	49,455
Other	6675	1809	8900	22,920

Source: **341**, 1920, pp. 48, 56, 58; 1979, pp. 20, 26–28.
[a] Foreigners included.

A number of treaties of friendship and reciprocal establishment were entered into in the 1850s, 1860s and 1870s between Switzerland and other States (see, for example, chapter 10). Except for a few qualifications, they granted to those citizens who were under the jurisdiction of one country an equality of rights in the other country (Switzerland). The treaties were reciprocal. In 1868, such a treaty between Switzerland and Italy assured a full equality of treatment between Italian citizens in Switzerland and the Swiss themselves (**329**, 1868, III, 478–87). One need hardly be reminded that Switzerland and her treaty partners, in course of time, felt obliged to enact legislation that severely limited to foreigners the right of establishment, of protracted residence, of freedom to exercise one's profession and of other rights enjoyed in the past. The two World Wars, especially that of 1914–18, were accompanied and followed by economic problems that precipitated such "unfriendly" legislation.

The concept of seasonal workers—foreigners whose work and residence permits were valid for only nine months of a year—was introduced in 1921. A popular votation in 1925, by means of an amendment to the Constitution (Article 69 ter), granted to the Confederation the right to legislate on the entrance, duration of sojourn, and establishment of foreigners in Switzerland.

A building boom, heightened industrial activity, substantial increases in tourism—the total "prosperity package"—ultimately had their effect. The demand for labor increasingly exceeded the domestic supply. Foreign workers entered Switzerland in such numbers that by the early 1970s the alien population constituted 17.2 percent of the total population, the highest percentage recorded for all European countries. Many Swiss feared that the characteristically Swiss qualities of their homeland would be diluted beyond recognition and ultimately lost if the foreignization of Switzerland was not brought under control. No less than five popular initiatives were introduced, the first in 1968, to stem the *Ueberfremdung*. All five were voted down by increasingly large majorities. A sixth attempt was initiated in mid-1983. This approach, a stabilization of the population at 6,200,000 would progressively reduce the immigration of foreigners until the population levelled off at about 6,200,000. This initiative was also defeated.

The Federal Government has sought to establish an acceptable balance—a stabilization—in the population mix, either by fixing the maximum foreign population as a certain percentage of the total population or as an absolute number. It has also realized that foreign policy and any resulting legislation must recognize humane and social considerations—the dignity, the liberties, the rights, as well as the duties, of the foreign population. Foreigners already in Switzerland must be able to enjoy a humane and sociable environment, and juridical security.

Parliament has been petitioned by a group of foreign-worker organizations to so ameliorate the status of all foreigners, such that after at least five years of residence in Switzerland and at least one year in a given canton they would be granted voting and electoral rights at the community and cantonal levels.

On April 5, 1981, a proposed constitutional amendment that would have removed virtually all of the restrictive limitations on the rights of foreign workers was voted upon. With a heavy turnout of the four million registered voters the measure, known as the *Mitenand* initiative, was rejected by an overwhelming ratio of five to one. All 26 cantons were also opposed. Adoption of the amendment would have extensively liberalized the existing legislation: (a) a foreign worker would enjoy the right to remain in Switzerland even if his services were no longer needed, unless expelled by a court order pursuant to conviction for a crime; (b) he would be entitled to full Social Security coverage, the right to be joined by his family, and freedom to change his job and place of residence.

The principal beneficiaries of the rejected amendment would have been the foreign seasonal workers, mostly Italian, Spanish and Portuguese—possibly totalling 100,000 but not included within the alien population as reported by the Swiss Statistical Office (893,000 in December, 1980). Note that a seasonal worker must leave the country each year after nine months of employment. After four nine-month periods, 36 months in all in four consecutive years, he can be granted a work and residence permit good for one year and renewable annually: he becomes a *Jahresaufenthalter*. An additional 15 months must elapse before entrance of his family is permitted. In ten years he can acquire the status of a foreign resident and may then remain in Switzerland even if unemployed: he has finally become a *Niedergelassene*.

Rejection of the *Mitenand* initiative has been followed, however, by a new proposal that would shorten by four months the time required for a seasonal worker to become a year-long permit holder. This minireform appears to be trifling but the heavy vote against the initiative indicated to the political parties that liberalization can only be achieved by one ministep at a time.

One other aspect of the foreign-worker problem disturbs officialdom in Switzerland, namely the flight of Swiss francs into other countires—in part, a result of the savings by the *Gastarbeiter* (guest worker) in Switzerland and his practice of sending the money home to his family. The seasonal workers and the "year-longers" (*Jahresaufenthalter*) earned in 1978 5.5 billion francs, of which 925 million were sent to their homeland. (In 1973, 1790 million francs were sent home.) The border-crossers in 1978 took to their homes across the border 2110 million francs and spent in Switzerland about 240 million.

Political Refugees

The foreign population of Switzerland includes not only the seasonal workers, the border-crossers, the many immigrants with year-long permits of work and residence, but the even larger group of long-time resident aliens who no longer require permits for work or residence. It includes also a second class of aliens, whose smallness in numbers belies their political and social significance. These are political refugees some of whom were admitted as early as 1975, from south-east Asia, especially Viet-Nam, Cambodia, and Laos. At the end of 1980, Switzerland was providing hospitality to a total of 6875 refugees from these countries.[4] This includes a few small groups who were accepted by other countries on a temporary basis. Switzerland was prepared to receive approximately 1000 more South-east Asia refugees in 1981.

Early in 1979 Switzerland sent a delegation to South-east Asia to arrange for the selection and transport of refugees. The four delegates represented the Swiss Red Cross, the Federal Office for Police Matters, the Evangelical Churches and *Caritas Schweiz* (Swiss Catholic Charity). Plans were made to accept about 60 persons per week during the last half of 1979—a total of 2000 for the whole year. The delegation returned with 90 "boat people" rescued from the coast of Malaysia, 120 refugees from Cambodia and 40 Vietnamese from camps in Thailand.

Though showered with gifts on arrival and received with compassion and friendliness, the initial warmth extended to the refugees frequently disappeared. Before long they might barely be noticed by their Swiss neighbours—a coolness which is not always meant to be unfriendly but which may be felt by many other foreigners until a real assimilation takes over. Other Swiss are genuinely in-hospitable, almost on principle, to incoming foreigners. They fear a loss of the native qualities of their homeland and of her people.

The new-comers are torn between pressures to adjust as quickly as possible to their new environment and, on the other hand, to maintain as long as they can their own traditions and their own way of life. What a dilemma! Switzerland poses another problem. The winters can be very cold and adjustment to such a hostile climate is not easy for people from warm, sunny and humid South-east Asia.

The first three months in Switzerland are usually spent in a refugee camp where, surrounded by their own people, the first steps in the adjustment process can be taken gradually. Later they are dispersed, to be received in small groups by various communities where local volunteers do what they can to find homes, and work, and to assist in many ways, including language instruction, in the difficult process of adjustment and assimilation.

In 1956 came the great freedom fight of the Hungarian people. We know the result: they lost and many had little choice but to flee the country. Thousands fled.[5] One week after the Russian invasion of Hungary, Switzerland initiated efforts to help the victims of the Soviet repression. One week later, Switzerland offered asylum to 2000 refugees—a number which was soon increased to 4000. By the end of 1957, asylum had been granted to 13,100 or a few hundred more. Of the total, 1700 went on to overseas destinations and about 1400 returned to Hungary. By 1976, 9000 of the remaining Hungarians had acquired Swiss citizenship. The absorption of the Hungarians into Switzerland received the full cooperation of the federal, cantonal and local authorities and relief organizations of various kinds. Assistance was given in finding employment for those who sought work and medical care was extended to many. The universities and student organizations did their part in arranging for 500 Hungarian students to continue their studies. Dozens of individual volunteers and all the political parties assisted in various ways to receive the refugees—with one exception: the Communist-oriented Workers' Party.

Over 100,000 Tibetans left their homes in the high mountains of Tibet in 1959 when their country was seized by the Chinese. A few of these reached Switzerland and found a new home in the Graubünden. The mountainous environment and the snows of winter have appealed to the new-comers. They are eager to preserve and to foster their Tibetan traditions and to maintain their cultural identity. However, they are too few in number to establish a social center where they could meet from time to time to celebrate festively their cultural and religious days of observance. The second generation of Tibetan refugees are alleged to find assimilation in their new Swiss homeland more difficult than that of other foreigners. This is hard to understand unless, in practice, the Tibetans are too isolated from their neighbours. China would like them to return but the promises of improved conditions offered by the Chinese have impressed few if any of the Swiss Tibetans.

Asylum

Early in 1981, 42 Turkish Kurds, seeking asylum in Switzerland, were permitted to occupy a building in the *Kirchgemeinde* (church community) of Les Eaux-Vives in Geneva. The refugees claim that they will be executed if forced to return to Turkey. A Turkish paper, in an article about the group, concludes with the sentence: "Death to these people in whose veins our blood does not flow." The Kurds have been received with compassion and generosity by the church officers and the local community, but official action on the refugees' request for asylum has been deferred pending the clarification of several questions. The death threats have added a new element in the case. The authorities propose a thorough inquiry into the applications: "You will be treated according to justice and the law: we are not inhuman."

At the end of December, 1980, 3020 foreigners from 65 countries had submitted applications for asylum.[6] The main groups of applicants were as follows: Czechoslovakia, 742; Turkey, 627; Hungary, 426; Roumania, 245; Chile, 185; Poland, 184; Afghanistan, 93; Zaire, 70; and Iran, 59. Of the 3020 applicants, 1265 were granted asylum. Still pending were 916 applications. Requests of 193 were withdrawn by the applicants, or the individuals concerned left Switzerland before action was taken on the applications. The requests of 646 persons were denied. On the grounds of special assistance to the needy, 3102 Indochinese refugees were admitted and received asylum.

Only one Chinese citizen has thus far sought asylum in Switzerland. In mid-1981, a circus artist of the "Peking Circus," during a two month European tour of the group, applied for asylum, according to an official in the Federal Justice and Police Department.

Assimilation of the refugees by Switzerland has presented many problems. Two groups of refugees from Sri Lanka have engaged in acts of violence against each other—something akin to a civil war among the refugees— with one group being actively hostile toward the others. Refugees from Zaire have also engaged in acts of violence. In these and other cases, the cause of the trouble resides in the long delays that are encountered in processing the many applications for asylum and in the resistance of the refugees to accept the rules of conduct laid down by the Swiss authorities in granting hospitality, frequently only temporary, to their many "guests." Serious difficulties in finding employment and fears generated by the uncertainties of their future add to the troubles that beset the refugees.

The Central Register

In a modern administration building in Bern is to be found the Federal Office for Questions concerning Foreigners (*Bundesamt für Ausländerfragen*). Since 1973 the office has operated a central register of foreigners in Switzerland (*Zentrale Ausländerregister*). The facilities are fully computerized. Data on about two million foreigners are in the register. In the meantime about half of these have left the country. In the same building the information register of criminals (*Kriminale-polizeilichen Informationssystem*) is located. There is little if any overlapping between the two registers because the central register stores no information on criminals within the foreign population.

A small but almost intractable source of error plagues the central register, in which the data comes from 26 separate cantons. Some cantons register the foreigners according to their place of residence, others according to their place of work. In two cantons that border one another it is possible for a person to reside in one, and to work in the other. Hence in the all-Swiss statistics he may be listed twice, or not at all. The error may involve 15,000 foreigners (**266**, Nr. 124, p. 35). The comings and goings of the tourist population also present a troublesome challenge to the register.

Switzerland also keeps track of her citizens. This, too, presents its problems. For example, among her citizens are some 3000 to 7000 gypsies who cling to their age-long migratory style of life. They are traditionally not a sedentary people and, here and there in Switzerland, they find themselves driven from a resting place where they have temporarily camped. In 1979 only Biel and Bern had set aside places for these wanderers and both places are too small. The gypsies also encounter legal problems pertinent to employment as handymen or peddlers. A cantonal commission in Bern has been studying the problems of the gypsies in the hope of finding mutually acceptable solutions which will not force these intra-Swiss migrants to abandon their way of life. They should not be described or treated as if they were work-shy good-for-nothing vagrants and thieves—as they were once regarded in the west.

Sale of Land to Foreigners

The foreigners in Switzerland include also a significant number of visitors who, for a variety of reasons, wish to purchase a bit of real estate. For 20 years or more, the Swiss, concerned lest their homeland fall into the possession of foreigners, have been imposing restrictions on the sale of real estate to foreigners. "Sell-out of the Homeland" has become a slogan, rich in political overtones, and constantly enlivened by disturbing statistics. Thus we learn that in 1979 over 5900 sales of real estate to foreigners were approved. Only 69 proposed sales were forbidden by the authorities.[7] Since 1961, when sales to foreigners began to require official approval, 52,000 sales (including 28,000 pieces of land for multi-story buildings) have been approved. A total of 5000 hectares (12,500 acres) were involved in these transactions at a sales price of more than eleven billion francs.

Some prospective purchasers seek a second home for vacation purposes in an attractive tourist spot. Others are speculators in search of an investment which will increase in value. Some, especially in parts of Europe that seem always to be threatened by war, or equally threatening national policies, seek a haven of safety to which they can turn if their worst fears are realized.

The federal policy against real estate sales to foreigners is clearly ineffective. The cantons differ widely in their enforcement of the law: in one year, Appenzell was the only canton that refused all applications for sales to foreigners. The inhabitants of the high mountain meadows are frequently eager to sell—for a price—and regard the restrictions on sale as a device to protect agricultural lands in the valleys. The regulations recognize a variety of exceptions which a purchaser may sometimes use to his advantage. It is clear that ways exist by which the law may be circumvented.

The federal ordinance of 1976 has been "sharpened" considerably in the hope that it will be more easily understood, will be more fully enforced, will be stripped of certain exceptions, and will define with some precision just how many approvals may be granted in the specified tourist areas. Parts of the Ticino are already heavily

Germanized—the result of real estate sales to German nationals in past years. Between 1968 and 1977 a Swiss company, through a circuitous and tricky device, managed to collect sixteen million francs from German nationals for the purchase of land in Switzerland. Some 28 parcels were acquired before the scheme was exposed. Unfortunately, some of the transactions were relatively old; the statute of limitations prevented legal action against the principals in such cases. In the remaining cases fines and imprisonment of one month were levied against two of the directors of the company.

Such happenings serve to disturb many Swiss and account for the wide-spread desire to limit still further the sale of land to foreigners. In early 1983 a federal law was enacted which hopefully will reduce property sales to foreigners, of apartment hotels and holiday residences (principally), to 2400 in 1985–86. Details of the law have to be worked out in consultation with the cantons, each of which will be granted a certain proportion of the total sales receiving approval.

Switzerland and the Right of Asylum: A Historical Review

During the Thirty Years War cargoes of neutral ships (Swiss) on the Rhine and Lake Constance were seized from time to time and charges were levied on the ships. Ultimately such ships were recognized as Neutrals and were no longer molested. Other ships continued to be harassed, seized, and plundered. Out of such experiences emerged the right of asylum for all ships, when driven into neutral waters.

As for rights of asylum for troops on land, the Swiss policy in the seventeenth century was to disallow entrance and asylum for an army in flight because of possible pursuit by a victorious army and resumption of combat on Swiss soil.

When the Edict of Nantes was revoked in 1685 by Louis XIV, thousands of Huguenots fled to the Protestant cantons of Switzerland—ultimately to the economic advantage of their new country. But this "tidal wave" of immigrants can hardly be interpreted as comparable to the entrance of a fleeing army. Even by 1796 the rights of asylum and the practice of internment of belligerents by a Neutral had not been established.

In some cases the difficulties experienced by Switzerland were attributable to relatively small numbers of refugees who can only be described as troublemakers who paid little respect to the domestic and foreign policies of their new homeland. French aristocrats who fled for their lives from France and sought refuge in Switzerland during the French revolution were speedily granted asylum. The incoming refugees could not be adequately screened at the border and not until they actively intruded into Swiss foreign policy with furious tirades and invectives against Bern could they be identified as hostile troublemakers.

Long after the end of the Napoleonic war and the Peace of Paris in 1815, Switzerland continued to be plagued by political activists among refugees and resident aliens who, more than once, brought her to the brink of war. Metternich, the Emperor of Austria, Bismarck, the King of Prussia, and the Tsar of Russia—the most conservative among the political leaders of Europe in the 1820s and 1830s— were eager to intervene in Swiss affairs. There was no end to their ingenuity in devising plans to force their desires upon independent, sovereign and neutral Switzerland. Spies, informers, and *agents provocateurs* were extensively used by the determined conservatives from without and by a significant number of conservatives from within. Even the highly respected Pictet and d'Ivernois were regarded as dangerous by the Paris police: they propagated "destructive principles."

Karl Ludwig von Haller questioned whether the Great Powers which had guaranteed in 1815 the neutrality and independence of Switzerland could be expected to honor such a guarantee if Switzerland became a workshop for revolution and an assembly point for all the German, French and Italian conspirators. But notice also the vigorous action taken by Switzerland against foreign soldiers in the Ticino, the retreat of an entire Italian army corps into Swiss territory and the policy statement by the Confederation regarding observance of a rigorous neutrality (see chapter 9). Of equal relevance is the expulsion of the leaders of 10,000 revolutionary troops from Baden who, beaten by Prussia, sought asylum in Switzerland.

In time, Switzerland recognized that her proclaimed right as an independent State to grant asylum to incoming refugees, as she and she alone might determine, was somewhat in conflict with her commitment to neutrality which would not permit her to tolerate and condone any hostile behaviour toward her neighbours by aliens within her midst.

The continuing flow of applications for asylum by individuals and groups of civilians will be processed under a universally applicable policy only with great difficulty, however detailed the regulations may be. Doubtless every application will have to be evaluated, as at present, on its individual merits. I believe we can regard the granting of internment to the huge French army of Bourbaki in January 1871, under the conditions imposed by General Herzog, as the final act in evolution of the policy of internment of foreign troops by Switzerland.

Notes and Comments

1. In 1588 no less than 77 days of rain were recorded in Lucerne during the months of June to August. (**287**, p. 480). The six decades, 1570 to 1629 became known as the "Little Ice Age," reminding one of 1816—referred to as the "Year without a Summer" (**287**, p. 486).

2. The Federal Statistical Office, in a comparison of 1970 population data with that of 1980, has reported a number of interesting observations (**266**, 24–25 July, 1982) of which a few have been singled out for mention here.

(a) The number of children under six years of age decreased from 701,300 to 500,300 during the decade.

(b) The total population of the country changed little; it must be regarded as stable.

(c) The life expectancy at birth, of women increased from 76.2 to 78.7 years; that of men from 70.3 to 72.1 years.

(d) The Swiss proportion of the total population increased by 4.5 percent (231,000 persons)—the result of marriage of foreign women to Swiss men (164,000) and a birth excess of 60,000.

(e) The foreign population decreased by 135,000—a result of the change in citizenship, of emigration (144,200), and a partially compensating effect of an excess of births over deaths of 173,800.

(f) In 1970, 140,000 persons indicated that they were not attached to any confession or religious denomination. In 1980, the number had increased to 478,700.

(g) Of the total population, those who were 65 years of age or older increased in number by 167,400. Those of 80 years or more increased by 59,100.

(h) Of the working population, 189,600 Swiss citizens were added to the work force during the decade. Foreign workers decreased in number by 86,400.

3. The law lost out in the referendum. It was rejected by the people by a very narrow margin and was approved by only ten of the cantons.

4. By mid-1979, the USA had accepted 215,000 of these homeless refugees. China claimed to have received 240,000. The data on Indochinese refugee-acceptance by other countries from 1975 to 1979 are as follows: France (52,000), Australia (20,800), Canada (12,000), West Germany (3400), Hong Kong (3000), Great Britain (1900), Belgium (1240), Norway (1060), New Zealand (1000), Taiwan (1000).

The USA, in 1979, was asked by an International Commission to double its quota of 7000 per month, thereby permitting the admission of 14,000 per month. At that time, 300,000 Indochinese refugees still remained in camps in Thailand, Malaysia, Indonesia and elsewhere. Many thousand exiles sought refuge along the shores of Malaysia, dumped from boats of all sorts, and hoping for transport of any kind to a hospitable country.

Switzerland granted temporary hospitality in 1982 to a small number of Russian soldiers who were taken prisoner by the Afghans in the Russian-Afghanistan conflict. Though under police supervision and having the status of internees, the soldiers are treated generously and have occasional week-end freedom with small amounts of spending money. Troubles with two or three of the internees, though minor, suggest that Bern may be unwilling to accept any more of the prisoners.

5. Austria, to which Hungary was once attached under a single monarchy, received 120,000 refugees, most for temporary residence only.

The total number of refugees in Switzerland increased by 4388 in 1980.

By December, 1980, 1500 persons from the earthquake-torn regions of southern Italy had been granted temporary residence in Switzerland.

6. By December 1981, the number of applications for asylum had increased to 4226. Most of the applicants may be classified as follows: Poles, 929 (the largest single nation group); other East bloc citizens, 1582; South America, 517; Africa 468. Of the 4226 applications, 1285 were granted asylum speedily. The rest are pending. Switzerland has declared that asylum will be granted to 1000 of the many Poles, temporarily admitted to Austria. Few difficulties in assimilation (housing, work) are anticipated because the Swiss people are, in general, sympathetic with the Poles who fled their country when "solidarity" was suppressed and a Communist military dictatorship took control of the country.

Among the many who seek asylum in Switzerland are some who claim economic hardships in their country. For example, in August 1982, 757 Turks and 705 Chileans were among the asylum applicants whose cases were pending. Most will be denied acceptance as refugees, because of lack of evidence of hardship on political grounds unless there be a high probability of imprisonment or other severe punishment if they return to their homeland. The mere fact that life is hard in the homeland because of a depressed economy, a troubled industry, and unemployment is not recognized by Swiss law as acceptable grounds for admitting foreigners as refugees.

Expulsion of those whose applications are denied presents humanitarian problems: some, on return, would certainly be punished by the authorities on various grounds. The problem facing Switzerland cannot easily be solved. To permit a reasonable stay in Switzerland would be humane but would only defer a final and difficult extradition.

7. In 1980, 5950 sales were approved (5906 in 1979) at a total sales price of 1.8 billion francs; 250 ha were involved in these sales (206 ha in 1979). In 1983, the number of approved sales fell to 2495, about 20% less than in 1982.

11.3 PUBLIC HEALTH

The Drug Problem[1]

The illegal entry of hard drugs into Switzerland, their distribution by "pushers" and their use, especially by the young, are problems of the greatest concern. Drug addiction and criminal pursuits—frequently to pay for the drugs—are inseparable parts of the family of drug-related problems that afflict society in many countries. That Switzerland is among the afflicted may surprise many of us who are prone to regard Switzerland as "among the blessed." I regard the drug problem as sufficiently serious to discuss it first before bringing together data on morbidity, mortality and life expectancies, which can be helpful in an overview of public health in Switzerland.

In the city and canton of Zurich alone there were 21 deaths from drug abuse in 1978 and 29 in 1979. The Hirschenplatz in Zurich Niederdorf and the neighbouring streets play a central role as the scene of traffic in drugs in Zurich.

More to the point are data pertinent to Switzerland as a whole. A drug report issued in early January 1981 by the Federal Public Health Service (*Drogenbericht des Bundesamtes für Gesundheitswesen*) examines in detail the Swiss drug scene. A full page summary, published a few days after the report appeared, is very informative.[2] In 1982, no less than 11,951 persons were charged with infractions of the Narcotics Law and, of these, 7676 were convicted. Of those charged with violations of the law, 166 were under 15 years of age, 10,992 were from 15 years to 29, and 713 were 30 years or older. A distinct trend toward the use of hard drugs, especially heroin and LSD (lysergic acid), frequently in combination with alcohol and other drugs, is being observed. The number of deaths in Switzerland from drug abuse was 85 in 1978, 109 in 1982 and 144 in 1983.[3]

The number of addicts, dependent on hard drugs (inclusive of repeated offenders), was estimated at 5774 in 1982 out of a total of 7717 charged with illegal consumption. Although in 1980 there were 24 therapeutic facilities in Switzerland for treatment of the severely addicted, only 258 of those requiring long-continued treatment could be accommodated. An East-Switzerland drug clinic for some 45 patients is planned for 1983. Of course there are in Switzerland many facilities for the care (and punishment) of the users of narcotics: 108 places for counselling and for contact- and ambulatory patients, 24 open therapeutic centers for long-continued treatment as mentioned above, 42 centers for psychiatric services, and 42 other specialized facilities for application of a variety of drug-related measures.

Concern is expressed over the dangerous wave of cocaine addiction, the youthfulness of more and more of the addicts and the increasing use of alcohol along with the drugs. Methadone is used for treatment of heroin-dependence but there is no agreement from canton to canton as to its efficacy. If one may generalize, apparently not more than 20 percent of the hard-drug addicts can be considered cured. Whatever treatment is used, the "relapse quotient" is as high as 80 percent.

Also reported is the disturbing fact that more and more of the addicts become dealers in the drugs, almost forced into the business by the high cost of the drugs on which they are dependent. Hence, the number of "pushers" increases and, inevitably, an increase in the number of addicts follows. Expansion of the market leads to an increase in sales to the young. Curiosity and a willingness to try anything once lighten the task of the pushers.

A long term study of narcotics consumption by young adults (19 to 20 years of age) has been conducted since 1971 by the research division of the Psychiatric Clinic of the University of Zurich. The study, as reported, reveals a marked increase in the use of alcohol, in the number of those who are heavily dependent on drugs, and an increasing trend toward initial use of drugs by an ever younger population. "Of those questioned, one half had experienced their first use of drugs by the age of 16. Seven years ago (1971) practically none of the young women of 19 to 20 years, and less than one-sixth of the young men had had any experience with drugs."

Class distinctions among drug addicts appears to be vanishing. Behavioral problems, common to many, indicate an increase in the proportion of those who are socially disturbed.

The report informs us that the young adults have tried a variety of drugs and other allegedly stimulating agents, some of which can certainly lead to addiction and even dependence. In 1978, hashish had been tried by 19.8 percent of the men, opiates by 3.3, Weckamine (a stimulant of the blood circulatory system) by 5.7, hallucinogens by 6.8, alcohol intoxication by 68.5 (40.8 in 1971), cigarettes by 42.5 (55.3 in 1971),[4] pain-killers by 33.7, and sleeping agents by 4.7 percent. The data for young women differed relatively little from the above except, as might be expected, that pain killers had been used much more than by men (65.5 percent instead of 33.7).

We also learn that the schools have been unsuccessful in prophylactic measures against the use of drugs by the young, and in instruction about the harmful consequences of a drug habit. The schools seem to have done their best; they have acted responsibly and with sincere concern for the welfare of the children. However, the difficulties in overcoming the curiosity of the young and their frequent willingness to experiment with drugs have been insuperable.

Border cities also present their problems. Because of its central position in

Europe, narcotics entering Switzerland illegally flow through to points beyond. Some, presumably originating in Central and South America, enter from the USA.[5] Much is seized by the control authorities, but the amount that escapes detection at control points and is locally consumed is alarming to the country. There is nothing about the problem as observed in Switzerland that sets it apart from drug-related problems in other countries. I know of no data that permit a quantitative comparison with "civilized" countries elsewhere. Professor Meinrad Schär reminds us that within Switzerland itself there is one significant statistic that permits a quantitative comparison: "Whereas in 1968 only 123 cases of illegal possession of narcotic drugs were registered in Switzerland, the number of cases rose to 5725 in 1975" (**315**, p. 223).

Hashish (either as the solid concentrate or as the oil) and the hard drugs are of greatest concern. Heroin, morphine and, as a comparative newcomer, cocaine, are the principal trouble-makers among the narcotics. Hard drugs flow northwards from Italy through the Ticino. Members of an international cocaine ring, based in a boutique in the Lugano area, were arrested in early 1981 in the attempted smuggling of 2.5 kg of cocaine. With the cooperation of the Italian and Ticino police many other arrests have been made but a significant decrease in the traffic in hard drugs on the Rome-Milan-Como axis had not been achieved by 1981. As in other countries, the drug handlers are extending the traffic by reaching down to quite young school children and creating drug dependence, with all its attendant ills, within a group that cannot readily resist experimentation.

LEGISLATION AND THE DRUG TRAFFIC   The legislation designed to regulate the drug traffic is detailed, abundant, and under frequent revision. Penalties for violations are generally severe but may vary from canton to canton. An American, arrested at Zurich/Kloten airport with 6.18 kg of cocaine in his possession was faced with eleven years' imprisonment. In Würzburg (Bavaria) a citizen of Lausanne was sentenced to $8\frac{1}{2}$ years' imprisonment for organizing the smuggling of 6.4 tons (!) of hashish from Syria to the Netherlands.[6] Basel is known to be a center for the smuggling of drugs. From Basel, the end of the important Italy-Basel drug line, drugs are smuggled in for export to the north (France and Germany). It is also a reception point for drugs coming in from Holland or from other countries with shipping up the Rhine. The Basel police, through their narcotics-control branch, have arrested a number of foreign drug handlers engaged in smuggling amphetamine, hard drugs, and other narcotics. The sentences of those convicted are sometimes heavy, e.g. six years' imprisonment for a Portuguese found guilty of the attempted smuggling of one kilogram of amphetamine—the prison term to be followed by life-long banishment from Switzerland.

Ten years' imprisonment and fifteen years' banishment from Switzerland were ruled by a court in Basel against a 38-year old Syrian who had participated in the smuggling and sale of about one kg of heroin. The severity of the sentence was partly due to the refusal of the Syrian to give to the authorities the names of his Syrian accomplices.

In 1982 four drug handlers—two Algerians, one Spaniard and one English woman—were sentenced to 14 to 17 years' imprisonment, having been arrested in Nyon in the act of transporting 4 kg of pure heroin, 600 kg hashish, and 100 kg amphetamine. The sentence, possibly the most severe of its kind in Switzerland, was handed down by a judge in Vevey (canton of Vaud). Through their business "they endangered the lives of some thousands of people" (266).

The number charged with traffic in various drugs in 1980 is alarming: 1875 for traffic in marijuana and/or hashish; 1393 for traffic in heroin (156 in 1973). Traffic in LSD, in contrast, has declined: 183 arrests in 1980 as compared with 702 in 1973.

The drug-related violence associated with the illegal traffic is no different than in other countries. Drug handlers are killed, the users are frequently beaten or killed because of inability to pay for the drugs, violent robberies are committed to obtain money to procure the drugs, prostitution increases for similar reasons, etc. etc. It is a familiar story in most industrialized and "civilized" countries.

The city and canton of Zurich have approved the financing of a home for drug-endangered school children. It is conceived of as a pilot project under medical direction, having as its purpose the breaking of drug dependence. In June 1980, the number of drug-endangered children to be cared for in the home was small—55 or so, but a trend toward increasing drug consumption by school children is recognized.

Baden-Württemberg shares with Switzerland the dubious distinction of being a transit land for the central European traffic in drugs—the axis being from Milan to Frankfurt. In Baden-Württemberg the deaths in 1979 caused by consumption of narcotic drugs totalled 106. Drug-related crimes increased by 26 percent over 1978. A working group of police and customs officials representing Switzerland, Italy, Austria, France and Baden-Württemberg has been organized to develop cooperative approaches in the fight against the illegal traffic.

A United Nations Conference on Narcotics designated India and Turkey as the principal sources of legally produced opium. International concern over the illegal distribution of narcotics has resulted in a reduction in opium production in some countries—even supplies for medical purposes. India, from 1970 to 1978, increased her production from 794 to 1616 tons and satisfied almost two-thirds of the world's opium requirements. But by 1980 the production fell back to 900 tons or less. In the meantime, Australia has entered this profitable business and India's four million opium farmers are under increasing competitive pressure.

MARIJUANA AND HASHISH   While Swiss law treats marijuana offences as severely as offences involving narcotics generally, some of the courts are currently inclined to lighten the sentences of those convicted of possession or traffic in marijuana. Even hashish, in small quantities, is open to question in respect to the punishment involved. In one specific case, the possession of 57 kg of hashish (a small quantity?) was regarded in Basel as deserving of leniency since this "cannot be regarded as an amount of a narcotic drug which can endanger the health of many people."[7] Also at issue in such cases is the belief that the social and psychic consequences, as well as the potential to induce dependence, are distinctly less with marijuana and hashish than with other drugs "(Morphine/heroin, amphetamine/cocaine, and alcohol/barbiturates)."[8] Some jurists have contended that the use of marijuana is less hazardous than alcohol. The Federal Narcotics Commission, in its concern with these problems, is loath to go very far in recommending any liberalization of the laws pertaining to marijuana, hashish, and other soft drugs. The Commission draws attention to the increased numbers of drug addicts, increased seizures of illegal drugs, and a broad increase in drug-dependence with a pronounced tendency among the "soft-drug" users to move on to heroin and other hard drugs. The Federal Office of Public Health, recalling that Switzerland signed an international convention which places hashish among the dangerous narcotics, refuses, on the recommendation of a group of specialists, to approve any action designed to legalize the possession and sale of marijuana and hashish.[9]

Alcohol Consumption (ref. 414 is also relevant)

We should note that in Switzerland, alcoholism is probably a greater health problem than drug addiction, at least there are many more cases of alcohol-induced illness (130,000)[10] than of recorded cases of illegal possession of narcotic drugs (5725 in 1975). Two percent of the Swiss population must be regarded as alcoholics with 1500 new cases per year that require treatment in psychiatric clinics or in special homes for alcoholics (315, p. 223). In 1981, 545 men and 148 women in Switzerland died of cirrhosis of the liver—a positive indication of severe alcoholism. In 1981 the consumption of alcoholic beverages, expressed as pure alcohol, amounted to 11.0 liters per capita (10.3 in 1976).[11] The consumption of distilled spirits equalled 5.3 liters of 40 percent alcohol per capita (4.6 in 1977). Wine consumption increased to 48.4 liters per capita against 43.2 liters in 1976. Beer consumption declined slightly to 70.5 liters per capita.

The statistical yearbook for 1979 reports as follows on the consumption of alcoholic beverages (yearly averages for the period 1971 to 1975): Wine 61.9 liters, cider 9.0 liters, beer 104 liters and distilled spirits (alcohol content, 40 percent on the average) 7.4 liters. These are not per capita data for the entire population but refer only to consumption by the average adult of 18 years or more (341, 1979, p. 163). The Swiss Institute for Prophylaxis of Alcoholism reports that 4.2 percent of the Swiss population consumed 30 percent of all alcoholic beverages in 1977. This would mean that at least one liter of wine or two liters of beer or 0.25 liters of spirits would have been consumed daily by every person in this group. It also follows that 10 percent of the population drink one-half of all the alcohol consumed in Switzerland.[12] Federal Councillor Chevallaz and Director Müller of the Federal Alcohol Administration have advocated restrictions in the advertising and sale of spirits. The Ständerat (Council of States) would amend the alcohol laws by forbidding the sale of spirits in self-service stores (still sold in 1983). They would go much further than was contemplated in a people's initiative against advertising materials for smoking and alcoholic beverages.[13]

The Federal Office of Public Health would like to see a campaign initiated against drug abuse. More and better information for drug-endangered young people would be the objective—not only directed against narcotics but also against alcohol.

The Swiss Organization for Alcohol Problems (SFA) in a survey of drinking and smoking among school children in 1978 obtained information on the habits of 341 young people. Four-fifths of the children between 12 and 16 years of age were reported to drink alcoholic beverages more or less regularly. About one-third of the 16-year old students of both sexes reported that they had been intoxicated at least once during the two months preceding the questionnaire. In German Switzerland about one percent of the 12-year old children drank alcohol daily, compared with two percent in French Switzerland, and six percent in Italian Switzerland (the Ticino). It was concluded that education of the young on the consequences and dangers of habitual consumption of alcohol is needed. While agreeing with the need to increase the dissemination of information on the hazards of habitual consumption of alcoholic beverages, one hesitates to accept evidence stemming from questionnaires that concern personal habits. It is well known that many young people take a curious delight in replying playfully to such questionnaires with little if any regard for the truth.

Drivers of motor vehicles are subject to arrest if their blood-alcohol content exceeds 0.8 parts per thousand. The Federal Council declined to act on a recommendation of two experts in legal medicine in which reduction of the permissible blood level of alcohol to 0.5 per thousand was proposed. The cantons, political parties, and various unions and other organizations recommended by a significant majority that the present limit of 0.8 parts per thousand be retained.

Infectious Diseases

Turning now to a wealth of statistics, we shall begin with infectious diseases (Table 17). These alone must be reported to the Federal Public Health Service. How much weight may we attach to the data? Probably not very much (**315**, p. 222).

Genital herpes, which is very contagious, is now well known in Switzerland. There are as yet no statistics available on the incidence of the disease: at present it is not listed as a disease that must be reported. In many instances, for example influenza, a doctor never even sees some of the victims. Even if there is a medical examination, the doctor may or may not report the case depending upon the type and severity of the disease.[14]

The mere mention of influenza will certainly remind some of us of the terrible epidemic that followed World War I. It appeared in 1918–19 and was probably the "most widespread and most deadly influenza epidemic in history. From 15 to 50 percent of the population were afflicted and the number of deaths was estimated at 20 million" (**1**, p. 45). This exceeds all the combat deaths in World War I. The disease had a high mortality and killed people in the prime of life—20 to 45 years of age. The very young and the very old were usually spared. The disease struck, world-over, in a single blow. In Switzerland, over 21,000 deaths from this epidemic influenza were recorded (**67**). As for morbidity, the number of cases reported to the medical authorities was 664,463. Recognizing that many suffering from influenza

Table 17 Cases of infectious disease reported to the Federal Public Health Service[h]

	1955	1959	1963	1967	Cases 1978	Cases per 10,000 of population in 1978
Acute gastrointestinal infections & bacterial food poisoning	23	130	831	1137	2117	3.3
Chicken pox[a]	3446	3955	3080	3749		
Diphtheria	144	109	49	7	6	0
Encephalitis lethargica epidemica[b]	3	1	0			
Epidemic cerebrospinal meningitis	109	88	187	62	68	0.11
Epidemic dysentery[a]	43	127	215	54		
Epidemic influenza[a]	44,158	39,457	41,185	8192	13,305	21.0
Epidemic hepatitis	3334	1132	1026	1115	262	0.40
Enteritis of young children	—	—	—	—	0	0
Exanthematous diseases	[c] 1293 / [d] 3741	866 / 3108	1358 / 1650	1467 / 2289	3562	5.6
Gonorrhoea[e]	95	67	38		1652[f]	
Infectious diseases of the nervous system					93	0.15
Leptospirosis	36	32	22	23		
Malta fever	3	1	0	0		
Mumps[a]	2577	2330	3097	4069		
Measles[a]	7808	6471	6081	6145	2	0
Paratyphoid fever	182	236	159	50	40	0.07
Parrot fever	1	12	15	3		
Poliomyelitis	919	272	12	1	2	0
Queensland fever	79	36	26	14		
Syphilis[e]	26	34	42		351[f]	
Tuberculosis	2949	2449	2449	1965	1581	2.5
Typhoid fever	102	56	389[g]	64	24	0.04
Undulant fever	170	57	24	31		
Whooping cough[a]	4967	5124	6603	1187		

[a] Plus many unreported cases.

[b] Deaths, averaging about 40 per year (1955 to 1963), were high, reflecting the acute stage, many years earlier, when epidemic sleeping sickness was more common.

[c] German measles.

[d] Scarlet fever.

[e] Cases refusing or interrupting treatment; plus reported but unexamined sources of infection.

[f] As reported from six cooperating hospitals in Basel, Bern, Geneva, Lausanne and Zurich (two hospitals).

[g] Year of the typhoid epidemic at Zermatt.

[h] Rabies is discussed on page 510. Data appropriate for inclusion in this Table are not available to the author.

never even bother to call a doctor (or the doctor does not consider it of sufficient importance to report to the cantonal authorities), the number of cases may actually have been as great as two million, about half of the total population of Switzerland in 1918 (**67**, p. 279).

The data, such as they are, nonetheless permit one to conclude that cases of acute gastrointestinal infections and bacterial food poisoning may be on the increase; this may also be true of mumps. But many infectious diseases are gradually disappearing and some, such as smallpox and poliomyelitis, belong only to the past. The incidence of diphtheria is declining rapidly, measles may be on its way out. Tuberculosis, once a very serious disease, is decreasing—a fact which is also supported by the conversion of more and more sanatoria for tuberculosis into rest homes, hotels, holiday resorts, etc. (**219**, pp. 200–06).

Hepatitis B, not included in Table 17 is, nonetheless, an infectious disease with which the Swiss have good cause for concern: the incidence is about 1500 to 2000 cases per year. Thanks to a new vaccine obtainable in limited quantities from the USA and France, a campaign of vaccination against this inflammatory disease of the liver is being instituted in Switzerland. For the moment, the program will be restricted to high-risk subjects. The persons to be vaccinated are individuals in contact with chronic carriers of the virus, some members of the medical profession, patients who are immuno-suppressed for a variety of reasons,[15] patients in certain other categories, drug addicts, homosexuals with frequent change of partners, and prostitutes. Pregnant women will not be vaccinated, as yet.

One is tempted to predict, and with good cause, that all of the communicable diseases may eventually disappear or be under total control.

Chronic Diseases and Death Rates

The chronic diseases of the heart and blood vascular system, the respiratory system, and the genito-urinary system and, of course, cancer are of greater public interest but data on their incidence are totally lacking. Hospital records, if readily available, would be very informative. At the moment, we must depend on mortality statistics for when one reaches the end of his days, the fact that he is dead, as well as the cause of his death, becomes a matter of record.

This brings us to Table 18. The first eleven entries pertain to diseases which, thanks to modern medicine, are rarely fatal. Smallpox, which has been known for at least 6000 years, is now regarded by the World Health Organization as eliminated. The Horn of Africa, possibly the last stronghold of the disease, has been officially declared to be smallpox-free: no new cases have been seen in the past two years or more. In Geneva and Delhi, vaccine for 200 million persons is in storage—a good precautionary measure. Also to be on the safe side, the WHO advocates a fifteen-year program for the obligatory vaccination of all children.

Not surprisingly, the death rates from leukemia, diseases of the heart and blood vessels, and cancer have increased in the past 50 years. Suicides and fatal accidents, especially traffic accidents, are alarmingly high and may be increasing. Schär reminds us that in describing the health condition of a population one should not rely on the number of deaths due to certain diseases. The age at the time of death must also be taken into consideration. The most reliable criterion is therefore not the mortality itself but the loss of "man-years."

I shall not reproduce the tabulated data presented by Schär but the Table is very informative and should be referred to by those interested (**315**, p. 223).

Poisoning

Poisoning presents a problem of considerable concern to the public health authorities. The Swiss Toxicological Information Center reported 386 deaths from acute poisoning in 1978 and 474 in 1979 (0.75 per 10,000 of 1979 population). Of the 474 deaths, 126 were attributable to exhaust gases and 102 to sleeping agents. Probably most of these deaths were suicidal.

The center responded in 1979 to 17,551 telephone requests for assistance. About half of these phone calls concerned young children up to four years of age. Of the total calls, 62.8 percent were the result of accidental poisoning and 24.7 percent pertained to attempted suicide. While only 1.4 percent of the cases of accidental poisoning had a serious or lethal outcome, 13.4 percent of the suicide attempts ended in death or severe illness. Accidental poisoning in the household is frequently the result of young children opening bottles of medicine or household chemicals and tasting the contents. Sometimes adults are poisoned because of the bad household practice of transferring medicaments and poisonous substances into unlabelled or mislabelled containers. Although poisoning is recognized as a serious problem, in 1981 there were only three fatal cases in the age group under 15.

Most of the poisonings were caused by tranquillizers such as valium and librium. Cleaning agents, as used for kitchen ware, plates, and glasses, were also involved in some cases. Even fertilizers, insecticides, washing agents, bath-water additives, and soap were causal agents. Among laboratory and industrial chemicals, benzene, heating oil, and gasoline were most commonly responsible for poisoning. Mushroom poisoning was not uncommon, and over 40 inquiries were received because of poisoning by bee, wasp, and hornet stings.

Medicaments

Because of the abuse to which medicaments, especially "pain-killers," are subject all analgesics are now (since March 1981) available only by prescription. Over 200 preparations are in the list affected by the decision of the Intercantonal Office for the Control of Medicaments. Exempted from the requirement of a prescription are small packages containing not more than ten doses; they may be sold openly.

Expenditures for medicaments are not inconsiderable. In 1979, the Swiss spent a total of 1.6 billion francs (roughly one billion USA dollars at December 1979 exchange rates). This equals 250 francs ($157) per capita. Sleeping agents, analgesics, tranquillizers and stimulants are the most abundantly used—frequently without a prescription. Insomnia is experienced by many, such that one person in four is a frequent user of sleeping agents. The use of the medicaments mentioned is

Table 18 Death rates in Switzerland[a] (numbers per 10,000 of population)

	1880	1930	1978
Diphtheria	6.12	0.55	0
Erysipelas[b]	0.42	—	—
Enteritis of young children	14.6	1.05	0
Measles	0.84	0.10	0
Puerperal fever	1.27	0.73	0
Poliomyelitis		0.05	0
Scarlet fever	2.66	0.10	0
Smallpox[c]	0.61	0	0
Typhoid fever (inc. paratyphoid)	3.68	0.10	0
Whooping cough	2.05	0.32	0
Tabes (locomotor ataxia)[d]		0.32	0
Other diseases of the nervous system		2.84	4.4
Syphilis		0.42	0.03
Tuberculosis, pulmonary[e]	19.4	9.4	
Tuberculosis, other respiratory	24.0	0.16	0.24
Tuberculosis, other locations		2.8	
Cerebrospinal meningitis		0.12	0.25
Influenza[f]		1.26	0.76
Apoplexy	7.80	5.02	
Pneumonia and other respiratory diseases	24.0	15.2	1.90
Heart disease		15.3	15.6
Arteriosclerosis	7.36	10.2	12.9
Other diseases of the blood-vascular system		1.1	3.21[g]
Blood metabolism		3.15	
Cancer		16.4	20.7
Other malignant tumors		0.73	
Ulcers of stomach & duodenum		0.80	0.60
Appendicitis		1.24	0.09
Nephritis		2.57	1.46
Other renal disease		0.65	
Sex organs		1.03	0.27
Congenital debility		2.50	0.03
Senility		4.20	0.42
Suicide[h]	2.47	2.60	2.40
Traffic accidents[h]	6.70	1.80	2.20
Other accidents[h]		3.90	2.49
Homicide	0.38		
Death by unknown causes		2.85	0.50
Other deaths, medically attested	85.2		
Other deaths, without medical attestation	34.4		
Total deaths from all causes	228	115	92[i]

[a] Sources: Ref. **341** (1894, 1932, 1979). The mortality tables are heavily footnoted. If interested in the detailed definitions of each disease or group of diseases one should consult reference **341** for 1979 (page 69) and 1950 (page 81).

[b] Erysipelas: An infection caused by *Streptococcus* bacteria and having conspicuous cutaneous symptoms. Until the advent of antibiotics it was a serious disease, sometimes being a more generalized infection and occasionally fatal. Not listed in the mortality tables for 1930 and 1978.

more common in women than in men and increases in both sexes with advance of age. (Report of an investigation conducted throughout Switzerland by the Swiss Institute for Prophylaxis of Alcoholism, based in Lausanne. The investigation focused on "drugs in daily life").

Life Expectancies

Tables 19 and 20 bring to our attention the good news. The death rate of infants during their first year of life has decreased enormously during the past 100 years, and life expectancies have increased greatly in the same time span. In all countries where modern medicine and good public health practices have been enabled to work their wonders the statistics tell the same story. Whether further improvements are in store for us in these "good health" countries is doubtful. Infectious diseases are mostly under control and life expectancies are not likely to increase significantly until much more progress can be made in the fight against cancer, leukemia and diseases of the heart and blood-vascular system.

Institutional Care of the Ill

In 1982, 462 nursing homes and hospitals with 76,334 beds were to be found in Switzerland—about 120 beds per 10,000 inhabitants. Admissions totalled 949,373. In other words, and on the average, one person in seven was admitted for institutional care. The average duration of institutional care was 24.4 days. About one-fourth were received in infirmaries and nursing homes and almost as many received specialized psychiatric care. About 6 percent of the beds were provided by health resorts (*Kurort*) where the principal treatment is based on copious drinking of evil-smelling waters from natural springs and restful bathing in warm water from such sources.

The average stay in hospitals was 14.3 days, in infirmaries and nursing homes 205.8 days, and in psychiatric clinics 188.3 days. The total number of employees associated with these institutions was over 101,000 or about 1.5 employed persons per bed (excluding doctors and university docents). This strikes one as a very high ratio. Expenditures for the year totalled 6.10 billion francs or about 280 francs per hospital-day. Expenses exceeded ordinary income by 576 million francs. Of the deficit, 509 million francs were covered by payments from the cantonal govern-

---

[c] Smallpox: Last reported death was in 1926. Not listed in the mortality tables since 1933.

[d] Tabes: not listed prior to 1921.

[e] Tuberculosis: In 1880 only pulmonary tuberculosis (phthisis) is listed; in 1930 and later, other forms and other locations of tubercular lesions are included.

[f] In the influenza pandemic of 1918, deaths from influenza totalled 21,491 (5.5 per 10,000 of population). The number of cases reported to the Federal Public Health Service was 664,463. Because many with influenza fail to see their doctor or the doctor considers reporting to the cantonal or federal authorities to be unnecessary, it is believed that the actual number of cases was probably as great as two million—about one-half of the total population of Switzerland in 1918 (67).

[g] Leukemia, all forms.

[h] In the age group 20 to 39, accidents were responsible for 40 to 42 percent of the deaths in 1974. Suicide came next with 19 to 21 percent of the deaths among women and men, respectively. In the age group 1 to 19, 41.4 percent of the deaths were due to accidents (11, 1978, p. 75).

[i] Deaths from all causes (1965–78): 87 to 93.

Table 19 Deaths of infants, 0 to 1 year of age (numbers per 100 live births)

1876–80	1900	1930	1970	1978
18.9	13.3	5.08	1.50	0.86

ments. The remainder was made up by payments from cities and towns, the Federal Government, corporations, foundations, and private sources (**15**).

For the year 1983, we learn that the number of patients receiving treatment in the Swiss hospitals, infirmaries and nursing homes was 453,183 (**235a**, p. 15). Of the grand total of patients, 137,928 were ambulatory (**235a**, p. 15). Of the total, some patients received more than one treatment. The number of treatments totalled

Table 20a Life expectancies (in years)[a]

At age	1881–88 M	1881–88 F	1921–30 M	1921–30 F	1968–73 M	1968–73 F	1978–79[b] M	1978–79[b] F
0	43.3	45.7	58.14	61.41	70.29	76.22	72.1	78.7
65	9.7	9.9	10.83	11.84	13.32	16.33	14.3	18.0

[a] Source: Ref. **341**, 1981, p. 74.
[b] Source: Personal letter from Professor Schär (13 October 1983).

Table 20b Life expectancies (in years)[a] an international comparison

Country	At age 0 M	At age 0 F	At age 65 M	At age 65 F
Switzerland (1968–73)	70.29	76.22	13.32	16.33
Australia (1965–67)	67.60	74.20	12.20	15.70
Canada (1975–77)	70.19	77.48	13.95	18.00
Chile (1969–70)	60.48[b]	66.01[b]	12.64	14.62[b]
Great Britain				
England & Wales (1976–78)	70.0	76.2	12.50	16.60
Scotland (1971–73)	67.23	73.61	11.90[b]	15.16
Ireland (1970–72)	68.77	73.52	12.41	14.98
Japan (1979)	73.46[c]	78.89[c]	14.75[c]	17.92
Sweden (1975–79)	72.30	78.41	14.10	19.60[c]
USA (1978)	69.50	77.20	14.00	18.40

[a] Source: **341**, 1981, pp. 584, 585.
[b] The lowest life expectancies at either age for all 23 countries listed in the Yearbook.
[c] The highest life expectancies at either age for all 23 countries listed in the Yearbook.

Table 20c Some internationational comparisons (infant deaths in first year of life)[a,b]

Country	1965	1974	1979
Switzerland	18	12	8[c]
Australia	18	16	11
Canada	24	15	14 (1978)
Chile	102	65	38[e]
Sweden	13	10	7[d]
United Kingdom[f]	20	17	13
USA	25	17	13

[a] Source: **341**, 1981, p. 579.
[b] Per 1000 live births.
[c] Also Finland and Japan.
[d] Lowest of all 21 countries listed in the Yearbook.
[e] Highest of all 21 countries listed in the Yearbook.
[f] England and Wales, Scotland, Northern Ireland.

Table 20d Some vital statistics for 1980[a,b] (an international comparison)

Country	Marriages	Live births	Deaths	Birth excess
Switzerland	5.6	11.6	9.3	2.3
Australia	7.3	15.3	7.3	8.0
Canada (1979)	7.9	15.5	7.1	8.4[d]
Japan	6.7	13.7	6.2[c]	7.5
Sweden	4.5	11.7	11.0	0.7
United Kingdom[e]	7.5 (1979)	13.5	12.0[d]	1.5
USA	9.7[d]	15.8[d]	8.7	7.1
West Germany	5.9	10.0[c]	11.5	−1.5[c]

[a] Source: **341**, 1981, pp. 582, 583.
[b] Per 1000 inhabitants.
[c] Lowest of all 20 countries listed in the Yearbook.
[d] Highest of all 20 countries listed in the Yearbook.
[e] England and Wales, Scotland, Northern Ireland.

666,682 (acute cases of which 18,984 were psychiatric) (**235a**, p. 15). For all acute cases, the average duration of institutional care was 14.8 days as contrasted with 280 days for the psychiatric cases (**235a**, p. 119). Chronic cases totalled 5862. The average duration of stay in an institution for this group was 140.3 days (**235a**, p. 355). The number of deaths among all patients was 14,775 (**235a**, p. 305). This voluminous publication of VESKA (*Vereinigung Schweizerischer Krankenhäuser*) lists all the diagnoses reported by the professional staffs in the Swiss institutions for medical care. The data are classified according to the sex and age of the patients, the principal diagnoses, plus any related diagnoses, duration of institutional care, acute cases, chronic cases and ambulatory patients.

Many patients, not in need of hospitalization, are treated in policlinics—a name given to outpatient departments. From rather simple facilities, when first introduced for the poor and to aid in the instruction of medical students, the policlinics have evolved into specialized centers. They are excellently equipped and commonly receive patients referred to them for prior examination by practising physicians: few doctors could afford the expensive and useful equipment found in a typical policlinic. There are at least 18 such specialized centers in Zurich alone.

Dispensaries, functioning as centers where medical or social advice is available, are very numerous and the service is frequently free of charge. Some policlinics, such as in obstetrics and gynecology, may also serve as dispensaries where, for example, advice may be given on nutrition in pregnancy, family planning, and birth control. Others give advice on tuberculosis control, rheumatic disease, or on problems of alcoholism and the heavy drinker. Minor dispensaries which are numerous in the rural areas are run, not by doctors, but by social workers, fully trained nurses, or even nurses' aids with a modest amount of training.

There are many differences among the dispensaries, from canton to canton, and even within a canton—especially in the larger cantons, such as Bern. This variety and lack of uniformity is to be expected in a federated country with 26 autonomous or sovereign cantons—small and large, rich in linguistic, cultural, confessional and historic differences. The health services, in structure and administration, also show considerable diversity for they too have evolved from rather simple beginnings and at different rates of development.

Voluntary organizations are numerous. Intervention by the state has not meant a governmental takeover, but rather the possibility of giving governmental financial assistance by first conferring a legal status upon these organizations. Wherever they have functioned well, it has been considered unwise to tamper with their structure and services. The role of government has mainly been to provide financial aid when an organization could not otherwise discharge its responsibilities well, faced, as they frequently are, with escalating costs and increasing memberships.

Cost of Health Services

Two sets of figures follow. One source reports that such services (*Gesundheitswesen*) in 1979, cost a grand total of 4848 million francs (3080 million USA dollars at the December 1979 exchange rate). This is the sum of expenditures by the Federal Government (33.9), the cantons (3551.7) and the communities (1788.2), corrected for duplicating entries (**341**, 1981, p. 408). The second source gives a much larger total since it includes nongovernmental expenditures for health services. I refer to the Swiss Society for Public Health Policy (*Schweizerische Gesellschaft für Gesundheitspolitik*, or SGGP). From a communication to the *Neue Zürcher Zeitung* (**266**, 3–4 July 1982) and referring to a forthcoming publication by Gygi and Frei and a brochure *Das Gesundheitswesen in der Schweiz* (Basel, 1982), we learn that the total expenditure on health services and facilities in 1980 was 12,364 million francs or 7 percent of the Gross National Product. The total is broken down as follows: hospitals (5673 million francs), doctors (2057 million), dentists, dental clinics, and dental technicians (1196 million), medicines (1733 million), medical faculties in the

Swiss universities (600 million), and other expenses (1105 million). On a per capita basis, the two totals amount to 763 and 1947 francs, respectively.

If expenditures for health services increase at the same rate as between 1979 and 1980, the 1982 expenditure would total 15.2 billion francs, with hospital costs being most heavily responsible for the increase (**266**, 3–4 July 1982). See also **266**, 30–31 October 1982.

A comparison of hospital costs in 1955 (280 million francs) with those of 1980 (5673 million francs) reveals a 25-year increase of over 1900 percent. This is truly an explosive increase attributable to an upsurge in costs of virtually every component of hospital maintenance and services. Although some of the increases may be difficult to justify, it must be admitted that the quality of medical care and of hospital services has improved enormously in the past quarter century.

Other Hazards to Life and Well-Being

Are there other hazards to health and well-being, fatal or nonfatal in outcome, that face the Swiss and the people of many other countries? I have before me a stack of Swiss newspaper clippings and reports of the Swiss Federal Public Health Service. From these one learns that the loud music in youth discotheques is an increasing risk to health: hearing may suffer and inner ear problems can arise; that about 20,000 persons in Switzerland suffer from Bechterev's disease—a chronic and painful inflammatory disease of the spinal column; that the number of drug addicts is on the increase and deaths from addiction or from related causes are distressing in number.

Accidents, leading to injuries of which many are fatal, are disturbing to the authorities in most countries. In Switzerland, from 1969 to 1978, approximately 700,000 traffic accidents were recorded by the police. The result: about 330,000 persons were injured, and 14,590 died from their injuries. In 1978, 33,573 persons were victims, including 4639 pedestrians and 1268 who were killed (352 were pedestrians). Damage to property totaled about 300 million francs (not including damage claims of less than 500 francs). The principal causes of the traffic accidents in 1978 were inattentiveness of the driver, refusal to yield the right of way, excessive speed, unfamiliarity with the road conditions, and drunkenness. The victims were mostly in the age group 15 to 49 (male) and 15 to 29 (female). The year 1972 was the worst in the past 30 years, 77,982 traffic accidents being reported. Of 6310 traffic accidents involving drunkenness of the driver or pedestrian, 5091 were caused by drivers of personal automobiles. Of this group 3320 were tested for blood alcohol content. An alcohol concentration of 1.0 to 1.5 per thousand was found in 1247, and 1.6 to 2.0 parts per thousand in 917 (**341**, 1979, pp. 257–65).

In 1979 over 20,000 drivers of cars had their driving licenses revoked; 43.5 percent because of drunkenness and 48.5 percent because of infractions of driving regulations. About 84 percent of the 20,000 drivers were between 21 and 60 years of age. Of these, one-half were between 21 and 30, the remainder between 31 and 60. Accidents involving railway trains, trams, trolleybuses, and air-borne vehicles are too few in number to discuss in detail: a total of 498 injuries (including fatalities) in 1977 (**341**, 1979, pp. 266–67). The traffic accidents in the streets of the cities and towns receive the greatest attention. From the above data, one may calculate that, on the average, there has been one traffic death on the Swiss streets every 6 hours in the decade 1969 to 1978. According to estimates by SUVA (Swiss Accident Insurance Institute), accidents, however caused, approximate one million per year, of which 3000 are fatal. About 25 percent of the accidents are in places of employment. Of the remainder, traffic accidents are the most common.

With the introduction of speed limits and the legally required wearing of safety belts (Referendum of 30 November 1980) the number of fatal motor-vehicle accidents has been reduced from 1800 in 1973 to 1200 in 1981.

Although society can introduce a number of precautionary measures to reduce pedestrian and vehicular accidents there is little, if anything, that it can do to reduce the number of deaths from avalanches and climbing the Swiss mountains—50 deaths from avalanches and 188 from falls while mountain-climbing in 1978. The Matterhorn alone claimed 15 of the victims.

If we consider only the total number of deaths caused by avalanches and falls while mountain-climbing, the statistics are certainly disquieting:

Year	Total deaths	Deaths per year
1913	36	36
1923–47	1853	74
1948–72	2667	107
1973–79	1089	155

The increase in fatalities appears to be attributable to (a) the increased number of skiers; (b) ignoring of avalanche warnings; (c) carelessness, recklessness, inattentiveness, and lack of experience in mountain-climbing; (d) exhaustion and heart attacks. Forests on the mountain slopes are the best protection against avalanches of snow and ice. Otherwise expensive steel barriers are necessary. The annual cost to Switzerland for avalanche protection approximates (1980) 35 million francs.

Skiing also presents its hazards. Serious accidents are all too common.[16]

Drowning, another cause of death, claimed 47 victims in 1977 and 94 in 1979. Most of these drownings were attributed to recklessness or foolhardiness. Carbon monoxide inhalation causes a few deaths every year among people who fall asleep in a car parked in a closed place with the engine running, or who were sleeping in a mobile holiday van equipped with a propane heater that happened to misbehave and discharged incompletely oxidized gases into the van. Other similar causes of death from exhaust gases or a heating unit have been reported.

Rabies

Rabies made its appearance in Switzerland in 1967. It entered Schaffhausen from southern Germany and now (1981) all of the cantons, with three exceptions, have contaminated zones where rabid animals have been found. In the single canton of Bern, where rabies was first reported in 1976, the Veterinary Office has reported no less than 1100 rabid animals. In Switzerland, 95 percent of the infected animals have been wild. Of these, 85 percent have been foxes. To date only three persons have died of rabies in Switzerland but the Cantonal Veterinary Office in Bern believes that 11,000 persons in the world succumbed to rabies in the 1950s and 1960s.

An unusual and somewhat controversial method of stemming the spread of rabies, especially by rabid foxes, has been used with considerable promise in Switzerland in the last few years. Chicken heads containing live rabies vaccine were widely distributed in a large experimental area extending from Lake Geneva to Lake Thun on the north and the Rhone River to the south and west. Over 30 rabid foxes were collected in this area in 1980 but none have been found in the ensuing 18 months. Presumably the foxes became immune to the disease after eating the bait, thus breaking the transmission cycle of the disease. There is no evidence, despite fears to the contrary, that the harmless rabies virus reverts to virulence in the wild. Over 60,000 inoculated chicken heads were used in the test, distribution being achieved by hand or by helicopter (in the mountainous areas north of the Rhone valley).

Food Additives

The role of additives, as used by the food industry, and their possible hazards are of interest to consumers and public health authorities in a number of countries. Switzerland has been prone to regard their incorporation in foodstuffs with considerable caution and, at the legislative level, to take quite a "hard look" at the problem. At the same time, the use of saccharin and cyclamate as sweetening agents, the latter forbidden in the USA and the former officially suspect, is permitted in Switzerland. The Delaney Amendment to the USA Food and Drug Act concerns carcinogens and leads to a good deal of "overkill," and, in the interest of scientific precision and realism, should be redrafted. I reproduce a Swiss appraisal of the Delaney Amendment, written by a competent scientist whose judgment can be respected:

> . . . the so-called Delaney amendment . . . says, that any food additive that has been shown to cause cancer in people or animals must be barred from commerce. . . . This clause, unfortunately, is scientifically a total absurdity, because by now it should be known that the term "carcinogen" is senseless [when used] without attention to dosage, species and experimental conditions (**39**).

However, the use of diethylstilbestrol in the fattening of cattle is not approved. I have before me a recent article originating in Switzerland which carries the heading "The Hormone Spectre—Toxicologically Disenchanted. Scientific Facts Pertaining to the Controversial Fattening of Calves." And it begins with the arresting statement "If one speaks today of hormones, it is as if one speaks of the most evil poison—of a hormone 'infection' as they say—which gives rise to vague, irrational fears that express themselves in vehement reactions" (**266**, 15–16 November, 1980, p. 35).

In the midst of all the clamor that stemmed from the use of several hormones [oestrogens and the highly active hormone-like diethylstilbestrol (DES)] for the fattening of cattle in feed lots, the voices of scientists could hardly be heard. What was at issue was the abundantly demonstrated fact that the hormones mentioned, added in small amounts to the cattle food, or subcutaneously injected or implanted, accelerate the gain in body weight and reduce the total food consumption.

Equally well known was the fact that DES (as a synthetic oestrogen) given in large doses (100 mg) to women in early pregnancy, induced vaginal cancer in several cases in the daughters born to these women. Years elapsed before the cancer manifested itself, usually in early adult life. Acquainted with this fact, women were quite understandably aroused when the use of DES in the fattening of cattle became widely publicized. Women's organizations and their representatives in government demanded that the use of DES and oestrogenic hormones in the fattening of cattle be forbidden. In 1970 the Swiss parliament reponded by forbidding the use of hormones and hormone-like substances to influence the body weight of growing cattle.

Overlooked in the public uproar was the scientifically demonstrated fact that the quantity of hormones used in the fattening of animals was too insignificant to pose any danger to the health of those who consumed the liver or the flesh of DES-treated animals. For quite some time chemists failed to find even traces of DES in muscle, and in liver the concentrations were barely detectable. But even this was enough, under the inflexible terms of the Delaney Amendment to the USA Food and Drugs Act, to require the Food and Drug Administration to forbid the use of DES in the fattening of cattle in the USA. As the methods used in quantitative analysis improved it became possible to detect less than a billionth part of DES in animal tissues, and these are the quantities to which all the uproar pertains. Overlooked is the fact that several kilos of such meat or liver would have to be eaten to produce readily detectable concentrations of DES. Overlooked also is the fact that several micrograms of oestrogens (50 or so) are produced daily by young girls (also boys) prior to puberty—quantities a thousand times greater than would be present in a kilogram of veal from a DES-fed male calf. It should also be noted that a contraceptive pill contains as much oestrogen as 200 kg of veal from an oestrogen-treated calf.

But the clamor and the turmoil live on. Even in 1980, Swiss women's organizations were calling loudly for a boycott of veal until the authorities could guarantee that veal sold to the consumer was free of added hormones and antibiotics. The law of 1970 is still on the books and is respected by cattle feeders generally but there are a few who defy the ban on DES, other oestrogens etc. The law is difficult to enforce because an inspector cannot stand beside each and every feeder of cattle. And "one bad apple can spoil the entire barrel." Nonetheless, one must ask whether the law is in harmony with the scientific evidence and whether it serves the public interest.

Tetracyclin—a wide-spectrum antibiotic—is used in some countries in the fish-canning industry as a protection against bacterial contamination. Because residues of the antibiotic were found in 1980 in the products of an Italian fish-canning firm, a judge in Modena ordered that the entire stock of the product on sale throughout Italy be seized. Swiss veterinarians on duty at the border were alerted to the problem. Swiss authorities, aware of possible dangers to health that may result from the chronic ingestion of antibiotics, are concerned about the use of antibiotics by industry in the preservation of food products.

Air Pollution

Switzerland, in the 1980s, had eight stations for measuring quantitatively those components of the atmosphere that are regarded as health hazards. Air pollution, caused by sulfur dioxide, oxides of nitrogen, carbon monoxide, ozone and some of the products of incomplete combustion of motor fuel, is a problem of increasing concern in Switzerland as automobile traffic congestion goes from bad to worse, especially in the cities and towns. Dust is a recent source of concern, although it has been emphasized as a health problem for many years. In the early 1980s, dust, originating in the Sahara Desert and some attributed to volcanic activity (Mt. St. Helens in the USA, and also from Mexico, Hawaii, and possibly Mt. Etna) is the newer component of the problem. This adds an unknown amount to the heavy burden of dust particles from traffic in the streets and roadways, and from heating appliances, industry and natural sources (e.g. pollen). Apparently there is no means of alleviating the air-borne contribution from the great African desert and from volcanic activity. Traffic dust and industrial dust are more amenable to reduction.

Abortion

The abortion problem is debated as vigorously in Switzerland as in any other country. The conditions under which a pregnant women may be permitted to have an induced abortion presents problems of considerable concern. Commissions of the Federal Parliament are sharply divided. Some insist upon a federal law to spell out the conditions under which an induced abortion may be permitted, and the punishment to be prescribed for violations of the law. Others insist that the whole problem should be left to the cantons for solution. Only by so doing can the catholic-oriented cantons impose the restrictive regulations and the severe penalties that are favored by the Church while the protestant cantons would be equally free to develop more liberal solutions. Two initiatives, designed to modernize the existing law, voted upon in September 1977 and May 1978, were defeated but the parliamentary debate lives on. Some kind of a compromise will eventually be reached, for in Switzerland compromise is a favored solution of many problems where sharp differences exist, and the Swiss have abundant experience in the art. In 1979 a new initiative under the title "Right to Life" was proposed which would anchor a restrictive solution within the federal constitution.

Homosexuality

Homosexuality, as a social problem, has become of concern to public authorities. Whether it is a public health problem is not conspicuously an issue. In late 1979 the Administrative Tribunal of Geneva ruled that a certificate of "good life and habits may not be denied to a person because of homosexuality." An officer of the police had refused to issue such a certificate to a man because "he was known to be a homosexual and had a [male] friend." The case was appealed, leading to the following decision by the Court:

> when the appellant does not disturb the public order in any way, as the police inquiry has revealed, he ought not to be a subject of prejudice on the sole grounds that he lives differently than the majority of citizens from the sexual point of view.

Concluding Remarks

I have not drawn attention to the wealth of legislation concerning public health which has been enacted in Switzerland. Nor have I discussed the responsibilities and functions of the Federal Public Health Service. The latter is expanded upon in "Science in Switzerland" (**219**, pp. 174–90) though the material is now out-of-date in a few matters of detail. Schär's essay on Public Health in *Modern Switzerland* (**245**, pp. 213–26) can be strongly recommended. It also lists some of the laws, decrees, ordinances and regulations that pertain to public health. The basic law on narcotics is that of 3 October 1951 which has been updated several times by amendments in the 1950s, 1960s and 1970s.

Notes and Comments

1. The statistics in this section pertain to Cannabis products (marijuana, hashish), opium, heroin, morphine, synthetic opiates, cocaine, LSD (lysergic acid), other hallucinogens, amphetamine.

2. Reference **266**, 10–11 January 1981, p. 35.

3. In the first ten months of 1980, West Germany (population 62 million) suffered 410 deaths from drugs. Italy (population 56 million) reported 145 drug-related deaths, while among the five million Danes there were 105 such deaths (**266**, Nr. 25, 1981, p. 9).

4. In mid-November 1981, a regulation concerning cigarette-package labelling came into effect. The Federal Office of Public Health now requires that each package carry the warning "Smoking can endanger your health." This must be printed on each package in at least two of the official languages and in an easily readable type size. Enforcement of this order is a responsibility of the cantons which are authorized to confiscate packages that do not carry the prescribed warning: the Federal Council declares that punishment will follow (**266**, 15–16 November 1980, p. 9).

5. The Middle East at present, is the most significant world-wide source of illegal opiates: opium itself in smoking preparations, morphine and heroin. The amount of heroin reaching Western Europe in the first half of 1980 was 150 percent greater than in the first six months of 1979. Drug abuse is common in the countries of origin. For example, the number of opiate addicts in Iran is estimated to be about one million. Bolivia is a rich and troublesome source of cocaine—partly as the dried leaves of the coca plant for smoking. Marijuana and hashish are the most widely used, or misused, substances within the very large group of drug users (**266**, No. 25, 1981).

6. Marijuana, not hashish (a potent extract of marijuana), judging by the quantity being smuggled, was probably the substance involved.

7. Reference **266**, 24–25 May 1980; **266**, 5–6 July 1980.

8. Reference **266**, 24–25 May 1980, p. 52.

9. Reference **357**, 22 April 1981.

10. Of the 130,000 alcoholics (suffering from alcohol-induced illness), 9 percent were women (**327**, p. 217).

11. Topping the list of 25 European countries is France: 16.4 liters per capita (**327**, p. 217).

12. The Federal Alcohol Administration derived a net income of 276 million francs in 1979–80 from the taxes on distilled spirits. One-half of such income must be distributed among the cantons, and these

are required to spend one-tenth (13.8 million francs in 1979–80) to combat alcoholism (Art. 32 bis, par. 9 of the Federal Constitution).

13. Reference **329**, 1978, I, pp. 1097–1108.

14. Some doctors consistently ignore the ordinance of the Federal Council on reporting communicable diseases, insofar as "grippe-like diseases" are concerned. It is alleged to be too much trouble, especially since "*grippeartigen Erkrankungen*" is too diffuse a term—so unprecise as to cover possibly 200 cases per week in the winter months in Zurich canton alone. Some doctors also resort to the argument that they work for their patients, not for the officials, and they refuse to spend the time required to fill out reports pertaining to something as vague as a grippe-like disease (**266**, 5–6 Feb. 1983).

15. From 1980 to May 1984, in Switzerland, the acquired immune-deficiency disease syndrome (AIDS) had been diagnosed in 28 persons—25 males and 3 females.

16. Head injuries from collisions and falls while skiing are all too common. In the six ski seasons 1974–75 to 1980–81, in the canton of Graubünden alone, 523 skiers required medical treatment because of head injuries: 51 required an operation and 12 died. In three recent ski seasons, 105 children under 16 years of age with head injuries were treated in a single clinic in the Graubünden. Because brain injuries are frequently associated with irreversible loss of certain functions, the wearing of protective helmets by skiers has long been urged by the International Ski Association (**266**, 29–30 January 1983).

11.4 THE PLAGUE

Introduction

In several of the preceding chapters, I have written much about the plague. Its pandemic nature, its malignancy, and the long-sustained ignorance as to its causation have combined to make bubonic and pneumonic plague the most feared of all the diseases that have afflicted mankind. At least this was so until the mid-twentieth century when most of the questions concerning the plague had been answered: proof that it is a communicable disase, the causal organism isolated and described, the rat proven to be the principal carrier, the rat flea identified as the transmitting agent from rat to man, and several antibiotics found to be effective in the therapy of both bubonic and pneumonic plague.

Although the disease ceased to be a problem in Switzerland in the early eighteenth century, years were to elapse before fears of a recurrence in epidemic proportions disappeared. In Asia the plague lived on and only the determined and stubborn use of quarantine measures—directed especially against vessels, from Asia particularly, entering European ports—saved Europe from further infestation. Rats, especially rats from ships, came under suspicion and rigorous protective measures, partly embraced by the quarantine, helped to save the day.

The ravages of the plague in Africa and Asia were well known in Europe.[1] Despite the precautions that were taken against a return of the plague in epidemic dimensions, the fact that millions died of the disease in Asia kept the public health authorities "on pins and needles" for decades. At least ten million people in India died of the plague between 1898 and 1918 (**386**). In 1894, the disease hit Canton and, in a short time, 60,000 people died. In 1910, an epidemic in Manchuria killed 65,000 people in three months. In May of 1894, Hong Kong experienced an invasion of the plague with terrible results. Alexander Yersin, about whom more will follow, was sent to Hong Kong to study the epidemic and learn what he could about the disease. In spite of many difficulties with officialdom, but with some bribery, he obtained a fresh bubo. With a minimum of equipment he found the bubo to contain a "veritable purée" of microbes, all identical in appearance. This was confirmed several times and was soon followed by his discovery of the same microbe in the cadavers of rats which in great numbers were dying in the city. On 30 July 1894, Yersin's findings were reported to the *Academie des Sciences* in Paris and published shortly thereafter (**398**). A little later, a more extensive report was published (**399**).

517

The discovery of the rat flea as the transmitter of the disease from rat to man was the work of Ogata (276), who also was able to confirm the important finding of Rennie (304) that in any epidemic the death of rats in great numbers preceded by two or three weeks an outbreak of the plague in the human population.

Since I do not intend to deal further with clinical questions it is sufficient to sum up the status of therapy in 1957 as reviewed by Bloomfield (44): "Immune" sera were studied for many years but none were very effective, unless used early, in which case they sometimes had a slight protective and therapeutic effect. Sulfonamides were effective, especially in mild cases and if used early in the disease. The antibiotics were by far the most potent weapons. They cured advanced septicemic cases of bubonic plague and were equally effective in the pneumonic form of the disease. In the latter, the rat flea may be innocent because transmission from person to person is through coughed-up sputum.

Alexander Yersin

And now we return to Yersin (1863–1943). It is appropriate to do so since he was born in Switzerland (Lavaux, canton of Vaud). He studied medicine in Paris. While doing an autopsy on a victim of rabies, Yersin was unlucky enough to cut himself. He was promptly inoculated with the anti-rabies vaccine developed by Pasteur just one year after it had been successfully used in the treatment of the first of Pasteur's patients. Possibly this experience explains his passionate interest in bacteriology. In 1887 he studied under Robert Koch in Berlin. On returning to Paris, Roux accepted him as an assistant. Three memoirs on diphtheria were published by Roux and Yersin in 1888, 1889 and 1890. Next we learn of him as a doctor on a ship in service around Saigon and Haiphong. He soon became attached to the Pasteur Institute of Indochina, headed by Calmette. Several trips into the interior introduced him to bubonic plague—a few isolated cases having appeared in the preceding ten years. This brings us to 1894 and his memorable research in Hong Kong described above.

Yersin died in Nha-Tsang, Indochina, in March 1943 at the age of 79. Most of the biographical material on Yersin has been drawn from a small book edited by Noel Bernard (36).

Plague in the Twentieth Century

Probably few parts of the world have escaped the plague. Even as late as 1920–23, isolated cases were reported in Trieste, Hamburg, Glasgow, Marseilles, Naples, Sydney (1903), Melbourne and Adelaide (1903) and New York (1900). A few cases were reported among the San Francisco Chinese in 1900 and again in 1907. But plague of the twentieth century was not in epidemic form, pehaps because rats do not migrate as they once did, and man has also succeeded in protecting himself from rats and rat bites. In the USA a full-blown epidemic has not been reported, but there are certainly a few near-misses on record. In 1924, there were 34 deaths from the plague in Los Angeles. In 1900 an outbreak in San Francisco achieved some notoriety because public officials refused to acknowledge the presence of the plague even when the disease had obviously appeared in their midst (278).

A great classic on the history of the plague is the monumental work of Georg Sticker (**348**). A short but well documented chapter on the plague is in the book by Bloomfield (**44**, pp. 47–60). Finally, reference should be made to the work by Pollitzer (**413**).

Notes and Comments

1. Some of the early records of the plague are confusing, but others are quite unambiguous. Many deaths, with typical swellings of the lymphatic glands, were described as early as 280 B.C. One of the most terrible epidemics of bubonic plague is known as the pestilence of Justinian (531–80). It originated in Egypt, and spread to Europe where it is alleged to have killed half the population (**1**).

11.5 TRANSPORTATION

In General

For an historical background on the railways please refer to Chapter 10. Data on 45 railway companies plus 20 subsidiaries are included in the *Statistisches Jahrbuch* for 1900 (ref. **341**).

It all started in 1847–50 in a line from Zurich to Baden with a total trackage of 25.2 km. By 1870 tramways came into being (5.7 km). Relevant information for 1880, 1898–1900, 1960, and 1980 is presented in Table 21. Reference should also be made to Table 22. Table 23 pertains to all transportation except by water and air. The tramways carried 295 million passengers in 1977 while trolley buses (city and regional) carried about 240 million passengers in 1977 and lost about 30 million francs in so doing. The railway system, in 1978, had an operating profit plus other income of 184 million francs. However, after taking into account capital costs, amounts written off to cover depreciation and improvement of facilities, the system showed a loss of about 620 million francs. The Swiss railways received a total federal subvention of about 1236 million francs in 1978 of which 756 million pertained to covering of deficits. In October, 1980, fares on the federal railways were increased an average of 6.1 percent and were to be increased a further 8.8 percent in March 1982 (decision of Board of Directors on July 2, 1981).[1]

Currently, the Confederation is deeply interested in arriving at an all-embracing policy which will rationalize and harmonize the interests of the Federal Government, the cantons, the politcal parties and the transport organizations in all aspects of transportation. The cost of the total transportation is staggering. How much of the cost should be borne by the Federal Government? To what extent should the cantons share the burden? Involved are all kinds of transport systems: by rail, by trolley buses, and on roadways, or water.[2] Attention focuses principally on the publicly owned systems, but there are pressures to include also the privately owned systems. Such matters of concern as energy conservation and protection of the environment are included in the study. The most serious issues are financial: sharing of the costs, planning of the highway network, and distribution of construction and maintenance expense between the federal, cantonal and local governments, the future of the cantonal motor-vehicle taxes, the tax on motor fuel, and the heavy-traffic tax.

Table 21   Federal railways

	1880	1898–1900	1960	1980
Length of lines (km)	2449	3091	2919[a,b]	2923[a,b]
Employees	—	—	40,934	38,367
Train-kilometers (in thousands)	—	—	79,553	96,287
Passengers (in thousands)	25,500	62,000	225,780	216,302
Passenger-kilometers[c] (in millions)	—	—	6998.4	9179.0
Freight (in thousands of tons)	5850	14,500	29,645	46,831
Operating income[d] (in thousands of francs)	—	—	1,079,541	2,651,615
Operating expense (in thousands of francs)	—	—	782,666	2,480,332
Operating profit (in thousands of francs)	—	—	296,875	171,283
Operating profit plus other income (in thousands of francs)	—	—	331,987	285,506
Total expense[e] (in thousands of francs)	—	—	300,600	878,958
Net income (in thousands of francs)	—	—	31,387	− 593,452
Accumulated debt (in millions of francs)	—	—	− 103.3[f]	6383.2[g]
Total accumulated railway debt[h] (in millions of francs)	—	—	453.0[f]	10,497.0[g,i]

Source: **341**, 1981, pp. 244, 245, 246.
[a] Includes railway lines owned or leased by the Federal Government and foreign lines in Switzerland.
[b] Almost entirely electrified.
[c] One passenger-kilometer means one passenger transported one kilometer.
[d] From passenger traffic, freight transport, and other sources.
[e] Including capital costs, amortization, and other expenses.
[f] 1965 year.
[g] 1979 year.
[h] Including privately-owned railways.
[i] The increases in railway debt in the 1970s have been rapid and large. The total accumulated debt in 1979 (10.497 billion francs) represents an increase of 6.08 billion francs in only four years.

Clearly repugnant to many Swiss is the vision of a new and ponderous bureaucracy that would certainly arise if all transport systems were to be brought under a single administrative roof. The legal and constitutional questions that would have to be solved are likewise recognized as thorny and very difficult. The optimism with which the upper levels of bureaucracy regard the whole scheme may rest on shaky foundations.

The relative importance of railway transport in going to or from a place of employment is of some interest. In 1974, only about 6.3 percent of the working population used the trains. About 30 percent of this group expended 30 to 60 minutes in getting to work, and 45 to 50 percent were aboard the trains for over one

Table 22 Number of railway transportation units

	1880	1898–1900	1977–78
Steam locomotives	524	1128	141
Electric locomotives	—	16	1056
		(in 1905)	
Motor carriages (rail)[a]	—	—	677
Passenger train coaches	1624	2797	4784
Passenger seats	72,165	129,300	373,000
Passengers transported by trains[b]			
(thousands)	25,500	62,000	297,000
Freight cars[c]	8,500	13,700	36,600
Goods transported (in thousand tons)	5,850	14,500	52,200

[a] *Treibwagen.*

[b] More accurately described as passengers × trips (number of different passengers multiplied by the average number of trips per passenger). Thus, for railway trains, 800 trips per year by the average passenger in 1977–78 is indicated: which is reasonable for a population of commuters, plus tourists and non-commuting inhabitants. For trolley-buses, the comparable figure is 3150, where the total number of rides in 1977–78 was 240 million, and seats plus standing room totalled only 76 thousand. For *Luftseilbahnen* the corresponding figure is 1060 which represents in large part, the number of trips on a ski lift which the average person in an active skiing population might make in the course of a year. This number is inflated because many ascents are made by people who are headed for a restaurant at the top (e.g. the Schilthorn) or who seek only a good vantage point to enjoy the view.

[c] *Güterwagen.*

Table 23 Length of lines (in kilometers)[a]

	1880	1898–1900	1977–78
Normal gauge railway lines	2449	3091	3600[b]
Narrow gauge railway lines	48	507	1389
Cogwheel trains[c]	27	105	97
Cable trains[d]	—	—	701[e]
Tramways[f]	12	276	168
Trolleybuses[f]	—	—	331
Autobus lines, privately owned[f]	—	—	1583
Autobus lines operated by the postal service			
(Postautos)[g]	—	—	7535
Automobile enterprises operated by concessionaires			
(regional and cross-country)	—	—	3371

[a] Source: **341**, 1980, pp. 241, 243.

[b] Includes privately owned railway lines.

[c] Most mountain railways operate by cogwheels and are electrified. One exception: the old-fashioned steam-engines train from Brienz up the Rothorn.

[d] *Seilbahnen, funiculaires.*

[e] Mostly aerial (*Luftseilbahnen*) for ascent of mountainsides. In 1977–78, they carried a total of 70 million passengers (please see footnote b, Table 22)—15 million in summer, 55 million in winter.

[f] For local traffic only.

[g] A total of 6500 stopping places in 1979.

hour en route to work. The private automobile in 1974 was used by 39 percent of the working population in going to work in trips of a few minutes to more than an hour. Trams, buses, and postautos were used by some 12.4 percent of the employed. Approximately 26 percent went by foot, most for less than 30 minutes but a small percentage kept it up for more than an hour. Ordinary bicycles and motorcycles were the favored transport vehicle[3] of about 16 percent (**11**, p. 47).

The postautobuses permit access to a host of villages which, otherwise, would be deprived of virtually all means of public transportation. The 1300 buses travelled a total of 45 million km in 1979 and carried 59 million passengers. Of course, one can go by foot, and, for many Swiss, walking is a pleasure, especially if on holiday.

There is also the lowly bicycle ("pushbike") and the motor cycle, though the topography of Switzerland is not conducive to their extensive use in mountainous areas. Even so, in 1978, the number of pushbikes was equal to about 30 percent of the population—one bike to 3.5 people. Motor cycles were in use by not more than nine percent of the population—one motorbike to eleven inhabitants. In late 1983, about 40 percent of the inhabitants had a car (22 percent in 1970). For all of Europe, only West Germany (the Federal Republic) was more heavily motorized.

The use of the streets by private cars, trams, buses, other motor vehicles, bicycles and pedestrians presents a variety of problems. In Switzerland noise is heartily disliked. It is a very distinct consequence of traffic in the streets, which is today the most important and obnoxious source of noise in Switzerland.

Traffic Accidents

Traffic accidents, especially among the young and middle-aged (15–50 years), claim many victims. Traffic deaths in 1930 totalled about 700. However, in 1978, 1268 were killed in street and highway accidents, and 32,305 were injured (**341**, 1979, p. 264). To appreciate the significance of these figures, one should note that the number of fatalities approximates the total number of deaths (1365) from infectious diseases (including tuberculosis). Current data suggest that the greatest danger is to be riding in an automobile or on a bicycle, or to be on foot. He who rides a bicycle in the heavy traffic turmoil of many city streets is a real gambler: his life is at stake. A number of journalists were led by the Velo Company on a hair-raising journey over the streets of Zurich's inner city. Out of this rather terrifying experience is emerging a series of proposed safety measures to add to the peace of mind and life expectancy of all concerned.

The number of victims from traffic accidents appears to have reached a peak in 1971 (38,950). Surprisingly it has since decreased, rather erratically, and was reported to total 33,573 in 1978 (**341**, 1981, p. 268); all of this despite a 60 percent increase since 1970 in the number of motor vehicles[4] (2,342,600 in 1978) (**341**, 1981, p. 235). The authorities attribute the decrease to the introduction of speed limits on the streets and many suburban roads. So, why not decrease the speed limit further? The compulsory use of safety belts in autos has had a somewhat favorable result, though this compulsion is resisted by many.

There is much voter opposition to a proposed 50 km/hr speed limit for urban traffic. Highway traffic now bypasses most population centers. Level crossings of railway lines are gradually being eliminated where road traffic is deemed to be too heavy. More traffic signals, security-oriented, are being introduced. Safety belts and the obligatory use of helmets by drivers and passengers of motor cycles is also contemplated. The 50 km/hr speed limit is currently being tried out in about 100 cities and towns, since most of the traffic accidents are in population centers. Exceptions to the reduced speed limit are necessary on some roads, but are too detailed for present purposes. The experiment was to continue until 1982. If successful, a further reduction to 40 km/hr was proposed by some. The obligatory use of safety belts by automobile riders has been a sort of "off again-on again" requirement. This and some of the other safety measures are opposed by many on the grounds of a bureaucratic infringement of personal freedom. On the other hand, it is clear that the auto driver and passenger must exercise more selfdiscipline and personal responsibility or the law will step in.

Air Pollution

Air pollution by partially oxidized hydrocarbons, carbon monoxide (CO), nitrous oxide, and lead compounds is a problem but less so than in many large cities in other countries. Even so, the output of CO by motor vehicles increased eightfold between 1950 and 1970 (**11**, pp. 50, 51). In May 1982, the Federal Council published a new ordinance pertaining to air pollution by the exhaust gases emitted from motor vehicles. Effective 1 October 1983, all new models of vehicles allowed in Switzerland may not emit more than 2.1 gm of hydrocarbons, 24.2 gm of carbon monoxide, and 1.9 gm of oxides of nitrogen per kilometer of travel. Four years later the permissible limits will be lowered to 0.9, 9.3 and 1.2 gm respectively. Importers of motor vechicles will be required to place at the disposal of the Federal Government, for testing purposes, a prescribed number of each new model imported (**357**, May 26, 1982).

Tunnels

In a country as mountainous as Switzerland, tunnels are essential. There are at least 12 Alpine tunnels, varying in length from 19.8 km to 3.7 km, for rail traffic. Simplon I and Simplon II are the longest in the world—each being 19.8 km. The well-known Gotthard tunnel (15.0 km), opened in 1882, is the second oldest railway tunnel in the world.[5] A second Gotthard tunnel (for motorized road traffic) was opened in September, 1980. It is 16.8 km in length and runs from Goeschenen in Uri to Airolo in Ticino. Eleven years, $416 million, and 19 fatal accidents to workmen constituted the cost in time, money and human lives.[6] The tunnel lies on the busy route from Italy to Germany and Scandinavia. It is a valuable commercial asset: heavy trucks no longer have to be loaded on trains for passage through the Alps. For better or for worse, this new autobahn link between the Ticino and the great transalpine part of Switzerland to the north will have a tremendous impact on the inhabitants of the Ticino.

Another tunnel through the Furka was to be completed by January 1982.

Construction was commenced in 1970 at an estimated final cost of 74 million francs. But the inevitable happened. Unanticipated costs and, in 1980, the inflationary spiral required several supplementary credits by parliament—most recently in January 1980, when a heated debate over the scandal-enveloped (*Skandalum-witterten*) tunnel ensued in the *Nationalrat*. The final estimate, then submitted, was 300.4 million francs. Extending from Oberwald in upper Valais to Realp in Uri, the 15.4 km tunnel was almost fully bored, with only 1.17 km remaining (January 1980).[7]

Finally, another railroad tunnel is under study. Either the Gotthard massif or the Splügen on the Italian border will probably be chosen. The latter would provide communication with Italy by a line from Thusis to Chiavenna. Discussions are under way with the many cantons that are interested and with Germany, Austria, and Italy. A decision had been expected in 1981. Another proposed tunnel that has aroused considerable controversy is the so-called Rawil tunnel. It would be required for the construction of part of the national highway network, N 6, which would connect the Bernese Oberland in Valais with Wimmis near Spiez in the canton of Bern. The highway would follow the beautiful Simmental and, after penetrating the mountain range by the Rawil tunnel, would emerge in the Rhone Valley. The building of the N 6 is vigorously promoted by the Valais government and the Pro Rawil Committee of Valais. The construction is vehemently opposed by the Association Pro Simental. The Association has launched a popular initiative which by 1 October 1982, had received over 135,000 signatures, including 5000 from Valais. The initiative reads: "Between Wimmis and the Rhone Valley a national highway through the Simmental may not be built or promoted." This would be an amendment to the Constitution. If the initiative is approved it would spell an end to the project.

Cable Cars

As one might expect, the *Luftseilbahnen* are very numerous. Carriages dangling from steeply ascending cables are to be seen on many mountainsides. They provide access to numerous ski slopes, to interesting places for hikers, and to spots that command magnificent views of the countryside. Several of them lead to a well-situated restaurant at the top of the ascent. Among these is one on the Schilthorn at an elevation of 2970 meters above sea level. It is served by the Stechelberg-Schilthorn *Luftseilbahn*, which is the longest in the Alps. It provides a "close-up" view of the Eiger, Mönch, and Jungfrau just across the Lauterbrunnen valley at a distance of 10 to 15 km from the Schilthorn.

Navigation

Navigation of the lakes, rivers and even on the high seas (by the Swiss maritime fleet of 29 ships) is reasonably impressive. A total of 123 ships plied the waters of 13 Swiss lakes in 1977. Steamships first appeared on the Swiss lakes in the 1820s (on Lake Geneva in 1823, Lake Constance in 1824, and Lake Maggiore in 1826). By 1899 104 steamships (mostly paddle-steamers) on 15 lakes transported a total of 4.97 million passengers. The 104 ships had a total freight-carrying capacity of 3900 tons. How much they actually transported is not reported in the Statistical Yearbook for 1900.

The statistics for 1940 do not include the Aegerisee, Lake Lugano and Lake Maggiore. The 13 reported upon were served by 108 ships with places for 49,350 passengers. The total number transported was 4.64 million, which suggests that the average passenger may have made 94 trips if all places were occupied.

Traffic on the Rhine is enormous. In 1978, a total of 8950 ship departures (motor ships, touring boats, and barges) from the port of Basel were recorded; almost half were attributable to some 438 ships of Swiss registry. Only eleven of these were passenger vessels. Virtually all but these eleven were tankers, barges, and freighters. The total number, 438, has remained almost constant for at least 20 years.

One must mention that Switzerland also has an ocean-going fleet of more than 30 ships with a total tonnage between 400,000 and 500,000.

Air Transport

Switzerland's central location in western Europe favors relatively heavy traffic by air. Of 40 European cities, Zurich ranks as eighth in air transportation, measured by either passengers or freight transported. London, with three commercial airports, is by far the largest with about three to four times as many passengers, or as much freight, transported. Zurich and Geneva have the principal airports, with Basel providing service to about one-tenth as many passengers as Zurich. In 1978, Swiss and foreign-based airlines carried to and from Switzerland a total of about 11.2 million passengers—about ten times as many as in 1955. Air freight transport approximated 320 thousand tons in 1978 as compared to 24 thousand tons in 1955. In 1922 Swiss and foreign airlines transported about 4600 passengers to and from Swiss airports. Freight transport was almost negligible until 1928, when it totalled a little over 4000 tons.

Chartered planes from the three airports carried, in 1978, a total of 1.8 million passengers and 6.4 thousand tons of freight. Privately owned planes carried 382 thousand passengers. We may conclude that a few more than 13 million persons were in the air over Switzerland at some time or other in 1978, uncorrected for the number of those who made multiple flights. We also learn that in 1978, the airplanes serving Switzerland had a total passenger-carrying capacity of 16,250,000. But the number actually carried was 10,149,000.

Because of airport noise at Zurich-Kloten and Geneva-Cointrin a surcharge was added to the landing fees for planes of many different types at these two airports. The surcharge became effective in late 1980, and runs from 100 to 300 francs for planes of Class 1 to Class 4. Some of the newer planes (DC-10, L-1011, B 747-200 and A-300) belong to Ideal class 5 and escape any noise surcharge.

Swissair is aggressively expanding its services and modernizing its fleet. Deliveries of DC9 "Super 80" jets began in late 1980, with Swissair receiving the first aircraft. Ten of Swissair's DC9-32s (half the fleet) were sold to Texas International Airlines for $62.5 million. The purchase of two extended range DC10-30s[8] and four Boeing

B747-257s with elongated upper decks at a cost of $600 million was approved in July 1980. Swissair took delivery of two DC-10s earlier in 1980. These are being refitted to match the capabilities of the DC10-30s. Four more B747-275s are on option for delivery in 1986–88. In early 1979, Swissair placed a firm order for ten wide-body A310-220 Airbuses with an option to purchase ten more. These will go into regular service between 1983 and 1987 on Swissair's busiest European routes and in the Middle East. Balair, based in Basel, added a new DC10-30 to its fleet of aircraft in February 1979. With a total seating capacity of 345, the plane was used initially for two special round-the-world trips via Zurich, Bangkok, Hong Kong, Tokyo, Honolulu and San Francisco.

Officialdom in Switzerland looks askance at the USA policy of airline deregulation and the possible elimination of price controls. The Swiss share the basic competitive philosophy of the former American civil aviation policy toward "a regulatory regime which does not unduly hamper competitive, innovative and flexible airline management." It is feared that USA policy would risk the degeneration of free competitive pricing into a catch-as-catch-can situation for survival, with a serious reduction in service and safety standards" (**158**). As for freight and merchandise transport, we learn from the same source that in 1977 a total of 319.1 million tons (90.8 million in 1950) were transported: 12.8 percent by rail (20.3 percent in 1950), 78.6 percent by street and highway vehicles (72.7 in 1950), 4.5 percent by ship (7.0 in 1950), 4.0 percent by pipeline (0.2 in 1963, none in 1950), and 0.1 percent by air (0.0 in 1950).

Highways

Construction of the national network of highways (*Autobahnen*), a major project of the Federal Government, was initiated in 1959. The total cost of the far-reaching system was estimated in 1963 at 12,500 million francs. In 1980 the estimate was revised upwards to 31,191 million. The enormous increase (150 percent) is largely attributable to inflation, but beyond this many other factors have done their bit: widening of highways—previously planned or in existence—to carry additional lanes of traffic, conversion of mixed traffic roads into *Autobahnen*, changes dictated by requirements to protect the environment, construction of more tunnels than first planned, unusual difficulties imposed by geography and geology in some areas and increased safety installation in the vicinity of large population centers.

Apart from cost, the legal and political difficulties are great. The cantonal governments treasure their "sovereignty," and must be wheedled and coaxed into acceptance of trans-cantonal routes and construction plans. The local governments of communities alongside these national highways must also be heard. Osogna, a small village in Ticino, has fought strenuously for eight years to prevent the autobahn reaching from Basel to Chiasso to use the 15 km stretch of valley between Biasca and Bellinzona. Near Osogna, the left bank of the valley is narrow and 56 percent of the Osogna soil will be absorbed by four great traffic arterials (road and rail). With the battle now won by the Federal Government, the last link in this north-south autobahn can be constructed. As the planner said, "Never, in my long activities as an expert in Switzerland and abroad, have I witnessed such a case" (**363**).

The system is developing slowly but surely. A national network of 1836 km had been planned, but the future will certainly bring additions. In 1972 the amount expended on the network was 2785 million francs. The net expenditure in 1979 was only 1160 million, and in 1984 it may be zero. This situation, pleasing to the Federal Government, results from new sources of income for highway construction: a motor-fuel tax and a special fuel-tax supplement to customs duties. Together the two contributed 1502 million francs in a 1980 surcharge, at a cost to the motorist of 0.57 francs per liter. As may be expected, the government refrains from adding to the national debt by a crash program of construction. Year by year, it builds as much as is financially prudent. The 1980 revenue of 1502 million francs exceeded the 1980 expenditures on construction, maintenance, and administration of the network by about 380 million francs—a source of income used to reduce the heavy advances by government in the years preceding the special supplementary motor-fuel tax.

The Federal Government, ever embarrassed by its fast-emptying treasury, warns all concerned of a parliamentary initiative which will eventually come before the people. If approved, there will be an increase in the charges imposed on cars and trucks for use of the national highways.[9] A charge for use of the tunnels in also contemplated. The overall result may be an addition of 500 to 600 million francs per year to the federal income (**329**, II, 1422–39, 1981).

Notes and Comments

1. The Federal Council, yielding to considerable pressure from the unions and the administrative authorities (*Direktionen*) of the postal/telephone/telegraph services and the railway employees, has agreed to reduce the work week for all Federal Government personnel from 44 hours to 42. The reduction which will be effected in 1984 and 1985 will add greatly to the expenses of the Federal Government. The 1982 deficit for the railway system, the SBB, is expected to add over one billion francs to the system's accumulated debts (cf. Table 21). Inflation, high wages, and generous vacation policies are having the anticipated effect. With respect to vacations, every federal employee receives an annual four weeks of vacation to age 49, five weeks to age 50, and six weeks to age 60. Wages, in terms of real francs, increased an average of three percent on 1 January 1982.

The Minister of Finance, concerned, as well he might, by the deterioration in Switzerland's financial situation, is determined to balance the country's budget by 1986. Without a drastic cutting of costs, the country's deficits will be increasing by over two billion francs per year by 1986. Administrative expenses, foreign aid, and spending for defense should all be reduced, so we learn, and the automatic mid-year increases for federal employees should be abolished. Revenue might be increased appreciably by higher fuel-import duties and higher license fees for heavy vehicles. Not mentioned, apparently, was the anti-competitive position in world trade created by wage scales that are the highest among possibly all industrial countries; her exports are threatened by high costs of production. Instability in the value of the Swiss franc in relation to foreign currencies certainly does not ease her import/export position. As long as the "float" persists, all countries—not simply Switzerland—cannot time their imports and exports without encountering the financial hazards encountered by constantly fluctuating exchange rates.

2. A mixed subway-surface system to serve the city of Zurich, its suburban communities and, ultimately, through regional lines, much of the canton, has been under consideration through the 1970s. The estimated cost in November 1980 was 653 million francs, of which the federal railway system would

provide 100 millions. The cantonal payment of 553 million was to be subject to a cantonal votation which might or might not express approval. The whole project, especially its financing and political problems, has been riddled with controversy from the very beginning.

3. The well-known Velo is increasingly popular for use within cities and towns.

4. "Motor vehicles," in this context, includes trolleybuses, motorcycles, motorized agricultural equipment, and motor vehicles of the army.

5. Completion of the tunnel and initiation of the Gotthard railway in 1882 were festively celebrated in 1982. Many changes have been made in the 100-year interval to improve the service afforded by the railway: much heavier locomotives (up to 10,600 horsepower) to enable heavier trains to travel at higher speeds; installation of equipment to permit trains to follow each other in more rapid succession; improvement of performance of fixed installations to permit two or more trains to travel in the same track between two stations, etc. It is now theoretically possible for as many as ten trains to travel simultaneously in the tunnel.

In the future, improvement of the service may necessitate a low-level tunnel through the Alpine massif which, in effect, would convert the mountain railway into a level-road line. The cost would be enormous but the savings in operating costs would possibly justify the investment.

6. By way of contrast, the 1882 tunnel led to the death, during construction, of 177 (or more than 300) workmen (two dubious estimates). Some died from an intestinal disease which afflicted many and was frequently fatal (**266**, 9–10 January 1982).

7. Completed and officially opened in July 1982. Final cost, 318.5 million francs.

8. Swissair and Balair are satisfied that the DC10-30 is one of the safest of machines. Compared with the orginal DC-10s (186 tons), one of which crashed in Chicago, the DC10-30s are heavier (252 tons) and the engine mountings are better.

9. An annual tax will be imposed on all heavy vehicles using Swiss national highways. All private cars must carry a vignette (cost Sfr. 30) to permit use of the national highways. Both measures, good for 10 years, applicable to cars of Swiss or foreign ownership, were approved by the people in February, 1984, for implementation on 1 January 1985.

11.6 COMMUNICATION

In Switzerland, as elsewhere, people communicate by letters, postcards, news-papers, magazines, other forms of printed matter, by telegrams, telephone, radio, television, and by the non-instrumented use of the spoken word.

The Postal Service

The inland postal service in 1978 handled a grand total of 1875 million pieces of letter mail, postcards, and printed matter. In 1899 the grand total was only 166 million. The population, meanwhile, had almost doubled. The service to and from other countries handled a total of 180 million pieces in 1978 as compared with 38 million in 1899.

Magazines and Newspapers

During the first 78 years of the century the number of magazine and newspaper subscriptions increased almost tenfold, from 116 million in 1899 to 1082 million in 1978.

Telecommunication

The most dramatic increase has been in telephone installations: from 35,300 in 1899–1900 to 4,292,000 in 1978. The Swiss data suggest that telephone usage began in 1882–85: 2596 telephones had, by then, been installed. The rapid increase in telephones had an adverse effect on traffic in telegrams. At the turn of the century the total number of telegrams sent and received inland and abroad, was approximately four million. Except for atypical increases in 1919 and 1920 to somewhat over eight million per year, the total reached a peak of about six million per year between 1910 and 1930. Thereafter the number steadily decreased to about three million in 1978, including about one million wireless dispatches (radio) to foreign destinations. This marked decrease in telegraph service is attributable to increased use of telephones and telex installations from 1955 onwards.

The Swiss post and telecommunication service provides a pervasive range of services. There are numbers for help with leaky central heating, for cars that break down in the middle of the night, for the nearest pharmacy open on a Sunday, or for the latest winning lottery number. There is also a number for tomorrow morning's wake-up call, and a number for election results. Financial-service numbers will give up-to-date foreign-exchange rates and stock-market bulletins. A "helping hand" service offers private, anonymous, and denominationally neutral advice if you find yourself in "moral distress." A call to 111 will also get you a mountain-rescue dog.

Radio

The radio in 1930 was found in only one household in ten. By 1973 the radio concessions had increased to an average of about 1.5 radios per household.[1] Television concessions, which totalled 920 in 1953, rose to almost two million in 1978–80, or about three for every ten inhabitants: approximately one per household. Except for the PTT (Post and Telegraph system), radio and television broadcasting is a monopoly of the Swiss Radio Corporation.

Control of the Airspace

How can a country regulate and control what goes on in its airspace which reaches infinitely upwards? Almost since the advent of program broadcasting by radio and television, national airspaces have been invaded by foreign transmitters. In Switzerland, "Radio 24," with its Italian-based broadcasting station only 6 km from the Swiss frontier, has been busily beaming POP programs, 24 hours per day, into Switzerland. These are being rediffused through many cable networks which have chosen to insinuate the programs into those of Swiss origin. The PTT and concerned Federal Government departments charge that "Radio 24" is in violation of international conventions. The legal position of the sender requires clarification. In 1979, the Italian department of post and telecommunications ordered "Radio 24" to broadcast its programs only into Italy. The promoter of "Radio 24" claims that there is no legal basis in Italy to justify any intervention against his project. The Swiss complaint has been received by the Milano Court of Administration which is expected to hand down a decision in the near future.[2]

Austrian television authorities have filed a complaint with the Swiss Federal Tribunal charging that the PTT and a cable network have been feeding the programs transmitted from Austria into Swiss cable networks without paying the appropriate charges—a form of piracy.

Beyond avoidance of payment, there are many cases on record wherein a sender in one country has offended another country by unfriendly, inaccurate or hostile broadcasting.

The problem is not new. During the Olympic games in 1924, a radio reporter, determined to report the football game between Switzerland and Uruguay, was expelled from the stadium by the Paris authorities. Resourceful, as reporters frequently are, he broadcast his comments from a balloon. Transmitters in ships anchored beyond the coastal waters of a State have also been used to feed programs or propaganda where the sender may wish. In World War II, USA Stations broadcast the "Voice of America" to other countries and Japan made frequent use of "Tokyo Rose" for anti-USA propaganda.

Direct Broadcasting Satellites

A major problem in competition stems from the Direct Broadcasting Satellites (DBS) which serve as super stations. The existence of local cable networks and "pay TV" systems may be in jeopardy. North and South America, for example, are served by a DBS sending facility that operates on a 400 Megahertz band between 12.3 and 12.7 gigahertz in addition to a band between 11.7 and 12.1 gigahertz. It is estimated that the antenna and apparatus industries would enjoy a USA market of 25 billion dollars if every TV household had its own satellite terminal. Some authorities regard satellite-television broadcasting as totally incompatible with the locally oriented structure of present-day television services. Nonetheless, Switzerland is much interested in the television-satellite project, Tel-Sat. Its proponents look upon Tel-Sat as a medium for the "European Mission of Switzerland," whereby many millions of French, German, and Italian television fans can happily tune in on the Swiss view of the world (**266**, 24–25 May 1980).

The international conventions governing the use of national air space by radio and television transmitters are known to be inadequate, because the problem constantly acquires new dimensions.

Copyright

Copyright, as generally understood, confers to an author the exclusive right to either permit or prevent any exploitation of his/her work. In Switzerland, the right to forbid is a principle of the current Federal Copyright Law of 7 December 1922; there are few exceptions that permit a breaking of the law. In 1980 the Federal Court decided that the transmission of radio and television broadcasts by big cable-TV companies to the subscribers represented re-broadcasting and was therefore subject to the permission of the author or his successor in title. Hence, the rights of an author extend to modern communication techniques. This is a logical consequence of the monopoly an author has over his work. A conflict clearly arises between copyright and the need for free access to protected works that are considered indispensable for public distribution. The question is whether copyright, i.e. the private interest in the control of works, has to capitulate to the public interest in unrestricted communication. The Federal Court has clearly denied this. Apparently, in Switzerland, this conflict of interest will have to be resolved by legislation. In certain cases a compulsory license to permit access to stated works of public interest may have to be granted. Whether or not an author shall enjoy, in all cases, a right to share in the profits accruing from re-broadcasting will have to be decided.

The Swiss Intellectual Property Office, with responsibilities in matters pertaining to copyrights and trade marks, is of the opinion that the contemplated legislation must provide for a functional royalty-collection system. The 1980 Annual Report by the Office, upon which this section is based, does not state whether the proposed royalty collection system should also be responsible for the collection of royalties on photocopies or other reproductions of works in print that are under copyright protection (**14**).

Use of the Spoken and Printed Word

And now we come to communication by the spoken and printed word. First of all we must examine the multilingual character of Switzerland. Table 24 provides the statistical data that are essential for an understanding of rather remarkable changes in the usage of various languages. Table 24.1 indicates that in 1960 and 1970 the census revealed a very substantial increase in the proportion of residents whose mother language was Italian or a language other than those listed. From Table 24.3 it becomes clear that the explanation resides in a substantial influx of Italians and others.

Switzerland experienced a serious labor shortage which became most severe in the 1960s and continued until the mid-1970s. It was a period of rapid economic growth. The incoming Italians were largely employed by the construction industry. The hotels employed many Spaniards. The columns headed "Other" point to an influx of non-Italians that was significant even in 1950.[3]

Government policy, beginning in 1959 and spurred on by two political parties and a series of popular initiatives, was directed to ending the threatened "foreignization" of the country. The total number of aliens declined from 1,064,562 (16 to 17 percent of the total population) in 1974 to 1,012,710 in 1975 (**168**). The various initiatives and government resolutions were all rejected by popular vote. It required an economic recession, including a moratorium on new construction, to achieve a substantial reduction in the number of aliens. By December 1980, the alien population fell to 883,837—about 14 percent of the total population.

The Federal Constitution declares that German, French and Italian are the

Table 24   Languages in Switzerland[a] (numbers per thousand of population)

24.1 Mother tongue of the resident population of Switzerland					
Census year	German	French	Italian	Romansh	Other
1900	697	220	67	12	4
1950	721	203	59	10	7
1960	693	189	95	9	14
1970	649	181	119	8	43
24.2 Mother tongue of resident Swiss citizens					
1910	727	221	39	12	1
1950	741	206	40	11	2
1960	744	202	41	10	3
1970	745	201	40	10	4
24.3 Mother tongue of resident foreigners					
1910	486	153	321	2	38
1950	401	157	362	3	77
1960	275	78	541	1	105
1970	191	82	497	1	229

[a] Source: **341**, 1979, p. 27.

official languages of the Confederation. Participants in parliamentary debates may speak in any of these three languages and all publications of the Federal Government must appear in all three. In the Federal Tribunal also, the three official languages receive equal recognition. In the army, "the language of command is the mother tongue of the men in the given unit," though when different linguistic groups are "together in larger units, orders are translated" (104). The rules and regulations of the army appear in the three official languages.

The Swiss, for whom French is their native language, have a problem which is not always appreciated. It besets especially those who are in Parliament or those who are obliged to visit the German-speaking parts of Switzerland frequently. In brief, they are at a serious disadvantage if they are not conversant in both German and the dialect (*Mundart*). In Parliament, not only is much of the business transacted in German but occasions arise when the speakers lapse into dialect. If one hopes to be fully accepted socially or be on the best of terms with his fellow Parliamentarians or business associates in industry and commerce, a knowledge of the *Mundart* helps mightily.

It will, of course, be apparent that this linguistic burden that seems to weigh heavily on the people of *Suisse romande* also has its counterpart with the Ticinesi. Italian, like French, is an official language, but to get along optimally in *Suisse allemande*, linguistic competence in both High German and *Schwyzerdütsch* is necessary.

Because Fascist Italy sought to have Romansh declared an Italian dialect, thereby establishing a claim, however dubious, to the canton to Ticino and the Romansh-speaking parts of the Graubünden, the Swiss Federal Constitution was amended in 1938 by a referendum which resulted in German, French, Italian and Romansh being declared national languages. By this act, the Romansh-speaking population, possibly numbering only 40,000 or so, gained political and national recognition. Although the Federal Government is not thereby obliged to publish its official documents also in Romansh with its two or three dialects, important orders-in-council appear in the official languages but also in one of the Romansh dialects (104).

Communication between the Federal Government and the individual cantons is conducted in the principal language of the canton. Thus, German is used for 19 of the cantons, French for six, and Italian for one. A number of the cantons are virtually unilingual (e.g. 80 to 90 percent). In such cases the dominant language is the official language of the canton and is used by the canton's schoolteachers.

Romansh

Obviously, Romansh is no longer the dominant language of the Graubünden. Between 1880 and 1970, about 40 communities in which Romansh had previously been the language of most of the inhabitants, became predominantly German- or Italian-speaking (11). At present, about 58 percent of the total population of the canton is German-speaking; 23 percent prefer to use Romansh and 16 percent are Italian-speaking (327, p. 89).

Persistent and tireless efforts are being made by concerned individuals and the Rhaeto-Romansh League to save Romansh from extinction. At present Romansh is the mother tongue of 40,000 to 50,000 of Graubünden's 162,000 inhabitants. In 1850, when the population of the canton was only 90,000, Romansh was the native language of more than half of the canton's population. By 1980, the absolute number of Romansh-speaking people in the canton remained almost unchanged, but the proportion had decreased to one-fourth of the cantonal population. What can be done to check the decrease and, hopefully, save the language from extinction? Several suggestions have been put forth: (a) persuade the Federal Government to recognize Romansh as an official language, thus permitting its use in parliamentary debates and before the Federal Tribunal, and also requiring the publication of many official documents in the fourth language;[4] (b) require the teaching of Romansh in the public schools; (c) create a Romansh university and provide government funding for a Romansh newspaper; (d) establish small factories in the Romansh-speaking areas to lessen the population drift into the towns where Romansh is replaced by German; (e) develop from the two dialects a single uniform Romansh language; (f) increase the annual federal subvention to the Rhaeto-Romansh League from the present level of 450,000 francs to 1.9 million francs;[5] (g) protect the children in the Romansh areas from television with its all-German-language programs.

It should be noted that Romansh is the oldest in Switzerland of the four national languages. The fear that the cultural heritage in this ancient language may be lost forever is widespread in parts of the Graubünden. The canton has taken steps to preserve the language by establishing kindergartens for three- to six-year old children in which Romansh is the language employed. This should provide a base for further instruction in Romansh in the primary schools. In early 1981 the Romansh-language kindergartens numbered 80 out of a total of 219 kindergartens of all sorts in the canton. Regrettably, many of these children never hear the language at home; their parents and the older children are usually German-speaking. Two hours in the morning and two in the afternoon (for three years) constitute the total exposure of these young children to their mother tongue (**266**, 24 March 1981).

Dialects

The linguistic structure of Switzerland would be far from adequately described if we considered only the four national languages. The dialects, which are numerous, are found principally in the German-speaking areas. A foreigner, even though well versed in German, would be justifed in concluding that these dialects must have originated among creatures from outer space.[6] Actually, these Swiss-German dialects are ancient residues of Middle High German (A.D. 1200 to 1500). Especially in the rather isolated mountain valleys, their original forms of pronunciation and vocabulary have been well preserved.

A peculiarity of the German Swiss is that he speaks his Swiss-German dialect not only in conversation but also in many cantonal parliaments, on public occasions and, sometimes, even in church. For the school-child, standard German is tantamount to being a foreign language. (104)

A Zürcher understands Basler Deutsch and vice-versa. And so on for Berner Deutsch, St. Gallen Deutsch, etc. The dialects may not be thought of as the language of only the so-called "common people." They are used at all social and professional levels when the true German Swiss are in conversation. In the presence of any to whom the dialects are incomprehensible, speech is likely to shift, politely, into German, French, or English. But note that linguistic assimilation, meaning a high level of competence in the dialect of the community, is required of those who seek Swiss citizenship.

The dialects are regarded as the *Mundart*—you speak them but you do not use them in writing. German is the *Schriftsprache* of the German Swiss but dialects are conversational. It is said that Swiss writers speak, think and dream *mundartlich* but, when facing the typewriter, their thoughts, feelings and dreams become *schriftsprachlich*: they emerge from the typewriter in High German (141).[7]

This is not to deny the existence of dictionaries of the dialects, of grammars unique for certain regions and dialects, of language atlases and of monographs which probe the depths of the dialects. Remarkable in this context is the "Friedli," a seven-volume work devoted to Berner Deutsch prepared by Emanuel Friedli (1846–1939). Friedli lived in seven different towns and villages in the canton of Bern and noted the varieties of Berner Deutsch as he moved from place to place; finally, with a subvention from the cantonal government, the first four of the seven volumes on Lützelflüh, Grindelwald, Guggisberg, Ins, Twann, Aarwangen, and Saanen were published between 1905 and 1914. Then came the First World War, costs sky-rocketed and additional financing was needed. A private foundation, the Berner Deutsch Society (*Bärndütsch Gesellschaft*), managed to raise the money, permitting "Twann" to appear in 1922, "Aarwangen'" in 1925, and "Saanen" in 1927. The seven places differ significantly from each other in physical environment, in the principal occupations of the people, and in folklore. Thanks to photo reproduction, the seven volumes in their original brown colour are again available (140).

Ticino also has its *Mundart* and *Schriftsprache*. Unlike German Swiss where the dialects are used by people at all social and occupational levels, the Italian Swiss dialects are basically used by those who do not seek a higher education. They constitute the forms of speech of the less educated. Entrance into various professions and occupations requires much more schooling and total competence in the use of good Italian, especially that of Tuscany. In respect to language, Ticino lies historically in the region radiating out from Milan. Its dialects are largely those of Lombardy (266, 31 May–1 June 1980, p. 37).

Notes and Comments

1. The per-household figures require a substantial, but undetermined correction for installations in business offices, hotel rooms, etc.

2. On 25 November 1980, Radio 24 was closed by order of the Italian authorities. But, on referral to

the highest Italian court of appeal for such cases, Radio 24 came away the winner and by January 1981 was again enjoying "business as usual."

3. The data for 1920, 1930 and 1941 are omitted: the first 40 years of the century reveal no significant changes in distribution of the linguistic groups.

4. Within the Graubünden, Romansh is recognized as an official language by the cantonal government.

5. The cantonal government in a supporting letter to the Federal Council requested also that the Italian-speaking minority be assisted by a corresponding increase in the modest support currently extended to Pro Grigioni. The cantonal government also declared its willingness to double its own subventions to these two organizations if the Federal Government would do likewise.

6. A Russian engineer with great competence in 38 foreign languages, overheard a conversation between two guests at an adjacent table in a restaurant in Irkutsk (Siberia). The sound of the peculiar language in which the strangers conversed bore no relationship to any of the 38 languages that the Russian knew so well. Later, in English, he asked the strangers about the conversation, only to learn that they had been speaking in their native Swiss dialect. He was amazed to learn that the dialect stemmed from German. "But German was the first foreign language that I learned. It is surely an unknown language from Asia or Africa." The Russian engineer, incidentally, was professionally engaged in Moscow as a translator of international scientific and technological articles appearing in a variety of foreign language periodicals (357, 9 June 1982). Swiss business people and diplomats have long since known that use of a Swiss dialect when abroad is the best protection against unfriendly or undesirable listeners.

7. But this requires some qualification. Despite the manifest difficulties in spelling out the strange-sounding words that characterize the dialects, the last two decades bear witness to valiant efforts by a dozen or so writers to do just that. Poetry is the principal literary form in which *Mundart* has appeared in print. Many of the jokes in the weekly *Nebelspalter* are also in dialect.

11.7 INDUSTRIAL PEACE, EMPLOYMENT AND UNEMPLOYMENT

Introduction

Since 1937, strikes and boycotts in Switzerland have been so few and so inconsequential that their impact on the economy has been negligible (Table 25). One can date the beginning of industrial peace with precision. It was ushered in auspiciously and formally on 19 July 1937, when a Peace Agreement in the Swiss Engineering and Metalworking Industries was signed by Konrad Ilg (1877–1954), on behalf of the employees' union and by Ernst Dübi (1884–1947), representing the corresponding association of employers. Later, other unions of employees and other associations of employees accepted, essentially, the rules of the Peace Agreement of 1937 in matters of mutual concern to employers and employees.

Unions of Workers

The unions were the first to appear in Switzerland. Toward the end of the 1880s, the Metalworkers' Union in Winterthur succeeded in forming an all-Swiss Metalworkers' Association. In 1915, the Association merged with the Swiss Watchmakers' Association. By 1919, the membership of the Swiss Metalworkers' and Watchmakers' Association (SMUV) had expanded to over 84,000[1] and by 1963 it exceeded 136,000—the largest association of employees in Switzerland.

For some years the union was aggressively antagonistic to the employers of their labor. Its long-term objective was proclaimed to be "the preparation, in collaboration with the international proletariat, of the workers' takeover of production and the elimination of class domination" (**360**, p. 12). The Rules of the Union, currently in force since 1948, have been purged completely of such political elements. They are limited to a safeguarding of the workers' economic interests within the existing economic order.

Associations of Employers

The combative attitude of the trade unions in the early days compelled the employers to form their own organizations. Strikes were numerous and the employers were powerless against the combined strength of the workers. In the chaos and unrest that characterized the times during the First World War, employers were entirely on the defensive. In 1918 a national general strike erupted. The firms constituting the Employers' Association suffered a loss of 215,000 worker-days. The striking workers lost in wages 2.5 million francs. Note that 31 strikes in 1930, involving 6397 workers, led to a loss of 265,695 worker-days (Table 25).

Table 25 Collective labor conflicts in Switzerland leading to strikes of one day or more from 1930 to 1982[a]

Years	No. of strikes	Enterprises involved	Workers involved	Worker-days[b] lost
1930	31	322	6397	265,695
1931	25	161	4746	73,975
1932	38	198	5083	159,154
1933	35	267	2705	69,065
1934	20	163	2763	33,309
1935	17	82	874	15,143
1936	41	302	3612	38,789
1937	37	404	6043	115,648
1938	17	38	706	16,299
1939	77	7	238	4046
1940	6	12	578	1480
1941	15	36	722	14,311
1942	19	31	822	4030
1943	19	114	1069	12,050
1944	18	186	1324	17,690
1945	35	179	3686	37,187
1946	55	443	15,173	184,483
1947	29	745	6963	102,209
1948	28	463	4277	61,408
1949	12	139	853	41,113
1950	6	68	288	5447
1951	8	70	985	8469
1952	8	47	1207	11,588
1953	6	513	2079	61,124
1954	6	283	2997	25,963
1955	4	4	430	1036
1956	5	15	286	1439
1957	2	3	71	740
1958	3	3	815	2127
1959	4	15	126	1987
1960	8	20	214	1016
1961	—	—	—	—
1962	2	2	163	1386
1963	4	73	1120	70,698
1964	1	4	350	4550
1965	2	2	23	163

Table 25—*continued*

Years	No. of strikes	Enterprises involved	Workers involved	Worker-days[b] lost
1966	2	2	38	62
1967	1	1	65	1690
1968	1	1	70	1785
1969	1	1	33	231
1970	3	3	320	2623
1971	11	13	2267	7491
1972	5	5	526	2002
1973	—	—	—	—
1974	3	34	299	2777
1975	6	6	323	1733
1976	19	492	2395	19,586
1978	10	13	1240	5317
1980	5	330	3582	5718
1982	1	1	55	550

[a] Source: *Bundesamt für Industrie, Gewerbe und Arbeit,* Federal Office for Industry, Crafts and Labor; **341**, 1981, p.403; **76**, p. 187.
[b] Number of strikers multiplied by the number of days that a strike lasted.

The General Strike

The strike broke out at midnight on 11 November 1918 in Zurich. The press reported that over 250,000 workers, men and women, participated. Police and elements of the militia were called out by the Federal Council to prevent the troubles that would ensue if any of the demonstrators gave violent expression to their feelings in an atmosphere wherein mob hysteria was to be feared. After three days the demonstrators capitulated and the strike ended abruptly.

What caused the strike and what did the participants hope to achieve? The causes were almost certainly rooted in the economic turmoil and social unrest that seized the whole of Europe as the World War of 1914–18 came to an end. Thousands of men, their military duties now terminated, were suddenly thrown into the labor market in countries, ravaged by war, in which industrial activity was totally disrupted, distorted by four years of war, and partly in shambles.

Switzerland was by no means untouched by the war. The loyalties of the German-speaking and French-speaking Swiss were severely shaken and challenged by moral and historic attachments to one side or the other. This aspect of the war as it affected Switzerland is expanded upon in the section on neutrality in this chapter (11.22).

But there were other effects of the war which were widely experienced throughout the country. Forced, as Switzerland was, to supply the belligerents with various supplies, shortages of this and that persisted throughout the war. All of this was aggravated by a desperate economic situation in which food prices and rents had doubled during the war while wages had only slightly increased.

In brief, we are concerned with effects of the war that shook the whole of Europe and which found expression in forceful demands on government to solve speedily the employment problems of the worker (jobs and wages) and the food shortages of entire populations. The strike, about which we are seeking answers, can only be regarded as a massive demonstration by a deeply troubled people determined to make government realize that solutions of the problems were urgently necessary. The so-called Action Committee in Olten had combined the call for a strike on 11 November 1918 with a general proclamation to the Swiss people in which nine demands on the Federal Government were set forth. Most of the demands were quite reasonable and one of them, the introduction of proportional voting in election of the *Nationalrat* (National Council), was soon accepted by government and became effective with the *Nationalrat* election of October, 1919. There was nothing in the demands that savored of an overthrow of democratic government and introduction of a dictatorship of the proletariat.

The latter is important to any analysis of the claim that the general strike was motivated by the bolshevists who were still struggling to consolidate their position in Russia. It is true that Lenin was in Switzerland for quite some time and did not leave for Russia until 9 April 1917, accompanied by 30 radical Russian immigrants. The revolution in Russia had begun on 15 March 1917 and the bolshevists assumed the power of government on 7 November 1917. As for Lenin, who despised Robert Grimm (one of the far-left Swiss activists),[2] it is by no means clear that he was pressing for an overthrow of democratic government in Switzerland. It is more likely that he wanted multinational and neutral Switzerland to be the seat of a European bolshevist information service—a distribution center for revolutionary propaganda to European workers, especially of the Entente States. Switzerland was also needed by Russia as a sort of window on events in western Europe.

Be all this as it may, Swiss revolutionaries were to be found who advocated an overthrow of the democratic government of Switzerland and establishment of a dictatorship of the proletariat. Fritz Brupbacher, for example, a practicing physician in Zurich-Aussersihl, was a co-editor of the *Revoluzzer* ("the Revolutionary"), and in the 1920s he served for some time as a communist member of the Zurich City Council. In his diary for 2 January 1918 he spelled out a detailed program for a takeover of the government, pursuant to indoctrination of minorities with the idea of a proletarian national strike in the bolshevist sense.[7] His program, in 15 or 16 parts, included the following: occupation of the telegraph facilities to permit communication between leadership groups in each of the large cities; seizure of munition depots and procurement of machine guns; imprisonment of the government; occupation of the police stations, the banks, food stores; rationing of houses, apartments, and clothing; takeover of railway stations, freight depots and grain in storage.

The handwritten diary, held in Zurich's social archives, appears as document 17 in Gautschi's publication of documents pertaining to the general strike (ref. **412**, p. 61). References **411** and **412** are indispensable as scholarly and thorough analysis of the general strike. Additional relevant information on the role of Lenin, his followers and opponents is to be found in the book by Senn (ref. **415**).

Economic Distress

1932 was a year of world-wide economic distress. In June of that year, demonstrations of workers in Zurich were attended by considerable violence and property damage. A country-wide treaty which gave promise of improving the wages and bettering the employment of members of one of the unions within the parent association of Swiss Metalworkers' and Watchmakers' unions, was opposed by a Communist-led membership in Zurich. This very active splinter group endeavoured for weeks by manifestos, fiery publications (e.g. *Kämpfer*), a strong supporting letter from Leo Trotsky, and many demonstrations in the streets to convert the workers and their unions to communism. The effort failed completely. A communist party, from 1967 to 1978, held 4 or 5 seats out of 200 in the *Nationalrat* (House of Representatives) but none in the *Ständerat* (Senate). It has ceased to be a threat to industrial peace.

Arbitration

A major dispute, apparently the last, arose in 1934 when the employers contemplated reducing wages to match the reduced cost of living. The Federal Ministry of Economics, through an *ad hoc* arbitration commission, succeeded in solving the dispute after long and difficult negotiations. However, this was followed in 1936 by a Federal Decree that empowered the Ministry "to resolve as final arbitrator, collective wages disputes which cannot be settled by agreement between the parties" (**360**, p. 14). This action by the government did not rest well with employees or employers. Contrary to the provisions of the Federal Factories Act, the decree called for compulsory State arbitration instead of a conciliation system on a voluntary basis.

This erosion of contractural freedom in employment relationships had the remarkable effect of bringing together the Employers' Association and the Employees' Union, SMUV, in a common resolve to work out an agreement covering working relationships. Discussions were held in March 1937, between National Councillor Konrad Ilg, President of the Employees' Union and Dr. Ernst Dübi, President of the Employers' Association. The ice was broken, the discussions were fruitful, and to the immense surprise of all interested parties, the Peace Agreement was signed on 19 July 1937.

The Peace Agreement

The time was ripe. Konrad Ilg, with many years of experience as a trade union leader, recognized that everything in the past achieved by the Union had resulted from negotiations. He also knew of "no single strike in the history of our Association that has been a major success in important trade union matters" (**360**, p. 15). Communist infiltration of the Union was constantly attempted and required the Union officials to be on the alert and to defend against such attempts by appropriate action. The seizure of power in Germany by the National Socialists introduced a new threat of infiltration against which defensive measures by the Union were required. But the Union survived and prospered.

On the employers' side, Ernst Dübi, as President of the Association held an unusual amount of power. During the economic crisis of 1932, and in the negotiations with Konrad Ilg in 1937 he emphasized the necessity of joint action by employees and employers; in their own self-interest and the overall interests of the country, they must work together. He regarded his position in the Employers' Association with a sense of mission. At the General Meeting of the Association on 9 July 1937, with 137 members present, the draft Agreement was approved with only three negative votes and six abstentions.

At the General Meeting of the Employees' Union, the draft Agreement was approved unanimously and in anticipation that "the whole labour force will put its weight behind its loyal and effective implementation" (**360**, p. 17).

This brings us to the Terms of the Agreement.

First, a preamble declares that the parties endorsing the Agreement are The Employers' Association of the Swiss Engineering and Metalworking Industrialists and The Union of Metallurgical Industrialists of the Canton of Geneva as one party, and four workers' unions [named in the Agreement] as the other party.

The two parties declare their intention to settle differences of opinion or disputes through the terms of this Agreement so as to maintain absolute peace for its entire duration. It is important to note that labour boycotts, strikes, and lockouts are ruled inadmissible—a slightly weaker declaration than to resolve never to resort to such measures.

Article 1 provides that disputes shall first be referred for settlement to workers' committees and the employers' representatives within the enterprise itself. Workers' committees shall be appointed in all enterprises sufficiently large to warrant such committees. Each committee shall be appointed by the workers within the enterprise.

Article 2 provides that a stated dispute shall be submitted next to the executives of the respective parties for examination and settlement if no amicable agreement has been reached by recourse to the first approach (Article I). The executives are restricted to disputes concerning general wage modifications, normal working hours, wage-fixing and piecework systems, and to the implementation of a variety of special agreements, including vacations and compensation for public holidays; employers' contributions to the workers' sickness insurance fund; payment during absence in consequence of marriage, birth, death and military service; working hours; and allowances for children.

Article 5 provides for referral of a dispute to a Conciliation Board if the executives are unable to reach a settlement satisfactory to the two parties. Questions concerning the interpretation of the Agreement shall also be referred to the Conciliation Board.

Article 6 deals with the structure of the Conciliation Board: a chairman of magisterial standing appointed jointly by the two parties, and two other members appointed by the chairman from separate lists of proposed persons, the lists being submitted by the parties in dispute.

Article 7 states that if the recommendations of the Conciliation Board are unacceptable to one of the parties in the dispute, an arbitration award shall be pronounced provided that this solution has previously been declared to be acceptable to both parties.

Article 8 sets up the machinery for the final step—in disputes that still remain unsettled, and wherein the difficulties are manifestly serious. In such a case, one of the parties may call for a special Arbitration Board whose terms of settlement of the dispute shall be declared binding without the previous consent of both parties. This special Arbitration Board shall consist of a chairman of magisterial standing appointed by the two parties and two competent judges appointed by the chairman from two lists of judges proposed by the two parties. No discussion of the matter by the press shall be permitted prior to pronouncement of the arbitration award.

Article 9 is worth noting: freedom of association (affiliation or non-affiliation to a workers' union) shall not be affected by this agreement.[3]

Article 10 states that if either party is found guilty of any breach of this Agreement, a specially appointed court shall impose upon the party at fault a conventional fine.

In July 1983, the Peace Agreement of 1937 was renewed for the tenth time. The principal amendments to the agreement of 1978 were as follows:

(a) Effective in January 1986 the work week shall be reduced from 42 hours to 41 hours.

(b) A further reduction to 40 hours shall become effective 1 January 1988.

(c) The cost of these reductions in the work week shall be shared equally by the two parties.

(d) Apprentices and young workers shall receive a fifth holiday week per year, commencing 1 January 1984.

(e) The monthly supplement for children of a worker shall be increased, retroactively to 1 July 1983, from 70 to 90 francs.

(f) When carrying out his obligatory military service, a married man shall receive 80 percent of his regular wages instead of 70 percent as at present.

(g) The cooperation of the factory commissions in settling disputes is extended to include work reductions, overtime plans, shift- and night work, equalization of wages for men and women engaged in equivalent work, health- and noise protection, personal insurance, and personal data protection.

(h) The supplement for overtime work shall be 25 percent of the regular hourly wage and shall be effective for time worked over and above 45 hours in any week.

(i) The solidarity payments of non-union employees shall be increased from seven to eight francs for men and from five to six francs for women and youths.

The new Peace Agreement is reported upon in great detail in *SMUV Zeitung*, the official weekly newspaper of the Swiss Metal- and Watchmakers' Union (issues of

20 July, 3 and 17 August 1983). I am indebted to Dr. Lukas Burckhardt for these issues of *SMUV Zeitung* and other documentation.

This is about all that need be mentioned about the Agreement except for three general observations: first that it is based on mutual agreements between associations of employers and employees and thus deliberately excludes all State intervention; second that while the Agreement of 19 July 1937, was of two years' duration, all subsequently renewed agreements, with occasional amendments, have been for terms of five years; third that in the first 28 years of the Agreement only 200 cases had to be referred to the executives of the organizations (Article 2). A Conciliation Board was required about 40 times (Article 5), and in fewer than half of these 40 cases was arbitration by mutual agreement necessary.

That Switzerland has enjoyed industrial peace for all these years and that strikes are virtually negligible, both in number—especially since the Second World War—and in economic impact (cf. Table 25) testify to the spirit of good will and cooperative endeavour that characterize employer-employee relationships in Switzerland. Both parties have come to realize that strikes, boycotts and lockouts fail to effect a solution of the fundamental issues from which employer-employee disputes arise. It should be understood that many other collective agreements, with corresponding measures for ensuring industrial peace, now exist in other Swiss industries.

Lukas Burckhardt, the author of an excellent survey of Swiss industry-labor relations, approaches the conclusion of his article with the following cautionary statement:

> Industrial peace in Switzerland is only possible if the parties want it. Even if they conclude a collective labor agreement, our law obliges them to abstain from strikes and lockouts only with regard to conflicts concerning matters explicitly mentioned and regulated in the agreement. Total—or, as we call it, "absolute"—industrial peace in the private sector of our economy depends entirely on the good will of the parties: without this, it would be abolished (**76**, p. 197).

Federal Employees

The status of federal employees is not crystal clear. There are at least ten unions of federal employees (**341**, 1981, p. 401). In May, 1978, the Central Committee of the Assembly of Delegates of the Swiss Association of Christian PTT Personnel[4] (about 8000 members in 51 sections throughout Switzerland) proposed that the prohibition of strikes by government officials, as incorporated in a federal law of 1927, be re-examined. Also that the right-to-strike, anticipated for inclusion in the European Social Charter be incorporated in the [Swiss] law pertaining to government officials. A minimal number of enterprises in life-important services should also refrain from strikes and lockouts in order that the responsibility of State employees toward the general population would be legally and morally correct. The Union should cooperate with its social partner in good faith and whenever possible seek solutions through negotiation.

It should be noted that the federal employees in 1980, numbering 129,022, included 51,592 employees of the federal postal, telephone and telegraph services, and 38,367 persons employed by the federally owned railways (**341**, 1981, p. 406).

May-Day Proclamations

The first day of May is recognized in Switzerland as the Day of Work (*Tag der Arbeit*). Employers' associations, trade unions and political parties usually busy themselves at such a time with pronouncements for public consumption on matters of common interest to all three. In 1979 one heard from the Central Committee of the Swiss Employers' Organizations, the Directorate of the Federation of Swiss Unions, and the Social Democratic Party of Switzerland. From the employer we learn that work is the real basis for the recognition and maintenance of human values in a free society. Hence, unemployment must be avoided so far as possible. The policy of the employer must be to strive for the employment of all who are capable of work and eager to be employed.

The leadership of the Unions applauded the technical revolution with its promise of much that is good. But while the technical revolution moves on it may also turn in the wrong direction, and thus bring about a loss of work places, increased unemployment, and separation of people into those who have work and those who are deprived and can find none. Another result, said the speaker, is the concentration of firms into larger impersonal enterprises and increasing control of the individual through economic forces and the power of the State. With this comes a loss of democracy and co-determination. Errors in regional development is another result attended by the weakening of whole regions and an enlargement of the gulf between the rich cantons and the poor—a distorted growth which leads neither to a more just distribution of goods nor to a better life. All of this can only lead to dissatisfaction and a lack of understanding of each other's needs. Production moves into the countries where labor is cheap. In the underdeveloped countries a large part of the workers are shamelessly exploited. The mighty are one in spite of competition. Workers, let us unite. Beyond the borders of branches, regions, and States let us seek to strengthen our influence to direct the technical revolution in favor of the workers of both sexes and of all races. The task, hard and difficult, requires an almost superhuman solidarity. We must not allow our land to become a country of profiteers, said the speaker. Let us build it into a true social State. Let us strengthen our joint efforts in the communes, the cantons and the federation. Let us fight for influence in the economy where decisions today are still in the dark and all too often are against us. If we do not join in the decision-making process decisions will be made without us. This is neither in our interest nor in that of people elsewhere in the world who have a pressing need of our help.

The Social Democratic Party, in its proclamation, summarized the attitude of the Party in these social concerns. The satisfaction over what has been attained in the past is overshadowed by the heavily weighing consequences of an uncontrollable High Technology. It has become ever clearer that the division of the world into rich and poor States and population groups will be increasingly sharp. Democratic socialism and the free-union movement are concerned to recognize this problem more earnestly and to solve it now. As in the past, it requires the overcoming of social needs, the fight for equal rights, and the shaping of personal freedoms within social responsibility in our lands. These struggles are all the more necessary, because up to the present neither the private capitalism of the West nor the State Capitalism of the East has been able to improve the dangerous relationship between the wasteful and the poverty-stricken countries. Instead, the power blocs of the East and the West have brought about a gigantic armaments race—the so-called "Equilibrium of Terror." Billions will be more easily appropriated for armaments than millions for more social justice in the world. A colder wind biows within Switzerland. Since 1975 a halt in social expenditures has been advocated by administrative authorities and the banks, while the armament program of 1979 should be such as to permit military expenditures to rise to a new record height. Despite the anticipated deficits, the military expenditures will be assured, but not the social, educational, cultural and environmental ones. Hence the present level of expense [for these social purposes] will be endangered and new commitments will be impossible. The Social Democratic Party of Switzerland is not ready to accept a social-political retreat in exchange for a military-political advance. The right to work, social security, equality of opportunity for the young and security for the old are the most important political aims of the Party. All is endangered if we produce a High Technology which places in question our environment, our human destiny and our jobs. Nuclear power plants have become a security risk beyond control. Data banks impinge ever more strongly upon our personal privacy. The Swiss Social Democratic Party pleads for economic discernment, for social justice and for personal freedom.

Comparable pleas for less interference by the State and, for strengthening of the social partnership between employers' associations and the unions of employees were to be heard at the twentieth anniversary celebration of the founding of the Swiss Society for Practical Social Research. The Society, founded in 1959, met in Zurich in October 1979 to celebrate the past and to re-examine the present. Dr. Alfons Burckhardt, in a review of the past, reminded his audience that social problems in Switzerland cause no blood to flow, only ink.

In addition to its own research problems, the Society has collaborated with the Institute for Sociology of the University of Bern in the study of problems such as those of the foreign worker, the aged, and voter participation. The speaker for the Employers' Associations pointed out that the employer has less free space in which to maneuver than is commonly believed. His maneuverability is determined and constrained by market forces, by the total economy and by State political responsibility. In its own interest he must defend the arrangement of the market economy and convince the citizen that bad as it may be, it could be worse. He must pay attention to the views of his colleagues even if they are not rational but only emotional. And, finally, the State limits further their freedom in decision-making. Intervention by the State is excessive and all too perfectionist. Opposing policies with respect to social and economic matters must be evened out and bridged. To achieve this objective all further restrictions of freedom in decision-making must be energetically opposed.

The general secretary of the Swiss Metal- and Watchmakers' Union (SMUV) pointed out that the economic position of the worker has significantly changed in recent decades. He regards the Employers' Association as an equal partner in negotiations. As a convinced adherent and believer in the collective bargaining agreements (*Gesamtarbeitsverträge*) he sees danger in the plundering tactics of outsiders who, in the smaller factories, conclude separate agreements under advantageous conditions—a practice which can quickly become disadvantageous. Those who are not protected by a collective bargaining agreement can soon lose out and thus lead to protective measures initiated by State interference. The State, so we learn, in its draft of a new Federal Constitution would like to limit the activity of organizations of employers and employees to employment and professional matters only, which would paralyze their important political and social work.

Schwarzarbeit

In Switzerland, as elsewhere, there is such a thing as "black work" (*Schwarzarbeit*), the meaning of which is not obvious. In part it is as follows. Foreign workers in Switzerland must be paid according to the same scale that applies to Swiss. Were they to receive less, the wage structure for the Swiss and all concerned would be lowered. However, if an applicant for a job is desperately in need of employment he may offer his services for less than the going rate. And the employer will be tempted to accept. His labor costs will be less and, since he will not report employment of the person(s) concerned, he will contribute nothing on their behalf to the social service funds. The new employee(s) are officially nonexistent among the country's work force, even though their presence in the country may have been recorded. Of course, the employee will have a work permit because evey foreign worker must have one.[5] But possession of the permit does not prove that the holder works. *Schwarzarbeit* is obviously incompatible with all the positive factors that contribute to industrial peace.

Strikes and Lockouts

Although strikes and lockouts are stated to be inadmissible in the original agreement, referred to earlier (ref. **360**) and in similar agreements in other industries, such work stoppages have occurred since 1937 but, thus far, have had little impact on the economy. Table 25 lists the number of strikes and lockouts since 1930, the number of enterprises and the number of workers involved, as well as the worker-days lost. The Swiss Statistical Yearbooks, however, go much farther and report on the industries involved. The relevant data for a number of industries are presented in Table 26, which covers the years 1965, 1970, 1972–80.

The Table provides the evidence that strikes and/or lockouts do occur. It also indicates that employers' and employees' associations in industries other than the founding associations of 1937 have negotiated collective bargaining agreements. Of unusual interest is the fact that during the eleven years covered by the Table there

Table 26   Strikes and lockouts in Switzerland in selected industries 1965, 1970, 1972–80

Industry	No. of strikes and lockouts	Enterprises involved	Participating workers	Worker-days lost	
				Number	Yearly average
Clothing	3	3	310	2127	193
Leather and rubber	1	1	560	840	76
Construction	15	488	1129	5235	476
Wood and glass	5	5	215	1606	146
Textiles	1	1	208	208	19
Paper	0	0	0	0	0
Chemical	1	1	55	55	5
Metals and machines	11	11	1682	18,930	1721
Watch and jewelry	4	4	301	2172	197
Others	29	433	6071	15,726	1430
Totals	70	947	10,531	46,899	4263

Source: **341**, 1981, p. 403.

were no strikes or lockouts in the paper industry and only one in the leather and rubber industry as well as one only in each of the large textile and chemical industries. The two industries that suffered the most from strikes or lockouts were the construction industry with its many small enterprises and the large metal and machine industry.[6] It should be pointed out that almost half of the total worker-days lost by these two industries in the years covered by Table 26 was in the two years, 1975 and 1976 (cf. **341**, 1981, p. 403). This was a time of economic crisis which was widely experienced. In Switzerland, foreign trade suffered a decline with an accompanying decrease in employment by the export industries. This was largely due to the strengthening of the Swiss franc against virtually all foreign currencies. For example, by 1973, the USA dollar, relative to the Swiss franc, had decreased to 75 percent of its earlier long-sustained value. By the end of December 1976 it was down to 55 percent of its pre-1970 value. However, by 1985, the dollar had regained its former strength (e.g. ~ 2.9 francs = 1 dollar). Purchase of American products by residents of Switzerland and many other countries is now discouraged by unfavorable and unstable exchange rates.

The construction industry also experienced an unemployment problem as a result of a government ban on most construction projects contemplated by the private sector. One speaks in Switzerland of the recession of 1975 and 1976, the effects of which lingered on longer than one might have expected.

A strike by the Union of workers in the Printing and Paper Industries against the Swiss Association of Enterprises in the Graphic Arts appeared imminent in 1980 but a vote of the members late in the year approved the collective bargaining agreement (*Gesamtarbeitsvertrag*) that was under consideration. The collective-bargaining contract had already been accepted by a rival union. Only the Printing and Paper Union delayed until the last minute when the employers refused to reopen negotiations for new demands.

A Policy of Full Employment?

The membership of the Swiss Metal- and Watchmakers' Union (SMUV) directed a petition with over 63,000 signatures to the Federal Chancellery to express their concern over such problems as the threat to employment resulting from transfer of some production facilities to the Far East where the employer takes advantage of cheap foreign labor, and to the decrease in exports attributable to exchange rates for the Swiss franc which were unfavorable to the Swiss export industries. The petitioners urged that a policy of full employment in Switzerland's industries be adopted, that measures be taken to strengthen economically threatened regions and branches of industry, and that currency transactions of multinational concerns and internationally active banks be controlled. Finally, they proposed in a supplementary letter to the Federal Council that a consultative commission be set up to consider a policy of full employment—the commission to consist of representatives of federal and cantonal authorities with assured representation of employer and employee organizations. This serious concern of the Union was an almost inevitable result of the economic crisis of 1975–76 which had such a serious impact on the export industries. See also section 11.9.

Firestone Inc. and its Problems

As an internal measure, designed to maintain industrial peace by lessening the number of lay-offs resulting from the economic downturn there appears to have been a trend in the late 1970s toward more part-time employment. This spreads out the available work among more people and clearly lessens the suffering that would otherwise have a serious impact upon those deprived of employment. In Switzerland, such an arrangement would be the result of negotiations between employers and employees; it would not be a unilateral decision by the employer.

In 1973, Firestone Inc. bought a Swiss tire-making plant in Pratteln, near Basel, in which Firestone tires had been produced under a licensing agreement with the American company. The troubles that followed were numerous. Some were associated with the problems that beset the series-500 radial tires introduced by the parent company, leading to substantial losses of revenue. Others arose from the strengthening of the Swiss currency which made it less expensive to export tires from Akron for the Swiss market than to manufacture them in Switzerland; allegedly, according to Firestone, Swiss labor had become too expensive. But another problem was rooted in the failure of an American company to understand the cooperative relationship that exists between employers and employees in Switzerland, whereby problems of mutual concern are analyzed, weighed, and solved, if possible, by honest discussions between the two parties. Early in 1978, the problems had attained such a magnitude and losses were mounting so rapidly that the parent company announced a unilateral decision to a startled Switzerland: the plant in Pratteln will be closed at the end of July and the employees (about 600) will be dismissed. Discussions aimed at averting a closing of the plant or making a financial settlement agreeable to the Pratteln employees were almost endless. Involved were the company's principals in Akron, the management and employee representatives in Pratteln, the Swiss government and the courts. In 1979 a Baselland court levied a conventional fine of 2.6 million francs against Firestone Schweiz A.G. for violating a collective-bargaining agreement. The judgment was sustained by the highest court of Baselland and by the Swiss Supreme Court.

Unemployment

Unemployment is a problem that besets almost every country at some time or other. It is of concern to government, to employees and, above all, to the unemployed whenever the percentage of the active (working) population that finds itself unemployed becomes appreciable.

If we compare Switzerland's experience in such matters with that of any other industrialized country, we have to conclude that Switzerland has been remarkably fortunate in maintaining unemployment rates as low as 0.2 or 0.3 percent for years at a time. But just how lucky has she been? Table 27, which pertains to the years 1920 to 1980, tells the story. In the pre-war years, 1931 to 1939, the number of workers seeking employment rose steadily from a yearly average in 1931 of 24,208 to a yearly average of 93,009 in 1936 and then steadily declined to 16,374 in 1940. As percentages of the working population the corresponding figures were 1.3 in 1931, 4.8 in 1936 and 0.8 in 1940. In 1976, because of an economic depression, the number seeking employment rose to 21,732 or 0.725 percent of the working population. Otherwise, the percentage of the working population seeking employment in all remaining years from 1925 to 1980 has been as low as 0.01 percent and never higher than 0.8. Were we to concentrate on the totally unemployed, essentially similar data would necessitate the same conclusion: unemployment is not a serious problem in Switzerland. The available data for the years 1925–35 are somewhat uncertain but we may still conclude that, with only two exceptional periods (1921 to 1923 and 1931 to 1939), the unemployment rate has not risen above 0.8 percent and was as low as 0.003 in 1971 and 1973. If we consider unemployment only among those who are paying members of a professional group with its own insurance fund against unemployment we would find that between 9% and 33% of the full-time members of the construction industry and the watch industry unemployment funds (*Arbeitslosenkassen*) were unemployed during the pre-war years 1931–39 (**341**, 1951, p. 350). The small increases in general unemployment, still less than 1 percent of the active population, observable from 1975 to 1979, are attributable to a very substantial decrease in construction as ordered by the Federal Government, and an adverse effect upon foreign trade.

In 1981, the OECD (Organization for Economic Cooperation and Development) predicted in its 1981–82 report that a slight recession in Switzerland was to be expected. The recession may have been somewhat more serious in 1982 than predicted and little, if any, improvement can be expected in 1983 according to a

Table 27 Twentieth-century unemployment in Switzerland[a]

Active (*Erwerbstätige*) population[b]	Year	Seeking positions[c,d]		Unemployed		No. of unfilled positions
		Average for the year	Percentage of active population	Average for the year	Percentage of active population	
1,871,725	1920		—	—		
	1921	—	—	58,466	3.1	1113
	1922	—	—	66,995	3.6	1629
	1923	—	—	32,605	1.7	2403
1,942,626	1930	12,881	0.7	12,881	0.7	3061
	1931	24,208	1.3	24,208	1.3	2639
	1932	54,366	2.8	54,366	2.8	1977
	1933	67,867	3.5	67,867	3.5	2417
	1934	65,440	3.4	65,440	3.4	2424
	1935	82,468	4.3	82,468	4.3	2057
	1936	93,009	4.8	80,554	4.2	1511
	1937	71,130	3.7	57,949	3.0	2127
	1938	65,583	3.4	52,590	2.7	1989
	1939	40,324	2.1	36,663	1.9	2543
	1940	16,374	0.8	14,784	0.8	3673
1,992,487	1941	10,550	0.5	9095	0.5	3802
2,155,656	1950	10,709	0.5	9599	0.5	3992
2,512,411	1960	1690	0.1	1277	0.1	6393
3,124,100[e]	1970	219	0.01	104[f]	0.004[f]	4777
3,017,000[e]	1975	11,111	0.37	10,170[g]	0.34	2813
2,918,200[e]	1976	21,732	0.73	20,703	0.69	4625
2,922,700[e]	1977	12,973	0.43	12,020	0.40	6478
2,939,900[e]	1978	11,777	0.39	10,483	0.35	8290
2,961,800[e]	1979	11,449	0.38	10,333	0.35	8921
3,012,200[e]	1980	7241	0.24	6255	0.21	12,312

[a] From data provided by the *Bundesamt für Industrie, Gewerbe und Arbeit* (BIGA), *Abteilung für Sozialstatistik.*

[b] Excludes, in general, international functionaries and their families; excluded also are those who live on unearned income (investments etc.)

[c] The dashes (—) indicate that data were not given in the report provided by BIGA.

[d] Among the job-hunters, it cannot now be ascertained whether for the years 1925 to 1935 the unemployed part-time workers are included. Also, the data for the unemployed among full-time workers (*Ganzarbeitslose*) for the same decade can only be approximated. It is assumed, however, that the approximations are reasonably close. We have chosen to omit the data for 1925–29.

[e] Source: **377**, 1981, pp. 284, 286; and **341**, 1981, pp. 364, 365. Part-time workers are included.

[f] From 1971 to 1974 the corresponding values were all very low (81 to 221 and 0.003 to 0.007). Against these very low pre-depression values, the increases from 1975 to 1980, though still less than one percent, appear startling.

[g] The unemployment data, from 1975 to 1980, pertain only to those who were formerly full-time workers: the "part-timers" are excluded.

prognosis by the Basler Study Group for Business Research and the ETH Zürich (**266**, 9–10 October 1982). See also Table 28.

As for employment we learn that the number of working places (*Stellen*) vacant in 1983 will be more than two percent greater than in 1981. This amounts to a loss of at least 60,000 working places. The official offices of employment may show not more than 25,000 to 30,000 persons registered as totally unemployed (i.e. those who draw unemployment compensation). The difference of 25,000 to 30,000 represents, in part, the foreign workers and others who, through retirement etc., are ineligible for unemployment relief. The gap will lessen when there are more working places open to the job-seekers.

Inflation reached a rate of 6.5 percent in 1981, the highest since the recession of 1975–76. In 1980 the inflation rate was 4 percent and in 1983 is expected to approximate an average for the year of 4 percent. Rents, according to the OECD, increased by about 4.5 percent in 1981 as compared with one percent in 1980. Wages and salaries increased in 1981 less than inflation, leading to a decrease of about two percent in real wages.

The Basler Group prognosis is more pessimistic than that of the OECD. Both reports are unavoidably rendered somewhat speculative by totally unpredictable fluctuations in the value of the Swiss franc which affects materially Switzerland's exports and imports. This, in turn, has a considerable impact on the level of employment by Swiss industries. The machine and metal industry and the textile industry have experienced an appreciable downturn. The electrical industry and heavy machine construction have suffered somewhat less than others. In general the small factories (less than 200 employees) have been hit worse than the middle-sized (200 to 1000 employees). The large, heavily-capitalized firms (more than 1000

Table **28**   The Swiss gross national product and its components (in millions of francs)

	1981[a]	1982[b]	1983[b]
Private consumption of goods and services	65,020	65,020	65,020
Purchases by government (including social insurance)	11,865	12,100	12,220
Gross domestic investment (total)	30,130	28,420	28,585
Investment in building	17,770	16,880	16,540
Investment in equipment and furnishings	10,360	9840	9545
Domestic demand	107,015	105,540	105,825
Exports (goods and services)	46,865	45,735	46,560
Total demand	153,880	151,275	152,385
Less imports (goods and services)	49,265	48,500	49,255
Gross national product at market prices	104,615	102,775	103,130
Capital- and work-income from abroad	9230	9135	8760
Less capital- and work-income for other countries	3530	3430	3290
Gross social product at market prices	110,315	108,480	108,600

[a] Source: Provisional calculation, Basler study group for business research (**266**, 9–10 October 1982).
[b] Estimates and prognosis by the business research section of ETH Zürich (October 1982).

employees), while experiencing decreases in sales and employment, are not too seriously troubled by the recession of the early 1980s. These conclusions rest principally on the work on hand, as measured by anticipated months of full or well sustained employment at comparable times (7.7 months for the large concerns, 6.2 months for the middle-sized, and 4.3 months for the small) (**357**, 9 June 1982).

A sudden termination of employment is possibly one of the most depressing and difficult situations to face a worker—it being understood that the employer, compelled to solve the problems of his company as it enters upon a deepening recession or a succession of operating losses, is obliged to reduce his work force. The employee is surely entitled to a reasonably long advance warning of the forthcoming dismissal, not an abrupt loss of his job. Employees should also be protected against termination of their jobs during unavoidable absence attributable to illness, accident, convalescence, pregnancy or the first few weeks or months of motherhood. Such are the opinions and recommendations of the "Democratic Jurists of Switzerland" as expressed at a press conference in Lausanne.

Notes and Comments

1. By the end of 1919 there were 20 trade unions in Switzerland with a total membership of 223,588, distributed through 390 localities (**341**, 1920, p. 126). By 1980, twelve federated unions of employees reported a total membership of 144,710. Ten other unions of salaried employees ended the year with a total membership of 280,868. One of the unions within this latter group of ten, includes the employers within its membership.

2. Here we have Lenin's description of Grimm, who saw to it that military questions (on the agenda for 11 February 1917) were postponed indefinitely, thereby angering Lenin: "Grimm is a Schurk. He is guilty of a flagrant *délit* and the mask must be removed from his face." In another letter, Lenin described Nobs and Platten—friends of Grimm in the leadership of the Olten Action Committee—"as people without character (if not worse) who fear Grimm more than fire" (from Document 11, "Lenin über Robert Grimm," ref. **412**, pp. 51, 52).

3. If an employee chooses not to join the union, he is required by the 1974 text of the agreement to pay a modest "solidarity" contribution, therby participating in costs involved in administration of the Agreement. The nonmember pays less than he would in membership fees but it is agreed that he should support the cause through the solidarity contribution because of the benefits gained for all employees of the enterprise by the collective action of the organized workers.

4. *Verband des christlichen PTT-Personals.*

5. This statement must be qualified. There is, or was, an unguarded access to Switzerland from Italy, through a part of Chiasso. The access route has been known as the "Chiasso Opening"—well known to smugglers who manage to bring in drugs and other prohibited items, as well as aliens who for a variety of reasons would be denied admission by the Swiss immigration officers at the recognized ports of entry. Aliens who are smuggled in, usually at night, are unknown to the Swiss authorities; they have no official existence. They would not venture to apply for a work permit and, faced with the problem of survival, become *Schwarzarbeiter*. A proposal in 1980 to illuminate brightly the Chiasso Opening is of dubious merit because, while it would facilitate the work of the immigration authorities it would also help the smugglers find their way into the city.

We must, however, recognize that *Schwarzabeit*, as it applies to the foreign worker, is only a small part of a much larger problem which has a serious impact upon the economy. I refer to what may be called the shadow economy of which *Schwarzarbeit*, as I have used the term, is only a small part. The shadow economy, present in most, if not all countries, is that part of the total economy characterized by an evasion of government charges for social services, nonpayment of income taxes and other practices, legal or illegal, by which government is cheated out of income which it regards as due from its citizens. The most common example is failure of a taxpayer to declare all of his taxable income. Some may be deliberately hidden. It can also include the fraudulent receipt of money from the State—e.g. by the fraudulent receipt of welfare payments, or of retirement income (social security benefits) etc. These practices, deliberate or otherwise, significantly distort the statistics of an economy. The reported per capita income data in the USA would probably be 10 to 15 percent higher, the unemployment figures would be somewhat lower, and poverty would be less widespread than officially reported if the relevant economic data could be corrected for the abuses mentioned. Any estimate of the loss to government by the existence of a shadow- or hidden-economy is an attempt to measure something that to a large degree is immeasurable. Switzerland has refrained from any official estimate of this kind of economic loss. There are fears that *Schwarzarbeit* is increasing in the foreign-worker portion of the Swiss economy. Possibly there are 30,000 to 50,000 more foreign workers in Switzerland than the statistics indicate (**266**, 19–20 December 1981).

6. The eleven enterprises in the metals and machines industry lost 18,930 worker-days during the eleven years—3204 more than the 433 miscellaneous enterprises lost during the same period. Each of the 433 had very few employees. It has been characteristic of Swiss industry that a great many enterprises each with very few employees, exist. Their survival is precarious, partly because of the predatory activities of the large enterprises—a gobbling-up of the small ones—but also because of the transfer of some operations to cheap-labor centers in Asia.

7. Brupbacher's autobiography has been published (ref. **418**).

11.8. AGRICULTURE, VETERINARY SERVICES, FORESTRY, FISHERIES

Introduction

How does Switzerland use the two million or so hectares* devoted to farming? To avoid any trespass upon von Ah's excellent article "Swiss Agriculture and Food Production" in *Modern Switzerland* (**7**), I shall restrict this present treatment to cows, pigs, cheese, apples and the like.

Swiss agricultural policy is defined in the Fifth Report of the Swiss Federal Council to Parliament on the State of Agriculture (*Fünfter Bericht über die Lage der schweizerischen Landwirtschaft und die Agrarpolitik des Bundes*, Bern, December 1976). A synopsis, in English, of the most essential portions of this Report has been provided by von Ah (**7**, pp. 82, 83). The Report is by no means outdated because government, almost necessarily, determines its agricultural policy on a long-term basis.

Farming Area

First of all, the area suitable for active farming—raising cereal grains, vegetables, fruits, and farm animals—is more restricted than may first appear. Of the total two million hectares, about 43 percent is suitable only for pasturage. This is open meadow land in the high mountains, or on the steep slopes reaching up from the valleys or plateau land below. The production of cereal grains and other crops in such areas is relatively trifling, determined in part by the shortness of the growing season.

Import and Export of Foodstuffs

Switzerland has never succeeded in producing within her own borders all of the foodstuffs that her people needed or demanded. What country has? As for imports,

---

* 1 hectare (ha) equals 2.471 acres.

we learn that Switzerland's expenditure in 1978 amounted to a goodly 42.3 billion francs. Of this grand total 3.32 billion francs were expended on imported foodstuffs, mostly vegetables, but including raw tobacco (**341**, 1979, pp. 183, 191). On the export side, there was a counterbalancing grand total of 41.8 billion francs of which 1.46 billion constituted the revenue from the export of foodstuffs and fabricated tobacco (**341**, 1979, pp. 183, 193). In detail, about the only foodstuffs that Switzerland exports are cheese[1] (453 million francs), preserved milk and baby foods (33 million), chocolate (123 million), soups and bouillon (104 million). The revenue from export of fabricated tobacco, usually included in the statistics with foodstuffs, amounted in 1978 to 313 million francs (**341**, 1979, p. 193). Of these products, cheese is by far the most important export item. The production is embarrassingly large—from 60,300 tons in 1955 to 121,000 tons in 1980 (**341**, 1981, p. 120). From time to time other products of the farm are in excess, such as fruit, eggs and veal. Fortunately, there is a good demand, especially within the Common Market countries for these additional exports. As for cheese, serious competition is arising as a result of massive increases in cheese production in the Common Market and the EFTA countries.[2] Even the home market is adversely affected: in 1975, Switzerland imported as much as 21,500 tons of cheese, presumably for domestic consumption.

Dairy Farming

The number of milk cows in Switzerland (880,000 in 1978) has remained relatively constant since 1955 at least. The number of milk goats, meanwhile, decreased by about 50 percent (to 50,000 in 1978). Total milk production, as a result of improved care and feeding of the dairy cattle, increased in the 25-year interval about 30 percent to 3,540,000 tons in 1978 (**341**, 1979, p. 120). For some years there has been an overproduction of milk which cannot be counterbalanced by substantial increases in the production of butter, cheese, and preserved milk for export. To achieve such increases in export would require drastic decreases in prices of dairy products and would have disastrous effects on the income of dairy farmers. One must almost conclude that despite the overproduction of milk the income of the dairy farmer is considered by government to be too low, because the dairy industry received in 1978 almost half as much in federal subventions as did agriculture (total for agriculture, 1,246 million francs; for the production and use of dairy products, about 550 million francs) (**341**, 1979, pp. 407, 408). Indeed, the labor income of the midland farmer in 1975 was reported, provisionally, to be 86 percent of a fair remuneration, as defined by government. The income of the mountain farmer may have been as low as 58 percent of a fair remuneration (reference 7: Table 4).

Wines

The excellent wines produced in Switzerland are exported in quantities too trifling to merit inclusion in the statistical yearbooks. To the contrary the domestic wines are insufficient to satisfy the demands of her people. In fact, bulk wine imports in 1979 cost the country 231 million francs[3] (**341**, 1981, p. 197). Domestic production from the Swiss vineyards in 1979 (as grapes or raisins) was valued at 412 million francs (**341**, 1981, p. 120).

More on Imports and Exports

There is not much to be reported for earlier years. For 1892 we learn that total imports cost the Swiss about 869 million francs against total exports of 658 million (**341**, 1932, p. 246). Of these totals, imports and exports of primary agricultural products amounted to 40.2 and 14.5 million francs respectively.[4] Imports and exports of foodstuffs totalled 258 and 83.4 million francs respectively (**341**, 1932, p. 248).

As might be expected, most of Switzerland's foreign trade is with her fellow Europeans. In 1978, 80 percent of her total imports were from European countries and only 8 percent came from North America (USA, Canada, Mexico). The corresponding percentages for 1910 were 88 and 4.4 respectively. Her exports present a similar picture. In 1978, 65 percent of Switzerland's total exports went to European countries and 8.6 percent to North America. In 1910, 76 percent of the total was exported to European countries and 14.5 percent to North America (**341**, 1979, p. 189).

In only two decades, several extraordinary changes in food consumption and food preferences have been observed, notably in such basic foodstuffs as meat, bread and potatoes. The per capita consumption of bread has decreased from 47.2 kg in 1960 to 25.6 kg in 1979; and for potatoes, a decrease from 46.5 kg in 1960 to 23.6 in 1979. The per capita consumption of meat, however, increased from 24.2 kg in 1960 to 35.1 kg in 1979. Unfortunately, these results emerge from studies of food consumption by only a few hundred families. Such data can hardly be collected from the entire population.

There are two foodstuffs and one beverage which Switzerland is obliged to import most heavily: sugar, wheat flour and coffee. In 1978 she produced 98,600 tons of sugar but imported 161,000 tons. Her own production of wheat flour was 397,000 tons, while imports totalled 275,000 tons (**341**, 1979, pp. 159, 191). Her raw coffee imports in 1978 were valued at 354 million francs. Of all imported foods and food beverages, the expenditure on coffee was the greatest. In 1977, coffee imports at 604 million francs stood out, even more conspicuously, at the top of the list (**341**, 1979, p. 191). Perhaps this may help us to understand why a cup of coffee in Switzerland (and elsewhere in Europe) is so expensive: in 1981, the equivalent of 90¢ to $1.00 a cup.

Use of Crop Land

Let us next consider the uses to which Switzerland puts her one million or so hectares[5] of good crop land—mountain pasturage excluded. We learn that in 1975, about 263,000 ha consisted of open agricultural land, cultivated by about 80,000 farmers; of the 263,000 hectares, 178,000 ha were given over to production of cereals by about 53,000 farmers. Potatoes, which always seem to be in abundance, were produced on 23,800 ha and sugar beets on 10,600. Other agricultural products were derived from 50,000 ha. Artificial and natural grazing land (not including the short-season summer pasturage in the mountains) amounted to no less than 763,000 ha. Vineyards covered about 11,600 ha, cultivated by about 20,000 operators. Thus, we have accounted for 1,038,000 ha, leaving a scant 17,000 ha for odds and ends.

Of the grand total of 1,055,600 ha it should be mentioned that 358,700 ha are lower mountain lands suitable for year-round use, unlike the high mountain meadows. These lower mountain lands consist mainly of pasturage, and are included in the 763,000 ha mentioned above. But, in addition, 10,600 ha of the large area given over to cereals (178,000 ha) are to be found in these lower mountain lands. Finally, about 11 percent of the crop land for potatoes, and 16 percent of the vineyard lands are to be found in these lower mountain areas.

In 1975 about 53,000 farmers produced cereal grains, compared with 182,000 in 1917 (**341**, 1977, p. 101). This does not mean a great decrease over the years in production of cereal grains. It signifies rather, an increase in size of the average farm. By 1975 there was a very significant increase, especially by the "professional" farmers, in the number of larger farms of 5 to 50 ha or more. Of 76,900 such professional farms in 1975, about 90 percent were over 5 ha in size (**341**, 1979, p. 97). Potatoes in 1917 were produced on 248,000 farms and in 1975 on 53,600 (**341**, 1979, p. 101). This reduction cannot be explained entirely by an increase in size of the average farm. It suggests, rather, a switch by the average farmer from potatoes to cereals or a trend from mixed farming to specialized crops: certainly very few farmers raise only cereal grains or potatoes or alfalfa.

Mechanization

Coincident with the increase in farm size there has been a great increase in mechanization and with this a substantial decrease in labor costs. The farmers with less than 5 ha, in order to overcome the economic disadvantage to which they were thus exposed, have formed farm-machinery cooperatives to permit the use in common of expensive tractors, motorized transport vehicles (some with self-loading trailers) and other farm machinery acquired by the cooperative. Alternatively, lending arrangements for the use of farm machinery have developed among farmers in the same region.

These signs of progress are accompanied by signals of distress that are discomfiting to the average farmer. To afford expensive farm machinery and to achieve the economic benefits that can accrue to the purchaser, the land to be worked must exceed a certain minimum size. This is a function of the cost of the farm implement and the extra income to be derived from its use. For example, a machine to be used in the harvesting of a certain variety of carrots may be purchased for 150,000 francs but requires a minimum holding of 40 ha if it is to pay its way.

A bush-bean harvester, costing about 250,000 francs, can collect the crop from one to three hectares per day. Under the best of conditions, this harvesting ability may amount to 15 tons per hectare per day, or as little as 3 tons per hectare per day under poor conditions. But a good hand picker usually harvests only about 30 kg an hour or one-fourth of a metric ton in 8 hours.

It is easy to see that if the investment is to be worth its cost the acquisition of such machines and still other useful farm implements may necessitate the acquisition of additional farm land by purchase or by rental. Or one may rent the equipment from time to time to his neighbours or enter into an agreement whereby the owner of the machine will operate the equipment on the land of neighbouring farmers for a stated remuneration.

Whatever else may happen it is clear that in recent years, mechanization has proceeded apace and farms have become larger, the increase in size being achieved by purchase or by rental. About 40 percent of all the farm land in Switzerland is rented, rather than owned, by the operator (**266**, 22/23 August, 1981, p. 33). To some, this is a disastrous turn of events. They reason that the new generation of owners consists of commercial firms and conserve- or food-processing and food-canning factories which eagerly buy up available land. Subsequent rental of such land may cost anywhere from 300 to 1200 francs per hectare per year. In effect, the farmer-operator becomes a tenant farmer or he may be hired by the corporate owner to work remaining lands, not rented out, and to do so under the direction and management of the corporation. The effects of these changes on food prices is not clear but it is suspected by some that in the long term they will push upwards the prices of farm products. Alternatively, the operators of large farms, through increased efficiency, may force prices downwards in a competitive economy. This could be a disaster to the small farmer. As an analogy, his problem would be similar to that of the small "mom and pop" grocery store in competition with a large chain store in the same block.

It will be understood that topography greatly restricts the use of machinery on the steep hillsides and mountainous agricultural areas which constitute 37 percent of Switzerland's 133,000 farms (**341**, 1979, p. 95).

Farm Workers

And who does the work on these many farms? In 1975, the number of permanent farm workers totalled about 148,000, of whom 17,000 were women. This permanent work force consisted of 77,000 heads of farms, 53,000 members of their families, and 18,000 non-family workers including 4100 foreigners. Finally, an occasional work force of 211,000 (including 124,000 women) helped when needed (**341**, 1979, p. 101).

Farm Animals

Now we come to the farm animals. Arranged according to numbers per category we find that in 1978, the following were Swiss "residents": Pigs, 2,115,000; cattle, 2,024,000; sheep, 383,000; goats, 80,000; horses, 46,000; and mules, 2000. Chickens, ducks, geese, turkeys and other birds raised on the farm totalled 6,730,000 (**341**, 1979, p. 106).

The number of owners of farm animals is not without interest. In 1979, the beef and dairy cattle[6] were owned by 84,900 farmers, approximately 24 head of cattle per owner (**341**, 1979, pp. 108, 109). In contrast, of the 215,000 owners of cattle between 1866 and 1901, each possessed only five or six head of cattle (**341**, 1920, pp. 98, 99). It is much the same in the case of swine, a great increase in the number per owner in the past 100 years. In 1979, swine numbering 2,062,000 were owned by 42,900 farmers (**341**, 1979, pp. 108, 109) as contrasted with about 430,000 swine in 1866–1901 owned by about 140,000 farmers (**341**, 1920, pp. 98, 99). In other words, each owner of pigs in 1979 possessed about 50 head as contrasted with three each in 1866–1901. From Table 29, it will be clear that, as with pigs and cattle, the numbers of almost all other kinds of farm animals owned by a farmer have steadily increased during the past 100 years. This is to be expected from the corresponding progressive increase in size of the average farm and the introduction of labor-saving devices and procedures for the care of farm animals.

And we must not forget the bees. There were 264,000 hives of bees in Switzerland in 1978 divided among 22,300 owners. The yield of honey, which varies greatly from

Table 29
Table 29A   Number of farm animals in Switzerland[a]

Farm animals	1866	1901	1951	1979
Cattle	993,000	1,340,000	1,607,000	2,038,000
Horses	100,000	125,000	131,000	45,000
Mules and donkeys	5480	4870	2550	1820[b]
Sheep	447,000	219,000	192,000	361,000
Goats	375,000	355,000	148,000	80,000[b]
Pigs	304,000	555,000	892,000	2,062,000
Chickens	—	—	6,240,000	6,337,000
Geese, ducks, etc.	—	—	68,400	41,600
Bee colonies	177,000[c]	243,000	339,000	264,000[b]

[a] Source: **341**, 1916, pp. 54, 55; 1932, p. 12; 1951, p. 105; 1979, pp. 107, 108.
[b] 1978; [c] 1876.

Table 29B   Number of owners of farm animals[a]

Animals	1866	1901	1951	1979
Cattle	192,000	214,000	170,000	84,900
Horses	51,700	64,800	70,700	19,900
Mules and donkeys	—	4500	2600	1300[b]
Sheep	89,000	40,000	25,000	22,300
Goats	127,000	121,000	45,000	13,900[b]
Pigs	115,000	152,000	139,000	42,900
Chickens	—	—	261,000	68,400
Geese, ducks, etc.	—	—	14,900	8000[b]
Bee colonies	41,000[c]	42,000	36,000	22,000[b]

[a] Source: **341**, 1920, p. 99; 1932, p. 12; 1979, pp. 105, 107, 109.
[b] 1978; [c] 1876.

year to year was 13,000 quintal* in 1977, compared with 70,000 quintal in 1976 from about the same number of bee colonies. The honey, however, is less important than the bees: without the bees, no pollenation, and without pollenation, no fruit—in fact nothing requiring pollenation.

Infectious Diseases of Animals

Mention must be made of the infectious diseases of animals. The list of such diseases was revised and greatly extended by a law that went into effect on 1 July 1966. The statistical yearbooks, reporting on animals that died or were slaughtered as a result of disease, list the highly contagious foot-and-mouth disease of cattle, swine pest, *Rauschbrand* (an infectious disease, usually fatal, of cattle and sheep), anthrax, myxomatosis of rabbits, scabies of sheep and goats, brucellosis of sheep and goats, rabies, poultry cholera, poultry pest and pseudopest (Newcastle disease). The law of 1966 adds mite (acarine) disease of bees, the dangerous foul brood (*Faulbrut*) and sack brood (*Sauerbrut*) of bees. Very important additions to the list are the rickettsial diseases, the leptospiroses, ornithosis/psittacosis (parrot disease), and the salmonella diseases. *Dasselkrankheit*[7] and scabies are now in the list, as well as several diseases which cause serious losses of fish. Most important, however, is the inclusion of a blanket clause which covers any unspecified disease which may suddenly break out and is dangerous, contagious, or widespread among animals. Switzerland, heavily engaged as she is in the cross-country transport of animals, has every reason to take all possible precautions against diseases that may be introduced from foreign countries. Tularemia, as an example, has never occurred in Switzerland—but the day may come.

Bovine brucellosis (Bang's disease) was eradicated from the Swiss herds by the end of 1963 at a cost to the cantons and Federal Government of 86 million francs. Bovine tuberculosis was officially declared in 1959 to be eradicated from Swiss herds. Cattle plague (*Rinderpest*) has not been encountered in Switzerland since 1872. Pulmonary disease of cattle had disappeared by 1895 and glanders has not been observed since 1938. The disease which continues to be the most difficult to eradicate is bovine foot-and-mouth disease but even this appears to be yielding to the aggressive use of vaccination.

A virus disease of cattle that has recently been publicized in Switzerland (**266**, 1–2 September 1984), deserves more than a passing mention. In the *NZZ* article the disease is described only as IBR/IPV and a Canadian breeding bull, as a source of semen, is charged with transmission of the disease into artificially inseminated cows in Switzerland. A reader, compulsively curious about many things, may be pleased to learn that IBR/IPV refers to Infectious Bovine Rhinotracheitis/Infectious Pustular Vulvovaginitis—once thought to be separate diseases, but now proven to be different manifestations of the same viral infection. Present terminology, somewhat less cryptic, permits us to shed the IPV and reduce the name of the disease to IBR. The causal agent is a herpes virus and cattle are believed to be the principal

* 1 quintal (metric system) equals 100 kg (220.46 pounds).

reservoir, although goats, mule deer, and possibly other ruminants can be infected. Vaccination against the disease is standard practice in dairy herds and, if done properly, is quite effective. I am greatly indebted to Dr. Stephanie Ostrowski of the Veterinary Medical Hospital, University of California in Davis, for the above information. For the benefit of those who want to delve more deeply, Dr. Ostrowski draws attention to papers on IBR/IPV in Morrow's *Current Therapy in Theriogenology*.

The Federal Veterinary Office[8]

For well over 150 years, losses attributable to animal diseases have been a subject of concern to the cantonal governments and Federal Government of Switzerland. Naturally, the cantons that were rich in livestock were the first to give official attention to the problem. The canton of Bern was among the first to institute police measures to prevent the spread of contagious diseases among domestic animals. A subsidy program designed to reimburse for losses sustained through the compulsory slaughter of infected animals was instituted in Bern in the early days, apparently around 1804. By 1873 the capital of the fund for such subsidies had increased to a half million francs.[9]

In the mid-1800s the supervision and execution of veterinary police measures against animal diseases lay solely within the competence of the cantonal health authorities, who could, and sometimes did, rely upon the advice of veterinarians. In several cantons a so-called Senior Veterinarian (*Obertierarzt*) was entrusted with enforcement of the measures against animal disease. The important task of training young veterinarians was also his. In some cases district veterinarians were appointed, and this device introduced a little more uniformity into the measures taken against the spread of animal disease.[10] Nevertheless, much remained to be done to make appreciable progress in the difficult struggle. Not enough was known about the causation and nature of disease—a "miasma" or a "contagion"—and the conviction grew that a cantonal or regional approach in the fight against epizootics was not enough.

LEGISLATION AFFECTING THE FEDERAL VETERINARY OFFICE[11]   The laws enacted by the Federal Government in connection with animal disease and the meat industry are too numerous to be discussed in toto, but a few of the laws serve as landmarks in these matters. The Constitution of 1848 authorized the Federal Council to take such police measures as were deemed necessary in the fight against diseases which constituted a general danger.[12] In 1872 the first federal law covering such measures was enacted. The law provided for a federal commissioner for the border control of animal disease, but it had hardly gone into effect before serious deficiencies in its provisions became apparent. The controls introduced by local authorities, in accordance with the law and inherited in part from earlier days, varied greatly from canton to canton and were generally inadequate. A new law, enacted 1 July 1886, provided for compulsory inspection at the Swiss border of all livestock entering the country as well as for the control of imported fresh and preserved meat.

A law now in force dates from 13 June 1917. Among its many provisions is the extension of the border veterinary inspection service throughout the Confederation. Through a federal law of 26 March 1914, and by decree of the Federal Council in November 1914, the veterinary inspection service was placed under a new division within the Federal Department of Public Economy, the Federal Veterinary Office. Until then, the service was administered by an inspectorate of animal disease, which functioned provisionally as a division of the then Department of Commerce, Industry and Agriculture.

A very important law which bears upon the functions of the Federal Veterinary Office was in effect long before the Office came into being and is still in force. This is the law of 8 December 1905, on foodstuffs, food products, food processing, food handling, and numerous other aspects of food preparation, preservation, transport, and commerce. Insofar as the federal competence to legislate in such areas rests upon Article 69 of the Constitution, the federal authorities, through the Federal Veterinary Office and Federal Public Health Service, concern themselves only with the possible transmission of contagious or dangerous diseases.

RESPONSIBILITIES OF THE VETERINARY OFFICE   It is tempting to think that the Federal Veterinary Office would be under a blanket obligation to enforce, throughout the country, the numerous provisions of the federal law on veterinary disease. But in Switzerland one must not yield to any such temptation. The niceties of cantonal autonomy require a quite different emphasis in matters of cantonal versus federal authority. Basically, enforcement of the law within the cantons is a responsibility of the cantonal authorities while the transport of animals and of meat across the Swiss frontier is subject to federal control, now exercised by the Federal Veterinary Office. Within the cantons, the Federal Veterinary Office extends advice to the cantonal veterinary police, and in some cases gives direct support to some phases of enforcement and control. Actually, the Office achieves much in unification of control practices throughout the country, for it distributes circular letters to local, cantonal, and federal officials interpreting in detail the various laws and ordinances and describing the regulatory practices which have been found to be most satisfactory.

The Office has many other specific responsibilities—too numerous to mention. But we might add that it also administers, financially and through the direct intervention of veterinary control officers, a program of control and of subsidies whereby the Federal Government participates with the cantons in the rigorous enforcement of such control measures as are required—the slaughtering of animals and quarantining of premises—and effects the payment of subsidies to farmers in partial reimbursement of losses sustained. It prepares many technical documents in the form of instructions, regulations, and technical information. These are widely distributed throughout the country. In collaboration with the Faculties of Veterinary Medicine in Bern and Zurich, the Office arranges for continuation courses of instruction for the country's veterinarians in official positions.

FINANCES[13]   The charges imposed at the frontier for veterinary services have yielded the Confederation a gross income of 173 million francs in its first 50 years. This served to cover the expenses of the Federal Veterinary Office and provided a surplus which went into a special fund against which the costs of fighting the epizootics were charged. Thus the total cost of freeing the Swiss herds of bovine brucellosis (Bang's disease) approximated 86 million francs by the end of 1963, of which the Confederation paid 27.3 million and the cantons 37.7 million. About 66,000 cattle were slaughtered during the eradication program; the incidence of the disease in Swiss cattle was 3.87 percent. In the 10 years between 1955 and 1964 the Federal Government expended a total of 100 million francs in subsidies to support the eradication programs for foot-and-mouth disease, bovine tuberculosis, bovine brucellosis, swine pest, and other diseases.[14] The amounts paid by the cantons during the same period appear to have approximated 150 million francs. During this ten-year period over 214,000 animals[15] were slaughtered in the successful program to stamp out bovine tuberculosis. This represented over 13 percent of the total number of cattle in Switzerland.

The role of animals, of meat, milk, and eggs, in the transmission to man of the Salmonella diseases, ornithosis, the leptospiroses, and the rickettsial diseases is extensively discussed in the message of the Federal Council previously mentioned.[14] In some of these diseases the animals themselves, far from being passive carriers of the vector, are susceptible to the disease.

The Veterinary Office contemplates an immediate campaign against three diseases of fish: infectious kidney swelling and liver degeneration of rainbow trout, the twisting disease (*Drehkrankheit*) of trout broods, and furunculosis of the *Salmonidae*.

The regulations governing the transport of animals from one inspection district to another—be it for market, for exhibition purposes, or for slaughter—are strengthened by making mandatory a traffic document in which the owner certifies that the animal is in good health and is not being transported from a district under animal quarantine. The summering-wintering movement of animals to and from the high mountain pastures is now controlled by special regulations. Horses used by the military department are excluded from the regulations governing animal transport.

Control by the veterinary police of animals for export is also covered by the new law. This follows upon agreement with various countries that the animals purchased for export from Switzerland will be certified as being sound, in good health, and free of contagious or dangerous diseases. The export of animal products and of immunobiological substances is also included within the regulations.

Persons and institutes concerned with the storage or use of dangerous organisms and viruses such as the tubercle bacillus, the virus of foot-and-mouth disease, and the virus of rabies become subject to stringent rules designed to minimize the possibility of the spread of disease through carelessness on their part.

THE FEDERAL VACCINE INSTITUTE   The federal law of 13 June 1917 gave the Federal Government authority to support research on animal diseases and to establish an institute suitable for such research purposes and other activities deemed necessary in the fight against the diseases of domestic animals.

A plan was approved in 1941 for a joint enterprise by the Sanitary Department of the cantonal government of Basel-Stadt and the Federal Government. A new slaughterhouse would be constructed by the authorities of Basel-Stadt, and adjacent to this the Vaccine Institute would be built by the Federal Government.

Foot-and-mouth disease, apart from being stubborn and costly,[16] is possibly the most contagious of all. The highly virulent tissues used in preparing the vaccine against this disease must be obtained from freshly slaughtered animals. Great care must be exercised, from the time of receiving an infected animal until the carcass goes to the disposal plant, that there be no transmission of virus to other animals or infection of clothing, premises, and equipment. It was with these considerations in mind that the facilities in Basel were designed. Although it is possible to prepare different vaccines from animals suffering from different contagious diseases, the Institute has concentrated on the vaccine against foot-and-mouth disease.

Few of those who are concerned with animal disease will have forgotten the disastrous epidemics of foot-and-mouth disease in 1919–21 and 1937–39. In Switzerland alone no fewer than 622,811 animals were infected or were suspect of infection in the outbreak of 1919–21, and 437,023 in that of 1937–39.[17] That such an incidence is disastrous can be appreciated by recalling that the first step in fighting foot-and-mouth disease is the long-practiced and officially approved method of immediately slaughtering the infected animals.[18] An outbreak in 1951–52 in Switzerland caused the infection of 9076 animals and a flare-up in 1960–62 involved 12,539 animals. These figures should be compared with 14,035 and 23,662 for the entire decennia of 1943–52 and 1953–62, respectively. And if both sets of figures are compared with those for 1919–21 and 1937–39, a great reduction in the incidence of the disease is evident.[19] This decrease can be attributed almost certainly to the introduction of vaccination.

The usual practice, in an outbreak of foot-and-mouth disease, along with immediate slaughter of the infected animals, is preventive vaccination of herds on neighboring farms. Usually all of the animals in the infected herd are killed and neighboring herds are vaccinated on the same day. Quarantine measures are commonly employed. In Switzerland these are very rigorous and are such that a farm may be totally quarantined for 75 days and the infected areas completely disinfected; the movement of animals, people, farm products, and all materials out of the quarantined area is strictly forbidden.

In most countries only cattle are vaccinated routinely, and in some countries the transport of unvaccinated cattle is prohibited. Foot-and-mouth disease is to be found in swine and small ruminants, but extensive vaccination programs for these animals are uncommon.

Fruit Trees and Horticulture

And now we shall turn to fruit trees and horticulture. As for apples and other fruits, some of the relevant information is to be found in Table 30. It will be seen that in

Table 30   Agriculture: Some international comparisons (1977)
Table 30A   Areas planted in fruit trees[a]

	1968	1978
Total agricultural area[b] (in hectares)	2,174,713[c]	2,019,530[d]
Total area in fruit trees (hectares)	4795	6867
Apples (hectares)	3634	5366
Pears (hectares)	647	885
Cherries (hectares)	262	357
Plums (hectares)		225
Peaches (hectares)		31
Apricots (hectares)		3
Other (hectares)	252	

[a] Source: **341**, 1979, p. 111; 1969, p. 109.
[b] Excluding forested areas but including pasture land.
[c] 1969; [d] 1975.

Table 30B   Fruit crops[a] (in tons)

	1955	1968	1977
Apples	280,000	270,000	260,000
Pears	310,000	191,000	112,000
Cherries	61,000	51,000	28,500
Plums	31,000	50,000	46,000

[a] Source: **341**, 1975, p. 142; 1979, p. 118.

Table 30C   Livestock (in thousands)[a]

Country	Horses (No.)	Horses (per 1000 of pop.)	Cattle (No.)	Cattle (per 1000 of pop.)	Pigs (No.)	Pigs (per 1000 of pop.)	Sheep (No.)	Sheep (per 1000 of pop.)
Switzerland	45	7	2038	314	2062	317	361	56
Australia	476	36	27,107	2023	2268	170	134,361	10,027
Canada	350	15	12,348	546	8025	354	430	18.5
United Kingdom	140	2.5	13,534	241	7873	140	29,967	533
New Zealand	74	24	8499	2750	503	163	12,894	4173
USA	10,024	47	110,864	522	60,101	283	12,224	58
USSR	5700	22	114,086	451	73,484	290	142,600	563
West Germany	378	6	15,007	240	22,641	363	1136	18

Source: **341**, 1981, p. 586; and estimated 1975 populations of the countries listed.

Table 30D   Products (in thousands of tons)[a]

Country	Potatoes	Tobacco	Milk	Meat	Cheese	Butter	Fish[b]
Switzerland	713	1	3511	418	116	34	—
Australia	—	—	5933	2722	106	118	—
Canada	—	104	7751	1687	162	116	1280
Great Britain	6621	—	15,212	2133	206	134	1004
Japan	—	—	—	—	—	—	10,733
New Zealand	—	—	—	—	81	277	—
USA	16,088	867	55,655	18,013	1842	492	3102
USSR	—	311	—	—	—	—	9352
West Germany	11,368	—	22,547	3999	692	535	—

[a] Source: **341**, 1981, pp. 588, 591–593.
[b] Source: **341**, 1981, p. 594.

recent years apples were the favored products of the Swiss orchards. Of three popular varieties (not mentioned in the Table), Golden Delicious, Jonathan, and Gravenstein, the farmer and the consumer regard the Golden Delicious as the outstanding favorite.[20] The farm products on sale in the open-air Swiss markets would suggest to the casual observer that fruits and vegetables beautifully and bountifully displayed must be the principal products of the farm. However, it is obvious from the relatively small part of the total farm land given over in 1978 to orchards (0.33%) and to root crops plus other garden vegetables (about 2.0%) that other products of the farm such as cereal grains, animal fodder, livestock and dairy products are of far greater economic importance in Swiss farming.

Inclement Weather and Pests

All farmers in all countries are plagued from time to time by inclement weather, insect pests, and fungus invasions. On the north side of the Alps, the winter of 1980–81 brought massive amounts of snow. But on the south side, in the Ticino, a terrible drought was experienced. In December and January only 4 mm of rain fell in Lugano, the lowest on record since 1864. Many forest fires broke out, the growth of grass and cereal grains on the southern slopes suffered, and many Ticinesi blamed the föhn from the north as the cause of headaches, rheumatic pains, and psychological ills.

Throughout Switzerland, the farmers found themselves in 1981 in combat with countless millions of plant lice whose voracious appetites caused considerable damage to plantings of rape, wheat, cabbage, cauliflower, lettuce and other leafy plants. The pests, resistant to the usual chemical sprays, had to be sprayed every week. As required by law the crops when harvested had to be kept off the markets for two weeks to reduce the amount of active pesticide on the plants.

Subsidies

Through subsidies, government has endeavoured to assist farming and related activities. The independent rural people working in the mountain pasture lands—usually with dairy cattle—have been recipients of government subsidies since 1975, and professional fishermen have been aided since 1976 (341, 1981, p. 315). Refer also to Table 31. Both groups are small in number but are of economic importance in Switzerland. Forestry and the fishing industry also receive subventions from the Federal Government (cf. 341, 1981, p. 419). Agriculture, in general, receives federal subsidies in excess of 1.4 billion francs (341, 1981, p. 417).

It is not difficult to understand the plight of the mountain people. At one time, they were able to supplement the family income considerably by participation in home-industry activities. But these industries have long since almost disappeared and, currently, contribute nothing to many of these people. Government has appreciated the problem for many years and, for some time, has come to the rescue. The slopes where the farmer may endeavour to raise pasturage are frequently very steep. In addition to other subsidies to aid these people, a law was enacted in 1980

Table 31   Persons professionally employed in agriculture (*Landwirtschaft*)

	Permanent	Occasional	Total
1888[a]			481,033
1910[a]			469,106
1950[a]			455,103
1965[b]	229,097	225,654	454,751
1975[c]	147,921	211,130	359,051
1980[d]	138,076	193,819	331,895

Source: [a] Ref. **341**, 1951, p. 35; [b] **341**, 1969, p. 95; [c] **341**, 1979, p. 101; [d] **341**, 1981, p. 103.

Note: The totals for 1888, 1910, and 1950 may not be strictly comparable with the totals for 1965, 1975 and 1980. Note also that of the total active working force (*Erwerbstätigen*) in 1980 (circ. 3,015,500) about 6 percent were employed in agriculture. The corresponding percentage for 1960 was 13.3.

Employment in horticulture, forestry and fisheries[a]

	Horticulture	Forestry	Fisheries (and professional hunting)
1950	21,354	8327	927
1960	20,140	7550	724
1970	19,646	7481	836

[a] Source: **341**, 1975, p. 36.
Note that thousands of extras are occasionally employed in forestry: for example 38,065 in 1965 (**341**, 1969, p. 94).

which provides for the payment of 200 francs per hectare where the slope of the land exceeds 18°.

Expenses of the cantons include a variety of payments in connection with agriculture; forestry, fisheries, and hunting which for the year 1979 totalled 668,672,000 and 171,995,000 francs respectively (**341**, 1981, pp. 426, 427).

The number of people professionally employed in agriculture and related activities is reported upon in Table 31. Forestry, professional fishing and hunting are also included. They appear in the statistics for economic sector one and the inclusion of the relevant data in Table 31 is appropriate.

Forestry

The number of persons engaged in forestry has remained as a permanent work force of 6000 to 8000 for at least 100 years (cf. Table 31) despite the tremendous importance of the Swiss forests.[21] The forested area (1,052,000 ha in 1972), over 70 percent of which is publicly owned, constitutes one-fourth of the total surface of Switzerland (4,129,000 ha). The forests are largely concentrated on the slopes of the Jura, in the cantons of Ticino and Graubünden and the ancient forest cantons of

Vineyards in Switzerland. At the head of the Visp valley in the Valais region, the walls of the vineyard plots run across the hills like contour lines, some reaching terraces at nearly 4,000 ft., the highest vineyards in Europe. The vineyards of *Visperterminen.* (Swiss National Tourist Office)

Driving cattle up to the alpine meadows of Schwägalp in Appenzell/Northeastern Switzerland. (Swiss National Tourist Office)

In Central Switzerland. When the summer grazing is over, the decorated cattle are driven down from their Alpine pasture to the valley. (Swiss National Tourist Office)

In the Canton Valais, the grain is stored in especially constructed huts that stand on granite poles, in order to prevent the rodents from entering the huts. (Swiss National Tourist Office)

The laboratories of the High Alpine Research Station of the Jungfraujoch, including the Observatory for Astronomy and Astrophysics on the very peak. In the background is the Eiger with the north face—a challenge to many climbers—in the foreground. (E. Schudel, Photo-Haus, Grindelwald)

Swearing-in of new Standeräte (Councillors of State), 1971. (Swiss National Library)

Wrestling, a national sport in Switzerland. The combatants grip each other by the belt and the special outer shorts made of tough canvas. (Swiss National Tourist Office)

Wrestling. The winner brushes the sawdust off his opponent; a traditional gesture to show that there are no hard feelings. (Swiss National Tourist Office)

Hornussen, a Swiss national game. With a powerful blow, the disk is sent off! (Swiss National Tourist Office)

The defending party scattered over the playground is awaiting the "Hornuss." (Swiss National Tourist Office)

The Mazza-club with a wooden head that is 18-20 cm long and cylinder-shaped, fixed at the end of a flexible rod-shaped handle. (Swiss National Tourist Office)

Bois de Chillon Viaduct (1.4 miles) of the Swiss motorway system above Lake Geneva. View of the Chillon Castle and Montreux. (Swiss National Tourist Office)

View of San Carlo north of Poschiavo. To the left, San Carlo Borromeo Church known for its 17th century wall-paintings with matching wooden plastics. (Swiss National Tourist Office)

Grindelwald in the Bernese Oberland. This famous glacier village is one of the oldest holiday resorts in Switzerland. In the background: The Fiescherhörner with Fiescherwand and the Grindelwald glacier. (Swiss National Tourist Office)

Hikers along the high-level trail from Grindelwald-First to the Bachalpsee can enjoy this view of the upper Grindelwald glacier and the Schreckhorn/Bernese Oberland. (Swiss National Tourist Office)

Guests can easily reach the First terminus by chairlift from Grindelwald and, after one hour's walk along the Alpine path, they arrive at the Lake of Bachalp/Bernese Oberland. (Swiss National Tourist Office)

The Bernese Alps in the evening light. The panorama from *the Chasseral* extends in clear weather from Mont-Blanc to the Säntis. (Swiss National Tourist Office)

Regular Postal Buses comfortably take travellers over the new Gotthard-Pass Road to the south. (Swiss National Tourist Office)

Uri, Schwyz and Unterwalden. In fact there has been little change since the Middle Ages.

As of 1 January 1980, the total productive area of forest land amounted to 991,866 ha. Of this total, only 302,492 ha were privately owned. The remainder belonged to the State (56,093 ha) and to communes and collectives under public law (633,281 ha) (**341**, 1981, p. 133).

The Swiss consumption of wood in 1979 totalled 5,342,000 m³, of which 2,809,000 m³ were cut from public forests, 984,000 m³ from private holdings and 1,550,000 m³ were imported.* On the average, the corresponding data for the decade 1970–79 were quite similar (**341**, 1981, p. 133). Comparison with the data for earlier years is difficult because the necessary statistics provided by the cantons were incomplete in the earlier years. Sometimes the forestry results are presented in terms of number of trees, or as subventions to support reforestation—8,467,000 francs by the Federal Government from 1872 to 1915 (**341**, 1916, p. 60), or as net profit from the public forests after allowing for subventions by government—24,609,000 francs in 1979; 71,491,000 francs in 1960; and an average net profit of possibly 42 million francs per year between 1960 and 1979 (**341**, 1981, p. 134). A profit of 3,426,000 francs per year was derived from the federal forests during 1912 to 1919 (**341**, 1920, p. 109). Note that the state-owned forests amounted to only 12.1 percent of the total publicly-owned forests or 17.7 percent of the total area of forest land.

Wood consumption for manufacture of newspaper and printing papers is about twice as great, on a per capita basis, as in the rest of Europe. Approximately 23 kg of newsprint and 45.5 kg of ordinary printing paper are consumed annually by the average Swiss but only 11.4 kg and 20.7 kg, respectively, are needed to satisfy the annual requirements of the average European. The Swiss use slightly less wood per capita from deciduous trees and also less raw wood than the rest of Europe but significantly more wood from conifers than other European countries. The data apply to the years 1974–76.

Switzerland imports annually about 1.5 million cubic meters of *Nutzholz* (timber for building). This is about twice as much as the annual imports from 1975 to 1977 when there was a ban on construction of all but the most necessary buildings (**341**, 1981, p. 133).

The importance of forests to Switzerland goes far beyond that of providing wood for construction and for fuel: as a fuel, it has ceased to be of much importance since late in the nineteenth century when oil and coal came to be imported. Their greatest value is in prevention of erosion, protection against avalanches and preservation of ground water resources. They also have an intangible value because of their intrinsic beauty which is dear to nature lovers and hikers and certainly not lost upon the Swiss. Many of the *Wanderweg* trails traverse the forests, not merely to avoid trespass upon cultivated farm land but to permit enjoyment of the restful peace and quiet that dwell within the forests. The forest types are principally spruce (40

---

* m³ denotes cubic meters.

percent), beech (25 percent), silver fir (20 percent), other conifers (10 percent) and leaf trees (5 percent).

There is much federal and cantonal legislation designed to control the use of the forests, to regulate cutting, and to protect the forests against misuse and wanton damage. The Federal Constitution, in Article 24, gives to the Confederation

> the right of high supervision[22] over the control of river embankments and forests. It shall lend its support to works for the control and the embanking of mountain streams as well as the reforestation of their source areas. It shall lay down the regulations required to maintain such works and to preserve existing forests.

Even in the fourteenth century some communities in the ancient cantons placed restrictions on cutting certain species of trees (e.g. oaks and pine), and in 1488 Bern forbade the further conversion of forest into arable land. In general, we may say that the forestry laws are designed to ensure preservation of the areas now in forests, to forbid deforestation and partitioning of the forests, to regulate the uses of the forests and to define reforestation policies. Cutting within the forests must always be compensated by at least an equal area of new planting. Much of what may happen to forests under private ownership is also rigidly controlled. The sale of publicly owned forest is sharply restricted and its transfer to private ownership is almost impossible. In short, the laws, federal and cantonal, recognize the forests as an asset to be treasured, and forest policy is directed toward increasing the forest land,[23] reforesting if at all possible the slopes denuded by avalanches, and increasing the total yield and quality of the forest products.

As a relic of original communal ownership, the right of access to forests and forest pastures may be denied to no one. The right to tramp through the forests, to gather mushrooms, pine cones and berries may be enjoyed by all. Enclosures, if called for on the grounds of silviculture, may not be made permanent.

In 1876 a Federal Forestry Service was established within the Department of Interior. The Service is, in effect, a division of the Federal Inspection Service for Forestry, Hunting and Fisheries. Its responsibilities extend into the collection of woodland statistics and the negotiation of timber-trade agreements. The day-to-day management of the forests is largely a responsibility of the cantonal forestry services.

A School of Forestry was established as a division of the Federal Institute of Technology (ETH) when this great institution was founded in 1855. In the same year a Central Federal Institute for Forestry Research was established by federal decree. The research institute was annexed to the Division of Forestry of the ETH and was empowered to carry out scientific research and basic studies in forestry practice and management. In 1958, the Institute was transferred to Birmensdorf, near Zurich, on about 19 acres of land and in buildings that gave promise of adequate space for some years to come. An experimental nursery was established to study the raising of plants in nurseries to provide the young stock.

The experimental work of the Institute extends beyond Birmensdorf. Distributed over the forest lands are several hudred experimental plots totalling about 160 or so hectares. One of the plots, 7 to 8 ha in area, is on a mountainside high up in the Dischma Valley which leads down to Davos. It is just above the timberline at 2000 to 2230 meters. Climatological conditions are unfavorable in the extreme. The area is typical of other Alpine regions where the mountainside has been denuded by erosion, rock and land slides, avalanches and mountain torrents. The general aim of the work is to restore the timberline zone in a region which is extremely susceptible to avalanches. Ecological data must be assembled and possible plant associations studied. Concurrent studies on climatology, the soil, and possible entomological and phytopathological hazards are essential parts of such research.

Of all European countries engaged in the production and sale of forest products, Switzerland made the largest forestry profits (**265**, 1967, pp. 1163–64). The profit in 1960, as earned by the State, the communes and collectives under public law, amounted to 71,491,000 francs. In 1979 a profit of 24,609,000 francs was reported. In the intervening years there were marked fluctuations—from a loss of 300,000 francs in 1976 to a profit of 78,472,000 francs in 1974 (**341**, 1981, p. 134).

Table 32 Subsidies for agricultural workers, small farmers, independent mountain people and professional fisherman (in thousands of francs)
Table 32A Source of funds[a]

Year	Agricultural employers[b]	Federal Government	Cantons	Misc.	Total
1965	2628	18,128	7772	1292	29,820
1974	3612	38,804	17,948	1454	61,818
1980	6404	41,516	19,304	1454	68,678

Table 32B Payments to families[a]

Year	Agricultural workers	Small farmers	Administrative expense	Total
1965	8392	20,400	1028	29,820
1974	9247	50,947	1624	61,818
1980	11,358	55,495[c]	1825	68,678

Table 32C Number of recipients[a]

	Agricultural workers			Small farmers		Mountain people		Prof. fishermen	
	Adult Benefic.	Households	Children	Adult Benefic.	Children	Adults	Children	Adults	Children
1965	10,092	8708	17,713	29,170	93,392				
1974	5814	4457	11,403	31,816	97,123	51[d]	139[d]	35[d]	88[d]
1980	5444	3969	9602	28,483	77,400	66	160	28	70

[a] Source: **341**, 1981, p. 315.
[b] 1.3 percent of wages paid (up to 1974); thereafter 1.8 percent.
[c] Including independent mountain people and professional fishermen.
[d] 1976.

Fisheries

In Switzerland, one must distinguish between professional fishing and sport fishing. To practice fishing as a profession, one must be certified through an acceptable school where fishing is taught for professional purposes. Currently, such a facility for professional fishery training does not exist in Switzerland. In the 1960s a fisheries school existed in Germany, and I recall that it was attended by a number of Swiss. Much more is taught than the art of catching fish. An important part of the industry in which sound professional instruction is necessary concerns the operation of fish hatcheries. In 1975, a hundred or so fish hatcheries were to be found in Switzerland. Over 700 professionals were in charge, assisted by an almost equal number of nonprofessional workers and an occasional work force of about 500. In 1948, the number of professionals was 1132. This included 289 for whom fishing was their chief profession and 360 part-time fishermen. Incidentally, to be certified as a professional fisherman, three years of instruction in school and two years of apprenticeship are required (**329**, 1970, I, pp. 290–306). Thirteen professional fishermen were officially recognized by the canton of Zurich in 1982.

In the four-year period, 1972 to 1975, the annual catch from 18 of the Swiss lakes amounted to 3,186,530 kg (**341**, 1979, p. 117). This would provide only 500 gm of fish per inhabitant per year. However, this is supplemented by imports which, in 1980, totalled 30,600 tons of fish, prepared and unprepared. This works out to about 5 kg per person per year or 100 gm per week—a modest 300 to 400 gm for the modern family of three or four members. In 1970, it was only about 84 gm per week for such a family (**329**, 1970, I, pp. 290–306).

In 1919, the domestic catch (from only two lakes: Constance and Neuchâtel) was reported to be 358,033 kg (**341**, 1920, p. 116). Imports of fish and shellfish totalled 4,171,300 kg (**341**, 1920, p. 240). While recognizing that the data for the Swiss catch pertain to only 2 lakes instead of 18, it becomes clear that the domestic supply plus imports would provide, as a minimum, only about 22 gm per person per week, or possibly 100 gm per family of 4 or 5 members.

At the present time, the commercial domestic catch from the Swiss lakes consists principally of perch and *Felchen* which may be regarded as a choice whitefish and a relative of salmon. But pike, trout, char, bream, other white fish, and even eels are also caught in the Swiss lakes. During the 10 years, 1969–78, the total commercial catch amounted to 28,728,000 kg (**341**, 1981, p. 119).

Commercial fishing is not well developed. On Lake Constance in the early '60s only about 30 families lived as commercial fishermen. But with many other lakes, though all are smaller than Lake Constance, it may not be difficult to account for an annual catch of 3,000,000 kg or so. At the turn of the century, a great many salmon were taken from the Rhine at Basel, but now relatively few ascend the river, and those that do are so heavily contaminated with the pollutants that abound in the river between Basel and the North Sea that the lower Rhine salmon have ceased to be a delicacy.

The effect of pollutants on the fish population of other lakes is also very harmful.

The "noble" fish (trout, char, salmon, *Felchen* and *Brienzlig*, for example) are also dying out in Lake Geneva (*Lac Leman*) and Lake Thun. Perch (*Egli* or *Barsch*) have almost disappeared from these lakes. The problem is aggravated by the fishermen themselves who have been using nets of a smaller and smaller mesh-size.

The number of certified professional fishermen in Switzerland is also diminishing. From 120 or some years ago, the number who now fish in Lake Geneva is only about a dozen. The total number of certified fishermen in all of Switzerland was reported to be 340 in the late 1970s (**357**, 7 May 1980).

The regulations that govern sport fishing vary from canton to canton. In the canton of Bern, fishing licenses are sold to anyone and the holder may fish at any time in the waters of the canton. In Zurich, auctions are held from time to time and fishing rights, that entitle the purchaser to fish exclusively in a stated portion of a river, are sold.[24] For example, your rights will apply to a specified 2 or 3 km of the river and you alone may fish there. To preserve a semblance of democracy you are also given 6 or 7 fishing-privilege cards which you must distribute to 6 or 7 others— usually gratis, though sale of the cards is permitted. You are also required to seed your portion of the river annually with a specified number of fingerlings which one buys from a fish hatchery.[25]

National Self-Sufficiency in Food Production[26]

In section 20 I have discussed Switzerland's defense strategy in the event of an invasion of the country, a serious crisis situation requiring protection of the civilian population against the most destructive weapons and methods of modern warfare. However, a defensive strategy for use in war is now supplemented by a strategy in food production to serve the country well if crises develop in the future, serious enough to cut off all food imports. Switzerland's agricultural policy must be so shaped as to guarantee adequate food supplies in crisis situations, such as war. Experts are concerned over Switzerland's very unfavorable man/land ratio: 0.31 ha of agricultural area and 0.059 ha of tillable area per capita (ref. **416**). Self-sufficiency in food production is what it's all about.

In summary, Food Plan 80 calls for the following changes in food consumption and in usage of arable land, theoretically and hopefully amenable to realization.

(a) A progressive decrease in food consumption from the present comparatively high level of 3400 kcal per person per day to 2400 kcal. At present, Switzerland's domestic production is about 55 percent of her total food requirements (in calories). It is relevant to point out that the Swiss Federal Commission on Nutrition considers 2400 kcal per day to be sufficient for maintenance of efficiency and good health. It is also estimated that 10 to 20 percent of food purchases are not consumed but are wastefully discarded.

(b) A progressive increase in the area of arable farmland from 278,090 ha in 1981 to an eventual area of 355,000 ha.

And here, we should be aware of the uncontrolled abandonment of agricultural land ("back to nature; no interference by man") and its deliberate conversion to non-agricultural uses (e.g. factories, highways, and an ever-expanding suburbia). Equally relevant is the probability that the mountain lands are far below their full potential of agricultural development. Ecological considerations may also have to be re-evaluated if they conflict with the attainment of national security in food supply (cf. ref. **416**).

(c) With the plan in full operation, milk, dairy products, potatoes and bread cereals would cover more than two-thirds of the people's food-energy requirements and protein needs. The country's potato-growing area would have been increased more than threefold over that of 1981 and the area for producing bread cereals would be 55 percent greater. Total meat consumption would be only 30 percent of the 1980 level of consumption. Milk and butter consumption would continue at present levels, while cheese would decrease by about one-third.

(d) As gm per person per day, Food Plan 80 would provide, when fully operational, 80 of protein (93), 63 of fat (149) and 366 of carbohydrate (372)—1980 consumption in parentheses.

(e) Stockpiling of foods for people and animals and material for agricultural production would be an essential part of the peace-time policy because any major crisis, such as war, requires that reserve stocks be available. Also, these reserves would bridge the period between the beginning of the emergency and attainment of complete self-sufficiency.

(f) The plan also recognizes that fuel supplies for farm machinery, for the transport and processing of the products of the farm and for household use in food preparation demand a high priority. Research into the production of fuel from renewable organic materials, such as straw and wood, and also from manure and other agricultural wastes requires continued support and emphasis.

(g) Finally, the plan also recognizes that the means of production—labour, farm machinery, seed, fertilizers, crop-protection materials, antibiotics etc.—are essential components for which provision must be made.

Notes and Comments

1. 1978 values in parentheses (millions of francs).
2. Real Swiss cheese, as made in Switzerland, is quite unlike so-called Swiss cheese produced in other countries. There are several reasons for the difference: 1. Fresh milk is used by the Swiss. Over 1500 small cheese factories are spread throughout the country, each being within easy reach of an adequate number of dairy farmers, thus permitting the delivery of milk immediately after the morning and evening milkings. 2. The only additive permitted is common table salt. Other substances designed to affect the color, texture, or flavor of the cheese may not be used. 3. Possibly the most important reason for the unique flavor and texture of the cheese results from a law that prohibits the use of ensilage as a foodstuff for cows whose milk is to be used in cheese making for export. The green forage plants stored in a silo undergo extensive fermentation. Butyric acid and several other related fatty acids are produced in the fermentation process and these during digestion of the ensilage are absorbed and, in part, pass into the milk. The flavor of the cheese made from such milk is adversely affected. The texture suffers because of gas that may be released during the curing of the cheese, and this, incidentally, militates against long curing—an essential requirement in Swiss cheese making.
   In preparing the ever-popular cheese fondue, the Swiss most commonly use a mixture of Emmental

and Gruyère. When boiled with white wine, a little garlic, and a dash of *Kirsch*, the cheese is transformed into a bubbling, delectable dish into which pieces of bread enjoy being immersed. The flavor of a fondue differs from place to place in Switzerland because various local cheeses may be used instead of Emmental and Gruyère.

3. As a counterbalancing item, food and wine imports in 1978 yielded 408 million francs in customs duties (**341**, 1979, p. 197).

4. Including live animals of all sorts.

5. 1,055,600 ha in 1975; 1,080,400 ha in 1965.

6. Excessive rain and cold weather in the summer months of 1980, conspired to reduce greatly the amount of hay needed to feed cattle, especially the many that graze in the mountain meadows and slopes. In the great middle land, the weather was equally bad. The hay required for winter feeding of cattle was lacking. Many beef cattle, more than usual, were slaughtered and the country found itself faced with a mountain of meat (*Fleischberg*).

7. A skin disease caused by the bot fly (*Dasselfliege*).

8. *Eidgenössisches Veterinäramt*, Nordring/Birkenweg 61, Bern.

9. W. Messerli, *Festschrift zum 50 jährigen Bestehen des Eidgenössischen Veterinäramtes*, September, 1964, p. 15.

10. E. Fritschi, *Geschichte der Veterinärmedizin in der Schweiz*, 17 September 1962; a report by the Director of the Federal Veterinary Office.

11. A. Nabholz and F. Riedi, *Die Geschäftskreis des Eidgenössischen Veterinäramtes wahrend seines 50 jährigen Bestehens und künftige Aufgaben*, pp. 4–14 of the Festschrift cited in note 9, above.

12. The competence of the Federal Government was extended by a revision of Article 69, approved by popular vote in May, 1913: "The Confederation is empowered to legislate in the struggle against contagious, widespread, or dangerous diseases of man and animals."

13. E. Hügly, *Die Organisation des Eidgenössischen Veterinäramtes im Wandel der ersten 50 Jahre seines Bestehens*, pp. 60–64 of the Festschrift cited in note 9.

14. *Botschaft 9298 des Bundesrates an die Bundesversammlung zum Entwurf des Bundesgesetzes über die Bekämpfung von Tierseuchen* (**329**, 16 September 1965, pp. 1058–83).

15. The entire stand of Swiss cattle was officially declared free of tuberculosis in 1959. The 13,000 cases of the succeeding five years were new infections, revealed by positive tuberculin reactions; very few of these animals showed any clinical manifestations of the disease. The number of these new infections has been steadily decreasing (from 3851 in 1960 to 1274 in 1964).

16. The Federal Government pays the cantons about one million francs annually as the Confederation's share of the costs involved in stamping out the disease.

17. G. A. Moosbrugger, "*L'Institut vaccinal fédéral de Bâle*," *Mémorial à l'occasion du 150e anniversaire de la Société des Vétérinaires suisses*, 1963, pp. 123–29.

18. Fogdby, European Commission (FAO) for the Control of Foot-and-Mouth Disease, Proceedings of Symposium on Vesicular Disease, Plum Island Animal Disease Laboratory (27–28 September 1956). Agricultural Research Service, USDA, publication number ARS-45-1, December, 1957.

19. Recent data report a total of 103 cases since 1968: 19 in 1969, 7 in 1973, 15 in 1978, and 62 in 1980 (**341**, 1980, p. 112).

20. In 1926, in the canton of Vaud, 230 varieties of apples for the table, and 44 varieties of cider apples were known. By 1976 five varieties accounted for 86% of the apples under cultivation (**357**, 20 August 1980). A station is being created by a private collector in Prangins for the preservation of fruit-tree varieties threatened with extinction. The purpose is to maintain an inventory of trees possessed of unique genetic qualities and from which varieties may be bred which may be unusually resistant to disease, frost, fungi, destructive insects, microfauna, etc.

21. Many thousands more are employed from time to time as occasional workers—e.g. about 53,000 in 1975 (**341**, 1979, p. 98).

22. High supervision, as used in this article, means a concurrent power of the confederation and the cantons in the same field. The confederation issues the general rules by which the cantons are bound, . . . whereas the cantons issue subsidiary rules (**186**).

23. During the 80 years ending in 1956, 28,000 ha of new forest were established at the modest cost of

96 million francs. At the same time, government made heavy investments in building forest roads, sledgeways, ropeways and avalanche barriers, and in stream and flood control in forest lands.

24. Fishing rights, thus sold at auction, are very expensive—e.g. Sfr. 6000 to 10,000.

25. I am indebted to the late Professor Hadorn, then Rector of the University of Zurich, for the information presented in this paragraph (May, 1962).

26. I am indebted to Professor Joseph von Ah (Project Head of Food Planning, Federal Office of Agriculture, Bern) for a copy of a summarized edition of Food Plan 80, in the development of which the University of Fribourg is also participating. I am also grateful to him for copies of other documents pertaining to agriculture in Switzerland.

11.9 INDUSTRIAL ENTERPRISE

Introduction

Switzerland, though small in size and in population as compared with most of her European neighbours, is right up there among the giants in industrial enterprises. Fourteen out of 500 of the world's largest industrial corporations outside of the USA and ranked according to sales, are Swiss. Three of the fourteen manufacture prepared foodstuffs (Nestlé, Jacobs, and Interfood); three are concerned with fine chemicals and pharmaceuticals (Ciba-Geigy, Hoffmann-La Roche and Sandoz); six are in the group of machine and metal industries (Brown-Boverie, Alusuisse, Sulzer Brothers, Oerlikon-Bührle, George Fischer and Schindler Holding), one is a watch industry group (ASUAG), and one is in the building materials industry (Holderbank Financière Glaris). Their employees within Switzerland numbered 136,425 in 1977 (**102**), while their world-wide total of employees, 558,760 in 1977, was 604,873 in 1980. Employment throughout Swiss industry from 1895 to 1980 is summarized in Table 33.

Switzerland's imports and exports of products of the machine and metal industries, and several other industries are summarized in Table 34. The imports and exports of the food industry are detailed in the section on agriculture (11.8) and also included in summary form in Tables 34 and 35.

Mergers and Takeovers

Mergers, takeovers, and purchase of part or all of the assets of other companies, foreign and domestic, have proceeded apace in recent years. Frequently, this is an expression of a diversification policy by a company. Diversification may proceed from within by establishment of a new division and the hiring of personnel with the technical "know-how." The easier route, however, may be through purchase of all or a substantial part of the assets of an established company in the field which is to be penetrated. In some cases, an acquisition is intended to preserve a near-monopoly situation in a given industry, hence to ward off the threat to its position by a vigorous competitor. In Switzerland, industry is less extensively fettered by government regulations than in many other countries, notably the USA where corporate monopolies and corporate bigness seem to be regarded as sinful. For

579

Table 33   Employment in Swiss industry

	No. of factories	Employees			Sources
		Total	Swiss	Foreigners	
1895	4994	200,199			**341**, 1951, p. 146
1901	6064	242,534			**341**, 1951, p. 146
1923	7871	337,403		·	**341**, 1951, p. 146
1941	8734	436,493			**341**, 1951, p. 146
1950	11,475	492,563			**341**, 1951, p. 146
1951	11,529	545,863	494,306	51,557	**341**, 1951, pp. 142, 143
1966	13,360	881,571	584,322	297,249	**341**, 1981, pp. 156, 157
1967	13,183	881,593	581,369	300,224	**341**, 1969, pp. 144, 145
1968	12,669	881,949	576,181	305,768	**341**, 1969, pp. 144, 145
1970	11,954	879,889	564,959	314,930	**341**, 1979, pp. 152, 153
1973	10,663	814,269	512,909	301,360	**341**, 1975, pp. 170, 171
1976	9609	683,200	455,125	228,075	**341**, 1977, pp. 152, 153
1977	9341	681,819	458,037	223,782	**341**, 1979, pp. 152, 153
1978	9160	683,692	458,452	225,240	**341**, 1979, pp. 152, 153
1979	8944	678,179	454,571	223,608	**341**, 1981, pp. 156, 157
1980	8818	691,761	459,810	231,951	**341**, 1981, pp. 156, 157

Table 34   Imports and exports of several Swiss industries[a]
Table 34A   Imports

Year	Machines & metals[c]	Chemicals & pharmaceuticals	Food for human nutr.[d]	Textiles & clothing	Motor vehicles[b]	Sources
1906	170	58	145	364	2.9	**341**, 1951, pp. 174, 17
1950	647	487	764	553	242	**341**, 1951, pp. 174, 17
1977	10,407	4606	3882	4227	3580	**341**, 1979, pp. 191, 19
1978	10,607	4321	3247	4007	4484	**341**, 1979, pp. 191, 19
1979	11,712	5275	3080	4552	4352	**341**, 1981, pp. 197, 19
1980	15,974	6282	3472	5345	4779	**341**, 1981, pp. 197, 19

Table 34B   Exports

Year	Machines & metals[c]	Chemicals & pharmaceuticals	Food for human nutr.[d]	Textiles & clothing	Motor vehicles[b]	Sources
1906	90	41	127	428	5.1	**341**, 1951, pp. 188, 18
1950	1282	587	153	624	28	**341**, 1951, pp. 188, 18
1977	17,729	8228	1590	3117	470	**341**, 1979, p. 193
1978	17,961	8444	1456	2984	375	**341**, 1979, p. 193
1979	19,017	8800	1403	3208	369	**341**, 1981, p. 199
1980	21,466	9459	1490	3534	409	**341**, 1981, p. 199

[a] In millions of francs.
[b] Personal automobiles, cars, trucks, motorcycles, other motor vehicles.
[c] Watches excluded from imports and exports.
[d] Raw tobacco included in imports; processed (manufactured) tobacco included in exports.

Table 35   Switzerland's foreign trade[a,b,c,d]

Year	Imports[e]		Exports		Excess of imports	
1886	799		667		132	
1893	828		646		182	
1900	1111		836		275	
1910	1745		1196		549	
1915	1680		1670		10	
1916	2379		2448		−69	
1920	4243		3277		966	
1930	2564		1762		802	
1944	1186		1132		54	
1945	1225		1474		−249	
1950	4536		3911		625	
1960	9648		8131		1517	
1970	27,873		22,140		5733	
1973	36,589		29,948		6641	
1976	36,871		37,045		−174	
1978	42,300	f	41,779	f	500	f
1979	48,730	44,803	44,024	40,186	4706	4617
1980	60,859	53,980	49,608	44,648	11,251	9332
1981		56,665		48,680		7985

[a] In thousands of francs.

[b] Sources: **341**, 1951, pp. 164, 165; 1975, p. 201; 1981, p. 189.

[c] Until 1927, all transactions in gold bars were included. After 1927, all bank transactions in gold bars were no longer included. From 1944 to 1950, import values of gold bars were excluded, and from 1936 to 1950 gold bars for export were excluded from the tabulated data in this Table.

[d] In 1966 Switzerland's foreign trade, on a per capita basis, for both imports and exports, was the second highest of the 12 principal industrial countries of the world (**419**). Comparable data for the 1980s is not at hand.

[e] A footnote to a Table on import duties in the 1981 Statistical Yearbook (p. 203) states that import duties on raw tobacco were suppressed in 1970. The customs revenue on tobacco, 195 million francs in 1969, fell to 24 million francs in 1970, and to 3.6 million in 1971. From this minimal level the customs revenue rose gradually to 6.9 million francs in 1979 (6.1 million francs in 1980). The continuing customs revenue from tobacco imports is derived from fabricated products (cigarettes, cigars, etc.). The raw tobacco, imported duty free, amounted in 1980 to 25,300 tons with a total value of 159 million francs (**341**, 1981, p. 197).

[f] Source: **377**, "*Die Wirtschaftslage*," p. 12 (supplement to *Die Volkswirtschaft*, vol. 55, no. 6, June 1982).

example, there is not even a flutter of a governmental eyelash when Nestlé, the biggest of them all, acquires another company. In the early 1980s, Nestlé purchased the entire assets of Alcon Laboratories—a USA pharmaceutical company. It also bought a major interest in Roco Conserven A.G. in Rorschach, Switzerland, and is reported to be negotiating for a takeover of the Hero Company—a large producer of preserved fruit preparations. In April 1984, Nestlé announced a prospective takeover of all the outstanding shares of Hills Brothers Coffee Inc. (San Francisco). In late 1984, Nestlé initiated an offer to acquire the Carnation Company Inc.

A few other examples of recent major investments by Swiss companies in other corporations may suffice. Ciba-Geigy Inc. (USA) and three other USA companies bought about 80 percent of Dupont's pigments business. Ciba-Geigy Inc. and Ciba-Geigy A.G. (the parent company in Switzerland) also bought the pigments business of Hercules Inc. with several dye factories in the USA and one each in Belgium and the Netherlands.[2] Oerlikon-Bührle purchased the Bally concern (principally shoes), thereby increasing its consolidated sales to 3.4 billion francs. It also took over Motch-Merryweather Inc.—a USA producer of machine tools. The Schindler group has entered upon a joint venture with the Chinese Construction Machinery Corporation. Emerging from the agreement is a new company, the Chinese Schindler Elevator Company with its head office in Peking. Three other Chinese elevator companies in Peking and Shanghai are drawn into the joint enterprise. Schindler Holding Co. also acquired in 1979 the Haughton Elevator Division of the Reliance Electric Company in Cleveland—a large manufacturer of elevators. It had 1500 employees in 1979 and many branch operations—all in the USA.

Buhler Bros. A.G., the sixteenth largest industrial concern in Switzerland has entered into a cooperative agreement with the Soviet State Committee for Science and Technology to participate jointly in machine construction for the flour milling industry, the production of animal food, construction of silos, and machinery for the loading and unloading of ships.

Sandoz A.G. has agreed to purchase the proprietary medicine division of the Culbro Corporation—makers of Ex-Lax. Sandoz is also becoming actively involved in the oil industry through collaboration with the English firm, KCA International Ltd. and KCA's subsidiary B.W-Mud Ltd. The agreement provides for research and development of chemicals required in drilling operations and the use of those chemicals in drilling for oil in the North Sea. The sale of these chemicals to the partner should bring to Sandoz a few hundred thousand pounds, according to estimates in 1979. KCA is. assured of a loan from Sandoz of two million pounds. B.W-Mud Ltd. will also benefit financially through the sale to Sandoz of its technical knowledge and experience in oil drilling. If all goes well a take-over of the British Company by Sandoz is conceivable.

Brown-Boverie A.G. is to construct a gas-turbine power plant in Saudi Arabia. It has also announced that it plans to mass-produce batteries and related equipment for electric-powered cars in Canada in the 1990s. The products will be marketed in North America. The plan involves a possible joint venture of BBCs Mannheim unit and Magna International Inc. of Toronto. Swiss investors have bought the Times Square Tower (formerly the Allied Chemical Building). A Swiss investor in Geneva has bought a 5.88 percent interest in Pullman Inc. Swissair has bought the Drake Hotel in New York City. Alusuisse has bought from Phelps Dodge Inc. its 40 percent interest in the Consolidated Aluminum Corporation, the remaining 60 percent being already owned by Alusuisse. Also, Alusuisse, through a subsidiary, has bought a 93 percent interest in the Maremont Corporation Inc.—an auto parts manufacturer. The takeover is almost complete. And Electrowatt A.G. (Zurich) has bought out the Gamewell Corporation Inc. (USA), a maker of fire alarms and fire extinguishers. Many other examples could be cited. The Swiss watch group known as ASUAG has acquired a majority position (85 percent of the capital) in Statek Inc., a California corporation that specializes in the production of extremely thin quartz-crystal resonators (0.1 mm). The acquisition will strengthen ASUAG in the production of electronic watches and in the development of microelectronic products. ASUAG is also engaged in a joint venture with the Chinese Stelux conglomerate based in Hong Kong which has a strong minority position in the American company, Bulova. Ebauches—Electroniques S.A., another Swiss firm, is also involved with ASUAG in Hong Kong operations. Another Swiss group, SSIH, proposes a joint venture in Singapore with a Japanese partner. Still other Swiss firms are interested in such developments, partly with technical cooperation in mind and also largely influenced by the cheap labor—the wages of female employees being only about 15 percent of the prevailing wage in Switzerland for female labor.

And, of course, substantial equity positions in Swiss companies are being acquired by companies in the USA and elsewhere. For example, Schuepach A.G., a Swiss packaging company, has sold a 75 percent interest to Reynolds Industries Inc. and I.B.M. has bought an interest in four European companies, including two Swiss, that manufacture spectrophotometers. The two American fast-food chains, McDonalds and Burger King, are becoming established in Switzerland through the sale of franchises to prospective restaurateurs whose operations under the Company name must conform to requirements specified by the licensing company.

An interesting cooperative agreement in investment banking was reported in 1979 between MM. Pictet & Cie of Geneva and Mellon National Corporation in Pittsburgh. The agreement calls for a joint enterprise based in London. The purpose is to seek out American pension funds for investment outside of the USA. Mellon will find the money and Pictet will arrange for its investment.

In January, 1983, the Geneva-based Trade Development Bank Holding S.A. was acquired by Shearson/American Express and merged into its international banking operations. The acquisition, at an estimated cost to American Express of 500 million dollars, will greatly expand and strengthen the role of American Express in international financing.

The Nestlé Company

As previously mentioned, Nestlé A.G. is the largest Swiss company—ranked in sales—outside of the USA. It was founded in 1865 by the chemist, Henri Nestlé, whose initial interest in the newly-founded company concerned the preparation of foods for infants and young children. From sales of 20.1 billion francs in 1977, the company derived a net profit of 830 million francs. In 1980, when sales rose to 24.5 billion francs, the net profit failed to keep pace with sales and fell to 683 million francs, but rose to about 1000 million francs in 1982 and to about 1276 million francs in 1983.[3] The geographical diversity of the company is evidenced by the number of employees world-wide (140,009 in 1979), of whom only 6661 were employed in Switzerland. This is an extreme example of the internationalization of corporate activities in which the total number of employees in the foreign branches of a company may considerably exceed the number of employees in the factories within the home country. As might be expected, Nestlé's sales follow the same pattern: sales in Switzerland in 1977 of 682 million francs as compared with total world-wide sales of 20.1 billion francs.

The company's principal products are its infant-food preparations for which a heavy demand exists, especially in Third World countries. Nestlé, the Federal Public Health Service and other agencies agree that, whenever possible, the infant should be breast-fed; only when breast-feeding is impossible should a prepared infant food—a milk substitute—be used.[4] A hazard that exists in many underdeveloped countries resides in the use of polluted water in preparing the food for bottle feeding of the infant. A consensus is emerging that high-pressure advertising of these breast-milk substitutes should be avoided, that breast-feeding should be resorted to whenever possible and its benefits stressed in all infant-feeding programs. Finally, if breast-feeding is impossible, and if an infant-formula substitute is used, the water employed should first be boiled unless it is known to be unpolluted by disease-producing micro-organisms. The contraceptive effect of breast-feeding should also be stressed; women cannot conceive when they are lactating.

In the 1980s Nestlé built a research center in Lausanne at a cost of 100 million francs or so. In the planning phase it was expected to employ about 400 persons. On a world-wide basis, the company employs over 2000 persons in research and development.

Problems of Business Enterprises

For business enterprises generally, the late 1970s and early 1980s were characterized by difficulties almost too numerous to mention. Switzerland was no exception. Swiss businesses complain of a shortage of qualified personnel, of uncooperative attitudes by the bankers, of the State applying the brakes instead of helping, of a general deterioration of business ethics, and of constantly changing rates of currency exchange. The medium-size and small businesses cannot borrow from the banks on terms that are as favorable as those extended to the large enterprises. The whole system of quantity rebates operates to the disadvantage of the retailer and owner of a small business. Payments by their customers are frequently delayed by months or, occasionally, even a year or more. They complain that the banks and even the State go too far to protect their own interests. Assistance programs for the economy, allegedly have done little to lessen the burdens of the small businesses. Action on their requests for aid may be deferred for months. All authorities for whom the small businesses are entitled to seek assistance or from whom approvals etc. must be obtained act with a promptness that can only be compared with the speed of a snail. The building industry complains that procurement of approval to initiate construction takes longer than the construction itself.

Perhaps the loudest complaint stems from the paper war in which industry tries to defend itself against the overpowering forces of government. The demands of the State for more and more information increasingly require more and more paperwork by business at considerable cost. One to two percent of the employees of business must now work for the State to satisfy government's hunger for more reports. Finally, the introduction of the added value tax (*Mehrwertsteuer*) would have imposed on the retailer and owners of a small business, administrative costs that are appreciable. It is not surprising that they opposed the tax. See also Note 9 in Section 11.11 on Taxation.

Research and Development

Expenditures for research and development (R and D) in the Swiss industries totalled 2.39 billion francs in 1977, broken down as follows: chemical industry, 1.15 billion francs; machine and metal industry, 972 million; watch industry, 79 million; food industry, 84 million; textiles and clothing, 42 million; other industries, 67 million. The total expenditure represents about 4.4 percent of sales by the 504 enterprises covered by the survey. These firms employed about 400,000 persons, of whom 28,130 were engaged in research and development within Switzerland for the private economy (**341**, 1981, p. 502). Omitted are the R and D expenses of the branches of Swiss industries in other countries, of the universities, of the Federal Government and of autonomous enterprises. It will have been noticed that about 90 percent of the R and D expenditures by Swiss industry are incurred by two of her major industries: the chemical industry (48 percent, 11.6 percent of sales) and the machine and metal industry (41 percent, 5.7 percent of sales). If the other industries mentioned above would invest more in R and D it is probable that their exports would be significantly increased. Of 41 countries reported upon, Switzerland in 1978 with total exports valued at 23.6 billion dollars, was in eleventh position (**341**, 1981, p. 604). It is improbable that she would be able to overtake number 10 (45.0 billion dollars) but sales at home might also increase appreciably, doing so at the expense of imported products from competing industries elsewhere.

It should be mentioned that 16,665 persons engaged in R and D by the private economy in 1975 represented about 26 per 10,000 of the total Swiss population. They were made up of graduates of universities and schools of engineering plus a miscellaneous category exclusive of administrative personnel (**341**, 1981, p. 501). As Cerletti pointed out, such a quotient (26 per 10,000 of population) would compare favorably with the corresponding figure for West Germany.

An excellent report on Research and Development in the Swiss Private Economy has been prepared by Prof. Aurelio Cerletti of Sandoz A.G. (**83**). A general observation on business enterprises in Switzerland pertains to the size of enterprises in terms of employment. Of industrial concerns totalling 62,738 over half (32,452) employed only one to three persons. In the service enterprises with a total of 204,959 undertakings, again more than half (135,889) employed three persons or less (**341**, 1981, p. 142). One may generalize in concluding that smallness is characteristic of the unit of employment in Swiss enterprises. In a sense this is historically rooted in the proliferation of home industries prior to the industrial age—a time when the family members worked in their own homes for the textile and watch industries especially (see Chapters 7 and 10, including Tables 1 and 2 in Chapter 10).

Patents (see reference 14)

The number of patents in force in a country reflects its activity in research and development. At the end of 1979, with 89,630 patents in force, Switzerland would be ranked as number eight in a worldwide comparison. However, if the number of patents be corrected for population differences, we find that Switzerland, with 14,200 patents in force per one million inhabitants (three times that of the USA), rises to the first position. A comparison should also be made by looking at the number of applications for patent protection in other countries ("patent exports"). In 1979, individuals in Switzerland filed a total of 15,650 patent applications in other countries. She also was on the receiving end ("patent imports"): 7099 applications were received from individuals in other countries for patent protection. To this we could add 4441 of her own nationals to give a total of 11,540. Were we to correct the data for population differences we would find that in "patent exports" and "patent imports" Switzerland again rises high on the list. This can only mean that Switzerland vigorously pursues her activities in research and development and that her "know-how" is fully recognized by other industrial countries. Were we to learn that three to four years are required to process an application for a patent, we should understand that this great time lag may be of little importance, and should not disturb the inventor. The filing date of the application is usually sufficient to establish priority and to ensure protection despite the long delay in judging the novelty of the invention.

Questions concerning patents are in the responsibility sphere of the Swiss Intellectual Property Office (*Bundesamt für geistiges Eigentum*). The office is also responsible for matters pertaining to copyrights and trademarks to which reference has been made in the section on "Communication" (11.6).

The office is also deeply concerned with the protection of geographical indications of source in Switzerland. This is of much importance to the export industries. For example, the name "Swiss cheese" is shamefully exploited. There is a so-called "Swiss cheese" made in Wisconsin. There is also "Swiss chocolate" which has never been exposed to Switzerland and her people, "Neuchâtel clocks" which never swung a pendulum in Neuchâtel canton, and "St. Gallen lace" which never originated in St. Gallen or even in Switzerland. Sometimes one can buy Swiss Swiss cheese and get the real thing or Swiss-type cheese which honestly confesses that it was not made in Switzerland. Fortunately there is an increasing recognition of the need to identify accurately the source of a given product. This must be done to avoid deception. Ideally, the adjective "Swiss" should connote origin and not serve as a generic name meaning merely "Swiss type." The Swiss Intellectual Property Office, in cooperation with other federal agencies, strives to do battle against the misuse of names and symbols, especially those that seem to attribute to Switzerland products that are non-Swiss in origin and often are of a lesser quality.

Fortunately there are domestic laws and international legislation pertaining to this problem and it is sometimes sufficient merely to advise the embassies and consulates in the country at fault, of the appropriate legal measures required to end any such acts that are contrary to fair commerce. "CUSCO," for example, may not be used as a trademark to designate chocolate from elsewhere than Peru. And "PILS" may not be used to designate beer that is not brewed in Pilsner. The multilateral treaties in this field, ratified by Switzerland, are the Paris Convention for the Protection of Industrial Property and the Madrid Agreement for the Repression of False or Deceptive Indications of the Source of Goods. Bilateral treaties to achieve the same end appear to be preferred by Switzerland which, by 1980, had concluded six such treaties: with the Federal Republic of Germany, Spain, France, Czechoslovakia, Portugal and Hungary. Additional bilateral treaties are planned. The six mentioned give better protection of the source country than the multilateral treaties referred to. For example, the use of qualifying terms such as "kind", "type", "make" or the like, disguises the indications of source and is declared unlawful in the bilateral treaties.

TECHNOLOGY TRANSFER   Among the well-established industrial enterprises, transfer of technology, of industrial "know-how", presents few problems. Well-recognized, internationally accepted, and excellent licensing systems are in operation. Holders of patents commonly sell rights to others to exploit to their advantage certain stated patents within stated limits and restrictions to which the two parties agree. In Switzerland in the 1980s, the annual income derived from sale of patent rights exceeded the annual expenditure on purchase of such rights by about one billion francs.

The developing countries, including the Third World, face a real dilemma. They need the know-how of the industrialized countries for their own development but they lack the financial resources required for purchase of patent rights. Hence they are prone to argue in technology debates in the United Nations that "technology is the heritage of mankind" to which everybody has a right. The General Secretariat of UNCTAD established an intergovernmental working group in 1974 to formulate a universal Codex for technology transfer. The group, after holding four conferences and recording little if any progress, set up an Interim Committee, which after several struggles appears prepared to admit failure.

The trouble is that the different viewpoints of the two parties—the haves and the have-nots—are irreconcilable. The developing countries realize that a stated product of a giant corporation may be assembled from many parts, the manufacture of which may be spread around among many subsidiaries of the parent company. And so, "let us obtain patent rights on one or two parts; we shall shop around for other parts." The proposal is received coldly and negatively by the patent holder. "We will sell a manufacturing license for the total product, but not for any parts of it." The product may not be "unbundled."

The patent holders have also expressed fears that the secrets of manufacture may not be well guarded, as they are required to be, if sold to some developing countries with a dubious record of treaty-observance integrity.

In late 1982 the Codex covered 27 pages of text. Few of the paragraphs had been accepted as "agreed text." Most of the text can only be described as expressions of differences of opinion, parts of which constitute an appendix of 17 pages of possible variants. Whether a universal Codex will ever emerge from the present mountain of words and the semantic dialogue is questionable. For some time to come, subsidiaries of companies in the industrialized world may continue to be set up in Third World countries to the mutual advantage of both parties. Perhaps they can achieve what needs to be done without a universal code governing technology transfer. For a thorough discussion of the problem, see ref. **266**, 11–12 September 1982.

The Pharmaceutical Industry

The three largest members of the Swiss pharmaceutical industry are Ciba-Geigy, Hoffmann-La Roche and Sandoz. The Swiss Statistical Yearbook does not report either on individual companies or on the pharmaceutical industry by itself. The published data pertain to the chemical industry as a whole, of which the pharmaceutical industry is certainly the largest segment. Imports and exports for selected years in the twentieth century are reported upon in Table 35.

Data on employment in the chemical industry are presented in Table 36. The three largest pharmaceutical companies mentioned above employed in Switzerland in 1977 a total of 38,692 persons. Worldwide employment by the same three pharmaceutical companies totalled 149, 728. If we now turn to the remaining Swiss companies engaged in the chemical industry (including pharmaceuticals) and restrict our inquiry to the 100 largest industrial companies in the country, we would find that in 1977 only 4811 additional persons were employed by the industry in Switzerland and 9275 additional persons worldwide (**102**). In other words, 87.6 percent of employees in the chemical industry in 1977 worked for the three largest pharmaceutical companies. The industry, including as it does many small enterprises, nevertheless is concentrated in large manufacturing units. Of the 357 factories in the chemical industry in 1980, each of 307 employed less than 200 persons. Almost 76 percent of the 63,089 employees worked in factories employing more than 200 persons, and over 55 percent of the total work force were employed in 9 large factories with over 1000 employees in each. The last mentioned group totalled 34,797 persons. One half of all employees in the chemical industry are concentrated in the Basel area (cantons of Baselstadt and Basellandschaft)—the base of operations of the largest companies that manufacture pharmaceuticals, dyestuffs, vitamins and fine chemicals.

The problems facing the pharmaceutical industry in the major countries are seldom concerned with diminished employment and decreased production and sales, such as have troubled the Swiss watch industry. Even the unfavorable exchange rates for the Swiss franc had no adverse effect on the Swiss pharmaceutical industry in either exports or employment in the 1970s and 1980 (Tables 35 and 36).

The industry in Switzerland and elsewhere is constantly plagued by a variety of suits at law. Hoffmann-La Roche, for example, has been charged in several countries with abusing its monopoly position in respect to the tranquilizers valium and librium, by marketing these at prices alleged to be excessively high. The Federal

Table 36   Employment in the Swiss chemical industry

		Employees			
Year	Factories	Total employees	Swiss	Foreigners	Sources
1895	117	3078			
1901	136	4196			**341**, 1951, p. 146
1923	213	9896	8169	1727	**341**, 1948, pp. 141–143
1951	381	25,350	24,032	1318	**341**, 1951, pp. 143, 146
1966	434	54,717	44,602	10,115	**341**, 1981, pp. 156, 157, 158
1968	432	59,761	46,930	12,831	**341**, 1969, pp. 144, 145
1970	433	64,701	49,156	15,545	**341**, 1981, pp. 156, 157, 188
1973	401	65,371	46,831	18,540	**341**, 1975, pp. 170, 171
1976	372	61,508	44,060	17,448	**341**, 1977, pp. 152, 153
1977	368	61,076	44,212	16,864	**341**, 1979, pp. 152, 153
1978	358	61,502	44,623	16,879	**341**, 1979, pp. 152, 153
1979	361	62,263	45,230	17,033	**341**, 1981, pp. 156, 157
1980	357	63,089	45,646	17,443	**341**, 1981, pp. 156, 157

High Court in Karlsruhe, West Germany, which is a court of last resort, has decided in favor of Hoffmann-La Roche. In so doing it has recorded a judgment which will be accepted without question as a precedent in several other countries, such as Holland, which have awaited the decision of the Federal High Court in West Germany.

In another action, Hoffmann-La Roche Inc. (the American subsidiary of F. Hoffmann-La Roche A.G. of Switzerland) and Genentech Inc. have been sued jointly by the University of California in a battle over the right to profits resulting from the "unauthorized" use of a human-cell line which Hoffmann-La Roche, in concert with Genentech, has used in gene-splicing experiments to produce interferon. Without discussing the details on which the case rests, it is sufficient to add that the court has been asked to order return of the cell line and to require the payment of compensation for damages.

The problems of the pharmaceutical industry is all countries are legion. One is the cost of production. From the time of conception of a new drug by the research department until it is synthesized, tested and approved by the appropriate authority (the Food and Drug Administration in the USA), ten million dollars, an average figure, will have been invested.[5] Although now believed to be safe for human use, provided the directions for its use are faithfully observed, a number of troublesome questions remain unanswered. Will the long-continued use of the drug lead to addiction? Will withdrawal problems arise if its long-term use is abruptly terminated? Will it produce insidious effects that remain obscured until many years have elapsed? If taken in conjunction with other drugs, as happens frequently, will seriously adverse results ensue? Will the industrial wastes from the company seep into the ground water and thereby contaminate important sources of drinking water, or if discharged into a river or a lake will they lead to the death by poisoning of fish and water fowl? Will an antitrust suit arise, which, if the company loses, may necessitate surrender of its patent rights on the drug, and dedication of the relevant patents to the public? Claims for damages by those who allege to have suffered certain ill effects from a drug approved for human use, may run into many millions. The cost of insurance against such suits for damage compensation can be almost prohibitive.

Without describing any such claims that have been made against the Swiss pharmaceutical companies, it need only be said that they encounter the same risks with their products as are faced by the pharmaceutical industry in other countries. Perhaps the pharmaceutical companies in Switzerland and several other countries operate at an even greater risk, if it be true that approval of a new drug for human use is obtained in the home country with less delay, less testing and at less expense than in certain other countries.

In spite of the many problems faced by the industry, the financial reports of the Swiss pharmaceutical companies indicate that few tears need to be shed over the state of their health. Table 37 reports on the 1980–83 operations of the Hoffmann-La Roche concern which suggest that the company is doing quite well. Ciba-Geigy reported that it did well in 1981 and possibly a little better in 1982. Sandoz also enjoyed profitable operations. Hoffmann-La Roche reported the purchase of

Table 37 Hoffmann-La Roche operations[a]

	1980	1981	1982	1983[d]
Employees at year's end	43,643	44,033	46,484[e]	
Total sales[b]	5855.8	6774.6	7103.4[f]	7506
Sales by divisions (in % of total)				
Pharmaceuticals	44.4	43.7	42.3	41.9
Diagnostic aids	3.6	4.4	6.2	8.9
Vitamins & fine chemicals	27.6	27.8	28.0	28.8
Cosmetics	11.0	11.2	10.5	10.3
Instruments	6.8	6.6	6.9	7.0
Miscellaneous	6.6	6.3	6.1	3.1
Total	100.0	100.0	100.0	100.0
Income[b]	231.6	253.1	281.2	
In percent of sales	4.0	3.7	40.0	
Expenditure on research[b,c]	692.6	808.0	920.7	

[a] Source: **357**, 2 June 1982: for 1982 and 1983, personal communication from Hoffmann-La Roche.
[b] In millions of Swiss francs.
[c] The company assigns about 13 percent of its total turnover to support research.
[d] Provisional.
[e] Attributable to business acquisition, 2869.
[f] Of this grand total, sales in Switzerland amounted to only 215.9 million; in Europe as a whole, 2831.9; and in North America, 2476.1 million francs.

Biomedical Reference Laboratories in North Carolina for 160 million dollars. The newly acquired company, with a staff of 1600, specializes in laboratory investigations for doctors and hospitals.

The Watch Industry

Though a small country in which agriculture and related activities are conspicuously large, Switzerland is also heavily industrialized. In terms of the export market, as measured in francs, the watch industry in 1975 was in the third position, with the machinery industry and chemical industry being first and second respectively. The Swiss excel in the production of products requiring high precision in manufacture. The conversion of a ton of metal into almost a ton of watches is an example. Until the early 1970s, the Swiss watch industry was the world leader, well ahead of the industry in Germany, Hong Kong, Japan, Taiwan, USA or elsewhere.

But, unfortunately for the Swiss watch industry, their ever-cautious approach to the new, seriously delayed their entry into the manufacture of the electronic watch. By the time they decided that the electronic watch was here to stay and Swiss industry had begun to enter this highly competitive market, they suffered another blow that hit every branch of the Swiss export trade. This was the appreciation of the Swiss franc which by 1977 contributed to a substantial increase over the 1970 price of the same item abroad.[6] Thus, a Swiss watch that might have cost 100 USA dollars in 1970 could have cost the USA purchaser as much as $156 in 1977.

However, it may be that there is a turn for the better. In the first nine months of 1980 Switzerland's sale of watches abroad reached 2.46 billion francs which was eight percent higher than in the corresponding nine months of 1979. In 1981 the Swiss Watch Chamber reported a further increase to 2.8 billion francs for the corresponding nine months—13.2 percent better than in 1980.

Hopefully, 1979 marked the low point in the industry. The monetary problem—a currency that was too strong—was the deciding factor. Shipments of watches and watch movements abroad fell seriously below the 1978 levels—decreases of six percent in value and 18.8 percent in quantity. The cheaper items, principally mechanical watches, fell the most, while top-of-the-line products and electronic watches increased in sales. Table 38 presents the industry data for selected years from 1970 forward. Hong Kong bought 14.3 percent of the total, the USA 12.1 percent and West Germany 9.3 percent. But foreign-made watches appeal to some Swiss. The 1980 imports of watches and watch movements were valued at 399.5 million francs. The biggest supplier by far was Hong Kong.

One important group in the Swiss watch industry is SSIH (*Société Suisse pour l'Industrie Horlogère*), manufacturer of the Omega and Tissot watches. It also has a USA subsidiary, the Hamilton Watch Company. SSIH has fallen upon hard times with heavy accumulated losses in the past several years. By the end of 1980 the firm's liabilities exceeded its assets by 25 million francs. Six of the leading Swiss banks, one or two of which are shareholders in SSIH, have come to the rescue with a package of 300 million francs—one third to cover written-off stocks of unsold watches and costs of restructuring the company, one-third to provide new capital and one-third

Table 38   Swiss watch industry exports

	1970	1973	1975	1977	1978	1979	1980	1983	1984
Watches Movements Raw works (*Ebauches*)[a]	73.262	86.229	68.619	71.070	64.748	53.184	59.064	40.8[d]	44.0[d]
Actual export value in millions of francs[b]	2629	—	3141	3379	3433	3260	3550	3400[d]	3800[d]
Export value in millions of USA dollars[c]	600	—	1217	1390	1918	1904	2126	1550[e]	1479[e]

[a] In millions of pieces (**341**, 1977, p. 192; 1981, p. 200).

[b] (**341**, 1981, p. 199). It is not clear from the *Jahrbuch* whether watch movements and raw works are included.

[c] For USA exchange rates (**341**, 1981, p. 279).

[d] Estimated from January–September data.

[e] Average end-of-year exchange rates: 1983 = Sfr. 2.189
1984 = Sfr. 2.564.

as new lines of credit. Cooperation with ASUAG (*Allgemeine Schweizerische Uhrenindustrie A.G.*), the largest Swiss watchmaker, in research, development and production is contemplated. Rescue of SSIH is important. At stake are the jobs of 5000 employees and the prestige of the Swiss watch industry.[7]

In early 1983, ASUAG appeared to be ready to market a cheap Swiss-made quartz analog watch. Though of good quality, it is expected to sell for about 40 Swiss francs. It is known commonly as a "Swatch" and is expected to penetrate deeply the huge market at home and abroad for inexpensive wrist watches. It may face competition with the M-watch sold by the huge Migros concern but ASUAG expects to outsell the M-watch handsomely.

ASUAG lost about 150 million francs in 1981 and expected a comparable loss in 1982.

The Swiss watch and jewelry industry employing in 1975 some 61,058 persons consisted of 2867 establishments of which 1537 employed only one to five persons. Only 128 had more than 100 employees each (**341**, 1981, p. 142). The watch industry, by itself, numbered 776 enterprises in 1980 with a total of 41,343 employees, located principally in the cantons of Neuchâtel, Bern, Solothurn and Jura. The jewelry industry by itself employed in 1980 in 53 facilities only 3401 workers, giving a combined total for the two industries of 829 units employing 44,744 workers (**341**, 1981, pp. 142, 154, 155). Unless the statistics have been misinterpreted, the data suggest a reduction of over 16,000 employees in the two industries between 1975 and 1980. However, a secondary source reports that employment in the Swiss watch industry fell from a peak of 85,000 in 1968 to 50,000 in 1978—a loss of 35,000 in the decade (**357**, 17 January 1979).

It is clear that the tiny workshop and the home-industry workers who assemble some components in their homes have suffered the most. The villagers are unable to compete with cheap labor in Hong Kong and Taiwan—sources of vast numbers of inexpensive watches. The Swiss government announced in 1978 a rescue program of up to 50 million francs to assist the industry in financing research and development in electronic components; loan guarantees of 250 million francs during the next ten years; and additional assistance in interest subsidies, tax rebates etc. This supplements the financial aid program of SSIH. See also Table 39.

Ebauches S.A., a member of the ASUAG group, plans to acquire as a partner an electronics company. The watch industry alone cannot flourish if it must maintain an electronics division that only produces for the watch industry. A manufacturer of the electronic watch must be wedded to a broadly based and versatile electronics company to compete effectively in the world market for electronic watches. Several different ways of joining forces with an electronics company are being explored.

Another problem that has beset the Swiss watch industry is falsification. Several factories in Italy have been manufacturing copies of Swiss watches, falsely identified

Table 39   Employment in the Swiss watch industry

Year	Workers[a] (*Berufstätige Personen*)	No. of factory workshops (*Fabrikbetriebe*)	Factory employees[b] (*Fabrikperson*)
1888	45,729	465[c]	16,334
1900	54,601	647[d]	24,858
1920	66,564	953[e]	33,438
1941	50,402 (51,005)[f]	850	39,248
1950	47,013 (65,419)[f]	1139	
1966	72,552	1278	
1968	73,521	1225	
1970	72,810	1177	
1973	64,044	1027	
1977	48,021	909	
1978	46,785	891	
1979	41,870	829	
1980	41,343	776	
1982	39,000[g]		

[a] Includes the home-industry workers and other nonfactory personnel.
[b] Factory personnel only.
[c] 1895.
[d] 1901.
[e] 1923.
[f] As reported in ref. **341**, 1969, p. 26.
[g] Estimated.
Sources: **341**, 1951, pp. 35, 146; 1969, pp. 26, 144; 1975, p. 170; 1979, p. 152; 1981, pp. 154, 156.

Table 40   Employment in the Swiss machine and metal industry

| Year | Factories | Employees | | | Sources |
		Total number	Swiss	Foreigners	
1895	617[a]	23,355[a]			
1901	884[a,b]	44,916[a,b]			
1923	1263[b]	81,857[b]			
1951	2795	192,414	175,867	16,547	**341**, 1951, pp. 143, 146
1966	4488	384,820	258,230	126,590	**341**, 1981, pp. 156, 157
1968	4207	383,171	253,148	130,023	**341**, 1969, pp. 144, 145
1970	3887	388,318	251,340	136,978	**341**, 1981, pp. 156, 157
1973	3447	358,884	230,825	128,059	**341**, 1975, pp. 170, 171
1976	3223	311,495	211,666	99,829	**341**, 1977, pp. 152, 153
1977	3157	311,586	213,764	97,822	**341**, 1979, pp. 152, 153
1978	3110	316,670	217,051	99,619	**341**, 1979, pp. 152, 153
1979	3085	318,954	218,380	100,574	**341**, 1981, pp. 156, 157
1980	3087	329,696	223,375	106,321	**341**, 1981, pp. 156, 157

[a] Including arsenal workshops.
[b] Including independent iron foundries.

with the names of the best known Swiss manufacturers of top quality watches. The products have been exported, with considerable damage to the Swiss firms falsely designated as the makers. In Chiasso in 1979 a customs official seized a shipment of 1600 such watches about to be sent to Paraguay. Another shipment of 500, marked for delivery within Italy, was seized shortly thereafter by the same customs officers.[8]

Table 41   Employment in the Swiss textile industry

| Year | Factories | Employees | | | Sources |
		Total number	Swiss	Foreigners	
1895	1673	86,593			**341**, 1951, p. 144
1901	1556	91,318			**341**, 1951, p. 144
1923	1533	92,711			**341**, 1951, p. 144
1951	1057	70,500	61,697	8803	**341**, 1951, pp. 138, 143
1966	850	68,371	36,222	32,149	**341**, 1981, pp. 156, 157
1968	761	64,172	32,873	31,299	**341**, 1969, pp. 144, 145
1970	727	59,990	30,077	29,913	**341**, 1981, pp. 156, 157
1973	651	50,805	25,086	25,719	**341**, 1975, pp. 170, 171
1976	580	41,178	20,784	20,394	**341**, 1977, pp. 152, 153
1977	556	40,068	20,159	19,909	**341**, 1979, pp. 152, 153
1978	544	38,262	19,279	18,983	**341**, 1979, pp. 152, 153
1979	521	36,682	18,021	18,661	**341**, 1981, pp. 156, 157
1980	501	36,425	17,519	18,906	**341**, 1981, pp. 156, 157

There is also the good news. In January 1979, Swiss industry introduced to the American public the world's thinnest wrist watch—1.98 mm inclusive of case and crystal. The sapphire crystal is 0.28 mm thick. The watch, highly prized by collectors and fashion-conscious clients, is more than a novelty. It is an expression of remarkable technological skills. The machinery used had to operate with a tolerance of only 0.001 mm. The entire watch—case, face and works—had to be a single integrated unit. Sections of the back had to be scooped out to accommodate components of the movement. Known as the Concord Delirium I, it was placed on the USA market by the North American Watch Corporation at a retail price of $4400.

Notes and Comments

1. Tables appropriate to this section on Swiss Industry are included.

In interpretation of these Tables, not all of which are mentioned in the text, it should be noted that Switzerland experienced a recession in 1975 and 1976. This had adverse effects on the building industry (cf. Section 11.2) and on the export industries—aggravated by the strengthening of the Swiss franc relative to other currencies.

2. Ciba-Geigy, through an acquisition of the Titmus-Eurocon group of West Germany, is entering the contact-lens and lens-care-product business (**381**, 30 March 1983). In 1980, the USA subsidiary of Ciba-Geigy contracted with Titmus to market the West German company's products in the USA.

3. Expressed in dollars, the Company reported the consolidated net profit for 1983 to have been $580.6 million, an increase of 15 percent over the $505.5 million reported for 1982. If one translates the 1983 net into francs at the end-of-the-year exchange rate of 2.175 francs to the dollar, an increase of over 27 percent is suggested.

4. Nestlé has declared its intentions to comply fully with the 1982 United Nations Code aimed at encouraging the breast-feeding of infants. The company proposes also to set up a committee in the USA to investigate any complaints that Nestlé is violating international codes.

5. The cost of introducing a new drug is seldom appreciated by many people. Dr. Dunant, the Chairman and Chief Executive Officer of Sandoz A.G. has discussed this quite effectively:

> In 1960, for every 2000 newly synthesized compounds . . . one would become a new drug after a development period of 3 to 5 years. By 1976 this "survival rate" had fallen to one in 10,000, while the average development time for a new drug had risen to ten years (**357**, 7 November 1979).

6. In mid-1970, one USA dollar was worth 4.31 Swiss francs. By mid-1977, the USA dollar had decreased in value to 2.40 Swiss francs or the Swiss franc had increased in value by 56 percent over the 1970 USA dollar. For various other currencies, decreases relative to the Swiss franc were quite different.

7. To the indignation and dismay of political parties and unions, SSIH announced in August 1982 its intention to dismiss 300 or 400 employees. As a result, Biel (population, 54,000) was expected to have 1000 unemployed by the end of 1982 (**266**, 21–22 August 1982).

The General Director of the Swiss Watch Industry predicted that employment in the industry would suffer a reduction of 2000 in the year ending September 1982 (**266**, 10–20 December 1981). Despite such bad news, the treaty negotiated between the principal unions in the watch industry and the association of employers, for the five-year period ending 31 December 1985, marks significant material and social progress.

A merger of the two main groups in the industry, SSIH and ASUAG, accompanied by additional financing by the Swiss banks, appears probable (**381**, 16 May 1983). Although separate marketing operations will be maintained, the new company (Industrie Horlogère Suisse S.A.) will undergo restructuring, redevelopment and, probably, further infusion of capital from the Swiss banks (**357**, 25 May 1983).

8. These small shipments are only the tip of the iceberg. We read that "in Hong Kong, in 1982 alone, 48,000 watches and 260,000 parts were seized and 42 persons were prosecuted" (**357**, 14 September 1983). Recent estimates suggest that ten million counterfeit watches are sold annually in a world-wide market. Wholesale distributors have been reported in Milan, Hong Kong, Dubai, New York, Miami, Los Angeles, Bombay and Panama.

11.10. FAMILY INCOME vs EXPENDITURES

Income

This is an important problem everywhere. What can be said about it in twentieth-century Switzerland? The Federal Office for Industry, Occupations and Work[1] makes an annual survey of the income and expenses of households of varying size [from one to six persons (or more)]. The number of households in the entire country was 2,062,000 in 1970, and, probably, about the same in 1978 because the 1978 population was only about 70,000 greater than in 1970. It is unfortunate that some of the following data pertain to only 431 households out of over two million but the cost of the surveys has not permitted the collection of information from a substantially larger sample. We learn, however (**70**, p. 312), that the average household size is 3.33 persons, that the average age of the head of the household is 41 years and that the 431 households consisted of 295 from German-speaking Switzerland (mostly Zurich and Bern cantons), 112 from the French-speaking areas (mostly the cantons of Geneva and Vaud) and 17 from the Italian-speaking Ticino. Most of the households, 186 in number, occupied four rooms and 115 lived in three rooms. The man of the house was ordinarily the provider of the earned income but in many cases additional earned income was derived from employment of the housewife and to a small extent from that of the children.

Among 258 of 424 families (1979 data) the earned income of the head of the family averaged 42,750 francs. Additional sources of income, fourteen in number and each relatively small, brought the total family income up to 48,340 francs (**70**, p. 316).

Expenditures

Next we must ask how this income was expended. In 1979, according to BIGA, consumer expenditures for all Switzerland averaged 15,830 francs per head of population. Considering only the major items of expense, we find that insurance of various kinds[2] cost the average family about 14.6 percent of the total income; the family foodstuffs, 12.8 percent; education and leisure-time activities, 12.9 percent; rent, 11.4 percent; transportation,[3] 10.2 percent; and taxes plus related charges,[2] 11.0 percent (**70**, p. 317).

After paying for nine other categories of expense, this left about 7.6 percent of the total family income for savings accounts. Table 42A and 42B, for the benefit of the

Table 42   Average consumer prices for selected items and services
Table 42A

Foodstuffs	Average unit price (francs)[a]	Amount consumed per person in one year (1978)[b]	Total expenditures per person (francs)
Milk, 1 liter	1.30	9.4 liters	122
Cooking butter, 1 kg	9.0	2.9 kg	27.1
Margarine, 1 kg	6.4	2.1 kg	13.4
Cheese, 1 kg	13.9	10.7 kg	149
Eggs (50–60 g per egg)	0.19	122 eggs	23.2
Beef shoulder, boneless, 1 kg	20.2	5.3 kg	107
Pork shoulder, boneless, 1 kg	16.5	9.7 kg	160
Sausage, 1 kg	12.3	10.7 kg	132
Bread, 1 kg	2.24	24.0 kg	53.8
Rice, 1 kg	2.36	4.8 kg	24.5
Spaghetti, 1 kg	2.74		
Sunflower oil, 1 liter	4.13	3.8 liters	15.7
Potatoes, 1 kg	0.78	24 kg	18.7
Other vegetables,[c] 1 kg		32.2 kg	59.2
Apples, 1 kg	1.79	21.0 kg	37.6
Oranges, Canned pineapple, Bananas } 1 kg	3.0	22 kg	66.0
White sugar, 1 kg	1.18	8.1 kg	9.6
Wine: red and white, 7 dl	8.15	15.1 liters	123.0
Beer, 5.8 dl	1.10	10.9 liters	21.0
Total			1163

[a] Unit prices (November 1978), including, also, prices for all non-food items (Table 42B) goods, and services as given (**69**).
[b] This column pertains to the four-member household.
[c] Weighted averages used for the following: onions, garlic, carrots and other root vegetables (except potatoes), cabbage, cauliflower, lettuce, cucumbers and other vegetables. Current prices (October 1980) at Migros, less 5 percent.

curious, gives the average consumer prices for selected foodstuffs, goods and services in November 1978. The list is quite incomplete. Note that coffee, tea, condiments, spices and many other items are excluded from the Table. For the complete list see reference **70**, p. 326. For consumer prices and earned incomes in April 1981 and 1982, see reference **377**, no. 55, May 1982, pp. 386–388 and 3*. In general, incomes and expenditures were fractionally higher than in November 1978.

Standard of Living

In Switzerland, as elsewhere, there have been tremendous changes in family income and expenditures during the twentieth century. The national index of the cost of

Table 42B   Other goods and services

	Average price (francs)[a]	Work equivalent[b]	
		Hours	Minutes
Men's Clothing			
1 All-year suit (syn.)	131.4	9	20
1 Summer suit (cotton)	120.6	8	45
1 Trousers (syn. & wool)	73.5	5	15
1 Jeans (cotton)	65.6	4	45
1 Shirt (syn. & cotton)	36.3	2	40
1 pr Shoes	85.6	6	10
Women's Clothing			
1 Skirt (syn.)	59.8	6	20
1 Pullover (long sleeve, syn.)	30.4	3	15
1 Cotton blouse	53.8	5	45
1 pr Shoes (closed pumps)	92.7	10	0
Shoe repair (soles & heels)	27.6	3	0
Rent, per month[c]			
One room apartment	279	20	0
Three room apartment	392	29	0
Five room apartment	611	44	0
Heating oil, one season			
Four room apartment	610	44	0
Miscellaneous			
1 Kitchen table	180	12	45
1 Kitchen chair	36.7	3	0
Wash and iron raincoat	17.2	1	5
Gasoline, 15 liters	17.1	1	0
12 V Battery	161	11	20
1 Bicycle	512	32	15
1 Motorcycle	1200	80	0
Haircut, men	10.1	0	45
Haircut, women	10.8	1	10
1 Pair skis, without bindings	319	23	0

[a] November 1978 (**69**).
[b] At 13.9 francs per hour (the average for male employees (**71**)) for most items.
  At 9.35 francs per hour (the average for female employees (**71**)).
[c] Nationwide averages, April, 1982; One room, 310 francs; 3 rooms, 445; 5 rooms, 720. Source: **377**, 1982, p. 387. In 1980, the corresponding rental costs were 282, 401, and 635 francs respectively. Rents are routinely revised in May and November.

maintaining a certain standard of living gives us some of the pertinent information. Taking 1914 as 100, the index, after rising to 113 in 1915, 131 in 1916, 163 in 1917, and 204 in 1918, peaked out at 224 in 1920, fell to 164 in 1922 and decreased gradually to 158 in 1930. The effect of World War I on living standards is evident from these data. The costs of food, heat, light and clothing increased sharply during the same period. On the average, house or apartment rental cost the householder in 1930 almost twice as much as in 1915. Principally because of cost increases in mortgage financing, rents increased about 2.9 percent between November 1980 and November 1981. Of 100,000 rental units reported upon throughout the nation in May 1981, the rates for 33 percent had been increased, 65 percent remained unaltered, and 2 percent had been reduced (Source: BIGA). The households

Table 43 Wages and cost of living in Switzerland (in 1888–91 and selected years in the twentieth century)

Table 43A Wages—average income earned (francs per day)[a,b]

Year	Master workman	Skilled workman	Unskilled	Laborer	Women (18 years and older)	Youths under 18
1888–91	6.97	4.29	3.71	3.24	1.62	1.53
1918	12.95	10.55	9.71	8.00	5.38	5.03
1919	14.10	11.79	11.19	9.07	5.83	5.51
1920	15.44	12.90	12.62	10.51	6.83	6.29
1921	17.96	13.11	12.16	10.44	6.98	5.88

Average hourly wage, 1939–1952[b,c]

Year	Skilled workman	Unskilled	Women (18 years and older)	Youths under 18
1939	1.40	1.08	0.73	0.52
1941	1.54 (0.14)	1.22 (0.14)	0.82 (0.09)	0.68 (0.16)
1943	1.81 (0.27)	1.50 (0.28)	1.00 (0.18)	0.91 (0.23)
1945	2.03 (0.22)	1.70 (0.20)	1.16 (0.16)	1.03 (0.12)
1947	2.42 (0.39)	2.04 (0.34)	1.49 (0.33)	1.29 (0.26)
1949	2.60 (0.18)	2.19 (0.15)	1.62 (0.13)	1.34 (0.05)
1951	2.67 (0.07)	2.25 (0.06)	1.66 (0.04)	1.37 (0.03)
1952	2.76	2.34	1.74	1.45

Table 43B Cost of living in 1920 (expressed as percentage of year's income)[d]

	Lowest income group (about 4000 fr/yr for head of family)	Highest income group (about 11,000 fr/yr for head of family)
Food	47.9	31
Clothing	11.6	16.2
Rent	8.8	9.9
Insurance	2.4	2.7
Education & free time	3.9	9.3
Heat & light	5.9	5.0

[a] *Sozialstatistische Mitteilungen* (Bern, August 1923, Heft 3, p. 22).
[b] Average work day, about 9 hours (in 1913, about 11 hours).
[c] To indicate the effects of World War II, the biennial increases in hourly wages are also shown.
[d] *Sozialstatistische Mitteilungen* 1923–24, p. 11: a study of 225 families.

Table 43C Cost of living in 1943, 1944, 1945[a]

	1943	1944	1945
Households studied	523	256	274
Average family income (approx.)			
(francs per year)	5800	6000	6000
Family size for this wage group	3.91		
Percentage of income earned by			
head of household	86		
Percentage of income expended on:			
Food	39	39.5	39.9
Clothing	8.8	9.6	9.5
Rent	14.2	14.6	13.2
Insurance	7.0	6.6	6.2
Taxes	4.1	3.4	3.5

[a] *Die Volkswirtschaft*, 1947.

surveyed by BIGA are not representative of all occupational groups. The study excludes the self-employed (11.4 percent of the active working population in 1970), the farm population and those who lived on income from investments and retirement income (pensions). The average wages reported for men and women (13.9 fr. per hour for male employees and 9.35 fr. per hour for females) presented in Table 42B (footnote b) are country-wide averages for 899,870 male and 316,669 female employees in all 26 cantons in 1979 (**72**), in short all who are covered by the public old age and survivors' insurance (AHV)—the largest social program in Switzerland and the nearest thing to the Social Security program in the USA. It applies to all employed personnel with the premium payments divided equally between employer and employee.

More on Family Income

Average monthly incomes of the employed are also tabulated (**72**). For 1979 we read that the country-wide average was 3569 francs per male employee and 2362 for female employees. Since the average hourly wage is stated to be 13.92 and 9.35 francs for men and women respectively[4] it would seem to follow that the average hours of work approximate 60 per week. Because the work-week is actually 44 for most employees, an explanation of such a discrepancy must be sought. The explanation resides in supplementary sources of income which contribute about 33 percent (an average figure) to the household income. Frequently the income of the chief provider is supplemented by the earnings of other members of the household. Overtime work would provide additional income. The base salary of an employee is increased as one, two or more children are born to the mother in the household unit. The salary will also be supplemented to cover the added expenses of the household attributable to inflation and other inescapable expenses related to the economy. There may also be a supplement which amounts to the wages that would be earned

Table 43D Working time required for procurement of various necessities[a,b] [in hours and minutes (0/00) unless otherwise stated]

Year	Average wage (Rappen/hr)	Bread (kg)	Potatoes (kg)	Milk (liter)	Butter (kg)	Beef (kg)	Eggs (each)	Beechwood (cord)	Shoes (pair)	Man's shirt	Woman's skirt	Rental of 3-room apartment
1830	10	3/40	0/25	0/50	12/30	5/50	—	—	—	—	—	—
1840	10	3/30	0/25	1/00	15/00	5/20	0/20	10 days	55/00	12/00	47/00	4½ months
1850	13	2/30	0/30	0/40	10/00	4/40	0/15	7½ days	50/00	21/00	31/00	—
1860	16	2/30	0/30	0/50	11/10	6/00	0/20	10 days	32/00	14/00	34/20	—
1870	21	2/10	0/20	0/25	10/20	5/40	0/20	9 days	52/00	13/30	—	—
1875	30	1/20	0/17	0/20	8/10	—	0/15	7 days	35/00	—	—	2½ months
1880	45	1/00	—	—	6/30	3/25	—	—	—	—	—	—
1920	134	0/35	0/10	0/20	6/00	4/15	0/15	—	—	—	—	—
1970	720	0/10	—	—	1/50	2/20	—	—	—	—	—	—
1979[c]	1273	0/10	0/03	0/05	1/40	1/45	0/02	—	6/45	3/00	7/00	2 months

[a] The Table indicates the remarkable extent to which real wages (expressed as purchasing power) have increased since 1830. The data for the nineteenth century are taken from Gruner (**155**, p. 133).

[b] An international comparison, involving 15 countries, of the time that one must work in order to buy unit quantities of bread, beef, butter and potatoes reveals that Norway was a "best-buy" in 1980 for these staple foodstuffs; Japan was the most expensive (**266**, 1, 2 September 1984).

[c] Calculated from *Die Volkswirtschaft* no. 53, August 1980, pp. 555, 559.

in a thirteenth month if the calendar gave us that extra month. It may be thought of as bonus equal to 8.33 percent of the 12-month basic income. Interest earned in a savings account and several other miscellaneous sources of household income also contribute to the apparent discrepancy mentioned above.

Wages and living costs in earlier years of the century are presented in Table 43.

Notes and Comments

1. *Bundesamt für Industrie, Gewerbe und Arbeit* (BIGA).
2. Exclusive of taxes and insurance on motor vehicles.
3. Inclusive of taxes and insurance on motor vehicles.
4. By 1981, the average hourly wage for men had risen to 15.58 francs and to 10.57 francs for women (**377**, no. 55, June 1982, p. 415).

11.11. TAXATION

Introduction

Section 11.10 reports that the average Swiss family in 1979 paid about 11 percent of the family income in taxes. To whom is the tax paid and how is the taxation system structured?

In Switzerland, the taxing authorities are the Federal Government, the cantons and the local governments. Until 1848, when Switzerland became a true confederation of its constituent parts, each canton had its own special tax system based on customs duties and tax revenue derived from purchases by its own people. Direct taxes were of little significance. After 1848 the cantons agreed to give to the Federal Government the exclusive right to levy customs duties. The cantonal governments resorted to direct taxation. From 1915 on the Federal Government was forced to supplement its income from customs duties by the imposition of direct taxes. Until then, as a generalization, the tax revenue of the Federal Government was indirect and that of the cantons was direct. It must also be understood that the 23 cantons (Jura, the new canton, is included) and three half cantons, in firm adherence to their sovereign rights, refrain from any suggestion of uniformity in their tax systems. The taxing authority of the local governments is conferred upon them by the cantons and may be described as a derived fiscal sovereignty.

Fiscal Income of the Federal Government

The Constitution (*Bundesverfassung*) defines with much precision the kinds of taxes that the Federal Government may impose. Table 44A lists these taxes as well as the income derived therefrom in 1950 and 1980. The income from customs duties is also included to round out the total fiscal income. The minutiae are such that it is impossible to calculate with any precision how much the average taxpayer might be obliged to pay to government, including his canton and his *Gemeinde* (community). A confusing diversity in rates for this and that, with many kinds of deductions and several extras, is bewildering, to say the least. But, as we shall see later, some fairly reasonable approximations can be made.[1] However, it must be admitted that the Internal Revenue Service of the USA is even more successful than the Swiss Tax Office in confusing the taxpayer.

Table 44A   Fiscal income of the Federal Government in 1950 and 1980[a] (in millions of francs)

	1950	1980
National Defense Tax[b]	457	3420
Anticipation Tax[c]	78	1249
Military Exemption Tax[d]	16	103
Stamp Tax[e]	100	696
Sales Tax[f] (*Warenumsatzsteuer*)	445	4772
Special tax on consumption	95	1209
Duties on imports and exports	323	923
Duties on motor fuel[g]	95	955
Duties on tobacco	47	6
Surcharge on motor fuel[g]	—	1263
Other supplementary duties	12	24
Total Fiscal income[h]	1668	14,620

Total Government Income in prior years (in millions of francs): 1921–25, 277 per year; 1931–35, 419 per year; 1941, 877; 1947, 1516.

[a] Source: **341**, 1981, p. 414; 1951, p. 397.

[b] Tax on income of natural persons; tax on profits and capital of juristic persons.

[c] Tax on interest, dividends, lottery winnings, insurance income, and other similar sources. Tax is 35% of such income. It is withheld at the source and is paid to the Federal Tax Office. On verification of the payment, the tax is refunded to the individual (if in Switzerland) or more commonly to the appropriate canton as a credit on cantonal and community taxes due by the taxpayer. The purpose of this fancy manipulation (introduced in 1944) is to minimize tax evasion. It has a control function rather than a revenue purpose, although if these various sources of income are not declared and itemized on his tax return, the tax evader will lose his 35% and will be subject to penalties. The tax is officially described as a *Verrechnungssteuer* which defies a brief definition. The portion reported in the Table as fiscal income pertains only to the amount retained by the Federal Government for the reasons stated above.

[d] Levied on all male Swiss of military age (20 to 50) who, for a variety of reasons, are exempt from their military service obligations, including Swiss residents abroad.

[e] A tax levied on many legal and economic transactions involving a great variety of documents: issuance and sale or purchase of bonds, stocks, foreign securities, bills of exchange, promissory notes, receipts of insurance premiums, etc. It is somewhat of a misnomer because, with a few exceptions, no stamps are involved.

[f] The sales tax, introduced in 1941, is payable on a host of consumer purchases of goods and services. Excluded from the tax are purchases of gas, water, electricity, and fuel; all foods and beverages (if non-alcoholic), meat, fish, poultry; grain, seeds and agricultural aids (e.g. fertilizers and agricultural improvements); plants and flowers; pharmaceuticals and medicinal products; newspapers, magazines and books. The taxes are collected from the wholesaler or retailer—in exceptional cases directly from the consumer.

[g] Article 36ter of the Federal Constitution requires that 60 percent of the basic customs revenue (*Grundzoll*) on motor fuel shall be used to finance the construction of the network of federal highways and certain other roads. The surcharge must be used in its entirety for this purpose. Because the construction of tunnels, and the building and maintenance of many other roads that feed ultimately into the federal network, involve additional costs to the cantons and local communities, the country is faced with a hot political issue. The Federal Government needs a larger percentage of the *Grundzoll* for roads because the income from the surcharge on motor-fuel duties is no longer adequate. The cantons also seek a larger piece of the pie. The automobile associations and heavy users of motor fuel are opposed to any increases. There will be no winner but a reasonable compromise among the contestants will probably emerge.

[h] The fiscal income for 1981 was estimated in the Federal Budget at 16,103 million francs and expenditures at 17,280 million francs, with an expected addition of 1177 million francs to the national debt. The result was far better than expected. The federal revenues increased more than had been estimated and the deficit for the year was little more than 170 million francs (cf. ref. **377**, 55, June 1982, p. 15*). It is improbable that more or less of a balance between income and expense will continue through the next fiscal period.

Cantonal and Local Government Taxes

Whether paid to the local or the cantonal tax office (usually the former), the taxes will be redistributed such that the canton, the local community, and the church (evangelical or catholic) each receives its share.[2] The revenue derived from a variety of sources for the years 1950 and 1979 is presented in Table 44B. Part of the federal revenue is diverted to the cantons as subventions and reimbursements.

Considerable care is taken to avoid or correct for the double taxation of taxpayers, partly by other cantons and partly by other countries. The former is covered by an all-embracing system of rules established by the Swiss Federal Supreme Court (the Federal Tribunal). A number of conventions between Switzerland and other countries deal with avoidance of double taxation at the international level.

Table 44B Fiscal revenues of the cantonal (and local) governments in 1950 and 1979[a] (in millions of francs)

	1950	1979
Income taxes	—	7255
Property taxes	603.1	699.5
Profit taxes		1146
Taxes on capital		416.0
Taxes on real estate	3.7	74.1
Capital gains taxes[b]	4.0	242.1
Inheritance and estate taxes[c]	38.7	365.5
Taxes on transfer of property	14.4	209.0
Motor vehicle taxes	50.2	718.8
Entertainment taxes	7.9	29.7
Taxes on dogs	1.8	7.7
Other luxury taxes	14.0	80.3
Regalien and patents	34.9	173.2
Interest and dividends	54.2	331.0
Rents and leases	9.7	115.4
From banks	18.0	46.6
From industrial corporations	9.3	18.3
Other miscellaneous profit	18.3	135.4
From the confederation	146.0	1208
From the communities	—	—
Contributions, federal and communal	221.2	4431
Cash sales and misc. receipts	242.3	2955
Alienation of property	0.1	57.9
Total fiscal income	1492	20,716

[a] Source: **341**, 1981, pp. 428, 429.
[b] A distinction is drawn by the fiscal authorities between capital gains on movable property (stocks, bonds, etc.) and capital gains on immovable property (real estate).
[c] Usually goes to the local governments.

In both Tables (44A & B), the taxes received from natural persons are not always separated from those of juristic persons (joint-stock companies, other business enterprises, cooperatives). Only the combined data are presented in such cases.

The Individual Taxpayer

How much of his hard-earned income must the average Swiss employee (and resident foreigner) pay in taxes to government—federal, cantonal, and local? The inquiry focuses only on natural persons, of whom in 1976 there were 2,288,182 persons liable for payment of taxes (*Steuerpflichtige Personen*). They paid a total of 1,978,956,078 francs as the national defense tax (**341**, 1981, p. 443). This amounted to 865 francs per taxpayer. The data refer to the 18th period of the *Wehrsteuer* (years 1975, 1976). So much for the national defense tax, which constitutes the second largest source of tax revenue received by the Federal Government.

The tax liability of a person is a function of his salary, his marital status, the number of his dependants, the amount of his capital (*Vermögen*), and the town and canton in which he lives.[3] Here we may make a few assumptions: we shall assume that a taxpayer in the city of Bern in the canton of Bern is an average taxpayer. There are differences from canton to canton and between towns in the same canton but for much of what follows we must put our average taxpayer somewhere. This brings us to consider his tax payments to his canton and his community. Assuming that his salary bracket was 40,000 francs in 1980, he would have paid the following as income tax to his canton and local government: if unmarried, 5563 francs; married, with no dependants, 4575 francs; married, with two children, 4116 francs; and if married, with four children, 3657 francs (**341**, 1981, 449, 450). The communities and the cantonal governments would each have taken almost one half of the payment, leaving perhaps 125 francs for the parish administration.[4]

A taxpayer with a salary of 200,000 francs would have paid about 44,000 francs[5] for the year 1980. On an income of one million or more, enjoyed or suffered by 588 taxpayers in all Switzerland, one would have paid as a national defense tax (*Wehrsteuer*) about 8.1 percent of his income (**115**).

Next, we come to the tax on capital or property. If the capital of our modestly endowed average taxpayer in Bern amounted to 200,000 francs, his tax in 1980 would have been 684 francs. But if his net fortune were five million francs, and if he were married but without dependent children, his tax on capital would have been almost 35,000 francs (**341**, 1981, p. 451).

All taxpayers benefit from a variety of so-called social deductions other than wives and children. The tax burden also includes the indirect or hidden taxes. The most important of these is the sales tax (*Warenumsatzsteuer*) which brought in to the federal treasury 4772 million francs in 1980. The tax, well buried in the retail or wholesale price of an item is about five to eight percent. (See footnote f, Table 44A.)

Although not thought of as a tax, customs duties, a final source of fiscal revenue, may not be overlooked. The duties have an obvious impact on the prices that the consumer will pay for some goods and services. The burden falls on both natural and juristic persons. If we include the duties on tobacco, beer and spirits, and the motor fuel surcharges, in fact all the additional fiscal charges on consumer goods, the average taxpayer in all Switzerland paid about 1440 francs in indirect taxes and duties for the year 1980 (from Table 44A).[6]

Cost of Living and Personal Incomes

The cost of living in Switzerland increased in 1980 some 63 percent over that of 1970, but in the meantime wages and salaries doubled (**341**, 1981, 609, 373). Hence the inflation in the cost of living was more than compensated by the increase in wages.

In 1980, the OECD (Organization for Economic Cooperation and Development) reported a study of per capita incomes among 24 of the leading industrial States of the west. Switzerland was the highest at $13,450. Denmark, Sweden and West Germany were next with per capita incomes of $10,950 to $10,420. The USA was in the ninth position at $9660. The data refer to total national incomes (combined private and public sectors) and must not be confused with earned income which for the average Swiss family may be regarded as 48,340 francs or 14,648 francs per capita ($9330 at the December 1979 rate of exchange). The OECD data may also be calculated from the Swiss Statistical Yearbook. The net national income (*Sozialprodukt*) was 139,600 million francs in 1979 which gives a per capita income of $14,002 (**341**, 1981, p. 351).

For a meaningful comparison of living costs, cognizance must be taken of currency exchange rates in relation to the USA dollar, as well as the purchasing power of the local currency. As for Switzerland, I have imposed a further restriction by excluding the self-employed and those who live on investments and retirement income (pensions).

Table 45 summarizes the payments of the average employed taxpayer in direct taxes and customs duties in 1980. The 6124 francs in direct taxes alone is more than 11 percent of family income reported earlier (Section 11.10). The discrepancy is partly due to the fact that some of the tax entries include payments by juristic persons. If it could be corrected, the second entry (4575 francs) would be lower.

Expenditures of Government

In the previous Section (11.10) we examined personal incomes and expenditures in Switzerland. Having discussed and tabulated in this present section the income of government, it is equally appropriate to report on the principal categories of expenditure by government. As an introductory generalization we should note that the typical Swiss lives within his means and is able to put something aside in his savings account. Governments seldom save anything. To the contrary, every government is a bureaucracy always suffering from an inability to restrain its growth. If it can't find enough to do in maintaining peace and harmony within its own jurisdiction and in living peacefully with foreign jurisdictions, it invents new responsibilities that invade ever more deeply the personal and private affairs of its people. The results are obvious. It grows like a metastatic cancer and ultimately gnaws away at the health, wealth, and happiness of the citizens. Instead of saving

Table 45   Summary: Fiscal liability of an average person (in francs)

	Year	Tax	
National defense tax	1975, 1976	865[e]	Countrywide average (natural persons only)
Cantonal and community tax	1980	4575[f]	Average for Bern[a]
Tax on capital	1980	684	Average for Bern[b]
Indirect taxes and customs duties	1980	1440	Countrywide average (Juristic persons[c] included)
Total		7564[d]	

[a] Married taxpayer with no dependent children; Salary in 1980: 40,000 francs.
[b] Married taxpayer with no dependent children; Capital in 1980: 200,000 francs.
[c] Juristic persons: Stock Companies (tax on net profit and capital); Cooperative societies (tax on net profit and capital); Associations, Unions, Foundations (tax on income and capital); Organizations under public law (tax on capital).
[d] Or 18.9 percent of income if a yearly salary of 40,000 francs be assumed as the 1980 income of the average employed taxpayer (15.4 percent of income if indirect taxes and customs duties are excluded). Obviously the data in the Table must be regarded as gross approximations because of the many variables involved.
[e] Reported to be 360 francs in 1978 if income was 30,000 francs and 1391 francs in 1978 if income was 50,000 francs (average, 865 francs—the assumed liability if income was 40,000 francs).
[f] Reported to be 3168 francs in 1978 if income was 30,000 francs, and 7135 francs in 1978 if income was 50,000 francs (average, 5152 francs, assumed to be the tax if income was 40,000 francs). Calculated from tabulated data in ref. **266**, 10–11 January 1981.

any of its fiscal revenue, government goes ever more deeply into debt. Amputation of parts of the burgeoning bureaucracy has frequently been promised, sometimes attampted, but rarely achieved. If government had to observe the operating rules of private enterprises most governments would have been in bankruptcy years ago. So it is that the present section will include with a tabular summary of the public debt of the Swiss Federal Government and comments on the debt problem.

In Table 46, the expenditures of the Federal Government are presented for the years 1950 and 1980 according to subject categories of a departmental or administrative nature. Table 47 consists of a gross summary of income, expenditures and surplus (or deficits) of the Confederation, the cantons and the communities for the years 1950, 1970, 1980. Included also (Table 48) are data on the National Income (or National Product, *Sozialprodukt*), consisting of a summation of the incomes generated by both the private and public sectors. Finally, Table 49 is added to report on the status of the Federal Government's debt over a period of years. It should be noted that from a post-war high of 8957 million francs in 1946, the government managed to reduce its debt to 5649 million in 1965. By 1970 it had risen to only 6360 million francs. Then came the disastrous recession of 1974/75 and ultimately the troublesome economic problems of 1979/82. Despite all of this the Federal per capita debt at the end of 1980 was only $1815 or so (**341**, 1981, p. 416) compared with a USA figure for 1980 of $5860 (**193**).[7] The difference is only partly attributable to Swiss economy in military expenditures. For Switzerland, the total

Table 46 Expenditures of the confederation[a] (in millions of francs)

	1950	1980
Authorities, general administration	69.5	487
Justice	12.8	129
Police	4.27	39.9
Special services	9.64	77.1
Foreign relations	39.6	687
National defense	536	3533
Education, research	40.3	1510
Culture, sports, leisure-time activities	6.58	110
Health	12.6	36.3
Environment	—	206
Social welfare	265	3581
Space planning	—	72.2
Transportation, energy	76.0	2722
Agriculture	120	1573
Forestry, hunting, fisheries	4.18	35.0
Stream control, avalanche barriers	15.3	55.2
Tourism industry, handicrafts, commerce	2.20	289
Financial services	423	2245
Total	1637	17,388

[a] Source: **341**, 1981, p. 412.

expenditure on defense in 1980 by the Confederation was $316 per capita[8] (calculated from **341**, 1981, p. 412) and using an exchange rate of 1.76 Swiss francs equal to one USA dollar (**341**, 1981, p. 280). The International Institute for Strategic Studies, in its publications on the Military Balance presents data which may be re-expressed as $290 per capita for Switzerland and $800 for the USA (**244**). For the USA, the expenditures of the Federal Government in 1980 were 135.9 billion dollars (**340**) or $599 per capita (USA population, circa 227 million). If we consider the total expenditures of government, we find that in Switzerland, government (federal, cantonal, and local) in 1980 expended a total of 44.7703 billion francs (**341**, 1981, p. 407). On a per capita basis, the expenditure amounted to $4001. In the USA, the corresponding total expenditure by the Federal Government and states combined was 934.6 billion dollars of $4117 per capita (**340**). Another source reports per capita expenditures of $4185 for Switzerland and $4460 for the USA (**193**).

If and when the economy returns to its traditional robust state and if the Swiss people retain their antipathy toward supporting government at more than minimal levels of expenditure, one may predict that once again the Federal debt will gradually diminish. If in doubt, take another good look at Table 49 (see also "Financial Policy" in Section 11.17).

Comparative data for Switzerland and the USA are recapitulated in Table 50.

Table 47   Finances of the confederation, cantons and communities[a] (in millions of francs)

	1950	1970	1980
Confederation			
Expenditures	1650.5	7834.5	17,532.0
Income	1987.2	8044.0	16,460.8
Income surplus	336.7	209.5	—
Income deficit	—	—	1071.2
Cantons			
Expenditures	1488.0	9533.2	21,926.3
Income	1491.7	9286.9	21,762.7
Income surplus	3.7	—	—
Income deficit	—	246.3	163.6
Communities			
Expenditures	1244.0	6840.3	15,473.4 ⎫
Income	1231.6	6411.6	15,960.9 ⎬ b
Income surplus	—	—	487.5 ⎪
Income deficit	12.4	428.7	— ⎭
Total (corrected for double payments)			
Expenditures	3896.5	20,285.4	44,770.3 ⎫
Income	4225.6	19,839.6	43,464.2 ⎬ b
Income surplus	329.1	—	— ⎪
Income deficit	—	445.8	1306.1 ⎭

[a] Source: **341**, 1981, p. 407.
[b] 1979 data for communities.

The policy of government in Switzerland is clear. Not only do the politicians seek to balance the budget, but they strive to do so without increasing taxes, partly because increases in existing sources of tax revenue and the introduction of new sources of tax revenue are difficult to achieve. Approval by the people and the cantons is required and they are not easily convinced that the proposed increases are necessary; witness the fate of the federal proposal for a turnover or added value tax (*Mehrwertsteuer*).[9] Government is forced by the taxpayers to exercise all reasonable economies. This leads to a system which, except for the executive bodies (e.g. the Federal Council) and the administrative personnel, recognizes the services of the members of parliament as part-time only. They are modestly compensated and, even in the Federal Parliament, the members manage to dispatch their duties without a great corps of personal secretaries, and elaborate suites of private offices—in sharp contrast with the USA. Extensive use is made at the federal level of a full-time staff of civil service employees. And here we should note that the federal personnel (all departments of government including the chancellery and the federal courts) have remained almost unchanged in number for nine years (33,022 in 1973 and 33,696 in 1980).[10] Were we to include the employees of the post, telephone and

Table 48 National income (*Sozialprodukt*)[a,b] (in millions of francs)

	1938	1950	1973	1980
Income of the employed				
Wages and salaries	3954	9790	64,945	89,140
Social payments by employers	237	890	8225	13,060
Military revenue	23	50	155	205
Business income				
Agriculture	603	1340	3875	4130
Industry, handcrafts, construction	691	1330	6200	6020
Commerce, banking, insurance, consultation	291	640	3310	
Hotels, restaurants, transportation	107	200	1310	7350
Liberal professions and services	181	380	1750	
Income on capital of households				
Interest			5765	7780
Dividends			3740	4560
Less: interest on consumer debt			−235	−390
Income from property (household)			695	1030
Undivided income from enterprises				
From private enterprises			6300	7870
From public enterprises			705	2150
Direct taxes on enterprises			3270	3850
Income from state capital and enterprises			1055	1540
Less: Interest on the public debt			−1950	−3150
Income from social insurance capital and enterprises			2630	4180
Net national income	8702	18,160	111,745	149,325
Indirect taxes	344	930	8765	11,900
Less: subventions	—	—	−1220	−2290
Provision for consumption of fixed capital	—	—	−15,250	−18,030
Gross national income (Gross national product)	—	—	134,540	176,965

[a] Source: **341**, 1951, pp. 320, 321; 1981, pp. 350, 351.
[b] See also Table 28 in Section 11.7.

telegraph services and the federal railways, the same conclusion would apply: no increase in nine years (130,108 in 1973 and 129,022 in 1980). Salary payments, however, have increased substantially; for example, federal employee remunerations in 1975 totalled 1669 million francs; in 1979, 1873.5 million; and in 1980, 1935 million (**341**, 1981, p. 413).[11]

The 26 classes of federal employees received annual salaries in 1980 which averaged about 26,500 francs for class 25 and 88,000 francs for class 1a. In 1950, the corresponding averages were about 6100 francs for class 25 and 22,200 for class 1; class 1a did not then exist. (Source: **341**, 1981, p. 379.)

Table 49   The debt of the Swiss Federal Government

Year	Total[a] (in millions of francs)	Per inhabitant (in francs)
1850	4.643	1.94
1880	35.000	12.36
1900	68.437	27.38
1910	117.150	3.137
1920	1605.857	414.2
1930	1883.271	464.8
1940	3373.9	799.5
1946	8957.0	2005
1950	7949.7	1693
1955	8058.8	1616
1960	6549.6	1221
1965	5648.7	950.5
1970	6360.4	1015
1974	10,038.8	1558
1976	16,227.7	2557
1978	16,397.1	2588
1980[b]	18,046.5	2835 ($1815)
1981	18,150.0[c]	2820 ($1805)

[a] Source: **341**, 1920, p. 354; 1951, pp. 392, 393; 1981, p. 416.

[b] Data provided by the Federal Finance Administration (courtesy of M. Galliker) on 2 August 1982, give the public debt of the Confederation in 1980 as 24,409 million francs (3834 francs or 2154 USA dollars per capita). If we include the cantons and communities, the total debt of government (all three jurisdictions), according to the same source, was 75,272 million francs (11,824 francs or 6643 USA dollars per capita). We should note, however, that the data provided by the Federal Finance Administration pertain to the consolidated debt of Switzerland. In consequence, beyond the direct debts of government, viz public borrowings, there are included the loans of insurance societies, loans of the AVS, floating debts, debts in internal accounts, etc. The consolidated debt of only the Federal Government in 1980 is reported by the Finance Administration as 24,409 million francs ($2154 per capita). Another source gives the Swiss public debt in 1980 as $4621 per capita (**193**).

[c] Estimated.

In October 1982 the then Swiss Finance Minister (Willi Ritschard) proposed a program to balance the country's budget by 1986. It was a cost-cutting, not a tax-raising, program. The shock therapy proposed by Ritschard called for cuts in defense spending, foreign aid and administrative expenses. The automatic midyear salary increases for federal employees would be ended and grants to health insurance programs would be finished off. In earlier proposals, the Minister suggested equally unpleasant means of attaining the budget balancing. This would be done, not through tax increases—politically difficult to achieve—but by increasing the duties on fuel imports and imposing special license fees on heavy vehicles.

Table 50   Per capita financial comparisons, USA and Switzerland[a,b] (in dollars)

	Switzerland		USA	
Gross national product	15,834	**(341)**	11,454	**(340)**
Public debt	1815	**(341)**	5860	**(193)**
	1222[c]	**(194)**	3001	**(194)**
Expenditure on defense	316	**(341)**	599	**(340)**
	290	**(244)**	800	**(244)**
Total expenditures of government	4000	**(341)**	4117	**(340)**
	4185	**(193)**	4460	**(193)**

[a] End of 1980 unless otherwise stated.
[b] Bibliographic references in parentheses.
[c] 1979.

In November, the voters approved a proposal by consumer groups to establish a price-supervision board. They voted down a counter proposal by the Federal Government and supported by conservative political parties, to have such supervision only during times of national emergency. Consumer organizations have maintained that too much price fixing has been going on by key industrial, business and consumer-goods sectors.

Raising of revenue by a government cut on gambling profits is out of the question: games of chance are prohibited by Article 35 of the Federal Constitution. The Swiss casinos are not permitted to allow games of over five francs per throw. These restrictions please the French and the Italians who provide an abundance of gambling facilities adjacent to the Swiss border. Several estimates suggest that tourists and the Swiss themselves invest annually some hundreds of millions of francs in gambling just across the border. So-called "number lotteries" (*Zahlenlotto*) are authorized. In 1980, almost 250 million francs of these lottery tickets were sold in Switzerland. Including several other less popular forms of approved gambling, the total investment in 1980 amounted to 352 million francs (**341**, 1981, p. 300). The Swiss Federation of Tourism has urged that the government review its no-gambling policy and bring to an end the ostrich-like behaviour of the present; despite Article 35, much gambling (above 5 francs per throw) does go on—so it is alleged. Hence, so the argument continues, let us make it legal and let the government take a substantial cut in the proceeds.

As for the general tax imposed by the cantons and communities, a married person without children would pay, in 1981, to the canton of Zug 4612 francs if in the 50,000 franc-income bracket, but Freiburg would demand 7642 francs. The Swiss average was 6439 francs. If we consider the property tax and income tax together and assign to Switzerland generally an index value of 100, Zug emerges as the lowest with an index value of 71 and Freiburg retains the top position at 127. For natural persons with middle or high incomes, Zug is a tax paradise. And it is favorably

Table 51[a]   Take-home pay in three income brackets, after federal taxes
and social security[b]

	$20,000	$50,000	$100,000
Switzerland	17,400	37,000	63,000
France	16,600	37,000	64,000
Luxembourg	16,200	36,500	53,000
United States	16,200	35,500	63,000
Spain	15,600	36,500	62,000
Greece	15,000	29,000	49,000
Ireland	13,800	26,500	46,000
Italy	14,200	32,500	58,000
Norway	14,000	24,000	39,000
West Germany	13,800	30,500	52,000
Belgium	13,400	26,500	42,000
Finland	13,400	24,500	40,000
United Kingdom	13,400	29,500	50,000
Netherlands	13,000	26,000	41,000
Austria	12,800	26,000	46,000
Portugal	12,600	21,000	31,000
Denmark	12,200	21,500	37,000
Sweden	11,600	17,000	24,000

[a] Source: Dow Theory Letters—848 (17 November 1982).
[b] For a married couple with two children.

disposed toward publicly owned stock corporations (*Aktiengesellschaften*), wherein, if the average for Switzerland is 100, Zug is only 72 (**347**, 1982 edition).

If we consider total Take-Home Pay, the Swiss employee has been reported to be in a most enviable position as compared with employees in 17 other industrialized countries. Please refer to Table 51.

Notes and Comments

1. If interested, one may obtain additional information from the *Informationstelle für Steuerfragen* (Monbijoustrasse 32, 3003 Bern) in a variety of photocopied documents, such as one on the *Warenumsatzsteuer*, another on the *Verrechnungssteuer*, and a third entitled "*Die Einkommensteuer Natürlicher Personen.*" The *Statistiches Jahrbuch der Schweiz* is also a rich source of information.

2. In some cantons the church receives no support from tax revenues.

3. To illustrate the variations: In Basel-Stadt the National Defense Tax in 1975–87 averaged 1681 francs per head of population, and in Zug, 1006 francs. The mountain cantons, at the other end of the scale, averaged 285 francs in Schwyz, 256 in Valais and 225 francs in Appenzell-Innerrhoden. Equally pronounced differences exist from canton to canton in the tax paid by juristic persons.

4. A popular initiative, seeking a separation of Church and State was heavily defeated in a votation on 2 March 1980. Had it have been approved, payments by the State to the parish administrations from taxes would no longer have been permitted (**73**, 1978, II, pp. 665–698).

5. In all Switzerland in 1974 there were 722 persons in the 500,000-franc-income category and 268 with incomes of 1,000,000 francs or more (**341**, 1975, p. 445).

6. Unquestionably, this is a high estimate. Other elements of the population not subject to direct taxation (including tourists and diplomatic personnel) share in this impost. Juristic persons are also included in some elements of the estimated charge: for example, many motor vehicles, subject to taxation and to motor-fuel duties and surcharges are owned by juristic persons. Also, some of the customs duties are paid on imported raw materials and unfinished products which are fabricated in Switzerland and exported as finished products. In general, the customs duties on exports add little to the fiscal revenue.

7. "International Economic Indicators, 1981-82," which reports $5860 as the per capita public debt of the USA, reports $4621 as the corresponding figure for Switzerland (**193**). This is almost three times as great as the figure calculated from data in the official yearbook of Switzerland—viz $1615. The International Monetary Fund reports the total debt of the USA to have been $679.24 billion dollars in 1979 which amounts to $3001 per capita. For Switzerland the total debt is given as 13.659 billion francs which equals $1222 per capita (**193**)—figures that cannot be reconciled with other data.

8. The cantons spend a small amount for defense, about 61 francs ($35) per capita in 1980, partly covered by a small federal subvention of about 25 per cent ($9 per capita) earmarked for civil protection (**341**, 1981, p. 419).

9. The Federal Government, much in need of additional revenue, proposed an added value tax (*Mehrwertsteuer*) which would have imposed a tax on the value added to a product or service at each stage of distribution, from producer to consumer. First submitted to the people as an obligatory referendum to support a proposed amendment of the Constitution, the contemplated tax was defeated on 12 June 1977. In a second attempt, the Federal Government lost again when the tax measure was even more heavily defeated in a votation on 20 May 1979.

> Since 1950 we have voted 13 times in all on Federal Tax proposals—that is, an average of once every three years. On seven occasions the people have voted against. The only times they have voted in favor of such proposals have been when tax concessions have punched new holes in the federal cashbox instead of filling it. (Federal Councillor Willi Ritschard, head of the Federal Department of Finance, in a speech at Lugano, 23 August 1980).

10. Source: **341**, 1981, p. 406. Note, however, that the Federal Government of the USA, prodigal as it may be in its operations, has held its total civilian employment at about 2,900,000 from 1970 to 1981 (**340**, p. 268).

11. Cost of living increases and supplements for community cost variations and number of children in the family lead to annual increases in total remunerations of federal employees.

11.12. BANKING

Number of Banks

The importance of Switzerland as a great financial center is suggested by the number of banks in a country of only 6.3 million or so inhabitants. In 1980, the number of large commercial banks, cantonal banks, regional banks, savings banks, other lending institutions and other banks with specialized services totalled 432 (**341**, 1981, p. 282). If we include 84 financial societies (**341**, 1981, p. 285) we arrive at a partial total of 516. However, this excludes the branch offices, the country's smallest banks, and these are numerous. At the beginning of 1971, Swiss banking statistics listed 473 banks with a total of 4409 offices. Among these 473 banks were 24 cantonal institutions, 39 that belonged to the communities, 305 corporations, 98 cooperative credit banks and 7 other types of institutions. Also subject to the Swiss Federal Banking Law are some 1185 agricultural cooperative credit institutions (*Raiffeisenkassen*) (**125**, p. 4).

Assets

However, there are other ways of measuring the importance of a country as a banking center of international significance. The assets of a country's banks are a useful indicator. The 432 banks in Switzerland in 1980 had total assets of 466.299 billion francs (about 280 billion USA dollars at the end of 1980 exchange rate). If we include the 1980 assets of the 84 financial societies, the grand total would be 477.39 billion francs (**341**, 1981, pp. 283, 285). In 1955 the assets of the 408 banks, then in operation, totalled 36.7 billion francs (8.55 billion USA dollars at the 1955 exchange rate). A comparison of the 1955 and 1980 totals indicates an average annual increase of about 16 billion francs in total assets of the banking system—an average annual growth rate of 8 percent since 1975. Incidentally, the assets of the banking system in 1980 were about 2.6 times as great as the gross national product of 177 billion francs (**341**, 1981, p. 347)—a surprising observation.

Size Comparisons

The size of the Swiss banks may also be considered in relation to the banks of other countries. *The Banker*, a London publication, published the results of a 1979 survey. At that time, France's Crédit Agricole with balances of 104.9 billion dollars was the largest. The Swiss Bank Corporation was then in the 28th position, the Union Bank of Switzerland in the 31st, and Credit Suisse in position 46. All 500 were the world's largest, if ranked according to balances (total assets or liabilities).

Foreign Business

Another observation that is significant but not so surprising is that "over two-fifths of total bank assets are accounted for by foreign business" (**230**, p. 114). Switzerland is a neutral country with her neutrality declared to be in "the true interests of the . . . whole of Europe" (cf. Chapter 8). This declaration by the European Powers in 1815, implicitly reaffirmed by the 100 or so signatories of the Treaty of Versailles in 1919, confers upon Switzerland the status of a country that will not become embroiled in the quarrels of other countries and in their wars. It is a haven of safety and security, which more than any other country, can serve as a peaceful center for international financial transactions. To the world's financial community, Switzerland is considered to be solid, conservative, politically stable and blessed by a citizenry of cautious, industrious and honest people. The interest of the foreign investor in Switzerland's banking services is evidenced by the fact that 35 to 50 percent of the total balances of the Swiss banking system for a 25-year span (1955 to 1980) have consisted of foreign money, expressed as deposits by foreign banks and other foreign creditors (**341**, 1981, p. 283: liabilities, *Passiva*).

For a great financial center engaged in international transactions language facility can be important. The Swiss banks enjoy total linguistic competence in English, French, German, Italian and usually in several other languages. This is certainly true of the largest banks, especially the big three, which transact most of the foreign business. Competence in the three official languages of Switzerland, and in English, is widely dispersed through the entire Swiss banking system.

Securities Transactions

But there are other aspects of the Swiss banking services that appeal to the domestic and foreign investor. In brief, the Swiss banks are full-service banks, prepared to satisfy most of the financial needs of their clients. Unlike the banks of the USA they go far beyond the acceptance of deposits and the lending of money. They do an extensive business in securities transactions. If you wish to buy or sell stocks, bonds and other equities you will go to a bank. Their stock exchanges are among the busiest—not merely in dealing with domestic securities but in foreign securities as well. Stocks of almost all the large international companies can be bought or sold in a Swiss bank. The lobby of Credit Suisse on Bahnhofstrasse in Zurich has on display a large multi-sided rotating quote board on which are displayed the current prices for many selected stocks from the world's principal stock exchanges.

> In the bond sector Switzerland is rated as the most important market for Eurobonds. On the basis of this intensive world-wide business, there has arisen a foreign exchange market of international importance; in terms of volume it is now reckoned to stand in third place in the world after London and New York (**230**, p. 115).

In international stock-market trading, the orders placed from Switzerland are indeed substantial though Swiss capital is used to a relatively small extent. In acting on behalf of foreign investors, foreign capital is used. It is as a capital market that Switzerland owes its prominence in international banking. Of equal, if not of greater importance, is Switzerland's position in the international gold market in which "possibly one half of the annual turnover of physical gold is now thought to be handled by the Swiss banks." It should be noted that the business of the Swiss banks in new issues, securities, foreign exchange and precious metals is not reflected in their balance sheets.

The Big Three

One seldom refers to the Swiss banks without special mention of the Big Three: The Union Bank of Switzerland, the Swiss Bank Corporation, and Credit Suisse. They must be singled out for a number of reasons. They stand apart from all other Swiss banks in sheer size. The smallest of the three had assets in 1977 of over 44 billion francs while the largest of the three had assets of over 56 billion. But the fourth bank, ranked in the same way, had assets of only 15.5 billion francs—only about one-third of number three in the list. The Big Three had total assets of about 156 billion francs in 1977 which is one-third of the combined assets of the entire Swiss banking system in 1980.

The size of the Swiss banks in terms of assets must not be misinterpreted. The largest of them with 29 billion dollars (56 billion francs) in total assets in 1977 was considerably smaller than the largest USA bank, the Bank of America, which ended 1981 with total assets of 120 billion dollars. This is about one-half of the combined assets of the entire Swiss banking system.

A Comparison with the USA Banking System

A comparison with the USA banking system may be of some interest. The total assets of the system (14,400 domestically chartered commercial banks, 1480 billion dollars; savings and loan associations, 629.8 billion; mutual savings banks, 171.6 billion; credit unions, 71.7 billion; and domestic finance companies, 150.1 billion) amounted to 2503.2 billion dollars[1] at the end of 1980 (**126**). On a per capita basis, it follows that Switzerland with a population of 6.3 million and banking assets of 244 billion dollars had total assets in her financial institutions equal to $38,730 per capita. The USA population approximated 223 million in mid-1980. A similar calculation, based on the total assets of her financial institutions, gives a value of $11,225 per capita.[2]

The Swiss National Bank

The Swiss National Bank, established in 1907, is quite unlike the Federal Reserve System of the USA. Although the Constitution in October 1891 gave to the Swiss Confederation the right to create a National Bank, the bank emerged in 1907 as a joint stock company. Almost sixty percent of the stock is held by the cantons, the cantonal banks, and 55 other public bodies and institutions; the rest is privately owned by a few thousand shareholders.

The Federal Reserve System of the USA

The Federal Reserve Banks of the USA, twelve in number, are owned by the approximately 6000 member banks spread over the twelve districts. These member banks are the shareholders, they appoint six of the nine directors of the Reserve Bank in their respective districts, they put up the necessary capital and receive the statutory dividend on the corresponding Federal Reserve stock purchased to satisfy the capital requirements of membership.

In Washington we find a Board of Governors of the Federal Reserve System. The members, appointed for 14-year terms, are beyond the pale of government. They do not serve at the pleasure of the president and may not be dismissed at his command. The Board receives no money from the Bureau of the Budget and serves in virtual independence of the Federal Government. Members may be impeached by the Congress but it has never happened.

Although decisions of the Federal Reserve Bank do not have to be ratified by the President or by one of his appointees in the executive branch of government, the Federal Reserve must report to the Congress and thereby, though indirectly, to the people as a whole. Appointments to the Board are made by the President by and with the consent of the Senate. The President designates two members of the Board to be the Chairman and Vice-Chairman respectively. A fairly accurate description of the System's role is to characterize it as "independent within Government."

The System is relatively complex. In addition to the 6000 or so banks that are members of the System through its 12 Federal Reserve Banks there are three bodies that have responsibility for making and executing monetary policy: The Board of Governors, the Federal Open Market Committee, and the Federal Reserve Banks. Their main responsibility is to regulate the flow of credit and money, but they also perform important supervisory and service functions for the public, the US Treasury, and the commercial banks. The Board's offices in Washington are a headquarters-type facility, and no operations are conducted from those offices.

Each Reserve Bank is separately incorporated with its own nine-member Board of Directors of which the Chairman and Deputy Chairman are appointed by the Board of Governors. Earnings of the Federal Reserve Banks go first to the payment of expenses (including assessments by the Board of Governors to defray expenses of the Board) to the statutory six percent dividend on the Federal Reserve stock required to be purchased by member banks, and to surplus. Remaining earnings are paid into the US Treasury. More than 80 percent of the Reserve Banks' earnings have been paid into the Treasury since the Federal Reserve System was established in 1913 when President Woodrow Wilson signed the Federal Reserve Act.

The Federal Reserve Banks operate Regional Check Processing Centers as a service facility to the member banks. The volume of checks handled has grown rapidly. In 1973, the Reserve Banks cleared about 10 billion of the estimated 26 billion checks drawn on banks in the United States.

The Chairman of the Board of Governors, representing the Federal Reserve System, meets frequently with the President, the Secretary of the Treasury and the heads of various Offices and Councils of the government to discuss matters of fiscal policy and to evaluate economic conditions and objectives. He is also an alternate governor of the International Monetary Fund.

As the USA central bank, the System can affect the availability of reserves to support bank deposits, doing so through its open market operations—purchases and sales for its own account of securities, mainly those issued by the US government—and by its authority to vary reserve requirements. The discount rate set by Federal Reserve Banks directly affects the cost of reserves borrowed by member banks from their Federal Reserve Bank. This and various administrative rules affect the total amount of each borrowing. By virtue of its powers and its monetary policies, the level of interest rates in the country is virtually determined by the Board of Governors in regulating credit and the money supply. For example it establishes the maximum interest rates that commercial banks which are members of the System may pay on savings and time deposits. The Federal Reserve also supervises State-chartered member banks and regulates the foreign activities of all USA banks (127).

The Swiss National Bank and the Banking Law

The Swiss National Bank is the sole issuer of bank notes and it participates in fixing the interest rates on demand deposits in commercial banks. Capital exports in loans or credits with a life of more than one year and in excess of ten million francs must be approved by the National Bank. In 1961, after German and Dutch currencies appreciated in value, the country was flooded with foreign money and about one billion francs were diverted into a blocked account in the National Bank. Money continued to flow in and a so-called "Credit Resolution" of the Federal Government, designed to control bank credits, was not effective. A bill proposed by the government to control issues, credits and reserves was not favorably regarded by a commission assigned to study the problem. There was much public opposition to the contemplated interference by government. A gentlemen's agreement was finally concluded whereby the banks themselves resolved the problem which the government would otherwise have attempted to solve by legislative intervention. The role of the National Bank was significantly strengthened by the measures adopted and the Federal Assembly took no further action in the matter.

In Switzerland, agreements between the parties concerned are greatly preferred over settlements achieved by force of law. It is the Swiss way of doing things. If problems between parties are not solved by gentlemen's agreements, government intervention may result with political interference that is seldom regarded with favor.

This is not to imply that the National Bank exists and operates splendidly and totally isolated from the Federal Government. Articles 31 quater, 38 and 39 of the Federal Constitution provide the base for banking legislation. The Federal Law of 8 November 1934, amended by the Federal Law of 11 March 1971, and again in 1978, is generally known as the Swiss Federal Banking Law. Its main purpose is to provide protection for bank depositors. It contains regulations pertaining to liquidity, reserves, priority calls on savings deposits in case of bankruptcy proceedings, the publication of annual accounts and verifications by an auditor. The responsibilities of bank management are also defined in detail. Penalties for violation of Swiss banking secrecy are covered in Article 47 of the Law which obligates all banks not to furnish any information to third parties about the financial circumstances and business connections of their customers. This provision of the Law stems from the traditional Swiss belief in adequate protection of the personal freedom of the individual. The Swiss are not inclined to discuss their financial affairs with others and for anyone in banking circles, who may be privy to such financial information and who divulges it to a third party, the penalty is severe: imprisonment for up to six months or a fine of up to 50,000 francs. The violation of professional secrecy remains punishable even after termination of the official's employment. Penal provisions pertinent to irresponsible acts, negligence, dishonesty, fraudulent assertions, or wilful violations of rules and regulations governing the conduct and duties of employees reach far and wide through the banking system. They are spelled out in Articles 39 to 51 of the Law. The word employee, as I have used it, may include the entire staff of a bank, a liquidator or commissioner of a bank, a representative of the Banking Commission and an officer or employee of an auditing company.

The highest supervisory and implementing authority for the Banking Law is the Federal Banking Commission, elected by the Federal Council and under its direct control. The functions of the Commission include the issuing of implementing regulations for the Banking Law,[3] the interpretation of that Law, the supervision of auditing procedures, the general supervision of the banking system and of the investment trusts. The Commission consists of 7 to 9 members. They must be experts but they may not be an officer or a member of the management of a bank, of a recognized auditing firm or of an Investment Trust.

Article 38 of the Federal Constitution confers upon the Confederation all rights pertaining to the State monopoly of coinage. The Confederation alone has the right to coin money. It shall determine the monetary system and, if necessary, shall enact regulations on the rates of exchange.

Article 39 of the Federal Constitution confers upon the Confederation the exclusive right to issue bank-notes and other types of paper money. The Article also permits the Confederation to exercise this monopoly by means of a State bank placed under a separate management.[4] The main function of such a bank (The Swiss National Bank) shall be to regulate the circulation of money in the country, to facilitate payment operations, and to conduct within the scope of federal legislation a credit and monetary policy beneficial to the general interest of Switzerland.

At least two-thirds of the net profits of the bank, after certain deductions such as statutory payments to the reserve fund, shall accrue to the cantons.[5] The bank and its branches shall be exempt from any taxation in the cantons. Bank notes issued must be covered by gold and short-term securities.

If interested in statistical data regarding the Swiss National Bank, please refer to Tables 52 and 53. Assets of the Swiss banks, not including the National Bank, are presented in Table 54. The Swiss are a thrifty people and the deposit of spare cash in savings accounts is widely practiced. Table 55 reports on the moneys held in Swiss savings accounts since 1825. The 1980 population was about 6,366,000 and, with savings deposits of 90,239.6 million francs, the per capita savings amounted to 14,332 francs—the highest for all of western Europe. A substantial portion of the 90,239 million francs is of foreign origin but the exact amount held to the credit of non-residents is not publicly recorded.[6] The number of American accounts in Swiss banks was rumoured in 1975 to be at least 150,000 (**204**).

Interest Rates

In Table 56, the interest rates since the mid-nineteenth century on savings deposits, obligation loans (usually bonds), and first mortgages are presented.[7] An examination of the Table at once raises several intriguing questions. Since the interest rates on savings deposits are relatively low, why do the Swiss not deposit such funds in money market accounts (see also Table 57)? There are several answers which, considered together, would convince the average Swiss to shun any such temptation. True, money-market paper has been traded in Switzerland since mid-1979

Table 52 The Swiss National Bank—total assets[a,b]

End of December		End of December	
1914	818.9	1975	34,991.0
1915	957.3	1976	39,324.0
1916	1080.6	1977	38,921.0
1919	1298.2	1978	46,421.0
1932	2743.5	1979	43,244.5
1955	7738.2	1980	44,318.7
1965	15,287.6	1981	44,584.5
1970	23,095.3		

[a] In millions of francs.
[b] Sources: **341**, 1916, pp. 142, 143; 1920, p. 143; 1932, p. 213; 1981, p. 290; **377**, February 1982.

Table 53   The Swiss National Bank—miscellaneous data[a,b,e]

Gold reserves	11,903.9[e]	1.	Notes and coins in circulation	20,587
Foreign bills of exchange	28,981.8	2.	Demand deposits	44,877
Foreign treasury bonds	2028.5		Monetary mass, M1	65,464
Total monetary reserves	42,914.2	3.	Term deposits plus demand	
Notes in circulation	22,499.1		deposits in foreign money	
Total liabilities	46,396.0		of residents	20,676
Domestic borrowings from the Bank[d]			Monetary mass, M2 (M1 + 3)	86,140
Confederation	201.3	4.	Savings deposits	103,836
Cantons	162.3		Total amount of money, M3	
Communities	186.7		(M2 + 4)	189,976
Electricity, gas, water	273.1			
Industry	354.5			
Commerce (merchandise)	36.3			
Banks	814.0			
Mortgage central	61.3			
Holding companies	247.9			
Other Enterprises	103.1			
Total domestic borrowings	2440.5			
Foreign borrowings[d]	2687.5			

[a] In millions of francs.
[b] End of December 1978.
[e] Unchanged since mid-1976. Valued at $72 an ounce, about one-fifth of the 1982 market price.
[d] January to July 1979. Residue of borrowings at end of July, after deduction of conversions.
[e] Sources: **359**, August 1979, pages 25, 26, 29, 56; Current data appear in *Die Volkswirtschaft* (**377**).

and on a regular basis since early 1980. But why not invest in an American money-market fund? Money so deposited would be fully as liquid as it would be in a commercial or savings account and would currently (June 1982) earn about 14 percent per annum. There is no legal deterrent, Swiss or American, that would prevent a Swiss citizen from making such an investment.

But there are several negative considerations which indicate clearly that he should "look before he leaps." His investment would be in dollars not in Swiss francs and there are too many potential vagaries in the exchange rates. An investment of 20,000 Swiss francs may be equal to 10,200 USA dollars today but if the dollar, vis-à-vis the Swiss franc, increased in value by ten percent the value of the original investment would fall to 18,000 francs. Most of the currencies of the world, subject to the instabilities of the "float," move up and down like a yo-yo and no one can predict with confidence the exchange rates of next month or next week. The minimum investment of $500 or $10,000 required to open an account in most money market funds would also discourage some, even though there are many Swiss to whom such an initial investment would be no deterrent. But it could be inconvenient; the Atlantic Ocean would be a troublesome barrier. For one who resides in the USA, funds may be withdrawn almost instantly: request a withdrawal today and the

Table 54 Assets of the Swiss Banks at the end of December[a,b]

	1919[d]			1932[d]	
	Number	Total assets		Number	Total assets
Cantonal banks	24	3940.4		27	7685.9
Large banks	9	4664.3		8	6429.5
Local & middle size banks	84	1537.1		181	4093.8
Savings & loans	67	403.7			
Credit Unions Central[c]	1	85.4		1	324.6
Mortgage banks	17	1730.5			
Savings banks	115	1090.6		92	1411.0
Financial trusts	24	1086.4		47	1752.1
Transatlantic banks	1	57.9			
Total	342	14,596.3		356	21,696.9

	1959[d]			1980[d]	
	Number	Total assets		Number	Total assets
Cantonal banks		18,261.3		29	101,201
Large banks		14,771.3		5	239,394
Savings banks	352	16,561.0	Regional & savings banks	37	32,862
All banks[f]		49,804.0[e]			373,457[g]
			Others		103,933
			Grand total		477,390

[a] National Bank not included (see Table 52).
[b] In millions of francs.
[c] Local branches: 250 in 1919, 571 in 1932.
[d] Sources: **341**, 1920, pp. 142, 143; 1932, p. 213; 1969, pp. 267–269, 274; **377**, February 1982.
[e] Of this total, banks with assets of 100 million francs or more had combined assets of 41,039.1 million francs. In 1980 the large banks (and financial societies) had total assets of 455,080 million francs as compared with 477,390 for the whole banking system.
[f] Except the Swiss National Bank.
[g] This is a partial total, because the total assets of Switzerland's 432 banks and 84 financial societies were 477,390 million francs at end of December (**341**, 1981, pp. 283, 285).

money is in your hands tomorrow. However, at least one week, and the cost of a bank draft would be obstacles to a transatlantic, transcurrency transaction.

This is where the large Swiss banks with decades of experience in international banking enter the scene. Much of the money held by the banks, well protected by substantial reserves, is reinvested abroad at the relatively high interest rates that prevail.[8] To appreciate the significance of the large and middle-sized banks (each

Table 55   Deposits in savings accounts (*Spareinlagen*)[a]

Year end	Number of banks[b]	Deposits	Sources
1825	44	6.79	**341**, 1920, p. 151
1835	100	16.79	**341**, 1920, p. 151
1852	163	60.37	**341**, 1920, p. 151
1862	235	131.9	**341**, 1920, p. 151
1872	312	288.8	**341**, 1920, p. 151
1882	487	513.7	**341**, 1920, p. 151
1897	458	984.7	**341**, 1920, p. 151
1908	1047	1592.7	**341**, 1920, p. 151
1918	1394	2646.6	**341**, 1920, p. 151
1938	327	6231.5	**341**, 1951, p. 271
1950	389	9274.4	**341**, 1951, p. 271
1955	408	11,120.7	**341**, 1981, p. 282
1965	472	22,628.0	**341**, 1981, p. 282
1975	455	64,767.6	**341**, 1981, p. 282
1980	432	90,293.6	**341**, 1981, p. 282

[a] In millions of francs.
[b] The number of banks reported after 1918 excludes the country's smallest banks which are, in fact, branch offices of the cantonal banks, large banks, and regional banks of all kinds, and may have numbered in 1980 about 4500.

with assets of 100 million francs or more) about 90 percent of the assets of the entire banking system are held by these banks. Including 25 financial societies, they numbered 271 out of a grand total of 516 (including 84 financial societies) in 1980.

Swiss Banks in the USA

In mid-1981 there were six Swiss banks in the USA and seventeen USA banks in Switzerland. If the Swiss banks have any unique advantages in the USA, they must be few in number, because both domestic and foreign banks in the USA are subject to the same corporation and tax laws. The Swiss banks are restricted in interstate operations, nonbanking activities and reserve requirements in the same way as USA banks. One curious difference, advantageous to a foreign bank is that while USA banks are generally not permitted to acquire banks in other states or to acquire large in-state banks (because of anti-trust problems), foreign banks are not restrained from the purchase of large USA banks. Whether USA banks should be at such a disadvantage is the subject of complaint and hoped-for relief. Adherence to the principles of a free market economy would certainly require that foreign banks in the USA be treated in exactly the same way as domestic banks. The taxation of branches of foreign banks by some states, e.g. California, is a disadvantage to foreign banks and expresses a questionable policy because it raises the ugly head of double taxation.

Mandatory reporting requirements imposed by the Federal Reserve Board would require that information be released by the foreign parent of the Swiss branches on

Table 56   Interest rates

Year	Savings accounts[a]	Swiss obligation loans[b]	First mortgages[a]	Source
1856/60	4.00		4.58	**341**, 1951, p. 273
1881/85	3.95		4.45	**341**, 1951, p. 273
1901/05	3.71		4.07	**341**, 1951, p. 273
1915		4.42		**341**, 1920, p. 150
1916/20	4.22		4.99	**341**, 1969, p. 275
1925	4.35	5.30	5.40	**341**, 1969, p. 275
				341, 1932, p. 231
1935	3.00		4.10	**341**, 1969, p. 275
1945	2.60	3.34	3.70	**341**, 1969, pp. 275, 283
1955	2.40	3.13	3.50	**341**, 1969, pp. 275, 283
1965	3.25	4.75	4.13	**341**, 1969, pp. 275, 279
1975[c]	4.95	7.47	6.00	**341**, 1979, pp. 285, 291
1980[d]	2.73	5.10	4.50	**341**, 1981, pp. 281, 293

[a] Average interest rates effective in the cantonal banks of Zurich, St. Gallen, Aargau, Bern and Vaud.

[b] Interest rates on domestic borrowings by the Confederation, Cantons, communities, public utilities, industry, commerce, holding societies, real estate companies, hotels, restaurants, agriculture, transport and communication services, etc. These rates varied with time, place, and nature of the bank (large, cantonal, regional and middle-sized, savings and loans, mortgage, savings, trust banks etc.). On foreign borrowings the average interest rates were higher: for example 5.89 percent in 1980 compared with 5.10 percent on borrowings within Switzerland by Swiss residents.

[c] Interest rates reached a peak in 1974/75: 5.00 percent on savings, 6.03 on first mortgages, and 7.58 on Swiss obligations (**341**, 1981, pp. 281, 293). Note that 1975–76 were recession years in Switzerland.

From 1930 on, domestic interest rates were at their lowest in the decade 1947–1956: 2.40 percent on savings and 3.50 percent on first mortgages (**341**, 1981, p. 281).

[d] Late in 1980, four of the large banks proposed to increase the interest paid on savings deposits from 2.5 to 3.0 per cent. The interest rate on first mortgages would, however, be raised from 4.5 to 5.0 percent. Public opinion and government displeasure with the proposals were sufficient to persuade the banks to leave the interest rates at existing levels. The Swiss Bankers' Association agreed to postpone until 1 January 1981, at the earliest, any increase in the mortgage rates for existing contracts and new mortgages on farming property. New nonagricultural mortgages might be subject to the higher rate after 1 October 1980.

losses from bad debts and ownership of shares by the Board of Directors. According to Swiss law this demand is economic espionage under the Swiss penal code. Release of such information would be a direct violation of the bank-secrecy laws. Assuming that the basic question revolves around the financial soundness of the Swiss banks' parents and the adequacy of the protection available to depositors in the USA branches, it would seem possible to accomplish this desirable objective without placing a foreign bank in the awkward and embarrassing position of a forced violation of its country's banking laws. The Federal Reserve Board also requires compulsory insurance of small deposit accounts and maintenance of a stated minimum of reserves. It should be noted that the Social Democratic Party in Switzerland is sponsoring an initiative measure which will require Swiss banks to provide insurance for the protection of small deposits in those cases where the banks do not offer the protection afforded by State guaranties.

A word about investment banking. Although the USA commercial banks may

Table 57 Interest rates on government obligations—some international comparisons

Country	Interest rate 1980[a]	1981[b]	1983, July[e]
Switzerland	4.73[c]	5.39[c]	4.53[c]
Canada	12.67	15.27	12.03
Denmark	17.57[d]	20.38	16.53
Great Britain	13.80	15.65	10.59
Italy	16.88	21.42[d]	17.87[d]
USA	12.49	13.73	11.59
West Germany	8.90	9.70	8.10

[a] Fourth Quarter, 1980.
[b] Source: 341, 1981, p. 606; 341, 1982, p. 604.[b]
[c] Lowest of the 12 countries reported upon in the Yearbook.
[d] Highest of the 12 countries reported upon in the Yearbook.
[e] Source: *International Financial Statistics*, Volume XXXVI, Number 10, October 1983.

not engage in the direct underwriting of securities they can go far, indeed, in the business of investment banking. They suffer no prohibition in private placements, advice on mergers and acquisitions, sale of commercial paper and advisory services to investment companies. Currently (mid-1982) it seems likely that USA savings and loan associations will be enabled to trade in stocks, bonds and other securities, in clear competition with the recognized brokerage houses. If the savings and loan associations engage in the securities business it will almost certainly follow that the banks will ultimately be permitted to do the same.

Just as Zurich is the financial center of Switzerland, New York has long been the center for USA banking. Incidentally the largest of the foreign banks in New York is a branch of the Swiss Bank Corporation with a 1979 staff of 120 or so. The Big Three are the most prominent, with major branches in New York City and branches or representatives in Chicago, San Francisco and Los Angeles. The New York branches of the Big Three also engage directly or through their own securities companies in equities trading.

Other Foreign Banks in the USA

For several years, the dollar has been cheap in relation to major currencies abroad. This has led to a large influx of foreign banks, principally to New York. There is still room for more and more will come—especially if the city develops the "free-trade" banking area of which one hears much. If the New York banks can carry out Eurodollar market transactions, instead of using off-shore centers for such business, an enormous shift in these transactions will follow. Grindlays Bank has estimated that between 1980 and 1990, London's share of the Eurodollar market will fall from 32 percent to 20 percent; and that of the Bahamas and Caymans from 11 percent to 2 percent. However, New York's share will rise from zero to 18 percent. Much of the above on "Swiss Banks in the USA" has been abstracted from the published remarks of Guido Hanselmann of the Union Bank of Switzerland and of Hubert Baschnagel of the Swiss Bank Corporation (**357**, 27 May 1981; **357**, 27 June 1979).

The Bank for International Settlements

The Bank for International Settlements, founded as a result of the Hague Agreements in 1930, was established in Basel by the terms of an International Convention signed by Germany, Belgium, France, the United Kingdom, Italy and Japan on the one hand and by the Swiss Confederation on the other. This, however, is almost the extent of government participation except for State treaties which spelled out many of the details, including the immunities that the Bank would require in the various countries. In brief, the Bank may not be regarded as an intergovernmental bank. It is, rather, a "central bank's bank" for one of its main purposes is to promote the cooperation of central banks. It achieves this, in part, by smoothing and facilitating the international settlement transactions of central banks.

The role of the Bank as a "central bank's bank" is exemplified by reference to the Statutes of the Bank for International Settlements. Article 21 describes in detail the particular powers of the Bank. With few exceptions, the thirteen clauses refer in detail to what the Bank may do for or on behalf of central banks. And from Article 24 we learn that the Bank "may not make advances to Governments" and also "may not open current accounts in the name of Governments" (**23**).

The Bank enters into transactions with central banks on all five continents, thus reaching beyond the 29 shareholding members (of which 24 are European central banks). It makes only short-term loans—usually not more than three to six months and, with deposits that are usually short-term, maintains a high level of liquidity. The Board of Directors consists of representatives of eight central banks in Europe. They meet ten times each year and can act quickly because of the non-political structure of the Board and its ready access to financial markets—the central banks to which they lend and from which they receive deposits.

The authorized share capital of the Bank amounts at present (November, 1981) to 1500 million gold francs. Of this, 1183 million gold francs has been issued in the form of shares, paid up to the extent of 25 percent. The balance sheet consequently shows the capital of the Bank as 296 million gold francs. The gold franc referred to here has a fine-gold content of just over 0.29 grams. The Bank uses the gold franc for balance-sheet purposes only. In its day-to-day business, assets and liabilities are converted at the rate of US $1.94 equals 1 gold franc.

The growth of the Bank has been phenomenal. From a balance-sheet total of 1901 million gold francs in 1931, the total rose to 19,029 million gold francs in November 1981. Understandably, balance-sheet totals fell greatly during the European chaos of World War II: 470 million gold francs in 1940 and 451 million in 1946 (**23**, pp. 140, 141).

The Bank served as the agent for carrying out the clearing operations under the

Intra-European Payments Agreements of 1948–50 followed by the European Payments Union in 1950 in which the Bank was actively involved in creating and operating the EPU. The Bank took on new functions on behalf of the European Economic Community and, later, as agent for the European Monetary Cooperation Fund. The Bank serves as a Depository, virtually as a Trustee, for the European Coal and Steel Community with its responsibilities as Depository continuing until 1986.

The Annual Report of the Bank for 1981, in a critical view of USA economic policy, refers to interest rates at very high levels as a result of Washington's "conflict between a clearly budgetary counterinflation monetary policy and a deliberately expansionary budgetary policy." The rigorous monetary-supply controls of the US Federal Reserve Board seriously disturb the "equilibrium of the world economy." Were it not for the high interest rates in the USA, the interest rates in West Germany and Japan in the spring of 1982 would have been at levels "more consistent with the requirements of domestic balance."

In late 1982, the Bank made short-term loans to Mexico (1.8 billion dollars) and to Hungary (500 million dollars), doing so as rescue operations to meet the urgent financial needs of these countries while they negotiated long-term loans from the International Monetary Fund. Pressure has been developing from commercial banks for the BIS to become a more permanent lender of last resort to debt-ridden countries. Whether or not the central banks and the BIS will assume a new bail-out responsibility of this nature is in doubt. Certainly the loans to Mexico and Hungary are not precedent-establishing. The BIS is not equipped to provide medium-term or long-term loans: Its investments are entirely short-term. Also it does not have the staff to mount a regular rescue program and its present operating guide lines would preclude implementation of such a program.

It is worth noting that in the third quarter of 1982, banks in 14 major western countries reduced their overall lending to non oil-producing countries of the Third World by 800 million dollars. The banks are jittery over the ability of these countries to repay their debts. This reporting area consists of the ten major industrial countries plus Switzerland, Austria, Denmark and Ireland. New lending outside the reporting area decreased to four billion dollars from 20 billion dollars in the second quarter. The BIS loans to countries in the reporting area increased to 115 billion dollars in the third quarter compared with nine billion dollars in the second quarter. Outstanding credits to Eastern Europe were reduced in the third quarter by 11.1 billion dollars while loans to OPEC countries increased by 2.8 billion dollars—a dramatic change from the previous year when the OPEC countries were adding to their deposits in Western banks (**381**, 19 January 1983).

Incidentally, the President of the Swiss National Bank is currently (1982) also the President of the Bank for International Settlements. He is reported as having told representatives of heavily indebted Third World Nations "that they would have to put their countries through periods of painful adjustment to restore their financial stability." The 500-million dollar bridging loan being prepared for Yugoslavia has been declared to be the last of its type. Leutwiler is also reported to have said that the

BIS was "tired" of having to provide bridging financing without being able to see "an end to the bridge." As for Venezuela allegedly seeking help from the IMF to restructure its debts, there is "no way" by which Venezuela will gain access to BIS funds (**381**, 2 February 1983).

The International Monetary Fund

In contrast to the Bank for International Settlements, which neither makes loans to governments nor maintains current accounts in the name of governments, the International Monetary Fund, based in Washington, confines its membership to States. Members are either original members, i.e. those countries listed in the Articles of Agreement (concluded in 1944 at Bretton Woods) and that adhered to the Articles before 31 December 1945, or other members that have adhered in accordance with resolutions adopted by the Board of Governors. By 1982 the number of members had reached 140. Drawing rights of a member are largely a function of the assets deposited by the member to the credit of his account with the Fund (**152, 164**). In this respect it operates somewhat like a bank in which the owner of an account deposits money and from which he can make withdrawals. The Fund uses different terms to describe its operations but the analogy is permissible.

As an international fund many different state currencies are handled in its multinational transactions. The Fund is an excellent vehicle whereby member States may have credited to their accounts the currencies of as many other member States as they may choose to purchase. It is a fund for international settlements, exclusively between State governments just as the Bank for International Settlements renders a somewhat parallel service—exclusively between the central banks of member countries.

Various political obligations limit access to IMF assistance. The rules require adherence to a code of good behaviour such as having IMF permission before introducing any foreign exchange restrictions, adhering to a minimum set of obligations in respect to foreign exchange policy and regular consultation with the Fund on economic and financial policies.

The member countries are required to make cash contributions to the Fund and to pledge further monetary contributions, within limits, when called upon. In case of need, member countries are entitled to borrow or receive credit, from the Fund. The more that a country with balance-of-payments difficulties seeks to borrow, the more are the questions asked and the more are the conditions attached to the loan. In general, the policy of the IMF is to encourage a member in trouble to make a very serious effort to stop living beyond its means. A weak government sometimes succeeds in forcing its parliament to accept financial orthodoxy by reminding the members of parliament that financial aid is not forthcoming unless they put their house in order. Sometimes the IMF is circumvented by a member country, which, displeased with the severity of the IMF rules and the political obligations that are built in, will borrow, though more expensively, on the open market.

Both the Bank for International Settlements and the International Monetary Fund provide services other than those described above to their members. In general, both institutions provide machinery for consultation and collaboration on many international monetary problems such as exchange rates, exchange stability, foreign exchange restrictions, maladjustments in balance of payments, and international trade.

A recent addition to the IMF is an emergency fund bearing the curious name "General Arrangements to Borrow." It must be regarded as a bail-out facility to assist countries that are on the verge of financial collapse. The ten largest industrial democracies, known as the Group of Ten, provide the credits for this emergency lending pool from which funds are available to all IMF members. It is, in fact, a crisis fund to help avert defaults by major borrowing nations.

In early 1983, Switzerland made the surprising request that she be admitted as a member of the Group of Ten.[11] If her request is approved, the Group of Ten will probably be known henceforth as the Group of Eleven. Hitherto, Switzerland has attended the Group-of-Ten meetings as an observer but has been contributing to the General Arrangements fund since the mid-1960s. A minor administrative problem that must be solved stems from the fact that Switzerland is not an IMF member.

There is hope that the overall resources of the IMF, including the emergency fund, will be increased to about 120 billion dollars from the present level of 76 billion dollars—the decision on this massive increase to be reached in the immediate future. As for the emergency fund, Switzerland will be obliged to contribute six percent of the total in the pool, instead of 5.6 percent which she has provided in the past. The USA share of the 19 billion dollar total in the emergency fund will be 25 percent instead of the present 28 percent. Contributors to the fund will have the final say on allocations (**381**, 19 January 1983).

Swiss Bank Secrecy

Swiss bank secrecy about which one hears much and which is greatly misunderstood by foreigners has been discussed briefly in the section on the Swiss National Bank, and, more extensively and authoritatively, by Hans Mast (**230**, p. 118). The secrecy law was enacted in 1934 when Nazi Germany was pressing the Swiss banks to reveal information on the accounts of Jewish clients in Germany, but as has already been emphasized, the law is fully in accord with the innate desires of the Swiss people. From time to time efforts are made by pressures from without or from within Switzerland to loosen up the tightness of the law. The Chiasso affair became quite a political issue and demands for more government regulation of the banks could be heard on all sides. The Social Democratic party talked about increasing the banks' responsibility toward the common good. The party called for a national referendum to relax somewhat the rigidity of the law on bank secrecy. It is significant that despite the hue and cry about the banks "misdeeds," the party was unable to obtain the 100,000 signatures required for an initiative. Surveys by the banks indicated that only 20 percent of the voters would support any such initiative (**357**, 20 June 1979). In a second attempt enough signatures (121,882) were obtained for an initiative measure which, by amendment of the Constitution, might lead to a somewhat weakened secrecy law (**381**, 23 June 1980).[12] Annual reports of the banks would be much more informative and "hidden" reserves, used in part to cover hidden losses, would be a required entry in the reports, if the Social Democrats had their way. The banks might get by with hidden reserves but not with hidden losses, according to some observers. Losses should be reported, so we learn, and not caused to disappear from sight by a hidden reserve cover-up.

The initiative also would require insurance of deposits by banks for which a State guaranty is nonexistent. The bankers, though concerned about the possible flight of deposits to Austria, inform us that Austrian accounts must be held in Austrian schillings only, while Swiss accounts may be held in any major currency. Allegedly, Austrian bank accounts can be so anonymous that the identities of the depositors are unknown even to the banks, and so untouchable that the heirs are not allowed to open the accounts after death of the depositors. This taxes the credulity of even the credulous a little too much.

A curious case involving France and the Swiss bank-secrecy laws was publicized in mid-1980. Two French customs officers were charged in a Swiss court with attempting to obtain computerized lists of French depositors in a large Swiss bank. The laws of France forbid its citizens to transfer money in a clandestine manner. Currency smuggling and tax evasion are facilitated, so it was claimed, by the Swiss secrecy laws. The two men were accused of economic espionage and of prohibited activities in favor of a foreign Power. The two were fined, and received prison sentences. Pierre Schultz, in absentia, was sentenced to 3 months in prison, with a two-year reprieve, fined 2000 francs, and expelled from Switzerland for three years. Bernard Rui, also in absentia, was sentenced to 12 months imprisonment, with a five-year reprieve, fined 7000 francs, and expelled from Swiss territory for five years. If the accused are absent when a trial is ordered, the courts in Zurich do not permit the attorney(s) for the defense to plead. The tribunal alone decides the case and issues its judgment. A second trial, at the request of the defendants, is possible. If the defendants are present the trial will proceed in a normal fashion with attorneys for the defense in action.

The bank, concerned with this attempted attack on its secrecy, and knowing of an earlier instance when information was obtained by the French, is demanding satisfaction. The confidence and trust of its clients in the integrity of the bank and its ability to protect fully customers' bank accounts against any disclosures of information is the crucial issue. The French government retaliated by temporarily closing the country's frontier crossings into Switzerland and suspended services by air or sea with Switzerland. The Swiss Federal Council described the attempts of the French customs officers to circumvent the country's secrecy laws as detrimental to Swiss banking and its French customers. The incident emphasizes the tension with other countries that can be attributed to the tight bank secrecy that prevails and to the tendency to think of the Swiss banks as a safe haven for the illegal profits of criminals and tax evaders.

The case, just described, reminds one of another instance of alleged economic espionage by the French authorities. In Geneva, a French citizen employed by a large bank in Geneva, but residing in France, deposited his wages in the bank instead of bringing them into France for deposit. The employee was a so-called border-crosser (*Grenzgänger*) who came into Switzerland each morning and returned home to France at the end of the day. His account in Switzerland was protected by the bank-secrecy laws. But French law, so it was claimed, requires that such border-crossers deposit their wages in France. The attempts of French authorities to probe into the man's Swiss bank account were futile and the effort to gain such information could only be regarded by the Swiss as economic espionage. In France, the man was fined 35,000 French francs, part of which was paid as a reward to his colleagues who informed against him.

A potential violation of the bank-secrecy laws came to light in an effort of the USA Securities and Exchange Commission to obtain information from a Swiss bank on insider trading in corporate acquisition situations. The SEC charged that clients of the Banca Della Svizzera Italiana in Lugano had advance knowledge of a takeover bid for St. Joe Minerals Corporation at $45 per share. The bank had placed orders to buy call options on St. Joe stock the day before the takeover bid was announced. Purchase of the options was executed on 10 March. St. Joe stock was then trading at less than $30 per share. By 13 March, the investment had risen enormously in value as a result of the announcement of the takeover bid. The SEC acted promptly and secured a restraining order from a US judge to freeze the assets of the Lugano bank in the Irving Trust Co.—a necessary action to provide time to investigate the affair. The SEC is investigating other possible violations of the US law by people presumed to have access to privileged information. To determine whether insiders placed the orders from the Lugano bank would be difficult because the bank, if it cooperated, would violate the bank-secrecy law were it to reveal the names of its clients. However, such cooperation is provided for in the USA–Switzerland treaty of 1977 by which the parties agreed to inform each other of the identities of the principals in criminal investigations. Whether the case at issue is criminal according to Swiss law may be a thorny matter requiring resolution by the courts.

In extending the scope of the investigation, efforts are being made to determine whether any corporation officials, their lawyers, accountants, investment bankers and printers had accounts with the Banca Della Svizzera Italiana. Heavy trading from foreign banks prior to the announcement of tender offers is alleged to be a frequent occurrence.

According to an interview with a long-experienced Swiss banker, we are told that "the Swiss have never been good investors, but they are very shrewd in takeover situations." "Very often" says the banker "before a merger is announced, we will see Swiss companies buying those stocks" (**381**, 25 August 1980). "Shrewdness or insider information?" one is tempted to ask.

The Treaty of 1973, which came into force in 1977, providing for US–Swiss cooperation in criminal investigations appears to have worked well. Seventy requests by the US for information from Swiss banks had been received by late 1980 and twenty had come to the USA from Swiss authorities. The USA requests pertained mostly to cases of fraud, embezzlement and breach of fiduciary obligations.[13] The Swiss inquiries centered on fraud and cases of violation of the Swiss laws on narcotics. Practically all requests have been honored by both parties. It should be added that tax evasion—a serious USA problem—is not a crime under Swiss law, and it seems improbable that insider trading in securities would be frowned upon as more than a misdemeanour by the Swiss courts. We learn, however, that legislation is being drafted in Switzerland which will make insider trading in securities illegal (**381**, 3 August 1982).[14]

While we hear much about the secrecy of the Swiss banks it is clear that a certain measure of secrecy pertains to bank-customer relations in many countries. And, as in Switzerland, increasing efforts are made by government to facilitate its penetration of bank operations—especially bank secrecy. Such intrusions by government are very possibly a part of government's determination everywhere to invade ever more deeply the private affairs of its citizens.

When Lord Hailsham was the minister of justice in Great Britain, he visited Switzerland for five days by invitation of Federal Councillor Furgler. In commenting on the Swiss bank secrecy he expressed an opinion that is much to the point; if British citizens use the Swiss banks as depositaries for money that is exported in violation of the laws of Britain, it is not the Swiss banks that should be treated as guilty parties. The British citizens who use the Swiss banks as a hideaway for such funds, and they alone, are the guilty ones. The same conclusion obviously applies to the citizens of other countries who attempt to use the Swiss banks as a haven for their "escape funds" resulting from tax evasion, fraud, theft and other illegal or criminal activities.

Important in respect to bank secrecy is a revised code-of-conduct agreement accepted by the Swiss National Bank and the Swiss Bankers Association. The code extends and strengthens a 1977 agreement to which the Swiss banks have voluntarily adhered. In future, the identity of clients who seek to transfer funds from one currency to another in amounts exceeding 500,000 francs must be checked. The National Bank sought to persuade the Bankers Association to agree on identity checks for clients changing currencies in amounts less than 500,000 francs but failed to gain the bankers' agreement. The access to secret data about clients and their accounts will be made available to fewer people within or without the banking industry. The use of safe-deposit boxes for the storage of illegally obtained items will be made more difficult. Banks will not be permitted to maintain accounts for people or Swiss-based companies when it is clear that the accounts are being used to facilitate the flight of capital into Switzerland from abroad. Compensation transactions—the transfer of capital from one country to another by book-keeping adjustments instead of the physical transfer of funds—are specifically forbidden.

The new code, while retaining the basic regulations of the existing code on bank secrecy, should make the laundering of "dirty" money more difficult. Tax evasion will be more difficult. Identity controls will also be extended to all clients who open new accounts or deposit securities in a Swiss bank. Formerly new accounts with deposits of less than 100,000 francs were exempt.

The Chiasso Affair

It is said that money corrupts. If so, financial institutions must be especially subject to the corrupting influence of money. Bank scandals are not uncommon and Switzerland, as a great financial center, has not been able to avoid her share. A number of such lapses from the paths of rectitude by those who concocted a variety of fraudulent schemes to rob the banks and fleece the depositors have been described at length in the book by Kinsman (204). The Chiasso affair, of vast dimensions, did not come to light until 1977 although it had been boiling and bubbling for 17 years. Kinsman missed it by a few years.

Credit Suisse, one of the Big Three, has a branch in Chiasso, located squarely on the border between the canton of Ticino and Italy. The two top officers of the branch and three lawyers operated for 17 years an "off-the-books" bank in Chiasso. Investors were offered an interest return that was attractively high. The moneys received originated in Italy and can only be described as "escape funds." The five crooks, as indeed they were, had meanwhile organized a holding company, *Texon Finanzanstalt*, with themselves serving as the board of directors. This conglomerate, based in Liechtenstein, received the incoming moneys from Chiasso and, in turn, invested the funds in a growing list of Texon subsidiaries in Italy.

The Italian investors assumed that *Texon Finanzanstalt* was owned by conservative Credit Suisse. Representatives of the head office of Credit Suisse in Zurich testified that they knew nothing of this off-the-books scheme and had had no reason for concern. True, the volume of Texon business was very considerable but a big bank is accustomed to the ebb and flow of large sums of money in some of its accounts. Hence, the mere size of the Texon account could not arouse any suspicions.

The scandal surfaced in April 1977 when the head office of Credit Suisse announced that its Chiasso branch had been illegally transferring Italian escape funds to a Texon holding company. By 1977, the *Texon Finanzanstalt* was bankrupt: the income generated by its ailing subsidiaries in Italy was far from adequate.

After languishing in jail for two years, the five accused were brought to trial in 1979.[9] The charges before the Court in Chiasso were fraud, mismanagement, embezzlement, and violation of banking laws and federal decrees against an influx of foreign funds. Kuhrmeier, the manager of the Chiasso branch and his deputy, Laffranchi, were each sentenced to prison terms of $4\frac{1}{2}$ years and fines of $6000. The three lawyers received suspended prison sentences but fines of $121,000 were imposed on each. Credit Suisse was awarded 12 million dollars in damages, the payment to be shared by all five. Kuhrmeier died a week or two later of a heart attack.

Credit Suisse honoured the obligations, which had been fraudulently incurred by Kuhrmeier and his mob, totalling about 2.26 billion Swiss francs (1.35 billion USA dollars at the end-of-December-1977 exchange rate). The bank became the owner of the *Texon Finanzanstalt*, its operating subsidiaries, and its many non-operating companies. It was a most curious conglomerate. The subsidiaries included a racehorse farm, a salami business, a cheese factory, a spice company, a plastics business, a textile-machinery factory, 135 gasoline stations in Italy, a restaurant in Milan, several hotels, Italy's biggest wine producer, food companies, and a baby-buggy factory—a total of some 150 companies. After the liquidation of Texon, and depreciation of 1.2 billion Swiss francs, the acquired assets were entered into the books of Credit Suisse at a value of 977 million francs. The bank has sold some of the Texon companies but until they are all disposed of, the net loss resulting from the Chiasso affair remains undetermined.

Two episodes stemming from the scandal deserve mention. On 7 December 1977, an article appeared in *Tat* magazine regarding the "Chiasso Scandal." Credit Suisse complained in court that the authors—two former journalists of *Tat*, Roger Schawinski and Hans Peter Bürgin—had damaged the credibility of the bank, had violated the Banking Law, and were subject to fines. The accused, so it was claimed, had made charges that were untrue, had damaged the reputation of the bank before the shareholders, customers and employees, and had implied that management of the bank had lied about the whole Chiasso affair. The case was tried before a municipal court judge of the city of Zurich, with Schawinski found guilty and Bürgin acquitted for technical reasons.

The second episode was a complaint of the Federal Council through its Finance Department that the negative interest ordinance for protection of the currency had been violated.[10] In effect, the customers of *Texon Finanzanstalt* had imported foreign currency into Switzerland and, in so doing, had violated an ordinance which sought to protect the Swiss franc against a massive inflow of foreign money. Foreign deposits at the time carried a negative interest rate of ten percent per quarter, which certainly tended to slow down deposits from foreign countries. The Federal High Court ruled that the Texon customers were responsible, the law had been violated and that interest must be paid on the deposits credited to Texon during a certain stated period.

The total involved, according to the letter of the ordinance, at ten percent per quarter was about 293 million francs. The Swiss National Bank decided that 49 million francs would be a proper settlement although the Ministry of Finance had demanded 175.6 million. The Court rejected such a claim, after Credit Suisse consented and proved that 21.6 million francs was a fair and reasonable settlement according to the law.

Following the Chiasso affair, the banks, initiating the necessary reforms, agreed to a uniform code of conduct and a more positive identification of those who wish to open accounts. They agreed also to submit to the Banking Commission consolidated accounts with uniform rules on external transactions. Liechtenstein also acted to strengthen its regulations regarding "shadow companies" and to limit abuses of its laws pertaining to corporations.

The Pinkas Affair

The reforms instituted by the Swiss banks after the dust had settled from the Chiasso affair were too few and too late to prevent the Pinkas loan scandal. Eli

Pinkas had a small company in Lausanne which, under the corporate name Socsil S.A., sold nitrous oxide, commonly known as laughing gas. However, the events to be related were not a laughing matter. Pinkas was a remarkable confidence man who to all comers, exuded an impression of trustworthiness and the utmost probity in his business affairs. He negotiated loans from some 20 banks, each of which was left with the assurance that Pinkas was not borrowing from any other bank. Banking secrecy would have prevented any banker, who might have been curious, from seeking verification or mentioning the name of Eli Pinkas to another bank. Loans were needed in increasing amounts to pay even the interest on his mounting indebtedness.

On his death, by suicide, the details of the fraud were revealed. His debts had escalated to a total of about 109 million dollars. The creditors were mainly Swiss and American banks and individual investors who had been deceived by Pinkas' use of forged documents and balance sheets. The annual sales were fraudently claimed to be about 27 million dollars, instead of four million or so. Large contracts, again nonexistent, with the US Army in West Germany were also reported by Pinkas. Among the banks that lost was the Vaud Credit Bank in Lausanne of which Pinkas was a director and a member of the loan-approval committee. Other defrauded banks were the Union Bank of Switzerland, Credit Suisse, the Cantonal Bank of Zurich, American Express International Banking Corporation, the First National Bank of Minneapolis, and Citicorp in New York. Untangling of the accounts and bringing the affair to a close will be a difficult and prolonged task. The President of the Swiss Banking Commission has suggested that the banks should create a central office to monitor the loans to major creditors. The banks resist the proposal because any such monitoring program would weaken Swiss bank secrecy and business would be lost to other countries where greater secrecy for depositors is claimed.

The future of Socsil is not clear. There are those investigating the affair who claim that the company is viable and to avoid panic should not be brought into receivership. Others insist that Swiss laws would be violated if bankruptcy proceedings were not initiated.

The Telex Swindle

There is no end to the ingenuity of swindlers. In the Telex Swindle of 1979 the Bank of Naples was defrauded of millions of Swiss francs and other European currencies. The so-called Telex band managed to arrange fraudulent transfers from the Bank of Naples through a number of Swiss and European banks. Payouts were in cash. The first swindle appears to have been made through the St. Margrethan branch of the Cantonal Bank of St. Gallen. By use of correct instructions, correct codes and keys, four million francs were paid out in cash to a member of the band. The St. Margrethan bank merely conveyed the instructions to the Bank of Naples which was the ultimate victim in the transaction. At least 16 million francs in all were embezzled through Telex-transmitted instructions to the Bank of Naples. It was a complicated and cleverly operated swindle which may have involved insider access in Naples to the Telex codes of the banks through which the transfers of money were made.

The People's Temple

In 1978, the Justice Department of the US government determined that more than ten million dollars of the People's Temple funds were on deposit in banks in Panama, including branches of the Swiss Banking Corporation and the Union Bank of Switzerland. The government, seeking to recover about 3.5 million dollars expended in removal of hundreds of bodies of mass-suicide victims from Guyana to the USA, requested the Panamanian government to freeze the Temple's assets. Because of a treaty between Switzerland and the USA, and being satisfied that a violation of the property laws was involved, the Swiss government cooperated in providing a limited amount of information, restricted, however, by the bank secrecy law against requiring the banks to reveal fully the status of the account(s).

The Citibank Case

A former bank officer in Paris accused Citibank (New York) of "cooking the books" by transferring profits from European branches to Nassau and other tax havens to avoid paying income taxes in the European countries where the profits were generated. An accountant in Switzerland supported the accusation by reporting to the Swiss authorities the transfer of profits from the bank's Zurich branch to a bank in Nassau. The amount owed to the Swiss government was under negotiation in 1978 when claims of back taxes amounting to possibly 50 million dollars were reported. Citibank initiated a study of its own into its money-trading operations in a number of European countries, the study being conducted by its own accountants and attorneys.

The Iranian Case

Here we are concerned with efforts made by the Iranian government to gain possession of property of the late Shah in St. Moritz and elsewhere and deposits of almost three million dollars in Swiss banks. The money and real estate holdings, including a villa in St. Moritz—worth possibly five million dollars—are claimed by the Iranian government as possessions of the Iranian people. Whether the heirs of the late Shah or the Iranian government are legally entitled to the properties must be decided by the courts. The arbitration commission of the Swiss National Bank and the Swiss Bankers' Association state that the Iranian government must prove before the Swiss courts that the money and properties at issue originated from thievery or crooked underhanded operations. The Shah's tax delinquencies in Iran would not be recognized by a Swiss court because a relevant treaty on such matters does not exist between the two countries. The original export of Iranian money to Switzerland by the Shah or his family was perfectly legal at the time of the transactions, according to the Iranian National Bank and the Swiss authorities. This would seem to strengthen the claim of the heirs of the Shah to retain possession of these properties.

Fiduciary Accounts

According to the Swiss National Bank, about 70 billion dollars were in fiduciary (trustee) accounts as assets in the Swiss banks in December 1980. The Federal Government, seeking to increase its income and fearful of its mounting indebtedness, proposed a 5 percent tax on the interest generated in these accounts. Swiss and many foreign bankers oppose the tax although there is no agreement on whether its imposition would divert fiduciary funds to foreign banks, especially in Austria and Luxembourg. The growth in Swiss fiduciary accounts has been phenomenal; in 1960 for example the total was only about 240 million dollars. The revenue derived from the 5 percent tax would amount to only about 75 million dollars. This may account in part for the mixed reception that the tax proposal received in parliament. The upper house opposed the tax, the lower house favored it. To be enacted into law, the tax proposal would have to gain acceptance by both houses. It should be noted that the fiduciary accounts are popular with foreigners because of the concealment that results through the bank-secrecy laws. The funds are invested by the Swiss banks in their own name; the identity of the customer is not revealed.

Although proposals of new or increased taxes never seem to die a natural death, it now appears (March 1981) that parliament has dealt the fiduciary tax proposal a knockout blow: the upper house by a vote of 24–14 decided not to consider the matter further. This kills the proposal for the time being but not without the possibility of a restoration to life at some later date.

Growth Limitations

By an agreement between the Big Three and the Volksbank, a limitation in growth in terms of numbers of branches was decided upon for the four-year period ending in December 1983. The restraint on growth was requested by the Bankers' Association at the suggestion of one of the Big Three and was accepted with some displeasure by the other big banks. One must assume that a gobbling-up process had been going on by which the big banks were absorbing a variety of local and regional banks, with two or three of the group being faster than the fourth.

The agreement operates through a point system. Each of the four big banks started out with a four-year allocation of 22 points. The takeover of new affiliates results in the loss of points. When all 22 points have been used, the bank in question must terminate its takeover program, at least until 31 December 1983.

From 1970 to 1978, each of the four large banks increased its places of business at an average rate of about six per year. The agreement referred to permits the four banks to continue their absorption of affiliates but evens out any disparities among the four in rates of takeover (**266**, 23–24 February 1980).

The Swiss Banks vis-à-vis South Africa

A three-day seminar in Zurich in the spring of 1981 concerned itself with Apartheid. The participants included a UNO special committee against Apartheid, representatives of the World Council of Churches, the Swiss Anti-Apartheid movement, and several other organizations. But how are the Swiss banks involved? The Swiss banks play the leading role in the gold trade and extend considerable support to South Africa. Without such help, Apartheid, we are told, could not exist. South Africa needs foreign help to circumvent the UNO weapon embargo and the embargo imposed by oil-producing States. The Swiss banks were requested by the seminar participants not to collaborate with South Africa in the credit sector and in gold trading. The Swiss Federal Government was also urged to introduce legal proscriptions to achieve the same end—the termination of Apartheid. Incidentally, neither the Federal Government nor the Big Three sent representatives to the seminar.

Early in 1980, the Federal Government protested to the Government of South Africa about the espionage activities of two South African citizens in Switzerland. One had been employed for three years by the International University Exchange Fund. The other was an officer in the South African secret service. Both men were accused of spying into the activities of anti-Apartheid groups. They escaped arrest by leaving the country before action by the Swiss government was initiated.

Propping up the Dollar

In January 1979, the Swiss National Bank announced that a US Treasury offering of 1.2 billion dollars in Swiss franc notes had been heavily oversubscribed. Purchase of the notes was restricted to Swiss residents—individuals and corporations—with 500,000 francs ($290,000) as a minimum acceptable order. Requests totalled 3.1 billion dollars. Two issues were sold: short-term notes of $2\frac{1}{2}$ years at an interest rate of 2.35 percent, and long-term notes of four years at 2.65 percent. The short-term notes were favored by the purchasers (2.19 billion dollars against 910 million dollars in long-term notes). The Big Three banks are believed to have covered the entire initial offering of Swiss franc notes by their own purchases. One must assume that very few personal orders by individuals were executed because of the 500,000 franc minimum.

A similar offering in West Germany, denominated in marks, and totalling 1.5 billion dollars was also well received. The purpose of these purchases by the Treasury was to have at hand a reasonable supply of Swiss francs and West German marks for use in purchase of dollars when the USA currency was weakening and needed to be propped up.

Notes and Comments

1. Omitted are the USA life insurance companies with total assets of 479.2 billion dollars. They lend money to their policy holders and accept money as premium payments on the policies. Such receipts can be regarded as technically equivalent to the deposits received by banks. However, for comparative purposes, their assets are not included, because of the omission of insurance companies from the Swiss data.

2. Lest this comparison be misunderstood, we must recognize that much foreign money is in the banking systems of both countries: 205,295 million dollars in the USA on 31 December 1980 (**126**, A 59, February 1982).

3. The Implementing Ordinance for the Bank Law was issued on 17 May 1972, as a Decree of the Federal Council. It is set forth in pages 24 to 53 of reference **125**.

4. This monopoly of the issuance of bank notes was conveyed to the Swiss National Bank operating under the general supervision of the Banking Commission.

5. In 1980 the net profits of the National Bank were 7,516,000 francs of which one million was allocated to reserves, 1.5 million to dividends, and 5.016 million to the Confederation and the cantons. The annual net profits appear to have remained constant at 7.516 million francs since 1971 (**341**, 1981, p. 290).

6. In 1980, the savings deposits of non-residents accounted for 5646 millions of the 90,294 million-franc total. If we exclude the deposits of non-residents the per capita savings of the average Swiss in 1980 would have equalled 7943 USA dollars instead of $8473. Bank savings defined by the Swiss National Bank as total deposits in savings and deposit accounts and books, plus outstanding medium-term notes, equalled at the end of 1980, $13,917 per capita if the non-residents are included, or $12,993 per capita if they are excluded (personal communication from Dr. Hans Mast, Executive Vice-President of Credit Suisse).

7. In May 1982 the four major Swiss banks (the Big Three plus the *Volksbank*) lowered interest rates paid on customer time deposits to the following: 3.25 percent on deposits of three to five months; 3.75 percent on six to eight month deposits; four percent on nine to eleven month deposits; and 4.25 percent on deposits of 12 months duration.

8. 1485 million dollars in US Treasury bonds and notes in 1980 (**126**, A64, February 1982) and much more in State and local government securities, securities of US government agencies and corporate bonds and notes. Possibly the grand total approximates 120 billion dollars if real estate is also included.

9. A long pre-trial imprisonment of the accused is not uncommon in Switzerland where *habeas corpus* is not exercised.

> Criminal procedure is based upon interrogation in solitary confinement, and this process for which special prisons are constructed, may last eighteen months without arousing public comment, and the prisoner may on occasion be charged for the expenses of lodging him in prison . . . one sometimes gets the impression that it is best to avoid even being accused (**187**, p. 147).

10. In December 1979, Switzerland eliminated the 40 percent annual charge (also known as negative interest) on Swiss bank holdings of francs for nonresident foreigners, which had applied to deposits received after 31 October 1974. In March 1979, banks were permitted to pay interest on deposits of three months or longer. Since the fall of 1980, nonresident foreigners may hold Swiss franc deposits. The purpose of this relaxation is clear: to draw major deposits from the Near East and thus help to strengthen the Swiss franc against the US dollar. Increases in USA interest rates had favored investments in USA dollars at the expense of the Swiss franc and other major currencies.

11. Admitted to membership, April 1984.

12. The Federal Council recommended that the initiative proposal be disapproved when it comes to a vote. The Council also decided against submitting a counter proposal for the votation. The reason appears to be that amendments to the Banking Law are already in preparation and amendment of the Constitution—the object of an initiative—is not needed to achieve any of the reforms sought by the Social Democrats.*

> Clients of the Swiss banks are now notified that orders for execution on American exchanges can be accepted only on the express understanding by the client that there is a possible exposure to the USA Securities and Exchange Commission if the client is suspected of trading on insider information. Swiss Bank secrecy is weakened almost inappreciably. Banks can be released from their obligation to protect their clients' privacy only by a court order in connection with an investigation into an act that is a crime under Swiss law. A high-level commission of three members must be satisfied with the legitimacy of the SEC's case, as well as with the bank's response, before it passes on information requested by the SEC.

---

* The initiative proposal, mentioned in the paragraph 12 above, was voted upon on 20 May 1984, and was heavily defeated.

In May 1984, the Swiss Federal Tribunal ordered five Swiss banks to release information requested by the USA Securities and Exchange Commission on insider trading in the purchase of Santa Fe International by Kuwait Petroleum Company in September 1981. The Tribunal at last agreed that a certain named individual had indeed tipped off the traders named in the complaint and several unnamed individuals that the acquisition would be consummated within a few days. This act of tipping such inside information was ruled by the court as a violation of a Swiss–USA treaty of mutual assistance in criminal matters concerning cases of insider trading.

13. A recent case of tax evasion that was heavily publicized in mid-1983 involves Marc Rich A.G., based in Zug, Switzerland, and its USA subsidiary, Marc Rich Inc. The company is essentially a commodities-trading firm. The American subsidiary, in oil-trading operations, is charged with evasion of US income taxes by transferring substantial profits to its Swiss parent with the deliberate intent of circumventing the US laws on corporate taxation. The transfer was achieved by selling low-priced oil to the parent and buying it back, now falsely identified as high-priced oil, at inflated prices. This is an example of "transfer pricing" in which goods are transferred among the subsidiaries of a multinational company. Such a transfer is not illegal unless a subsidiary based in the USA pays inflated prices for the goods when resold by a foreign subsidiary to its American branch. In the Marc Rich case, the trading operation transferred profit from the USA to Switzerland and resulted in a case of tax evasion on an impressive scale, more than 100 million dollars of taxable revenue being involved. The grand jury indictment of Marc Rich and a fellow conspirator states that the taxes evaded approximate 48 million dollars but the US authorities suspect, in the light of additional evidence, that the amount may be considerably more—possibly twice as much as presently charged. The case goes back to the years of federal control of oil prices (1973 to 1981) when domestic oil was classified into several different price categories. The Rich indictment charges that the defendants conspired with other traders to certify low priced oil as being in a high-priced category when, by so doing, an additional substantial profit could be generated.

Documents pertinent to the case were demanded by the USA authorities. The Swiss government, faced with an additional request to extradite the principals, currently in Switzerland, declares that tax evasion, which is not a punishable offence in Switzerland, is not sufficient in itself to approve an extradition request. Nor will Switzerland release the pertinent documents, now in the possession of the Swiss government, because this would violate the Swiss secrecy laws that protect banks, other corporations, and even individuals against intrusions into their private affairs. In the meantime Marc Rich is being fined $50,000 a day for failing to turn over to the USA authorities the requested documents. The indictment claims that the defendants evaded taxes on more than 100 million dollars of income. Based on a review of the lists descriptive of the documents the USA government believes it could prove a much higher level of tax evasion. The documents themselves have not been seen by USA government officials.

14. On 1 May 1985 a bill to this effect was prepared by the Federal Council for submission to Parliament.

11.13. SOCIAL SECURITY AND OTHER INSURANCE PROGRAMS

Introduction

When the Federal Government, in the nineteenth century, took the initial steps to found a welfare State, it had in mind a system of social insurance which, as it became defined in later years, would financially protect its people against many of the economic hazards that face the living and would ensure adequate retirement pensions. It did not contemplate a system of welfare such as is in vogue in some countries in the late twentieth century, in which the citizen expects and may receive, at a price, near-total care by his government from the cradle to the grave.

Federal Legislation

The responsibilities of government in Switzerland in matters of social security are defined in legislation which rests solidly on the Federal Constitution. For example, Article 31 (bis) states that "... the Confederation shall take measures to promote the general welfare and the economic security of its citizens." The constitutional base for the appropriate legislation is detailed in subsequent Articles.

> The Confederation . . . is entitled to enact regulations in order to protect the workers against the operation of unhealthy and dangerous industries (Article 34). The Confederation shall institute by means of legislation, an insurance against illness and accidents, taking due account of existing insurance funds. It may make adherence thereto compulsory for all or for specific categories of citizens (Article 34 bis). The Confederation is entitled to legislate on . . . adequate compensation for loss of wages and earnings due to military service . . . insurance against unemployment and relief for the unemployed. The right to institute public funds and to declare unemployment insurance compulsory for all remains with the Cantons (Article 34 ter).

The Confederation shall introduce an old age and survivor's insurance by means of legislation. It is also entitled to introduce an invalidity insurance at a later date. It may declare these insurance schemes compulsory for all or for specific categories of citizens. The insurance schemes shall be implemented with the cooperation of the Cantons; public and private insurance funds may be called upon to cooperate (Article 34 quater).

The Confederation is entitled to legislate in the field of family compensation funds. It may declare adherence thereto compulsory for all or for specific categories of citizens.... It may make its financial contributions dependent on adequate participation of the Cantons. . . . The Confederation shall institute maternity insurance by means of legislation . . . and it may even require persons to contribute financially who are not eligible for insurance benefits . . . (Article 34 quinquies).

Role of the Cantons

A very active and responsible role of the cantons in implementing and enforcing social security laws may be inferred from the preceding excerpts from the Federal Constitution. Indeed, it is the cantons that have established the varied institutions that deal with such matters. Beyond the institutions required by law, the cantons also organized some social insurance schemes of their own. Ultimately this became too great a task for many of the cantons. The small cantons were quite unable to create and operate compulsory insurance plans, varied and expensive as they are, for social security. Although the cantons still have the responsibility of enforcing federal laws, only the regulations on family allowances continue to be cantonal matters except for their involvement in application of most branches of insurance.

Goal of Social Insurance

The Federal Constitution undergoes a continuing revision and it should be noted that of the 80 or more revisions in the past 100 years, many of these pertain to social legislation. The federal legislation now in force requires that the aged, the survivors of the insured, and the disabled shall be provided with a standard of living that harmonizes with the previous level. The far-reaching goal of social insurance in Switzerland is that retirement from the labor force should not require abandonment of one's social standing. The old and disabled should not be forced into subsistence on a mere minimum: they should be enabled to maintain their previous standard of living. The goal of such social insurance is laudable. Despite the increasing cost of attaining and maintaining the requisite kinds of insurance, one can only hope that such an admirable system of social insurance will be able to survive far into the future.

The Beginnings

The Swiss are cautious about changing anything, especially if it involves expenditure by government, unless the proposed change is clearly necessary or its promise of future benefits is solidly founded. It was not until 1911, after a faltering start around the turn of the century, that a modest federal law on health and accident insurance was accepted. Insurance against occupational and nonoccupational accidents for employees in a number of basic industries was made compulsory to the great relief of employers who hitherto were held responsible for occupational accidents. But health insurance was something else and the authorities had to be content with a law that merely provided subsidies. Various insurance funds, already existing or newly created, were eligible under certain conditions for Federal Government subsidies.

Unemployment Insurance

A somewhat similar arrangement was made for unemployment insurance. It was not satisfactory: at the time of the 1974–75 recession only about 20 percent of the labor force was covered by unemployment insurance. As a result of changes in the law, unemployment insurance became compulsory for the entire labor force as of 1 April 1977. Self-employed persons are permitted to join if they so wish.

Military Service and Social Insurance

Under special war-time authority granted by parliament to the Federal Council for the duration of World War II, an insurance plan was introduced to give financial relief to persons liable for military service. Financed entirely from the federal budget, it is almost a complete insurance package for persons on military service. They are relieved of premium payments because their occupation is required of them by law, and the risks entailed are not entered upon voluntarily. There is, however, a second social security plan for persons on military service or civil defense and this involves modest payments by both the employee and the employer. It is an income compensation plan and is designed to make up for income lost during service. Under the plan, compensation is paid for (a) household allowances to servicemen, whether married, single, widowed or divorced, who live with children and are forced by professional or official duties to maintain a separate household; (b) allowances for single persons; (c) children's allowances; (d) support allowances; and (e) operating allowances to servicemen who, as owners of a business or farm from which their earnings are derived, incur considerable expense through salary payments to employees who replace them and do their work while they, the owners, are on military service. The special compensation funds, created by the employer associations and the cantons, serve as administrators of the insurance. The system served later as an operating model for the old age and survivors' insurance (AHV), and disability or invalidity insurance (IV) and the family allowance plan for agricultural employees, small farmers, and two other categories.

AHV and IV

The AHV, adopted in 1947 by popular vote, came into effect in 1948. It covers the entire population, working and nonworking, employees and the self-employed, and is compulsory for inhabitants of Switzerland. In 1960 the IV was introduced, also as a compulsory national plan applicable to the total population. In subsequent years all the existing plans have been revised, new forms of insurance have been created, and, in general, coverage has been broadened and benefits increased.

The Swiss National Insurance Institute

As for accident insurance the Swiss National Insurance Institute (*Schweizerische Unfallversicherungsanstalt*, or SUVA) covers about two-thirds of the labor force, specifically for occupational and nonoccupational accidents and for occupational diseases caused by certain materials or by specified occupations. The benefits include medical care: doctors' bills, hospital care and medicine. Also, 80 percent of the lost earnings are paid and, if it seems probable that the accident or occupational disease will lead to permanent incapacity for gainful employment, a disability pension is paid. If the disability is total, the pension is fixed at 70 percent of the pre-disability income. In case of accidental death, survivor pensions are paid to the widow and to the children (up to the age of 18). The owner of an enterprise is responsible for the payment of the premiums, subject to the premiums on nonoccupational accident insurance being deducted from the employee's wages.

The competence and responsibility of SUVA extends beyond mere administration of the accident insurance plan. SUVA is also entrusted with the responsibility of doing what can be done in the prevention of accidents and occupational disease. Enterprises that are reluctant to introduce the necessary prevention measures that are recommended by SUVA can be charged with higher premiums.

Health Insurance; Loss-of-income Insurance

Health insurance, though voluntary, is very widespread—at present exceeding 90 percent of the population. One type of health insurance covers medical care (doctors' bills, hospital care and medicine); a second covers loss of income during illness. The same person may carry both types. For the medical care insurance he will pay a portion of the effective costs. As for loss of income, the insured will receive daily payments that normally amount to 50 percent of his/her salary, if covered by a collective agreement; otherwise the payment may amount to as little as two francs per day—a long-outdated minimum. Compared to the accident insurance plan, insurance against loss of income is seriously inadequate. The needs of the two, in respect to loss of income, are identical. Health insurance, however, is not compulsory and therefore is not universal. A compulsory health insurance plan would provide higher benefits for loss of income, but thus far has not been accepted.

Health insurance is administered mostly by private insurance funds with the legal status of cooperatives, associations or foundations. There are also public insurance schemes usually designed for the compulsory insurance plans of cantons and communes. The number of health insurance funds with many types of membership totalled 1812 in 1903 and 1135 in 1955. In 1977 the number had fallen to 529, presumably, in most cases, the result of amalgamations (**341**, 1920, p. 170; 1979, p. 309).

Some Financial Aspects

Benefit payments have risen from 12 million francs in 1919 to 374.0 million in 1955 and to 4675 million in 1977 (**341**, 1979, p. 309). The income of the funds, which totalled 4982 million francs in 1977, included federal subsidies of 856 million francs, cantonal subsidies of 259.6 million and community subsidies of 26.8 million; employers contributed 42.5 million francs. The insured persons contributed the "lion's share"—3672 million francs (341, 1979, p. 310). The enormous increases since 1955 are due to a doubling of the number of persons insured and to the fanciful increase in costs of medical care. In summary, the public authorities pay almost 30 percent by covering hospital deficits and the patients pay the rest.

Maternity Insurance

Legislation to provide for maternity insurance has not yet been approved by the people. Fortunately, health insurance covers pregnancy and childbirth, hence the usual charges by the doctor and the hospital are paid by the funds. Health insurance also reimburses the working mother for loss of income up to ten weeks, six of which follow delivery. Additional benefits are needed but may have to await the acceptance of an effective maternity insurance plan.

More on the AHV

The Old Age and Survivors' Insurance (AHV) mentioned earlier, has grown into the country's largest social program. The Federal Constitution now stipulates that AHV must provide for adequate subsistence of the insured. The present provisions of 525 to 1050 francs per month for single persons and 788 to 1575 for couples are not yet at the level of adequacy. Under certain circumstances the payments may be increased somewhat. The old and infirm must be able to live without help from public welfare. Premiums in 1978 were 8.4 percent of the entire income, with the payments shared equally between employer and employee.[1] The premium must be paid on the full income although premiums paid on incomes in excess of 36,000 francs do not add to the pension to be received on retirement. Two points about AHV should be emphasized: (1) the total population is covered, there are no exceptions; (2) the whole pension system favors the less fortunate since the maximum pension is only double the minimum. A central fund guarantees the country-wide solidarity, maintains a register of all insured persons and calculates the amount of the pension to be paid when it falls due. Though relatively complicated, the bookkeeping or computer records seem to be maintained satisfactorily and the system functions well. There is the ever-present problem of adapting pensions and premiums to changing price and wage levels but a scheme for a more dynamic adjustment of pensions is contemplated.

Voluntary Pension Funds

Switzerland also has thousands of voluntary pension funds which cover about two-thirds of all employed persons. Benefits may be in the form of modest lump sum payments to generous annual pensions. If this system is made compulsory, as may indeed happen, it will add a "second pillar" to the retirement provisions, and employers and self-employed shall have an opportunity to purchase the insurance if they so wish. This optional plan, designed especially for the self-employed, constitutes a so-called "third pillar." The Federal Government is more or less obliged to encourage this third pillar through its tax and ownership policies.

Security for the Disabled

Another insurance plan provides security for the disabled. It endeavours to integrate the disabled into the economy and society. To obtain that goal, the plan resorts to medical measures, vocational training and retraining, special schooling, care for helpless minors, and distribution of appliances for the disabled. Daily allowances are paid during this integration period to cover living costs. There is no legal limit to the amount or duration of these payments. An invalid with a two-thirds disability, which cannot be corrected and which continues to his age of retirement, is entitled to the same pension as an AHV pensioner. The disability insurance is a nation-wide plan, like the AHV, with premiums fixed at 0.5 percent of the pre-disability income and shared equally by employer and employee.

More about Unemployment Insurance

Since 1 April 1977, all employees are covered by compulsory unemployment insurance. The AHV administration collects the premiums which are shared half and half between employer and employee. At present they amount to 0.8 percent of salary up to a maximum monthly income of 3900 francs. Persons with dependents are entitled to receive 70 percent of the insured income with supplements for each dependent person. The maximum daily payment is 85 percent. Those persons without dependents or persons to support receive 65 percent of the insured income. Payments per year may not extend beyond 150 days of unemployment.

Children's Allowances

To 1978, at least, the Federal Government has not been able to draft uniform regulations on children's allowances. However, a reasonably satisfactory plan has been worked out for agriculture. Employed agricultural laborers are entitled under federal law to receive monthly household allowances of 100 francs and, in the flat lands, children's allowances of 50 francs per month for each child. The children's allowances increases to 60 francs for farmers in the mountains. Self-employed small farmers receive the same allowances for children, but no household allowance. Premiums for the allowances to employed agricultural laborers are paid by the employers (1.8 percent of the paid wages) and the remaining half or more by public funds. The premiums applicable to the allowances paid to small farmers are charged entirely to the Federal Government and the cantons.

The cantons have laws of their own that prescribe payment of children's allowances to nonagricultural employees—somewhere between 50 and 85 francs per child. Childbirth and educational allowances are also provided by the cantons, but the premiums are paid by the employer—1.5 to 3.0 percent of wages received by the head of the family.

General Observations and Costs

Switzerland has sought for many years to attain comprehensive national insurance plans. At present, it has all the types of insurance demanded by Internationsl Conventions: sickness, accident and occupational disease, old age, unemployment, maternity (in part), care for the family, disability, loss of the provider. The regulations are essentially the same as those decreed by the European Human Rights Convention which Switzerland has ratified. The high degree of decentralization in administering social security insurance is possibly unique, as is to be expected in a federation of sovereign cantons. The work to be done, however, devolves upon a variety of public funds or funds of associations, with the cantons playing a very important role in applying the social security laws and in enforcing those that are federal in origin.

Reference was made earlier to the escalation of costs and the heavy burden that the economy now carries. Again "we must ask ourselves . . . whether we have not reached the bearable and reasonable limit to which social security can go" (**371**, p. 210). I have appended four Tables for the benefit of those who are interested in figures as well as facts.

From Table 58 it might appear that social insurance is financed in such a way as to

Table 58 Income and expense of social insurance in Switzerland in 1979[a] (in millions of francs)

	Income	Expense
Old Age and Survivors Insurance (AHV)		
Federal AHV	9910.2	10,103.3
Supplementary AHV	329.6	329.6
Invalidity Insurance (IV)		
Federal IV	1953.4	2010.0
Supplementary IV	69.9	69.9
Cantonal AHV and IV	86.7	55.2
Professional Social-Aid Organizations[d]	10,411.0	3098.0
Recognized Sickness Funds	5424.5	5261.0
Accident Insurance (SUVA)[b]	1432.2	1416.3
Military Insurance	166.6	166.6
Special allowances to servicemen (employers)[c]	595.8	508.6
Unemployment Insurance	626.0	209.6
Family allowances to farm workers, small farmers, independent Alpine families and professional fishermen	60.2	60.2
Cantonal family allowances	371.9	361.8
Total	31,438.0	23,650.1[e]

[a] Source: **341**, 1981, p. 302.
[b] *Schweizerische Unfallversicherungsanstalt.*
[c] To cover operating losses (e.g. salaries to replacements) resulting from time given to military service.
[d] Pension funds, group insurance, savings funds, social assistance funds.
[e] This total is substantially less than that reported in **341**, 1981, p. 334 which tabulates the total expenditure on social insurance of all kinds; in 1979: 35,413 million francs.

generate a handsome income excess. Some of the funds operate year by year with a comfortable surplus of revenue but in 1979, the surplus was mostly attributable to the single item, professional social aid organizations. Otherwise, the deficit portion of federal AHV and IV was covered by the modest surpluses from other insurance sources.

Table 59 shows that the expense of government in social insurance is a small part of the total. The cost of social insurance to the employer and the insured persons is five times as great as the cost to the federation, and the cantons. The cost of social insurance to all three levels of government (federation, cantons, communes) was 4505.8 million francs in 1979, 4257.3 million in 1977, 1118.9 million in 1967, 160 million in 1950[2] (**341**, 1981, p. 408; 1979, p. 398; 1969, p. 441; 1951, p. 298). If social assistance (*Fürsorge*) be included, though it is not to be regarded as a form of insurance, we would have to increase the 1979 figure by 1317.9 million francs, that of 1977 by 1250.7 million, and the 1967 figure by 707.1.

Whatever may be the state of the financial health of the entire social security insurance system, the pension funds of the federal personnel are expected to have an accumulated deficit of 2.9 billion francs by the end of 1982. In the 1950s and 1960s everything was much better and the deficit was down to 156 million in 1968. By the end of 1982 the pension fund of the federal railway personnel will probably have an accumulated deficit of 1.5 billion francs. Such are the consequences of inflation and

Table 59   Social insurance in 1979:[a] Sources of income (in millions of francs)

| | Payments by insured & by employers | Subventions | | Interest & other | Total |
		Federal	Cantonal		
Federal AHV	7964.3	1111.4	505.2	329.3	9910.2
Supplementary payments to AHV	—	165.8	159.2	4.6	329.6
Federal IV	955.9	759.4	253.1	−15.3	1953.4
Supplements to IV	—	34.8	32.6	2.5	69.9
Cantonal AHV and IV	48.3	—	0.8	37.6	86.7
Professional health facilities	7149.0	—	—	3262.0	10,411.0
Recognized sickness funds	4086.5	895.0	296.3	146.7	5424.5
Accident insurance (SUVA)	1071.8	—	—	360.4	1432.2
Military insurance	—	166.6	—	—	166.6
Military income compensation plan[b]	571.4	—	—	24.4	595.8
Unemployment insurance	598.6	—	—	27.4	626.0
Family & children allowances[c]	5.8	36.3	18.1	—	60.2
Cantonal family allowances	363.2	—	—	8.7	371.9
Total	22,814.8	3169.3	1265.3	4188.6	31,438.0

[a] Source: (**341**, 1981, p. 302).

[b] To cover operating losses (e.g. salaries to replacements) resulting from time required for military service.

[c] Described in Table 58 as family allowances to farm workers etc.

escalation of costs in the late 1970s. The Federal Government, by means of an employment freeze, especially on the most highly paid categories of employees, and other measures, has made an effort to combat this adverse trend in federal social security expense.

As for the insurance industry generally, investment income is of major importance in an endeavour to counter the negative effects of inflation and cost escalation. The internationally oriented insurance companies tend to invest in some foreign countries where interest rates on such investments are appreciably higher than in Switzerland. Insurers are faced with the problem, especially difficult in an inflationary economy, of calculating premium payments "of today in order to meet the claims of tomorrow" (Portmann, ref. **97**, vol. 85, p. 32, 1979–80).

From the very nature of compulsory insurance plans, costs must be constantly supervised and premiums must be rather frequently increased in an inflationary economy. So it is that the Old Age and Survivors Insurance (AHV) as well as the Invalidity Insurance (IV) have been frequently revised. Emergency measures adopted in June 1975 were amended in the ninth AHV revision of 24 June 1977 whereby the Federal Government increased its share of total costs of the AHV and IV programs from 9 percent to 11 percent, while the costs to be borne by the cantons were fixed at 5 percent of the total. This decree of the government was approved by the people and the cantons in a referendum of 26 February 1978.

By mid 1979 the AHV Commission took preliminary steps for the tenth revision of the AHV law. Two subcommittees were organized to concentrate respectively on those aspects of AHV that are of special concern to women, and the expressed desire of many that a flexible retirement age for commencement of pension benefits be introduced. The special committee to consider the problems pertaining to women was faced with at least three matters requiring attention: the equal-rights problem in relation to AHV, the biological fact that the life expectancy of females is six to eight years greater at birth than the life expectancy of males. To these must be added the complicated and intricate problem of AHV benefits for Swiss women who live abroad, or who no longer are in the work force, or separated, divorced, etc.

At the political level there was much concern in the early eighties over future financing of the AHV. Can the payments to the insured be steadily, even modestly, increased as in the past? Are the deficits such that the benefits might even have to be reduced somewhat if the economy does not permit increased contributions by the Federal Government, the cantons and the communities? Postulates by members of parliament to do something or other to the AHV are introduced with considerable frequency. The problems, whatever they may be, are of great importance to the people and to their representatives in parliament.

An equalization fund (*Ausgleichsfond*) maintained by government is required by law to have funds on hand at least equal to one year's expenditures for the three principal programs. At the end of 1981 the capital of the AHV amounted to only 95.8 percent of the expenditures. Because of increases in AHV payments mandated for 1982, the relationship between capital and payments to the insured will deteriorate further unless there is a fresh infusion of money into the fund.

I hasten to recommend to the reader the authoritative article on Social Security by Hans Peter Tschudi (371) who served for 13 years as a Federal Councillor in charge of the Interior Department and two terms as President of Switzerland. Without constant reference to Tschudi's article, I would have despaired of attempting any discussion in depth of Swiss social security. I have included much additional material and various interpretations for which I alone am responsible. I have also omitted much detailed information and all reference to the changes resulting from recent legislation, effective in 1984 and 1985. For an excellent update and many details of the Social Security System, I recommend "Focus on Switzerland" (*Employee Benefit Plan Review*, August 1983, pp. 46–60. Publisher: Charles D. Spencer & Associates, 222 W. Adams St., Chicago, Ill 60606).

Other Insurance

The preceding sections describe almost exclusively those insurance programs that are relevant to Social Security. There are, however, many other kinds of insurance that have little, if anything, to do with social security but which relate to a great variety of risks against which the prudent member of society seeks financial protection. The Swiss are a prudent people and, in general, are heavily insured.

Some of the insurance companies to which they turn have been in business for many years: five of the Swiss life insurance companies were founded between 1857 and 1881. In Table 60 the number and kind of specialized private insurance companies, and their dates of foundation are presented. As indicated in the Table, most, if not all of these, have been "going strong" for many years. As early as 1886, the Confederation introduced a system of surveillance of these many companies. Some cantonal societies were much older, preceding the 1848 Act of Confederation. One in Bern (fire insurance) was founded in 1806.

Many societies concerned with sickness insurance, with memberships of less than 50 per society to others with memberships of 1000 or more, were organized in the

Table 60   Private insurance companies

Specialty	No. of Swiss companies by 1901	Dates of formation[a]
Life	6	1857 to 1881
Accident	5	1864/1898
Water damage	1	1887
Transport	6	1858/1883
Reinsurance	3	1864/1875
Fire	4	1826/1874
Glass breakage	1	1887
Cattle	0	—
Hail	1	1880

[a] Source: (341, 1903, pp. 174/79).

early 1900s and in later years. In 1914 there were 453 such societies (*Krankenkassen*) with a total membership of 121,000. By 1932 the societies had increased to 1154 with a total of 1,789,000 members (**341**, 1933, p. 245). The number of societies showed little change until the 1950s when a decrease set in: presumably the result in many cases of amalgamation. By 1979 the number had decreased to 491 but the total membership had reached 6,735,000, which suggests that many members were resident elsewhere than in Switzerland (**341**, 1981, p. 311): the total population of the country in December 1979, approximated 6,356,000.

Of the specialized kinds of insurance against various illnesses, tuberculosis insurance once played a most important role. But for quite some years, a decline in the incidence of tuberculosis has been evident. The number of cases of tuberculosis reported to the public health authorities in 1979 was less than one half of the number in 1955. The number of sanatoria decreased in the same time span from 55 to 21 and the number of first-time admissions decreased from 5807 to 659. Likewise the

Table 61   Private insurance in Switzerland

	Premium income[a]			Payments on claims[a]		
				5-Year avg.		
	1901[b]	1945[c]	1979[d]	1961–1965[f]	1945[f]	1979[d]
Life	29.10	340.2	5035.3	18.85	186.2	1443.3
Accident	10.56 ⎫	93.0	1001.4	8.63 ⎫	54.0	572.4
Civil responsibility	— ⎭		1411.7	— ⎭		853.9
Fire	9.53	34.9	548.8	5.46	18.4	330.1
Transport	1.79[h]	36.4	184.0	0.761	9.10	103.3
Vehicle damage	—	2.23	570.5	—	1.00	353.8
Hail	0.702	10.45	36.9	0.583	5.85	16.8
Animal	0.354	—	3.5	—	—	3.1
Robbery	—	6.50	250.3	0.013	1.71	170.2
Glass breakage	0.197	2.48	96.5	0.099	0.79	38.3
Water damage	0.031	4.37	184.7	0.010	2.02	122.7
Credit	0.134[g]	—	30.1	—	—	7.5
Machines	—	—	107.7	—	—	57.2
Legal protection	—	—	55.2	—	—	17.2
Illness	—	—	604.6	—	—	367.4
Other kinds	0.368	5.80	48.8	0.313	3.43	25.7
Total	52.40[e]	536.3	10,170.0	34.70	282.5	4483.6

[a] In millions of francs.
[b] Source: (**341**, 1903, p. 173).
[c] (**341**, 1952, p. 293).
[d] Source: (**341**, 1981, p. 330).
[e] 1886 total equals 22.00 (**341**, 1903, p. 173).
[f] (**341**, 1952, p. 294).
[g] Robbery included.
[h] As given in **341**, 1933, p. 239.

number of patients discharged fell from 7968 in 1955 to 1112 in 1979 (**341**, 1981, p. 520). I suspect that the number of institutions specializing in tuberculosis insurance has also decreased considerably.

Pension funds are numerous. The principal risk against which such insurance operates is the three-fold combination of old age, disability, and death. The number of organizations serving in this large field of social assistance totalled 17,060 in 1978, a few operating under public law, and over 16,000 under private law (**341**, 1981, p. 320). Total premium income in 1978 was 11,339 million francs. Expenses totalled 5887 million (**341**, 1981, pp. 324–25). There are federal pension funds that take care of the retirement income needs of federal employees and their surviving widows and orphans. Retirement because of disability is a part of the "package." The employees of the federal railway system are covered under a policy that differs somewhat from that which is applicable to other federal employees.

As might be expected, the total insurance coverage in Switzerland against fire is relatively enormous. Including private, local, and cantonal fire insurance institutions, the coverage in 1979 totalled 1,017,652 million francs or, in other words 1.018 trillion francs. This total may be compared with that of 1910, viz. 18,955 million francs less than one-fiftieth of the 1979 total (**341**, 1981, p. 329).

Table 61 pertains to the income and expense of private insurance institutions in 1901, 1945, and 1979. Pension funds are not included in the Table.

Notes and Comments

1. Payments by the insured in 1984 were as follows: Self-employed persons, 5.06 percent to 9.4 percent of income; employed persons, 5 percent of their salary plus 0.3 percent for unemployment insurance. Employers are required to make a matching contribution of 5.3 percent of an employee's salary.

2. This is the expenditure by government on the Old Age and Survivors' Insurance (AHV) program, which became effective in 1948, Disability Insurance (IV) and the special allowances to servicemen, who, as employers, had to pay wages to those who temporarily replaced them at work (EO). In 1960 public funds for social insurance totalled 350 million francs as contrasted with 5.2 billion francs in 1980 (**371**, p. 211).

In 1933, the total federal expenditure on social "welfare" was 63,287,000 francs, of which 16,518,872 francs were for illness, accident, and life insurance and 29,089,506 francs were for unemployment insurance (**341**, 1933, p. 335).

Chronic excessive smoking, use of drugs, and addiction to alcohol can lead to a reduction of 10 percent or more in the payments to the insured under the IV program. This is a penalty, approved by the Federal Insurance Court, suffered by those whose habits endanger themselves and indirectly penalize the innocent by imposing upon them the financial burden of sharing the IV costs of these chronic addictions.

On record is the case of a heavy smoker of cigarettes (20 to 30 per day for 25 years) whose capacity for work was greatly reduced and his income from employment was substantially lessened. The IV Commission decided that, because of the failure of the insured to reduce his consumption of cigarettes, even after medical advice, insurance payments to the person would be reduced by 20 percent. In cases of the long-continued misuse of alcohol through excessive consumption, IV payments have been reduced by as much as 50 percent.

11.14. EDUCATION

Role of the Federal Government

Like many other institutional activities in Switzerland, education of her people is a sovereign right and responsibility of the cantons, not preempted to the Confederation by the Constitution. True, Article 27 of the Constitution[1] empowers the Confederation to establish and maintain the ETH (*Eidgenössische Technische Hochschule*)[2] which it has been doing for many years. The ETH provides the high-level training required by diploma engineers and architects. A sister group of institutes, known as *Techniken*, provide much practical instruction and somewhat less of the theoretical and academic. They are scattered throughout the country and help to satisfy Switzerland's needs for people with good practical training in engineering and architecture. The graduate of a *Technikum* receives the professional title *Ingenieur-Techniker HTL*[3] or *Architekt-Techniker HTL*—as distinct from Diploma Engineer or Diploma Architect, granted by the ETH. The titles are embodied in a federal law for professional education.

The Confederation also exercises control over professional education and vocational training generally. It does so largely by prescribing the training required, and by examination of those who have completed the training program and who seek the necessary certification. Almost all professions and vocations are covered, from entrance requirements, courses of instruction and granting of degrees in medicine (including veterinary medicine), dentistry and pharmacy to training and certification of those who plan to be barbers, shop assistants in retail stores, bricklayers, professional fishermen, etc. The operational details in respect to the training programs, course work, examination of the candidates and certification are taken care of by many commissions responsible to the Federal Government, usually through the Federal Office for Industry, Trades, and Labor (BIGA).[4] The relevant statistics are presented in Tables 67 and 68.

Preschool and Primary Education (see Table 62)

But let us go back to the lower levels of education. Primary school education is compulsory and, in the public school system, is free of charge.[5] Preschool education, meaning thereby in kindergartens, is widespread. It is designed for young children of four, five or six years of age, specifically during the two or three years that precede the beginning of compulsory schooling. Preschool education is not obligatory but in the larger cities and towns well over 90 percent of the young children attend kindergarten.[6] These schools are usually supported by the cantons or communes as a part of public education but private kindergartens also exist.

Most Swiss children terminate their student days at 14 or 15 years of age. The duration of compulsory schooling varies, however, from canton to canton. Indeed, if one may generalize, some 26 different systems of primary education are possible— an inevitable result of cantonal autonomy in education and the existence of a school bureaucracy, headed by a cantonal director of education, in every canton. In many of the cantons further education in school, or training for a trade, is obligatory beyond the so-called school-leaving age which ordinarily marks the end of compulsory schooling. Equally, or more serious, is the actual or potential existence of 26 different curricula at the primary school level, because if a family changes its place of residence by moving into a different canton, or, in some cases, to a different town in the same canton, the children may experience troublesome delays in adapting to a new curriculum. There is also the problem of beginning and ending of the school year, and vacation periods. These differ somewhat among the cantons and efforts to resolve the difficulties that ensue have been pursued for some years. Uniformity of the school calendars throughout Switzerland is the ultimate objective.[7]

Table 62 Primary school education[a]

Year	No. of primary schools	Pupils	Teachers	Cost to the cantons & communes (Million francs)	Cost per inhabitant (cantonal avg.) (francs)	Cost per pupil (cantonal avg.) (francs)	Federal subventions (Million francs)
1900	4663	471,713	10,362	32.8[b]	9.9	69	—
1932–33	—	476,382	13,368	—	—	—	13.55[c]
1951–52	—	476,331	14,476	285.0[g]	—	—	18.75[d]
1979–80	—	468,531[e]	—	4516.7[f]	—	—	52.8[f]

[a] Sources: **341**, 1903, pp. 215–217, 232; 1933, pp. 335, 363; 1952, pp. 405, 415, 433; 1981, pp. 408, 470, 473.
[b] Expenses of the cantons and communes for compulsory schooling in general: 49,971,126 francs.
[c] Federal subvention for education generally, of which 4,600,000 francs appears to have been for the primary schools.
[d] 1951 expenses include subventions for Swiss schools abroad, education at all levels and occupational training; 3,847,000 francs appear to have been designated for the primary schools.
[e] Inclusive of lower secondary schools, i.e. all pupils under compulsory schooling, total is 872,934.
[f] Includes lower middle schools.
[g] Cost of education at all levels in 1951.

Table 63   Secondary schools[a]

Year	No. of schools	Pupils	Teachers	Cost to the cantons & communes (Million francs)	Cost per student (francs)	Federal subvention (Million francs)
1900	549	37,945	1619	5.20	137	—
1932–33	—	46,199	1834	—	—	13.55[b]
1951–52	—	56,166[c]	2365[d]	285.0[h]	—	18.75[e]
1979–80	—	366,792[f]	—	4516.7[g]	—	52.8[g]

[a] Sources: **341**, 1903, pp. 218–220; 1933, pp. 335, 363; 1952, pp. 415, 434; 1981, pp. 408, 470.

[b] Paid to the cantons in 1933; includes 7,127,289 francs for occupational training (*gewerbliche* and *kaufmännische Schulen*).

[c] Inclusive of lower middle schools (district schools, nonclassical secondary schools, and pre-gymnasia): 80,207.

[d] Teachers for the lower secondary schools (925 in number) included in upper middle school teacher group.

[e] Includes primary schools (3,669,573 francs), agricultural schooling (1,454,127 francs), occupational and household training (12,759,761 francs).

[f] Including primary and all schools engaged in compulsory education, there were 872,934 pupils of whom 137,608 were foreigners.

[g] Inclusive of costs and subventions of primary schools.

[h] Cost of education at all levels in 1951.

Although primary school education is a cantonal responsibility, this, in practice, is usually delegated to the communes.

Additional Education and Training

To return to the requirement of many of the cantons that additional schooling or vocational training be obligatory beyond the years of compulsory schooling, we

Table 64   Upper middle schools and gymnasia[a]

Year	Divisions and schools	Pupils	Teachers	Federal maturity certificates issued	Maturity certificates of cantonal origin	Cantonal expenditures (Million francs)	Federal subventions (Million francs)
1900	116[b]	9805	770	718	—	—	—
1931–32	36	11,038	1098	1459	358	18.16	13.55[c]
1951–52	—	12,576	1170	1902	503	50.0[g]	18.75[d]
1979–80	—[h]	68,935	—	9379	996	1081.0[e]	359.0[f]

[a] Sources: **341**, 1903, p. 221; 1933, pp. 335, 363, 364; 1952, pp. 403, 415, 435; 1981, pp. 420, 425, 471.

[b] In 1901.

[c] Total to the cantons in 1933 for educational purposes.

[d] For education at all levels, including occupational training.

[e] 1979 expenses.

[f] For education at all levels, including occupational training; 1980 expenditure.

[g] In 1951.

[h] Maturity schools are to be found in 91 communities—some of the cities having more than one (Reported by the Federal Office of Statistics).

should note that continuation into the upper middle school or a gymnasium[8] satisfies the cantonal requirement. Otherwise, the student will be obliged to serve an apprenticeship for two, three or four years and take the ancillary schooling provided in a trade school, or corresponding training in agriculture in regular agricultural schools, or in agricultural continuation schools with their associated apprenticeship system. Finally, he may satisfy the requirement of further education by attendance for two or so evenings a week at a continuation school for general studies. In most of the cantons, young women, before attaining the age of 21, must receive at least five

Table 65   The universities[a]

	1900–01	1932–33	1951–52	1980–81
Students (Swiss)	2229	5717	9150	41,922
Male	2116	4840	7884	27,316
Female	113	877	1266	14,606
Students (foreign)	1979	2161	3529[j]	9907[b]
Male	1238	1816	2857	5753
Female	741	345	672	4159
Student totals				
Humanities &				
Soc. Sci.	2790	4182	6443	34,178
Exact & Nat.				
Sciences	—	1358	2770	9779
Medicine[d]	1418	2216	3466	10,263
Doctorates	—	614	964[e]	1436[e]
Teaching staff[f]	—	1059 (in 1933–34)	1428	5067
Expenses[g]	—	—	73.0[k]	1230.1
Principal sources of funds[g]				
Confederation	—	—	19.0[k]	1174.4
Cantons	—	—	37.4 (in 1950)	965.7
Stipendia	—	—	—	178.37[l]
Number of				
Stipendiates	—	—	—	60,392
R & D expense[h]	—	—	—	424.5[i]

[a] Source: **341**, 1933, pp. 370–376; 1952, pp. 438–455; 1981, pp. 408, 412, 424, 488–490, 493, 495–497, 500, 501.
[b] 35 percent in the University of Geneva.
[c] In 1952.
[d] Including veterinary medicine, dentistry, pharmacy.
[e] In 1979; includes the ETH.
[f] Excluding assistants.
[g] In millions of francs.
[h] Research and development.
[i] In 1975.
[j] In 1952–53; 777 from USA; 674 from Germany; 246 from Greece; 232 from Iran; 232 from France.
[k] In 1950; includes ETH.
[l] Only 21.7 percent of this total was extended to university students. Apparently most of the stipendial support went to students in the middle schools, the institutes of technology and the *Techniken*. The total reported represents the contributions of the Federal Government, the cantons and the communes. Many private foundations participate in aid to students through stipendia, loans, and by other means. The aggregate annual disbursement from the private sector is not recorded.

weeks of general household training, elsewhere than in their own home. Not uncommonly she will seek the training in a different linguistic region in order to practice her French, German, or Italian—as the case may be.

Information Centers

Two central offices collect and disseminate information on the Swiss schools and the educational regulations: a center in Geneva which is concerned with primary and secondary education, and a center in Zurich which performs a similar function at the university level. The centers, which come under the administrative direction of the Federal Department of the Interior, are extremely useful since education at all levels is a cantonal responsibility and the regulations, the facilities, and the practices differ significantly from canton to canton (**219**, p. 14).

Prerogatives of the Federal Government

The Federal Government intervenes in primary and lower middle school education only in requiring adherence to the second and third paragraphs of Article 27 of the Constitution.[1] At higher levels of education, the federal government exercises three prerogatives: (a) conferring of the federal maturity certificate, which qualifies one

Table 66   Federal institutes of technology[a]

	1866–67	1900–01	1932–33	1951–52	1980–81
Students (Swiss)	206	642	1280	2424	7724
Male	—	—	—	—	6802
Female	—	—	—	—	922
Students (foreign)	265	362	500	493	1821
Male	—	—	—	—	1593
Female	—	—	—	—	228
Student totals					
Exact & Natural Sci.	70	⎱ 212	228	596	2145
Pharmacy	—	⎰	104	139	476
Engin. Sci.[b]	401	792	1448	2182	6785
Doctorates	—	—	56	125[f]	239
Diplomas granted	—	—	238	575[f]	—
Teaching staff[c]	63	100	125	168	875
Expenses[d]	—	—	—	9.21 (1950)[g]	454.5[e]
Federal subventions[h]		1,132,327			

[a] Source: **341**, 1903, pp. 233, 241; 1933, pp. 377–379; 1952, p. 446; 1969, p. 479; 1981, pp. 488–490; 493–497.

[b] Including forestry, agricultural science, military science, architecture & planning, as well as the usual divisions (civil, mechanical, electrical etc.).

[c] Includes part-time teachers; excludes assistants.

[d] In millions of francs; covered almost entirely by the Confederation.

[e] In 1979. In April 1983, the Federal Council allocated almost 290 million francs to the ETH and associated institutes for building purposes alone.

[f] In 1951.

[g] In 1960; 40.1 million francs; In 1970, 230 million francs; 1950 expense (from reference **219**, p. 62).

[h] In francs.

for admission to the universities, to the ETH and to all of the Swiss medical schools and related professional schools; (b) authority, granted in 1965–66, to extend financial support to all seven of the cantonal universities and the Hochschule St. Gallen; and (c) the federal control of professional education and vocational training. The authority to control vocational training derives from Article 34 ter of the Federal Constitution:

> The Confederation is entitled to legislate on . . . (g) vocational training in the fields of industry, crafts, commerce, agriculture and domestic service.

It should be noted that in 1980, 2889 students were granted diplomas certifying to their completion of training in some 50 or so different professions (Tables 67 and 68). Of the diplomats, 206 were granted diplomas in banking—the most popular course. Conversely only 3 chose to be blacksmiths, and 6 were certified as bakers.

> The full-time vocational schools are cantonal, communal or private institutions, but are subsidized by the Federal Government. Also—though to different extents—many professional organizations share in the financing of these schools (113, 238).

Vocational training involves both theoretical and practical training, the latter being oriented toward specific vocations. Apprenticeships are of prime importance and for many vocations an apprenticeship may be the only way to learn the trade. BIGA (the Federal Office for Industry, Trades and Labor) establishes the extensive

Table 67 Vocational training[a]

	1901	1932–33	1952–53	1979–80
Students	16,105	29,846	—	317,309[b]
Agricultural schools	605	2281	—	8127
Teacher training	2327	2633	—	18,709[c]
Commercial training	1696	6984	—	—
Domestic economy & occupations for women	—	13,500	—	—
Industrial training	4397	2709	—	—
Higher technical (HTL)	7080	1739	3274[g]	8029
Federal expenditure[e]	1.686	7.127	15.528[d]	221.15
Schools	—	268	—	—
Diplomas issued	—	—	960[f]	2889
Instructors	—	1882	—	—
Apprenticeship contracts[h]	—	—	79,389[b]	—

[a] Sources: **341**, 1903, pp. 223–233; 1933, pp. 335, 365; 1952, pp. 405, 449, 453; 1969, p. 458; 1981, pp. 412, 420, 475, 486.
[b] Including teacher training.
[c] Included in above total.
[d] In 1950; (in 1960, 29.5 million francs; in 1970, 84.4 million francs).
[e] In millions of francs.
[f] In 1952; 143,065 apprenticeship contracts at end of 1974 (**113**, p. 251).
[g] In 1956.
[h] Including terminal examinations passed on completion of apprenticeships.

Table 68   Vocational and professional certification (*Meisterprufungen*)[a,b]

Year	No. of diplomas issued	No. of professions represented	Most popular professions[c]	Least popular professions[c]
1948	1328	39	Barber (125) Butcher (105)	Photographer (2) Bookbinder (3)
1965	1381	31	Commercial traveler (110) Female farmer (121)	Baker (2) Harness-maker (5)
1980	2601	44	Banking (206) Female farmer (186)	Blacksmith (3) Harness-maker (3) Baker (6)

[a] 50 different vocations and professions are listed in the Statistical Yearbook, including, however, a "catch-all" entitled *Übrige Berufe* (other professions). "Up to now, BIGA has established regulations for 270 vocations" (**113**, p. 237).

[b] Source: **341**, 1952, p. 449; 1969, p. 488; 1981, p. 483.

[c] Number of certifications (in parentheses).

and detailed regulations governing apprenticeships. They usually last for two, three, or four years, after which there is a final examination which, if passed, permits issuance of a federal certificate of vocational proficiency.

University Education

There are eight universities in Switzerland, including the School of Economics, Business and Public Administration in St. Gallen.[9] The responsibility for university education is vested in the cantons.[10] Rising costs forced the cantons involved to seek financial aid from the Federal Government. As early as 1888 efforts were made to persuade the Federal Government to come to the rescue. At least seventy years had to elapse before parliament responded to the needs of the university cantons. The National Science Foundation, founded in 1952, with operational responsibility almost entirely a university matter, but funded by the Federal Government, might be regarded as a first step in supporting the university cantons. On the contrary, new obligations fell upon the cantonal universities, for the moneys derived through the National Science Foundation could be used only for the direct costs of research. Overhead expenses and building additions or renovations to accommodate the expanding research programs could not be charged against the grants from the Foundation.

The granting of stipendia by the Federal Government to aid foreign students and others in need of financial assistance was initiated in 1961 and extended by enactment of a Stipendia Law in 1965. This did not get to the heart of the problem because its effect was to increase the student population without adequate compensation to the universities for the increased cost of providing and maintaining facilities.

However, in late 1965, the Federal Council recommended to the Federal Assembly that grants be made to the university cantons in partial support of their universities. The recommendations received a positive response and interim grants were made for the years 1966, 1967 and 1968 with the understanding that a permanent plan for federal subsidies would be developed before the interim period expired. This much-needed plan for federal support followed upon an excellent study by the Labhardt Commission, representing and responsible to the Federal Department of the Interior.[11]

The status of the universities, including the ETH, over the years is described statistically in Tables 65, 66, and 69. Private universities and municipal or city universities are not to be found in Switzerland. The closest approach to being a city institution is the Hochschule St. Gallen which derives its basic support from both the canton and the city.

Each of the seven other universities possesses its own unique qualities. Bern has seven faculties, Geneva and Zurich six, Basel and Lausanne five, and Freiburg and Neuchâtel only four. Veterinary medicine is taught only in Bern and Zurich. Each university has a faculty of medicine with the exception of Freiburg and Neuchâtel. Dental institutes are affiliated with all the medical schools except Lausanne. Faculties of humanities and social science (Philosophy I), and exact and natural sciences (Philosophy II) are to be found in all seven. Engineering was also recognized as a faculty at Lausanne where the faculty was semi-autonomous, as EPUL. Now, however, engineering is restricted to the Federal Institutes of Technology where it is taught in nine or so divisions within the engineering sciences.

Table 69   Student enrollment in the universities and the ETH in 1980–81[a]

University	Swiss	Men	Women	Foreigners	Men	Women	Total
Basel	5160	3599	1561	555	343	212	5715
Bern	7135	5106	2029	466	308	158	7601
Freiburg	3092	1984	1108	1018	763	255	4110
Geneva	6533	3325	3208	3516	1698	1818	10,049
Lausanne	3967	2389	1578	1526	870	656	5493
Lucerne[b]	173	131	42	25	17	8	198
Neuchâtel	1556	951	605	372	209	163	1928
Zurich	12,860	8537	4323	1926	1118	808	14,786
St. Gallen	1446	1294	152	503	422	81	1949
Subtotal	41,922	27,316	14,606	9907	5753	4159	51,829
ETH, Zurich	6520	5696	824	868	757	111	7388
ETH, Lausanne	1204	1106	98	953	836	117	2157
Grand total	49,646	34,118	15,528	11,728	7341	4387	61,374

[a] Source: **341**, 1981, p. 488.
[b] Theological faculty; not a full-fledged university.

Pharmacy is also taught in the ETH. The two faculties, Phil. I and Phil. II, found in all seven universities, embrace about 25 different subjects.

In 1980–81, 31 percent of the Swiss students in the universities were women. But in 1900–01 only 5 percent of the Swiss university students were women (two percent in 1890–91). Of the foreigners in the universities 42 percent in 1980–81 were women, compared with 37 percent in 1900–01. It should also be noted that in Geneva, a truly international city, 35 percent of the university students in 1980–81 were foreigners, whereas in Bern, despite the presence of many foreign diplomats, this being the capital of Switzerland, only six percent of the Bern university students were foreigners. Geneva is also atypical in that 50 percent of the university students (Swiss plus foreigners) in 1980–81 were women as compared with 29 percent in Bern (Tables 65 and 69).

The Federal Institutes of Technology

The preceding section may leave the impression that the Federal Government's interest in higher education is rather shallow and that its financial support is grudgingly given. If so, a correction is in order.

The Federal Institutes of Technology (ETH Zurich, ETH Lausanne) derive almost their entire support, and generous at that, from the Confederation. ETH Zurich, was founded by federal law in February 1854 and opened for instruction in October 1855. In Lausanne, the *Ecole polytechnique de l'université de Lausanne*[2] became more closely affiliated with the ETH Zurich when, in 1968–69, the two institutions were placed under a central administration. Apart from the instruction offered in the engineering and related sciences in Zurich and Lausanne there are several closely affiliated institutes, such as the Federal Forestry Experiment Station at Birmensdorf near Zurich, the Federal Laboratory for Material Testing (EMPA) at Dübendorf near Zurich, the Federal Institute for Reactor Research at Würenlingen in Aargau canton and the Swiss Federal Institute for Water Supply, Waste Water Purification and Water Protection (EAWAG) in Dübendorf.[12]

Special Schools

Data should also be presented on a number of schools that we may describe collectively as Special Schools.[13] They include: (a) schools for the reform and correction of the young who have gone astray, the mentally deficient, the deaf and dumb, the blind and the orphans; (b) schools for the training of laboratory technicians, paramedics, nurses and nurses' aides. For this last-mentioned group, the schools require recognition by the Swiss Red Cross. Students numbered 9077 in 1980. The programs of study are for three years (six semesters) (**341**, 1981, p. 478). The Special Schools mentioned initially [group (a)] had 2936 students in 1901, 6952 in 1932–33 and 26,606 in 1979–80 (**341**, 1903, pp. 244–48; 1932–33, p. 315; 1981, p. 475).

Private Schools

Private schools of several different types are to be found in Switzerland. They serve quite different functions and are permitted in all of the cantons. Some of the schools are for Swiss children of six or so to about 15 years of age. This is the group for whom school attendance is compulsory and for whom the official curriculum and textbooks conform to the requirements of the canton in which a school is located. Unlike the public schools, schooling is rarely free.

Another group of schools serves the needs of young people from foreign countries, such as the USA. Some are sent by their parents to learn French or German. Others come to a "classy" institution as a "finishing school". In either case, Switzerland is regarded abroad as a well-ordered, trouble-free country and her private boarding schools are usually believed to be clean, the students are well disciplined and the curricula are stripped free of trivia and anything that does not contribute to a sound education in the fundamentals. Of course, the schools are free to organize their curricula and teaching methods as they may choose. The selection of textbooks, duration of the school year, hours of instruction and other aspects of school operation are determined by school management.

From personal experiences I entertain a few doubts about this group of schools. They operate with a profit-making motive, the teachers are not generally dedicated and may not even be adequately trained. Some of them accept an appointment for a year or two, only to enjoy some of the fringe benefits that life in Switzerland may have to offer. I doubt that many of the schools provide the quality of instruction and environment that was anticipated by the parents. Despite the high cost of tuition and maintenance in these schools it is open to question whether a school can be an institution of high quality and still generate a profit.

Other private schools, operated at the expense of commercial enterprises or industrial undertakings, serve as special training centers in language, business administration, marketing, management etc. Some of these are fully independent and are designed for foreign adults who have been sent to Switzerland for a few months or longer by their home company and require instruction in French, German or Italian. For this subgroup of schools tuition is not free and is charged to the student or, indirectly, to his home company.

A few private schools adhere to curricula closely patterned after those of the middle school (high school) of those countries from which most of the students come and to which they will probably return. With one of these I have had first-hand experience and found it to be excellent in all respects. In some cases the students are children of members of the diplomatic corps who, because of a lack of competence in French or German, are unable to attend a regular Swiss school.

Of the many vocational schools, some are private and, like the publicly supported vocational schools, are obliged to comply with cantonal or federal requirements concerning vocational training.

Swiss schools abroad, subsidized by the Federal Government, are also private institutions. Curricula and instruction are largely patterned after those of schools in

Switzerland, thus facilitating ultimate transfer to schools in the homeland with a minimum of interruption in the continuation of schooling.

Some private schools are secular and are usually found in the cantons that are principally catholic. As a rule they provide only primary and secondary school education and, therefore, are subject to the requirements of government regarding compulsory education.

A number of "Special Schools" operate as private institutions but are well subsidized by the cantons and the Federal Government in accordance with provisions of the law on disability insurance.

The Teachers

The cantons are responsible for the training of teachers including, usually, formulation of admission requirements to teacher-training institutions, programs of instruction, and final examinations. Teachers are classified and trained at several different levels depending upon their ultimate teaching responsibility. Kindergarten teachers are trained in cantonal, communal or private institutions. Ten years of schooling plus a practical training period in a family or day nursery is the usual admission requirement. The training lasts for two or three years with emphasis on art, music, handicrafts, sociology and child psychology.

Elementary (primary) school teachers are usually trained in the cantonal teachers' colleges. A maturity certificate may be required before the students are admitted to the didactic training. The programs last four or five years from an entering age of 15 or 16 to a leaving age of 19 to 21.

Secondary school teachers receive their training only after maturity certification or diploma recognition as an elementary teacher. Specialization in training is necessary, either as a future teacher of humanities or mathematics and science. This preadmission training may be received in a university (psychological and pedagogical faculty) or at a special institute for advanced pedagogical studies—of which there are at least three in Switzerland. The training period is of three years duration.

Gymnasium teachers are required to have a licentiate or a doctorate degree—and to have completed their university studies in either humanities or mathematics and science. This must be followed by training in pedagogy and psychology in cantonal courses of one or two years duration, or in a university. As gymnasium teachers they will be expected to teach two or three subjects. For several special subjects attendance at a special teacher-training college may be necessary. To teach in a special school for the handicapped, instruction in rehabilitation and child guidance is required.

To teach in a trade school or one for industrial vocations, a teacher must have gained adequate experience as a teacher in primary or secondary schools or in a gymnasium. In the professional schools for higher technical education, a teacher must be a diploma engineer with professional experience as well. The pedagogical training will be given by the Swiss Institute for Vocational Pedagogy.

Continuation courses, either voluntary or compulsory in participation, are offered to the elementary school teachers by the cantons. These may be given at various times during the school year (school-free periods) or for two or three weeks during the summer vacation. With the recognition that education is a continuing process that does not end when formal schooling is finished, extension programs of one kind and another have developed remarkably in the recent past. The Federal Government is empowered by law to support vocational extension programs. Continued education in general studies is, however, a cantonal responsibility with participation in some instances by private institutions.

CANTONAL DIFFERENCES   Switzerland is still far from a unification of her 26 different cantonal school systems. Progress is slow because of Swiss caution in accepting changes in customs and institutions and because of the stubborn determination of many cantons to give their cantonal autonomy and decision-making powers the top priority. As far as the teachers and school organization are concerned, the Concordat on School Coordination has made a number of recommendations which, if not accepted today, some may be adopted tomorrow. In general, the school structure and practice in Switzerland are somewhat as follows:

(a) A school year of 38 weeks, as stipulated by the Concordat.

(b) Distribution and dates of vacations are determined by the cantons or their communities.

(c) In some cantons there is no schooling on Saturdays. In others, Thursday is a free day. Still others, prefer two free half-days each week, usually the afternoons of Wednesday and Saturday.

(d) The hours of instruction are from 20 to 30 per week in the elementary and lower secondary schools (the compulsory grades) and between 30 and 36 in the higher grades of the secondary schools.

(e) In the compulsory grades, teachers are on duty from 20 to 30 hours per week. Teachers in the higher grades are typically on duty from 20 to 26 hours per week.

Language Instruction and Maturity Certificates

Competence in several languages is of prime importance in Switzerland because of its multilingual cantonal structure. The three official languages are French, German and Italian. Romansh is recognized as a national language but is not involved in this present discussion of language instruction. In the lower grades of the secondary schools, a student is introduced to the first foreign language: German if he lives in *Suisse romande*; French if in *Suisse Allemande* and French or German if his school is in the Ticino where Italian is the cantonal language. By the time the student is in an upper middle school (gymnasium), he is probably preparing for his maturity examinations and entrance to a university. Additional linguistic competence is now necessary. There are five different maturity certificates recognized by the Federal Council. Whatever type the student may elect, the gymnasium curriculum, with eleven subjects selected by the student, must be completed. The types of maturity certificates are as follows:

(i) Type A, requiring Greek and Latin;

(ii) Type B, requiring Latin and modern languages;

(iii) Type C, less emphasis on language. Mathematics and science are emphasized;

(iv) Type D, requiring several modern languages;

(v) Type E, with emphasis on economics.

Language looms large in upper school instruction. For all five types of certificate, examinations in eleven subjects are required, including the mother tongue (German, French or Italian), and a second official language (French, German or Italian). Depending on the type of maturity certificate, the student may also have to possess a satisfactory knowledge of Latin and Greek; or Latin and the third official language (or another foreign language); or graphic geometry and the third official language (or another foreign language); or the third official language (or two other foreign languages); or economics and the third official language (or another foreign language).

Any one of the five certificates is adequate for admission to any of the faculties of a university (including medicine) or to the two Federal Institutes of Technology. The Federal Council also recognizes religious boarding schools (e.g. catholic) as equivalent to public gymnasia in preparing students for maturity examinations. Some public or private gymnasia in the larger towns have evening schools which also prepare students for university entrance. The minimum age for admission to an evening school is 20 years. Some maturity certificates are recognized by the cantons but not by the Federal Council. They include certificates in the arts and the pedagogical or commercial sciences.

Finally, there are higher secondary schools in some of the towns which grant a diploma after two or three years of general education and preparation for professional schools in which training is offered in paramedicine, social work or pedagogy.

Social Services

In a number of countries, the universities and some schools at various educational levels have found the provision of social services, medical and psychological aid, and special counseling for the student body to be advisable, if not a necessary function of the institution. In Switzerland, the responsibility of providing these services rests with the cantons—frequently delegated to the communes with cantonal financial support. The services consist in (a) medical checkups for students and teachers at specified times; (b) observance of the federal law pertaining to tuberculosis; (c) inspection of hygienic conditions in the schools; (d) provision of dental care; (e) detection and treatment of endangered and handicapped or mentally retarded children; (f) arrangements for the transfer of children in this last-mentioned group to the appropriate special school; and (g) educational and vocational counseling.

Problems of the Universities

The problems of the cantons and the Confederation with regard to their responsibilities in education are largely financial; if it cannot be solved with money, it is not a problem. One of the ever-recurring complaints of the universities focuses on the escalating costs of instruction, and of expansion or rebuilding of their facilities. The university clinics in the medical schools are faced with rapidly soaring costs. The science departments of the universities (Philosophy II) are far more expensive in their operations than the humanities and the social sciences (Philosophy I).

Increases in tuition charges would never solve the problem: the highest fees that could be imposed upon the students at a level that might be bearable would fall far short of meeting the actual costs.[14] In a typical private American university, despite the high tuition charges at the better-known universities, tuition income is usually less than one-third of the actual costs incurred by the university.

In Switzerland the problem has been partly solved by the introduction of federal aid to the cantonal universities. The program was initiated in 1965–66 with grants of 45, 65 and 80 million francs to the eight cantonal universities for the years 1966, 1967, and 1968 respectively. The allocations were divided among the cantons according to a formula which took into account the student enrollments and the relative financial strengths of the eight cantons. The program has been continued by renewal of grants of increasing size for additional three-year periods and use of the original formula (size of the student body and financial strength of a canton) for distribution of the funds.

The most promising sources of financial support might appear to be a special charge assessed against foreign students, and an assessment against the non-university cantons whose young people may attend one of the eight cantonal universities without their home cantons contributing anything to relieve the university cantons of a fair portion of their costs of operation and maintenance.[15] The first proposal, if implemented by charging each foreign student 27,500 francs per year (as calculated from Tables 65 and 66, 1980–81) would yield 322.5 million francs instead of the 11 or 12 million francs assumed to be currently derived as tuition income from the 11,728 foreign students in the universities and the ETH.

The annual loss of about 310 million francs must be regarded as an investment in international good will. The Swiss universities have refrained from any discrimination against the foreign student by charging higher tuition and I doubt that any such surcharge is even contemplated. The common reply to the obvious question is "Other countries do not have discriminatory tuition policies directed against the foreign student, and we would never, in Switzerland, endorse such a policy; we believe in the international exchange of students and we prefer to encourage the practice." In fact, Switzerland granted 178.37 million francs in stipenda in 1980–81 to 60,392 students, of whom 21.7 percent were at the university level.

In 1961 a special federal commission was established to administer a stipendium program for foreign students. The enabling legislation provided for the support of about 100 students per year (60 from the underdeveloped countries and 40 from the more developed). In 1965, 289 stipendiates under this program were at Swiss universities, including 43 at the ETH. Most of the stipendiates remain at a Swiss university for four years. Students from the more developed countries receive stipendial aid for only one year. Fifteen countries, or more, reciprocate by granting similar scholarships to Swiss students. Of the total funds from the public purse (178.37 million francs) only a portion was directed to the foreign student program. Swiss students may also receive grants.

The prevailing opinion in Switzerland appears to be that stipendia should be regarded as qualitatively akin to salaries, not as alms to the needy. An applicant should not be required to give evidence of penury, so we are told. Receipt of a stipendium should be regarded as a scholastic honor, entirely divorced from questions of financial stress.

The participation of nonuniversity cantons in the support of their young people attending educational facilities in the university cantons is another matter and one may assume that such financial participation will eventually be achieved. Certainly it is not feasible for each and every canton to have its own university, although Aargau and Lucerne have been trying for years to establish their own universities.

For quite some time, the universities have been troubled by an ever more serious threat of an inability to accept the steadily increasing number of entering students.[16] On the surface it would seem that more universities would be the obvious and probably the ultimate solution. However, the space problem is not yet an embarrassment to all faculties or departments. It focuses sharply on the medical schools where the pressures for admission have been steadily mounting. Rather than invoke the protection offered by the *numerus clausus* by which the universities would inform qualified applicants, "Sorry we have run out of space: we cannot accept your application," the *Nationalrat* (House of Representatives) has approved a decree by which 60 million francs would be appropriated to provide more places in the medical schools. The opposition used as an argument the belief of some that there are too many physicians in Switzerland: there is no need for more. But if we examine the Labhardt report, we find that a medical school enrollment (including veterinary medicine) of 7000 students was estimated for 1975 (**219**, p. 49). Actual enrollment was 7229 in 1973–74, 7713 in 1976–77 and 8097 in 1980–81.

More to the point is the number of practicing physicians: 6085 in 1974, 6379 in 1976, and 7473 in 1979–80 (**341**). In 1970 the *Jahrbuch* (**341**) reports the presence of 5508 practicing physicians. The Schultz Commission, not looking farther into the future, concluded that 5620 to 6050 would be required by 1970.

The number of applicants for admission to medical studies (human and veterinary medicine, and dentistry) was 1839 in 1982. The number of places open for first semester students has been officially placed at 1447 (**294**, No. 3, p. 121, October 1982).

In the 1950s and 1960s several *ad hoc* commissions were established by the Federal Government to study the problems of higher education in Switzerland: the Schultz Commission, to concern itself with the important problem of forecasting the number of students for whom Switzerland should be prepared by 1975, and the number of teachers needed; the Labhardt commission to study the problem of federal grants to the university cantons for the specific purpose of helping the universities meet their rapidly increasing costs; and three study groups responsible to the Federal Delegate for Employment (*Delegierter für Arbeitsbeschaffung*) to recommend a specific course of action with respect to the apparent shortage of engineers and scientists available to meet the expanding needs of the economy. Their findings were published in 1959 as the Hummler report (Dr. Hummler was then the Federal Delegate). Portions of the report were updated in 1964. For an analysis of the reports of these commissions and study groups please see reference **219**.

Costs of Education

For other than the expenses incurred by government, this subject is much too complicated to explore in depth.[15] Although education of children to the school-leaving age is compulsory, free secondary schools are not sufficiently numerous in some cantons to permit a student to live at home during the school year. If parents have to pay for room and board for their school-age children attending school in a fairly remote town, the expense may be beyond the family's ability to pay. In some cantons, especially the mountain cantons, the school-leaving age is 13 or 14, and environmental pressures and family income are not conducive to further schooling. A common complaint in the not-too-distant past in some cantons also expressed the thought that higher education, even middle school education, was unsettling and disturbing to children. After all, their parents had decided that the help of their children was urgently needed on the farm and further education was totally unnecessary. Nevertheless, exodus of the young people from the mountain villages and from the countryside generally to the cities and towns became a continuing phenomenon. As mercenary service began to fade away and finally ended in the latter part of the nineteenth century, the young Swiss men lost the opportunities of the past to visit a foreign country, and to share in the booty of warfare and the excitement of life as a mercenary. But the industrial revolution was by then well under way, and the industries of the cities and towns served as a magnet to drain young men from the countryside.

Boredom, monotony and a dull existence experienced by many of the young would be replaced by excitement, new acquaintances and thrills galore in those wonderful cities and towns where the action was—so they hoped.

Acknowledgement

In preparing this chapter I have made extensive use of the article on "Education in Switzerland" by Prof. Eugene Egger (**113**) who, as Secretary General of the Swiss Conference of Cantonal Directors of Education, is a widely recognised authority on the subject. I have also drawn upon my own experiences and observations, especially with respect to higher education, and science and engineering in Switzerland (**219**). Finally, for detailed information on each of the Swiss universities and the ETH, a publication in English by the Swiss National Tourist Office, "The Swiss Universities," can be recommended.

Notes and Comments

1. The Confederation is empowered to set up, in addition to the existing polytechnic school, a federal university and other establishments for higher education or to subsidize such institutions.

The cantons shall provide for adequate primary education which shall be placed wholly under state control. Such education shall be compulsory and, in public schools, free of charge.

The adherents of all religious beliefs shall be enabled to attend public schools without being affected in any way in their freedom of creed or conscience (Article 27, Federal Constitution).

As a matter of historical interest, the original Constitution of 1848 stated only "The Confederation is empowered to establish a university and a polytechnic school." The competence of the Federal Government was significantly extended in 1874 by addition of the clause "and to establish other higher educational institutions or to support such institutions."

2. Literally, Federal Technical University. The ETH Zurich was founded in 1854. EPUL (*Ecole polytechnique de l'Université de Lausanne*) functioned in *Suisse romande* as a corresponding institution for the training of engineers. EPUL, in turn, was a successor to the *Ecole spéciale* which was founded in 1853. In 1968–69 EPUL was taken over by the Confederation. As the ETH Lausanne, it was placed with the ETH Zurich under a small administration to centralize the contacts of both the ETH Zurich and ETH Lausanne with the Federal Government, and to unify curricula and other aspects of the two institutions.

The creation of the ETH was envisaged much earlier than 1854. Indeed, at the time of the Helvetic Republic, 1798 to 1803, plans for establishment of a central university were much to the fore. However, nothing came of the original proposals, largely because of the distractions of the Napoleonic Wars and because the federal authorities did not have the legal competence to found a university (granted by the first Federal Constitution of 12 September 1848).

3. *Höheres Technisches Lehranstalt*—Higher Technical Training Institution.

4. One must not over-emphasize the role of the Federal Government, because education is basically a responsibility of the cantons.

Important cantonal bills are normally prepared by commissions nominated by the executive council of the government (*Regierungsrat*) and then submitted to the legislative authority (*Grosser Rat*, Cantonal Council) for acceptance. In most cantons, however, bills concerning school matters must be acted upon by popular vote. Only legislation of minor importance can be enacted directly by the executive, either the board of education or the cantonal department of education. In all important matters, the voter has the last word. . . . Innovations in the Swiss educational system are introduced with great caution, and . . . coordination between the cantons is often lacking (**113**, p. 229).

5. Prior to the early nineteenth century, education, such as it was, was a responsibility of the church. In the spring of 1831, the constitution of Zurich canton was amended by vote of the people to make instruction of children a responsibility of the canton. In consequence, a cantonal law of 1832 led to the introduction of compulsory all-day schooling for children of six to twelve years of age with a school year for all the cantonal primary schools of 27 weeks. Good schools require well-trained teachers. Hence, a teacher-training school was established in Küsnacht (Zurich) in the same year. I assume that the introduction of compulsory schooling in Zurich in 1832 marked the beginning of compulsory schooling throughout Switzerland.

Resulting from compulsory schooling, a fringe benefit of great importance to child welfare resided in the further reduction of child labor in factories (please refer to "Factories" in Chapter 10).

6. In the country as a whole, 113,814 children in the age group 4 to 6 attended kindergartens in 1979–80. This is almost exactly 50 percent of the total number of children in the same age group in all Switzerland (**341**, 1981, p. 472). Even in 1900, when the total population of Switzerland was 3,315,000 there were 40,344 children in kindergartens (**341**, 1903, p. 214).

7. A Concordat on School Coordination, established in 1970 by the Swiss Conference of Cantonal Directors of Education has as a declared purpose the search for country-wide uniformity in various portions of school legislation [age of school entrance (at least six years), duration of compulsory

schooling (nine years), and length of schooling up to the maturity examination (12 to 13 years)].
Recommendations are also being developed concerning curricula, mutual recognition of cantonal
examination results and easing of transfer of pupils between schools of equal level.

Over 20 of the cantons have ratified the agreement by which the Concordat was established.

Mention was made of intercantonal differences in the beginning and ending of the school year. In both
the cantons of Bern and Zurich, the school year begins in the spring. In Lucerne canton, school starts in
August. In most cantons the school year begins after the summer vacation. Discussion of the problem,
for it is a real problem if a family with school-age children moves into another canton, seems always to be
enlivened by emotional and passionate arguments presented by those adults who have survived the
system. A similar problem exists at higher levels of education: requirements for beginning studies in a
gymnasium; termination dates at the gymnasium level; etc. etc.

8. A gymnasium carries one an additional year or two beyond the American or Canadian high school
which seem to terminate at about the beginning of the Swiss upper middle school. As such, a graduate of a
gymnasium is commonly admitted to the sophomore year of many American universities if his
competence in English permits. In general, gymnasia serve the needs of those students who require
maturity certificates for professional training in the universities in medicine, veterinary medicine,
dentistry, pharmacy or entrance to a university for other types of study.

9. The eight cantonal universities are as follows (founding dates in parentheses): Basel (1460), Bern
(1528), Freiburg (1889), Geneva (1559), Lausanne (1537), Neuchâtel (1838), Zurich (1833) and the
Hochschule St. Gallen (1898).

The student enrollment in each of the eight in 1980–81 is presented in Table 69 which also includes the
two Federal Institutes of Technology.

10. Although an unwritten rule, it has long been understood that this responsibility does not include
the right to appoint professors without first seeking the recommendations of the community of
professors in the disciplines concerned. In the spring of 1982, the cantonal government of Basel-Stadt
elected to a full professorship in history in the University of Basel someone who had not even been
proposed by the Faculty. Twenty-eight professors of history from the other cantonal universities and the
ETH Zurich considered this to be a violation of the unwritten rule and joined in a protest to the cantonal
government of Basel-Stadt.

11. André Labhardt, Professor of Letters at the University of Neuchâtel, was chairman of the
commission. The other members, eight in number, were drawn from the remaining six universities, the
Hochschule St. Gallen and the Federal Institute of Technology.

12. Mention should also be made of a number of institutions that are associated with the universities.
In Geneva, several are almost an integral part of the university. These three are quite closely associated:
the School of Architecture, the Institute of the Educational Sciences, and the School of Interpreters. Four
others are rather remotely associated: the University Institute of International Studies, the University
Center for Ecumenical Studies, the Center for Industrial Studies and the International Institute for Social
Studies.

In Basel there is the Swiss Tropical Institute which is loosely affiliated with the University of Basel.
Associated with the Faculty of Science in the University of Neuchâtel is the Swiss Laboratory for
Research on Horology.

13. Another type of special school for which a need is recognized is a sort of transitional school,
designed to meet the needs of newly arrived foreign children who are about to enter a regular Swiss
school. A knowledge of the language—French, German or Italian—used in the school, is frequently
lacking by the would-be entrant. The Conference of Cantonal Directors of Education, the Federal Office
for Science and Education, as well as the Federal Commission for Problems of Foreigners have finally
come together in study-group sessions to solve the problem. The Council of Europe is also interested
because, basically, the problem is common to all the countries of Europe.

Over 150,000 foreign children are in Swiss schools. They constitute an excessively high proportion of
the scholars in so-called special classes. Special preschool courses in language are now recommended,
including a modest amount of elementary instruction (two hours each week) in the culture and
characteristic qualities of Switzerland itself. To be avoided are such unsatisfactory solutions as after-

school instruction in language, or private tuition outside of the school hours. It is hoped that the program now advocated will achieve a real integration of the foreign children into the life of the school and community. Some parents have already expressed the fear that the program will convert their children into "little Swiss." I assume that the plan, if fully implemented, will be supported by grants from government—principally cantonal and communal.

14. In 1958 to 1962, tuition in Swiss universities appears to have been about 250 francs a semester, which for a medical student would amount to 2850 francs as his total outlay for tuition in the required 13 semesters of instruction (219, p. 18). The actual cost to a canton was more nearly 10,000 francs per student per year and about 13,000 francs per year for a student in medicine, science or engineering, as contrasted with possibly 500 francs of actual tuition income per student per year. For the benefit of those who wish to convert all these francs into dollars, note that throughout the 1960s, one franc was equivalent to a little more than 23 USA cents (341, 1981, p. 480). For the source of the above data please refer to reference 212.

15. For an attempt to explore this problem, please see reference 219 (pp. 78–88). Note that about one-half of the students attending the eight cantonal universities are from the 18 cantons and half-cantons that are without universities (341, 1981, p. 488).

16. The number of students enrolled in the Swiss universities (inclusive of the ETHs) was 54,198 in 1977 and 61,374 in 1981 (Tables 65 and 66). The estimated enrollments for 1984, 1985, 1986, and 1987 are 68,300, 69,900, 71,200, and 72,100 respectively (294, Supplement 30, 1983, p. 56).

11.15 SCIENCE AND TECHNOLOGY

Introduction

The importance of science and technology in Switzerland may be inferred from the fact that the machine and chemical industries hold the two top positions in amount of net income generated by world trade.[1] The watch industry, though seriously depressed, is in the third position.

Significant also is the proportion of students in the universities and the Federal Institutes of Technology who are studying subjects directly concerned with science and technology. In 1980 the percentage was about 40 in the universities and, as may be expected, almost 100 in the Federal Institutes of Technology (from Tables 65 and 66 in Section 11.14). Both totals exclude the *Techniken* students who in 1980 numbered 8029 (**341**, 1981, p. 486).

An examination of the research grants allocated in 1981 by the Swiss National Science Foundation[2] (*Schweizerischer Nationalfonds zur Förderung der Wissenschaftlichen Forschung*)—the principal source of support for research conducted in the universities and the ETH—also demonstrates convincingly the importance of science and technology in Switzerland. First of all we must recognize that science (*Wissenschaft*) embraces the entire field of learning and is not restricted to the natural and physical sciences (*Natur- und Physikalische Wissenschaft*) as in the English-speaking countries. In 1983, (as reported in Table 72) the Foundation expended 162,416,000 francs in support of research. Of this total, 43.2 percent was allocated to research in the Exact and Natural Sciences and 36.5 percent to Biology and Medicine. The Humanities and Social Sciences received 20.3 percent; it should be pointed out that research in these fields of learning is far less expensive than in the natural and physical sciences, including medicine (**294**, July 1982, p. 66).

I propose to concentrate on the support of research, and with only one exception, to mention briefly several agencies other than universities that conduct research or provide money for the direct or indirect support of research. The exception, deserving of special mention, is the Swiss National Science Foundation.

The Swiss National Science Foundation

During World War II the Swiss Federal Government extended modest support to science through the office of the Delegate on Employment Opportunities

(*Delegierter für Arbeitsbeschaffung*). A wartime credit of four to five million francs was voted by the Federal Government to aid in the fight against unemployment which, with the inflow of refugees, threatened to become a serious problem. In a decree of 6 August 1943, it was stipulated that these funds could be used to support applied research in the universities and the research and development programs of broad interest pursued within Swiss industry. Although this was conceived of as an emergency program, the office continued in being and sums of about 1.4 million francs per year were allocated for its work.

In 1943 the Swiss Academy of Medical Sciences was founded. Professor Alfred Gigon was the initiator, assisted and encouraged from the beginning by Professor Alexander von Muralt. Even in 1942, largely because of von Muralt's great interest in education in general, and in the biological-medical sciences in particular, a foundation had been created to provide stipendia to those promising young scientists who wished to further their training through advanced study in Europe or abroad. The foundation promptly became associated with the Academy for Medical Sciences. In its first 20 years it expended approximately 2.2 million francs for stipendia.

That all too little was being done to support scientific research and to assist in the advanced education of its scientists was clear to the leaders of Swiss science and scholarship. In November, 1945, the General Assembly of the Union of Swiss University Teachers devoted its attention to these problems. Director O. Zipfel (Federal Delegate for Employment Opportunities), in the principal address, described the efforts of himself and Professor Rohn (President of the Board of the ETH) to organize a foundation for the promotion of scientific research. The foundation would serve as a bridge between the technical sciences and the humanities. Because of objections which evidently originated elsewhere than in the Federal Government, the plan came to naught—described by Zipfel as "belonging to the area of lost opportunities."

Von Muralt and several others pointed out that the desired objectives could not be attained through the federal appropriations for *Arbeitsbeschaffung*. Such credits had been voted by the Federal Assembly to support only research and development, expansion of existing industries, and development of new industries which would afford employment opportunities. "The fight against tomorrow's unemployment is our foremost responsibility."[3] It was certainly transparently clear that such funds could not be used to support research in the social sciences and humanities.

Von Muralt's contribution to the discussion was much to the point and almost prophetic, for only a few years were to elapse before the Swiss National Science Foundation, under his able leadership, was to come into being.

Through granting a payment of four million francs (for *Arbeitsbeschaffung*) the Confederation has taken a first step of fundamental importance, in which for the first time in our country scientific research is supported to some extent by the Confederation. Thus it is a beginning which justifies our highest hopes. On the expiration of a trial period, it will be possible through this very gratifying action to so prepare the soil that we shall succeed through a parliamentary decree in attaining a national science foundation. At present it is still not possible to support in any general way research in the social sciences. But developments of the future must and will lead us to a solution in which the presently existing limitations can be put aside and the active promotion of research in all scholarly fields of endeavor in our cultural life will be possible. As long as the funds are made available from credits for *Arbeitsbeschaffung* one cannot demand more than today can be given. However, if we can achieve a special national foundation for scientific research—a foundation such as has long existed in Belgium—it will then be possible to do justice to all needs and points of view. But this can only be realized if corresponding sums are made available by the Federal Assembly exclusively for the purposes of science in general.

The need for such a Foundation was brought to public attention in a document prepared by the Central Committee of the *Schweizerische Naturforschende Gesellschaft* and signed by von Muralt, then President of the Society. This document, published in 1949, was directed to the rectors and members of the faculties of the seven cantonal universities, the President of the Board and the rector and professors of the ETH, the rector and professors of the St. Gallen Graduate School of Economics and Social Sciences, and the members of the senate of the Swiss Natural Science Society (*Schweizerische Naturforschende Gesellschaft*).

At the time of this report, scientific research in Switzerland, exclusive of research in industry, was supported by the various private foundations (including occasional grants from the Rockefeller Foundation), by the major industries of Switzerland, by the cantons insofar as provision of some of the basic facilities was concerned, by two of the three major scientific organizations, and by the Federal Government. It is important to note, however, that the support extended by the Federal Government (4 million francs in 1943) was restricted to such types of applied research as would be presumed to generate new industries and expand opportunities for the employment of labor. The Federal Government in 1949 was also expending about one million francs annually for research in nuclear science, but federal funds for the support of basic research in general were not provided. In the light of later developments it should be noted that stipendia were nonexistent in the social sciences, and the Swiss Society for the Humanities and the Social Sciences (*Schweizerische Geisteswissenschaftliche Gesellschaft*) did not have funds available for research support. The document emphasized, *inter alia*, the pressing need for the federal support of pure basic research throughout the sciences, including the social sciences and humanities.

It raised such provocative questions as whether the funds for basic research were really inadequate, whether a better coordination of research effort was feasible, whether the independence of the cantonal universities would be jeopardized by the proposed project, and whether the funds would be equitably distributed among the universities.

The establishment of an enlarged commission representative of the universities and of the scientific societies was proposed, as well as local advisory commissions within each university. Possible statutes for the Foundation were drafted, and the proposals were submitted in 1949 to the members of the faculties of the Swiss universities.

On 21 December 1950, a representative delegation of scientists presented the final draft of the proposal to the Federal Council, and on 1 August 1952, the National Science Foundation came into being as an extragovernmental agency designed to disburse federal funds allotted for support of research. By the end of December, 1961, almost ten years of work had been accomplished. The regular contributions of the Federal Government had steadily risen from 2 million francs in 1952 to 7 million in 1961—a total of 44 million francs for the ten-year period. The regular contributions were supplemented by a special grant of 600,000 francs for the purposes of the International Geophysical Year, and two special grants totaling 50.5 million francs to support fundamental research in nuclear science for the period 1958 to 1962.

Since the inception of the National Science Foundation and up to 31 December 1961, 2312 grants for research and publication had been made in an amount of 75,136,221 francs. In addition, through the local commissions, 851 stipendia totaling 4,038,681 francs had been granted to promising students in the social and general sciences, and 38 stipendia (388,845 francs) to students in nuclear science.

Summarized in Table 70 are the total expenditures in research grants, stipendia, and for publication purposes for the first 14 years of the Foundation and for 1983.

Late in 1962 and again in 1965, the Foundation underwent an expansion and

Table 70   National science foundation expenditures

	Category	1952–65 Grants	1952–65 Amount[f]	1983 Amount[f]
A[a]	Research grants in Social Science, Natural and Physical Sciences (exc. Nuclear Science), Engineering and Agriculture	3058	123.8 ⎫	
B[b]	Nuclear Science (basic research)	529	49.3 ⎬ 145.3[e]	
C	Publication	448	4.6	1.8
D	Stipendia	1360	8.0	10.7
E	Administration and miscellaneous	n.a.	3.8[c]	3.9
F	Appointments to University posts	40[d]	4.0	—
	Personnel payments	—	—	4.1
	Services of experts	—	—	0.9
	Apparatus, equipment, and depreciation	—	—	0.5
	International cooperation	—	—	0.4
	Total expenditures		193.5	167.6

[a] Nuclear Science included in Category A after 1962.
[b] 1962 only.
[c] Approximation.
[d] Number of appointees.
[e] Including National Research Programs (nonexistent prior to 1976).
[f] In millions of francs.
n.a. Not applicable.

reorganization coincident with substantial increases in the Confederation's appropriations. In the category of research grants, the subjects of major support were as indicated in Table 71, with 1983 data added for comparative purposes.

The Foundation operates through two bodies: the Foundation Council (*Stiftungsrat*), which serves as an intermediary between the Research Council (*Forschungsrat*), and the Federal Government, and which, according to certain rules, appoints most of the members of the *Forschungsrat*, the second body. The *Stiftungsrat*, by statute, consists of stated representatives of government agencies and of a specified number of representatives of various nongovernmental scientific agencies, including universities. It meets at least twice a year. In addition to general advisory functions, the *Stiftungsrat* extends advice regarding grant requests for unusually large sums. It is essentially the legislative organ of the *Nationalfonds*. The members serve for four years and are eligible for re-election. The membership of the *Stiftungsrat* as of 31 December 1981, consisted of two representatives from each of the ten universities (*Hochschulen*), two each from four of the principal science organizations and one each from three other organizations. The Federal

Table 71 Major divisions of science receiving researching support (1952–65) and in 1983[a,b]

	Number of grants		Expenditures (in francs)	
	1952–65	1983	1952–65	1983
Mathematics	—	10	—	723,416
Human medicine	673	182	27,658,436	29,791,937
Biology	516	123	18,883,383	20,826,585
Chemistry	307	64	14,802,032	11,433,797
Physics	253	61	29,690,390	18,070,351
Astronomy, astrophysics	42	16	2,088,812	5,820,375
Earth sciences	131	24	4,918,789	2,883,947
Engineering sciences	—	27	—	3,058,843
Environmental sciences	—	19	—	1,751,670
Language, literature, folklore	217	17	4,490,093	2,440,375
History	259	28	4,917,478	2,956,040
Prehistory, archaeology ethnology, beaux-arts, musicology, theater	—	35	—	3,903,192
Philosophy, religion, church history, education, psychology	—	35	—	3,475,096
Sociology, political science, economics, law, geography	—	33	—	2,792,847
Fine arts	100	—	1,688,733	—
National programs	—	16[c]	—	29,764,128
Other	—	12	—	2,012,252
Total	2498	702	109,138,146	141,729,851

[a] Inclusive of humanities, social sciences, engineering and national programs.
[b] Source: **219**, p. 107; **134**, 1983, pp. 38–57.
[c] Number of programs.

Government had eight representatives and the cantonal governments, three in all. Nine others represented various cultural and economic institutions—giving a total membership of 51.

The *Forschungsrat* is the executive body within the *Nationalfonds*. It has been expanded several times since 1962 from an original membership of 11. In 1984 the membership totalled 58. The representation from the Federal Government was thereby increased to 14, most of whom are scientists. The nongovernmental members consist of scientists selected by the *Stiftungsrat*, on a very broad basis, from throughout Switzerland. The *Forschungsrat* makes grants in support of research in the humanities, the social, natural, physical, and medical sciences—indeed the whole broad field of scholarly investigation.

Until 1962 research in nuclear science was uniquely supported, a subcommission on atomic science serving as the advisory body. This commission came into being in 1958 with two appropriations of 10.5 million and 40 million francs for the support of basic research in nuclear science through the period ending in December, 1962.

Each of the universities and learned societies embraced by the Foundation has a local research commission and these assist, *inter alia*, in an advisory capacity. The local commissions do, in fact, play an important role in the work of the National Science Foundation. Incoming applications must be routed through these commissions, which must give a preliminary rating to the applications from their universities. They also disburse Foundation funds for stipendia.

The ensemble of local commissions includes also commissions set up within the principal scientific, cultural, and humanistic organizations of Switzerland. These extra-university commissions act upon applications received from scholars who are outside of universities. They also receive funds for stipendia.

Members of the *Forschungsrat,* the *Stiftungsrat* and the various local commissions serve on a part-time basis, deriving their income very largely from their principal activity—e.g. as a professor or in private employment in industry, law, medicine, or other kinds of business. In Switzerland, an arrangement of this kind, which applies also to members of parliament, is known as a militia system (*Milizsystem*). The secretariat, in contrast, is employed by the Foundation on a full-time basis.

In response to various proposals with additional international collaboration (e.g. European Science Foundation), the National Science Foundation has established a special group of studies described collectively as National Programs of Research. In 1981, fourteen of these received a total of 11.4 million francs. Some of the programs are cross disciplinary and others fill in gaps between some of the research areas listed in Table 71. All of the national programs may be thought of as either short-term programs of an ad hoc character, or programs in areas of applied science to be supported, if need be, for three or four years.

The Annual Report of the Foundation for 1981 lists the individual research grants, 861 in number, inclusive of 85 within the division of National Research Programs. The grants are reported upon by author, institution, subject of investigation, and funds allocated (**134**, pp. 57–150, inclusive of subsidies for publication, and bursaries). Other grants, including international collaboration, totalled 739,484 francs.[4]

Government and Industrial Support of Science

The cantonal universities are financed basically by the cantons in which the universities are located. In 1979, the cantons expended about 966 million francs for support of their universities including some of the research conducted therein. The amount actually used for research purposes is not recorded but I would be surprised if it were less than 100 million francs. Under the general heading of instruction and research, we learn that in 1979 the cantons expended 5.482 billion francs. Of this total, 4.335 billion francs were expended to support the public schools, the middle schools, and vocational training (**341**, 1981, p. 427).

Also in 1979, the Federal Government expended about 449 million francs for science and research.[5] Of the total, the universities received 190 million francs for basic expenses plus 101 million as subsidies for buildings and major equipment.

After granting 136 million francs to the National Science Foundation in response to its needs, there was relatively little remaining. However, about 7.5 million francs were allocated for "seed" programs (*Impulsprogramm*).[6] Six million francs were also allocated for the encouragement of applied research (**341**, 1981, p. 420).

Of the 1.685 billion francs expended for higher education in 1979 (**341**, 1981, p. 497), 422.3 million constituted expenses incurred by the Federal Institutes of Technology (ETHZ and ETHL). The covering of these ETH expenses is entirely a financial responsibility of the Federal Government, with about 29 million of the total arising from work done by divisions of the ETH for third parties. As a prime contributor to science and technology in Switzerland, the ETH is of utmost importance. Its activities focus almost entirely on engineering and the basic sciences that are relevant, such as mathematics, physics and the earth sciences. The social sciences, humanities, and law are excluded from the curricula.

Were we to consider the total requests of the various scientific and technological organizations seeking federal support, we would find that for the four-year period 1984 to 1987 the requests totalled 901.56 million francs. The Science Council recommended to the Federal Government a total appropriation of 789.70 million francs (Table 73). See also Table 72.

The role of Swiss industry in the pursuit of science and technology is of obvious significance. The expenditure of the major industries on research and development is not clearly revealed in the annual reports of the companies involved. In the pharmaceutical industry, it probably approaches 10 or 12 percent of the total turnover. In addition, industry supports a considerable amount of extramural research pursued in the universities. Again, the amount so expended cannot readily be determined. It is apparent, however, that the support expended is appreciable and does not necessarily require that the investigator pursue a problem of unique interest to the donor.

Other governments also participate in science activities in Switzerland. In the early 1960s, for example, agencies of the USA government expended about 4.5

Table 72   Research subsidies and bursaries in 1982, 1983[a,b]

		Humanities	Exact and natural sciences	Biology and medicine
Research grants	1982	16.805	43.118	48.148
	1983	17.499	43.823	50.644
Publication subsidies	1982	1,562	0.086	0.043
	1983	1.734	0.051	—
Personnel subsidies	1982	1.766	1.021	1.273
	1983	1.770	1.071	1.324
Stipendia for advanced	1982	1.279	0.853	2.030
investigators	1983	1.237	1.023	2.105
Stipendia for beginning	1982	2.100	1.722	2.365
investigators	1983	2.060	1.855	2.482
Acquisition of	1982	—	—	—
apparatus	1983	—	1.919	1.084
Other subsidies	1982	0.220	0.346	0.442
	1983	0.183	0.355	0.433
National research programs[c]	1982	10.082	2.827	1.451
	1983	8.553	20.008	1.203
Totals	1982	33.814	49.973	55.752
	1983	33.036	70.105	59.275
Grand total	1982	—	139.539	—
	1983	—	162.416	—

[a] In millions of francs.
[b] Source: **134**, 1982, p. 17; **134**, 1983, p. 17; **294**, July 1982, p. 66 (corresponding data for 1981).
[c] In 1983, the Federal Council approved a five-year grant of 15 million francs for a new National Research Program in microelectronics.

Table 73   Subventions requested by various organizations and those recommended by the Swiss Federal Science Council for the period 1984 to 1987[a,b]

	Requested	Recommended
National science fund	849	739
Federal public health office for research on cancer	26.25	26.08
Swiss society for natural science	12.00	11.05
Swiss society for the humanities	10.70	9.96
Swiss academy of medical sciences	1.60	1.60
Swiss academy of technical sciences	2.01	2.01
Total	901.56	789.70

[a] Source: **294**, supplement 30, 1983 ("Requêtes au Conseil fédéral . . . 1984–1987," p. 196).
[b] In millions of francs.

million francs for research grants and fellowships awarded to American scientists pursuing research in Switzerland. At that time 25 to 30 American scientists were doing research at the facilities in Meyrin (near Geneva) of the European Organization for Nuclear Research (CERN). Switzerland is a member and, as determined by the formula for membership payments, contributes 3.2 percent of the annual budget.

BURSARY-SUPPORTED PROGRAMS   In 1983, approximately 680 bursaries were granted by the Swiss National Science Foundation to senior Swiss investigators for support of their research projects in Switzerland (**134**, 1983). The number includes a few grants for attendance on scientific conferences, and 20 or so for various commissions, museums, and special organizations. In addition, 100 or so grants were made to support the studies pursued within 16 National Research Programs. Other bursaries, 310 in number, supported the studies of advanced students, some of whom went to another Swiss university or research facility. At least 165 of the total went to universities or research institutes in the USA. Also included in the group of 310 are bursaries in the category of international exchange (8 from the USA, 2 from Japan and 4 from Hungary). Under other subsidies of the National Science Foundation (Programs of International Exchange), the 1983 report (**134**, p. 157) mentions eleven exchanges with Great Britain, seven with Italy, seven with China, one with Bulgaria, three with Poland, three with the USSR, and seven with Hungary.

Other Science Organizations

THE SWISS SOCIETY FOR NATURAL SCIENCE   The organization that deserves special mention is the Swiss Society for Natural Science (*Schweizerische Naturforschende Gesellschaft* or SNG) which I have described elsewhere in detail (**219**, pp. 97–100). The Society is also mentioned as an important eighteenth century invention in a preceding section devoted to Swiss science and scientists of the eighteenth century (Chapter 7). The SNG does not have a limited membership of individuals, restricted to a relatively small number of distinguished scientists.

The SNG is also the principal medium through which scientific relations are maintained at the national level with foreign academies and foreign scientific societies. Its delegates represent officially the Swiss Federal Council in International Scientific Congresses and in the General Assemblies of the International Scientific Unions. The Federal Government reimburses the SNG for its expenditures on membership fees paid by the Society to the many International Scientific Unions to which Switzerland adheres. In 1980 the Government paid to the SNG, 1.490 million francs as reimbursement for these and a variety of similar or related expenses (**341**, 1981, p. 420).

In 1828, the first topographic map of Switzerland was prepared under SNG auspices. Out of this enterprise grew the Swiss Federal Topographical Bureau. In 1860, the SNG created twelve recording meteorological stations, from which, in 1880, through a Federal Decree, the Swiss Central Institute for Meteorology

(*Schweizerische Meteorologische Zentralanstalt*) emerged. This replaced the weather bureau of the SNG. The Federal Institute for Hydrometry likewise originated in the SNG Commission on Hydrography and Hydrometry.

THE SWISS ACADEMY OF MEDICAL SCIENCES   Founded in 1943, the Academy was planned to serve as a national research council in the medical sciences—a service which was later assumed, almost in its entirety, by the Swiss National Science Foundation. For specific assignments, various commissions are appointed by the Senate of the Academy from among the medical and veterinary medical faculties, the Swiss Medical Association and other interested bodies. Many proposed projects that are of mutual interest to the Academy and the *Nationalfonds* have been studied by the Academy and reported upon to the Swiss National Science Foundation, for example:

(a) The possible establishment of a Swiss Institute for Virology.

(b) Grants from the *Nationalfonds* to assist young clinicians in completing their work for a degree; to assist, through travel grants, in attendance upon biomedical scientific congresses; and to expand stipendia support in the biomedical sciences.

(c) Subventioning of academic posts for recognized investigators.

(d) An inquiry into the experience of young Swiss physicians who receive postgraduate training in USA hospitals.

In the 1960s eleven study commissions were organized for the study of specific scientific questions. The commissions were dissolved on submission of final reports. These included a Commission on Isotopes which cooperated with several federal agencies in the study of problems of mutual interest, for example with the Federal Public Health Service and the Federal Commission on Radioactivity. Other commissions deserve mention, although the details of their studies will be omitted: the Commission for Brain Research, the Commission on Deficiency Diseases in Man and Domestic Animals, the Tuberculosis Commission, the Commission for Human Genetics, the Fluorine Commission, and the Commission for the Psychological Study of the Problems of Refugees. In general these study commissions may be regarded as workshop conferences for groups of scientists with research interest and experience in specific problems.

In the 1960s, and earlier, the Academy also served as a center for advice, on request, to government agencies and others on matters important to the public health. For this purpose, ad hoc advisory commissions were organized. For example, in response to a request from the Federal Public Health Service a commission of 13 members and several consultants in the 1940s and 1950s studied the question of vaccination against smallpox. Pursuant to its recommendations, the Federal Council ordered that all children between 14 and 18 months of age be vaccinated against smallpox and revaccinated between their twelfth and fifteenth years. The Federal Nutrition Commission sought the advice of the Academy on the permissibility of using antioxidants for the preservation of foodstuffs. Again, the task was referred to an advisory commission. Similar advisory commissions studied the fortification of milk with Vitamin D, milk hygiene in particular reference to bacteriological control measures against tuberculosis and brucellosis, specialized training in anesthesiology and in industrial medicine.

The Academy organized many symposia and conferences. Some of these were broadly based conventions for the presentation of a great variety of papers on medical topics. Others focused rather sharply on specific topics such as the adrenal cortex, fluorosis, radiation injury and protection, and chronic alcoholism. The major conferences were frequently international, being jointly organized by the Academy and a corresponding scientific body in another country. Thus, a scientific conference in Geneva in October 1945 involved participation by the French Academy of Medicine and the French Academy of Surgery. This marked the resumption of scientific relations between the two countries, long interrupted by World War II.

Many miscellaneous questions and projects have come before the Academy: the toxicology of insecticides and insecticide residues on foodstuffs; the use of antibiotics in the preservation of foodstuffs; the misuse of phenacetin-containing analgesics; the use of lead additives in motor fuel and the attendant dangers to health; and the status of Swiss medical school credentials in the USA. These are mentioned only as examples: there are many others.

A major post-war project was that of helping to restore the library services and scientific periodicals in neighbouring countries ravaged by the war. Periodicals and books were collected from various sources and freely donated. Book and instrument funds were established to assist medical faculties and institutions in specific countries where the need was clearly recognized.

The Academy also assisted in 1944–45 in founding a Swiss Center for the Collection of Type Strains of Microorganisms. With support from the World Health Organization (WHO) this developed into an international undertaking. It has been recognized since 1955 by the International Union of Microbiology.

In 1957 the Swiss Life Insurance and Annuity Institute celebrated its 100th anniversary by establishing a Jubilee Foundation for Public Health and Medical Research. The Institute provided the Foundation with capital of one million francs and a further 250,000 francs in 1962. The Academy names three members to the seven-man Governing Council of the Foundation. Grants have been made to hospitals for purchase of laboratory equipment and for research.

When the Academy was launched, it was the recipient of good financial support: three of the leading pharmaceutical houses dontated one million francs. With this as an example to others many more substantial gifts were received from a variety of sources. Free housing for the Academy was provided by the cantonal government of Basel-Stadt and the Wildt House Foundation.

THE FOUNDATION FOR BIOLOGICAL-MEDICAL STIPENDIA This Foundation was established in 1942 through capital donations totalling 229,000 francs contributed by the pharmaceutical industry, several firms in the food industry, the Swiss Medical

Association, and the Swiss Chemical Society. The Swiss National Science Foundation has made annual grants since 1962 with matching contributions from the industrial donors.[7] Stipendia are granted on a rather generous scale for study in Europe, USA and Canada.

OTHERS   There is little need to describe in detail the many other scientific and technological organizations that contribute to Swiss science and technology. Industry itself, where technology flourishes, is treated in other chapters (7, 9, 10, and 11.9) and, hence, is omitted from further consideration.

There is no need to even list the many other academies, societies, organizations and federal or cantonal offices and institutes that focus their activities on science and technology. Switzerland is fully as interested in all the sciences that are pursued in other industrialized and developed countries. Doubtless every country has a few specialized interests in some branches of science and technology that are of unique interest to that country. In some, we find organizations that focus their activities on deserts or arid lands; others are devoted to many aspects of petroleum and natural gas; others pertain to the mining and exploitation of mineral resources; and so forth. Switzerland has none of these unless it be a rather small institutional interest in peat and coal of which small deposits exist, or in exploring for oil and minerals that the super-optimists hope to find in Switzerland.

There are, however, a few institutes and organizations that may be lacking in most of the other industrialized or developed countries: A Swiss Tropical Institute in Basel with field operations in Tanzania (or Tanganyika); an Institute for Snow and Avalanche Research on the Weissfluhjoch (2670 meters above sea level) above Davos; and the High Alpine Research Station on the Jungfraujoch (international but nongovernmental).

Many institutes, experiment stations and other organizations are concerned with agriculture, dairying, viticulture and enology, garden crops, fruit and plant protection. Many schools exist for education and practical training in agriculture, horticulture, etc. In general they fall into the vocational training organizations, embraced by Article 34 ter, of the Federal Constitution. All of this is unusually important in Switzerland and is described in considerable detail in sections 11.8 and 11.14. See also ref. **219**, pp. 265—281.

International Organizations

Switzerland, though cautious in joining international organizations—obviously steering clear of any that might compromise her commitment to permanent neutrality—adheres to many international organizations in science and technology: most, if not all, of the International Scientific Unions; UNESCO; the World Heatlh Organization (WHO); the European Space Agency (ESA); the Food and Agriculture Organization (FAO); the International Atomic Energy Agency; CERN; the International Commission for Protection of the Border Waters Against Pollution; and many others.

Most of the international organizations to which Switzerland adheres are not based in Switzerland. It is appropriate to mention the High Alpine Research Station on the Jungfraujoch because it is located in Switzerland and is the only facility in Western Europe for high-altitude research, excluding the use of satellites. It is also unusual in that the Station, though international, is nongovernmental in structure. The membership consists of scientific organizations in Austria, Belgium, France, Germany, Switzerland, and the United Kingdom. It is described elsewhere in great detail (**219**, pp. 351–356).

For a small country, she is more active in the forefront of research in science and technology than might be expected: plasma physics, space research, nuclear research and particle physics, molecular biology, chemistry and pharmacology—all are mentioned as conspicuous examples of her activities on the leading edge of modern science.

Several international organizations devoted to applied research on a contract basis are actively represented in Switzerland. Those that I know best are the Batelle Memorial Institute in Geneva with a staff of over 400, including 160 university graduates. It is one of the four major research centres of Battelle Memorial Institute (Columbus, Ohio; Richland, Washington; Frankfurt, Germany; and Geneva, Switzerland). It includes six other specialized research facilities and 14 offices throughout the world, the number of employees totaling about 7400. Battelle at Geneva is known to operate currently on an annual budget of 50 million Swiss francs.

There is also the Stanford Research Institute, with a small office in Zurich. The staff solicits projects from various parts of Europe, the Middle East and Africa, and pursues the studies in the home laboratories in California, as well as in Zurich and other parts of Europe.

Finally, over 400 American companies have branch or affiliated operations in Switzerland. International Business Machines has an excellent laboratory, beautifully located in Rüschlikon near Zurich. The site is a magnificent hill overlooking Zürichsee. This laboratory, inaugurated in 1962, is devoted to pure research, but in the expectation that something of practical value to the company will emerge. All such findings are transmitted to industrial development laboratories of the Company for further study.

The head of the laboratory in Rüschlikon is a Swiss. The staff consists of 80 to 90 senior scientists (postdoctorates) and about 40 technicians and assistants. Studies are pursued in solid state physics, device technology, communications and computer science and other fields of interest. The scientists are drawn from Western Europe generally.

In the early 1980s, several other American companies had research facilities in Switzerland—principally for applied research of direct company interest, including RCA corporation and Varian Associates.

Research in science and technology has many different facets. We learn, for example, that an efficient oral vaccine against typhoid fever has been developed in Switzerland and that field tests in the Middle East establish its efficacy. By "genetic engineering," bacteria can now be used to manufacture human interferon, a discovery also reported from Switzerland. In joint USA-Swiss experiments conducted in Geneva, the successful cloning of mammals (mice) has been reported. These three achievements, exciting and promising as they are, require independent confirmation by others, like all scientific discoveries, before they gain acceptance by the world-wide community of scientists.

We mention also an achievement in science that will certainly be important to botanists and environmentalists. I refer to the publication of an atlas in two volumes and three languages that brings together descriptions of the Swiss flora as observations that have accumulated during 250 years. These descriptions, involving some 400,000 pieces of information, are currently dispersed in many publications, and in collections of universities and museums. The publication is described as an Atlas of Distribution of the Pteridophytes and Phanerograms in Switzerland.

In the field of applied science, considerable interest attaches to the role of Switzerland, more specifically of the firm of Sulzer Brother in Winterthur, in the manufacture and export, of artificial hip joints as prostheses for the diseased members that they replace. In 1980, the company manufactured over 50,000 total joint prostheses of which about 90 percent were exported. Work is also pursued by the company on the manufacture of other joint prostheses, especially of the elbow, finger, knee and hand joints.

The products of Wild-Heerbrugg should not be overlooked. Their microscopes, cameras for aerial photography, and other sophisticated optical instruments have gained international acclaim. Their research, leading to products wherein the highest precision and reliability are demanded has placed the company in a leading position world-wide.

International cooperation in science and in other activities that are compatible with world peace and harmony and not a potential threat to Switzerland's commitment to perpetual neutrality has long been dear to Swiss officialdom. In science, she is a member of many international scientific organizations to which reference is made earlier in this subsection. Of added interest is a five-year agreement between the Swiss *Nationalfonds* and the National Science Foundation of the USA, entered into in the early 1980s, to provide for close cooperation in general and in certain specific activities in particular: an increased exchange of scientists in the exact and natural sciences especially; the pursuit in common of research projects of mutual interest; and arrangement of work-table conferences on projects of interest to both parties.

The European Space Research Organization, in cooperation with NASA, proposes to investigate the effect of weightlessness on the growth of lymphocytes— white cells in the blood which contribute to defense of the body against foreign and infectious agents such as viruses and bacteria. The experiment is of importance to any program that envisages the long-time maintenance of astronauts in space. Other space-exploration programs, important in geology, hydrology and supervision of the earth's land and water resources, apparently by use of space satellites, have been planned.

LEGISLATION   On 1 August 1952, the Swiss National Science Foundation came into being as a disbursing agency of federal funds provided for the support of research. Although the foundation is extragovernmental, the Confederation has been represented from the beginning in the Foundation Council (*Stiftungsrat*) which serves as an intermediary between the Research Council (*Forschungsrat*) and the Federal Government. In 1984 the Confederation was represented by ten appointees and the cantons by three. The remaining nine members of the *Stiftungsrat* represented various cultural and economic institutions.

The Confederation, for years, has been contributiong to the support of research within the ETH and its annexed institutes. Likewise, federal subventions to the universities (since 1968) have helped to support research. Under the aegis of a number of scientific organizations (the Swiss National Science Foundation most conspicuously), a great many research programs have received federal support. But it was not until October, 1983, that a Federal law on research was enacted.

The law, based on Article 27 sexies of the Federal Constitution, first defines its purposes:

1. To promote scientific research and to support the application of the results.
2. To watch over the cooperation of research organs and, if necessary, to regulate the collaboration.
3. To assure the economic and efficient use of federal research funds.

The research organs are specified in Article 5:

(a) Institutions for the Promotion of Research:
   1. The Swiss National Science Foundation.
   2. The Swiss Natural Science Society, the Swiss Social Science Society, the Swiss Academy of Medical Sciences, and the Swiss Academy of Technical Sciences.
   3. Other scientific institutions recognized by the Federal Council.
(b) The organs for research within the universities:
   1. The Federal Institutes of Technology and their associated (annexed) institutes.
   2. The recipients of subventions pursuant to the Federal Law of 28 June 1968, concerning university promotion (assistance).
(c) The Federal Administration, insofar as:
   1. For the discharge of its responsibilities, it itself performs research.
   2. It commisions research, or directly supports or is concerned with further research measures.

The importance of the law resides in its recognition of the responsibility of the Federal Government to promote and support research. The respective responsibilities of government and of the recipients of its subventions for research are set forth in great detail in the 33 Articles that constitute the law.

Ammann and Einstein

As we think of Switzerland's contributions to advances in science and technology, it is appropriate to mention that in 1981 the Golden Anniversary of the opening of the spectacular and beautiful Bayonne bridge which joins New York to New Jersey was festively celebrated. The bridge was designed by Othmar H. Ammann, the renowned Swiss-American bridge builder. Among his many other achievements, Ammann designed the George Washington bridge which the Port Authority of New York/New Jersey also opened in 1931. Thirty-three years later, the Verrazano-Narrows bridge, designed by Ammann, was opened. The bridge spans the Narrows between Staten Island and Brooklyn and consists of a single span suspension of record length. In 1964, President Johnson conferred upon Ammann the National Medal of Science. He died ten months later. The Bayonne bridge in 1931 was the longest single-span steel-arch bridge in the world—1675 feet long—a record which it held for 46 years.

Ammann, born in Schaffhausen in 1879, lived in New York from 1904 until his death in 1965. Although a naturalized American, Switzerland never ceased to lay claim to Ammann. In February, 1979, Switzerland issued a commemorative 20-centime stamp in his honor.

If Ammann deserves special mention, as indeed he does, in engineering and technology, another Swiss, Albert Einstein (1879–1955), must be singled out as one of the world's greatest scientists of the century. Born in Ulm, Germany, he came to Switzerland after finishing his gymnasial studies in Munich and, at the age of $16\frac{1}{2}$, applied for admission to the Federal Institute of Technology in Zurich. Although he failed to pass the qualifying examination, the rector of the ETH advised the young Einstein to spend a year in the Cantonal School in Aarau in preparation for a second application to the ETH. Einstein was impressed by the liberal spirit that prevailed in the Aarau school, in sharp contrast to the rigid authoritarian system of education that he had known during six years of schooling in Germany. In 1896 he reapplied to the ETH, passed the entrance examinations and emerged four years later with mathematical physics as his recognized specialty. In that same year, 1900, he was admitted to Swiss citizenship and, in Bern, accepted a position in the Federal Office for Intellectual Property (Patent Office). The years that followed were characterized by remarkable intellectual activity as evidenced by four publications in 1905 in volumes 17 and 18 of the Annalen der Physik, and pertaining to the most fundamental problems in the physics of the universe. He was promptly recognized as the leading theoretical physicist of his time. At the age of 30 he was honored by the University of Geneva with the degree of *Doctor honoris causa*. In 1921 he received the Nobel prize in physics. If we omit the years from 1905 on, spent in Bern, Zurich, and Berlin we come finally to 1933—the year in which Hitler came to power. Einstein happened to be visiting the California Institute of Technology at the time, and realized that a return to Germany was out of the question. He accepted the offer of a professorship in the Institute for Advanced Studies at Princeton and remained there until his death in 1955. Although he became an American citizen in 1940 through naturalization, he maintained his Swiss citizenship to which he affectionately referred from time to time. As such, Einstein is claimed by Switzerland with almost as much determination and pride as if he had spent his entire life in Switzerland (**258**).

Acknowledgements

In 1978, the Union Bank of Switzerland published a booklet of 25 pages descriptive of the largest enterprises in Switzerland, *Die Grössten Unternehmen der Schweiz* (**102**). It presents the appropriate data for adequate statistical descriptions of the 100 largest industrial enterprises, the 50 largest commercial companies, the 25 largest transport and service undertakings, the 50 largest banks and the 30 largest insurance companies. I suspect that the Union Bank of Switzerland would gladly make copies available to interested individuals. A multi-author volume on research and technology in Switzerland, published in 1978, can also be recommended. The articles are mostly in German; a few are in French. It is a *Festschrift* in honour of Dr. Jakob Burckhardt, the then President of the Council of the Federal Institutes of Technology (**135**). In 1974 the Swiss Office for the Development of Trade (Lausanne) published a small work by Credit Suisse which describes concisely much of interest about Switzerland, Switzerland and its Industries (**361**). Copies are also available in French, German and Spanish. Another work in English (**112**) is excellent though largely out of date—published in 1950. Of greatest importance to those with enough curiosity about Swiss science and technology are the authoritative and informative articles (in English) by Professors Hugo Aebi (**3**) and A. P. Speiser (**336**) in *Modern Switzerland* (**245**). I have deliberately avoided any mention in detail of substantive aspects of Swiss science and technology—in other words, an account of the specific contributions by Swiss scholars and engineers to the ever-expanding body of knowledge in science and technology. However, personal interest and background in the biomedical sciences demand a single exception. This is the Swiss discovery of a fungus in soil samples that produces the remarkable substance, cyclosporine, which possesses the unique property of greatly reducing, if not preventing, the ability of the body's immune defense system to reject a foreign tissue implant, such as a transplanted heart, kidney or liver. The substance was isolated by a team of microbiologists in the laboratories of Sandoz A. G. in Basel. Its efficacy, as reported by surgeons, is such that cyclosporine must be included with antibiotics as possibly the most important of all the substances added to the medical armamentarium in the twentieth century.

Notes and Comments

1. The net income generated by tourism is of great importance but the actual revenue, corrected for expenditures by Swiss on holiday in foreign countries, is rich in uncertainties and inevitable "guesstimates" and, hence, lacking in the precision needed if we were to attempt a meaningful comparison with the income from world trade in tangible products.

2. To be more accurate in translation, this should be described as "The Swiss National Fund for the Promotion of Scientific Research."

3. Federal Councillor Kobelt.

4. The Federal Government grants to the *Nationalfonds* for the early 1980s amounted to 139.7 million francs for 1980, 134.1 million for 1981, 140.4 million for 1982 and 146.7 million for 1983. In addition, the Swiss Institute (in Lausanne) for Experimental Research on Cancer received 13.3 million francs to support research from 1980 to 1983 on the causes and action mechanisms of cancer. A number of regional centers for clinical studies on cancer received a total of 7.5 million francs for the same period. An International Cancer Research Center in Lyon received a four-year grant of 600,000 francs. Possible adherence to the center will be considered at a later date.

Ten years earlier, Parliament approved grants to the *Nationalfonds* at about one-half of the early 1980 levels, viz 70 million francs for 1970, with annual increases of five million francs to a level of 90 million for 1974. Subject to proof of need and availability of funds, Parliament also promised additional appropriations of ten million francs per year for 1972, 1973 and 1974.

5. Because science (*Wissenschaft*) embraces scholarship generally, the total allocation includes grants to universities.

6. A variety of measures designed to promote technological development and education. For example: to assist the lagging watch industry by encouraging and assisting its expansion into the field of electronics, research on materials, computer-supported fine-technical manufacturing techniques for production of parts of the electronic watch; further development of information research in the technical scientific area and accelerated search of patent literature; research in building-construction technology, insulation materials, heating technology, etc. (**59**).

7. The principal supporter of this foundation is now the Swiss National Science Foundation.

11.16. LAW AND ORDER

The Swiss Judicial System

Switzerland is a federal State, which means that the 26 sovereign cantons have transferred certain of their powers to the Federal Government. In general, the Federal Government legislates and the cantons administer and execute the laws. In greater detail, the Federal Government legislates in civil and criminal law, in much of the economy, in military affairs and external relations with other States. The Federal Constitution is extremely fluid, and in the past 100 years (to 1975) has undergone 86 partial revisions, of which one-third apply to transfer of cantonal powers to the Federal Government—all of this amid unending discussion and slow progress toward a total revision.

The cantons exercise a great deal of power in financing, planning, governing, or administering federal law. They can, and frequently do, delegate some of these powers to the communes (local government authorities). Enforcement of federal legislation by the cantons is not always observed. One is tempted to conclude that, in some cases, a given law is ignored because of cantonal disapproval or a lack of adequate means for enforcement.

Unlike the USA judicial system, federal courts are not patterned after a parallel or dual system of cantonal courts. The Swiss system is pyramidal: the administrative, civil and criminal courts of first and second instance are cantonal, and the Federal Tribunal, located in Lausanne, is the court of last resort. It is at the top of the pyramid. Uniformity in the execution of federal laws is highly desirable and to strive for its attainment, the Federal Tribunal has the power to decide on appeals from cantonal courts.

Civil and criminal courts are to be found in each of the cantons. Administrative tribunals have also been instituted by most of the cantons. While almost all civil and criminal law is federal, most of the administrative and tax law is cantonal. As a rule, commercial and labor law is federal. Apart from international treaties, procedural law is exclusively cantonal.

Civil lawsuits in most cantons must be preceded by a conciliation procedure before a justice of the peace who may also adjudicate minor cases. As the court of first instance, there is either a single judge or a district court usually consisting of a lawyer-president and several lay members. Appeals are possible in certain categories of cases wherein errors of fact or law are alleged. In certain other cases only a petition of nullity is admissible. In such cases questions of fact may not be introduced. In the major cantons the court of second instance is a professional tribunal, of which the members are elected in most cantons by the people. It is called a Cantonal or Superior Court. Appeals and petitions for nullity (sometimes directed against its own appeal decisions) are within the powers of these courts which sometimes also function as courts of first instance.

In criminal investigations, several authorities with different functions are involved. Most conspicuous are the public prosecutor, who is a career civil servant with power to initiate the formal public accusation or to carry out the pretrial investigation, and the investigating judge who is not a civil servant and has a measure of independence. In felonies or certain other cases he decides whether a charge shall be entered. Misdemeanors such as traffic offences are usually dealt with by the communes, which can inflict fines. But if more than a misdemeanor is involved, the case must be brought before the criminal court of first instance which is usually a district court. The Cantonal or Superior Court becomes involved if there is an appeal, a petition for nullity or a petition for cassation (annulment, abrogation or reversal of a legal judgment). Jury trials have an erratic record and are exceptional. They are gradually disappearing.

As for administrative law, more and more cantons have introduced Administrative Tribunals for controversies involving cantonal administrative law. In some cantons, the Cantonal Court exercises such a function, or the tribunal may include judges from the Cantonal Court, or it may be independent of the Cantonal Court. Sometimes a tribunal may exercise the power of judicial review and may declare invalid any cantonal statutes that appear to violate the cantonal consti- tution. But this is exceptional because, in general, the courts do not have such power. Cantonal Courts may refuse to apply cantonal statutes or ordinances if in violation of federal law but not because they violate cantonal law. Where administrative courts do not exist, a petition to the executive branch is the rule.

A few cantons have commercial courts for disputes pertinent to commercial undertakings. About half of them have a labor or industrial court to handle employer/employee disputes (see also section 11.7 on industrial peace).

The Federal Tribunal

The highest Swiss Court is the Federal Tribunal. Located in Lausanne, it consists of 26 to 30 full members and 12 to 15 substitute justices. Elections are made by the Federal Assembly for terms of six years. Re-election is possible and usual. Although every Swiss citizen can be a candidate, the federal justices who are elected are either cantonal judges or law professors or federal parliamentarians. The Tribunal, in its composition, reflects reasonably well the several languages, the regions, the confessions and the major political parties in respect to their quantitative distribution in Switzerland. The Tribunal sits in various divisions and chambers—

some seven or eight in number—constitutional and administrative law, civil law, bankruptcy and seizure, the Accusation Chamber, the Criminal Chamber, the Federal Criminal Court and the Criminal Cassation Chamber. There is also the Federal Insurance Tribunal for social security questions. It sits in Lucerne and, though an independent division, it is organizationally a part of the Federal Tribunal. In addition, we find at the federal level about 20 special tribunals concerned with administrative law. They are called Appeal Commissions and deal with such specialized areas as tolls, alcohol, grain, the watch industry, and nationalization indemnities. Among the busiest are the Military Tribunals which must handle the problems incident to traffic accidents by soldiers, and the unsolved problem of the conscientious objector.

In 1980 the Federal Tribunal acted on 474 civil cases, 605 penal code violations, 1298 interpretations of public law, 500 of administrative law, and 118 cases of debts and bankruptcies—a grand total of 2995 as compared with 1846 in 1960, 2288 in 1950, 1595 per year in 1926–30, and 1056 per year in 1901–05 (**341**, 1951, p. 502; 1981, p. 530).

The Federal Assembly

A certain division of responsibility between the Federal Assembly (legislative) and the Federal Tribunal requires description. The Federal Assembly decides on the constitutionality of federal statutes, the Federal Tribunal being prevented by the Federal Constitution from exercising such judicial review. The Assembly also decides upon the compatibility of cantonal constitutions with federal law, and upon the validity of federal initiatives. The Federal Tribunal, however, decides on conflicts of competence between federal and cantonal authorities or between two or more cantons, but not on disputes between various federal organs (e.g. between the executive and the legislature). The Federal Tribunal adjudicates most constitutional complaints. Every citizen whose constitutional rights have been violated by any cantonal act may raise a constitutional complaint with the Federal Tribunal: fundamental rights and freedoms, violations of the guaranty of property or the freedom of commerce and industry, encroachments upon political voting rights, the referendum or initiative, and, indeed, any inequality. Any interpretation of cantonal law which is judged to be arbitrary or capricious amounts to an inequality before the law. The constitutional complaint may be lodged only against cantonal acts not against federal acts—the adjudicational province of the Federal Assembly.

In civil and criminal matters, almost all applicable substantive law is federal, not cantonal. Administrative law is sometimes predominantly federal and sometimes predominantly cantonal. Procedural law is within the power of the cantons, so that the civil, criminal and administrative proceedings, the execution of penal sentences and the organizational structure of the courts may vary from canton to canton.

As a result of certain minimal procedural standards derived from the Federal Constitution and imposed on the cantons by the Federal Tribunal, the cantonal courts must respect the right to be heard. In criminal proceedings the accused has the right to prove his innocence with all reasonable means. In administrative proceedings, the right of the individual to be heard is similarly protected.

While important parts of the civil law have been codified, there is much that has not been codified although it exists as written statutory law. The essence of cantonal legislation consists of statutes dealing with specific subjects within the power of the cantons. Important parts of the Swiss law system are formed, above all, by case law. The relationship between written and unwritten law is set forth in Article I of the Swiss Civil Law Code:

1. Statutory law is applicable to all legal questions to which it refers either in the text or according to the interpretation.

2. If no rule can be deduced from the statute, the judge shall apply customary law and, if there is no such customary law, he shall decide in accordance with the rule which he would set up for himself if he were the legislator.

3. In so deciding he follows the approved teaching and tradition.

Although precedents are not binding, they are of great importance in the daily routine of the attorney, the administration and the courts. The Federal Tribunal regularly invokes its own precedents and if, exceptionally, it deviates from them, it explains such a decision thoroughly and at some length.*

Trial by Jury

In Zurich, a jury is chosen for a six-year period, the selection being made by the Municipal Council (*Gemeinderat*) or by direct popular vote. On the basis of population of the community, the cantonal government (*Regierungsrat*) determines the number of jurymen to be chosen for a given community. In the canton as a whole, 1134 persons of whom 16 percent were women, were chosen for the six-year period, 1 January 1978 to 31 December 1983. The names are recorded on a master list from which 28 will be drawn for a stated session. Both the defense and the prosecution have the right to challenge four of the 28 without giving any reasons. After further challenges, nine will be selected to serve as the jury for that particular session. In addition to the jury, the court consists of a president (a superior judge) and two local judges who practice full or part time. Before the proceedings begin, only the president will know the case to be tried. The members of the jury must vow that they will discuss the case with no one and the voting will be kept secret. While the views of the president and the other judges certainly influence a jury inexperienced in law, a typical juryman respects his own independence and his ability to form his own judgment. For agreement on the question of guilt of the accused, a majority of eight votes is necessary. On the other questions, for example that of punishment, a simple majority is sufficient. It should be noted that the nine

---

* In all of the above on the organization and operation of the Swiss law system I have drawn heavily upon the informative and authoritative article by Luzius Wildhaber (**388**) which should be consulted for a more extensive description.

lay members of the court and the three judges—12 persons in all—participate in the voting.

Jury trials are infrequent in Switzerland, and virtually occur only in Geneva and Zurich. They are decreasing in number and may disappear from the scene in a few years.

International Relations and the Law

The law of 1892 regarding help to other States in search of information on various misdemeanours or crimes committed by their citizens (*Rechtshilfegesetz*) has long been in need of revision. Six European agreements pertaining to harmonization of laws in this area were overdue for ratification by Switzerland. Tax evasion, the flight of foreign money to Switzerland, alleged criminal activities of various kinds, and other acts that are illegal in a foreign country constitute the problems that face the Swiss when help from the Federal Government is sought in cases involving foreigners, whether resident in Switzerland or residing in their home country.

In 1977 there was the case of Peter Menten, a Dutch citizen in Switzerland, charged by the Netherlands government with war crimes. Switzerland extradited him at Holland's request, even though a strict enforcement of the law would not have permitted extradition because of the statute of limitations. This suggests that an amendment to this portion of the law might be forthcoming. Of even greater concern to other States is Swiss bank secrecy and the flight of clean or dirty money to Swiss banks where the funds and the depositor enjoy protection from scrutiny.

For Switzerland to be of any help to an inquiring government requesting information about one of its nationals or seeking his extradition, the questionable act, whatever it be, must be punishable according to the laws of both countries. Also no Swiss citizen can be extradited to another country without his consent. One differentiates between the "greater" cases such as extradition of persons and those of "lesser significance" such as tax avoidance and exchange of information and documents. In some instances *Rechtshilfe* is routinely denied: for example, if the proceedings would be a violation of the Human Rights Convention or if the person's race, religion, or political affiliation is the point at issue. The political exceptions, however, are not applicable if the act is that of a terrorist or a war criminal.

Simple tax evasion in Switzerland is considered as a *Kavalierdelikt*—a gentle-manly offence. But if fraud is involved and tax documents are falsified the offender can be severely punished. And so it follows that if a foreign country seeks *Rechtshilfe* in cases involving tax fraud, the offence would be regarded as a crime in both countries. The problem, heavily debated in Parliament, resulted in a compromise presumably acceptable to all, except, possibly, the Social Democrats.

Rechtshilfe is assured if tax fraud and falsification of documents occur, but not if ordinary holding back on tax payments (*Steuerhinterziehung*) is the issue. The compromise also makes it clear that no one will be extradited for offences of "lesser significance."

Parliament appears also to have been in agreement on the following:

1. In cases of war criminals and acts of terrorism, where extradition is sought, the Statute of Limitations will no longer apply.

2. Terrorists, those who seize hostages, and other persons engaged in acts of violence should, in future, be punished or extradited. This decision permits ratification of the corresponding Europa Council Agreement. See p. 712.

3. The private or secret sphere in human affairs must be exactly defined.

Disorder and Illegalities

A random sampling of a great variety of acts in Switzerland that constitute offences against the laws of the country follows. Qualitatively, they are no different from the illegalities that are reported *ad nauseam* by the public information media of many countries: robbery; murder; beatings; mugging; possession, sale and transport of narcotics; extortion; fraud; arson; kidnapping; obscene acts; espionage, etc. If there are any categories of illegal acts that are committed only in Switzerland, they must be few in number: I can recall only one, viz. the stealing of Chaplin's body from its Swiss grave on 1 March 1978, for which a young Polish refugee was convicted and sentenced to $4\frac{1}{2}$ years imprisonment. Illegal acts by and against the Swiss banks and attempted violations of the bank-secrecy laws, with one exception, are excluded from all that follows: they have been discussed elsewhere (see section 11.12 on Banking).

1. Armed robbery of an employee in Regensdorf who was carrying the day's cash receipts to the night depository of a bank. In Effretikon on the same day, a branch of Denner's stores was robbed by two armed men who forced the three employees into the air shelter.

2. A well-known robber and escape-artist, Walter Sturm, who escaped many times from different prisons is again in prison (1982). Several escapes were accompanied by a serious beating of, and injury to, a prison guard. Sturm was commonly known as the *Ausbrecherkönig* (King of Prison Escapers).

3. The brutal robbery of an 87-year-old woman in her home in Solothurn Canton by two young thugs, 20 and 18 years of age respectively. They were caught in the Vorarlberg (Austria) and extradited to Switzerland.

4. Taking advantage of the bank-secrecy laws, and knowing of wealthy French citizens who were depositing money in a Swiss trust company in violation of French law, several employees of the trust company blackmailed at least one of the French clients. They demanded one million French francs as the price of silence. The victim was told to pay 500,000 francs and, later, another 400,000, but he reported the extortion attempt to the police who arrested the four principals. To avoid publishing the names of the French client(s) and thereby violating the bank-secrecy law, the trial was held behind closed doors. Two of the accused were sentenced to $5\frac{1}{2}$ years in prison and two others to two years each. Fines were also imposed (see also section on Swiss Bank Secrecy in 11.12).

5. A 32-year-old Russian civil servant, on a diplomatic mission, was found dead in his hotel room in Aarau. The police reported the death as a suicide. Russia

claimed, after a post-mortem investigation in Moscow, that the victim had been drugged and killed by western intelligence agents who had tried to enlist him as a counterspy.

6. Throwing of Molotov cocktails against a former military installation in Zurich used for weapon storage. The damage was negligible.

7. Attempted murder by a hired killer of a wealthy woman whose 33-year-old son was heavily in debt. The first attempt was frustrated by a barking dog. A second attempt was planned but came to naught when the police learned of the plot.

8. A former bank director who fraudulently manipulated the books of his two finance companies in Zurich in 1974 and thereby swindled his 7000 clients of millions of francs in their savings accounts. He was apprehended in Panama and returned to Zurich. The Zurich Superior Court ordered a repayment of 6.3 million francs, the payment of a fine, court costs totalling 7000 francs and imprisonment for $4\frac{1}{2}$ years.

9. The widely publicized Cornfeld case came to trial in Geneva in the fall of 1979. The charges arose from the collapse of his I.O.S. (International Overseas Services) mutual-fund empire. Cornfeld was head of I.O.S. until control of the collapsing company was taken over by Robert Vesco, the fugitive American financier. The principal charge was the sale in 1969 by Cornfeld and 490 other insiders of 3.9 million shares of I.O.S. Ltd. (the parent company) at $10 each to persons employed by I.O.S. The sale was alleged to be fraudulent because Cornfeld, it was claimed, knew the company was in a bad situation which was rapidly worsening. The sale to employees coincided with a public offering and sale of another 5.6 million shares. After a rapid climb to $20 per share, the stock quickly declined in value. Vesco's takeover of the company was soon followed by Vesco's looting of I.O.S. to the extent of 200 million dollars. The I.O.S. stock became worthless and the company was liquidated. Arrested in May 1973, Cornfeld was released in 1974 on a bail of five million francs. At its high point, the fund managed 2.2 billion dollars of its investors. Allegedly, the top executives, Cornfeld and Vesco among them, purchased stock at preferential prices and sold out at $20 per share, thus precipitating collapse of the company. Cornfeld faced a maximum sentence, if convicted, of 10 years in prison. Vesco fled with his millions and attempts of the USA government to have him extradited from Puerto Rico have failed.

10. In an extraordinary case of mail fraud, a couple from the USA, resident in Zurich for ten years or more, submitted 72 income-tax returns carrying false and fictitious names, and thereby obtained from the Internal Revenue Service more than $500,000 during the years 1970 through 1978. According to an indictment issued by a federal grand jury, the couple received through the mails 131 government cheques totalling $501,443. Neither of the defendants, charged with fraud, worked in the United States during the period in question.

11. In still another case of fraud, a Swiss court ruled that a certain European journalist and film producer be extradited from the United States to Switzerland on charges of business fraud involving millions of dollars. Although the defendant claimed that the extradition demand was politically based rather than relevant to a

criminal offence, the charges suggest that the offence was indubitably criminal. The defendant, a Swiss citizen, induced a business associate to guarantee large loans to finance television films. The films, so it was charged, were never made and the defendant, furthermore, impersonated a bank official to authorize the withdrawal of substantial funds.

12. "Whoever, in public, performs an obscene act shall be punished by imprisonment or a fine": so reads Article 203 of the Swiss Penal Code. A man and woman found guilty of bathing in the nude in the presence of children (also naked) and of sunbathing in the nude on a beach at Vidy (Lake Geneva) were acquitted by the Cassation Court in Vaud: "complete nakedness, according to present-day concepts, is no longer an obscenity in every case."

13. Switzerland has experienced many cases of espionage on behalf of the Soviet Union. Russian diplomats have rarely been declared *personal non grata* because of espionage. Smaller "fry" are used by the Soviet Union for such purposes, especially diplomatic representatives of Czechoslovakia. From time to time, one or more Czechs in the diplomatic corps are ordered to pack their bags and leave the country immediately because of espionage. Occasionally a Swiss citizen is found guilty of spying for a foreign power and is severely punished. Perhaps the most heavily publicized case involving a Swiss was that of Brigadier J. Louis Jeanmaire. As a high-ranking army officer Jeanmaire had access to top secret information which he was charged with transmitting to the Soviet Union. The trial was held behind closed doors, Jeanmaire was found guilty as charged and was sentenced to 18 years imprisonment. Much has been written about the case, for it involved a man of prominence who, had he behaved himself, would have been eligible for honorable retirement in another year or two.

14. Theft of motor vehicles. In 1981, 67,000 "Velos" or "Mopeds" were stolen in Switzerland—approximately 183 per day—according to the West-Swiss Office of Insurance Information. Over 21 million francs were claimed from the insurance companies in compensation for these losses.

15. In May 1979, the Spanish Embassy in Bern was severely damaged by a bomb explosion. Two terrorist groups claimed responsibility but the police question the credibility of the reports.

16. Arson. A fire in the airplane factory at Stans destroyed four planes and caused a loss of over one million francs in damage to the building and destruction of the planes. A group claiming responsibility for the act reported they were trying to draw public attention to the export of weapons, it being further claimed that these civilian planes are filled with weaponry on arrival in South America and subsequently used against the civilian population (see also section 11.20).

17. In early 1983, two Swiss citizens, having been found guilty of providing a member of the terrorist "Red Army Fraction" with almost 90 kg of explosives, including equipment and a variety of weapons, were sentenced to seven years imprisonment.

18. In September 1982, the Polish Embassy in Bern was seized by four gunmen, identified as Poles, who threatened to blow up the Embassy unless Poland

terminated martial law, freed all political prisoners and ended the repression of the Polish people. After three days of negotiations, a special Swiss police squad stormed the Embassy, captured the gunmen and freed the hostages (including five Polish diplomats). Not a shot was fired. Tear gas was used in the attack, after blowing down the door with explosives.

Discontent

Demonstrations in Switzerland by groups of people concerned about something or other are not new. In the 1960s they were relatively peaceful,[1] as were most of the student demonstrations in the USA. What is new about the Swiss demonstrations of the early 1980s is the resort to violence, if not terrorism, by some of the demonstrators.

To be specific, we must remind ourselves of the opera-house precipitated demonstration of 30 May 1980 on Zurich's Bahnhofstrasse, and the attendant massive property damage. Other similar demonstrations occurred in the weeks and months that followed. The police, present in considerable numbers, used water hoses, truncheons, and tear gas against the demonstrators.

Demonstrations, stressful, noisy, and frequently threatening to erupt into something worse were experienced in Bern, Basel, Lausanne, and other towns in Switzerland. Nothing can be gained by reviewing the particular incidents that allegedly triggered the various demonstrations, nor do we know for a certainty whether they were centrally organized and directed or, to the contrary, quite spontaneous. If the latter were the case we must assume that one or more serious causes of unrest were surfacing throughout the country.

Who were the "troublemakers"? The media and the public authorities seemed always to imply that the demonstrators were young. They were on the streets because they had no other place to go. They demonstrated against this or that because of the misdeeds and selfishness of the older generation, which contributed to the craziness, the distortion in values, and the social instability of the world in which the younger generation was forced to live. Somewhat surprising are the results of a study of 2488 participants questioned by the Zurich police in the nine-month period following the riotous demonstration of 30 May 1980. There were many other demonstrations in that nine-month period. Table 74 presents the results of the study. If that data be accepted at face value, they would shatter the widely held belief that only young people were involved.[2] The rumour that the trouble-makers were mostly foreigners is also without any foundation in fact, although it may be true that at the center of things was a hard core of experienced rioters or revolutionaries from other countries. This may be so but it has never been proven to be true.

In Zurich, Bern and elsewhere there were insistent demands among the demonstrators for a house or a meeting place where they would be sheltered from the police and could enjoy an autonomy that would permit them to entertain themselves as they alone might wish. The authorities in Zurich provided a youth center on the Limmatstrasse, and Bern made available the Reithalle for the same

Table 74   The Zurich demonstrators in 1980[a]

A. Age Groups	
Adults: 1450 men; 375 women	1825
Youths: 16 years of age to 25,[b] 479 men; 173 women	652
Children: under 16 years	11
Total	2488
B. Swiss Citizens, According to Residence	
City of Zurich	1153
Canton of Zurich	627
Rest of Switzerland	383
No fixed place of residence	45
Total	2208
C. Foreigners, According to Residence	
City of Zurich	79
Canton of Zurich	50
Rest of Switzerland	33
Other countries	118
Total	280

[a] Source: **266**, 21–22 February 1981.
[b] 25 is assumed.

purpose and under similar conditions.[3] In Basel and in Zug, houses standing empty were taken over by the *Unzufriedenen* (the discontented ones). In Lucerne, the empty Hotel Einhorn, owned by one of the big banks, was occupied by a group of young demonstrators.

The Zurich youth center was opened on 25 April 1981, but for many months it was the focus of discord between the occupants and the police. Many citizens strongly objected to the cave-in by the authorities when faced with continuing riots and violence: force rather than yielding to the demonstrators' demands was called for, so we were told. Others complained that the city authorities and the police were much too brusque—even stupidly so—in handling the outbreaks. Zurich's political parties carried on a war of nerves. The "solution" displeased everyone, including the demonstrators, the authorities and the ordinary citizens. The occupants of the center were incensed by the failure of the authorities to grant the total autonomy they desired. The police raided the center on a number of occasions, complaining of accumulated filth, gross untidiness, numerous violations of the narcotics laws, housing of stolen property, presence of drug peddlers, trade in hashish and hard drugs, and use of the center by terrorists and 20 or so foreigners—possibly a spill-over from Zurich's overcrowded youth hostel. The ordinary citizen, proud of the good behaviour of the Zurchers, of the great reputation of the city as a clean, orderly and well-managed center for financial services and the transaction of business, was totally unprepared for the series of violent demonstrations against authority. The image of the city suffered to an incalculable degree and the physical damage and related costs—a serious concern—amounted to many millions of francs.

Did unemployment play a role? Probably not. Of the total working population, of Switzerland, only 6255, an average figure, were unemployed in 1980 (cf. Table 27 in section 11.7). Of these, about 27 percent were less than 25 years of age—perhaps 1700 in all. Between 25 and 50 years of age, about 53 percent of the unemployed were to be found—possibly 3300 in all. Only a fraction of these would be residents of the cities and towns that suffered such violence, and only a fraction of the fraction would have been in the demonstrations.

Local governments, cantonal authorities, and the Federal Government became involved in seeking solutions. The Federal Government proposed credits to support work by youths outside of school hours. Money would be made available to associations of youth, organizations and movements wherein the chief purpose was development of young people and their responsibility to society. Specifically, payments were promised to the Swiss Work Organization of Youth Associations and to other organizations that have the same purpose. The conditions for support were spelled out: A resident organization must be:

a. All Swiss or super regional;
b. Able to carry part of the financial load;
c. If possible, in receipt of cantonal funds also.

The activities to be supported were described as sports, games, health and social activities; cultural education; political education; and international concerns of an appropriate kind (**73**, III, pp. 181–182, 29 September 1981).

The causes of the many demonstrations that broke out from time to time during 18 months or longer were many, and the specific incidents that triggered each demonstration were just as numerous and just as varied. Perhaps a common denominator is to be found in expenditures by the older generation—the establishment, if you will—that was regarded as selfish and wasteful when viewed in the light of the needs of the young—principally youth centers where, collectively, they could live their own lives, sheltered from the police and free of the restraints imposed by the stiffness, rigidity and conservatism of the Swiss social order.

But there were many other causes, sometimes insidious and frequently unyielding. There was and still is the problem of housing, extremely critical for those young people who were determined to leave the parental home but, usually, totally unable to find a decent room that they could afford to rent in any of the cities. And why did they choose to leave home: an honest and understandable urge to be independent, to escape the all too-loving clutches of benevolent parents, to get away from the quarreling, the in-fighting, and the hostile atmosphere of a broken home? Indeed, all this happens—not only in Switzerland but in other countries. Equally insidious, and not always appreciated, is the damage done to a citizenry, especially to the young, by the questionable pursuit of material things as an end in itself—

money and whatever money will buy. Has Switzerland forgotten the spiritual values that are the bedrock of a solid, peaceful and enduring society? Dissatisfaction with the world about them, a determination to right the wrongs, and to reconstruct the social order from its very foundations are a common manifestation among the young—a part of the complex business of growing up. The violent "hell-raising" that broke out was an infection that intruded itself and rapidly spread from a few "carriers" to the excited and semi-hysterical members of the mob. In Zurich, a street sign read "Turn the State into cucumber salad." Many were immune and did not join in the violence.

Federal Councillor Ritschard interviewed seven or eight who were seized by the police after the demonstration of 30 May 1980. He agreed that there were wrongs that should be righted, imperfections and injustices in the social order that call for correction, and that peaceful demonstrations by concerned citizens cannot be condemned or disallowed. But, he added, society cannot condone the violence and the damage to people and to property that was so conspicuous in the demonstration. Participation in such violence achieves no good and weakens enormously the cause of the *Unzufriedenen*.

Not everyone regards the rioters with even an iota of tolerance. There are many who look upon the riotous youngsters as a spoiled, bored, undisciplined aggregation of "brats" who need to be "roughed-up" and whose violence must be answered with equal violence—truncheons, water cannon, imprisonment and forced labor.

A serious and wide-ranging study funded by the Swiss National Science Foundation (*Nationalfond*) was initiated in 1979 by the *Institut für Praxisorientierte Sozialforschung* and continued through 1982. In the spring of 1980, 1076 young people—18 to 26 years of age, in the German-speaking part of Switzerland, were interviewed, each for about an hour, using a battery of 83 questions.[4] Of 1076 responses to a question about the use of free-time, only 6 individuals (0.6 percent) stated they were dissatisfied with things as they are. Five percent were not very satisfied. In general, quite satisfied were 43 percent, and fully satisfied with their use of free time, about 50 percent of those who were questioned.

Related to opinions on free-time were attitudes toward work. Of apprentices and full-time workers embraced by the study, 85 percent found their work to be "always very interesting" or "mostly interesting." The inquiry is conceived as a long-term study—addressed to various aspects of "Problems of Social Integration in Switzerland." It focuses on the broad question "How discontented are the youth?" (**266**, 13–14 December 1980).

A detailed account of the troubles in Zurich, from 30 May 1980 when it all started, to the end of May 1981, has been published (**266**, 30–31 May 1981). In summary, there were 60 confrontations between the demonstrators and the police, 3000 persons were arrested, 1000 convictions resulted with punishment by imprisonment and/or fines. Property damage was estimated at 15 million francs ($8 million). Apparently this is not the end of the story. In mid-1982 cases were still being tried. The legal and procedural difficulties are troublesome. Some years may have to elapse before the riots of the "discontented ones" fade into the past.[5]

If the young men of times past felt frustrated, bored, or experienced a life style that was very restrictive they had abundant opportunities to become mercenaries in the military service of a foreign Power. Happily, this kind of escape is no longer open to the young Swiss. One must not press the comparison too far but the youthful rebels of today are partly motivated by the same kind of a deep-seated urge for adventure and a radical change in the simple life style to which they may have become accustomed.

Terrorism

The heavily publicized activities of terrorists in Germany and Italy in the 1970s were not confined to these countries. Switzerland was caught in the middle. Shortly after the Schleyer murder, two German terrorists, Gabriele Kröcher and Christian Möller, were convicted in the killing of two Swiss border guards in the Jura and sentenced to imprisonment, Kröcher for 15 years, Möller for 11.

Why was the death penalty not ordered by the court? Article 65 of the Federal Constitution states quite clearly "No one may be sentenced to death for political crimes." The attorneys for the defense had only to convince the court that the accused were members of a gang that was politically oriented and politically motivated.

Although many Swiss are against the death penalty, there appears to be an articulate majority that calls for the death penalty in cases of murder, the violent seizure of hostages, and various other crimes. In October 1979, a member of the *Nationalrat* (the lower House of Parliament), called for introduction of the death penalty in the case of terrorists, using the argument that punishment must bear some meaningful relationship to the crime. He was supported by two other members of the House and opposed by fourteen others. However, an amendment of Article 65 to the effect that murder and the seizure of hostages by terrorists may not be regarded as political crimes was approved, in the sense that a constitutional initiative for such an amendment will be drafted and submitted for a vote by the people.

The death penalty appears in the Swiss military penal code and was carried out 17 times in World War II.

Scattered representative reports on incidents of terrorism in Switzerland follow:

1. The murder of a border guard and a cantonal police officer in Bottstein (Aargau) on 25 December 1980 by a German extremist.

2. Murder of the Turkish ambassador in Bern in February 1980.

3. A number of bombings by members of secret Armenian organizations in Geneva and elsewhere, directed against Turkish consulates and Swiss diplomatic posts. The Swiss maintain friendly relations with Turkey and this invites violent acts by the Armenian organizations. By mid-1981 a total of 17 murderous acts committed against Switzerland by Armenians had been recorded (**357**, 5 August 1981).

4. Support centers in the Ticino, established by two middle-school teachers and

several others, to assist Italian terrorists by procurement, concealment and transport of explosives and weapons. The Swiss group functioned more or less autonomously, but also in close association with Italian terrorists who, in Italy and in the Ticino, carried out acts of violence including kidnapping and theft of weapons and munitions from a military depot near Locarno. A number of the Italian terrorists captured in the Ticino have been extradited to Italy.

5. Theft of Swiss identity cards from the Federal Printing Office, used with other blank forms of official documents to prepare forged papers, essential for some activities of terrorists.

6. The Italian terrorist, Petra Krause, who was under arrest in Switzerland, and because of ill-health was held in detention for many months. Subject to a much-delayed trial in Switzerland and extradition proceedings, deportation to Italy is to be expected. Swiss justice is such that the accused may not be brought to trial if a doctor certifies that the health of the accused is too impaired to permit the heavy strain of a trial. But it is also so that the accused may not be tried in absentia. There are those who predicted in 1979 that the trial of Petra Krause may never be concluded.

7. Attempted bombing of an Israeli passenger plane at Zurich-Kloten airport in May 1980. The bomb was discovered before takeoff and was detonated in a special building. The affair was described as a second Würenlingen (Aargau) with reference to an explosive device which in February 1969 had been placed in a Swissair plane scheduled to fly to Tel Aviv. The plane exploded over Würenlingen. All 47 occupants of the plane were killed. The person arrested in the incident of 1980 was not a known terrorist. It is believed that he had been paid to smuggle "something" and needed the money for narcotics.

8. Attempted burning of Philips A.G. in Basel by "Commando Willi Stoll" as a protest against the extradition of a number of German terrorists to West Germany.

Arming of Swiss officers in the diplomatic service has been proposed frequently. The murder of a Swiss diplomat in San Salvador led to renewed discussion of the problem. Kidnapping, occupation of a diplomatic post, and murder of the officers have happened too often. Protection of an embassy or consulate and of the diplomats assigned to the post is recognized in international law as a responsibility of the government of the host country. Switzerland, in recognition of this, continues to refuse to arm her representatives in foreign countries. Diplomatic officers, on their own responsibility, are not denied the right to carry their own private weapons.

Terrorist bands in Europe are well organized and well equipped through an international network, with weapons, munitions, and the means to acquire or assemble explosive devices. Wherever they exist they constitute a threat to many institutions, to people in high positions, and to the peaceful conduct of affairs in democratic States. The seizure of passenger planes and the holding of passengers as hostages in order to acquire, as a ransom, large sums of money, the release of imprisoned terrorists, or transport of the principals to a "friendly" country, was a frequent occurrence for a decade or more.

Protection of a visiting head-of-state or of a high-ranking government official against the ever-present danger of a terrorist act became more and more of a burdensome responsibility of the local police. In Switzerland, the federal security police can call upon the cantonal police who, with the consent of the cantonal government, are able to help.

Beyond the security risk stemming from visits of persons, other security problems have arisen: protection of people and property against the terrorism and violence that characterize some demonstrations; the threatened occupation of nuclear power plants; and political confrontations in which an undisciplined mob may engage in acts of violence.

The security risk in any given instance cannot be well determined in advance. Should 100 or 1000 police be instantly available to restore order or to minimize the risk of a violent outbreak? To the present, Switzerland appears to be unwilling to increase substantially the size of her federal security police force. The cost is regarded by some as prohibitive. On political and social grounds, the parties to the left of center are opposed to the establishment of a large, and hence powerful, federal police system. A telling argument against the proposal has been the fear that it would be the first step in converting the nation into a police state with a progressive loss of personal freedoms and privileges. A referendum to authorize a federal security police force, equal to the task of protecting the people against the mounting outbreaks of violence and terrorism, came to a vote in December 1978 and was defeated.

The Federal Council has been urged by some members of parliament to draft whatever legislative measures may be necessary to provide help to the victims of violent crimes, for example, by reimbursement of expenses incurred in restoration of premises or property damaged, sabotaged, or burned during a violent terroristic act, as well as expenses entailed in medical and hospital services to injured persons.

Several initiatives to this end have been drafted by members of parliament. Much has been made of the fact that the punishment of the guilty person is frequently too light, especially when the victim may sustain injuries that cripple him for life. Sometimes the guilty one is never apprehended—he cannot be found—or he is so destitute that a fine large enough to cover a substantial part of the loss sustained by the victim is out of the question. Apparently the existing private institutions in Switzerland such as Pro Infirmis and *Rechtsdienst für Behinderte* (in Zurich) have neither the experience nor the means to help financially the victims of violent crimes. A special fund to assist the victims has also been proposed. The existing insurance programs that operate under a broadly conceived policy, appropriate to a social State, are not sufficient to provide adequate protection, if any, for the victims of violent crimes. The issue seems to reduce itself to the question whether the help which is clearly needed should be provided by the State or by private sources. There is enough public concern over the problem that a solution will certainly be found, very probably as a program that recognizes the responsibility of government itself in providing appropriate financial aid.

In several European States terrorists have received little punishment for their misdeeds if they claimed they were politically motivated and inspired by a deep concern over human rights. The Council of Europe, disturbed over the spread of terrorism in Europe, prepared an agreement whereby a terrorist on conviction in a signatory country must be extradited or punished in the country of his arrest and conviction. Switzerland signed the Agreement in 1977 but five more years had to elapse before the Federal Council requested Parliament to ratify the document. Haste is seldom evident in Switzerland's decision-making procedures wherein the parliamentary machinery grinds slowly but surely.

Miscellaneous

RIGHTS OF ATTORNEYS   (a) *Is an attorney free to express publicly his personal opinions?* The Superior Court of the Canton of Uri censured an attorney in Erstfeld because he had stated in a letter to the press that the proportion of decisions of the court, subsequently reversed or corrected (*Durchfallquote*) by the Federal Court was very high. The Superior Court of Uri claimed that the attorney had violated his professional responsibilities by publishing such a letter. Without informing the attorney, the Supervisory Commission of the Superior Court of Uri carried out a disciplinary proceedings and punished the attorney in May 1980 with a censure. The attorney filed a complaint with the Federal Court and requested that the reprimand by the cantonal authorities be rescinded because of his constitutional rights to a free expression of his opinions. The attorney won his case. (b) Somewhat similar is the case of four attorneys whose permission to practice their profession was withdrawn by the Chamber of Attorneys of the Canton of Bern. The decision of the Chamber has been set forth in a 36-page comprehensive statement of explanation. The confrontation with the Chamber arises from the attack on the customs station at Fahy in the Jura by two German terrorists and the killing of two Swiss border guards. The four attorneys were charged with the holding of press conferences and the wide distribution of untrue assertions and biased unworthy statements. They were charged with violating the law and standing regulations of the Chamber regarding the conduct of attorneys. As a result "they no longer deserved the trust of the people and the authorities." A complaint against the decision of the Chamber was filed with the Federal Court. If the Court has acted on the complaint, I am unaware of its decision.

HOUSING AND THE LAW   The small canton of Geneva contains more than 800 registered houses for week-end rental. Of these, over 700 do not conform to the regulations spelled out in the applicable laws or ordinances. Most are in the business without legal approval. Organizations for the protection of Nature and the Homeland now demand their destruction. Precedents, however, tie the hands of the authorities who, also, as elections approach, fear the wrath of the organized owners of these premises. Zone planning exists in various Swiss towns and cities, but, over the years, the authorities in some communes, including Geneva, have chosen to overlook some infractions of the rules. After years of silence and tolerance, the authorities are now urged by the owners to be less inflexible and politically more lenient. They claim that fines and recommendations of a Commission on Architecture as to which of the week-end houses are aesthetically attractive and which are hideous—hence inviting destruction—might be the basis for an acceptable solution.

AN INSTITUTE FOR COMPARATIVE LAW   A Swiss Institute for Comparative Law was made possible by a gift in 1978 of the near-total residue (3.67 million francs) of the Samuel Schindler Fond—a Glarus Foundation. The gift will cover about half the costs, inclusive of furniture and necessary equipment. The Institute, by agreement with the Canton of Vaud will be on university land at Lausanne-Dorigny.

Statistical Data

To answer a variety of questions that have been posed regarding crime and punishment in Switzerland, some of the pertinent data is appended in Tables 75 to 78. As an introduction to the tabulated data, we should note that the violations of the penal codes and other problems that likewise require the services of people trained in the law have been increasing for decades. Increases in the density of population, especially in urban areas, have brought with them more and more friction and personal conflicts, innocent or deliberate. The increased "rubbing of shoulders" with others does not always lead to friendly interchanges: litigious acts increase and the services of "gentlemen of the law" have become increasingly necessary. In 1930–35 Switzerland managed somehow with one attorney to 2484 inhabitants. But by 1950 the ratio became one to 2224, and by the end of 1980 there was one practicing attorney to 1726 inhabitants (**341**, 1951, p. 494; 1981, p. 528). Similar increases in the number of practicing physicians could also be reported, doubtless for several reasons—all of which have little to do with criminal acts: in 1934–35, one practicing physician to 1253 inhabitants; one to 1150 inhabitants in 1950 and one to 852 inhabitants in 1980 (**341**, 1951, p. 453; 1981, p. 505).

From Table 75, we find that the number of young adults convicted of penal code violations in 1979 is more than fourfold that of 1960. The increase in population

Table 75 Persons guilty of penal code violations in 1960 and 1979[a]

	1960	1979
Women	2957	3573
Foreigners	3496	4945
Adolescents[b]	2051	1300
Young adults[c]	1790	7666
Total	22,003	20,459

[a] Source: **341**, 1981, p. 529.

[b] 14 to 17 years of age. After 1974, 15 to 17 years of age. After 1971, reprimanded but offence not recorded.

[c] 18 to 24 years of age. Prior to 1970, 18 and 19 years of age.

Table 76 Number of persons guilty of stated violations of the law (1941, 1950, 1965, 1979)[a]

	1941	1950	1965	1979
Against "life and limb"	1926	2290	2169	1911
Against property	8842	9575	9811	13,275
Against honour	545	929	381	303
Against freedom	263	264	275	375
Against morality	1106	1873	3152	1078
Against family	331	757	564	524
Against public communications	127	1419	502	539
Against public authority	747	1104	952	566
Offences creating a collective danger	—	—	—	473
Falsification of documents	119	240	413	714
Other violations	403	1002	1025	701
Total	14,409	19,453	19,244	20,459

[a] Source: **341**, 1951, p. 501; 1981, p. 531.

during the 20-year span was less than one million. Expression of the data on a per capita basis would contribute almost nothing to an explanation of the great increase. It will have been noted that the totals reported substantially exceed the sums of their parts. The yearbook omits any mention of convictions of adult men; perhaps one may conclude that 11,709 adult men in 1965 and 2975 in 1979 make up the unexplained deficiency.

The data in Table 76 (**341**, 1951, p. 501; 1981, p. 513), with the entries in Column 1 literally translated from German or French into English, may be as confusing to the

Table 77 Punishments (1941, 1950, 1965, 1979)[a]

	1941	1950	1965	1979
Penitentiary	562	515	469	497
House of correction	1920	—	—	—
Imprisonment to 14 days	4547	3455	2934	4460
Imprisonment, 15 days to 3 months	2883	5497	5291	5456
Imprisonment, over 3 months	575	3158	3514	3331
In custody	282	792	896	841
In detention	—	—	969	958
Fined	3317	5064	4293	4480
Reprimanded	—	—	116	—
Other punishments	323	972	762	436
Total	14,409	19,453	19,244	20,459

[a] Source: **341**, 1951, p. 501; 1981, p. 531.

Table 78 Cancellation of permission to drive a motor vehicle[a]

	1951	1960	1980
Contravention of traffic rules			
Without an accident	186	681	3447
With an accident	857	2054	7827
Tipsy from alcohol			
Without an accident	1038	2187	4550
With an accident	813	2643	5098
Theft of vehicle	—	64	90
Illness	82	197	483
Alcoholism and other addictions	—	69	232
Bad character	85	190	105
Flight after accident	—	58	10
Other grounds	112	178	1014
Total	3173	8321	22,856

[a] Source: **341**, 1951, p. 503; 1981, p. 535.

reader as they are to me. I suspect that to accuse a person publicly as a liar, a thief, a wastrel or a woman-chaser may be an "offence against honour." To hold a person in bondage, or as a slave, or as a forced hostage, is surely an "offence against freedom." Obscenity, pornography, adultery are obvious "offences against mortality." Incest, child abuse, interparental violence and desertion can be regarded as "offences against family." "Offences against public authority" may be difficult to explain. Refusal to bow before a monarch or a high official, or to rise in court when the judge enters, or to salute the flag, are not offences at law, surely. Deliberate failure to pay taxes (*Steuerhinterziehung*) or to send your young child to school when education of the young at public expense is mandatory may be examples of violations that belong in this category. Offences against property (theft, arson, wilful damage, etc.) stand out conspicuously as the most common violations of the law.

Table 77 concerns the punishment of the guilty. In general, during the forty-year period to 1980, they have been imprisoned or fined, sometimes imprisoned and fined. There is no provision for capital punishment except in the military penal code.

Table 78 pertains to loss of permission to drive a vehicle. It will be noticed that violation of the ordinary traffic regulations (e.g. excessive speed) and drunkenness are the most common grounds for loss of a driver's permit. Loss of permission to drive may be from 3 months or less up to a loss of unlimited duration. In 1980, 14,518 cancellations were for three months or less and 1637 were unlimited. In 1955, the corresponding figures were 3202 and 645 respectively. In 1980 out of a grand total of 22,856 cancellations, no less than 9648 were because of drunkenness. Of the 22,856 drivers involved, 11,877 were under 30 years of age (**341**, 1981, p. 536).

Notes and Comments

1. Peaceful usually, but a violent demonstration occurred in Zurich in 1968—the *Globus Krawalle*.

2. If the participants in the Zurich May-Day demonstration were included, the study would be heavily slanted toward the older adults. Many members of three or four unions, teachers and others were present who came to hear the leftist National Councillor from Geneva, Jean Ziegler. There was a great parade and then the chaos. Masked and painted demonstrators intruded; they broke windows on Uraniastrasse and Bahnhofstrasse and smeared the buildings with paint. Slogans were shouted and stones were thrown. Chaos and confusion dominated the scene for some time. If we exclude the May-Day parades there can be little doubt that most of the demonstrators were young and most of the violence in Zurich and elsewhere was an expression of frustration, hysteria, and a profound lack of understanding between the young and the old, and between authority and undisciplined, irresponsible youthful participants.

Somewhat surprising is the report that Geneva, almost alone among the major cities of Switzerland, suffered none of the demonstrations and violence that Zurich and other cities in Switzerland experienced (**266**, 24–25 July 1982). It may be argued that Geneva is not a typical Swiss city because of the very high proportion of residents from many foreign countries. Children and young adults grow up in a remarkably cosmopolitan environment and their attitudes toward the establishment may be quite different than elsewhere. Doubtless many explanations of Geneva's escape from the violent demonstrations experienced elsewhere could be advanced and have, indeed, been discussed in the long article cited above.

3. Zurich is also committed to the expenditure of 15 million francs for the reconstruction of a building which will serve as a youth center: Drahtschmidli (**266**, 12–13 December 1981).

4. Addresses of subjects for the study were obtained from 65 communities. Unfortunately, Zurich was excluded, not by intent but only because addresses could not be made available.

5. Two religious organizations of the youth and certain political parties demanded that the youthful participants in the demonstrations, beginning with the violent incident of 30 May 1980, be granted amnesty. The request was referred to a special commission of the *Nationalrat*. The question of a partial amnesty was considered, for example, applicable to demonstrators under 25 years of age who satisfied other criteria of selection, was defeated by a close vote of nine to seven. After prolonged debate in the two Houses of Parliament, the negative vote of the Commission was sustained and the request for amnesty was denied. Of some 1250 demonstrators who were possibly subject to punishment, only a few dozen would have been eligible for amnesty after the more dedicated participants and "professional" troublemakers from outside Switzerland had been eliminated. The close vote within the Petitions Commission and the negative decision of Parliament suggest that among the Swiss people there would have been a close division of opinion on the wisdom of granting amnesty.

11.17 THE POLITICAL SYSTEM AND SOME POLITICAL PROBLEMS

The Political Parties

There is nothing simple to a foreigner about the Swiss political system. There are eight or nine political parties with the ever-present possibility that one or two may fade away and a new one may appear. This might suggest a high level of instability with occasional shifts in position such that one or more of the government parties suddenly join the opposition: hence much wrangling in parliament and a touch of chaos from time to time. Not so in Switzerland. Only four of the parties succeed year after year in gaining enough representation in parliament to be significantly influential. In 1981, these four parties held 85 percent of the 200 seats in the House of Representatives (*Nationalrat*).[1] The same four parties held 42 of the 46 seats in the Council of States (*Ständerat*). There is no organized opposition. Whatever dissent exists among the representatives of the four major parties, as indeed it does on major issues, permits a parliamentary decision after prolonged debate and much give and take. The Swiss parliament moves slowly and cautiously and usually generates little excitement beyond the walls of the parliament buildings.

The Federal Assembly

Enactment of legislation is a function of the Federal Assembly. According to Article 71 of the Federal Constitution, the "supreme power of the Confederation shall be exercised by the Federal Assembly which consists of two sections or councils, to wit: A. The National Council; B. The Council of States." The Federal Assembly, inserted as it is between the strong Federal Council, which it cannot overthrow, and the people, does not appear to an outsider as if it is supremely powerful. The people, by means of the ballot, can challenge the decisions of the Federal Assembly through the optional referendum and can occasionally achieve a change in the constitution itself through the popular initiative. The Federal Council, a body of seven who serve as the heads of the seven ministries (government departments) exercises a great deal of power by formulating and proposing legislation to the two councils and by use of its executive powers.

> The Federal Assembly compensates for some of its deficiencies by the vigorous use of motions, postulates and interpellations. During each session there are hundreds of such thrusts and their number has doubled during the last 25 years. If one may characterize the British Parliament as a debating parliament and the American parliament as a cooperating one, the Swiss parliament merits the adjective threatening.
>
> Another reason for the weakness of the Swiss Federal Assembly lies in the fact that down to the present day it has remained an assembly of notables, a nonprofessional parliament. In imitation of the expression "militia army" the Federal Assembly is usually called a "militia parliament." Switzerland still cherishes the illusion that parliamentary work is not so demanding as to exclude the exercise of an ordinary occupation, and that the individual parliamentarian can continue to make a living from his usual occupation despite the loss of time involved. In recent years the balance between duties and privileges has shifted onesidedly toward a full-time job, but this has not been accompanied by an adequate parliamentary salary. Swiss parliamentarians do not have offices, assistants, or secretaries. Thus the work style of the Swiss members of parliament is characterized by chronic lack of time and by conflict between occupational and parliamentary demands (156, p. 341).

The obligatory referendum and the optional referendum, as discussed later, were introduced in 1874 when the Federal Constitution was completely revised. The popular initiative for constitutional amendments was built into the federal system in 1891. Legislative initiatives are not a direct prerogative of the people, rather, their use is limited to the individual cantons.

Majority rule prevailed until 1919 when proportional representation was introduced. Seats are assigned to the parties in proportion to the number of votes each party receives. Hence, each vote for a candidate is first credited to the party.

Elections

The system of elections is too complicated to describe in all its details. Each party may have its list of candidates for the two councils but the voter is free to vote for candidates from several such lists. Sometimes the parties propose candidates jointly, thus affording to the voter an opportunity to vote for a given candidate more than once. "In the 1975 elections to the National Council no less than 2000 candidates presented themselves on 170 lists" (156), which would seem to be enough to baffle each and every voter. There are additional complexities and oddities in the system such that Swiss elections have been compared to a lottery (Christopher Hughes as quoted by Gruner 156).

We must admit, however, that the system works. This is quite an achievement in a country with many diversities: 20 cantons and six half cantons that contribute to the Confederation linguistic, confessional and cultural differences as well as profound variations in economic activity and strength. Integration of her people has not been a problem in Switzerland,[2] as it has been in the USA which is commonly regarded as a melting-pot of ethnically mixed, highly mobile people.

Referenda and Initiatives

A discussion of Swiss politics might well include an outline of the issues that have come before the voters in recent years. In general, they give us a picture of the concerns of government and of the people in matters relevant to the body politic. Shall we, the people, approve or disapprove what the government is trying to do to the constitution or what it is seeking to achieve by legislative enactments? Or shall we, the people, seek an amendment to the Constitution that will thus provide a base for enacting into law something that we believe will redound to the country's best interests. There are, of course, hundreds of such issues and all that I shall attempt will be a random selection. Voting is usually on Sunday and so many questions come before the people in this very democratic country that almost every other Sunday will find the concerned voter in his polling booth. I have excluded the cantonal and local community votations—concentrating only on the federal issues.

These fall into several categories: (a) the obligatory referenda pertaining to amendments of the Constitution introduced by the Federal Government; (b) the optional referenda regarding laws and decrees of the Federal Government; (c) initiatives by the people seeking specific amendments of the constitution; (d) counter proposals of the Federal Assembly pertinent to some of the popular initiatives.

We must note that if anyone chooses to challenge a federal law or decree he must do so within a stated time, for example, six months after parliament has enacted the "questionable" decision, and he must be supported by at least 50,000 like-minded voters. If he is proposing a popular initiative for an amendment of the constitution, no less than 100,000 signatures will be required to achieve a votation.

Of 1141 federal laws, of which 78 were submitted to referenda, only 48 (4.2 percent of the laws) were rejected. Of 102 obligatory referenda, the voters rejected 20. As for the popular initiatives, 67 in number, the voters rejected 49 (73 percent) including counter proposals by government. Were the counter proposals excluded, the rejections would increase to 60 (90 percent) (**156**, p. 342).

Motions, Postulates, and Interpellations

In addition to discussion of measures proposed for legislation and voting on numerous bills, the members of parliament through motions, postulates and interpellations do much to pave the way for enactment of legislation. A "motion," according to Swiss parliamentary procedure, is a polite command to the Federal Council to submit a report, to initiate a stated project, to study the advisability of certain legislative actions by the Federal Assembly. A motion requires agreement of both Houses: the National Council and the Council of States. The motion is disposed of when the requested report is received, or when the motion lapses or is withdrawn. A "postulate" is of a somewhat lower order. Again it is a request or an invitation for information or action by the Federal Council, but, unlike a motion, it requires agreement by a majority vote of only one House. Postulates are submitted in writing and automatically lapse if ignored by the Federal Council. Somewhere near the bottom of the list is the "interpellation." This is a written question addressed to the Federal Council and signed by a number of deputies from either House. The questioner or "interpellant" customarily expands upon his concern in a brief address to his fellow deputies. The answer, which will be verbal, will be given by a Federal Councilor and may not be debated except by a resolution of the Council (**219**, p. 78).

The Federal Council

I have made frequent mention of the Federal Council, which, according to Article 95 of the Constitution, is the "supreme directing and executive power in the Confederation." This body of seven resembles the US Cabinet in the sense that each member is the head of a government department; but at this point the comparison ceases and the contrasts begin to loom large. The members are chosen for four years by the Federal Assembly (a joint session of the National Council and the Council of States). Any Swiss citizen eligible for membership in the National Council is eligible for election to the Federal Council but it is probably obvious, although an unwritten requirement, that any candidate, to receive serious consideration, shall have previously held some high elective office, such as a deputy in the National Council or Council of States as well as some correspondingly high office in his own canton.

Every fourth year (December 1963, 1967, etc.) all seven seats in the Federal Council must be filled. It is customary to reelect all of the Federal Councilors who wish to continue in office, and, in practice, only one or two seats need to be filled with new members at any one time. The filling of such vacancies is of great public interest, for the field of candidates is more circumscribed than may first appear: the seven members must be from different cantons; it is customary that one be from the canton of Zurich, one from Bern, and two from French Switzerland; and the four major political parties, the two principal linguistic groups, and the two confessions customarily must be represented in the Federal Council.

The president of the Swiss Confederation, who holds office for one year, acts as chairman of the Federal Council and is elected by the Federal Assembly from among the members of the Federal Council. The vice president, who is similarly elected, succeeds the president on completion of the presidential term of office. Actually, these offices are filled by a system of rotation from within the Federal Council, newly elected Federal Councilors being placed at the bottom of the list, thus waiting six or seven years before being elected to the presidency. The retiring president moves to the bottom of the list, and so on.

The president has very limited emergency powers, a general supervisory power, and responsibility for the Federal Chancellery (general secretariat). Otherwise, his duties are mostly limited to those of representing the Confederation at home and abroad, and presiding over the meetings of the Federal Council.

Federal Councilors may attend the sessions of both Houses and, indeed, one or two are usually present. They have the constitutional right to give advice, to propose resolutions, and to speak whenever they consider it appropriate to do so.

The powers and responsibilities of the Federal Council are detailed in the Constitution. They are very numerous and I have no intention of listing them here. Legislative power is largely vested in the Federal Assembly. That body enacts the legislation and the Federal Council administers and supervises its enforcement. In foreign affairs, the over-all direction is given by the Federal Assembly but the day-to-day conduct of foreign affairs is within the competence of the Federal Council.

In internal affairs, the maintenance of peace and order is a cantonal responsibility. As has been previously stated, the cantons, in the exercise of their autonomy, regulate many aspects of the economic and cultural phases of the national life. Here, the Federal Council has the important responsibility of examining those laws and ordinances of the cantons that specifically require federal approval or which may be presumed to be in conflict with federal law.

As a generality, the Federal Council should be thought of as the executive body, and the two Councils that make up the Federal Assembly as the legislative body. Their powers are in effect, coordinate, and neither is subordinate to the other (**219**, pp. 8–10).

The Federal Constitution

The Constitution is basically that of 1848 as revised in 1874. (Please refer to chapters 9 and 10 and, most importantly, to reference **18**.) It is a very fluid document: "up to December 31, 1976, the Federal Constitution of 1874 had been partially revised by 88 amendments. Changes are thus . . . more frequent than in the United States and France, but less so than in California" (**18**, p. 300). The US Constitution was amended only 24 times in 175 years, and ten of the amendments were adopted almost before the ink was dry on the basic document.

The Constitution of Switzerland constantly adds new bits and pieces and strikes out a few others, as the Federal Government makes ceaseless and untiring efforts to extend its competence under the law. Centralism gains at the expense of federalism. However necessary this may appear to be, these intrusions upon cantonal sovereignty and the powers of local government do not rest well with many Swiss.

Some Political Issues

What are some of the issues calling for political action that have come before the voters in recent years? To simplify the task, the following symbols will be used:

Obligatory Referenda: O
Facultative (optional) Referenda: F
Popular Initiatives: I
Counter Proposals re Popular Initiatives: X

REFERENDA AND INITIATIVES

Date	Symbol	Title	Action
26 Oct. 1958	I	*Introduction of the 44-hour week* (a shortening from 48 hours or so).	Defeated
		Eventually the 44-hour week was generally observed. A popular initiative in Nov. 1973 to reduce the 44-hour week to 40 hours of work was heavily defeated.	
1 Feb. 1959	O	*Introduction of voting rights for women.*	Defeated
7 Feb. 1971	O	*Introduction of voting rights for women.*	Approved
1 April 1962	I	*Interdiction of atomic weapons*	Defeated
26 May 1963	I	*Right of the people to decide on equipping the Swiss army with atomic weapons.*	Defeated
24 Sept. 1972	I	*Increased control of the armaments industry and interdiction of the export of arms.*	Defeated by a very slim margin (49.7% for; (50.3% against)
16 Oct. 1966	I	*For the fight against alcoholism*	Defeated
19 May 1968	F	*Taxation of tobacco.*	Defeated
6 June 1971	O	*Protection of the environment.*	Approved
5 March 1972	O	*Protection of renters.*	Approved
25 Sept. 1977	I	*Protection of renters.*	Defeated
25 Sept. 1977	X	*Protection of renters.*	Defeated
4 June 1972	O	*Stabilization of the construction industry.*	Approved
4 June 1972	O	*Protection of the currency.*	Approved
12 June 1977	O	*Introduction of an added value tax (Mehrwertsteuer)*	Defeated
20 May 1979	O	*For an added value tax.*	Defeated
12 June 1977	O	*Tax harmonization* ("Soak the rich; relieve the poor")	Approved
4 Dec. 1977	F	*Measure to equilibrate the federal finances*	Approved
8 June 1975	F	*Financing of the national highways*	Approved
26 Feb. 1978	I	*Democracy in construction of the national highways.* (Decisions of the Federal Assembly on conception, location and construction of the national highways must be submitted to the people for approval or rejection if 30,000 voters or eight cantons so request).	Defeated
28 May 1978	I	*Twelve Sundays each year free of motor vehicle traffic* (the second Sunday of each month would be closed in all Switzerland with respect to use of private motor vehicles on land, water and in the air).	Defeated
3 Dec. 1972	O	*Agreement with the European Common Market.*	Approved
4 March 1973	O	*Promotion of scientific research.*	Approved
2 Dec. 1973	O	*Supervision of prices, salaries, wages & profits*	Approved
20 May 1973	O	*Abrogation of the constitutional proscription against the Jesuits and convents.*	Approved
25 Sept. 1977	I	*Air pollution by motor vehicles* (specifies how much carbon monoxide, hydrocarbons and nitrous oxide are permitted in exhaust gases).	Defeated
30 Nov. 1980	F	*Security belts* (motor-vehicle drivers & passengers) *and protective helmets* (motorcycle riders) *to be required.*	Approved
4 Dec. 1977	O	*Civil service as a replacement for military service by religious and ethical objectors.* More heavily defeated in a second votation in Feb. 1984	Defeated

Date	Symbol	Title	Action
20 Oct. 1974	I	*Against over-foreignization (Überfremdung)* and overpopulation of Switzerland.	Defeated
13 March 1977	I	*"Over-foreignization".* (For protection of Switzerland—*Zum Schutze der Schweiz).*	Defeated
13 March 1977	I	*"Over-foreignization"* (for limitation of naturalizations).	Defeated
5 April 1981	I	*A new Foreign-Worker Policy* (the *Mitenand Initiative).*	Heavily defeated
26 Feb. 1978	I	*Reduction of the AHV age from 65 for men and 62 for women to 60 and 58 respectively* (the age at which one is eligible for pension benefits under the AHV program).	Defeated
28 May 1978	F	*Adoption of summer time.* (Winter time plus one hour or standard time plus two hours).	Defeated
		Approved in 1980 for introduction in 1981. The most determined opponents of summer time were the farmers and their cows. In 1979 cows outnumbered their owners 24 to 1. In 1886 it was only six to one. Swiss pride may also have come into play, some contending that the clock was invented by the Swiss and it is quite inappropriate for foreigners to tell them what to do about time.	
14 June 1981	X	*Equal rights for men and women.* Men and women are entitled to equal rights. The law is concerned for their equality, before all in the family, in education and in work. Men and women are entitled to equal pay for equivalent work.	Approved
24 Sept. 1978	O	*Creation of the Canton of Jura.*	Approved
3 Dec. 1978	F	*Creation of a federal security-police force.* While recognizing that the maintenance of inner security in Switzerland is a cantonal responsibility, outbreaks of terrorism, protection of delegates to international conferences in Switzerland and protection of federal property suggested to some that a special federal security police force of unstated size should be organized. The opposition emphasized that such a move would be counter to the preservation of federalism. The creation of a federal police force could also be regarded as the first step on the dangerous path that leads to a police state.	Defeated
18 Feb. 1979	O	*Voting rights at age 18.*	Defeated (49.2% for; 50.8% against)
18 Feb. 1979	X	*Footpath network for hikers.* The Federal Government would be required to plan, construct and maintain a national *Wanderweg* net and to ensure the coordination, erection and maintenance of regional footpaths in the whole of Switzerland.	Approved
18 Feb. 1979	I	*Atomic installations.* (Protection of people's rights and security measures to be required in the building and operation of atomic reactors).	Defeated
20 May 1979	F	*Revision of the law on atomic energy.*	Approved
	I*	*For a future without more atomic energy plants.* This initiative was designed to end the atomic energy program: No more atomic power plants to be placed in operation: building and operation of industrial plants for obtaining, enriching and recovery of atomic fuels to be forbidden on Swiss soil; until these and other measures come into force, existing atomic power plants must cease operaton, etc.	Heavily defeated

REFERENDA AND INITIATIVES—*continued*

Date	Symbol	Title	Action
	I*	*For a safe, economical and environmentally directed energy provision.* (Much less radical and much less negative than some earlier initiatives).	Defeated
28 May 1978	F	*Legalization of induced abortions.* Mention should also be made of a popular initiative, voted upon in Sept. 1977 (and defeated) that was concerned with the "protection of pregnancy and the punishment for inducing abortions." The negative vote by the people was very close but the cantonal vote was more decisively negative. Another popular initiative entitled "the Right to Live" was introduced by the anti-abortionists on Sept. 9, 1980. The opening paragraph: "Every person has the right to live in physical and spiritual entirety. The life of a person begins with conception and ends with his natural death."	Defeated
		The Federal Council, on juristic and political grounds, and in dissatisfaction with the lack of precision in the concluding sentence, proposed a counter initiative: "Every person has the right to live in physical and spiritual entirety with freedom of movement and personal security." (See also subsection on "Abortion" in 11.3.)	
	I	*For an active protection of motherhood.* An obligatory and general motherhood insurance to be provided: complete birth (medical care and hospital costs); a maternal leave of at least 16 weeks with payment of wages in full to employed women during this period; unemployed women to receive a payment; for employed parents a parental leave of at least nine months. For the father this leave shall begin at the birth of the child; financing by the cantons and the Federal Government; payments to employed people to be financed according to the AHV model (one-half by worker, one-half by employer). *Bundesblatt*, 1980, I, pp. 821–824.	Heavily defeated
		The Federal Council proposed rejection of the initiative and did not offer a counter-proposal. (*Botschaft* of 17 November 1982, p. 66). Initiative rejected in the votation of December, 1984.	
2 March 1980	I	*For complete separation of Church and State.* Defeat of the initiative means that each canton will decide for itself the preferred relationship with the Church. Had the initiative been approved, the cantons would no longer be empowered to levy taxes in support of churches.	Defeated
14 June 1981	X	*Protection of the rights of consumers.*	Approved

---

*In May 1984, both of these initiatives were formally disapproved by Parliament. A counter proposal to the initiatives was not adopted. Both initiatives were defeated in the votation of September, 1984.

A few of the many motions, postulates and interpellations introduced by members of the National Council (*Nationalrat*) in recent years may be of interest. The sample is very small indeed, because, as Gruner has pointed out, hundreds of such "thrusts" are introduced at each session of parliament. I find the postulate by National Councillor Schalcher (November, 1969) of unusual interest because it antedates by a year or two any serious expression of concern in the USA over the possible dangers inherent in ill-considered tampering with genes, including their transplantation.

MOTIONS   Ziegler (26 September 1969). A global credit of 100 million francs for three years is proposed to supply excess foodstuffs (cheese, powdered milk) to starving people in food-short countries.

Schaller (19 March 1969). Cancer research and cancer clinics. According to Schaller, about 12,000 die of cancer each year in Switzerland. About 30,000 to 40,000 incurable cases are believed to exist. The Federal Council is requested (a) to study whether special integrated clinics for research amd medical care should be established; (b) to report on the state of research; in particular, clinical research, and to determine if it should be broadened, etc.

Schmidt (13 May 1969). Establishment of an office for emission protection. Air pollution in the cities and industrial areas is increasing. The Federal Council is asked to determine if such an office should be set up.

Binder (27 co-signers, March, 1970). The Federal Council is requested to report to Parliament on the possible organization of a central toxicological institute in the ETH, to be concerned, inter alia, with traffic in poisons.

Dubois (March, 1970). Contending that Switzerland, among the 14 EFTA and EWG (Common Market) countries is the only one without an institute for advanced studies in social and preventive medicine, requests that the Federal Council consider the establishment of such an institute in Switzerland for the training of specialists.

Schalcher (23 June, 1970). Requests the Federal Council to propose appropriate action to stem the flow of poisons of all sorts into Switzerland.

POSTULATES   Schalcher (26 November, 1969). Security against dangers in alteration of genetic materials. Schalcher states that in the near future it will certainly be possible to alter at will the genetic code and to produce mutants of a pre-determined kind. Legislation to protect against misuse and unhealthy developments in this field is desirable in advance of such developments (in gene transplantation)—not afterwards, as happened in the case of organ transplantation. Action by the Federal Council is requested.

Tissières (9 December, 1969). Concerns occupational diseases. Tissières reports that drivers of motor vehicles, including construction machinery vehicles, frequently develop spinal column disease. The Federal Council is requested to include this occupational disease among the diseases covered by accident insurance.

Blatti (March, 1970). A request to the Federal Council to consider the formation of a permanent consultative commission on water protection.

Schürmann (March, 1970). Ocean Technology. Schürmann requests of the Federal Council information on whether Switzerland can participate (with other countries) in procurement of raw materials, proteins, drugs, minerals, etc. from the oceans and also join in the manufacture of machinery and navigation control systems for surface- and underwater ships. Are there international organizations in this field that Switzerland should join?

Leu (18 June 1970). A proposed veterinary-medical research facility. Leu claims that the Swiss dairy industry loses annually well over 100 million francs through a number of destructive diseases of cattle. The origin, transmission and course of these diseases requires study but the present veterinary-medical institutions are too overloaded or too understaffed to pursue such research. Leu requests the Federal Council to study the possible provision of a veterinary-medical research facility exclusively for research on the significant health problems of cattle.

Dubois (22 June, 1970). Federal Law concerning medical agents provides legislative control over narcotics. As for ordinary drugs, Dubois reports that their control, if any, is left to the cantons. Procurement of a given drug requires a medical prescription in some cantons but not in others. Painkillers are greatly misused and, as in Sweden, should be under Federal control. Dubois requests the Federal Council to propose a law for control of medical substances (*Arzneimittel*).

INTERPELLATIONS   Akeret (26 June, 1969). Encouragement of research on free-living animals and their environment. A federal law of 1962 makes the Federal Government responsible for the pursuit of such research. Akeret claims that the Confederation has done nothing to finance the necessary research. Requests the Federal Council to take appropriate action.

Financial Policy

Like finance ministers generally, Willi Ritschard, once Head of the Federal Department of Finance, painted a doleful picture of the Confederation's financial problems. With a current debt of almost 20 billion francs, the Confederation has to borrow about one billion francs per year to pay only the interest on its debt. And every year the Federal Government must pay about 55 to 60 million francs more in interest on its debt than it paid the year before. It is indeed an amazing phenomenon that Switzerland, by 1982, had experienced at least 15 years of very favorable business, of excellent economic growth and a high per capita income but now must agonize over its burden of debt which has tripled since 1966–67. It also worries over a current unemployment rate of about one percent of the working population (0.1 percent unemployment in 1979–80 and in many earlier years), an inflation rate of over 5 percent and a 20 percent increase in bankruptices in 1982 over the 950 or so in 1981. Exports declined about 5 percent in 1982 and many expect a further decline in 1983. Much depends on the strength of the Swiss franc. Should the franc weaken, exports should improve; but a strong franc, while easing the cost of imports, has an adverse effect on exports. Switzerland labors also under the fear that West Germany and France may introduce trade barriers directed against imports, doing so to combat their own unemployment. These two countries are Switzerland's principal export markets. The tourist industry, one of the three most important sources of income, is not expected to strengthen in 1983. The near-term outlook is not rosy. As the Finance Minister pointed out, the Confederation lives not merely from hand to mouth: it must also eat the spoon; and, as they say in Appenzell, it may also have to eat the plate. The people must know, continued the Finance Minister, that in the past ten years they have lived beyond their means.

In principle, it would seem that the Confederation might partially solve its financial problems by increasing taxes. However, the central government is limited by its arrangement with the cantons, whereby direct taxation rests principally with the cantons while the Federal Government must depend principally on customs revenue and a few sources of indirect taxation. The only direct taxes of any consequence to which the Federal Government may resort are the military tax (*Wehrsteuer*) and the sales tax (*Warenumsatzsteuer*). Parliament speaks of a "cold progression" in the military tax. To make any tax increases palatable it has also been pointed out that they must be sweetened with some kind of a compensating benefit such as an improvement in social programs. By late 1981, a goodly amount of juggling with possible tax increases had reduced the hopes of the Finance Minister for an increase of 800 million francs in federal income from the military tax to a more probable increase of 300 million francs from all sources.

In 1980 the upper House (*Ständerat*) voted to mitigate the financial plight of the Federal Government by reducing all federal subventions by 10 percent. This would effect an annual saving of 560 million francs, of which 200 million might be set aside for alleviation by the Federal Council of hardship cases. A transport tax on heavy vehicles, if approved, would add to the federal income from 1983 forward about 500 to 600 million francs per year—roughly half of the average annual deficit since 1970 (cf. Table 49 in section 11.11). Imposition of a charge for use of the main expressways by ordinary motor vehicles has also been considered.

The pervasive financial gloom is deepened by the following predictions of the cost to the country of a number of programs set forth in several initiatives: the motherhood insurance program, 400 million francs; reduction of the age at which AHV pension benefits would begin, 1.1 billion francs; the 40 hour-work week, some hundreds of millions (**266**, 13/14 October 1979).

All three initiatives were defeated but one can predict that, in time, they will again come before the voters. Perhaps it is significant that this financial alarm reached the people just before the federal votations of October 21. Did the voters over-react?

Foreign Policy

Pierre Aubert, the Federal Councilor in charge of the Federal Foreign Affairs Department since 1 February 1978, has outlined in an interview the main goals and objectives of Swiss foreign policy (**19**).

> The main objective of our foreign policy is to preserve our independence and to remain a free nation. The basic means to guarantee this is our traditional and permanent neutrality. Important components of this policy are the concepts of solidarity (e.g. cooperation with developing countries), of universality (our diplomatic relations extend to all countries) and of our readiness to render good offices (for instance Switzerland has looked after US interests in Cuba since 1961). Another example of our readiness to serve the international community is the presence of many international organizations in Geneva and the many multilateral conferences which take place in this same city.

In the interview, Aubert pointed out that her neutrality does not permit Switzerland to take sides in disputes between other governments. However, Switzerland cannot survive in splendid isolation, aloof from the sometimes entangled affairs of other countries. Her almost total dependence on imported raw materials dictates otherwise. Switzerland must participate in the dialogue between quarreling countries, if so invited, and must encourage cooperation among nations in the interest of peaceful and harmonious relations.

Aubert also discussed at length Switzerland's relations with the United Nations Organization and the possibility of Switzerland becoming a member (cf. United Nations in this section, and see note 9 in 11.22).

Switzerland's participation in the European Space Program is important because experience in high technology is necessary to the Program. Switzerland has such experience and her participation can be of mutual benefit—to the Program and to Swiss industry.

The interview also touched on the Swiss abroad and their relations with the mother country. This subject is discussed elsewhere in the present section.

On another occasion, in mid-1980, when on the same platform with the Austrian Minister of Foreign Affairs, Aubert had much more to say about Swiss foreign policy. Although a part of western Europe, heavily export-oriented and with her economy integrated into the economy of the world at large, Switzerland always strives to remain as independent as possible in political affairs. Traditionally, the Swiss are cautious and very skeptical about any increase in the political power of individual persons. They are equally distrustful of any regimentation by the State. The collegial system of government, the autonomy of communities and the near-sovereign power of the cantons, federalism, and direct democracy do not facilitate in any way the conduct of foreign policy. In no other country have the people so much to say about foreign policy as in Switzerland, even though foreign policy is typically the business of government. But despite these inner-political problems, Switzerland cannot sit aside during these difficult years in world affairs, waiting for better times. She must participate still more in international dialogues and in international cooperation as further opportunities are presented: adherence to the United Nations Organization would be a logical consequence of this necessary collaboration.

Relations with the Third World

Switzerland has long been interested in extending aid to developing countries. Her motives are partly humanitarian and partly an expression of self-interest. The Foreign Minister has reminded his fellow Swiss of the incredible poverty under which some hundreds of millions of people try to eke out a bare existence. In 1980 Parliament approved an appropriation of 1650 million francs (increased to 1800 million francs for 1985–87) for technical collaboration and development help to Third World countries for the period 1981 to 1983. This is about double the sum voted in 1978 (735 million francs) for the years 1978 to 1980—an amount equal to 0.23 percent of the gross national product. The latter has been regarded by the recipient countries, as well as by industrial nations, as niggardly and has not escaped criticism by the OECD. The new appropriation amounts to 0.31 percent of the GNP which approaches the average 0.34 percent of the GNP granted by other industrialized countries. The OECD criticism rested on the fact that Switzerland, one of the richest of countries, enjoys the highest per capita income of all western countries and should appropriate for Third World assistance much more than she currently grants. Parliament is well aware of the fact that poorer countries may be obliged to reduce substantially their imports if increased aid is not forthcoming. This, in turn, would affect adversely Switzerland's export industries. Generous financial assistance to the Third World is, therefore, not only a moral responsibility of a rich country but is of economic importance to her own industries. A part of the grants is earmarked specifically for humanitarian purposes and food procurement, a part is for financial aid and a third part is for technical cooperation. In general, the credits are administered through the Interamerican Development Bank (IDB), the Asiatic Development Bank (ADB) and the African Development Bank. Switzerland is a member of the IDB and the ADB. The African Bank consists of African country members only, but the admission of non-African States to membership is under consideration.

Problems with Iran

When the monarchy came to end in Iran and the Shah sought refuge elsewhere, the new Islamic government of the country called for freezing of all assets in Switzerland of the exiled Shah and members of his family. The assets included a large villa at St. Moritz and other properties and bank deposits. A survey of 25 leading Swiss banks disclosed that they held, at the end of 1978, 1.2 billion dollars in deposits from Iranian banks, individuals and private companies. A portion of these assets was the property of the Shah and his family. The Swiss government refused an Iranian request to freeze the assets of the Pahlewi family. Although the Constitution would permit the government to grant Iran's request, the Iranian government was advised that the validity of claims against funds in Switzerland would be determined by the courts.

The Iranian Republic demanded that all documents pertinent to ownership of the villa be transferred to the Iranian government. Also demanded was a prohibition of transfer of assets from Switzerland by any members of the Pahlewi family. The Shah meanwhile declared that he would not come to Switzerland again unless the Swiss authorities guaranteed total security and protection of his person.

In the meantime the Swiss government invited its citizens in Iran and any others under Swiss jurisdiction to leave Iran. About 300 Swiss were involved. Swissair was prepared to fly them back to their homeland. Economic contacts between the two countries were also suspended.

Representation of Interests of Foreign Governments

Switzerland, in accordance with its policy of offering its good services to other governments, agreed to a request of the USA government in 1980 to represent its interests in Iran—the USA embassy in Teheran was already occupied by Iranians. Iran agreed to the Swiss representation. In 1979 a total of 15 similar mandates in which Switzerland agreed to represent the interests of various countries were in force: Iran in Israel (since 1958), USA in Cuba (1961), Guatemala in Cuba (1962), Great Britain in Guatemala (1963), Honduras in Cuba (1963), Brazil in Cuba (1964), Israel in Hungary (1967), Poland in Chile (1973), Israel in Madagascar (1973), Israel in Ghana (1973), Israel in Liberia (1973), Ivory Coast in Israel (1973), Iran in Egypt (1979), South Africa in Iran (1979), Iran in South Africa (1979).

Such representation can be quite a burden: to protect the USA interests in Cuba, Switzerland found she had to expand her embassy in Cuba by an additional 30 persons.

The former foreign minister of Iran and Iranian Ambassador to the USA, Ardeschir Sahedi, now living in Switzerland, sought asylum of the Swiss authorities. The request was granted. Sahedi was known to be a close friend of the former Shah and would probably have been severely punished had he returned to Iran.

Relations with Israel

Switzerland, in the 1980s, experienced two thorny problems in its relations with Israel. (1) Switzerland expressed its readiness to sign a social convention with Israel, doing so in Bern, in Tel Aviv, or anywhere else except in Jerusalem (as the Israeli government desires). The Swiss consider transaction of the business in Jerusalem would be tantamount to recognition of Jerusalem—notably the eastern part—as the capital of the Hebrew State. The intention was to sign the document much earlier, but delay has resulted from the intransigent position of Israel on Jerusalem. Switzerland contends that the action of the Knesset in declaring Jerusalem as the capital of the Hebrew State is not compatible with international law. The Swiss-Israel Association has deplored the negative policy of the Swiss government and Israel's ambassador in Bern has personally presented the protests of his government to the Swiss Ministry of Foreign Affairs. (2) The Federal Council expressed its intention to invite the PLO "foreign minister" to come to Switzerland on an official visit. The "Israelitische Wochenblatt" criticized the Federal Council's action, pointing out that an official meeting with a representative of the PLO in the House of Parliament would be regarded as an offence against the honour of Switzerland. The Federal Council replied to this criticism by reminding the *Israeli Weekly* that such a meeting would permit once again an unconditional disavowal by the PLO of any terroristic acts of violence. At issue also are those aspects of policy which are important to the security of Switzerland. The Council also expressed its approval of the opening of a PLO office in the United Nations premises in Geneva.

Farouk Kaddoumi, a member of the PLO Executive Committee, was received by Federal Councilor Aubert on an official visit in June 1981. The position of the Federal Government on the vexing questions concerning the PLO appears to be friendly but very reserved.

The Helsinki Conference

In a meeting in Helsinki, the Foreign Minister of Finland agreed with Aubert that a conference of the four foreign ministers of the neutral countries of Europe was desirable. The proposed discussions would be held prior to the impending KSZE conference in Madrid (November 1980). The preliminary meeting of the Neutrals would be to seek a common course of action on several of the KSZE agenda items. As for a European Disarmament Conference, the Swiss delegation held to the position that such a conference would be futile unless, in advance, a feeling of mutual trust could be restored between East and West. To the Swiss there appeared to be a political solution. Proof of the USSR's sincerity and good intentions resided in a solution of the Afghanistan problem, viz a return of Afghanistan to the status of a free, sovereign and unattached nation. The Finnish proposal of a disarmament conference was acceptable to the Swiss provided the conference be a part of the KSZE Conference and the participants be amply prepared in advance. A preliminary meeting of delegates should be held, e.g. in 1981, at which a Steering Committee would be appointed. The Finnish Minister expressed the opinion that Finland could not accept the Swiss position that the holding of a disarmament Conference must depend on the course of events in Afghanistan.

Incidentally, Parliament, through a unanimous vote of the lower House (*Nationalrat*) in March, 1980, condemned the intervention of the USSR in Afghanistan. In the presence of representatives of Embassies of East Germany, the USSR, Hungary, France and the USA, Aubert described the Swiss position on the relaxation of international tensions (*Entspannung*) and expressed concern that the ideas of the Soviet Union constitute a deviation from the fundamental concepts of *Entspannung*. The easing of international tensions and the restoration of harmony require the recognition of certain elementary principles of international morals. It is in this light, added Aubert, that the planned KSZE Conference in Madrid should be regarded. An important step forward would be in the furtherance of, and return to, a recognition of human rights. He greeted warmly the agreement between the Federal Council and Parliament on Swiss participation in the Madrid Conference.

Relations with the Soviet "Bloc"

Relations with the Eastern Communist Bloc of countries have been strained for many years. Officially, Switzerland, as a neutral country, strives to avoid discrimination between the communist East and the capitalistic West. This is admittedly difficult because the Swiss dislike heartily the Communist system of government—the all-powerful State. The Swiss subscribe to a policy of maximum individual freedom and human rights compatible with the maintenance of national security and peaceful relations with other States.

It is not surprising that the Federal Council condemned the USSR deportation of Andrei Sacharov as a violation of the concluding Act of the European Conference in Helsinki on Security and Cooperation and, in particular, the principle of respect for human rights and basic freedoms.

Economic and military espionage is a frequent cause of concern. In the 1960s, 1970s, and 1980s the complaints of Switzerland have been numerous. Although one is inclined to suspect that the USSR has been the ultimate recipient of the forbidden information and/or materials, much of the "dirty work" has been done by Bulgaria, Czechoslovakia, Hungary, Poland and other fringe countries, from whose embassies and commercial missions in Switzerland people with diplomatic passports have been frequently ordered out of the country. Even a high official of the permanent Soviet Mission to the United Nations in Geneva was extradited for illegal activities. In the early 1980s several high-ranking Russian diplomats were ordered out of Switzerland because of espionage. The Polish Military Attaché who was rescued after seizure of the Polish Embassy by gunmen, was found guilty of espionage and was deported. Late in 1982 the commercial counselor of Hungary was ordered out of Switzerland because of espionage. Also involved and extradited were an engineer from Budapest and several diplomatic couriers.

In March 1980, the Ambassador of the Soviet Union, accredited to Switzerland, formally protested to the Federal Department of Foreign Affairs against the anti-Soviet campaign allegedly conducted by the Swiss press, television and radio. The protest was directed also against some members of Parliament and Swiss officials who participated in the dissemination of anti-Soviet propaganda, doing so, according to the Soviet Ambassador in a spirit that was contrary to the final Act of the Helsinki Conference on Security and Cooperation in Europe. The protest was verbal and, as such, was not accepted by the Swiss Department of Foreign Affairs. The Constitution, in an Article on the separation of powers, also casts doubt on the propriety of receiving such a protest.

The Swiss Federation of Journalists replied to the Russian accusation by pointing out that the protest rested on a total misunderstanding of Swiss democracy in general and the independence of the media in particular.

In January 1982, Caritas Schweiz (a Swiss Catholic Charity) announced a plan to send monthly to Poland 120 tons of foodstuffs, serious shortages having resulted from economic boycotts and poor harvests.

Switzerland is also concerned with the problem of granting asylum to Poles who fled their country when the Communist military dictatorship took over the reins of power. Some came directly to Switzerland and others entered after a temporary stay in Austria. By December 1981, 929 applications for asylum had been received from Poles—the largest single nation group (see also 11.2, note 5).

Relations with the USA

Aubert, as the Swiss Minister for Foreign Affairs, has been busily visiting his counterparts in many other countries—possibly spending more time "on the road" than in Bern. This may, indeed, be commendable: bilateral discussions, in advance, between the Swiss Minister and the Foreign Office heads of each of the 30 or so countries involved in the Madrid Conference of November, 1980, might have achieved a greater understanding of the problems involved, but such a hope could only be partly fulfilled.

Aubert's official visit to the USA in 1979 is noteworthy for other reasons. Apparently, this is the first time that a Swiss Minister for Foreign Affairs has made an official visit to Washington. This surely testifies to the fact that major political problems rarely arise between Switzerland and the USA. Those that do arise, major or minor, are customarily left to the American Embassy in Bern and the Swiss Embassy in Washington to resolve. Problems having to do with finance and trade stand out in bold relief as compared with the less evident political problems. In fact, Switzerland is regarded by some observers as underdeveloped politically and overdeveloped in its economy. She has been described also as a dwarf with an oversized head (her financial and commercial power) resting on underdeveloped legs (her political status). As an extreme position there are those, including some Swiss, who contend that Switzerland has no foreign policies, only financial and commercial interests.

In an atmosphere clouded with such extreme points of view, one is inclined to ask what Aubert did in Washington. He met his counterpart in Washington and other high officials with whom an exchange of views would certainly be helpful. It is known that the discussions concerned developments in Iran, problems in South Africa such as the Swiss ban on shipment of certain materials to Rhodesia, events of mutual concern in South East Asia (Vietnam and the emigrés), Third World problems as, for example, in South Africa, Latin America, South Korea and the Philippines—countries in which the USA is regarded as somewhat of a protector of Switzerland's economic interests. The USA is even beneficently thought of as a stabilizing influence in these countries where governments may be greeted abroad with mixed emotions: friendly to capitalism but all too often repressive against their own people.

Relations with the Swiss Abroad

CITIZENSHIP[3]   Children born to a foreign couple in Switzerland receive the nationality of their parents. In many countries, especially in the Anglo-Saxon States, children born therein automatically obtain the nationality of the country in which they are born and may also acquire the nationality of the parents. If a child is born of a woman who is Swiss by descent and is married to a foreigner, the child will receive Swiss citizenship if the parents are resident in Switzerland at the time of the birth.[4] But if the parents are resident abroad when the child is born, Swiss citizenship cannot descend through the Swiss mother to the infant. But it can descend to the newly born child through a Swiss father. The Swiss laws governing the conferring of citizenship upon the newly born are clearly discriminatory. The residence requirement imposed upon the parents is regarded as unfair and is the subject of study by the federal authorities. The studies are carried out in consultation with the cantons because citizenship is acquired through a commune and hence becomes a concern of the cantons. The various provisions of the law governing nationality in the family appear to require extensive revision and are included as a part of the study. The remedy of the problem presented by the laws on citizenship will require an amendment of the Federal Constitution which, in turn, must be approved by the people and the cantons through an obligatory referendum. Dual citizenship is very common. For example, on marriage to a foreigner, a Swiss woman acquires her husband's citizenship and becomes a dual national provided that she declares in writing before marriage her intention to retain her Swiss citizenship. At the end of 1977 more dual nationals than purely Swiss citizens were living abroad, the ratio being 52 to 48 (**357**, 3 October 1979).

EDUCATION   Swiss, living abroad, may now enter upon programs of study in preparation for the federal maturity examinations or for the diploma of commerce, supplementing the study programs with participation in special seminars for two to four weeks a year. The scheme is helpful to young Swiss living abroad who plan to return to Switzerland to enter a Swiss university for professional training. It is also conceived as a program of adult education for the adult Swiss who wish to further their education, perhaps indeed with the thought of returning to Switzerland eventually. Purely individual studies may also be pursued by selection of individual subjects from the maturity or commerce programs, thus permitting an expansion of one's knowledge of certain areas of learning which happen to interest the participant. A student (young or adult) on entry into the program must give evidence of having had at least eight school years of basic instruction and of having a very good knowledge of German. Development of these programs resulted from twelve years of research into new teaching methods for students abroad and for systematic checking of a student's progress.

SOCIAL SECURITY   In July 1979 a Convention between the USA and Switzerland relative to social security was signed by the two parties.[5] The principal purpose of the Convention is to solve the double-payment problem faced by Americans employed in Switzerland or by Swiss who are gainfully employed in the USA. In the former case the Swiss employer and the American employee are obliged to participate in the federal old age and survivors' insurance program and the corresponding federal insurance program against invalidity (disability). However, he may also be still included in the USA social security system which requires payments into the system by the employer and the employee. A corresponding requirement of double payments has been experienced by Swiss citizens employed in the USA. It is true that the problem was partly resolved by an exchange of notes in 1968 between the Federal Political Department of Switzerland (renamed in 1979, the Federal Department for Foreign Affairs) and the USA Embassy in Bern. The Convention replaces the accord of 1968 and, in great detail, describes the arrangement between the USA and Switzerland. It is much too complicated to permit a presentation here of its many provisions. Detailed information can be provided by any Swiss Consulate in the USA, by the Social Security Administration of the USA, or, for questions pertaining to the Swiss Federal Old Age and Survivors' Insurance and the companion Invalidity Insurance Program, inquiries may be directed to the Swiss Compensation Office in Geneva.

FEDERAL OFFICES IN THE SERVICE OF SWISS ABROAD   There are at least ten such offices of the Federal Government that concern themselves with problems that from time to time, are confronted by Swiss residing in a foreign country. Although tempted to list them all and to give a thumb-nail sketch of the responsibilities of each in relation to Swiss citizens living abroad, it is probably better to resist any such temptation. In addition to the federal offices there are a few other organizations that deserve mention: The Auxiliary Committee for Swiss Schools Abroad (an advisory committee to assist the teaching staff and administrators of the 19 Swiss schools in foreign countries); the Schnyder von Wartensee Foundation (extends help as far as possible to Swiss abroad who have suffered as a result of national catastrophes); the Kiefer-Hablitzel Foundation (to help those Swiss who, in commercial enterprises abroad, have lost their livelihood and have had to return to Switzerland); the Swiss Evangelical Union of Churches and the Conference of Swiss Bishops (each has an office that specializes in certain aspects of the religious needs of Swiss abroad such as the choice of ministers and pastors); the Swiss Tropical Institute in Basel (of interest to Swiss in tropical countries and to repatriated Swiss suffering from tropical diseases); the Pro Helvetia Foundation (among a variety of activities, the Foundation organizes cultural events of interest to Swiss in foreign countries).[6]

The Foundation for Young Swiss Abroad (*Stiftung für junge Auslandschweizer*) has an interesting program in progress (1981) that focuses upon young Swiss, of age 7 to 15 years, resident in foreign countries. The purpose is to provide 500 of these children with a summer vacation of four to six weeks duration in the mother country, thereby to introduce some who were born of Swiss parents abroad to the homeland of their parents. To others who were born in Switzerland, life with a Swiss family or in a holiday colony for a few weeks would renew and, hopefully, strengthen their ties with Switzerland. The program is carried out in collaboration with the well-known Swiss organization, Pro Juventute. The Foundation also helps to support Swiss schools abroad and to extend financial aid through stipendia to young Swiss in foreign countries who propose to return to Switzerland for their schooling. For the financing of its activities, the Foundation is heavily dependent upon donations from the general public.

Among the economic organizations, mention should be made of the Swiss Office for the Development of Trade, the Union of Swiss Chambers of Commerce Abroad and the Swiss National Tourist Office. The last-mentioned has branch offices in many cities abroad and renders useful services to Swiss in foreign countries and to foreigners who contemplate visits to Switzerland.

Finally there is the Secretariat for Swiss Abroad, operating under the aegis of the *Neue Helvetische Gesellschaft*. The Secretariat publishes a quarterly bulletin and accomplishes a useful coordination between Swiss in the homeland and those living in foreign countries.

MISCELLANEOUS   Many other matters of concern to the Swiss abroad have been subject to constant examination and the pertinent legislation has been undergoing ceaseless study and revision: diplomatic and consular protection of the Swiss in foreign countries; their military obligations; their political rights; social assistance (welfare); taxation; investments in the homeland and abroad; the rights and obligations of Swiss women abroad; insurance, especially against accidents and sickness and unemployment; vocational training possibilities.

In many cases, the problems revolve around the rights and obligations of dual nationals (a) to their country of adoption (b) to Switzerland especially, resulting from visits of long duration or on permanent return to the mother country. The problems are just as complicated for Swiss citizens abroad who are not dual nationals. It is not feasible to expand upon any of these because of the exigencies of space and the fluid state of the relevant legislation.

Jura, a New Canton

An important event in Switzerland in the late 1970s was the creation of the canton of Jura by detaching a portion of the most northerly part of Bern and conferring upon it the privileges and responsibilities of sovereignty, as possessed by other States (cantons) within the Swiss Confederation. The number of seats in the House of Representatives (*Nationalrat*) hitherto possessed by Bern was reduced from 31 to 29 and two seats were thereby transferred to the new canton. The obligatory referendum by which the canton of Jura came into being had been approved on 24 September 1978.

The separatist movement had a long and turbulent history. If one attempts to date its beginnings, a proposal of the Federal Military Department in the late 1940s to acquire 197 km^2 in the mountainous area midway between Porrentruy and Delémont for artillery practice aroused massive opposition. Although the proposal was modified in the mid 1950s to use of the property for tank exercises (no shooting) the opposition increased. Representatives of 15 villages in the area concerned met in Saignelégier in 1956 and adopted a strongly negative position, including advice to the land owners in the affected area to refrain from signing any sale documents. This was soon followed by an assembly of some 5000 people who vigorously protested the proposals of the Military Department.

The opposition, under the leadership of several experienced agitators and politically inspired theoreticians, quickly became transformed into a separatist movement, determined to establish in the Jura a new canton, sovereign and independent of Bern. The movement, unfortunately, resorted to a great many acts of violence and terrorism from the burning of military barracks in 1962 and 1963 to the use of explosives, and destruction, by other means, of property owned by some of the antiseparatists. The terrorism continued to March 1980 at least.[7] Acts of violence, numbering 21, have been described in detail (**114**).

The head of the *Rassemblement jurassien* and acknowledged leader of the separatists was Roland Béquelin[8] whose contempt for the antiseparatists was ill concealed. In the agreements between the Confederation, the canton of Bern and the Jura is to be found a clause whereby the cantons of Bern and Jura agree to respect the territorial integrity of the other and to behave peacefully toward each other. Despite this understanding, Béquelin and his followers have ceaselessly endeavoured to join the southern Jura (especially Moutier) to their new canton.

The existing canton of Jura consists more or less of the old Bishopric of Basel which was seized by Napoleon and remained under French rule from 1792 to 1813. It consists of about 837 km², populuated by about 67,000 people. Of the working population, 11 to 12 percent work the land, 50 to 58 percent are in industry and the remainder are employed in the service sector. The watch industry, greatly depressed in the late 1970s, is the principal industrial employer. In Choindez, south of Delémont (the capital), there is an iron foundry and in Courfaivre a small motor-cycle factory is to be found. A few other small factories exist in the Jura but two-fifths of the industrial employees are in the watch industry. Factory development suffers from the location of the canton—remote from the main Swiss highways.

In general, the canton faces impoverishment: it is a poor canton. Doubtless it would be strengthened by absorption of the south Jura, whose people have indicated clearly their desire to continue as a part of Bern canton. Tourism is being vigorously promoted as a potential source of additional revenue. Parts of the Jura are well worth a visit by any tourist who is interested in places of natural beauty.

The arms of the new canton consist of a bishop's crozier on the left half and three silver horizontal bars on the right half on a red field. The crozier is in red on a white field and, obviously, is a reminder of the canton's past as the Bishopric of Basel. The right half with its seven horizontal bars was intended to symbolize the seven districts which originally made up the Jurassian territory. It is important to note that when the people in the Jura voted on remaining with Bern or joining the new canton, only three of the seven (Porrentruy, Delémont and Les Franches-Montagnes) voted to join the new canton. The area is heavily catholic and is almost entirely French-speaking. The other four including Laufen and Moutier (Protestant) voted to remain with Bern. Much of the South Jura is German-speaking. In 1949, the three principal Jurassian groups demanded that Bern officially recognize the new flag. Probably to appease the belligerent separatists, Bern in 1951 recognized the arms as a regional flag only. As of 1 January 1979, when the new canton became officially separated from Bern, the regional flag became the cantonal flag of Jura.

Citizens originating in any of the 92 communes of the canton of Jura, residing in any other part of the world have the right to vote in federal matters, like other Swiss abroad, and a similar right to vote in cantonal matters. They must, however, be at least 18 years of age and must have applied to their Commune Secretariat for placement on the voting register. The administrative authorities of the canton are studying the voting rights of Jurassians abroad in the hope of facilitating their exercise of the vote.

A most informative article on the canton—its past and its present—appeared under the authorship of Rudolf Maurer in the *Neue Zürcher Zeitung* (30/31 October 1982, pp. 77–80).

Revision of the Federal Constitution

For years, Parliament has talked about a total revision of the Federal Constitution. The present document, heavily loaded with innumerable amendments, would probably benefit from such a revision.

It now appears that something is being done. A section of the Constitution,

Chapter III, provides the main outlines of the procedure to be followed. Three subcommittees have been involved in the task since 1974, each concerned with an assigned section of the Constitution. By 1977, a draft had been prepared[9] for submission to the Federal Council which would next decide whether to propose a total revision or be satisfied with partial amendment, the latter being the procedure to which the country has adhered since 1874. Professor J. F. Aubert, a member of the Federal House of Representatives (*Nationalrat*), and the author of a concise, informative and authoritative article on the Swiss Federal Constitution (**18**) concludes the chapter by pointing out that, under the most favorable conditions, six or seven years, at least, would elapse before the necessary referendum could reach the people for approval or disapproval—"at present it looks as if the idea of a total revision is of greater interest to the professors than to the general population." I doubt that anything further will be done about the total revision before the mid-1980s at the earliest: the Federal Council in the early 1980s is faced with a variety of problems of much higher priority.

In 1979, the cantonal government of Vaud, convinced that a revision of the Federal Constitution would lessen further the powers of the cantons, thereby violating the important principle of federalism, expressed itself as opposed to the contemplated revision. Much more important, the cantonal government concluded, would be a redefinition of the specific powers of government, those of the Federal Government and those of the cantons, This, in itself, would achieve a revison of the Constitution which might be more fairly accomplished than if the revised draft emerged as the product of committees appointed by the federal authorities.

Federalism

Switzerland is a federation of 20 cantons and six half cantons. Is the Confederation, apart from its small size, comparable to the neighbouring States? Is it, in all respects, a confederation that enjoys total sovereignty? The Federal Constitution, after an introductory declaration of intent begins (Article 1): "Together, the peoples of the . . . sovereign cantons of Switzerland united by the present alliance . . . form the Swiss Confederation." In Article 3 we read "The Cantons are sovereign insofar as their sovereignty is not limited by the Federal Constitution and, as such, exercise all rights which are not entrusted to the federal power." Article 5 continues in a similar vein: "The Confederation shall guarantee the cantons within the limits set forth in Article 3 . . . ."

During the brief period of the Helvetic Republic (1978 to 1803) when Napoleon forced upon the Swiss a Constitution which declared in its first article "The Helvetic Republic is one and indivisible," the conqueror soon discovered that the basic principle of centralism was so foreign to the Swiss that a radical constitutional change was necessary. Hence, in 1803 Napoleon introduced the "Act of Mediation" which was tolerated by the Swiss with less hostility.

For centuries the Swiss have treasured their cantonal autonomy and independence. Indeed, until 1848 when the Confederation was reconstructed into an operational entity, each canton was truly a separate State with its own currency and its own customs barriers. The 26 differ in many ways: in language (four national languages), confession, cultural qualities and the principal occupations of their people. Even the cheeses and wines differ noticeably from canton to canton.

It should be noted that the loyalties of the Swiss are directed first of all to their community, then to their canton, and last of all to the confederation. They have a reluctant and modest respect for federalism but a deep distance for centralism. The cantons yield bits of their sovereign power to the Federal Government grudgingly. The government, however, has devised a happy compromise by concluding many of its laws and decrees with the statement: "Enforcement shall be a responsibility of the cantons."

The reader should be referred to "Swiss Federalism in the Twentieth Century" — an article by Dr. Max Frenkel (138) in *Modern Switzerland* (245) in which the author discusses this important subject much more comprehensively.

The problem is that governments everywhere become top-heavy with administrators and bureaucrats who hunger for increases in their discretionary authority and an accompanying lessening of constitutional restraints. Switzerland is no exception. The draft of its totally revised constitution would elevate social rights to constitutional status and infringe upon or remove the present constitutional guarantees of private property rights. The State, for example, "shall prevent an excessive concentration of wealth, combat economically—or socially—damaging pursuits of profit, and provide for a just redistribution of the surplus value of land" (Article 30 of the draft). This brings us from clearly definable private property rights into the foggy region of social rights where the professional bureaucrat exercises a presumed authority to interpret. The six French-speaking cantons have already expressed their disapproval of any such tampering with the Constitution that would clearly increase the centralistic power of the bureaucrats in Bern and reduce the power of the people and their cantonal governments to cooperate under a federalism which has served the country ponderously, cautiously and slowly, but well.

The Half Cantons

Twenty full-fledged cantons, each with two representatives in the Upper House (*Ständerat*), and six half cantons, each with one representative in the *Ständerat*, constitute the territorial subdivisions of Switzerland. Two of the half cantons, Basel-Stadt and Basel-Landschaft, each with a population somewhat in excess of 200,000, exceed in population nine or ten of the full-fledged cantons. Uri, for example, has a population of about 34,000 but has two representatives in the Upper House. All of the half cantons are eager to be elevated in status to that of the full-fledged cantons and to have a second representative in the Upper House. Representations to this effect have been made to the Federal Council. Several rounds of discussion have been held but have not progressed to definitive action by the Council. The smallest of the half cantons, Appenzell Inner Rhodes with a population of only 13,000, has indicated its willingness to continue, if necessary, with only one representative in the Upper House.

Switzerland and the United Nations

Although Switzerland is a member of UNESCO and of other organizations that constitute a part of the United Nations family of affiliated or subordinate organizations, she is not a member of the United Nations (UNO). When the UNO came into being in 1945 it was, in effect, a coalition of the Powers that emerged victorious from World War II. The adherence of Switzerland at that time would have compromised her position as a country committed to permanent neutrality and so recognized the world over. Switzerland would never have agreed to the system of sanctions as provided for in the UNO charter. However, even the Great Powers have been loath to resort to sanctions. Indeed, the system has proved itself to be ineffective because of disagreement among the Powers as to its use. As a result the UNO has never invoked sanctions against a misbehaving member.

Whatever happens we should be aware of Switzerland's current practice, and good intentions for the future, of rendering all possible financial support to UNO activities. Thus in 1982 she contributed 59.4 million francs to the United Nations: 36.2 million to the developmental program of the UNO, 8.2 million to the children's fund, and 15 million for the special fund of the UNO, designed to help the least developed countries of the Third World. Beyond this, Switzerland makes extra-UNO contributions to the economically needy countries of the Third World. She has also converted a loan of 65 million francs for construction of an international conference center in Geneva to a gift and agreed to pay two million francs per year for five years to assist in its maintenance. This action by the Federal Council, in 1980, did not receive the hearty approval of the *Nationalrat* which, concerned about the precarious financial position of the Confederation, greeted the announcement with loud murmurs of disapproval.

Something should be said about Switzerland and the League of Nations for her experiences in the League account in part for the hesitancy of some Swiss to approve the proposed adherence of their country to the United Nations.

Anyone interested in a comprehensive and authoritative analysis of Switzerland's relation to the UNO can do no better than to refer to Professor Haug's article in *Modern Switzerland*. **(166)**. See also section 11.22 note 9.

Switzerland and the League of Nations

The ending of World War I in 1918 was followed in 1919 by the Treaty of Versailles. Article 435 of Part XV begins with the following declaration:

> The High Contracting Parties ... recognize the guarantees stipulated by the Treaties of 1815, and especially by the Act of November 20, 1815, in favour of Switzerland, the said guaranties constituting international obligations for the maintenance of peace ...

There can be little doubt that this clause in the Treaty of Versailles, supported by the guarantes of 1815, strengthened greatly Switzerland's application for entry to the League of Nations as one of the founding members. Her case certainly needed such support for she sought admission to the League without being required to join in military sanctions if the League determined that such sanctions must be invoked against any member which violated the Charter of the League. It emerged that she was the only member—her application was approved unanimously—to receive such special treatment. This, in turn, weakened the League's solidarity, though solidarity of action is dear to Swiss policy.

The situation of Switzerland vis-à-vis the League of Nations is given official recognition in the Minutes of the League of Nations Council, 13 February 1920, p. 45, Annex 18:

> The Council of the League of Nations, while affirming that the conception of neutrality of the Members of the League is incompatible with the principle that all Members will be obliged to co-operate in enforcing respect for their engagements, recognises that Switzerland is in a unique situation, based on a tradition of several centuries which has been explicitly incorporated in the Law of Nations; . . . signatories of the Treaty of Versailles have rightly recognised by Article 435 that the guarantees stipulated in favour of Switzerland by the Treaties of 1815 and especially by the Act of 20th November, 1815, constitute international obligations for the maintenance of peace.

The Swiss commitment to solidarity is set forth in the following excerpt from the same set of Minutes:

> . . . Switzerland recognises and proclaims the duties of solidarity which membership of the League of Nations imposes upon her, including therein the duty of co-operating in such economic and financial measures as may be demanded by the League of Nations against a Covenant-breaking State and is prepared to make every sacrifice to defend her own territory under every circumstance, even during operations undertaken by the League of Nations, but will not be obliged to take part in any military action or to allow the passage of foreign troops or the preparation of military operations within her territory.
>
> In accepting these declarations, the Council recognises that the perpetual neutrality of Switzerland and the guarantee of the inviolability of her territory as incorporated in the Law of Nations, particularly in the Treaties and in the Act of 1815, are justified by the interests of general peace and as such are compatible with the Covenant.

We should note Switzerland's recognition of her duty to cooperate in such economic and financial measures as may be demanded by the League of Nations. However, in 1938 the Swiss Government asked the Council of the League "to recognize that Switzerland will not particpate in any sanctions whatsoever." The Council agreed (Report by the Representative of Sweden, American Consulate, Geneva, Switzerland, received 16 May 1938).[10] The Council formally approved the report of the Swedish representative and declared that Switzerland will not be invited to participate in sanctions (*L. of N. Journal* 19, 369, 1938).

But things were different in 1920 and Switzerland, eager to be an original member, may not have forseen the difficulties posed by sanctions. We learn that M. Ador, a former President of Switzerland, declared in a statement to the Council of the League "complete neutrality in everything economic and military is clearly inconsistent with the position of a Member of the League (League of Nations

Official Journal, 1, p. 57, 1920) . . . it is a question of making a certain exception in favour of Switzerland (Council Minutes, 11 Feb 1920, p. 3). Nonetheless, Switzerland was accepted as a member.

It was not long before Switzerland's membership in the League of Nations proved embarrassing to both Switzerland and the League. A problem arose from the decision of the Council to send international troops to Vilna to maintain order during a plebiscite relating to a dispute between Poland and Lithuania. Switzerland was invited by the President of the League in early 1921 "to appoint delegates, in order that Switzerland might be represented during the Sessions at which the dispute between Poland and Lithuania was to be discussed" (*League of Nations Official Journal* 2, p. 170 (1921)).

At the Council Meeting of the League on 26 February 1921, M. Dunant (the Swiss Minister in Paris) reported the decision of the Federal Council on the matter at issue. In brief, the Swiss Government, faced with a possible encroachment on Switzerland's neutrality if the passage of troops through Switzerland was permitted, decided in the negative. M. Léon Bourgeois, speaking on behalf of the League Council, then described the decision of the Swiss Federal Council as causing "great moral injury to the League of Nations . . . a preliminary exchange of views would have prevented the incident from arising" (*L. of N. Journal* 2, p. 171 (1921)).

Beyond the embarrassment to the two parties caused by this incident, with its trespass upon protocol and diplomatic niceties, Switzerland may have added fuel to the fire by appealing to her right of independent judgment. But if every member State invoked such a right "continuous cooperation between the nations would be difficult" [M. Bourgeois, *L. of N. Journal* 2, p. 172 (1921)]. The Swiss position, as set forth by Guiseppe Motta, then Head of the Federal Political Department, is clearly expressed in his letter of 12 February 1921 to the Secretary General of the League [(*L. of N. Journal* 2, pp. 173, 174 (1921)] and need not be reproduced here.

The next problem, somewhat late in maturing, concerned damage suffered by Swiss nationals resident in the belligerent countries, or possessions thereof, during World War I. Switzerland claimed, on behalf of her nationals, reparations for damages suffered as a result of the war. Basically, it was contended that her nationals had the same rights to reparations for war damages as did the citizens of the countries involved. In some cases any claim by foreigners for war-time reparations must be sustained by treaties between the belligerent country and the neutral country of which the foreigner who claims damages is a national. In other cases, the claims, if they are to be legally recognized, must satisfy a variety of requirements imposed by the "debtor country." These are too numerous and too varied to discuss in detail.

The Swiss case, essentially against France, Germany, Italy and the British Empire, was built up over several years by the Federal Council and reinforced by a legal statement prepared by Professor Sauser-Hall of the Faculty of Law, University of Geneva. Switzerland, inviting the Council of the League to declare itself competent in the matter, therby desired that the Permanent Court of International Justice be asked to submit an "advisory opinion as to the various legal points arising in connection with reparations for war damage incurred by nationals of neutral countries during the world war" (*L. of N. Official Journal* 15, 1510, November 1934).

The war damage sustained in the belligerent countries consisted in part in requisitions or seizures of property by the armies of occupation or of requisitions of property independently of any military occupation.

The observations of the Federal Council, followed by the legal statement prepared by Sauser-Hall are to be found, in extenso, in the *League of Nations Official Journal* 15, 1479–1510, November 1934. This, in turn, is preceded by the verbatim report (pages 1436–49) of the discussion between the members of the League Council which focused on three fine points of the law: was there a dispute; to which Article, if any, of the Covenant of the League did the Swiss case apply; and was there, in fact, a legal case.

Although "the representatives of the United Kingdom, France and Italy contended that the claims of the war victims were well founded and submitted, . . . for various reasons, the Council ought not to deal with them" (*L. of N. Journal* 16, 620, 1935).

A committee of three, duly appointed to make a final recommendation to the Council of the League following the Council's refusal to seek an advisory opinion from the Permanent Court of International Justice, reported that "the probable results of conciliation are insufficient to justify maintaining the matter on the Council's agenda" (*L. of N. Journal* 16, 621, 1935).

Switzerland was greatly disappointed. Motta expressed the fear that public opinion . . . would look upon the League of Nations as a siren, very beautiful and splendid, but one to whom might be applied the words of the poet: "Desinat in piscem mulier formosa superne"[11] (*L. of N. Journal* 16, 622, 1935).

By 1949, much had changed. The League of Nations had faded away: the United States had not joined the League despite President Wilson's pleading; three members of the League withdrew; the remaining members virtually ignored their responsibilities under the Covenant of the League. By 1945 the League of Nations had quietly expired, leaving behind a beautiful world headquarters building in Geneva, and a world that had just suffered through another terrible war. International sentiment was ready for another committment to peaceful relations and good will among nations and internaional cooperation in almost everything conducive to the welfare of all.

These great hopes and aspirations gave birth to the United Nations Organization. The United Nations Organization came into being in 1945. The problem of reparations for war damages suffered by nationals of a neutral country in a belligerent country had been settled and the propriety of claims for such damages was recognized, at least by some countries. Thus, we find that the Government of the USA in 1949 agreed to pay to Switzerland over 62 million Swiss francs in full payment of claims submitted by Swiss nationals for damages suffered in World War II (*British State Papers* 155, 916–17). Switzerland's claim for damages suffered by her nationals would necessarily be honoured by virtue of the "Convention of

Friendship ... between the United States and Switzerland", 25 November 1850 (*Br. State Papers* 38, 285–90)].

Apparently much patience will be required before Switzerland's claims are settled for reparations covering wartime damages suffered by individual Swiss and Swiss companies with respect to properties owned by them in Communist East Germany. The amount that is claimed, 700 million francs, is the approximate total in reparations sought by 10,000 persons and a number of corporate enterprises.

Not until 1972 was it possible for the two parties even to discuss the problem because diplomatic relations between Switzerland and East Germany were nonexistent.

Since then, at least eight discussions between experts of the two countries have taken place and, sooner or later, a settlement of the claims appears to be probable. The Foreign Minister of the DDR visited Bern in November 1980 and had an official discussion with Federal Councillor Aubert on the state of the problem. The solution may be quite complicated and both parties, aware of the complexities, are determined that every step must be legally correct. Poland, faced with smaller claims for reparations, seems to have settled her debts to Switzerland with trainloads of coal.

Notes and Comments

1. The percentage representation of these four parties in the *Nationalrat* has held firm at 80 to 87 percent since the 1943 electoral year. The four parties are the Radicals, the Christian-Democrats, the Social Democrats, and the Swiss People's Party which are represented in an approximate 2 : 2 : 2 : 1 proportion. The 1979 election made no significant change in the composition of the *Nationalrat* as determined by the election of 1975. From 1919 on, proportional representation was used in determining the number of members in the lower House (*Nationalrat*) to which the various cantons were entitled.

2. Integration of her foreign population is something else. Assimilation, even of those who become naturalized, proves to be a formidable problem in which patience and caution are rewarded by gradual progress.

3. For the Swiss Nationality Law (29 September 1952) please refer to *British State Papers,* **160,** 771–785. It appears in French. Although I have not seen an English translation of the Law, the following publication can be recommended: *The Swiss Review*, Special Issue, 1979, pp. 8–12, obtainable from Secretariat of the Swiss Abroad, Alpenstrasse 26, CH-3000, Bern 16, Switzerland.

4. The concept "Swiss by descent" excludes women who acquired Swiss citizenship by independent naturalization or by marriage. A Swiss woman who marries a foreigner and who wishes to retain her Swiss citizenship must make a written declaration to this effect when the marriage is officially announced. If she loses her Swiss citizenship by failing to fulfill this requirement, procedures do exist whereby, subject to still other conditions, she may be renaturalized. A popular initiative, approved in late 1983, will improve somewhat the equal rights' status of women in matters concerning citizenship. The attainment of Swiss citizenship by their newly born children will also be facilitated.

5. Similar Conventions pertaining to social security have been signed between Switzerland and many other countries.

6. The Feris Foundation of America deserves mention, even though it is a USA Foundation. It supports the Albert Gallatin Fellowship in International Affairs through which an American candidate for an advanced degree (Ph.D.) in International Affairs is enabled to spend a year at the Graduate Institute of International Studies in the University of Geneva. There are plans afoot to expand the Fund in order to permit Swiss scholars in international affairs to spend a year of study in the USA. Albert

Gallatin, born in Geneva in 1761, emigrated to America in 1780. His distinguished career in politics, and as a private citizen, is summarized in reference 357 (13 June 1979).

7. Acts of violence have continued. At La Ferrière in August 1979, five people were wounded by separatists in a shooting incident when a number of cars carrying visitors were passing through La Ferrière from the canton of Neuchâtel. Other less serious acts of violence have been reported. Serious disturbances of the peace also broke out in Cortébert in the South Jura where the *Rassamblement jurassien* held a delegate assembly in March 1980. To convene this assembly in the South Jura (a part of Bern) was a deliberately provocative act. However, the maintenance of peace and order is an inner security problem which rests with the cantons, not with the Federal Government. Bern clearly failed in its responsibility to restrain the demonstrators, to maintain peace and order and to protect the town against such hostile and dangerous demonstrations.

8. The first president of the cantonal government of Jura was François Lachat, less inflammatory in public than Béquelin. Lachat was succeeded in 1982 by Pierre Boillat, a jurist and one of the original five members of the government.

9. *Verfassungsentwurf* (Expert Commission for the Drafting of a Total Revision of the Federal Constitution, 33, pp. 1977).

10. This document contains the draft resolution of the Council which declares that Switzerland will not be invited to put into operation the provisions of the Covenant relating to sanctions.

11. "The body of a beautiful woman ending in the tail of a fish" (i.e. a mermaid) from Horace's "Ars Politica".

11.18. LEISURE-TIME ACTIVITIES AND TOURISM

Introduction

This chapter is intended to cover sports, hiking and games requiring physical activity. Sedentary activities such as watching television programs, attending cinema, theatrical and musical performances are excluded, not because of any adverse value judgments but because of an unusual dedication of the Swiss to developing and maintaining a good physique and a strong healthy body. Even if one's working hours are spent in fairly heavy physical labor there is something about participation in sports and games that contributes a value other than that of mere muscle building.

> Anyone with more than an armchair interest in Switzerland will have been impressed by the encouragement she gives to the physical fitness of her people. Government at all levels participates in supporting the variety of activities that are involved—physical education and gymnastics in the schools, organized sports . . . and a great deal of hiking with exhausting charges up and down the mountainsides. An ascent of 1500 meters on a *Wanderweg* hike hardly deserves mention. To many of her people, a high degree of physical fitness is an inevitable result of the environment, of life in a country with high mountains, rolling hillsides, valleys that ascend steeply into the mountain pastures and an economy in which agriculture, despite much forbidding terrain, plays a very important role.
>
> But there is more to this than meets the eye. Switzerland depends for her defense on a nonprofessional army. Hers is a militia in which all men of military age must always be in readiness to respond instantly to a military emergency. They must be physically fit at all times; theirs must be a state of body readiness for which they have been prepared by physical education and sports—later supplemented by an annual course of military training (**220**, p. xii).

And, to quote from Brunner's excellent and authoritative article on Leisure-Time Activities (**66**, pp. 255–58):

> To the Swiss, sport is a leisure-time occupation. It must not interfere with, let alone endanger, education at schools or on the job. Nevertheless, physical education, sports, and games are considered of such value that more recently one has even come to connect

747

them with youth policy and to esteem them highly because of that. Also, in the course of the past few decades, a wider public has become aware that some sportive activity is necessary to the health of the sedentary population of our time. . . . For boys and girls of school age, exercise and sport are an intrinsic part of their total education which must bring together soul, mind and body. . . . Sport is considered to be primarily the domain of non-governmental sports clubs. . . . The Federal Government assists moderately where the private organizations lack the proper means. However, the government is vitally interested in a widespread popular development in the interests of youth, public health and physical fitness; it provides encouragement through appropriate measures and financial support. . . . The federal law . . . since March 17, 1972 effectively regulates government promotion and provides the legal basis for financial credits and other encouraging measures. . . . Even if the Constitution of the Swiss Confederation of 1874 made no provision for physical education and sports . . . the Federal Government, based on its constitutional duty to develop military defense, reserved to itself the right to make rules with regard to one branch of learning of military relevance, viz physical education and sports, and significantly enough only for boys: The primary aim was quite obviously to make sure that the young Swiss were kept physically fit for military service.

Sports Federations

In 1980, some 68 federations with a total membership of over 2,650,000 covered most of the gymnastic activities and sports in Switzerland. Not too much significance should be attached to the grand total because it is reasonably certain that some members would belong to more than one association. Incidentally the three largest associations were the Swiss Rifle Association (*Schweiz Schutzenverein*) (562,780 members), the Federal Society of Gymnasts (*Eidg. Turnverein*) (442,702 members), and the Swiss Football Association (*Schweiz. Fussball-Verband*) (310,244 members). With only a few exceptions they are also the oldest of the 68, being founded in 1824, 1832 and 1895 respectively (**341**, 1981, pp. 524, 525).

Youth and Sports

In addition to the 68, there is a large organization known as Youth and Sports (*Jugend und Sport*) which is administered centrally by the Federal Government. As the name implies, its membership consists of young people from 14 to 20. Relatively few of this age group belong to the associations listed above. Each canton has a local office to cooperate with the youth organizations within the canton. Courses and tests are given in most of the sports of interest to the youth. Training is offered at three levels: beginners, further training for the average person, and advanced courses for athletes in particular sports.[1] Instructors are also trained in three programs: one for group instructors, another for course instructors and a third for instructors attached to large organizations.

The salaries of the instructors and other relevant expenses are paid by the Federal Government: 3.71 million francs for the gymnastic and sport associations, and 2.00 million francs for construction of sport facilities were contributed by the Federal Government in 1980.

A federal law in 1972 empowered the Federal Government to issue rules and regulations on physical education and sports instruction in schools. Instruction is compulsory for three hours each week. Specified half days or full days are also covered by the physical education rules, as well as camps devoted to sports. Toward the cost of this compulsory physical training, the Federal Government contributed 2.33 million francs in 1980.[2]

Since, in many cantons, compulsory schooling ends at age 14 or 15, the Youth and Sports programs must be regarded as "fillers" to maintain the country's youth in good physical condition between the end of compulsory schooling and the years of compulsory military training which commence at age 20 and continue for the next 30 or 35 years—an overall total of about 52 weeks, inclusive of 17 weeks in recruit school at age 20. Somewhat anomalously, for they are not subject to compulsory military service, girls are included in the Youth and Sports programs.

Organization of Sports

Although the Federal Government intrudes itself minimally in the organization and regulation of physical education and sports, the present system is a bit complicated but it seems to work tolerably well.

NONGOVERNMENTAL AUTHORITIES   First of all there are the nongovernmental authorities with important responsibilities:

(a) The Swiss Association for Physical Education (SAPE) is the top organization of the Swiss sports association. Through a central committee of 13 members representative of the sports associations, the Swiss Olympic Committee and two other organizations, SAPE endeavours to co-ordinate the activities of all the participating groups and to serve as a liaison with the governmental authorities. It operates through a secretariat with a director, a press chief, and researchers. In matters concerning the Olympic Games, SAPE functions through the Swiss Olympic Committee.

(b) There is also the Swiss Committee for Top Athletes (SCTA). With a membership of nine, SCTA represents the Executive Board of SAPE, the International and Swiss Olympic Committees, the Swiss School for Physical Education and Sports, the Swiss Committee for Physical Education and Sports and the Swiss Football Clubs. SCTA maintains a central management and a corps of full-time experts. As the name implies it focuses on training and development of the best Swiss athletes.

GOVERNMENTAL AUTHORITIES   The interest of the Federal Government in physical education and sports has been mentioned in the introduction. The rules and regulations of government provide for financial help where needed, and require that physical education and sports be a compulsory part of the lower school curricula. Finally, through Youth and Sports, government encourages programs of physical fitness to fill in the seven-year gap between the end of compulsory schooling and the beginning of military training with its arduous demands on the body as a result of much strenuous physical activity. Two quasi-agencies of the Federal Government serve as the administrative authorities.

(a) The Swiss School for Physical Education and Sports (SSPES). As the executive organ for the Federal Government, the school serves as a training center, a center for research, and an administrative office to handle the responsibilities of government in physical education and sports. In cooperation with the Swiss Committee for Physical Education and Sports (SCPES), the School disposes of all the tasks in this field assumed by the Federal Government. The School is located at Magglingen (high above Biel) on a large and magnificent site with all of the facilities that appear to be necessary: the school building; six dormitories; one guest house; a center for research; a large-indoor stadium for games and athletics; two gymnasia (40 × 25 m and 25 × 15 m); one pavilion each for rhythmical gymnastics and for boxing, judo, and wrestling; one 400 meter track; one training track of 300 meters; one playing field with a synthetic surface; six lawn-covered playing fields; one field for javelin and discus throwing; one soccer field; one covered and one heated open-air swimming pool; and still other miscellaneous facilities. Its budget comprises all expenditures of the Federal Government for physical education and sports. In 1976 "it amounted to about 40 million Swiss Francs" (**66**, p. 260). Please refer also to Notes and Comments—No. 2.

(b) The Swiss Committee for Physical Education and Sports (SCPES). This committee serves in an advisory capacity for the government. Its 21 members represent the cantons, schools, the SAPE, the nongovernmental research organization and sports associations by whom they are appointed. The SCPES operates through subcommittees of experts. The secretariat is maintained at Magglingen.

International Competitions

Despite this tremendous interest of government and people in sports, the Swiss have not fared well in Olympic games. But there are exceptions. In skiing, the Swiss women have done brilliantly in international competitions. Without meaning to downgrade several others, Lise-Marie Morerod, Marie-Therese Nadig and Erika Hess should be mentioned. The first two are winners in the overall competition for the World Cup. Nadig was a double Olympic champion in 1972 and came in third in the 1980 Olympics.[3] Erika Hess won the bronze medal in the Lake Placid Olympic slalom. In 1981, 18 or 19 years old, she won every slalom event in which she was entered, including the World Cup competition. She was also the World Cup champion in 1984 and, in 1985, won the gold medal at the World Alpine Championships in Bormio, Italy, in the women's combined event. If Liechtenstein may be thought of as part of Switzerland, as it almost is, we can include the remarkable Hanni Wenzel who, at Lake Placid, won two gold medals and one silver medal. Her brother, Andreas, is almost as good.

Two or three Swiss men have good records in international events but, in this person's opinion, they have been outclassed by the women in skiing.

The USA boycott of the Olympic Games in Moscow, proclaimed by President Carter on political grounds, did not receive extensive support. The Swiss Olympic Committee by a close vote of 24 against 22 decided to be represented but left the troublesome question of participation open for decision by individual sporting groups. When all was decided, riders from Britain, France, and Switzerland refrained from entering the Moscow event. The shooting contestants from France and Switzerland also decided to remain at home. Two other sports (gymnastics and fencing) were represented by mini-delegations from Switzerland. Although Switzerland could only be classified as a partial participant, 81 Swiss athletes were selected by the Swiss Olympic Committee for the Games in Moscow—26 more than were sent to the Montreal Olympics in 1976.

Other international contests in which Switzerland has fared well deserve to be mentioned. Tug-of-war (*Seilziehen*) is a great sport in some of the cantons in which a number of communities have tug-of-war teams of which they are very proud. A heavyweight team from Engelberg (Unterwalden) represented Switzerland in an international contest at Santa Clara, California in the World Games of 1981. The team emerged undefeated and won the gold medal. In the lightweight class, the Swiss team proved to be second best of the seven national teams and won the silver medal.

Dressage is a sport requiring consummate skill in riding and a remarkable ability of the horse to respond to sensitive and almost imperceptible guidance by the rider. Christine Stückelberger of Switzerland was the recognized world champion in the dressage events for women in the 1970s.

Sports for Adults

The various federations mentioned in preceding sections organize the adult sporting activities. Almost all of them belong to SAPE, with a few, such as the Swiss Association of Swiss Wrestlers,[4] remaining outside of SAPE as independent organizations. All of the associations are autonomous and independent of the government. In choosing the Swiss members of Olympic teams and any other world-wide or European championship contest, SAPE becomes involved as well as SCTA—the special Swiss committee for top athletes. The Swiss Olympic Committee is very actively concerned with Swiss participation in Olympic games. The Federal Government's role is largely that of providing financial aid. It does so, through annual subsidies to SAPE, and to the sports associations. The funds must be used for the training of instructors and of participants in championships. SAPE also receives 25 percent of the net profits of the football pools—an important source of income to the association.

The Swiss Rifle Association, with a membership of over 500,000 is unusual. A considerable number of its members are in the militia and are required to join a shooting club for their compulsory practice. Ammunition is provided free of charge to the members of the militia each of whom has a rifle or pistol provided by the military department. The regulations require attainment of a certain standard of performance. Failure to achieve this is followed by obligatory participation in additional shooting courses.

The 68 associations referred to earlier in this section embrace almost every sport of which one can conceive plus a few that are atypical for one reason or another. One of these, with some 66,000 members, is the Swiss Association for Company Sports

(*Schweiz. Firmensport-Verband*). Its members provide a large number of splendid facilities for sports, made available by industrial firms, banks and insurance companies for the benefit of their employees.

Typical Swiss Games[5]

I suspect that every winter sport of which one has heard is known, practiced and enjoyed in Switzerland. Some winter sports are even practiced in the summer. Skiing, for example, is possible in the high mountains—notably on some of the glaciers, if one has the necessary expertise and is not deterred by exceptional risks such as crevasses. All the usual indoor and open-air sports of summer are well known in Switzerland.

One need only mention a few that appear to be uniquely Swiss. I shall avoid detailed descriptions of each for they are well described by Brunner (**66**, pp. 265–272).

SWISS WRESTLING (*SCHWINGEN*)   Unlike ordinary wrestling the two contestants are first required to take hold of his opponent's trunks (short leather-belted cotton or linen) in a formally prescribed manner. The contest begins when the umpire calls out *Gut* (good) and a contestant strives mightily, while holding firmly his opponent's trunks to hoist his opponent in the air before throwing him to the ground. *Schwingen* is a very popular sport among the Alpine herdsmen of central Switzerland and the Bernese *Oberland*, with its origins believed to be in the sixteenth century. Each year there is a Federal Swiss Wrestling and Alpine Festival. The victor in the wrestling becomes the King of Swiss Wrestlers (*Schwingerkönig*) and receives a young bull as the traditional prize.

STONE-PUTTING   The Festival also features a stone-putting competition in which a contestant lifts an egg-shaped granite boulder of 83 kg (185 lb) as high as his head and throws the stone as far as possible. The record is about 10 feet. The boulder, known as the Unspunnen Stone, carries the date of the first festival which was held at Unspunnen in 1805.

HORNUSSEN   This game, popular in the Bernese Emmental particularly, is playfully known as farmers' tennis, each of the receivers being armed with a catching board on a long handle, used to knock down the *Hornuss* (hornet) if it is about to enter the valid zone, 100 to 300 meters beyond the batter. The game might equally well be described as farmers' golf because the *Hornuss*, shaped like a hockey puck, is driven from a fixed tee by use of a long whip-like club. The batting boards may be thrown in the air if desired—anything to intercept and knock down the oncoming *Hornuss*. The batting party consists of 16 men, each entitled to three attempts to drive the *Hornuss* for a landing in the valid zone. There is a Federal Hornuss Association with about 9000 members.

MAZZASPIEL   This game, played in parts of the Graubünden, can best be described as a form of baseball without bases.

CROSS-COUNTRY HIKES, MARCHES AND SKIING   Organized cross-country hikes of any distance from 10 to 100 km are very popular. A 100 km hike, in 1976, attracted almost 4000 starters. In addition, popular marches are much in favour and in the 1970s, received a total participation of 20,000 to 30,000 people.[6] The Military Department arranges a variety of competitive events. For the marching courses the participants must be fully equipped and armed. "Each year nine such traditional courses with 600 to 1500 participants are held; the oldest and most important of them is that of Frauenfeld which covers a distance of 42 km." (**66**, p. 272).

As for cross-country skiing, at least 60 cross-country ski courses are held each year. The Engadine Ski Marathon covers 42 km and enjoys the participation of about 10,000 men and women.

Several games deserve mention, not because of the physical activity involved, but because they may be typically Swiss. Also they are enjoyed in the great outdoors.

MÜHLE   *Mühle* is a game played with large wooden counters, each on the end of a 10″ or 12″ handle. It reminds one somewhat of checkers. The game is played on three concentric squares painted on a firm base such as a concrete slab. It is illustrated in Figure 1 which also shows the spots to which the players may move their counters (pieces). Each player is provided with nine pieces, one set of one colour, the other set

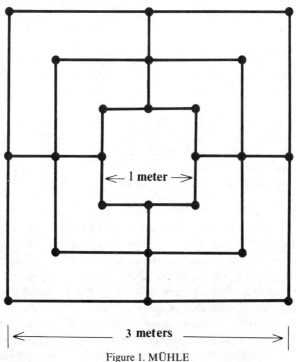

Figure 1. MÜHLE

of nine being of a different colour. In turn, each player places a piece on one of the unoccupied spots until all 18 are placed. If, however, a player in so doing completes a row of three, his opponent must sacrifice one piece already on the grid. The game continues with two players alternately moving one piece at a time and striving to complete a row of three (diagonals excluded). Whenever this happens he may remove from the grid any one of his opponent's pieces that he may choose. The game becomes slightly more complicated when a player has only three pieces left and ends when a contestant is reduced to two.

It is obvious that the game could equally well be played indoors on a grid no larger than a checker board and with ordinary checkers as the playing pieces. I am acquainted only with the outdoor game which alone is relevant although it certainly requires very little physical activity.

OUTDOOR CHESS   Another popular game is outdoor chess. The pieces, beautifully carved, are 18" to 24" in height. The chess "boards" are permanently ruled off by painting appropriate areas approved by the authorities. In Bern several public squares have facilities for chess and *Mühle* and are well patronized by the many who enjoy these games.

ARCHERY   Championship contests in cross-bow shooting are also held in various localities, the most important being under the patronage and supervision of the Swiss Archery Association (*Schweizer Bogenschutzen-Verband*) or the Swiss Cross-Bow Association (*Eidg. Armbrustschützenverband*). The latter holds a grand *Armbrustenfest* every few years (usually five). The sixteenth was held at the recognized center of the sport in the Bernese Oberland community of Ringgenberg-Goldswil on the right bank of Lake Brienz. Eighteen or more separate village organizations are embraced by the association and its steering committee of 30 members.

RIFLE SHOOTING   Rifle shooting contests with many participants arouse much interest. Practice shooting on innumerable rifle ranges goes on every Sunday. As mentioned earlier, the Swiss Rifle Association is the largest and oldest (1824) of the federations for sports and gymnastics. The Military Department lends all possible assistance and encouragement for these contests.

Conclusion of "Leisure-time Activities"

As a concluding thought, it should be emphasized that sports in Switzerland are of unusual importance. Although they are leisure-time activities they are an essential part of the national policy toward youth, young adults of pre-military age, and adults in military training. The many associations specializing in every conceivable sport are independent and autonomous. Membership is voluntary. The Federal Government encourages physical education and sports and provides modest financial support. But it does so unobtrusively for the typical Swiss dislikes anything that smacks of centralization. Independence and minimal intrusion of government in his daily life are cherished ideals that are partly realized. He understands the need for federalism, because Switzerland, despite its many complexities and inter-cantonal differences is still one country—happily unified in spite of its diversities. He knows full well that the 26 cantons could not survive in the modern world, if each were to insist upon the total independence and sovereignty of the distant past.

Tourism

The tourist industry is probably among the oldest of the Swiss industries. As Krippendorf has pointed out, Romans travelled 2000 years ago to Helvetia (now known as Switzerland) most as members of the military forces, but others to enjoy the pleasures of the thermal baths (**210**). Even then, tourism may have been an important industry but it is impossible to compare it in economic terms with the revenue derived from foreign trade (please refer to Chapter 1). In 1960 Switzerland's income from tourism was reported to be 1.580 billion francs as compared with 6.870 billion francs in 1980. After correcting for the cost to Switzerland of the many tourists (7.75 million in 1960; 10.94 million in 1980[7]) the net income derived from tourism is reported to have been 0.940 billion francs in 1960 and 2.010 billion in 1980 (**341**, 1981, pp. 226, 232). After making allowances for margins of error in the financial data, it follows from the gross income that "the tourist industry (ranks) third among Switzerland's five leading export industries, after the machine and chemical industries and ahead of the watch and textile industries" (**210**, p. 287). About 40 percent of the guests arriving at hotels, motels, pensions and health resorts (*Kurorte*) are from Switzerland and Liechtenstein. The health resorts receive about 0.7 percent of the incoming guests, most of whom are Swiss in search of the thermal baths and the evil-smelling waters which are copiously consumed.

The average tourist, according to the *Statistical Yearbook*, appears to spend about three to four days on holiday (35.72 million nights lodging for 10.937 million guests).[8] Krippendorf has tabulated the data on guests and guest-nights from 1910 to 1975 (**210**, p. 278).

During the 1970s, the Graubünden was consistently the most favored holiday region for the Swiss. Freiburg, Neuchâtel and the Jura were the least popular, with the Bernese Middleland and Zurich only slightly more in favor. Foreign visitors, with equal consistency throughout the 1970s, picked the Geneva region as their first choice, the Graubünden came in second and Zurich was a strong third (**341**, 1981, p. 228). The preferences are different in the winter when the winter-sport fans prevail among the tourists. As may be expected, most of the foreign visitors in Switzerland come from Germany, with France, Great Britain and the USA high up on the list. The data expressed as millions of guest-nights, are presented in Table 79. See also Table 80. The currency exchange rate and other factors in the late 1970s had a serious depressing effect on the inflow of tourists, except from the USA and Germany, as shown by the data for 1977, 78, and 79.

The cost of hotel accommodations reported in the 1981 Yearbook (p. 227) covers the range of less than 20 francs per room per day to 80 francs and over. Most of the Swiss guests (52.8 percent) chose accommodations within the range of 20 to 39.50 francs per room per day (data for 1980). A curious exception would be guests who

Table 79   Foreign tourists in Switzerland[a] (millions of guest-nights)

Years	Germany	France	Italy	Great Britain	USA
1960	4.178	2.654	0.987	2.913	1.489
1977	6.685	1.964	0.770	0.956	2.553
1978	6.804	1.705	0.686	1.083	1.931
1979	6.246	1.623	0.700	1.051	1.440
1980	7.789	1.800	0.802	1.354	1.731

[a] Source: **341**, 1981, p. 225.

went to Zurich: 23.6 percent of the group preferred rooms at 80 francs or more; only 33.7 percent behaved like average Swiss (20 to 39.5 francs per day). Guests from foreign countries spent somewhat more than the Swiss: 36.8 percent of the total paid 30 to 49.50 francs per room per day; of those who settled down in Zurich, 45.6 percent paid 80 francs per day or more. There are many hotels and motels in Zurich but travel agencies abroad are inadequately informed, as a rule, about the lesser known (and inexpensive) hotels—not only in Zurich but elsewhere in Switzerland. A publication is available from the Swiss National Tourist Office that reports year by year on hotel accommodations in most of the cities, towns and resort areas: number of rooms, baths, price per day, etc. (**358**).

Youth hostels, popular for many years in Switzerland were heavily patronized in the 1970s and early 1980s. As the name implies, they provide hospitality for young travellers—in Switzerland up to 25 years of age. Older people are usually accepted if space is available. Again, the Swiss National Tourist Office or any of any of its many branch offices in foreign countries has an abundance of information about the youth hostels.

Camping out has also been much in favor. In 1980, for example, 7.66 million guest-nights were chalked up by visitors with tents or private motor vans. This is more than 21 percent of the guest-night total attributable to hotels, motels, and health resorts (**341**, 1981, p. 231). Over 450 camping places are available for tourists who prefer these outdoor accommodations; most are located within easy reach of the main thoroughfares. Surprises may await the campers: in July 1980 a sudden snow storm brought plenty of snow above 1000 meters and the collapse of many tents unable to support the load. Chains were required of motorists at the high mountain passes such as the Flüela (altitude 2383 m).

Tourists, in the late 1900s, traveled around Switzerland by almost all the known methods of transport, except by camel or elephant. The Swiss get about on foot, by bicycle, motorbike, automobile, autobus, airplane, train, or boat. In 1978 I was having dinner in a small hotel restaurant in an out-of-the-way village. The place was packed. I asked my Swiss friend, "Who are all these people?" "Oh, they are Swiss people on holiday." "But what do they do here? There's nothing in sight except forests, hills, meadows and cows." "They eat, sleep, and walk—a good breakfast

Table 80 Tourism—international comparisons[a]—Number of tourists in 1979

Country of residence	Country of arrival							
	Switzerland	West Germany	Great Britain	Canada	Spain	USA	France	Oceania
Switzerland	—	401,978	296,000	28,000	398,068	89,000	1,780,000	—
West Germany	1,857,400	—	1,379,000	125,200	3,210,649	369,000	6,650,000	—
Great Britain	324,400	634,584	—	340,600	2,762,851	533,000	2,800,000	—
Canada	112,900	120,405	528,000	—	—	12,083,000	400,000	—
Spain	122,300	117,698	267,000	8500	—	59,000	730,000	—
USA	1,020,900	1,350,566	1,686,000	11,460,000	2,352,202	—	1,200,000	—
France	636,200	544,399	1,324,000	77,900	—	216,000	—	—
Oceania	96,500	94,238	442,000	54,400	—	221,000	220,000	—

[a] Source: **341**, 1980, pp. 598, 599.

followed by a two- or three-hour stroll; a hearty lunch, possibly a siesta, another walk of several hours; an even heartier dinner and off to bed."

The Swiss love to walk. Several times in Grindelwald I have taken the chair lift up to Grindelwald First. Below me, a number of hardy natives, young and old, were to be seen scrambling up the mountain side.

Foreigners also walk—sometimes. The *Wanderweg* movement, doubtless of special appeal to the Swiss, has also proved inviting to the foreigner who, wherever he is based for his holiday, can use any one or more of many *Wanderweg* books with footpaths, changes in elevation (ups and downs for every walk) and time required, clearly laid out. The Federal Government, following upon a request of the people and a popular vote in February 1979, agreed to increase its financial support of the *Wanderweg* movement.[9]

Despite the extensive coverage of Switzerland by train, autobuses and private cars which give access to most towns and villages in the land, quite a few small villages are to be found which are accessible only by foot, horseback, dog cart or possibly by motorbike. I remember walking up the Tsmutt valley from Zermatt to take a look at Tsmutt itself—a village(?) of six or so buildings with no public transport facilities, about 5 or 8 km from Zermatt by an uphill footpath of a sort.

Travel by train or autobus is remarkably good. The tourist, since spring 1972, has been able to avail himself of the Swiss Holiday Card, good for eight days, two weeks, or one month and providing unlimited travel by rail, boat, and postautobus—the entire network of the Swiss Federal Railways, most of the private railways, the lake boat routes, and the entire postauto system. The cards are not available to the Swiss, except to those who reside in a foreign country. Several other reduced fare schemes exist that are tempting to young and old, and to Swiss and foreigners alike.

As one might expect, holiday tours by air, train, and bus have been increasing in number and variety throughout the decade. They have been bewildering to travel agents, the carriers, the travelers and all concerned, mainly because of fluctuations in exchange rates, USA deregulation of this and that, and frequent changes in costs of transport.

One of the great attractions of Switzerland is that the tourist may enjoy its natural pleasures throughout the year. November has stood out as the month when tourism falls to its lowest level: no exceptions since 1953 at least (**341**, 1962, p. 220; 1969, p. 213; 1981, p. 229).

Notes and Comments

1. Participation in the Youth and Sports programs is not compulsory.

2. The subventions of the Federal Government for physical education and sports are somewhat obscure. On page 421 of the 1981 Yearbook (**341**) the relevant entry suggests that the total subvention for 1980 was 15.27 million francs. On page 408 we find that the expense of the Federal Government for Culture, Recreation and Sports was 97.7 million francs. The same category on page 412 appears as an expense of 109.7 million francs. The portion specifically devoted to physical education and sports is not indicated.

3. She retired from the competitive sport in mid-1981 and became official trainer for the women's football club of Bad Ragaz.

4. Swiss wrestling is quite unlike ordinary wrestling with which it should not be confused: the rules and techniques differ greatly. Both kinds of wrestling are practiced in Switzerland.

5. In Basel, a Swiss Sports Museum is located. Documents, equipment and outfits applicable to typical Swiss sports are in the museum. In 1984 an exhibition entitled National Games of Switzerland, such as *Hornussen* and *Schwingen*, was opened.

6. In June 1984 about 12,500 persons from 22 countries took part in the twenty-fifth Swiss two-day march. Approximately one-half of the participants were children and young people. A military contingent also engaged in the march, with soldiers from Denmark, West Germany, Holland, Austria, France, South Africa, the USA and Switzerland (379 young men from 8 recruit schools). Civilian participants were required to cover 20, 30 or 40 km per day. The soldiers had a daily assignment of 30 or 40 km, each man carrying his weapon and a pack weighing 8 kg.

7. Other tables in the 1981 Yearbook report 16.862 million guests and 75.282 million nights of lodging (pp. 230, 231). These data include the parahotels (holiday chalets, tents and camping vans, youth hostels and other modes of accommodation) instead of only hotels, health resorts, motels, pensions and sanatoria (so-called *Hotelbetriebe* and *Kurbetriebe*) to which the smaller figures (10.94 million guests and 35.72 million guest-nights) pertain. Krippendorf's article on tourism includes a Table that compares the statistical data on Swiss tourism in 1970 and 1975. All types of lodging are listed, their capacity (expressed as number of beds), numbers of Swiss guests and foreigners (expressed as thousands of guest-nights). The figures are impressive: in 1975, 284,133 beds were available in hotels and health resorts, and 636,308 (mostly estimated) available in other lodgings (the parahotels), giving a grand total of 920,441 available beds. Guest-nights in 1975 totalled 68.23 million (**210**, p. 279).

8. Four to seven days if we include the parahotel facilities (cf. preceding comment).

9. The expansion of roads and highways seriously encroaches upon the foot and *Wanderweg* network, leading to a current annual loss (early 1980s) of about 1000 km of footpaths (**226**, 10–11 March 1984, p. 35).

11.19. THE RED CROSS

Origins

One is tempted to date the origins of the Red Cross from the battle of Solferino in 1859, the suffering of the wounded, Henri Dunant's widely distributed booklet "Memories of Solferino," and what appeared to be a sudden world-wide determination to do something humane about battle-field casualties. But, however, sudden the awakening may have seemed, there is a long history of the introduction of more and more merciful practices into the conduct of war.

For centuries, the Swiss were regarded as heroic but merciless fighters. There were two rules only: "Take no prisoners, kill all enemies on the field of battle" and "never retreat, never surrender, fight to the death." The relatively few Swiss who escaped the slaughter of 26 August 1444, at St. Jakob on the Birs were treated as cowards who deserted the field of battle instead of fighting until they were killed.

The teachings of the Church—we are all God's children—eventually had an effect. Soldiers were permitted to bury their dead and care for their wounded. Some of the old Chronicles picture weaponless attendants who helped the wounded, gave them water to drink, and carried them away from the field of battle. The Sempacher Brief, which was concerned with warfare, gave protection to churches, cloisters and chapels. They may not be burned, robbed, or entered by force. Women must be spared and fully protected against war-time violence.

Early in the history of the Confederation, the Swiss appeared as mediators, not only in the resolution of intercantonal strife but also in efforts to resolve the problems of neighbouring belligerents who were fighting it out or threatening to do so. A peaceful solution was sought. Rather late in Swiss history we learn of the Swiss view of asylum—a handmaid of neutrality—to which the Swiss clung stubbornly against the arch conservatism and threats of Metternich and the European monarchs. Somewhat related was the Swiss acceptance of refugees from confessional wars (e.g. Huguenots) and later of political refugees who harbored ideas that were anathema to the monarchs.

With the Enlightenment (*Aufklarung*) came the belief that the rules of warfare must protect elementary human rights and decency. Thus, the wounded among the enemy, as well as your own, must be treated humanely. Treaties were negotiated between belligerents providing for the proper care of the dead and wounded.

Bonjour tells us (**57**, p. 125) that 300 such treaties had been negotiated prior to the Geneva Convention. The imprisoned sick and wounded were entitled to care.

Certain personnel categories of both belligerents must not be imprisoned: doctors, field surgeons, pharmacists, army chaplains and various kinds of service personnel. The idea of neutralizing hospitals was introduced in the eighteenth century. But in 1809, during the Napoleonic wars, a doctor made the comment "Unfortunately we have not yet reached that degree of humanity." It came about, however, that food, clothing, building materials and money were procured by private and governmental contributions for humanitarian purposes—even apart from war. Strengthened by Dufour's orders in 1847–48 at the start of the Sonderbund war, the concept became accepted that the wounded and injured of all countries deserve humanitarian treatment.

By 1859 the time was ripe for Henri Dunant's vision of well organized procedures for the humane treatment of the wounded and provision of ancillary services in time of war. Dunant himself was a young man of 31 when a business trip led him directly to the battlefield near the small city of Castiglione where over 6000 wounded were laid out. Doctors, attendants, nurses and essential medical supplies—even bandages—were lacking. Forgetting about his business, Dunant organized a volunteers' service to care for the wounded. Following Dunant's "Memories of Solferino" in 1862, the *Société génévoise d'utilité publique* asked the following question:

> Should it not be possible in all European lands to found societies with the purpose of using volunteers to care for the wounded in time of war without reference to nationality?

A committee of five, all from Geneva, with Dufour as chairman, studied the problem, and, in 1863, a small preliminary international conference was held: 14 governments sent 36 persons—doctors and diplomats—to study the idea further. The Federal Government gave the project its official blessing by calling 25 countries to a second conference. At first the military people objected to the idea: they did not favor the use of volunteers. But, despite various objections, the conference reached, in unanimity, a successful conclusion—the Geneva Convention—"*Convention pour l'amélioration du sort des militares blessés dans les armées en campagne.*" The Convention, in ten Articles, provided for neutralization of field hospitals and their personnel, return home of the healed soldiers incapable of further combat, designation of field hospitals, service vehicles and personnel by a red cross on a white field.

All countries may belong. The universality of the organization is inseparable from its neutrality. It shall be unconditionally nonpartisan. It shall have two functions: in war it shall concern itself with the wounded, the prisoners, the interned and the impact on the civil population; apart from war it shall minister aid in civil catastrophes to the homeless, the sick and the starving.

The Geneva Conventions

The Convention of 1864 was followed by a second in 1929. These two were revised in 1949 and supplemented by a third and a fourth in the same year. The Convention of

1929 defined the treatment to be accorded prisoners of war. As applied to the millions of captives in World War II, the mortality rate during the five-year period did not exceed 10 percent wherever the Convention was observed. In camps for detention of the political outcasts where legal protection was lacking the mortality rate was as high as 90 percent (**292**, p. 478).

The third Convention applied humanitarian practices to the victims of war at sea, while the fourth extended these principles and practices to the civilian victims of war. To each of the Conventions, a new Article 3, concerned with civil war, was added.

In general, it may be said that the protection, care and humane treatment required under these Conventions must be extended without any kind of discrimination—be it of nationality, religious confession, or belligerent status. The victims of war, including those who take no direct part in the hostilities, are embraced by the Conventions. The hospitals, field stations, vehicles used for the transport of the sick and wounded, medical personnel, hospital ships, and the victims of naval combat are all included under these Conventions. The Fourth Convention requires that all civilians, deprived of their liberty by war-time internment, must be given a status at least equal to that of prisoners of war. Places of internment must be open to inspection by the Protecting Power and the International Committee of the Red Cross (ICRC). Deportation, the seizure of hostages and looting are specifically banned.

The Red Cross and Neutrality

It is important to note that the Red Cross must adhere rigorously to the practice of neutrality. It may not take sides in hostilities nor engage at any time in controversies of a political, racial, religious or ideological nature. This is but one of a number of fundamental principles proclaimed by the Twentieth International Conference of the Red Cross in Vienna in 1965.

The International Committee of the Red Cross (ICRC)

The ICRC, the founder of the Red Cross, is a private and independent organization of Swiss citizens, 15 to 25 in number. It is self-perpetuating: the members select and appoint new members, including replacements on the Committee. Although national in composition, its activities are international. Because its members are citizens of a small perpetually neutral country with no political ambitions and a history of non-interference in the affairs of other countries—unless it be as a mediator—the countries of the world have complete confidence in the impartiality of the ICRC. Its relief actions are aloof from the political arena. Wherever there is war, the ICRC is to be found, provided only that the national authorities permit entry of the ICRC representatives: they may not cross a frontier without permission, nor may they force their services on those who may not want them. In general, however, the ICRC is well received: the interests of the governments concerned are well served, for example in the many prisoner-of-war problems that confront a nation at war. The ICRC operates a Central Tracing Agency for prisoners of war and civilians. During World War II the Agency processed 40 million information cards and provided news to several thousand families a day. The Agency is now a permanent institution.

The National Red Cross Societies

From 1865 on, national Red Cross societies have been founded throughout the world. As is well known, the national societies engage in a multitude of peace-time activities: relief in epidemics of disease, in teaching hygiene, in organizing relief for the homeless and starving—the victims of such natural disasters as floods, tornadoes, and earthquakes. The Red Cross movement concerns itself with almost all forms of human suffering, the world over. It is a world-wide voluntary relief institution in which all national societies have equal status and share equal responsibilities and duties.

Charles Dickens and the Red Cross

In discussing the origins of the Red Cross, a paragraph or two must be added about Charles Dickens, his anguish over the horrors of battlefields and the absurdity of warfare. He visited Switzerland in 1844, 1846, and 1853, falling in love with a country in which he found both tranquillity and stimulation. In Lausanne he wrote "The Battle of Life," a part of which pertains to the suffering and folly of war. In his "Seven Poor Travellers," Dickens asks himself how men, noble in character, killed in battle at Waterloo or in the Crimea, "could find the path of duty leading them to kill each other, sometimes in hand-to-hand combat." These were men in the opposing armies who, in fact, harboured no feelings of personal hatred toward each other.

From Switzerland, Dickens received a copy of Dunant's eye-witness account of the battle of Solferino and the horrible aftermath of suffering by the wounded. He wrote an eloquent eulogy in which he extolled Henri Dunant who, on the day after the battle, though a "travelling amateur, a tourist, entirely stranger to and disinterested in the mighty struggle . . . had worked on under the scorching sun to bring hastily improvised relief to the worst cases of the wounded, mostly in vain. . . . For three days and three nights a pitifully inadequate number of carts took away the dead and the dying." Dickens' review of Dunant's book was widely read and made a great impression upon the English public. One may assume that Dickens' strong endorsement of Dunant helped to engender support for founding the International Red Cross. His tribute to Dunant was published in May 1863. The first and most fundamental of the Geneva Conventions was formulated in 1864.

In the preparation of this section, I have drawn heavily upon Bonjour (57) and Pictet (292). The concluding paragraphs about Charles Dickens are based on Schazmann's booklet "Charles Dickens in Switzerland" (318).

11.20. ARMAMENTS AND NATIONAL DEFENSE

Introduction

Unlike the military policies and systems of other countries, the Swiss military forces are organized as a militia for the defense of the homeland. Her military policy precludes offensive operations into a neighboring country. Defense of the independence and neutrality of Switzerland is the prime objective. A permanent standing army is not a part of the Swiss military system. Rather, Switzerland depends upon the universal training for military service of all her citizens of military age, women being excluded from combat service but enabled to participate as volunteers in other essential services.

The chapter by Dr. Kurz on "Swiss National Defense" in *Modern Switzerland* describes adequately and authoritatively those aspects of the subject that are sufficient to provide a well-rounded background (**211**, 403–18). I propose only to discuss the weapons industry, defense strategy, and one or two miscellaneous topics that came to one's attention in the mid-1980s.

Weapons

Switzerland's neutrality is an armed neutrality which reflects the country's determination to defend herself against any violation of her borders by a foreign Power. Implementation of this policy requires heavy expenditures for the military equipment that is indispensable for modern warfare. If possible, a country prefers to be independent of all other countries in weapons procurement, hence able to manufacture for its own needs all the weapons and sophisticated gadgets that one can conceive as indispensable for war.

EXPORTS   Obviously, there are few countries, if any, that are so independent. For a small country such as Switzerland, the maintenance of a total-weapons industry capable of producing the aircraft, the tanks, other surface-based weaponry, the munitions and all ancillary equipment and facilities required for modern warfare would be quite impossible unless sustained by a huge volume of exports.

Herein we face the first of the problems encountered by a small country. In Switzerland, the law requires that an end-use certificate be obtained before an export of arms can be permitted. This is a document wherein the purchaser declares that the specified weapons are for his own use and will not be transferred elsewhere

765

without the supplier-country's consent. By use of another document, the import certificate, which the exporting country may demand of the country of destination, as official proof of the country's intention to import a particular consignment of arms, an additional safeguard is provided against diversion of the weapons, during transit, to another country (**338**, pp. 39, 40).

Swiss policy, set forth in a 1968 law (Federal Law concerning War Materials, Articles 1, 2 and 11) does not permit the export of arms to a country at war or where there is a threat of war. In April 1967 the Swiss Political Department learned that a group of Nigerian army officers would be visiting several countries, including Switzerland, to procure weapons. The Military Department was promptly advised that export licenses for the contemplated purchase could not be granted because of the threat of civil war in Nigeria. By January, 1968, the Swiss Embassy in Lagos had evidence that some of the anti-aircraft guns being used in Nigeria were of Swiss manufacture. By July 1968, the Political Department became convinced that the anti-aircraft guns, manufactured by Oerlikon-Bührle, were recent exports shipped illegally to Nigeria. The Office of the Federal Attorney confirmed this and pursued the inquiry further. The illegal sales to Nigeria were valued at 5.4 million Swiss francs. Illegal sales to other countries began in 1965 but were not discovered until 1968 by which time the grand total reached 88.7 million francs. The sales are broken down in Table 81. See also Table 82.

These illegal shipments were received finally by countries under an arms embargo. Oerlikon-Bührle arranged the sales by employing end-use certificates obtained from officials in non-embargoed countries. The signatures were forged. The Swiss government was not involved directly in these illegal shipments: the documents seemingly in order, gave false destinations, namely to non-embargoed countries.

Table 81   Arms exports[a] (presumably illegal)

Purchaser		Value—in millions of francs
South Africa	35 mm AA guns	52.7
Israel	30 mm ammunition	
	(for aircraft cannons)	19.5
Egypt	AA guns	6.5
Nigeria[b]	AA guns (mostly 20 mm)	5.4
Saudi Arabia	8 cm air-to-ground rockets	4.5
Lebanon	20 mm ammunition	0.15
	Total[c]	88.75 mill. francs
		($20.5 million)

[a] Source: **338**, p. 46.
[b] 87.9 million francs in 1983.
[c] Total exports of war materials in 1983 approximated 471 million francs. Shipments were made to 69 countries (**357**, 7 December 1983).

Table 82 Total weapons exports and weapons exports to Third World Countries[a,b]

Exporter	Weapons exports		Percentage of total to the Third World
	Total	To Third World countries	
USA (average 1962–68)	2500[d]	930	35
USSR (average 1962–68)	(2000)	(800)	40
Great Britain (average 1964–68)	4000	(200)	50
France (average 1965–68)	470	(200) ·	40
Italy, 1967	(75)	40	50
West Germany, 1967	75	20	25
Sweden (average 1965–69)	30	5	15
Switzerland (average 1967–68)[c]	30	5	15
Canada (average 1965–68)	(80)[e]	(30)	40
Others	(180)	(110)	60
Total	5840	2340	40

[a] In millions USA dollars.

[b] Source: "Die International Handel mit Waffen" (**266**, 26 March 1972). See also reference **338**.

[c] In the 1970s, Switzerland exported to Iran weapons valued at over 500 million francs.

[d] USA sales of war materials in 1975 totalled 9500 million dollars through government channels and 600 million in direct commercial transactions. The 1974 total was between 9000 and 10,000 million dollars with about 80 percent representing purchases by Middle East countries (testimony of Lt. General Fisk before a subcommittee of the House of Representatives).

[e] Canada's exports of war materials to the USA, about 300 million dollars per year, are not included.

When the dust had settled, three employees of Oerlikon-Bührle were found to be the principals in the scandal. One of those arrested was sentenced to five years imprisonment and a second to one year. The third, Dr. Dieter Bührle, received only a slap on the wrist—a fine of 20,000 francs ($8750). The Oerlikon-Bührle affair, a shameful incident that discredits a great Swiss manufacturing company, is described because it indicates how arms may be exported if the seller is determined to circumvent the law by the use of falsified documents (**266**, 20 and 22 December 1968; 1 February 1969).

Troublesome also is the formulation of a crystal-clear and unambiguous definition of a "threat of war" or of a military menace to human rights. Also the definition of war materials is anything but simple and, with little difficulty, can be circumvented. For example, civilian aircraft can usually be exported anywhere with few restrictions. Received ultimately in a high-risk country (possibly by a re-transfer) they may be fitted with enough weaponry to convert them into fighter planes or bombers. Cameras for aerial photography, the operating parts of watches, and even barbed wire, with little stretch of the imagination, can be defined as war materials. The Pilatus-Porter planes, manufactured by Bührle at Stans, were civilian aircraft and were not listed as war material, but with appropriate mountings they could be equipped with 20 mm anti-aircraft cannon. In 1979, according to press reports (**357**, 3 September 1980) war material valued at 18 million francs was sent via Italy to Ecuador. Whether this re-transfer to Ecuador received the full approval of the Federal Council appears to be in question. Ecuador and its neighbours were known to be chronically troubled by civil disturbances and even civil war. The export of Pilatus-Porter planes from Italy to Ecuador and other high-risk countries such as Chile, Bolivia, Guatemala, Burma, Iraq, Jordan etc. was never questioned because they were not listed as war material. The Chief of the legal division of the Federal Military Department contends that the export of the Pilatus-PC7 planes did not violate the law against export of war materials (**357**, 5 December 1984). Allegedly, the export of Swiss-made 20 mm anti-arcraft cannon through Italy to Ecuador was approved by the Federal Council.

Tanks, armed or unarmed, assault vehicles and ancillary equipment are listed as war materials and their export to the high-risk countries of South America is strictly forbidden. It is alleged, however, that Mowag tanks (Swiss-made) and assault weapons have been reaching these countries, unhindered, for years (**357**, 3 September 1980). In many cases it is extremely difficult to verify such allegations: the statistics themselves are not easily interpreted and some unpleasantries are glossed over by the authorities. Note also that the export of parts of weapons is permissible and this loophole, if fully exploited, circumvents the main intent of the law. One may also suspect that foreign subsidiaries, such as branches of Swiss firms in Italy, may be beyond any effective control by the Swiss government. For example, Egypt purchased anti-aircraft weapons at a cost of 600 million francs from an Italian subsidiary of Oerlikon-Bührle. The weaponry was used to strengthen Egypt's defenses on the Egyptian–Lybian border. The Swiss weapons-export law, applicable only to weapons made in Switzerland, could not be used to restrain sales of armaments by a foreign subsidiary of a Swiss firm.

The export of arms, presumably in full accordance with the law, is not inconsiderable. In 1977 it amounted to 513 million francs with West Germany as the principal purchaser. The sale of arms fell to 426 million francs in 1978 ($231 million) and by 1980 had declined to $186 million. This decrease is attributed by arms-industry officials to a lack of new products. West Germany continues to be the principal purchaser of Swiss weaponry ($96.6 million in 1983). Purchases by Western Europe accounted for all but $27.8 million of the remainder.

During the war in Vietnam, specifically in 1967, the government of the USA was instructed by the Swiss government that Swiss military equipment sold to USA forces in West Germany must not be transferred to Vietnam. Relatively small quantities were involved.

The export of arms by Switzerland is not readily accepted by the people. The foreign policy hazards involved in the sale of armaments are recognized. But it is also clear that without such exports the domestic arms industry would perish. The 1968–69 inquiry into the sale of arms by Oerlikon-Bührle led to new restrictions on the company's operations. The most serious was a prohibition of any new export contracts. It was soon established that the resulting decrease in production would jeopardize the supply to the Swiss army of Oerlikon guns and ammunition. This proved to be a cogent argument for removal of the restriction because the company was about to receive a substantial order, in accordance with the 1969 budget, for 35 mm anti-aircraft guns needed by the Swiss armed forces. The restriction against issuance of new export licenses to Oerlikon-Bührle was promptly rescinded.

But the Bührle affair was not forgotten and by 1971 the popular pressure to prohibit the export of arms received expression in a popular initiative to increase control of the arms and to forbid the export of arms. The relevant clause concerning exports was as follows: "The export of military weapons, munitions and explosives is forbidden, including all materials serving war-technology purposes and the integral parts [of military weaponry]." The status of the problem and arguments pertinent to the initiative are discussed in a report of the Federal Council (73, 16 July 1971, 1585–1633). In March 1972, Parliament debated the problem at length, including the report of the Federal Council and that of a commission of the *Nationalrat* which recommended, 13 to 1, that the popular initiative be disapproved. The many arguments, mostly against the initiative, have been presented, *in extenso*, in the *Neue Zürcher Zeitung* (7, 8, 9 and 11 March 1972).

The parliamentary debates also included a discussion of the possible collaboration of the three Neutrals (Belgium, Sweden and Switzerland) in policy and in cooperative manufacture of armaments for their own needs.

When the initiative came to a vote on 24 September 1972 the result was even closer than expected: 584,726 votes in favor; 593,205 votes against, 7 cantons for, 15 cantons against.

The Swiss position on the export of arms can be partially summarized: (a) the domestic manufacture of arms and munitions is necessary for protection of her independence, defense against aggressors, and maintenance of her neutrality; (b) a domestic industry adequate for these purposes can not be sustained unless the substantial export of arms and munitions to countries at peace is permitted and the necessity of heavy imports of some weapons is recognized.

Table 81 summarizes exports in the 1960s to the Third World, including arms and munitions, by the principal industrialized countries. The high percentage devoted to purchase of weapons is discomforting. Should the money (borrowed) not be used for better purposes?

IMPORTS   In 1979 the government approved an expenditure of 1.44 billion francs ($900 million USA dollars) for the Swiss armaments program. In the fall of 1980 the *Nationalrat* commenced the study of an armaments program which would cost 1.55 billion francs.[1] Of this total 382 million francs would be represented by contracts with Swiss private industry, while 187 million would be for arms manufactured by Swiss government installations. This would leave about 980 million francs for imports consisting principally of self-propelled howitzers, guided anti-tank missiles, rocket launchers, anti-radar electronic devices, military planes and helicopters.

Much of the aircraft is purchased in the USA. In 1976, the Northrop Corporation sold to Switzerland fighter planes with a total value of 400 million dollars. In return, Northrop agreed to return to Switzerland by 1983 no less than 143 million dollars in the form of direct purchases of Swiss products, by producing certain aircraft parts in Switzerland or by assisting Swiss companies to expand their exports into new or existing markets. By 1980 this counter-assistance program had returned the equivalent of 150 million dollars to Switzerland. In effect, Northrop became a sales representative for more than 200 Swiss concerns, and helped them secure many new sales contracts in world markets. Of the Swiss exports under this program about 35 percent are for the USA and 65 percent go to other countries. Well satisfied with this arrangement with Northrop, Switzerland, in 1980, contracted with Northrop for another supply of fighter planes valued at $335 million dollars. In an offset contract, Northrop is pledged to obtain $140 million of business for Swiss companies in nondefense activities (for example, aerial photography, wine presses, interior design, X-ray equipment).

Some of the planes purchased by Switzerland are partly or totally assembled at the Swiss federal aircraft factory in Emmen near Lucerne. This part of the Northrop contract helps to satisfy the demand of the Swiss worker for increased assistance to the domestic industry. Such assistance has also been urged as a means of reducing unemployment which in early 1983 reached 0.8 percent of the work force, in contrast to the 0.1 percent to which Switzerland has long been accustomed. Military trucks are manufactured in Switzerland and proponents of the program to fight unemployment insist that many more could be made by the domestic industry. Licensing arrangements with German, American and British firms are under discussion and, if realized, will permit the building of army tanks of foreign design in Switzerland.[2] This would supplement the domestic production of Swiss Mowag tanks.

Under President Carter, a reduction in the export of weapons to non-allied countries was planned. The allies were defined as the NATO lands, Japan, Australia and New Zealand. Switzerland fell into a second category which might suffer restrictions in the purchase of USA weaponry. Switzerland, proud of its long history of friendship with the USA and of its status within Europe, was said by some Swiss to have suffered reduction to the level of a "Banana Republic." Aided by a visit to the USA of the Swiss Minister of Defense, Rudolf Gnägi, in February 1979, the possible restrictions on purchases by Switzerland proved to be more imaginary than real.

PROTESTS   The export business in weapons does not rest well with many Swiss. A petition calling for a total ban on weapons exports was circulated within the Federal Institute of Technology in Lausanne and received the signature of 346 professors, research associates and assistants. The signatories deplored the participation of Switzerland in an industry the products of which are used for the "massacre of human beings." The economic, political and social arguments advanced in favor of the sale of arms were deplored as an "indignity unworthy of our people and incompatible with humanitarian ends."

The close vote on the popular initiative to forbid the export of arms and to increase the controls by government over the armaments industry proves that a great many Swiss disapprove of Swiss participation in the export of weapons and are strongly in favour of increased restrictions on the operations of the domestic arms industry.

Protests take still other forms: (a) the people of Rothenthurm (canton of Schwyz), by popular vote have expressed by a heavy majority their disapproval of the proposal of the Military Department to construct in their neighbourhood a place for weapons storage, parking of army vehicles, and rifle practice;[3] (b) a somewhat similar proposal by the Military Department to construct an all-year rifle range with ancillary facilities at Champéry (western Valais) has led to vigorous protests by the people and local government of Champéry. They object to the presence of military personnel in substantial numbers, and the adverse effect of the proposal on tourism and pleasurable use of the well-developed and heavily patronized facilities for skiing; (c) early in 1983 a group calling themselves the "Group of Radical Ecologists" succeeded in penetrating by night an area developed in Frauenfeld (Thurgau) by the army as a parking area for military motor vehicles. They set fire to a number of the vehicles and did extensive damage. Inscribed on a nearby wall was to be found "Rothenthurm never!" In a letter to the media the group protested the destruction of the environment by the army's extensive use of concrete (*Verbetonierung*) in developing the motor park; (d) the Social Democrats, protested i n Parliament in 1981 the plan of the Federal Council to spend 880 million francs for the purchase of 38 additional fighter planes and 40 training planes. The protests focussed not on any questioning of the important principle of ensuring the security of the country against an aggressor. The concern of the party was directed against the magnitude of the funds available to the Military Department at a time when the national debt was soaring and the financial health of the Confederation was considered by many to be precarious. The protest of the party was expressed by members withholding their votes when endorsement by Parliament of the proposed expenditures was sought. The same tactics were used in 1980 when the voting credits amounting to 1.2 billion francs for acquisition of weaponry came up for approval. As would be expected, not all members of the party joined in these parliamentary protests.

CANTONAL LAWS CONCERNING WEAPONS   It has long been recognized that legislation governing the acquisition and carrying of weapons in Switzerland is inadequate and what there is of it at the federal level is too liberal and is even lax in enforcement. When the citizen commences his military duties at the age of 20 he is provided with his military equipment which he must keep in his home. This is convenient, for he is required to engage in frequent practice on an army rifle range, and need only, on a Sunday for example, throw his rifle over his shoulder and cycle over to the nearest rifle range. It is also helpful to have his weapon at home in case he is suddenly called up for maneuvers or actual wartime service: in uniform and with his rifle he can reach his pre-assigned place of duty on very short notice. When he finishes his years of military training the weapon remains with the service-man. It is alleged that during these years of retirement some of the weapons may be siphoned off, ultimately appearing in the hands of terrorists. Machine pistols and semi-automatic rifles of Swiss manufacture have been found on a number of occasions in the possession of terrorists.

Although the weapons used by the army are controlled by federal legislation, the cantons under their own laws regulate the procurement and carrying of weapons acquired by civilians for their private use, in contrast to the weapons issued by the military authorities. In some cantons, rifles may be purchased legally with few if any restrictions. The weapon that killed a high German official in Karlsruhe in April 1977 was a semi-automatic small caliber rifle (HK43) which had been legally purchased in Malters (Lucern canton). Federal Councillor Kurt Furgler once described Switzerland as a "self-service weapon-supply store for terrorists" (**266**, 8–9 March 1980).

Trade in weapons was first regulated by an Intercantonal Concordat in 1944. Ultimately all the cantons adhered to the Concordat. After 20 years it was replaced by another which included tear-gas pistols and tear-gas spraying equipment. The Concordat was approved by the Federal Council in 1970. Licenses were required for some weapons. The issuance of licenses for weapon purchases by some applicants could be denied if, for example, the use of the weapon could endanger themselves or a third party.

In all cantons the acquisition of revolvers and pistols is regulated but not necessarily by the same set of rules. Indeed the regulations governing purchase, -carrying on one's person, or transport in a vehicle, differ so much from canton to canton that the upright citizen while obeying the law on such matters in his own canton, must think twice about driving across Switzerland with any kind of a weapon, especially a revolver, in his car—e.g. in the glove compartment. Security guards and inquisitive police can show up unexpectedly.

While acquisition of weapons is one thing, the carrying of weapons is something else. In 16 cantons the carrying of weapons is regulated and a license to carry a weapon is required. In Zurich—a large city—only 493 persons in 1979 held licenses. A weapon silencer is regarded as something desired only by persons of criminal intent. In Zurich and several other cantons their possession is illegal. However, thedetermined Zurcher need only to step into a neighbouring canton and the purchase can be made. The carrying of rifles is not a punishable offence. The party in question may be on his way to a rifle range, to a hunting expedition, or to a gunmaker.

Some of the regulations are not easily enforced. In Zurich, in 1979, 262 persons were apprehended and fined for carrying forbidden weapons—revolvers, pistols, tear-gas weapons, knives of a certain kind, and daggers. A considerable number of these weapons were discovered and seized by security guards at the Zurich airport.

The weapon of a criminal is usually a revolver or a pistol, seldom acquired legally, almost always stolen. In 1970 to 1979, 2836 pistols and revolvers were stolen in Switzerland. Less than half as many rifles were lost to thieves. A great deal of ammunition (203,937 rounds) was also stolen (**266**, 8–9 March 1980).

LOSSES[4]   The Swiss Air Force has been plagued by losses of aircraft through accidents in the air attributable to a variety of causes, some of which remain unexplained. In 1951, 16 planes and helicopters were lost; in 1960, eleven; in 1965, ten; in 1967, nine; in 1979 and 1980, two; and in 1981 the military aircraft losses totalled nine: three Mirage IIIs, two Vampires, two Tigers, one Venom and one Hunter. Three pilots and one civilian lost their lives in these accidents. Flying with fighter planes and helicopters in the necessary training exercises and simulated air combats is an unavoidable high-risk activity especially in view of the restricted air space available above Switzerland. Much is being done by the Air Force to reduce these unfortunate accidents.

Defense Strategy[5]

In World War II, after the fall of France, Switzerland found herself surrounded on all sides by the Axis Powers. Granted that Switzerland could speedily summon several hundred thousand men "to the colours," the defense of her frontiers against aggression would be extremely difficult, if not impossible. With a total length of 1860 km (**341**, p. 3, 1981) and a male population of about 735,000 between 20 and 34 years of age (**341**, p. 27, 1981), it may be assumed that 350,000 elite forces could be rushed to Switzerland's defense in the first call-up. If every kilometer of the entire frontier was subject to an equal threat of penetration by the enemy every man of the "Elite" force would have to defend about 5 meters of the frontier.

Obviously, and fortunately, this is not what would happen. Long stretches of the border are mountainous and almost self-protective against an invading land force. The northern and western frontiers are less impregnable. Fewer men need be committed to defense of the south and east.

Shortly after his election as Commander-in-Chief, General Guisan altered radically the defense strategy.

> He concentrated the core of the army in the interior of the country, so that, sacrificing for the time being the bulwarks of the frontiers and the midlands, he could carry on the defence of Swiss independence in and along the Alps (**58**, p. 367).

This strategy—resort to a *réduit* system—with heavy dependence upon mobile defense forces in the deep interior of the country has led to another development since 1950 or so. This has involved the construction, on an enormous scale, of bomb-proof and radiation-proof underground installations equipped with thousands of tons of ammunition, food, clothing, and medical facilities designed to sustain the army during a conventional or nuclear war. A group of journalists privileged to have a glimpse of one of the installations—a three-story underground supply base—was informed by Divisionär Edmund Müller, Vice Chief-of-Staff for logistics that the overall length of the supply caverns was about 100 km exclusive of fortresses, hangars and other underground facilities that could house the entire army plus their aircraft, artillery, ammunition, food and fuel. This concept of defense assumes that supplies from abroad could not be obtained in wartime and domestic production would be reduced to the vanishing point—hence the necessity of vast reserves (252).

By 1990, almost the entire civilian population will have war-time protection in well-stocked underground shelters, including hospitals and first-aid posts with 72,400 beds. The shelters offer protection against nuclear radiation, chemical weapons and near hits by conventional weapons. They are equipped with foot-thick double-armoured doors, generators, air filters and other essential equipment. Food is stocked for three days instead of 14 days as once contemplated. The total cost of the project is currently estimated at $2.79 billion. The Federal Government provides currently (1980) about $100 million per year and this is matched by an equal sum contributed by the cantons and communities.

Implementations of the program comes under the Civil Defense Service which is compulsory for men between 20 and 60 who are not subject to combat duty. Participation by women is voluntary. At present the Civil Defense Service involves about 250,000 people.

Also very relevant to defense strategy is a description by Kurz of the organization of the Swiss army (211, p. 411):

> A recently issued troop ordinance anticipates the distribution of the armed forces according to the following territorial breakdown: (a) the border areas, in which the access routes to the interior plains are blocked, and which protect the army's mobilization and deployment capabilities; (b) the interior of the country, where war is waged flexibly with modern, partially mechanized units; (c) the alpine areas, which are secured by a special alpine corps; and (d) airspace, which is defended by airborne and anti-aircraft troops—which, however, do not form an independent part of the army, but rather are subordinated to the armed forces.

The actual field army, consisting of 12 divisions, is mobile, in principle, and is not confined to specified localities. It consists mainly of the "Elite" forces (age 21 to 32). In addition there are many brigade units which defend fixed positions. They consist principally of the *Landwehr* troops (age 33 to 42). Finally there are the *Landsturm* troops (age 43 to 50) who constitute the territorial service. Its members support and relieve the army of certain localized duties and are responsible for military protection of the civilian population, As a result of the militia system and for democratic reasons the army does not have a general in peace-time. The highest peace-time rank is that of corps commander.

Switzerland is not under any illusions as to the outcome of a war in which she would be forced to defend to the utmost her people and their country.

> ... the defensive combat which Switzerland would have to conduct would not be a war for a victory in the conventional sense. Switzerland would be struggling to preserve as much as possible of the substance of her population and to retain the maximal portion of her national territory. She would have to struggle to hinder the opponent as much as possible in his plans by putting up an obstinate, long-lasting resistance which for the aggressor should be as costly as possible. .... In a direct attack, waged in relentless combat, the aggressor must be effectively prevented, by means of aggressive tactics, from

achieving his goals for as long as possible. Such a combat is a defensive war, ultimately waged by the entire nation for survival. Far beyond the resistance of the organized army, a bitter war of resistance would be waged against the invading enemy in all admissible forms, which would delay the control of occupied areas and serve as effectively as possible to make all of the enemy's actions difficult. In these later phases of a defensive war the various forms of small-scale and guerilla warfare would come into effect. This would not only be intended to combat the enemy's immediate operations—but also to provide a starting position, as favorable as possible, for a new beginning after the war— for only a nation which has fought to preserve her freedom deserves to obtain it once again after the war. (**211**, pp. 415, 416.)

CIVIL DEFENSE Switzerland's elaborate system of civil defense is described above. Supplementing the system is a number of alarms which are described on the penultimate page of Swiss telephone books: a general alarm of one minute duration; an alarm of two minutes against radioactive emissions from a nuclear catastrophe; a six-minute flood alarm (dash to the nearest high ground). Brief instructions on what to do for self protection are given in the telephone book. Test warnings, twice a year, will give the residents of Switzerland's 3029 communities a chance to practice survival in a world threatened by all too many major hazards to the existence of mankind.

Women and Military Service

Article 18 of the Swiss Constitution states that "Every Swiss is obliged to perform military service." Military service certainly includes combat duty, from which women are excluded, as may be inferred from subsequent Articles. For example, Article 19 states "The Federal Army consists of

(a) the troops from the cantons;

(b) All Swiss who, though not belonging to those troops, are nevertheless subject to military service."

Combat duty is a responsibility of the troops. Women would belong to category (b). Article 22, par. 5 states that "Women may engage in voluntary civil protection; the details of such service shall be regulated by law." From this we may conclude that military service, so far as women are involved, means participation in the Civil Defense Service as volunteers. I suppose this could change, e.g. if it became legally possible for the cantons to include women in their troop contingents, or if the inclusion of women in the Civil Defense Service became mandatory rather than voluntary.

The role of women in military service has become a subject that deserves clarification. This stems, in part, from the need to define as precisely as possible, what we mean by equal rights for women. Does this mean that equality of rights as between men and women implies an equality of responsibilities which could be literally interpreted to mean combat duty for women and military training, equal to that of men, for those who are physically capable of being in the armed services? From the results of a questionnaire that originated in Swiss women's organizations one is permitted to conclude that if women are not to be trained for military service, they should receive obligatory training in first aid, civil defense, etc., including what may be called a right-to-survival training (**357**, 24 May 1980).

Objections to Military Service

In 1977, a popular initiative to permit civil service duty instead of military service by conscientious objectors and by those who have ethical objections to the bearing of arms, came before the people and was heavily defeated in a December votation. However, the same question, possibly modified, can come before the voters again and again. Initiatives dealing with *Überfremdung* and what to do about the growing proportion of foreigners in Switzerland, came before the people five times and were defeated with increasing majorities. The proponents appear to have given up, at least for the time being: the last defeat was in April 1981.

And so, without surprise, we learn of a second attempt to so amend the constitution that civil service could be performed in lieu of military service. In the first attempt (December 1977) a popular initiative to this end was introduced and defeated. In a second effort the proponents extended considerably the scope of objections. Anyone who objected to military service would be free of military responsibilities if he engaged in appropriate civil services, doing so for $1\frac{1}{2}$ times as long as would be required of him in the active militia. A commitment to peace; removal of the causes of gigantic confrontations, as in war; recognition of human values; and the strengthening of international solidarity were all cited by the proponents as arguments in favor of the initiative. As civilian duties, in place of military service, we find that work in hospitals, in old folks' homes, service in refugee organizations, and assistance to the economically depressed inhabitants of the higher mountain slopes (the mountain-farm population) were proposed. The initiative was heavily defeated (February 1984). Military service is required of all men who are physically acceptable and between the ages of 21 and 50 years. For this group an alternative civil service is not permitted. Transfer into the civil defense service occurs after attaining 50 years of age.

Defeat of the popular initiative, mentioned above, would seem to close the door against any who seek exemption, because of religious belief and conscientious objections, from the existing obligation to bear arms. In general, there is no permissible form of alternative service which exempts men from the requirement to bear arms at some time or other.

But there are occasional exceptions. On record is the case of Jürg Merk who, like his father and grandfather, belonged to the evangelical community of New Baptists (*Neutäufer*). When called up for military service in June 1979 he presented a written request that, because of his religious beliefs and his conscience, he be permitted to serve in the medical corps: he would not carry a weapon. Although Merk's two brothers, his father and his grandfather had been allowed to perform weaponless service in the medical corps, his own request was denied. In July 1979 he was ordered into the artillery corps' communication services as an *Ubermittlungssoldat*. He replied that he categorically refused to use or be concerned with weapons, even at the risk of punishment by imprisonment. The case dragged on for two years. Finally a military court ordered a five-day arrest and two years' probation. The President of the Court has indicated that one may assume that Merk will now be permitted to discharge his military duties in some form of weaponless service (**357**, 25 February 1981).

Notes and Comments

1. In April 1983, the Military Commission of the *Nationalrat* approved an appropriation of about 1390 million francs for equipment procurement in the fiscal year 1983. Of this sum, 180 million francs would be for a new series of assault weapons and ammunition required for new 5.6 mm weapons.

2. By mid-1983, the Federal Government decided to purchase military tanks from West Germany (the Leopard 2). By means of a licensing contract the tanks would be manufactured in Switzerland with Contraves A.G. as the principal licensee. Estimates suggest that subcontracts will involve the participation of several hundred Swiss firms. Initially, 420 tanks were to be purchased at a cost of 4.5 billion francs. In September 1984, Parliament was considering a downward revision of the number. Whether the final order will call for 380, 390 or 400 tanks was undecided at the end of 1984.

3. In the spring session of 1983, Parliament approved construction of the proposed military facility at Rothenthurm at an estimated cost of 108 million francs. Despite local objections, it must be assumed that the Military Department now has the necessary permission to go ahead with the project; qualified, however, by the launching of a wide-ranging popular initiative "For Protection of the Moors" which could delay construction of the facility. Initiants claim that in the past hundred years 90 percent of the natural moors and moorland has been lost by draining or overbuilding. The high moor of Rothenthurm, 10 km^2 in area, is reported to be the largest in Switzerland and, unique in nature, is of general European significance.

4. Several factories in Switzerland are engaged in the manufacture of explosives, gunpowder, and related munitions, the principal customer being the Military Department. The Federal Government is the owner of at least two of these factories. Although security procedures to protect employees against injury or death from explosions or fires are believed to be thorough and rigorously enforced, occasional fires and explosions cannot be totally avoided. Several such untoward events in the early 1980s at factories in Wimmis (Bern canton), Isleten (Uri canton), and in at least one other installation, have claimed seven or eight lives and caused property damage of some millions of francs.

5. The general defense of Switzerland is conceived by the Federal Council as "merely the instrument" of the country's security policy. To be adequately informed about the many elements that enter into Switzerland's security policy and hence her general defense strategy, the reader should refer to the English-language publication "General Defense." This 55-page document is the Interim Report of the Federal Council to the Federal Assembly, dated 3 December 1979. It can be obtained from the *Zentralstelle für Gesamtverteidigung*, 3003 Bern, Switzerland.

11.21 ENERGY

Conventional Sources

Currently, hydropower is generated in more than 400 plants scattered throughout the country. For the average hydrographic year, the total hydroelectric production amounted in recent years to about 36–37 TWh,[1] of which roughly one-third is accumulation energy, mainly from Alpine dams, and two-thirds is run-of-river energy.

By the 1970s, Switzerland had virtually exhausted her reserves of undeveloped sources of hydroelectric power. In 1981, representatives of several communities on the Rhone river proposed development of ten small power plants on a stretch of the Rhone between Chippis (near Sierre) and Bouveret (at the mouth of the Rhone on Lac Leman (Lake Geneva). The two communities are about 65 km apart and differ by about 150 meters in altitude. The proponents claim that this fall in the river would permit the development of about 730 million kWh of energy—i.e. about 40 percent of the present annual increase in Switzerland's energy consumption. In early 1981 Motor-Columbus A.G. sought a concession to build five hydroelectric power plants on the 30-mile stretch of the Rhine between Trübbach and Sennwald (St. Gallen canton). In an average year, these plants should produce about 440 million kWh of energy. Many objections, which need not be described, have been advanced by the local population again the project. Doubtless there are other spots where small amounts of hydropower could be developed if the capital investment could be justified, but the country's energy policy has had to be directed toward other sources of energy. The total capacity of undeveloped sources of hydroelectric power amounts to about two-thirds of a one-GWe[1] nuclear power plant. Apart from the cost of exploiting marginal sources of hydropower, the Swiss are concerned for fear that new sources of energy, especially atomic, might require installations that would be destructive to the environment.

In the early 1960s, Switzerland, in planning future sources of power for electricity production, had to choose between oil-fired and nuclear plants; coal production abroad was declining and natural gas was not then available. A small oil-fired plant of only 40 MW capacity had been built in 1948–49 and, though several more conventional power plants using oil were proposed, only one was constructed—at

Chavallon. This is of 300 MW capacity and started up in 1965–66. At the time there was tremendous resistance by those who resided near the proposed sites. They objected on environmental grounds, claiming a serious threat of air pollution if oil-fired plants were to be in operation. Oddly enough, in the light of later developments, the same population groups called for nuclear reactors, arguing that they would not pollute the atmosphere and would be almost competitive with the oil-fired turbines. This reaction of the people pleased the Federal Government which feared any substantial increase in Switzerland's dependence on petroleum— already being used for space heating, industrial processes and road transportation. As is well known, Switzerland has no petroleum or coal resources of her own.

Atomic Power

This brings us to the role of atomic power. At Beznau, north of Baden, two nuclear reactors, each of 350 MW, were constructed and began operations in 1969 and 1971 respectively. A third, of 320 MW, was built at Mühleberg (Bern canton) and was in operation by 1972. The three produce about seven billion kWh each year which approximated 20 percent of Switzerland's electricity consumption (in 1978). In their first 20 years of operation they produced a total of about 60 billion kWh of electricity, doing so without any problems that impaired the technical security of the plants or exposed any person to radiation in excess of the legally permissible levels. They also reduce petroleum imports by 1.4 million tons per year, which would otherwise have been necessary to produce an equivalent amount of electricity. Beznau I and II and Mühleberg are operating at nearly 90 percent of that which is theoretically possible. In 1979, a nuclear reactor of 920 MW, constructed at Gösgen (in Solothurn canton) began producing electricity. A fifth plant at Leibstadt (Aargau) of 945 MW capacity began operations in 1984.

ADDITIONAL NUCLEAR REACTORS   Another plant of 925 MW, proposed at the end of the 1960s for construction at Kaiseraugst (near Basel) has been the focal point of almost endless controversy. Demonstrations against the project have been numerous. Unfortunately, there has also been resort to violence. An occupation of the site of the proposed Kaiseraugst reactor was reported in 1975. Opposition to other new projects increased by leaps and bounds following the much publicized problem with the Three Mile Island reactor near Harrisburg, Pennsylvania. Outbreaks of violence flared up at various places. The cantons of Aargau, Basel-land, St. Gallen, Solothurn and Ticino experienced the burning of automobiles owned by industrialists, politicians and others who were widely known as leading proponents of atomic power. Bombings have caused damage at Gösgen, and destruction of the information center at Kaiseraugst. The close defeat in February 1979 of the popular initiative on atomic installations touched off a wave of demonstrations and violence of one kind and another directed against those in positions of authority who favored atomic power and opposed the initiative measure.

However, it must be remembered that the majority of the Swiss voters are in favor of the use of atomic power to decrease the country's dependence on petroleum.

Some are aware of the fact that nuclear reactors produce electricity without, at the same time, producing acid rain or adding to the atmospheric burden of carbon dioxide.[2] This cannot be said of power plants fired by fossil fuels—coal, petroleum and gas.

Apart from the militant groups who are found throughout Europe, the USA and elsewhere, the opposition in Switzerland is largely localized in communities along the Rhine and, especially, around the sites proposed for construction of new reactors. This opposition is to be expected. The Kaiseraugst area is near Basel. The population density is great: a nuclear catastrophe in the area is regarded as a potential threat to the lives of thousands. The two cantons of Basel-Stadt and Basel-Land have joined in opposition to the Kaiseraugst project. Attention is drawn also to the earthquake sensitivity of the area (Basel was almost totally destroyed by an earthquake in 1356), to the possible catastrophe if an aeroplane were to strike the plant (as nearly happened at Würenlingen),[3] to the damage to the landscape through the presence of a concrete monstrosity, and potential loss of fish and plant life in the streams that carry away the huge quantities of heated effluent waters from the plant, and, of course, to the troublesome problem of nuclear waste disposal.

The sit-ins, the protest marches, other demonstrations, and even the militancy of obscure groups of individuals characterize the opposition to the peaceful use of atomic energy, not only in Switzerland, but also in the USA, West Germany and in various other countries. The opponents, though frequently highly emotional in their protests, have been able to resort to a number of very reasonable objections. One of these focuses on the seemingly unsolved problem of the disposal of the radioactive atomic waste by means that will neither endanger the health of future generations of mankind nor be environmentally destructive, for example, to life in the oceans. This problem will be considered later in this section.

To return to the program calling for construction of more nuclear reactors in Switzerland, there may be enough opposition to the Kaiseraugst project to prevent construction on the proposed site[4] but the overall program is certainly not in jeopardy. There is indeed a recognition that a 1000 MW nuclear reactor will be required in the early 1990s.[5] Zangger reported in 1978 that nuclear power plant projects were being studied in at least four other locations: Graben (Bern canton), Verbois (Geneva canton), Rüthi (St. Gallen canton) and Inwil (Lucerne canton) (**401**, p. 57). The Graben reactor, as planned, will have a capacity of 1140 MW. The site received official approval in October 1972. Construction, twelve years later, had not commenced: the usual demonstrations against the project have taken place; the small local population has recorded a negative vote; the Canton of Bern in June 1981 approved a cantonal initiative, favoring by a very thin margin (87,888 in favor, 87,128 against) construction of the Graben reactor; the building plans have not yet received approval of the cantonal authorities etc. The construction of a nuclear reactor now requires approval at so many levels that years must elapse before construction can proceed. Such is the temper of the times in Switzerland and elsewhere.

Much of the objection to the nuclear reactor programs is irrational, highly emotional, and stems from fears that are not well-founded. There is also the insistent demand of many that they be assured of life in a risk-free environment. Realization of such a desire is unattainable. We must be satisfied with the concept of "acceptable risks" which will vary in degree with the nature of the risk to which one is exposed, and the benefits received by the country at large.

Export of Nuclear Technology

Under the Carter administration, the USA government adopted a policy of blocking, if possible, the sale of nuclear technology by European countries to a number of countries, e.g. Argentina. Switzerland had approved the export of a heavy-water production plant to Argentia following West Germany's approval of an export license for a 740 MW nuclear reactor to Argentina. The USA urged both countries to deny the export of the nuclear facilities because Argentina had not signed the treaty on the non-proliferation of nuclear weapons or had not agreed to full-scope nuclear safeguards. Switzerland replied to the USA protests by referring to Argentina's assurance that the plant and its technology would be used only for peaceful purposes, and would be placed under IAEA safeguards. It would not be re-exported without the prior consent of the Swiss government. USA policy would have required that all past, present and future nuclear facilities in Argentina be subject to the controls and periodic inspection regulations of the International Atomic Energy Agency based in Vienna. However, West Germany and Switzerland had accepted a code of conduct to which 15 major countries, including the United States, the so-called London Nuclear Suppliers Club, had agreed. In the export of nuclear plants and materials, they had only to assure that adherence to international safeguards on the use of the exported goods had been received. The USA, meanwhile, had resumed shipments of enriched uranium to India.

Pakistan has also presented problems to countries that export nuclear materials and nuclear plants. Switzerland, in late 1980, terminated the export of certain equipment to a uranium-enrichment facility in Pakistan pending the formal agreement of that country to accept the controls and periodic inspections of the International Atomic Energy Agency (IAEA). Although Pakistan has repeatedly given assurance that she proposes only to use imported nuclear technology for peaceful purposes, she has refrained from accepting any control by the IAEA. Formerly, Pakistan had illegally acquired the technology of centrifuge-enrichment of uranium from the Netherlands, and, subsequently, bought certain parts for the centrifuge, piece by piece, on the black market from countries employing, or not employing, the centrifuge technology.

Swiss sales to both Argentina and Pakistan had been made with the knowledge and approval of the Swiss government, acting in accordance with export regulations to which members of the "London Club" are obliged to adhere. Whatever mis-understanding exists between the USA and Switzerland apparently derives from the more restrictive regulations in the USA Nonproliferation Act (Carter, 1977), a law that is applied by the USA to the whole world.

The USA, however, became adamant in approving the transfer of nuclear material of USA origin out of Switzerland for reprocessing in France or Great Britain, but was reluctant to approve the re-use of plutonium in Switzerland, presumably to pressure the Swiss into acceptance of USA policies concerning the sale of nuclear materials and technology to countries on the USA black list. These measures were counter-productive because the Swiss operators of nuclear power plants are now drifting away from USA suppliers to other suppliers.

In 1977 Canada had boycotted the sale of uranium to Switzerland; the boycott was still in effect in 1984. With diversification of uranium supplies as the óbjective, Switzerland entered into negotiations with Australia in the spring of 1981 for establishing a nuclear cooperation agreement. In February 1983, negotiations on this agreement were terminated. In addition to the supply of uranium, the agreement would also provide for information exchange between the two countries, and research and cooperation in matters pertaining to safety and security in the peaceful use of atomic energy. Because of a change of government in Australia, this agreement had not been signed by mid-1984.

However, Switzerland does not intend to abandon the Canadian source. Relations between the two countries are not unfriendly. Canada has been embarrassed by her sale of a research reactor to India which was subsequently employed for the production of plutonium used in an explosive device experimented upon in 1974. In consequence, the Canadian government tightened considerably the rules governing its sale of nuclear materials to other countries. Switzerland is faced with the more restrictive Canadian policy but has difficulties in speeding up her own cautious and slow-moving machinery for adoption of agreements proposed by foreign governments.

Disposal of Nuclear Waste

In June 1980, Switzerland disposed of nuclear waste of low level radioactivity from medical centers, research units, and nuclear reactors by dumping it in the Atlantic, within the framework of OECD recommendations. In accordance with regulations prescribed by OECD, the waste was imbedded in concrete in steel drums which were transported to Belgium or the Netherlands, transferred to a special ship, and sunk in a trench, 4500 meters deep, in the Atlantic Ocean, some 900 km southwest of the English coast. Due to problems in the countries that executed the dumping operation (strikes of the ship personnel) this method has been temporarily suspended.

Through a company called NAGRA (*Nationale Genossenschaft für die Lagerung radioactiver Abfälle*), Switzerland is studying the feasibility of burying such nuclear waste of all types in the Swiss underground, particularly in the granite formations which lie 600 to 2000 meters below the surface of the Swiss middle land. This company, in support of the program which was initiated in 1979, has approved an expenditure of 200 million francs, and expects a preliminary report in 1985.[6] After 1995 the first disposal sites will be available, so it is planned, for depositing weak and medium radioactive waste from medical centers, research institutions and nuclear reactors. Highly radioactive waste contained in spent fuel elements will be processed abroad—England and France have been mentioned. Alternatively, the reprocessing wastes can also be returned to Switzerland for final disposal. Such are the plans and the perspectives.

For highly active wastes, NAGRA sought permission to make 12 deep borings as test sites, it being clearly understood that approval of this request would be preliminary to, and independent of, approval for burial of any radioactive waste. The initial request requires for consideration by the Federal Council, which has the last word, a small mountain of documents (site plans, geologic reports, cantonal and community approvals, etc.). An allowance of 60 days was made for receipt of objections from all interested parties—the 12 communities selected by NAGRA, interested organizations and individual persons. All 12 communities advanced certain objections, 15 other communities objected, 12 organizations and many individuals joined in the opposition—a grand total of nearly 1000 objections. Swiss geologists have voiced a certain amount of skepticism about the safety of disposal of highly radioative waste underground in selected geological formations and about selection of drilling sites.

For disposal of waste of low and medium activity, three sites had been given, in early 1983, a top priority for further study and evaluation. Five others were listed as a second priority group, and twelve, tentatively considered for further study, were dropped from the list. On conclusion of a vast amount of investigation and paper work and, assuming that the necessary approvals are received from the community of first choice, the canton(s), the Federal Government etc., NAGRA hopes to make the first burial of waste in 1995. Of greatest importance is the established safety of the site in respect to protection against radioactivity leakage from the deposited waste. NAGRA proposes to employ special security barriers. These will be designed in collaboration with Sweden, West Germany, and the USA. Belgium and the "European Community" based in Brussels, also interested in the safe disposal of nuclear waste, will be collaborating with NAGRA and other Swiss institutions in various phases of the project.

The underground cavern(s) to be constructed for wastes of low and medium activity will consist of two parallel galleries each of 100 meters in length. With the approach, and cross-connecting galleries, a construction cost of 90 to 170 million francs, and a construction time of three to six years are estimated. The storage volume of such a cavern will approximate 330,000 to 430,000 cubic meters. The volume of waste of low and medium level radioactivity occurring yearly amounts to about 700 cubic meters (mostly waste from power plant operations and spent fuel reprocessing, as well as, on a yearly pro-rata basis, from future plant decommissioning). For the storage of highly radioactive waste, at least four special security barriers and separately located caverns are contemplated for use in the deep underground in the northern part of Switzerland.

Research

In July 1980, 97 million francs were allocated by the Swiss public authorities (Federal Government, ETH School Council, cantons, communities and *Nationalfonds*) and the National Energy Research Fund. Sixty-one percent of the total (about 60 million francs) was earmarked for research on atomic energy (nuclear fission with and without breeders, and thermonuclear fusion). Renewable energy sources received 14.2 million (e.g. solar energy research, 9.6 million; biomass (wood, etc.) research, 3.3 million; and geothermal research, 1.0 million). Research support by industry for energy research was estimated at an additional 300 to 400 million francs.

Eleven power and engineering companies together with two agencies of the Federal Government have planned a solar energy station in the Swiss Alps. Construction should begin in 1985 and electric power should be in production by 1988. The plant is intended to be a demonstration model rather than for the development of electric power for domestic sale. As a "model" it is hoped to be attractive to foreign buyers seeking to acquire similar facilities. The cost of this 5 MW pilot plant is estimated to exceed 50 million francs. It would consist of 500 heliostats (automatic swivel-mounted mirrors) of about 50 m^2 surface area per mirror. The incident solar radiation would be concentrated by reflection on a boiler (steam generator) mounted on a tower about 100 m high. The steam would drive a turbo-generator for production of electricity. The ground surface required for the installation would be about 125,000 m^2 (five times the total area of the 500 mirrors). Several places in the Alpine regions are being considered for location of this solar facility. Hours per year of sunshine are estimated at 1750.

A water-pumping station, powered by solar energy, on Mt. Pélerin (near Lake Geneva) pumps about four or five cubic meters of water daily to a reservoir with a pressure head of 70 m. The water is used to meet the needs of about 170 head of cattle that spend the summer on Alp Chesau near Puidoux. The solar energy installation at a cost of about 100,000 francs was constructed as an economic measure to avoid the use of electric power provided by an ordinary utility. For this conventional source of power an underground high tension cable would have been required; the cost of merely laying such a cable would have been 380,000 francs.

The interest of Swiss scientists in research on breeder reactors is evidenced in part by an international conference on breeder reactors held in Lucerne in 1979. Participants numbered 160, representing 19 countries, including the USSR. The conference expressed the hope of many that, thanks to the efficient use of uranium in these reactors, Europe might become independent of external sources of energy.

Voll Roll Ltd., a Swiss company, developed a process for the efficient generation of steam by the combustion of garbage. The process was licensed to Wheelabrator-Frye Inc in the USA. The American company opened a plant in October 1975 on a garbage dump and produced in the next four years some 6 to 8 billion pounds of steam. According to a newspaper report (357) the plant incinerates three million pounds of garbage daily at a temperature of 1650° and under controlled pressures. Scrap iron is removed magnetically from the ash. The final residue is used for highway resurfacing. Steam is produced from boilers heated by the incineration process and sold as a clean source of energy. Two-unit sewage- and garbage-disposal plants are to be found in Switzerland, with methane and steam as the energy-yielding products of the disposal processes.

Apart from the European Center for Nuclear Research at Geneva, the principal, purely Swiss research center is the Federal Institute for Reactor Research (EIR) at Würenlingen in Aargau. The Institute was founded in 1955 as Reaktor A.G. by 171 Swiss enterprises to study the technical aspects of the peaceful use of atomic energy. The Federal Government, which also supported the enterprise, in 1960 transferred the center to the Federal Institute of Technology as an affiliated or annexed organization. In the intervening 25 years the EIR has become the main national center for energy research. Service functions and training of personnel in the handling of radioactive isotopes (e.g. medical personnel) are important ancillary functions. The effects of different sources of energy on the environment and the study of new energy sources are among the activities of the center. In 1979, nearly 10 percent of public funds at the disposal of EIR were used for solar energy research. In the EIR school for radiation protection, 3200 participants received training in 1979. As an annexed facility of the Federal Institute of Technology, EIR has an important liaison function between industry and the universities in the field of energy research.

As much as 100 kg of plutonium was held by the EIR in the late 1970s for research purposes. As is to be expected, there were those who voiced their fear that this might be used by Switzerland for the construction of atomic bombs. The fears were unfounded: the plutonium was owned by Great Britain and was on loan to the EIR. Half had been returned by 1979–1980 and the remainder was scheduled for return shortly thereafter.

Mention should also be made of a joint research program to be undertaken between EIR and the USA national laboratory at Los Alamos. Uranium oxide, currently used as reactor fuel will be compared with uranium carbide which, according to EIR, has a higher utilization capacity. EIR hopes also to engage, under the agreement, in uranium-recovery research and in the preparation of new fuel elements. The studies, initiated in April 1981, are expected to continue for eight years.

An authoritative description of the EIR and its many activities in the early 1960s has been published by Professor Urs Hochstrasser, formerly Delegate of the Federal Council for Atomic Energy Questions (180).

A large electron-positron machine has been under construction at the European Center for Nuclear Research (CERN) near Geneva. In a tunnel, 20 miles in circumference, positrons and electrons circle the huge ring in opposite directions at the speed of light. They collide in a mutual annihilation reaction and present an opportunity to study three long-sought particles that should be emitted, and whose existence has been predicted by a generation of physicists. The tunnel extends under the Jura and in places is 3000 feet underground. Much of the tunnel is under rolling farmland on the French side of the Franco-Swiss border.

Another important institute involved in basic energy problems, pure and applied, is the *Schweizerisches Institut für Nuklearforschung* (SIN) i.e. the Swiss Institute for Nuclear Research.

Planning for SIN was actively pursued in 1962–63 by a group of experts at the ETH Zurich. SIN was conceived as a national research facility for studies in nuclear and particle physics at high energies, including applications in other fields of science and technology. The institute would be located at Villegen on the other side of the river Aare from the EIR. The research facility would be equipped with a 500 MeV ring accelerator of high intensity. As planned, SIN would serve research groups in all Swiss universities and various international and foreign interests.

In 1968, when construction began, the institute was annexed to the ETHZ as a new section under the administrative supervision of the governing board of the ETH (*Schweizerischer Schulrat*). An ordinance of the Federal Council on the Organization and Operation of the Swiss Institute for Nuclear Research (10 November 1967) specified in detail the responsibilities of the *Schulrat* in respect to SIN. The institute would be under the on-the-spot governance of a director and the heads of its three divisions. They, in turn, would enjoy the advice and consultative support of a scientific commission of 14 to 20 representatives of the Swiss universities and cognate institutes as well as from foreign and international institutes (e.g. CERN).

Work at the institute was commenced in January 1974 when the first 590 MeV* proton accelerator was installed. A second injector cyclotron, receiving ionized hydrogen (protons and electrons), accelerates the protons from 0 MeV to 72 MeV, and the ring cyclotron further accelerates the protons from 72 MeV to 590 MeV. Protons of 600 MeV travel with a velocity of 240,000 km/sec (80 percent of the velocity of light). The instrumentation provides for a collision, at this point, of the highly accelerated protons with a resting proton (carbon, whose nucleus contains 6 neutrons and 6 protons, is the actual target for the accelerated proton). A product of the collision is a pion, also known as a meson.

The institute, overall, can be regarded as a meson factory of which, in 1984–85, only two or three other comparable facilities existed elsewhere in the world. Research problems presently contemplated concern e.g. (a) the physics of elementary particles and processes—an area which will be more deeply penetrated if the building of a proton accelerator of still higher energy (20–30 GeV) and higher intensity, is achieved; (b) superconductivity and the building of superconducting coils as believed to be necessary for the next generation of fusion reactors; (c) production of medically important radioisotopes; and (d) destruction of tumors by simultaneous radiation with mesons entering through multiple pathways.

A technical description of the institute (in German) is to be found in "Schweizerischer Institut für Nuklearforschung," a well-illustrated booklet of 35 pages, published in 1984 and available from the institute at Villgen, Aargau Canton, Switzerland.

Legislation

A national referendum on May 20, 1979, approved a revision of the atomic energy law of 1959 to achieve the following desiderata: that a license to proceed with construction may only be granted if the applicant provides evidence that the plant is

---

* 1 MeV = 1 million electron volts.

necessary to help satisfy the country's needs for electricity; that the safe disposal of its nuclear waste is assured; and that the final decision on issuance of the construction permit be made by Parliament, not by the Federal bureaucracy. Environmentalists, generally opposed to the new law, favored much more stringent limitations on the development and use of atomic energy. It is worth noting that 982,723 votes were recorded in favor of the proposed changes in the existing law, against 444,156 votes in opposition.

The Federal Energy Commission has pointed out that the proof-of-need requirement should be expanded upon to answer a number of relevant questions that are of concern to the Commission.

The Federal Law of 1959 on atomic energy is based on Article 24 quinquies of the Federal Constitution. The Article is all-inclusive: "Legislation on atomic energy is a federal concern." The law based on this Article pertains to the peaceful use of atomic energy and protection against atomic radiation. It is now considered to be inadequate and in need of total revision. At issue, *inter alia*, is the troublesome problem of competence. To what extent is the construction and location of nuclear reactors a concern of the cantons rather than of the Federal Government? Should the Constitution be revised to recognize the insistent claim of those who argue that legislation on atomic energy is also a concern of the cantons? Is the law of 1959 too centralistic?

Rather than discussing the question, it is important to mention two initiatives which on 23 September 1984 were voted upon. The first of these, entitled "For a Safe, Economical and Environmentally Acceptable Source of Energy," would add a new section to Article 24 of the Federal Constitution. With this as the necessary legislative base, an energy policy would be developed by the Confederation in collaboration with the cantons and communities. The policy would focus upon many aspects of the energy requirements of the consumer, effects of the means of production upon environment and safety of the people, the preferential use of nationally acceptable, renewable energy sources that do minimal violence to the natural beauty of the countryside, decentralization of production, etc. etc. The Federal assembly has recommended that this initiative be voted down.[7]

Table 83   Net production of electricity[a,b]

	1932	1945	1955	1977	1980	1983
Hydroelectric	4760	10,060	15,255	36,290	33,542	36,002
Conventional thermal plants	30	13	132	1885	957	996
Nuclear power[c]	—	—	—	7728	13,663	14,821
(Less pumping usage)	(66)	—	(141)	(1277)	(1531)	(1346)
Net production, total	4801	10,130	15,246	44,626	46,631	50,473

[a] Source: **341**, 1962, p. 177; **341**, 1933, p. 143; **420**, 1983, p. 5.
[b] In GWh.
[c] From Beznau I (350 MW), Beznau II (350 MW), Mühleberg (320 MW) and Gösgen (920 MW).

Table 84 Energy consumption[a]

	1950	1960	1977	1980
Light heating oil[b]		—	6098	6204
Heavy heating oil[b]	1000	—	1309	1084
Gasoline[b]		—	2582	2744
Diesel fuel[b]		—	645	759
Electricity[c]	9600	15,891	31,289	35,252
Gas[d]	4510	5380	26,800	33,740
Coal[b]	2500	2400	360	482
Wood[e]	2500	1700	950	1100
Remote heating[d]		—	—	7920
Industrial waste[b]		—	—	295
Total[d]	172,700	295,720	638,890	683,870[f]

[a] Source: **341**, 1981, p. 184.
[b] In thousands of tons.
[c] In GWh = millions of kWh.
[d] In billions of joules.
[e] In thousands of cubic meters.
[f] About one-half by households, agriculture, service and businesses (non-industrial); about one-fourth by industry; and about one-fourth by transport facilities.

The second initiative was based upon the belief of the sponsors that the use of nuclear reactors to develop energy should be discouraged, that the construction of new reactors should be prohibited and replacement of existing reactors should not be permitted. This initiative, rejected by the Federal Council, would also, as a plebiscite, assuredly prevent construction of the Kaiseraugst plant. Clearly, the results of the voting would determine the fate of nuclear power plants now in operation, and of those now being planned or proposed for the future.[7]

Data

Data on the production, consumption, cost, and import and export of energy carriers for selected years in the 1900s are presented in Tables 83 to 87. According to press reports from the Federal Office of Energy, the total expenditure on energy in 1979 was 13 billion francs (updated in Table 86).

From 1977 to 1981 the average annual increase in electricity consumption was about four percent, which leads to the startling result that an additional large nuclear reactor might be required every four years to keep up with the increased demand. Switzerland has benefitted considerably by a continued reduction in imports of petroleum and petroleum products. The amount imported in 1982 was 0.64 million tons less than in 1981 (− 5.7 percent). As a result of unit price decreases, the 1982 cost of such imports fell by 7.1 percent (to 6.39 billion francs) below that of 1981 (**266**, 19–20 February 1983).

Table 85A   Energy imports (I) and exports (E)[a]

	1970			1977			1980		
	I	E	Net imports	I	E	Net imports	I	E	Net imports
Petroleum and petroleum products[b]	13,359	256	13,103	13,287	109	13,178	12,705	47	12,658
Coal[b]	827	64	763	315	—	315	773	0	773
Gas[c]	1800	90	1710	28,910	200	28,710	40,960	650	40,310
Electricity[d]	3594	9619	−6025	5046	15,231	−10,185	9947	18,128	−8181

[a] Source: **341**, 1981, p. 183.
[b] In thousands of tons.
[c] In billions of joules.
[d] In millions of kWh.

Table 85B   Coal, petroleum and petroleum products, lubricating oil[a,b]

	Cost of imports	Income from exports	Customs revenue[c]
1960	773	3.7	322.6
1970	1456	41.2	1224
1977	3954	60.8	2055
1980	6496	60.7	2242

[a] Source: **341**, 1981, pp, 196, 203.
[b] In millions of francs.
[c] Including surcharges (*Zollzuschläge*).

Table 86   Overall cost of energy to consumers[a] (in millions of francs)

	Petroleum products		Electricity	Gas	Coal	Wood	Remote heating	Total
	For heating	For vehicles						
1979	3912	4821	3978	378	104	47.0	88.4	13,328
1980	4005	5662	4227	475	141	61.3	151	14,722
1981	4377	6321	4412	628	196	75.0	167	16,176

[a] Source: **417**, 1982, p. 44.

Table 87   Energy usage by consumer groups in 1950, 1965, 1982[a,b]

	1950	1965	1982
Households	94,550 }	225,200 }	206,520
Artisans, agriculture, services			139,860
Industry	52,740	124,330	133,990
Transport	25,410	98,450	186,920
Total	172,700	447,980	667,290

[a] Source: Ref. **417**, 1982, pp. 45–49.
[b] In terrajoules; one joule = 0.7375 foot-pounds.

Insurance

As has been suggested for some years by opponents of nuclear reactor installations and by members of the legal profession, the financial responsibility of government and the utility companies in damage claims should be unlimited. Until recently the utility companies carried insurance up to 200 million francs as protection against personal claims for damage sustained in a nuclear accident. The Gösgen reactor is insured for 650 million francs against damage sustained by the reactor itself.

A new law accepted by Parliament in 1983 provides unlimited responsibility of the plant operator with one-billion-franc liability, funded in part by private and public insurance, and with federal responsibility also for financial coverage of any additional damage claims. This includes damage through earthquakes, war, and acts of sabotage.

Acknowledgment

I have made extensive use of the article by Professor Claude Zangger in *Modern Switzerland* for much background material (**401**). It is warmly recommended to those interested in Switzerland's energy problems. I am also indebted to Professor Zangger for several publications of the Swiss Federal Office for Energy.

Notes and Comments

1. TWh (Terrawatthour) = 10^{12} kWh; 1 GWh (Gigawatthour) = 10^9 kWh; 1 MWh (Megawatthour) = 10^6 kWh. 1 GWe = 1 billion watts, electrical.

2. Switzerland "imports" a moderate amount of acid rain which has its most serious impact in the Ticino in the Maggia and Verzasca valleys. Several small lakes in these valleys have become too acid to sustain any life in the waters. Waters to the north of the Alps are scarcely affected, possibly because of neutralization by limestone in the riverbeds.

3. Site of the Swiss Federal Institute for Reactor Research.

4. If the nuclear reactor at Kaiseraugst is not constructed, the loss to the shareholders of *Kernkraftwerke Kaiseraugst AG.* would amount to 800 to 1000 million francs, as of December 1982. The Federal Government authorities, as early as 1974, informed the investing corporations that they are proceeding with the project entirely at their own risk. This cautionary declaration strongly suggests that

the government would not share in reimbursement for accumulated losses if a bail-out were ever proposed.

5. Early in 1983, the Ständerat (Senate) approved the general outline of plans for construction of the nuclear power plant at Kaiseraugst. This was followed by a tumultuous demonstration by some thousands of Basel opponents of the project. Elsewhere in the Basel area, violence erupted and two high-tension electricity transmission towers were levelled.

Subject to the successful implementation of certain energy-saving measures and the operation of the Leibstadt reactor at full power, construction of the Kaiseraugst reactor before the year 2000 would not be necessary, according to the President of the Federal Energy Commission in an April 1984 address.

6. Delays at administrative and organizational levels will probably require an extension of time beyond 1985.

7. Defeated in the votation of 23 September 1984.

11.22. SWISS NEUTRALITY IN THE TWENTIETH CENTURY

Introduction

Whatever may have been the challenges and problems that faced neutral Switzerland in earlier years, we are forced to conclude that they were infinitely greater during the two World Wars of the twentieth century. Such a conclusion must be tempered by considering the fate of Switzerland during the Napoleonic wars. The country was overrun by the armies of Napoleon, several cantons were declared to be a part of France and were so incorporated by a simple decree of the Emperor. When peace was restored, Switzerland returned to her pre-war state except for the loss of the Valtellina to Austria and, some years later, Northern Savoy, to which she had a precarious claim, to France.

The two great wars of the twentieth century have been described as wars "to make the world safe for democracy" or as "wars to end war." A reorganization of the world was attempted, first by the League of Nations and later by the United Nations Organization, to weld together into a world family all nations committed to the restoration and maintenance of an enduring peace and to international cooperation in attainment of harmonious international relations. Solidarity in achievement of these great objectives was an important but fragile component of the rules by which the member nations were to cooperate.

Switzerland's participation in the League of Nations and her relationship to the United Nations Organization have been described in other sections and need not be expanded upon.

World War I

As might be expected from precedents of the past, the outbreak of the First World War was followed promptly, or even preceded by, Switzerland's declaration of neutrality. On 4 August 1914, the Federal Council at the behest of the Federal Assembly announced the firm determination of Switzerland to preserve and maintain her independence and neutrality by all the means at her disposal. After an introductory high-sounding paragraph the Powers were reminded that:

> the Swiss Confederation will maintain and defend by every means at its disposal, its neutrality and the inviolability of its territory such as they were recognized by the treaties

of 1815; she herself will observe the strictest neutrality vis-à-vis the belligerent States. Relative to . . . the Act of recognition and guarantee of the Swiss neutrality.

In implementation of this declaration, the Federal Council declared that Switzerland would summon to the task all the means at her disposal to protect and maintain her neutrality and the inviolability of her territory. As a reminder to France, the Federal Council drew attention to the declaration of the Powers in 1815 that Northern Savoy falls within the compass of Swiss neutrality and that she possesses the right to occupy the provinces of Northern Savoy as though they were a part of Switzerland. The Federal Council added that Switzerland would exercise this right if events rendered it necessary to do so to secure the neutrality and inviolability of Swiss territory (see also Chapter 10).

The outbreak of the war, which followed so speedily after the assassination of the Austrian archduke, caught Switzerland and the whole of Europe with surprise. The assassination and the subsequent events were totally unexpected. The economic and political problems which Switzerland now had to resolve were accompanied by a deep rift between the two main linguistic groups of the French-speaking Swiss to the west and the German-speaking Swiss to the east—a dividing line that clung closely to the linguistic frontier.

In French-speaking Switzerland, with its moral and historic attachments to France, the rape of Belgium and fears of a German victory brought about a near-unanimity of opinion that pious declarations of neutrality must be subordinated to a vigorous national policy of condemnation of Germany by word and by deed. Eastern Switzerland, without being conspicuously Germanophile, hesitated to take sides between the belligerents. The German-speaking Swiss preferred to adhere to a policy of strict neutrality, as in the past, and to ready the country for defensive operations by manning the frontiers—the historic expression of armed neutrality.

Western Switzerland (the French-speaking cantons), convinced that the chiefs of the Swiss army were too Germanophile, demanded the retirement of the general (Ulrich Wille) and his Chief-of-staff. In August 1917, a vote of want-of-confidence in the military leaders was proposed in parliament. Although this and other similar proposals were rejected, they throw light on the discontent of the French-speaking Swiss.

Of course we must understand that German-speaking Switzerland had problems that were uniquely hers. Apart from the Swiss citizens who were attached to Germany by linguistic bonds and a common Alemannian ancestry, there was a substantial representation of German citizens in eastern Switzerland. Determined efforts were made by Germany to enlist the aid of her subjects in Switzerland in espionage and subversive activities and in strengthening by any and all means Swiss support for the German cause.

FOREIGN TRADE   It is difficult to recall a time, if ever, when Switzerland was materially self-sufficient and, in glorious independence, able to live contentedly on her own resources. Even in the distant days of ancient Helvetia, trade with the outside world was important (see Chapter 1). But during the two World Wars of the twentieth century, Switzerland's dependence on the outside world became glaringly evident. Landlocked as she is, she must turn to her neighbours for some supplies and for use of their transit facilities to reach the sea or other European countries. In World War I, the Federal Council, which had persuaded the Federal Assembly to grant it full and unrestricted powers, even in financial matters, to rule the country, negotiated an agreement with France in respect to Switzerland's need for grain, and a similar agreement with Germany for coal, iron, steel, etc. Much more was required such as foodstuffs for her people, fertilizer for the farms, and a wide variety of products for maintenance of her manufacturing industries. But the imports had to be compensated by exports: payment in goods necessary to the life of the belligerent countries.

For her very existence, Switzerland had no alternative to the continuation of trade with her pre-war trading partners. Germany repeatedly demanded a cessation of, or heavy reduction in, Switzerland's trade with the Allies (the *Entente*) and the Allies, in turn, made every effort to terminate Switzerland's commercial relations with Germany and her Triple Alliance. That Switzerland managed to maintain her tight-rope balancing act between the belligerents for the duration of the war was a tribute to her diplomatic skills and much more. As a perpetual Neutral she felt obliged to treat the two groups of belligerents equally. A unilateral favoritism, expressed by restriction of her economic relations to Germany and Austria-Hungary only, could have led to her treatment as an enemy by the *Entente*, her occupation by Germany and Austria-Hungary, and the probability of Switzerland becoming another field of battle. Despite her military policy and determination to defend her borders against an enemy penetration there were grave doubts whether she would be able to repel a massive enemy attack on her north-west frontier. Italy entered the war in 1915 as an ally of Britain and France but it is also doubtful whether she would have been able to contribute enough military aid to prevent a German conquest of Switzerland. It must be remembered that until mid 1916 Germany and her allies appeared to be the prospective victors; the opening of a new front on the Swiss frontier was a possibility that could not be ignored.

But would the attempted seizure of Switzerland by either of the belligerents have been worth the effort? Apart from the commitment of substantial forces to the military operation there was much to be said in favor of maintaining and sustaining a neutral country in the heart of Europe. Granted that Switzerland required a continuous and substantial inflow of materials for the survival of her own people, which was clear to all concerned, there was a certain trade-off that was extremely valuable to the belligerents. Swiss agriculture and Swiss manufacturing industries were well worth preserving. Switzerland could be forced to export some foodstuffs and some products of the machine and watch industries in return for the coal, iron, steel, grain, potatoes, sugar and fertilizers that were indispensable for her survival. Incidentally, dairy cows were exported to Germany and Austria-Hungary in such numbers as to induce from time to time a milk famine—and subsequent rationing of milk. The milk ration fell as low as one-third liter per person per day. The milk famine has been described as one of the greatest calamities suffered by Switzerland during the entire war (**116**, 12th edition, Vol. 32, p. 644). Doubtless, it was aggravated by a devastating outbreak of foot-and-mouth disease which called for the slaughter of all affected cattle. In April 1920, the rationing of milk and other necessities came to an end.

Early in World War I, the export of various foodstuffs, such as bread and milk was prohibited. Farmers had learned that dairy farming and the sale of milk, cheese and butter were more profitable than raising cereal grains. In January 1915, the Swiss government introduced a provisional monopoly of grain and issued a decree relating to limitation of grain exports. This action was followed in 1916 by a government monopoly of rice imports. From November 1915 on, only small amounts of cheese could be exported and licenses to export butter were no longer granted. Potatoes, and other such produce, were also rationed and each householder was required to plant them on his land. Flower gardens disappeared to permit replacement by potatoes and other edible products.

One of the most important and necessary imports was coal which was chronically in short supply, expensive, and had to be rationed. The coal-supply problem was so serious that Switzerland decided to electrify her railroads with, in time, tremendous savings in coal purchases.

When war broke out in 1914, many people, fearing the worst, laid in huge food supplies, in some cases enough for several years. In general, as the duration of the war lengthened, food shortages became more and more severe. Speculation was rife. Profiteers bought foodstuffs and other necessities—some smuggled in—in huge quantities and exported to Germany at fancy prices. This illegal trade was difficult to stop, although from time to time considerable quantities of coffee, cocoa, chocolate, rice, fat etc. were seized from smugglers, speculators and profiteers. The difficulties were aggravated by Germany's counter action: threats to terminate all exports to Switzerland unless she continued to receive from Swiss sources the supplies needed by Germany. The *Entente*, in turn, threatened to punish Switzerland by severe rationing of the consignments of grain that were being shipped in, unless she ended all exports to Germany and Austria-Hungary. Britain and France were able, if they wished, to impose and enforce a naval blockade of the ports of entry. The Swiss government argued that some exportation to Germany was necessary to ensure even minimum supplies of coal, iron, steel for Swiss industry, fertilizers for agriculture, and sugar and potatoes for the Swiss people. At one time the importation of grain from the USA and elsewhere was completely cut off by an allied blockade. It was quite impossible for Switzerland to please both sides since each strove to have Swiss exports to the other belligerent group terminated. A saying that became prevalent in Switzerland ran somewhat as follows: "A neutral Power is kicked from the left and whipped from the right."

The Statistical Yearbook of Switzerland, a rich source of information on all sorts of things, lists the sources of Switzerland's imports and also the countries to which she exported products during 1913, 1917, and 1920. Unfortunately, the corresponding information for 1914, 1915, 1916, 1918 and 1919 is not included. From the data pertinent to the three years mentioned, tentative conclusions may be drawn regarding specific items of import and export during the years of World War I. Tables 88 and 89 report on Swiss imports and exports during World War I. On the average, imports from six of the countries listed were maintained virtually at pre-war levels. Imports from Austria-Hungary, however, decreased to about half the pre-war levels from 1915 forward, continuing at the reduced level through the *Anschluss* in 1938. Imports from Russia, which were modest in the pre-war years, fell to a mere trickle during the war. Exports to the countries listed in Table 89 were maintained at about pre-war levels, or even greater, except to Russia. The Bolshevik revolution of November 1917 and Switzerland's termination of diplomatic relations with Communist Russia in 1918 adversely affected Swiss exports to that country from 1918 forward.

EMERGENCY POWERS OF GOVERNMENT   A comment on the emergency powers granted to the Federal Council—full and unlimited authority to run the country—is in order. Such a transfer of power from the people to an executive body of seven was a tremendous departure from the process of decision-making to which the Swiss were accustomed. The cantons were unable to check the actions of the central authority—in fact the voice of Parliament itself was stilled. The popular initiative could not be used by the people to invoke changes in the Constitution, and the decisions of the Federal Council could not be challenged by the cantons or the people: use of the referendum was suspended. The unlimited powers of government vested in the Federal Council—and, hence, in a number of administrative officials—may have been almost unavoidable: time for the leisurely and deliberate decision-

Table 88   Swiss imports (1910–1930) from selected countries[a,b]

Year	Germany	Austria-Hungary	France	Italy	Great Britain	Russia	USA	Argentina
1910	566	111	347	203	113	85.6	68.8	16.4
1911	581	114	340	181	100	89.6	75.1	29.2
1912	647	122	376	193	117	80.2	83.8	36.0
1913	631	109	348	207	113	71.5	118	36.9
1914	481	103	221	194	76.2	53.5	108	24.4
1915	418	65.7	189	259	112	8.4	324	49.5
1916	472	44.7	236	390	160	0.9	565	128
1917	483	43.7	305	369	269	0.3	459	82.9
1918	620	61.0	280	222	248	0.3	354	52.8
1919	483	69.2	407	273	363	2.9	788	198
1920	809	71.5	603	325	466	7.7	865	121
1921	440	32.3	321	200	156	3.1	385	50.8
1925	471	41.1	499	266	281	10.0	227	85.3
1928	624	57.1	491	200	203	6.7	244	80.7
1930	709	50.5	447	185	139	18.7	205	73.0

[a] In millions of francs; uncorrected for war-time price increases.
[b] Source: **341**, 1933, pp. 257–59.

Table 89   Swiss exports (1910–1930) to selected countries[a,b]

Year	Germany	Austria-Hungary	France	Italy	Great Britain	Russia	USA	Argentina
1910	270	80.1	130	85.6	200	41.8	144	26.8
1911	275	85.0	133	85.2	213	48.1	142	28.4
1912	307	88.7	138	90.6	230	47.8	136	29.8
1913	306	78.4	141	89.2	236	58.7	136	29.9
1914	275	67.2	115	82.8	234	41.5	122	15.6
1915	457	157	221	89.5	355	29.3	107	16.5
1916	709	195	401	150	424	61.1	133	22.4
1917	699	93.1	462	136	362	49.6	120	21.7
1918	445	101	466	96.7	269	5.1	99.3	18.8
1919	698	242	502	209	347	121	183	27.7
1920	253	106	522	166	646	1.3	283	76.2
1921	195	87.8	239	74.2	349	0.3	586	28.6
1925	368	70.3	173	104	422	0.5	206	37.9
1928	386	70.8	157	141	308	7.1	195	38.4
1930	278	54.5	183	120	265	16.3	144	32.2

[a] In millions of francs; uncorrected for war-time price increases.
[b] Source: **341**, 1933, pp. 267–69.

making procedures of pre-war Switzerland was a thing of the past. Some of the decisions, almost by virtue of the machinery that was used, added to the strength of centralism at the expense of federalism with results that had an impact on post-war Switzerland. The unlimited powers of the Federal Council were not ended until long after peace was declared. During those interminable years the Federal Council tried to limit freedom of expression by imposing a censorship. This un-Swiss policy was doomed to failure: it irritated many, including even some foreign governments, and added nothing to whatever popular respect remained for the war-time system of government.

WAR-TIME PROFITS   While it may be true that huge fortunes were made by Swiss manufacturers of war materials and other products exported to the belligerents there is no evidence that the Swiss people, generally, enjoyed material benefits from the neutrality of their country. To the contrary they experienced many food shortages, nutrition of the people suffered, the cost of living increased[1] and the many restrictive regulations, frequently quite petty, imposed by government contributed to a general malaise and depression aggravated by the realization that they were compelled to suffer for a cause that was not their own and from which neither Switzerland nor any of the belligerents would benefit.

HUMANITARIAN SERVICES   At the same time, Switzerland rendered humanitarian services of inestimable value to the whole of Europe, almost in fulfillment of the 1815 expectations of the Powers who, in the Treaty of Paris, made the memorable declaration that the perpetual neutrality of Switzerland is in the interests of the whole of Europe. Almost 70,000 internees were given shelter in Switzerland between 1916 and the end of the war. The International Committee of the Red Cross, based in Geneva, rendered magnificent services in many ways: operation of a clearinghouse for military personnel missing in action, and prisoners of war, was one of the most noteworthy services. Inquiries were made concerning missing persons and families were informed about their health and whereabouts[2] (please refer also to Section 11.19). Many charitable organizations were created which rendered a variety of services to the needy from all of the belligerent countries and continued their ministrations far into the post-war era.

The Swiss Red Cross joined in the training of female Red Cross nurses (Red Cross sisters). At the very beginning of the war 900 sisters, to assist in the care of sick soldiers, were sought. The influenza epidemic of 1918 which spread widely and rapidly among all (soldiers and civilians) required the assistance of many volunteers. The Samaritan Association, somewhat connected with the Red Cross, urged its members, partially trained, to help the afflicted families. The principal burden fell on the professionally trained nurses of the Red Cross, of whom 10 percent died of their exertions.

WAR-TIME SCANDALS   As might be expected some questionable, even scandalous, incidents in the military and political arenas arose in Switzerland. Two colonels on the General Staff, Egli and von Wattenwyl, were found guilty of regularly supplying the Austrian and German military attachés with copies of the Bulletin of the Army Staff. The bulletins contained summaries of the military operations of the belligerents but were not informative on any Swiss military secrets. There was, however, a tremendous public uproar. The colonels were censured and suspended from their civil and military duties.

More serious was the case of Federal Councillor Hoffmann who, in May 1917, on his own initiative, travelled to Petrograd to initiate negotiations on a separate peace between Russia and Germany. A telegram intercepted by the Russian government stating that Germany would undertake no offensive operations as long as a peaceful settlement with Russia seemed possible, was published by the Russians and Hoffmann was promptly expelled. Hoffmann resigned at once and his singlehanded action in Russia was unanimously condemned by the Federal Council. It is to be noted that while a neutral State may try to bring about peace it must contact each of the belligerent Powers: it may not intervene unilaterally in the war policy of one of the Powers.

The War ended in November 1918 and might have terminated sooner if Germany had not stubbornly refused to surrender earlier in the year: it was clear to all, especially after the USA entry in 1917, that further military operations by Germany would be futile and the continued loss of life and property was senseless.

Post-war Events

A number of post-war events with which Switzerland was concerned must be mentioned.

THE RUSSIAN REVOLUTION   The Russian Revolution left an indelible imprint on Switzerland. Lenin who had resided in Bern and Zurich during part of the war was permitted in 1917 to return to Russia with a few of his followers. To do so, travel through Germany was necessary and this was achieved by use of a sealed train, as required by the authorities. The Bolshevik revolution reached its climax in November 1917.

THE GENERAL STRIKE   Lenin left behind a large number of devoted adherents who received jubilantly the news of the political and social revolution in Russia. They strove to achieve in Switzerland a similar dictatorship of the proletariat. In their machinations against the State they found substantial support from the Diplomatic Mission of the Soviet Republic which was received and established in Bern in 1918. But the Swiss peasant, most of the workers in industry, and the men in the army could not be won over to revolution.

Nonetheless the government feared the worst and when the Social Democratic party planned a great demonstration in Zurich to celebrate the first anniversary of the Russian Revolution, the government ordered a military occupation of the city. A demand of the party's executive to withdraw the troops immediately was refused. This led to a general strike, announced for 11 November 1918 and planned to continue until the most important of the workers' demands had been granted. Over 200,000 men and women participated. Two or three days later the Federal Council ordered the Social Democratic party to call off the strike by evening. The Federal Assembly declared their readiness to introduce social and political reforms but only by constitutional means. The party executive bowed to the order of the Federal Council and surrendered unconditionally. The Federal Council on November 12 promptly expelled the Soviet legation and terminated all diplomatic relations with the USSR. Not until 1946 did Switzerland permit the return of a Soviet diplomatic mission to Switzerland and resumption of diplomatic relations.

In Section 11.7 on Industrial Peace I have described other aspects of the strike and the events that led to the Peace Agreement of 1937.

THE INFLUENZA EPIDEMIC OF 1918–1919   This, the most widespread and deadly influenza epidemic on record, is reported to have afflicted 15 to 50 percent of the world's population and to have caused 20 million deaths (1, p. 45). In Switzerland, over 21,000 deaths were recorded among 664,463 cases reported to the medical authorities (67). If we recognize, however, that many influenza sufferers fail to call a doctor, it is reasonable to suspect that two million may have had influenza—about half of Switzerland's 1918 population (67, p. 279). The Chief of the Army Medical Staff was accused of preferential treatment of the sick among the interned soldiers of the belligerent armies: Swiss soldiers, it was alleged, were treated negligently. His resignation was demanded by an articulate pressure group. The officer was finally acquitted of want of attention to the Swiss soldiers (116, 12th edition, Vol. 32, p. 641). The epidemic has no direct bearing on Swiss neutrality but was one of the inter-war events of singular importance because of its impact on the Swiss people.

THE VORARLBERG   The Vorarlberg is the most westerly of the Austrian *Länder* (provinces), with little Liechtenstein sandwiched in between a short stretch of the Vorarlberg border and Switzerland. As World War I drew to a close and the Austrian monarchy collapsed, the Vorarlberg adopted a democratic constitution and, expressing a right to self-determination, the Vorarlbergers expressed their desire to unite with Switzerland. But the desire of Vorarlberg to secede from Austria and become an easterly canton of Switzerland did not receive a welcoming response from the Swiss. Switzerland's policies did not favor territorial expansion. Beyond the policy question, the Vorarlberg was impoverished and Catholic, facts which gave rise to misgivings among the Swiss. A racial and linguistic kinship encouraged some Swiss to favor the absorption of the Vorarlberg. While the Federal Council, aware of the difficulties in reaching a consensus, stood aloof, the people of the Vorarlberg voted 45,566 in favor of, against 11,209 opposed to the proposed union. The Austrian Government vigorously opposed the secession. The peace of St. Germain in September 1919 left the old western border of Austria intact and ended the clamor of the Vorarlbergers to unite with Switzerland. Had the Vorarlberg been taken over by Switzerland without the free consent of the Austrian government, the act could surely be interpreted as an intrusion of Switzerland into the internal affairs of another country—a clear violation of her commitment to neutrality.

LIECHTENSTEIN   This small mountainous country of 160 km², with a population of over 21,000 in 1970 has had a long and fascinating history (**302**). Its sovereignty and territorial integrity were upheld by the Congress of Vienna in 1815. Its borders have remained unchanged to the present day—its sovereignty, tainted somewhat until 1866 by its close relationship to Austria. Not until 1842 did a ruling prince take the time or trouble to visit his principality. In that year, Prince Alois II visited Vaduz. The Liechtenstein family was Austrian by birth and lived in Vienna. It was natural that Austria should be the protector of the small principality.

The fall of the Austrian Empire in 1918 had a great impact on Liechtenstein. Her ties with Austria were gradually relinquished and those with Switzerland were strengthened. It should be mentioned that in the Middle Ages Liechtenstein had belonged to the Bishopric of Chur, and in subsequent years a variety of treaties began to forge a close relationship with Switzerland. And so it happened that Switzerland was requested to take over the Principality's diplomatic relations abroad because Austria, as a former belligerent, was no longer able to do so. Liechtenstein next entrusted Switzerland with the administration of its postal services. Finally, in 1923, the Customs Union of the two countries was agreed upon and supplemented by a border-police agreement. The effect of this was to move the customs border of the two countries to the Vorarlberg frontier and to terminate the pre-existing customs border between Switzerland and Liechtenstein. The political and economic developments resulted in the opening of a Liechtenstein legation in Bern, diplomatic representation of Liechtenstein abroad by the Swiss Ministry for Foreign Affairs, and conclusion of a number of treaties to give effect to the close association between the two countries.

In 1924, the Swiss franc became accepted as Liechtenstein's currency. As for the postal services, Liechtenstein issues its own stamps—an excellent source of income. Swiss stamps may not be used in Liechtenstein unless the Principality's stamps are not available.

Nationals of the two countries receive equal treatment when living in the other's country. One may conclude that Liechtenstein is a sovereign State which has limited the exercise of its sovereignty by transfer of some of its powers to Switzerland. It has had no army since 1868 although it became necessary to enlist a supplementary police force of 50 men to maintain surveillance over the many refugees, objectors and deserters who streamed into Liechtenstein during World War II.

Liechtenstein is necessarily neutral. It is much too small to be aggressive in its international relations and carefully avoids political alliances, except for the close association with Switzerland. It is not, however, a part of the Swiss defense system and the Liechtensteiners are not subject to the military training that is a conspicuous element in the Swiss defenses. In World War II, "Vaduz could . . . have fallen to the Germans within a quarter of an hour after the border was crossed" (302, p. 145). The 50 or so members of the auxiliary police corps were not under any orders to offer resistance: it would have been futile and suicidal (see also 226).

THE ITALO-ABYSSINIAN AFFAIR   When the war was entering its last year or two, the League of Nations came into being with Switzerland as an original member (Section 11.17). Her experiences in the League presented several conflicts with her status as a permanent Neutral. The final blow came in 1938 when the League declared economic sanctions and a boycott against Italy, because of her invasion of Abyssinia. Switzerland refused to apply other sanctions but boycotted the sale of armaments to both Italy and Abyssinia equally. This angered Abyssinia and her friends but the refusal to sell weaponry to the two belligerents was an understandable expression of Switzerland's responsibility as a neutral Power.

World War II

Possibly the first events involving Switzerland, as the curtain began to rise on World War II, concerned her relations with Italy. In general, attempts to draw the Ticino into much closer relations with Italy led to espionage, unjustified arrests and pro-Italian demonstrations arranged by the irredentists. Politically, Switzerland managed to rebuff these clumsy, though troublesome, attempts to join the Ticino to Italy. Policies of friendship were adopted between the two countries and re-affirmed from time to time. Mussolini was not commonly regarded as a dangerous megalomaniac but simply as a clever politician. With German nationalism in the ascendancy it was argued that Mussolini's political goal was only the maintenance of a European balance of power—of sorts.

It took the *Anschluss* of 1938—Germany's seizure of Austria—and the attack on France in June 1940 to awaken Switzerland to the mounting dangers that confronted her. Comforting reassurances of their pacific intentions, from both

Goebbels and Hitler, were greeted with the same mistrust and disbelief as were comparable assurances of friendship and peace, conveyed by Hitler through Neville Chamberlain to the British people.

Germany made every effort to enlist the support of the many German nationals in Switzerland in aiding the Reich. Espionage and attempts to subvert the German-speaking Swiss, with their common language and ethnic background, became seriously troublesome and dangerous almost as soon as Hitler's totalitarian regime came into being. As early as 1933 the Swiss press, because of its hostile treatment of Hitlerian Germany, so inflamed the German government that the Swiss Federal government decided, regretfully, to impose a press censorship in an effort to appease their powerful neighbour to the north.

If the Swiss people were at all divided on policy matters concerning Germany, they became one when they learned that German training regulations regarded Switzerland as a part of the Reich. Official German maps impudently showed Switzerland as an incorporated part of the new Germany. When war broke out, the Federal Assembly elected Henri Guisan from French-speaking Switzerland as General and Supreme Commander of the Swiss armed forces. His election was greeted enthusiastically throughout Switzerland. The Federal Assembly proclaimed the determination of the Confederation "to preserve its neutrality in all circumstances and against all Powers." On 31 August 1939, the Federal Council issued a formal declaration of neutrality similar in form and content to that of 4 August 1914. Mobilization was ordered at the same time and general labour conscription followed two days later. When war broke out on 3 September 1939, Switzerland had 400,000 men under Guisan's command. Including additional troops who were later called up, members of the home guard, and auxiliary services, a total of 850,000 were called to the colours with at least 100,000 in active service at any one time. Defense strategy has been discussed in section 11.20 and need not be repeated here, although it is well to be aware of General Guisan's fundamental changes as described in the section mentioned.

FOREIGN TRADE As for the impact of the war on Switzerland's economy, above all on her imports and exports, she was in a more desperate situation than during World War I. In June 1940, France fell and Italy joined the enemy. Switzerland then found herself completely surrounded by hostile belligerents except for a narrow corridor through the outskirts of Geneva into "Free France" to permit trade with non-Axis Powers. Germany lost no time in imperiously ordering Switzerland to terminate all trade relations with the British Empire. Otherwise the coal and iron imported from Germany and Vichy France would no longer be available—possibly an idle threat because Germany needed the Swiss-made machinery and armaments for which coal and iron had to be provided. Germany also demanded credits from Switzerland and imposed tight controls on Swiss exports to the Allies through the Free-France corridor. Britain responded with a blockade which reduced Swiss food imports to very small amounts. Britain herself, struggling for survival, was desperately short of food—a situation that improved with the USA entry into the war in December 1941. Meanwhile, but unwillingly, Switzerland had become economically more dependent on Germany.

Tables 90 and 91 report on Switzerland's imports and exports from eight selected countries. It will be noticed that imports from Germany were maintained at a high level through the first six years of the war and decreased sharply in 1945 and 1946. Swiss exports to Germany were correspondingly relatively substantial for the period 1939 to 1944, and underwent a sharp reduction in the last two years. Great Britain exported only modest amounts to Switzerland throughout the war except for a significant increase in 1946. Her imports from Switzerland were likewise modest, and fell sharply in 1943 and 1944. Trade with the USSR virtually terminated. Pierre Béguin reports that Swiss "exports to Germany and Italy, as well as to the countries dependent on them totaled 5.3 thousand million francs while . . . imports reached 7.1 thousand million." The same source reminds us that the Allies received Swiss exports worth 1.7 thousand million francs and sent to Switzerland, in turn, goods worth 2.0 thousand million (**32**).

THE END OF THE WAR   The war came to an end in 1945–46 leaving behind a Europe devastated by bombing, and Japan with two of her cities destroyed by the most terrible weapon known to mankind, the atomic bomb. The survivors determined that the nations of the world would never again resort to war to settle their problems. Country by country entered the United Nations Organization, always in the hope that here would be found the means, through international cooperation and solidarity, to attain a lasting peace and an end to the insanity of war. In 1945, when the UNO was born so auspiciously, its predecessor, the League of Nations, faded quietly away (please refer to section 11.17).

Table 90   Swiss imports (1938–1947) from selected countries[a,b,c]

Year	Germany	France	Italy	Japan	Great Britain	USA	Canada	Australia and N. Zeal.	USSR
1938	373	229	117	12.0	95.0	125	24.1	11.1	29.0
1939	440	275	135	11.8	109	133	30.6	11.9	9.1
1940	411	139	165	10.1	88.0	199	19.5	2.7	10.6
1941	656	75.5	245	10.4	14.3	151	21.8	0.3	50.7
1942	660	77.3	154	1.7	20.0	235	13.1	0.2	1.7
1943	532	78.4	131	0.7	3.6	56.4	80.2	0.0	0.1
1944	433	51.8	28.6	0.4	1.2	21.2	14.3	0.0	0.0
1945	54.3	130	47.1	0.4	21.5	137	104	2.8	0.9
1946	45.4	355	228	4.0	197	548	111	18.5	4.6
1947	133	459	321	5.7	323	1032	55.8	30.8	8.6

[a] In millions of francs.
[b] Source: **341**, 1952, pp. 168, 169.
[c] Switzerland's imports from all countries (1938–1947) totalled 21,804 million francs (**341**, 1952, p. 157). The nine countries listed above, all of which were belligerents for all or part of the war, exported to Switzerland products valued at 11,412 million francs during this ten-year period, i.e. about one half of her total imports.

Table 91 Swiss exports (1938–1947) to selected countries[a,b,c]

Year	Germany	France	Italy	Japan	Great Britain	USA	Canada	Australia and N. Zeal.	USSR
1938	206	121	91.2	32.9	148	90.8	14.7	20.7	10.1
1939	192	140	80.7	13.3	165	130	15.2	19.1	15.8
1940	285	112	142	14.1	94.9	140	15.5	11.6	19.5
1941	577	92.6	186	4.5	23.0	108	12.5	4.3	14.5
1942	656	67.4	159	22.2	21.6	102	13.6	5.1	0.2
1943	598	51.5	93.5	3.0	35.7	153	19.5	15.8	0.0
1944	294	23.6	4.9	0.2	34.0	141	17.0	6.7	0.3
1945	11.2	165	11.1	—	31.7	385	35.1	13.2	0.8
1946	7.9	282	156	0.0	58.1	453	39.8	16.9	2.9
1947	15.5	298	210	0.0	117	395	53.9	33.0	4.9

[a] In millions of francs.
[b] Source: **341**, 1952, pp. 184, 185.
[c] Switzerland's exports to all countries (1938–1947) totalled 17,142 million francs (**341**, 1952, p. 157). The nine countries listed above, all of which were belligerents for all or part of the war, imported from Switzerland products with a total value of 8699 million francs during this ten-year period again, about one-half of her total exports.

The Palestinian Problem

On 14 June 1981, Farouk Kaddoumi, representing the Executive Committee of the Palestinian Liberation Organization (PLO) made an official visit to Switzerland to discuss with the Minister for Foreign Affairs and others the Swiss position in respect to the Middle-East conflict and the fate of the Palestinian people.

To the surprise of Switzerland and other nations, Austria had already recognized the PLO, and Kaddoumi, doubtless, hoped that Switzerland would do likewise. But this was not to be. Switzerland's policy in such matters is clear. She interprets her responsibility as a Neutral to adhere to the recognition of States, not of a People. According to international usage, a State consists of three essential elements: a defined territory, a population within the territory, and a government. It follows that the PLO, not being a State, cannot be recognized by Switzerland. But were she to do so by a departure from her present policy, peace in the Near East would not be furthered: Israel would certainly be greatly disturbed and the Arab States might also be displeased.

Switzerland can maintain an information exchange through the PLO's observer office at the UNO branch in Geneva or, again in Bern, with an accredited visitor to the Department of Foreign Affairs. Information exchange, but not diplomatic representation, appears to be Switzerland's policy for the present.

The EEC Boycott of Iran

In May 1980, the European Economic Community declared a boycott of goods ordered by Iran from the member States. Switzerland refused to join in the boycott because such economic sanctions are incompatible with her neutrality and also because of her special status as the diplomatic representative for USA interests in Iran. Not wishing to profit more than at present from her continued trade with Iran, she sought a voluntary limitation of exports by Swiss industry. Alternatively, a system of export approval by government may be required. Swiss exports to Iran are principally machinery, apparatus, pharmaceuticals and other chemicals. Imports are mostly carpets and petroleum.

Human Rights and Basic Freedoms

That such matters have any relevance to neutrality would be disputed by any State whose concept of neutrality is merely abstention from war. Switzerland, however is committed to perpetual neutrality and this commitment has meant to the Swiss the acceptance of a number of peacetime responsibilities which are uniquely hers. The most striking example is the International Red Cross, Swiss in origin and in administration, with its manifold activities (cf. Section 11.19). A second example which will be discussed is her zeal for human rights and basic freedoms.

A comprehensive definition of human rights defies a straightforward presentation. Sometimes it is easier to say what it is not rather than to say what it is. It is also easy to itemize a number of restrictions that society is obliged to place upon so-called basic freedoms. For example: Freedom of expression: Society, with some exceptions, does not permit the use of obscenities in the printed word, and in public statements, and nudity in public places is seldom condoned. In popular demonstrations society cannot permit those who feel so disposed to express themselves by hurling bricks through windows or by other acts of violence that are obviously anti-social and can induce others among any peacefully-inclined demonstrators to do likewise. Robbery cannot be condoned by society even though the guilty party may claim he is determined to correct social inequities by taking from the rich to give to the poor. Many other examples could be given but all of us with little effort can think of various restrictions that society must place on various freedoms.

It would be a difficult exercise to determine when and where in the long history of mankind society began to reveal and to put into practice an interest in human rights. The Bible is rich in exhortations about brotherly love, of doing unto others as we would be done by, of caring for the poor and so forth. The Magna Carta, signed by King John at Runnymede on the Thames in June 1215, and the Petition of Rights of June 1628 are political documents which paved the way for much legislation in England on human rights. In the USA on 4 July 1776, Congress declared as a principle which the newly emerging nation should recognize and honor: "that all men are born equal; that they are created with certain inalienable rights including life, freedom and the pursuit of happiness." The French declaration of 26 August 1789, on human and civil rights was impressive and influential but failed to carry the protection of human rights to the level of international concern. Indeed, until the recent past the view prevailed that the treatment of their citizens was entirely a concern of the individual States. When the presence of foreigners loomed large within their borders, the question of human rights took a different turn.

International law and custom obliges a State to grant at least a minimum of protection to the foreigners in its midst. At the diplomatic level, a foreign Power has the right to demand protection of its nationals, subject to certain reasonable conditions wherever international law and customs are known and recognized. After World War II an internationalization of basic rights came to be perceived, in the sense that the legitimate interests of the individual should be protected, irrespective of his citizenship.

One of the first great projects of the United Nations was a General Declaration of Human Rights, proclaimed by the General Assembly through Resolution 217A(III) of 10 December 1948. The Declaration appears as an appendix to a report by the Federal Council on Switzerland's human rights policy (**188**). The Declaration embraces most of that which is pertinent to human rights and basic freedoms and, as such, serves as the basis for the UNO universal pacts of 1966, for legislation at the international and national levels, and for regional conventions such as the European Human Rights Convention of 1950.

Another important body that embraces all the States of Europe, except Albania, and is external to the United Nations Organization is the Conference on Security and Cooperation in Europe (KSZE, i.e., *Konferenz über Sicherheit und Zusammenarbeit in Europa*). With its beginnings in 1972 and its final Act in Helsinki in 1975 it gave to the representatives of the 35 member States (including Canada and the USA) an opportunity to deliberate upon such questions as national togetherness (*Zusammenleben*), economic relations, and security in Europe. Subsequent conferences of the member States in Belgrade and Madrid have been less fruitful, largely because of the distrust between East and West. Trust between member States is indispensable, for, in its absence, any meaningful debate and progress in achieving good will, however small, can hardly be expected. The Russian intervention in Afghanistan in 1979, and the more recent usurpation of power by a military dictatorship in Poland, contributed most strongly to failure to resume the Madrid conferences on a hopeful note.

Without listing in detail the contents of the 30 Articles that constitute the UNO Declaration of Human Rights, and of other international instruments that pertain to single aspects of human rights, such as torture, genocide, and discrimination because of race, sex, or religion, it is sufficient for present purposes to discuss the place of Switzerland in relation to human rights and basic freedoms.

There is no doubt about her zeal for human rights, tersely expressed in a report by the Federal Council:

> today, we should no longer fail to recognize the close connection that exists between respect for human rights and the maintenance of peace and security in the world (**188**).

We also learn from the report:

> that an active Swiss human rights policy demands the adherence of Switzerland to the pacts of the United Nations. That international agreements on human rights, especially if they contain a control mechanism for their application, and are signed by as many

States as possible, constitute one of the basic preconditions for strengthening the protection of human rights in the world (**188**, p. 29).

Amnesty International, serving as a watchdog in respect to violations of human rights and basic freedoms, wherever they arise, comments briefly on the behavior of Switzerland. "The imprisonment of conscientious objectors to military service and the lack of any alternative civilian service remained the main concern of Amnesty International" (**13**).[5] See also section 11.20.

Somewhat related is a request for amnesty, originating within two religious organizations in Switzerland, for youthful participants in the demonstrations that commenced on 30 May 1980 in Zurich, but continued in the months that followed in Zurich, Basel, Bern, Lausanne and elsewhere. If the federal authorities adhere to the letter of the law, it is improbable that a federal amnesty would be granted. When specific cantonal laws are broken, cantonal authorities would be in a position to consider requests for amnesty. Indeed, the federal authorities may turn the whole "sticky" problem over to the cantons. It should be noted that many of the demonstrators were under 25 years of age, and not all who were rounded up by the police were guilty partners in the violence that erupted. See also section 11.16.

Are there other actual or alleged violations of human rights in Switzerland? Not all citizens of voting age are permitted to vote. There are no exclusions in the federal elections, but in the cantonal elections women are denied the right to vote in one of the two half cantons of Appenzell. In 30 of 215 communities in the Graubünden, women could not vote until recently in the local community elections. However, beyond persuasion, the Federal Government is powerless to correct these infringements of human rights: cantonal sovereignty in such matters as elections to cantonal governments and the high level of self government in the local communities would not permit any interference by the Federal Government.[6]

There is also the matter of equal pay for equal work, without any discrimination based on sex, religion, or race. In Switzerland, the average pay for women is 25 to 30 percent lower than that of men. It is possible that equality exists among federal employees, men and women alike. However, it is apparent that in private industry, in agriculture, and among cantonal employees there may indeed be a problem. Government in Switzerland is loath to assume a dictatorial attitude toward industrial enterprises, and interference in their operating policies is minimal.

There are also among the zealous proponents of human rights those who insist that in the elections for public office, voting should be by secret ballot. By inference they condemn the electoral procedure in the *Landsgemeinden*—still adhered to in several of the cantons—whereby electoral decisions are reached in public by voice vote or by a show of hands. But, again, the Federal Government does not have the power to force the *Landsgemeinde* cantons to change their ways. Although Article 21 of the UNO General Declaration of Human Rights specifies the use of secret voting it also suggests an alternative "or with an equivalent free electoral procedure." The Federal Council respects the UNO Declaration of Human Rights. Although Switzerland is not a member of the organization, she strives to be exemplary in behaviour[7] and sooner or later may find herself a member of the UNO.

As for her good behaviour, the question has been raised as to whether Switzerland should not refrain from making loans and extending economic help to countries, underprivileged or otherwise, wherein violations of human rights are blatant:[8] imprisonment for expression of opinions that are unacceptable to government, punishment for defending "prisoners of conscience," for practising their religious beliefs, for distributing religious literature, for belonging to unofficial groups that monitor government observance of human rights, as defined in conventions to which the government has adhered, disappearance of people regarded by government as enemies of the State, torture, etc. Switzerland's policy of divorcing business from human rights is the focus of such a criticism arising from within Switzerland herself through the Swiss Section of Amnesty International.

A second criticism contends that Switzerland in such matters tries to shield herself by claiming that her commitment to neutrality does not permit her to interfere in the internal affairs of other countries. To deny economic aid to a country because it constantly violates human rights or to refuse to do business with a country because of Swiss disapproval of its social policy is tantamount to interference in its internal affairs.

We should recall that the Lower House (*Nationalrat*) of the Swiss Parliament in March 1980 unanimously condemned the intervention of the USSR in Afghanistan. A purist, who interprets rigidly the obligations of a perpetual neutral to avoid any entanglement in the internal affairs of another country, would insist that the action of the *Nationalrat* is an example of such an *Einmischung*.

The USSR and its block of fringe States approve the policy of noninterference by any State in the internal affairs of another. In so doing they interpret the Helsinki document, to which they have subscribed, as declaring it to be a right of all States to be free to choose and to develop their own political, social, economic and cultural systems without any *Einmischung* from outside. Freely interpreted, the USSR declares to the world that whatever goes on in the USSR is not subject to criticism by outsiders. The heavy hand of the communist government over its people, the absence of many basic freedoms and the persistent violation of human rights by the government are strictly and exclusively affairs of the USSR. Such a conclusion does not rest well with any individual or government dedicated to human rights, solidarity, peace, and international good will.

It should be noted that the Federal Council approves a policy of humanitarian interventions, provided that it rests on coherent and objective criteria. In the observance of such a policy, the Federal Council undertakes to intervene on humanitarian grounds in the internal affairs of other States irrespective of the political orientations of the governments concerned (**188**, p. 13).

A possible solution of the dilemma is for the government of neutral Switzerland to refrain from any condemnation of the policies of other States which do not have any bearing on Switzerland herself, leaving to organizations such as Amnesty International, the UNO, other organizations and concerned individuals, the responsibility of condemning other countries for violations of human rights. But it must also be recognized that at the diplomatic level much more may sometimes be quietly accomplished than through a widely publicized, and sometimes provocative, outburst by concerned individuals and well-meaning organizations.

A final solution to the problems that confront Switzerland in these matters may have to await her admission to membership in the United Nations Organization (UNO).[9] The UNO outlined a human rights policy in 1948. Somewhat later came the UN pact for human rights through the European Convention for the Protection of Human Rights and Basic Freedoms (the EMRK). Much of this is confirmed and strengthened by the final Act of the Helsinki Conference (KSZE). All of this emphasizes the international status of the human rights problem and, in one way or another, has a significant impact upon the foreign and domestic policies of many States.

In conclusion a few words should be added about Swiss foreign policy. Its first and most important objective is the maintenance of Switzerland's independence. Her state of readiness for the nation's defense is expressed by her commitment to permanent armed neutrality—the chief instrument for ensuring her continued independence. She is also deeply committed to international solidarity as expressed by her cooperation with many other States in seeking the achievement of all humanitarian objectives that are conducive to international peace and good will. Herein lies her consuming interest in the world-wide recognition and observance of human rights and basic freedoms.

Notes and Comments

1. With an index of 100 in June 1914, the cost of foodstuffs (selected list) rose to 213 in 1921 and declined to 152 in 1930 (**341**, 1933, p. 283). The national index for the cost of living (food, heating and lighting, clothing, rent) rose from an index value of 100 in June 1914 to 224 in 1920 (**341**, 1933, p. 282) and fell gradually to 158 in 1930. It reached a minimum of 128 in 1935 and rose to 138 in 1939. By the end of World War II in 1945–46, the index had climbed to 208 (**341**, 1952, p. 335).

2. During World War II the Central Tracing Agency of the ICRC processed 40 million information cards and provided news regarding prisoners of war and civilians to several thousand families a day.

3. Germany is not mentioned in the Yearbook as a source of potatoes for Switzerland, though another source states that in 1916 Germany exported 1600 truck loads of potatoes to Switzerland (**116**, 12th edition, Vol. 32, p. 642). This is very little if we recall that in 1917, thanks to her domestic program, Switzerland's home production was 120,000 truckloads. Thousands of families raised potatoes (**116**, 12th edition, Vol. 32, p. 643).

4. The export of dairy cattle to Germany and Austria, though not mentioned in the Yearbook, is reported in reference **116** (12th edition, Vol. 32, pp. 639, 642).

5. The report covers the period January to December 1981—not the year 1982.

6. In the cantonal elections in the Graubünden in late 1982, the right of women to vote and hold office in the local communities throughout the canton was approved.

7. Since 1974, a control mechanism has been in operation, whereby the European Human Rights Commission, the European Court of Justice for Human Rights and the Ministerial Committee of the Council of Europe keep track of alleged violations of human rights by individual member States. Up to the end of 1981, 238 complaints had been registered against Switzerland. Of these, 176 were dismissed by the Commission as inadmissible and 19 were declared to be admissible—not unfounded. Some 54 complaints were awaiting action. Of these, three fell within the jurisdiction of the European Court of

Justice for Human Rights and six were within the competence of the Ministerial Committee of the Council of Europe.

8. For the period 1981–83, Switzerland allocated 350 million francs for economic help to Third World Countries. This contrasts with 200 million francs appropriated for the 1978–80 period. Of the 350 million francs, 110 are chiefly for balance-of-payments adjustments, while 240 million are reserved for so-called mixed credits, principally for the purchase of Swiss industrial products. In the financing of these purchases the Swiss banks also participate. The total allocation for developmental help in 1981–83 was 1.65 billion francs. For 1985–87, the Federal Council recommends an appropriation of 1.80 billion francs.

9. The question of Switzerland's accession to the United Nations has been debated for years in Switzerland. (Please refer to section 11.17.) In mid-1983 it was again actively under discussion and the time appeared to be at hand for Switzerland to initiate the appropriate request for membership. Should the application be introduced through a restrictive reservation (*Vorbehalt*) that in seeking accession to the UNO, Switzerland does so with the firm intention of adhering resolutely to her policy and practice of perpetual neutrality as declared by the signatory Powers of the Treaty of Paris and the Congress of Vienna in March 1815 to be in the true interests of the whole of Europe? Alternatively, and by whatever means would be most effective, should the member States of the UNO be directly informed that Switzerland, while seeking accession to the UNO, will neither abandon her centuries-old policy of armed and perpetual neutrality nor will she engage in any act which may jeopardize her neutral status within the family of nations? One is almost forced to conclude that unless the UNO fully understands and accepts the Swiss position and unless the Swiss voters also understand that the Federal Government will not jeopardize the neutrality of their country, there is little chance that a treaty of accession to the UNO would be ratified by the people and the cantons.

11.23 THE ENVIRONMENT

Introduction

Three aspects of the environment are of great concern to the Swiss. One of these recognizes the natural beauty of the country. By voluntary measures and by legislation, efforts are constantly made to preserve and protect the magnificent works of nature with which Switzerland is generously endowed. Even any of the works of man that call for preservation because of their historical or artistic value fall within the compass of *Heimatschutz* (protection of the homeland). All of this pertains to qualities of Switzerland that are of great touristic value: the economics of it all cannot be overlooked. Government at all levels seeks to exploit to the full the economic values inherent in the majestic grandeur of the mountains and the storybook charms of the countryside.

A second aspect is that of land planning—the rational determination of the uses to which land may be put, including restrictions on new building construction and on additions or major changes to existing structures. In Switzerland, these planning decisions are made by the communities. Elaborate plans may emerge; their observance by property owners is compulsory. Relatively few of the 3209 communities have established mandatory plans but there is general agreement that only by such measures can the open lands, the forests, and other natural beauties of the country be preserved. I have made many visits to Arni (near Bieglen in the canton of Bern). From Arniberg, for some kilometers in all directions, the landscape resists change: the natural beauty of the area bears witness to the value of land planning, mandatory controls over land use and protection of the environment.

The third aspect concerns the threats to the environment and pollution of the air we breathe, of the water we drink, and of the soil and water upon which we depend for our food production. As Hans Weiss puts it, "Man endangers his natural environment by his very existence" (**382**).

Pollution of the Environment

Every country that is heavily industrialized and motorized pays a tremendous price in damage to man's environment, the magnitude of which is only beginning to be appreciated. Switzerland is acutely aware of the problem and is actively in search of the answers. The atmospheric pollutants are principally sulphur dioxide (SO_2) and oxides of nitrogen, designated collectively as NO_x. The SO_2 is largely derived from the oxidation of sulphur in fossil fuels, especially coal. The oxides of nitrogen are partly the emission products from motor vehicles. The hydroxyl radical (OH), hydrogen peroxide (H_2O_2), and ozone (O_3) are ubiquitous in the atmosphere and each can oxidize SO_2 and NO_x to products which in the presence of water as vapor, rain, snow or fog are converted to sulphuric acid and nitric acid respectively. These are the substances that are commonly believed to be responsible for acid rain. NO_x can destroy atmospheric ozone, of which the stratospheric component provides a vital shield for the earth against ultraviolet radiation.

Quantitatively, and assuming the number of people on earth to be about four billion, the mass of the entire atmosphere is about 1.3 million tons per person, that of carbon dioxide in the atmosphere approximates 670 tons per person, the ozone burden is 1.2 tons per person, and the mass of oxides of nitrogen (calculated as NO_2) in the stratosphere is about 2.4 kg per person (**421**). Human enterprise cannot alter the total mass of the atmosphere but it does increase the burden of carbon dioxide. The atmospheric burden of the oxidation products of nitrogen and sulphur is also increasing as a result of human enterprises. In the USA the emissions of SO_2 and NO_x have doubled since 1960 (**422**).

The existence of acid rain and the damaging effects of the constituent acids have been known, but largely ignored, for over a century. In 1872, R. A. Smith reported a 20-year study of acid rain (a) on buildings, (b) on trees, shrubs, grasses, and moss. The grasses disappeared, the moss continued to grow (**423**). In Canada, the USA, and in the Scandinavian countries some lakes have become so acid that they cannot support life. The effects on vegetation are minimized where limestone and alkaline carbonates are abundant, and, hence, able to neutralize the acidic pollutants.

As for Switzerland, pollution of the environment is a most important, though depressing, topic of the news media. Every major newspaper has something to report, at least once or twice a week, on the damage being caused by acid rain. The disposal of chemical wastes by industry, the accidental spillage of petroleum and dangerous chemicals while in transport on the highways, the emission of toxic gases by industry,[1] and everything else in the environment that is dangerous or seriously unpleasant to man are reported upon almost daily.

A report issued by the Federal Office for Protection of the Environment for the year 1982 states that the three principal pollutants in Switzerland's atmosphere are hydrocarbons (incomplete oxidation products of petroleum), sulphur dioxide (SO_2), and oxidation products of nitrogen (NO_x). The quantities of these three groups of chemicals discharged into the Swiss atmosphere in 1982 are impressive and startling: hydrocarbons, 193,000 tons; NO_x, 182,000 tons; SO_2, 9000 tons. Table 92 presents a breakdown of these three totals to reflect the contributions of transport, household heating and cooking, and industry, regarded as the three principal sources of these noxious chemicals.

The report regards these three groups of chemicals or their oxidation products (notably sulphuric and nitric acids) as the substances responsible for the damage to the forests. The dying forests may be saved, so we are told, only by reducing the

Table 92 Emission in Switzerland in 1982 of atmospheric pollutants[a,b]

Origin	Hydrocarbons	Oxides of nitrogen	Sulphur dioxide
Transport	100,000	150,000	7000
Household heating and cooking	5000	15,000	32,000
Industry	88,000	17,000	51,000
Total	193,000[c]	182,000[c]	90,000

[a] Source: 1982 report of the Federal Office for Protection of the Environment.
[b] In tons.
[c] A tenfold increase since 1950.

emission of these substances to the 1950/1960 levels, in other words an average reduction of 80 percent.

A word of caution is necessary at this point. Acid rain may not be the sole cause of the death of forest trees. Include also drought, fungi, bark-loving beetles, a leaching from the forest soils of mineral elements essential for growth and well being of the trees, atmospheric dust, damaging chemicals brought into solution from inert precursors by acid rain, etc. etc. The eruption of Mt. Saint Helens in May 1980 was accompanied by a tremendous discharge of volcanic ash that was carried vast distances by wind. The canton of Geneva has received no less than 200 tons according to measurements made in 1981. Deposition of the ash may not have been complete even by 1983. Other sources of a particulate pollutant are the great deserts of North Africa from which clouds of sand particles, finely and minutely ground by abrasion, may be carried great distances by wind.

An international problem arises from the failure of a nation's atmosphere to remain confined within the national boundaries. Norway, for example, produces relatively little of the atmospheric pollutants mentioned (reported to be only about 8 percent of the total atmospheric burden of pollutants).[2] However, great masses of air move in from elsewhere. Pollutants originating in Great Britain, and in Norway's neighbors in the rest of Europe, are brought to Norway by the ever restless winds that blow and give to the country a burden of atmospheric pollutants far in excess of its own production. This is also true of Switzerland where only 10 percent of the atmospheric burden of sulphur pollutants originates within Switzerland; 90 percent is "imported" from elsewhere. The average monthly deposition of "sulphur" is reported to be 141 metric tons (**424**). Insofar as Norway and Switzerland may seek to reduce such troublesome burdens to more tolerable levels, one may well ask why they should be obliged to pay the cost of cleaning up an atmosphere that others have polluted. As a homely analogy, they are involuntarily forced to "take in other people's washing." It presents a problem in international ethics that defies any simple solution.

Apart from pollution of the atmosphere, Switzerland has a family of pollution problems which are well known in every industrialized country and need not be discussed here: disposal of any industrial wastes that are known to be detrimental to the well-being of man, other animals, and plants; accidental spillage of dangerous chemicals and petroleum while in transit, leading to localized pollution of soil, ground waters, rivers, streams and lakes; the widespread use of various herbicides, insecticides, fungicides etc., some of which have undesirable side effects that were unexpected and unpredicted.

What is Switzerland's answer to environmental pollution? Specifically, what solutions are being considered? The federal governments of Switzerland, West Germany and Austria agreed in late 1984 that the use of lead-free gasoline would become mandatory in their countries by early 1986. This would be followed by the mandatory installation of catalytic converters to complete the oxidation of the hydrocarbons in the effluent gases of motor cars and trucks. The rationing of gasoline has also been considered by the Swiss authorities as a means of reducing the volume of motor traffic and thereby decreasing the amount of pollutants discharged into the atmosphere. This proposal has not been well received and its implementation is improbable.

It appears likely that legislation will be enacted to require that those who are polluting the atmosphere will have to pay for their "sins." This conclusion emerges from a special session of the *Nationalrat* convened in February 1985 to formulate possible solutions to the increasing damage to the forests by atmospheric pollutants.

Legislation and Legislative Proposals

Although pollution of the environment by harmful chemicals is certainly the major concern of those who seek to legislate us into a clean and healthy environment, noise was the first damaging component of the human environment to receive the attention of the Federal Government of Switzerland. In 1957, a postulate by a member of parliament asked that, in cooperation with the cantons, a study be made of the measures that could be taken to limit noise. By a decree of the Federal Council on 21 October 1957, an expert commission was entrusted with the study of the noise problem from the medical, technical, and legal points of view, and to propose specific measures for reducing noise emissions to levels deemed unobjectionable to the general public. Sonic booms, *inter alia*, were then becoming a source of complaint by many who also found that building-construction noises should be combatted or restrained by appropriate legal measures. It was even proposed that a Division on Acoustics and Noise Control be organized within EMPA (the Federal Institute for Material Testing and Industrial Research located in Dübendorf near Zurich).

In March 1958, as a result of a postulate and again in 1960, through questions in parliament concerning air pollution, an ad hoc Commission on Air Hygiene was set up in January 1961 and replaced by a permanent Commission in January 1962. In the early 1960s the primary task of the Commission was to advise the federal authorities on the nature and magnitude of the emerging problems in air pollution.

In February 1964 the Commission proposed that Article 24 quater[3] of the Federal Constitution be supplemented to provide a legislative basis for protection against air pollution, whatever be the source: industrial and commercial installations and processes; domestic fires for heating and cooking; motor traffic, oil refineries; thermal energy works; garbage burning installations etc. In June 1971, by popular vote, Article 24 septies was added to the Federal Constitution.[4]

Following upon a message of the Federal Council in 1979, addressed to parliament, and based on Article 24 septies of the Constitution, the Federal Assembly passed a comprehensive law on 7 October 1983.[5] Its purpose is stated as follows:

> To protect mankind, animals, and plants, their group associations in life, and their living space, against dangerous or undesirable substances and effects, and to preserve the fruitfulness of the soil. In the sense of precautionary measures, such substances are to be limited by appropriate timely action.

In 66 Articles, the law covers everything that appears to be relevant to protection of the environment: the impact of this new law on other federal legislation; its coverage (pollution of air, water and soil; noise; vibrations; and radiation); the limitation of emissions and their permissible limits; control of pesticides, fungicides, fertilizers, growth regulators, and exhaust gases; disposal of human and industrial waste and chemical poisons; implementation, supervision, and coordination of enforcement measures; allocation of expenses attributable to the law; equipment and installations for waste disposal; processing of complaints; penalties for violation of the law; rights and responsibilities of the cantons; and amendment of existing laws that are relevant to this law.

Foreign and International Actions

Were we to return briefly to the past, we would find that pollution of the environment failed to evoke any action by the governments of industrialized countries until the 1960s.

The British government in 1963 issued a special report on noise, and Germany, in 1965, enacted a law against building-construction noise. The British government, also concerned about air pollution, passed Clean Air Acts in 1956 and 1968. A Royal Commission on Environmental Pollution was set up late in 1969 and a National Council for Environmental Research also came into being.

In Germany there was no federal legislation in the 1960s against air pollution. North Rhine-Westphalia in 1962 enacted a general Emission Protection Law against air pollution, offensive odors and vibrations, insofar as persons or objects were suffering damage. Other States in Germany soon adopted a similar pattern and prepared laws like the Westphalian model.

In the USA, in 1963, a Clean Air Act was passed by the Congress. This, in 1967, was replaced by the Air Quality Act. In 1969, President Nixon set up the Environmental Quality Council to recommend action against all kinds of environmental pollution. In January 1970, a Bureau for Condition of the Environment came into being and, in February 1970, proposed a broadly conceived program against air pollution and aviation noise.

It was also a time when international organizations took action in such matters. The OECD proposed a research program on city-generated noise and on sonic booms. The European Economic Commission of the United Nations initiated a study of measuring techniques and norms for motor noise, important to the problem of traffic noise. The International Civil Air Transport authority proceeded to study aeroplane noise. Noise in general became a problem of interest to the European Transport Ministers Conference and to the World Health Organization.

Conclusion

Futile as the exercise may be, it is enlightening to reflect upon man's environment in the industrialized countries of 100 years ago. Motor vehicles propelled by petroleum products were not in use. We had no occasion to worry about the gaseous emissions of such vehicles. The aeroplane had not been invented. The noise generated by aeroplanes and helicopters would not be a source of complaint for many years to come. Sonic booms were believed to be impossible. How can any airborne vehicle exceed the speed of sound? Coal was burned for household use and as fuel for the young and growing railway transportation systems. Then, as now, the coal-burning locomotives did their bit to pollute the atmosphere. The industrial revolution, still in its infancy, was dependent upon coal or wood as the final source of power for its industries. Water power was diminishing in importance.

Returning now to Switzerland of the present, we find that, with few exceptions, the railway trains are now electrified. Electricity is generated in three ways: (1) by hydrosystems, which were almost fully exploited in the 1970s and now offer very few opportunities for future development; (2) by generating systems using petroleum as the fuel for propulsion; (3) by atomic reactors which, when the Liebstadt reactor is in full operation, will provide some 40 percent of Switzerland's energy requirements. For household heating and cooking, Switzerland is still heavily dependent on petroleum, natural gas and, to a diminishing degree, on coal and wood.

Were we to look into the future we might reasonably anticipate that the day will come when Switzerland's source of electricity for heating, lighting and motor power will be (a) from falling water, as at present—a source that is now almost fully exploited and (b) from atomic reactors which will generate electricity in amounts that may satisfy almost the total requirements of industry and of the private sector. Petroleum and coal, which are the principal sources of the worst atmospheric pollutants, will surely diminish in use. They are not among Switzerland's few natural resources, an economic consideration that makes their progressive abandonment as sources of energy increasingly desirable. This leaves us with motor vehicles, which now, dependent as they are on petroleum products, constitute an expanding source of atmospheric pollutants. Can Switzerland exploit electricity as a source of power for the passenger cars and trucks that now clutter up her highways? The only hope for clean air in the future rests with the use of electricity as the energy source, provided further that the energy is developed by the exploitation of atomic power wherever hydro sources are inadequate to satisfy Switzerland's total needs. She must also hope that atomic fusion will be fully developed for commercial use to provide her people with a clean source of energy with none of the troublesome radioactive waste products that are generated in atomic fission reactors.

Notes and Comments

1. An emission of toxic gases (dioxin) in 1976 at a factory of Givaudan S.A., in Seveso, Italy, forced the evacuation of more than 700 people. In 1980, an agreement between the Italian government and Hoffmann-La Roche (the owners of Givaudan S.A.) was reached whereby the company paid in compensation claims a total of 109 million dollars. At the same time, the Italian government and the region of Lombardy terminated all civil actions against Givaudan in Italy and abroad.

2. The report pertains only to sulphur pollutants (**424**).

3. Article 24 quater empowers the Confederation to legislate on protection of surface and underground waters against pollution.

4. This (Article 24 septies) empowers the Confederation to issue regulations for protection of man and his natural environment against dangerous or undesirable substances and effects—in particular air pollution and noise. The enforcement of the regulations is entrused to the cantons except for any legislation that is reserved for the Federal Government. Federal legislation is deemed to be necessary because the problem is country-wide, intercantonal and intercommunity. Also, the cantons, in general, lack the necessary scientific and technical personnel.

Incidentally, what happened to Articles 24 quinquies and 24 sexies? The former (Article 24^5, or quinquies) gives the Confederation constitutional authority to legislate on protection against the dangers of ionizing radiation—indeed, the whole field of atomic energy is declared to be within the legislative competence of the Federal Government.

Article 24^6 gives to the cantons constitutional authority to legislate on protection of Nature and the Homeland—discussed in the first two paragraphs of this Section on the Environment.

5. Published: 18 October 1983 (*Bundesblatt III*, pp. 1040–1061, 1983).

11.24 THE SWISS WOMAN

Acknowledgment

As an introduction to much of this section, one cannot do better than to read the informative and authoritative chapter by Margrit Baumann and Judge Marlies Näf-Hofmann entitled "The Status of Women in Society and in Law" in *Modern Switzerland*, pp. 361–80 (**29; 264**).

Political Rights

On 7 February 1971, following an obligatory referendum, Swiss women of voting age, resident in Switzerland, were granted the right to vote in Federal elections and to be members of Parliament if so elected. In the autumn of 1971, ten women were elected to the House of Representatives (*Nationalrat*) out of a total of 200 members. One woman was elected to the Senate (*Ständerat*) with its total in 1971 of 45 members. Fourteen years later, 19 women held seats in the *Nationalrat*, three were in the *Ständerat*, and one woman, the first ever, was elected to the Federal Council in 1985.

Except for the two half cantons of Appenzell, women of voting age may also vote in the cantonal elections and, if elected, become members of the cantonal government. In 1981, 256 women, out of a total of 2871 cantonal parliamentarians, were members of cantonal governments. The canton of Geneva topped the list with a 22 percent female membership. As for representation of political parties, 84 of the 256 women in cantonal governments belonged to the Social Democratic party.

At the local or community level, women now, in 1982, vote in all local elections. In April, 1980, about 30 communities out of 215 in the Graubünden still denied to women the right to vote and to be elected to local offices. In the cantonal elections of late 1982, an amendment to the cantonal constitution was approved whereby the right of women to vote and be elected to local offices gained acceptance throughout the Graubünden. Opponents argued that the amendment, initiated by the Great Council (*Grossrat*), infringed upon the autonomy of the *Gemeinden* (local communities).

Any discussion of the equal rights problem of women in Switzerland should recognize the impact of topography. There are alpine communities with a total population of only forty to fifty; the smallest one, Rasa in Canton Ticino, numbers eleven inhabitants (**307**, p. 72). The problems of residents of these small alpine communities with a few cows, goats and hens differ greatly from those of city dwellers who frequently suffer from crowding, traffic density, noise and air pollution and are prone to turn to government to make their living conditions more endurable. This is not to overlook the economic problems that chronically bear heavily upon the "mountain people" and necessitate the continuing help of government in providing financial aid.

Another set of problems arises from the different life expectancies of men and women. As of 1 January 1980, about 162,000 residents of Switzerland were over 80 years of age. Of this age group, the number of women exceeded the men by 56,000. In fact, after the age of 45 or 50, women increasingly exceeded the number of men in each age grouping (**341**, 1981, p. 27). This numerical advantage of the women in elections more than counterbalanced the slight numerical advantage of men in the age group 20 to 45. There is no evidence that women over 45 have attempted to use their numerical advantage in hastening the attainment of certain kinds of equal rights such as equal pay for equal work.

MARRIAGE AND THE FAMILY   In 1975, the Federal Council established a federal commission to examine the status of women and of the family, especially in relation to the problems of equal rights. The first report, "On the Position of Women in Society and in the Economy," appeared in 1979 (**137**). A second report was expected to appear in 1980 on "Familiar Areas of Concern: the Incomplete Family and the Dissolution of the Family as it Affects the Wife." "An Inventory of the Inequalities in the Treatment of Men and Women as revealed in the Federal Laws" was scheduled for publication in 1981, and a fourth report, "An Overview of the Problems of Women and the Contributions of Art, the Mass Media, Politics and the Social Partner to make People Conscious of the Problems and to Point the Way to Solve Discrimination against Women" which would follow, would probably terminate the Commission's assignment.

All of this led to an on-going revision of the marriage law of 1907. The central concept of the new law is that marriage is a partnership in which the wife becomes a full and equal partner of her husband. Article 34 quinquies of the Federal Constitution empowers the Confederation to legislate in matters that "have due regard for the needs of the family." Article 4 is also relevant.[1] Areas of tension exist within the family and it is considered desirable that these be defined and perhaps regulated: the rights of children, child labor and the responsibility of schools are conspicuous examples.

Equally, if not even more conspicuous focal points of the new marriage law, are those aspects of the marital relationship that directly affect the husband and wife. No longer, according to the new law, is the husband the dictatorial head of the family. The husband-wife relationship shall be that of real partnership in which the premarital assets and current income and debts of the husband may not be concealed from his wife; and decision-making, household duties, and responsi-

Table 93 Statistical information, 1979 census

Married women	1,466,985
Divorced	74,882
Widows	270,950
Unmarried (ledig)	1,367,640[a]
Total female population	3,180,457[b]
Married women without children	495,721
Married women with children over 18	155,499
Married women with children under 18	758,720
Married women, separated[c]	57,045
Married women, total	1,466,985
Wives, professionally employed:	
Without children under 18	233,497
With children under 18	193,204
Total	426,701

[a] Inclusive of female children; unmarried adult females without female children are 430,754 in number.
[b] 50.7 percent of the total 1970 population; increased to 51.1 percent in 1980.
[c] Not living with husband.

bilities toward the family shall be equally shared. Who shall decide the living place? The husband and he alone? Not at all. The decision of the wife shall be as important as that of the husband. If they cannot agree, a judge will settle the argument. Shall the husband and he alone "bring home the bacon," leaving his wife to care for the children, prepare the meals, and take care of the house? Not if his wife prefers otherwise. She shall be as free as her husband to earn an income by work outside of the home. The joint income shall be community property, and the work of the household shall be a joint responsibility to be shared under a mutually acceptable arrangement.

And what happens if there is a dissolution of the marriage as a result of divorce or the death of one of the partners? By existing law, the wife or her descendants receives one-third of the bénéfice or true community property[2] and the husband or his heirs receives two-thirds. The new marriage law will ensure an equal division. Brothers and sisters of the two principals will no longer have a legal right to a share of the property.

Stepchildren brought into the family by either the husband or wife from a previous marriage shall be entitled to equal treatment in all respects with the children of the newly consummated marriage. Although children who are born as the result of a sexual indiscretion with an outside party by either the husband or wife are not entitled to the equal treatment provision, it is not yet clear how this problem will be solved.

Then there is the question of the family name. At present, if Frau Schneider marries Herr Gaebler the family name becomes Gaebler-Schneider or, possibly, just

Gaebler, Under the new law the family name can be Schneider-Gaebler if the parties agree, but probably not Schneider.[3] The new law may go a little too far and could invite endless genealogical problems that would create havoc, after a few generations, with the public birth and marriage records.

"Save the Family" is the title of a 160-page report, released in late 1982. It consists principally of recommendations by a special commission of the Department of the Interior. Starting from the high incidence of divorce—allegedly every third marriage in Switzerland ends in divorce—the report moves into specific recommendations to help save the family:

(a) Employers should create more part-time work and provide flexible working hours to permit a satisfactory balance between family and professional life.

(b) Family apartments are steadily being converted into higher-paying bachelor flats or offices. A resident family should be protected against loss of their living quarters through such conversions.

(c) Parents should be granted a leave-of-absence by their employer in the first year after a child's birth.

(d) To grant a measure of relief in respect to the heavy financial burden of rearing children and, hence, the generations of the future, child allowances and tax deductions should be extended to parents.

(e) Give both parents a chance to work through providing child-care centers, more kindergartens and day schools.

The "Save-the-Family" recommendations remind one of the initiative "For an Active Protection of Motherhood," the rejection of which was recommended by the Federal Council in November 1982. (Please refer to section 11.17—last item—or to the message of the Federal Council, 82.074, "*Über die Volksinitiative für einen wirksamen Schutz der Mutterschaft*" of 17 November 1982.)

Citizenship and Equal Rights

Until 1977, children received Swiss citizenship through their Swiss mothers only if they were born illegitimately or if the father was stateless. Legislation in 1978, and interpretation by the courts in 1979, extended the ground rules for citizenship rights of children. It is now agreed that if the father is Swiss and the mother is not Swiss, children born of such a marriage are indisputably Swiss. But if a child has a Swiss mother and a non-Swiss father, Swiss citizenship can be granted to the child only if the parents are living in Switzerland when the child is born. This rule applies only to those cases where the father is a foreigner. It is also necessary that the mother be Swiss by birth, not by naturalization or by marriage.

A number of postulates and motions in Parliament express the desire of the politicians to correct the existing inequalities which stem from Article 44, paragraph 3 of the Federal Constitution. The Council of Europe has also recommended to its members that all discrimination in this area of concern be eliminated. A commission of the *Nationalrat* drafted a constitutional amendment designed to rectify the problem by granting equal rights to the child of a Swiss woman and a man,

From the Swiss satirical weekly *Nebelspalter*.

irrespective of the origin of the mother or the place of residence at the time of birth.

In fact, the measure that came before the voters on 14 June 1981 as a counter initiative by the Federal Government, and was approved by 60.3 percent of the voters and by $15\frac{1}{2}$ of the cantons, goes much farther than the citizenship problem. It covers the entire constellation of equal rights:

> Men and women are entitled to equal rights. The law is concerned for their equality, before all in the family, in education and in work. Men and women are entitled to equal pay for equivalent work.

Let us summarize the potential effects of this constitutional amendment.

(a) Wherever women have been denied the right to vote in local elections, as in Appenzell Outer Rhodes, women may now be able to bring legal action against local officials who refuse to permit them to vote. Presumably, women will also enjoy the right to resort to legal action against any cantonal officials who attempt to deprive them of voting rights in cantonal elections. In the *Landsgemeinde* cantons, it is presumed that women of voting age may henceforth receive the legal right to participate in these open elections.

(b) A Swiss woman may henceforth obtain the right to pass on Swiss citizenship to a foreign husband. The citizenship problem of children, as described above, is also presumed to be solved.

(c) In all cantons, a working wife may now have the right, for tax purposes, of separating her income from that of her husband.

(d) In many cantons, schoolgirls must take courses in sewing and in other kinds of domestic work, thus depriving them of the opportunity to spend as much time as boys in preparing for a professional life outside the home. This kind of discrimination may also be amenable to elimination by virtue of the constitutional amendment.

(e) The equal-pay provision, if enforceable, will add substantially to production costs and to labor costs generally. Especially by virtue of its specific mention in the amendment, the courts will be obliged to rule against any who are found guilty of non-observance of the provision.

(f) In 1981, the canton of Jura included in its constitution an equal-rights clause which reads "Men and women are entitled to equal rights." The cantonal Delegate for Questions Concerning Women, by virtue of this constitutional imperative, succeeded in blocking the proposed structuring of a cantonal commission because not even one woman had been included in its membership.

If this serves as a precedent elsewhere in Switzerland, women throughout the country could insist on representation in a host of commissions which hitherto have been all-male in membership. Women are heavily under represented in leadership positions in many organizations and decision-making bodies. At the policy-making level in unions, for example, women are barely represented, if at all (137).

Opponents of the federal amendment have stressed the point that the way is now open for a veritable flood of new laws that may penetrate deeply into the private lives of the individual and of the family.

Whether the cantons can be compelled by the courts to respect and observe any pertinent legislation that stems from this equal rights amendment of 14 June 1982, is an open question. Many of the federal laws conclude with a sentence which says, in effect: "enforcement of this law is a responsibility of the cantons." Occasionally some of the cantons have ignored the enforcement responsibility, either because they disapproved of the law or for several other reasons that need not be discussed.

It would not be difficult to mention many other kinds of discrimination some of which may be readily amenable to elimination. We may take note of one which suggests that the rights of men and women in prison are sometimes unequal. A husband and wife, condemned in St. Gallen to $5\frac{1}{2}$ years imprisonment, were sent to different prisons. The husband received his mail unopened. Letters to his wife were opened, read, and censored. The husband, with approval, could use a telephone. This privilege was usually denied to his wife. The husband had his first "leave"

(*Urlaub*) after three months. His wife had to wait over two years for her first *Urlaub*. But it is relevant to note that the husband was imprisoned in St. Gallen, his wife in Hindelbank (Bern Canton). A petition by 66 inmates of Hindelbank sought an improvement in the treatment they received which suggests that this specific problem stems from inter-prison differences in the treatment of inmates, not from sexual discrimination in any one prison (**357**, March 1979).

Many Swiss women are married to foreigners. Under the anticipated legislation that will soon follow, the children of these women would be entitled to Swiss citizenship. There is a strong feeling in Switzerland against *Überfremdung* (over-foreignization), and any easing of the rules by which citizenship may be granted to children of a non-Swiss father may meet considerable opposition. Please refer also to 11.17.

The desire to become a Swiss citizen is expressed by some foreign women in a straightforward cash-purchase scheme. We read that in Zurich, girls from Thailand have been known to be accepted in a "paper marriage" with Swiss men by paying the prospective husband 15,000 Swiss francs or a white Mercedes and agreeing to co-habit one night per month. In another case, a businessman in Zurich married a Thai girl in return for a monthly payment to him of 600 francs. Six months later he died and the "Swiss" widow received from the State a monthly widow's payment of 496 francs (**357**).

National Mixed Marriages

The problems that arise from marriage of a Swiss woman to a foreigner are not obvious from the citizenship laws governing mixed marriages. Until recently the men involved were usually from neighbouring countries—Austria, France, Germany and Italy. In the 1980s an increasing proportion of the mixed marriages are being contracted with men from Third World countries. In these cases the cultural gap may be greatly increased and the matrimonial bond subjected to increased tension.

Foreign men frequently have to accept jobs for which they are overqualified. A work permit is not automatically granted and the applicant may have to accept menial employment or work that overtaxes his physical ability. Chances of promotion into something better have not been good. Difficulties in language and cultural differences may contribute greatly to the discontent of the foreign husband both on the job and at home. The Swiss wife requires much more tolerance and sympathetic understanding than in a Swiss-Swiss marriage.

Social problems are much in evidence. The foreigner frequently is not accepted in her social circles and the Swiss wife, in turn, may not be at all comfortable among his friends—usually his fellow-countrymen. Frequently she may not even meet the members of his family—his parents, his brothers and his sisters.

The employment of the husband, as a foreigner, is not solidly established. It may be terminated, as has been experienced by many foreign workers, and he finds himself obliged to return to his homeland. This can result in a family separation. Otherwise she moves with him into a strange environment that can enhance the tension of the marriage. And, according to the marriage law of 1907, if children are born to the couple, especially when the parents are not in Switzerland, the children cannot receive Swiss citizenship.

Economically and politically, the Swiss wife is factually the head of the family. She, it is, who must deal with officialdom, the owner of the apartment, insurance representatives and, sometimes, she must also be the chief provider.

In brief, the conjugal relationship may prove to be exceedingly difficult.[4] The new marriage law, if it permits a foreign man to become a Swiss citizen through marriage to a Swiss woman, may eliminate many of the existing problems, leaving unresolved the very difficult situations that frequently arise because of deeply rooted cultural differences.

Women Living Alone

In 1920, about half of all women of marriageable age lived by themselves (*alleinstehend*). By 1970, following a massive increase of marriages in the years after World War II, the proportion fell from about 50 percent to 37 percent. While 50.7 percent of the total population in 1970 was female, the percentage increased to 51.5 by 1980. This increase is attributed to the increased life expectancy at birth of the female population from 76.2 years in 1970 to 78.7 in 1980. That of the male population increased by only 1.8 years during the decade, i.e. from 70.3 years in 1970 to 72.1 years in 1980. The proportion of single-person households in Switzerland increased from 14 percent of all households in 1960 to 30 percent in 1980. An appreciable number of the "singles" is attributable to the fact that the life expectancy of women is greater than that of men. The same explanation is suggested by the fact that of all single-person households in 1980, 62.5 percent were female in occupancy and 37.5 percent were male. Relevant also is the observation that 36.2 percent of the total number of people involved were over 65 years of age.

But it should also be noted that 31.2 percent of the "singles" were less than 35 years of age, and 32.6 percent were in the age group 35 to 64. For these people of less than 65 years who live by themselves in single bliss (?), the causes appear to be the fragility of the marriage bond, evidenced by an increase in the number of divorces and separations (6700 in Switzerland in 1970, and 12,250 in 1982—not to be attributed to population growth, because the population increase was almost negligible). Of 123,000 women in 1980 who had been divorced since 1960, only 42.3 percent remarried. The remainder had had enough of marriage and, somewhat like those who had never married, disliked or feared marital responsibilities.

The statistical picture would be misleading if we implied that "single" in the present context connotes living alone. An estimate for Switzerland places the number of unmarried couples who share the same apartment or domicile at 100,000. In some of these cases the relationship may lead to marriage. In other heterosexual cases, the arrangement is only for convenience, marriage being neither contemplated nor desired. Many homosexual arrangements are likewise only for convenience and economic benefits, such as sharing the rent. The statistics are from ref. **266** (7–8 July 1984).

Cohabitation under Common Law

In some cantons, for example Baselland and St. Gallen, concern is publicly expressed over the practice of young men and women to live together in a *de facto* marriage. This common-law relationship is regarded as endangering the long-accepted social structure wherein the family is the bed-rock upon which social institutions rest. But in a specific case, a young child was involved and in the interests of justice, the law against "concubineage" was not invoked. In fact, the district court before which the young couple appeared, absorbed the costs of the hearing and paid the parents of the child 600 francs in damages.

Equal Rights for Men

A federal official over 62 years of age who had paid his federal insurance premiums for 40 years complained that he was still not qualified to receive a pension. His case rested on a discrimination against men in that the pension system provided that a woman need only be 60 years of age or have paid her insurance premiums for 35 years to be eligible for a pension. The complaint came before the Federal Court in Lausanne which recognized that under the existing regulations exceptions are permissible only under pressing physiological-biological considerations. The Court invited the Federal Council to re-examine the statutes of the Federal Insurance System (**266**, 26–27 March, 1983).

Article 4 of the Federal Constitution to which the claimant and the Court referred states that: "All Swiss citizens are equal before the law. In Switzerland, there shall be no subjects, and no privileges of place, birth, family or person."

In respect to the pension system, the regulations provide a clear use of reverse discrimination against men. In 1980, the life expectancy at birth was 78.7 years for women and 72.1 years for men. But despite the fact that, statistically, a Swiss woman lives 6.6 years longer than a Swiss man, women are entitled to their AHV pension at age 62 while men have to continue to age 65.[5] If life expectancy alone, was to be the base on which a pension system rested, men should be pensioned off a few years earlier than women.

Miscellaneous

There are many other topics pertaining to women in Switzerland which, in the following paragraph, are mentioned by subject only. A detailed exposition of each is excluded because of space limitations:

(i) Women and Military Service (discussed in section 11.20)
(ii) Employment of Women, including Prohibition of Night Work
(iii) Women's Organizations
(iv) Demonstrations to promote Specific Causes of Interest to Women
(v) Alcoholism
(vi) Abuse of Women
(vii) Illegitimate Children

(viii) Special Public Meeting Rooms for Women
(ix) "Frau" instead of "Fraulein"
(x) Conditional Imprisonment of a Female Member of Parliament

Notes and Comments

1. Article 4 of the Constitution, based on that of 1848, was concerned only with the abrogation of the special privileges enjoyed by the old aristocratic families.

2. *Bénéfice*. In effect, the community property or net assets accumulated during marriage, i.e. after the separately owned property that each partner brought to the marriage has been deducted from the total assets at the time of marriage dissolution. Existing law permits an equal division of the *bénéfice*, provided that this is spelled out in the marriage contracts.

3. It is unlikely that this compromise will satisfy the ardent feminists who would argue that Schneider has as much right to be the family name as Gaebler.

4. From 1972 to 1979, about 35 percent of the marriages of Swiss women to foreigners ended in divorce (**266**, 12–13 December 1981).

5. Late in 1983, the Federal AHV/IV Commission recommended that women be eligible to receive their AHV pension at age 63 instead of age 62. See also section 11.13 re Social Security.

11.25 CULTURAL ACTIVITIES

Introduction

I would have learned much about Swiss literature, music, and art had I decided to review this subject with the thoroughness that it deserves. To do so would require a separate substantial volume, a special kind of competence, and much more time than I can summon to the task. And, surely, one cannot do justice to the subject with a mere listing of the names of its recognized and more-or-less established contributors.

Without any apology, however, we shall resort to a compromise: a recommendation to the readers of four sources of information (in English) that may be sufficient to satisfy their curiosity, somewhat, and to serve the needs of those interested in the overall history of Switzerland.

The first to be mentioned is an informative illustrated article by Dr. Hans Lüthy on "Modern Art in Switzerland" (**222**). The second is a book by Walter Sorell, *The Swiss* (a cultural panorama of Switzerland), published in 1972 by Oswald Wolff, London. It is a volume of 303 pages, comprehensively written, and a pleasure to read.

The third, on Swiss literature, is by Heinz K. Meier. The article appeared in the 1980 edition of the *Columbia Dictionary of Modern Literature*, and has been reprinted in the *Newsletter of the Swiss American Historical Society* (Vol. 18, June 1982, pp. 4 to 9) and in the *Swiss American Review*, September 22, 1982, page. 7. The article in the Newsletter of the SAHS is supplemented by 22 biographical and literary sketches (pp. 10 to 39) of twentieth-century Swiss writers of prose and poetry. Nine Swiss authorities prepared the 22 articles.

Also to be mentioned is an article by Hans Christoph von Tavel entitled "Art in Switzerland from Hodler to the Present Day," published in the *Swiss American Review*, July 11, 1979.

Both Meier and von Tavel refer the reader to many other publications of which only two are in English—Sorrel's book and one by E. Wilbert-Collins (*A Bibliography of Four Contemporary German-Swiss Authors: Dürrenmatt, Frisch, Walser, Zollinger*). The Lüthy article lists 12 publications in English in the bibliography.

The two serial publications mentioned may not be well known except to the Swiss and Swiss-Americans. Hence, the addresses of the publishers of these two very useful and readable publications, with other relevant information, are in Notes and Comments (item 1).

As an afterthought, it may be of interest to touch on such matters as the prizes that are awarded for contributions to culture—mostly to writers of prose and poetry, and to the many musical events that constantly attract the Swiss and their many visitors. A few paragraphs on archaeology are also added, probably because of a personal interest in the distant past.

Awards

Many prizes and other kinds of recognition are awarded in various countries, including Switzerland, to honor those whose cultural contributions have been judged to be especially meritorious. A random selection in literature follows in which the award was either of Swiss origin or the recipient was Swiss:

Alfred Döblin Prize (West Berlin) to Gerold Späth, 1978.
Goncourt Prize in Literature (Paris) to Jacques Chessex (1973). Chessex was later honored by election to membership in the Académie Goncourt.
SWF Prize in Literature (Germany) to Otto F. Walter.
Innerschweiz Prize in Culture (Canton of Schwyz) to Hans Schilter (1979).
Art Prize (Basel City) to Klaus Huber (1979).
Prizes in Literature (Bern City) to Walther Kauer, Jean Rudolf von Salis, and Walter Vogt (1980).
Johann Peter Hegel Prize (Baden in Württemberg) to Erika Burkart (1978).
Schiller Foundation Prizes in Literature (Switzerland) to Walter M. Diggelmann, Lukas Hartmann, Klaus Merz and Anne Cuneo (1979).
Prize in Literature (Bern City) to Friedrich Dürrenmatt (1979).
Prize in Literature (Zurich City) to Adolf Muschg (1984).
Prizes for Books (Bern City) to Guido Bachmann, Lukas Hartmann, Kurt Marti, Rosalia Wenger, and Gertrude Wilker (1979).
Droste Prize for Women Writers (Meersburg in Germany) to Gertrud Leutenegger (1979).
Bündner Culture Prize from the Canton of Graubünden to J. R. von Salis (1984).

Musical Events

Many music festivals are held annually in Switzerland. The programs and the location of some of the festivals differ from year to year. A partial listing of the summer offerings in a specific year may help to convey an understanding of the wide-spread interest in music. In 1979, for example, the following events were among those that were well publicized:

Bernese Oberland Music festivals in Meiringen and Interlaken.
The 23rd Yehudi Menuhin festival in Gstaadt.
Concerts in the castle at Spiez.
A musical summer academy in Lenk in the Simmental.

Summer concerts in Wengen.

An internationally famous music festival in Lucerne.

The 14th annual concert weeks in Engelberg.

The 39th Engadine concert weeks in the Graubünden.

The 13th organ and chamber music festival in Arosa.

A week of music in Braunwald.

The International Tibor Varga festival in the old Valeria church in Sion (Valais) where the oldest playable organ, of remarkable beauty and quality, is to be found.

The 18th "Musical Hours" in Champex.

Church concerts in Zermatt.

A week-long music festival in Gruyères.

The 34th music festival in Ascona.

The 34th Montreux-Vevey music festival.

All of the musical events listed are intended to attract tourists and, in this, some of the festivals are conspicuously successful. However, music continues to be of consuming interest to the native populations in all four seasons of the year.

The Show "Heidi"

That immortal classic "Heidi" by Johanna Spyri, first published in 1880, was dramatized about one hundred years later by two Swiss women in Texas. The musical, "Heidi", premiered in Berne, Indiana, and, subsequently, was presented in New Bern, North Carolina where it received acclaim as the "Best Show of the Year." It played also in Fresno, California, and is greeted with delight in Swiss-American communities.

The Alphorn

The alphorn, with a history that takes us back to the sixteenth century at least,[2] is played at many events throughout Switzerland, largely as a tourist attraction. Swiss composers of the late twentieth century have been introducing the alphorn to the world of classical music, and have created a number of works for the alphorn and an orchestral accompaniment. One of these was performed by the Philadelphia Symphony Orchestra under Eugene Ormandy and another by the Houston Symphony Orchestra in late October 1981, following the Swiss festival in that city.

Archaeology

Archaeology is a lively activity in Switzerland. Seldom does a year go by without a discovery of great popular interest that carries us back to the remote past. The twentieth-century excavations have yielded many items that testify to the skills of the very early goldsmiths, silversmiths and artistic craftsmen who used other materials. For example, a beautiful necklace of 24 karat gold was discovered in 1970 at a depth of 11.5 meters near Augst. The museum at Augst, by the site of the magnificent Roman amphitheater, houses a wealth of sculpture, mosaics, silver plate, silver drinking vessels, and intricate golden jewelry recovered during the extensive excavations. A large and beautifully designed silver platter, housed in the Augst museum, was found in 1962. It is strikingly similar to a platter found in England, now displayed in the museum at Colchester. In 1975 the remains of a Roman temple came to light at Martigny in Valais. Large quantities of gold and silver, jewelry and sculptures were found in the temple excavations (see Chapter 1, Note 16). Golden bowls of Celtic origin discovered in the mid-1900s in Zurich and in Uri are on view in the Landesmuseum in Zurich. In the late 1970s, along the shores of Lake Murten, discoveries of archaeological interest were made that originated in the Horgen period (circ. 3000 B.C.). The findings included a harpoon carved from the horns of a stag, a very primitive axe and weapons. Hundreds of objects—intact or in fragments—have been recovered. Divers in Lake Zurich have retrieved, since the 1960s, clay pots of the New Stone Age, textiles, basketry, and sundry other objects, all better preserved under the slime on the lake bottom than on land. Bronze Age finds include necklaces, bracelets, pendants, looms, farming utensils, and charms made from boar fangs, bear teeth and from skulls of the wild boar. The ancient lake dwellers to whom these objects belonged lived in dwellings which were constructed on pilings at a time when the surface of the lake must have been at least four meters lower than at present (346). By mid-summer, 1981, some 34 New Stone Age and Bronze Age sites had been identified around the lake shore. The lake-dweller culture of Zurich dates from 4000 or 4500 B.C., according to tree-ring chronological studies.

In the late 1970s an archaeological discovery was made in Geneva that has aroused sensational interest. It consists of a fifth- or sixth-century mosaic of superb beauty. The original colours appear to be perfectly preserved. The find is regarded as a treasure that is unique in quality among the mosaics retrieved in northern Europe. It was found during work on restoration of the St. Pierre Cathedral. Removal of the mosaic to another site for exhibition purposes is not considered to be feasible. Consideration is being given to construction of a roof over the walls with the mosaics intact, accompanied by a raising of the street which passes over the site.

In Basel, archaeological research in the 1970s has contributed greatly to our knowledge of the ancient Celtic-Roman settlements beneath the present Münsterplatz. The discoveries were made possible by extensive work and much excavation necessitated by a program for complete renovation of the Cathedral.

Notes and Comments

1. *Newsletter of the Swiss American Historical Society* published by Old Dominion University. Editor: Professor Heinz K. Meier, Old Dominion University, Norfolk, Virginia.

Swiss American Review published weekly by the Swiss Publishing Company Inc., 608 Fifth Avenue, Suite 609, New York, NY 10020. Editor: A. K. Maier.

2. The account books of the Monastery of St. Urban (Lucerne canton) record a payment in 1527 of "two pennies to a man from Valais with an alpine horn" (357).

APPENDIX

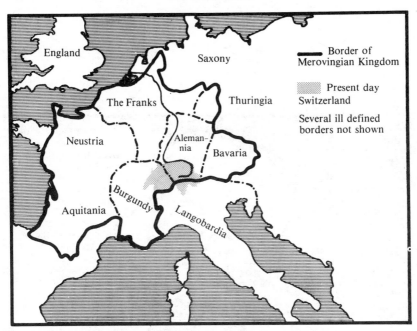

Map 1. Western Europe, circ. 700 A.D.

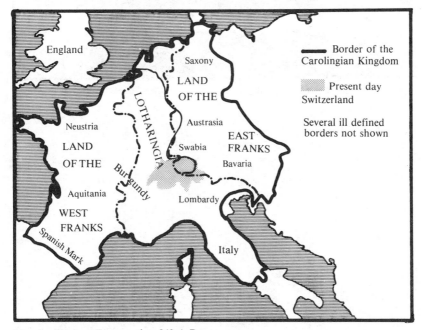

Map 2. Western Europe, circ. 843 A.D.

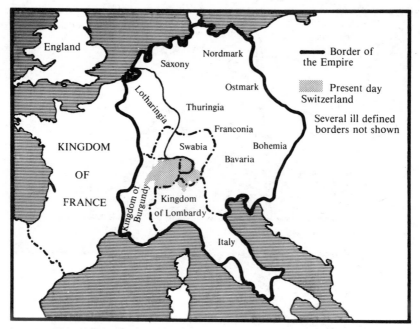

Map 3.   Western Europe, circ. 1033 A.D.

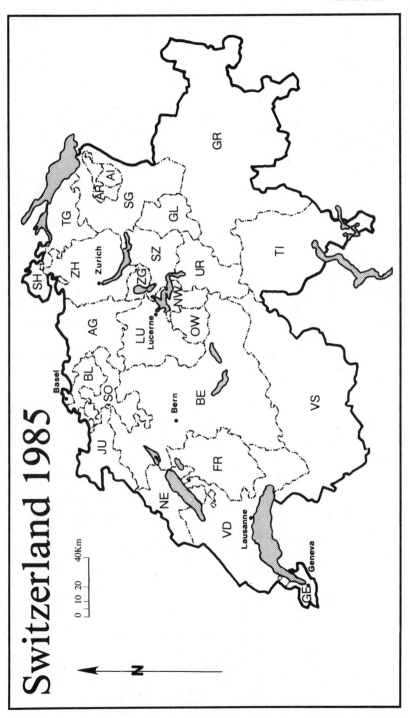

Switzerland 1985

DIAGRAM 1

The Merovingians and Early Burgundians

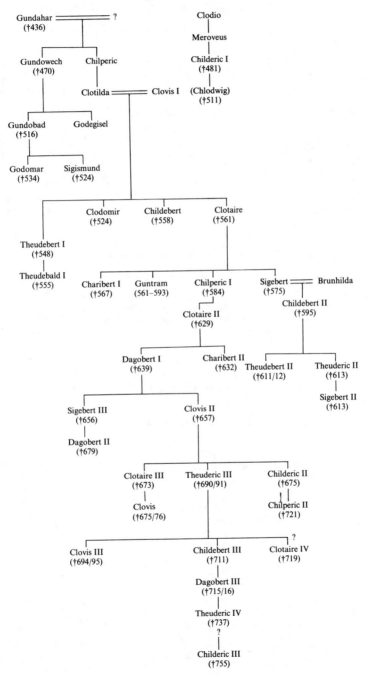

DIAGRAM 2

The Burgundians[a]

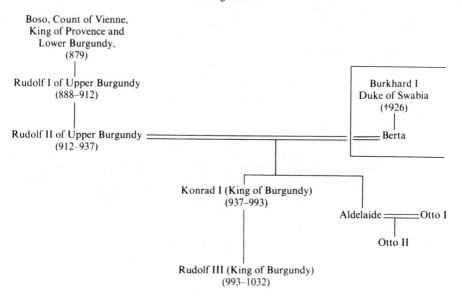

Boso, Count of Vienne,
King of Provence and
Lower Burgundy,
(879)

Rudolf I of Upper Burgundy
(888–912)

Rudolf II of Upper Burgundy
(912–937)

Burkhard I
Duke of Swabia
(†926)

Berta

Konrad I (King of Burgundy)
(937–993)

Aldelaide ═══ Otto I

Otto II

Rudolf III (King of Burgundy)
(993–1032)

[a] For the early Burgundians, see Diagram 1; the later Dukes of Burgundy, Diagram 4.

DIAGRAM 3

The Carolingians

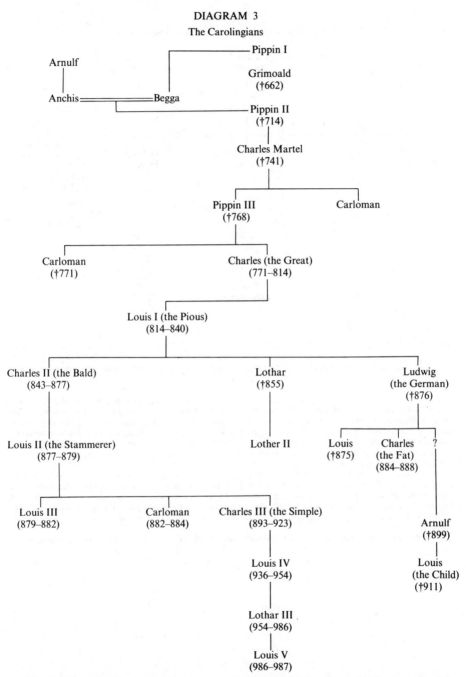

Note: The Carolingian dynasty reigned in France from 751 to 987. The Capetians then came to power. The Carolingians ruled in Germany until the death of Louis the Child in 911; they remained in power in Italy until Charles the Fat was deposed in 887.

DIAGRAM 4

The Kings of France and the Dukes of Burgundy

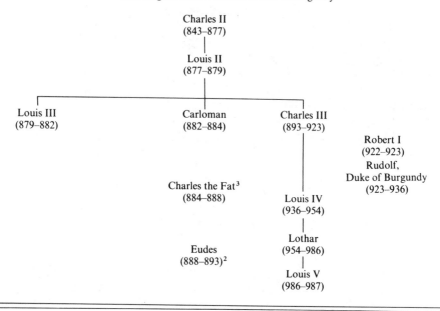

Charles II
(843–877)

Louis II
(877–879)

Louis III   Carloman   Charles III
(879–882)   (882–884)   (893–923)

                                              Robert I
                                              (922–923)
                                              Rudolf,
                     Charles the Fat[3]   Duke of Burgundy
                     (884–888)   Louis IV   (923–936)
                                  (936–954)

                                  Lothar
                     Eudes   (954–986)
                     (888–893)[2]
                                  Louis V
                                  (986–987)

---

[1] Son of Hugh the Great (brother-in-law of Rudolf of Burgundy). Hugh Capet, while a minor, bore the title Duke of France.

The early Capetians, from Hugh Capet to Philippe II Augustus, consistently pursued the policy of circumventing the selection of their successors by any kind of electoral process controlled by others. This they accomplished by naming their successor, usually their eldest son, and having him crowned and consecrated as king during their own reign. This can be thought of as a monarchial association of the designated heir, bordering on an actual transfer of the royal authority. The motives are not crystal clear but it appears safe to assume that a determination to perpetuate the rights and powers of the ruling dynasty must have been a compelling consideration. Even more to the point, this practice of anticipatory association ensured to the monarch the exclusive privilege of selecting his successor. Similar practices were pursued in the tenth and eleventh centuries by the great nobles. For an expanded treatment of this subject one should refer to an informative article by Lewis (216) who also points out that "Five German emperors of the tenth and eleventh centuries, then four Hohenstaufen, insecure in their hereditary titles, had their sons elected or crowned king during their own lifetimes" (216, p. 907). The structure of government during the Capetians and especially the administration of Philippe Augustus, one of the most remarkable of the Capetians, are described at length by Hollister and Baldwin (183).

[2] Son of Robert the Strong (†866), ancestor of the House of Capet, and duke of the lands between the Loire and the Seine.

[3] Nephew of Charles II and son of Louis the German; succeeded Carloman. See Diagram 3 (the Carolingians).

DIAGRAM 4

The Kings of France and the Dukes of Burgundy

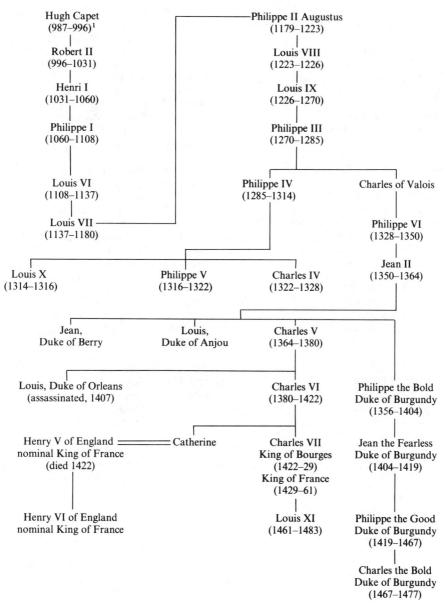

DIAGRAM 5
Rulers of the Holy Roman Empire*

800–814	Charles the Great
816–840	Ludwig I
843–855	Lothar I
855–875	Ludwig II
875–877	Charles the Bald
884–887	Charles the Fat
896–899	Arnulf
901–905	Ludwig III
915–924	Berengar[1]
900–911	Ludwig the Child
911–918	Konrad I[2]
919–936	Heinrich I[3]
936–973	Otto I, the Great
967–983	Otto II
983–1002	Otto III
1002–1024	Heinrich II, The Holy
1024–1039	Konrad II,[4] son of the Count of Speyer
1046–1056	Heinrich III,[5] son of Konrad II
1084–1093	Heinrich IV[6]
1105–1125	Heinrich V[7]
1125–1137	Lothar of Saxony
1138–1152	Konrad III
1152–1190	Friedrich I, Barbarossa[8]
1190–1197	Heinrich VI
1198–1208	Philipp of Swabia
1198–1214	Otto IV
1212–1250	Friedrich II[9]
1250–1254	Konrad IV
1247–1256	William of Holland[10]
1256–1273	The Great Interregnum
1273–1291	Rudolf I[11]
1292–1298	Adolf of Nassau
1298–1308	Albrecht I, son of Rudolf I
1308–1313	Heinrich VII of Luxembourg
1314–1326	Friedrich the Beautiful[12,13]
1314–1347	Ludwig IV of Bavaria[13]
1346–1378	Karl IV
1378–1400	Wenzel, son of Karl IV
1400–1410	Ruprecht III, Count of the Pfalz
1410–1411	Jodokus, Markgraf of Brandenburg
1410–1437	Sigismund, Elector of Brandenburg[14]
1438–1439	Albrecht II of Austria[15]
1440–1493	Friedrich III of Inner Austria[16]
1493–1519	Maximilian I[17]
1519–1556	Karl V, grandson of Maximilian[18]
1556–1564	Ferdinand I, brother of Karl V
1564–1576	Maximilian II
1576–1612	Rudolf II
1612–1619	Matthias, brother of Rudolf II
1619–1637	Ferdinand II
1637–1657	Ferdinand III
1658–1705	Leopold I
1705–1711	Joseph I, son of Leopold I
1711–1740	Karl VI
1742–1745	Karl VII, Elector of Bavaria
1745–1765	Francis I[19]
1765–1790	Joseph II
1790–1792	Leopold II
1792–1806	Francis II[20]
1806–	Title lapsed

*Source: Ross, Martha. "Rulers of Governments of the World; vol. I. Earliest Times to 1491," (Bowker, London, New York, 1978).

[1] Berengar was a grandson of Ludwig the Pious, and King of the Lombards. He exercised little power outside of Italy. After Berengar the title was always associated with kings of Germany.

[2] Also Duke of Franconia.

[3] Also known as Henry the Fowler, Duke of Saxony.

[4] Nephew, by marriage, of Rudolf III of Burgundy.

[5] Crowned German King in 1028, emperor in 1039, and crowned by Pope Clement II in 1046.

[6] Son of Heinrich III. Surrendered to the papal authority (Gregory VII) as a penitent in 1077 and was absolved. Crowned emperor in 1084 by Pope Clement III.

[7] Crowned as emperor in 1111 after a bitter quarrel over investiture (selection of the pope by the king/emperor). Renounced the right of investiture in 1122.

[8] Nephew of Konrad III.

[9] Also King of Sicily.

[10] A counter-king.

[11] Rudolf IV of the House of Habsburg, son of Albrecht IV.

[12] Son of Albrecht I of the House of Habsburg.

[13] Double election in 1314, resulting from a divided electorate.

[14] Also King of Hungary.

[15] Stepson of Sigismund.

[16] Cousin of Albrecht.

[17] Son of Friedrich III.

[18] Also King Carl I of Castille and Aragon. In 1530 crowned in Rome as Kaiser. This was the last of the kaiser coronations in Italy.

[19] Son of Duke Leopold of Lorraine.

[20] Renounced the title of Holy Roman Emperor.

GLOSSARY*

Ammann—a local administrator once appointed by the Habsburgs as their *Vögt*, later appointed by the people.

Aufklarung—the Age of Enlightenment, when, in the eighteenth century, scholarship and an interest in learning seized the whole of Europe.

Bacchant—a mediaeval travelling scholar.

Brief (pl. *Briefe*)—letters and documents of many kinds.

Büchsen—all kinds of fire weapons.

Bund—a federation.

Bundesbrief—a treaty of alliance between the corporate members of a *Bund*.

Burg- und Landrecht—a form of unequal association in which nobles, ecclesiastical houses, cities, towns, and counties entered. It was, in effect, a defensive alliance in which one party assumed a protective relationship to the other. But the second party was not in subject status. It enjoyed unconditionally the protection of the first party but it could not begin a war without the knowledge and consent of its protector. The Permanent Burgrecht of 23 May 1477 was multiple in character. It involved the cities of Zurich, Bern, Lucerne, Freiburg and Solothurn. They enjoyed mutual protection but none could begin a war without the consent of the others.

Bürgermeister—mayor.

Diet—see *Tagsatzung*.

Durchmarsch, Durchzug—a passage of foreign troops through another jurisdiction.

Eid—an oath; in the present context a solemn oath taken by individual persons, sometimes as representatives of the corporate States which constitute the *Eidgenossenschaft*.

Eidgenossen—the people within the *Eidgenossenschaft*.

Eidgenossenschaft—the Swiss equivalent of *Bund*.

Erbeinung or *Erbeinigung*—a hereditary accord.

Ewige Richtung—meant a permanent peace, not permanent direction (or policy). *Richtung*, in this context, meant a definitive peace agreement, the ending of a strife.

Freibrief—a document which conferred certain freedoms and special rights and privileges upon the recipient.

Freiheiten—means freedom from specific obligations to single *Orte*, cities, ecclesiastical houses etc. In matters concerning warfare, the *Freiheiten* were volunteered troops and should not be confused with *Reisläufern* who, without permission, engaged in foreign wars.

Friede—appears to have meant, originally, an armistice. *Richtung* corresponded to our present concept of *Friede* as peace—more lasting than an armistice.

Gau—a district or province. Aargau and Thurgau ultimately came to be identified as cantons of the same name. Zurichgau lost the suffix and town and canton alike became identified as Zurich.

Gemeinde—a community (village or town) from the adjective *gemein* (common, or belonging to, in common).

Graf—a count. The counts, originally replaceable officials, because of weak royal administrations, and sometimes under the favor of the king himself, entrenched themselves and transferred their office into an inheritable property. It became, in the hands of the rich and powerful families, an office which was passed down through the family, like any kind of real property.

Hochschule—literally, a high school; actually a university (or college with several faculties of university-level quality).

Innerschweiz—usually the four or five cantons that surround Lake Lucerne. Sometimes the term refers only to the three forest cantons—Schwyz, Unterwalden and Uri.

Landammann—the principal *Ammann* in a district or country. Napoleon Bonaparte designated the head of government in the whole of Switzerland as the Landammann of Switzerland.

---

* From Dändliker (**99**, vol. 1) and the *Abschiede* (vol. II).

Landmarchen—border lands.

Landschreiber—county clerk.

Landsgemeinde—literally, the aggregate of communities within the *Land* (or more narrowly, the county). In time it came to mean an assembly, commonly in the principal square of the county seat, of the males of voting age for the transaction of business pertaining to the county. Peculiar to a few cantons.

Oberland—the higher lands reaching into the Alps.

Ort (pl. *Orte*)—a place. The member cantons of the Swiss Confederation were referred to in official documents for many years as *Orte*.

Pfalzgraf—an overseer of the Grafs: a kind of permanent royal messenger, delegate, envoy, ambassador of *Königsboten*.

Schultheiss—mayor.

Schwurverband—an association or union in which the members are joined together under a solemn oath. In early times the sworn agreements were frequently only oral, not always supported by a written document.

Stammvater—ancestral line.

Stadtschreiber—town clerk.

Tagsatzung—from *Tag*, the coming together of delegates or fully-empowered representatives of *Orte*. *Tagsatzung*, which referred literally to the seating arrangements for the *Tag*, came to mean the meeting itself with restricted reference to an assembly of cantonal delegates for the transaction of federal parliamentary business. I have used "Diet" as an acceptable and commonly used synonym.

Überfremdung—an excessive proportion of foreigners in the population of a city, a canton or the State.

Vogt—a district governor; *Landvogt*, a cantonal governor; a *Reichsvogt* was a high appointee of the kaiser; a *Schirmvogt* was a protector of the people in a district or county—usually a count or a high official.

BIBLIOGRAPHY

1. Ackerknecht, E. H. *History and Geography of the Most Important Diseases*. New York/London: Hafner. 210 pp. (1965).
2. Addison, J. *Remarks on Several Parts of Italy, etc. In the years 1701, 1702, 1703.* London. 304 pp. plus index. 3rd ed. (1726).
3. Aebi, H. Research. In *Modern Switzerland.* See Ref. **245**, pp. 129–56.
4. Aebischer, P. Nyon: Noviodunum. *Rev. Hist. Vaudois* 66: 61–66 (1958).
5. Agassiz, L. *A Journey to Switzerland.* London. 288 pp. (1833).
6. Aglionby, W. *An Account of my Negotiation in Suizzerland in the years 1702, 1703, 1704, and 1705 with some remarkes on the people and Gouvernment of the 13 Cantons calld the Helvetick bodye.* London: Public Record Office. S. P. 96 10X/K. 3546.
7. von Ah, J. Swiss Agriculture and Food Production. In *Modern Switzerland.* See Ref. **245**, pp. 71–90.
8. von Ah, J. J. *Die Bundes-Briefe der alten Eidgenossen. 1291–1513.* Einsiedeln: Benziger. 168 pp. 2nd ed. (1891).
9. von Alberti, H. J. *Mass und Gewicht.* Berlin: Akademie Verlag. 580 pp. (1957).
10. Alexander, J. T. *Bubonic Plague in Early Modern Russia: Public Health and Urban Disaster.* Baltimore: Johns Hopkins Univ. Press. xvii, 385 pp. (1980).
11. *Almanach der Schweiz.* Bern: Peter Lang. (1978).
12. Ammann, H., Schib, K. *Historischer Atlas der Schweiz.* Aarau: Sauerländer. 36 pp. of text, 67 pp. of maps. 2nd ed. (1958).
13. *Amnesty International, 1982 Report.* London: Amnesty Int. Publ. 367 pp. (1982).
14. *Annual Report (1980) of the Swiss Intellectual Property Office.* (In English, French, and German). Einsteinstrasse 2, 3003 Bern. 44 pp. (1980).
15. Annual Report. *Die Vereinigung Schweizerischer Krankenhäuser.* See also Ref. **357a**.
16. Anshelm, V. *Die Berner Chronik des Valerius Anshelm*, (an edition publ. by Historischer Verein des Kantons Benzin, 6 vols., 1884–1901); another edition publ. by L. U. Haller, Bern. 439 pp. (1825).
17. Arbeitsgruppe "Verkehrsprognosen" der Kommission für die Schweiz. Gesamtverkehrskonzeption und Generaldirektion SBB, Statistik.
18. Aubert, J. F. The Swiss Federal Constitution. In *Modern Switzerland.* See Ref. **254**, pp. 297–310.
19. Aubert, P. An Interview. *Swiss Am. Rev.* (May 16, 1979).
20. Bächler, E. *Das Alpine Paläolithikum der Schweiz im Wildkirchli, Drachenloch, und Wildenmannlisloch.* Basel: Birkhauser. 263 pp. (1940).
21. Bächler, H. *Die ersten Bewohner der Schweiz.* Bern: Francke. 176 pp. (1947).
22. Baier, M. The Early Naturalists and Anatomists during the Renaissance and Seventeenth Century. In *History of Entomology*, pp. 81–94. Palo Alto, Calif.: Annual Reviews. 517 pp. (1973).
23. *The Bank for International Settlements.* Basel. 153 pp. (May 1980).
24. Barclay, T. Neutrality. In *Encyclopedia Britannica*, 19: 441–50. New York: Encyclopedia Britannica, Inc. 11th ed. (1910–1911).
25. Barclay, T. State. See Ref. **24**: 799—801.
26. Barrett-Hamilton, G., Hinton, E. *History of British Mammals*. London: Gurney & Jackson. Published in 21 parts (1910 to 1921).
27. Barth, H. Jean Jacques Rousseau/zum 250.Geburtstag(28. Juni). *Neue Zürcher Ztg. Sonntagsausgabe* (24 Juni 1962).
28. Bauer, H. Die Geschichte der schweizerischen Eisenbahnen. In *Ein Jahrhundert Schweizer Bahnen*, Vol. I. Bern: Swiss Federal Railways. 329 pp.
29. Baumann, M. The Status of Women in Society. In *Modern Switzerland.* See Ref. **245**, pp. 361–72.
30. Baumgartner, G. J. *Die Schweiz in ihren Kämpfen und Umgestaltungen von 1830 bis 1850.* In 4 volumes. 2: 296. Zurich. (1853–1866).
31. de Beer, G. R. *Early Travellers in the Alps.* London: Sidgwick & Jackson. 204 pp. (1930).
32. Beguin, P. In *Switzerland* by W. Martin, p. 311. London: Elek Books. (1971).
33. Bentwich, N. *Declaration of London.* Effingham Wilson; London: Sweet & Maxwell. 179 pp. (1911).
34. Benziger, J. C. Das Schweizerische Archiv. In *Mitt. Hist. Vereins des Kantons Schwyz* 16: 99–127. (1906).
35. Benziger, C. Die Schweiz in ihren Beziehungen zu den Vereinigten Staaten von Nordamerika. In *Schweizerische Konsular-Bulletin*, 19: 28. (Jan. 1931).
36. Bernard, N., Alexandre Yersin (1863–1943) pp. 15–40 in *Yersin et la peste.* Lausanne: Rouge et cie. 246 pp. (1944).

37. Besson, H. R. *Manuel pour les Savans et les curieux qui voyagent en Suisse*. Bern: Haller. 198 pp. (1786).
38. Biaudet, J. C. *Echos du Sonderbund, Lettres choisies de Samson Vuilleumier*. Lausanne: Editions de l'eglise nationale vaudoise. 252 pp. (1847).
39. Bickel, M. H. Zum Cyclamat-Verbot. *Medical Tribune*, p. 19 (12 June 1970).
40. Bickel, W. *Bevölkerungsgeschichte und Bevölkerungspolitik der Schweiz*. Zurich: Büchergilde Gutenberg. 333 pp. (1947).
41. Billigmeier, R. H., Picard, F. A., eds. *The Old and the New, the Journals of two Swiss Families in America in the 1820s*. Minneapolis: Univ. Minn. Press (1965).
42. Bloch, M. *Feudal Society*. Univ. Chicago Press. 2 vols. 499 pp. 12th impression (1974).
43. Bloch, M. The Feudal World. In *Mediaeval Society: 400–1450*, ed. N. F. Cantor, M. S. Werthman, pp. 37–83. New York: Crowell. 295 pp. (1972).
44. Bloomfield, A. *Communicable Diseases*, p. 58. Univ. Chicago Press. 560 pp. (1958).
45. Bluntschli, C. Der Tag zum Stans um Weihnachten 1481. *Arch. Schweiz. Gesch.* 4 : 117–42 (1846).
46. Bluntschli, J. K., Brater, K. *Bluntschli's Staatsworterbuch*. Zurich: Friedrich Schulthess. A three-volume edition of the original eleven-volume work by Bluntschli & Brater. This three-volume work was edited by Dr. Loning. Vol. 1 (1869); 2 (1871), 3 (1872).
47. Bohnenblust, E. *Geschichte der Schweiz*. Zurich: Eugen Rentsch. 590 pp. (1974).
48. Bonjour, E. Johannes von Müller, Erbe des Aegidius Tschudi. In *Studien zu Johannes von Müller*, pp. 237–54. Basel/Stuttgart: Benno Schwabe. 306 pp. (1947).
49. Bonjour, E. *Geschichte der Schweizerischen Neutralität*. Basel: Helbing & Lichtenhahn. 6 vols. 5th ed. (1970) (8 vols. by 1976, 9 vols. by 1978).
50. Bonjour, E. *Die Schweiz und Savoyen im Spanischen Erbfolgekrieg*, p. 14. Bern (1927).
51. Bonjour, E. Die Idee des Europäischen Gleichgewichts bei Johannes von Müller. See Ref. **48**, pp. 213–35.
52. Bonjour, E. Die Schweiz und England, eine geschichtliche Rückschau. In *Die Schweiz und Europa*, 2 : 11–60. Basel: Helbing & Lichtenhahn (1961).
53. Bonjour, E. Der Charakter der bernischen Bauernbewegung im Reformationszeitalter. In *Die Schweiz und Europa*, 1 : 329–39. Basel: Helbing & Lichtenhahn (1961).
54. Bonjour, E. Das Ende des Söldnerdienstes. See Ref. **52**, pp. 93–101.
55. Bonjour, E. Werden und Wesen der Schweizerischen Demokratie, See Ref. **52**, pp. 303–36.
56. Bonjour, E. *Swiss Neutrality*, London: Allen & Unwin. 155 pp. 2nd ed. (1952).
57. Bonjour, E. Die Entstehung des Inter-

nationalen Roten Kreuzes. See Ref. **52**, pp. 123–32.
58. Bonjour, E., Offler, H. S., Potter, G. R. *A Short History of Switzerland*. Oxford: Clarendon Press. 388 pp. (1952).
59. Botschaft über Massnahmen zur Förderung der technologischen Entwicklung und Ausbildung. Message from the Federal Council to Parliament. 60 pp. (3 Feb. 1982). See Ref. **329**.
60. Bourrit, M. T. *Description des Cols ou Passages des Alpes*. Genève: Manget. 490 pp. (1803) (two parts in one volume).
61. Bourrit, M. T. *Nouvelle description des glacières, vallées de glace, et glaciers*. Genève: Manget. 3 vols. (1787).
62. Bucher, E. *Die Geschichte des Sonderbundkrieges*. Zürich: Berichthaus. 595 pp. (1966).
63. Büchi, H. Vorgeschichte des helvetischen Revolution. In *Mitt. Hist. Vereins des Kantons Solothurn*, Section 13, *Die Schweiz in den Jahren 1789–98*. Solothurn. 622 pp. (1925).
64. Bresslau, H. Das älteste Bündnis der schweizer Urkantone. *Jahrb. Schweiz. Gesch.* 20 : 3–36 (1895).
65. *Brockhaus Encyclopedia*.
66. Brunner, H. Leisure-time Activities. In *Modern Switzerland*. See Ref. **245**, pp. 255–74.
67. *Bulletin des Bundesamtes für Gesundheitswesen, Bericht des Schweizerischen Gesundheitsamtes über seine Geschäftsführung im Jahre 1918*. p. 277 (1919).
68. Bullinger, H. *Schweizerchronik*, including "Epitome oder Kurtze Verzeichnuss des Alten Zürichkriegs" (1531). In 1568, Bullinger completed his *Historie gemeiner loblicher Eydtgnoschaft*, which covered ancient times to 1516. In 1574, his *Historie* was redone as a revised text under the title *Von den Tigurinern und der Stadt Zürich Sachen*. Zentralbibliothek. Zürich.
69. Bundesamt . . . Arbeit (BIGA). *Die Volkswirtschaft* 52 : 796–98 (1979).
70. Ibid. 53 : 311–33 (1980).
71. Ibid. *Lohn und Gehaltserhebung vom Oktober 1979*, p. 13. (27 pp.) (Separate publication from *Die Volkswirtschaft*, No. 6, June 1980).
72. Ibid. *Die Volkswirtschaft* 53 : 550–60 (August 1980). (This pertains to 1,216,539 salary recipients in all 26 cantons and in the five largest cities.)
73. *Bundesblatt*.
74. Burckhardt, A. *Demographie und Epidemiologie der Stadt Basel während der letzten drei Jahrhunderte 1601–1900*. Basel (1908). Cited by Bickel in Ref. **40**, p. 81.
75. Burckhardt, J. R. Untersuchungen über die erste Bevölkerung des Alpengebirgs. *Arch. Schweiz. Gesch.* 4 : 1–116 (1846).
76. Burckhardt, L. F. Industry-labor Relations: Industrial peace. In *Modern Switzerland*. See Ref. **245**, pp. 173–98.
77. Burckhardt, P. *Geschichte der Stadt Basel*

von die Zeit der Reformation bis zur Gegenwart. Basel: Helbing & Lichtenhahn. 407 pp. 2nd ed. (1957).

78. Burnet, G. *Some Letters containing an Account of what seemed most remarkable in Switzerland, Italy, etc.* Rotterdam: Abraham Rocher. 306 pp. (1686).

79. Businger, J. *Die Geschichten des Volkes von Unterwalden ob und nid dem Wald von dessen frühester Abkunft an bis auf unsere Zeiten mit Hinsicht auf die Geschichten seiner Nachbarn von Uri und Schwyz,* 1 : 456. Luzern: Xavier Meier. 2 vols. (1827).

80. Casanova, G. *Meine Erlebnis in der Schweiz.* Bern: Hallwag (1940).

81. Castell, A. *Die Bundesbriefe zu Schwyz.* Einsiedeln: Benziger. 112 pp. (1963).

82. Catalogue of Cometary Orbits, 1960. *Mem. Br. Astron. Assoc.,* Vol. 39, No. 3 (1961).

83. Cerletti, A. Forschung und Entwicklung in der Schweizerischen Privatwirtschaft. *Sandoz Bull.* 52 : 1–13 (1979).

84. Chapuisat, E. *La Suisse et les Traités de 1815.* Genève: Edition Atar. 95 pp. (1917).

85. Charlick, C. Diplomatic Caretaker. In *Foreign Service Journal.* Am. Foreign Serv. Assoc. (Oct. 1955).

86. Chastellain, H. *Le Major Duval.* Lausanne (1923).

87. Chastellain, L. *Histoire de Romainmôtier.* Lausanne: Georges Bridel. 270 pp. (1902).

88. Coolidge, W. A. B. *Swiss Travel and Swiss Guide Books.* London: Longmans Green. 336 pp. (1889).

89. Cooper, J. F. *Correspondence of James Fenimore Cooper.* New Haven: Yale Univ. Press. 396 pp. (1922).

90. Ibid. Excursions in Switzerland. In *Collection of Ancient and Modern British Authors,* Vol. 138. Paris. 323 pp. (1836).

91. Ibid. *A Residence in France with an Excursion up the Rhine, and a Second Visit to Switzerland.* Paris. 320 pp. (1836).

92. Ibid. *Sketches of Switzerland,* Part I. Philadelphia. Vol. I, 244 pp.; II, 239 pp. (1836).

93. Ibid. *Sketches of Switzerland,* Part II. Philadelphia. Vol. I, 219 pp.; II, 226 pp. (1836).

94. Cost Studies in European Forestry. Reviewed in *Nature,* pp. 1163–64. (Dec. 23, 1967).

95. Coxe, W. *Travels in Switzerland.* London: T. Cadell. 3 vols. (1789).

96. Cramer, L. *Correspondance diplomatique de Pictet de Rochemont et de Francois d'Ivernois 1814–16.* Genève: Kündiz; Paris: Champion. 2 vols. (1914).

97. Credit Suisse *Bulletin.*

98. Curti, T. *Geschichte der Schweiz im XIX. Jahrhundert.* Neuenburg: Zahn 714 pp. (richly illustrated) (1902).

99. Dändliker, K. *Geschichte der Schweiz.* Schulthess. 3 vols. 4th ed. (1901).

100. Ibid. 2nd ed. (1885–1904).

101. *Dictionnaire historique et biographique de la Suisse.*

102. *Die grössten Unternehmen in der Schweiz.* Schweizerische Bankgesellschaft (1978).

103. Dierauer, J. *Geschichte der Schweizerischen Eidgenossenschaft.* 5 vols. 3rd ed. Gotha: Perthes (1919–22) (from Roman Times to 1848).

104. Doka, C. *Swiss Am. Rev.* (Jan. 3, 1979).

105. Droz, N. *Politische Geschichte der Schweiz im neunzehnten Jahrhundert,* ed. P. Seippel, Vol. 1. Bern/Lausanne (1899).

106. Dufour, G. H. *Campagne du Sonderbund et événements de 1856.* Paris. 250 pp. (1876).

107. Du Mont, J. *Corps universal diplomatique du droit des gens contenant un Recueil des Traitez d'Alliance, de Paix, de Treve, de Neutralité. . . .* Amsterdam à la Haye (1731).

108. Dürrenmatt, P. *Schweizer Geschichte,* p. 98. Zürich: Schweizer Verlagshaus. 736 pp. (1963).

109. Durrer, R. *Der Tag zu Stans.* In *Bruder Klaus,* 1 : 115–70. Sarnen: Buch- und Kunstdruckerei Louis Ehrli. 2 vols. (1917, 1928).

110. Durrer, R. Die ersten Freiheitskämpfe der Urschweiz. In *Schweizer Kriegsgeschichte,* 1 : 83–102. Bern (1915).

111. Ebel, J. G. *Manuel du Voyageur en Suisse et en Savoie.* Paris. 480 pp. (1833–34).

112. Edwards, R. S., La Roche, C. *Industrial Research in Switzerland.* London: Pitman. ix, 111 pp. (1950).

113. Egger, E. Education in Switzerland. In *Modern Switzerland.* See Ref. **245,** pp. 227–54.

114. *Eidgenoss* (24 July 1978) (a quarterly Winterthur publication).

115. *Eidg. Wehrsteuer. Statistik der 17. Periode (1973–74).* From *Stat. Quellenwerke der Schweiz,* No. 16 : 33. Bern: Eidg. Stat. Amt (1978).

116. Encyclopedia Britannica.

117. Encyclopedia Canadiana.

118. *Entwicklungsperspektiven und Probleme der Schweizerischen Volkswirtschaft.* Bern: Eidg. Drucksachen und Materialzentrale. 130 pp. (1974).

119. Escher, H. Reisebericht des Chronisten Johannes Stumpf aus dem Jahr 1544. In *Quellen zur Schweizer Geschichte,* Vol. 6 (1884).

120. Etter, P. In *Grosse Schweizer,* pp. 23–28. ed. M. Hurlimann, E. Winkler, et al. Zürich: Atlantis Verlag, 2nd ed. (1942).

121. Etterlin, P. *Kronikon von der loblichen Eidgnosschafft har komen und seltzamen striten und Geschichten.* 123 pp. (1507).

122. Ettinger, E. Handel und Gewerbe. In *Die Romer in der Schweiz,* pp. 21–25. Part 4 of *Repertorium der Ur- und Fruhgeschichte der Schweiz.*

123. Evelyn, J. *The Diary of John Evelyn,* with an introduction and notes by A. Dobson, New York/London: MacMillan. 3 vols. (1906).

124. Faust, A. B., Brumbaugh, G. M. *Lists of*

Swiss Emigrants in the Eighteenth Century to the American Colonies, 1:3. Baltimore: Genealogical Publ. (1976). Faust's scholarly introduction (pp. 1–25) is especially informative.

125. *Federal Law Relating to Banks and Savings Banks, Including the Implementing Ordinance* (English edition). Zurich: Union Bank of Switzerland. 53 pp. (1972).

126. *Federal Reserve Bulletin*, Feb. 1982. Washington, D.C.: Board of Governors, Federal Reserve System (1982).

127. *Federal Reserve Bulletin*, Washington, D.C.: Federal Reserve System. 6th ed. 125 pp. (1974).

128. Feller, R. *Die Schweiz und das Ausland in Spanischen Erbfolgekrieg*. Bern: K. J. Wyss. 156 pp. (1912).

129. Feller, R. *Jakob Stämpfli*. Bern. 32 pp. (1914). Considerable material on Wilhelm Snell, who was Stämpfli's most influential mentor, is to be found in this publication.

130. Feller, R. *Geschichte Berns*, Vol. 1, 618 pp. Bern: Herbert Lang. 4 vols. (1974).

131. Feller, R. Bonjour, E. *Geschichtsschreibung der Schweiz*. Basel: Benno Schwabe. (2 vols.) (1962). Helbing & Lichtenhahn. (2 vols.) 2nd ed. (1979).

132. Ferguson, C. W., Huber, B., Suess, H. E. Determination of the Age of Swiss Lake Dwellings as an Example of Dendrochronologically-calibrated Radiocarbon Dating. In *Z. Naturforsch.* 21a : 1173–77 (1966).

133. Fleming, O. *Instructions for Oliver Fleming our Agent resident with the Protestant Cantons in Switzerland*. London: Publ. Record Off. S. P. 96 3 X/K 3546.

134. *Fonds national suisse de la recherche scientifique*, Report annuel. Nationalfonds, Wildhainweg 20, 3001 Bern (1982).

135. Cosandey, M., Ursprung, H., eds. *Forschung und Technik in der Schweiz*. Bern: Paul Haupt. 182 pp. (1978).

136. Franscini, S. *Neue Statisk der Schweiz*. 3 vols. Bern (1848–1851) (transl. from Italian). Cited by Bickel in Ref. **40**, p. 121.

137. Frauenfragen Bericht der eidg. Kommission für Frauenfragen. *Stellung der Frau in der Schweiz*. First Rep. (Oct. 1979).

138. Frenkel, M. Swiss federalism in the Twentieth Century. In *Modern Switzerland*. See Ref. **245**, pp. 323–36.

139. Frey, E. *Die Neutralität der Schweiz*. Winterthur: Buchdruckerei Geschwister Ziegler. 35 pp. (1900).

140. Friedli, E. *Bärndütsch als Spiegel bernischen Volkstums*. Bern: Francke-Verlag.

141. Fringeli, D. Des Schweizers Deutsch. *Swiss Am. Rev.* (Oct. 25, 1979).

142. Fueter, E. *Geschichte der exakten Wissenschaften in der Schweizerischen Aufklärung (1680–1780)*, Graphische Werkstatten. Aarau: Sauerländer. (1941).

143. Fueter, E. *Grosse Schweizer Forscher*. Zürich: Atlantis. 340 pp. (1941).

144. Fullerton, W. M. *The Great Problems of World Politics* (1913). Quoted in French by Edouard Chapuisat in *La Suisse et les Traités de 1815*. Genève: Edition Atar. 95 pp. (1917).

145. Gäbler, U., Zsindely, E., eds. *Bullinger-Tagung* (1975). Under the auspices of the Institut für Schweizerische Reformationsgeschichte, Zurich. 142 pp. (1977).

146. Gagliardi, E. *Geschichte der Schweiz*. Zürich-Leipzig: Orell Füssli Verlag. 3 vols. 4th ed. (1939).

147. Gallati, F. *Gilg Tschudi und die ältere Geschichte des Landes Glarus*. Glarus: Kommissionsverlag J. Barschin. (1938).

148. Geigy, A., von Liebenau, T. Aus den Papieren des französischen Botschafters Franz Karl du Luc. *Archiv des historischen Vereins des Kantons Bern*, 12 : 375–448 (1889).

149. Geiser, K. Bern unter dem Regiment des Patriziats. *Arch. Hist. Vereins des Kantons Bern*, Vol. 32 (1934).

150. Gerbel, L. Paper read to the Class d'industrie et de commerce, 12 April 1858, by L. A. Grosse. *Bulletin de la Classe d'industrie et de commerce de la Societé des Arts de Genève*.

151. Gingins La Sarra, F. Episodes des guerres de Bourgogne. In *Memoires et documents publiés par la société d'histoire de la Suisse romande*, Vol. VIII, footnote 3, p. 101. Lausanne: Georges Bridel, pp. 113–510 (1849).

152. Gold, J. *The International Monetary Fund and International Law*. Washington: Int. Monetary Fund. 26 pp. (1965).

153. Grote, G. *Seven Letters on the Recent Politics of Switzerland*, pp. 58–60. London: 182 pp. (1847).

154. Grotius, H. *De jure belli ac pacis*. 1st ed., Amsterdam (1625); *Le droit de la guerre et de la paix*. French trans. from Latin by M. de Covertin, Amsterdam (1688); *The Law of War and Peace*. English transl. from Latin by W. Evats, London (1682).

155. Gruner, E. *Die Arbeiter in der Schweiz im 19. Jahrhundert*. Bern. 1136 pp. (1968).

156. Gruner, E. The Political System of Switzerland. In *Modern Switzerland*. See Ref. **245**, pp. 339–60.

157. Guggenheim, K. *Philipp Emanuel von Fellenberg und sein Erziehungstaat*. Bern. 2 vols. (1953).

158. Guldimann, W. Civil Aviation: The Swiss Position. *Swiss Am. Rev.* (May 30, 1979).

159. Haas, L. Die Schweiz und die Vereinigten Staaten von Nordamerika. *Z. Schweiz. Gesch.* 20 : 228–63 (1940).

160. Haasbauer, A. *Basler Beitr. Geschichtswiss.* 35 : 1–213 (cf. pp. 37–53) (1949).

161. *Hague Peace Conference of 1907*, Volume I, *Plenary Meetings of the Conference*. Carnegie Endowment for International Peace, New York: Oxford Univ. Press (1920). Convention respecting the rights and duties of neutral powers and persons in case

of war on land, pp. 632–36 of the *Proceedings*. Also reproduced, with annexes, in *Br. State Papers* 100 : 281–93.

161a. *Handbuch der Schweizer Geschichte*. Zürich: Berichthaus. 2 vols., 13 authors. 1320 pp. (1972–1977).

162. von Haller, K. L. *Die Freymauerey und ihre Einfluss in der Schweiz, dargestellt und historisch nachgewiesen von Carl Ludwig von Haller*. Quoted by Adolphine Haasbauer in Die historischen Schriften Karl Ludwig von Hallers. *Basler Beitr. Geschichtswiss.* 35 : 1–213 (1949).

163. Häne, J. Die Kriegsbereitschaft der alten Eidgenossen. In *Schweizer Kriegsgeschichte*, Vol. 1, Pt. 3. Bern: Eidg. Militärdept. 4 vols. (1915).

164. Harrod, R. *The International Monetary Fund, Yesterday, Today and Tomorrow*. Institut für Weltwirtschaft an der Universität Kiel. 27 pp. (1966).

165. Hauduroy, P. Comment Alexandre Yersin découvrit le microbe de la peste, pp. 41–66. In *Yersin et la peste*. Lausanne: Rouge et Cie. 246 pp. (1944).

166. Haug, H. Switzerland and the United Nations. In *Modern Switzerland*. See Ref. **245**, pp. 457–72.

167. Hauser, A. *Vom Essen und Trinken im alten Zürich*. Zürich: Verlag Berichthaus. 271 pp. 3rd ed. (1964).

168. Hauser, J. A. Demography and Population Problems. In *Modern Switzerland*. See Ref. **245**, pp. 1–25.

169. Heeren, A. H. L. *Der Deutsche Bund in seinen Verhältnissen zu dem europäischen Staatensystem*, p. 35. Göttingen (1816).

170. Ibid. *Cours d'histoire moderne d'après le manuel de Heeren*. Neuchâtel. 183 pp. (1836).

171. Helbling, H. Gehalt und Deutung der Schweizer Geschichte. In *Handb. Schweiz. Gesch.*, p. 1026.

172. Hertslet, E. *The Map of Europe by Treaty; showing the various political and territorial changes which have taken place since the general peace of 1814*. London: Butterworths. 4 vols. (1875).

173. Hescheler, K., Kuhn, E. Die Tierwelt. In *Urgeschichte der Schweiz*, ed. O. Tschumi, 1 : 121–368. Frauenfeld: Huber. 751 pp. (1949).

174. Hidber, B. *Schweizer Urkundenregister*. 2 vols. Bern (1863). German language translations of 2875 Latin documents from 700 to 1200 AD.

175. Hill, T. G. *Report of the British Association for the Advancement of Science* (1931).

176. Hilty, C. *Die Neutralität der Schweiz in ihrer heutige Auffassung*. Bern: K. J. Wyss. 91 pp. 2nd ed. (1889).

177. Hilty, C. Eidgenössische Politik. *Polit. Jahrb. Schweiz. Eidg.*, pp. 477–81 (1889).

178. Hirzel, J. C. Ä. Beantwortung der Frage: Ist die Handelschaft . . . die Sitten des Volks. *Höpfners Magazin für die Naturkunde*

Helvetiens, Vol. 3. Zürich (1788). Cited by Bickel in Ref. **40**, p. 54.

179. *Historisch-biographisches Lexikon der Schweiz*.

180. Hochstrasser, U. The History and the Present Organization of the Swiss Efforts in the Field of Atomic Energy. In *Science in Switzerland*, Appendix VI, pp. 391–400. See Ref. **219**.

181. Hoffmann, G. Die grossbritannische Schweizer-Legion im Krimkrieg. *Z. Schweiz. Gesch.* 22 : 573–95 (1942).

182. Hohlenstein, W. ab. *Urschweizer Bundesbrief 1291*. St. Gallen: Staatsarchiv. 575 pp. (1956).

183. Hollister, C. W., Baldwin, J. W. The Rise of Administrative Kingship: Henry I and Philip Augustus. *Am. Hist. Rev.* 83 : 867–905 (1978).

184. Huber, A. *Die Waldstätte Uri, Schwyz und Unterwalden bis zur festen Begründung ihrer Eidgenossenschaft*. Innsbruck (1861). Mit einem Anhange über die geschichtliche Bedeutung des Wilhelm Tell.

185. Huber, A. *Geschichte Hüningens von 1679–98*. Inaugural dissertation. Basel. 138 pp. (1894).

186. Hughes, C. *The Federal Constitution of Switzerland*. Oxford: Clarendon Press (1954).

187. Hughes, C. *Switzerland*. London: Ernest Benn. 303 pp. (1975).

188. *Human Rights Policy Report 82.043* of the Federal Council (2 June 1982).

189. Hungerbuhler, H. *Etude Critique sur les traditions relatives aux origines de la Confédération suisse*. Genève (1869). Ext. from Bulletin de l'Institut National Genevois, Vol. 15.

190. Hürlimann, M. In *Grosse. Schweizer*. Zürich: Atlantis. 768 pp. (1938).

191. Iklé, M. *Switzerland: an International Banking and Finance Center*. Stroudsburg, Penn.: Dowden, Hutchinson & Ross. 156 pp. (1972). Transl. from German by Eric Schiff.

192. Im Hof, U. Ancien Regime, Aufklarung, Revolution und Fremdherrschaft (1648–1825), *Quellenheft zur Schweizergeschichte*, No. 6. Aarau: Sauerländer. 64 pp. (1954).

192a. Im Hof, U. *Die Helvetische Gesellschaft*. Frauenfeld: Huber. 388 pp. (1983).

192b. Im Hof, U., et al. *Geschichte der Schweiz und der Schweizer*, 3 vols. in French, German, and Italian editions. Basel: Helbing & Lichtenhahn (1983).

193. *International Economic Indicators, 1981/82*. Köln: Institut der deutschen Wirtschaft.

194. *International Monetary Fund. Government Finance Statistics Yearbook*, Vol. 5, pp. 586, 636 (1981).

195. Iselin, I. *Philosophische und politische Versuche*. Zürich: Drell. 319 pp. (1760).

196. Isler, A. *Bundesrat Dr. Jonas Furrer 1805–61*. Winterthur. 224 pp. text and 68 pp. of notes (1907).

197. Jaggi, A. *Die alte Eidgenossenschaft und ihr Untergang.* Bern: Haupt. 128 pp. (1945).
198. Jenkinson, C. *A Collection of all the Treaties of Peace, Alliance, and Commerce, between Great Britain and Other Powers from 1648 to 1783.* 3 vols. London: J. Debrett. (1785).
199. Justinger, K. *Die Berner Chronik des Conrad Justinger,* ed. G. Studer. Bern (1871).
200. Kaiser, D. Bunder Zuckerbäcker, Cafetiers und Handelsleute in der Fremde. *Neue Zürcher Z.* 8/9 (32): 68–69 (Feb. 1975).
201. Kasser, P. Der Durchmarsch der Alliierten durch die Schweiz im Winter 1813 auf 1814. In *Schweizer Kriegsgeschichte* 4 : 38, cf. also pp. 20–21 and 34–35. Bern. 4 vols. (1915).
202. Kaufmann, H., Nabholz, P. *Verzeichnis schweizerischer Inkunabeln und Frühdrucke,* Fazikel I. Zürich. 40 pp. (1968); *Die Inkunabeln von Basel,* Fazikel II. Grenchen. 62 pp. (1974); *Die Drucke von Luzern, Serrières/Neuchâtel, Bern und Poschiavo 1501–50.* Zürich. 33 pp. (1969).
203. Keate, G. *A Short Account of the Ancient History, Present Government, and Laws of the Republic of Geneva.* London: R & J Dodsley, 218 pp. (1761).
204. Kinsman, R. *Your Swiss Bank Book.* Homeward, Ill.: Dow Jones-Irwin. 283 pp. (1975).
205. Kipfer, H. Vom Säumerpfad zur Handelsroute. *Der Bund.* Bern. (25 Aug. 1975).
206. Klebs, A. C., Sudhoff, K. *Die ersten gedruckten Pestschriften.* Munich. (1926). 224 pp. plus 24 tables and the text of Heinrich Steinhöwel's *Pestbuch* (1473).
207. Kopp, J. G. *Geschichte der eidgenössischen Bünde,* Vol. 2, p. 327, footnote 1. Published in five volumes plus four parts. Leipzig: Weidmann's Buchhandlung (1845–1888).
208. Kopp, J. G. *Urkunden zur Geschichte der eidgenössischen Bunde.* 2 vols. Vol. 1, Luzern (1835); Vol. 2, Vienna (1851).
209. Kossuth, L. Ein Brief Kossuth's an die Eidgenossenschaft von 1853. *Polit. Jahrb. Schweiz. Eidg.* 9 : 695–702 (1895).
210. Krippendorf, J. Tourism in Twentieth Century Switzerland. In *Modern Switzerland.* See Ref. **245,** pp. 275–95.
211. Kurz, H. R. Swiss National Defense. In *Modern Switzerland.* See Ref. **245,** pp. 403–18.
212. Labhardt, A., chairman. Report of the Federal Expert Commission on Questions of University Development. *Bericht der Eidgenössischen Expertencommission für Fragen der Hochschulförderung.* Bern: Fed. Dept. Interior (June 29, 1964).
213. Lasserre, D. *Etapes du Federalisme, l'Experience suisse.* Lausanne. 303 pp. (1954).
214. Lerner, R. E. The Black Death and Western European Eschatological Mentalities. *Am. Hist. Rev.* 86 : 533–52 (1981).
215. Lepionka, L. Purrysburg, an Archaeological Survey. *Newsl. Swiss Am. Hist. Soc.* XVI : 18–29 (June 1980).
216. Lewis, A. W. Anticipatory Association of the Heir in Early Capetian France. *Am. Hist. Rev.* 83 : 906–27 (1978).
217. von Liebenau, T. *Geschichte der Freiherren von Attinghusen und von Schweinsberg.* Aarau: Sauerländer. 220 pp. (1865).
218. Lienhard, H. *From St. Louis to Sutter's Fort,* English transl. of Lienhard's diary by Erwin G. and Elizabeth K. Gudde. Norman, Okla.: Univ. Okla. Press (1961).
219. Luck, J. M. *Science in Switzerland.* New York: Columbia Univ. Press. 419 pp. (1968).
220. Ibid, ed. *Modern Switzerland.* Palo Alto, Calif.: SPOSS Inc. xvi, 515 pp. (1978).
221. Ibid. Swiss Scientists of the 18th Century. Unpublished.
222. Lüthy, H. A. Modern Art in Switzerland. In *Modern Switzerland.* See Ref. **245,** pp. 489–503.
223. Lüthy, H. *Die Tätigheit der Schweizer Kaufleute und Gewerbetreibenden in Frankreich unter Ludwig XIV. und der Regenschaft.* Aarau (1943).
224. Lüthy, I. C. E. General Sir Frederick Haldimand: A Swiss Governor General of Canada (1777–1784). *Can. Ethnic Stud.,* Vol. III : 63–75 (1971).
225. Maag, R. *Die Freigrafschaft Burgund und ihre Beziehungen zur Schweiz. Eidgenossenschaft von 1477–1678.* Zürich (1891).
226. Malin, G. Principality Liechtenstein. *Swiss Am. Rev.,* special issue, No. 31 (March 1982).
227. de Martens, G. F. *Recueil des principaux traites.* Suppl. 4, p. 217 (1808).
228. Martin, C. 1958. Monnaies romaines trouvées à Nyon. *Rev. Hist. Vaudois* 66 : 67–75.
229. Martin, W. 1971. *Switzerland.* London: Elek. 335 pp. This is an English translation of *Histoire de la Suisse* to which was added an appendix (pp. 272–326 in the translated edition) by Pierre Béguin to cover the period from 1928 to about 1970.
230. Mast, H. J. The Swiss banking industry. In *Modern Switzerland.* See Ref. **245,** pp. 113–28.
231. Mattmüller, H. Carl Hilty (1833–1909). *Basler Beitr. Geschichtswiss.* 100 : 322 (1965).
232. May, M. E. *Histoire militaire de la suisse et celle de suisses dans les différens services de l'Europe.* Lausanne: J. P. Heubach. 8 vols. (1788).
233. Mayer, Th. Die Königsfreien und der Staat des fruhen Mittelalters. In *Das Problem der Freiheit (Vorträge und Forschungen),* ed. Th. Mayer, 2 : 7–56. Lindau/Konstanz: Jan Thorbecke (1953).
234. Mazzini, G. *Selected Writings,* p. 55. Edited and arranged by N. Gangulu. London. 253 pp. (1945).
235. Mazzini, G. L'Egoisme. *La Jeune Suisse,* No. 60. (23 Jan. 1836). Unsigned article, initialled M. F.
235a. *Medizinische Statistik Gesamtstatistik 1983.* Aarau: VESKA. 357 pp. (1984).
236. Meier, M. Die diplomatische Vertretung

Englands in der Schweiz im 18. Jahrhundert (1689–1789). *Basler Beitr. Geschichtswiss.*, Vol. 40. Basel (1952).

237. Meyer, B. 1953. Freiheit und Unfreiheit in der alten Eidgenossenschaft. See Ref. **233**, 2:123–58.

238. Meyer, B. Die Entstehung der Eidgenossenschaft. Der Stand der heutigen Anschauungen. *Schweiz. Z. Gesch.* 2:153–205 (1952).

239. Meyer, E. Römische Zeit. In *Handbuch der Schweizer Geschichte*, 1:53–92. Seven authors. Zürich: Berichthaus. 672 pp. (1962–1965, 1972).

240. Meyer, K. Der Ursprung der Eidgenossenschaft. *Z. Schweiz. Gesch.* 21(3):285–652 (1941).

241. Meyer, K. *Das weisse Buch. Die älteste Chronik . . . neu herausgegeben.* Zürich (1939).

242. Meyer von Knonau, G. *Die Sage von der Befreiung der Waldstätte Die Ausgangsstelle, das Erwachsen und der Ausbau derselben.* Basel (1873).

243. Meyer, W. Der Chronist Werner Steiner 1492–1542. *Geschichtsfreund, Mitt. Hist. Vereins der V Orte Luzern, Uri, Schwyz, Unterwalden, und Zug* 65:59–215 (1910).

244. *The Military Balance, 1981/82*, London: Inst. for Strategic Studies, pp. 5, 45.

245. *Modern Switzerland*, ed. J. M. Luck, Palo Alto, Calif.: SPOSS Inc. xvi, 515 pp. (1978).

246. Mohr, J. C. B. *Religion in Geschichte und Gegenwart*, 1:1539–41. Tubingen: 3rd ed. (1957).

247. Mojonnier, A. *Histoire de la Confederation*, ed. E. T. Rimli, Zürich, Lausanne, Paris: Stauffacher. 562 pp. (1967).

248. Du Mont, E. *Corps diplomatique V*, Vol. II, pp. 26 ff.

249. Monter, E. W. *Witchcraft in France and Switzerland.* Ithaca/London: Cornell Univ. 232 pp. (1976).

250. Montaigne, M. de *The Diary of Montaigne's Journey to Italy in 1580 and 1581.* Transl. by E. J. Trechmann. London: Hogarth Press. 297 pp. (1929).

251. Mühlemann, A. *Studien zur Geschichte der Landschaft Hasli.* Bern: Jakob Stämpfli. 144 pp. (1895).

252. Müller, E. *Kriegsbereitschaft.* Documentation for an Information Conference by the Federal Military Department. Bern. (3 May 1979).

253. Müller, G. Der amerikanische Sezessionskrieg in der schweizerischen öffentlichen Meinung. *Basler Beitr. Geschichtswiss.* 14: 7–209 (1944).

254. Müller, H. R. Johann Jakob Scheuchzer und seine Drachen. *Neue Zürcher Z.*, pp. 58, 59 (20 May 1973).

255. von Müller, J. *Die Geschichte der Schweizer*, in 18 volumes. Volume I, which appeared in 1780, records Boston as the place of publication. Actually, the book was printed in Bern; as explained by Feller and Bonjour,

Boston was designated as the place of publication in order to circumvent the censor. See Ref. **131**, 2:634.

256. Münster, S. *Cosmographia Universalis*. Basel. (1550). Many later editions.

257. Münzwesen. *Historisch-biographisches Lexikon der Schweiz*, 5:201–3. Neuchâtel (1929).

258. von Muralt, A. *Albert Einstein, 14.III.1879–18.IV.1955.* Vortrag anlässlich der Einstein Gedenkfeier in Bern am 14.III.1979.

259. von Muralt, C. *Hans von Reinhard, Bürgermeister des eidgenössischen Standes Zürich und Landammann der Schweiz.* Zürich. 591 pp. inclusive of 140 pages of appended material (1838).

260. von Muralt, L. *Bismarck's Politik der europäischen Mitte.* Wiesbaden: Steiner Verlag. 47 pp. (1954).

261. van Muyden, B. *Histoire de la nation Suisse.* Lausanne: Mignot. 3 vols. (1896–1899).

262. Nabholz, H. *Die Helvetische Gesellschaft 1761–1848.* Zürich: Atlantis. 61 pp. (1961).

263. Nabholz, H., von Muralt, L., Feller, R., Dürr, E., Bonjour, E. *Geschichte der Schweiz.* Zürich: Schulthess. Vol. I, 525 pp.; Vol. II, 691 pp. (1938).

264. Näf-Hofmann, M. The Status of Women according to Swiss Civil Law. In *Modern Switzerland.* See Ref. **245**, pp. 372–79.

265. *Nature Magazine.*

266. *Neue Zürcher Zeitung.*

267. *Neujahrs-Blatt für Basels Jugend*, Vol. XV, 23 pp. (1837). *Das grosse Sterben in den Jahren 1348 und 1349.* Unknown authorship.

268. von Noorden, C. *Europäische Geschichte im 18. Jahrhundert.* Dusseldorf: Julius Buddeus. 2 vols. (1874).

269. Oaklander, H. *The Swiss call it "The Firestone Affair".* A case study originating in the Graduate School of Business of Pace University, New York (1978).

270. Ochs, P. *Geschichte der Stadt und Landschaft Basel.* Basel (1822).

271. Ochsenbein, A. Die Entwicklung des Postwesens der Republic Solothurn 1442–1849. *Mitt. Hist. Vereins des Kantons Solothurn*, No. 12:33. Solothurn. 296 pp. (1925).

272. Oechsli, W. *Die Anfänge der Schweizerischen Eidgenossenschaft.* Zürich: Ulrich. 357 pp. (1891).

273. Oechsli, W. *Geschichte der Schweiz im neunzehnten Jahrhundert.* Leipzig: Hirzel. Vol. 1, 1903 (1798–1813, 781 pp.); Vol. 2, 1913 (1818–1830, 848 pp.).

274. Oechsli, W. *History of Switzerland 1499–1914.* Cambridge. 480 pp. and 3 maps (1922).

275. Oechsli, W. Eine Denkschrift über die geheimen Verbindungen in der Schweiz 1824. *Polit. Jahrb. Schweiz. Eidg.* 63 pp. (1912).

276. Ogata, M. Ueber die Pestepidemie in Formosa. *Centralbl. Bakteriol.* 21:769–77 (1897).

277. Ogley, R. *The Theory and Practice of*

Neutrality in the Twentieth Century. New York: Barnes & Noble. 217 pp. (1970). On p. 35, Ogley cites the "remain-quiet" quotation from Kelsey's translation of Hugo Grotius' *On the Law of War and Peace.* See also Ref. **154.**

278. Onesti, S. J. Plague, Press and Politics. *Stanford Med. Bull.* 13 : 1 (1955).

279. Pearson, L. B., chairman. *Partners in Development,* Rep. of the Commission on Int. Devel. New York (1969).

280. Peel, R. *France, Savoy and Switzerland. Speeches by Sir Robert Peel 1860–61.* Printed for private circulation, London: Hatchards. 135 pp. (1898).

281. Pelichet, E. Autour de la fondation de la Colonie équestre de Lyon. *Rev. Hist. Vaudois* 66 : 49–60 (1958).

282. Pestalozzi, H. *An die Unschuld, den Ernst und den Edelmuth meines Zeitalters und meines Vaterlandes.* Iferten. 276 pp. (1815).

283. Pestalozzi, L. *Die Münzwirren der westlichen Schweiz.* Zürich: Drell, Füssli. 55 pp. (1839).

284. Petitpierre, M. Is Swiss Neutrality Still Justified? In *Switzerland, Present and Future,* ed. T. Chopard, pp. 48–63. Bern: Verlag Buri. 216 pp. (1962).

285. Peyer, H. C. Frühes und hohes Mittelalter; Die Entstehung der Eidgenossenschaft. See Ref. **239,** Vol. 1.

286. Pfister, C. Franks. See Ref. **24.**

287. Pfister, C. Die Fluktuationen der Weinmosterträge im schweizerischen Weinland vom 16. bis ins frühe 19. Jahrhundert klimatische . . . Bedeutung. *Schweiz. Z. Gesch.* 31 : 486/87 (1981).

288. Piccolomini, A. S. *Beschreibung Basels zur Zeit des Conzils* (Ein Sendschreiben des Aeneas Silvius an den Kardinal Julian St. Angeli, papstlichen Legaten). This fascinating description of Basel appears as an appendix to *Die Kirchenversammlung zu Basel (1431–1448).* See also *V. Neujahrs-Blatt für Basels Jugend* (1825).

289. Pictet de Rochemont, C. *De la Neutralité de la Suisse dans l'intérêt de l'Europe.* Geneva. New edition. 110 pp. (1860).

290. Pictet de Rochemont, C. *Lettres de M^r. Ch. Pictet à ses collaborateurs de la Bibliotheque Britannique, sur les établissements de M^r. Fellenberg, et spécialement sur l'école des pauvres à Hofwyl.* Paris, Genève: Paschoud. 35 pp. (1812).

291. Pictet, E. *Biographie, travaux et correspondance diplomatique de C. Pictet de Rochemont.* Genève: H. Georg. 444 pp. (1892).

292. Pictet, J. The International Committee of the Red Cross and the Geneva Conventions for the Protection of Victims of War. In *Modern Switzerland.* See Ref. **245,** pp. 473–87.

293. Ploetz, K. *Auszug aus der Geschichte.* Würzburg: Ploetz-Verlag. 27th ed. (1968).

294. *Politique de la Science.* Inform. Bull. Swiss Agency for Science Policy, Wildhainweg 9, 3001 Bern.

295. *Portrait du Jura.* First volume of a planned encyclopedia of the Jura; Porrentruy: Societé jurassienne d'Emulation. 220 pp. (1980).

296. *Quellenwerk zur Entstehung der schweizerischen Eidgenossenschaft,* Part I, Urkunden, 1 : 197–98, Item 422. Aarau/Leipzig: H. R. Sauerländer. (1948).

297. See Ref. **296,** Sect. 3, Vol. 1; Wirz, H. G. *Das Weisse Buch von Sarnen.*

298. *Quellenwerk,* Part I. Urkunden, Item 1092 (5 May 1273).

299. Radding, C. M. Superstition to Science: Nature, Fortune, and the Passing of the Medieval Ordeal. *Am. Hist. Rev.* 84 : 945–69 (1979).

300. Ramp, E. *Das Zins Problem.* Zürich: Zwingli Verlag. 121 pp. (1949).

301. Rappard, W. E. *La revolution industrielle et les origines de la protection légale du travail en Suisse.* Bern: Jakob Stämpfli. 343 pp. (1914).

302. Raton, P. *Liechtenstein, History and Institutions of the Principality.* Liechtenstein: Verlag, Vaduz. 151 pp. (1970).

303. Ray, J. *Travels through the Low Countries, Germany, Italy, and France.* London (1673). Cited by Gavin de Beer in Ref. **31,** p. 67.

304. Rennie, A. The Plague in the East. *Br. Med. J.* 2 : 615 (1894).

305. Reports on Plague Investigations in India: Epidemiological Investigations in Bombay City. *J. Hygiene* 7 : 724–989 (1907).

306. Reymond, M. *Histoire de la Suisse.* Lausanne: Haeschel-Dufey. 3 vols. (1931–1933); and *Supplement.* Lausanne: NOVOS. (undated).

307. Ribi, M. Swiss Women in Swiss Politics. In *International Issues—Swiss Views.* Zürich: Credit Suisse. 79 pp. (Nov. 1976).

308. Ridgeway, W. Celts. See Ref. **24.**

309. Riggenbach, A. *Die Marchenstreit zwischen Schwyz und Einsiedeln und die Entstehung der Eidgenossenschaft.* Zürich: Fretz & Wasmuth. 160 pp. (1966).

310. Rimli, E. T., ed. *Histoire de la Confédération.* Text: Arthur Mojonnier. Zürich: Stauffacher. 562 pp. 2nd ed. (1967).

311. Ruchat, A. (pseudonym Gottlieb Kypseler de Munster). *Delices de la Suisse.* 4 vols. Leyden (1714).

312. Rutz, M. *Die Walzmuehle in Frauenfeld.* Zürich: aku-Fotodruck. 198 pp. (1973).

313. Saint-Pierre, C. *A Discourse on the Danger of Governing by one Minister.* Printed for T. Warner at the Black-Boy in Paternoster Row, London. 140 pp. (1728).

314. de Saussure, H. B. *Voyages dans les Alpes. Précédés d'un essai sur l'histoire naturelle des environs de Genève.* 8 vols. Neuchâtel: Fauche-Borel. Vols. 1–4 (1803); Vols. 5–8 (1796).

315. Schär, M. Public health. In *Modern Switzerland.* See Ref. **245,** pp. 213–26.

316. Schaufelberger, R. *Die Geschichte des*

Eidgenössischen Bettages. Zürich: Beer. 183 pp. (1920).

317. Schaufelberger, W. Spätmittelalter. See Ref. **239**, Vol. 1.

318. Schazmann, P.-E. *Charles Dickens in Switzerland.* Swiss National Tourist Office. 46 pp. (1972).

319. Schelbert, L. *Einführung in die Schweizerische Auswanderungsgeschichte der Neuzeit.* Zürich: Stäubli. 443 pp. (1976).

320. Schenk, A. *La Suisse préhistorique.* Lausanne: Rouge. 632 pp. (1912).

321. Schilling, D. *Die Berner Chronik 1468–84.* Bern: H. J. Wyss. 2 vols. Tobler edition. (1901).

322. Schleiniger, E. *Die Gesundheitsverhältnisse der Bevölkerung des Eifischtales.* Inaugural dissertation for M.D. degree. Basel: Laupen/Bern. 28 pp. (1938).

323. Schneider, H. *Geschichte des schweizerischen Bundesstaates 1848–1918.* Zürich: Waldmann. 857 pp. (1931).

324. Schmid, F. V. *Allgemeine Geschichte des Freystaats Uri* 1 : 112, 212. In two small volumes. Zug: Johann Michael Aloiş Blunschi (1788).

325. Schütz, E. *Unsere Eisenbahnen im Dienste des Landes.* Luzern. 92 pp. (1944).

326. Schwarz, F. Briefwechsel des Basler Ratschreibers Isaak Iselin mit dem Luzerner Ratsherrn Felix Balthasar. *Basler. Gesch. Alterumskd.* 24 : 1–311 (1925).

327. *Schweizer Almanach '80.* New York: Transbooks (1980).

328. Schweizer, P. *Geschichte der schweizerischen Neutralität.* Frauenfeld: J. Huber. 1030 pp. (1895).

329. *Schweizerisches Bundesblatt.*

330. von Segesser, P. A. *Sammlung kleiner Schriften* 3 : 173. Bern. 4 vols. (1879). The Foreword (pp. v to xxxx) contains much material about Stämpfli and Druey.

331. Seippel, P. *Die Schweiz im neunzehnten Jahrhundert.* Bern: Schmid & Francke; Lausanne: F. Payot (1899, 1900). 3 vols., many illustrations.

332. Senebier, J. *Memoire historique sur la vie et les écrits de Horace Bénédict de Saussure.* Genève: l'Imprimerie de Luc Gestie. 219 pp. (1801); see also Montgolfier biographies in *Biographie universelle.* Paris: Michaud (1858).

333. Sidler, P. W. Die Schlacht am Morgarten. Published by the cantonal government of Schwyz, Zürich, pp. 248–44. Zürich: Füssli (1910).

334. Siegenthaler, H. The Economy. In *Modern Switzerland.* See Ref. **245**, pp. 91–112.

335. Sinner, J. R. *Voyage dans la suisse occidentale.* 2 vols. Neuchâtel. (1781).

336. Speiser, A. P. Technology. In *Modern Switzerland.* See Ref. **245**, pp. 157–71.

337. Stähelin, F. *Die Schweiz in Römischer Zeit.* Basel: Benno Schwabe. 549 pp. (1927).

338. Stanley, J., Pearton, M. *The International Trade in Arms.* New York–Washington: Praeger. For the Institute for Strategic Studies. 244 pp. (1972).

339. Stanyan, A. *An Account of Switzerland.* London. 216 pp. (1714). The volume contains an appendix (pp. 219–47), "An Account of the Allies of the Switzers".

340. *Statistical Abstracts of the United States.* Washington: US Dept. Commerce, Bureau of the Census (1981).

341. *Statistisches Jahrbuch der Schweiz.*

342. *Statistisches Jahrbuch der Stadt Zürich,* p. 2. (1939). Cited by Bickel in Ref. **40**.

343. *Statistik der Schweizerischen Nahrungsmittelindustrie,* No. 10. Swiss Food. (1979).

344. Stauffer, P. Die Idee des europäischen Gleichgewichts im politischen Denken Johannes von Müllers. *Basler Beitr. Geschichtswiss.* 82 : 60ff. (1960).

345. Steiner, G. *Napoleon I: Politik und Diplomatie in der Schweiz während der Gesandtschaftszeit des Grafen Auguste de Talleyrand* 1 : 162. Zürich. 366 pp. (1907).

346. Steinert, H. Pfahlbauer oder nicht Pfahlbauer. *Swiss Am. Rev.,* p. 7 (Jan. 7, 1981).

347. Steuerbelastung in der Schweiz. In *Statistische Quellenwerke der Schweiz, 1977.* No. 612 : 11, 29. Bern: Eidg. Stat. Amt. (1978).

348. Sticker, G. *Abhandlungen aus der Seuchengeschichte und Seuchenlehre.* Giessen: Alfred Töpelmann (1908).

349. Strahm, H. Zur Verfassungstopographie der mittelalterlichen Stadt mit besonderer Berücksichtigung des Grundungsplanes der Stadt Bern. *Z. Schweiz. Gesch.* 30 : 372–410 (1950).

350. Strickler, J. *Grundriss der Schweizergeschichte* 2 : 163. 2 vols. Zürich (1867–68).

351. Strickler, J. *Aktensammlung aus der Zeit der helvetischen Republik* 9 : 876–78. 11 vols. (1866–1911).

352. Stumpf, J. *Gemeiner Loblicher Eydgnoschaft Stetten, Lander und Völckern Chronikwurdiger Thaaten Beschreibung.* Zürich: Froschauer. 1463 pp. (1586).

353. Stumpf, J. *Reisebericht von 1544.* Zürich: Froschauer. About 75 pp.

354. Suess, H., Strahm, C. The Neolithic of Auvernier, Switzerland. *Antiquity* 44 : 91–99 (1970).

355. Sully, M. de B. *Memoires of the Duke of Sully during his Residence at the English Court* and containing "A Relation of the Political Scheme, commonly called the Great Design of Henry IV". Dublin: G. & A. Ewing (1751).

356. Sulzer, J. G. *Tagebuch einer von Berlin nach den mittäglichen Ländern von Europa in den Jahren 1775 und 1776 getanen Reise und Rückreise.* Leipzig. 414 pp. (1780).

357. *Swiss American Review.*

357a. *Swiss Hospitals,* Vol. 47 (1983).

358. *Swiss Hotel Guide.* Swiss Hotel Assoc., 3001 Bern.

359. Swiss National Bank *Monthly Report.*

360. Swiss Pioneers of Economics and Technology 2. In *The Peace Agreement of July 19, 1937*. Zurich: (1967). See also *Fortune Mag.*, pp. 206–16 (Aug. 10, 1981).

361. *Switzerland and its Industries*. Lausanne, Zürich: Swiss Office for the Development of Trade. 215 pp. (1974).

362. Tafur, P. *Travels and Adventures 1435–39*, pp. 182–89. Transl. Malcolm Letts. London: Routledge. 262 pp. (1926). This contains a chapter about Switzerland.

363. Tessiner Dorf wehrt sich gegen N2. *Swiss Am. Rev.* (July 30, 1980).

364. Thornbrough, G., ed. *The Correspondence of John Badollet and Albert Gallatin: 1804–1836*. Indianapolis: Indiana Hist. Soc. (1963).

365. von Tillier, A. *Geschichte der Eidgenossenschaft wahrend der Herrschaft der Vermittlungsakte 1803–13*. Zürich: Schulthess. Vol. 1, 508 pp. (1845); Vol. 2, 470 pp. (1846).

366. von Tillier, A. *Geschichte . . . vom Anfange des Jahres 1814 bis zur Auflösung der ordentlichen Tagsatzung von 1830* 2: 135–43. Bern/Zürich. 3 vols. (1849).

367. von Tillier, A. *Geschichte der Eidgenossenschaft wahrend der Zeit des sogeheissenen Fortschrittes 1830–1848*. Bern: Körber. 3 vols. (1854, 1855).

368. de Tribolet, M., Archiviste d'Etat adjoint. Letter of 1 Sept. 1976 to the author.

369. Troxler, P. I. V. *Die Verfassung der Vereinigten Staaten Nord Amerikas als Musterbild der Schweizerischen Bundesreform.* Schaffhausen (1848).

370. Tschudi, A. *Chronicon Helveticum.* Basel. 2 large vols. (1734). Mention should be made of a new study of this famous chronicle, *Quellen zur Schweizer Geschichte*, published by Allgemeinen Geschichtforschenden Gesellschaft der Schweiz. Vol. VII.1. "Aegidius Tschudi, Chronicon Helveticum," First Part (1001–1199), by P. Stadler, B. Stettler. Bern: Stadt & Universitätsbibliothek. 355 pp. (1968). The study has been made difficult, we are told, by missing pages here and there (sometimes torn out), by marginal corrections (sometimes by Tschudi and sometimes by unknown persons), and by mice that ate into the margins.

371. Tschudi, H. P. Social Security. In *Modern Switzerland*. See Ref. **245**, pp. 199–212.

372. Tschumi, O., ed. *Urgeschichte der Schweiz*, Vol. 1. Frauenfeld: Huber. 751 pp. (1949).

373. Ueber 10,000 Menschen demonstrieren gegen Saissonierstatut. *Swiss Am. Rev.* (Nov. 12, 1980).

374. de Vattel, E. *Les droits des gens ou principes de la loi naturelle, appliqués a la conduite et aux affaires des nations et des souverains*, Vol. 3, Ch. 7, Sects. 103, 104. London (1758).

375. Verzár, F., Gsell, D. *Ernahrung und Gesundheitszustand der Bergbevölkerung der Schweiz.* St. Gallen: Tschudy. 521 pp. (1962).

376. Vogt, E., Urgeschichte. See Ref. **239**, pp. 27–52.

377. *Die Volkswirtschaft* 53: 585 (Sept. 1980); 55: 386–88, 3* (May 1982).

378. Wackernagel, R. *Geschichte der Stadt Basel.* Basel: Helbing & Lichtenhahn. 5 vols. (1907).

379. Waddell, L. M. The American Career of Henry Bouquet. *Newsl. Swiss Am. Hist. Soc.* 17: 13–38 (1981).

380. Wain, H. *A History of Preventive Medicine.* Springfield, Ill.: Thomas. 407 pp. (1970).

381. *Wall Street Journal.*

381a. Wehrli, M. Aegidius Tschudi, Geschichtsforscher und Erzähler. *Schweiz. Z. Gesch.* 6: 433–55 (1956).

382. Weiss, H. The Swiss Landscape. In *Modern Switzerland.* See Ref. **245**, pp. 27–48.

382a. Wartmann, H. Die Königlichen Freibriefe für Uri, Schwyz und Unterwalden von 1231–1316. *Arch. Schweiz. Gesch.* 13: 107–60 (1862).

383. Weiss, T. *Jakob Stämpfli.* Bern: Wyss Verlag. 572 pp. (1921). Considerable material on Wilhelm Snell, who was Stämpfli's most influential mentor, is to be found in this publication.

384. Weissenbach, P. Der Rückkauf der Gotthardbahn. *Arch. Eisenbahnwes.*, p. 13 (1912).

385. Welti, F. E. *Die Pilgerfahrt des Hans von Waldheim im Jahre 1474.* (1925).

386. White, N. Twenty years of plague in India with special reference to the outbreak of 1917–18. *Indian J. Med. Res.* 6: 190 (1919).

387. Wickham, W., ed. *Correspondence of the Rt. Hon. William Wickham*, 2 vols. edited by his grandson William Wickham. London: Richard Bentley. 961 pp. (1870).

388. Wildhaber, L. The Swiss judicial system. In *Modern Switzerland.* See Ref. **245**, pp. 311–21.

389. Williams, H. M. *A Tour in Switzerland; or, a view of the present state of the Governments and Manners of the Cantons, with Comparative Sketches of the Present State of Paris.* London: G. G. & J. Robinson. 2 vols. Vol. 1, 354 pp.; Vol. 2, 278 pp. plus Appendix of 74 pp. on "Observations on the Glacières and the Glaciers" by M. Ramond. (1798).

390. Williams, H. M. *Eindrücke einer Engländerin auf ihrer Schweizerreise von 1794.* Transl. P. E. Scherer. Sarnen: Louis Ehrli. 89 pp. (1919).

391. Winkler, A. *Metternich und die Schweiz. Z. Schweiz. Gesch.* 7: 127–63 (1927).

392. Wirz, H. G. *Das Weisse Buch von Sarnen im Spiegel der Forschung* (cf Ref. **297**).

393. Wurstinen, C. *Basler Chronick*, Vol. III, Ch. XI, p. 131 (1580).

394. Wyss, A. *The Gotthard—Switzerland's Lifeline.* Lausanne: Ovaphil S. A. (1980).

395. von Wyss, G. *Die Chronik des weissen Buches im Archive Obwalden*, pp. 1–22. Zürich (1858).

396. von Wyss, G. *Ueber die Geschichte der drei*

Länder Uri, Schwyz und Unterwalden in den Jahren 1212–1315. Zürich: Meyer & Zeller. 32 pp. (1858).

397. Yeames, A. H. S. The Grand Tour of an Elizabethan. *Papers of the British School at Rome* 7 : 92–113 (1914).

398. Yersin, A. Sur la peste de Hong Kong. *C. R. Acad. Sci.* 119 : 356 (1894).

399. Yersin, A. La peste bubonique. *Ann. Inst. Pasteur* 8 : 962 (1894).

400. Yosy, A. *Switzerland, as now Divided into Nineteen Cantons.* 2 vols. 50 colored engravings. London: Booth & Murray (1815).

401. Zangger, C. Energy resources and development. In *Modern Switzerland.* See Ref. **245**, pp. 49–70.

402. Zeller, W. Switzerland and the Common Market. In *Modern Switzerland.* See Ref. **245**, pp. 439–56.

403. Zellweger, J. K. *Geschichte der diplomatischen Verhältnisse der Schweiz mit Frankreich von 1698 bis 1784.* St. Gallen/Bern: Huber. 2 vols. I, 322 pp.; II, 612 pp. (1849).

404. Zguta, R. Witchcraft Trials in Seventeenth-Century Russia. *Am. Hist. Rev.* 82 : 1187–1207 (1977).

405. Ziegler, A. *Adrian von Bubenberg und sein Eingreifen in die wichtigsten Verhältnisse der damaligen Zeit.* Inaugural dissertation. Bern: Jakob Stämpfli. 135 pp. (1887).

406. Zinsser, H. *Rats, Lice, and History.* Boston: Little, Brown & Co. 31st printing. 301 pp. (1963).

407. Zurlauben, B. F. A., le Baron de Zur-Lauben. *Histoire Militaire des Suisses au service de la France.* Paris. Vols. 1–5 (1751); 6–7 (1752); 8 (1753).

Addenda

408. *Dictionnaire biographique des Genevois et des Vaudois.*

409. Lätt, A. *Zwei Schweizer General-Gouverneure von Kanada.* Brugg (1925).

410. Cosandey, M., Ursprung, H. See Ref. **135**.

411. Gautschi, W. *Der Landesstreik 1918.* Zürich: Benziger (1968).

412. Gautschi, W. *Dokumente zum Landesstreik 1918.* Zürich: Benziger. 455 pp. (1971).

413. Pollitzer, R. *Plague.* Geneva: World Health Organization (1954).

414. *Zahlen und Fakten zu Alcohol- und Drogenproblemen 1983/84.* Lausanne: Schweizerische Fachstelle für Alkoholprobleme (1983).

415. Senn, A. E. *The Russian Revolution in Switzerland, 1914–17.* Univ. Wisc. Press, Madison. xvi, 250 pp. (1971).

416. von Ah, J. Food Security and Ecology in Conflict? Minimum Data Needs for Pragmatic Problem Solving in Switzerland. In *Mountain Research and Development,* Vol. 4, No. 1. Boulder, Colorado (1984).

417. *Schweizerische Gesamtenergiestatistik.* Bundesamt für Energiewirtschaft. 54 pp. (1982).

418. Brupbacher, F. *60 Jahre Ketzer.* Zürich: Limmat Verlag. 376 pp. (1981).

419. *Die Schweiz im Zahlenbild,* p. 41. Bern: Eidg. Stat. Amt. (1968).

420. *Schweizerische Elektrizitätsstatistik.* Bern: Federal Office for Energy (1983).

421. Weiss, H. The Swiss Landscape. In *Modern Switzerland.* See Ref. **245**, pp. 27–48.

422. Johnston, H. S. Human Effects on the Global Atmosphere. *Ann. Rev. Phys. Chem.* 35 : 481–505 (1984).

423. Gould, R. H. Energy and Acid Rain. *Ann. Rev. Energy* 9 : 529–59 (1984).

424. Cited by Cowling, E. B. Acid Precipitation in Historical Perspective. *Environ. Sci. Technol.* 16 : 110A–23A (1982).

425. O'Sullivan, D. A. *Chem. Eng. News,* pp. 12–18 (28 Jan. 1985).

INDEX

A

Aarau, peace of, 227
Aargau
 conquest of, 87-8
 seizure of
  and early Swiss neutrality,
   119
Aargau Convents
 suppression of, 356
 illustration, 53A
Abbey of St. Gallen, 50
 in ninth-tenth centuries, 9
Abbot Gero
 and dispute with forest district, 42
Abbot of St. Gallen
 military force of, 180
 and revolutionary unrest, 281
 and the Toggenburg road, 226
Abbot Rudolf
 of Einsiedeln, 43
Abortion
 issues, 513
Accident insurance
 federal law on, 648
Accidents
 statistics, 510
Acid rain, 791
 damaging effects of, 814
Act of Mediation
 and laws of the State, 267
 and Napoleon, 312
 termination of
  1814 AD, 322
Act of Union
 and the Federal Pact, 324
Addiction
 drug problems, 495
Addison
 description of Swiss temperament, 178
Administrative tribunals
 in the cantons, 697
Adultery
 as offence against morality,
  715
 punishment for
  17th century, 180-1
Advertising
 and alcohol, 499
 and breast-feeding, 584
Agassiz, Louis
 distinguished emigrant, 430
Age of Enlightenment
 education in, 264
Agents provocateurs
 and refugees, 492
Aglionby, William, 217, 223

Agreement of Stans
 dissension in the Waldstätte,
  105
Agricultural production
 and the peasant revolt, 138
Agriculture
 in the 20th century, 557-78
 and economy
  post Napoleonic, 344
 and emigration, 428
 experimental farm
  of Johann Rudolf Tschiffeli,
   252
 and the fattening of cattle
  parliament law, 512
 and land divisions, 469
 and the new Swiss nation, 412
 and population increase, 259
Air craft
 losses of, 773
 as war material, 767
Air pollution
 oil-fired plants, 780
 quantitative measures, 513
 from transportation, 525
Air transport, 530
 passenger and freight, 527-8
Airline deregulation
 Swiss policy on, 528
Airspace
 control of, 532
Albrecht I, Emperor
 murder of, 77
Alcohol intoxication
 and drug abuse, 496
Alcoholism
 as a health problem, 499, 514
Alemannia
 600 AD, 20
Alemannians, 33
 invasion by, 6-7
Aliens
 population data
  figure, 474
Alliances
 11-12th century, 37-41
 with foreign Powers, 456
 and neutrality, 118
Allied Armies
 occupation by, 321
Allied troops
 and right of passage, 330
Alphorn
 in the world of classical music, 833
Alpine regions
 and erosions, 573
Alps
 as barrier to invasion, 216

and recruitment from the
 Graubünden, 187
Alsace
 as a duchy, 24
 French expulsion from, 289
 and the Prussian Federation,
  404
 seizure of, 401
 and the treaty of 1777, 294
Alt-Rapperswil
 destruction of castle of, 60
American Civil War
 Swiss in combat forces, 409
American colonization
 by the Swiss, 212
American companies
 and research, 691
American Constitution
 Swiss influence on, 365
American War of Independence
 and Swiss banking, 437
Ammann, Othmar H.
 and the George Washington
  bridge, 694
Amnesty International
 and human rights, 808
Anabaptists
 exodus of
  and Bern, 260
 in the reformation, 146
 religious persecution of,
  183
Andiron of clay
 illustration, 2A
Animals
 diseases of, 563-4, 577
 early domestication of, 2
 farm, 561
Annexation
 of Savoy, 398-9
Annexed territories
 under Napoleon, 334
Anschluss
 1938 AD
  and imports, 797
Anshelm, Valerius
 as chronicler, 115
Apartheid
 and Swiss banking, 642
Apartment rental
 statistics, 600
Apartments
 occupancy rate, 478
Appenzell
 admittance to the Bund, 119
 associations with the Confederation, 73-5
 as a grass-roots democracy,
  312